BIOGRAPHICAL DICTIONARY OF REPUBLICAN CHINA

VOLUME III: MAO–WU

BIOGRAPHICAL DICTIONARY OF REPUBLICAN CHINA

HOWARD L. BOORMAN, *Editor*
RICHARD C. HOWARD, *Associate Editor*

VOLUME III: MAO–WU

COLUMBIA UNIVERSITY PRESS

1970   NEW YORK AND LONDON

COPYRIGHT © 1970 COLUMBIA UNIVERSITY PRESS
SBN 231-08957-0
LIBRARY OF CONGRESS CATALOG CARD NUMBER: 67-12006
PRINTED IN THE UNITED STATES OF AMERICA

BIOGRAPHICAL DICTIONARY
OF REPUBLICAN CHINA

HOWARD L. BOORMAN, Editor
RICHARD C. HOWARD, Associate Editor
O. EDMUND CLUBB
RUSSELL MAETH

STAFF

ANNE B. CLARK

SHEN-YU DAI

LIENCHE TU FANG

PEI-JAN HSIA

YANG-CHIH HUANG

MELVILLE T. KENNEDY, JR.

DONALD W. KLEIN

ROBERT H. G. LEE

BERNADETTE LI

ALBERT LU

SUSAN H. MARSH

YONG SANG NG

LORETTA PAN

A. C. SCOTT

PEI-YI WU

CONTRIBUTORS

John S. Aird
Cyril Birch
Scott A. Boorman
Conrad Brandt
Robert A. Burton
C. M. Chang
K. N. Chang
Kwang-chih Chang
Fu-ts'ung Chiang
Tse-tsung Chow
M. W. Chu
Samuel C. Chu
Wen-djang Chu
James I. Crump, Jr.
John Dardess
James E. Dew
John Philip Emerson
Albert Feuerwerker
Yi-tsi Feuerwerker
Wolfgang Franke
Donald Gillin

Merle Goldman
Jerome B. Grieder
Marus Fang Hao
James P. Harrison
Judy Feldman
    Harrison
David Hawkes
Nicole Hirabayashi
Ping-ti Ho
C. T. Hsia
Ronald Hsia
Kung-chuan Hsiao
Francis C. P. Hsu
Kai-yu Hsu
Chün-tu Hsüeh
Paul V. Hyer
Chalmers A. Johnson
Paula S. Johnson
William R. Johnson
Olga Lang
Kan Lao

Shu-hua Li
C. T. Liang
H. H. Ling
Arthur Link
Chun-jo Liu
Ch'ung-hung Liu
James T. C. Liu
Wu-chi Liu
John T. Ma
Meng Ma
Eduardo Macagno
Robert M. Marsh
Harriet C. Mills
Donald Paragon
Robert W. Rinden
David T. Roy
Harold Schiffrin
Stuart R. Schram
William R. Schultz
T. H. Shen
Tsung-lien Shen

James E. Sheridan
Stanley Spector
E-tu Zen Sun
Rufus Suter
S. Y. Teng
Te-kong Tong
T. H. Tsien
T'ung-ho Tung
Lyman P. Van Slyke
Richard L. Walker
Farrell Phillips
    Wallerstein
Chi-kao Wang
Y. T. Wang
Holmes H. Welch
Hellmut Wilhelm
Hsiang-hsiang Wu
K. T. Wu
William C. C. Wu
William A. Wycoff
Isabella Yen

Editor for the Columbia University Press: Katharine Kyes Leab

EXPLANATORY NOTES

NAMES

The romanization systems used are the Wade-Giles (with the omission of some diacritical marks) for Chinese and the Hepburn (with the omission of some macrons) for Japanese. The major exception to this rule is Chinese place names for large cities, which are given according to the Chinese Post Office system. In the case of Kwangtung province, Cantonese spellings often have been indicated: Nanhai (Namhoi). For place names in Manchuria and in the case of Peking, we generally have followed contemporary usage. In such outlying areas as Sinkiang, Mongolia, and Tibet, any given place might have several names. For convenience, we have standardized the place names in all outlying areas according to the dictates of common sense.

Chinese personal names are given in the Chinese order, that is, with the surname first. In general, the articles are arranged alphabetically by the Wade-Giles romanization of the subject's surname and given personal name (ming). However, the biographies of Chiang Kai-shek, Eugene Ch'en, H. H. K'ung, T. V. Soong, Sun Yat-sen, and a few others appear under the name most familiar to Western readers. The courtesy, literary, Western, alternate, and common pen names of subjects of biographies are listed at the beginning of each article (see ABBREVIATIONS). The reader should note that the ming and the tzu (courtesy name) frequently are confused in modern Chinese sources.

THE CALENDAR

Dates are given according to the Western calendar, converted in many cases from the Chinese calendar. The word sui often is used in referring to age. In China, a person is regarded as being one year old at birth and two years old at the beginning of the next Chinese calendar year. Thus, a person's age by Western calculation will be less than his sui. We have retained the sui form in many articles because of the difficulties of conversion and, frequently, the lack of precise information about month and day of birth.

MEASURES OF MONEY AND LAND

From 1911 to 1949 the values of Chinese monetary units varied so greatly that it is impossible to assign them standard values in Western terms. Until 1933 the official unit of value was the Customs tael (Hai-kuan liang). Other monies, such as silver dollars (yuan), also were current. In 1933 the silver dollar (yuan) became the standard legal tender of China. In 1935, by law, a managed paper currency (fapi) replaced the silver. A gold dollar unit (yuan) was briefly introduced in 1948, but the Chinese monetary system remained unstable until after the establishment of the Central People's Government at Peking in October 1949.

Standard units of land measurement used in this work are li and mu.

1 li = 1/3 mile
1 mu (or mou) = 733 sq. yards
6.6 mu = 1 acre

MILITARY ORGANIZATION

We have used Western military terms to describe the organization of Chinese armies. Thus:

chün = army   ying = battalion
shih = division   lien = company
lü = brigade   p'ai = platoon
t'uan = regiment

The reader should note that the organization of Chinese armies was not so standardized as that of Western armies, and the size of units varied considerably. During the second phase of the Northern Expedition (1928) armies were combined for field operations to form larger units, although they retained their individual designations (e.g., First Army). The combined forces were known variously as army groups (chün-t'uan), direction armies (fang-mien chün), and route armies (lu-chün). Above this level was that of group army (chi-t'uan-chün). Although these were temporary designations, they achieved the permanence of organizational categories.

PROVINCIAL ADMINISTRATION

The administrative divisions, in ascending order, of each province at the end of the Ch'ing period were:

> hsien = districts or counties
> chou = departments
> fu = prefectures
> tao = circuits composed of
>   2 or more fu

We have used the terms military governor and civil governor in referring to provincial rulers of the 1912–28 period. At the beginning of the republican period the Chinese title for the military governor of a province was tutuh. The official designation was changed to chiang-chün in 1914 and to tuchün in 1916. Beginning about 1925, the title was changed in some areas to tupan, a designation which implied that the governor's primary responsibilities were demilitarization and social rehabilitation.

We have used the term governor in referring to the top-ranking officer of a provincial government after 1928, rather than the more literal rendering of the Chinese (sheng cheng-fu chu-hsi) as chairman.

The term tao-t'ai refers to the official in charge of a circuit. A number of the men who held this office during the Ch'ing period were important in foreign relations because often the tao-t'ai was the highest Chinese official available for negotiations with foreigners.

Mention should be made of the likin, an inland tax on the transit of goods which was introduced by the imperial government at the time of the Taiping Rebellion (1850–64). Likin stations soon proliferated throughout China.

The tax revenues were beyond Peking's control and often were used to finance regional armies. The likin tax on local trade was not suppressed officially until 1933.

THE EXAMINATION SYSTEM

In the Ch'ing period, the official class was defined by statute, and its composition was determined by the results of examinations in literary and classical subjects. Although the examination system was abolished in 1905, a brief discussion of it is necessary because many prominent people in the republican period were members of this class by achievement or purchase and because the examinations and degrees have no Western equivalents.

Preliminary examinations were conducted on three successive levels: the hsien; the fu; and the sheng, which was conducted at the prefectural capital. Successful candidates received the sheng-yuan degree, which entitled them to assume the dress of the scholar and exempted them from forced labor. However, they had no legal right to or opportunity for official appointment. They were subject to sui-k'ao, examinations given regularly in the prefectural capitals under provincial supervision. Success in the sui-k'ao meant that they received a small stipend annually to further their studies. Roughly equivalent to the sheng-yuan degree was the chien-sheng degree, which, however, could be purchased. Accordingly, holders of the chien-sheng degree were not subject to periodic examination. Holders of the chien-sheng and the sheng-yuan degrees, who were neither commoners nor officials, comprised a large and changing group.

Those who wished to qualify for official status took the provincial examinations, composed of a preliminary examination, or k'o-k'ao, and a hsiang-shih, or provincial examination. Successful candidates received the degree of chü-jen, which made the holder eligible for office. The kung-sheng degree was roughly equivalent to the chü-jen, but was acquired by appointment, by examination, or by purchase.

The examinations for the highest degree, the chin-shih, which brought appointment to the middle levels of the imperial bureaucracy, were held at Peking. They were composed of the hui-shih, or metropolitan examination; the tien-shih, or palace examination; and the ch'ao-k'ao, an examination in the presence of the emperor which led to specific appointment. Chin-shih who ranked near the top of their group usually were appointed to the Hanlin Academy, where their duties included drawing up government documents and compiling materials for official histories. Service at the Hanlin Academy frequently afforded access to the highest positions in the imperial government.

Candidates who passed the examinations in the same year were linked in the t'ung-nien (same year) relationship, a bond somewhat similar to that linking, for example, members of the Class of 1928 at Harvard College.

FINAL DATE FOR VOLUME III

The final date for inclusion of information about the subjects of biographies in Volume III was March 1969.

BIBLIOGRAPHY

The final volume of this work will contain a comprehensive bibliography. It will list the published writings, if any, of the subject of each article and the sources, both personal and written, used in preparing the article. A brief bibliography of basic sources for twentieth-century Chinese biography is to be found at the end of each volume.

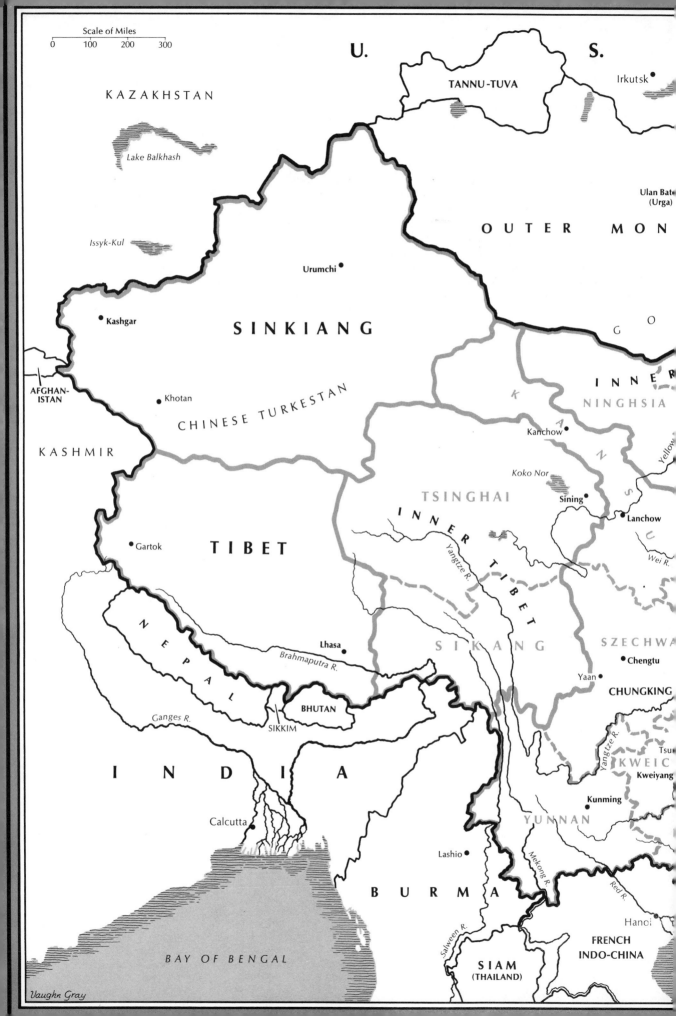

Scale of Miles
0   100   200   300

U.   S.

KAZAKHSTAN   TANNU-TUVA   Irkutsk

Lake Balkhash   Ulan Bat
                                                                            (Urga)

Issyk-Kul   OUTER   MON

                        Urumchi   G   O

                                                                    INNER
KASHGAR   SINKIANG   NINGHSIA

AFGHAN-   Kanchow
ISTAN   Koko Nor   Yellow
            Khotan   CHINESE TURKESTAN
                                                        Sining
KASHMIR   TSINGHAI   Lanchow

                                                                    Wei R.
            Gartok   TIBET   INNER   TIBET

                            Yangtze R.   SZECHWA

            NEPAL   SIKANG   Chengtu

                    Lhasa   Yaan
            Brahmaputra R.   CHUNGKING
    Ganges R.   BHUTAN
            SIKKIM   Yangtze R.   Tsu
                                                    KWEIC
    INDIA   Kweiyang

    Calcutta   Kunming
                                            YUNNAN
                    Lashio
                                    Mekong R.   Red R.
                    BURMA
                                                        Hanoi
    BAY OF BENGAL   Salween R.
                                            SIAM   FRENCH
                                        (THAILAND)   INDO-CHINA

Vaughn Gray

S. R.

LAKE BAIKAL

Shilka R.

Argun R.

Amur R.

Khabarovsk

HEILUNGKIANG

Kerulen R.

LIA

Nonni R.

Tsitsihar

Sungari R.

Harbin

MANCHURIA

KIRIN

Ussuri R.

L. Khanka

MONGOLIA

CHAHAR

Changchun

Kirin

LIAONING
(FENGTIEN)

Vladivostok

JEHOL

Mukden   Fushun

Anshan

Yingkow

Antung

SEA OF
JAPAN

UIYUAN   Kweisui

Kalgan

Chengte

T'angshan

Shanhaikuan

Yalu R.

KOREA

J A P A N

otow

Tatung

PEKING
(Peiping)

TIENTSIN

Chinwangtao

KWANTUNG
(Japan)

Dairen
Port Arthur

Seoul

Tokyo

SHANSI

Shihchiachuang

Paoting

HOPEI
(CHIHLI)

Tangku
Taku

Weihaiwei

Taiyuan

Yellow R.

Chefoo

(Hwang Ho)

Tsinan

SHANTUNG

Tsingtao

YELLOW
SEA

Quelpart I.

Nagasaki

ENSI

Sian

Loyang

Chengchow

Kaifeng

Grand

Hsuchow

HONAN

Canal

PACIFIC

Han R.

Hwai R.

Hofei

KIANGSU

Yangchow

Pukow

Chinkiang

Nant'ung

Woosung

EAST

HUPEH

Hankow

NANKING

Wusih

Soochow

SHANGHAI

CHINA

Ichang

Hanyang

Wuhan

Wuchang

Wuhu

Anking

Hangchow

SEA

RYUKYU ISLANDS

OCEAN

Yochow

Kiukiang

Ningpo

Tungting
Lake

Nanchang

*Poyang
Lake*

CHEKIANG

Changsha

KIANGSI

HUNAN

Hengyang

Foochow

Kweilin

Juichin

FUKIEN

Formosa Strait

Taipei

NGSI

Amoy

TAIWAN
(FORMOSA)

West R.

KWANGTUNG

CANTON

Swatow

ning

HONG KONG (Br.)

Macao (Port.)

KWANGCHOWAN
(Fr.)

HAINAN
(to Kwangtung)

SOUTH
CHINA
SEA

PHILIPPINES

REPUBLICAN CHINA
IN 1928

BIOGRAPHICAL DICTIONARY OF REPUBLICAN CHINA

VOLUME III: MAO-WU

ABBREVIATIONS

Alt. = alternate name
H. = hao, a literary name
Orig. = original name
Pen. = pen name

Pseud. = pseudonym
Studio. = pieh-hao (alternate hao)
T. = tzu, courtesy name
West. = Western name

ECCP = *Eminent Chinese of the Ch'ing Period*, ed. by
Arthur W. Hummel. Washington, 1943–44.

Mao Tse-min　　　毛澤民

Alt. Chou Pin　　　周彬

Mao Tse-min (1895–27 September 1943), Chinese Communist economic expert who became Sinkiang commissioner of finance in 1938. The intrigues of Sheng Shih-ts'ai (q.v.) resulted in Mao's execution in 1943.

Shaoshan village in Hsiangt'an hsien, Hunan, was the birthplace of Mao Tse-min, the second son of Mao Jen-sheng and the younger brother of Mao Tse-tung (for family details, *see* Mao Tse-tung). Little is known about his early life except that he received his early education in the village school and that he learned the rigors of peasant life by laboring on the family farm.

In 1922, having been influenced by his elder brother's political activities, Mao Tse-min joined the Chinese Communist party. He worked with Mao Tse-tung as a labor organizer in Hunan and came to know such other Hunanese Communists as Li Li-san and Liu Shao-ch'i (qq.v.) while attempting to organize workers in the Anyuan coalfields. In 1925 Mao Tse-min went to Shanghai, where he received a new assignment from the Central Committee of the Chinese Communist party: traveling through various cities in the Yangtze valley and in Hunan to organize a distribution network for party propaganda materials. Toward the end of that year, he was in Canton, where he enrolled in the fifth class (October–December) at the Peasant Movement Training Institute.

Late in 1926 Mao Tse-min went to Wuhan, then newly occupied by the Northern Expedition forces, and became the editor of the *Min-kuo jih-pao* [republican daily]. Although Mao fled Wuhan when Wang Ching-wei (q.v.) broke with the Communists in July 1927, he did not escape arrest. He was detained in Kiangsi for a time, but he somehow managed to secure his freedom. Mao then made his way to Shanghai, where he again assumed responsibility for the printing and distribution of Chinese Communist propaganda literature. These

activities led to his arrest at Shanghai in 1930, but he was set free because the Nationalist authorities failed to discover his identity. Because increasing Nationalist pressure made it virtually impossible for Communists to operate in the Shanghai area, Mao moved in 1931 to the Fukien-Kiangsi-Kwangtung border region, where he served as director of the general affairs department of the Communist military forces in that base area. Later that year, he moved to the central Communist base in Kiangsi, where he took part in the preparations for the first All-China Congress of Soviets. At that meeting, held at Juichin in November 1931, Mao Tse-tung was elected chairman of the provisional central government of the Chinese soviet republic.

When Lin Po-ch'ü (q.v.) became commissioner of finance in the central soviet government in 1932, Mao Tse-min was assigned to work under him in the treasury office and was given responsibility for note issue in the base area. Thus, he also controlled the soviet's gold and silver reserves. After the Chinese Communists were forced to evacuate the Kiangsi base late in 1934 and to undertake the Long March, their financial problems became increasingly complex. Mao Tse-min had the triple assignment of preserving specie reserves, collecting gold and silver from unpopular landlords in areas through which the Communist columns passed, and issuing paper currency to pay for purchases when possible. After the Long March forces arrived in northern Shensi late in 1935, Mao Tse-min formulated programs and policies designed to support the primitive financial structure of the Paoan base area and to pay for essential imports. In 1937 Mao became a member of the Shensi-Kansu-Ninghsia Border Region Government's economic commission, serving under Lin Po-ch'ü once again.

The outbreak of the Sino-Japanese war in the summer of 1937 and the establishment of a Nationalist-Communist united front in China wrought political and military policy changes in Sinkiang province. In 1937 the governor, Sheng Shih-ts'ai (q.v.), invited the Chinese

Communists to send cadres to Sinkiang for development work. The Chinese Communists accepted the invitation and sent a group of cadres headed by Teng Fa (q.v.) to Sinkiang. Early in 1938, when Mao Tse-min was passing through Sinkiang on his way to the Soviet Union for medical treatment, he was ordered to stop at Urumchi and to help reorganize the financial structure of Sinkiang. Under the name of Chou Pin, Mao became provincial commissioner of finance. His wife, Chu Tan-hua, headed a local middle school for girls.

Early in 1942 military developments in Europe led Sheng Shih-ts'ai to question the desirability of maintaining close relations with the Soviet Union. Ch'en T'an-ch'iu (q.v.), who had replaced Teng Fa in 1939, became suspicious and asked that the Communist cadres in Sinkiang be permitted to return to Shensi. Sheng refused this request, and he transferred Mao Tse-min to the office of commissioner of civil affairs. In the autumn of 1942 Sheng demanded the withdrawal from Sinkiang of Soviet troops and representatives, and ordered the arrest of Chinese Communists in Sinkiang. A public announcement in December stated that the Chinese Communists had been involved in an international Communist plot to overthrow Sheng Shih-ts'ai's regime in Sinkiang. By that time, Sheng had made arrangements with the National Government to permit the extension of Kuomintang authority into Sinkiang.

Mao Tse-min, Ch'en T'an-ch'iu, and many of their associates were executed in secret on 27 September 1943. After the Chinese Communists took control of Sinkiang in 1951, four men were executed publicly on 29 April, reportedly for the murder of Mao Tse-min and his associates. Representatives of the Chinese Communist party and the Sinkiang provincial government held a memorial service at Urumchi in April 1954 to honor the Communist martyrs. A full account of their death did not become available until September 1963, when Saifudin (q.v.) published an authoritative article at Peking to commemorate the twentieth anniversary of the death of Mao Tse-min and his comrades.

Mao Tse-tung   毛 澤 東
   T. Jun-chih   潤 之

Mao Tse-tung (26 December 1893–), leader of the Chinese Communist party and founder of the

People's Republic of China.

Shaoshan, Hsiangt'an hsien, Hunan, was the birthplace of Mao Tse-tung. This agriculturally productive and culturally advanced section of Hunan produced two of the outstanding scholar-generals of the late Ch'ing period, Tseng Kuo-fan (ECCP, II, 751–56) and Tso Tsung-t'ang (ECCP, II, 762–67), and contributed soldiers to the Hsiang-chün, which played a leading role in the defeat of the Taiping rebels in the 1860's. Mao Tse-tung's family background was undistinguished. His father, Mao Jen-sheng (d. 1927) was what Communist social analysis would term a rich peasant. The tile-roofed family house, though more spacious than many of its neighbors, was typical of the area. Mao Jen-sheng owned about 15 mou of land, and he later acquired additional land and operated a small grain business. A rough, autocratic man for whom existence was measured by the gap between buying cheap and selling dear, he embodied the narrow, grasping prejudices of the poor peasant once removed. His wife, Wen Ch'i-mei (d. 1919), an illiterate and superstitious woman from a nearby village, was known for her warmth and generosity. Mao Tse-tung was the eldest of their four children. The others were two boys, Mao Tse-min (q.v.) and Mao Tse-t'an (d. 1935), and a girl, Mao Tse-hung (d. 1930).

Mao Tse-tung received his early education at the village school in Shaoshan between 1901 and 1906. At the age of 13, he left primary school and began work on the family farm, laboring in the fields by day and keeping accounts for his father in the evening. He soon began to rebel against his father's authority. He disliked his father, despised his avariciousness, and feuded with him regularly. One point of contention was the young Mao's fondness for reading novels. Like countless other schoolboys in China, Mao devoured the *San-kuo yen-yi* (*Romance of the Three Kingdoms*) and the *Shui-hu chuan* (*Water Margin*). The adventure-filled tales of heroic deeds, clever stratagems, and righteous rebellion gripped the young Mao and stirred his imagination. He also was influenced by Cheng Kuan-ying's *Sheng-shih wei-yen* [words of warning to an affluent age], a contemporary reformist tract which advocated industrialization, improved communications, parliamentary government, and public libraries for China; it also denounced foreigners' treatment of the

Chinese in Shanghai.

In 1909 Mao Tse-tung defied his father by leaving the family farm and going to nearby Hsianghsiang, the home of his mother's family, to enter the Tungshan Higher Primary School. Mao was somewhat of an outcast at school, for he was six years older than most of the students, ragged in appearance (he had only one decent suit), and lacking in social graces. However, the school's modern curriculum provided some compensation for his personal unhappiness. His knowledge of Chinese affairs expanded as he studied the writings of K'ang Yu-wei and Liang Ch'i-ch'ao (qq.v.), while a book called *Heroes of the World* introduced him to George Washington, Napoleon, Wellington, and Peter the Great. Washington aroused Mao's enthusiasm because he had shown such admirable patriotism and military valor in eight bitter years of fighting for his country's independence. The American Revolution was distant, however; that in China was just approaching. Mao soon left his home district and walked to Changsha, the political, intellectual, and commercial capital of Hunan, to enter middle school. In Changsha, he became an avid reader of the *Min-li pao* [people's strength], edited by Yü Yu-jen (q.v.).

The revolution that finally toppled the Ch'ing dynasty took place when Mao Tse-tung was not quite 18. On hearing of the Wuchang revolt of October 1911, Mao enthusiastically cut off his queue and set out for Wuchang, but he got no farther than the outskirts of Changsha before fighting broke out in Hunan. He joined a volunteer unit which was composed primarily of Changsha students and served under the direct command of Chao Heng-t'i (q.v.) and the over-all command of T'an Yen-k'ai (q.v.). With the agreement of January 1912 between Sun Yat-sen and Yuan Shih-k'ai, Mao decided that the revolutionary surge had ended, and he returned to his books. After attending classes at the First Provincial Middle School for six months, he spent several months reading independently in the Hunan provincial library. Through the translations made by Yen Fu (q.v.) and others of such works as Thomas Henry Huxley's *Evolution and Ethics*, John Stuart Mill's *On Liberty*, Adam Smith's *Wealth of Nations*, and Charles Darwin's *Origin of Species*, he came to know something of Western political and social thought.

In the spring of 1913 Mao Tse-tung enrolled at the Hunan Fourth Provincial Normal School.

This institution was merged into the First Normal School that autumn, and Mao thus became a student at one of Changsha's most prosperous and intellectually competitive schools. As the provincial capital of Hunan, Changsha reflected the tensions between old and new that characterized the early republican period in China. A center of classical Chinese studies as early as Sung times, when the great Chu Hsi (1130–1200) had lectured there, Hunan long had produced traditional scholars known both for their personal dedication and for their intellectual conservatism. Hunan also had a strong reformist tradition, a radical outlook that encouraged examination of new ideas and action based on new premises. Indeed, Hunan had produced three of the most famous revolutionary leaders of the early twentieth century: Huang Hsing, Sung Chiao-jen, and Ts'ai O (qq.v.). All three of them died while Mao was a student in Changsha.

As a patriotic young Hunanese, Mao Tse-tung was conscious of Hunan's fading significance in China's national politics and of China's declining influence in Asian politics. Thus, when the *Hsin ch'ing-nien* [new youth] of Ch'en Tu-hsiu (q.v.) first appeared in 1915, he responded enthusiastically to its bold ideas and vigorous literary style. The April 1917 issue of this journal contained Mao's first significant published article, "T'i-yü chih yen-chiu" [a study of physical culture]. A product of Mao's ardent interest in physical fitness (an interest which was itself of Western influence), this essay was notable for its spirit of elemental nationalism. It proposed a series of athletic exercises which, by helping to stimulate a new national ethic blending civil and military virtues, would serve to remedy China's weakness. As Mao put it: "The principal aim of physical education is military heroism." He objected to Confucianism because of its emphasis on family loyalty at the expense of nationalism and its deprecation of military virtues, but he cited the Hunanese scholar-official Tseng Kuo-fan as an outstanding example of a worthy Chinese statesman who maintained bodily fitness.

At the same time that Mao Tse-tung found his central goal to be nationalism, as distinguished from the culturalism characteristic of traditional Chinese civilization, he sought a broader intellectual foundation for his mood of social protest. He was strongly influenced by such liberal-minded faculty members of the

First Normal School as Yang Ch'ang-chi and Hsü T'e-li (qq.v.). Yang, whose daughter Mao later was to marry, was a respected scholar known locally as "Confucius." Under his tutelage, the students absorbed some Western ethical theory as well as the precepts of major Chinese thinkers of the Ming and Ch'ing periods. The Western book that most influenced Mao at this time was Friedrich Paulsen's *System of Ethics*, translated into Chinese by Ts'ai Yuan-p'ei (q.v.) and used by Yang Ch'ang-chi as a textbook. In teaching traditional Chinese values, Yang emphasized self-discipline, self-cultivation, patriotism, and resistance to alien rule. Mao, who was Yang's favorite pupil in ethics, once wrote an essay on "Hsin chih-li" [the power of the mind] for which Yang awarded him the maximum mark of 100 points with a special added "plus 5."

Yang Ch'ang-chi's socially oriented individualism affected Mao Tse-tung's extracurricular activities as well as his classroom work. Mao was secretary of the Changsha student association in 1915–16 and its director in 1917–18. He also created a committee for student self-government to deal collectively with the school authorities. In the summer of 1917 he began working to form a new student organization dedicated to "strengthening China through strengthening Chinese youth." Ts'ai Ho-sen (q.v.), a fellow-student at the First Normal School who was three years older than Mao, played a leading role in this effort. The resulting Hsin-min hsüeh-hui [new people's study society] held its first meeting at the Ts'ai residence in Changsha on 18 April 1918. When news reached Changsha of the work-study program (*see* Li Shih-tseng) sponsored by several older Kuomintang leaders with European connections, the Hsin-min hsüeh-hui sent Ts'ai Ho-sen to Peking in June 1918 to investigate the situation.

In June 1918 Mao Tse-tung was graduated from the First Normal School. During the summer, Ts'ai Ho-sen wrote to suggest that more members of the Hsin-min hsüeh-hui go to Peking to study French so that they could participate in the work-study program; Yang Ch'ang-chi, who had accepted an invitation to teach at Peking University, also wrote to urge Mao to go to Peking. In September 1918 the 24-year-old Mao left Changsha for his first extended journey outside Hunan. He arrived in Peking to encounter a broader and more complex intellectual world than that offered by Changsha. Through Yang Ch'ang-chi, he gained an introduction to Li Ta-chao (q.v.), the recently appointed chief librarian at Peking University. Li's influence on the students of that period stemmed from his willingness to lend a sympathetic ear to their personal problems as well as from his writings and lectures. Because Mao appeared to be in straitened circumstances, Li arranged for his employment as a clerk in the university library. Like many other young men, Mao was deeply influenced by Li Ta-chao's dedication to the vision of a new, self-reliant China and by his personal thoughtfulness. Mao also met Ch'en Tu-hsiu and Hu Shih (qq.v.), but he failed to gain their attention. After spending the winter working in the library and auditing some courses at Peking University, Mao went to Shanghai in the early spring of 1919. On the way, he paid a visit to the birthplace of Confucius in Shantung province. In Shanghai, Mao assisted in the final preparations made by friends from Hunan before they embarked for France on the work-study program. Mao left Shanghai in April when he learned that his mother had become seriously ill and had been moved to Changsha for medical treatment. He returned to Hunan and cared for his mother until her death a few weeks later.

In the spring of 1919 Changsha was affected by the May Fourth Movement, and Mao Tse-tung responded by attempting to mobilize the Hunan students. He played an active role in the creation, on 3 June, of the United Students' Association of Hunan. The situation in Changsha provided Mao, then an obscure normal-school graduate, with new opportunities for action, influence, and prestige. On 14 July 1919 he founded the weekly *Hsiang-chiang p'ing-lun* [Hsiang river review], published by the United Students' Association and patterned on the *Mei chou p'ing-lun* [weekly critic] edited by Li Ta-chao in Peking. The *Hsiang-chiang p'ing-lun*, which advocated "democracy and new culture," attained national recognition among young intellectuals as it gained local disfavor among the Changsha authorities. Between 1918 and 1920 Hunan was controlled by Chang Ching-yao, a Peiyang warlord of the Anhwei faction whose brutal tyranny won him the hatred of the Hunanese. Mao strongly opposed Chang and all that he represented in his writings during the summer of 1919. Mao's most influential article of this period, an anti-imperialist and anti-militarist essay entitled "The Great Union of the Popular Masses," appeared in the *Hsiang-chiang p'ing-lun* in July and August. The magazine was banned after its fifth issue, and Mao then began to write for another student journal, the *Hsin Hunan* [new Hunan], which he also edited. When the *Hsin Hunan* was banned, he took to writing for the *Ta Kung Pao*. Although Mao's political views in 1919 were somewhat primitive, his activities among the students and teachers of Changsha constituted a threat to the rule of Chang Ching-yao. After Mao organized a general student strike in December 1919, Chang banned student publications and suppressed the United Students' Association.

Because it was dangerous for him to remain at Changsha, Mao went to Peking in January 1920 at the head of an anti-Chang delegation. He thus had the opportunity to see Yang Ch'ang-chi once again before Yang's death on 17 January, and he renewed his acquaintance with Yang's daughter, Yang K'ai-hui. Mao soon joined the Young China Association, a group formed in mid-1919 by Tseng Ch'i (q.v.), Li Ta-chao, and others to mobilize opposition to the pro-Japanese government of Tuan Ch'i-jui (q.v.). As Li Ta-chao moved leftward in his political thinking, Mao followed him, reading the *Communist Manifesto* for the first time (the Chinese translation appeared in book form in April 1920) and exploring the elementary tenets of historical materialism.

In May 1920 Mao went to Shanghai to coordinate the activities of the Hunanese student delegations working to overthrow Chang Ching-yao. He supported himself by working as a laundryman, and he spent much of his free time talking with Ch'en Tu-hsiu, then at the center of a cluster of self-styled Marxists, socialists, and anarchists whose youthful enthusiasm often exceeded their political consistency. Mao's conversations with Ch'en were crucial in his movement toward Communism, and he later (1936) stated that these talks "deeply impressed me at what was probably a critical period in my life."

Chang Ching-yao finally was forced out of Hunan in June 1920, primarily because of friction between the Chihli and Anhwei factions of the Peiyang warlords. Mao Tse-tung returned to Hunan in June 1920 to seek employment and opportunities for political organization. That autumn, in an attempt to restore the Hunan educational system to its pre-Chang level, T'an Yen-k'ai (q.v.) appointed Yi P'ei-chi (q.v.) to head the First Normal School at Changsha. Yi carried out a thorough reform of the school's faculty, and he invited his former student Mao Tse-tung to teach Chinese literature and to head the primary school attached to the First Normal School. Mao accepted the offer, thus gaining material security for the first time. This post, which he held until the winter of 1921–22, gave him new channels for his political activities and enabled him to consider marriage seriously. Yang K'ai-hui had returned to Changsha, and she and Mao were married in the autumn of 1920.

Mao soon began to distribute materials on Marxism to students through such outlets as the Wen-hua shu-she [culture bookstore], which was established at Changsha in September 1920. "From this time on," he later wrote, "I considered myself a Marxist." When Bertrand Russell, on a visit to Changsha in 1920, excoriated the Bolshevik dictatorship in Russia and advocated an evolutionary approach to socialism through education and economic reform, Mao vigorously opposed his views and argued that political power should be seized by force if necessary. In October 1920 Mao received from Peking the charter of the Socialist Youth Corps, a precursor of the Chinese Communist party, and instructions for the establishment of a branch in Hunan. With Ho Shu-heng (q.v.), who had assumed direction of the Hsin-min hsüeh-hui in the absence of Mao and Ts'ai Ho-sen, he organized a branch of the Socialist Youth Corps at Changsha in January 1921.

THE CHINESE COMMUNISTS AND THE KUOMINTANG

In July 1921 Mao Tse-tung and Ho Shu-heng went to Shanghai, where they represented Hunan at the founding meeting of the Chinese Communist party. The other delegates to the First National Congress were Tung Pi-wu, Ch'en T'an-ch'iu, Li Ta, Li Han-chün, Chang Kuo-t'ao, Liu Jen-ching, Ch'en Kung-po, Chou Fo-hai (qq.v.), Wang Ching-mei, and Teng En-ming. The congress also was attended by two Comintern delegates: Gregory Voitinsky and Maring (Henricus Sneevliet). Upon his return to Changsha, Mao began the arduous task of developing the Hunan branch of the Chinese Communist party. As secretary of this provincial party organ, Mao worked to spread the Marxist message and to organize urban workers and miners in accordance with Comintern directives and Marxist-Leninist doctrine. The activities of the Hsin-min hsueh-hui came to an end, and its radical members joined the Communist party branch. Mao, Ho Shu-heng, and several of their associates who were teachers used the school system as a major propaganda channel. Paradoxically, an important center of Communist activity was the Wang Fu-chih Study Society (Ch'uan-shan hsueh-she), an institute which had been founded at Changsha in the early years of the republic to study the works of Wang Fu-chih (ECCP, II, 817–19), a seventeenth-century Hunanese nationalist and classical scholar whose writings had been used at the beginning of the twentieth century to support the anti-Manchu movement. The society, which was supported by the government and directed by traditionalist scholars, granted Mao permission to use its facilities for the establishment of a Marxist study group and for the dissemination of Marxist literature. In August, Mao established the tzu-hsiu ta-hsueh [self-study university] at the society's headquarters, and many future Chinese Communist leaders were trained there. As Mao's biographer Stuart Schram has pointed out, this and other undertakings of the 1921–23 period illustrate Mao's "genius for exploiting respectable people and institutions for radical ends."

After Chao Heng-t'i, the governor of Hunan, ordered the execution of two anarchist labor leaders in January 1922, Li Li-san, Liu Shao-ch'i (qq.v.), and Mao Tse-tung organized a series of strikes throughout Hunan. In September, they led the important strike in the Anyuan coal fields and the strike on the Canton-Hankow railroad. These Communist successes led the provincial authorities to order the suppression of labor unions. In November, Mao was elected head of the Hunan branch of the China Trade Union Secretariat. Chao Heng-t'i responded to Mao's continued activity in the labor field by issuing an order for his arrest. Mao made a precipitate departure for Canton in April 1923.

During this early period of the Chinese Communist movement, the Soviet Union's China policies were based on the decisions of the Second Comintern Congress of 1920 regarding revolutions in underdeveloped countries, and thus upon the analyses of Lenin, who held that Asian nationalism could be a useful ally of the Western proletariat in the common struggle against imperialism and capitalism. Lenin's theory called for an alliance between the proletarian revolution and the nationalist revolt against imperialism in "the East." The application of this general theory in China resulted in an alliance between the infant Chinese Communist party and the Kuomintang. In the summer of 1922, when approached by Russian agents in Shanghai, Sun Yat-sen agreed to cooperate with the Chinese Communist party to the extent of permitting Communists to join the Kuomintang on an individual basis. This possibility was discussed at the Second National Congress of the Chinese Communist party, held at Shanghai in July. Mao Tse-tung was absent from the congress, allegedly because he could not find the meeting place. In August, a special plenum of the Central Committee of the Chinese Communist party, meeting at Hangchow under the guidance of Comintern representative Maring, confirmed the party's decision to cooperate with the Kuomintang and stated that "part of the party members" should join the Kuomintang "in their personal capacity." The general terms of the Kuomintang-Communist alliance were set forth in a joint manifesto signed on 26 January 1923. Details of the new alliance, as well as plans for the reorganization of the Kuomintang along Leninist lines, were worked out in discussions between Adolf Joffe and Sun Yat-sen's trusted lieutenant Liao Chung-k'ai (q.v.).

The Third National Congress of the Chinese Communist party, meeting at Canton in June 1923, voted to relinquish control of the labor movement to the Kuomintang and declared that the Kuomintang "must be the central force in the national revolution and assume the leadership of the revolution." At this congress, Mao Tse-tung was elected to the Central Committee and was named to succeed Chang Kuo-t'ao as director of the organization department. When the reorganized Kuomintang held its First National Congress at Canton in January 1924, three Communists who had become members of the Kuomintang—T'an

P'ing-shan (q.v.) Li Ta-chao, and Yü She-te—were elected to the Central Executive Committee. Mao Tse-tung, Lin Po-ch'ü, Yu Fang-chou, Ch'ü Ch'iu-pai, Han Lin-fu, and Chang Kuo-t'ao became alternate members of the Central Executive Committee. Mao also was elected to the committee charged with examining the Kuomintang party constitution. His enthusiasm in cooperating with the Kuomintang led such Communists as Li Li-san to criticize him and to refer to him as "Hu Han-min's secretary" during the time he worked under Hu in the organization department of the Kuomintang. Toward the end of 1924 Mao became ill and returned to Hunan for a rest. Accordingly, he was absent from the Fourth National Congress of the Chinese Communist party, held at Shanghai in January 1925. Because he did not attend the congress, he was not reelected to the Central Committee.

In the early months of 1925 Mao worked to organize peasant associations in central Hunan. He also helped organize a sympathy strike at Changsha after the May Thirtieth Incident, when police fired on Chinese in the International Settlement at Shanghai. His activities came to the attention of Chao Heng-t'i that summer, and he was forced to flee Hunan. He arrived in Canton in October or November and became secretary, under Wang Ching-wei (q.v.), of the Kuomintang Central Executive Committee's propaganda department. In this post and later as deputy chief of the department, he was its *de facto* head. He made a report on propaganda at the Second National Congress of the Kuomintang in January 1926. He was reelected to alternate membership on the Central Executive Committee, and he became editor of the political department's weekly magazine, *Cheng-chih chou-k'an* [political weekly].

Early in 1926 Mao Tse-tung wrote his "Analysis of the Classes in Chinese Society," an attack on influential anti-Communist tracts written by Tai Chi-t'ao (q.v.) in 1925. Ch'en Tu-hsiu refused to print the essay in the official Chinese Communist journal on the grounds that it was doctrinally immature. Mao succeeded in having it published in the February 1926 issue of *Chung-kuo nung-min* [China peasant] at Canton. It later became the first text in the official canon of Mao's *Selected Works*.

Mao Tse-tung's most important post at Canton in 1926 was the directorship of the Peasant Movement Training Institute, a school supervised by the peasant department of the Kuomintang (then headed by the Hunanese Communist Lin Po-ch'ü), which had been founded in 1924 to train students from south China to work among the peasants. As the time for launching the Northern Expedition drew near, many of the institute's trainees were sent to the rural areas of Kwangtung, Kwangsi, and other provinces to mobilize peasant support, to organize peasant associations, and to serve as assistants and guides for the National Revolutionary Army. Mao personally directed the training of the institute's sixth class, which was graduated on 5 October. He then went to Shanghai to head the Chinese Communist party's peasant department. By mid-December he had returned to Hunan. In a speech to the First Provincial Peasant Congress at Changsha on 20 December 1926, Mao declared that the peasant problem was the central issue in the national revolution. Unless this problem were solved, he argued, it would not be possible to deal with such matters as imperialism, warlordism, and the backwardness of industry and trade.

At the beginning of 1927 Mao Tse-tung was in Hunan surveying conditions in his native Hsiangt'an and the four adjacent hsien of Liling, Changsha, Hengshan, and Hsianghsiang. In February, he wrote a "Report of an Investigation into the Peasant Movement in Hunan," in which he predicted that the peasants of China "will rise like a tornado or a tempest—a force so extraordinarily swift and violent that no power, however great, will be able to suppress it. They will break through all the trammels that now bind them and push forward along the road to liberation." In assessing the accomplishments of the national revolution, he gave 30 percent of the credit to urban dwellers and the military, and 70 percent to the peasants. He defined the rural revolution as "one in which the peasantry overthrows the authority of the feudal landlord class." In later years, Mao's report evoked acrimonious debate among Western scholars of Chinese Communism about what it revealed of Mao's position with reference to the doctrinal authority of Lenin and to the organizational authority of the Comintern in the world movement. In any event, the type of political revolution that Mao would lead in the rural areas of China, in substantial isolation from the Kremlin, was prefigured in this report. It also contained an appeal to the leaders of the Kuomintang and the Chinese Communist party to appreciate that social revolution, though it requires elite leadership, is generated by mass discontent. Mao's emphasis on the revolutionary potential of the peasantry was to become the most salient characteristic of his political style as he rose to leadership in the Chinese Communist party.

In 1927 the Kuomintang split into factions over the question of cooperation with the Communists. Mao participated in the Kuomintang Central Executive Committee's third plenum at Wuhan in March, when Wang Ching-wei (q.v.) was named to head both the Kuomintang and the National Government. On 2 April, Mao was named to the newly established central land committee of the Kuomintang. He presented his report on the Hunan peasant movement to the Fifth National Congress of the Chinese Communist party, but his ideas were not accepted. Despite strong personal reservations and despite Chiang Kai-shek's purge of Communists at Shanghai in April, Ch'en Tu-hsiu was attempting to maintain the coalition with the Kuomintang, important elements of which were opposed to any radical program of land redistribution. P'eng Shu-chih (q.v.), Ch'en's personal assistant, reportedly refused to allow the official Chinese Communist journal to publish Mao's report. Ch'ü Ch'iu-pai, who had been elected to succeed Mao as head of the peasant department, thereupon wrote a preface to Mao's report and published it as a pamphlet. About this time, Mao was elected head of the newly established National Peasant Association.

The Chinese Communist party was brought close to annihilation in the summer of 1927. In July, Wang Ching-wei, the head of the Kuomintang faction at Wuhan, broke with the Communists. Arrests and executions followed immediately. After the August 1927 emergency conference which deposed Ch'en Tu-hsiu and installed Ch'ü Ch'iu-pai as general secretary of the Chinese Communist party, Mao was ordered to return to Hunan. There, in what the Communists referred to as the Autumn Harvest Uprising, Mao attempted to mobilize peasant discontent over taxes and exorbitant rents imposed by landlords. Mao later told the American journalist Edgar Snow that the purposes of this uprising were: the organization of a revolutionary army, the confiscation of landlords' property, the establishment of independent Communist power in Hunan, and the formation of soviets (prohibited by Comintern policy). The uprising began on 9 September with the severing of railroad lines leading to Changsha. On 15 September, faced with superior provincial military troops, Mao called off the siege of Changsha. The Central Committee of the Chinese Communist party, meeting in November, punished Mao for his failure by removing him from both the Central Committee and the Hunan provincial committee.

Official Chinese Communist histories written after 1949 state that during the decade after "the defeat of the Great Revolution of 1925–27," Mao Tse-tung's principal function was "leading the anti-Kuomintang revolutionary war, with the rural areas as its base." The 1927 debacle in China was largely Moscow's responsibility, for Stalin had assumed that the Kremlin should control the Chinese Communist party and that the Chinese party should concentrate on the cities and proletariat. Mao's reaction to this debacle was a recognition that seizure of urban areas meant little if the rural areas were not secured. Accordingly, he set about building a peasant-based organization which nevertheless called itself the party of the proletariat and which proposed to play the role attributed by Lenin to the Communist party elite, that of a "vanguard of the proletariat" spurring the masses to action. And he began fighting a protracted "revolutionary war," using military action to gain political objectives.

THE KIANGSI YEARS

After the Autumn Harvest Uprising failed, Mao Tse-tung reorganized his remnant forces as the 1st Division of the Chinese Workers and Peasants Red Army and instituted a system of political representatives. In October, he led his men to the Ching-kang mountains on the Hunan-Kiangsi border. After surviving a difficult winter in this remote area, Mao's forces were bolstered in April 1928 by the arrival of troops under Chu Teh (q.v.) which had fled from Nanchang the previous year and had established a small base area in southern Hunan. The two men combined their military forces to form the Fourth Red Army, with Chu as commander and Mao as political commissar. They remained in the Ching-kang mountain refuge throughout 1928, during which time they evolved the famous tactical slogan: "The enemy advances, we retreat;/The enemy camps, we harass;/The enemy tires, we attack;/The enemy retreats, we pursue." On 14 January 1929 Nationalist military pressure forced them to retreat. Leaving P'eng Te-huai (q.v.) to fight a rearguard action, Chu and Mao made their way across Kiangsi and settled at Juichin, a small jute and hemp center in southeastern Kiangsi. They gradually built what came to be the central Soviet base. In relative isolation from the Central Committee of the Chinese Communist party at Shanghai, Mao began to formulate independent theories regarding organization, leadership, territorial bases, and other political-military problems. These theories, the foundation of his method of operation in China after 1935, were set forth in a lengthy report of December 1929 (part of which later was published as "On the Rectification of Incorrect Ideas in the Party") and in a sharply critical letter to Lin Piao (q.v.) of January 1930 (later published as "A Single Spark Can Start a Prairie Fire").

Although Mao Tse-tung was elected *in absentia* to the Central Committee when the Chinese Communist party held its Sixth National Congress at Moscow in the summer of 1928, he was not an important figure in the central party structure. During the period from 1928 to 1931, when Li Li-san and Ch'en Shao-yü (qq.v.) dominated the party, it enjoyed Moscow's support in continuing attempts to base the revolution in China on the urban proletariat and on the capture of cities. In contravention of this policy, Mao and his associates created the territorial base in Kiangsi province that eventually became a refuge for the remnants of the Central Committee at Shanghai.

In 1929–30 Mao Tse-tung participated in campaigns and peasant agitation in western Fukien and along the Kan River in southern Kiangsi. In mid-1930 Li Li-san called for frontal attacks on cities in central China with the purpose of gaining control over the strategically important Yangtze Valley. The Chu-Mao forces attacked Nanchang, but soon abandoned their efforts; P'eng Te-huai's attack on Changsha in July was repulsed quickly. When

it became apparent that a joint attack on Changsha in September would fail, Mao and Chu ignored party orders and returned to their base, thus withdrawing their support of the Li Li-san group in Shanghai. Soon afterwards, Yang K'ai-hui, who had remained in Hunan when Mao fled to the Ching-kang mountain area in 1927, was arrested and executed by the order of Ho Chien. In December, Mao suppressed a local rebellion against his authority at Fut'ien, Kiangsi. The Fut'ien incident resulted in one of the most extensive purges in the pre-1949 history of the Chinese Communist party.

On 7 November 1931, the fourteenth anniversary of the Bolshevik Revolution, the Chinese Communists convened the first All-China Congress of Soviets at Juichin. The congress elected a central executive committee which, in turn, elected a council of people's commissars, with Mao as council chairman and Hsiang Ying (q.v.) and Chang Kuo-t'ao as vice chairmen. Although Mao headed the government in the most important Communist base in China—an area with an estimated population of 4,000,000 in 1934—he did not have control of the party apparatus. Li Li-san had fallen from power in November 1930, and the group associated with Comintern representative Pavel Mif had gained control of the central party organs in January 1931 and had appointed Ch'en Shao-yü general secretary. The political situation within the Chinese Communist party in 1931–33 is unclear; after 1949 it was said at Peking that an erroneous leftist line dominated the party during that period. In the autumn of 1932 Ch'en Shao-yü went to Moscow as Chinese representative to the Comintern, and another of the so-called 28 Bolsheviks, Ch'in Pang-hsien (q.v.), succeeded him as general secretary.

As Communist strength in the rural areas of south-central China grew, the Kuomintang, having completed the Northern Expedition and having established a new National Government at Nanking in October 1928, worked to achieve the political unification of China under its aegis. High on Chiang Kai-shek's agenda was the task of crushing the Communists by force of arms. Beginning in the winter of 1930, Chiang undertook five successive campaigns in an effort to annihilate the Communists. Even when confronted with Japanese aggression in

Manchuria beginning in September 1931, Chiang continued to allocate most of his military resources to the anti-Communist campaigns. Although numerically inferior to the Nationalist forces, the Communist troops survived these attacks by using tactical maneuvers that combined carefully calculated withdrawals and counterattacks. Chiang Kai-shek's problems increased when the Fukien revolt was launched at Foochow in November 1933 by a number of senior Kuomintang officials, with military support from the Nineteenth Route Army (for details, *see* Ch'en Ming-shu). The Communist leadership in Kiangsi, divided over policy toward the anti-Chiang revolt in Fukien, agreed to aid the rebels but took no practical steps in that direction. When the dissident regime at Foochow collapsed in January 1934, Mao Tse-tung denounced the Communist failure to unite with the Fukien rebels.

Throughout the 1931–33 period, Mao Tse-tung's power was limited by his superiors and by the competition among factions for leadership of the Chinese Communist party. His authority over the Red Army also was weakened in May 1933, when Chou En-lai (who then supported the 28 Bolsheviks) was appointed political commissar of Chu Teh's First Front Army. Mao did secure reelection as chairman of the central soviet government when the Second All-China Congress of Soviets met at Juichin in January 1934, but the Nationalists encircled the base area later that year and forced him and his associates to begin a year-long forced march for survival. In October 1934 the central soviet government at Juichin dissolved as the Long March began.

THE LONG MARCH

When the Chinese Communists left their Kiangsi base at the beginning of the Long March, they knew only that they were marching westward to establish a new soviet. An early plan, which called for joining forces with Ho Lung (q.v.) in northwestern Hunan, involved crossing the Hsiang River in northern Kwangsi. This measure resulted in the loss of nearly two-thirds of the 100,000 troops that had begun the march. At Mao Tse-tung's urging, the Hunan plan was abandoned and the First Front Red Army moved westward into Kweichow, where it crossed the Wu River at year's end. In January 1935 they took the city of Tsunyi.

Immediately afterwards, at an enlarged conference of the Political Bureau, military policies were changed so that henceforth a strategy based on mobile and guerrilla warfare would be used. Chang Wen-t'ien (q.v.) replaced Ch'in Pang-hsien as the party's general secretary. The party line of Pavel Mif and the 28 Bolsheviks thus was discarded as Mao became the first, and for many years the only, leader of a major Communist party to achieve his position without investiture by Moscow.

At the Tsunyi conference, the Chinese Communist leadership also decided to join the Fourth Front Army of Chang Kuo-t'ao and Hsü Hsiang-ch'ien (q.v.) in Szechwan, a province that was not under the direct control of the National Government. Unfortunately for the Communists, this course of action also seemed logical to Chiang Kai-shek, who sent troops to attack both the First Front Army and the Fourth Front Army. After a successful engagement at Loushan pass, Mao decided to go by way of Yunnan and Sikang to western Szechwan. The First Front Army crossed the Wu River and marched toward Chiang Kai-shek's headquarters at Kweiyang. When he called for reinforcements from Yunnan, the Communist columns suddenly turned west and marched into Yunnan toward Kunming. Changing direction again, they crossed the Chinsha River and moved northward. The last great obstacle that faced them was the Tatu River. In an extremely difficult and hazardous operation, a small band of soldiers captured the Luting suspension bridge at the end of May. On 12 July, the First Front Army, having struggled through the Chiachin mountains, reached Maokung hsien in Szechwan, the base area of the Fourth Front Army. Mao and Chang Kuo-t'ao then joined forces and marched northward to Mao-erh-kai.

Although Mao Tse-tung had gained control of the central apparatus of the Chinese Communist party, his position was not yet beyond challenge by such other leaders as Chang Kuo-t'ao. The two men came into conflict in the summer of 1935, the basic issues being control of the Communist military forces and delineation of future political strategy. Chang Kuo-t'ao proposed moving west to establish a new base in Sikang; Mao Tse-tung proposed moving north to Shensi, where a Communist base under Kao Kang and Liu Chih-tan (qq.v.) already existed. As a result of this controversy, the Communist forces split. Chu Teh and Liu Po-ch'eng accompanied Chang on his westward trek, while Mao, P'eng Te-huai (q.v.), Lin Piao, and the First Front Army moved toward Shensi. The last phase of the march was the most dangerous: the non-Chinese minority peoples were hostile, and the boggy region known as the Grasslands was nearly impassable. Having braved these dangers, the First Front Army headed eastwards to the Latsek'ou pass, moved northward over the Minshan mountains, traversed the Liu-p'an mountains, and reached Shensi. They arrived at the remote village of Wa-yao-pao, just south of the Great Wall, in October 1935. In assessing the significance of the Long March, Mao Tse-tung later stated that: "The Long March is a manifesto. It proclaims to the world that the Red Army is an army of heroes . . . . The Long March is also an agitation corps. It declares to the approximately two hundred million people of eleven provinces that only the road of the Red Army leads to their liberation . . . . The Long March is also a seeding machine. It has sown many seeds in eleven provinces, which will sprout, grow leaves, blossom into flowers, bear fruit, and yield a harvest in the future."

When Mao Tse-tung and his 7,000 or so remaining troops arrived in the loesslands of Shensi, they represented a relatively minor force in the national politics of China. Nevertheless, by surviving the Nationalist encirclement campaigns and the Long March, they gave rise to a belief in their indestructibility. This legend was to be useful to the Chinese Communists in the next few years, as was the political and military experience they had gained in the Kiangsi soviet. Even the remote location of the Shensi base was to prove advantageous, for it provided a geographical base from which the Communists could extend their influence and authority into the traditionally conservative but highly important north China plain. However, the development of the Shensi base proceeded slowly, and the last of the Long March forces did not reach there until the spring of 1937.

MAO TSE-TUNG AT YENAN

The career of Mao Tse-tung from 1935 to 1949 is inseparable from the rise to power of the Chinese Communists. During these years Mao came to be the supreme planner and director of what the Communists termed the "revolutionary war," an unorthodox type of conflict which utilized the crisis created by the Japanese invasion and the discontent of the peasantry to project the Chinese Communist party as the most effective spokesman for China. The Japanese invasion, and the violence and social disorganization that it created, challenged both the Kuomintang and the Chinese Communist party, raising the basic political question of which party was the most responsible leader of the Chinese nation in its efforts to resist Japanese aggression. The Kuomintang, which had the advantage of controlling the National Government, in effect evaded that challenge and sought the aid of allies outside China to bolster its political power. The Chinese Communist party, as an insurgent force, blended flexibility, pragmatism, and increasingly skillful coordination of political and military measures in meeting the challenge. Mao Tse-tung's major political achievement during the Sino-Japanese war was the astoundingly rapid expansion of a competing administrative system behind the Japanese lines that showed itself to be more effective and more efficient than the National Government.

The Seventh Congress of the Comintern, meeting at Moscow in the summer of 1935, elected Mao Tse-tung *in absentia* to its central committee at the same time that it called for Communist parties throughout the world to pursue a united-front program in domestic politics. However, the key to Communist victory in China was not furnished by the Comintern, but by the Japanese, whose troop movements in north China created a wave of opposition to the continuance of the Kuomintang-Communist conflict. The Chinese Communists were quick to exploit this shift in public opinion. On 25 December 1935 the Political Bureau, meeting at Wa-yao-pao, called for the creation of an "Anti-Japanese National United Front." At a meeting of party activists two days later, Mao Tse-tung gave a report, "On the Tactics of Fighting Japanese Imperialism," in which he analyzed the political situation in class terms, stating that the Japanese "want to change the whole of China from a semicolony shared among several imperialist powers into a colony monopolized by Japan" and that the basic task facing the Chinese Communist party was "none other than to form a broad national revolutionary united front."

Political programs had to be integrated with military measures if full use were to be made of the Japanese threat as a catalytic agent of social change which could benefit the Communists. Mao Tse-tung's military doctrine was essentially pragmatic, influenced directly by his experience in the Kiangsi campaigns and indirectly by his knowledge of Chinese history and of such traditional Chinese military works as the *Sun-tzu ping-fa* (for further information, *see* Kuo Hua-jo). His first major statement in this field was *Strategic Problems of China's Revolutionary War*, a series of lectures given at the Red Army Academy in December 1935 and published in 1936. In this work, Mao declared that: "a vast semicolonial country that is unevenly developed politically and economically and that has gone through a great revolution; a powerful enemy [the Kuomintang]; a weak and small Red Army; and the agrarian revolution—these are the four principal characteristics of China's revolutionary war." With these as a basis, he analyzed the strategy (primarily defensive) and the tactics required to combat Nationalist military operations. To adapt themselves to the new situation created by the Japanese threat, the Communists had only to modify the details of Mao's analysis, making Japan the "powerful enemy." The resulting doctrine was simple and direct: because Japan was the national enemy of China, all responsible Chinese were duty-bound to support the "anti-Japanese national salvation movement." Guerrilla and mobile warfare techniques would permit the Chinese Communists to avoid positional engagements unless they chose to undertake such battles.

On 10 February 1937, less than two months after the Sian Incident (*see* Chiang Kai-shek) the Central Committee of the Chinese Communist party set forth the terms under which it would agree to cooperate with the Kuomintang in opposing the Japanese. Because party members had reservations about this policy, a national conference was held at Yenan in May 1937 to discuss the matter of collaboration. Mao Tse-tung delivered a report entitled "The Tasks of the Chinese Communist Party in the Period of Resistance to Japan," in which he affirmed that the Kuomintang and the Chinese Communist party could find a basis for co-operation. After the Sino-Japanese war began in July 1937, Mao began to stress differences of policy between the Chinese Communist party and the Kuomintang in responding to the national emergency. On 25 August 1937 the Political Bureau, meeting at Loch'uan, Shensi, endorsed a ten-point program intended to ensure that "the Communist party give leadership to the people throughout the country to win the anti-Japanese war and to oppose the Kuomintang's anti-popular policy." Although final agreement on terms of cooperation between the Kuomintang and the Chinese Communist party was not reached until 22 September 1937, by mid-August the Chinese Communist forces in north China had become the Eighth Route Army, with Chu Teh as its commander and P'eng Te-huai as his deputy. In January 1938 the National Government designated this force the Eighteenth Army Group. Communist forces in central China were reorganized as the New Fourth Army, with Yeh T'ing (q.v.) as commander and Hsiang Ying (q.v.) as deputy commander and political commissar. The Kuomintang-Communist alliance, though an uneasy one, lasted until January 1941, when units of the New Fourth Army came into conflict with Nationalist forces at Maolin in southern Anhwei. The battle, which lasted from 6 to 14 January and which resulted in an almost total rout of the Communists, is known as the New Fourth Army Incident.

Mao Tse-tung issued several major pronouncements on military doctrine in 1938. *Basic Tactics*, a collection of lectures on the day-to-day conduct of guerrilla warfare given at the Anti-Japanese Military and Political University, was published in book form in March. Another series of lectures, "On the Protracted War," appeared in *Chieh-fang* [liberation] in July. In it, Mao stated that "in the course of the prolonged, ruthless war, guerrilla warfare should not remain its old self but must develop into mobile warfare." On 7 July, the first anniversary of the war, the Society for the Study of the Anti-Japanese War published *K'ang-Jih yu-chi chan-cheng ti i-pan wen-t'i* [on all the problems of the anti-Japanese guerrilla warfare]. Its seventh and final chapter was Mao Tse-tung's "Questions of Strategy in the Anti-Japanese Guerrilla War," which stated that the war would be a three-phase conflict: strategic defense, strategic stalemate, and a Chinese offensive in which guerrilla tactics would be abandoned in favor of large-scale mobile warfare. Implicit in Mao's analysis was the assumption of ultimate victory over both the immediate foreign enemy, Japan, and the long-term domestic foe, the Kuomintang. That assumption was based on Mao's perception of the interaction of military and political factors in revolutionary war. He never lost sight of the practical objective of destroying the enemy's armed forces, but he viewed the political mobilization of the Chinese population as a matter of equal importance. Civil-military relations and the extension of territorial control were highly significant. To Mao, military conflict was a function of politics, and military victory was but a precondition of the radical transformation of a society.

During this period, Mao met his first Westerners. In the summer of 1936 the American journalist Edgar Snow made his way to the Communist headquarters at Paoan, interviewed Mao and other Chinese Communist leaders, and wrote a report on Mao's pre-1936 career that remains an important source of information. According to Snow, Mao was then a tall, pale figure, still gaunt from the strains of the Long March, with "large, searching eyes, wide, thick lips, and a strong chin with a prominent mole. His black hair was thick and long, on a head for which the Generalissimo was offering 250,000 silver dollars." In Mao, the earthiness and lively sense of humor of the peasant blended with the aloof and introspective qualities of the intellectual. He was an omniverous reader, an able writer, a man of boundless energy, a military and political planner of "considerable genius," and a man who was careless in personal habits and appearance but meticulous about details of duty. The American reporter Agnes Smedley, who first met Mao at night in his Yenan cave in 1937, offered another view: "The tall, forbidding figure lumbered toward us and a high-pitched voice greeted us. Then two hands grasped mine; they were as long and sensitive as a woman's.... His dark inscrutable face was long, the forehead broad and high, the mouth feminine. Whatever else he might be, he was an aesthete.... Despite that feminine quality in him he was as stubborn as a mule and a steel rod of pride and determination ran through his nature. I had the impression that he would wait and watch for years but eventually have his way.... His

humor was often sardonic and grim as if it sprang from deep caverns of spiritual seclusion." The publication and translation into Chinese of the writings of these and other Western journalists had a strong impact on public opinion, strengthening Mao's image as a patriotic and a highly moral man.

Mao Tse-tung's personal life during the 1930's also was interesting to many Chinese. After the execution of Yang K'ai-hui at Changsha in 1930, he had married Ho Tzu-chen, a graduate of the Hunan Normal School and a Communist. After the Long March, which Ho was one of the few women to survive, she and Mao separated. In an action that elicited sharp criticism from some of his colleagues in the Chinese Communist party, Mao sent his wife to Moscow, reportedly for medical treatment, and their separation became permanent. About 1939 he married Chiang Ch'ing, a film actress who had come to Yenan in 1937 from Shanghai, where she had been known as Lan-p'ing. Mao lost two of his siblings in the 1930's: Mao Tse-hung was executed at Changsha in 1930, and Mao Tse-t'an was killed in Kiangsi in 1935.

Mao Tse-tung gave considerable thought to the future beyond the Sino-Japanese war. Nearly a decade before he gained power, he attempted to place Chinese Communism within the framework of modern Chinese political history and to explain the "new democracy" he projected for China's future. He presented his analyses in "The Chinese Revolution and the Chinese Communist Party" (December 1939) and in "On New Democracy" (January 1940). Writing within the framework of conventional Leninist doctrine, Mao called for a two-stage revolution, first "national-democratic" and then "socialist." Mao recognized that the circumstances of an anti-imperialist revolution in a technologically backward land like China made it both possible and desirable for the Communists to gain the support of several classes. The "new democracy" principle, therefore, called for the Chinese Communists to champion a united front composed of workers, peasants, petty bourgeoisie and national bourgeoisie. These essays proved to be stimulating intellectual fare for many thoughtful Chinese—men who were weary of domestic strife and parochial leadership, frustrated by the rigid structure of political and social controls imposed by the Kuomintang, and anxious for a new sense of national purpose and direction.

Mao Tse-tung spoke to them, not as a theorist with a dream but as a political leader in the prime of his career as a professional revolutionary. "The aim of all our efforts," he said, "is the building of a new society and a new nation of the Chinese people."

At the Yenan base, the capital of the Shensi-Kansu-Ninghsia Border Region Government, Mao Tse-tung also began to assemble a brain trust, composed of Ch'en Po-ta (q.v.) and others, and to define the intellectual and cultural aspects of the Chinese Communist revolution. Mao's reputation as a Marxist theoretician, much touted after 1949, rests on two essays that were drawn from lectures he delivered in 1937: "On Practice," published in 1950; and "On Contradiction," published in 1952. These essays, both of which reflect Mao's basic lack of interest in systematic Marxist philosophy, are primarily notable in that they contain the seeds of Mao's theory of permanent revolution. Two installments of an essay entitled "Dialectical Materialism" appeared in a Shanghai journal in 1940 before Mao, dissatisfied with it, decided to stop publication. This essay was neither reissued nor referred to in later years by Mao or his adherents.

In both propaganda and program, the Chinese Communist leadership placed strong emphasis on the "cultural front." Mao Tse-tung set forth the party's cultural policy at the Yenan Forum on Literature and Art in May 1942. Quoting from Lenin's 1905 statement on "Party Organization and Party Literature," Mao defined the ideological basis of revolutionary literature, saying that literature must be shaped by a clear "party spirit" and must be designed for the masses—specifically for the workers, peasants, soldiers and petty bourgeoisie. Literature should come from the masses and should be consciously native; authors should draw material from China's rich storehouse of "revolutionary tales" and other folk tales which could be interpreted in an appropriately socialist manner. Literary language should be the language of the common people, and writing should reflect everyday Chinese life. Bourgeois themes and subjective inspiration should be rejected. Mao then turned to a consideration of the relationship between literature and politics, arguing that literature exists primarily for "class politics and mass politics," not for entertainment.

However, he recognized that literary works had to be artistically effective in order to serve the Chinese Communist party's political ends: "What we demand is unity of politics and art, of content and form, and of revolutionary political content and the highest possible degree of effectiveness in artistic form. Works of art, however politically progressive, are powerless if they lack artistic quality." In large part, Mao's Yenan talks represented a summation of theories which had been discussed in leftist literary circles in the 1930's. His call for linguistic and literary reforms echoed programs advocated by leaders of the League of Left-Wing Writers. His stress on the necessity for "popularization" was as much pragmatic as political, a reflection of the fact that pai-hua [vernacular] literature had become almost as incomprehensible to the average reader as the classical wen-yen. Nor did Mao's ideas go unchallenged, for a small but influential group of left-wing writers and literary critics opposed his dictates throughout the 1940's (see Hu Feng). Moreover, Mao's own attitude toward modern Chinese literature remained ambiguous. Despite his 1942 statements, he continued to use the classical tz'u form when writing poetry, and his political writings contained few references to modern works.

Even while busily planning strategy, exploring Marxist theory, and drawing designs for China's "revolutionary literature," Mao Tse-tung did not lose sight of his primary responsibilities as the leader of a rapidly growing political party. During the Yenan period, the Chinese Communists launched the cheng-feng [rectification] campaign, an ideological remolding movement designed to sharpen discipline in a geographically scattered organization which was becoming increasingly heterogeneous in social background as it recruited students from petty bourgeois families to supplement its predominantly peasant membership. In launching the campaign on 1 February 1942 with a statement on "Rectification of the Party's Style of Work," Mao said that "for the complete overthrow of the enemy, our ranks must be in order, we must all march in step, our troops must be seasoned, and our weapons fit. Unless these conditions are fulfilled, the enemy will not be overthrown." Thus, he indicated the emphasis on the "new democracy" was not to eclipse the essential role of the party as a professional elite controlling a mass movement. This cheng-feng campaign was not a blood purge on the Stalinist model, though it was aimed in part at members of the party elite who had incurred Mao's displeasure as Moscow-trained "dogmatists." In Mao's opinion, such men as Ch'en Shao-yü lacked sufficient experience in practical politics in China to balance the theoretical knowledge they had gained in the Soviet Union. Basically, however, the cheng-feng campaign involved the intensive indoctrination of all party members and cadres in Marxist-Leninist precepts as selected and interpreted by Mao Tse-tung and other senior leaders at Yenan. In the ensuing 12 months, more than 30,000 Chinese Communists received this training in small study groups. Nominally, the principal aim of the cheng-feng campaign was the unification of doctrinal standards so that directives issued by the party leadership would be understood clearly and implemented effectively at all levels. In practical terms, however, the movement was designed to consolidate the power of Mao Tse-tung as leader of the Chinese Communist party.

As a distinctive mechanism linking organization and ideology, the Chinese Communist party as it developed during the early 1940's was not intended to exist as an end unto itself. The party's main organizational purpose was to serve as a transmission belt, communicating party policies downward to people living in the Communist base areas and relaying their reactions upward to the top command at Yenan. An authoritative statement about the so-called mass line of political operations was Mao Tse-tung's 1943 statement "On Leadership." The key function of political leadership, as outlined by Mao, is to attain a pattern of continuous, organized interaction between party and populace—a pragmatic process aimed at increasing popular support. Though the Communist party in China, as elsewhere in the world, was by definition an authoritarian, hierarchic structure, its operations were based on planned, sustained, and flexible attention to points of direct contact between the party's representatives and the Chinese people.

Although the chronology of Mao's advance to full power over the party structure remains murky, the result is clear. In 1943 and 1944 he was elected chairman (chu-hsi) of the Central Committee and the Political Bureau. Mao also headed the five-man Secretariat of the Central Committee, then the party's top policy-making body. By the spring of 1945, when the Chinese Communist party held its Seventh National Congress at Yenan, party membership estimates had reached 1,200,000, with another 900,000 in the armed forces. This congress, the first to be held in China in nearly 20 years, reviewed wartime developments; elected a new Central Committee and a new Political Bureau, both of which were composed overwhelmingly of men who had proven their ability and their loyalty to Mao during the difficult war years; and adopted a revised party constitution. The preamble to the constitution stated that the Thought of Mao Tse-tung was necessary "to guide the entire work" of the party. A highlight of the meeting was Mao Tse-tung's "On Coalition Government," a statement that summed up Mao's political thought as it had evolved during the Yenan years, and that stated the conditions under which the Chinese Communists would cooperate with the Kuomintang in the postwar period.

Chiang Kai-shek was still the acknowledged national leader of China—the National Government was recognized by both the Western powers and the Soviet Union as the legitimate government of China—but by war's end the Yenan government controlled 19 Communist-organized bases with a population of over 90,000,000. The position in China of Mao Tse-tung and the Chinese Communists had changed drastically since the executions of 1927 and the exhaustion of 1935; Yenan's resolute anti-Japanese stand, lack of venality, and Spartan way of life had bred new vigor and self-assurance.

THE RACE TO POWER

Between 1944 and 1946 the United States government entered Chinese political life directly in an attempt to bridge the gap between the Kuomintang and the Chinese Communist party. With Communist consent, a United States Army observation group, headed by Colonel David D. Barrett and accompanied by the diplomat John S. Service, went to Yenan in 1944. In pursuit of its principal policy objective in China, the creation of a coalition government, Washington pressed for direct talks between Chiang Kai-shek and Mao Tse-tung. The Chinese Communists issued orders immediately after the announcement of Japan's surrender for troops under their command to "step up the war effort," accept the surrender of Japanese and puppet troops, and take over their arms and other equipment. Two telegrams from the commander of the Eighteenth Army Group to Chiang Kai-shek (13 and 16 August) stated that the Communists were proceeding independently in handling Japanese surrender and take over arrangements. Thus, the race for control of the vitally important regions of Manchuria and north China began. Despite this overt competition for authority, the Americans tried again. Ambassador Patrick J. Hurley flew to Yenan, greeted Mao at the airport with an Indian war whoop, and personally escorted Mao, Chou En-lai, and Wang Jo-fei (q.v.) to Chungking for discussions with Chiang Kai-shek about postwar government in China. The journey from Shensi to Szechwan was Mao's first airplane flight, and at its end he met Chiang Kai-shek for the first time since 1926. Mao and his party remained at Chungking for six weeks, 28 August–10 October, but the meetings held during this period had no practical results. In March 1946 General George C. Marshall, special representative of the President of the United States, flew to Yenan for conferences with Mao and other Chinese Communist leaders, but again the results were negative.

Mao Tse-tung remained in Shensi after the breakdown of American mediation efforts and the outbreak of full-scale civil war in China in the summer of 1946. He had been saddened in April 1946 when Ch'in Pang-hsien, Teng Fa, Yeh T'ing, Wang Jo-fei, and other Communists had been killed in a plane crash between Chungking and Yenan. By this time, he had formulated the famous slogan "all reactionaries are paper tigers," and he had become known as an innovator who had transformed traditional Marxism-Leninism into a practical creed for an underdeveloped Asian country. The English writer Robert Payne, who met Mao at Yenan in 1946, wrote of the elusiveness of the essential Mao: "then Mao came into the room. He came so quietly that we were hardly aware of his presence. He wore a thick brown Sun Yat-sen uniform which seemed to have been woven of goat's hair, and as he stood beside the towering P'eng Te-huai he looked slighter and smaller than I had imagined him . . . . There is hardly a photograph of him which resembles any other photograph, so strangely and so suddenly does he change. Today, he looked like a surprisingly young student, a candidate for a doctorate, and perhaps he played for his college: the shoulders were very heavy. The hair was very slick and long, the eyes large, the lips pursed, and he had no mannerisms. There was about him a kind of quietness such as you will find among people who have lived much alone . . . . He was fifty-three and looked twenty."

The sense of impending victory remained strong in Mao Tse-tung even though a Nationalist drive forced the Communists to evacuate Yenan in March 1947. The Communist top command split into two groups for safety. Mao Tse-tung, Chou En-lai, and Jen Pi-shih (q.v.) remained in northern Shensi, while Liu Shao-ch'i, Chu Teh, and an alternate working committee moved to the Communist-controlled Shansi-Chahar-Hopei base. Mao's command post during the winter of 1947 was the small town of Yang-chia-k'ou in Michih hsien. There, at a special meeting of the Central Committee on 25 December 1947, he summarized the methods of the People's Liberation Army in a report entitled "The Present Situation and Our Tasks." The ten principles of operation set forth in this statement included: "To attack dispersed, isolated enemy forces first; to attack concentrated, strong enemy forces later . . . . To take small and medium cities and extensive rural areas first; to take big cities later . . . . To make the wiping out of the enemy's effective strength our main objective . . . . To wipe out the enemy through mobile warfare, at the same time paying attention to the tactics of positional attack and capturing fortified enemy points and cities . . . . To make good use of the intervals between campaigns to rest, train, and consolidate our troops." This report, as well as other political and military estimates of the 1947–48 period, provides impressive evidence of Mao's analytic and planning capacities.

By early 1949 the top party leaders had been reunited in Hopei, where the North China People's Government under Tung Pi-wu had been established in August 1948 to unify all areas in the north that were under Communist jurisdiction. The seventh Central Committee of the Chinese Communist party held its second plenum on 7–24 March 1949 at Shih-chia-chuang. Meeting after the Communist capture of Tientsin and Peiping, this plenum stated that the center of gravity of the Communist effort in China was shifting from the rural areas to the cities, and announced that, henceforth, national industrialization would be the central objective of Chinese Communist economic policy. On 25 March, the Central Committee and other top party organs moved to Peiping.

In the context of national politics, Mao Tse-tung had established his supremacy over the now-vanquished Chiang Kai-shek, and in the context of international communism, he had established his independence from Comintern control. It was hardly surprising that Mao should view the interests of world communism from the standpoint of China, even as Stalin consistently viewed them from the standpoint of the Soviet Union.

THE PEOPLE'S REPUBLIC OF CHINA

In the spring of 1949 Li Tsung-jen (q.v.), then acting President at Nanking, made a final attempt to negotiate a peace settlement. Fighting resumed on 20 April, when the Chinese Communists crossed the Yangtze. By the end of May, both Nanking and Shanghai had fallen to the Communist forces. June saw the formation of a preparatory committee which was called upon by Mao Tse-tung to "convene a Political Consultative Conference, proclaim the founding of the People's Republic of China, and elect a democratic coalition government to represent it." On 30 June, the twenty-eighth anniversary of the founding of the Chinese Communist party, Mao published the celebrated essay "On the People's Democratic Dictatorship," a distillation of much of his earlier thinking about government. He wrote with a new frankness, made possible by the Communist military victory, in stating that the working class, the peasantry, the urban petty bourgeoisie, and the national bourgeoisie, "led by the working class and the Communist party, unite to form their own state and elect their own government; they enforce their dictatorship over the running dogs of imperialism— the landlord classes and the bureaucrat-bourgeoisie . . . . The combination of these two aspects, democracy for the people and dictatorship over the reactionaries, is the people's democratic dictatorship." What Mao did not make explicit, however, was as significant as what he did say. The power of the dictatorship in the new regime was to be exercised by the Chinese Communist party elite, a fact that was cloaked but not concealed by the concept of the people's democratic dictatorship.

The Chinese People's Political Consultative Conference, an "organization of the democratic united front of the entire Chinese people," met from 21 to 30 September 1949 and adopted the Common Program, a restatement of the ideas expressed in "On the People's Democratic Dictatorship" and in "On New Democracy," and the Organic Law of 27 September, which set up the Central People's Government of the People's Republic of China. On 27 September, Peiping was redesignated Peking and was named as the capital of the new regime. The Central People's Government was inaugurated on 1 October, with Mao Tse-tung as chairman and (in order of rank) Chu Teh, Liu Shao-ch'i, Soong Ch'ing-ling, Li Chi-shen, Chang Lan, and Kao Kang as vice chairmen. The new regime's highest policy-making body, the Central People's Government Council, was composed of these leaders and 56 other members elected by the Chinese People's Political Consultative Conference. The council was assigned responsibility for "leadership of the state apparatus at home" and for representation of the People's Republic of China in international affairs. Subordinate to the Government Council was the 20-man Government Administration Council, headed by Chou En-lai. It had jurisdiction over ministries, commissions, and committees. In addition to his government and party posts, Mao Tse-tung served as chairman of the People's Revolutionary Military Council.

The major domestic challenges Mao Tse-tung faced in 1949 were the rehabilitation of a country ravaged by hyper-inflation and war and the consolidation of authority throughout China. As Mao stated in "On the People's Democratic Dictatorship," the "serious problem is the education of the peasantry." The traditional greed for land and the individualism of the peasants needed to be overcome, as did the backwardness of rural areas with reference to modern agricultural methods. Beginning with the Agrarian Reform Law of June 1950, Mao worked to increase production in the rural areas. At the same time, a law of July 1950 was used to suppress potential sources of opposition. The holdings of landlords were confiscated in campaigns that were carried out at great human cost; by Mao's later admission, some 800,000 people lost their lives during the rural upheaval in China. Other suppressive movements of the early 1950's were the Three-Anti Movement, which tightened party control and rid the bureaucracy of former Kuomintang officials so that newly trained Communist cadres could replace them; the Five-Anti Movement, which was directed against urban businessmen; and the "study campaign for ideological reform," which imposed thought reform on intellectuals, reorganized the schools, and worked to create a variety of mass organizations.

The People's Republic of China made its debut in international Communist society near the end of Stalin's life. The Chinese Communist view of the international status of the new regime had been outlined by Mao Tse-tung in his 30 June 1949 essay and by Liu Shao-ch'i in his statement *On Internationalism and Nationalism* of 1 November 1948. To Stalin, however, Mao Tse-tung and his cohorts were unconventional and unpredictable men who in the past had opposed such Moscow-oriented Communists as Ch'en Shao-yü. In December 1949 Mao made his first trip outside China, traveling to Moscow to hammer out political, security, and economic arrangements with Stalin. His goals were the gaining of maximum Russian support for his country's projected industrialization program and the regaining of Chinese rights that had been compromised by the Sino-Soviet treaty of 1945. Nine weeks of negotiation with the aging but obdurate Stalin resulted in the signing, on 14 February 1950, of the Sino-Soviet Treaty of Friendship, Alliance, and Mutual Assistance. This thirty-year alliance provided for Soviet support of China in the event of attack by Japan or allies of Japan and for annual Soviet credits to China of US $60 million for five years. The Russians would remain in Port Arthur and Dairen until 1952, and the Chinese would recognize the independence of the Mongolian People's Republic. Having reached this compromise agreement, Mao left Moscow for China on 17 February.

Mao Tse-tung recognized the superiority of the Soviet Union in "socio-historic development" and technology; and he realized that China's dependence on the Soviet Union for aid in development required that ideas differing from those of the Russians not be expressed publicly. The alliance benefitted Peking during the Korean war (1950–53), providing China with war material and the United Nations forces with a source of deterrent concern. Although the Korean war severely drained China's resources and forced the temporary abandonment of the agricultural reform program, it served Mao Tse-tung's political purposes in Asia because it was regarded there as a conflict between East and West. The war ended with an armistice agreement on 27 July 1953. Peking claimed a psychological victory, saying that the so-called Chinese People's Volunteers, hastening to the aid of their North Korean brethren, had fought the Western world's strongest military and industrial power without being defeated. Within China, the Korean war permitted more rapid consolidation of political control and mobilization of human and material resources. It also allowed Mao to demonstrate to the Chinese people that "American imperialism" was a real and dangerous threat to the perimeters of their nation.

In 1954 the Central People's Government was reorganized according to the provisions of the new constitution. The highest organ of state authority became the National People's Congress, which was to meet every year and which consisted of 1,226 members, who were elected to four-year terms. The First National People's Congress, convoked in September 1954, elected Mao Tse-tung Chairman of the People's Republic of China. The congress theoretically had broad powers, but because it met but once a year, these powers actually were vested in the congress's Standing Committee, headed by Liu Shao-ch'i. The highest administrative organ was the State Council, headed by Chou En-lai. The Council of National Defense, chaired by Mao Tse-tung, was responsible for the direction of military affairs. Other important organs included the Supreme People's Court and the Supreme People's Procuratorate. Under the new constitution, Mao Tse-tung had wide-ranging and undefined powers. The most important administrative change made at this time was the return to a system of provinces, autonomous districts, and municipalities. The regional administration system was abolished, thus removing a source of potential challenge to the leadership of Mao Tse-tung.

The death of Stalin in March 1953 brought greater flexibility to Moscow-Peking relationships. The Soviet Union granted increased financial and technical assistance to China, and Nikita Khrushchev visited Peking in October 1954. In February 1956, however, Khrushchev stunned Chinese and other delegates to the Twentieth Congress of the Communist party of the Soviet Union when he bitterly denounced Joseph Stalin. Disunity in the Communist bloc increased after Soviet military force was used to suppress the Hungarian revolt in the autumn of 1956. Mao Tse-tung, though irritated by Khrushchev's surprise action in February, supported the Moscow leadership. For the first time, he played a part in international affairs that affected European as well as Asian Communism. Mao's public reaction to "de-stalinization" was expressed in "On the Historical Experience of the Dictatorship of the Proletariat," which appeared as an editorial in the *Jen-min jih-pao* of 5 April 1956. A second editorial, "More on the Historical Experience of the Dictatorship of the Proletariat," was published on 29 December 1956. Within the Chinese Communist party, the standard technique for dealing with deviant leftist or rightist influences was the so-called unity-struggle-unity formula. Mao Tse-tung was convinced that nothing similar to the Hungarian revolt could occur in China because the Chinese people understood their freedom and its limits. In 1956 Peking launched the Hundred Flowers Campaign (based on the slogan "let a hundred flowers bloom and a hundred schools of thought contend"), which ostensibly was designed to mobilize support for the Central People's Government among the intellectuals of China by permitting open criticism of political conditions.

In 1957 Mao Tse-tung produced a new analysis of "contradiction" to explain social relationships and the process of social change. The ideographs used to express this concept (mao-tun) meant spear and shield; they were derived from the traditional Chinese story of the man who boasted that he could supply both spears that could penetrate anything and shields that nothing could pierce. Mao had been fascinated by the concept for many years, and his 1937 essay "On Contradiction" had been published at Peking in the early 1950's. His

"On the Correct Handling of Contradictions Among the People" of February 1957 reiterated the view that human society develops through a continuous process of creating and resolving contradictions. In analyzing social contradictions in China and the ways in which the Chinese Communist party should seek to resolve them, Mao stated that "non-antagonistic" contradictions among the people should be resolved by education and by discussion aimed at showing deviants the error of their criticism and the validity of Communist policy. Contradictions "between ourselves and our enemies," on the other hand, could only be resolved by drawing a firm line "between ourselves and our enemies." Mao affirmed his belief that contradictions pervade society not only during the stage of transition to socialism but also after the establishment of a socialist system. They could only be resolved by "permanent revolution." Soviet leaders were, of course, reluctant to accept this idea. Mao's statement, though made in February 1957, was not released publicly until June of that year, a delay that gave rise to speculation outside China about the possibility of changes being made in it. By the time of its release, the Hundred Flowers Campaign, which had occasioned a surprising amount of strong criticism of both party and government, had been succeeded by an anti-rightist campaign which marked a return to censorship.

The launching of Sputnik I in 1957 and the gains made by the Russians in developing intercontinental ballistic missiles indicated, in Mao Tse-tung's view, a decisive military and psychological shift in world politics. He concluded that the Communist bloc, with its new military lead over the West, could take advantage of that imbalance to extend its authority in Asia, Africa, and other underdeveloped areas. He also believed that such an effort could help offset economic weaknesses and political tensions then manifesting themselves in China. The increasing importance of China in the Communist bloc was confirmed by the signature in October 1957 of a Sino-Soviet agreement on "New Technology for National Defense" under which the Soviet Union agreed to supply China with a sample atomic bomb and with relevant technological data. When in Moscow for meetings in November 1957 Mao gave strong public support to the Soviet leadership: "the socialist force has surpassed the imperial force. Our socialist camp should have a leader, and this is the Soviet Union. The enemy also has a leader, and this is America. If there is no leader, the strength will be weakened." In a speech to Chinese students at Moscow University on 17 November 1957 Mao said of the Communist bloc's strategic ascendancy that "the east wind prevails over the west wind."

Mao Tse-tung's role in the tangled history of Chinese domestic and foreign policies of the years after 1957 is difficult to determine or assess. Generally successful economic performance during the period of the first Five Year Plan (1953–57) generated efforts to launch a new phase of "socialist construction" in China. In the agricultural sector, this phase was marked by the program of drastic acceleration known as the Great Leap Forward, which was initiated by Mao Tse-tung in 1958 in connection with the undertaking of a second Five Year Plan. This program, which involved the mobilization of underemployed rural labor on an unprecedented scale, led to the collectivization of the rural population and the creation of communal farms and public works projects.

Radical experimentation in domestic planning was paralleled by commitment to a bolder and more bellicose strategy in foreign affairs. Mao's hostility to Khrushchev's plan to call a summit meeting in the hopes of settling the Middle Eastern crisis caused Khrushchev to make a hasty trip to Peking on 31 July 1958 for talks with Mao. Khrushchev then withdrew his summit offer. Mao increased international tensions in August by shelling the off-shore islands. The Peking Government later (September 1963) charged that at the time of the Sino-Soviet talks the leadership of the Communist Party of the Soviet Union had made "unreasonable demands designed to bring China under Soviet military control." Soviet reaction to Mao's harder line was indicated in June 1959, when the Soviet Union scrapped the October 1957 nuclear accord with China, seriously retarding Peking's nuclear program.

In December 1958 Mao Tse-tung announced his intention to relinquish his executive responsibilities. Liu Shao-ch'i succeeded him as chief of state and chairman of the National Defense Council in April 1959. At the same time, Chou En-lai replaced Mao as chairman of the Chinese People's Political Consultative Conference, with Mao becoming honorary chairman. Mao retained his top party posts, and he concentrated much of his time and attention on foreign affairs.

In the autumn of 1959, soon after his conversations with President Eisenhower at Camp David, Khrushchev went to Peking for discussions of such matters as the Sino-Indian border conflict that had broken out in August. When he and Mao stood side by side atop the Gate of Heavenly Peace to witness the celebrations on 1 October that marked the anniversary of the foundation of the People's Republic of China, it was clear that the occasion belonged to Mao Tse-tung alone. Mao's position in China was not affected seriously by the economic difficulties by then apparent in China or by the deterioration of Sino-Soviet relations. The Great Leap Forward ground to a halt, but adulation of Mao increased steadily.

Mao Tse-tung's approach to the international situation in the late 1950's and early 1960's was determined by concepts he had developed years before. In the 1927–37 period he had written that "we are to despise all enemies strategically and to take account of all enemies tactically." Strategically, with respect to the general situations of conflict and competition, revolutionaries must "despise the enemy," struggle with him, and dare to seize victory. Tactically, with respect to specific engagements, revolutionaries must take the enemy seriously and prudently select the forms of struggle that will isolate, fragment, and annihilate enemy power. In an August 1946 interview with Anna Louise Strong, Mao made another statement that was to have important effects on Chinese Communist political doctrine: "All reactionaries are paper tigers. In appearance, the reactionaries are terrifying, but in reality they are not so powerful. From a long-term point of view, it is not the reactionaries but the people who are really powerful." In the 1960's Mao stated that "American imperialism" should be despised strategically but respected tactically. The short-term potency of United States military power must be recognized in specific conflict situations. However, the long-term effectiveness of American power is illusory because that power rests on vulnerable political bases. By gaining active or passive support among anti-colonialist new nations of the Third World and by eroding the political bases on which the United States military position in these areas must rest, communism, Mao said, will triumph over the "paper tiger."

Similarly, Mao Tse-tung's attitude toward the Soviet Union continued to be shaped by both nationalistic and ideological considerations. He realized that Russian economic aid and technical advice had been important to China before and during the first Five Year Plan, but he also recognized that after the Soviet decision in 1960 to withdraw technical experts and to suspend shipments of equipment, the People's Republic of China had no prospect of receiving Soviet aid in its effort to alleviate adverse pressures on its economic development programs. Nor would Moscow offer Peking any prospect of direct, sustained assistance in China's efforts to develop nuclear weapons and intercontinental ballistic missiles. Impatient with the recalcitrance and "revisionism" of the Soviet leaders, Mao in the early 1960's made increasingly violent verbal attacks on the Soviet leadership, saying that the Chinese Communists were the true revolutionaries and guardians of Leninist orthodoxy and that Soviet polices were inconsistent and even pro-Western. At no point, however, did Mao argue that China was equal to the Soviet Union in industrial, military, or scientific capabilities. He confined his attacks to ideology and policy. The emergence of Peking as an aggressive and articulate center of neo-orthodoxy in the international Communist system made it impossible for the Soviet leadership to maintain the unity and direction that the Kremlin had symbolized for four decades. Such pronouncements and presumptions as those expressed in the Central Committee's highly critical letter to the Soviet party of 14 June 1963 created problems for Communist leaders throughout the world. The replacement of Khrushchev with Breznev and Kosygin in 1964 failed to alleviate Sino-Soviet tensions.

Disunity in the top command of the Chinese Communist party became apparent in the mid-1960's, culminating in the so-called Cultural Revolution of 1966. The summer of that year brought reports of the first mass rally in Peking of the Red Guards, most of whom were young people who were intent on expressing their frenzied adoration of Mao Tse-tung. The new

movement seemed to bear the imprint of Mao in that its dominant characteristics were an emphasis on revolutionary voluntarism and an impatience with bureaucratic constraints. The stated aim of the Cultural Revolution was to root out "old" customs, habits, and ways of thought and to rid China of lingering bourgeois and Western influences. Its major targets were those institutions in Chinese society that appeared to hinder "permanent revolution." The Chinese Communist party structure itself became a prime target in the drive to purge so-called revisionist leaders and tendencies. Teng Hsiao-p'ing, P'eng Chen and other senior Communist leaders were vilified as revisionists; Liu Shao-ch'i, for two decades the second-ranking party leader and Mao's apparent successor, also was subjected to public condemnation. At the same time, Mao's wife, Chiang Ch'ing, emerged from a quarter-century of seclusion to take a prominent public role as deputy chief of the group directing the Cultural Revolution. Perhaps the most important results of this political disarray and economic disruption were the designation of Lin Piao as Mao's heir apparent and the emergence of the People's Liberation Army, headed by Lin Piao, as a locus of authority in China.

In 1967 Mao Tse-tung made a number of public appearances, received several foreign delegations, and made two tours into the Yangtze valley. To a degree, his public appearances belied reports of his ill health. By the time of Mao's seventy-fourth birthday, in December 1967, the Cultural Revolution seemed to have subsided somewhat, and salvage and reconstruction activities seemed to have begun. Praise of the leadership and wisdom of Mao Tse-tung continued to permeate the mass media, and it was apparent that a major segment of the paper and metal industry was devoted to the production and distribution of materials contributing to the perpetuation of the Cult of Mao Tse-tung. In 1967 alone more than 76,000,000 sets of the *Selected Works of Mao Tse-tung* were published, along with some 47,000,000 copies of Mao's *Selected Readings* and 57,000,000 copies of his poems. Even more notable was the report that 350,000,000 copies had been produced of the little red booklet entitled *Quotations from Chairman Mao Tse-tung*. In addition, Mao Tse-tung badges by the hundreds of millions and portraits in all shapes and sizes contributed to the canonization process.

BASIC RECORDS OF MAO'S CAREER

To understand the Thought of Mao Tse-tung it is necessary to study his writings. Unfortunately, there is no comprehensive, critically edited edition of Mao's published writings available in Chinese. The Peking-published *Selected Works of Mao Tse-tung* is a bowdlerized series which virtually ignores Mao's pre-1927 writings and which provides the reader with notes that often are instructive but rarely are objective. The official Chinese version of the *Selected Works* was published in four volumes between 1952 and 1960, and an official English translation in four volumes appeared in the early 1960's. A volume of 29 articles, speeches, and directives from the 1928–49 period, *Selected Military Writings of Mao Tse-tung*, was published in 1963. The following year saw the issuance of a two-volume *Selected Readings from Mao Tse-tung's Works. Mao Tse-tung on Art and Literature* appeared in 1960. Beginning in 1957, Peking began to issue new editions of Mao Tse-tung's poetry. Most of the 40 or so poems that appeared in the next few years also were translated into English and French.

An important source of information about Mao Tse-tung's early career is Li Jui's authorized biography, *Mao Tse-tung t'ung-chih ti ch'u-ch'i ko-ming huo-tung*, published at Peking in 1957. Mao's autobiography, as told to Edgar Snow in 1936, is contained in Snow's *Red Star Over China*, published in 1937. One of Snow's later books, *The Other Side of the River: Red China Today* (1962), contains a section on Mao as Snow saw him at Peking in 1960. The most recent and most comprehensive account of Mao's career is Stuart Schram's *Mao Tse-tung*, published in England in 1966 and in the United States in 1967. Schram's introduction to his 1963 collection of documents, *The Political Thought of Mao Tse-tung*, provides a fine introduction to the mind and political personality of Mao. Other full-length studies of Mao are Jerome Ch'en's *Mao and the Chinese Revolution*, published in 1965, and John E. Rue's work on the Kiangsi period, *Mao Tse-tung in Opposition, 1927–1935*. Information about Mao Tse-tung appears in virtually every serious book and in most articles dealing with Chinese Communism. Although assessments of his career and inter-

pretations of his thoughts and actions vary, most scholars agree that the career of Mao Tse-tung and the rise of Chinese Communism are aspects of a single subject.

Mao Tun: *see* SHEN YEN-PING.

Masud Sabri
Alt. Mai-ssu wu-te

Masud Sabri (1886–April 1951), Uighur educational reformer in Sinkiang who served the National Government in the 1930's and 1940's. He was governor of Sinkiang in 1947–48. Because he refused to support the People's Republic of China, he was arrested and executed in 1951.

Born into a Uighur family in the Ili district of northwest Sinkiang, Masud Sabri was the son of a prosperous merchant and landlord who was a devout Muslim. After studying at the Muslim Technical School at Ining, the boy was sent to Turkey, where he enrolled at a military school. Upon graduation in 1907, he entered the natural science department of the University of Constantinople; and in 1910 he also became a student in the university's medical college. He completed his science courses in 1911, and he received a medical degree in 1914.

In 1915 Masud Sabri returned to Sinkiang to practice medicine. Having been influenced by progressive ideas during his student days in Turkey, he began to devote much of his time to the creation of educational opportunities for the Uighurs of Sinkiang. These efforts were viewed with suspicion by Yang Tseng-hsin (q.v.), the provincial governor of Sinkiang, who was attempting to consolidate Chinese rule in the Ili district and to prevent the spread of unrest from adjacent Russian areas. Thus, Masud Sabri's first modern school, established in Ili in 1916, was closed by order of the provincial authorities soon after the Russian Revolution. Masud Sabri established new schools, but all of them were closed by the authorities at Urumchi. In 1924 he was charged with having engaged in revolutionary activity and was imprisoned for ten months at Urumchi, but after his release he promptly returned to his eductional projects in Ili. By placing his schools under the nominal direction of men who were deemed conservative, he managed to avoid further confrontation with the provincial government. About this time, he decided to allow a few young men to study under him at his home-clinic; and by 1926 he had trained several young men in basic medical procedures and techniques.

The assassination of Yang Tseng-hsin in 1928 signaled the beginning of a new period of turmoil in Sinkiang. To protect his son and his nephew from possible harm, Masud Sabri sent them to Turkey to study in 1928. Discontent with Chinese rule soon led to movements and uprisings aimed at obtaining a degree of political autonomy for the minority groups of Sinkiang. Masud Sabri became involved in one of these movements early in 1934, when he left Ili for Aksu to serve as a political worker in a Uighur military force commanded by a local leader named Mahmoud. Later that year, when Ma Chung-ying (q.v.), the young Chinese Muslim leader from Kansu, fled to southern Sinkiang, Mahmoud's forces were defeated in battle. Masud Sabri fled to India and sailed from there to Tientsin, which he reached in November. He then went by train to Nanking, where he was welcomed by the city's Sinkiang community and by representatives of the National Government. He served as a Sinkiang delegate to the Fifth National Congress of the Kuomintang in 1935 and became a member of the party's Central Executive Committee. Masud Sabri established residence at Nanking, where younger members of his family, including those who had studied in Turkey, enrolled at Central University and the Central Military Academy.

After the Sino-Japanese war began in July 1937, Masud Sabri accompanied the National Government to Hankow and then to Chungking. In 1938–40 he served on the People's Political Council, and in 1942 he became one of two Muslims (the other being Ma Lin, a former governor of Tsinghai) on the 36-member State Council. Toward the end of the war period, when the National Government succeeded in removing Sheng Shih-ts'ai (q.v.) from his position of authority in Sinkiang, Masud Sabri was named supervisory commissioner for Sinkiang. His mission was to explain Nationalist policies to the ethnic minorities of the province and to win their support for the National Government. His task was made more difficult by the so-called Ili rebellion of November 1944. The insurgents soon won control of three northwestern districts adjacent to the Soviet Union, and they established the so-called East Turkestan Republic. In response to this new threat to Chinese rule in Sinkiang, Chiang Kai-shek sent Chang Chih-chung (q.v.) to Urumchi for negotiations with the rebels. In March 1946 Chang became governor of Sinkiang.

After Chang Chih-chung assumed office, Masud Sabri and his associate Mohammed Emin became leading spokesmen for that segment of the Uighur nationalist movement which stood for self-determination within the political framework of the Chinese republic. They worked with Chang in attempting to rally the Sinkiang populace against the Ili rebels. That the two men had considerable political influence was confirmed by the fact that the Ili insurgents were more hostile in condemning them than in criticizing Chang and the other Chinese officials. Chang's plan to name Mohammed Emin deputy governor of a reorganized Sinkiang provincial government was so strongly opposed by the Ili group that he named Burhan (q.v.) to the post instead.

In the summer of 1946 a new Sinkiang provincial government, headed by Chang Chih-chung and including representatives of the Ili group, was established at Urumchi. Masud Sabri continued to work for self-determination under Chinese rule, and in May 1947 he became the first non-Chinese governor of Sinkiang. His appointment, designed to placate the non-Chinese groups in Sinkiang, served only to increase the hostility of the Ili group and other politically active Uighurs, who regarded Masud Sabri as a tool of the Nationalist authorities at Nanking. New disturbances soon wracked southern and eastern Sinkiang. Although Chinese military forces led by Sung Hsi-lien (q.v.) were deployed to sustain the Urumchi government, the coalition fell apart in the summer of 1947. The Ili leaders demanded that Masud Sabri be removed from office, but the Nationalist authorities refused. The situation remained deadlocked throughout 1948. At the end of December, the National Government, then under extremely heavy pressure because of the rapid expansion of Communist power in China, removed Masud Sabri from the governorship and named Burhan to succeed him. In the autumn of 1949 Chinese Communist forces commanded by P'eng Te-huai (q.v.) moved through northwest China and occupied Sinkiang. Masud Sabri refused to support the new regime. In April 1951 he was arrested, charged with being a counter-revolutionary plotting against Communist rule, and executed.

Mei Kuang-ti   梅 光 廸
  T. Ti-sheng   廸 生
  Chin-chuang   董 莊

Mei Kuang-ti (22 January 1890–27 December 1945), scholar and editor of the conservative literary journal *Hsueh-heng* [the critical review]. Though a pioneer in the introduction of Western literature to China, he was an uncompromising opponent of the Chinese literary movements of the 1920's. He taught Chinese at Harvard University from 1924 to 1936.

Hsuancheng, Anhwei, was the native place of Mei Kuang-ti. His father, a schoolmaster and a firm believer in memorization of the Chinese classical texts, instilled in the young Mei a genuine love of traditional Chinese literature and learning. Mei Kuang-ti took the first level of civil-service examinations at the age of 12. After completing his secondary education in Anhwei, he went to Peking, where he attended Tsinghua College. He learned English in a single year of solitude and diligent study, competed for a government scholarship in 1911, and won both a scholarship and admission to the University of Wisconsin. After spending two years in Madison, Wisconsin, he transferred to Northwestern University, from which he was graduated in 1915. He then entered the graduate school of Harvard University.

Mei Kuang-ti's four years at Harvard deeply influenced his intellectual development. Of primary importance was his association with Irving Babbitt, professor of literature and prophet of the New Humanism, the philosophical and critical movement which flourished briefly in the United States during the 1920's under the influence of Babbitt and Paul Elmer More. In the New Humanism, Mei Kuang-ti saw affinities with China's cultural heritage and possible approaches to the uncertainties that beset the contemporary intellectual scene in China.

Soon after his arrival at Harvard, Mei began a lengthy and often turbulent correspondence with Hu Shih (q.v.), then a graduate student of philosophy at Columbia University. The only record of this literary debate, which concerned the pros and cons of literary reform in China, is contained in Hu Shih's published diaries. Even that fragmentary and admittedly one-sided account reveals the deep seriousness of these young Chinese students, newly exposed to Western learning and distressed by conditions in their homeland, and their earnestness in seeking out solutions. It was through these arguments, Hu Shih wrote, that he gradually formulated his ideas regarding literary reform and began to experiment with the writing of poems in pai-hua [the vernacular]. Mei Kuang-ti was opposed to Hu's position, not because he was unaware of the moribund state of the old Chinese literary tradition, but because he believed that Hu Shih's theories and practices were based on fallacious literary premises. Mei argued that Hu oversimplified the complex relationship between language and literature and underestimated the importance of tradition in the process of poetic composition. In 1917 Hu Shih returned to Peking to raise the banner of literary reform with his articles in the *Hsin ch'ing-nien* [new youth], and Mei Kuang-ti remained at Harvard to continue his literary studies with Irving Babbitt.

Although Professor Babbitt had no direct access to Chinese sources, and had not studied Chinese, he impressed Mei Kuang-ti with his profound understanding of Confucius as a moralist and humanist, his interpretation of the early Taoists in the light of modern Western naturalism, his vision of the essential unity of the cultures of East and West, and his interest in working for a "humanistic international." Babbitt's devotion to classicism and his impatient opposition to the philological approach to the study of Western literature made him a controversial scholar. Mei Kuang-ti regarded Babbitt as a man who shared his own deep appreciation of traditional Chinese culture, a fellow visionary who looked forward to a synthesis of the central and enduring elements in both Eastern and Western traditions, and a kindred spirit who also was waging a lonely but heroic crusade against current literary fads.

In 1920 Mei Kuang-ti returned to China and became chairman of the English department at Nankai University. He moved to Nanking in 1921 to head the English department at

Southeastern University (after 1927, Central or Chung-yang University). Among his students was Ching-ying Lee, who had traveled from Canton to become one of the eight women in the first coeducational class at the university. She and Mei were married in 1927, after which she went to the United States for graduate work at Radcliffe College and returned to China to teach English language and literature courses.

In 1922 Mei Kuang-ti, together with Wu Mi (q.v.) and other colleagues at Southeastern University, founded *Hsueh-heng* [the critical review] to oppose the Chinese literary revolution. In the first issue of *Hsueh-heng*, Mei wrote a scathing indictment of the advocates of the new literary movement. By that time, pai-hua had been established as a medium of instruction in Chinese elementary schools and had begun to gain wide acceptance as a medium for communication and writing. The rapid success of the "literary revolution" inevitably encouraged charlatanism. Some of the new writers were ignorant of their own literary heritage, and their understanding of Western literature was similarly shallow and limited. Mei criticized the writers of the new literary movement for their fondness for self-aggrandizement, their lack of objectivity and humility, their fanaticism, their intolerance, and their increasing indulgence in personal, vituperative attacks on those who disagreed with them. Mei Kuang-ti never opposed Western learning, but he did oppose the indiscriminate iconoclasm of the literary reformers who wanted to replace or destroy everything in the Chinese tradition and who, without sufficient knowledge of the central and enduring features of Western philosophy or literature, emphasized much that was peripheral, transient, or decadent. Mei did not oppose the use of pai-hua; he had a great appreciation of many Chinese literary works written in the colloquial language and recognized it as a legitimate style of writing. However, he did not subscribe to the view that pai-hua should completely supersede classical Chinese, although he realized that the classical language needed to be stripped of archaisms and empty rhetoric in order to become a more flexible instrument capable of expressing modern ideas.

As part of their efforts to provide perspective and balance to Chinese understanding of Western literature, the editors of the *Hsueh-heng* devoted many pages to translations and to essays about the Western writers they deemed important. Mei Kuang-ti's contributions dealt chiefly with literary critics who, not content with analyzing the formal aesthetic qualities of a literary work, used literary criticism to express their moral and philosophical insights in such a manner that they became critics or prophets of their age—writers such as Carlyle, Arnold, and, of course, Irving Babbitt. This concept of the man of letters was one which for Mei Kuang-ti had been confirmed by the New Humanists in the United States; but it also was profoundly Confucian, central to the Chinese literary tradition. For Mei, the heroes in his own culture were those who were able to exemplify the high moral life both in writing and in action—men such as Ou-yang Hsiu in the eleventh century and Tseng Kuo-fan in the nineteenth, who were at once statesmen, moralists, and men of letters.

What Mei and his colleagues of the *Hsueh-heng* group refused to accept was that the literary reform movement in China was motivated chiefly by a desire for social and political reform. The urgent demands and the convulsive changes of the republican period made a true appreciation of the best in both Eastern and Western cultures, much less their attempted synthesis, a luxury that Chinese intellectuals could no longer afford. Nevertheless, Mei Kuang-ti saw more clearly than some of the leaders of literary reform the probable consequences of undermining literary principles and of debasing literary values for political ends. His opposition to the modern literary movement was based on this uncompromising refusal to view literature as a response to the practical needs of the time.

While he was introducing Western literary thought to Chinese readers through the pages of *Hsueh-heng* and other journals, Mei Kuang-ti was simultaneously playing the role of cultural ambassador on the other side of the Pacific. From 1924 to 1936, except for an interval of one academic year (1930–31) when he was acting dean of the college of arts at Central University, he taught Chinese at Harvard University. Y. R. Chao (Chao Yuen-ren, q.v.) had preceded Mei as instructor of Chinese at Harvard from 1921 to 1924. Mei's relatively long tenure in the post had an important influence on the early study of Chinese language and literature in the United States. In his courses, Mei attempted to impart to his students what he felt to be the essential elements of China's traditional civilization.

In 1936 Mei Kuang-ti returned to China to become head of the English department at National Chekiang University and assistant dean of its college of arts and sciences. The Sino-Japanese war broke out in July 1937, and Chekiang University was moved to Tsunyi, Kwei-chow, in 1939, where it remained until the end of the war. In 1939 Mei Kuang-ti became dean of the newly independent college of arts. As an important administrator in the university, he devoted much energy to maintaining high educational standards in the face of great hardships. In addition to his regular adminis-trative duties, greatly complicated by material shortages and by psychological uncertainties, he had to be concerned with the personal welfare and physical survival of his students. Many of Mei's students stood in awe of him and were ill at ease in his presence, but he was unstinting in his efforts to encourage and support students in whom he saw promise. He also was known for acts of personal kindness that at times bordered on impulsive generosity: emptying his pockets for a student who had to go on a journey; raising funds for one who required an operation; or risking his own safety to rescue one who had been secretly arrested on false political charges.

At Tsunyi, Mei Kuang-ti continued to give courses on English literature, concentrating on the critics and essayists of the eighteenth and nineteenth centuries. His published writings included articles about these writers and analyses of twentieth-century events in Europe with reference to their historical and intellectual backgrounds. From 1938 to 1945 Mei also served on the People's Political Council at Chungking.

By February 1945, Mei Kuang-ti had become seriously ill. His diary for 1945 contains many references to writings which he now began to feel that he would not live to complete. He died on 27 December 1945. Among the many notes and drafts of incomplete manuscripts he left were outlines for books on Han Yü, which were to be written in both English and Chinese. Mei also intended to write an intellectual history of the West for Chinese readers, including biographical and critical studies of 20 or 30 outstanding figures from Voltaire to Nietzsche. These plans were consistent with the pattern of Mei Kuang-ti's career. His mission was to introduce Western literature to China and Chinese literature to the West, treating his subjects in historical perspective and with a sense of tradition, and to uphold a concept of literature which related it to the moral and philosophical life, a concept both Confucian and neo-Humanistic.

Mei Lan-fang   梅 蘭 芳
  T. Wan-hua   畹 華

Mei Lan-fang (22 October 1894–8 August 1961), Peking opera star who was the outstanding figure in the Chinese theater during the first half of the twentieth century and who was the last link with the great old acting tradition of imperial China.

Yangchow, Kiangsu, was the native place of Mei Lan-fang. His grandfather, Mei Ch'iao-ling, a well-known actor in the late Ch'ing period, directed a popular Peking opera troupe and played the *tan* [female] roles. He had two sons and one daughter. The elder son, Mei Yü-t'ien, was a theater musician of note. The younger son, Mei Chu-fen, the father of Mei Lan-fang, was an actor. He died when Mei Lan-fang was only three, leaving him to be brought up by Mei Yü-t'ien.

Mei Lan-fang received his first lessons in dramatic art at the age of seven. After a year of private study, he was sent to the household of another relative to continue his studies with a group of boys. Their teacher was Wu Ling-hsien, a friend and former professional colleague of Mei Lan-fang's grandfather. Wu Ling-hsien took interest in the young Mei and gave him extra coaching. In 1904, at the age of ten, Mei Lan-fang made his first stage appearance in Peking. Three years later, he enrolled as a senior student at the famous Hsi-lien-ch'eng (Fu-lien-ch'eng) Dramatic Training School and began to appear regularly with the school's troupe in the principal Peking theaters. At the same time, he became the private pupil of the *tan* actor Wang Yao-ch'ing (q.v.). Mei's later stage technique incorporated a number of Wang Yao-ch'ing's ideas.

After completing his training at the Hsi-lien-ch'eng school, Mei Lan-fang joined a profes-sional troupe and began to appear regularly. By 1913, he had begun to attract the attention of the theater audiences of Peking through the quality of his acting, the charm of his stage personality, and his attractive appearance in make-up. Although he still was ranked as a second-grade actor, his services as a performer of *tan* roles were in constant demand for both public and private performances. In the autumn of 1913 Mei was invited to go to Shanghai by the management of the Tan-kuei ti-i wu-t'ai, a well-known theater in the great port city. His senior partner on that occasion was Wang Feng-ch'ing, an actor of the *sheng* [male] roles with whom Mei had appeared regularly in Peking. The two northern players enjoyed a resounding success in Shanghai, and Mei Lan-fang's reputation as a new star in the Peking-style drama was made during their 45-day appearance.

Upon his return to Peking, Mei staged a number of new plays which he had learned in Shanghai. These included several *tao ma tan* [sword, horse, woman] dramas. Until then it had not been customary for a Peking actor of the woman's roles to combine the fencing, dancing, and singing techniques as Mei did in these new plays. The conservative Peking audiences received his innovations with enthusiasm. Mei also began to experiment with a new style of contemporary costume drama, then in vogue in Shanghai, which had impressed him with its spirit and novelty. He staged his first modern play of this kind in 1914 in Peking. Entitled *Nieh-hai po-lan* [the waves of the evil sea], the play dealt with the problems of women forced into prostitution. Mei continued to experiment with this type of drama until 1916, when he abandoned these adventures in a semi-Western idiom to concentrate solely on the classical techniques.

Mei Lan-fang paid his second visit to Shanghai in December 1914. His brilliant interpretation of traditional roles further enhanced his reputation. It was during this period that Mei first met Ch'i Ju-shan (q.v.), a scholar and drama expert who had traveled in Europe and who was deeply concerned with the problems of the old Chinese theater in an age of transition. Ch'i Ju-shan was destined to have a great influence on Mei's artistic development and stage career. He became the actor's adviser, playwright, impresario, and constant companion, and his name is inseparable from any serious discussion of Mei's art. The first important result of this collaboration was the staging of a new play based on an ancient legend, *Ch'ang-o pen-yueh* [Ch'ang-o flies to the moon] for the autumn festival of 1915. In the production of this play, devised by Ch'i Ju-shan, traditional stage garb was abandoned for authentic ancient models, and old dance forms were used. It was an immediate success. Soon afterwards, Mei performed the new play before an audience of American university alumni in Peking, the first public indication of an awakening foreign interest in Mei's art. *Ch'ang-o pen-yueh* was one of the more popular plays in Mei's repertoire for several years. Ch'i soon produced another new dance play for Mei called *Tai-yü tsang-hua* [Tai-yü buries the blossoms]; it was based on an episode from the great Chinese novel, *Hung-lou-meng* (*Dream of the Red Chamber*), and it created a furor during the actor's third visit to Shanghai in the autumn of 1916.

In the spring of 1919 Mei Lan-fang was invited to Japan to appear at the Imperial Theater in Tokyo. This was the first time that a Chinese actor had been asked to perform outside his own country. Mei appeared for a season of four weeks in Tokyo and Kobe, and the Japanese, much impressed by his acting, received him with tremendous enthusiasm. In April 1922 the Chinese community of Hong Kong invited Mei to perform there before the Prince of Wales, who was scheduled to visit the colony. It was a signal honor for the 27-year-old actor, but his appearance had to be cancelled when a general strike completely paralyzed Hong Kong. The disappointed Chinese community renewed its offer in the autumn, and in October 1922 Mei appeared in Hong Kong at the T'ai-p'ing theater. In December 1922 Mei was asked to appear with other actors at a series of command performances given in the imperial palace in Peking on the occasion of the marriage of P'u-yi (q.v.), the last of the Manchu emperors. In 1924 Mei returned to Japan at the invitation of the management of the Imperial Theater in Tokyo and again scored a great success.

By this time, persons as diverse as the Crown Prince of Sweden and Rabindranath Tagore had seen Mei Lan-fang perform in Peking and had carried enthusiastic reports of his brilliance to their own countries. At a banquet in 1926 John van Antwerp MacMurray, the retiring American minister to China, expressed the hope that Mei would visit the United States with his troupe. This was one of an increasing number of suggestions that the actor should display his talents in the West, and Mei was eager to go if means could be found. In 1929 Li Shih-tseng (q.v.), who was a prominent patron of the Chinese drama and an old friend of Ch'i Ju-shan, prevailed upon several prominent Chinese bankers to finance a tour of the United States for Mei and his troupe; the actors sailed from Shanghai on 29 December 1929.

After his arrival in the United States, where he first gave a private performance at the Chinese embassy in Washington, Mei was advised to put himself under the direction of F. C. Kapakas, a professional producer. Mei wisely decided to take this advice. Kapakas insisted upon a month of hard rehearsals and adaptations of staging before he would permit Mei to make his debut on Broadway. A special program was prepared in English, and an English-speaking Chinese commentator was trained to explain details to an American audience completely unfamiliar with Chinese stage traditions. In presenting this program to the American public, Mei was assisted by Chang P'eng-ch'un, a younger brother of Chang Po-ling (q.v.) and a devotee of the Chinese drama, who handled the troupe's public relations during its American tour. Mei's first public performance in the United States took place on 16 February 1930 at the 49th Street Theater in New York. It was an outstanding success, and the drama critics were unanimous in their praise of the troupe. Mei played for five weeks in New York, the last three at the Imperial Theater, after which he performed in Chicago for two weeks and in San Francisco. He then went to Los Angeles for a 12-day appearance at the Philharmonic Auditorium. At the conclusion of this triumphant tour, Mei was awarded honorary degrees by both the University of Southern California and Pomona College. On his way back to China, he appeared for 12 days in Honolulu. The troupe reached Peiping in September 1930.

When the Japanese attacked Mukden in September 1931, Mei Lan-fang, because of professional obligations to his troupe and personal obligations to his young family, decided to move to Shanghai even though such a move would end long-established partnerships with people like Ch'i Ju-shan and Wang Feng-ch'ing. Shanghai knew Mei well and offered him greater scope as a professional base. The next few years were very active ones for Mei, who was then at the height of his powers, and his fame and reputation grew steadily.

In 1935 Mei was invited to visit Russia with his troupe, as was Miss Butterfly Wu (Hu Tieh, q.v.), China's leading film star. They traveled together to Russia and then visited Italy, France, Germany, and England. It had long been Mei's ambition to play in Europe, particularly in London, but because of the uncertain political situation, no theatrical producer was willing to finance such a venture. He disappointedly left London and returned to China.

In the autumn of 1936 Mei performed in Peiping for the last time before the Sino-Japanese war. With the outbreak of fighting in north China in July 1937, he left Shanghai with his family and moved to Hong Kong. In May 1938 he played at the Lee Theater in Hong Kong for 18 days, his last appearance before world war broke out. He continued to live quietly in Hong Kong until the Japanese seized the colony in December 1941. After the occupation, the Japanese invited Mei to resume his career again and promised the necessary financial assistance. Mei had long before decided that he would never consent to appear before the enemies of his country, and he refused to accede to the repeated Japanese requests. He even grew a mustache to emphasize his refusal to perform the *tan* roles for the Japanese. The Japanese authorities finally granted Mei and his family safe conduct and a special plane to return to Shanghai. For the remainder of the war, Mei lived in quiet seclusion, devoting his time to teaching private Chinese pupils and keeping himself in rigid training for his return to the stage.

The end of the War in the Pacific in 1945 found Mei's old troupe widely scattered. Gradually he was able to reassemble his company and to begin to stage large-scale productions. Mei had lost none of his appeal, and his appearances invariably drew full houses. However, the chaotic economic conditions of the postwar period made the successful running of large theatrical troupes virtually impossible. Like others in his profession, Mei was faced with difficult financial problems, and between 1945 and 1948 his stage appearances steadily diminished. In 1947 he made his first color film, *Sheng-ssu-hen* (translated as *The Wedding in a Dream*), a play from his personal repertoire which he had made famous many years before. His last stage performance before the Communists came to power in China was in April 1947.

The establishment of the Central People's Government in Peking in 1949 marked the beginning of a new period in Mei's career. The Chinese Communists, recognizing Mei as one who commanded a unique affection in China both for his artistic accomplishments and for his patriotic behavior during the Japanese occupation, made every effort to utilize his name and his achievements to support the prestige of the regime. Mei was given honorary positions in the new cultural hierarchy. He became a member of the national committee of the All-China Federation of Literary and Art Circles, and in 1951 he was named president of the Chinese Drama and Ballad Research Institute. He was encouraged to resume an active stage program and was asked to take his troupe on tour, giving performances to workers and military groups in many parts of China as well as making more orthodox stage appearances. He made a film entitled *Wu-t'ai i-shu Mei Lan-fang* [the stage art of Mei Lan-fang], which presented a summary of his life story and excerpts from some of the plays he had made famous, including *Kuei Fei tsui-chiu* [the drunken beauty], *Pa Wang pieh-chi* [the emperor's farewell to his favorite], *Yü-chou feng* [the sword of the universe], and *Pai-she chuan* [the legend of the white snake]. In 1956 Mei and a troupe of 80 went to Japan, where they performed these plays in all the principal cities. Mei also visited the Soviet Union by official request.

Mei Lan-fang died at Peking on 8 August 1961, at which time his accomplishments and contributions were highly praised by the Chinese Communist authorities. A year later, the first anniversary of his passing was marked by a series of commemorative activities, including a major exhibition dealing with his theatrical career, the holding of special meetings, the issuance of commemorative postage stamps, and the publication of a collection of his post-1949 writings. T'ien Han (q.v.), chairman of the Union of Chinese Stage Artists, wrote a special article for the *Jen-min jih-pao* [people's daily] in which he said that many Westerners knew of only two Chinese personages, Confucius and Mei Lan-fang.

Mei Lan-fang was the outstanding figure of the Chinese theater during the first half of the twentieth century and the last link with the old acting tradition of imperial China. Conservatives have sometimes criticized his debasement of traditional forms, and it is true that the spectacular presentations of some of his earlier theatrical experiments were over-elaborate, but such errors in judgment were unavoidable during a period of transition and experimentation. Mei Lan-fang's career coincided with a crucial period in the history of the Chinese classical theater and he played a major cultural role in preserving the essential heritage of Chinese dramatic art in a period of great social change during which many of his countrymen were confused and frustrated by the impact of the West upon China. The story of Mei Lan-fang's life is, in a sense, the story of the turbulent decades which defined the emergence of a modern China. Mei's professional contributions to the Chinese theater were diverse. The creation of female roles in which singing, dancing, and acrobatic techniques are combined in the performance of a single actor—a development for which Mei was largely responsible—has had a profound effect on the art of his successors. His revival of old dancing techniques infused new vigor and charm into the classical theater, while his innovations in make-up and costume substantially enhanced stage presentation.

Mei Lan-fang was a man of great personal integrity and strength of character, and these qualities, together with his artistic genius, earned him a position in Chinese society unknown to any previous actor. His first wife died, as did the son she bore him. His second wife, Fu Chih-fang, was a talented actress before her marriage. She bore him a son, Pao-chiu, and a daughter, Pao-yueh, both of whom pursued theatrical careers.

Mei Yi-ch'i　　　　　　梅 貽 琦
　T. Yueh-han　　　　　月 涵
　West. Y. C. Mei

Mei Yi-ch'i (29 December 1889–19 May 1962), engineer and educator who headed Tsinghua University from 1931 until 1949. He later served as minister of education in the National Government in Taiwan.

Tientsin was the birthplace of Mei Yi-ch'i, the eldest son of a sheng-yuan and salt administration official who traced his ancestry to Mei Yin, a brigand general who served the first emperor of the Ming dynasty. After a childhood that was uneventful except for the family's flight to Paoting in the summer of 1900 to avoid the turbulent aftermath of the Boxer Uprising, in 1904 Mei Yi-ch'i entered the First Private Middle School at Tientsin, the forerunner of the Nankai Middle School (*see* Chang Po-ling), as one of its first students. After graduation in 1908, he entered the Kao-teng hsueh-t'ang in Paoting, where he prepared for the Boxer Indemnity Fund Scholarship examinations in 1909, thus becoming one of the forty-seven candidates chosen that year for study in the United States.

From 1910 to 1914 Mei Yi-ch'i studied electrical engineering at the Worcester Polytechnic Institute in Massachusetts, earning a B.S. degree. He then returned to China and, after a brief period of service with the YMCA, in 1915 began teaching at Tsinghua College, an institution which had been established specifically to prepare students for study in the United States on Boxer Indemnity Fund scholarships. He was universally liked and respected as a teacher, and in 1926 he was elected dean of the faculty. Two years later he was made director of the Chinese Education Mission in the United States and was charged with supervision of the scholarship students.

In 1931 Mei Yi-ch'i's career at Tsinghua was crowned by his appointment as president, a post he was to hold for more than 20 years. At the time of his appointment, Tsinghua had not grown much beyond its original preparatory-school status. Under Mei's administration, it developed into one of China's most important universities. To Tsinghua's three colleges of arts, sciences, and law, he soon added a college of engineering, consisting of departments of civil, mechanical, and electrical engineering. Mei Yi-ch'i also instituted a policy of holding competitive examinations, open to the graduates of all Chinese colleges and universities, for Tsinghua scholarships for advanced study in the United States. To meet the specific needs of China, fields of specialization were specified for scholarship recipients, and 25 students were sent abroad each year on this basis.

After the outbreak of the Sino-Japanese war in 1937, the fall of Peiping, and the closing of Tsinghua University, the National Government at Nanking directed Peking University, Tsinghua University, and Nankai University to amalgamate temporarily as Changsha lin-shih ta-hsueh [Changsha emergency university]. Mei and the other two presidents constituted the executive committee of the new institution at Changsha. Japanese advances soon necessitated the removal of the university to Kunming, where it became Southwest Associated University (Kuo-li hsi-nan lien-ho ta-hsueh). The executive committee continued to administer the university, but the burden of direction fell on Mei Yi-ch'i because the other two presidents, Chiang Monlin (Chiang Meng-lin) and Chang Po-ling (qq.v.), were busy with other responsibilities. Under his leadership, the three universities that constituted Southwest Associated University worked harmoniously and conscientiously together so that high academic standards were maintained throughout the war. In recognition of Mei Yi-ch'i's achievements, he was awarded an honorary degree by the Worcester Polytechnic Institute in 1940.

After the Japanese surrender in August 1945, Southwest Associated University continued to operate in Kunming for another year while the three constituent universities began the work of restoring their campuses. Mei Yi-ch'i flew to Peiping in November 1945 to supervise work on the Tsinghua campus, which had been commandeered during the war by the Japanese army and had been damaged seriously. Mei and his hard-working colleagues managed to reopen Tsinghua University for classes on 10 October 1946. Although Mei's restoration efforts achieved notable results in 1946–47, his work was made increasingly difficult by the developing civil war between the Nationalists and the Chinese Communists. In December 1948 the Chinese Communists advanced on Peiping and took control of the Tsinghua campus. Mei flew to Nanking on 21 December, where he served on a committee which gave aid to professors who had escaped from Communist-occupied areas. Early in 1949 he went to Shanghai and then to Canton. In June, he went to Paris to participate in a conference on science information and remained there to attend a UNESCO meeting in September. At year's end, he went to New York to confer with members of the China Foundation for the Promotion of Education and Culture about the safeguarding of the Tsinghua endowment fund. He remained in the United States for six years, working to make the best use of the proceeds from the endowment fund. Some of this money was used to establish teaching fellowships for Chinese scholars in the United States and graduate scholarships for American students specializing in Chinese studies, and some was used to purchase books and equipment for colleages and institutions in Taiwan.

In 1953 the National Government in Taiwan established a cultural affairs advisory committee in the United States and appointed Mei Yi-ch'i its chairman. Mei went to Taiwan in March 1954 to participate in the elections and returned to New York the following month. In November 1955 he went to Taiwan to plan the establishment, with American aid, of a nuclear science research institute as part of Tsinghua University. The construction of buildings for the institute at Hsinchu began in 1956, and the first group of buildings was ready for use in June 1957. Classes for the 18 students admitted to the first class began in 1956 on the campus of National Taiwan University. Class work began at Hsinchu in the autumn of 1957. Under the auspices of the Nuclear Science Research Institute, Taiwan's first atomic reactor, an open-pool type of one-megaton capacity, went into operation on 2 December 1961. Mei was appointed minister of education in the National Government in July 1958, and he held this post until early 1961, when illness forced him to retire. He also served as deputy chairman of the Kuo-li ch'ang-ch'i fa-chan k'o-hsueh wei-yuan-hui [national council on science development]. Mei Yi-ch'i died at Taipei on 19 May 1962.

Mei Yi-pao   梅 貽 寶
West. Y. P. Mei

Mei Yi-pao (5 November 1900–), philosopher and educational administrator who was associated with Yenching University for many years. After 1949 he taught in the United States, becoming chairman of the Chinese and Oriental studies program at the State University of Iowa in 1955.

The fifth son and the second-youngest child in a family of ten children, Mei Yi-pao was born in Tientsin. His father, a sheng-yuan and a minor official in the Tientsin salt administration, was determined, despite limited means, to provide his children with fine educational opportunities. The young Mei received a primary education in the Chinese classics, and a fine secondary education at the Nankai Middle School (see Chang Po-ling). In his early teens, he was converted to Christianity. Upon completion of his studies at the Nankai Middle School, he went to Peking, where he enrolled at Tsinghua University. After graduation in 1922, he spent a year as a traveling secretary for the national committee of the YMCA in China. He then went to the United States, where he received a B.A. degree from Oberlin College in 1924 and a Ph.D. in philosophy from the University of Chicago in 1927. In the course of his doctoral studies he worked under such noted philosophers as John Dewey at Columbia and Alfred North Whitehead at Harvard. He spent 1927–29 in Cologne, Germany, where he was the only Chinese student at the University of Cologne. His advanced studies, which focused on the ancient philosopher Mo Tzu, culminated in the publication of *The Ethical and Political Philosophy of Motse* (London, 1929) and *Motse, the Neglected Rival of Confucius* (London, 1934).

On returning to China in 1928 Mei Yi-pao joined the faculty of Yenching University, a Christian institution in Peking. For eight of the next ten years he taught philosophy at Yenching while successively serving as registrar, director of admissions, dean of studies, and dean of the college of arts and letters. In 1934–36 he was acting president of the Ming-hsien School (Oberlin-Shansi Memorial School) at T'aiku, Shansi, a post which he accepted at the behest of H. H. K'ung (q.v.), who was a prominent member of the controlling boards of both the school and the university.

Following the outbreak of the Sino-Japanese war in July 1937, Mei Yi-pao was drawn into the administration of several enterprises which reflected the broadening interests of the National Government and the increasing pressures of the national defense effort. As director of the newly created Kansu Science Education Institute at Lanchow in 1938–39, he administered extensive research and survey operations throughout northwest China as well as the local educational programs. From 1940 to 1942 he served as secretary general of the Chinese Industrial Cooperatives, supervising the work of three regional headquarters which, in turn, governed the activities of more than fifteen hundred cooperative societies in eighteen unoccupied provinces.

On 8 February 1942, Yenching University having been closed by the Japanese, H. H. K'ung called a meeting of members and former members of the Yenching board of managers at Chungking. In response to the expressed desires of many alumni, this body voted to reopen Yenching University in Free China. Mei Yi-pao was appointed director of the office on preparations for reopening the university. With the assistance of H. H. K'ung and such other important officials as Chang Ch'ün (q.v.), the governor of Szechwan, and with the aid of government and relief funds, Mei established cooperative relations with West China Union University at Chengtu, which already was playing host to three other Christian institutions. Yenching was permitted to rent buildings belonging to the Hua Mei Girls School and the Chi Hua Primary School and was given the use of the Confucian Temple of Chengtu. A faculty was assembled, and the refugee university opened its doors in the autumn of 1942. From 1942 to 1946 Mei Yi-pao served as acting president and acting chancellor of Yenching University in Chengtu.

At war's end Mei Yi-pao returned to the Peiping campus of Yenching University to resume teaching and research as a professor of philosophy. In mid-December 1948, as Communist forces reached the outskirts of Peiping, he fled by plane with his family to Shanghai, where he taught for a term at St. John's University. He then accepted an invitation to teach for a year at the University of Chicago. In the United States he also served as a visiting professor at such institutions as Indiana University, Oberlin College, Princeton University, the University of Cincinnati, Wabash College, Bowdoin College, and Purdue University. In 1955 he became professor and chairman of the Chinese and Oriental studies program at the State University of Iowa.

Mei Yi-pao received an honorary LL.D. degree from Oberlin College in 1945 and an L.H.D. from Wabash College in 1951. In addition to his two works on Mo Tzu, he wrote and published more than twenty philosophical papers and made substantial contributions to six chapters in *Sources of Chinese Tradition*, which was published in 1960 by the Columbia University Press.

Mei married Nyi Yong-kyih in 1929. The daughter of a Hangchow pastor, she was a 1924 graduate of Smith College and a librarian. A son, Tsu-lin, born to them in 1933, studied at Yale University and later taught modern Chinese at Harvard. Mei Yi-pao's elder brother Mei Yi-ch'i (q.v.) for many years was the president of Tsinghua University.

Meng Sen 孟 森
Pen. Hsin-shih 心 史

Meng Sen (1868–14 January 1938), supporter of constitutional government and a leader of the Chin-pu-tang. He became an authority on the Ming-Ch'ing transitional period and a professor of history at Peking University.

A native of Yanghu hsien, Kiangsu, Meng Sen was born into a prominent family in a region where scholars abounded. After becoming a salaried sheng-yuan, he abandoned the traditional course of study leading to a civil service career and devoted his time to the study of current affairs. The words and deeds of Cheng Hsiao-hsü (q.v.) after his return from diplomatic duties in Japan in 1894 impressed Meng so much that he decided to study in Japan. From 1901 to 1904 he studied law at Hosei University in Tokyo.

In the spring of 1905 Meng Sen accepted an invitation from Cheng Hsiao-hsü, then commissioner of border defense in Kwangsi, to join his military staff at Lungchou. Meng soon learned the art of poetry from Cheng, who had won acclaim for his poetical accomplishments, and he also exhibited a talent for historical writing. After combing through the official and private documents he found at the Lungchou post and doing additional research, he wrote the *Kuang-hsi pien-shih p'ang-chi* [addenda to the history of Kwangsi border defense affairs]. It was published in August 1905, with a commentary by Yen Fu (q.v.).

When Cheng resigned from the service in 1905, he and Meng Sen went to Shanghai, where they helped organize the Yü-pei li-hsien kung-hui [society for the preparation of constitutional government]. In July 1908 Meng Sen became the chief editor of the *Tung-fang tsa-chih* (*Eastern Miscellany*); it was published by the Commercial Press, of which Cheng Hsiao-hsü was a director. Meng overhauled the magazine's format and added such features as a column on constitutional government.

Meng Sen resigned from the *Tung-fang tsa-chih* after being elected to the Kiangsu provincial assembly in May 1909. That October, Chang Chien (q.v.), the chairman of the assembly, sent him to visit the provincial assemblies of Fengtien, Kirin, Heilungkiang, Chihli (Hopei), and Shantung to urge them to join with the assemblies of Kiangsu and other provinces in petitioning the Ch'ing court for the formation of a national constitutional government. Three such petitions later were presented to the imperial authorities, but they were ignored. In June 1911 Meng accompanied Chang Chien to Changteh for discussions with Yuan Shih-k'ai. He then went to Manchuria to reestablish contact with the leaders of the provincial assemblies in that region. In November of that year, he drafted the proclamation for the attack on Nanking by the revolutionary forces of Kiangsu and Chekiang under the command of Ch'eng Te-ch'üan.

After the provisional republican government was established, a large number of parties and cliques began to clutter the political scene in China. Meng Sen became executive secretary of the Kung-ho-tang [republican party], led by Li Yuan-hung (q.v.), and an enthusiastic supporter of the movement to amalgamate the small groups to form large political parties. In September 1912 Meng and Chang Chien, who had recommended the establishment of a Sino-American bank and the reform of the salt administration as means of alleviating some of the new government's financial problems, were invited to Peking for consultation with Yuan Shih-k'ai. Meng Sen remained in Peking for some time before returning to Kiangsu to become a candidate in the national elections for the Parliament. He was elected to the National Assembly, and in April 1913 he went to Peking

to assume office. The following month, the campaign for the amalgamation of political groups bore fruit when the Kung-ho-tang and two other parties which opposed the Kuomintang merged to form the Chin-pu-tang [progressive party]. Meng, who advocated the establishment of a responsible cabinet system (*see* Sung Chiao-jen) which would limit the powers of the presidency, was elected in July 1913 to the National Assembly committee charged with drafting a constitution. Four months later, Yuan Shih-k'ai paralyzed the Parliament by ordering the dissolution of the Kuomintang. Disheartened by this turn of events, Meng Sen left Peking and gradually divorced himself from political life.

After the publication of the essay "Chu-san-t'ai-tzu shih shu" [the accession of Emperor Yung-lo], which appeared in the Shanghai *Shih-shih hsin-pao* (*China Times*) in November 1913, Meng Sen came to be recognized as an authority on the history of the Ming-Ch'ing transitional period. In 1915 the *Hsiao-hsueh yueh-pao* [the short story] published his "Tung Hsiao-wan k'ao" [inquiry into Tung Hsiao-wan], which purported to identify a number of characters in the *Hung-lou-meng* (*Dream of the Red Chamber*) as members of the court of an early Manchu emperor. The Commercial Press published a three-volume collection of Meng's writings, the *Hsin-shih ts'ung-k'an*, in 1916.

Meng Sen became an associate professor of history at National Central University in Nanking in 1929. The following year, the Commercial Press published his *Ch'ing-ch'ao ch'ien-chi* [predynastic history of the Ch'ing], a pioneering work which aroused considerable interest in the academic world because of the methods Meng used to sift out propaganda and legend in reconstructing the history of that period. Meng's appointment as professor of history at Peking University in 1931 enabled him to utilize the rich documentary treasures of the old capital to advance his researches into the Ming-Ch'ing transitional period. The first part of his *magnum opus*, the *Ming-yuan Ch'ing-hsi t'ung-chi* [predynastic history of the Ch'ing in accordance with the chronology of the Ming] was published by Peking University in September 1934. By July 1937, when the Sino-Japanese war began, 16 volumes of this work had appeared, covering the period from 1371 to 1524. The *Ming-yuan Ch'ing-hsi t'ung-chi*, based mainly on the *Ming shih-lu* [veritable record of the Ming dynasty] and the Korean *Yijo sillok* [veritable record of the Yi dynasty], describes in detail the rise of Manchu power and its effect on the Ming empire. In this work, Meng corrected many errors of fact and interpretation made by earlier Chinese and Japanese scholars. Meng's *Pa-ch'i chih-tu k'ao-shih* [factual inquiry into the system of the eight banners], published in 1936, was an important study of early Manchu political organization.

In the spring of 1937 the students and faculty of Peking University held a celebration in honor of Meng Sen on his seventieth birthday. He responded by writing an essay, the "Hsiang-fei k'ao-shih," on the legendary Fragrant Concubine. In August 1937 Meng wrote the "Haining Ch'en-chia" [the Ch'en clan of Haining] to show that the Japanese occupation of Peiping would not force him to abandon his research. He also worked to improve his English and wrote poems to his friends which expressed his confidence that the Chinese would achieve victory. Meng fell ill in 1937, and Cheng Hsiao-hsü, who had become prime minister of Manchoukuo, came to visit him. Meng gave Cheng some poems in which he rebuked Cheng for cooperating with the Japanese. His illness gradually worsened, and he died on 14 January 1938.

In 1959 two collections of Meng Sen's works appeared. These were the *Ming Ch'ing shih lun-chu* [collected works relating to the history of the Ming and Ch'ing periods], compiled by Shang Hung-kuei and published in Shanghai, and the *Ch'ing-tai shih* [history of the Ch'ing period], compiled by Wu Hsiang-hsiang and published in Taipei.

Miao Ch'üan-sun 繆荃孫
T. Yen-chih 炎之

Miao Ch'üan-sun (1844–22 December 1919), the foremost Chinese bibliographic scholar of his day and the founder of several excellent libraries.

Chiangyin, Kiangsu, was the birthplace of Miao Ch'üan-sun. He was a sixth-generation descendent of Miao Sui (d. 1716), whose rule as magistrate of Tinghai, Chekiang, from 1695 until his death was so benevolent that the local inhabitants erected a sheng-tz'u [living shrine] in his honor. Miao Ch'üan-sun's grandfather was Miao T'ing-huai, a chin-shih of 1805 who became magistrate of the P'ingliang district in Kansu; and his father was Miao Huan-chang, a chü-jen of 1837 who served in the military headquarters of Chang Kuo-liang. In 1855 Miao Ch'üan-sun's mother, *née* Chu, died of malaria; his father soon remarried.

In September 1860, a few months after Miao Ch'üan-sun passed the examinations for the sheng-yuan degree, the Taiping rebels took Chiangyin. Soon afterwards, he and his stepmother fled to Huaian, Kiangsu, where he studied at the Licheng Academy. He and his stepmother later joined his father at Huayang, Szechwan. In 1867 Miao passed the examinations given in Szechwan for the chü-jen degree, but he was not awarded the degree because he was not a permanent resident of Szechwan. About this time, Miao came to know the leading Kwangtung bibliophile Li Wen-t'ien (ECCP, I, 494–95), who encouraged him in his pursuit of a scholarly career.

A chance to utilize his bibliographic knowledge presented itself to Miao Ch'üan-sun in 1874, when Chang Chih-tung (ECCP, I, 27-32), then the minister of education in Szechwan, invited him to participate in the compilation of the *Shu-mu ta-wen* [questions answered on bibliography], which appeared in 1875. At the time of the invitation, Miao was teaching at the Tsunching Academy, of which Chang was the founder and the principal. The two men soon became friends.

In 1876 Miao Ch'uan-sun achieved the chin-shih degree and became a compiler in the Hanlin Academy. In the meantime, Chang Chih-tung had returned to Peking to serve as the editor in chief of the gazetteer of the Peking metropolitan area, then known as the *Shun-t'ien fu-chih*. General principles of compilation were laid down by Chang, but the editorial work apparently was entrusted to Miao, who also wrote the treatises on topography, temples, economics, officials, literature, and stone-inscriptions. The gazetteer was completed in 1884 and published in 1886.

Except for a brief period during which he served as an examiner for the Peking metropolitan area, Miao Ch'üan-sun served the Hanlin Academy primarily by compiling a biographical dictionary of prominent Chinese of the Ch'ing period, under the supervision of P'an Tsu-yin (ECCP, II, 608–9) and later of Hsü T'ung. For a short time, T'an Chung-chün (1846–1888) served as co-compiler. After his departure from the project, Miao and Hsü T'ung came into conflict over the nature of the contribution to classical scholarship made by Chi Ta-k'uei (1746–1825), who had written a treatise on the *I-ching* (*Book of Changes*) which had less to do with textual criticism than with possible applications of this classic to divination. Miao maintained that Chi should be classified as a practitioner of fortune telling, not as a scholar.

After Miao's stepmother died in 1888, he withdrew from government service and went home to observe the traditional mourning period. He taught classics and literature at the Nan-ching Academy, which was headed by Wang Hsien-ch'ien (q.v.). At the end of the mourning period he went back to Peking, but he soon had to leave again because of his father's death in 1890. During this second period of mourning, he was chief lecturer at the Loyuan Academy in Shanghai. He then returned to Peking, where, as a compiler of the Hanlin Academy, he received an excellent rating from his superiors, who ranked him at the top of the third grade. However, the board that later reviewed these rankings demoted him more than 100 places at the insistence of Hsü T'ung. Miao responded by resigning from his post. At the invitation of Chang Chih-tung, then the governor general of Hupeh and Hunan, he went to Wuchang to compile a provincial gazetteer for Hupeh. During Chang Chih-tung's brief tenure of office as acting governor general at Nanking, Miao was asked to become chief lecturer at the Chung-shan Academy. He held that post from 1896 to 1901.

In 1901 Chang Chih-tung called a conference of prominent Chinese scholars in Wuchang to discuss ways and means of modernizing China. One result of that conference was the establishment at Nanking of the Chiang-ch'u pien-ishu-chü [Kiangsu-Hupeh compilation and translation bureau], with Miao Ch'üan-sun as its director. Miao headed this organization until its dissolution in 1910, and it published his biographical work *Hsü pei-chuan chi*, which he had begun compiling in 1881.

Miao Ch'üan-sun became known as China's leading authority on bibliography, and two of

his country's best libraries were founded and developed under his guidance. These were the Chiang-nan t'u-shu-kuan (later known as the Nan-ching kuo-hsueh t'u-shu-kuan and the Chiang-su sheng-li kuo-hsueh t'u-shu-kuan) and the Ching-shih t'u-shu-kuan (later known as the Kuo-li Pei-p'ing t'u-shu-kuan). In 1906, soon after he founded the Chiang-nan t'u-shu-kuan, Tuan-fang (ECCP, II, 780–82), then the governor general of Liang-Kiang, learned that the descendents of Ting Ping (1832–1889) were about to sell his fine collection of rare books, the Pa-ch'ien-chuan lou. He ordered Miao to buy it for the new library so that this collection would not suffer the fate of the rarities collected by Lu Hsin-yuan (ECCP, I, 545–47), which had been sold a short while earlier to Baron Iwasaki Yanosuke of Japan. The Ching-shih t'u-shu-kuan was established as a result of recommendations made to the Ch'ing court in 1909 by Chang Chih-tung, then the chairman of the Board of Education in Peking. Miao published some of the rarities he found at Peking, including books from the court library of the Southern Sung dynasty (1127–1279) at Hangchow which had been moved to Peking by the Mongols and forgotten. He enriched the holdings of the Ching-shih t'u-shu-kuan by buying the private collection of Yao Chin-yuan. Miao prepared a catalogue of rare books, the *Ch'ing hsueh-pu t'u-shu-kuan shan-pen shu-mu*, and a catalogue of local gazetteers, the *Ch'ing hsueh-pu t'u shu-kuan fang-chih-mu*. These works later were published in the *Ku-hsueh hui-k'an*.

After the republic was established in 1911, Miao Ch'üan-sun lived in Shanghai and devoted most of his time to bibliographic studies. In 1914 he was invited to take part in the compilation of a history of the Ch'ing dynasty (*see* Chao Erh-sun). During a two-year stay in Peking, he rewrote many of the biographies he had prepared some thirty years before and wrote treatises on the T'u-ssu [aborigines] and the Ming i-ch'en [Ming officials who survived under the Ch'ing]. Miao then helped complete the treatise on inscriptions for a provincial gazetteer of Kiangsu and supervised the compilation of the local gazetteer of Chiangyin. On 22 December 1919 he died. He was survived by his second wife, *née* Hsia, and by two sons and two daughters.

Miao Ch'üan-sun was the author of many books as well as the compiler and editor of major collections. The phrase "I-feng-t'ang" [hall of literary breeze] appears in the title of several collections of his own works. As a poet, he was known as the embodiment of the Sung style, characterized less by literary splendor than by depth of feeling. His contributions as a historian include chronological tables of high-ranking officials of the Nan-pei period (420–589) and a treatise on the literature of the Liao dynasty (907–1125). Miao edited a number of ts'ung-shu, including the *Tui-yü-lou ts'ung-shu* of 1905 and the *Shih-yuan ts'ung-shu* of 1914. He is best remembered, however, for his biblio-graphic contributions, including the *I-feng-t'ang tu-shu-chi* [record of books read in the hall of literary breeze]. Because of his enthusiastic efforts and obvious success in this field, the collation of texts and the publication of ancient and rare books became fashionable enterprises in twentieth-century China.

Miao Pin 繆 斌
T. P'ei-ch'eng 丕 成

Miao Pin (1899–1946), Kuomintang official who served in the Japanese-sponsored government at Nanking in the early 1940's. Although he allegedly served as a Nationalist agent during the Second World War, he was executed by the Nationalists in 1946.

Wusih, Kiangsu, was the birthplace of Miao Pin. He was the son of Miao Chien-chang, a Taoist priest. Miao Pin received his early education in the Chinese classics at the local primary school, where he showed great promise. About 1918 he enrolled at Nanyang University (later Chiaotung University) in Shanghai, where he studied electrical engineering. After gradu-ation in 1923, he went to work for the railway administration. Early in 1924 he went to Canton, where he joined the Kuomintang and became a radio instructor at the Whampoa Military Academy. He later served as a political instructor.

By the time the Northern Expedition was launched in 1926, Miao Pin had become an alternate member of the Kuomintang's Central Executive Committee. He participated in the first stage of the Northern Expedition as party representative to the division commanded by

Wang Po-ling in the First Army, and he soon became friendly with Ho Ying-ch'in (q.v.), who had succeeded Chiang Kai-shek as commander of the First Army. When Chiang Kai-shek undertook a purge of Communists in the spring of 1927, Miao Pin was arrested as an alleged member of the Chinese Communist party. The intervention of Wu Chih-hui (q.v.) and Ho Ying-ch'in saved him from the executioner. At Ho Ying-ch'in's behest, he was appointed director of the Nanking government's commissariat of army headquarters in April 1927. Later that year, he served on the Central Special Com-mittee of the Kuomintang, which worked to settle the differences that had split the Kuomin-tang into factions based at Wuhan, Nanking, and Shanghai. Miao became a member of the newly organized Executive Yuan in the autumn of 1928.

When Niu Yung-chien (q.v.) became governor of Kiangsu in 1928, Miao Pin was appointed civil affairs commissioner, with control of the hsien magistrates and police chiefs throughout the province. However, Miao soon became known as a corrupt administrator, and early in 1930 he was impeached. He then returned to Wusih, where he became associated with local industrialists. About this time, his wife (about whom little is known) fell from the upper floor of their home and died. Soon afterwards, Miao married the niece of the industrialist Jung Tsung-ching, who operated the Sing Sung chain of textile and flour mills. Jung then appointed Miao Pin chief engineer of his group of mills. Miao still hoped to return to political life, however, and he began to advocate Sino-Japanese cooperation, thus winning the approval of a few Kuomintang leaders and retired Peiyang politicians. However, his suggestions won him the enmity of many Kuomintang leaders, some of whom questioned his patriotism.

After the Sino-Japanese war began in 1937 and a puppet regime was established at Peiping, Miao Pin went to the old capital, where he was given funds for the organization of the Hsin-min-hui [new people's society]. Miao became the vice president of this pro-Japanese propaganda group. However, some of the leaders of the puppet regime came to consider him a threat to their authority. In 1940 Miao learned that his life would be in jeopardy if he remained in Peiping, and he fled to Nanking, where Wang Ching-wei (q.v.) headed another puppet regime. Wang appointed Miao vice president of the examination yuan and a member of the central political council at Nanking. A year or so later, Miao also became vice director of the cultural committee of the East Asia League, a Japanese-sponsored organization formed to promote the "Greater East Asia Co-Prosperity Sphere."

In the early 1940's, as it became evident that Japan would eventually lose the War in the Pacific, many members of the Nanking government, from Chou Fo-hai (q.v.) down to functionaries at the lowest levels, established contact with National Government authorities at Chungking, and offered their services to Tai Li (q.v.), the head of intelligence operations, as underground agents. Miao Pin gave information and funds to Nationalist agents in Shanghai; he also sent his two sons to Free China, where they sought the assistance of Ho Ying-ch'in and eventually joined the Nationalist forces.

Early in 1945 it was rumored that Japan would seek to conclude a separate peace with China. Miao Pin promptly offered his services to the National Government as an emissary to Japan to initiate preliminary peace talks. He went to Tokyo, representing himself as a Nationalist agent, in March 1945 for talks with Premier Koiso Kuniaki, but it is not clear whether or not the National Government authorized this trip. He and Premier Koiso met twice in March. However, the Japanese Supreme War Council opposed Koiso's efforts at diplomacy and suspected that Miao was a fake, and this affair contributed to Koiso's overthrow in April 1945. Miao returned to China and reported on the failure of his mission to the Nationalist authorities at Chungking.

At war's end, many officials of the puppet regimes were placed under arrest, but Miao Pin was not among them. When he entered a Shanghai prison camp early in 1946, it was as a person in protective custody, not a prisoner. Three days later, he was transferred to a camp at Nanking, where he lived in the commandant's office. Suddenly, everything changed. For unexplained reasons, Miao Pin was moved to Soochow, where the top-ranking officials of the Nanking puppet regime were being held. He was rushed to trial, sentenced to death, and executed in the early summer of 1946.

Mo Te-hui　　　　　　　莫 德 惠
T. Liu-ch'en　　　　　　　柳 忱

Mo Te-hui (1881–17 April 1968), Manchurian official who served as China's chief representative in the 1930–31 Sino-Soviet negotiations concerning the Chinese Eastern Railway. From 1954 to 1966 he served as president of the Examination Yuan in Taiwan.

Born in Sinkiang, Mo Te-hui was the son of a general in the imperial forces who came from Shuangch'eng, Kirin. He received a traditional education in the Chinese classics, and he passed the examinations for the sheng-yuan degree at the age of 20 sui. After being graduated from the Peiyang Higher Police Academy in Tientsin, he was made chief of police at Harbin. He held that post until 1912, when he was elected to the provisional National Assembly in the new republican government. Little is known about his career between 1914, when Yuan Shih-k'ai dissolved the Parliament, and 1921, when Mo was appointed intendant tao-t'ai at Ilan, Kirin. In 1922 he became an adviser in the headquarters of the peace preservation force for the Three Eastern Provinces.

Because of his association with Chang Tso-lin (q.v.) and his administrative abilities, Mo Te-hui was appointed vice minister of agriculture and commerce in the Peking government. He returned to Manchuria in 1926 to become civil governor and commissioner of finance of Fengtien province. He worked to improve educational facilities in the province and served for a time as dean of Northeastern University. In 1927 he was appointed minister of agriculture and commerce in the Peking government. He held that post until June 1928, when Chang Tso-lin decided to leave Peking before the forces of the Northern Expedition occupied the old capital. Mo was aboard the train that was wrecked by a bomb explosion on 4 June 1928 as it was carrying Chang Tso-lin and his party back to Manchuria. Chang was killed, and Mo was seriously injured. When he recovered from his wounds, Mo entered the service of Chang Tso-lin's son Chang Hsueh-liang (q.v.).

After the political-military disaster that resulted from the mid-1929 Chinese attempt to seize the Chinese Eastern Railway and oust its

Soviet employees, Mo Te-hui was appointed director general of the railway early in December. The Khabarovsk Protocol, signed on 22 December, provided for the restoration of the *status quo ante*. Mo then was made president of the railway and China's chief delegate to a conference at Moscow, scheduled to open on 25 January 1930, which was to settle all important questions relating to the administration of the Chinese Eastern Railway. Early in January 1930 the Chinese decided that Ts'ai Yun-sheng, their plenipotentiary representative at Khabarovsk, had exceeded his instructions; and they began to work for the voiding of part of the Khabarovsk Protocol and the basing of the conference agenda on the 1924 treaties between Moscow and Peking and between Moscow and Mukden. Instead of going to Moscow as planned, Mo Te-hui went to Nanking for consultation with National Government authorities. He finally reached Moscow in May 1930, and his first official meeting with Leo Karakhan, the chief Soviet negotiator, did not take place until October. After a second bargaining session in December, Mo went to Nanking to report on the sessions. He returned to Moscow in March 1931 and participated in 22 fruitless meetings between April and November. The conference then lapsed into inactivity because of the Japanese invasion of Manchuria, although it technically remained in session. Mo stayed in Moscow, and he reportedly played a role in the negotiations that led to the restoration of diplomatic relations between China and the Soviet Union in December 1932. By this time, Manchoukuo had been established, and there no longer was any apparent purpose in continuing a conference designed to resolve a Sino-Soviet dispute that had arisen in territory that now was under Japanese control. Accordingly, the Moscow conference adjourned in 1933, and Mo Te-hui returned to China.

Little is known about Mo Te-hui's activities from 1933 to 1938, when he became a non-partisan member of the People's Political Council at Chungking, the National Government's wartime seat. He was named chairman of the council's presidium in 1942. After the War in the Pacific ended he served in January 1946 as a nonpartisan delegate to the Political Consultative Conference. He was a delegate to the National Assembly when it reconvened later in 1946, and he was elected vice chairman of the commission for supervision of the enforcement of constitutional government, becoming its chairman in September 1948. In 1947–48 he served on the State Council; and in 1948 he ran as the government-approved candidate for the vice presidency of the republic, but he lost to Li Tsung-jen. He then was appointed adviser to the presidential headquarters, and in 1949 he was made a minister without portfolio in the cabinet of Ho Ying-ch'in (q.v.). Soon afterwards, with the Nationalist defeat in the civil war with the Chinese Communists for control of the mainland, he went to Taiwan and helped establish the National Government at Taipei.

In Taiwan, Mo Te-hui was prominent in the National Assembly that met in early 1954, and from mid-1954 to mid-1966 he served as president of the Examination Yuan. During this period, he also continued to serve as chairman of the commission for supervision of the enforcement of constitutional government. He died at Taipei of a cerebral thrombosis on 17 April 1968.

Mu Hsiang-yueh　　　　穆 湘 玥
　T.　　Ou-ch'u　　　　藕 初
　West. H. Y. Moh

Mu Hsiang-yueh (18 June 1876–1942), known as H. Y. Moh, entrepreneur who was noted for his work in developing the cotton industry in China.

The youngest of six children, four boys and two girls, H. Y. Moh was born in Shanghai. His mother, *née* Chu, was the third wife of Mu Cho-an, a successful cotton merchant who had founded the cotton firm Mu Kung Cheng. In 1881, at the age of six sui, H. Y. Moh began to receive a traditional education in the Chinese classics. His formal schooling ended in 1888, and he then became an apprentice in a cotton firm. As he learned the trade, he noted that many of the traditional methods and practices of the Chinese cotton merchants were inefficient. Mu Cho-an died in 1892, leaving H. Y. Moh and his brother Mu Shu-tsai to care for their mother. H. Y. Moh determined to further himself by acquiring modern knowledge, a determination that was strengthened by China's defeat in the Sino-Japanese war of 1894. In 1897 he began to study English, and by 1900 he had acquired sufficient fluency to pass the examinations for entrance into the Chinese Maritime Customs Service. That year, he married a girl whose surname was Chin.

His work in the customs service exposed the young H. Y. Moh to a large variety of people and ideas, and he soon began to study Western political and scientific ideas. He also worked to become a good public speaker. In 1904 he joined the Hu-hsueh-hui [Shanghai scholastic society] and became an active participant in its various enterprises. His dream was to go abroad and study economics. In 1905 he served as a director of the Customs Employers Club in Shanghai, and he enthusiastically promoted club support of a Chinese boycott of American goods to protest reported persecution of Chinese workers in the United States. This campaign led to his resignation from the Chinese Maritime Customs service, and he became an English teacher at the Lung-men Normal School in Shanghai in 1906. Throughout this period he slowly made plans for his trip abroad to study. In 1907, thinking that he was ready for the venture, he resigned from the school. At the last moment, he had to postpone the trip. He then accepted a commission from the Kiangsu provincial railway company to undertake a study of railway policing methods in north China. He did such a good job that the company offered him the post of chief of railway police, which he accepted and held for a year. His trip to north China affected H. Y. Moh's plans for advanced study. The underdeveloped state of China's vast northwestern region convinced him that industry was China's pressing need and that agriculture was the basis of industrial development. He therefore decided to study agriculture instead of economics.

H. Y. Moh's lack of formal education was an obstacle to his admission to a foreign college or university. In an attempt to compensate for this deficiency, he enrolled in the International Correspondence School, concentrating on English and mathematics. In 1909, at the age of 33, he left China for the United States. His friends and relatives helped finance the trip, and one of his former colleagues in the customs service helped him to enroll at the University of Wisconsin as a special student.

On the strength of his good showing during that academic year, H. Y. Moh became a regular student in 1910. He also received a scholarship from Kiangsu province, which relieved him of financial worries and enabled him to devote all of his time to study. In 1911 he transferred to the University of Illinois, from which he was graduated with a B.S. in agriculture in 1913. He then entered Texas A & M to study the textile industry, and he received an M.S. degree in 1914.

After returning to China in the summer of 1914, H. Y. Moh began preparations for the establishment of a cotton mill. At this time, the cotton-spinning industry in China was dominated by British interests, but British attention was focused on the outbreak of the First World War. H. Y. Moh took advantage of the situation by establishing the Hou Sheng Cotton Mill in Shanghai in 1915. A year later, he organized the much larger Tak Da (T'e-ta) Mill as a public company. As these mills grew, the supply of cotton from nearby Tsungming and Tung-chow had to be supplemented with cotton from other areas. Having learned that industries should be built near producing or distribution centers, H. Y. Moh decided to build a branch of the Tak Da Mill at Chengchow, Honan. However, his plans were frustrated by a group of stockholders. These men knew nothing of modern industrial management methods, and they refused to allow the establishment of a mill far from their Shanghai base of operations. H. Y. Moh then decided to establish a privately owned mill in Honan. The Yu-feng Cotton Mill commenced production in 1920, and it developed quickly because of its proximity to cotton supplies and the availability of cheaper labor. In the meantime, H. Y. Moh had begun to experiment with various strains of cotton. He rented a ten-acre site near the Hou Sheng Mill, planted cotton seeds imported from Georgia, and made detailed observations of the growth of the Sea Island and other strains of cotton.

In 1920 H. Y. Moh made an important contribution to the Chinese cotton textile industry by helping to found the Cotton Yarn and Cloth Exchange (also known as the Chinese Cotton Goods Exchange) in Shanghai, of which he served as president until 1926. Also in 1920 he was appointed an honorary adviser on industry to the Peking government by Hsü

Shih-ch'ang (q.v.), the president. H. Y. Moh's famine-relief activities in Honan and the surrounding region during 1920 heightened his vision of that area's potentialities. H. Y. Moh entered still another field in 1921, when he founded the Chuan-kung Bank, a bank for the promotion of industry. The following year, he served as the delegate of the Shanghai Chinese Chamber of Commerce to the Pacific Trade Conference at Honolulu.

By 1923 Chinese-owned textile mills, which had enjoyed booming business during the First World War, had suffered a decline in profits because of renewed Japanese and British competition. Because the Tak Da Mill was in serious financial troubles, H. Y. Moh attempted to increase its capitalization. Conservative stockholders opposed him, and he resigned from that company. The Chinese textile industry continued to decline, and H. Y. Moh lost control of the Yu-feng Cotton Mill in Honan. However, he managed to retain ownership of the Hou Sheng Mill and to aid the industry through his work as president of the Cotton Yarn and Cloth Exchange. In these troubled years, he found comfort in Buddhism, to which he was converted in 1923 by the great Chinese religious leader T'ai-hsü (q.v.). His clear memories of the difficulties he had encountered in his search for a modern education led H. Y. Moh to provide a number of students with scholarships for foreign study. Among the young men he aided were Lo Chia-lun, Tuan Hsi-p'eng (qq.v.), and the economist H. D. Fong.

From October 1928 to July 1931 H. Y. Moh served under H. H. K'ung (q.v.) as administrative vice minister in the National Government. He then returned to Shanghai. When the Sino-Japanese War began in July 1937 he was among the Chinese leaders living in the foreign-controlled areas of Shanghai who organized and worked for the Civic Federation (see Tu Yueh-sheng), which made a number of contributions to China's war effort. He later moved to Chungking, where he served on the Executive Yuan's commission for the promotion of agriculture production. When the National Government established a cotton, yarn, and cloth control bureau in 1940, H. Y. Moh was appointed its director. He held this post until his death in 1942.

New, W. S.: *see* Niu Hui-sheng.

Nieh Erh　　　聶 耳

Nieh Erh (1911–17 July 1935), composer who wrote the music for "March of the Volunteers," which was adopted as the official national anthem of the People's Republic of China in 1949.

The son of a practitioner of Chinese medicine, Nieh Erh was born in Kunming. His father died when he was only four years old, leaving his mother to bring him up in Yunnan. Nieh was fond of music as a child, and he learned to play the violin at the Kunming Provincial Normal School. At the age of 17 sui, he went to Canton and enrolled at the Kwangtung Dramatic School under Ou-yang Yü-ch'ien. After a brief stint as a soldier in Hunan and Kwangsi, he went to Shanghai, where he joined the Anti-Imperialist League in 1929 and found a job as a violinist in the orchestra of the Bright Moon Variety Company, directed by the popular composer Li Chin-hui.

In 1931 Nieh Erh met T'ien Han (q.v.) and joined a music group known as the Friends of the Soviet Union Society. He obtained a job as a clerk for the Lotus Motion Picture Company (Lien-hua ying-p'ien kung-ssu), and he soon began collaborating with T'ien Han on songs for the film *Glorious Motherhood*, including "The Miners' Song." Between 1932 and 1935 Nieh wrote the music for more than 30 film songs, including "Graduation Song" for the film *Students in Trouble* and the title song for *Big Road*. At meetings of the Friends of the Soviet Union Society and in the course of his work, Nieh Erh met a number of politically conscious writers, musicians, and film people. His own political outlook gradually became more radical, and in 1933 he joined the Chinese Communist party.

In 1934 Nieh Erh collaborated with T'ien Han on an opera, *Storm on the Yangtze*. Its story was based on an episode that had taken place on the Shanghai waterfront during the Japanese attack on that city in 1932, and Nieh Erh himself played the role of an old stevedore whose grandchild had been killed in the fighting. His best known work, however, was his setting for "March of the Volunteers," a song written in 1934 by T'ien Han for his scenario, *Children of the Storm*, just before his arrest. Its stirring opening lines and music— "Arise, all you who refuse to be slaves . . ."— enjoyed continued popularity in China, particularly in left-wing and Communist circles. In 1949 this song was adopted as the official national anthem of the People's Republic of China.

Before Nieh Erh completed this last film score, his name reportedly was placed on the police blacklist. Early in 1935 he escaped to Japan with the aim of going to the Soviet Union for formal training in music theory. A left-wing variety troupe in Japan gave him work, and on an outing with them, he was drowned while swimming at Kuganumia on 17 July 1935, at the age of 23.

Nieh Erh came to be known in Chinese Communist terminology as a "pioneer of proletarian music." Although he lacked the formal training and the maturity that might have made him a musician of the first rank, his songs were charged with a spontaneity and an emotional vigor that attested to the high degree of talent he possessed. A biographical film made in 1959 bears little relation to the facts of Nieh Erh's life or character.

Nieh Jung-chen   聶 榮 臻

Nieh Jung-chen (1899–), marshal of the People's Republic of China. After serving as commander of the Shansi-Chahar-Hopei military district during the Sino-Japanese war, he became acting chief of staff (1950) and vice chairman (1954) of the People's Revolutionary Military Council. He was made chairman of the Scientific Planning Commission in 1957 and director of the Scientific-Technological Commission in 1958.

Little is known about Nieh Jung-chen's family background or early life except that he was born into a well-to-do farming family in Chiangching, Szechwan, and that he participated in the May Fourth Movement of 1919 while a student at a Chungking middle school. After graduation in 1919, he became interested in the work-study movement (*see* Li Shih-tseng), and in 1920 he went to France as a member of a work-study group that also included Teng Hsiao-p'ing (q.v.). Nieh attended school in Grenoble for a year and then went to Charleroi, Belgium, to enroll at the Université de Travail, a tuition-free institution sponsored by the Belgian Socialist party. After studying chemical engineering for two years, Nieh returned to Paris in 1923 to work as an engineer at the Schneider-Creusot arms factory and the Renault automobile plant. He joined the Chinese Socialist Youth Corps in the winter of 1921 and became a regular member of the Chinese Communist party's newly established Paris branch in 1922. In 1924 Nieh went to Moscow, where he studied at the Communist University for Toilers of the East and the Red Army Academy.

Nieh Jung-chen returned to China in the summer of 1925 to serve under Chou En-lai (q.v.) as general secretary and instructor in the political department of the Whampoa Military Academy. In 1926, the year that the Northern Expedition was launched, he was a special representative of the Chinese Communist party on the military committee of the National Revolutionary Army. In the early months of 1927 he served under Chou En-lai as a labor organizer in Shanghai. After the Kuomintang-Communist alliance came to an end in 1927, he participated in the Nanchang uprising of 1 August (*see* Ho Lung; Yeh T'ing) as a political commissar in Yeh T'ing's 24th Division, and he took part in the Canton Commune (*see* Chang T'ai-lei) that December. With the suppression of the Canton Commune on 14 December, he fled to Hong Kong.

Little is known about Nieh Jung-chen's activities in 1928–29, but some reports indicate that he went to the Soviet Union. In any event, he served on the Hopei military committee of the Chinese Communist party in 1930, and he apparently worked in Shanghai with Chou En-lai in the early months of 1931. He later moved to the central soviet area in Kiangsi, where he became deputy chief of the general political department of the Chinese Workers and Peasants Red Army. In 1932 he was appointed political commissar of the First Army Group, commanded by Lin Piao (q.v.). He held this post until 1937, when, as part of the Kuomintang-Communist alliance against the Japanese, the Chinese Communist forces in north China were reorganized as the Eight Route Army.

There he became deputy commander and political commissar of Lin Piao's 115th Division, in which capacity he conducted the battle of P'inghsingkuan in Shansi, the first Chinese victory of the Sino-Japanese war. The Japanese 5th Division of Itagaki Seishiro suffered almost 5,000 casualties and lost much equipment and many weapons. After the battle, Nieh Jung-chen was ordered to work behind the Japanese lines in Hopei to develop a base for guerrilla warfare in the Wut'ai mountains.

In November 1937 Nieh Jung-chen was appointed commander of the Shansi-Chahar-Hopei military district by the Chinese Communist government at Yenan. Earlier, the National Government had created a military district in Hopei under Ch'eng Ch'ien and one in Shansi under Yen Hsi-shan (q.v.). Discussions between Nieh and local leaders resulted in plans for the creation of a regional government. Yen Hsi-shan opposed the idea, but Ch'eng Ch'ien approved it, and Nieh made preparations for a conference at Fup'ing. Delegates from 39 hsien of Hopei and Shansi met on 10–14 January 1938 and selected a committee to form a border region government. Nieh Jung-chen and Lü Cheng-ts'ao were the only two Communists on the nine-man committee. By the summer of 1938, the new government, headed by a non-Communist, had won the approval of the National Government and had restored Chinese administration to a considerable portion of north China. At first, it controlled only 36 hsien, but its authority expanded steadily as Nieh used his recruiting and organizing skills to swell the ranks of his military forces with patriotic Chinese from the Peiping-Tientsin area. By war's end, he had amassed an army of about 150,000 men. His troops thrust southward in 1939 to aid Wang Chen, a brigade commander in Ho Lung's division, in the defense of the Wut'ai mountain region. They also took part in the so-called Hundred Regiments Offensive of August–September 1940, the major Chinese Communist effort of the war.

Nieh Jung-chen was elected to the Central Committee of the Chinese Communist party at the party's Seventh National Congress in 1945. After the War in the Pacific ended, his troops moved rapidly into Inner Mongolia. They were forced to evacuate Kalgan late in 1946, but they established a firm base at Shihchiachuang in 1947. Nieh was elected a

member of the standing committee of the party's Shansi-Chahar-Hopei bureau and commander of the Shansi-Chahar-Hopei Field Army in 1947. When the military balance in north China shifted in favor of the Chinese Communist forces in 1948, Nieh was appointed commander of the north China military district of the People's Liberation Army and second secretary of the Chinese Communist party's north China bureau. He served on the presidium of the north China provisional people's congress and became a member of the north China people's government at Shihchiachuang. When Fu Tso-yi (q.v.) surrendered Peiping in January 1949, Nieh made the arrangements for the peaceful takeover of the old capital. Nieh then became garrison commander of the Peiping-Tientsin area, in which capacity he participated in unsuccessful negotiations with the Nationalists in April 1949. He became mayor of Peiping on 8 September 1949, and he held that post until February 1951. He also served as a delegate to the Chinese People's Political Consultative Conference.

When the People's Republic of China was established on 1 October 1949, Nieh Jung-chen became a member of the Central People's Government Council and deputy chief of staff of the People's Revolutionary Military Council. He was promoted to acting chief of staff early in 1950 when Hsü Hsiang-ch'ien (q.v.) resigned, and he served briefly as vice chairman of the People's Revolutionary Military Council in 1954. Also in 1954, he represented the North China Military District at the National People's Congress and became a member of the congress's Standing Committee. Soon afterwards, he was made a vice chairman of the National Defense Council.

Nieh Jung-chen was rewarded for his military contributions to the Chinese Communist cause in September 1955, when he was named one of ten marshals of the People's Republic of China and was accorded the nation's three highest military orders: the Order of August First, first class; the Order of Freedom and Independence, first class; and the Order of Liberation, first class. In September 1956 he was reelected to the Central Committee of the Chinese Communist party at the party's Eighth National Congress, and in October of that year he became a vice premier of the State Council, once again working closely with Chou En-lai. When the Scientific Planning Commission of the State Council was reorganized in May 1957, Nieh replaced Ch'en Yi (1901–; q.v.) as its chairman. The Scientific Planning Commission was merged with the National Technological Commission in November 1958 to form the Scientific-Technological Commission, with Nieh as chairman. The new commission worked to coordinate the activities of the armaments ministries. Nieh served as a delegate from Szechwan to the National People's Congresses in 1958 and 1964, and he was elected to the presidium at the latter congress.

Throughout the 1950's Nieh Jung-chen, who spoke French and Russian fluently, visited foreign countries on behalf of the People's Republic of China. In December 1955 he was a member of a Chinese delegation which went to Rumania and, in January 1956, to the German Democratic Republic on the occasion of President Wilhelm Pieck's eightieth birthday. Nieh then visited Hungary and Czechoslovakia and attended the Political Consultative Committee meeting of the Warsaw Pact powers as an observer. After a brief stopover in Moscow, he returned to Peking. In April 1956 Nieh headed the Chinese delegation to the Third Congress of the North Korean Workers' party; in 1957 he headed a delegation to the independence celebrations in Ghana; and in October 1959 he led a delegation to East Germany for the tenth-anniversary celebrations of the German Democratic Republic.

Little is known about Nieh Jung-chen's personal life except that he was married and was the father of at least two children.

Niu Hui-sheng 牛惠生
West. Way-sung New
W. S. New

Niu Hui-sheng (14 June 1892–4 May 1937), known as W. S. New, founder of the Shanghai Orthopedic Hospital, devoted his life to the improvement of conditions in hospitals and the raising of standards in the medical profession in China.

Shanghai was the birthplace of W. S. New. He was the son of Shangchow New (Niu Shangchou), an American-educated engineer, and the former Ni Kuei-chin, a teacher at the Bridgman Girls School in Shanghai. Both of his parents were devout Congregationalists. After receiving his early education in the Chinese classics from private tutors, W. S. New attended the Anglo-Chinese Public School and the St. John's Middle School. In 1907 he enrolled at St. John's University.

In 1910, having received a B.A. degree from St. John's University, W. S. New went to the United States to study at the Harvard University Medical School. He was admitted to the Boylston Medical Society in 1913 after presenting a paper on "Acute Anterior Poliomyelitis" in March of that year. After receiving an M.D. degree from Harvard in 1914, New served as a house physician and surgeon at St. Luke's Hospital in New Bedford, Massachusetts, and worked in its Floating Hospital for pediatrics. He returned to Shanghai in August 1915 to assume charge of the department of anatomy at the Harvard Medical School of China. In 1915 he surveyed the state of orthopedic care in government and missionary hospitals in China and decided to specialize in orthopedics so that he could improve the plight of the crippled and maimed in China. He went to the United States on a Rockefeller Foundation fellowship in 1916 and became an assistant in orthopedics at Massachusetts General Hospital and the Children's Hospital. He also served in the out-patient department of the Carney Hospital in Boston and taught bacteriology at the Harvard Medical School. In 1917 he became a licensed physician, and he was appointed orthopedic house surgeon at Massachusetts General Hospital. He held that post until May 1918, when he went to Baltimore to serve briefly as an orthopedic assistant at the Johns Hopkins University Hospital. During the 1917–18 period, he joined the American Medical Association, the Massachusetts Medical Society, and the American Orthopedic Association.

In 1918 W. S. New returned to China as head of orthopedic surgery at the Peking Union Medical College, a post he held until June 1920. He served as secretary of the Peking Medical Society in 1919–20, and he also was an officer of the St. John's University Alumni Association of Peking, the Harvard Club of North China, and the American University Club of North China. In 1920 he moved to Shanghai and established a private practice, which he maintained until 1929. He also became a visiting surgeon at the Margaret Williamson Hospital in Shanghai and a consulting surgeon at hospitals in Soochow and Hangchow. In 1922–26 he was superintendent of the Red Cross Hospital at Shanghai, and in 1928–29 he was surgeon general of the Chinese Red Cross. He was elected a fellow of the American College of Surgeons in 1927, thus becoming the first Chinese to receive that honor. In 1929 he founded the Orthopedic Hospital of Shanghai, then the only hospital of its kind in East Asia. He planned every detail of its design and operation, and it came to be regarded as a model institution.

In the 1930's W. S. New devoted most of his time and energy to the operation of the Orthopedic Hospital of Shanghai, of which he served as superintendent and chief surgeon. He was pleased when, in 1931, it came to be used as a Red Cross hospital for the teaching of orthopedic surgery. New also found time to serve as professor of anatomy and medical jurisprudence at the St. John's University Medical School and the Women's Christian Union Medical School in Shanghai and as a lecturer at the medical school of Central University. He organized a chain of clinics for factory workers, and at various times he served as a member of the medical board of the Shanghai Municipal Council, medical officer of the Yangtze River and Whangpoo River conservation commissions, medical adviser to the Shanghai-Nanking and the Shanghai-Hangchow-Ningpo railways, honorary superintendent of the Chinese Infectious Diseases Hospital, and medical director of the National Child Welfare Association.

W. S. New was an able administrator who worked assiduously to improve conditions in hospitals and standards in the medical profession in China. He was a charter member of the National Medical Association of China, founded in 1915, and a member since 1915 of the China Medical Missionary Association (later the China Medical Association). When these two organizations were merged in 1932 to form the Chinese Medical Association, W. S. New was elected president of the new body. He took a leading role in the direction of an energetic financial campaign which enabled the association to acquire its own building in Shanghai. New's health never had been robust, and the burdens he assumed in preparing for the association's 1934 conference at Nanking

brought on a severe illness from which he never recovered. Despite his poor health, he assumed even heavier responsibilities in 1935, when he agreed to serve as general secretary of the Chinese Medical Association until a suitable younger man could be trained for the post. He founded a crippled children's ward at the Kwangchi Hospital in 1935, served as chairman of that hospital's board of directors in 1936, and became superintendent of Chungshan Memorial Hospital in Shanghai in 1937. He died of nephritis at Shanghai on 4 May 1937.

W. S. New was respected by both Chinese and Western medical colleagues as a major force in the development of modern medicine in China and as a man who strove to create a more humane and scientific attitude toward such patients as factory workers and children than had been characteristic of the Chinese medical profession in the past. He also was known as a civic leader in Shanghai. He was a leader in the alumni affairs of St. John's University, a Mason, and a Rotarian.

W. S. New was survived by his wife, *née* Hsü I-chen, and his son, Peter Kong-ming New (Niu K'ang-min, 1928–). The daughter of Hsü Hui-ch'eng, a professor of Chinese history at St. John's University, Hsü I-chen was a graduate of Ginling College and Teachers College, Columbia University. She and W. S. New were married in Shanghai on 24 February 1924 at a Congregational church which his family had helped support for many years. Peter New was schooled in the United States after his father's death; he became a medical sociologist.

Niu Yung-chien　　　鈕 永 建
T. T'i-sheng　　　　　惕 生

Niu Yung-chien (1870–24 December 1965), republican revolutionary and military associate of Sun Yat-sen who later served as governor of Kiangsu (1927–29) and vice president of the Examination Yuan (1933–40, 1949). He became acting president of the yuan in 1949 and continued to hold that post in Taiwan until his retirement in 1952.

Little is known about Niu Yung-chien's family background or early years except that he was born in a village near Shanghai. After passing the examinations for the sheng-yuan degree in 1889, he was selected by the Kiangsu provincial commissioner of education for admission to the Nan-ching Academy in Chiangyin. In 1895, having been angered by the signing of the humiliating Treaty of Shimonoseki with Japan, he abandoned a promising civil-service career to enroll at the Hupeh Military Academy. After being graduated, he won a scholarship in 1900 for advanced military studies in Japan. Among his associates in Tokyo, where he was active in Chinese student groups, was Tsou Jung (ECCP, II, 769), whose provocative work, *Ko-ming chün* [the revolutionary army], was polished by Niu before its publication in 1903. In this book, Tsou Jung advocated the overthrow of the Manchus and the establishment of a Chinese republic. About this time, Niu met Sun Yat-sen, who was living in Yokohama.

In March 1903 Chinese students who were indignant about the Russian occupation of Manchuria held meetings to discuss ways of resisting Russian aggression. A large group of students decided to form the Association for Universal Military Training and to volunteer for military service. They dispatched Niu Yung-chien and T'ang Erh-ho (q.v.) to Tientsin to discuss the matter with Yuan Shih-k'ai (q.v.), who, however, refused to receive them. In the winter of 1903 Niu Yung-chien returned to China and established a military academy, the Tzu-kang School, in Shanghai. In addition to its primary function, the school also served as a cover for Niu's revolutionary activities.

In 1906 the military commissioner for the Taiping and Ssuen districts of Kwangsi, Chuang Yung-k'uan, a schoolmate of Niu at the Nan-ching Academy, invited Niu to become chief clerk at the Kwangsi border defense headquarters and commandant of the training corps at Lungchou. Niu accepted the offer and went to Lungchou with a dozen of his own men. He devoted several hours each day to drilling the training corps, and he continued to work secretly for the overthrow of the Manchus. He later was entrusted with the task of establishing a military preparatory school in Kwangsi.

Niu Yung-chien's activities became known to the Manchu court in 1910, and orders for his arrest were issued. Niu fled to Hong Kong and boarded a ship bound for Germany. He returned to Shanghai in the summer of 1911, and that November he served under Ch'en

Ch'i-mei (q.v.) during the capture of Shanghai by the republican revolutionaries. The 7th Battalion of the imperial army, stationed between Shanghai and Nanking and commanded by Hsü Shao-chen, staged an anti-Manchu uprising. It was suppressed by troops loyal to the Ch'ing government, but the rebels held on in areas around Chengchiang and sent Niu Yung-chien an appeal for help. Niu persuaded the Shanghai merchant Yü Hsia-ch'ing to lend him a large amount of money, and the revolutionary forces put these funds to good use. Before long, the magistrate of Chengchiang had cast his lot with the revolutionaries, and Hsü Shao-chen had become commander in chief of the Kiangsu-Chekiang allied forces. Niu Yung-chien went to Sungchiang to rally support for an assault on Nanking; Sungchiang soon declared independence, and Niu was elected to head the district.

When the provisional republican government was established at Nanking in January 1912, Niu Yung-chien was appointed assistant chief of staff in the general headquarters of the republican army. Sun Yat-sen soon decided to resign from the presidency in favor of Yuan Shih-k'ai (q.v.), and Niu was one of the special envoys dispatched to Peking to welcome Yuan and accompany him to Nanking for his inauguration. During the riots engineered by Yuan's supporters so that he would not leave the northern capital, Niu's hotel was looted by Yuan's soldiers. After Yuan assumed the presidency at Peking on 10 March, Niu resigned from office.

Niu Yung-chien was elected an honorary adviser of the Kuomintang when that party was founded in 1912. During the so-called second revolution of 1913 (*see* Li Lieh-chün) Ch'en Ch'i-mei ordered Niu to seize the Kiangnan Arsenal with a small squad consisting largely of students from Sungchiang. The attack was a failure, however, and Niu and his comrades fled to Japan. About this time, Niu became a convert to Christianity. In Japan, he reportedly joined the European Affairs Research Society, a group within the Kuomintang composed of men who did not support Sun Yat-sen's plans for reorganizing the Kuomintang. He left Japan in the winter of 1914 and traveled to the United States and England, where he continued to work against Yuan Shih-k'ai. He returned to Shanghai after Yuan died in June 1916.

Sun Yat-sen launched the so-called constitution protection movement and assumed the post of generalissimo of the southern revolutionary government at Canton in August 1917. On Sun's orders, Niu Yung-chien arrived in Canton that November, assumed command of about 15 battalions, and reorganized them as a division. Niu later served as assistant chief of staff in Sun's headquarters and as director of the Canton arsenal. An attempt on his life was made in November 1918, and he was hospitalized for several weeks. After recovering from his wounds, he resigned his posts and went back to Shanghai. In the summer of 1922, at Sun's behest, Niu traveled north in an attempt to persuade Feng Yü-hsiang (q.v.) to support the Kuomintang. Niu went north again in the winter of 1924, when Sun, then in Peking, appointed him and Wu Chih-hui to his political committee. Niu remained in Peking after Sun's death in April 1925, but returned to Canton in 1926.

After the Northern Expedition was launched, Niu was sent to Shanghai as the Kuomintang's special agent in charge of Kiangsu. He directed underground activities from a hideout in the French concession, and his efforts contributed a great deal to the peaceful takeover of Shanghai by the Kuomintang. When Chiang Kai-shek established a national government on 18 April 1927 in opposition to the one at Wuhan, Niu was appointed secretary general of the government. He resigned soon afterwards to become a member of the provincial government committee of Kiangsu and director of the bureau of civil affairs. Later in 1927 he became governor of Kiangsu, a post he held until March 1930. He reorganized the militia and public security forces of Kiangsu and brought order to even the most remote villages of the province; he initiated a program of land survey and registration; he reorganized the police system and set up a police academy; and he established a teachers college and worked to promote adult education.

Niu Yung-chien was appointed minister of the interior in the National Government in 1930, and about six months later he became minister of civil service in the Examination Yuan. In 1933 he was made vice president of the Examination Yuan, and in 1938 he resumed office as minister of civil service, retaining the yuan vice presidency. For reasons that are unclear, he resigned from these offices in December 1941. A month later, he was appointed chairman of the National Government's committee on the impeachment of civil servants, a post he held until 1948. Niu resumed the vice presidency of the Examination Yuan in March 1949, and he became its acting president in April 1949. He continued to serve as acting president of the yuan after the National Government moved to Taiwan. In April 1952 he retired from public life. The following year, he went to the United States for medical treatment, returning to Taiwan in 1957. He went back to the United States for surgery in 1958 and decided to stay there. Thereafter he lived in Lake Success, New York, with his daughter Mrs. Lewis Li. He died of pneumonia on 24 December 1965, at the age of 96. In addition to Mrs. Li, he was survived by his wife, *née* Huang Mei-sien; a son, Thorndike C. T. New; two daughters, Mrs. Sien-Wah Shen and Mrs. Samuel O. Moy; ten grandchildren; and eight great-grandchildren.

Osman

Alt. Usman Batur

Chinese. Wu-ssu-man 鳥 斯 曼

Osman (1899–April 1951), Kirei Kazakh military leader. He was executed in 1951 for opposing the Chinese Communists.

A Kazakh of the Kirei tribe, Osman was born in an encampment in the Altai region of northeast Sinkiang. The Kazakhs of Sinkiang were nomadic herdsmen, and Osman received his basic Islamic education in various encampments. He was introduced to warfare at the age of 12, when Boko Bator, a blood brother of Osman's father, took him along on an anti-Chinese campaign. With the failure of this uprising, Osman returned to his father's encampment. Much of his later education was devoted to riding, fighting, and learning to drink kumis; and he developed into a vigorous fighting man, noted for his large size and great strength.

Osman won fame among the Sinkiang Kazakhs during the administration of Sheng Shih-ts'ai (q.v.) in Sinkiang. Between 1937 and 1940 Sheng antagonized the Kazakhs by arresting many of their leaders and executing some of them. In 1940 Osman worked to mobilize resistance to Sheng's oppressive rule, but he and his rebel band were not strong enough to overcome the Chinese authorities. By the winter of 1942 Osman's small force, which had been driven out of Sharasume (Ch'enghua) had withdrawn to the upper reaches of the Bulgan River, on the Sinkiang-Mongolian border. Osman established his headquarters at Tayingkul, just inside the border of Outer Mongolia. He worked to foster Kazakh-Mongol cooperation, and he secured some arms and equipment from the Mongols. Before long, he had formulated a political program that called for Kazakh autonomy in the Altai region and for the barring of Chinese military and civilian officials from that region. Sheng Shih-ts'ai, meanwhile, strove to suppress Kazakh resistance through military action, including the use of aerial bombing, to destroy the Kazakhs, their yurts, and their livestock. Sheng asserted publicly that Osman was receiving Soviet aid and direction, and that Sinkiang would know neither prosperity nor peace until the Kazakhs were suppressed.

The Kazakh movement in Sinkiang gained support in November 1944, when open revolt against Chinese rule broke out in the Ili district of northwest Sinkiang. Osman apparently concluded an agreement with the Ili military leader Ali Khan Türe, and his Kazakh cavalrymen took advantage of Chinese preoccupation with the Ili revolt to capture Sharasume and Chugachak (T'ach'eng), leading towns in the Altai district. With the establishment of the so-called East Turkestan Republic at the beginning of 1945, Osman received the post of special executive officer for the Altai district, with headquarters at Sharasume. In November 1945 he severed relations with the Mongols of Outer Mongolia even though he was beginning to have difficulties with the Ili rebels.

In January 1946 Chang Chih-chung (q.v.) succeeded in working out an agreement that called for a coalition government in Sinkiang in which the non-Chinese nationalities of the province would gain representation. The Naiman Kazakh tribes continued to support the Ili group after this agreement was signed, but the Kirei Kazakhs, whom Osman represented, soon became restive. In April 1946 Osman, acting in the name of his Kazakh followers, denounced the Ili regime as Russian-dominated, struck camp, and marched into the mountains on the Sinkiang-Mongolian border. Later that year, after receiving a representative of Sung Hsi-lien (q.v.), the Chinese Nationalist military commander in Sinkiang, Osman came to terms with the Chinese authorities, his erstwhile enemies. He and his men clashed that summer and autumn with the Ili forces in the remote Baitak Bogdo (Peitashan) district. By 1948 Osman had demonstrated firm opposition to the Ili regime, the Mongolian People's Republic, and the Soviet Union. His continued support of the Chinese in Sinkiang won him command of three Paoan squadrons as a reward. In 1948 Osman's headquarters were located in the T'ienshan range, where he claimed power over 4,000 yurts and 15,000 Kazakhs. In the autumn of 1948 such American and British correspondents as A. Doak Barnett, Henry R. Lieberman, and Ian Morrison visited Osman at his T'ienshan encampment.

Osman took to the field again in 1949 when T'ao Chih-yüeh, who had replaced Sung Hsi-lien as top Nationalist commander in Sinkiang, switched allegiance to the Chinese Communists. After moving his forces toward Hami, Osman joined with Yolbars (q.v.) in organizing anti-Communist resistance. By September 1950, Osman had been forced to withdraw to a new base in the Gezkul district of Tsinghai. About this time, Yolbars decided that it was useless for the Kazakhs to attempt to maintain themselves against Chinese Communist power. He and many of his followers departed for India on the first leg of their journey to Taiwan. Osman, however, decided to remain behind. In February 1951 Chinese Communist military units, operating from bases in Hami and Urumchi, attacked the remnant Kazakh forces in their Gezkul encampment and captured Osman, one of his daughters, and some of his followers. Osman was taken to Urumchi, where he was executed as a counter-revolutionary in April 1951.

Ou-yang Ching-wu	歐 陽 竟 無
Orig. Ou-yang Chien	歐 陽 漸

Ou-yang Ching-wu (20 November 1871–23 February 1943), leading Buddhist layman and scholarly representative of the wei-shih school.

The son of an assistant department director

in the Board of Civil Affairs, Ou-yang Ching-wu was born in Ihuang, Kiangsi. His father died when Ou-yang was six, and he was raised by his mother and other female relatives. In 1890 he earned the sheng-yüan degree, but he did not study for higher degrees because he had abandoned the style of writing required in the examinations. Later on, Ou-yang attended the Ching-hsün Academy in Nanch'ang, where he specialized in Han Learning, the study of reaching truth through concrete facts. He also studied mathematics and astronomy. After the Sino-Japanese war of 1894–95 ended, he spent much of his time studying the writings of Lu Chiu-yuan (1139–1192) and Wang Yang-ming (1472–1529), two Neo-Confucian scholars who had opposed the rationalism of the Confucianist Chu Hsi. Ou-yang attempted to find principles of national salvation for China in these texts.

In 1904 Ou-yang Ching-wu sat for the metropolitan examination at Peking, but did not pass it. On his way back to Kiangsi, he stopped in Nanking and visited Yang Wen-hui (1837–1911; T. Jen-shan), who was the director of the Chin-ling k'o-ching ch'u (Nanking Buddhist Press). Ou-yang was so impressed by Yang that he began a study of Buddhism. Soon afterwards, he established the Ching-chih School in Ihuang, where he taught for one year. In 1906 he became inspector of schools at Kuang-ch'ang, but he left the post almost immediately because his mother was gravely ill. After her death, he was so grieved that he took the vows of a Buddhist chü-shih [lay-monk], which prohibited the eating of meat, sexual activity, and acceptance of official appointment. He retired to a mountain retreat at Chiu-feng-shan to mourn his mother's death and to attempt to achieve enlightenment. A year later, he returned to Nanking and began studying under Yang Wen-hui.

At Yang Wen-hui's suggestion, Ou-yang Ching-wu went to Japan in 1907 to study Shingon, or Japanese tantric Buddhism. In Tokyo he became acquainted with the scholars Chang Ping-lin and Liu Shih-p'ei (qq.v.), who also were interested in Buddhism. He returned to China in 1908, where he taught at the Canton Higher Normal School. A few months later, he was compelled by ill health to retire to Ihuang. Ou-yang went to Nanking in 1910 to study both wei-shih, or "consciousness-only,"

Buddhism and classical yoga under Yang Wen-hui. In 1911, after Yang died, he assumed the editorship of the Buddhist Press. He organized China Buddhist associations in 1912 at Nanking and Peking after proposals were made in the Parliament to make Confucianism the state religion; the pronouncements of the Buddhist associations bitterly criticized the inability of the Buddhist clergy to uphold their beliefs. As editor of the Buddhist Press, Ou-yang began in 1914 to publish "consciousness-only" scriptures brought to China from India and translated from Sanskrit into Chinese by Hsüan-tsang (602–64).

Ou-yang Ching-wu soon became a well-known editor and scholar, and he attracted a large following of Buddhist students. His teaching method in leading students to a comprehension of "consciousness-only" Buddhism was to acquaint them first with earlier Hinayana and Mahayana Buddhist writings in chronological and developmental sequence. In 1918 Ou-yang Ching-wu, Chang Ping-lin, Ch'en San-li (q.v.), and others established the China Institute of Inner Learning at Nanking, where much valuable research on Buddhism was done during the next ten years. In July 1922 Ou-yang was appointed chancellor of the Nanking Buddhist Academy; his inauguration was attended by such Buddhist laymen as Liang Ch'i-ch'ao, Carsun Chang (Chang Chia-sen, qq.v.), and others. In 1925 Ou-yang Ching-wu and about 40 of his students at the academy began to edit and publish more than 100 volumes of Buddhist scriptures which had been translated from Sanskrit into Chinese during the T'ang period (618–907). However, work on the project had to be suspended during the political disturbances of 1927 (*see* Chiang Kai-shek) when Nationalist soldiers encamped on the academy grounds. In 1928 Ou-yang traveled to Lushan, Kiangsi, to discuss Buddhism with Ch'en San-li and Liang Ch'i-ch'ao. After order and political stability had been restored in Nanking, he returned to the academy.

During the 1930's Ou-yang Ching-wu continued to pursue his editorial, scholarly, and teaching activities. In 1931 he founded the *Nei-yüan nien-k'an* [academy annual] and the *Nei-yüan tsa-chih* [academy magazine] to discuss and propagate "consciousness-only" doctrine. He also became agitated about the threat of Japanese aggression in north China, and in

January 1932 he called upon Ch'en Ming-shu (q.v.), who had been one of his students and who had become minister of communications in the National Government, to urge strong military resistance to Japan. After the Sino-Japanese war began in the summer of 1937, Ou-yang moved the Buddhist Academy from Nanking to Chiangchin, Szechwan. He continued to direct the academy until his death on 23 February 1943.

Ou-yang Ching-wu married at an early age, and he continued to live with his wife and children after taking Buddhist lay vows in 1905. His daughter, Ou-yang Lan, died in 1914, and his second son, Ou-yang Tung, drowned in 1923; his wife *née* Hsiung, died in 1940. His eldest son, Ou-yang Ko, was captain of the gunboat Yung-feng, the vessel in which Sun Yat-sen took refuge after the June 1922 coup of Ch'en Chiung-ming (q.v.).

Ou-yang Ching-wu was one of the foremost Buddhist laymen of his day, and he achieved fame for his leadership of the movement to revive the "consciousness-only" school of Buddhism. This school, which was founded in India by Asanga (c. 410–c. 500), was a dominating influence on Chinese scholars from the fifth to the seventh century. Ou-yang Ching-wu's major contributions to the literature of "consciousness-only" Buddhism were his prefaces for the classical Buddhist texts published by the China Institute of Inner Learning and his "Wei-shih chueh-tse t'an" [a decisive analysis of idealism], in which he attacked the doctrine of *The Awakening of Faith*, upheld by the Ching-t'u sect and the T'ien-t'ai and Hua Yen schools. Ou-yang's well-known statement that "Buddhism is neither religion nor philosophy" reflects his view of Buddhism as a unique system which includes all branches of human discipline. In the 1920's he engaged in a number of polemical arguments with T'ai-hsü (q.v.), who believed that a broad synthesis of Buddhism and Western thought was necessary. Ou-yang opposed synthesis and advocated strict adherence to the tenets of "consciousness-only" Buddhism. He also disagreed with Hsiung Shih-li (q.v.), who reconstructed idealistic Neo-Confucian philosophy to include "consciousness-only" concepts. Ou-yang Ching-wu's collected works, *Ching-wu nei-wai-hsüeh*, were published posthumously.

Ou-yang Yü-ch'ien   歐 陽 予 倩
Orig.   Li-yuan   立 袁
T.   Nan-chieh   南 傑

Ou-yang Yü-ch'ien (1887–21 September 1962), teacher, actor, playwright, and director whose career reflects the development of drama and cinema in twentieth-century China.

Liuyang, Hunan, was the birthplace of Ou-yang Yü-ch'ien. His paternal grandfather, Ou-yang Chung-ku, was provincial treasurer of Kwangsi during the last years of the Ch'ing dynasty, and his maternal grandfather, Liu Jen-hsi, was the military governor of Hunan during the early years of the Chinese republic. When Ou-yang Yü-ch'ien was ten, a family servant took him to a private Peking opera performance given in the house of one of his grandfathers for some festive occasion. Because the boy was intrigued by the performance, the family servant, an avid theater-goer, taught him a hua-tan [young woman] role from the play *Mei-lung-chen*. Thereafter, Ou-yang often amused himself by pretending to be an actor.

About 1899 Ou-yang went to Peking to attend school for a year. He then spent one term in Changsha at the Ching Cheng Middle School before going to Japan to study military science at a Tokyo middle school. Except for a visit to his family in 1905, he remained in Japan until 1911. Ou-yang later recalled that during his school days in Peking he had seen the great T'an Hsin-p'ei (q.v.) in a traditional role, but the performance had made little impression on him. Not until he went to Tokyo was his interest in the theater aroused. In February 1907 he saw an adaptation of *La Dame aux camélias* entitled *Ch'a-hua Nü*, staged by the Ch'un-liu chü-she [spring willow dramatic society] to aid the Hsuchou Relief Fund. The Ch'un-liu chü-she had been founded by Chinese students under the strong influence of the Japanese modern drama movement (*see* Li Shu-t'ung), and this production gave Ou-yang his first experience of non-operatic drama. In the winter of 1907 Ou-yang was invited to become a member of the Ch'un-liu chü-she and was given a part in its second production, an adaptation of *Uncle Tom's Cabin* called *Hei-nu yü-t'ien lu* [the black slave's cry to heaven]. He soon became a leading member of the dramatic group, and he began to study stage technique under the guidance of teachers. Women were not yet seen on the stage, and Ou-yang decided to specialize in hua-tan roles.

In 1911, having been graduated from the literature department of Waseda University in Tokyo, Ou-yang Yü-ch'ien returned to China. He went to Shanghai in 1912 and became a member of the Hsi-chü t'ung-hui [drama league], newly organized by Lu Ching-jo to encourage hua-chü [spoken drama]. This group performed at the Chang Yuan, a well-known entertainment center of the period. Ou-yang spent 1913 at his family's home in Changsha, but he returned to Shanghai in 1914 to join the Ch'un-liu chü-ch'ang [spring willow drama company], established by Lu Ching-jo with the help of several former members of the Ch'un-liu chü-she. The troupe performed for nearly a year at a theater on Nanking Road in Shanghai, but it disbanded after Lu Ching-jo died.

Ou-yang Yü-ch'ien gradually rose to prominence as an actor of hua-tan roles on the Shanghai stage. This achievement was particularly noteworthy because he was the first of his family to become an actor. At this time, many of the actors in Peking opera productions came from famous theatrical families. Like Mei Lan-fang (q.v.), Ou-yang experimented with traditional-style plays, incorporating new costumes and techniques. In 1918 Chang Chien (q.v.), who had created a model community in Nant'ung, Kiangsu, invited Ou-yang there to direct the Ling-kung hsueh-she, a school for actors. Ou-yang accepted, and he proceeded to modernize the school's curriculum and methods. Corporal punishment was abolished, and students were required to study a variety of subjects so that they would have a good general education in addition to training in stagecraft. The school came to have its own theater and a musical research department. After spending three years at Nant'ung, Ou-yang returned to the Shanghai stage.

In September 1923 Ou-yang Yü-ch'ien joined the Shanghai hsi-chü hsieh-she [Shanghai dramatic association], which had been established by Ku Chien-ch'en and others to present modern hua-chü dramas. The association staged two of Ou-yang's plays: *P'o-fu* [the shrew] and *Hui-chia i-hou* [after returning home].

In 1925 Ou-yang left Shanghai briefly to organize a modern drama group at Changsha. He left Shanghai again two years later, this time to take charge of the newly established Kuo-min hsi-ch'ang [national theater] at Nanking, working with T'ien Han (q.v.) and his associates. In 1929 he assumed direction of the Kuan-yueh hsi-chü yen-chiu-so [Kwang-tung musical and dramatic institute].

By 1930 Ou-yang Yü-ch'ien had abandoned his career as an actor in traditional dramas. He traveled to Europe, and in 1933 he went to Russia twice and to Germany, where he met leading film-makers. After taking part in the Fukien revolt in the winter of 1933, he took refuge in Japan for six months. Upon his return to China in 1934 he became associated with the Hsin-hua ying-yeh kung-ssu, a Shanghai film company. In 1936 he joined the Star Motion Picture Company as head scriptwriter. He went to Hong Kong in 1938 to prepare the script for *Mu-lan ts'ung-chün* [Mu-lan enlists], a costume picture based on the adventures of a famous Chinese heroine. He also found time to edit editions of ancient plays and to organize a drama group in Hong Kong.

In the autumn of 1939 Ou-yang went to Kweilin, where he became director of the Kuang-hsi i-shu kuan [Kwangsi institute of art], and chairman of the Kweilin branch of the All-China Resistance to the Enemy Federation of Writers and Artists. He remained in Kweilin until the Sino-Japanese war ended and wrote several propaganda plays during his stay there. He returned to Shanghai in 1946, where he worked with the Hsin Chung chü-she [new China drama company] and wrote the script for a film entitled *Kuan-pu-chu ti ch'un-kuang*. In 1947 he accompanied the Hsin Chung chü-she on a tour of Taiwan, and in 1948 he went to live in Hong Kong.

Ou-yang Yü-ch'ien went to Peiping in April 1949 and immediately received membership on the Chinese delegation to the World Peace Conference in Paris. He became a member of the preparatory committee of the Chinese People's Political Consultative Conference in June and a member of the standing committee of the All-China Federation of Literary and Art Circles in July. After the Central People's Government was established, he served as director of the Central Institute of Drama, becoming its president when it was reorganized in 1950 in a merger with the Nanking National Drama School and the drama department of North China University. He also was vice chairman of the first national committee of the All-China Federation of Literary and Art Circles (1949–52), a member of the All-China Drama Workers Association (1953–61), a member of the culture and education committee of the Government Administration Council (1949–53), and a member of the cinema guidance and drama reform committees of the ministry of culture. In 1955 he was listed as a member of the Chinese Communist party. He accompanied Mei Lan-fang's troupe to Japan in 1955, and he continued to devote much of his time to theatrical endeavors. On 21 September 1962, after a long illness, he died in Peking.

In the course of his career, Ou-yang Yü-ch'ien was actor and playwright in both the traditional opera and the modern hua-chü drama, a teacher of actors, a reformer, and an actor, director, and producer of motion pictures; his career reflects the development of drama and cinema in twentieth-century China. He consistently used his talents and knowledge to preserve the dignity of the old dramatic forms while working to develop new theatrical movements.

Pa Chin: *see* LI FEI-KAN.

Pai Ch'ung-hsi   白 崇 禧
  T. Chien-sheng   健 生

Pai Ch'ung-hsi (1893–2 December 1966), general of the Kwangsi clique, which also included Li Tsung-jen and Huang Shao-hung. In 1946–48 he was minister of national defense in the National Government. At the end of 1949 he went to Taiwan, where he became vice director of the strategic advisory commission in the presidential office.

The second of three sons, Pai Ch'ung-hsi was born into a Chinese Muslim family in Shanwei village, Linkuei hsien, Kwangsi. The Pai clan, whose members had been farmers for generations, was said to have come to Kwangsi from Szechwan many years before Pai Ch'ung-hsi's birth. After receiving a traditional primary education in the Chinese classics, Pai Ch'ung-hsi was sent to a modern school in the town of Huihsien. In 1906, at the age of 14 sui, he enrolled at the Kwangsi Army Primary School, where his schoolmates included Li Tsung-jen and Huang Shao-hung (qq.v.). He later withdrew from the academy at the request of his family and entered a civilian institution, the Kwangsi School of Law and Political Science. Late in 1911, after the Wuchang revolt and the declaration of independence in Kwangsi, he left school and joined the Students Army Dare-to-Die Corps, of which Huang Shao-hung was a squad commander. This unit marched northward to Wuchang, but arrived there too late to participate in the fighting. It then was transferred to Nanking and disbanded. The discharged student-soldiers entered the Nanking Enlistment Corps, and they later were transferred to the Second Military Preparatory School at Wuchang.

After being graduated in the winter of 1914, Pai Ch'ung-hsi and some of his classmates went to Peking and received six months of "pre-cadet training." In June 1915 Pai entered the third class of the Paoting Military Academy, where his classmates included Huang Shao-hung and Hsia Wei. Soon after graduation late in 1916, he organized a group of 36 fellow graduates and petitioned the Peking government to accept their services in the frontier region of Sinkiang. Although the Peking government accepted his petition and gave him a commission, the project had to be abandoned in 1917.

Pai Ch'ung-hsi returned to Kwangsi as a probationary officer in the 1st Kwangsi Division. In the summer of 1917 the Kwangsi Model Battalion was established by the provincial government. Its commander was Ma Hsiao-chün, a graduate of the Shikan Gakkō [military academy] in Japan, and its officers included Pai Ch'ung-hsi, Huang Shao-hung, and Hsia Wei. The Model Battalion soon was ordered to Hunan to participate in the so-called constitution protection movement as a guard unit serving under T'an Hao-ming, tuchün [military governor] of Kwangsi and commander in chief of the Hunan-Kwangtung-Kwangsi Constitution-Protection Army. A machine-gun company was added to the Model Battalion, and Pai Ch'ung-hsi, Huang Shao-hung, and Hsia Wei all volunteered as deputy commanders. The three men received joint command of the company.

Early in the autumn of 1918 T'an Hao-ming, having been defeated by Wu P'ei-fu (q.v.), reorganized the Model Battalion. Pai Ch'ung-hsi and Huang Shao-hung each received command of a company. The Kwangsi forces returned home early in 1919, and the Model Battalion then saw a year of garrison service in western Kwangsi, where it proved effective in the so-called bandit-suppression campaigns. That winter, Ma Hsiao-chün, because of his success in these campaigns, was given command of the Model Battalion, which then was ordered to Chaoch'ing in western Kwangtung to replace the local garrison force. Later in 1920 it marched eastward to garrison Canton on orders from Lu Jung-t'ing (q.v.). The Kwangsi troops were defeated in October by the Kwangtung Army of Ch'en Chiung-ming (q.v.) and were forced to retreat to Kwangsi along the northern bank of the West River. The Model Battalion, in cooperation with the forces of Li Tsung-jen, served as the rear guard.

After their return to Kwangsi, Pai Ch'ung-hsi and Huang Shao-hung followed Ma Hsiao-chün to Paise (Poseh) in February 1921. The war between Kwangtung and Kwangsi began again in June, and Kwangtung troops commanded by Ch'en Chiung-ming soon occupied Kwangsi. The Model Battalion endeavored to remain aloof from the conflict and to recruit men. Ma reorganized it as a five-battalion army, with Pai Ch'ung-hsi as commander of the 2nd Battalion. When the army was surrounded by Liu Jih-fu's Kwangsi Antonomous Army, Pai escaped with some of his men. After he had recruited new troops, Ma appointed him commander of the 2nd Regiment. Liu Jih-fu's force was defeated by the Kwangtung Army later in 1921, and Ma and his men then returned to Paise. About this time, Pai fell from a cliff during a night inspection tour and suffered a broken leg and other injuries. He gave command of his regiment to Huang Shao-hung and went to Canton for medical treatment.

Pai Ch'ung-hsi arrived in Canton in the summer of 1922. After Sun Yat-sen returned to Canton in February 1923, he asked Pai to return to Kwangsi and persuade Huang Shao-hung to accept appointment as commander in chief of the Kwangsi Anti-Rebel Army. The purpose of the new force was to defeat Shen Hung-ying, under whom Huang then was serving at Wuchow. Huang seized Wuchow

that autumn after Shen's expeditionary force had been defeated in Kwangtung. He then proceeded to organize the Kwangsi Anti-Rebel Army, with Pai Ch'ung-hsi as his chief of staff. The new force cooperated closely with Li Tsung-jen's Kwangsi Pacification Army at Yülin to defeat other forces in the province. After Lu Jung-t'ing and Shen Hung-ying began to vie for control of Kwangsi, Pai Ch'ung-hsi, Huang Shao-hung, and Li Tsung-jen decided to ally themselves with Shen. In June 1924 their forces took Nanning, and the following month the two armies were combined to form the Kwangsi Pacification Anti-Rebel Army, with Li as commander in chief, Huang as his deputy, and Pai as field commander and chief of staff. Lu Jung-t'ing's forces were defeated in September, and the Kwangsi Pacification Anti-Rebel Army was abolished on 1 December. Pai, Li, and Huang all joined the Kuomintang about this time. Li then became Kwangsi pacification commissioner and commander of the First Kwangsi Army, with Huang as deputy commissioner and commander of the Second Kwangsi Army, and Pai as chief of staff of the pacification commission and the Second Kwangsi Army. Early in 1925 these forces joined with the Kwangtung 1st Division, commanded by Li Chi-shen (q.v.), to drive Shen Hung-ying into Hunan. A short time later T'ang Chi-yao (q.v.), the military governor of Yunnan, tried to send troops through Kwangsi to Canton so that he could succeed Sun Yat-sen, who had died on 12 March. During the ensuing battles in northern Kwangsi, Pai Ch'ung-hsi participated in a general counteroffensive at Shap'u which ended in victory for his troops. T'ang's battered forces soon retreated from Kwangsi. Pai also helped in the suppression of Szechwan troops under Hsiung K'o-wu (q.v.) which had marched into Kwangtung. By this time, Pai's tactical abilities had won him the nickname Hsiao Chu-ko, signifying that he was deemed a worthy successor of the great military strategist of the Three Kingdoms period, Chu-ko Liang (181–234).

By the end of 1925 Kwangsi had come under the control of the three men who became known as the Kwangsi clique, and negotiations for closer cooperation between Kwangsi and Kwangtung had begun. In March 1926, after lengthy discussions, the Kwangsi forces were reorganized as the Seventh Army of the National

Revolutionary Army, with Pai Ch'ung-hsi as chief of staff and commander of the 2nd Brigade, Li Tsung-jen as commander, and Huang Shao-hung as party representative. Later that month, Pai Ch'ung-hsi and Ch'en Ming-shu (q.v.) were sent to Changsha to persuade T'ang Sheng-chih (q.v.) to ally himself with the Nationalists. Their success in winning T'ang's support enabled the National Revolutionary Army to make a decisive start on its move northward. After the Northern Expedition began, Pai served as deputy chief of staff of the National Revolutionary Army. In November 1926, after the Nationalist capture of Nanchang, he was given command of a pursuit force. He later served with Ho Ying-ch'in (q.v.) in the East River district of Kwangtung and participated in the overthrow of Chou Ying-jen, the military governor of Fukien.

Early in 1927 Pai Ch'ung-hsi was appointed field commander of the Eastern Route Army. After his forces captured Hangchow on 18 February and Shanghai on 22 March, he received the concurrent post of Woosung-Shanghai garrison commander. In April, he was given the authority to purge the Communists in Shanghai. On 12 April, he struck, disarming the volunteers of the Workers General Union, demolishing underground Communist organs, and ordering the execution of known Communists and other leftists. Thus the vigorous Communist movement in Shanghai was crushed. When Chiang Kai-shek established a national government at Nanking on 18 April in opposition to the government at Wuhan, Pai accepted an appointment from Chiang as acting commander of the Second Route Army. Pai participated in the capture of Hsuchow in June, moved into Shantung, and then pulled back to northern Kiangsu as military and political pressures mounted.

Chiang Kai-shek announced his retirement in the interest of party unity and went to Japan in August 1927. The headquarters of the commander in chief of the National Revolutionary Army then was reorganized as the Military Affairs Commission, with Pai Ch'ung-hsi, Li Tsung-jen, and Ho Ying-ch'in constituting the standing committee. Late in August, the trio won a victory over Sun Ch'uan-fang (q.v.), whose troops had crossed the Yangtze at Lungt'ang in an attempt to recapture Nanking and Shanghai. On 15 September, the Central

Special Committee was formed by the leaders of the Nanking, Wuhan, and Western Hills factions to serve as an interim government. T'ang Sheng-chih, then at Wuhan, objected to the reunification measures, and the authorities at Nanking launched a campaign against him in October, with Pai Ch'ung-hsi as field commander and Li Tsung-jen as commander in chief. Pai occupied Wuhan early in November, forcing T'ang into temporary retirement. Early in 1928 he extended his offensive into Hunan province in pursuit of T'ang's remaining troops. They soon surrendered, and in February 1928 they were combined with other forces to form the Fourth Group Army, with Li Tsung-jen as commander in chief and Pai Ch'ung-hsi as his deputy. About this time, Pai also received command of the newly established Thirteenth Army, composed of troops from the Fourteenth Army and the 2nd Brigade of the Seventh Army. Pai participated in the drive on Peking in June 1928 which brought the Northern Expedition to completion. After Peking fell to the Nationalists, he was given command of a mixed force from the four group armies and was ordered to destroy the remnants of Northern forces inside the Great Wall. Having completed this task, he returned to the northern capital with his troops. He then became a member of the Peiping branch of the Political Council. At his own request, Pai Ch'ung-hsi then was sent to the northwestern frontier region at the head of troops from the Fourth Group Army.

Early in 1929 the Kwangsi clique came into conflict with Chiang Kai-shek, who sent T'ang Sheng-chih to north China to recover control of the Hunan troops under Pai's command. T'ang's coup was successful, and Pai fled to Kwangsi. On 26 March, Li Tsung-jen and Pai Ch'ung-hsi were relieved of their official posts and denounced as plotters against the government; on 27 March, they were expelled from the Kuomintang. Pai Ch'ung-hsi and Huang Shao-hung launched an unsuccessful attack on Kwangtung, following which they were set upon by Liu Chien-hsü, who occupied Kweilin. The forces of Yü Tso-po, who had been appointed to succeed Huang as governor of Kwangsi, occupied Nanning on 27 June. Pai and Huang then went to Hong Kong, by way of Indo-China, to join Li Tsung-jen. In November, the three men returned to Kwangsi and established the Party-Protecting National Salvation Army at Nanning, with Li as commander in chief, Huang as deputy commander and governor of Kwangsi, and Pai as field commander.

In January 1930 the Kwangsi forces and the Fourth Army of Chang Fa-k'uei (q.v.) made an attempt to capture Canton, but they soon were defeated and forced back to Kwangsi. In May, the four generals decided to support the northern coalition of Feng Yü-hsiang and Yen Hsi-shan (qq.v.) by invading Hunan and capturing Wuhan. This move ended in defeat at Hung-chiao, and the remnants of the Kwangsi forces returned home to regroup. Huang Shao-hung, who opposed the policy of continuing the civil war, then broke with the Kwangsi clique.

The arrest of Hu Han-min (q.v.) at Nanking on 28 February 1931 and the formation in May 1931 of an opposition government at Canton by such political leaders as Wang Ching-wei, Eugene Ch'en, and Ch'en Chi-t'ang (qq.v.) opened the way for a reconciliation of Kwangsi and Kwangtung. A military alliance was formed, and a joint Kwangsi-Kwangtung force moved to challenge the National Government by invading southern Hunan in early September. On 18 September, the Japanese attacked Mukden, and the National Government called for national unity. The Canton regime dissolved itself after gaining the release of Li Chi-shen and Hu Han-min and the temporary retirement of Chiang Kai-shek. In November, Pai Ch'ung-hsi was elected to the Central Executive Committee of the Kuomintang.

In April 1932 Li Tsung-jen was appointed pacification commissioner of Kwangsi, with Pai Ch'ung-hsi as deputy pacification commissioner. The two men then began the work of reconstructing Kwangsi by putting into practice the san-tzu cheng-ts'e [three-self policy] of self-government, self-defense, and self-sufficiency and the san-yü cheng-ts'e [three-reservation policy] of building military power. The vehicle used to put these policies into effect was the min-t'uan system. In 1932 Pai Ch'ung-hsi was appointed commander in chief of the Kwangsi provincial militia and was placed in charge of the administration of the min-t'uan system throughout the province.

Min-t'uan was an old term which meant little more than "militia" until Pai Ch'ung-hsi put the new program into effect. The new system was built into the provincial political structure. In the early 1930's, the province of

Kwangsi consisted of 94 (later 99) hsien, with a total population of approximately 12,800,000. Each hsien was composed of ten ch'ü, which, in turn, consisted of about ten hsiang. The basic unit of political administration was the ts'un, of which there were ten in each hsiang. There were approximately 24,000 ts'un in Kwangsi.

According to the Kwangsi law of conscription, adopted in June 1933, every able-bodied male adult between the ages of 18 and 45 was subject to compulsory draft. Those who were not drafted were required to serve in the min-t'uan. Its basic unit was the squad, which contained nine to thirteen militiamen. Three or four squads constituted a platoon, of which there were several in each company. The chief of a ts'un held a concurrent appointment as commander of the company organized under his jurisdiction. Several companies constituted a battalion, with the chief of the hsiang as battalion commander. A column was composed of several battalions, and the column commander was the chief of the ch'ü. In each hsien there was a min-t'uan headquarters, and the hsien magistrate served as commander of all the columns in his district. The district headquarters were organized into about a dozen divisional headquarters, each of which was headed by a professional soldier who held no civilian appointments. The divisional headquarters were under the over-all command of Pai Ch'ung-hsi.

Each militiaman had to undergo, in his leisure time, fundamental military training totaling 180 hours a year. According to Pai's personal estimate, all the able-bodied male adults in Kwangsi would be trained soldiers. In an emergency, an enormous army could be mobilized overnight, with the assistance of an efficient radio network throughout the province. The min-t'uan system also was interwoven with the provincial educational system. Because most of the militia commanders in the lower ranks were unpaid volunteers, they supported themselves by teaching in primary schools. Thus, a trained person appointed to a position in the min-t'uan had to perform a three-fold public duty: political administrator, military commander, and teacher. During large-scale public construction, min-t'uan commanders would serve as directors and foremen in a huge corvee labor system.

Under Pai Ch'ung-hsi's direction, the min-t'uan system turned Kwangsi into a military polity which was relatively free from crime. At the same time, Kwangsi began to develop itself industrially and to undertake the construction of public works. These achievements helped to make Pai Ch'ung-hsi and Li Tsung-jen nationally famous as capable administrators and efficient mass organizers.

In June 1936 Pai Ch'ung-hsi moved Kwangsi forces into southern Hunan and issued an order for the general mobilization of Kwangsi and Kwangtung forces. This order in part was an attempt to forestall the possibility of National Government action to end the semi-independence of Kwangtung following the death of Hu Han-min. However, the announced purpose of the mobilization was a northward march to protect China because Chiang Kai-shek was not resisting the Japanese. Pai Ch'ung-hsi and Li Tsung-jen became deputy commanders of the First Anti-Japanese National Salvation Forces, serving under Ch'en Chi-t'ang. The movement collapsed in early July after the Kwangtung air force defected to the National Government. On 25 July, the National Government appointed Pai Ch'ung-hsi governor of Chekiang, but he rejected the post as an attempt to remove him from Kwangsi.

At the end of July 1936 Pai Ch'ung-hsi and Li Tsung-jen organized a military government in Kwangsi and appointed Li Chi-shen its chairman. Through mediation efforts of Huang Shao-hung and Ch'eng Ch'ien, however, the Kwangsi leaders resolved their differences with Chiang Kai-shek. Kwangsi then accepted the authority of the National Government, and the Kwangsi forces were reorganized as the Fifth Route Army, with Li Tsung-jen as commander in chief and Pai Ch'ung-hsi as deputy commander.

Soon after the Sino-Japanese war began in July 1937, Pai Ch'ung-hsi went to Kuling for a conference with Chiang Kai-shek. He then became deputy joint chief of staff in the Military Affairs Commission and a member of the National Aeronautical Council, in which posts he played a major role in the formulation of battle strategy for the Nanking-Shanghai area. He accompanied the National Government to the wartime capital of Chungking, where he continued to participate in strategy planning for such actions as the Taierhchuang campaign

of 1938. On occasion, he was sent to help field commanders win their battles. He also helped organize the Chinese Islamic National Salvation Federation (later the China Islamic Association), which helped mobilize the Muslims of China in support of the war, and he served as its president.

In November 1938 Pai was appointed director of the Kweilin field headquarters to unify the command of the three war zones south of the Yangtze. When Japanese troops landed at Kwangchouwan and invaded Kwangsi in 1939, Pai personally commanded the Chinese forces which fought the Japanese in the vicinity of the K'unlun pass. Because he failed to drive the Japanese back as ordered, he was recalled to Chungking, where he served until war's end as deputy joint chief of staff, director of the military training board, and chairman of the military inspection committee in the Military Affairs Commission.

With the creation of the ministry of national defense on 1 June 1946 to replace the ministry of war, Pai Ch'ung-hsi was appointed minister, with Ch'en Ch'eng as chief of general staff. In 1948 Pai also became director of the Strategic Advisory Commission. By this time, the Nationalist-Communist struggle for control of the mainland was reaching its height. Pai proposed that the Nationalist troops between the Yellow River and the Yangtze River be placed under a single commander. Chiang Kai-shek, however, decided that the area should be under two commanders—a commander in chief for bandit suppression in east China and another in central China at Wuhan. Pai was removed from office as minister of national defense and was transferred to the Wuhan post. As the Nationalist position in the Hsuchow sector deteriorated, Pai was called upon to reinforce it, but the request came too late. As the situation worsened, Pai in late December sent Chiang a series of telegrams advising negotiations with the Chinese Communists. Those telegrams, together with others sent by provincial authorities in Honan and Hunan, were a factor in Chiang Kai-shek's decision to retire from office on 21 January 1949, leaving Li Tsung-jen to serve as acting President. Li and Pai evolved a plan to defend the Yangtze River line, but Chiang, who continued to issue orders as tsung-ts'ai [party leader], refused to authorize the plan. By this time, Chiang had already begun to move troops to the offshore islands. Pai Ch'ung-hsi lost battles with the Chinese Communists in Hupeh, Hunan, and Kiangsi after some of his troops were shifted to other areas. In October, when the National Government moved from Canton to Chungking, Pai withdrew to Kwangsi. He planned to make a last stand at the Luichow peninsula and on Hainan Island, but Chiang Kai-shek ordered a large part of his force to Kweichow. At the end of 1949, Pai fled from Nanning to Taiwan.

In 1950 Pai Ch'ung-hsi became vice director of the strategic advisory commission in the presidential office. A member of the Central Executive Committee of the Kuomintang, he also belonged to the committee charged with carrying out party reorganization in Taiwan in 1950–52. On 2 December 1966 he suffered a heart attack and died in Taipei, at the age of 74. He was survived by his wife, Ma P'ei-chang, whom he had married in 1925, and by seven sons and three daughters.

Pai Yang   白 揚

Pai Yang (c. 1920–), leading film actress known for her performances in such productions as *I-chiang ch'un-shui hsiang-tung liu*.

Little is known about Pai Yang's family background or personal life. According to some sources, she was born in Peking in 1920, and she began her stage career at the age of 12 when she passed the entrance examinations for the Peking branch training school of the Lien-hua ying-yeh kung-ssu [united photoplay service]. Other sources give her birthplace as Hsiangt'an, Hunan, and her birthdate as 1916. In any event, she was a graduate of the Peiping Institute of Dramatic Art, and she began her professional career as a member of the Chung-kuo lü-hsing chü-t'uan [China traveling dramatic troupe], headed by T'ang Huai-ch'iu. She also took part in some of the rural productions staged by Hsiung Fo-hsi (q.v.). Her vivacious acting and personality soon brought her recognition, and it seems likely that she would have become China's premier legitimate actress if she had not decided to enter the film world.

The first film in which Pai Yang appeared was made in 1936 and was shown in Shanghai in 1937. Entitled *Shih-tzu chieh-t'ou* [at the cross-roads], the film was directed by Shen Hsi-ling and produced at the Ming-hsing ying-p'ien kung-ssu [star film company studios], with Chao Tan as the male lead. The film, which was concerned with unemployment problems, contained much implicit social criticism. Its anti-Japanese bias was sufficiently strong for the Shanghai Municipal Council to order one scene cut in deference to possible Japanese sensitivity. *Shih-tzu chieh-t'ou* brought Pai Yang to the forefront as a screen actress, and she became a favorite of a more critical public than had existed previously. She and Hu Tieh (q.v.) became the two leading stars of their day, and a number of critics and other intellectuals preferred the performance of Pai Yang to those of her colleague.

Some of Pai Yang's more popular feature films were *She-hui-chih-hua* [the flower of society], of 1937; *Chung-hua erh-nü* [daughter of China], of 1939; and *Ch'ing-nien Chung-kuo* [young China], of 1941. Perhaps the film for which she is best remembered by the postwar generation was the marathon production (really two films), *Pa-ch'ien li-lu yün-ho-yüeh* [eight thousand leagues away lie the clouds and the moon] and *Pa-nien wan-luan* [eight years of chaos], the first being made in 1946 and the second in 1947. The double production was screened in 1947 under the title *I-chiang ch'un-shui hsiang-tung liu*, rendered in English as *The Tears of the Yangtze*. The film depicted the vicissitudes of the people in wartime China against a background of corrupt government administration. It took four hours to screen, and it broke all box-office records in Shanghai by running for eighty-four consecutive days. The producer was the K'un-lun ying-yeh kung-ssu [K'un-lun film company].

During the Sino-Japanese war years, which she spent in Chungking, Pai Yang married the playwright and Western theater specialist Chang Chün-hsiang (q.v.). They later were divorced. After the Chinese Communists came to power, Pai Yang remained in China and continued to appear in films. Two notable ones were *Wei-liao ho-p'ing* [in the cause of peace], which was made in 1954, and *Chu-fu* [the blessing], which was released in 1956.

An honored figure in the People's Republic of China, Pai Yang was voted the nation's most popular screen actress in a public poll taken in the mid-1950's. She took part in public affairs in the 1950's by reading poetry before large audiences in Shanghai, going abroad as a member of various cultural missions, and serving as vice chairman of the China Film Workers Union. During this period, Pai Yang married Chiang Chün-ch'ao, a film director and former actor. They had two children, a girl and a boy.

Pai Yun-t'i: *see* BUYANTAI.

Panchen Lama (Ninth)
>   Tibetan. Lop-sang Tub-dan Ju-gye I-ma
>   Go-lok La-mu-gye
>   Secular. Erdeni Chuyi-Geltseng

Panchen Lama (1883–1 December 1937), earthly manifestation of the buddha Amitābha. When the thirteenth Dalai Lama (q.v.) was in exile (1904–9, 1910–12), the ninth Panchen was *de facto* ruler of Tibet. The Panchen was forced into exile by the Dalai in November 1923.

The eighth Panchen Rimpoche [precious sage], the earthly manifestation of the buddha Amitābha, died late in 1882, and the search for his infant successor, the new incarnation of Amitābha, began immediately under the direction of high ecclesiastical dignitaries. Among the candidates was Erdeni Chuyi-Geltseng, a child born in the province of Tak-po about whom rumors of miraculous signs and gifts were circulating. A committee of high lamas investigated the child when he was three. In 1888 his name was selected from a golden urn in a traditional ceremony at Lhasa, and on 1 February 1892 he took his seat on the holy couch at Tashi Lhunpo as the ninth Panchen Lama.

The Panchen Lama's youth was devoted to studying the Buddhist doctrines traditionally expounded at the Tashi Lhunpo monastery and to mastering the administration of the monastery's extensive land holdings. The Tashi Lhunpo monastery was second only to the Dalai Lama's capital of Lhasa in territorial and political importance. The thirteenth Dalai Lama helped guide the Panchen Lama's academic and spiritual education, and in 1902 the Panchen Lama made a pilgrimage to Lhasa to take the most solemn religious vows at an ordination ceremony presided over by the Dalai Lama. This event, which occasioned several weeks of celebration throughout Tibet, marked the Panchen's coming to spiritual maturity and to full control of the secular affairs of the Tashi Lhunpo monastery.

In 1903 a British expedition led by Colonel Francis Younghusband, bent on forcing Tibetan compliance with the provisions of a Sino-British treaty, made camp at Khamba, which was within the jurisdiction of the Tashi Lhunpo monastery. Although the Panchen Lama sent an emissary to demand the immediate withdrawal of the expedition from his territory, Younghusband remained. The following year, he continued his advance on Gyantse and at Geru inflicted an overwhelming defeat on the motley Tibetan troops which had been assembled to bar his passage. As a result of the Younghusband expedition's advance, the Dalai Lama fled the country, leaving the Panchen Lama as the highest ranking authority in Tibet.

The years of the Dalai Lama's absence were trying ones for the Panchen Lama, for he was caught between foreign (Chinese and British) ambitions and the jealous intrigues of both the Lhasa monks and his own followers. On the recommendation of the Chinese amban [imperial resident], Yü-t'ai, the Peking government invited the Panchen Lama to act as regent during the Dalai Lama's absence. Because such an action would have violated Tibetan hierarchical practice and because the Panchen Lama stood in a student-teacher relationship to the Dalai Lama, he declined this invitation.

Soon afterwards, in September 1904, the Tibetan kashag [grand council] was obliged by the Younghusband expedition to sign a convention that, in effect, established a British protectorate. Although this agreement settled the dispute between Tibet and the British government of India, it did not lead to the immediate return of the Dalai Lama. In his continued absence, the Panchen enjoyed increased power and prestige, buoyed up by the successful settlement of the international dispute. His position rose higher still in the winter of 1905 when he visited India at British invitation to meet the Prince of Wales. The Panchen Lama and the British viewed the trip as voluntary, but the Peking government interpreted it as a bow to the dictates of foreign imperialists with designs on Tibet. Accordingly, the Peking government requested that the

British minister at Peking inform the British authorities in India that the Chinese would refuse to recognize any agreement that the Panchen Lama might make in the course of his visit. The Panchen, however, was not importuned in any way by the British. He returned to Tibet early in 1906. Charles A. Bell, the British official in charge of the relations of the government of India with Sikkim, Bhutan, and Tibet, visited the Panchen in 1906 and found him eager to be independent of Lhasa and to deal with the British government as the ruler of an independent state.

Unfortunately for the Panchen Lama, he did not have sufficient room or power to maneuver in Tibet even with the Dalai Lama out of the country. The secular power of the Tashi Lhunpo monastery was limited to its own holdings. The Dalai Lama controlled even Shigatse, which was no more than a mile from the Panchen Lama's seat of power. Even though he was the incarnation of the buddha Amitābha, the Panchen wielded less ecclesiastical power than the Dalai, the incarnation of a mere bodhisattva. The Dalai Lama's line had been established before that of the Panchen Lama, and he was the earthly manifestation of Chen-re-zi, the patron deity of Tibet. In sum, the Panchen was in no position to challenge the Dalai's power. Nevertheless, there existed areas of potential disagreement between the two holy men, especially in the realm of politics. The monks of the great lamaseries traditionally were much given to jealousy and intrigue, and the respective followers of the Panchen Lama and the Dalai Lama contributed substantially, by their scheming, to the development of a rift between the two. There was no time for either deterioration or improvement of relations between them after the Dalai's return to Tibet in December 1909, for the Dalai was forced to flee Lhasa again in February 1910. The new Chinese amban, Lien-yü, asked the Panchen Lama to come to Lhasa and administer Tibet in the Dalai's absence. The Panchen went to the capital as requested, but he asked the Dalai, then in India, for instructions. At the Dalai's behest, he left Lhasa and returned to Tashi Lhunpo.

At the time of the Chinese revolution of 1911, the Dalai Lama, still in India, ordered that strong action be taken against the Chinese garrison troops occupying Lhasa. The Panchen Lama's followers and the disgruntled monks of the Ten-gye-ling lamasery in Lhasa paid little attention to these orders, and it was only through British intervention at Peking that the Chinese forces were repatriated. The Panchen courteously met the Dalai ten days' journey from Lhasa at the end of 1912 to accompany the Dalai back to his capital, but the Panchen's association with the Chinese amban and his inaction in face of virtual Chinese occupation in 1910–11 brought him sharp criticism from the Dalai. The Dalai's supporters charged that the Panchen had hoped to assume power in Tibet, citing the traditional rules which he had broken in establishing a political relationship with Lien-yü. Other incidents may have contributed to the estrangement. For one thing, the Panchen had erred in permitting his retinue to continue beating the drums when passing the Potala during the Panchen's 1902 visit to Lhasa. The Dalai fined his coreligionist 150 taels for this offense.

In 1914 the Panchen Lama sent a message to Lhasa requesting that the Dalai Lama receive him at Lhasa and give him benediction. The Dalai replied in September 1915 that the visit should be postponed because he was busy with affairs of state and because the Panchen Lama was overseeing the construction of an image of the buddha Maitreya. For various reasons, it was not until December 1919 that the Panchen finally was able to go to Lhasa and receive the Dalai's benediction. By that time, the Dalai had decided to divorce Tibet from its traditional relationship with China, to build up a modern army, and to centralize control over domestic affairs. He therefore began to apply increasing political and economic pressure on the Panchen Lama's domain, especially by attaching his revenues. In November 1923 the Dalai demanded that the Panchen pay him 5 million taels and a large quantity of grain, provide men and animals for official use, and appear in Lhasa for consultation. The Panchen responded by fleeing Tibet.

Little is known about the Panchen Lama's activities in the year following his flight. Having barely escaped a cavalry force sent after him by the Dalai Lama, he apparently spent the first several months of 1924 in Outer Mongolia. About June 1924 he went to Lanchow. After sending two representatives to Peking, presumably for negotiations concerning his future, he went to Taiyuan, Shansi, arriving there early in January 1925. He received a representative of Tuan Ch'i-jui (q.v.), the chief executive at Peking, and left Shansi for Peking. On arrival at the capital, he was accorded a state welcome by the Peking government and was provided with a residence, a modest subsidy, and the title "Propagator of Sincerity and Savior of the World." He remained in Peking for over a year, departing when the Peking government came under the challenge of the Northern Expedition. Then he undertook a religious pilgrimage into Manchuria and Eastern Inner Mongolia. In 1928–30, at the invitation of various banner leaders, he held four Shih-lun chin-kang fa-hui [great Buddhist convocations].

During his religious exercises the Panchen Lama had learned by divination that "chairman Chiang [Kai-shek] can unify China and bring forth happiness and benefit for the people," and the National Government at Nanking evidently had divined that the Panchen Lama could prove very useful in connection with its aim of reestablishing Chinese control over Tibet. Accordingly, in January 1929 the Panchen Lama was made a member (*in absentia*) of the Mongolian and Tibetan Affairs Commission. A month later his lieutenant Lo-sang Chien-tsan was appointed director of Tibetan affairs in the commission and director of the Nanking office of the Panchen Lama.

In February 1931 Chiang Kai-shek invited the Panchen Lama to Nanking for the nominal purpose of making inquiries regarding conditions in the borderlands. The Panchen left Liaoning by special train for Nanking, where he was warmly welcomed by high officials. He vowed adamant support for the National Government and reputedly declared that "the Three People's Principles are one with the spirit of Buddhism." The National Government responded in June 1931 by endowing the Panchen Lama with a respectable subsidy and the title of Hu-kuo hsuan-hua kuang-hui ta-shih [great teacher, protector of the country, and propagator of universal enlightenment]. A month later, in response to the joint invitation of leaders of the Mongol banners in the Hulun Buir region, the Panchen returned to Eastern Inner Mongolia to "propagate reform" (hsuan-hua) and to proclaim the National Government's "virtuous intent" (te-i). With the beginning of Japanese

aggression in Manchuria in September, he left Hulun Buir and took up residence in the palace of Te Wang (Demchukdonggrub, q.v.). In April 1932 the Panchen went to Pailingmiao, Suiyuan, to prepare for his fifth Buddhist congress, held there in July 1932. On such occasions, the faithful were called upon to make rich gifts to the Tibetan religious potentate, and his visitations tended to impoverish the regions in which they took place. The form of his religious progress was fixed, however, and in October 1933 he held his sixth congress in the T'ai-tsu-tien at Peiping, with an estimated 100,000 Buddhists in attendance.

On 1 September 1932 Kung-chüeh Chung-ni, the Dalai Lama's representative at Nanking, transmitted to Chiang Kai-shek a strong protest from the three leading Tibetan monasteries and the Tibetan consultative assembly demanding withdrawal of the titles and honors accorded the Panchen Lama. This action merely served to strengthen the National Government's support of the Panchen. When he visited Nanking in December 1932 he was appointed Hsi-ch'ü hsuan-hua shih [propagator of reform for the western regions]. His mission was to mollify the Mongols of Western Inner Mongolia so that they would remain loyal to Nanking. Te Wang and his supporters were pressing for autonomy with Japanese support. In January 1933 the Panchen Lama made his way to Pailingmiao for discussions with Te Wang, who then was appointed defense commissioner at P'angchiang and was given some responsibility for training Mongolian military forces. Throughout the first half of 1933 the Panchen Lama exercised a restraining influence on the ruling princes of Western Inner Mongolia, but on 14 August 1933 they sent a telegram to Nanking announcing their intention to establish an autonomous government.

The death of the Dalai Lama on 17 December 1933 set the stage for the Panchen Lama's final attempt to win power in Tibet. As the senior lama at Nanking, he presided over the National Government's memorial service for the Dalai, and he dispatched his deputies to various parts of China "bearing heavy gold" for holding memorial services in monasteries. Moreover, he requested the National Government to award posthumous honors to his old antagonist.

In January 1934 the Panchen Lama was elected to the State Council at Nanking, and on

20 February 1934 he was sworn in. He held his seventh Buddhist congress at Hangchow in April, visited Shanghai in June, returned to Nanking, and then flew to Peiping. Before long, he moved to the Paotow area, where he resided with the Ikechao League for about two months. At the invitation of Da Wang, the ruling prince of the Alashan Special Banner, he then proceeded to Ninghsia. In February 1935 he set up office as Hsi-ch'ü hsuan-hua shih at the headquarters of Da Wang. Three months later, he flew to Sining, Tsinghai, where he established residence in the T'a-erh monastery. In due course he held his eighth Buddhist congress, again taking the occasion to proclaim the National Government's "virtuous intent." After a year's residence at Sining, he went on to the famous Labrang monastery; he held his ninth Buddhist congress at Labrang.

The Panchen Lama throughout this period was moving slowly but steadily toward the borders of Tibet, and the issue of his return to Tibet assumed increasing significance in the 1930's. In probing for the conditions under which Tibet might accept the restoration of its earlier suzerain-vassal relationship with China, the National Government had asked questions bearing on the Panchen Lama and his acceptability in Tibet. The Dalai Lama had replied that it would be difficult to welcome the Panchen Lama and his followers "unless they can give a satisfactory explanation for taking flight [in 1923]."

Two of the proposals carried by the National Government's 1931 mission to Lhasa were that the thirteenth Dalai Lama should welcome the Panchen Lama back to Tibet and that the secular and religious authority of the Dalai and the Panchen "should be maintained as before." Nanking's envoy, Hsieh Kuo-liang, died only one day's march from Lhasa, but the National Government proposals presumably reached Lhasa. In any event, the Panchen Lama was informed soon afterwards by a representative from Lhasa that the Dalai Lama was willing to invite him back to Tibet and to restore all his privileges. The Panchen then sent two representatives to Lhasa, but they were informed on arrival at Lhasa that the Dalai would have to consult the Tibetan assembly about the Panchen's return. At the meeting called to consider the issue, two men who were hostile to the Panchen Lama dominated the pro-ceedings, and the assembly ruled against his return. The Panchen Lama sent the An-ch'in Hutukhtu to Lhasa for further negotiations, but the death of the thirteenth Dalai Lama put an end to this attempt. In January 1934 the National Government appointed Huang Mu-sung (q.v.) Chinese high commissioner in Tibet. He held negotiations with the Ka-dreng Hutukhtu, who had become regent at Lhasa; the regent finally decided that the Panchen Lama would be allowed to return to Tibet if he did not bring a large Chinese escort with him and if he would not attempt to exercise any political authority at Lhasa.

On his return to Nanking in October 1934 Huang Mu-sung proposed that the Panchen Lama be provided with a military force for his return to China. In February 1935 the Panchen was assigned a military escort of some 500 troops. Huang Mu-sung became head of the Mongolian and Tibetan Affairs Commission a month later, and plans for the Panchen's return to his homeland began to take shape. In May 1936, about the time the Panchen moved to Labrang, the National Government dispatched a special envoy, Chao Shou-yü, to accompany the Panchen on his journey. With an enormous amount of treasure, the Panchen Lama's aide Nong-yong made his way to Tachienlu in Sikang, with orders to proceed to a point of rendezvous. The time for the fulfillment of the Panchen Lama's destiny seemed to have come. In September, he left Labrang. Proceeding by way of various monasteries, he finally arrived at Jyekundo in southern Tsinghai.

The Panchen Lama's movements were of particular interest to the British and Tibetan authorities. In 1935 and 1936 the British had protested the Panchen's planned return; in 1937, as the return party stood poised at the Tibetan border, they protested again. In the meantime, the Lhasa authorities had decided to offer armed resistance to the Panchen's return, for they viewed it as a threat to Tibetan autonomy. The outbreak of the Sino-Japanese war in July 1937 overshadowed this issue, but in mid-August the Panchen and his party moved to the La-hsiu monastery on the Tsinghai-Tibetan border. On 24 August, a message reached Jyekundo from Nanking, stating that the National Government, in view of the national emergency, urged the temporary postponement of the Panchen's return to Tibet. Chao Shou-yü dispatched the message to the La-hsiu monastery, and it reached the Panchen on 28 August. Discussions and deliberations followed. In early October, during a snowstorm, the Panchen Lama and his party made their way back to Jyekundo. As a result of this journey, the Panchen developed a serious respiratory ailment. On 1 December 1937 he died.

On 24 December 1937 the National Government accorded the Panchen Lama the posthumous title Hu-kuo-hsuan-hua kuang-hui yuan-chueh ta-shih [all-perspicacious great teacher, protector of the country, and propagator of the universal enlightenment]. His spirit-coffin was kept at Jyekundo until February 1941, when officials from Lhasa finally came to accompany the Panchen Lama back to Tashi Lhunpo.

P'an Kuang-tan   潘 光 旦
  T.   Chung-ang   仲 昂
  West. Quentin Pan

P'an Kuang-tan (1898–), sociologist, essayist, and propagandist for national betterment through eugenics. He was noted for his studies of family and clan genealogies.

Born in Paoshan, Kiangsu, P'an Kuang-tan was the son of P'an Hung-ting, a chin-shih who was a member of the Hanlin Academy. According to P'an Kuang-tan, his family "belonged half to the scholar class and half to the merchant class, though no member of the family had achieved high official rank or had become really wealthy." After receiving a traditional education in the Chinese classics, P'an entered Tsinghua College. Although he sustained an athletic injury which resulted in the amputation of one of his legs, his handicap did not prevent him from attaining an outstanding academic record. Upon graduation in 1922, he was awarded a Boxer Indemnity Fund scholarship for study in the United States. He enrolled at Dartmouth College, where he ranked seventh in his class, became a member of Phi Beta Kappa, and received a B.A. degree with honors in zoology in 1924. From Dartmouth, P'an proceeded to Columbia University, where he studied for two years. After receiving an M.A. degree in 1926, he returned to China

to become a professor and director of studies at Wu-sung kuo-li cheng-chih ta-hsüeh [Wusung national university of political science] near Shanghai.

In the course of his scientific studies in the United States, P'an Kuang-tan had become interested in the possible applications of biological principles to the problems of human society. He spent much of his time during the next two decades refining and teaching the concepts of eugenics and studying their influences on Chinese social history. In 1927 alone he published four books on the subject: *Jen-wen shih-kuan* [the humanist view of history], *Jih-pen Te-i-chih min-tsu-hsing chih pi-chiao yen-chiu* [a comparative study of the national traits of Japan and Germany], *Yu-sheng yü k'ang-chan* [eugenics and the will to resist], and *Jen-wen sheng-wu-hsüeh lun-ts'ung* [collected essays on a humanistic biology], which later was reissued as *Yu-sheng kai-lun* [general theory of eugenics]. In 1928 P'an temporarily abandoned eugenics to write *Feng Hsiao-ch'ing chih fen-hsi* [the psychoanalysis of Feng Hsiao-ch'ing], in which he sought to refute Bertrand Russell's charge that China lacked data for psychological analysis by doing a Freudian case study with the famous Ch'ing poet and musician as its subject. The following year, he published *Chung-kuo chih chia-t'ing wen-t'i* [Chinese family problems]. For this book he made a survey of readers of the magazine *Hsueh-teng* [lamp of learning] concerning their marriage and family status; the survey revealed that in Shanghai compromise patterns of marriage and family life were more common in the late 1920's than fully traditional or fully modern patterns. Also in 1929 he produced the "Chung-kuo chia-p'u-hsüeh lüeh-shih" [a brief history of the study of Chinese clan records], which appeared in the *Tung-fang tsa-chih (Eastern Miscellany)* and which set forth P'an's views on the importance of the large corpus of genealogical material available in Chinese for Chinese social history.

Two main arguments emerged in P'an's writings during this period and continued to dominate his work for two decades. The first concerned the necessity for bettering mankind, and the population of China in particular, through the improvement of biological inheritance; the second was the use of Chinese history, particularly family and clan genealogies, as evidence in support of eugenics. The combining of these two interests led to a number of highly interesting studies of Chinese social history which pioneered in the use of genealogical materials. P'an also wrote widely in the related fields of population and birth control, the role of women in society, sex education, and "national health" (min-tsu chien-k'ang). In the period immediately following the successful completion of the Northern Expedition, there was much talk in a Spenglerian vein of the "health" or "sickness" of China in relation to Japan and the West. P'an equated "national health" with eugenics and argued that it could be achieved only if the population of China developed according to eugenic principles. He insisted that while "national vitality" (min-tsu huo-li), another catchword of the day, might have metaphysical connotations for some, it also had definite scientific meaning with respect to the quality of the nation's genetic resources. China's strength as a nation, P'an held, would be tested in the coming struggle with Japan. P'an then translated and published several works by the British psychologist Havelock Ellis, including *Hsing t'i chiao-yü* [sex education] and *Hsing ti tao-teh* [sexual morality], both of which appeared in 1934.

During this period, P'an Kuang-tan became active in the Crescent Moon Society. His associates in this group included Hu Shih, Liang Shih-ch'iu, Wen I-to, and Hsü Chih-mo (qq.v.). He contributed articles to the *Hsin-yüeh tsa-chih* [crescent moon monthly] and founded the Hsin-yüeh shu-tien [crescent moon book company], which published works by a number of leading authors before succumbing to financial difficulties. For a while, P'an also was editor of the *Hsüeh-teng*, the literary supplement to the Shanghai *Shih-shih hsin-pao*.

In 1930 P'an was appointed professor of sociology at Tsinghua, and in 1936 he became dean of faculty. He held these posts until 1946, serving out the war years at Southwest Associated University in Kunming. During this period, P'an published two notable books. *Tu-shu wen-t'i* [thoughts on reading], published in 1930, was a collection of P'an's essays; *Chung-kuo ling-jen hsüeh-yuan chih yen-chiu* [blood kinship among Chinese actors], published in 1941, analyzed the transmission of theatrical talent through the study of the family records of several famous acting families and purported to show that the large number of famous actors

produced by a very few families was the result of preserving desirable genetic qualities. However, P'an avoided the worst extremes of the eugenics school by stressing social environment and biological inheritance equally.

As the Second World War drew to a close, P'an Kuang-tan began to take a greater interest in the immediate political and social future of China than in the distant prospects envisioned by eugenic theory. At Kunming, he often addressed student groups on political topics, and he wrote a number of essays in which he criticized the political and educational policies of the National Government. After Wen I-to (q.v.) was shot on 15 July 1946, P'an was among the intellectuals who took refuge in the United States consulate at Kunming. Soon afterwards, he published his own plan for the development of a new China, *Tzu-yu chih lu* [the road to freedom]. In this book P'an expressed his urgent concern for the realization of democracy, which he characterized as hsien-jen cheng-chih [government by virtuous men]. Contrasting such Chinese traits as passivity with those of the English and the Americans which he deemed conducive to the growth of liberty, P'an argued that democracy could only be developed in China through the adaption of its principles to the conditions and characteristics of Chinese life.

Late in 1946 P'an Kuang-tan returned to Peiping to become director of the Tsinghua University library. The following year, he published two of his most important works. The first, "K'o-chü yü she-hui liu-tung" [the examination system and social mobility], was written jointly with Fei Hsiao-t'ung (q.v.) for publication in the magazine *She-hui k'o-hsüeh* [social science]. It challenged traditional opinion by arguing that the Ch'ing examination system was a narrow way, not a wide road, of mobility for men of non-official background. It also revealed that successful candidates in the examinations tended to come from cities and towns in provinces with a high rate of absentee landlordism rather than from rural areas in provinces with a high rate of peasant proprietorship. The second notable work published by P'an in 1947 was *Ming-Ch'ing liang-tai Chia-hsing ti wang-tsu* [the leading clans of Chiahsing during the Ming and Ch'ing periods]. This study indicated that once a clan gained prominence, it tended to retain its influential status for several generations. During this period, P'an also collaborated with Fei Hsiao-t'ung in editing two collections of Fei's essays: *Jen-hsing yü chi-ch'i* [human nature and the machine] of 1946 and *Sheng-yü chih-tu* [systems of child rearing] of 1947.

Both "K'o-chü yü she-hui liu-tung" and *Ming-Ch'ing liang-tai Chia-hsing ti wang-tsu* were read—and probably were intended to be read— as covert criticism of the ruling Kuomintang elite and of China's social structure as a whole. It surprised no one, therefore, that P'an Kuang-tan elected to remain in China when the Chinese Communists took control of the mainland in 1949. Shortly after the fall of Peiping in January 1949, P'an was appointed a member of the university affairs committee of the newly established Peiping municipal military control commission. With the establishment of the Central People's Government, he became a member of the Government Administration Council's culture and education committee. In December 1949 he represented the China Demo-cratic League at the second session of the National Committee of the Chinese People's Political Consultative Conference.

At a mass meeting held in Peking during the Korean conflict P'an declared that the aim of the United States was "to turn Chinese into both spiritual and material parasites of the American way of life . . . and thus to destroy China's culture." He also castigated American friendship for Chinese as being nothing more than a mask for "cultural aggression." About this time, P'an rejected his ideas about democracy and eugenics, confessing that he had over-emphasized members of "the feudal elite" in his studies. He made a full confession of his errors in *Su-nan t'u-ti kai-ko fang-wen-chi* [an account of a tour of inspection of land reform in southern Kiangsu], written in collaboration with Ch'uan Wei-t'ien and published in 1952. He inter-polated a long list of ideological inadequacies and offenses into an account of the land reform then being carried out in the T'aihu region of Kiangsu, confessing that because his family had lived in towns for the past 16 generations as scholars or merchants, his ancestors had known nothing about the conditions of peasant life. He himself had left home at the age of 13 and thereafter had lived in Peking, Shanghai, Kunming, or foreign cities. He therefore wel-comed the opportunity to gain a better under-standing of peasant life by touring Kiangsu.

In 1954 P'an became a member of the national committee of the Sino-Soviet Friendship Associ-ation. In 1957 he was sent to observe the T'u-chia, a non-Chinese minority group living in western Hunan. P'an's assignment was to make recommendations for the handling of the minorities problem as a whole on the basis of his study of the T'u-chia. His recommendation that autonomous chou [districts] be set up for each minority group led to his condemnation as a rightist in 1958 along with such other members of the minority peoples department of the Chinese Academy of Sciences as Lei Hai-tsung (q.v.). P'an was charged with deciding the minorities question solely on the basis of sociological theory "with not one reference to Marxism and without taking notice of the present needs and desires of the people." This criticism notwithstanding, P'an was appointed deputy director of the department of history in the Chung-kuo min-tsu hsüeh-yuan [academy for the study of minority peoples]. He was elected to the National Committee of the Chinese People's Political Consultative Confer-ence in April 1959, and the order designating him a rightist was rescinded in September of that year.

P'an Kung-chan   潘 公 展

P'an Kung-chan (1895–), journalist and pub-lisher who founded such newspapers as the *Ch'en Pao* and the *Hsin Yeh Pao* and who served the National Government as vice minister of information (1939–41) and director of the Executive Yuan's publications screening com-mittee (1942–45). In 1950 he went to New York and became editor of the *China Tribune*.

Wuhsing, Chekiang, was the native place of P'an Kung-chan. He was born into a family of moderate means in Ling-hu-chen, near the silk-producing center of Nanhsün. About 1901 he enrolled at a school where the curriculum included such modern subjects as English, mathematics, and physical education, as well as the Chinese classics. He later attended the First Middle School at Hangchow, where one of his classmates was Hsü Chih-mo (q.v.). In 1910, the year before the republican revolution, P'an went to Shanghai to matriculate at St. John's University. While studying literature at St.

John's, he joined the Nan-she [southern society], a literary group which also was a peripheral organization of the T'ung-meng-hui. Membership in the Nan-she enabled P'an Kung-chan to become acquainted with such talented writers and revolutionaries as Liu Ya-tzu, Yeh Ch'u-ts'ang, and Su Man-shu (qq.v.).

At the time of the May Fourth Movement of 1919, P'an Kung-chan was teaching at the Shih-pei Middle School in Shanghai. He participated in the mass meetings and strikes that were staged in Shanghai and became the editor of a daily newspaper published by the students' union of Shanghai. The T'ai-tung Book Company commissioned him to write a comprehensive history of the May Fourth Movement, and the resulting *Hsueh-sheng chiu-kuo ch'uan-shih* [complete history of national salvation by the students] was published in 1920.

These activities established P'an Kung-chan's reputation as a writer, and Ch'en Pu-lei (q.v.), the chief editor of the newly established *Shang Pao*, invited him to become telegraph editor of that newspaper. P'an held that post from 1920 to 1925, and he continued to teach school. The *Shang Pao* had a conservative editorial policy, for its principal financial backers were such merchants' organizations as the Kuang-chou kung-so [Cantonese guild] and the Ning-po t'ung-hsiang hui [Ningponese guild]. Nevertheless, Ch'en Pu-lei and P'an Kung-chan published a number of articles and editorials which gave support to the Nationalist cause. In 1925 P'an accepted an offer from the *Shun Pao*, one of the two oldest newspapers in Shanghai, to become its telegraph editor. He worked there until the summer of 1926, when he resigned because of the entrenched conservatism of the owner and most of the staff. In the meantime, the *Shang Pao* had been reporting with enthusiasm on the progress of the Northern Expedition. P'an accompanied Ch'en Pu-lei to Nanchang, the temporary headquarters of Chiang Kai-shek, in the autumn of 1926. They were received warmly by Chiang, who joined with Ch'en Kuo-fu (q.v.) in sponsoring their admission to the Kuomintang.

In the spring of 1927 P'an Kung-chan was appointed to membership in the Shanghai branch of the Central Political Council. For the next decade, he utilized his journalistic associations and talents and his familiarity with conditions in Shanghai to become an important party and municipal leader. From 1927 to 1937 he served the municipality of Shanghai as director of the bureau of social affairs, the bureau of education, and the bureau of agriculture, industry, and commerce. In these posts he made important contributions to social welfare, education, and the development of commerce. He represented Shanghai at the Third National Congress of the Kuomintang, held in Nanking in 1929. After the Shanghai hostilities between the Chinese and Japanese armies took place in 1932, P'an temporarily left politics to launch the *Ch'en Pao* [morning post], the *Hsin Yeh Pao* [new evening post], the *Erh-t'ung Ch'en Pao* [children's morning post], and the *T'u-hua Ch'en Pao* [pictorial morning post]. In 1935 he was elected to the Central Executive Committee of the Kuomintang.

After the Sino-Japanese war broke out in July 1937, P'an Kung-chan edited a series of books about the war of resistance for the Commercial Press. The Japanese soon occupied Shanghai, and P'an went to Wuhan in the spring of 1938. He became a member of the Military Affairs Commission, and in October 1938 Chiang Kai-shek appointed him secretary general of the Hunan provincial government. He held the Hunan post for about a month. In November, Chang Chih-chung (q.v.), the governor of Hunan, made an error in judgment which led to the burning of Changsha. P'an then went to Chungking, the wartime capital of the National Government. From 1939 to 1942 he served as vice minister of information, doing propaganda work. In 1942 he became a member of the standing committee of the Kuomintang's Central Executive Committee. He also found time to serve as director of the Tu-li ch'u-pan she [independent publishing company] and the Cheng-chung Book Company, both of which were affiliated with the Kuomintang. In 1942–45 P'an was the director of the Executive Yuan's committee for the screening of publications, which was concerned with the censoring of potentially seditious books and magazines. Because P'an was required to adhere to the cultural and educational policies of the National Government in making his decisions, he inevitably offended such leftist writers as Kuo Mo-jo and T'ien Han (qq.v.). His censorship activities soon won him the enmity of the Chinese Communist party, which later branded him a "war criminal."

At war's end, P'an Kung-chan returned to Shanghai to become the publisher of the *Shun Pao*, which had passed into the hands of collaborators during the Japanese occupation of Shanghai. Ch'en Shun-yu, a younger brother of Ch'en Pu-lei, became chief editor of the *Shun Pao* late in 1945. From 1946 to 1949 P'an Kung-chan also served as chairman of the board of the *Hsin Yeh Pao* and vice chairman of the board of the *Shang Pao*. When the Shanghai-shih ts'en-i-hui [Shanghai municipal council] was inaugurated in 1946, P'an was elected its speaker. Because of the retrocession of the International Settlement and the French concession under the terms of the treaties of equality concluded between China and her principal Western allies, the council had jurisdiction over a very large area. Thus, the speakership was a job of high importance. P'an discharged his duties with efficiency and resourcefulness. Toward the end of 1948 it became clear that the Chinese Communist would win their struggle with the Nationalists for control of the mainland. In mid-November, P'an's close friend and colleague Ch'en Pu-lei committed suicide in Nanking because of the impending crisis. A few months later, in May 1949, the Chinese Communists reached the outskirts of Shanghai, forcing P'an to leave his home and career. He went to the United States, where he took up residence in New York in 1950. He became the editor of the *China Tribune*, a Kuomintang organ published in New York's Chinatown. Although he was staunchly loyal to the Nationalist cause, he occasionally wrote articles which were critical of the National Government in Taiwan.

P'an Kung-chan was married to an accomplished painter, *née* T'ang Yun-yu, who also was a native of Wuhsing, Chekiang.

Pei Tsu-yi   貝 祖 詒
T. Sung-sun   淞 蓀

Pei Tsu-yi (1893–), banker who was known for his pioneering work in developing the foreign-exchange business of the Bank of China and for helping to plan the managed currency system that China adopted in 1935.

Born into a merchant family in Wuhsien, Kiangsu, Pei Tsu-yi received his early education in the Chinese classics at a local school maintained by the Lu family. At the age of ten sui, he was sent to study at the Ch'en-chung Middle School in Shanghai, where he remained until 1907, when he returned home to attend Soochow University. After being graduated in 1911, he went to north China for a two-year stint at the T'angshan College of Railways. In 1913 he moved south to work in the accounting department at the Shanghai office of the Han-yeh-p'ing Iron and Coal Company.

Pei Tsu-yi embarked on his banking career in 1914 when he joined the accounting department at the Bank of China's head office in Peking. He was transferred to the Canton branch in 1915 as acting head of the accounting department. After serving as chief accountant and as head of the business department, he became assistant manager of the Canton branch in 1917. About this time, Sun Yat-sen's newly established military government at Canton began to make incessant and excessive demands on the resources of the Canton branch of the Bank of China. The branch manager proved unable to cope with the situation, and he soon left for Peking to tender his resignation at the head office. Pei Tsu-yi was made acting manager. He soon incurred the wrath of the local military authorities by ignoring their demands for funds. They retaliated by ordering his arrest, and he was forced to flee to Hong Kong.

By this time, the Kwangtung provincial note issues had lost much of their value, and Hong Kong bank notes had found their way into Canton in increasing numbers. Pei Tsu-yi had learned much about foreign exchange because of this situation, for the principal activities of Canton bankers had come to be the handling of remittances between Canton and Hong Kong and the exchange of currency. In 1918 the Bank of China transferred its Canton branch to Hong Kong and appointed Pei to manage it. The Canton establishment was maintained as a sub-office under the control of the Hong Kong branch, which was to direct the bank's activities throughout south China. However, the development of the new branch was hampered by the smallness of capital appropriations from the head office and the slowness of people to place their confidence in a new banking operation. Pei Tsu-yi therefore decided to specialize in arbitrage, exploiting the regional differences in the exchange rates among the major currencies of the world. Because of its complete lack of banking restrictions, Hong Kong was admirably suited to arbitrage activities. Pei's faultless handling of foreign-exchange operations enhanced both his reputation and that of the Bank of China.

In 1927 Pei Tsu-yi became the manager of the Bank of China's Shanghai branch. When the Bank of China was reorganized in 1928 as a specialized bank handling foreign-exchange transactions, Pei was elected a director of the bank (representing private stockholders) and was appointed chief of the business department at the head office, now located at Shanghai. He was elected to the Shanghai Municipal Council in 1929 as a representative of the Chinese Ratepayers Association. In 1930 he was named director of the newly created foreign-exchange department at the Bank of China. Before assuming his new duties, he made a tour of England and the United States to study banking practices in those two countries. On returning to China in 1931 he ordered all branches of the Bank of China in treaty or commercial ports to undertake foreign-exchange operations. Credit facilities were extended to Chinese importers and exporters; and guarantees were furnished for National Government agencies and for merchants in the interior who wished to place orders with manufacturers abroad. In branches which handled remittances from overseas Chinese, every effort was made to improve these facilities. Before long, Pei also secured the admittance of Chinese brokers to the previously all-Western Foreign Exchange Brokers Association in Shanghai.

The reserves accumulated by the foreign department enabled the Bank of China to create new branches and agencies abroad. It came to have offices in New York, London, Tokyo, Osaka, Havana, Sydney, Singapore, Penang, Kuala Lumpur, Bombay, Calcutta, Karachi, Chittagong, Jakarta, Saigon, Bangkok, Phnom Penh, and Rangoon. Pei Tsu-yi's role in breaking the foreign monopoly of the business of foreign remittances in China was of great importance. The Bank of China enjoyed an ever-increasing volume of business in the 1930's, and it handled all public and private foreign-exchange transactions during the Sino-Japanese war, for there were no foreign banks in Free China.

In 1934–35 Pei Tsu-yi participated in the planning which resulted in the monetary reform of November 1935 (for details, *see* H. H. K'ung), when the National Government abandoned the silver standard in favor of a managed paper currency. The new legal tender notes were known as fapi. In the years following, Pei was called upon for aid and advice whenever measures were needed for the maintenance of the fapi system. Thus, when the outbreak of the Sino-Japanese war in July 1937 caused financial panic and strong demands for the redemption of fapi with foreign exchange, Pei Tsu-yi, representing the Bank of China, collaborated with the Central Bank of China in sales of foreign exchange in order to maintain public confidence. When the Central Bank of China suspended the exchange of foreign currency for fapi at fixed rates in 1938, Pei's department collaborated with a British bank, the Hong Kong and Shanghai Banking Corporation, in supplying foreign exchange at current open rates, thus preventing a drastic fall in the value of the fapi.

By 1939 inflation in China had become so serious that it no longer was possible to maintain the value of the fapi through ordinary measures. At the urging of the Hong Kong and Shanghai Banking Corporation, the British Government agreed to cooperate with the National Government in establishing the Sino-British Stabilization Board. The Bank of China and the Bank of Communications joined with the Hong Kong and Shanghai Banking Corporation and the Chartered Bank of India, Australia, and China in subscribing a total of £10 million as the stabilization fund for the maintenance of the fapi. Pei Tsu-yi served as the principal Chinese representative on the five-man management committee. With the exhaustion of this fund in 1941, the Sino-British-American Stabilization Board was established with the subscribing of US $50 million by the United States Government, £5 million by the British Government, and US $20 million by the National Government. Pei Tsu-yi was one of the three Chinese representatives to the five-member board, the other two being Hsi Te-mou of the Central Bank of China and the board's chairman, K. P. Ch'en (Ch'en Kuang-fu, q.v.).

Pei became acting general manager of the Bank of China in 1941. In this post, he did much to promote agricultural and industrial production by providing financial assistance and by participating in the operation of various enterprises. In June 1944 he accompanied H. H. K'ung to the United States as a member of the Chinese delegation to the United Nations Monetary and Financial Conference at Bretton Woods, New Hampshire. He made a second trip to the United States in 1945, when he held discussions with American officials about the possibility of floating a postwar rehabilitation loan of US $500 million for use in maintaining the value of the fapi. The outbreak of hostilities between the Nationalists and the Chinese Communists put an end to these negotiations.

From March 1946 to April 1947 Pei Tsu-yi served as governor of the Central Bank of China. He was handicapped severely in his attempts to stabilize the Chinese economy by the huge and irreducible Nationalist military budget and by galloping inflation. In 1948 he was made head of the Chinese Technical Mission to Washington, which went to the United States in 1949 for discussions on problems connected with proposed American aid to China. In November 1952 he became a director of C. V. Starr and Company in New York as an adviser, a post he held until 1959. He then became a director of K. P. Ch'en's Shanghai Commercial Bank of Hong Kong, and thereafter he divided his time between New York and Hong Kong.

One of Pei Tsu-yi's sons, Pei Yi-ming (1917–), better known as I. M. Pei, went to the United States in 1935 to study architecture. He later became an architect of international renown.

P'ei Wen-chung
T. Ming-hua

裴 文 中
明 華

P'ei Wen-chung (1903?–), discoverer of Peking Man (*Sinanthropus pekinensis*). Long associated with the Choukoutien excavations, he worked after 1950 in association with the Chinese Academy of Sciences at Peking.

Little is known about P'ei Wen-chung's family background or early years except that he was born in Luanhsien, Hopei, and that he majored in geology at Peking University. At the time of P'ei's graduation in 1928, there was much excitement in the archaeological world about the discovery of paleontological specimens, including two hominid teeth, in the limestone caves at Choukoutien, near Peking. In 1927 the Geological Survey of China, in cooperation with the Peking Union Medical College and with the financial assistance of the Rockefeller Foundation, undertook large-scale excavations at the Choukoutien site. The Laboratory of Cenozoic Research was established, with such distinguished scientists participating in its work over the years as Davidson Black, Franz Weidenreich, O. Zdansky, W. Granger, B. Bohlin, R. W. Chaney, Henri Breuil, and Pierre Teilhard de Chardin. P'ei Wen-chung joined the China Geological Survey as a field assistant at the Choukoutien site. Because many of the Western scientists worked there for short periods of time and because circumstances required that a Chinese serve as the principal field coordinator, P'ei soon became the field director of the Choukoutien excavations. Thus, he participated in all field seasons from 1928 until 1939 at all the fossiliferous stations.

In 1929 P'ei Wen-chung unearthed the first Peking Man skull. His article "An Account of the Discovery of an Adult *Sinanthropus* Skull in the Choukoutien Deposit," which appeared in the *Bulletin of the Geological Society of China* later that year, made him famous overnight. In the next decade, the fossil remains of more than 40 individuals were uncovered on what proved to be the richest paleoanthropological site of the Middle Pleistocene age known to the world. P'ei also helped focus attention on the artifacts of Peking Man, describing in a series of reports the paleolithic implements from Choukoutien. These reports included the "Notice on the Discovery of Quartz and Other Stone Artifacts in Lower Pleistocene Hominid-bearing Sediments of the Choukoutien Cave Deposit" and (with Teilhard de Chardin) "The Lithic Industry of the Sinanthropus Deposits in Choukoutien," of 1931; "Palaeolithic Industries in China," which appeared in G. G. MacCurdy's *Early Man* in 1937; "New Fossil Material and Artifacts Collected from the Choukoutien Region During the Years 1937 to 1939"; and "The Upper Cave Industry of Choukoutien," of 1940. These works earned him a well-deserved reputation as the foremost Chinese scientist in the field of Early Man in China.

In 1933 P'ei directed the excavation of the upper cave at Choukoutien which resulted in the discovery of the fossil remains of a family group of seven, examples of *Homo sapiens* of the later Pleistocene or earliest post-Pleistocene period. This discovery filled an important gap in the knowledge of human forms between the appearance of *Sinanthropus* and Modern Man in north China. In 1935 P'ei was a member of a reconnaissance team of geologists working in Kwangsi which located four caves in which mesolithic implements were found. These were among the first such sites to be investigated in southwest China. A summary of the Kwangsi expedition was contained in P'ei's "On a Mesolithic Industry of the Caves of Kwangsi," published in the *Bulletin of the Geological Society of China* in 1935.

On National Government orders, P'ei remained in Peiping after the outbreak of the Sino-Japanese war in 1937 and continued to work at Choukoutien until 1939. For the next few years, he taught Chinese archaeology at a number of universities in occupied Peiping and did research on the neolithic archaeology of China. His interest in this field led him to make brief investigations in the Peiping area of later prehistoric sites and a major archaeological reconnaissance trip to Kansu in 1947. These researches led to two books, *Shih-ch'ien shih-ch'i chih hsi-pei* [northwest China in prehistoric times] and *Chung-kuo shih-ch'ien shih-ch'i chih yen-chiu* [researches on prehistoric China], both published in 1948.

After Peiping fell to the Chinese Communists in January 1949, P'ei Wen-chung decided to remain there and support the new regime. In the latter part of March, he became a member of the Chinese delegation to the World Peace Conference. He returned to Peiping in the latter part of May and joined a training class for political cadres. He then was assigned to a study group for technical personnel. During his three months of political indoctrination, he participated in class discussions and attended public meetings. In September 1949 he declared in writing that he had discovered the applicability of the theory of dialectical materialism to the study of geology, palaeontology, and archaeology. In 1952 he contributed an article entitled "Wo hsueh-hsi-le shemma" [what I studied] to the symposium *Wo-ti Ssu-hsiang shih tsemma-yang chuan-pien-kuo-lai-ti* [how I came to accept communism], which told of his acceptance of Marxism as a guide for his specialized studies.

P'ei Wen-chung held a number of scientific posts in the People's Republic of China. In 1951 he served as president of the Chinese Palaeontological Association and as a director of the All-China Federation for the Dissemination of Scientific and Technical Knowledge. The following year, he was elected to the board of directors of the Chiu-san-hsueh-she, a political organization which had been founded in 1944 at Chungking by scientists and other intellectuals who were critical of the National Government's policies. P'ei became a member of the society's central committee in 1953 and its deputy secretary general in 1958. He represented the Chiu-san-hsueh-she at the 1954 and 1959 sessions of the Chinese People's Political Consultative Conference. In 1955 he was appointed to the department of biological and earth sciences in the Chinese Academy of Sciences and to the scientific committee of the academy's institute of vertebrate palaeontology.

Beginning in 1949 P'ei Wen-chung directed excavations at Choukoutien under the auspices of the Chinese Academy of Sciences. In 1951 he took charge of a dig at Tzuyang, Szechwan, where a skull of *Homo sapiens* of the Upper Pleistocene period was found by railroad workers. This skull was of particular interest to archaeologists because it was one of the earliest Modern Man fossils unearthed in East Asia and because it bore some morphological resemblance to both Upper Cave Man and Peking Man. In 1954 P'ei directed the Tingts'un excavations at Hsiangfen, Shansi, where a new paleolithic assemblage, including three hominid teeth, was found. An analysis of the teeth revealed that Tingts'un Man was phylogenetically situated between Peking Man and Modern Man and was close to the Neanderthals, especially Ordos Man. A summary of the Tingts'un finds, by P'ei and others, appeared in 1958 under the title *Shan-hsi Hsiang-fen hsien Ting-ts'un chiu-shih-ch'i shih-tai i-chih fa-chueh pao-kao* [report on the excavations of the paleolithic site at Tingts'un in Hsiangfen hsien, Shansi]. A Dutch palaeontologist, G. H. R. von Koenigswald, had discovered three giant teeth in a Hong Kong drug shop in 1939 and had identified them as belonging to a species of giant ape, which he named *Gigantopithecus blacki* in honor of Davidson Black. Controversy arose in the 1940's when Franz Weidenreich and some other European scientists decided that the teeth had belonged to a giant ape-man. In 1956 a peasant, Tan Hsiu-huai, discovered a *Gigantopithecus* lower jaw, with 12 teeth in place, in a limestone cave at Liucheng,

Kwangsi. P'ei Wen-chung and other scientists undertook excavations in Kwangsi and recovered, among other fossil remains, about 50 *Gigantopithecus* teeth. After studying these remains, P'ei concluded that "it is fundamentally a giant ape; therefore, I endorse Koenigswald's original idea." He described the ape as having been about 12 feet tall and a contemporary of Peking Man. The teeth indicated that the ape ate a mixed meat and vegetable diet and that it was "perhaps approaching the status of man." P'ei's report on the Kwangsi remains, "Discovery of Gigantopithecus Mandibles and Other Material in the Liu-ch'eng District of Central Kwangsi in South China," was published in *Vertebrata Palasiatica* in 1957.

P'ei Wen-chung's discoveries and his studies of Pleistocene palaeontology, human fossils, and paleolithic cultures were important scientific contributions. He aptly described himself as a quarternary geologist by training and profession, a paleolithic archaeologist on the side, and a neolithic archaeologist as an amateur.

P'eng Chen　　　　　彭　眞
Orig. Fu Mao-kung　　傅　茂　功

P'eng Chen (1899–), Chinese Communist official who held the top administrative and party posts in the Peking municipal government in the 1950's and early 1960's. He was one of the first high-ranking officials to be removed from office in the Cultural Revolution of 1966.

Little is known about P'eng Chen's family background or early life except that he was born into a peasant family in Ch'uwu, Shansi, and that the necessity to work left him little time for study. At the age of 21, however, he managed to gain admittance to an old-style normal school in Taiyuan. He soon encountered such periodicals as *Hsin ch'ing-nien* [new youth] and the Chinese Communist party organ *Hsiang-tao chou-pao*, which introduced him to the precepts of Marxism-Leninism. After joining the Socialist (later Communist) Youth Corps, he worked to organize the students at Taiyuan. In 1925 he helped plan a boycott of Japanese goods at the time of the May Thirtieth Incident at Shanghai.

P'eng Chen joined the Chinese Communist party about 1926 and became director of the labor union on the Taiyuan-Shihchiachuang railroad. The party later ordered him to attempt to increase its influence in north China by organizing miners at T'angshan and industrial workers at Tientsin and Peiping. These activities led to his arrest and imprisonment at Tientsin in 1929. After being released in 1935, he became an assistant to Liu Shao-ch'i (q.v.) at Peiping, organizing student demonstrations against the National Government. When the Sino-Japanese war began, he moved to Taiyuan and then to the Chinese Communist wartime capital, Yenan. He soon was assigned to return to Shansi and work with the 115th Division of the Eighth Route Army, commanded by Nieh Jung-chen (q.v.). P'eng remained in north China until 1942, serving as secretary of the Shansi-Chahar-Hopei border region committee of the Chinese Communist party and as a member of the regional soviet's government council; he also worked for a period in the Jehol-Liaoning area of southern Manchuria.

In 1942 P'eng was recalled to Yenan to become director of the Central Party School, the principal institution guiding the training and indoctrination of cadres during the war years. Thus, he played a key role in the cheng-feng [rectification] campaign of 1942–43 (for details, *see* Mao Tse-tung), which affirmed the Marxist-Leninist orthodoxy of the Chinese Communist party within its native environment and which helped tighten the party structure. P'eng Chen's prominent position in the Chinese Communist party was confirmed at the Seventh National Congress, held at Yenan in the late spring of 1945. He was elected to the congress's 15-man presidium and to the Central Committee of the Chinese Communist party.

From 1946 to 1948 P'eng Chen served in Manchuria with Lin Piao (q.v.) as senior political commissar. He also worked under Ch'en Yun (q.v.) in the Northeast bureau of the Chinese Communist party. In 1948 he became deputy director, under Liu Shao-ch'i, of the Chinese Communist party's organization department. Early in 1949 he also was made secretary of the party's Peking municipal committee, a post he held until June 1966.

With the establishment of the Central People's Government in October 1949, P'eng Chen assumed new and important responsibilities at the national level, becoming a member of the Central People's Government Council and vice chairman of the Government Administration

Council's political and legal affairs committee. In 1951 he succeeded Nieh Jung-chen as mayor of Peking, thus coming to hold the top administrative as well as the top party position in the municipal government. Later that year, he was elected to the Political Bureau of the Chinese Communist party. From 1952 to 1954 he served on the State Planning Commission. He was a delegate from Peking to the National People's Congress in 1954, and he was elected a vice chairman of the congress and secretary general of its Standing Committee. Later that year, he was elected vice chairman of the National Committee of the Chinese People's Political Consultative Conference. His senior rank in the party was confirmed by the Eighth National Congress, held in September 1956, at which he was reelected to the Political Bureau and was elected to the party's Central Secretariat, in which he ranked just below Teng Hsiao-p'ing (q.v.). P'eng served as vice chairman and secretary general of the National People's Congress in 1959, and as vice chairman in 1965.

P'eng Chen also played an increasingly important role in foreign affairs. He made his first trip abroad in 1956, when he led a delegation from the National People's Congress and the Peking municipal government. He also traveled to Italy as head of the Chinese delegation to the Eighth Congress of the Italian Communist party. In 1960 he led a delegation to the Rumanian Workers Party Congress in June and made a fiery statement denouncing President Tito of Yugoslavia as a revisionist. Sino-Soviet relations became strained in 1960. Although P'eng and other Chinese met with Soviet officials at Moscow later that year in an attempt to settle their differences, the Russians withdrew their technical aid and personnel from China at the year's end. P'eng returned to Moscow in October 1961 as a member of the Chinese delegation, led by Chou En-lai (q.v.), to the Twenty-second Congress of the Communist Party of the Soviet Union. Chou left the congress abruptly to express dissatisfaction with Soviet Premier Khrushchev's policies, and P'eng became acting head of the Chinese delegation. P'eng went to Moscow with Teng Hsiao-p'ing in July 1963 to discuss the Sino-Soviet dispute, but they accomplished nothing. On their return to Peking, they were welcomed at the airport by Mao Tse-tung. In May 1965, at the forty-fifth anniversary celebrations of the Indonesian

Communist party, P'eng gave a speech at Jakarta in which he strongly attacked Khrushchev's successors.

On 3 June 1966 P'eng Chen was removed from his official posts. He thus became one of the first high-ranking officials to be purged in the Cultural Revolution of 1966.

P'eng P'ai　　　　　彭 湃

P'eng P'ai (22 October 1896–30 August 1929), the first Chinese Communist leader to organize peasants for political purposes and the founder of the short-lived Hai-lu-feng soviet. He was executed by the Nationalists at Shanghai.

Born into a well-to-do landlord family in Haifeng (Hoifung), Kwangtung, P'eng P'ai received a traditional primary education in the Chinese classics. After he had completed his middle-school education, he and several other local youths were encouraged to continue their studies in Japan by Ch'en Chiung-ming (q.v.), a prominent native of Haifeng and at that time the commander of the Kwangtung Army stationed at Swatow. In Japan, P'eng enrolled in the department of political economy of Waseda University in Tokyo in September 1918. His three years in Japan coincided with the rapid growth of the socialist movement among Japanese professors and students at Waseda, and P'eng himself became an active member of a socialist group primarily interested in problems of agrarian reform. His socialist connections and his participation in the Chinese student demonstration held in Tokyo on 7 May 1919 to protest the decision of the Paris Peace Conference regarding the Shantung question brought him to the attention of the Japanese authorities. After being graduated from Waseda in the summer of 1921, he returned to China.

P'eng appears to have joined the nascent Chinese Communist organization in Shanghai (*see* Ch'en Tu-hsiu) before proceeding to Canton and Haifeng in the autumn of 1921. By that time, Ch'en Chiung-ming had gained control of the entire province of Kwangtung and had become its governor, under the nominal authority of Sun Yat-sen. Ch'en, who was favorably disposed to moderate reform, had taken steps to implement a new educational program for the province in 1920, when he had invited

Ch'en Tu-hsiu (q.v.) to head the provincial department of education. On 1 October 1921 Ch'en Chiung-ming appointed P'eng P'ai superintendent of education in Haifeng hsien, where he had established several new schools. Utilizing the authority of his new position, P'eng began to propagate socialist ideas among the students and other local people. He and a colleague set up a radical paper, the *Ch'ih-hsin chou-k'an* [sincere mind weekly], which advocated agrarian revolution among the peasants. With several Chinese students who had studied in Japan, he formed an association for the study of socialism. In 1922 he organized a student May Day parade in Haifeng. This overt demonstration of radicalism incensed the local gentry, at whose insistence Ch'en Chiung-ming removed P'eng P'ai from his educational post.

Shortly after his dismissal, P'eng began to organize Communist-led peasant associations in the East River area of Kwangtung. Donning peasant clothes, he started agitation among the peasants of his native town of Haifeng, many of whom were tenants of his own family. Although his activities resulted in his being ostracized by his outraged family, he continued his work. In January 1923 he formally opened the Haifeng Federation of Peasant Associations (Hai-feng tsung nung-hui) at a ceremony attended by some 20,000 people. The federation's central organization maintained departments of sanitation, education, general affairs, arbitration, agriculture, information, and external relations. It also sponsored free public schools and medical facilities for the peasants, made strenuous efforts to reduce agricultural rents in the area, and established contacts with ricksha coolies in Hong Kong, most of whom were former peasants from the East River area. The peasant associations movement soon spread to Lufeng, Huiyang, P'uning, Tzuchin, Huilai, and other neighboring hsien, and membership was said to have exceeded 130,000. Such was the success of the peasant movement that by May 1923 the Kwangtung Provincial Peasant Association was organized, with P'eng P'ai as its chairman.

As the peasant associations in the East River area became more powerful, they encountered growing opposition from the landlords and local authorities. Although Ch'en Chiung-ming, who had been ousted from Canton late in 1922 by supporters of Sun Yat-sen, appears to have been well disposed toward P'eng P'ai and to have tolerated the peasant associations, he eventually was persuaded that because of their connections with Sun Yat-sen's Kuomintang-Communist regime at Canton they represented a threat to his hold on the East River region. In March 1924, when Ch'en issued orders to break up the peasant associations, P'eng P'ai decided to depart from Canton, leaving his colleagues in Haifeng to carry on the peasant movement underground.

Two months previously, in January 1924, the Kuomintang had held its First National Congress at Canton and had carried out a full-scale reorganization, thereby inaugurating a policy of collaboration with the Soviet Union and the Chinese Communist party. In February, the Central Executive Committee of the reorganized Kuomintang had set up a peasant department under the Communist Lin Po-ch'ü (q.v.). Soon after his arrival in Canton, P'eng P'ai was named secretary of this department. He held this post for almost a year, serving under a succession of department heads, and was chief of the department's training institute during the summer of 1924. P'eng played a key role in the rapid expansion of the Communist-dominated peasant movement in the areas under Kuomintang control.

In February 1925, during the Kuomintang's first so-called eastern expedition, members of the peasant underground in Haifeng cooperated with the Kuomintang troops in driving Ch'en Chiung-ming's forces from the area. P'eng returned to Haifeng in March, set up a local branch of the Chinese Communist party with himself as its secretary, and began to redevelop the peasant associations there and in other localities that had recently come under Kuomintang control. However, with the withdrawal of Kuomintang troops to Canton later in the spring and the reoccupation of the East River area by Ch'en Chiung-ming's troops, the renascent peasant movement was mercilessly crushed, and P'eng fled to Canton. Not until October 1925, when the triumphant second eastern expedition under Chiang Kai-shek had reestablished Kuomintang control over all of eastern Kwangtung, did P'eng return to Haifeng and resume the task of rebuilding the peasant associations. Although the top Chinese Communist leaders, anxious not to antagonize their Kuomintang allies, officially discouraged "excesses" among the peasants, the increasingly powerful peasant organization in the Haifeng area took over most of the functions of local government. Under P'eng's direction it pursued a radical policy of land expropriation, rent reduction, and execution of landlords. Meanwhile, in addition to his positions as head of the district committee of the Chinese Communist party and a member of the party's Kwangtung regional committee, P'eng had become a member of the Kuomintang's provincial executive committee and head of that party's provincial peasant department.

In the spring of 1927 P'eng P'ai went to Hankow and took part in a joint conference of leaders of the peasant movement in several provinces, including Fang Chih-min and Mao Tse-tung. At the Fifth National Congress of the Chinese Communist party, held in Wuhan in late April and early May, P'eng was elected to the Central Committee and was named a member of the temporary executive committee of the All-China Peasant Association, then headed by Mao Tse-tung.

With the collapse of the Kuomintang-Communist entente in the summer of 1927, P'eng P'ai went to Nanchang, where he joined the revolutionary committee organized by Chang Kuo-t'ao, Chou En-lai, Li Li-san (qq.v.), Lin Po-ch'ü, and other Chinese Communist leaders immediately after the 1 August uprising led by the troops of Ho Lung and Yeh T'ing (qq.v.). A few days later, however, these troops were compelled to withdraw from the area by strong anti-Communist forces. P'eng accompanied Ho Lung and Yeh T'ing to Kwangtung, and after the defeat of their forces at Swatow, he made his way with some 800 of their troops to the Hai-lu-feng (Haifeng and Lufeng) area.

As early as April 1927, while P'eng P'ai had been in Wuhan, the East River region had been occupied by anti-Communist troops of the Kuomintang. Peasant associations had been suppressed, and the local Communist organization had withdrawn with a few hundred peasant militia to an inaccessible mountain base. When P'eng reached the area in October, he combined his forces with the peasant militia to form the 2nd Division of the Worker-Peasant Revolutionary Army. Following the withdrawal of Kuomintang troops from Haifeng early in November, the 2nd Division recaptured most of the towns in the hsien of Haifeng and Lufeng. Two weeks later, a soviet government, known as

the Hai-lu-feng soviet, was established with P'eng P'ai as its chairman. Immediately thereafter P'eng initiated a policy of land confiscation accompanied by violent retaliation by the peasants against "anti-revolutionary" landlords.

After the collapse of the Canton Commune in December 1927 (see Chang T'ai-lei) remnants of the Communist troops commanded by Yang Yin (d. 1929) escaped from Canton and made their way to the Hai-lu-feng soviet. P'eng P'ai incorporated them into his forces as the 4th Division of the Worker-Peasant Revolutionary Army and made Yang Yin deputy chairman of the soviet government. Ringed by hostile forces, the Hai-lu-feng soviet was able to maintain itself for only a few months. By February 1928 National Government forces under Yü Han-mou (q.v.) had defeated the troops of the Hai-lu-feng soviet and had occupied Haifeng. The soviet troops staged revolts in March and in May 1928, but they were crushed by the National Government forces.

With the fall of the Hai-lu-feng soviet, P'eng P'ai and Yang Yin fled to Shanghai. At the Sixth National Congress of the Chinese Communist party, held in Moscow in the summer of 1928, P'eng was elected (presumably *in absentia*) head of the Central Committee's peasant department. In 1929 the party appointed him to its Kiangsu provincial committee and assigned him to work in Shanghai. Betrayed by a fellow Communist, P'eng and a few of his comrades were arrested by the Shanghai concession police on 24 August and extradited to the National Government authorities. A few days later, on 30 August, P'eng P'ai was executed near Shanghai.

P'eng P'ai married Ts'ai Su-p'ing in 1912, and she bore him three sons. Ts'ai later was arrested and executed by Kuomintang military authorities.

While secretary of the Kuomintang peasant department in Canton, P'eng prepared at account of his experiences in organizing peasant associations in Haifeng from 1921 to 1924. *Hai-feng nung-min yün-tung* [the peasant movement in Haifeng] appeared serially in the department's official organ, *Chung-kuo nung-min*, between January and May 1926 and was published in book form later that year. After P'eng's death, Communist historians wrote of his martyrdom and praised his important contributions in mobilizing Chinese peasants. Through Russian-language accounts of his early activities in Kwangtung written by his friend Hsiao San (Emi Siao), P'eng's name became well known in the Soviet Union during the 1930's. Russian Communist sources of that period credited P'eng with establishing the first soviet government in China, while in China itself, that distinction was reserved for P'eng's more durable, and subsequently more famous, contemporary, Mao Tse-tung.

P'eng Shu-chih   彭述之

P'eng Shu-chih (1896–), close associate of Ch'en Tu-hsiu who left the Chinese Communist party with Ch'en and became a leader of the Trotskyist movement in China.

Born in Hunan, P'eng Shu-chih came from a peasant family which was relatively well-to-do by Chinese rural standards. After receiving his early education in Hunan, he went to Shanghai in 1920. There he joined the Socialist Youth League organized in August of that year by the Comintern representative in China, Gregory Voitinsky. Another Hunanese youth, Liu Shao-ch'i (q.v.), joined the league about the same time.

P'eng Shu-chih and Liu Shao-ch'i both studied Russian at a small language school established at Shanghai by Gregory Voitinsky and his Chinese assistant Yang Ming-chai. In January 1921, on a visit to Changsha, P'eng helped Mao Tse-tung form a local branch of the Socialist Youth League. P'eng then returned to Shanghai to join a group of about 20 young Chinese (including Liu Shao-ch'i, Jen Pi-shih, Hsiao Ching-kuang, and Lo I-nung) preparing to go to Russia. This was the first group recruited in China by the Comintern to study Marxism and to observe Socialist practice in the Soviet Union. Under difficult conditions, the group spent three months traveling from China to Moscow by way of Vladivostok.

After reaching Moscow in the spring of 1921, P'eng Shu-chih and his Chinese associates enrolled at the Communist University for Toilers of the East. That institution had been established by the People's Commissariat of Nationalities to train cadres from "eastern nationalities" of the Soviet Union and from "colonial countries," especially those of Asia and the Middle East. The school was poorly organized, and the Chinese students there were handicapped further by their language inadequacy. These drawbacks and the drab living conditions in Moscow notwithstanding, the Chinese students were impressed by the revolutionary spirit found in the Soviet Union. P'eng was elected secretary of the Moscow branch of the Chinese Communist party. He also joined the Communist Party of the Soviet Union.

On his return to China in 1923, P'eng Shu-chih was assigned by the Chinese Communist party to work in the propaganda department, then headed by Ts'ai Ho-sen (q.v.), of its Central Committee. P'eng contributed numerous articles to the Chinese Communist journals of the period, notably *Hsiang-tao chou-pao* (*Guide Weekly*) and *Hsin ch'ing-nien chi-k'an* [new youth quarterly]. Through his writings he established a reputation as one of the more articulate Chinese Communist theorists of the period. He became associated with Ch'en Tu-hsiu (q.v.) and was regarded as a faithful young lieutenant of Ch'en, who then was the party's general secretary.

The years 1924 and 1925 marked P'eng Shu-chih's rise to a position of authority in the Chinese Communist movement. In 1924 he visited Moscow for the second time as an official Chinese delegate to the Fifth World Congress of the Comintern. In 1925, at the Fourth National Congress of the Chinese Communist party, he was elected to the Central Committee. Meanwhile, he had also become a member of the party's Political Bureau. When Ts'ai Ho-sen left China to attend the sixth plenum of the Executive Committee of the Comintern late in 1925, P'eng succeeded him as head of the propaganda department and as chief editor of the *Hsiang-tao chou-pao*. The year 1925 was also a significant year in P'eng's personal life, for he met Ch'en Pi-lan, who was to become his wife. She came from a scholarly family and had attended school in Hupeh during the period of the May Fourth Movement. In 1922 she had joined the Chinese Communist party, and in 1923 she had gone to Peking to work for the party under Li Ta-chao (q.v.). She had enrolled at Shanghai University in 1923 and had gone to Moscow to study in 1924. After returning to China in the spring of 1925, she worked under Hsiang Ching-yü (q.v.) among women students and factory workers in Shanghai. She was also an editor of *Chung-kuo fu-nü tsa-chih* [Chinese women], a journal with which Hsiang Ching-yü was then associated.

Beginning in 1926, P'eng Shu-chih and Ch'en Tu-hsiu began to follow policies that ran counter to Comintern policy for China. After the coup of 20 March 1926 when Chiang Kai-shek dissolved a Hong Kong strike committee and removed many Communists from prominent posts, Ch'en Tu-hsiu sent P'eng to Canton to consult Borodin, then a Comintern representative. P'eng, following Ch'en's instructions, suggested that all Chinese Communist members should withdraw from the Kuomintang. He also asked Borodin to give Soviet arms to the Chinese peasants. Borodin refused both suggestions and reaffirmed the Comintern policy of Communist party collaboration with the Kuomintang in China.

In the spring of 1927 P'eng, Ch'en, and Lo I-nung (q.v.) were reportedly "shocked" by the Comintern order that the Shanghai workers bury their weapons and avoid clashing with Chiang Kai-shek's forces. By that time the Comintern had decided to remove Ch'en Tu-hsiu from party leadership by inciting defection of a group within the Central Committee led by Ch'ü Ch'iu-pai and Chang Kuo-t'ao (q.v.). Ch'en and P'eng seemed to be aware that such action was impending. According to Pavel Mif, a Comintern representative, they "plotted" to postpone the Fifth National Congress of the Chinese Communist party in order to forestall a possible crisis. In April 1927, the congress convened in Hankow. The meeting was marked by the ascendency of the Ch'ü Ch'iu-pai faction backed by Comintern representatives, and Ch'en Tu-hsiu was forced to make a confession of past errors. In July 1927, at an enlarged meeting of the Central Committee, Ch'en and P'eng Shu-chih proposed that Chinese Communist members withdraw from the Kuomintang. This motion reportedly was passed by the majority but vetoed by the Comintern. On 13 July, Ch'en Tu-hsiu, in the name of the Chinese Communist party, issued a declaration at Hankow denouncing Kuomintang members there. The Kuomintang faction at Wuhan led by Wang Ching-wei (q.v.) decided on 21 July to purge the Communists in areas under its control. After the final

rupture in the Kuomintang-Communist alliance, Stalin's group in the Comintern was forced to shift its policy, and it ordered the Chinese Communists to encourage peasant uprisings. Ch'en and P'eng both resolutely opposed this drastic change of policy, but their views went unheeded.

In the intraparty struggle of the mid-1920's, P'eng Shu-chih's principal antagonist was Ch'ü Ch'iu-pai, who was jealous of his favored position as well as opposed to many of his ideas. P'eng's view of the Chinese revolution stemmed from his belief in the prime revolutionary role of the proletariat. As early as 1924 he had expounded the view that the Chinese bourgeoisie had become anti-revolutionary and that the peasantry could not lead the revolution because it was backward by nature. The proletariat, therefore, was the natural leader of the revolution. The Kuomintang, according to P'eng, was a coalition of "bureaucratic and compradore" elements and "new warlords." The proletariat should not submit to its leadership, for the Kuomintang was essentially a reactionary political and military apparatus. On the basis of these arguments, P'eng worked to end the alliance between the Kuomintang and the Chinese Communist party. Along with Ch'en Tu-hsiu he opposed Communist participation in the Northern Expedition, saying that the Chinese Communist party should devote itself to educating and organizing the masses in preparation for the proletarian revolution. P'eng set forth these views in a pamphlet entitled *Chung-kuo ko-ming chih chi-pen wen-t'i* [basic problems of the Chinese revolution].

P'eng's views were denounced by Ch'ü Ch'iu-pai, who acted as a spokesman for the Stalinist group in the Comintern in condemning Ch'en Tu-hsiu's leadership of the Chinese Communist party. In a polemical pamphlet written in March 1927, Ch'ü Ch'iu-pai accused P'eng Shu-chih of understating the strength of the national bourgeoisie and the peasantry. He said that P'eng's analysis of the class composition of the Kuomintang was false because militarists could not be regarded as a social class in the Marxist sense. Ch'ü branded P'eng's views as "sheer Trotskyism."

The 1926–27 controversy over revolutionary strategy also affected Mao Tse-tung. As editor of the *Hsiang-tao chou-pao*, P'eng Shu-chih published only a portion of Mao's "Report of an Investigation into the Peasant Movement in Hunan," which stressed the key role of the peasantry in the revolutionary struggle in China. When P'eng refused to print the rest of the article, Ch'ü Ch'iu-pai recommended its publication as a separate pamphlet and wrote an introduction to it.

On 7 August 1927 some 20 Communist delegates met in a secret emergency conference at which Ch'ü Ch'iu-pai replaced Ch'en Tu-hsiu as general secretary of the Chinese Communist party. P'eng Shu-chih was removed from his party posts and was assigned to work in north China to incite uprisings in the Peking-Tientsin area. Because he postponed his trip north, he was dismissed from the Political Bureau. He then went to Shanghai to join Ch'en Tu-hsiu.

In the summer of 1928 Stalin summoned Ch'en Tu-hsiu and P'eng Shu-chih to the Sixth World Congress of the Comintern in Moscow, but both men declined the invitation. In early 1929 they came into contact with a number of Chinese students, who had returned from Sun Yat-sen University in Moscow with Trotsky's new essays, "Summary and Perspective of the Chinese Revolution" and "The Chinese Question After the Sixth World Congress." Stimulated by Trotsky's views, they wrote to the Central Committee demanding that the Chinese Communist party's "adventurous" policy be changed. Furthermore, they persuaded some 80 party members to sign a manifesto that charged Stalin with having replaced Lenin's democratic centralism with bureaucratic dictatorship. After the publication of the manifesto in December 1929, P'eng Shu-chih, Ch'en Tu-hsiu, and other signers, including P'eng's wife, were expelled from the Chinese Communist party. A month prior to his expulsion, P'eng had been dismissed from the Kiangsu provincial committee.

Embittered, P'eng, Ch'en Tu-hsiu, and their followers, now branded as the ch'ü-hsiao p'ai [liquidation faction] by the Central Committee of the Chinese Communist party, organized a pro-Trotsky opposition group, the Wu-ch'an-che she [proletarian society] and began to publish a journal, Wu-ch'an-che [the proletariat]. Aside from Ch'en Tu-hsiu's group, three other Trotskyist societies also existed in Shanghai: the Wo-men ti hua [our words] group, the Chan-tou she [combat society], and the Shih-

yueh she [October society]. In May 1931, on advice received from Trotsky in Turkey and with funds from Trotskyist organizations in Europe, these rival groups merged to form the Chinese Communist Party Left Opposition Faction (Chung-kuo kung-ch'an-tang tso-p'ai fan-tui-p'ai).

The new organization was dominated by Ch'en Tu-hsiu's Wu-ch'an-che she. As Ch'en's trusted aide, P'eng Shu-chih became a member of the standing committee. P'eng contributed many articles to Huo-hua [the spark], one of the organization's publications. Before long, however, the Opposition party was torn by internal dissension and by police interventions. On 15 October 1932 Ch'en Tu-hsiu was arrested. P'eng and others were imprisoned about the same time. After being given a trial, which lasted two years and was much publicized in China, Ch'en and P'eng were sentenced to fifteen years in prison, but the sentence later was reduced to eight years. After the outbreak of the Sino-Japanese war, the National Government declared a general amnesty for political prisoners, and in August 1937 P'eng, Ch'en, and their associates were released on parole.

After regaining his freedom, P'eng Shu-chih sought refuge in the International Settlement of Shanghai. When Ch'en Tu-hsiu declared that he was independent of any political group, P'eng began to gather together the forces of the Chinese Trotskyists. He published several clandestine magazines and translations of Trotsky's works, notably his *History of the Russian Revolution* and *The Revolution Betrayed*. Despite his best efforts the movement failed to gain momentum. After the Japanese occupied Shanghai, they imprisoned many Chinese Trotskyists. P'eng escaped arrest. From 1941 to 1945, he taught under an assumed name at Shanghai University, where he lectured on Chinese history and on Western literature and philosophy. At war's end, P'eng reestablished connections with Trotskyists and published journals in the name of the Chinese Communist Party Left Opposition Faction. One of these journals, Ch'iu-chen [searching for truth] reportedly attained a monthly circulation of nearly 5,000 copies. In the inaugural issue of that magazine in 1946, P'eng sought to synthesize the views of Lao-tzu with those of Trotsky. In August 1948, the Opposition party held a third national convention, attended by some 300 members.

In late 1948, when the victory of the Chinese Communists on the mainland appeared imminent, P'eng Shu-chih and his wife fled to Hong Kong, where P'eng published a Chinese language edition of the *Fourth International* of the Socialist Workers party in the United States. In 1949, fearing arrest by the Hong Kong authorities, P'eng fled to Viet Nam and thence to Europe. He and his wife arrived in France in the summer of 1951 and took up residence in Paris as political refugees, sustained by friends and sympathizers. They continued to produce Trotskyist analyses of Chinese politics while working on their memoirs. Ross Dowson interviewed them and wrote "Chinese Revolutionists in Exile," which appeared in the summer 1963 issue of the *International Socialist Review*, published in New York. P'eng Shu-chih's views on the background of contemporary developments in China were reported in interviews with Antonio Farien which appeared in *World Outlook* (12 August 1966 and 10 February 1967 issues). These interviews were incorporated in a pamphlet, *Behind China's "Great Cultural Revolution,"* which was published in New York in May 1967.

P'eng Te-huai   彭 德 懷

P'eng Te-huai (1898–), Chinese Communist general who served as minister of national defense at Peking from mid-1954 to mid-1959, when he was removed from office and replaced by Lin Piao.

Hsiangt'an hsien, Hunan, the native district of Mao Tse-tung, was the birthplace of P'eng Te-huai. His mother died when he was six, and, after several unhappy years in the care of a stepmother, P'eng left home. He undertook a variety of occupations: helper to a cowherd, bunker boy in a coal mine, and apprentice to a shoemaker. After supporting himself for five years, he went to live with a maternal uncle. Two years later, he left his uncle's prosperous household to join the Hunan provincial forces, in which he soon became a platoon commander. About 1916, he was imprisoned after participating in an attempt to assassinate Fu Liang-tso, the governor of Hunan. After his release, he enrolled in the provincial officers' training school. He received a commission in the Hunan provincial army in 1918.

By the time the Northern Expedition began in 1926, P'eng Te-huai had become a major and the commander of the 1st Regiment in the 5th Division of the Thirty-fifth Army. When the army's commander, Ho Chien (q.v.), began to purge it of leftist elements at the time of the Kuomintang-Communist split in 1927, P'eng and his men were driven into Shih-shou-kung, a wild lowland area along the Yangtze north of Tung-t'ing Lake. By then, P'eng had become active in the Hunan peasant association of which the Chinese Communist T'eng Tai-yuan was chairman, and he had married a middle-school graduate who belonged to the Socialist Youth Corps. Through his wife's influence, he began reading Marxist literature, and he joined the Chinese Communist party in April 1928.

By the beginning of 1928 P'eng and his guerrillas had retreated northward to P'ingchiang, an important junction on the Hankow-Changsha road. P'eng led attacks on the Nationalist troops in the area and forced the magistrate at P'ingchiang to release some imprisoned leaders of the Hunan peasant association. These actions were referred to as the P'ingchiang uprising by Chinese Communist historians. About this time, P'eng organized his men as the Fifth Army of the Chinese Workers and Peasants Red Army, with himself as commander and T'eng Tai-yuan as political commissar. Moving from P'ingchiang north to the Hupeh-Hunan-Kiangsi border, P'eng directed guerrilla activity in the area until the winter of 1928, when he and his men were driven south by Nationalist troops to the Ching-kang mountain refuge of Chu Teh (q.v.) and Mao Tse-tung. Soon after P'eng's arrival, Chu and Mao were forced to retreat into Fukien province, leaving P'eng to fight a rearguard action. He was driven out of the area in April 1929, and he spent the rest of that year rebuilding his army.

In the summer of 1930 Li Li-san (q.v.), who then dominated the Chinese Communist party organization, called for concentrated attacks on the industrial cities of central China. On 28 July 1930 P'eng Te-huai's forces, now known as the Third Army Group of the Chinese Workers and Peasants Red Army, took Changsha, the capital of Hunan. They held it for ten days, and they recaptured it in September only to lose it again a few days later.

With the dismissal of Li Li-san and the failure of the Chinese Communist party to capture and hold any of the major industrial cities, P'eng Te-huai returned to his old headquarters at P'ingchiang. Beginning in September 1930 he served under Yang Yu-lin as the deputy chairman of a small Hunan soviet in the Hunan-Hupeh-Kiangsi border area. The Third Army Group was merged with the First Army Group of Chu Teh in October 1930 to form the First Front Army. Some of P'eng's men continued to support the policies of Li Li-san until December 1930, when Mao Tse-tung had them arrested at Fut'ien, Kiangsi. About this time, P'eng became a member of the People's Revolutionary Military Council, and in November 1931 he was named to the central committee of the newly established central soviet government at Juichin, Kiangsi.

Some of P'eng's forces began to move eastward into Fukien after the Kuomintang undertook its fifth campaign against the Communists in September 1933. These troops offered their support to the leaders of the Nineteenth Route Army at the time of the Fukien revolt (see Ts'ai T'ing-k'ai, Ch'en Ming-shu), but the people's government at Foochow was suppressed by the National Government before any plans for cooperation could be discussed.

In October 1934 Chiang Kai-shek's troops forced the Chinese Communists to evacuate the central soviet base area and begin the Long March. The forces from Kiangsi met the Fourth Front Army of Chang Kuo-t'ao in western Szechwan at Moukung in June 1935, but here policy debates broke out which resulted in the separation of the Communist forces, with Chang Kuo-t'ao, Chu Teh, Liu Po-ch'eng, and Hsü Hsiang-ch'ien moving westward into Sikang. Mao Tse-tung, P'eng Te-huai, Lin Piao, and the First Front Army continued to advance toward Shensi, with P'eng serving as commander of the First Front Army. Before arriving at the Communist base in Shensi, this army fought bitterly with Kuomintang forces in Ninghsia and Kansu. P'eng retained command of the First Front Army until October 1936, when Chu Teh finally arrived in Shensi.

After the Sino-Japanese war began in July 1937, the Chinese Communist forces in north-west China were reorganized as the Eighth Route Army (later redesignated the Eighteenth Army Group), with Chu Teh as commander and P'eng Te-huai as deputy commander. Except for a brief period of activity on the Shansi front in the winter of 1937, Chu remained at Yenan, the Communist wartime capital, and P'eng served as field commander. In 1942 P'eng went to Yenan to assume charge of the movement to correct unorthodox tendencies in Red Army members. Also in 1942 he married P'u An-hsiu, a sister of the prominent leftist reporter P'u Hsi-hsiu.

In recognition of his military accomplishments during the Second World War, P'eng Te-huai received full membership in the Central Committee of the Chinese Communist party and alternate membership in the Political Bureau at the party's Seventh National Congress, held at Yenan in April–June 1945. He also served on the congress's presidum. In 1947 he commanded the Northwest People's Liberation Army; in 1948 he received command of its successor, the First Field Army. His forces soon won control of Ninghsia, Kansu, and Sinkiang. Although he held office as commander and political commissar of the Sinkiang Military District from 1949 to 1951, his vice commanders, Wang Chen and Saifudin (qq.v.), were more active in Sinkiang than he.

Of the four such armies created in 1948, the First Field Army was by far the smallest, poorest, and least important. Stationed in an economically backward area in which it met with little resistance from Nationalist forces, the army had few opportunities to capture valuable war material. For example, after it took control of Yenan from the Nationalists in April 1948, the First Front Army discovered that the Nationalists had not built up a strong and well-supplied garrison during the short time they had held the Communist wartime capital. The First Front Army also posed special command problems because its ranks included large numbers of non-Chinese troops—Kirghiz, Kazakhs, Tatars, Mongols and Muslims from northwest China. P'eng continued to hold command of the First Field Army until September 1954.

With the establishment of the People's Republic of China in October 1949, P'eng Te-huai assumed additional responsibilities as chairman of the Northwest Military and

Administrative Committee, a member of the Central People's Government Council, and a member of the National Committee of the Chinese People's Political Consultative Conference. He also served on the executive board of the Sino-Soviet Friendship Association. For a time after 1950 P'eng was chairman of the Northwest Military and Administrative Committee's finance committee, but the post must have been little more than titular, for he took charge of the Chinese People's Volunteers in Korea in October 1950. He signed the armistice agreement at Panmunjom on 27 July 1953, and he was given a triumphal reception in Peking on 12 August 1953. Throughout the Korean conflict, he had continued to hold such high civil posts as membership in the State Planning Commission. Upon his return to China in the summer of 1953 he resumed the chairmanship of the Northwest Military and Administrative Committee and became a member of the committee charged with drafting a constitution. He also retained his Korean command until September 1954, when he relinquished it to Teng Hua.

In the governmental reorganization of 1954 P'eng Te-huai became minister of national defense, a vice premier of the State Council, and a vice chairman of the National Defense Council. In May 1955 he led a delegation to East Germany and Poland. In September 1955 he was one of the ten military leaders who received the rank of Marshal of the People's Republic of China. He was a delegate to the First and Second National People's congresses, and in 1956 he served on both the presidium and the standing committee of the Eighth National Congress of the Chinese Communist party, at which he was reelected to the Central Committee and the Political Bureau. He led delegations to the Soviet Union in 1957, and during the latter trip he also visited Eastern European countries.

In September 1959 P'eng Te-huai suddenly was removed from office as minister of national defense and replaced by Lin Piao. Other high officials dismissed at this time were Huang K'o-ch'eng and Chang Wen-t'ien (qq.v.). The reasons for P'eng's dismissal are not clear, and various explanations have been offered by Western observers. Some have stated that P'eng was purged because he advocated the creation of a professional army free from party

control and non-military tasks, thereby opposing Mao Tse-tung's theory of people's warfare. Another explanation alleged that P'eng was dismissed because of his strong opposition to the "Great Leap Forward" and the creation of people's communes. Whatever the reason, it is interesting to note that when the historian Wu Han (q.v.) was criticized during the so-called Cultural Revolution in 1966, he was accused of implying in his historical drama *Hai Jui pa-kuan* [the dismissal of Hai Jui] that P'eng Te-huai, like Hai Jui, was an upright official who had the courage to speak against the bad policies of a tyrant for the good of the people.

Ping Hsin: *see* HSIEH WAN-YING.

Po I-po 薄一波

Po I-po (1907–), subordinate of Yen Hsi-shan who later became known as a Chinese Communist economic planner. He served as minister of finance at Peking in 1949–53.

Tinghsiang, Shansi, was the birthplace of Po I-po. Little is known about his family background or his early life. About 1926 Po went to Taiyuan, the provincial capital of Shansi, and enrolled at the Kuo-min Normal School. He soon was exposed to the more radical publications of the day, and in 1927 he joined the Chinese Communist party. After being graduated from the Kuo-min Normal School about 1930, Po and some of his classmates became active in radical student movements in the Peiping-Tientsin area. Po is said to have taken courses at Peking University, but he received no degrees from that institution. His radical activities led to his arrest and imprisonment in 1932. He was released in 1935 through the efforts of his schoolmate Liang Hua-chih, a nephew of Yen Hsi-shan (q.v.).

At the invitation of Yen Hsi-shan, Po I-po went to Taiyuan in 1936 as a leader of the Hsi-sheng chiu-kuo t'ung-meng [league for national salvation through sacrifice] and of its "Dare-to-Die" units, both of which were established to organize resistance to the Japanese. Soon after the Sino-Japanese war began, the Japanese occupied Taiyuan. Po and other guerrillas took refuge in the Taiyueh and Taihang mountains. Major Evans Carlson, an American military observer who traveled through Chinese Communist territory in 1938, met Po at Ch'inchow, a small city in the Taiyueh district. Ch'inchow was the administrative center for the ten surrounding counties, of which Po was magistrate. Po's Communist affiliation apparently was unknown to Major Carlson, who spoke of him as "the local representative of Yen Hsi-shan." Some sources of information about Po's activities during the late 1930's state that Po was a secretary to Yen Hsi-shan and director of the southeastern Shansi administrative office. However, his own account of the period, as told to the American journalist Jack Belden in 1947, tells only of Communist affiliations and posts. Po commanded a force known to the Chinese Communists as the New Army. It was formed about 1939 when Po and some of the Dare-to-Die forces left the service of Yen Hsi-shan and joined the Communist 129th Division of Liu Po-ch'eng (q.v.).

From 1939 until 1947 Po I-po commanded the so-called New 1st Division of the Shansi-Hopei-Shantung-Honan Border Liberated Area and served in the region's government. In 1944–45 he also commanded the Taiyueh military sub-district. He became deputy chairman of the border region government in 1945 and chairman in 1946. He held the chairmanship until 1948, during which time he also served as deputy political commissar of the Shansi-Hopei-Shan-tung-Honan Military District. At the Seventh National Congress of the Chinese Communist party, held at Yenan in the spring of 1945, Po was elected to the Central Committee. Thereafter, he rose rapidly in the Chinese Communist political and administrative hierarchy. In 1948 he became political commissar of the North China Military District, secretary of the party's north China bureau, first vice chairman of the North China People's Government, and vice chairman of that government's finance and economics committee.

When the Central People's Government was established in October 1949, Po I-po became minister of finance, a post he held until September 1953. His other posts in the 1949–53 period included: vice chairman of the Government Administration Council's economic-financial committee, member of the Government Council, executive board member of the Sino-Soviet Friendship Association, member of the

State Planning Commission, and standing committee member of the All-China Federation of Cooperatives. In 1953 he served on the committee charged with drafting a constitution, and in 1954 he served on the presidium of the National People's Congress, at which this new constitution was promulgated. Po was chairman of the State Construction Commission from September 1954 to May 1956 and director of the heavy industry and construction office of the State Council from October 1954 to September 1959.

Po I-po's importance in both government and party was confirmed in 1956, when he became chairman of the National Economic Commission and a presidium member of the Eighth National Congress of the Chinese Communist party. At the congress, he gave a report on the "Relationship Between Accumulation and Consumption in Socialist Construction," and he was elected to alternate membership in the Political Bureau. In November, he became a vice premier of the State Council. He attended the National People's Congress in 1958 as a delegate from Hopei. In 1960–61 he headed the State Council's industry and communications office, and in 1962 he was appointed vice-chairman of the State Planning Commission. Po represented Shansi at the National People's Congress in 1964 and served on the congress's presidium. Throughout this period, Po made speeches about various aspects of Chinese Communist programs for economic development. In the field of economic planning, he served for several years under Ch'en Yun (q.v.). Little is known about Po I-po's activities after 1964 or his status with reference to the Cultural Revolution of 1966.

Po Ku: *see* CH'IN PANG-HSIEN.

P'u-ju   溥 儒
   H. Hsin-yü   心 畬

P'u-ju (1896–18 November 1963), painter, calligrapher, and poet.

Born in the town of Wanp'ing, near Peking, P'u-ju was the second son of Tsai-jung, a brother of Tsai-feng (Prince Ch'un). Thus he and his two brothers, P'u-wei and P'u-hui, were cousins of P'u-yi (q.v.), the last Manchu emperor. After receiving a traditional education in Peking, P'u-ju went to Germany about 1914 and enrolled at the University of Berlin. He returned from Europe about 1917 with a Ph.D. in astronomy and a bit more pride in his accomplishment than his mother thought proper. He soon discovered that astronomers were not in demand in China. At his mother's behest, he retired to the Buddhist temple Chieh-t'ai-ssu in the Western Hills near Peking. He remained apart from the world for several years, filling his days with poetry and painting. During this time he referred to himself as the Hsi-shan i-shih [retired scholar of the Western Hills].

In 1926 P'u-ju exhibited some of his paintings at Peking and established a fine reputation as a painter. Because he was a traditionalist, he held that the writing of poetry, painting, and calligraphy should be developed equally. P'u-ju was an ardent student of poetry and an accomplished calligrapher, following the chuan-li style of Yen Liu until he became a master calligrapher in his own right. P'u-ju's other interests included chess, music, and good food. Because of his extravagance, improvidence, and impracticality, his inheritance gradually melted away. To maintain his standard of living, he taught painting at Peking Normal University and at the Peking Institute of Fine Arts. He also accepted private pupils.

P'u-ju reportedly remained in Peiping throughout the Sino-Japanese war. In 1947 he abandoned his apolitical role to the extent of accepting election to the National Assembly as a Manchu delegate. Later in 1947 he left Peiping and went to Hangchow, where he resided with a friend. He made preparations for a trip to the sacred mountains of China, but had to abandon his plans because of the Kuomintang-Communist struggle for control of the mainland. In May 1949 Mao Tse-tung reportedly invited P'u-ju to return to Peiping. P'u-ju responded by boarding a ship and sailing to the Chusan Islands, then still in Nationalist hands.

In 1950 P'u-ju went to Taiwan, where he supported himself by teaching at Taiwan Normal University and by selling his paintings and examples of his calligraphy. He also became a director of the China Spinning Construction Company. In Taiwan, as on the mainland, he wore the traditional long gown of the Confucian scholar, insisted that his students pay him proper Confucian deference (including ritual prostration), and smoked cigarettes constantly. In March 1963 P'u-ju underwent a medical examination and learned that he had cancer of the throat. Because he had little faith in Western medicine he refused to undergo an operation. He consulted various practitioners of native medicine, but to no avail. P'u-ju died on 18 November 1963. He was survived by his wife, Li Mo-yun, and by their two sons. Hsiao-hua and Yü-ch'i.

The publication of P'u-ju's *Han-yü-t'ang Lun-chi* [collected essays] in 1963 was subsidized by the ministry of education in Taiwan. Just before his death, he published the two-volume collection *Hua-lin Yun-yeh*. After his death, the National Museum of History in Taiwan set up a permanent exhibition of his paintings and his painter's tools.

P'u-yi 溥儀
T.　　　　　Hao-jan 浩然
Reign Title. Hsuan-t'ung 宣統
West.　　　Henry Pu Yi
Manchu.　　Aisin Gioro

P'u-yi (1906–17 October 1967), the last Manchu emperor.

Born in Peking, P'u-yi was the son of Tsai-feng, the second Prince Ch'un and the nephew of the Kuang-hsü emperor. As the emperor neared death in 1908, some members of the Manchu hierarchy pressed the claims of P'u-lun and P'u-wei, older great-grandsons of the Tao-kuang Emperor in the P'u generation, saying that they had priority as successors to the childless Kuang-hsü. But the indomitable Empress Dowager Tz'u-hsi on 13 November informed a conference of high officials that P'u-yi would be emperor because, at the betrothal of the daughter of her favorite courtier, Jung-lu (ECCP, I, 405–9), to Prince Ch'un, she had decided that their eldest son would inherit the throne.

P'u-yi, not yet three years old when he succeeded the Kuang-hsü emperor on 14

November 1908, was formally enthroned on December 2. Following tradition, the first Hsuan-t'ung reign year began in 1909 with the new lunar year. Prince Ch'un acted as regent. As a device to straighten out the tangled web Tz'u-hsi had woven around the imperial succession since the death of the Hsien-feng emperor in 1861, however, it had been stipulated that P'u-yi was to be regarded as the adopted son of the T'ung-chih emperor and the ritual heir of Kuang-hsü. Kuang-hsü's widow, the Empress Dowager Lung-yü, thus stood in the official relationship of mother to P'u-yi.

A struggle for power ensued between Lung-yü and Prince Ch'un, and Lung-yü won. Under the combined pressure of the Chinese republican revolutionaries, the demands of foreign powers, and the machinations of Lung-yü, Prince Ch'un retired on 11 December 1911. It was Lung-yü who authorized the issuance of the imperial decree of 12 February 1912 by virtue of which the Manchu emperor abdicated. Although he relinquished political authority in China, by stipulation of the "Articles of Favorable Treatment" in the abdication agreement he retained his status and the dynastic title Ta-Ch'ing huang-ti. He was even permitted, "as a temporary measure," to remain in residence in the Forbidden City, with the understanding that he would move in due course to the Summer Palace, outside Peking's walls. The republican government, for its part, agreed to provide an annual subsidy of 4 million taels for the support of the emperor's establishment.

After Lung-yü died in 1913, Yuan Shih-k'ai requested that the emperor and his entourage move to the Summer Palace. But the imperial household resisted because such a move might have reduced personnel and sources of revenue. P'u-yi and his entourage remained in the Forbidden City.

During the early years of the republican period, some Manchu nobles and officials of the republican government still supported the traditional imperial system. One of these was Chang Hsün (q.v.), who had been among the original petitioners for Manchu abdication. In the spring of 1917 Li Yuan-hung (q.v.), then the president, called upon Chang, who commanded a strong military force at Hsuchow, to mediate between the contending political factions of Li and Tuan Ch'i-jui (q.v.). Chang arrived in Peking with 5,000 troops and forced the dissolution of the Parliament so that he could restore the monarchy. One of the imperial tutors, Ch'en Pao-ch'en, who had been sub-chancellor of the Grand Secretariat and vice president of the Board of Rites, was among the promoters of the restoration attempt, but P'u-yi and his entourage apparently had no knowledge of the scheme. On 1 July, the 11-year-old Hsuan-t'ung emperor was installed upon the throne, reportedly with some reluctance. Chang Hsün and K'ang Yu-wei (q.v.) had the imperial seal affixed to some 19 "edicts" announcing the restoration of the Manchu dynasty and the imperial administrative system. Chang intended to dominate the new regime, and he had himself made Chung-yung ch'iu-wang [Prince Chung-yung], governor general of Chihli (Hopei), high commissioner of military and foreign affairs for north China, and minister of war. The restoration movement collapsed when Tuan Ch'i-jui assembled an army and stormed Peking on 12 July. No action was taken against P'u-yi for his role in the attempt, but the followers of Sun Yat-sen at Canton campaigned thereafter for the cancellation of the "Articles of Favorable Treatment" and the reduction of P'u-yi's status to that of an ordinary citizen.

After Hsü Shih-ch'ang (q.v.) became president in 1918, he decided that P'u-yi should receive a modern education. Until then, P'u-yi had studied under three imperial tutors. Hsü appointed British civil servant Reginald F. Johnston tutor to P'u-yi in March 1919. Somewhat later, P'u-yi and his younger brother P'u-chieh began to study English together. Because of the traditional taboo on addressing the emperor by his given name, P'u-yi decided that the name "Henry" would be used in addressing him in connection with his studies. He chose the name from a list of English kings. However, journalists began using both names, and he became known to Westerners as Henry P'u-yi.

P'u-yi continued to live in his private little world—the Forbidden City. His mother died in 1921; reportedly, she committed suicide after having been scolded by High Consort Tuan-kang. In 1922 it was decided that the time had come for P'u-yi to marry. P'u-yi dutifully selected a wife, Wen-hsiu, from a collection of photographs of suitable young women. A conflict ensued between Tuan-kang and Ching-yi, and P'u-yi then selected Tuan-kang's candidate, Wan-jung, the daughter of Jung-yuan, a hereditary nobleman of the sixth rank. The problem of two selections was solved by having Wen-hsiu designated imperial concubine, with the ceremony performed on 30 November, just in time for the imperial concubine to head the welcoming party for the new empress on her wedding day. The imperial bridal procession, on 1 December 1922, was magnificent.

Belatedly, after a mysterious fire in June 1923 had destroyed the Palace of Established Happiness with its accumulated treasures (which were about to be inventoried), P'u-yi decided to put an end to the corruption that pervaded his establishment in the Forbidden City. In 1923 he expelled most of the 1,000 eunuchs remaining there and enlisted the services of Cheng Hsiao-hsü (q.v.) to renovate the imperial household. However, the former chief of the imperial household, Shao-ying, launched a public campaign against Cheng and replaced him three months later. In early 1924 P'u-yi entrusted Johnston with administering the Summer Palace and with making arrangements for the imperial household to move there. P'u-yi went outside the walls of Peking for the first time to visit his future residence. However, P'u-yi did not move to the Summer Palace. Feng Yü-hsiang (q.v.) turned against his superior, Wu P'ei-fu, and on 23 October 1924 occupied Peking. On 5 November a detachment of Feng's troops entered the Forbidden City, demanded that P'u-yi sign a "revision" of the Articles of Favorable Treatment, removed him to Prince Ch'un's palace outside the Forbidden City, and held him there under guard. According to an explanation given by C. T. Wang (Wang Cheng-t'ing, q.v.), the new foreign minister, the removal was undertaken in response to the demand of "Chinese public opinion." The Peking authorities assured foreign envoys that P'u-yi's life and property would continue to receive protection. The revised agreement, besides providing for abolition of the imperial Manchu title and removal of the Ch'ing household from the imperial palace, stipulated that P'u-yi would continue to receive an annual subsidy, that sacrifices at the Ch'ing ancestral temples

would continue "forever," and that the Ch'ing household would retain its private property.

P'u-yi and his entourage were not content to remain quietly at his father's northern mansion. In 1923 P'u-yi had undertaken the piecemeal removal of palace treasures to Tientsin for deposit in foreign banks for safekeeping. He also had purchased a residence in the British concession in Tientsin. On 29 November, when strained relations between Chang Tso-lin and Tuan Ch'i-jui on one side and Feng Yü-hsiang on the other had brought about a relaxation of Feng's watch over the palace of Prince Ch'un, P'u-yi, with the aid of Reginald Johnston, escaped into the Legation Quarter, where he was given refuge by Japanese Minister Yoshizawa Kenkichi. P'u-yi rejected his father's plea that he return. Yoshizawa secured Tuan Ch'i-jui's permission for the empress and the imperial concubine to join P'u-yi the following day. Rumors of impending restoration attempts increased. According to Johnston, "the young emperor had not the slightest inclination to take part in any monarchist conspiracy." P'u-yi continued to reside in the Japanese legation until 23 February 1925. Then, disguised as a student, he made his way to Tientsin and established residence in the Japanese concession. This second "escape" was engineered by Cheng Hsiao-hsü.

Reginald Johnston stated that, contrary to a commonly held belief that the Japanese at this time endeavored to induce the Emperor to proceed to Manchuria or to Japan, P'u-yi was given to understand (through Johnston himself) that his presence in either Japan or the Kwantung Leased Territory would "seriously embarrass" the government at Tokyo. For five years, P'u-yi resided (without being required to pay rent) at the Chang Garden, the property of a former Ch'ing general, and made a number of political contacts. In June 1925 P'u-yi called on Chang Tso-lin, and later that year he received Chang Tsung-ch'ang (q.v.) and Grigori Semenov, a White Russian adventurer in the pay of the Japanese and Chang Tso-lin. In the years that followed, P'u-yi gave Semenov considerable financial support. However, the possibility of benefitting from political contact with Chang Tso-lin and Chang Tsung-ch'ang was ended by the second stage of the Northern Expedition in 1928. Chang Tso-lin was killed by the Japanese shortly after the Nationalists occupied Peking in June. When Chang Tsung-ch'ang appealed to P'u-yi for financial aid to rebuild his army, he was refused.

In July 1928, despite provisions in the "Articles of Favorable Treatment" guaranteeing the protection of the tombs of the Manchu emperors, the tombs of the great Ch'ien-lung emperor and of the Empress Dowager Tz'u-hsi were broken into and looted, and the remains of these two royal persons were thrown to the ground and mutilated. The Nationalists made little effort to apprehend and punish those responsible for the desecration. P'u-yi later described his reaction to the desecration by saying that his heart had "smouldered with a hatred I had never known before" and that he had sworn to avenge this wrong. His father, Prince Ch'un, moved to Tientsin at this time because he was afraid to remain in Peking.

P'u-yi's three principal advisers in Tientsin were Cheng Hsiao-hsü, Ch'en Pao-ch'en, and Lo Chen-yü (q.v.). They often disagreed, and Cheng and Lo long had vied for preeminence. Lo had established close ties with the Japanese garrison at Tientsin; and after the events of June-July 1928 Cheng Hsiao-hsü also became convinced that Japanese policies favored the P'u-yi fortunes. In August, he made a trip to Japan and met with representatives of the nationalist Black Dragon Society and the Japanese general staff and broached the subject of restoration. He returned well satisfied with his mission. At the end of the year, Lo Chen-yü moved to Japanese-controlled Dairen.

In July 1929 P'u-yi moved to the Quiet Garden, which also was located in the Japanese concession in Tientsin. He was living there when a domestic crisis of major dimensions occurred. One day, Wen-hsiu entered the Chinese city of Tientsin on a shopping tour and never returned. P'u-yi, his imperial dignity outraged, refused to grant the divorce until Wen-hsiu in early 1931 finally entered suit against him. He then granted the divorce, and Wen-hsiu became a primary-school teacher. She died in 1950.

In July 1931 P'u-yi was informed by his brother P'u-chieh (upon the latter's return from a trip to Japan) and by Viscount Mizuno Katsukuni that the rule of Chang Hsueh-liang in Manchuria was unsatisfactory to the Japanese, and that the possibility of P'u-yi's returning to power had increased. The Mukden Incident of 18 September 1931 that marked the beginning of the Japanese military occupation of Manchuria thus had a special significance for P'u-yi, and he sent emissaries to Manchuria to see Uchida Yasuda and Honjo Shigeru, commander of the Kwantung Army. On 30 September he and Lo Chen-yü met in Tientsin with a representative of Colonel Itagaki Seishiro of the Kwantung Army general staff. At the beginning of November, Doihara Kenji, the head of the Kwantung Army's secret service organization, visited P'u-yi to assure him that Japanese military action in Manchuria had been directed solely against Chang Hsueh-liang and that Japan had no territorial ambitions in Manchuria and wished to help the people of Manchuria establish an independent state. He said that Japan would sign a treaty of mutual assistance with an independent state headed by P'u-yi. When assured, in response to his question, that the new state would be monarchical in form, P'u-yi consented to assume the projected role. He did not change his mind when approached by emissaries of Chiang Kai-shek who offered to revive the "Articles of Favorable Treatment" if he would promise not to live in Japan or Manchuria.

On 10 November 1931, during disorders in Tientsin which had been organized by Doihara to justify the imposition of martial law, P'u-yi, accompanied by Cheng Hsiao-hsü, secretly left Tientsin, boarded a Japanese ship, and went to southern Manchuria. The party took up residence in the house of the son of Prince Su at Port Arthur. In a later interview with the British editor and writer H. G. W. Woodhead, P'u-yi condemned the National Government for violating every provision of the abdication agreement and confirmed that he had gone to Manchuria of his own free will. Plans for restoration of the monarchy, however, were far from being as advanced as Doihara had indicated. It was being proposed that P'u-yi should become head of a republic comprising Manchuria and Mongolia. Lo Chen-yü strongly urged insistence on the promised monarchy; Cheng Hsiao-hsü, on the other hand, adjusted more readily to the idea of a republic.

On 18 February 1932 the "Administrative Committee for the Northeast," headed by Chang

Ching-hui, declared Manchuria independent and resolved on the establishment of a republic. P'u-yi later stated that although Cheng Hsiao-hsü agreed with the Japanese that the new state should be a republic, he had refused agreement until Colonel Itagaki Seishiro said menacingly that the Kwantung Army would view rejection of its plan as "evidence of a hostile attitude" and promised that an imperial system would be introduced within a year if the plan were accepted. P'u-yi accepted, and Itagaki gave a banquet that evening for the future chief executive of Manchuria.

The state of Manchoukuo was formally established on 1 March 1932. On 5 March P'u-yi accepted the repeated invitation of a delegation of prominent Manchurians to head the new state. P'u-yi went to the capital, Hsinking (Ch'angch'un), on 7 March, and he was formally installed as chief executive on 9 March, with Cheng Hsiao-hsü as premier. The National Government at Nanking declared that, because he had "allowed himself to be employed as a puppet," P'u-yi was liable to punishment for high treason. On 15 September, Cheng Hsiao-hsü and General Muto Nobuyoshi, who was governor general of the Kwantung Leased Territory, commander of the Kwantung Army, and Japanese ambassador to Manchoukuo, signed a protocol of recognition and a treaty of mutual assistance. However, it soon became apparent that the government of Manchoukuo was constituted to give Japan the deciding voice in the affairs of the region.

In May 1932 P'u-yi was interviewed by the Lytton Commission, which had been created by the League of Nations to investigate the circumstances surrounding the creation of Manchoukuo. P'u-yi informed the investigators that he had come into power with the support of the Manchurian people and that his state was independent.

Manchoukuo had two reign periods: Ta-t'ung, during the time that P'u-yi was chief executive; and K'ang-te, which began in March 1934 when P'u-yi was installed as emperor. On 1 March, Manchoukuo became the constitutional monarchy Man-chou ti-kuo [the Manchu imperial state], and P'u-yi, then 28, was enthroned. He was not a ruler, but a figurehead, and his official role was ceremonial rather than administrative. P'u-yi's personal life was equally unsatisfying, for Wan-jung, his empress, had become addicted to opium. She was kept in seclusion, appearing for ceremonial occasions only.

In 1935 P'u-yi decided to make a state visit to Japan. Prince Chichibu had attended his enthronement as emperor in 1934, and he wished to return the courtesy. He sailed on the Japanese battleship Hiei and on 6 April disembarked at Yokohama, where he was met by Prince Chichibu. His visit was described by a Japanese chronicler as "a personal expression of gratitude by His Majesty to the Japanese nation for the great and constant assistance extended to Manchoukuo since that state's creation." Similar sentiments were expressed by P'u-yi himself on the occasion of his reception by the Emperor Hirohito. He was the first foreign ruler ever to be received by the Mikado.

P'u-yi returned to Hsinking on 2 May 1935. Soon afterwards, Minami Jiro, then the Kwantung army commander, suggested that Cheng Hsiao-hsü be replaced as premier. Cheng asserted that Manchoukuo should be permitted a degree of independence from Japanese guidance. P'u-yi acceded to the proposal, and Minami informed him that the Kwantung Army had already chosen a man for the post, Chang Ching-hui. Cheng Hsiao-hsü resigned on 21 May, and Chang succeeded him.

On 3 April 1937, P'u-yi's brother P'u-chieh married Hiro, the daughter of Prince Saga and a second cousin of the Mikado, in Tokyo. Within a month, upon the recommendation of the Kwantung Army, a law of succession had been passed, providing that in the event of the death of the emperor, his son would succeed him; if there was no son, the grandson would be the successor. If the emperor had neither sons nor grandsons, his next younger brother (this violated the Confucian rule of succession) would inherit the throne. The son of the younger brother was next in the line of succession. P'u-yi thought the law a plot to replace him, and after P'u-chieh's return to Hsinking he refused to eat any food Hiro brought into his household or to talk freely with his younger brother. He began to develop an aversion to Yoshioka Yasunao, the Japanese aide assigned to him. In 1937 P'u-yi took as secondary consort a Manchu girl, Tatala (T'an Yü-lin), but no issue resulted from this union. She died in 1942.

In accordance with established Japanese strategy, Manchoukuo in 1939 adhered to the Anti-Comintern Pact. P'u-yi made an eight-day visit to Japan in May 1940. Generally speaking, he had nothing to do. He was not permitted to seek out his ministers for discussion, and was unable even to inquire about governmental affairs, to say nothing of contributing to "allied" policy. Japan's affairs were becoming too critical to be referred to or discussed with the puppet "emperor." But the fate of Japan would determine the fate of P'u-yi.

The outbreak of the War in the Pacific in December 1941 increased the importance of Manchoukuo in the Japanese scheme of things. However, P'u-yi's account of the 1942–44 period relates only to the trivia with which his days were filled. Then, on the morning of 9 August 1945, he was informed that the Soviet Union had declared war on Japan. On the evening of 11 August, accompanied by his family, P'u-yi left Hsinking and went to Tunghua, which was to have served as a "temporary capital." When he learned of Japan's surrender, P'u-yi issued an imperial rescript renouncing the Manchoukuo throne.

Yoshioka informed P'u-yi on 16 August that they would leave for Japan the following day. P'u-yi selected a few people to accompany him on the small plane provided to take them to Korea (where they were to board a larger plane): P'u-chieh, his two sisters and their husbands, three nephews, a personal physician, and the servant Big Li. P'u-yi's empress and P'u-chieh's wife Hiro were left behind. Wan-jung died miserably at Tumen, in June 1946; Hiro, who had been imprisoned with Wan-jung, lived to write her memoirs.

Because of the adverse weather conditions prevailing in Korea, the small plane carrying P'u-yi was forced to land in Mukden. On 18 August, while P'u-yi and his party were waiting at the airfield, a Soviet plane landed. Shock troops emerged and disarmed the local Japanese guards. P'u-yi and his company were put under arrest. The next day, the whole group was sent by plane to Chita, in the Soviet Union. One of P'u-yi's first acts on the way to Chita was to inform the responsible Soviet officer that he much disliked his longtime aide Yoshioka and

wished to be relieved of the latter's company. His wish was granted. From Chita, P'u-yi was taken to Khabarovsk and was imprisoned for five years. The tedium was relieved by his appearance, in August 1946, as a prosecution witness at the war crimes trial in Tokyo. He testified eight times, saying that he had been forced to do everything he had done with reference to Manchoukuo. He placed the blame for his becoming emperor and for Manchoukuo's collaboration with Japan on the shoulders of Itagaki and the other Japanese who had been his advisers, aides and co-workers.

On 1 August 1950 P'u-yi and other "war criminals" were handed over by the Soviet authorities to representatives of the new Central People's Government at Peking. They were taken to Fushun, near Mukden, and imprisoned. After P'u-yi and the others had been at Fushun for two months, they were removed to Harbin to a prison built during Manchoukuo times for the incarceration of opposition elements. P'u-yi remained there for two years, undergoing the exhausting and exhaustive Chinese Communist process called hsueh-hsi or learning and practice. He was told that he must reform and that he should write out the story of his misdeeds and his reformation. P'u-yi duly composed the first draft of his autobiography, in which he claimed that he had been "forced" by Reginald Johnston to take refuge in the Japanese Legation at Peking in 1924, and that he had been "kidnapped" by the Japanese to become emperor of Manchoukuo. The Chinese Communists, however, did not follow the practice of accepting a man's first telling of his political sins as the full truth, and P'u-yi was told to continue his reform efforts.

A while later, in July 1956, P'u-yi testified at the trial in Mukden of Japanese who had served in important posts in the Manchoukuo regime. Before the trial began, as a part of their "confessions," the Chinese prisoners and P'u-yi set forth details of the Japanese "oppression." At the trial, P'u-yi testified in detail and confirmed what had been obvious years before: that he had lacked power in Manchoukuo and that it had been administered by the Japanese director of the general affairs board and the Kwantung Army.

P'u-yi later said that his "transformation," after which he began to tell the truth as a good Maoist, began on 1 January 1955. By 1956 both his own destiny and that of the Manchu race had been fixed in accord with Maoist precepts. After his exemplary performance at Mukden, P'u-yi began to receive foreign visitors and mail. In August 1956 he was interviewed at the Fushun prison by David Chipp of the Reuters news service, who described him as being "a forlorn looking figure in his drab black jacket, with his name sown over the pocket, and his matching trousers."

Mao Tse-tung issued an order on 24 September 1959 granting amnesty to P'u-yi and a number of other "war criminals" and "counter-revolutionaries." By order of the Supreme People's Court on 4 December 1959, P'u-yi was released from prison after five years' internment in the Soviet Union and nine years' imprisonment in "his" Manchuria.

P'u-yi arrived at Peking, which he had left 35 years before, on 9 December 1959. His father, Prince Ch'un, had died at Peking in 1951, but an uncle, Tsai-t'ao, was still alive, Tsai-t'ao held various posts in the new regime, including membership on the Nationalities Affairs Commission of the State Council. P'u-chieh went to Peking after being released from prison in November 1960. He was rejoined there by Hiro; they took up residence in a commodious establishment once owned by Prince Ch'un.

A report of April 1960 stated that P'u-yi was working in the mechanical repair shop of a botanical garden. The chairman of the Supreme People's Court, who issued the report, quoted him as saying: "The P'u-yi who was once Emperor is now dead. The present one is the P'u-yi of the new life given to me by the Communist party." On 1 May 1962 P'u-yi married a 40-year-old woman named Li from Hangchow, who was a trained nurse. In March 1963 he received an appointment to the National Political Library and Historical Materials Research Committee. P'u-yi died of cancer on 17 October 1967, at the age of 61.

An edited and expanded version of P'u-yi's memoirs was published in Peking in 1964 as *Wo-ti ch'ien-pan-sheng* [the first half of my life]. In 1964–65 a two-volume translation by W. J. F. Jenner, *From Emperor to Citizen: The Autobiography of Aisin-Gioro Pu Yi*, was published by the Foreign Languages Press in Peking.

Quo T'ai-ch'i: *see* KUO T'AI-CH'I.

Sa Chen-ping   薩 鎮 冰
T. Ting-ming   鼎 名

Sa Chen-ping (1859–10 April 1951), commander in chief of the imperial fleet who later served the republican government at Peking as president of the Woosung Maritime Academy, director general of the Shanghai police forces, director general of arsenals, minister of the navy, and governor of Fukien.

A native of Foochow, Fukien, Sa Chen-ping was born into a moderately wealthy family which had a strong scholastic background. After receiving a traditional education in the Chinese classics and passing the examination for the sheng-yuan degree, he decided to pursue a naval career, a choice facilitated by the fact that Foochow was one of the major naval training centers in China. In 1877 he was graduated from the Foochow Naval Academy. His brilliant academic record soon came to the attention of Shen Pao-chen (ECCP, II, 642–44), the minister of naval affairs, who selected Sa and Yen Fu (q.v.) as recipients of government scholarships for advanced naval training in England. Sa enrolled at the Royal Naval College in Greenwich, England, and he successfully completed a tour of duty at sea as well as the course of study.

After returning to China in 1879, Sa Chen-ping joined the imperial navy. He also served as an instructor at the Tientsin Naval Academy, where one of his students was Li Yuan-hung (q.v.). Sa participated in the Sino–Japanese war of 1894–95 as the commander of a cruiser. After seeing duty in several parts of China, he served from 1903 to 1906 as commander of the naval forces in Kwangtung. In 1906 he was appointed to the commission charged with studying the possibilities for naval reorganization. The commission soon completed its study, however, and he returned to active duty. By the end of 1908 Sa had attained the rank of admiral.

In 1909 Sa Chen-ping accompanied Prince Tsai-chün on a naval mission to Japan, Europe, and North America. In England, he was knighted by King Edward VII. On his return to China in 1910, Sa was designated commander in chief of the imperial fleet. It was in this capacity that he led naval forces against the insurgents at Wuchang after the revolution of 1911 began. Although the naval forces led by Sa initially proved to be of considerable help to such imperial commanders as Feng Kuo-chang (q.v.), the Chinese captains in Sa's fleet soon overpowered the Manchus on board and declared their support of the revolution. Li Yuan-hung, who revered Sa as his teacher, sent a message to the defecting naval commanders to afford Sa protection. Sa left the navy at Kiukiang and took refuge in the British consulate. He later fled to Shanghai. In recognition of his apparent loyalty to the Ch'ing government, he was appointed minister of the navy.

In 1912, the first year of the republic, Sa Chen-ping was appointed president of the Woosung Maritime Academy, which trained men for the merchant service. The following year saw him serving as director general of the Shanghai police forces on both land and water. His achievement in creating a modern police force in Shanghai's Chinese city won him high praise from Yuan Shih-k'ai, who appointed him director general of arsenals in August 1914. Sa remained loyal to the Peking government after Yuan Shih-k'ai's monarchical ambitions became apparent. He frustrated an attempt by Ch'en Ch'i-mei (q.v.) in December 1915 to incite an insurrection of naval forces at Shanghai. The gunboat Chao-ho, controlled by Ch'en's forces, started the uprising according to schedule on 5 December. However, the plot was frustrated when a vessel which was supposed to give support to the Chao-ho failed to do so because of Sa's intervention. Although the pro-Yuan forces emerged triumphant from this engagement, their ascendency was short-lived. With the death of Yuan Shih-k'ai in June 1916, Sa Chen-ping withdrew from active service. In June–July 1917 he served briefly as minister of the navy during the so-called constitution protection movement.

Sa returned to public life in 1918, when he became commissioner of bandit-suppression in Fukien. Early in 1919 he was sent on a naval mission to Europe, and in December of that year he was appointed minister of the navy in the cabinet of Chin Yun-p'eng (q.v.). After the Chihli-Anhwei war of July 1920 and the downfall of Tuan Ch'i-jui (q.v.), he served briefly as acting premier. He then returned to his native province, where he served from 1922 to 1927 as provincial governor.

On 20 November 1933 Ch'en Ming-shu (q.v.), with the support of the Nineteenth Route Army, launched the Fukien revolt. Sa Chen-ping was drawn into the affair, serving as a delegate to the provisional assembly which was convened on 21 November to establish a people's government at Foochow. The rebels denounced Chiang Kai-shek and called for resistance to the Japanese. Sa was appointed a member of the regime's state council and governor of one of the four provinces created in Fukien. By January 1934, however, the rebels had realized that they could not withstand Nationalist military pressure. Ts'ai T'ing-k'ai (q.v.) decided not to risk the destruction of Foochow, and he ordered its evacuation. Sa Chen-ping supervised the rebel withdrawal and the Nationalist takeover of the city.

Sa Chen-ping lived quietly in Fukien until the Sino-Japanese war broke out in July 1937. He spent the war years in Southeast Asia, returning to Fukien in 1945. When the Chinese Communists took control of the mainland in 1949, he served as a specially invited delegate to the Chinese People's Political Consultative Conference and as a member of the conference's National Committee. On 10 April 1951 he died at Foochow, at the age of 92.

Saifudin

Alt.　　Saifuddin Azizi
　　　　Seyfudin Azizof
　　　　Saif-al-Din 'Aziz
Chinese. Sai-fu-ting　　　賽福鼎

Saifudin (c. 1914–), Uighur political leader who served the so-called East Turkestan Republic as minister of education and head of the Ili youth organization. In December 1949 he became vice chairman of the Sinkiang provincial government, and in February 1950 he joined the Chinese Communist party. He was elected chairman of the Sinkiang Uighur Autonomous Region in October 1955.

Born into a Uighur merchant family of Artush in the Kashgar district, Saifudin received his early education in Sinkiang. He then went to the Soviet Union, where he studied law and politics at the University of Tashkent, became fluent in Russian, and reportedly joined the Russian Communist party. After returning to Sinkiang, he took part in the Uighur independence movement at the time of the disorders that accompanied the intrusion of Ma Chung-ying (q.v.) into Sinkiang. With the downfall of Ma Chung-ying and the consolidation of power by Sheng Shih-ts'ai (q.v.), Saifudin went to the Soviet Union. He later moved to Afghanistan, where he spent several years.

The withdrawal of Russian representatives from Sinkiang, the political demise of Sheng Shih-ts'ai, and the extension of the authority of the National Government into Sinkiang in 1943–44 prompted Saifudin's return to political activity in his native province. In November 1944 a major anti-Chinese revolt broke out in the three northwestern districts of Sinkiang that were adjacent to Soviet Central Asia. This so-called Ili revolt led in January 1945 to the establishment of the so-called East Turkestan Republic, with Saifudin as minister of education and head of the Ili youth organization. The political orientation of the Ili regime was patently anti-Chinese, and it enjoyed Soviet support stemming from Russian interest in encouraging anti-Kuomintang unrest among the non-Chinese ethnic groups of Sinkiang.

In an effort to bring peace to Sinkiang, the National Government appointed Chang Chih-chung (q.v.) provincial governor. After protracted negotiations, agreements were signed in January and June of 1946 between the Chinese Nationalists at Urumchi and Akhmedjan and other senior leaders of the Ili rebel regime. In the coalition government established in Sinkiang under these agreements, Saifudin became commissioner of education at Urumchi and a member of the provincial assembly. The coalition was short-lived, however, and Saifudin soon became one of the leaders of the movement that developed in early 1947 in opposition to continued Chinese domination of Sinkiang. The coalition fell apart after the appointment of Masud Sabri (q.v.) as provincial governor. Saifudin resigned his post and left Urumchi in June; Akhmedjan and others also departed for Ili in July; and

the Ili regime resumed its strongly anti-Kuomintang stance. From the time of the November 1944 revolt the Ili area, for all practical purposes, had been independent of Chinese authority, be it Nationalist or Communist. In August 1948, however, the Ili leaders announced the establishment of the Sinkiang League for the Protection of Peace and Democracy (Hsin-chiang pao-wei ho-p'ing min-chu t'ung-meng); its name had a definite Chinese Communist ring. Saifudin was prominent in the new league, which issued a proclamation attacking both past and present Chinese rulers of Sinkiang. Despite this statement, the Ili leaders continued to disagree about what their future relationship with the Chinese Communists should be. In September 1949, following the defection of the senior Chinese Nationalist military commander in Sinkiang, Burhan (q.v.) and other leaders at Urumchi surrendered to the Chinese Communists. By this time, a three-man Ili delegation led by Saifudin had arrived in Peiping to participate in the establishment of the Central People's Government of the People's Republic of China. At year's end, the Chinese Communists quietly announced that another Ili delegation had been lost in August when the plane in which it was traveling had crashed in Manchuria. It is interesting to note that this delegation included Akhmedjan, the chief Ili spokesman for true Uighur autonomy in Sinkiang, and several other prominent Uighur nationalist leaders whose attitudes toward the Chinese Communists were unclear.

At the Chinese People's Political Consultative Conference in September 1949, which he attended as a "specially invited" delegate, Saifudin articulated the new Chinese Communist analysis of the Sinkiang political situation. He now interpreted the Ili uprising as a "movement of liberation" rather than a rebellion of Sinkiang's non-Chinese peoples against Chinese rule. True liberation, he said, came only with the Communist victory in China proper: "the victory of the People's Liberation Army is also the victory of the liberation movement of the Sinkiang people." With the problem of Sinkiang's political orientation "basically solved," he added, the area henceforth would be "an independent Sinkiang under the leadership of the Central People's Government." Saifudin was elected to the Central People's Government Council and the nationalities affairs commission of the Government Administration Council. In December 1949 he was named vice chairman of a new Sinkiang provincial government, headed by Burhan. He also became a member (later vice chairman) of the Northwest Military and Administrative Committee, vice chairman of that organ's nationalities affairs committee, a member of the National Committee of the Chinese People's Political Consultative Conference, and a member of the national committee of the Chinese People's Committee for World Peace.

In February 1950 Saifudin led a Sinkiang delegation that went to Moscow to participate in Sino-Soviet negotiations directed, for the Chinese, by Mao Tse-tung and Chou En-lai. He thus was concerned with the agreements bearing on Sinkiang that were concluded at the time of the signing of the 1950 Sino-Soviet Treaty of Friendship and Alliance. On his return to China, Saifudin was admitted to membership in the Chinese Communist party on 28 February 1950. He also became vice chairman of the Sinkiang branch of the Sino-Soviet Friendship Association. In 1952 he was made a vice chairman of the Government Administration Council's nationalities affairs commission.

In September 1954 Saifudin attended the National People's Congress as a delegate from Sinkiang, and he later was elected vice chairman of the congress's Standing Committee. In the governmental reorganization of 1954, he was confirmed as vice chairman of the Sinkiang provincial government and was named to membership on the newly established National Defense Council at Peking, and in December of that year he was made a vice president of the Sino-Soviet Friendship Association. When Sinkiang province became the Sinkiang Uighur Autonomous Region in October 1955, Saifudin was elected chairman and was appointed deputy commander of the Sinkiang military district. He also became second secretary of the Chinese Communist party committee of the Sinkiang Uighur Autonomous Region. At the party's Eighth National Congress in September 1956, Saifudin was elected to alternate membership in the Central Committee.

Saifudin's role as a leading non-Chinese in the People's Republic of China also led to his participation in international affairs. In April 1955, having become a member of the board of directors of the Sino-Indian Friendship Association, he visited New Delhi. In 1956 he became a member of the newly formed Asian (after 1958, Afro-Asian) Solidarity Committee of China. He visited Moscow in July–August 1957 and then went to Finland to head a Chinese delegation representing the National People's Congress. Three months later, in November 1957, Saifudin was again in Moscow, this time as a member of the Chinese delegation headed by Mao Tse-tung that participated in the fortieth-anniversary celebrations of the Russian Revolution. At that time, he also visited Prague as a member of the Chinese delegation, led by Li Hsien-nien, that attended the funeral of Antonin Zapotocky.

Saifudin continued to enjoy prominence in both Sinkiang and national affairs in the 1960's. He participated in the second and third National People's congresses as a delegate from Sinkiang, continued to serve as a vice chairman of that body's Standing Committee, and continued to hold membership on the National Defense Council at Peking. In September 1962 he was deputy chairman of a National People's Congress that visited North Viet Nam. Saifudin was reelected chairman of the Sinkiang Uighur Autonomous Region in 1959, and he was named president of Sinkiang University in 1964.

Shang Chen   商 震
T. Ch'i-yü   啓 子

Shang Chen (c. 1884–), military subordinate of Yen Hsi-shan who later served as governor of Hopei (1928–29), Shansi (1929–31), and Honan (1936). He headed the Chinese Military Mission to the United States in 1944–45.

Little is known about Shang Chen's family background or early life except that he was born in Paoting, Chihli (Hopei) and that his native place was Shaohsing, Chekiang. After receiving a military education, he became a divisional staff officer in Fengtien, where he became active in the anti-Manchu revolutionary movement. With the establishment of the republic in 1912, he received command of a mixed brigade in Shantung. Later that year, he was transferred to an advisory post in the ministry of war. During the so-called second revolution of June–September 1913 he was arrested on suspicion of complicity in the anti-Yuan plot, but he was released soon afterwards and was given a post in Mienchih, Honan. In 1914 he received command of a regiment in the forces of Feng Yü-hsiang's uncle Lu Chien-chang. He spent 1914 and 1915 campaigning against bandits in northern Shensi.

In 1916 Shang Chen led his regiment into Shansi and entered the service of Yen Hsi-shan (q.v.). He soon rose in rank and power from commander of the Shansi 1st Mixed Brigade to commander of the Shansi Temporary 1st Division, director of the Taiyuan arsenal, and defense commander for southern Shensi. In September 1926 Yen Hsi-shan appointed Shang military governor of the Suiyuan special district. When Yen decided to support the Northern Expedition, Shang received command of the First Army of the Northern Route of the National Revolutionary Army. When Yen's forces were reorganized in 1927 as the Third Army Group, Shang became field commander of that army's northern route. He served as field commander of the entire Third Army Group during the final stage of the Northern Expedition in 1928, and his own First Army led the way into Paoting and Peking.

At the end of June 1928 Shang Chen was rewarded for his services during the Northern Expedition with appointments as governor of Hopei, bandit-suppression commander in Hopei, and deputy (under Yen Hsi-shan) Peiping-Tientsin garrison commander. Soon afterwards, he became a member of the Peiping branch of the Political Council. When Yen Hsi-shan became minister of interior in the new National Government established at Nanking in October 1928, Shang assumed full command of the Peiping-Tientsin garrison forces. In 1929 Shang was appointed governor of Shansi in September and was elected an alternate member of the Kuomintang's Central Supervisory Committee at year's end. About this time, he apparently decided that his future prospects would be enhanced if he dissociated himself from Yen Hsi-shan. Thus, he did not take part in the activities of the so-called northern coalition (*see* Yen Hsi-shan; Feng Yü-hsiang) in 1930.

Shang Chen received command of the Fourth Army in 1930 and of the Thirty-second Army in 1931. He was succeeded as governor of Shansi by Hsü Yung-ch'ang (q.v.) in August 1931, at which time he received command of the Third Army Group of the so-called northern bandit-suppression forces. Early in 1933 he was appointed commander in chief of the Second Army Group in north China and was dispatched to the Great Wall, where his forces performed well in turning back the Japanese at Langkow. Beginning in June 1934, Shang served as adjutant of the Lushan Officers Training Corps. He was reassigned to north China in June 1935 as Tangku-Paoan commander and mayor of Tientsin. After the Ho-Umezu agreement (*see* Ho Ying-ch'in), he was appointed governor of Hopei and was elevated to full membership on the Central Supervisory Committee of the Kuomintang. He was transferred to the governorship of Honan in January 1936, but later that year he left that post to assume command of the Twentieth Army Group in north China.

In 1939, the second year of the Sino-Japanese war, Shang Chen became deputy commander of the Ninth War Area. He was appointed commander of the Sixth War Area and director of the executive office of the Military Affairs Commission in 1940 and was given the additional post of director of the commission's foreign affairs bureau in 1941. He held these posts until 1944, when he was made chief of the Chinese Military Mission to the United States. The mission's chief function was to obtain supplies of war matériel, and Shang was chosen to head it because of his military knowledge, command of English, and prowess at polo. In 1946 he also served as chief Chinese delegate to the Military Staff Commission of the United Nations. Ho Ying-ch'in succeeded him in these posts in October 1946, and Shang then returned to China to become chief adjutant to Chiang Kai-shek.

Shang Chen went to Japan in April 1947 as Chinese delegate to the Allied Council and head of the Chinese mission in Japan. With the Chinese Communist victory on the mainland and the withdrawal of the National Government to Taiwan in 1949, Shang left public life to embark upon a comfortable retirement in Japan.

Shao Chen-ch'ing: *see* SHAO P'IAO-P'ING.

Shao Li-tzu   邵 力 子
  T. Chung-hui   仲 光 軍

Shao Li-tzu (1882–29 December 1967), teacher and journalist who became a veteran leader of the Kuomintang. He served as governor of Shensi in 1933–36 and as ambassador to the Soviet Union in 1940–41. After 1949 Shao held a variety of posts in the People's Republic of China.

The son of a government official, Shao Li-tzu was born in Shaohsing, Chekiang. As a child, he traveled with his father from post to post and studied the Chinese classics under private tutors. His father died about 1897, and he went to live with his maternal grandparents. After passing the examinations for the chü-jen degree in 1903, he studied briefly at Aurora University in Shanghai and then transferred to Futan University, where he taught in the lower grades while pursuing his own studies. Upon graduation in 1907, he went to Japan to study journalism. About 1908 he joined the T'ung-meng-hui. Information about the precise date of his return to China is lacking, but it is known that he taught school in Shensi in 1910.

With the establishment of the Chinese republic in 1912 Shao Li-tzu went to Shanghai where he worked as a reporter on the *Min-li pao* and the *Min-hsin pao*. He also became associated with the new literary movements of the time. In 1915 he and Yeh Ch'u-ts'ang (q.v.) collaborated to launch the *Min-kuo jih-pao*, and Shao served as its chief editor for ten years. During this period, Shao also lectured at the Yu Chi Normal School and at Futan University. He joined the Kuomintang, took part in the May Fourth Movement of 1919, and studied Marxism in the company of Ch'en Tu-hsiu (q.v.). As a prominent intellectual with an interest in Marxism, he met the Comintern agent Gregory Voitinsky in the spring of 1920 and participated in the formation of a Communist group at Shanghai that summer. However, he broke with this group before the Chinese Communist party took form. In 1923

he joined with Yeh Ch'u-ts'ang and the poet Liu Ya-tzu (q.v.) in organizing the Hsin Nan-she [new southern society], which hoped to create a new literature for China.

In the summer of 1925 Shao Li-tzu went to Canton, the seat of the National Government, where he was appointed chief secretary of the Whampoa Military Academy. He attended a Kuomintang conference at Kalgan in August 1925 as a representative of the Central Executive Committee, and he became a member of the party's Central Supervisory Committee in January 1926. After going to Moscow in November 1926 to attend the seventh enlarged plenum of the Comintern as a Kuomintang "fraternal delegate," he remained there for a time to study at Sun Yat-sen University. He returned to China soon after the conservative Kuomintang faction at Nanking, led by Chiang Kai-shek, broke with the left-Kuomintang at Wuhan. In February 1928, after Chiang's return to power over a united Kuomintang, Shao became a member of the Central Political Council and secretary general of Chiang Kai-shek's military headquarters. He also worked with Ch'en Pu-lei and Chou Fo-hai (qq.v.) in drafting Chiang Kai-shek's state papers.

In February 1931 Shao Li-tzu married Fu Hsueh-wen, a native of Ihsing, Kiangsu. (Shao's first wife, *née* Wang, who had borne him a son and a daughter, had died in Shanghai in 1919.) Fu had been one of Shao's students at Shanghai University, and they had studied together at Sun Yat-sen University in Moscow. Also in 1931 Shao relinquished his post as secretary general to Chiang Kai-shek to become principal of the China Academy and director of the Futan Experimental Middle School. He was named governor of Kansu in December. The previous governor, Ma Hung-pin (q.v.), had been detained by rebellious forces at Lanchow in August, and the situation in Kansu remained troubled. Shao resisted the appointment, but he finally acquiesced and assumed office in April 1932. He was replaced by Chu Shao-liang (q.v.) in April 1933, whereupon he became governor of Shensi.

During the Sian Incident of December 1936 (*see* Chiang Kai-shek; Chang Hsueh-liang) Shao Li-tzu was among those detained by the rebels. With the formation of a new national strategy, the united front against the Japanese, at the close of the Sian Incident, Shao assumed new political roles. In 1937 he relinquished the Shensi governorship to become director of the Kuomintang central publicity department, a post he held until 1938. After the Sino-Japanese war began in July 1937, he became vice president of the China branch of the International League Against Aggression. He also served as chairman of the Chinese People's Foreign Relations Association, vice president of the Sino-Soviet Cultural Association, secretary general of the Military Affairs Commission's war area and political affairs committee, and a member of the administrative committee of the Central Political Institute. Shao's wife, Fu Hsueh-wen, was active at Chungking during the war as head of the Women's Aid Institute of the National Relief Commission. From 1940 to 1942 Shao served as China's ambassador to the Soviet Union. In 1943 he became secretary general of the People's Political Council and secretary general of the Commission for the Promotion of Constitutional Government. He held these posts for the remainder of the war.

As secretary general of the People's Political Council, Shao Li-tzu played an important role in the 1945–46 negotiations with the Chinese Communists. He was one of the three Kuomintang members, the other two being Chang Ch'ün and Wang Shih-chieh (qq.v.), who participated in working-level discussions with the Chinese Communists Chou En-lai and Wang Jo-fei (qq.v.) during Mao Tse-tung's trip to Chungking in August–September 1945. He also served as a Kuomintang delegate to the Political Consultative Conference in January 1946. Even as he had promoted Sino-Soviet cooperation during the early years of the Sino-Japanese war, he now worked to achieve an understanding between the Kuomintang and the Chinese Communist party.

When the civil war resumed in the summer of 1946, Shao Li-tzu was serving as chairman of the National Assembly preparatory committee and a member of the committee charged with drafting a constitution. When the National Assembly convened late in 1946, Shao participated in its work as a Kuomintang delegate. In 1947 he was elected to the State Council and the Chinese Association for Social and Economic Research, and in 1948 he was made a member of the National Government's national policy

advisory committee. On 22 January 1949, the day after Chiang Kai-shek announced his retirement from the presidency, Shao was appointed chairman of a five-man peace mission. The Chinese Communists refused to negotiate with this group, and Shao then became a member of an unofficial delegation headed by W. W. Yen (Yen Hui-ch'ing, q.v.) that went to north China in February for an exchange of views with Mao Tse-tung and Chou En-lai at Shihchiachuang. He also served on the official National Government delegation that went to Peiping in April (for details, see Chang Chih-chung). With the failure of this mission, Shao, whose wife had joined him at Peiping, decided to remain there. He became a member of the preparatory committee of the Sino-Soviet Friendship Association, a delegate to the Chinese People's Political Consultative Conference, a member of the conference's presidium, and a member of the Standing Committee of the conference's National Committee.

With the establishment of the Central People's Government of the People's Republic of China on 1 October 1949, Shao Li-tzu received membership in the Government Administration Council, the Overseas Chinese Affairs Commission, the standing committee of the Kuomintang Revolutionary Committee's central committee, the standing committee of the Chinese People's Committee for World Peace, the national committee of the All-China Federation of Literary and Art Circles, and the board of directors of the Chinese People's Institute of Foreign Affairs. In 1952 he became a member of the Government Administration Council's labor employment committee, and in 1953 he was made a member of the board of directors of the Chinese Youth Publishing House.

Shao Li-tzu participated in the work of the National People's Congress of 1954 as a delegate from Chekiang and a member of the Standing Committee. Also in 1954 he was reelected to the Standing Committee of the National Committee of the Chinese People's Political Consultative Conference, and he was made a vice chairman of the Sino-Soviet Friendship Association. He also became known for his strong advocacy of birth control.

In 1955 Shao served on the Chinese delegation to the World Peace Congress. That year, he became a member of the World Peace Council and the People's Parliamentary Group for Joining the Interparliamentary Union. In March 1956 he attended the meeting of the World Peace Council in Stockholm. Upon his return to China he was made vice president of the Institute of Socialism of the Chinese People's Political Consultative Conference. He also served on the committee for the reformation of the Chinese written language, the central work committee for the popularization of standard spoken Chinese, and the committee for examination and formulation of the Han language phoneticization program. In 1957 he became chairman of the Kuomintang Revolutionary Committee's committee for the liberation of Taiwan and social contacts work committee. At the National People's Congress of 1959, which he attended as a delegate from Chekiang, Shao was reelected to the standing committee and was elected chairman of the liaison committee and a member of the bills committee. In the 1960's the aging Shao Li-tzu severely curtailed his activities. He died on 29 December 1967, at the age of 86.

Shao P'iao-p'ing   邵 飄 萍
Orig. Chen-ch'ing   振 青

Shao P'iao-p'ing (1889–26 April 1926), journalist and editor of the Peking newspaper *Ching Pao* [Peking report]. He was executed for allegedly treasonous activities in 1926.

The Chinhua district of Chekiang was the birthplace of Shao P'iao-p'ing. Little is known about his background or early years except that he entered the Chekiang Higher School at Hangchow about 1907. Among his schoolmates were Ch'en Pu-lei and Shao Yuan-ch'ung (qq.v.), both of whom later achieved prominence in the Kuomintang. After being graduated in 1911, the year of the republican revolution, he became an editor of the *Han-min jih-pao* at Hangchow. At the time of the so-called second revolution in 1913, he was imprisoned by supporters of Yuan Shih-k'ai for having written strong editorials supporting Sun Yat-sen's cause. Upon his release several months later, he fled to Japan, where many Kuomintang leaders had taken refuge. In Tokyo, Shao came to know the prominent

Hunanese journalist Chang Shih-chao (q.v.), who then was editing a monthly publication called *Chia-yin tsa-chih* (*The Tiger Magazine*).

After the death of Yuan Shih-k'ai in June 1916, Shao P'iao-p'ing went to Peking and became a correspondent for such newspapers as the Shanghai *Shun Pao* and the *Shih-shih hsin-pao* (*China Times*). When Chang Shih-chao revived his Tokyo magazine in Peking as a daily newspaper, *Chia-yin Jih-k'an* (*The Tiger Daily*) in January 1917, Shao became one of its most enthusiastic contributors. He also assumed responsibility for editing and publishing the paper whenever Chang was absent from the northern capital.

Shao P'iao-p'ing, who had "a nose for a good story" and a forceful style, soon became one of the best-known journalists in Peking. In 1920 he launched the *Ching Pao* [Peking report]. Although the paper became popular as a result of its criticism of the Anhwei clique (*see* Tuan Ch'i-jui), official reaction to it obliged Shao to flee to Japan. He returned to China in 1921 to accept an appointment as professor of journalism at Peking University. In 1923 he published a textbook on modern journalism, *Hsin-wen-hsueh tsung-lun*. In the early 1920's Shao flourished in the unstable political climate of Peking. By offering the editorial support and influence of the *Ching Pao* for sale, he was able to indulge his extravagant tastes.

In 1925 Shao P'iao-p'ing attempted to win the favor of Feng Yü-hsiang (q.v.) by supporting him in the *Ching Pao*. About the same time, he commissioned several radical professors at Peking University to prepare a series of literary supplements for his paper. The Chinese Communist party and the Kuomintang then were joined in a political alliance supported by the Comintern, and Shao's actions somehow gave rise to the rumor that he was linked with the propaganda apparatus of the Soviet embassy at Peking. The very existence of this rumor, regardless of its truth or falsity, placed Shao's life in danger when, in the spring of 1926, Chang Tso-lin (q.v.) defeated Feng Yü-hsiang's forces and took control of Peking. Shao sought refuge in the Legation Quarter at the Hotel des Wagons-Lits. On 24 April, having been assured of his safety by an intermediary, he left the security of the Legation Quarter. He immediately was seized by the police and was charged with treason for allegedly having been on the payroll of the Soviet embassy at Peking. Despite his friends' efforts to save him, he was executed on the morning of 26 April 1926 at the T'ien-ch'iao [bridge of heaven] in Peking. Although some newspaper accounts implied that he might have been guilty as charged, others eulogized him as a martyred victim of warlordism. His widow, *née* T'ang Hsiu-hui, assured the continued appearance of the *Ching Pao* by becoming its publisher.

Shao Yuan-ch'ung　　　　邵 元 冲
T. I-ju　　　　　　　　　　　翼 如

Shao Yuan-ch'ung (1888–14 December 1936), close associate of Sun Yat-sen and Chiang Kai-shek who served as confidential secretary and aide to Chiang at Nanking beginning in 1928. He was accidentally shot and killed by snipers at the time of the Sian Incident in 1936.

A native of Chekiang, Shao Yuan-ch'ung was born into a family which had a strong tradition of scholarship. His father died when the boy was but nine sui, and thereafter he was raised by his teacher, Shu Keng-tieh. In 1906 he enrolled at the Chekiang Higher School (later Chekiang University) at Hangchow, from which he was graduated in 1909. During his student days, Shao joined the T'ung-meng-hui. After passing an examination in 1909, Shao was appointed a judge of the local court in Chinkiang, Kiangsu. He resigned a few months later and went to Japan to meet Sun Yat-sen. Late in 1911 he returned to China and went to Wuchang to take part in the revolt that sparked the republican revolution. Shao soon won recognition as a journalist, and in 1912 he became chief editor of the Min-kuo News Agency in Shanghai. When the Kuomintang was created, Sun Yat-sen appointed him editorial director of the party's Shanghai office, with responsibility for liaison work in that city.

When the so-called second revolution began in the summer of 1913, Shao Yuan-ch'ung was serving as chief secretary at the headquarters of the Kuomintang forces at Huk'ou, Kiangsi. With the failure of the second revolution in September, he fled to Japan, where he served as editor of the *Kuo-min tsa-chih* and assisted Sun Yat-sen in the reorganization of the Kuomintang as the Chung-hua ko-ming-tang in 1914. He returned to Shanghai in 1915 with Ch'en Ch'i-mei (q.v.), who worked to extend Sun Yat-sen's power into the Yangtze provinces and to plan anti-Yuan uprisings. In December, Shao and Chiang Kai-shek participated in the bold but unsuccessful attempt, engineered by Ch'en Ch'i-mei, to seize the gunboat Chao-ho at Shanghai.

When Sun Yat-sen established a government at Canton in 1917, he named Shao Yuan-ch'ung director of general affairs of the generalissimo's headquarters, later promoting him to acting chief secretary. By mid-1918, however, the balance of power in the southern regime had shifted in favor of the Kwangsi clique and Sun Yat-sen had gone to Shanghai. Shao took advantage of this lull in Sun's political career to go abroad, and he spent the years from 1919 to 1924 outside of China. He went first to the United States, where he studied at the University of Wisconsin and at Columbia University. He later worked on several Chinese newspapers in the United States (San Francisco and Seattle) and in Canada (Victoria and Toronto). In the summer of 1923 Shao went to Europe, where he inspected Kuomintang branch organizations in England, France, and Germany. By this time, Sun Yat-sen had decided to foster Kuomintang-Communist cooperation and to send a special mission, headed by Chiang Kai-shek, to Moscow to study questions of military organization. On Sun's orders, Shao went to Moscow in November 1923 to participate in the work of the mission. He returned to Germany at the end of November.

After the reorganization of the Kuomintang in January 1924, Shao Yuan-ch'ung rose rapidly in the party hierarchy. Although he was still in Europe when the First National Congress convened in January 1924, he was elected an alternate member of the Central Executive Committee. Soon afterwards, he was elevated to full membership, and upon his return to Canton that summer he was named to the Central Political Council. He also became acting director of the party's overseas department and a political instructor at the Whampoa Military Academy. He later was appointed acting director of the academy's political department. In September, Shao married Chang Mo-chün (q.v.) in Shanghai, with Yü Yu-jen (q.v.) officiating at the ceremony and Tai Chi-t'ao (q.v.) present as matchmaker.

Near the end of 1924 Sun Yat-sen left Canton for Peking to attempt to work out arrangements with the military authorities in north China for national unification. Shao accompanied Sun on this trip, serving as a confidential secretary and handling correspondence, interviews, and various travel arrangements. In Peking, Shao also served on the Peking branch of the party's Political Council and edited the *Min-kuo jih-pao*. He remained close to the ailing Sun and witnessed his final testament just before his death in March 1925. In November 1925, at the Western Hills conference, Shao aligned himself with Chang Chi, Hsieh Ch'ih, Tsou Lu (qq.v.) and other conservatives in the party in opposition to Wang Ching-wei (q.v.) and the Russian adviser Borodin at Canton. Shao remained distrustful of those in the Kuomintang who supported the policy of alliance with the Communists. In 1926 he became director of the Kuomintang's youth department at Canton.

After the Northern Expedition began, Shao Yuan-ch'ung became prominent in the political affairs of his native Chekiang, serving as a member of the provincial branch of the party's Political Council and as mayor of Hangchow in 1927. He returned to south China in 1928 to become chief secretary of the Canton branch of the Political Council and editor of the *Chien-kuo chou-pao* [national reconstruction weekly]. At year's end, he moved to Nanking, where he was active in the formulation of economic and labor legislation as a member of the Legislative Yuan and chairman of its economics committee. At the Third National Congress of the Kuomintang in 1929, he was reelected to the Central Executive Committee and the Central Political Council. He also served as vice chairman (chairman after 1930) of the examinations committee of the Examination Yuan and as editor of the *Chien-kuo tsa-chih* [national reconstruction monthly]. When the split between Hu Han-min (q.v.) and Chiang Kai-shek took place early in 1931, Shao was named vice president of the Legislative Yuan, a post he held until December 1935. After 1931 he also served on the State Council and its foreign affairs committee. He took time off from his duties in the spring of 1935 to

travel with his wife through Shansi, Shensi, Kansu, Tsinghai, and Ninghsia. Their record of the trip, *Hsi-pei lan-sheng* [viewing the grandeur of the northwest], was published later that year. In December 1935 Shao was appointed director of the party history compilation committee.

Amidst the persistent political strife of the early 1930's, Shao Yuan-ch'ung remained a staunch ally of his fellow provincial Chiang Kai-shek. He enjoyed Chiang's trust and served him as confidential secretary and public relations assistant, his role being somewhat similar to that played later by Ch'en Pu-lei (q.v.). Shao continued to write voluminously, providing orthodox interpretations of Sun Yat-sen's political theories and showing special interest in Sun's concept of national psychological reconstruction (hsin-li chien-she). He also found time to practice the arts of poetry and calligraphy.

At the end of 1936 Shao Yuan-ch'ung accompanied Chiang Kai-shek to Sian for conferences with the Manchurian generals who then were pressing for the formation of a united front against the Japanese. He broadcast a speech to the nation on 10 December in which he appealed to the patriotism of the Chinese people to resolve the national crisis. Four days later he was shot and killed by snipers at the time of the Sian Incident, during which Chang Hsueh-liang and Yang Hu-ch'eng (qq.v.) seized Chiang Kai-shek and held him captive for 11 days. Shao was survived by his wife and by a son and a daughter.

Shen Chia-pen 　　　沈 家 本
　　T. Tzu-tun　　　　子 惇
　　H. Chi-i　　　　　寄 簃

Shen Chia-pen (20 July 1840–27 April 1913), the foremost scholar of the late Ch'ing period in the field of Chinese law. He was best known for his efforts to modernize the traditional legal system, and his reforms served as inspiration for the law codification programs of the 1920's and 1930's.

Born into a prominent scholar-official family, Shen Chia-pen was a native of Wuhsing, Chekiang. His grandfather, Shen Ching-yuan, was a chü-jen of 1801 who taught in a hsien school; and his father, Shen Ping-ying, received a chin-shih degree in 1845 and spent much of his career in the Board of Punishments, where his legal knowledge won him the respect of his superiors. However, in 1864, having served for a time as prefect of Anshun, Kweichow, Shen Ping-ying was dismissed from office on charges of insubordination. Shen Chia-pen received a traditional education in the Chinese classics, and he acquired an interest in law from his father.

About 1860 Shen Chia-pen became a department director in the Board of Punishments, in accordance with a regulation that permitted sons of high officials to serve in the government. His formal career in the field of law began at this time. In 1865 Shen received the chü-jen degree, and for the next two decades he worked in minor offices of the Board of Punishments. He became known for his ability to draft opinions for difficult cases, and he was promoted to more important sections of the board soon after 1883, when he obtained the chin-shih degree. From 1883 to 1893 he is said to have spent "not one day without working at making compilations and editing books on law."

Shen Chia-pen was appointed prefect of Tientsin in 1893. On first taking office, he was lenient in his application of the law, but he later became more severe and once ordered four leaders of a riot beheaded "so that no one would dare to violate the law again." In 1897 Shen was appointed prefect of Paoting, where he gained experience in dealing with foreigners. One of the problems he faced was conflict between the local population and Christian missionaries. A group of Chinese soldiers had destroyed a foreign church outside the city walls, and it was Shen's responsibility to make a settlement. In negotiating he insisted on following the land records of the district and thus prevented the missionaries from taking land belonging to the prefectural yamen as a new site for their church. In later years, Shen often commented on the danger to China of the "religious cases," stressing that the situation had worsened largely because most Chinese officials knew nothing about the law and therefore could not handle conflicts with foreigners.

At the turn of the century, as a consequence of the earlier dispute, Shen Chia-pen was falsely accused by some missionaries of sup-porting the Boxer Uprising. When the Allied armies occupied Paoting in 1900, Shen was arrested and questioned. After being released for lack of proof, he joined the imperial court at Sian, for the turmoil in China prevented him from taking office as provincial judge of Shansi, the position to which he had just been appointed. In Sian, he was given the post of junior vice president of the Board of Punishments and the honorific title of kuang-lu ssu-ch'ing. He returned to Peking with the imperial court in 1902.

In January 1901 the Empress Dowager Tz'u-hsi had issued an edict asking her high officials to suggest reforms. In response, Liu K'un-i (ECCP, I, 523–24) and Chang Chih-tung (ECCP, I, 27–32), who then controlled central China, presented four memorials to the empress dowager in 1901. Liu and Chang, though loyal to the empress dowager, probably were responsible for keeping the Boxer Uprising from spreading southward. Thus, they were in an especially strong position with regard to the imperial court on the eve of the defeat of the Boxers. Two of the memorials pertained to law, discussing abuses of present laws and suggesting the need for new regulations to cover the legal complexities of dealing with foreign powers and their nationals. In January 1902, after the empress dowager returned to Peking, she asked Yuan Shih-k'ai (q.v.), Liu K'un-i, and Chang Chih-tung to recommend officials who would assume responsibility for revising the law. At their suggestion, Shen Chia-pen and Wu T'ing-fang (q.v.) were appointed. Because Wu then held a number of posts, each of which demanded time and attention, Shen became almost solely responsible for the entire law reform program.

Administrative difficulties caused a delay of two years in organizing the law reform program. During this time, China signed new commercial treaties with Great Britain, the United States, and Japan in which these powers took official notice of the new interest in modernizing the law and agreed to relinquish their extraterritorial rights when the state of Chinese law warranted such action. Accordingly, after the fa-lü pien-tsuan-kuan [bureau for the compilation of the law] finally was opened in May 1904, the reformers worked rapidly in the hope of securing the abolition of extraterritoriality.

Before making any recommendations of their own, the members of the newly established bureau hired scholars who had studied abroad to translate foreign books on law and government, studied Western and Japanese law, and invited such Japanese legal experts as Okada Asatarō and Matsuoka Yoshimasa to come to China as advisers to the bureau. Shen and Wu soon realized that they could not continue to look abroad for the necessary legal talent, and they obtained permission to establish a law school. The Fa-lü hsueh-t'ang, China's first modern law school, opened at Peking in 1906.

The Ch'ing code of law that was to be revised, the *ta-Ch'ing lü-li*, consisted of two types of laws: the lü [fundamental laws], of which there were 436, most of which dated from the T'ang dynasty; and the li [supplementary provisions], of which there were about 1,800. The Ch'ing code was arranged in seven sections. The first section, entitled "ming-li" [general provisions], included rules about such things as the names of punishments, the ten heinous crimes, offenses by officials, mitigation of punishment, and pardon. The remaining six chapters, named for the six boards of government, contained specific laws governing the bureaucracy, family matters, taxation, rites, the army, criminal matters, and public works. The code included both criminal and civil law provisions, but no distinction was made between them. Confucianism provided the philosophic basis for the code. Loyalty and filial piety were emphasized, and crimes against the emperor and senior members of the family were considered more serious than other offenses.

Shen first proposed a series of changes in the Ch'ing code in April 1905. These, of all his suggestions, were the most favorably received and the easiest to implement. He called for the abolition of 344 supplementary provisions on the grounds that they were redundant. He wanted to discard laws inflicting corporal punishment in favor of fines or prison work; torture was to be eliminated from trial procedure except in capital cases where the offender refused to confess; also to be abolished were branding and the crueler forms of capital punishment. In addition, there was to be individual rather than collective responsibility in criminal matters. The reform program was successful in all of these areas, although some cases involving torture continued to be reported, and such punishments as banishment and wearing the cangue continued to be meted out.

During the winter of 1906 attempts were made to reorganize the entire Ch'ing administration according to the principle of separation of powers. The ta-li-yüan [supreme court] was formed at this time. It was based on the old ta-li-ssu [court of revision], but, unlike its predecessor, it was independent of the executive branch of the government. Shen Chia-pen was named president of the ta-li-yüan, and Chang Jen-fu succeeded him as vice minister of the ministry of justice, the former Board of Punishments. Within six months, however, the two men had switched positions. This shift apparently was motivated by the fear that Shen would become too powerful heading the independent ta-li-yüan. Another factor was the general confusion over separation of powers. After Chang became president of the ta-li-yüan, he proposed that the revision of the laws be undertaken jointly by the ministry of justice (executive branch) and the ta-li-yüan (judicial branch), using the fa-lü pien-tsuan-kuan (legislative branch) in an advisory capacity only. Shen responded to this suggestion by resigning from the fa-lü pien-tsuan-kuan. At the same time, the recently established cheng pien-ch'a-kuan [constitution committee] attacked Chang's proposal on the grounds that it violated the principle of separation of powers. This committee suggested that an independent organ be created to draft codes. This suggestion met with the emperor's approval, and Shen Chia-pen and Yü Lien-san were appointed hsiu-ting fa-lü ta-ch'en [imperial commissioners for the revision of the laws]. At the same time, the hsiu-ting fa-lü-kuan [codification committee] was established. Shen, at last, had the authority and the independence to pursue his main concern, the modernization of Chinese law.

In the spring of 1906 Shen Chia-pen submitted to the throne the first Chinese code of law governing procedure in criminal and civil cases, the *hsing-shih min-shih su-sung-fa*. This code was revolutionary in three respects: clear distinction was made between civil and criminal law; trial procedure was broadened to allow the parties to confront each other in cross-examination; the jury system was introduced as a way of counterbalancing the power of the magistrates. The code was misrepresented by its opponents as an attack on Confucian values, and the very radicalness of its proposals doomed it to failure.

Although Shen Chia-pen now had learned that it would be necessary to move slowly in changing the law, he submitted another proposed code to the throne in 1907. This code, called the *hsin-hsing-lü* [new criminal law] violated or ignored the traditional Confucian principles of law to an even greater extent than had the 1906 draft. Ethical considerations were separated from legal ones so that the severity of a crime was determined by the act itself, not by the person who committed it; offenses against morality were not included in the law at all, for education was felt to be the proper method of coping with them; and acts which were not clearly stated to constitute a criminal offense were not punishable even if they resembled other acts which were stated to be criminal. For the first time, the judge was given the right to exercise his discretion in imposing sentence in both capital and non-capital cases. The law established maximum and minimum sentences for each offense, and the judge was to weigh the importance of such special considerations as the degree of relationship between criminal and victim in making his decision. The provisions of the code were comprehensive in nature, and the old Chinese notion of "one case, one rule" was abandoned. The proposed code was based almost entirely on the suggestions of Shen Chia-pen's chief criminal law adviser, the Japanese scholar Okada Asatarō, who, in turn, had been influenced strongly by the German code of 1889. In adopting Japanese and German principles of law, Shen committed himself to the principle that all people, with the exception of the imperial family, are equal before the law. This commitment (evident not only in the new code but also in his memorial on the abolition of legal distinctions between Manchus and Chinese and in his essay on the abolition of slavery) irreconcilably separated him from the conservative Confucian officials who thought that distinctions based on status, age, and sex should remain at the heart of the Chinese legal system. The proposed code was submitted to the throne in two parts, the general provisions on 3 October 1907 and the specific provisions on 30 December of that year. The general

provisions section was circulated among the high officials in the capital and in the provinces for their criticism. Led by Chang Chih-tung, then minister of education, and Lao Nai-hsuan (q.v.), a member of the cheng pien-ch'a-kuan, the bureaucracy uniformly denounced the code and even made personal attacks on its author. As a result, the hsiu-ting fa-lü-kuan was ordered to compile a code which hewed to the principles of Confucian morality. Under Shen's leadership, however, the committee balked, and only a few technical changes were made. The minister of justice, T'ing-chieh, countered by proposing five provisional articles which incorporated the main points made by the conservatives. Partly because of this gesture of opposition, in March 1908 Shen asked the emperor for permission to revise the *ta-Ch'ing lü-li* without changing its basic characteristics. As a result, he came to write two quite distinct criminal codes, one an outgrowth of the Chinese legal tradition, the other, alien to it.

The revision of the *ta-Ch'ing lü-li* proceeded smoothly. In October 1909 Shen submitted his *hsien-hsing hsing-lü* [criminal law in force] to the cheng pien-ch'a-kuan. After certain changes were made, the document now called the *ho-ting hsien-hsing hsing-lü* [revised criminal law in force] was approved without further delay. It was promulgated on 15 May 1910. The most important principle that was established by this code was the distinction between criminal and civil law. The memorial that accompanied the final version of the code clearly stated that all cases dealing with succession and inheritance, division of estate, marriage, land and tenements, and debts should be considered civil cases. This code remained in force until 1929, when the first special civil law code was promulgated.

The revised code was a step closer to modernity than the old *ta-Ch'ing lü-li*. The system of punishments was changed; the number of fundamental laws and supplementary provisions was reduced; and the articles were rearranged and systematized. In the final analysis, however, the revised code continued the tradition of the *ta-Ch'ing lü-li*, since there was no attempt to deviate from accepted legal principles. Shen Chia-pen continued to be concerned about the lack of procedural law in China. In 1910 he submitted to the throne the *ta-Ch'ing hsing-shih su-sung-lü ts'ao-an*, which set forth procedural law for criminal cases, and the *ta-Ch'ing min-shih su-sung-lü ts'ao-an*, which set forth procedural law for civil cases. No mention was made of trial by jury, and certain provisions were intended as a compromise between Chinese and Western court practice. At the same time, these proposed codes were more modern in that they defined the proper sphere of procedural law much more sharply than the earlier attempt. Once again, Shen failed to win support for his views.

Shen Chia-pen, disillusioned by the attacks made upon him and disappointed by the failure of his most cherished plans for law reform, resigned from all his government offices late in 1910. As the political situation became more and more acute, Shen's attention was diverted from the problems of law reform to those of dynastic survival. When Yuan Shih-k'ai, in a last attempt to halt the revolution, organized a cabinet at the end of 1911, he appointed Shen Chia-pen minister of justice. Again, Shen lacked the opportunity to make any changes in the legal structure. When the republic was established, Shen's proposals were enacted, but after Yuan Shih-k'ai became president, the supplementary provisions were again made part of the law, thus defeating Shen's attempts to create an entirely new criminal code for China. Shen Chia-pen, who had gone into retirement with the downfall of the Ch'ing dynasty in 1912, died at Peking on 27 April 1913.

The dominant motif in Shen Chia-pen's career was his conviction that China should adopt a modern legal system. He hoped that the change could be made without rejecting the entire Chinese legal tradition, but by distinguishing between law and morality and by treating all people as equals under the law, he came into conflict with basic Confucian principles. Most of his efforts, therefore, were unacceptable to the vast majority of his fellow officials. Nevertheless, Shen made important contributions to Chinese jurisprudence. He humanized the system of punishments, brought about legal equality between Manchus and Chinese, and helped bring about the abolition of slavery. He formulated China's first modern codes in both criminal and procedural law, and thereby paved the way for the codification efforts of the National Government. He called attention to the importance of law and to the proper roles of judges and lawyers. Through

his efforts, a law school was opened, countless foreign books on law were translated into Chinese, and old editions of Chinese law books were brought up to date and reissued. Shen also trained and inspired such younger jurists as Tung K'ang, Wang Hsi-chih, and Chang Tsung-hsiang.

The works of Shen Chia-pen were collected and published by his followers as *Shen Chi-i hsien-sheng i-shu*. His most important writings are the *Li-tai hsing-fa k'ao* [a historical study of Chinese criminal law] and *Wen-ts'un* [selected works—memorials, letters, criticisms and prefaces].

Shen Chia-pen married twice. He had four sons, two of whom were adopted by his brothers. All of the sons became government officials, and one of them was educated in England. Shen also had two daughters, both of whom married officials.

Shen Chün-ju   沈　鈞　儒
T. Heng-shan   衡　山

Shen Chün-ju (1874–11 June 1963), legal scholar and official in the Ch'ing, National, and Central People's governments. A prominent member of the China Democratic League, he became its chairman in 1956.

Chiahsing, Chekiang, was the birthplace of Shen Chün-ju. Little is known about his family background or early years. After passing the chü-jen examinations in 1903 and the chin-shih examinations in 1904, he served for a time as a secretary of the seventh rank in the Board of Punishments at Peking. He then went to Japan, where he studied at Tokyo Law College and came to know a number of T'ung-meng-hui members. As the movement toward constitutional government gained momentum in China at the end of the Ch'ing dynasty, Shen returned to Chekiang. In 1909 he became the vice chairman of the Chekiang provincial council, which aimed to lay the foundations of self-rule in the province, and superintendent of the Chekiang Higher Normal School at Hangchow.

After the 1911 revolution and the establishment of the Chinese republic, Shen Chün-ju became commissioner of education for Chekiang, general secretary of the National Assembly at

Peking, and a member of the Kuomintang. After the so-called second revolution of 1913, he was among those members of the Kuomintang who left the party in October 1913 to join with members of the Chin-pu-tang [progressive party] in forming the Min-hsien-tang [people's constitution party]. Shen's action, which coincided roughly with Yuan Shih-k'ai's order for the dissolution of the Kuomintang, reflected his belief that China needed reconstruction, not revolution, and that Yuan Shih-k'ai represented a stabilizing force. However, when Yuan suppressed the Parliament, Shen, who opposed Yuan's plan to become monarch, went to Shanghai and established a law practice. When a military government headed by Sun Yat-sen was established at Canton in September 1917, Shen became its procurator general. He later returned to Peking to serve in Parliament once again, but little is known about his activities in the 1920's.

After the National Revolutionary Army occupied Chekiang on the first leg of the Northern Expedition, Shen Chün-ju became secretary general of the Chekiang provincial government in 1927. Beginning in 1930 he served as dean of the Shanghai Law School. That he soon won the esteem of Shanghai lawyers was evidenced by his election as chairman of the Shanghai Lawyers Association. Although he no longer held any official posts, Shen continued to be active in politics. He helped found the China League for the Protection of Civil Rights (Chung-kuo min-ch'üan pao-chang t'ung-meng) in December 1932 and the Shanghai Association for National Salvation in December 1935. Together with Tsou T'ao-fen (q.v.) and some 200 writers, newspapermen, and lawyers, he participated in the formation of the Cultural Workers' National Salvation Association in January 1936. Finally, at the end of May, the All-China Federation of National Salvation Associations (usually referred to as the National Salvation Association) was established. This national organization soon issued a statement, reportedly written by Shen, entitled "The First Political Principles in Resisting Japan and Saving the Nation." In July, Shen joined with Chang Nai-ch'i, T'ao Hsing-chih (qq.v.), and Tsou T'ao-fen in writing and publishing "A Number of Essential Conditions and Minimum Demands for a United Resistance to Invasion," which advo-cated cessation of the Kuomintang-Communist civil war, negotiations with the Red Army, release of political prisoners, and establishment of a united front against the Japanese. Mao Tse-tung, then in Yenan, responded in August with an open letter in which he stated that the Chinese Communists were willing to cooperate with the Kuomintang. This response led some National Government officials to believe that the National Salvation Association was working with the Chinese Communists.

On 23 November 1936, after supporting strikes in Japanese-owned factories at Shanghai, Shen Chün-ju was arrested on charges of associating with Communists and attempting to overthrow the government. Others arrested at the same time were Tsou T'ao-fen, Chang Nai-ch'i, Wang Tsao-shih, Li Kung-p'u, Sha Ch'ien-li, and Shih Liang, all of whom were active leaders of the National Salvation Association. They became known as the Ch'i chün-tzu [seven gentlemen]. Altogether, Shen and his associates spent about 250 days under surveillance, first at the Shanghai municipal police station and then (after 4 December) at the detention house of the higher court at Soochow. In the Shanghai prison, Shen practiced calligraphy in the morning without interruption; in Soochow, where he had many relatives and former students, he was kept busy by visitors. During the trial in April 1937 Shen, because he was the eldest of the seven, was regarded as the leader of the group. On 31 July, after the Sino-Japanese war had begun and a united-front policy had been put into effect, Shen and his fellow prisoners were released on bail.

With the Japanese invasion of Shanghai and east China, Shen Chün-ju moved with the National Government to Hankow, where in December 1937 he organized the All-China Association to Support Activities for Resistance and National Salvation. He was responsible for the publication of the *Ch'üan-min chou-k'an* until Hankow fell to the Japanese. After moving with the National Government to Chungking, he became a member of the People's Political Council. In February 1939 he was appointed to the Supreme National Defense Council. He and his associates in the national salvation movement joined the League of Chinese Democratic Political Groups in 1941. After it became the China Democratic

League in 1944, Shen continued to be a leading member, second only to Chang Lan (q.v.) in age and prestige. He represented the Democratic League at the Political Consultative Conference at Chungking in January 1946. When the National Government ordered the dissolution of the Democratic League in 1947 on the grounds that it was a Communist front organization, Shen and other league leaders fled to Hong Kong. In January 1948 the Democratic League pledged its support to the Chinese Communist party.

Shen Chün-ju served as vice chairman of the preparatory committee for the Chinese People's Political Consultative Conference. He attended the conference in September 1949 as a representative of the China Democratic League, and he was elected vice chairman of the conference's National Committee. With the establishment of the Central People's Government of the People's Republic of China on 1 October 1949, he became a member of the Government Council, a member of the Government Administration Council's commission on political and legal affairs, and president of the Supreme People's Court. He continued to be responsible for financial matters and the youth movement of the China Democratic League, and he became national vice president of the Sino-Soviet Friendship Association when it was organized later that year. In April 1951 he was deputy chief of a Sino-Soviet Friendship Association delegation to Moscow for the May First celebrations. He then went to East Berlin as head of the Chinese delegation to the opening ceremony of German-Chinese Friendship Month on 6 June. He went to East Berlin once again in September to attend a council meeting of the International Democratic Lawyers Association, and he was elected vice chairman of the association's council. Shen was appointed to the committee for drafting the constitution in 1953. The following year, he was a delegate from Shanghai to the National People's Congress, and he was elected vice chairman of the congress's Standing Committee. In the governmental reorganization that followed the congress, Shen was replaced by Tung Pi-wu (q.v.) as president of the Supreme People's Court. Toward the end of 1954, Shen was elected chairman of the National Committee of the Chinese People's Political Consultative Conference and reelected vice chairman of the

Sino-Soviet Friendship Association. By this time, he also had become vice chairman of the All-China Association of Social Science Workers.

At the memorial meeting for Chang Lan, who died in February 1955, Shen Chün-ju was elected acting chairman of the China Democratic League. He was formally elected chairman in February 1956. During the anti-rightist campaign of 1957 many of the "democratic" personages who had spoken frankly during the Hundred Flowers Campaign were reprimanded for their criticisms of party and government. On 17 June, Shen issued a statement concerning the China Democratic League and the "mistaken" views expressed by Chang Po-chün and Lo Lung-chi (qq.v.). He said, in part: "with reference to matters in the Democratic League in recent years, owing to ill health, I very seldom have a hand in the handling, but I do have the responsibility. The Democratic League held a national work conference in March 1957 and after that date, Chang and Lo, the two vice chairmen, took greater charge of the affairs of the league. I thought this a very good arrangement, but I did not anticipate their having ulterior motives. I was very indignant recently on seeing in the press the mistaken views of Chang and Lo . . . ." He promised that an enlarged meeting of the standing committee of the Democratic League would clarify the political stand of the league. In November 1958 he addressed the Third Congress of the China Democratic League, pointing out that the league was a political party of bourgeois character and that most of its members had not entirely relinquished their bourgeois standpoint. Therefore, he said, it was necessary for the league to accept the leadership of the Chinese Communist party in all of its work.

Shen Chün-ju served as a delegate to the 1959 National People's Congress, and he was reelected vice chairman of its Standing Committee. He died in Peking on 11 June 1963. He was survived by four sons and a daughter.

Shen Hung-lieh   沈 鴻 烈
T. Ch'eng-chang   成 章

Shen Hung-lieh (1882–), naval officer who commanded the Northeast Sea Defense Squadron in the 1920's. He later served as mayor of Tsingtao (1931–37), governor of

Shantung (1938–41), minister of agriculture (1942–44), and governor of Chekiang (1946–47).

T'ienmen hsien, Hupeh, was the birthplace of Shen Hung-lieh. His father, Shen Chi-ch'ang, was a noted scholar, and the younger Shen soon became a diligent and accomplished student of the Chinese classics. At the age of 18 sui, he passed the examinations for the sheng-yuan degree and became a salaried licentiate. He was given a teaching post at the prefectural academy, where he encountered modern publications from Japan. Shen soon decided to pursue a military career, and in 1904 he joined the Tzu-ch'iang chün [self-strengthening army]. In 1905 he won a government scholarship for military study in Japan, and he entered the Japanese naval school the following year. While in Japan, he reportedly joined the T'ung-meng-hui. He returned to China immediately after graduation in the summer of 1911. At the time of the Wuchang revolt of October 1911, Li Yuan-hung (q.v.), who had been Shen's commanding officer in the Tzu-ch'iang chün, offered him the post of naval commander. Shen declined Li's offer so that he could undertake a mission to incite naval units on the middle and lower reaches of the Yangtze to defect to the revolutionary cause. Shen also participated in the occupation of Nanking.

After the republic was established in 1912, Shen Hung-lieh was appointed a section chief in the staff headquarters in charge of naval operations. In 1914 he was commissioned to carry out an investigation of naval ports and forts along the coasts of China, and in March 1916 he was appointed naval attaché to the War Observation Mission to Europe. He was assigned to the British fleet. After returning to China by way of the United States in the autumn of 1918, he resumed his duties at staff headquarters and became naval instructor at the army college.

Shen Hung-lieh's involvement in Manchurian affairs began in 1920, when he served on a delegation, headed by Wang Hung-nien, charged with investigating border incidents. Shen took four gunboats up the Sungari River, and these vessels enabled the Kirin-Heilung-kiang river defense bureau, established in 1920, to enforce its policies. Wang Ch'ung-wen was bureau commander, with Shen as chief of staff. The new patrol put an end to illegal Russian interference with merchant shipping in the area, and Shen's work attracted the attention of Chang Tso-lin (q.v.), the self-proclaimed commander in chief for peace preservation in the Three Eastern Provinces.

In 1922 the ministry of the navy at Peking transferred jurisdiction over the river patrol to Chang Tso-lin, thus placing Shen Hung-lieh under Chang's command. Chang then began to build a naval force for Manchuria. In July 1923 he formally established the Northeast Sea Defense Squadron and made Shen its commander, with the rank of vice admiral. After being defeated in October 1924 in his war with the Chihli clique headed by Ts'ao K'un (q.v.), Chang Tso-lin transferred control of the Po-hai fleet at Tsingtao, the strongest fleet in the Northeast Sea Defense Squadron, to his ally Chang Tsung-ch'ang (q.v.). This transfer led to considerable unrest within the Po-hai fleet. In the summer of 1927 Shen Hung-lieh, now commander in chief of the vanguard forces of the Northeast Sea Defense Squadron, arrived in Tsingtao to learn of a plot being hatched within the fleet to bombard the city. To forestall such action, he called upon Chang Tsung-ch'ang and had the officers of the two largest vessels in the Po-hai fleet replaced. The fleet was restored to the Northeast Sea Defense Squadron, and a joint command was established with Chang Tso-lin as commander in chief and Shen Hung-lieh as deputy commander in chief and field commander. When Chang Hsueh-liang (q.v.) came to power in Manchuria after his father's death, Shen reportedly urged him to pledge Manchuria's allegiance to the National Government. Chang did so on 29 December 1928, whereupon Shen attacked and subdued Chang Tsung-ch'ang's recalcitrant forces. Shen continued to command the Northeast Sea Defense Squadron, and he helped repel Soviet attacks in 1929 after China and the Soviet Union severed diplomatic relations over the Chinese Eastern Railway.

When the Japanese attacked Mukden in September 1931, Shen Hung-lieh realized that he could do nothing more in Manchuria. Accordingly, he returned to his naval command at Tsingtao. In November, the National Government gave him the concurrent post of mayor of Tsingtao. He resigned from his naval command in June 1933, after the Tangku truce (*see* Ho Ying-ch'in) was signed, so that he could devote his full attention to municipal development. After the Sino-Japanese war began in July 1937, he was appointed to the joint command of the land and naval forces then concentrated in the Tsingtao area. Shen secretly ordered the removal of guns from warships and had these weapons placed on mountain tops and aimed at the nine Japanese cotton mills in Tsingtao. When the Japanese learned of this threat to their property, they evacuated all civilian and military personnel from Tsingtao on 1 September 1937. On orders from the National Government, Shen destroyed all Japanese factories in the Tsingtao area on 18 December.

Shen Hung-lieh succeeded Han Fu-chü (q.v.) as governor of Shantung in the spring of 1938. He established his headquarters in Ts'ao hsien, for the greater part of the province had been occupied by the Japanese. Shen slowly reestablished Chinese authority in more than 40 hsien and organized guerrilla operations. Toward the end of 1941, he was appointed minister of agriculture in the National Government. He assumed office at Chungking in January 1942 and received the additional post of secretary general of the National General Mobilization Council in December of that year. In August 1944 he left these posts to become secretary general of the committee for the examination of work records of central party and administrative organs. At the request of Hsiung Shih-hui (q.v.), he also took charge of the Northeast Committee of the Central Planning Board. Because of his familiarity with conditions in Manchuria, he was called upon to accompany T. V. Soong (q.v.) to the Soviet Union for the negotiations that resulted in the Sino-Soviet Treaty of Friendship and Alliance in August 1945.

At war's end, Shen Hung-lieh was appointed governor of Chekiang, and he assumed office at Hangchow in April 1946. He held this post until July 1948, when he became minister of personnel in the Examination Yuan. In 1949 he moved to Taiwan, where he held a sinecure post as an adviser to the President's office.

Throughout his career, Shen Hung-lieh took the time to write about his experiences and about such subjects as municipal government in Tsingtao, agricultural development under wartime conditions, and the provincial adminis-

tration of Chekiang. Although he wrote much, he published little. In 1953 his *Tung-pei pien-fang yü hang-ch'üan* [border defense and navigation rights in Manchuria] appeared in Taipei.

Shen Tse-min   沈 澤 民

Shen Tse-min (1898–1934), writer and translator who worked to introduce Western concepts to the readers of the *Hsiao-shuo yüeh-pao* [short story magazine] and other journals. He later joined the Chinese Communist party and spent four years studying in the Soviet Union.

The younger brother of Mao Tun (Shen Yen-ping, q.v.), Shen Tse-min was born in T'unghsiang, Chekiang. His father, an advocate of modern education, specifically stated just before his death in 1906 that his sons should take up technical studies in order to make themselves fit for a world increasingly dominated by the Western countries. Shen Tse-min, honoring his father's wishes, became a student at Ho-hai Engineering College at Nanking in 1917. He did not complete his technical studies, however; in 1919 he joined his brother in Shanghai.

At Ho-hai Engineering College, Shen Tse-min met Chang Wen-t'ien (q.v.), and the two young men became close friends. Both had something of a literary bent, and both, while at college, became members of the Young China Association (Shao-nien Chung-kuo hsueh-hui). Branches of the association in various cities kept in close touch with each other with regard to their activities and membership. Shen thus learned about the activities of such members as Mao Tse-tung, Li Ta-chao, Yün Tai-ying, Teng Chung-hsia and Chao Shih-yen. This knowledge made him restive and caused him to seek a new life in Shanghai.

Shen Tse-min joined the Socialist Youth Corps at Shanghai in 1920. That autumn, he and Chang Wen-t'ien went to Japan to study. Shen returned to China in time to attend the first conference of the Young China Association, held at Nanking in July 1921. Soon afterwards, he joined the newly formed Chinese Communist party. Also in 1921, Shen joined the editorial staff of the *Hsiao-shuo yüeh-pao* [short story magazine], then headed by his brother. In the following years, Shen became an important member of the Society for Literary Studies, which promoted "literature for life's sake" in the *Hsiao-shuo yüeh-pao* in opposition to "literature for art's sake," advocated by the Creation Society. Addressing himself seriously to the task of translating Western literary works into Chinese, he worked to introduce Western concepts to the readers of the *Hsiao-shuo yüeh-pao* and other journals. From 1921 to 1925 his contributions consisted of translations of, commentaries on, and criticisms of such Western authors as Oscar Wilde, Romain Rolland, Kropotkin, Andreiv, and the Swedish poet Heidenstam. He relied on English versions of all Western works, for he had a good command of English. He later became fluent in Russian. His translations into pai-hua [the vernacular] won him an important place in the ranks of the "new literature" pioneers in China.

In 1923 Shen Tse-min attended Shanghai University, where the Communists Yün Tai-ying and Ch'ü Ch'iu-pai (qq.v.) were instructors. When Ch'ü became an alternate member of the Central Executive Committee of the Kuomintang in 1924, he secured Shen a post in the propaganda department of the Kuomintang's Shanghai executive headquarters. Shen also served as editor of the *Min-kuo jih-pao* and as an instructor at the middle school of Shanghai University.

Late in 1925 Shen Tse-min and such other Shanghai University students as Ch'en Shao-yü and Ch'in Pang-hsien (qq.v.) were chosen by the Communists to go to Moscow for study at Sun Yat-sen University. Up to this time, Shen's affiliation with the Chinese Communist party had not seemed to have influenced his literary activities. The four years he now spent in Moscow, however, steeped him in Marxism-Leninism and caused his literary production to dwindle in both quantity and quality. Leadership of the Chinese group in Moscow went not to Shen, but to Ch'en Shao-yü, a much younger man who was ambitious and highly skilled in political maneuvering. This group, under the tutelage of Pavel Mif, the rector of Sun Yat-sen University, became known as the 28 Bolsheviks. In 1930, having returned to China with Mif, who had been appointed Comintern representative to China, the 28 Bolsheviks strove to wrest control of the Chinese Communist party from

Li Li-san (q.v.). Shen Tse-min went to work in the propaganda department of the Chinese Communist party in Shanghai. Although he made no appreciable contribution to the overthrow of the Li Li-san leadership, he was made head of the propaganda department when Ch'en Shao-yü became general secretary of the party in the summer of 1931. Shen also became a member of the Political Bureau.

Shen Tse-min went to the Kiangsi soviet area in November 1931 to attend the first All-China Congress of Soviets, at which he was elected to the central executive council of the central soviet government at Juichin, headed by Mao Tse-tung. Shen then went to the O-yü-wan soviet area as a member of the party committee of which Chang Kuo-t'ao (q.v.) was secretary. Chang later recalled that Shen constantly quoted Marx and Lenin, thus indicating his basic unsuitability for a life that depended more on guerrilla maneuvers than on the fine points of Communist theory. When Chang Kuo-t'ao and Hsü Hsiang-ch'ien evacuated the O-yü-wan soviet under Nationalist pressure and moved westward into northern Szechwan, Shen Tse-min, who was in poor health, was left behind with Hsü Hai-tung (q.v.). Shen's wife, Chang Ch'in-ch'iu, was in charge of the women's department of the Fourth Front Army, and she therefore went with Chang Kuo-t'ao and Hsü Hsiang-ch'ien to northern Szechwan. Shen was made secretary of the O-yü-wan special committee later in 1933. His health continued to decline, however, and he died in 1934, at the age of 36.

Shen Tsung-han   沈 宗 瀚
West. T. H. Shen

Shen Tsung-han (15 December 1895–), agriculturalist noted for his work in establishing and developing a national agricultural research bureau and for his service on the Joint Commission on Rural Reconstruction, of which he became chairman in 1964.

The fourth of six children, Shen Tsung-han was born in Yuyao, Chekiang. He received his early training in the Chinese classics from his uncle and from his father, a sheng-yuan who taught school for a living. At the age of 13, Shen won a scholarship to a senior primary school. Upon graduation in 1912 he decided to study agriculture in the hope that he could help strengthen China and better the lot of the peasantry. With this idea in mind, he spent two years at an agricultural vocational school in Hangchow and then went to Peking to study at National Agricultural College. During this period he was strongly influenced by his eldest brother, a devout Christian; and in 1919, a few months after his graduation, he joined the Chinese Episcopal Church in Peking.

In 1919–22 Shen worked on a cotton farm and taught at agricultural vocational schools. The many problems he encountered caused him to think of going abroad for further training. With US $800, some of which he borrowed from friends, he went to the United States in September 1923 and enrolled at the University of Georgia at Athens to study the cotton industry. He received an M.A. degree in June 1924. With the help of a partial scholarship from Tsinghua College and, later, a research fellowship from the International Education Board of New York, he went to Cornell University, where he chose plant breeding as his area of concentration and worked under the supervision of Professor H. H. Love. He received a Ph.D. degree in 1928.

Upon returning to China, Shen Tsung-han became a professor at Nanking University and did research on wheat genetics. An extremely popular teacher, he trained many outstanding Chinese agriculturists. Shen also took charge of wheat, rice, and kaoliang breeding in the Nanking-Cornell cooperative crop improvement program, a venture which was supported by the International Education Board of New York. He made annual inspection trips to the ten Christian institutions which undertook experimental work in areas that were representative of north, central, and east China. One result of this cooperative program was the development of No. 2905 wheat, which yielded at least 40 percent more than the ordinary variety. A new rice variety and a new kaoliang variety improved farmers' yields by 20 percent. During his annual inspection trips to various parts of China, Shen studied other aspects of China's agricultural problems. In 1931 he and a few other agriculturalists prevailed upon the National Government to establish a national agricultural research bureau under the ministry of industry. Shen joined the bureau as chief

technician in 1934, retaining his Nanking post.

As part of his work in the agricultural research bureau, Shen Tsung-han made a study of China's imports of rice, wheat, and cotton from foreign countries in the 1920–33 period. He found that the heavy concentration of population in the coastal industrial cities, inadequate transportation facilities from the interior, and the high cost of marketing were the principal causes of importation; and he and other experts recommended improvements in grain production, marketing, and milling to attain self-sufficiency. These recommendations led to the establishment of a national cotton improvement bureau and a national rice and wheat improvement bureau, with Shen as head of the wheat division. When inspection services for these three crops were established in 1937, Shen also became director of the one for wheat, which set up offices in the wheat-marketing centers to inspect the moisture content and foreign matter of wheat as a first step toward standardization. As a result of these improvements, the imports of cotton, wheat, and rice dropped sharply in 1933–36. In 1937, however, China's economic development was disrupted by the outbreak of the Sino-Japanese war. Shen resigned from his Nanking University post so that he could devote more of his time to work in the agricultural research bureau, concentrating his efforts on wartime food and cotton programs.

In December 1937 Wu Ting-ch'ang(q.v.), governor of Kweichow, invited Shen Tsung-han to work out an agricultural program for his province. After studying the work of the provincial agricultural stations in the Kweiyang vicinity, he recommended that all independent small stations be dissolved and that a provincial agricultural improvement bureau be established in order to reduce administrative expenses and coordinate agricultural programs. He also recommended that emphasis be placed on a few projects that would be helpful to the war effort: extension of wheat, rape, tobacco, and cotton crops to replace opium poppies; improvement of irrigation by digging ponds and building small dams; improvement of rice, wheat, and cotton strains; control of hog cholera and cattle rinderpest; and the creation of a rural credit loan system. Shen's recommendations were adopted, and a Kweichow provincial agricultural improvement bureau was created in the spring of 1938. The national agricultural research bureau set up a field station at Kweiyang with a working staff of 20 specialists which also served the provincial bureau. The close cooperation between these two bureaus helped effect a significant increase in Kweichow's agricultural production.

In the course of a governmental reorganization in February 1938 all national agriculture organizations were abolished and their work transferred to a national agricultural research bureau, of which Hsieh Chia-sheng was director and Shen Tsung-han was deputy director. With about 150 specialists and an administrative staff of 20, this organization gave the provincial bureaus both technical and financial assistance. Shen paid frequent visits to the provincial bureaus and advised them on how to improve research work and extension services.

After returning from the Postwar World Food and Agricultural Conference in Hot Springs, Virginia, in 1943, which he attended as a National Government delegate, Shen Tsung-han discussed with Owen L. Dawson, agricultural attaché of the American embassy in Chungking, the need for technical cooperation between the U.S. Department of Agriculture and the Chinese ministry of agriculture and forestry. In 1946, partly as a result of Shen's efforts, a joint China–United States Agricultural Mission was formed to study agricultural conditions in China, to outline a comprehensive program for agricultural development, and to suggest the types and forms of public services necessary for its implementation. With Dr. C. B. Hutchison as its chairman and Shen Tsung-han as deputy head of the Chinese section, the mission—composed of ten American and thirteen Chinese specialists—spent several months touring fourteen mainland provinces and the newly retroceded island province of Taiwan. The report of the mission, which was published by the Office of Foreign Agricultural Relations of the U. S. Department of Agriculture in May 1947, provided valuable information for the 1948 discussions in the U.S. Congress about economic aid to China; it also contributed to the development of the joint commission idea.

At the suggestion of Secretary of State George C. Marshall, Dr. James Y. C. Yen (Yen Yang-ch'u, q.v.) prepared a memorandum in which he proposed the establishment of a joint commission to administer a program of rural reconstruction, and he recommended that ten percent of American economic aid be earmarked for this program. In accordance with the authority provided by Section 407 of the 1948 China Aid Act (P.L. 472, 80th Congress), an agreement was entered into by the United States and China through an exchange of notes on 4 August 1948 whereby the Joint Commission on Rural Reconstruction (JCRR) would be established. The commission became operative on 1 October 1948. It was composed of two American commissioners, John Earl Baker and Raymond T. Moyer, and three Chinese commissioners, Shen Tsung-han, James Yen, and Chiang Monlin (Chiang Meng-lin, q.v.). Chiang was elected chairman, and he held that office until his death in 1964.

The basic objectives of JCRR were to increase agricultural production, promote rural welfare and fair distribution, and strengthen government and private agencies in their service to agriculture. Because of the agricultural crisis in China, high priority was given to projects that would bring direct benefits to great numbers of people as soon as possible. Accordingly, the basic programs of JCRR were: (1) increase of food production through flood control, irrigation, the multiplication and distribution of improved grain varieties and seeds, and the control of animal diseases and plant pests; (2) land reform programs in Fukien, Szechwan, and Taiwan; and (3) a mass education program in Szechwan. A number of JCRR specialists were recruited from the national agricultural research bureau, of which Shen Tsung-han had been the director since 1947.

With the fall of the Chinese mainland to the Chinese Communists in 1949, the JCRR moved to Taiwan, where it continued to provide technical and financial assistance to government and private agencies concerned with agricultural development. Shen Tsung-han's chief concern was helping the National Government in Taiwan to plan and coordinate agricultural programs for the economic development of Taiwan. He served on the Economic Stabilization Board (later the Council for International Economic Cooperation and Development), which promulgated four successive four-year plans from 1953 to 1968 and which formulated agricultural, industrial, trade, transportation,

financial, and educational policies and programs. Government and private agencies at
all levels took part in carrying out various
agricultural projects, and it was Shen Tsung-han
who coordinated their activities and promoted
interagency cooperation. With the death of
Chiang Monlin in 1964, Shen became chairman
of the JCRR. Although American economic
aid to Taiwan ended in June 1965, the JCRR
continued to operate as a bi-national organization with funds provided by the Sino-American
Development Fund.

In the course of his career, Shen Tsung-han
wrote more than 180 articles on many aspects
of agriculture, including wheat genetics and
crop improvement, agricultural policy and
planning, land reform, and farmers' organizations. His two books in English, published by
the Cornell University Press, were *The Agricultural Resources of China* (1951) and *Agricultural
Development on Taiwan Since World War II* (1964).
He wrote two autobiographical works in Chinese, both of which were published by the
Cheng-chung shu-chü in Taipei.

Shen Tsung-han married four times. His
first wife, *née* Wu, was a girl from his native
village. They were divorced in 1930. The following year, Shen married Shen Li-yin, a graduate of Wellesley who was an agriculturalist.
She died in October 1941, after suffering a
stroke. Shen's third wife, Ch'en Pin-chih,
whom he married in June 1942, died of stomach
cancer on 3 January 1944. He married Liu
T'ing-fang, a historian, on 2 July 1944.

Shen Ts'ung-wen　　　　沈 從 文

Shen Ts'ung-wen (1903–), professor of literature,
editor, and writer of fiction celebrating everyday
life and the dignity of the common Chinese.

Fenghuang, on the western border of Hunan,
was the birthplace of Shen Ts'ung-wen. He
was born into an old military family which had
lost its money during the Boxer Uprising. Shen
was an indifferent student, known chiefly for
his truancy. After studying at a military school
for two years, he was assigned to a regiment at
Yuanling when he was 15. He spent most of
the next three years in observing army life,
bandits, and the local Miao tribesmen and in
pursuing a program of self education which

included classical and modern literature and
politics. After leaving the army, wandering
awhile, and holding a variety of jobs, he went
to Peking in 1922 for further study.

At Peking, Shen Ts'ung-wen registered as a
non-matriculating student and found lodgings
in a boardinghouse frequented by young
writers. Many of his new friends were venturing
to publish their own stories and essays, and
Shen soon followed suit—the more eagerly
because writing constituted his only possible
source of income. From 1922 to 1927 he
wrote scores of stories, most of them concerning
his Hunan adventures. He gradually won a
reputation as a sound craftsman and an effective
stylist. As almost the only young writer of
recognizable talent who was not a radical, he
soon became part of the circle of liberal intellectuals that was dominated by Hu Shih
(q.v.). Shen also met and became deeply
attached to Ting Ling and Hu Yeh-p'in
(qq.v.), and the three of them lived together
until Hu's death in 1931.

Late in 1927 Shen Ts'ung-wen, Ting Ling,
and Hu Yeh-p'in left Peking for Shanghai and
various publishing ventures (for details, *see* Hu
Yeh-p'in). None of the three was possessed of
a business head, however, and by September
1929 all of their enterprises had ended in
bankruptcy. Faced with large debts, Shen
became a professor of Chinese literature, in
which capacity he was to serve off-and-on for
the next 20 years at Shanghai, Wuhan, Tsingtao,
Kunming, and Peiping. He also took up
editing and served from 1933 to 1937 as editor
of the literary supplement of the Tientsin *Ta
Kung Pao*. At the same time, Shen continued
writing so prolifically that by 1935 his collected
works totalled some 35 volumes.

With the outbreak of the Sino-Japanese war
in 1937, Shen Ts'ung-wen traveled to Yunnan
by way of western Hunan and joined the staff
of Southwest Associated University at Kunming. He remained there until the war ended,
using his leisure time to revise and correct old
pieces and to rework some of his early war
notes into new form. In 1945 Shen left
Kunming for Peiping, where he had been
appointed professor of Chinese literature at
Peking University. After the Chinese Communists came to power in 1949, his serene life
was shattered and he was subjected to severe
ideological attacks by groups of leftist students.

When forced to undergo "thought reform," he suffered a nervous breakdown and attempted suicide. Subsequently, he was transferred to the institute of folk music and then to the staff of the palace museum. By 1955 he seemed to have recovered his health. In February 1956 he served as a special delegate to the Chinese People's Political Consultative Conference, and he also attended the 1959 and 1964 meetings of this body. Shortly after his recovery, Shen resumed teaching. In 1957 a book summarizing his work in the palace museum and a collection of his stories were published at Peking. Although Shen wrote no original fiction after 1949 and although he was subjected for a time to "reform through labor," his career ended on a positive note, in ironical contrast to that of his old friend Ting Ling. She had denounced Shen as apolitical and pro-bourgeois and had received a Stalin Prize in 1952 only to vanish a few years later after being accused of a variety of ideological crimes.

As a writer, Shen was known above all for his independence and his prodigious output. Although he knew no foreign languages, he developed a remarkably "Europeanized" style which contributed a new flexibility and variety to the emerging pai-hua [vernacular]. Shen's favorite theme was the courage and dignity of the common Chinese, and his techniques were drawn largely from the traditional Chinese novel. However, he also read Western literature in translation and frequently adapted Western conventions to his own purpose.

Shen Ts'ung-wen's earliest writings appeared in the literary supplements (wen-hsüeh fu-k'an) of such Peking newspapers as the Ch'en-pao [morning post]. Before long, his stories began to appear in the Hsien-tai p'ing-lun [modern critic] and the Hsin-yüeh [crescent moon], while a number of his critical essays were published in the Wen-i yüeh-k'an [literature monthly], notably a study of the poetry of Chu Hsiang (q.v.). Shen's earliest successes were exciting stories of border fighting and Miao life which earned him a reputation as "the Dumas of China." In 1926 a volume of his stories, Ya-tzu [ducks] was published, and in 1937 Mi-kan [oranges] appeared. Studies of Chinese soldiers and rural inhabitants followed in 1928, in Ju-wu-hou [in the army] and Lao-shih jen [an honest man]. That year also saw the

publication of the satirical Hao-kuan hsien-shih-ti jen [the man who understood leisure] and of A-li-ssu Chung-kuo yu-chi [Alice's adventures in China], a fanciful continuation of the Lewis Carroll classic. In addition, Shen wrote a Chinese adaptation of the Decameron under the title Yüeh-hsia hsiao-ching [shadows in the lamplight].

In 1929 Shen published Shih-ssu yeh-chien [14 nights] and Shen wu chih ai [love of a witch]. Shen Ts'ung-wen chia-chi [the collected works of Shen Ts'ung-wen, first volume] appeared in 1930, as did Lü-tien yü ch'i-t'a [the hotel and other matters], a collection of six stories about city life. In 1931 Shen published further installments of his collected works and two volumes of short stories entitled Shih-tzu ch'uan [marble boat] and Chiu-meng [old dreams]. The following year saw the appearance of Hu-ch'u [tiger cubs], Ni-t'u [mud], Tu-shih i fu-jen [a woman of the city], and I-ko nü-chü-yüan-ti sheng-huo [life of an actress]. In 1933 Shen published I-ko mu-ch'in [one mother] and Chi Hu Yeh-p'in [reminiscences of Hu Yeh-p'in], and in 1934 he published Mo-mo chi [spume], Yu-mu chi [wherever the eye roams], and Ju-jui chi, the last of which contains some of his best descriptions of city life and his most famous Miao piece, "Hsiao-hsiao." Also in 1934 he published Chi Ting Ling [reminiscences of Ting Ling] and his first novel, Pien-ch'eng [border town].

In 1935 Shen began superintending his monster 35-volume edition of his collected works and published Fu-shih chi [this floating world] and Pa-chün-t'u [the eight steeds], the latter containing some frank descriptions of brothel life which aroused considerable comment at the time. Hsin yü chiu [the old and the new] and three volumes of selections from his earlier writings appeared in 1936. The following year, Shen collaborated with Hsiao Ch'ien on a volume of essays entitled Fei-yu ts'un-kao [letters we never sent]. During the war years, Shen's production slackened somewhat. In 1940 he published a second volume of reminiscences concerning Ting Ling, Chi Ting Ling hsü-pien, as well as a collection of five stories entitled Chu-fu chi [housewives]. In 1943 he published the best of his wartime writing in two volumes entitled Hsiang-hsi [western Hunan], a book of fact, and Ch'ang-ho [the long river], a book of fiction. Both of these were based on his 1937 visit to western Hunan. Episodically constructed around the theme of permanence and change, *Ch'ang-ho* is generally considered the best of Shen's longer fiction. To the same period belong *Ch'un-teng chi* [lamp of spring] and *Hei-feng chi* [black phoenix], Shen's most important collections of stories. In 1946 Shen completed his autobiography, *Ts'ung-wen tzu-chuan*, and in 1947 he published four chapters of what appeared to be a long romance about feuding Miao tribesmen. These chapters, which appeared in Chu Kuang-ch'ien's *Wen-hsüeh tsa-chih* [literary magazine], were entitled "Ch'ih-mo" [the red incubus], "Hsüeh-ch'ing" [snow and sunshine], "Ch'iao-hsiu ho Tung-sheng" [Ch'iao-hsiu and Tung-sheng], and "Ch'uan-ch'i pu-ch'i" [a romance quite ordinary].

Following the Communist takeover in 1949, Shen Ts'ung-wen stopped writing fiction. An historical study of Chinese textile design entitled *Chung-kuo ssu-ch'ou t'u-an*, based on his work in the palace museum, appeared in 1957, as did a selection of his stories, *Shen Ts'ung-wen hsiao-shu hsüan-chi*. *T'ang Sung t'ung-ching* [bronze mirrors of the T'ang and Sung periods] appeared in 1958. Shen's last published articles, which appeared in the *Kuang-ming jih-pao* in 1961, stressed the need to check written sources against artifacts when elucidating obscure classical texts.

Shen Tuan-hsien 沈 端 先
Pen. Hsia Yen 夏 衍

Shen Tuan-hsien (1900–), known as Hsia Yen, writer and dramatist who was prominently associated with the left-wing literary movement that began in the 1920's. His best-known works were his war plays.

Born in Hangchow, Chekiang, Hsia Yen came from a family of prominent landowners. He received his early education at the Hui-lan Middle School, a Baptist institution, and later attended the Chekiang Industrial School, from which he was graduated in 1919. He then went to Japan and studied electrical engineering at the Kyushu Engineering School. After being graduated in 1925, he returned to China and taught school in Shanghai. He also lectured at Chinan University. In 1926–27 he took part in the Northern Expedition. After that, he devoted himself to writing. He played a prominent part in the left-wing literary movement and was one of the original sponsors of the League of Left-Wing Writers, inaugurated on 2 March 1930. The same year, Hsia Yen collaborated with Chang Po-ch'i and others in forming the Shang-hai i-shu chü-she [Shanghai dramatic society], the aim of which was to provide contemporary drama with revolutionary content and to spread it through the medium of traveling troupes. During this period, Hsia Yen also edited *I-shu yüeh-k'an* [art monthly], wrote scripts under a pen name for the Star Motion Picture Company, and translated Gorky's *Mother* and Tolstoy's *Resurrection*.

In 1935 and 1936 Hsia Yen produced two important plays: *Shang-hai wu-yen-hsia* [under a Shanghai roof], which was about the hard lot of tenement dwellers in a great city; and *Sai Chin-hua*, which concerned the famous Ch'ing dynasty courtesan of that name, whose gallant actions saved Peking from destruction during the Allied intervention that followed the Boxer Uprising. *Sai Chin-hua* was a great success and was lauded for its masterly and novel handling of a historical theme. The Dramatists Association held a forum to discuss it and acclaimed it as the first major play to be produced after the pronouncement of the League of Left-Wing Writers that drama should be dedicated to the cause of national revolution and defense.

During the Sino-Japanese war Hsia Yen wrote seven realistic war plays. Among these were *Ch'ou-ch'eng-chi* [city of sorrow], which satirized life in the occupied areas; *Fa-hsi-szu hsi-chün* [fascist bacteria], which analyzed the contradictions between science and fascism through the wartime tragedy of a Chinese doctor trained in Japan; and *Fang-ts'ao t'ien-yai* [fragrant grass on the horizon], which portrayed the wartime lives of intellectuals.

In the early years of the war, Hsia Yen also edited the left-wing newspaper *Chiu-wang jih-pao* [salvation daily], founded by Kuo Mo-jo. The paper originally was published in Shanghai, but moved to Changsha and then to Kweilin as the Japanese advanced. In 1941, to avoid detention by the Nationalist authorities, Hsia Yen fled to Hong Kong, where he edited a monthly called *Keng-yün* [culture] in collaboration with Yeh Ch'ien-yü, Tai Wang-shu, and

Chang Kuang-yü. When the Japanese occupied Hong Kong in 1942, Hsia Yen escaped to Kweilin and thence to Chungking, where he remained until 1945. He returned to Shanghai in 1946 and founded the newspaper *Chien-kuo jih-pao*, which was suspended by government order after the twelfth issue. In September 1946 Hsia Yen went to Hong Kong, where he was associated with the *Hua-shang pao* [Chinese commercial news] until May 1949.

After 1949, Hsia Yen ceased writing for production or publication. He held a number of cultural posts in Shanghai and east China, and he was a delegate, representing Shanghai, to the First National People's Congress. In 1951 he headed the delegation of the Sino-Soviet Friendship Association to the May Day celebrations in Moscow. He held office in the Central People's Government as director of the Asian affairs department of the ministry of foreign affairs and as vice minister of culture in charge of the film industry.

The writing and supervision of films was the most important cultural and political activity of Hsia Yen from 1932, when he headed the Chinese Communist party's film team, until April 1965, when he was removed from his post as vice minister of culture. For more than three decades his scenarios did much to keep the Chinese cinema a force in Chinese intellectual life. Films that he wrote include *Wild Torrent* (1933), *Twenty-four Hours in Shanghai* (1934), *Spring Silkworms* (1934), *A Bible for Daughters* (1934), *New Year Coin* (1936), *White Cloud Village* (1940), *The Way to Love* (1949), an adaptation of Lu Hsün's "Hsiang Lin's Wife" as *New Year Offering* (1956), *Lin's Shop* (1959), and *A Revolutionary Family* (1960). Even after his ministerial appointment, he continued his work on scenarios and film theory. The public criticism that followed his dismissal used his 1959 film adaptation of Mao Tun's "Lin-chia p'u-tzu" as proof of his sins and errors.

Hsia Yen married the painter Ts'ao Shu-hsin. They had two daughters.

Shen Yen-ping
Pen. Mao Tun

沈 雁 冰
茅 盾

Shen Yen-ping (1896–), known as Mao Tun, the foremost realist novelist in republican China. He ceased to function as a creative writer in 1949, and he served from 1949 to 1965 as minister of culture in the Central People's Government.

Ch'ingchen, a suburban district of T'ung-hsiang hsien, Chekiang, was the birthplace of Mao Tun. He is known to have had one younger brother, Shen Tse-min (q.v.). His father, a member of the gentry who was interested in Western mathematics, encouraged Mao Tun to prepare for a career in science and technology because he believed that a traditional education in the Chinese classics would be of no help in the eventuality of the partition of China by foreign powers. However, he died when Mao Tun was nine years old, and the boy soon began to devote most of his time to the study of Chinese literature. He attended middle schools in Huchow, Chiahsing, and Hangchow.

At the age of 17, Mao Tun went to Peking, where he enrolled in the preparatory college course at Peking University. He completed the three-year course in 1916, at which time financial difficulties compelled him to discontinue his schooling and accept a position as a proofreader at the Commercial Press in Shanghai. He soon was promoted to editor and translator, and, during the period from 1917 to 1920, he contributed many articles and translations to the *Hsüeh-sheng tsa-chih* [student magazine], a Commercial Press publication.

In November 1920 Mao Tun, along with Chou Tso-jen, Cheng Chen-to, Yeh Sheng-t'ao, Hsü Ti-shan (qq.v.), and seven other writers, founded the Wen-hsüeh yen-chiu hui [literary association]. The group persuaded the Commercial Press to give them editorial control over the *Hsiao-shuo yüeh-pao* [short story magazine], a monthly devoted to traditional Chinese writing, and Mao Tun became its new editor. The renovated magazine began publication in January 1921, and it became one of the most influential publications in China.

Although the Wen-hsüeh yen-chiu hui was popularly known for its advocacy of realism and "literature for life's sake," the primary task of its founding members was to establish writing as a serious profession and to counter the spirit of playful dilettantism prevalent among the more traditional writers. As editor of the *Hsiao-shuo yüeh-pao*, Mao Tun wrote a monthly summary of foreign literary news, critical essays on modern Chinese literature, and introductory articles on such foreign authors as Tolstoy, Chekhov, Bjornson, Petofi, Sienkiewcz, Balzac, Flaubert, Zola, Byron, Keats, and Bernard Shaw. Because he knew only Chinese and English, he used secondary sources for his information about most of these authors. Nonetheless, he endorsed Emile Zola's naturalism and made frequent use of Hippolyte Taine's theory of race, milieu, and moment as determining factors of literary expression. He became convinced of the spiritual vitality and technical superiority of Western literature, and he had little use for traditional Chinese literature. In his two essays on the national literary heritage, included in the *Hua-hsia-tzu* [chatterbox] of 1934, he expressed doubts about whether modern practitioners of fiction could learn much from such classical novels as the *Shui Hu Chuan (The Water Margin)* and the *Hung Lou Meng (Dream of the Red Chamber)* because he thought that their narrative techniques were too elementary. He condemned more recent traditional-style fiction as being degenerate and the new pai-hua [vernacular] literature as being sentimental in his 1922 essay "Tzu-jan chu-i yü Chung-kuo hsien-tai hsiao-shuo" [naturalism and modern Chinese fiction].

In 1923 Mao Tun resigned from the *Hsiao-shuo yüeh-pao*, but he continued to contribute critical essays and news articles to it. According to one source, the Commercial Press was dissatisfied with his editing; other accounts state that he quit voluntarily in order to engage more actively in politics. However, other than the fact that in 1923–24 he taught a course in fiction at Shanghai College, a newly opened center of Marxist training staffed by such leading Communists as Ch'en Tu-hsiu, Ch'ü Ch'iu-pai, Yün Tai-ying, and Teng Chung-hsia (qq.v.), there is little evidence that he participated in any political activities at that time. During the May Thirtieth Movement of 1925 he protested, more as an indignant patriot than a political organizer, with many other writers against the presence of foreign powers in China. Although he moved in Communist intellectual circles, he did not see any need to modify his literary beliefs to accommodate his political radicalism. It is believed that he never joined the Communist party.

Mao Tun left Shanghai in 1926 and went to

join the Northern Expedition at Canton, where he served under Wang Ching-wei as secretary to the propaganda department of the Kuomintang Central Executive Committee. He later returned to Shanghai to serve as chief editor at the Kuo-min t'ung-hsin-she [national news agency], and in late 1926 he joined the victorious Northern Expedition forces in Wuhan, serving as editor of the Hankow *Min-kuo jih-pao* [national daily]. After Chiang Kai-shek began to purge the Kuomintang of Communists in April 1927, the left-wing Kuomintang members followed suit and broke with the Chinese Communist party. Mao Tun fled Wuhan and went to Kuling in July, supposedly to recuperate from an illness. In August, he secretly returned to Shanghai with his wife, *née* K'ung Te-chih, whom he had married some years before.

In the period between September 1927 and June 1928 Mao Tun wrote three novelettes: *Huan-mieh* [disillusion], *Tung-yao* [vacillation], and *Chui-ch'iu* [pursuit], which were immediately serialized in the *Hsia-shuo yüeh-pao* and which were published as a trilogy in 1930 under the title *Shih* [eclipse]. Because he could not then disclose his identity, he adopted the fashionable Communist term Mao Tun [contradiction] as his pseudonym. The new name achieved immediate national fame upon the public's enthusiastic reception of the three works. In *Shih*, Mao Tun wrote about Chinese youth's participation in the Northern Expedition: its initial fervor, its ineffectual idealism, and its eventual despondency and despair. *Huan-mieh* depicts its young heroine's recoil from the revolutionary experience, with all its frivolity and anarchy, and her resignation to the romantic delirium of personal happiness. *Tung-yao* tells of the paralysis of the well-meaning hero, Fang Lo-lan, as he vainly attempts to steer a middle path between reactionary and revolutionary demagoguery in a liberated small town in Hupeh. *Chui-ch'iu* portrays the futility and bitter nihilism of a group of intellectuals in Shanghai, once participants in the Northern Expedition.

The great success of the trilogy prompted Communist critics to launch an attack on the author for his so-called petty-bourgeois decadence and unwarranted pessimism. In the essays "Ts'ung Ku-ling tao Tung-ching" [from Kuling to Tokyo] and "Tu Ni Huan-chih" [on reading *Ni Huan-chih*], Mao Tun admitted that the novelettes reflected a period of crisis in his own life, but defended his right to depict truth as he saw it. He countered the charges of decadence by arguing that the revolutionary writer should regard the petty bourgeoisie as his primary audience because the proletariat is illiterate and therefore beyond the reach of literary communication, but he agreed that disillusionment and nihilism are inherently undesirable states of mind.

Mao Tun lived in Tokyo from the summer of 1928 until the spring of 1930. In addition to the essays defending his trilogy and several largely unfavorable sketches of Japanese life, he wrote five short stories in the style of *Shih* which were collected and published in 1929 as *Yeh-chiang-wei* [the wild roses]. These stories record the vacillation and exasperation of young women caught in the conflict of old and new. During this period, Mao Tun also wrote a second novel, *Hung* [rainbow], published in 1930, which traces the evolution of Chinese youth during the May Fourth and May Thirtieth movements. Although the novel begins in the literary style of *Shih*, its latter half shows the influence of Chinese Communist rhetoric. *Hung* is a study of an earnest idealist, Mei, and her quest for a meaningful life. The first third of the book, which depicts the protagonist's struggle against feudalist tradition (in the person of her detested husband), is a masterpiece of psychological realism.

Upon his return to Shanghai in the spring of 1930, Mao Tun became a founding member of the League of Left-Wing Writers. By this time, he had recovered from his earlier despondency, had enthusiastically come to the support of proletarian literature, and had discarded his ornate style for a simpler prose. A few of his political fables written in the early 1930's in the guise of historical tales (about Ch'en She, the anti-Ch'in rebel, and about the heroes of *Shui Hu Chuan*) were of some literary interest, but his two novelettes *San-jen hsing* [three men] and *Lu* [the road] were of negligible value. Because Mao Tun was forced by illness in 1930 to limit his activities, he began to take a keen interest in the stock market in Shanghai and associated with relatives and friends in the business world. He also learned of Communist activities in Shanghai. Later, he embodied these observations and researches in a novel entitled *Tzu-yeh* [midnight]. The first edition, published in 1933, also bore the English title *The Twilight, a Romance of China in 1930*. *Tzu-yeh* was immediately acclaimed by Communist critics as Mao Tun's masterpiece. Its protagonist, Wu Sun-fu, a powerful industrialist with strong faith in national capitalism, is determined to consolidate his silk empire during a period of world-wide depression. However, his investments in his home town have been destroyed by Communist-organized banditry, and his main silk factory is plagued by continual Communist-led strikes. To offset his losses, he speculates on the stock market, only to be ruined by a formidable rival strongly backed by foreign capital. The novel is an impressive study of the complex life of Shanghai, with its capitalists, factory workers, bourgeois youths, and stranded feudalists, even though the proletarian material sometimes is inadequately presented in the absence of personal knowledge. Despite its wide range, *Tzu-yeh* has been called a very different and much less impassioned work than Mao Tun's earlier *Shih*. Whereas *Shih* vibrates with felt life, *Tzu-yeh* is a piece of Zolaesque research, a naturalistic confirmation of the Communist thesis about China's foredoomed endeavor to build national capitalism while in a semi-feudal, semi-colonial state. Its large number of capitalist and feudalist characters are nearly all caricatured to support this thesis.

During the Sino-Japanese conflict at Shanghai in 1932, Mao Tun lived for a short time in his native town of Ch'ingchen. Although Mao Tun had always excelled in his depiction of city life and had rarely touched upon the rural and small-town experience of his childhood, he now decided to write about peasants and tradesmen. The resulting stories were ranked by Communist critics with *Tzu-yeh* as outstanding examples of socialist realism in the 1930's. Some of these stories, especially "Lin-chia p'u-tzu" [Lin's shop] and "Ch'un-ts'an" [spring silkworms], both written in 1932, are notable for their compassionate quality and for their portrayal of doomed modes of traditional existence. Another story, "Hsiao-wu" [little witch] of 1932, although it received less Communist acclaim because of its frank references to sex, is a grim story of a brutally abused concubine. Because all of the stories are propagandistic in purpose, Mao Tun's essays of this period, collected in 1934 as *Ku-hsiang tsa-chi* [home town sketches], provide more candid and truthful reporting of a harassed peasantry suffering the economic consequences of the Sino-Japanese conflict in Shanghai.

Mao Tun did not produce any memorable writing during the years 1934–36. He produced a short novel in 1936, *To-chueh kuan-hsi* [polygonal relations] and two collections of short stories, *P'ao-mo* [froth] of 1935 and *Yen-yün chi* [smoke and cloud] of 1937. Most of the stories are satires on Shanghai businessmen, their wives, and their secretaries. One exception is "Ta-pi-tzu ti ku-shih" [the story of big nose], which is about a young beggar in Shanghai living on garbage and occasional thieving. The story was written in the jocular, anecdotal style of Lu Hsün's "The Story of Ah Q," with further obvious borrowings from Ch'ang T'ien-yi, who was noted for his comic stories about city children.

When Chou Yang (q.v.) disbanded the League of Left-Wing Writers in the spring of 1936 and, in support of the united front campaign, established the Writers' Association, Mao Tun joined the new group. It called for a realistic style, the use of resistance to the Japanese as the central theme of writings, and the slogan "Literature for National Defense." In July 1936, however, Mao Tun joined Lu Hsün, Hu Feng (q.v.) and the 64 other writers who formed the Chinese Literary Workers Association in issuing a rival declaration which called for "People's Literature for the National Revolutionary Struggle," for he had come to believe that the directors of Communist literary policy in Shanghai were subverting literature to accommodate whims of the Chinese Communist party. After a prolonged, bitter feud that become known as the Battle of the Slogans, the two writers' groups resolved their differences sufficiently to issue a proclamation of unity in October 1936.

After the Sino-Japanese war began in 1937, Mao Tun went to Changsha by way of Hong Kong and then to Wuhan, where he and his friends founded a magazine called *Wen-i chen-ti* [the literary front]. He moved, along with the magazine's headquarters, to Canton in February 1938; not long after, he moved to Hong Kong, where he also began to edit the literary page of the daily *Li Pao*. A new novel, eventually titled *Ti-i-chieh-tuan ti ku-shih* [story of the first stage of the war], about the siege of Shanghai in the summer of 1937, was serialized in the *Li Pao*. Although industrialists, financiers, bourgeois intellectuals, Trotskyites, and feudal remnants were again his characters, the book was not considered a success. At the end of 1938 he went to Urumchi to serve as dean of the college of liberal arts at Sinkiang University and possibly to promote Sino-Soviet relations in that border region. According to Communist sources, he went there at the invitation of a good friend, the journalist Tu Chung-yuan (q.v.).

In May 1940 Mao Tun left Urumchi for Yenan, where he lectured at the Lu Hsün Institute. In October of that year he left the Communist capital and traveled to Chungking. In the spring of 1941, following the New Fourth Army Incident, he left Chungking for Hong Kong, where he arranged for the serial publication in the journal *Ta-chung sheng-huo* [life of the masses] of his novel *Fu-shih* [putrefaction], with the purpose of exposing the National Government's role in bringing about the New Fourth Army Incident (*see* Ho Lung). The novels also accused the Kuomintang of employing secret agents to trap Communist underground workers in the Nationalist interior. Although *Fu-shih* lacks the vitality of *Hung* and *Shih*, Communist critics termed it the author's second greatest novel, inferior only to *Tzu-yeh*.

At the end of 1941 Mao Tun and his family went to Kweilin, where he wrote a series of sketches of life in Hong Kong before and after its Japanese occupation entitled *Chieh-hou shih-i* [jottings after the ordeal], published in 1942, and the first part of a trilogy, *Shuang-yeh hung-ssu erh-yüeh-hua* [maple leaves as red as February flowers], published in 1943. Although, according to the author's postscript to a recent edition, the completed work will show the progress of Communist youth from the May Fourth period through the Kuomintang purges of 1927, the first volume has little to do with Communism. It studies the careers of several tradition-bound and reformist youths against the economic background of a small town in Chekiang during the early republican period. Temporarily disengaged from his propagandist concerns, Mao Tun showed a surprising recrudescence of psychological skill in depicting the marital difficulties of two young couples and the thwarted idealism of the hero, Ch'ien Liang-ts'ai.

Late in 1942 Mao Tun moved to Chungking, where he served under Kuo Mo-jo (q.v.) on the cultural work committee of the political training board of the National Military Council. He did little serious writing in the years 1942–44 except for several short stories later collected in the volume *Wei-ch'ü* [grievances] and published in 1945. Though they have received little critical attention, they are ironic and compassionate studies of the impoverished middle class in the interior done in a style suggestive of Chekhov. In the spring and summer of 1945 Mao Tun completed a play, *Ch'ing-ming ch'ien-hou* [before and after the Ch'ing-Ming festival], which proved to be his last major creative effort. It is a study of the tribulations of average Chungking citizens against the background of the war-profiteering officials and industrialists in the last year of the war.

Mao Tun returned to Shanghai soon after the War in the Pacific had ended. From December 1946 to April 1947 he toured the Soviet Union with his wife, and he subsequently published a record of impressions of the trip entitled *Su-lien chien-wen-lu* [what I saw and heard in the Soviet Union]. Upon his return to Shanghai, he soon left for Hong Kong, where in 1948 he founded the pro-Communist *Hsiao-shuo yueh-k'an* [fiction monthly]. Following the Communist capture of Peiping in 1949, Mao Tun, along with Kuo Mo-jo and many other Communist and leftist writers then in Hong Kong, was invited to attend the All-China Congress of Writers and Artists. Kuo Mo-jo was elected chairman and Mao Tun vice chairman of the All-China Federation of Literary and Art Workers. Mao Tun also became chairman of the Association of Literary Workers (subsequently renamed the Writers' Union). Soon afterwards, he was appointed minister of culture in the Central People's Government. In 1954 he was elected a deputy to the First National People's Congress. A founding editor of the leading literary journal of the 1949–53 period, *Jen-min wen-hsüeh* [people's literature], and of *I-wen* [translations], he later joined with Yeh Chün-chien in editing the English-language journal *Chinese Literature*.

Mao Tun ceased to function as a creative writer after 1949. Moreover, he had not completed any serious work in the 1946–48

period: the novel *Tuan-lien* [discipline] was partially serialized in the Hong Kong *Wen Hui Pao* and then abandoned. And yet when the War in the Pacific ended, he had been only 49 years old, a writer in his prime. The works he produced during his residence in Kweilin and Chungking—*Shuang-yeh hung-ssu erh-yüeh-hua*, *Ch'ing-ming ch'ien-hou*, and *Wei-ch'ü*—have been called markedly superior to his novels and stories of 1934–41. Writing under the shadow of a vigilant censorship during this period, he had to refrain from overt political propaganda. On the other hand, one critic believes that the new note of artistic restraint and sympathetic realism was due more to individual choice than to external political pressure, especially in view of the fact that his creative silence coincided with the new Communist era. Despite his undoubted Communist sympathies, Mao Tun was a writer deeply committed to the literary ideals of Western realism and one who drew his creative sustenance mainly from the capitalist and feudalist life that he knew. He was particularly noted for his competent grasp of city manners, his preoccupation with sensuality and finance, his romantic idealism tinged with melancholy and pessimism, and his extreme superficiality whenever he depicted ideal characters and situations in the expected style of socialist realism. During the Hundred Flowers campaign, Mao Tun, in his official capacity as minister of culture, attacked the conformity of the Communist literary product, but he was criticized for his outspokenness during the ensuing anti-rightist campaigns.

After the establishment of the People's Republic of China in 1949, Mao Tun delivered many reports and addresses at conventions of literary and art workers, one of which was his long address entitled "Reflect the Age of the Socialist Leap Forward, Promote the Leap Forward of the Socialist Age," to the Third Congress of Chinese Literary and Art Workers in July 1960. He traveled abroad many times to attend cultural or literary conferences of Communist or Afro-Asian nations. As an older and well-established writer, he advised young writers to write well and learn the rudiments of literary art, and he has encouraged and praised many new writers of fiction. *Mao Tun wen-chi* [the works of Mao Tun], an eight-volume collection published in 1958, includes all of his novels and short stories.

In December 1964 Mao Tun was removed from office as minister of culture on charges of ideological heresy in connection with a film, by Hsia Yen based on his "Lin-chia p'u-tzu." The film allegedly weakened the class struggle by generating sympathy for a bourgeois shopkeeper.

Shen Yi　　　　　沈　怡
 T. Chün-yi　　　　君　怡

Shen Yi (1901–), German-trained hydraulic engineer who served as secretary general of the National Resources Commission (1937–40), general manager of the Kansu Agricultural Development Corporation (1941–44), mayor of Nanking (1946–47), and chief of the Bureau of Flood Control and Water Resources Development of the United Nations Economic Commission for Asia and the Far East (1949–60). After serving in Taiwan as minister of communications (1960–67), he became ambassador to Brazil (1968).

Kashing (Chiahsing), Chekiang, was the native place of Shen Yi. After receiving his early education in Chekiang, he studied at Tung-chi University in Shanghai, where he was graduated from the department of civil engineering in 1920. He then went to Germany for graduate work at the Technische Hochschule at Dresden, where he studied hydraulic engineering under Professor Hubert Engels and received a doctorate of engineering in 1925 after writing a dissertation, *Der Flussbau in China*, which dealt with the problem of flood control in China. Shen visited the United States in 1925 and inspected many rivers and river control projects.

After his return to China, Shen Yi was appointed director of the public works department of the Shanghai municipal government in 1927. The post was important because the new National Government, which was establishing its authority in that part of China, had ambitious plans for development of a major new metropolis with a civic center in Kiangwan. Known as the Greater Shanghai plan, the project aimed at eventual transfer of the hub of activity in China's leading city from the foreign-controlled concessions to a new urban complex under Chinese jurisdiction. This ambitious undertaking finally had to be abandoned because of the continuing political and military turmoil in China after 1928.

Despite the obstacles which confronted urban planning, Shen Yi established an unusual record among the public functionaries working under the authority of the National Government, for he remained director of public works in Shanghai uninterruptedly for more than ten years. Among his undertakings was the improvement of public works facilities in the Chinese-administered areas, sometimes referred to as the Chinese City, of Shanghai. Although his Shanghai work did not call upon his special training in hydraulic engineering, he continued to keep abreast of world developments in the field of river control. His admiration of the Tennessee Valley Authority in the United States led him to formulate a similar plan for the Yangtze River in China, the so-called YVA project.

After the outbreak of war between China and Japan in the summer of 1937 and the withdrawal of Chinese authority from Shanghai and the lower Yangtze area, Shen Yi moved to Chungking, the wartime capital of the National Government. There he became a senior official of the National Resources Commission, serving as secretary general of the commission and head of its industry section.

It was not until the summer of 1941 that Shen Yi found an opportunity to work as an engineer. In that year, the Bank of China transferred certain enterprises that it had operated in the Tientsin area to northwest China. Chang Hsin-yi, an agricultural expert on the bank's staff, was appointed director of the reconstruction department of the Kansu provincial government, an appointment designed to facilitate Bank of China investment in the agricultural development of that province through the newly established Kansu Agricultural Development Corporation. The corporation's tasks were primarily connected with promotion of water conservation, and Shen Yi was offered the position of general manager. He accepted the appointment and moved to Lanchow.

Water conservation projects had been undertaken earlier in Kansu province, but it was only with the formation of the Kansu Agricultural Development Corporation and the appointment of Shen Yi to direct its work that the programs gained impetus and direction. The corporation took over and improved one large-scale dam, and it completed construction of a second. Under Shen's direction, new dams were planned and constructed, and a network of irrigation projects was developed. These major projects were designed to provide irrigation for more than 260,000 mou of land; and, with completion of a projected system of branch canals and small reservoirs, the Kansu project was intended to irrigate more than a million mou in China's arid northwest.

When the war ended in 1945, Shen Yi was called away from his post in Kansu. By that time he had laid the groundwork for a sound provincial irrigation system, and many additional reservoirs later were completed and put into service. The National Government appointed Shen vice minister of communications to help with the complex problems of demobilization and economic reconstruction in the immediate postwar period. On the return of the National Government from Chungking to Nanking in 1946, Shen Yi was appointed mayor of Nanking. He held that post until 1948, during which period he also served as chairman of the public works committee of the Supreme National Economic Council.

In 1949 Shen Yi was appointed chief of the Bureau of Flood Control and Water Resources Development of the United Nations Economic Commission for Asia and the Far East (ECAFE), with headquarters in Bangkok, Thailand. He held that post for 11 years. His outstanding accomplishment was the series of studies undertaken by his bureau on the potential of the lower Mekong river basin. These studies, initiated in 1951, led to the adoption of a United Nations program for development of that vast Asian river and to the establishment of a unique cooperative system embracing the Mekong's four riparian nations. The program was praised by economic development experts, and Shen's work was particularly commended by United Nations Secretary General Dag Hammarsjold.

In 1960 Shen Yi returned to the service of the National Government in Taiwan. He held the post of minister of communications for seven years, during which period he frequently traveled abroad as an official delegate to international meetings. Shen relinquished his post as minister of communications in November 1967 and became a presidential adviser to Chiang Kai-shek. In February 1968 he was designated ambassador to Brazil.

Shen Yi had three sisters, all of whom married prominent men. The eldest was the wife of Huang Fu (q.v.), friend and adviser of Chiang Kai-shek. Another sister married Ch'ien Ch'ang-chao, sometime vice chairman of the National Resources Commission and chief aide to Wong Wen-hao (q.v.); and the third married T'ao Meng-ho (L. K. T'ao), a sociologist who later served as a vice president of the Chinese Academy of Sciences at Peking until his death in 1959.

Shen Yin-mo　　　沈尹默

Shen Yin-mo (1887–), professor of history and literary man who later won fame as a calligrapher.

Wuhsing, Chekiang, was the native place of Shen Yin-mo. After receiving a traditional primary education in the Chinese classics, he attended the Chiahsing Normal School and later joined his brothers, Shen Shih-yuan and Shen Chien-shih, in Japan for advanced studies. Their funds soon ran short, however; and Shen Shih-yuan returned home to teach school so that he could support his younger brothers. Shen Yin-mo was graduated from Kyoto Imperial University in 1912.

From 1914 to 1928 Shen Yin-mo served as a professor of history at Peking University. Under the chancellorship of Ts'ai Yuan-p'ei (q.v.), the university had become a center of a movement against traditionalism in Chinese literature and philosophy, and Shen was an ardent supporter of this movement. He became a frequent contributor to the *Hsin ch'ing-nien* [new youth], and in 1919 he joined Ch'en Tu-hsiu, Ch'ien Hsuan-t'ung, Hu Shih, Li Ta-chao and Liu Fu (qq.v.) on its board of editors.

Shen Yin-mo left Peking University in 1928 to become commissioner of education for Hopei province. He soon discovered, however, that administrative work did not suit his independent temperament. He resigned in 1930 and assumed the presidency of the newly established Peiping University. After holding that post for two years, he moved to Shanghai and attempted to associate himself with Lu Hsün (Chou Shu-jen, q.v.) in the League of Left-Wing Writers. Because of his past connections with the National Government, however, he was not allowed to play a significant role in the activities of this radical organization.

From earliest youth, Shen Yin-mo had practiced the art of calligraphy. He had displayed remarkable talent even as a young man, and he had already become known as a calligrapher at the time of his return from Japan. Shen cultivated this talent assiduously in the following decades. After grounding himself carefully in the seal (chüan) and clerical (li) styles, he became equally proficient in the standard (k'ai), running (hsing), and "grass" (ts'ao) styles through rigid personal discipline involving the writing of at least 500 characters every morning before breakfast. His mastery of many styles earned Shen a unique place in the annals of modern calligraphy. In the early 1930's Shen decided to make calligraphy his profession. His writings were prized for their elegance as well as for their versatility. Some critics, however, discerned in his work a certain lack of originality, a deficiency which, they held, debarred Shen from a place in the roster of all-time calligraphic greats. During this period, Shen also took up the composition of classical poetry, but only as an avocation.

During the Sino-Japanese war, Shen Yin-mo was a member of the Control Yuan. The office was little more than a sinecure, but it suited him, for it left his time free for calligraphy. At war's end he established residence in Shanghai. In 1948 he divorced his wife of many years and married a girl who was 20 years his junior. After the Chinese Communists took control of the mainland in 1949, he was offered the post of deputy mayor of Shanghai. He declined the office, but consented to serve instead as an adviser. Thereafter, he led a quiet life, practicing the art of calligraphy and exhibiting his works.

Shen Yin-mo wrote voluminously on the theory and practice of calligraphy. In 1962 he produced *Mao chu-hsi shih-tz'u erh-shih-i shou* [21 poems by Chairman Mao], executed in the small k'ai style, to serve as a calligraphic model for the new simplified orthography. In 1963 Shen started the series *Li-tai ming-chia hsueh-shu ching-yen chi-yao shih-i* [a compendium of the experience of famous calligraphers throughout the ages in their study of the art, with explanations].

Sheng Hsuan-huai   盛 宣 懷

Sheng Hsuan-huai (4 November 1844–27 April 1916), industrial promoter who developed the concept of company organization known as kuan-tu shang-pan [official supervision and merchant management].

Wuchin hsien, Ch'angchou, Kiangsu, was the birthplace of Sheng Hsuan-huai. His father, the gentry-official Sheng K'ang (1814–1902), was a chin-shih of 1844 who held several minor provincial posts before becoming salt tao-t'ai at Wuchang in 1861. As a youth, Sheng Hsuan-huai undertook the traditional course of study in the Chinese classics as preparation for the civil-service examinations, and in 1866 he passed the first examination for the sheng-yuan degree. Three times (1867, 1873, and 1876) he participated unsuccessfully in the provincial chü-jen examinations. By the time of the last failure, however, he was well on his way to prominence by another route.

Like a number of other men who became important at the end of the Ch'ing period, Sheng Hsuan-huai entered public service as a member of the entourage of Li Hung-chang (ECCP, I, 464–71). After serving as a minor functionary in the Huai Army in 1870–71, Sheng rose to become Li's chief deputy for economic affairs in the years prior to the Sino-Japanese war of 1894–95. His first major assignment was an administrative post in the newly founded, semi-official China Merchants' Steam Navigation Company (Lun-ch'uan chao-shang chü). Until his death in 1916, Sheng was intimately associated with this enterprise as shareholder and officer. He served as assistant manager from 1873 to 1875, left the company, and then returned in 1883. From 1885 until 1902, as its chief executive and largest stockholder, he was in complete personal control of the company.

In the last three decades of the nineteenth century, Sheng Hsuan-huai also carried out several diplomatic assignments for Li Hung-chang. The most important of these were the negotiations for the recovery of the unauthorized Shanghai-Woosung railroad, the first in China, which had been completed in 1876 primarily with funds from Jardine, Matheson and Company. In 1879 Sheng briefly held a substantive official post as military-administrative tao-t'ai for the Tientsin-Hochien district. In 1880 he planned the organization of a joint stock company (under the official supervision of Li Hung-chang) which undertook the construction of China's first telegraph lines. This enterprise, known as the Imperial Telegraph Administration (Tien-pao tsung-chü), like the shipping company with which it had close financial ties, was to be Sheng's personal preserve until the telegraphs were nationalized after 1902.

From July 1886 until June 1892 Sheng Hsuan-huai was tao-t'ai and superintendent of customs at Chefoo in Shantung province. In June 1892 he reached the apex of administrative authority under Li Hung-chang with his appointment to the office of Tientsin customs tao-t'ai, the key financial post in Li's Chihli (Hopei) satrapy. In addition to controlling the Tientsin customs and serving as director-general (tu-pan) of the kuan-tu shang-pan [official supervision and merchant management] shipping and telegraph companies, Sheng in October 1893 undertook the reorganization of Li Hung-chang's Shanghai Cotton Cloth Mill, which had been completely razed by fire. This enterprise was refinanced with private capital, in large part invested by Sheng and his business associates, and established on a kuan-tu shang-pan basis with Sheng as director-general. Renamed the Hua-sheng Spinning and Weaving Company, it became the first successful modern cotton mill in China and served to enhance Sheng's position as industrial entrepreneur. Since 1877 Sheng also had controlled valuable iron deposits in Tayeh hsien, Hupeh, which were later to form a component of the famous Han-Yeh-P'ing Coal and Iron Company.

With the fall of Li Hung-chang, resulting from the defeat of the Peiyang Army and Navy by Japan in 1894–95, Sheng Hsuan-huai's industrial and commercial enterprises gradually came under the aegis of the powerful Hu-Kuang governor general, Chang Chih-tung (ECCP, I, 27–32). During the decade of his association with Chang, Sheng's independent influence in Peking was significantly augmented and his economic empire considerably expanded. The

first accretion to his industrial holdings occurred in 1896 when Chang Chih-tung placed under his direction the nearly bankrupt Hanyang Ironworks, which Chang had organized in 1889 as a government industry. With Sheng as a major shareholder as well as its chief officer, the Hanyang Ironworks and its associated mines were operated on a kuan-tu shang-pan basis until 1908. Because of its continued inability to raise adequate domestic capital even with a monopoly franchise to supply iron and steel to government railroads and arsenals, the company increasingly was forced to turn to the Yokohama Specie Bank and other Japanese sources for loans in order to enlarge and modernize its plant. This development led eventually to the inclusion of a Japanese demand for control of the company in the Twenty-one Demands of 1915. Sheng continued to head the Hanyang Ironworks after its kuan-tu shang-pan status was terminated in 1908 at the time of its amalgamation with the Ta-yeh Iron Mines and the P'ing-hsiang Coal Mines—both developed by Sheng—to form the privately owned Han-Yeh P'ing Coal and Iron Company.

In October 1896 Sheng Hsuan-huai, with the backing of Chang Chih-tung, was appointed director general of the imperial railway administration, a new official agency charged with planning and constructing a railroad network as part of a renewed effort at "self-strengthening," prompted by Japan's easy victory in the 1894–95 war. Sheng continued to hold this post until the end of 1905, during which time the railway administration arranged for loans from European investors amounting to China $300,000,000 for the construction of 3,000 miles of railroad. When the agency was dissolved in 1906, a trunk line between Peking and Hankow had been completed, and a line from Shanghai to Nanking was well under way. Together with the lines constructed in Manchuria, which were not controlled by Sheng, these formed the basis of China's pre-republican railroad network. His position as director general of railroads brought Sheng Hsuan-huai into extensive contact with Western businessmen and diplomats and also brought him closer to the upper echelons of the Peking bureaucracy.

In 1896 and 1897 Sheng Hsuan-huai was rewarded by the emperor with sinecures carrying high court rank; in 1900 he was made vice director of the imperial clan court, and he gained the upper-third rank; in 1901 the empress dowager, from her self-imposed exile in Sian, appointed Sheng imperial commissioner to conduct the renegotiation of commercial treaties with the Western powers as provided by the Boxer Protocol. In recognition of his role in arranging the "Yangtze Compact," which secured the neutralization of southern China during the Boxer Uprising, Sheng was made a junior guardian of the heir apparent (t'ai-tzu shao-pao) in December 1901. It is because of this title that he is often referred to as Sheng Kung-pao in Western-language sources. In February 1902 he was given the post of vice president of the ministry of works and the upper-second rank.

During the years that he filled these numerous entrepreneurial and official posts, Sheng also found time to organize China's first modern bank in Shanghai in 1897 (the Chung-kuo t'ung-shang yin-hang, known in English as the Imperial Bank of China); to found and finance with funds from his shipping and telegraph companies two important centers of Western-style education, Peiyang College in Tientsin (1895) and Nanyang College in Shanghai (1896), both of which later developed into good technical institutions at which such political leaders as Ch'en Li-fu and Wang Ch'ung-hui (qq.v.), as well as many Chinese engineers, were educated; and to promote the organization of Chinese chambers of commerce in Shanghai and elsewhere.

Sheng Hsuan-huai was at the peak of his power in September 1902 after the conclusion of the (later abortive) Mackay Treaty, which was intended to set a new pattern for commercial relations between China and the West by raising import tariffs and abolishing transit duties (likin). It was just at this point, on 24 October 1902, that the death of his octogenarian father set loose a train of events that cost Sheng his official posts and the control of several of his kuan-tu shang-pan enterprises. The prime mover behind Sheng Hsuan-huai's discomfiture was Yuan Shih-k'ai (q.v.), who, having succeeded to Li Hung-chang's military and political power in north China, sought also to bring under his control the economic components of Li's regional domain. The

telegraphs were nationalized; Yuan's appointees assumed control of the China Merchants' Steam Navigation Company; and only the strong support of Chang Chih-tung enabled Sheng to maintain his post as director general of railroads until 1905. Despite his losses, however, Sheng was able to protect his position in those enterprises, such as the Hanyang Ironworks and mines and the bank, which had not been associated with Li Hung-chang.

Until the dismissal of Yuan Shih-k'ai in 1909, Sheng was embroiled in a complex struggle to regain his power and position. With the aid of his enormous personal wealth and in alliance with Yuan's enemies in Peking, he eventually was successful. In 1907 Sheng recovered control of the China Merchants' Steam Navigation Company, and in 1908 he received the nominal appointment of junior vice president of the Board of Posts and Communications. But only toward the end of 1910 did Sheng return to official prominence in Peking and to de facto control of the board, of which he was appointed president in January 1911.

As head of the Board of Posts and Communications, Sheng Hsuan-huai again dominated the modern means of communications in China. His principal endeavor during 1911 was to seek the establishment of a national railroad system by bringing under the control of the Peking government uncompleted railroad projects which had been undertaken in the provinces by local gentry and merchant interests. Sheng's memorial of 1911 particularly condemned the delays and corruption on the Canton-Hankow and Hankow-Szechwan lines as being injurious to the Manchu reform movement and to the national defense. The close association of the railroad centralization program with large-scale borrowing from the Four-Power Consortium contributed to a fusion of provincial xenophobia with growing anti-Manchu sentiments; and both were aggravated by extreme dissatisfaction with the proposed method of compensation to those who had invested in the railroads. Rioting in Szechwan and elsewhere through the summer of 1911 culminated in the Wuchang revolt on 10 October, which brought about the collapse of the dynasty.

Sheng Hsuan-huai was dismissed from office in the last days of Manchu rule and was forced to flee for his life to Japan. He returned to his home in the Shanghai International Settlement in October 1912. Until his death in 1916 he lived in retirement, but retained control of the China Merchants' Steam Navigation Company, the Han-Yeh-P'ing Coal and Iron Company, and his textile interests.

The career of Sheng Hsuan-huai and the history of his enterprises are useful indices to China's response to the West in the last part of the nineteenth century. At the same time, the kuan-tu shang-pan formula foreshadowed the "bureaucratic capitalism" of more recent decades, one of the obstacles to the modernization of China within a democratic framework. Despite their pioneering character and the fact that they were few in number, the kuan-tu shang-pan companies controlled by Sheng showed a remarkable range and diversity. Heavy industry (coal and iron mines, a steel plant), light manufacturing (textile mills), communications (a steamship company, telegraphs, railroads), and finance (a modern bank) were all represented. It was undeniably a substantial achievement for one man to have pioneered in all these fields, especially in the unpropitious environment of late Ch'ing China. It was all the more notable that Sheng was able to undertake and manage these enterprises while pursuing an active official career. His industrial enterprises, however, did not signify the beginning of a basic transformation of the Chinese economy. On the contrary, their constitution represented a compromise with traditional Chinese institutions and patterns of behavior. Their opportunities for expansion were circumscribed by foreign economic pressure, by official indifference if not outright rapacity, by capital and personnel shortages, and by a framework of values that emphasized personal and family ties rather than rationalized economic activity. These enterprises inevitably were forced to depend upon the monopoly patents their official patrons had been able to secure for them. These monopolies could be relied upon to sustain the profits and perquisites of the promoters and to protect the capital of the promoters, but they were not compatible with reinvestment of profits and long-range growth. In short, after an initial period of expansion, the modern enterprises founded by Sheng Hsuan-huai tended to be transformed into institutions for the protection of bureaucratic capital.

Sheng Shih-ts'ai 盛 世 才
T. Chin-yung 晉 庸

Sheng Shih-ts'ai (1895–), military adventurer from Manchuria who seized power in Sinkiang in 1933 and ruled that province for nine years with Soviet aid. In 1943 he switched allegiance to the Chinese Nationalists, who, however, dislodged him from his seat of power in 1944.

The Kaiyuan district of Liaoning in southern Manchuria was the birthplace of Sheng Shih-ts'ai. His father, who owned a small amount of land, belonged to the local gentry. After completing his early education in the Chinese classics at local schools, Sheng Shih-ts'ai went to Mukden. He attended the provincial college of agriculture and forestry until 1912, when he went to Shanghai to become a student of political economy at the Chung-kuo kung-hsueh [China college] at Woosung. When he completed his course work in 1915, some of his teachers advised him to go to Japan for further study. With financial assistance from relatives and friends, Sheng sailed for Japan in 1917 to study political economy at Waseda University in Tokyo. He returned to China in 1919 to participate in the May Fourth Movement as a representative of the Liaoning students. The political disarray in which he found China caused him to abandon the study of political economy and to pursue a military career.

After spending a brief period at the Shaokuan military training school in Kwangtung, Sheng Shih-ts'ai returned to his native Manchuria, where he received further training at the Northeast Military Academy. He entered active military service under Kuo Sung-ling and soon rose to become a staff officer with the rank of lieutenant colonel. In 1924 Kuo sponsored his admission to the Shikan Gakkō [military academy] in Japan for advanced military studies. When Kuo Sung-ling joined with Feng Yü-hsiang (q.v.) in an attempt to overthrow Chang Tso-lin (q.v.) in November 1925, Sheng returned to Manchuria to participate in the revolt as a battalion commander. With the defeat and execution of Kuo Sung-ling in December, Sheng went back to Japan to continue his training, but he was suspended from the Shikan Gakkō at the request of Chang Tso-lin. Feng Yü-hsiang then secured his reinstatement, and Chiang Kai-shek provided him with sufficient funds to complete his military studies in Japan.

Upon graduation from the Shikan Gakkō in 1927, Sheng Shih-ts'ai returned to China to join the National Revolutionary Army on the Northern Expedition. He received the rank of colonel and a post on the general staff under Ho Ying-ch'in (q.v.). He later became a staff officer in Chiang Kai-shek's field headquarters, and he held that post until the Northern Expedition came to an end. In the summer of 1928 he was made chief of the war operations section of the general staff at Nanking, but he resigned in 1929 after coming into conflict with his superiors. He then joined the Survival-First Study Society, which concerned itself with national unity and the strengthening of border defenses.

In 1929 Lu Hsiao-tzu, the secretary general of the Sinkiang provincial government, arrived in Nanking on an official mission. He was under instructions from Chin Shu-jen (q.v.), who had seized power in Sinkiang in 1928, to find an able military man to help effect the consolidation of Sinkiang's military establishment. P'eng Chao-hsien, a leading member of the Survival-First Study Society, recommended and introduced Sheng Shih-ts'ai to Lu, who, in turn, recommended Sheng's employment to Chin Shu-jen. Sheng then traveled by way of Siberia to Sinkiang, arriving in Urumchi in late 1929 or early 1930.

Sheng Shih-ts'ai's first assignment in Sinkiang was as director of the general staff, with the rank of brigadier general, in the office of the border defense commander (Chin Shu-jen). He undertook an officer-training program, but it had to be abandoned when the Hami rebellion of 1931 forced Chin Shu-jen's troops into the field. At the request of the Turki natives of Hami, Ma Chung-ying (q.v.) and his cavalry force advanced into Sinkiang from Kansu in June 1931. Although Ma was forced to withdraw in defeat to western Kansu that autumn, the Hami situation remained unsettled. Sheng Shih-ts'ai went to the Hami area as commander of one of two bodies of provincial reinforcements, but he failed to find the rebel

troops. In July 1932 he led a larger force into the mountains around Hami, but this attempt to find and destroy the Muslim dissidents also failed.

In August 1932 Ma Shih-ming entered the fray, and T'ung-kans and Sarts joined forces to capture Shanshan and Turfan. Sheng moved his men from Hami to Turfan and captured Turfan in a bloody two-day battle. This victory, however, failed to stem the tide of revolution in southern Sinkiang. Ma Shih-ming assumed the position of commander in chief of the rebel forces at Karashar, and Khoja Niaz and Yolbars (q.v.) strove to bind the Sarts and the T'ung-kans together in defiance of Chinese role. In the winter of 1932 the rebels advanced on Urumchi, defeated the force that Chin Shu-jen sent to intercept them, and pressed on to the provincial capital. They attacked Urumchi at the end of February 1933, but were beaten off. At this juncture, several thousand Manchurian troops from the commands of Su Ping-wen and Li Tu arrived in the Urumchi area to help lift the rebel siege. Ma Shih-ming then took the nearby town of Santaopa, thereby cutting off Urumchi's grain supply. Sheng Shih-ts'ai advanced from Turfan and succeeded in recovering Santaopa with the aid of the Northeasterners. Sheng then moved his men to Urumchi, where he became a major general, commander of the 1st Division, and Chin Shu-jen's chief of staff.

As the Muslim disorders spread throughout Sinkiang and Urumchi came under intermittent siege, fear, ineffectiveness, and official corruption became rife in the capital. In these circumstances, the return of Sheng Shih-ts'ai to the Urumchi area had considerable significance. The core of Sheng's military force was a White Russian group led by a General Antonov, and the White Russians of Sinkiang had become increasingly dissatisfied with Chin Shu-jen. The Northeastern troops also preferred Sheng to Chin, for Sheng, like the Northeasterners, was a Manchurian. Chin Shu-jen finally was forced to flee Urumchi on 12 April 1933, whereupon Liu Wen-lung, the provincial education commissioner, was made provisional governor. On 14 April, Sheng Shih-ts'ai became provisional border defense commissioner, in which post he held control in Urumchi. Sheng's authority soon came under challenge by the Turki peoples of the province and by Ma Chung-ying. In mid-May Ma moved against Urumchi once again. Sheng Shih-ts'ai took the field with a force of some 5,000 men, and he protested Ma's actions to the National Government at Nanking. After being beaten in an encounter with Ma near Kucheng, Sheng recaptured Turfan and bested Khoja Niaz and his men at Karashar. The Ili commander Chang P'ei-yuan indicated that he would join the rebels, and Sheng then decided to negotiate a compromise settlement. At this juncture, the National Government appointed Huang Mu-sung (q.v.) pacification commissioner of Sinkiang. He arrived at Urumchi on 10 June 1933 and issued an order forbidding military action. Sheng and Ma ignored this directive, and Sheng soon drove Ma eastward to Kucheng.

After returning to Urumchi, Sheng Shih-ts'ai accused Huang Mu-sung of plotting to overthrow him and placed Huang under house arrest. Sheng soon obtained what he considered to be sufficient proof of evil-doing, and he executed three National Government officials— T'ao Ming-yueh, Li Hsiao-t'ien, and Ch'en Chung—for allegedly plotting with Huang. P'eng Chao-hsien was dispatched from Nanking to Sinkiang to investigate the situation for the Military Affairs Commission, and Huang Mu-sung was ordered by the Executive Yuan to return to Nanking immediately to report on the matter. After Huang wired Nanking recommending that Sheng Shih-ts'ai and Liu Wen-lung be confirmed in their posts, Sheng permitted Huang to leave Sinkiang. On 1 August, ten days after Huang reached Nanking, the National Government confirmed Sheng's and Liu's authority. They were formally installed in office by Lo Wen-kan (q.v.) on 7 September. Another part of Lo's mission to Sinkiang was to mediate between Sheng Shih-ts'ai and Ma Chung-ying. After effecting a compromise distribution of authority among Sheng Shih-ts'ai, Liu Wen-lung, Ma Chung-ying, and Chang P'ei-yuan, Lo Wen-kan returned to Nanking by way of the Soviet Union. Soon after Lo's departure, Sheng announced the discovery of a new plot against his authority. He forced Liu Wen-lung from office and caused him to be replaced by Chu Jui-hsi. (When Chu died early in 1934, he was replaced by another figurehead, Li Yung.) In December 1933 Sheng ordered the execution

of some 20 officers in the Northeastern forces, saying that they had conspired against him.

At the end of 1933 Ma Chung-ying launched another drive on Urumchi, and Chang P'ei-yuan advanced from Ili with 3,000 troops to assist him. Sheng Shih-ts'ai, who had been negotiating with Moscow for the delivery of arms promised to Chin Shu-jen, now appealed for Soviet aid on the grounds that a Ma Chung-ying victory would harm Soviet interests in Sinkiang. Soviet military units attacked Ma's forces on 24 January and forced them to retreat southward; Chang P'ei-yuan's army was ambushed and almost completely destroyed near Manas, whereupon Chang committed suicide. These two actions brought northern Sinkiang under Sheng's control, but he still had to contend with the so-called East Turkestan Republic which had been proclaimed at Kashgar, with Khoja Niaz at its head and Sabit Mullah as premier. These two men soon fell into disagreement; the retreating Ma Chung-ying attacked and destroyed the weakened political organization at Kashgar; and Khoja Niaz decided to support Sheng Shih-ts'ai. In July 1934 Ma Chung-ying unexpectedly transferred command of his troops to Ma Hu-shan and disappeared into the Soviet Union, leaving southern Sinkiang to Sheng Shih-ts'ai by default.

Sheng Shih-ts'ai proclaimed "Eight Great Declarations" as the political bases of his rule and formulated "Six Great Principles," two of which were anti-imperialism and friendship with the Soviet Union. His armed forces became the Anti-Imperialist Army, and his political party was the Anti-Imperialist Society. On 16 May 1935 he signed an agreement with Moscow by virtue of which he obtained a large loan and technical assistance in the fields of public health, mining, petroleum extraction, and road construction. He received military aid once again in May 1937, when a rebellion led by Ma Hu-shan showed strong promise of succeeding.

Ties between Sinkiang and the Soviet Union, which had been formed because of Sheng Shih-ts'ai's need for political and economic support, strengthened with the outbreak of the Sino-Japanese war in 1937. Moscow stationed a regiment at Hami, granted Sheng a new loan, increased the number of Soviet technicians in Sinkiang, and increased trade. In 1938, during a trip to Moscow, Sheng joined the Communist Party of the Soviet Union. On his return, though he still refused to allow the Chinese Communist party to operate as an organization in Sinkiang, he accepted a number of Chinese Communists from Yenan as officials in the provincial government. Among the newcomers was Mao Tse-min (q.v.). Sheng's pro-Soviet policy reached its peak with the signing, on 24 November 1940, of the so-called Tin Mines Agreement, which granted the Soviet Union extensive economic rights in Sinkiang for a period of 50 years.

If Sheng Shih-ts'ai's principle of "friendship for the Soviet Union" had continued to guide Sinkiang's foreign policy, Soviet influence might have become pervasive. In April 1941 the National Government at Chungking appointed Sheng governor of Sinkiang. The following year, as the Germans advanced on the Soviet Union and it appeared that Russian resistance might collapse in time, an imposing delegation from Chungking went to Urumchi in July. It soon became evident that Sheng had agreed to switch allegiance to the National Government. On 29 August 1942 a Nationalist delegation that included Soong Mei-ling (q.v.), the wife of Chiang Kai-shek, came to Sinkiang to celebrate Sheng's conversion. On 5 October, by his own account, Sheng demanded Soviet withdrawal from Sinkiang within three months. Early in 1943 the Russians complied with this demand. Sheng joined the Kuomintang in January 1943, and a Kuomintang provincial headquarters was established at Urumchi. Sheng soon received appointments as director of the Sinkiang party branch, commander of the Northwest Cadre Training Corps, member of the Kuomintang Central Supervisory Committee, director of a branch school of the Central Military Academy, deputy commanding officer of the Eighth War Area, and special officer for foreign affairs for Sinkiang. Also in 1943, Sheng caused the execution of Mao Tse-min and other Communist and "pro-Soviet" officials; their places in the provincial government were taken by Nationalists.

The National Government patently intended to achieve what Huang Mu-sung and Lo Wen-kan had failed to do: to bring Sinkiang under its direct control at the expense of Sheng Shih-ts'ai's power. The encroachments on his authority by Nationalists, combined with

a series of Soviet victories over the German invaders, convinced Sheng that he had made the wrong choice. Beginning in February 1944 he began to absent himself from official meetings in Urumchi; in April, he began to arrest Kuomintang officials on the timeworn charge that they were plotting against him. He reportedly contacted Moscow in August and asked that Stalin incorporate Sinkiang into the Soviet Union, but to no avail. At the end of August, he was named minister of agriculture and forestry at Chungking, and the National Government sent a special plane to fetch him. In September, Sheng left Urumchi forever to take up a sinecure post. He was removed from this office in July 1945 because of criticism of his past record. He had caused the arrest, imprisonment, or execution of thousands of persons during his rule in Sinkiang, and public outcry caused the National Government to move him to an obscure post as counsellor in the Wuhan headquarters of the Military Affairs Commission. In 1949 he followed the National Government to Taiwan. His past misdeeds were given formal consideration by the National Assembly in 1954, but the deliberations were kept secret. Sheng continued to live in comfortable retirement with his wife, Ch'iu Yü-fang, who had borne him a daughter and three sons.

Sheng Shih-ts'ai and the American scholar Allen S. Whiting wrote *Sinkiang: Pawn or Pivot?*, published in 1958. Sheng's contribution to that work is essentially an apologia for his administration of Sinkiang; it stands in radical contradiction to parts of his earlier works, *Liu ta cheng-ts'e chiao-ch'eng* [lectures on the six great policies] and *Cheng-fu mu-ch'ien chu-yao jen-wu* [present tasks of the government].

Shih Chao-chi   施 肇 基
T. Chih-chih   植 之
West. Sao-ke Alfred Sze

Shih Chao-chi (10 April 1877–3 January 1958), known as Sao-ke Alfred Sze, diplomat who became Chinese minister to the Court of St. James's in 1914 and who spent most of the rest of his life outside China. In addition to serving as China's chief envoy to Great Britain and the United States, he was plenipotentiary delegate to many international conferences.

After 1941 Sze maintained residence in the United States.

Ch'unhsiaoli, Chentsechen, Kiangsu, was the birthplace of Sao-ke Alfred Sze, the son of Shih Tse-ching, a chü-jen who was a buyer of silk for export. At the age of five, Sze was sent to a local school to begin his training in the Chinese classics. He enrolled at the T'ung-wen-kuan at Miaohsiangan in 1886, but he contracted rheumatism after studying there for a year. Accordingly, he went to Shanghai in 1887 and enrolled at St. John's Academy (later St. John's University), where he studied for three years. During the last year of his residence there he served as editor of the student publication, *St. John's Echo*. In 1890 he transferred to the Kuo-wen hsueh-yuan [Chinese literature academy], where he studied for two years.

In 1893 Sao-ke Alfred Sze was appointed a student interpreter at the Chinese legation in Washington. He proceeded to his post in the company of Yang Ju, the newly appointed minister to the United States, Spain, and Peru. After arriving in Washington in August, Sze enrolled at Central High School. He continued to serve as a legation attaché until the summer of 1897, when he resigned to enroll at Cornell University. His studies were interrupted in 1899 when Yang Ju, who had become minister to Russia, requested that Sze serve as an interpreter at St. Petersburg. Sze accepted the appointment, went to Russia, and then accompanied Yang Ju to the First Hague Conference. He received a B.A. in 1901 and an M.A. in 1902, thus becoming the first Chinese to be educated at Cornell. He was elected to Phi Beta Kappa and Phi Kappa Phi.

Sze returned to China in the summer of 1902 and went to Hankow to visit his elder brother Shih Ch'eng-chih, who then was assistant manager of the China Merchants Steam Navigation Company. At that time, Tuan-fang (1861–1911; ECCP, II, 780–82), was looking for people with modern training and Sze, on his brother's recommendation, was appointed English secretary in the governor's office at Wuchang, superintendent of the Northwestern High School, and supervisor of Hupeh students in the United States. He accompanied a group of students to the United States to take up their studies. While he was there, Jeremiah W. Jenks, a Cornell economics professor, was invited to visit China for the purpose of studying its currency system and suggesting reforms. Sze, on the recommendation of the Chinese legation at Washington, was appointed Jenks's interpreter by the Ch'ing government, and he returned to China in 1903 with the Jenks mission. In the course of the mission's tour of various provinces, Sze met such important officials as T'ang Shao-yi and Hsü Shih-ch'ang(qq.v.).

In the autumn of 1902 Sao-ke Alfred Sze escorted a second group of Hupeh students to the United States. This group included Tuan-fang's son and V. K. Wellington Koo (Ku Wei-chün, q.v.). From 1902 onwards, in the absence of Chang Chih-tung (1837–1909; ECCP, I, 27–32), Tuan-fang had been acting governor general of Hupeh and Hunan. In 1904, however, Chang returned to Wuchang, and Tuan-fang became governor of Hunan. When Sze returned from the United States, he reported to Chang Chih-tung's office in Wuchang. He was appointed English secretary in the office of Wang Feng-tsao, the secretary general. He became friendly with Pi Kuang-tsu, a chü-jen who was a secretary in Chang Chih-tung's office. Pi profoundly influenced Sze's development as an official. After dealing successfully with a case involving the importing of goods without payment of likin tax, Sze received appointment to seven new positions, the most important of which was that of commissioner of the copper mint.

In July 1905 Hsü Shih-ch'ang (q.v.) asked Sze to accompany a five-man mission being sent abroad to study Western systems of government. When Chang Chih-tung heard of this development, he dismissed Sze from his posts. Sze then accepted the invitation. Because of a bombing incident at the Peking railway station, the departure of the mission was delayed. Three of the ministers, including Hsü Shih-ch'ang, withdrew from participation, leaving Tuan-fang and Tai Hung-tz'u to head it. Tuan-fang confirmed Sze's appointment, and the mission finally left China in December. In the meantime, on 27 November, Sze had married Yü-hua Alice T'ang (b. 1886), a daughter of T'ang Chieh-ch'en and a niece of T'ang Shao-yi. The mission spent several months in the United States and Europe, returning to China in mid-1906. In September, Sze took the government examinations in law and obtained the coveted chin-shih degree.

T'ang Shao-yi, now senior vice president in charge of railway administration of the newly established Board of Posts and Communications, appointed Sao-ke Alfred Sze director general of the Peking-Hankow Railway and junior secretary of the board in 1906. After Sze refused to give the Liu-ho-kou Coal Mining Company preferential treatment, shareholder pressure forced his removal from the junior secretaryship on grounds of loss of public confidence and nepotism on the part of T'ang Shao-yi. It was assumed that he would resign the directorship of the Peking-Hankow Railway, but he did not. After T'ang Shao-yi became governor of Fengtien in April 1907, Sze was transferred to the post of assistant director general of the Peking-Mukden Railway, serving under Shouson Chow (Chou Ch'ang-ling, q.v.). In 1908 Sze became tao-t'ai of the Kirin northwestern circuit, superintendent of customs at Harbin, and director of the Kirin bureau of forestry. Among the important cases he handled in Harbin was the investigation of the assassination of Ito Hirobumi in 1909. The following year, he resigned from his Kirin posts to become junior counsellor in the Board of Foreign Affairs at Peking. He was made senior counsellor in August 1911, and later that year he was appointed minister to the United States, Mexico, Cuba, and Peru. Before he could leave China to assume the ministership, the Wuchang revolt broke out. The republican revolution left him jobless in Peking.

In the spring of 1912 T'ang Shao-yi, the premier in the new republican government, appointed Sao-ke Alfred Sze minister of communications and acting minister of finance. When T'ang resigned in June, Sze also left his post. Sze subsequently was named minister to the United States, but the Parliament refused to confirm his appointment. In November 1913 Sze was made chief of protocol in the presidential office, and in June 1914 he was named minister to the Court of St. James's. Sze arrived in London in December, and he remained there throughout the First World War. He served as a Chinese delegate to the Paris Peace Conference in 1919, but played a less prominent role in it than did Wellington Koo and C. T. Wang (Wang Cheng-t'ing, q.v.).

Sao-ke Alfred Sze was appointed minister to the United States in September 1920, and he assumed office in February 1921. That autumn, he was designated chief of the Chinese delegation to the Washington Conference. It presented China's "Ten Points," which included a definition of China, its territorial and administrative entity, and its right to participate in international conferences affecting its interests. Although the Chinese delegation, which also included Wellington Koo and C. T. Wang, did not achieve all of its aims, it obtained substantial benefits from the negotiations: the Nine Power treaty signed in February 1922 and the settlement of the Shantung issue.

In January 1924 Sze assumed the post of minister of foreign affairs, but he resigned in February after the Senate refused confirmation of his appointment. He then returned to his post as minister to the United States and negotiated an exchange of letters with the Department of State governing the use of remitted American Boxer Indemnity funds for the education of Chinese students in the United States. He later was appointed a trustee of the China Foundation for the Promotion of Education and Culture, the body charged with allocating these funds. In the summer of 1924 and again in 1925 Sze was China's chief delegate to meetings of the International Opium Conference, held at Geneva under the auspices of the League of Nations. When the Customs Tariff Conference convened at Peking in October 1925 in somewhat tardy fulfillment of an agreement reached at the Washington Conference, Sze was appointed to a special commission to advise the Chinese delegation. His contributions to the work of the conference were speeches made in the United States. Sze's only trip outside the United States in 1926 was a brief journey to Turkey.

During the Northern Expedition, Sao-ke Alfred Sze's legation communicated with the Chinese Nationalists, but he maintained a technically proper attitude by stating that his official representation was "confined to the Peking Government." In May 1928 the Nationalists implicitly challenged his standing by sending C. C. Wu (Wu Ch'ao-shu, q.v.) to Washington as a special envoy. On the eve of the entry of Nationalist forces into Peking and the dissolution of the Peking government,

Sze advocated that foreign powers adopt a "hands-off" policy. Sze's appointment as minister to the United States was confirmed by the National Government at Nanking in mid-July. In November, however, C. C. Wu was appointed to the Washington post, and Sze was named minister to the Court of St. James's. Sze returned to China for a visit before proceeding to his new post. He reached London in time to represent China at the International Postal Union Conference in May 1929. He held the London post for three years, and in December 1930 he also became chairman of the Sino-British Purchasing Commission. In July 1931 he was appointed China's chief delegate to the Assembly of the League of Nations. After Japan invaded Manchuria in September, he also represented China on the League Council. When a Kuomintang-sponsored mass meeting of Chinese residents of Paris voiced bitter complaint against the League Council's handling of China's case and criticized Sze's representation as being weak, he offered to resign. His resignation was refused. Nevertheless, W. W. Yen (Yen Hui-ch'ing, q.v.) replaced him as China's representative to the League Council in January 1932. Sze resigned from his London posts in April, saying that his health was poor. Because W. W. Yen was kept from his duties as minister to the United States by his League of Nations responsibilities, Sze became acting minister to the United States in October. When Yen became ambassador to the Soviet Union, Sze succeeded him at Washington. In June 1935 China and the United States raised the status of their respective missions, and Sze became China's first ambassador to the United States. He held this post until May 1937, when he was succeeded by C. T. Wang.

Sao-ke Alfred Sze retired from his country's diplomatic service in 1937 and took up residence in Shanghai. He remained there after the Sino-Japanese war broke out in July. He served as director of the propaganda section of the International Relief Committee, and he founded the Anti-Tuberculosis Association, which supported a hospital at Shanghai. In July 1938 he was appointed to the People's Political Council at Chungking, but he did not go to Free China to play an active role in the work of that advisory body. He took up residence in Shanghai in 1940, and he went to the United States in June 1941. On 12 July 1941 President Franklin D. Roosevelt appointed Sze "American non-national commissioner" on the five-man United States–Union of South Africa International Peace Commission. In December, after the United States entered the War in the Pacific, Sze became vice chairman of the China Defense Supplies Commission, stationed in Washington to handle Chinese procurement. At war's end, he served as senior adviser to the Chinese delegation at the United Nations Conference on International Organization at San Francisco in June 1945. From 1948 to 1950 he served on the advisory committee for the International Bank for Reconstruction and Development. He suffered a stroke in October 1954 and was incapacitated for several months, but he made a gradual though partial recovery. Sao-ke Alfred Sze died in Washington, D.C., on 3 January 1958. He was survived by his wife, two sons, four daughters, and twelve grandchildren.

In the course of his career, Sao-ke Alfred Sze received several honors from the National Government, including the First Order of Wenhu in September 1921 and the First Class Tashou Paokuang Chiaho and the Second Order of Merit in March 1922. Such educational institutions as Columbia University, the University of Toronto, Syracuse University, Lafayette College, Grinnell College, and St. John's University in Shanghai awarded him honorary degrees. In 1954, before his stroke, Sze told Anming Fu the story of his life up to 1914 for publication after his death. *Sao-ke Alfred Sze: Reminiscences of His Early Years* was published in English in 1962.

Shih-fu: *see* LIU SSU-FU.

Shih Liang-ts'ai　　史 量 才
　Orig. Chia-hsiu　　家 修

Shih Liang-ts'ai (1879–13 November 1934), owner and publisher of the *Shun-pao*. An entrepreneur with many business interests in Shanghai, he was also a civic leader. He was assassinated in 1934.

Although his native place was Nanking, Shih Liang-ts'ai was born in Ssu-ching-chen, near Shanghai, where his father, Shih Ch'un-fan, had moved during the Taiping Rebellion. The young Shih received a traditional education in the Chinese classics to prepare him for a career in the Ch'ing civil service. In reaction to the Boxer Uprising, however, he decided to take up more practical subjects. He spent 1901-3 at the Sericultural School in Hangchow. Immediately after being graduated, he began teaching at several schools in Shanghai. In 1904 he helped to found the Women's Sericultural School at Kao-ch'ang-miao. The school soon moved to Soochow, where some of its graduates worked to develop sericultural enterprises in the fertile T'aihu area. Shih also was instrumental in promoting the General Association of Educational Affairs in Kiangsu, and he became chief editor of the *Shih-pao* [eastern times] in Shanghai. His agricultural interests led him to found the China Agricultural Association in Nanking and to serve as its general secretary. It was probably in this connection that he was chosen to head a group of experts which appraised the agricultural exhibits at the Nanyang ch'uan-yeh hui [Nanyang exhibition] at Nanking in 1910.

Soon after the Wuchang revolt began in October 1911, Shih Liang-ts'ai, who had become prominent in civic affairs, was made a member of the provincial council by Ch'eng Te-ch'uan, the military governor of Kiangsu. Shih became the director of the bureau charged with liquidating customs revenues in Shanghai to meet the pressing financial needs of the revolutionary regime in Kiangsu. In 1912, soon after the republic was established, he was made director of the Sungchiang salt bureau.

Also in 1912 Shih Liang-ts'ai became co-owner and general manager of the *Shun-pao*; in 1915 he became its sole owner. The *Shun-pao* had been founded in 1872 by a British business-man named Ernest Major. At first, it met with an indifferent reception, but its circulation began to pick up when it published vivid and detailed accounts of the Japanese invasion of Taiwan. In 1884, when a dispute arose between China and France over Indo-China, the *Shun-pao* provided its readership with on-the-spot coverage. In subsequent years, the fame and popularity of the *Shun-pao* increased after each major national or international crisis. Major left China and entrusted the *Shun-pao* to a group of Englishmen. In 1909 they sold the paper to Hsi Yü-fu for China $75,000. Three years later, Shih and his friends acquired it for China $120,000. By this time, the *Shun-pao's* daily circulation had reached 7,000 copies. Under Shih's management, the paper's circulation reached 20,000 in 1917, 30,000 in 1918 and 50,000 in 1921. By 1928 it was claiming a paid circulation of 140,000, the largest in China.

Because of the political instability of China in the 1920's and the embryonic state of Chinese journalism, such major Chinese newspapers as the *Shun-pao* and its chief rival in Shanghai, the *Sin-wen-pao* [the news] avoided political involvement and devoted much space to news of a non-political nature. Under Shih Liang-ts'ai's guidance, the *Shun-pao* gradually shifted its reportorial emphases and increased its coverage of political affairs. Shih worked constantly to keep abreast of the times and to improve the *Shun-pao*. In 1929 he established a planning department to devise ways to streamline operations, and he persuaded Huang Yen-p'ei and Ko Kung-chen (qq.v.) to serve as co-directors. Also in 1929 he and a group of his friends acquired control of the *Sin-wen-pao*. Shih soon became interested in subsidiary enterprises and established the *Shun-pao Yearbook*, the *Shun-pao Monthly*, a movable library, and supplementary schools. When the paper celebrated its sixtieth anniversary in 1932, Shih commissioned the geologists V. K. Ting (Ting Wen-chiang) and Wong Wen-hao (qq.v.) and the cartographer Tseng Shih-ying to prepare the *Shun-pao* map of China, which turned out to be the best general and provincial map ever published by a private enterprise in China.

After the Mukden Incident in September 1931, the *Shun-pao* became highly critical of the National Government's Japan policy. Early in 1932 Shih Liang-ts'ai, who had become a prominent civic leader in Shanghai, began to organize the citizens of Shanghai in an effort to maintain peace and order during a period of great panic and much confusion as the Japanese forced their undeclared war on Shanghai. Shih later became the first chairman of the provisional municipal council of Shanghai. His influence in the economic and industrial life of Shanghai was great, for, in addition to his newspaper enterprises, he had helped to found or expand the China and South Seas Bank, the Min-sheng Cotton Mill, the Wu-chou

Dispensary Company, and the Chung-hua Book Company. He also served as a member of the Rural Rehabilitation Committee, a vice director of the Wen-ch'i Paper Mill, and a director of the China Merchants' Steam Navigation Company.

Late in 1934 Shih Liang-ts'ai, who suffered from stomach ulcers, went to Hangchow to rest. On his way back to Shanghai on 13 November, he was shot by assassins at Wang-chia-pu near Haining, Chekiang. Although the assassins were never identified, it was generally assumed that they had been inspired by Kuomintang authorities who resented the *Shun-pao*'s strong criticism of the National Government's Japan policy. Shih was survived by his wife and a son, Shih Yung-keng.

Shih Mei-yü　　　　　石美玉
West. Mary Stone

Shih Mei-yü (1 May 1873–30 December 1954), known as Mary Stone, American trained physician and Methodist medical missionary. She was best known for her work as superintendent of the Elizabeth Skelton Danforth Hospital at Kiukiang.

The parents of Shih Mei-yü were among the earliest and most devout Protestant converts in central China. Her father was for many years a minister of the Methodist church at Kiukiang, Kiangsi, and her mother was principal of a day school for girls operated by the Methodist mission at Kiukiang. The young Shih Mei-yü thus was reared in an atmosphere of Christian piety and of radically nonconformist attitudes toward certain traditional Chinese values. Her parents refused to bind her feet, for example, and she had the reputation of being among the first "big-footed" girls in central China. She was tutored by her mother in the Chinese classics and in Christian literature. Her father, who had been impressed by the work of an American medical missionary, Dr. Kate Bushnell, further defied convention by deciding that his daughter should be trained for similar service. On Dr. Bushnell's advice that a basic grounding in the liberal arts should precede medical training, he enrolled Shih Mei-yü at the Rulison-Fish Memorial School, a mission school for girls

at Kiukiang. She studied there for ten years under the guidance of Gertrude Howe, a Methodist missionary from Lansing, Michigan.

On completing her middle school education in 1892, Shih Mei-yü went with Miss Howe to the United States to begin medical training. With them was K'ang Ch'eng (q.v.) who was later to win acclaim for her work as a pioneer Chinese woman doctor. In the United States, Shih Mei-yü adopted the name Mary Stone, and K'ang Ch'eng became Ida Kahn. Having passed entrance examinations in mathematics, rhetoric, history, physics, and Latin, the two girls were admitted to the medical school of the University of Michigan in the autumn of 1892. Upon graduation in June 1896, they became the first Chinese women to receive medical degrees from an American university.

After spending the summer of 1896 in Chicago hospitals observing procedures and techniques, Dr. Stone received a commission as a medical missionary in China from the Women's Foreign Missionary Society of the Methodist Church. Accompanied by Dr. Kahn, she returned to China that autumn as a representative of the society's Des Moines, Iowa, branch. The two young physicians set up practice at Kiukiang, where the suspicion with which the local inhabitants regarded them soon gave way to confidence. Dr. Stone later reported that during their first ten months at Kiukiang she and her associates treated more than 2,300 dispensary patients, made almost 300 house calls, and kept their one-room hospital filled.

Within two years the problem of inadequate facilities had been solved through the generosity of I. N. Danforth, a Chicago physician who had befriended Dr. Stone in the United States. He provided funds for the Elizabeth Skelton Danforth Hospital at Kiukiang, a memorial to his wife, equipped with 95 beds in wards and 15 rooms for private patients. Almost as soon as it was ready for occupancy, the new hospital had to be abandoned in the summer of 1900 because of the Boxer Uprising, which claimed Dr. Stone's father as a victim. Dr. Stone and Dr. Kahn took refuge in Japan. They returned to China in 1901 and formally opened the Danforth Memorial Hospital on 7 December, with Dr. Stone as superintendent.

Two years later, Dr. Kahn responded to an urgent appeal to establish a similar medical center in Nanchang, leaving Dr. Stone to administer the rapidly expanding Kiukiang hospital program alone. However, when Dr. Danforth offered Dr. Stone assistance in the form of an experienced and highly recommended American nurse to share the executive burdens, Dr. Stone graciously but firmly declined in order to demonstrate that Chinese women could become efficient administrators as well as competent medical practitioners.

In 1907 Dr. Stone spent seven months in the United States undergoing surgery at the Wesleyan Hospital in Chicago under Dr. Danforth's supervision, resting and recuperating in the homes of friends throughout the country, and making appeals for support of the Danforth Memorial Hospital. Her success as a fund-raiser enabled the hospital to expand its facilities considerably in the next few years. Demands on the Kiukiang facilities continued to increase as Dr. Stone's reputation as a physician and surgeon spread throughout central China. Records indicate that almost 3,000 patients a month were treated there in the busiest seasons, an increasingly large proportion of cases requiring "the largest operations known to surgery." After observing Dr. Stone's performance in the operating room, Dr. Danforth reported that "no Chicago surgeon is doing work superior to hers."

In addition to administering the hospital and practicing medicine, Dr. Stone supervised the training of more than 500 Chinese nurses during her tenure of more than 20 years at Kiukiang. Because modern medicine was new to China, she had to prepare Chinese transla-tions of textbooks and training materials for her nurses. Despite growing responsibilities at the Danforth Memorial Hospital, she also found time to supervise a home for cripples in Kiukiang. And she brought four adopted sons into her own home—two from families of relatives and two from destitute families.

Dr. Stone spent the academic year 1918–19 doing postgraduate work at the medical school of The Johns Hopkins University on a Rocke-feller Foundation scholarship, and she remained in the United States until June 1920. In an address to the Women's Foreign Missionary Society at Des Moines on 12 May 1920, she expressed her concern at the manner in which American brewers were "hurting China" through introducing foreign alcoholic beverages to her homeland. Dr. Stone also spoke on

behalf of Chinese students in the United States, expressing her desire that Christian homes be opened to young Chinese so that they might receive the best that America had to offer. "I wonder," she said, "if they are left adrift here in your large cities to settle down with the foreign element there that is causing so much trouble in America today." Dr. Stone also expressed dismay that her younger sister, Dr. Phoebe Stone, had been denied the privileged status in American missionary circles that she herself enjoyed. Her sister, a graduate of Goucher College who had received her medical training at The Johns Hopkins University, took charge of the Danforth Memorial Hospital while Dr. Mary Stone was in the United States.

Because her sister was able to carry on the work in Kiangsi, Dr. Mary Stone, whose interests had never been confined solely to medicine, sought a new base of operations. Her increasingly literalist religious views led her, on her return to China from the United States, to sever ties with the Methodist Board of Missions and to settle at Shanghai. She founded the Bethel Hospital and established the Bethel Mission in cooperation with Jennie V. Hughes, an American missionary. In the 1920–37 period, the Bethel nurses' training program was one of the best-known in China, drawing students from all parts of the country and graduating hundreds of trained nurses to assist in the expansion of modern medicine. The Bethel complex also included primary and secondary schools, an evangelical training department, and an orphanage. Dr. Stone herself conducted a Sunday morning Bible class with senior nurses and a Thursday evening Bible class with new students. Her aim was to have the young women accept Jesus Christ as their savior before leaving Bethel so that they would work as nurse-evangelists. Miss Hughes and Dr. Stone brought up 36 Chinese children in their Shanghai home. Throughout this period, Dr. Stone was more prominent as a Christian evangelist than as a physician. She became the first woman to be ordained a Christian minister in central China, the first president of the Women's Christian Temperance Union in China, and a member of the China continuations committee of the National Mis-sionary Conference.

The Japanese attack on China in 1937 forced

the Bethel Mission to move to Hong Kong. Dr. Stone worked indefatigably to gain support for its work. She spent much of her time in the United States, where the Bethel Mission headquarters was established at Pasadena, California. She was in Shanghai soon after the Japanese surrender, but she returned to Pasadena in her last years. She died at Pasadena on 30 December 1954, in her eighty-second year.

Shih Ying   石　瑛
T. Heng-ch'ing   桁　青

Shih Ying (1879–4 December 1943), engineer, administrator devoted to the modernization of China, and member of the Western Hills faction of the Kuomintang. As mayor of Nanking in 1932–35 he instituted impartial law enforcement and enacted sumptuary measures.

Yanghsin, Hupeh, was the birthplace of Shih Ying. His great-grandfather and grand-father had been scholars, but a decline in the family fortunes had forced his father into trade. Shih received a thorough education in the Chinese classics. After passing the examinations for the chü-jen degree in 1903, he decided to study at a modern school in Wuchang. He soon became friendly with such other students as Chü Cheng (q.v.) and T'ien T'ung (d. 1930; T. Tzu-ch'in), who later became anti-Manchu revolutionaries.

In the autumn of 1904 Shih Ying won a Hupeh provincial scholarship for study abroad, and he decided to study at a French naval academy. He and another Chinese student at the academy, Hsiang Kuo-hua, became angry when they discovered that they had been excluded from lectures on new tactics and weapons. They rashly removed a number of maps and papers from the academy and took them to a small studio near Brussels to have them copied. When the photographer dis-covered the origin of these materials, he informed the academy authorities of their whereabouts. When Shih and Hsiang took the materials back to France, they were followed and apprehended in Paris. Because the Chinese legation inter-ceded for them, they were expelled from France instead of being prosecuted as spies. Shih then went to England, where he came to know Wu

Chih-hui (q.v.) and found a place to live next door to Wu. Shih acquired a working knowledge of English in less than three months. After auditing classes at the University of London for a time, he became a regular student there, majoring in railroad engineering.

At the end of October 1911, after the republican revolution had begun in China, Sun Yat-sen went to England from the United States to conduct negotiations with the British government and private banking interests. His assistants in these negotiations were Shih Ying, Wu Chih-hui, and Li Shu-ch'eng. In November, Sun and Li returned to China by way of France while Shih and Wu took the way of Berlin and Rome. On arrival at Nanking in 1912, Shih was appointed director general of the opium-suppression campaign. He resigned in April 1912 to become chief of the T'ung-meng-hui branch in Hupeh. He joined the Kuomintang later that year and made a successful bid for election to the National Assembly.

After the failure of the so-called second revolution in 1913 and the outlawing of the Kuomintang by Yuan Shih-k'ai, Shih Ying fled to England. He remained there for nine years, studying mining and metallurgy at the University of Birmingham and depending on friends to supply him with food and money. When he sailed for China in 1923, Shih could not afford a full fare. Accordingly, he bought space on the deck and slept in the hold when it rained. Because he was big and rugged, with a frank and uncompromising character, his friends nicknamed him Shih T'ou [the rock].

Shih Ying had hoped to organize a machine factory in Kwangtung after his return from abroad, but the plan did not work out. He then accepted an invitation from Ts'ai Yuan-p'ei (q.v.) to teach at Peking University. In 1924 Hsiao Yao-nan, the military governor of Hupeh, invited a number of Kuomintang members to assist him in developing Hupeh. Shih accepted an invitation to become president of Wuchang University, but he held that post for less than a year. After returning to Peking University in 1925, he spent much of his time working to increase Kuomintang membership in the Peking area. At the First National Congress of the Kuomintang, held in January 1924, he was elected to the Central Executive

Committee. After Sun Yat-sen's death, he and other conservatives called a so-called fourth plenum of the Central Executive Committee at Peking, later known as the Western Hills Conference. The Western Hills group advocated the purging of Communists from the Kuomintang and the impeachment of Wang Ching-wei.

In the summer of 1926, at the start of the Northern Expedition, Shih Ying went to Canton to work as an engineer at the Shih-ching Arsenal. By thoroughly reorganizing the arsenal, he doubled its output and cut its expenses in half. By so doing, he made an important contribution to the northward advance of the National Revolutionary Army.

In 1928 Chang Chih-pen, the governor of Hupeh, appointed Shih Ying head of the provincial department of construction, Chang Nan-hsien head of the department of finance, and Yen Chung head of the department of civil affairs. These men ushered in a new era of provincial administration in Hupeh. Their lack of bureaucratic habits and their unostentatious appearance earned them the designation of "the three eccentrics of Hupeh." In the winter of 1929 Shih resigned his government post to become dean of the newly established college of engineering at Wuhan University (the successor to Wuchang University). Before long, however, Chang Nan-hsien, now governor of Chekiang, pressed him into service as head of the Chekiang department of construction. Shih soon concluded that priority should be given the Hangchow-Chiangshan railway and the Hangchow electric plant. Because the provincial treasury was virtually empty, he obtained loans from Shanghai bankers for these projects. He also cut costs by dismissing several foreigners who drew large salaries as water conservation experts without doing any work.

Shih Ying's fine reputation as an administrator led the National Government to appoint him mayor of Nanking. In his new post, Shih was not satisfied with merely improving the appearance of the capital. He regulated taxation and other matters and applied the new rules to all classes, including political leaders who hitherto had been inclined to consider themselves above the law. To promote the habit of thrift and the sale of Chinese products, Shih always wore clothes made of Chinese fabrics and required the same practice of all officials in the city

government and the public schools. Because he believed that the young should be trained in frugality, he stationed policemen at the entrances of public schools to discourage affluent officials from transporting their children to and from school in automobiles. He increased the number of private schools, raised the salaries of the teachers, and searched for the most qualified men as school principals. He also served the citizenry by making government loans available to traditional, small-scale industries. During Shih's term as mayor, Sino-Japanese relations entered a critical stage. Shih maintained a rigidly anti-Japanese posture, refusing even to meet socially with the Japanese consul general at Nanking. When a private Japanese group arrived at Nanking for a visit in March 1935, Wang Ching-wei ordered all high-ranking city officials to greet the visitors at the airport. Shih, infuriated by what he considered to be a national humiliation, resigned from office. On 24 July 1935 he was appointed chief of the bureau of civil appointments in the Examination Yuan. This post gave him an opportunity to bring order to China's chaotic civil service system.

When the Sino-Japanese war broke out in 1937, the Hupeh provincial government was reorganized because of the strategic importance that province was likely to have. Shih Ying was asked to head the province's department of construction, and he accepted the offer without hesitation. For military reasons, his job involved destruction as well as construction, particularly with regard to highways. He also helped plan the evacuation of industries and the establishment of cooperative enterprises. In the autumn of 1938, however, the overworked Shih was forced by ill health to resign from office. The following year, he was elected speaker of the Provisional Hupeh People's Council, which met at Enshih, the wartime capital of Hupeh. At Enshih, he also organized a cotton and hemp weaving cooperative. Its products were sold cheaply to the government or to soldiers, and its profits were used to aid education. Shih's health continued to decline. In July 1943 he died at Chungking. He was survived by his wife, *née* Hsü, and his son, Hsien-tsung. Feng Tzu-yu (q.v.), the unofficial historian of the Kuomintang, judged Shih as "the foremost incorruptible and honest official since the founding of the republic."

Shu Ch'ing-ch'un   舒 慶 春
Pen. Lao She   老 舍

Shu Ch'ing-ch'un (3 February 1899–October 1966), known as Lao She, novelist and short-story writer with a flair for using the Peking dialect in a comic-satiric vein. During and after the Sino-Japanese war he also wrote propaganda plays. He was known by Americans as the author of *Rickshaw Boy*, an unauthorized and bowdlerized translation of his novel *Lo-t'o Hsiang-tzu*.

Peking was the birthplace of Lao She, who was of Manchu descent. When he was still an infant, his father died during the suppression of the Boxer Uprising. After attending an elementary school and the Pei-ching shih-fan hsueh-hsiao [Peking normal school], he decided to pursue a career in education. At the age of 17, he became principal of a municipal elementary school. He later was sent by the Peking school authorities to visit schools and to study educational practices in Kiangsu and Chekiang. On his return to Peking, he was promoted to ch'üan-hsueh-yuan [supervisor of education] for the Peichiao district of Peking. Lao She did not like this sort of work, and he soon resigned to become secretary to the Pei-ching chiao-yü hui [Peking education society], organized by Ku Meng-yü (q.v.). He eked out his livelihood by teaching Chinese literature in a high school, and he managed to support himself and his mother, finance his studies at Yenching University, and save money for a trip abroad.

In 1924 Lao She left China and went to England, where he found a job teaching Mandarin at the School of Oriental and African Studies in London. For the next five years, he spent most of his time at the home of Clement Egerton, then Gilchrist scholar in Chinese at the school, whom he assisted in the translation of the Ming novel *Chin-p'ing-mei*, a work which was published under the title *Golden Lotus* in 1939. The novels of Charles Dickens, which Lao She read while working to improve his English, inspired him to write a work of fiction, *Lao Chang-ti che-hsüeh* [Lao Chang's philosophy], which he completed early in 1926. This story of conflict between two honest boys and a wicked schoolteacher owed a great deal to Dickensian methods of characterization. Although it revealed Lao She's talents as a humorous writer and as a defender of the underdog, the work failed to commend itself to the author in later years. However, Hsü Ti-shan (q.v.), a pioneer member of the Wen-hsüeh yen-chiu-hui [literary association] who then was a student at Oxford, read it and recommended it to the *Hsiao-shuo yüeh-pao* [short story monthly], which began to serialize it in July 1926.

Lao She wrote two more novels during his stay in England. The first was *Chao Tzu-yüeh*, which has been characterized as the first serious comic novel in China. This work, which was a marked improvement over Lao She's first novel in style and construction, was serialized in *Hsiao-shuo yüeh-pao* in March–November 1927. Centered on Chao Tzu-yüeh, a college student in Peking, the novel zestily flays the corruption and ineffectualness of the new breed of Chinese student. Lao She portrayed this new breed as venal, lecherous, stupid, and deceitful—the antithesis of the heroic ideal which Lao She was to proclaim as the only salvation for China. Lao She's third London book, *Erh Ma* [the two Ma's], was serialized in the *Hsiao-shuo yüeh-pao* in May–December 1929 and was published in book form in April 1931. The two central characters are a Cantonese father and son who manage a curio shop in London. In the course of writing about their adventures with English and Chinese acquaintants, Lao She managed to explore the attitudes and reactions of both Chinese and Englishmen of differing viewpoints and experience to the phenomenon of revolutionary China and more explicitly to the conflict between personal happiness and national duty as it confronts the younger Ma.

In 1929 Lao She left England and spent three months on the continent before going on to Singapore, where he remained for six months teaching Mandarin in a middle school and beginning a novel. This slight tale, *Hsiao P'o-ti sheng-jih* [little Po's birthday], was inspired by the children he saw in the streets. It was published serially in *Hsiao-shuo yüeh-pao* in January–April 1931 and in book form in 1934.

By the time Lao She returned to China in 1930, he had acquired a considerable reputation as a comic novelist. However, he soon found that he could not live by his writing alone, and he took a teaching post at Cheeloo University in Tsinan, Shantung. He remained there until 1934, during which time he wrote several works of note. His first novel of this period, "Ta-ming hu" [Ta-ming lake], never was published. The manuscript was destroyed when the offices of the Commercial Press were bombed during the Japanese attack on Shanghai in January 1932. *Mao-ch'eng chi* [cat city], published serially in 1932–33 in the *Hsien-tai*, was a satirical fantasy based on China's failure to take her rightful place in the modern world. In a third novel, *Li-hun* [divorce], which appeared in 1933, Lao She continued his exploration of the endemic weaknesses in Chinese character and society which he considered to be the cause of China's low rank among the nations of the world. The plot revolves around Lao Li, who takes his country wife to the city and tries to transform her into a sophisticated woman. In the end, he is forced to return to the country to curb her extravagance.

Lao She also began writing short stories during this period. These were published in three collections: *Kan-chi* [collection of hastily executed stories], in 1934; *Ying-hai-chi* [cherries and the sea], in 1935; and *Ko-tsao-chi* [clams and weeds], in 1936. These collections contained some of Lao She's best writing, including the well-known story "Hei-pai Li" [dark Li and fair Li], a story of two brothers. After a life of constant sacrifice for his younger brother, the elder Li finally is executed in his stead.

In 1934 Lao She decided to leave the teaching profession and to devote all of his time to writing. He soon finished *Niu T'ien-tz'u chuan* [the life of Niu T'ien-t'zu], described as "the education of a little hero of the petty-bourgeois class." The book, though slight in literary merit, throws considerable light on a significant change in Lao She's thinking. *Li-hun*, by implication, had suggested that an assertion of individualism was the key to delivering China from corruption and apathy. In *Niu T'ien-tz'u chuan* this thesis is questioned, and the paramount importance of social environment, against which it is useless for the isolated individual to struggle, is stressed. The full implications of this change of heart were to be worked out in Lao She's later works.

Because the returns from his writing were still too meager to support him, Lao She returned to teaching, this time at Tsingtao University. He soon completed his greatest masterpiece, *Lo-t'o Hsiang-tzu* [Hsiang-tzu the camel], which first appeared in 1936–37 in serial form in *Yü-chou feng* [cosmic wind], edited by Lin Yü-t'ang (q.v.). In this moving story of the corruption and doom of a strong and good-hearted ricksha puller in Peking, Lao She gave clearest expression to what now seemed to him the tragic futility of individual effort in a society hostile to human values. Publication of the novel was halted by the Japanese attack of July 1937, and it did not appear until 1939. In 1937 Lao She did publish *Lao-niu p'o-ch'e* [old ox and worn-out cart], a collection of essays dealing with the genesis of a number of his novels and with matters of language and style.

After the Sino-Japanese war began, Lao She went to Hankow, where in March 1938 he was elected head of the All-China Anti-Japanese Writers Federation, a post he retained throughout the war. With Yao P'eng-tzu, he edited the federation's journal, *K'ang-chan wen-i* [literature for national resistance]. Of all the Chinese writers of this period, only Lao She seems to have maintained good relations with both Communists and anti-Communists; he was elected unanimously to this important information and propaganda post. Lao She spent the greater part of the war years in Chungking, where he was active in organizing writers and encouraging them to use literature in promoting the war effort. He also continued to produce works of his own. He associated himself with theater groups and began to write plays. *Ts'an-wu*, his first drama, was followed by such works as *Kuo-chia chih-shang* [the state above all], a fervently patriotic piece depicting cooperation between Muslims and Chinese in common support of the national cause. He wrote this play in collaboration with the young playwright Sung Chih-ti. Participating in a then-current fad, he also wrote a long poem for recitation in the ta-ku [popular ballad] style, *Chien-pei-p'ien* [north of Chienmenkuan]. Throughout the war period he wrote many short ballads and ch'ü-i. He published a collection of short stories, *Huo-ch'e chi* [the train] in 1939. The following year, the Tso-che shu-she in Hong Kong published an unauthorized edition of

Hsuan-nien [the citizen], which had appeared in 1936–37 in the *Lun-yü*, under the title *Wen po-shih* [Dr. Wen]. This was a mordant study of a student with an American Ph.D. degree who ends up marrying a rich girl and wondering why he went to the United States to study in the first place.

In a letter written from Wuhan and published in the *Yü-chou feng* a few months after the outbreak of the Sino-Japanese war, Lao She urged young writers to guard their good health so that they would work for their country, and complained that he was not getting enough sleep and was damaging his health because he could not rest for thinking that he must devote every hour to the anti-Japanese struggle. His health soon deteriorated, and toward the end of the war he was hospitalized for some time.

Lao She published a play, *Kuei-ch'ü-lai hsi* [return], in 1943. The following year saw the appearance of the novel *Huo-tsang* [cremation], a melodramatic and romanticized tale of traitors and patriots in a fictitious Chinese city. In the preface to this naive and propagandistic tale, Lao She confessed that he never would have published it in normal times, blaming economic pressures for forcing its appearance. Also, in 1944 he published a collection of short stories entitled *P'in-hsueh chi* [collection of anaemic stories]. *Tung-hai Pa-shan chi* [sea and mountain], a collection of stories selected from *Huo-ch'e chi* and *P'in-hsueh chi*, appeared in 1945. During this period, he also began working on a trilogy, *Ssu-shih t'ung-t'ang* [four generations under one roof], a saga of Peiping during its eight years of occupation by the Japanese. The first two parts, *Huang-huo* [bewilderment] and *T'ou-sheng* [ignominy], were published in 1946. The third part, *Chi-huang* [famine] did not appear until 1950. Like *Huo-tsang*, the trilogy *Ssu-shih t'ung-t'ang* suffers from its conception as a species of propaganda.

In 1945 an English translation of *Lo-t'o Hsiang-tzu* by Evan King (pseudonym of Robert S. Ward) was published under the title *Rickshaw Boy*; it became a Book-of-the-Month Club selection and a best-seller in the United States. Lao She and the dramatist Ts'ao Yü (Wan Chia-pao, q.v.) went to the United States in 1946 on a cultural cooperation grant from the American Department of State. During their sojourn, Lao She gave lectures on Chinese literature and helped with the translation into English of several of his novels. *Rickshaw Boy* had been translated and published without his authorization, and he was unhappily surprised to discover that the tragic ending of the original had been discarded in favor of a happy reunion. *Li-hun* also presented problems. An unauthorized translation of this work by "Venerable Lodge" (a literal rendering of Lao She) had appeared, and Lao She had to seek legal redress before the authorized version, translated by Helena Kuo as *The Quest for Love of Lao Lee*, could be published. Lao She remained in the United States for three years, during which time he wrote his last novel, *The Drum Singers*, which was translated by Helena Kuo and published in 1952. This work never appeared in Chinese.

After returning to China, Lao She was given a formal welcome in Peking by the All-China Literary Workers Association. He soon set to work writing plays and participating in government literary organizations and committees. His play *Fang Chen-chu* was followed in early 1951 by *Lung-hsü kou* [dragon beard ditch], a drama concerning the successful reclamation of a slum district in Peking which received enthusiastic critical and popular acceptance. In 1951 P'eng Chen (q.v.), then the mayor of Peking, awarded Lao She the title of "People's Artist." He soon became chairman of the Peking Municipal Federation of Literature and Arts. In 1953 he became vice chairman of the Union of Chinese Writers, and in 1956 he was made vice chairman of the central work committee for the popularization of standard spoken Chinese. Throughout the 1950's he was active in the promotion of such political and cultural movements as the Hundred Flowers campaign. In March 1958 he was among the 50 writers and artists who issued a statement of determination to bring about a "great leap forward" in literary production.

Lao She also continued to be active as a writer. In addition to the plays already mentioned, he published *Pieh mi-hsin* [don't be superstitious] in 1951; *Lung-hsü kou* in 1953; the influential *Ho kung-jen t'ung-chih-men t'an hsieh-tso* [discussions on writings held with worker comrades] in 1954; *Wu-ming kao-ti yu-le ming* [that high ground has a name now], a collection of Korean war fiction, in 1955; *Hsi-wang Ch'ang-an* [looking westward toward Ch'angan], a satirical play, in 1956; and

Shih-wu kuan [fifteen strings of cash], based on a well-known theme in ancient Chinese literature, in 1956. *Ch'a-kuan* [the teahouse], a three-act play published in 1957, was a fine drama and a masterpiece of linguistic skill and command of various strata of the Peking dialect. In this play, Lao She attempted to summarize his human and political experience. Other works of Lao She were *Fu-hsing chi* [the lucky stars], a collection of historical and critical essays, published in 1958; the play *Ch'üan-chia fu* [the whole family happy], published in 1959; *Pao-ch'uan*, a children's play, which appeared in 1961; and *Ch'u-k'ou Ch'eng-chang* [essays on the use of literary language], published in 1964.

In October 1966 Lao She's death as a result of Red Guard harassment was reported.

Shu Hsin-ch'eng   舒 新 城
Orig. Wei-chou   維 周

Shu Hsin-ch'eng (5 July 1893–1960), editor and publisher. He was best known as the chief editor of the famous encyclopedic dictionary *Tz'u-hai*, published by the Chung-hua Book Company in 1936.

Born at Hsüp'u, Hunan, Shu Hsin-ch'eng came from a long line of impoverished tenant farmers. His father had been to school for a few years and had learned to read, write, and keep accounts. His mother, *née* Hsü, was known for her shrewd and frugal management of the family's meager income. She went to work soon after Shu Hsin-ch'eng's birth so that he would be freed by education from otherwise obligatory agricultural labor. By 1898 Shu's parents had saved enough money for him to begin his studies at the local primary school, where he received elementary training in the Chinese classics. He was betrothed in 1898 to a girl three years older than he, and she came to live in the Shu household in 1899. Because she and Shu did not get along, the engagement was broken in 1903, and the girl returned to her family. Shu studied at the clan school in 1903 and spent his spare time working in his father's newly opened general store and studying commercial accounting. In 1904 the clan school was moved to the mountains of western Hunan, where Shu enjoyed greater freedom from parental control.

In 1905 Shu Hsin-ch'eng left the clan school to study with a scholar at Shuitung named Chang Huan-ch'üan. Chang did not ask his students to compose traditional eight-part essays; instead, he explained to them the meanings of the classics and their relevance to current events. He also introduced them to such topical publications as the *Hsin-min ts'ung-pao* (*see* Liang Ch'i-ch'ao). Under Chang's guidance, Shu's education progressed rapidly, and the influence of this remarkable teacher probably was a cause of Shu's interest in education as a profession and a subject of study. In 1907 Shu was admitted by examination to the tuition-free Lu-liang Academy, which in 1908 became a prefectural higher primary school. Because his scholastic level was higher than that attained by most of his classmates, he spent most of his time reading political tracts and novels, training in Chinese boxing, and practicing calligraphy, seal carving, and painting. He remained at this school until April 1911, when he was dismissed for leading a student strike and demanding that the school provide real instead of dummy rifles for military training.

Shu Hsin-ch'eng submitted to an arranged marriage in the winter of 1911. The match was not a happy one, owing largely to Shu's mother's strict supervision of her new daughter-in-law. In 1912 Shu sent his wife home to her family and went to Ch'angte, where he studied for several months at a teacher-training school. After spending the winter of 1912 in Changsha, he went to Wuchang in June 1913 and entered the Hunan Higher Normal School. To obtain his first term's tuition he sold his winter bedding and clothing as well as samples of his calligraphy. After being graduated from the Higher Normal School in 1917, he moved to Changsha, where he was reunited with his wife.

At Changsha, Shu taught for a while at the Tui-tse Middle School and spent much of his time in the library of the local YMCA. He also worked for the *Hu-nan jih-pao* [Hunan daily], which he had helped to found in 1916. In 1918 he became a Presbyterian and an instructor in education at the Fu-hsiang Girls School, a Presbyterian institution. He also served as director of social services at the Changsha YMCA and as instructor in music at the Provincial First Middle School, but he left both of these jobs in 1919 to devote all his energies to teaching at Fu-hsiang, where he had been appointed dean of studies. In November 1919, however, he was obliged to resign after coming into conflict with the American missionary staff over an indignant article he had contributed to *Hsüeh-teng* in which he had denounced the staff's action in dismissing a student from the school because she had received a letter from a male cousin. About this time, he also left the Presbyterian Church.

Soon after his departure from the Fu-hsiang Girls School, Shu joined with some friends to found the *Hu-nan chiao-yü yüeh-k'an* [Hunan education monthly], which they were obliged to publish clandestinely because of the oppressive censorship rules then being enforced by the military governor of Hunan, Chang Ching-yao. Among the contributors to this magazine was Mao Tse-tung. Publication of the *Hu-nan chiao-yü yüeh-k'an* ceased after only five issues. Shu, possibly to avoid unpleasant political repercussions, left Changsha in June 1920 for Shanghai, where he joined the staff of the *Shih-shih hsin-pao (China Times)*. After Chang Ching-yao was overthrown that summer by T'an Yen-k'ai (q.v.), Shu returned to Changsha, where he secured a teaching job at the First Provincial Normal School. In June 1921 Chang Tung-sun (q.v.), the editor of the *China Times* and the director of studies at the Chung-kuo kung-hsueh (China Institute) in Woosung, invited Shu to take charge of the institute's middle school. Shu accepted the invitation and went to Woosung, where he soon became involved in a bitter dispute that resulted in a school strike. With its settlement after long negotiating sessions, Shu decided to put into practice some of the educational theories he most admired, notably the Dalton Plan. This program of progressive education, which had been introduced by Helen Parkhurst in the school system of Dalton, Massachusetts, in 1919, emphasized the necessity for classroom teaching according to the varying requirements of individual students and subdivided the work of the traditional curriculum into contract units for individual completion. Near the end of 1922, however, increased opposition to the Dalton Plan among his colleagues at Woosung forced Shu to resign. Despite this unhappy ending, Shu's 18-month sojourn at Woosung was important to his later career, for he came to know such prominent intellectuals as Chang

Po-ling, Yeh Sheng-t'ao, and Chu Tzu-ch'ing (qq.v.). Another important acquaintance made during this period was that of K'uei Lu-fei, the founder of the Chung-hua Book Company in Shanghai.

In 1923 Shu taught at the Middle School of Tung-nan University and at the Provincial Middle School in Nanking. In the summer of 1924 he made a lecture tour of 35 schools in Kiangsu, Anhwei, and Chekiang to urge adoption of the Dalton Plan. Later that year, he published a book on the plan entitled *Tao-erh-tun-chih yen-chiu-chi* [studies on the Dalton plan]. These activities resulted in his appointment in October 1924 as professor of educational methods and psychology at the Chengtu Higher Normal School. Reactionary colleagues at the school seized on the fact that a girl student, Liu Fang, visited Shu often, and they cast aspersions on his character. Although the student body supported him, the pressures on him became such that he fled to Nanking in June 1925. Despite offers from the Honan Normal School and the Normal University of Peking, he decided to give up teaching and enter publishing.

As early as 1924 K'uei Lu-fei of the Chung-hua Book Company had invited Shu to become editor in chief of the Chung-hua Book Company's middle school textbook division. Shu had refused this offer but had accepted an invitation to write a series of primers for adults, *Kung-min tu-pen* [the citizen's reader]. In 1925 Shu received and declined another offer from K'uei Lu-fei. He spent the next three years writing and publishing books based on his research and lectures on education. These included *Chung-kuo chiao-yü chih-nan* [a guide for Chinese education] and *Chiao-yü ts'ung-kao* [articles on education], both of 1925; *Shou-hui chiao-yü-ch'üan yün-tung* [the movement to regain educational sovereignty] and *Chin-tai Chung-kuo liu-hsüeh-shih* [history of study abroad in modern China], both of 1927; and *Chiao-yü t'ung-lun* [the complete theory of education], *Chung-kuo hsin-chiao-yü kai-k'uang* [the situation of China's new education], *Chung-kuo chiao-yü tz'u-tien* [dictionary of Chinese education], *Chin-tai Chung-kuo chiao-yü shih-liao* [materials toward a history of education in China in modern times], and *Chin-tai Chung-kuo chiao-yü ssu-hsiang-shih* [a history of educational thought in modern China], all of 1928. Having completed these works, Shu accepted an offer from the Chung-hua Book Company to become chief of the editorial board and editor in chief of the encyclopedic dictionary *Tz'u-hai* [sea of words].

China's first encyclopedic dictionary, the *Tz'u-yüan* [fountain of words], edited by Liu Erh-k'uei of the Commercial Press, had been published in 1915. Its instant success inspired other publishing companies to undertake similar projects. The Chung-hua Book Company began work on an encyclopedic dictionary in 1915, but very little had been accomplished by the time Shu assumed charge of it. At first, Shu's other duties at Chung-hua impeded his participation in the project, but after 1930 he was able to devote his full attention to it. Working with a team of 50 associate editors, Shu planned a reference book which would be both larger and more selective than the *Tz'u-yüan*. As published in two volumes in 1936, the *Tz'u-hai* contained 13,000 characters and well over 100,000 phrases; it covered modern drama, fiction, and slang as well as more traditional fields; and it included many Sino-Japanese coinages. In format also the *Tz'u-hai* contained many valuable innovations. A one-volume edition appeared in 1947.

During his years as editor of the *Tz'u-hai* Shu Hsin-ch'eng also managed to continue his own writing. In 1930 he wrote the *Hsien-tai chiao-yü fang-fa* [modern methods of education] and edited the *Chung-hua pai-k'o tz'u-tien* [Chung-hua encyclopedic dictionary], a brief compendium of technical terms used in various academic fields. In 1931 he wrote *Chih ch'ing-nien shu—t'ao-lun chi-chien kuan-yü tu-shu-ti shih* [letters to young readers—concerning some matters related to study], and *Chung-kuo chiao-yü chien-she fang-chen* [a policy for the reconstruction of Chinese education]. In 1936 he published a book of memoirs, *K'uang-ku-lu* [looking back in anger], and a volume of travel sketches, *Shu-yu hsin-ying* [impressions of Szechwan].

Shu remained in Shanghai throughout the Sino-Japanese war except for a brief trip to Hong Kong in 1939. In 1945 he published two more books: another volume of memoirs, *Chiao-yü ho wo* [education and me], and a second travel book, *Man-yu jih-chi* [diary of a leisurely ramble]. He also published his collected letters for the previous decade under the title *Shih-nien shu*. Shu remained in China after the Communists took power in 1949, and in 1954 he served as a delegate from Hunan to the National People's Congress. He served in a similar capacity in 1959, this time as a Shanghai delegate. Shu's last years were devoted to the compilation of source materials bearing on the history of Chinese education between the Opium War and the May Fourth Movement (published in 1961 as *Chung-kuo chin-tai chiao-yü shih tzu-liao* [materials toward a history of education in modern China]). Shu Hsin-ch'eng died in 1960. He was survived by Liu Fang, whom he had married in 1931, four years after the death of his first wife.

Siu, Fat-sing: *see* HSIAO FO-CH'ENG.

Soong family

The Soong family, often regarded as republican China's first family, emerged in a single generation from obscurity to prominence in the political, economic, and social life of China. T. V. Soong instituted many important reforms in the financial structures associated with the National Government and became an important link between China and Western political and financial men. The Soong sisters, Ai-ling, Ch'ing-ling, and Mei-ling, became the wives, respectively, of H. H. K'ung, Sun Yat-sen, and Chiang Kai-shek.

The origins of the Soong family were as marginal as its later rise was spectacular (for details, *see* Charles Jones Soong). The eight years Charles Jones Soong spent in the United States as a youth laid the foundations for various relationships with Americans in China. However, Soong became so Westernized during this period that, after his arrival in Shanghai, he had to study local Chinese customs and dialects before he could perform effectively as a Methodist missionary in the lower Yangtze valley. After he was appointed to the K'winsan circuit in the Soochow district, he renewed his acquaintance with New Shan-chow, whom he had met in Boston. New, a brother of W. S. New (Niu Hui-sheng, q.v.), had married one of the three daughters of the Ni family of Yuyao, Chekiang. They were descendants of Hsü Kuang-ch'i (ECCP, I, 316–19), one of the first

Chinese converts to Christianity. New Shan-chow introduced Charles Jones Soong to his sister-in-law Ni Kwei-tseng (1869–23 July 1931). She had been educated at home by tutors and at the Pei-wan Girls Higher School. That her home environment had been marked by Western influences was indicated by her fondness for playing the piano. Soong's new social status, buttressed by his Christian training in the United States, was confirmed when his proposal of marriage to Ni Kwei-tseng received her family's approval. They were married in 1887 in a ceremony performed by Clarence Reid, a Southern Methodist missionary. Their first child, Ai-ling, was born in 1890; a second daughter, Ch'ing-ling, arrived in 1892.

Financial pressures created by his growing family responsibilities and conflict with his superintendent, Dr. Young J. Allen, caused Soong to turn from missionary work to business in 1892. He remained active in Methodist affairs in Shanghai, however, and one of his enterprises was the Mei-hua Shu-kuan [Sino-American press], which published Chinese editions of the Bible and translations of religious tracts. Another daughter, Mei-ling, and three sons, Tzu-wen (T. V.), Tzu-liang (T. L.), and Tzu-an (T. A.), were born into the Soong family in the next decade.

In 1905 Charles Jones Soong went briefly to the United States to enroll his eldest daughter at Wesleyan College for Women, a Methodist institution in Macon, Georgia. Three years later, Ch'ing-ling and Mei-ling joined their sister in Georgia. Ch'ing-ling became a college student, and Mei-ling studied privately until she was old enough to go north and become a member of the class of 1917 at Wellesley. By that time, T. V. Soong had enrolled at Harvard, from which he was graduated in 1915. All of the Soong children received their higher education in the United States. T. L. Soong was graduated from Vanderbilt in 1921, and T. A. Soong received a B.A. degree from Harvard in 1928.

Soon after the Chinese republic was established, the Soong family became directly involved in Chinese political affairs. After discussions in 1912 between Charles Jones Soong and Sun Yat-sen, who had become acquainted in 1894, Soong Ai-ling, who had returned to Shanghai in 1909, became Sun's English-language secretary. The two elder Soongs and Ai-ling accompanied Sun to Japan after the so-called second revolution of 1913. When Ai-ling left Sun's entourage to marry H. H. K'ung (q.v.), she was replaced by her sister Ch'ing-ling, who married Sun Yat-sen in October 1914.

With the death of Charles Jones Soong in May 1918, his widow assumed direction of the Shanghai household. Although her English was limited, Mrs. Soong made many friends among the Western missionaries. She participated in charitable activities and was a devoted worker at Allen Memorial Church in Shanghai. At this time, T. V. Soong and Soong Mei-ling were in Shanghai, and Soong Ch'ing-ling moved between Canton and Shanghai as her husband's political fortunes fluctuated. Soong Ai-ling and H. H. K'ung were based in K'ung's native Shansi province. He divided his time between a prosperous family business and the affairs of the Ming-hsien School, which in 1919 became affiliated with Oberlin College.

In the early 1920's H. H. K'ung began to work for the Kuomintang; and T. V. Soong moved to Canton in 1923 to participate in the republican government and to strengthen its shaky financial structure. The final illness of Sun Yat-sen in early 1925 brought most members of the Soong family to Peking to attend him. After Sun's death on 12 March, Soong Mei-ling and Eva Macmillan, registrar of the Peking Union Medical College, made the arrangements for the private Christian funeral service that was held in the college chapel a week later. The death of Sun Yat-sen created a succession crisis within the Kuomintang and gave rise to factionalism which eventually split the Soong family itself.

During Sun Yat-sen's lifetime, Soong Ch'ing-ling had not been active in political affairs. As the living symbol of the founder of the Chinese republic, however, she was thrust into politics at a time when the Kuomintang was splitting into factions and the Kuomintang-Communist alliance was becoming fragile. The situation was complicated by the emergence of Chiang Kai-shek as the dominant military leader of the Northern Expedition launched from Canton in the summer of 1926. By the end of that year, both Soong Ch'ing-ling and T. V. Soong were in Wuhan, participating in the joint Kuomintang-Communist regime established there. The tumultuous events of 1927 increased the frictions that had developed within the Soong family, and the situation became critical when Chiang Kai-shek made a proposal of marriage to Soong Mei-ling, whom he had met in 1924 at Sun Yat-sen's home in Canton. Chiang, who was married and who was not a Christian, hardly seemed an appropriate suitor for a Wellesley alumna of Christian missionary background who was one of Shanghai's most attractive and eligible socialites. The union was strongly supported by Soong Ai-ling, but it was vigorously opposed by Soong Ch'ing-ling, who left China in August 1927 for Moscow because she believed that the new Kuomintang policies were perversions of her husband's principles. Chiang Kai-shek finally won the all-important approval of Mrs. Charles Jones Soong, and he and Soong Mei-ling were married in December 1927 at Shanghai.

The years 1928–36 in China marked a period of unprecedented effort at national unification, modernization, and reform under the auspices of the Kuomintang. T. V. Soong became minister of finance in the National Government at Nanking in 1928, and he enabled that regime to secure the financial support of the leading Chinese bankers of the lower Yangtze provinces. He also worked to gain tariff autonomy for China and to abolish obstructive internal tax restrictions. Soong Ai-ling was regarded as a power behind her husband, H. H. K'ung, who then served as minister of industry and commerce at Nanking. But the key to influence over Chiang Kai-shek was held by Soong Mei-ling, who quickly enlarged the scope of her impressive abilities as civic activist and club woman from Shanghai to the Chinese nation. Only Soong Ch'ing-ling remained adamant in opposing the new leadership of the Kuomintang. She remained in the Soviet Union until 1929, when she returned to China to attend the state burial of her husband at Nanking.

In order to marry Soong Mei-ling, Chiang Kai-shek had promised that he would investigate Christianity. He was baptized by Z. T. Kaung (Chiang Ch'ang-ch'uan) at Allen Memorial Church in Shanghai on 23 October 1930. Soong Mei-ling stood beside her husband at that ceremony and repeated vows with him to dramatize their joint dedication to Christian principles and to the rejuvenation of China. Chiang's baptism constituted a triumph for his mother-in-law, who had elicited the promise to study Christianity from him three years earlier. Mrs. Soong, who was less Westernized than her late husband, to some extent based her appraisal of Chiang Kai-shek on the fact that they both were natives of Chekiang. Some informed observers believed that Chiang was her favorite son-in-law. Not long after the baptism, in July 1931, Mrs. Soong died at her summer home at Tsingtao.

From 1932 to 1937 Soong Ch'ing-ling resided in Shanghai. She steadfastly opposed Chiang Kai-shek and the Nanking-based Kuomintang on the grounds that their political policies were reactionary; their economic measures, superficial; and their social programs, repressive. These charges (which were echoed by the Communists) notwithstanding, the National Government did effect reforms in China during the years when members of the Soong family held official posts at Nanking. T. V. Soong played a major role in the establishment and direction of public finance until the autumn of 1933, when he resigned because of his opposition to soaring military expenditures and to floating bond issues to finance economically unproductive military campaigns against Chiang Kai-shek's opponents. H. H. K'ung succeeded his brother-in-law and held the top financial post in the National Government for a decade thereafter. In 1934 the so-called New Life Movement was launched, and it stressed Christian as well as traditional Chinese principles, thus reflecting the influence of Soong Mei-ling in the National Government. She also recruited into government service a number of American-educated Chinese who had Protestant backgrounds and outlooks.

The Sian Incident of December 1936 (*see* Chang Hsueh-liang; Chiang Kai-shek) created a new crisis for the Soong family as well as for the Kuomintang. While T. V. Soong and Soong Mei-ling participated in the negotiations that led to Chiang's release and, paradoxically, to confirmation of his role as China's wartime leader, H. H. K'ung temporarily assumed political authority at Nanking by order of the Central Political Council. The united front and the spirit of patriotism after 1937 even led to a degree of reconciliation among the Soong sisters. In the spring of 1940 they flew together from Hong Kong to Chungking, where Soong Ch'ing-ling was the guest of honor at a lawn party given by Chiang Kai-shek. The influence of the Soong family on the style of political life in Nationalist China was strongest in the early 1940's. In particular, T. V. Soong began to emerge once again as a prominent figure about 1940. After negotiating credits in the United States, he flew to Chungking in 1942 to become minister of foreign affairs. About this time, Wei Tao-ming (q.v.), whose wife, Cheng Yü-hsiu (q.v.), was a close friend of Soong Mei-ling, became ambassador to the United States. T. V. Soong continued to be a major figure in China's diplomacy and international relations throughout the Second World War. During these years, many of the government-related business enterprises in which T. V. Soong had important interests were directed by his two younger brothers.

The image of the Soong family was at its best abroad, at least in North America, in 1942–43, when Soong Mei-ling made a triumphal and much-publicized trip to the United States and Canada to win popular support for Nationalist China and Chiang Kai-shek. The highlights of her journey were an address to a joint session of the United States Congress in February 1943 and an address to the Canadian Parliament in June of that year. After her return to Chungking in the summer of 1943, Soong Mei-ling continued to function as her husband's English interpreter and adviser in wartime dealings with Western officials.

At war's end, T. V. Soong became president of the Executive Yuan and chairman of the Supreme National Economic Council. The postwar period, however, brought a general decline in the influence of the Soong family. H. H. K'ung, then nearly 65, in effect retired from public life. T. V. Soong, now the target of widespread criticism because of the deteriorating economic situation in Nationalist-controlled areas, resigned to become governor of Kwangtung in September 1947. Soong Mei-ling's magic touch also failed, and a whirlwind flight to Washington late in 1948 on a mission to secure American aid had no result. Soong Ch'ing-ling remained at her home in Shanghai, becoming the moving spirit in the China Welfare Fund, which channeled funds to Communist-related organizations, and the center of a small group of people who were opposed to Chiang Kai-shek and who supported the policies of Mao Tse-tung. H. H. K'ung and his wife moved to the United States in 1948, for Soong Ai-ling had become ill.

With the establishment of the Central People's Government at Peking in October 1949, Soong Ch'ing-ling was rewarded with a number of official posts. Her role in the People's Republic of China after 1949 was basically symbolic, representing the continuity of Sun Yat-sen's revolutionary movement and the Chinese Communist revolution. Soong Mei-ling left the United States in January 1950 to join her husband in Taiwan. H. H. K'ung and his wife remained in the United States, although K'ung made two trips to Taiwan before his death in August 1967. T. V. Soong and T. L. Soong also established residence in the United States. T. A. Soong served as chairman of the board of directors of the Bank of Canton; he traveled frequently between San Francisco, where he maintained a residence, and Hong Kong, where the bank was registered. He died in February 1969.

The fortunes of the Soong family reflect the social reorientation of republican China during the period between the world wars. Within the context of Chinese politics, the Soongs' rise to power was not unrelated to the fact that they had family roots in two provinces that were of key importance in Kuomintang politics —Kwangtung and Chekiang. That rise also was spurred by Soong Ch'ing-ling's marriage to Sun Yat-sen. Without that relationship, it is doubtful that other members of the family could have achieved such a high level of prominence as they did. On the other hand, it is also doubtful that the political leaders who married into the family could have established firmly based governments without the cooperation of the family's financial men, especially T. V. Soong. The prominence of the Soong family also was related to its personal ties to the United States through education and religion. However, the prominence of the Soong family in public life was not sustained into the next generation. The two most prominent Soong sisters, Ch'ing-ling and Mei-ling, were childless; the children of Soong Ai-ling made no impact on the affairs of China; and the three daughters of T. V. Soong married Chinese who lived outside China and outside the mainstream of Chinese affairs.

Soong, Charles Jones

Orig. Han Chiao-shun
Alt. Sung Chia-shu   宋 嘉 樹
      Sung Yao-ju   耀 如
      Soon Chai-jui

Charles Jones Soong (1866–3 May 1918), American-trained missionary who became a successful businessman and industrialist in Shanghai as well as the patriarch of the influential Soong family.

The Wench'ang district of the island of Hainan, off the coast of Kwangtung province, was the native place of Charles Jones Soong. He was the youngest of three sons born to Han Hung-i, who, like many other poor people in Kwangtung, eventually sent his boys abroad to work. About 1875 Charles Jones Soong was sent to the East Indies with one of his brothers. Three years later, a childless maternal uncle adopted him, took him to the United States, and had his name changed from Han Chiao-shun to Soon Chai-jui. After working for a time as an apprentice in his adoptive father's tea and silk shop in Boston, he decided to run away.

For many years it was believed that the young Soong stowed away on the American revenue cutter Colfax in Boston harbor and that the ship's captain, Charles Jones, employed him as a cabin boy, converted him to Christianity, and made arrangements for his higher education. According to this story, the boy adopted the Christian names Charles Jones at the time of his baptism as an expression of gratitude to his benefactor. Through repetition, this story came to be accepted as fact, and it was not disproved until 1949, when Ensign A. Tourtellot, a journalist who had served in the United States Coast Guard during the Second World War, published an article entitled "C. J. Soong and the U.S. Coast Guard" (U.S. Naval Institute, *Proceedings*, Volume 75). This article established that Soong shipped aboard the American revenue cutter Albert Gallatin at Boston early in 1879. Captain Eric Gabrielson, the commanding officer, enlisted him as a cabin boy. Thus, Soong became a member of the Coast Guard; his name first appeared on the muster list on 8 January 1879. In May 1880 Captain Gabrielson was transferred to the cutter Schuyler Colfax, based at Wilmington, North Carolina. Soong requested a discharge in July and made his way to North Carolina, where he joined Captain Gabrielson and reenlisted on 1 August. Gabrielson, a devout Methodist, talked to him about Christianity and took him to church whenever the cutter was in port. On 7 November 1880 the boy was baptized at the Fifth Street Methodist Church in Wilmington by the Reverend Thomas Page Ricaud. At that time he took the name Charles Jones Soon (the final letter was not added until he returned to China in 1886).

Charles Jones Soong, who had expressed his wish to secure an education and to return to China as a missionary, received the help of General Julian S. Carr, a prosperous Durham manufacturer who decided to finance his education. Captain Gabrielson arranged for Soong's discharge from the Coast Guard, and in April 1881 Soong became "a special and preparatory student" at Trinity College, the forerunner of Duke University. At Trinity, which then had two buildings, six professors, and fewer than 200 students, Soong studied under Dr. Braxton Craven, its president. In the autumn of 1882 Soong entered the theological seminary of Vanderbilt University in Nashville, Tennessee. During his summer vacations he made and sold hammocks and assisted ministers at revival services in Tennessee and North Carolina. After being graduated in the spring of 1885, he expressed a desire to remain in the United States so that he could study medicine, saying that this knowledge would increase his usefulness as a missionary. General Carr was willing to pay for his medical studies, but Bishop Holland N. McTyeire, then the president of the board of trust of Vanderbilt, opposed this idea on the grounds that Soong might become used to the comfortable life he lived in the United States and might lose all desire to live the more difficult life of a missionary in China. Soong was admitted to the North Carolina Annual Conference of the Methodist Episcopal Church (South). In response to a special request from Bishop McTyeire, Soong was ordained by the conference and appointed a missionary to China.

After arriving in Shanghai in January 1886, Charles Jones Soong began to study the local customs and dialect. This study was necessary not only because his native dialect was different from that of Shanghai but also because he had become thoroughly Americanized—so thoroughly that he never recovered his taste for Chinese food, and he later sent all six of his children to the United States for their educations. When the China Mission Conference held its inaugural session in November 1886, Charles Jones Soong was appointed to the K'winsan circuit in the Soochow district. The following year, he married Ni Kwei-tseng (1869–23 July 1931), a descendant of Hsü Kuang-ch'i (ECCP, I, 316–19), a prominent official of the early Ch'ing period and one of the first Chinese converts to Christianity. After being transferred to the Ts'ipao circuit in the Shanghai district in 1889, Soong found time to teach English in several schools. Among his students was Hu Shih (q.v.).

Charles Jones Soong continued to serve as a missionary until 1892, when he resigned. Apparently, there were two primary reasons for his resignation: conflict with his superintendent and money. According to Soong, Dr. Young J. Allen, his superintendent and the editor of the *Wan-kuo kung-pao* (*The Globe Magazine*), lacked Christian charity in dealing with his subordinates; for example, he refused Soong permission to visit his parents. Allen also had a low opinion of Soong's education and considered him a "denationalized Chinaman." By 1892 the Soongs had one child and were awaiting the birth of a second; Soong believed and wrote to an American friend that he could not support himself and his family "with about $15.00 of U.S. money per month."

Although he resigned from missionary work, Charles Jones Soong continued to be a devout and active Christian. He founded a publishing house, the Mei-hua Shu-kuan [Sino-American press], which published Chinese editions of the Bible. Although some of his highly successful commercial activities were unrelated to religious pursuits—for instance, he became manager of the Fou Foong Flour Mill in Shanghai—they helped him to achieve greater prominence and influence as a Methodist lay leader in Shanghai. A founder of the YMCA in China and a close associate of the American Bible Society in Shanghai, Soong also taught Sunday-school classes and gave generous financial support to the Methodist Church. His wife was noted in Shanghai for her church work, and their home was always open to foreign missionaries.

In addition to being a lay leader and a businessman, Charles Jones Soong was credited with being a revolutionary. About 1894 he met Sun Yat-sen in Shanghai and became one of the first Chinese to hear Sun's revolutionary ideas. Although details about the extent of his participation in the revolutionary movement are lacking, he was known to be an ardent supporter and close friend of Sun Yat-sen. After the republic was established in 1912, his eldest daughter, Soong Ai-ling, became Sun's English secretary. Soong, his wife, and Ai-ling accompanied Sun to Japan in 1913. After Ai-ling married H. H. K'ung (q.v.), the second daughter, Soong Ch'ing-ling (q.v.), became Sun's English secretary. She and Sun were married on 25 October 1914.

Although Charles Jones Soong had great affection for the United States, he made only one trip there after 1896. He went to Durham in 1905 to spend a few weeks with his old friends and benefactors and to arrange for his eldest daughter's college education. When General Carr returned the visit in 1916, he was given splendid receptions in Shanghai by Soong's two sons-in-law, Sun Yat-sen and H. H. K'ung.

Charles Jones Soong died of stomach cancer on 3 May 1918 in Shanghai. He was survived by his wife and their six children: Ai-ling, Ch'ing-ling, Tzu-wen (T. V. Soong, q.v.), Mei-ling (Soong Mei-ling, q.v.), Tzu-liang, and Tzu-an (for further information about the importance of the Soongs as a family in China, *see* the article on the Soong family). On 1 November 1942 his contributions to Methodism and to China were recognized in the United States with the dedication of the Charles Jones Soong Memorial Building of the Fifth Avenue Methodist Church in Wilmington, North Carolina.

Soong Ch'ing-ling　　　宋慶齡

Soong Ch'ing-ling (1892–), wife of Sun Yat-sen. She was active in social welfare work, and after 1949 she held a variety of posts in the People's Republic of China.

The second daughter of Charles Jones Soong (q.v.), Soong Ch'ing-ling was born in Shanghai. Like her elder sister, Soong Ai-ling, she received her early education at the fashionable McTyeire School for Girls. In 1908 she accompanied her younger sister, Soong Mei-ling (q.v.), to the United States and entered Wesleyan College for Women, a Methodist institution in Macon, Georgia, where Soong Ai-ling was a senior. In 1913, having been graduated from Wesleyan, Soong Ch'ing-ling returned to China.

By the time of Soong Ch'ing-ling's return, Soong Ai-ling had become Sun Yat-sen's English-language secretary. Sun's political fortunes were at a low ebb. Yuan Shih-k'ai had turned against the revolutionaries, and the so-called second revolution launched by the republican forces against Yuan had failed almost as soon as it had begun in mid-1913. Sun had to leave China to take refuge in Japan in August 1913. When Soong Ai-ling decided to marry H. H. K'ung (q.v.) in Tokyo, she relinquished her position in Sun's entourage to Soong Ch'ing-ling. Direct contact with Sun Yat-sen soon transformed admiration and respect into love. Soong Ch'ing-ling agreed to marry Sun even though he was 26 years her senior and had two children from a previous marriage. The ceremony took place on 25 October 1914 in Tokyo.

From the time of their marriage until Sun Yat-sen's death in 1925, Soong Ch'ing-ling was his constant companion, aide, and confidante. As the wife of Sun Yat-sen, she spent most of her married life in Shanghai and Canton as Sun traveled between the two cities in his struggle against a variety of political and military opponents. For a time, Sun was actively in control of the revolutionary military regime at Canton, established as a center of political opposition to the government at Peking. This period was followed by an interlude of enforced retirement in his Rue Moliere residence in the French concession at Shanghai, where Sun devoted much attention to formulation and refinement of his political doctrines. During these ten years, Soong Ch'ing-ling played the varied roles of political assistant, personal secretary, and wife with grace and dignity.

As the ranking woman associated with the government in south China, Soong Ch'ing-ling had a harrowing experience at Canton in June 1922. Toward the end of 1920, with the aid of the army of Ch'en Chiung-ming (q.v.), Sun Yat-sen had returned to Canton to resume charge of the revolutionary government there.

In May 1921 he assumed the post of president extraordinary of China on election by the rump parliament meeting in Canton. He then turned to planning a northern expedition; but Ch'en Chiung-ming, his chief military lieutenant, opposed the scheme. The disagreement eventually led to Ch'en's open revolt. In the early hours of 16 June 1922, shortly after midnight, the rebels laid siege to Sun's presidential headquarters. Sun, unprepared, had to rely on his small bodyguard, which was no match for the attackers. In her reminiscences, Soong Ch'ing-ling recalled that she was awakened by her husband after he received the report of the siege. She refused to leave the house with him because her presence might complicate his escape, and she insisted that he leave first and proceed to the gunboat Yung-feng for safety. Sun left hurriedly for the safety of a warship. By then, Ch'en Chiung-ming's forces had reached the presidential mansion which was located on a small hill. Soong Ch'ing-ling remained there until noon on 16 June, when three guards escorted her out of the house by way of the back courtyard. They mixed with the crowd that had gathered, and the few possessions she carried soon were taken by the rebel soldiers. Fortunately, Soong Ch'ing-ling was not identified, and she eventually took shelter in a small house, where she collapsed from the strain. She finally reached safety in Shameen and went to Whampoa on 18 June.

Sun Yat-sen had to leave the warship for Shanghai again in August 1922. At that time, he started measures for a major reorganization of the Kuomintang. A manifesto in the name of the Kuomintang was issued on 1 January 1923 restating the Three People's Principles as the party's basic platform. Later in January, Sun had his historic meeting with the Soviet Union representative Adolf Joffe, and the two men issued a joint declaration. Soong Ch'ing-ling participated in all these events, but, being of a retiring character, she neither took part in politics nor expressed any opinion which would show her own political orientation at the time.

Meanwhile, forces loyal to Sun Yat-sen had ousted Ch'en Chiung-ming from Canton. Sun and his wife returned there, and once again Sun assumed charge of the military government, with the title of Generalissimo. The reorganization of the Kuomintang moved forward steadily, and the move was institutionalized at the party's first congress in January 1924. The establishment of the Whampoa Military Academy, with Chiang Kai-shek as president, soon followed. In August the Central Bank of China was inaugurated at Canton, and Soong Ch'ing-ling's younger brother, T. V. Soong (q.v.), was named its general manager.

Although Sun Yat-sen was again preparing for the long-awaited northern expedition from Canton, in November 1924 he accepted the invitation of the political and military leaders in Peking to pay a visit to north China to discuss national affairs. Accompanied by Soong Ch'ing-ling and a sizeable staff, which included Wang Ching-wei, Eugene Ch'en, Li Lieh-chün (qq.v.) and others, Sun left Canton on 13 November 1924, traveling to Peking by way of Hong Kong, Shanghai, and Japan. He arrived at Tientsin on 4 December. Then already ill, he proceeded to Peking for medical treatment, and he died there on 12 March 1925. From the time they left Canton in mid-November 1924 until his death, Soong Ch'ing-ling was constantly at the side of her husband. Her stepson, Sun Fo (q.v.), hastened to Peking at the news of Sun Yat-sen's serious illness, and he was with his father during his last days.

On his deathbed, Sun Yat-sen left a political will in which he called on his followers to continue his unfinished revolutionary work. He also left a family will bequeathing all his personal possessions and books, as well as his house in Shanghai, to Soong Ch'ing-ling.

While Sun Yat-sen lived, Soong Ch'ing-ling had not openly taken part in the political affairs of the day. In 1925, as the widow of the founder of the Chinese republic—the living representative, in a sense, of the leader of the Kuomintang —circumstances soon forced her to assume a more active political role. This change in role was also required because of signs of factionalism within the party which her husband had led. At the Second National Congress of the Kuomintang in January 1926, she was elected to the Central Executive Committee. Ho Hsiang-ning (q.v.), the widow of Liao Chung-k'ai (q.v.), was also elected to that group; while Ch'en Pi-chün (q.v.), the wife of Wang Ching-wei, was elected to the Central Supervisory Committee. Soong Ch'ing-ling was reelected to the Central Executive Committee of the Kuomintang at every successive congress

through the Sixth National Congress at Chungking in 1945, the last held on the mainland.

In November 1926, after the Northern Expedition had captured Wuhan, the National Government at Canton sent an advance party of five men—Sun Fo, Eugene Ch'en, T. V. Soong, Hsü Ch'ien (q.v.), and Comintern representative Michael Borodin—to Wuhan to investigate the question of moving the government there. Soong Ch'ing-ling accompanied the group, which proceeded northward by way of Nanchang, then recently captured by Chiang Kai-shek. The group was given a great welcome to Nanchang by Chiang, and it finally arrived at Wuhan by boat on 10 December 1926. Soong Ch'ing-ling herself preceded them by two days, for she flew by plane from Nanchang to Wuhan on 8 December.

On 13 December 1926 members of the Kuomintang Central Executive Committee and of the State Council of the National Government who were in Wuhan met and decided on the establishment of a joint council to serve as the interim authority pending the complete removal of the government to Wuhan. The joint council was headed by Hsü Ch'ien, and Soong Ch'ing-ling was a member. This post marked her first official participation in the government as distinguished from the party. In March 1927 the National Government was established in Wuhan, and Soong Ch'ing-ling became a member of the State Council.

By this time, differences between the Wuhan leaders and those who had moved forward from Nanchang to Nanking had become pronounced. Following the beginning of a purge of Communist elements at Shanghai and elsewhere in the lower Yangtze valley, a rival national government was set up in Nanking on 18 April 1927. Although Hu Han-min (q.v.) was chairman of that government, Chiang Kai-shek controlled it. For a time, the Wuhan and Nanking factions threatened to settle their differences on the battlefield. The situation was saved when the Wuhan group also started to rid itself of Communists. On 13 July 1927, the Chinese Communist party declared that it would withdraw from the Wuhan government, though its members would remain in the Kuomintang. The next day, ostensibly because of her disapproval of this Wuhan development, Soong Ch'ing-ling issued an announcement stating that she would no longer be actively associated with the new policies, which she believed were doing "violence to Sun Yat-sen's ideas and ideals." She then returned to her home in Shanghai. In late August, she slipped aboard a Russian steamer and sailed, together with Eugene Ch'en and others, to Vladivostok. The group then proceeded by train to Moscow. Judging from her public statement at Shanghai before she left for Moscow, it was clear that Soong Ch'ing-ling identified herself with the left-Kuomintang, the branch of the party which she regarded as the true bearer of Sun Yat-sen's spirit, and that she had become pro-Communist in her political outlook. When the Chinese Communists staged a revolt at Nanchang on 1 August 1927, they used the name of a so-called revolutionary committee to attempt to legitimize the action. The names of Soong Ch'ing-ling, Eugene Ch'en, and Teng Yen-ta (q.v.) were included on the list of committee members, but it was generally believed in China that Soong Ch'ing-ling had not authorized the use of her name.

Personal as well as political frustrations marked the year 1927 for Soong Ch'ing-ling. In December, her younger sister, Mei-ling, married Chiang Kai-shek. This union was as strongly opposed by Soong Ch'ing-ling as it was supported by Soong Ai-ling. Soong Ch'ing-ling remained in the Soviet Union for nearly two years. She returned to China by way of Berlin in May 1929 to attend the state burial of Sun Yat-sen in the impressive mausoleum built for him at Nanking. On the eve of her return, she issued a statement in which she made it clear that her attendance at the burial ceremony was not to be interpreted as in any sense implying a modification of her views. She said that she would continue to abstain from direct or indirect contact with the Kuomintang as long as its leadership was opposed to the so-called "three great policies" of Sun Yat-sen, namely, alliance with the Soviet Union, cooperation between the Kuomintang and members of the Chinese Communist party, and the advancement of the interests of Chinese workers and peasants.

After the burial ceremony, Soong Ch'ing-ling retired to Shanghai, but she remained there for only a short time. During 1930 and 1931 she toured Europe. She then returned to China, where she resided in Shanghai from 1932 through 1937. When Teng Yen-ta was arrested by the National Government late in 1931, she tried unsuccessfully to save his life. With Ts'ai Yuan-p'ei (q.v.) and others, she organized the China League for Civil Rights and constituted herself a champion for that cause. She also attempted to intervene on behalf of Chinese Communists arrested by the National Government, notably Ch'en Keng and Liao Ch'eng-chih (qq.v.). After the outbreak of the Sino-Japanese war in July 1937, Soong Ch'ing-ling moved to Hong Kong, where, in June 1938, she founded the China Defense League for wartime medical relief and child welfare work. Through the league organization, some outside medical aid was channeled to the Communist base areas in the hinterland of China. Notable in this connection was the International Peace Hospital, established in Shensi by a Canadian surgeon, Dr. Norman Bethune.

Although family relations among the Soongs remained strained for a number of years after 1927, the spirit of wartime patriotism led to a measure of reconciliation. In April 1940 Soong Ch'ing-ling and her two sisters flew from Hong Kong to the wartime capital of Chungking. There, as the widow of Sun Yat-sen, Soong Ch'ing-ling was honored at a lawn party given by Chiang Kai-shek. The three Soong sisters traveled about Chungking and nearby areas of Szechwan to visit schools and hospitals and to inspect orphanages and air defense dugouts.

At war's end, Soong Ch'ing-ling returned to Shanghai. In late 1945 she organized the China Welfare Fund, a continuation of the wartime China Defense League established in Hong Kong. Beneficiaries of the fund were virtually limited to Communist-related organizations. While living in Shanghai in the postwar period, Soong Ch'ing-ling also attracted a small but active group of Western admirers in China, all of whom were opposed to Chiang Kai-shek and the Nationalists and were increasingly sympathetic to the Chinese Communist cause. In 1948, when a Kuomintang splinter group was organized in Hong Kong as the Kuomintang Revolutionary Committee under the leadership of such prominent anti-Chiang figures as Li Chi-shen, Ho Hsiang-ning, Feng Yü-hsiang (qq.v.) and others, Soong Ch'ing-ling was named honorary chairman of the group.

In September 1949 Soong Ch'ing-ling was in Peiping as a delegate to the Chinese People's Political Consultative Conference "by special invitation." That meeting led to the establishment of the Central People's Government of the People's Republic of China. In the new political structure, Soong Ch'ing-ling became one of three non-Communist vice chairmen of the government (the other two being Li Chi-shen and Chang Lan). In 1954, when the Peking government underwent reorganization at the time of the adoption of a new national constitution, Chu Teh became the sole vice chairman of the government, and Soong Ch'ing-ling became a vice chairman of the standing committee of the National People's Congress, then headed by Liu Shao-ch'i. In the reorganization of 1959, when Liu Shao-ch'i succeeded Mao Tse-tung as chief of state, two vice chairmen, then both well into their seventies, were elected: Soong Ch'ing-ling and Tung Pi-wu (q.v.), who represented the eldest generation of leaders in the Chinese Communist movement.

Soong Ch'ing-ling was elected deputy, from the municipality of Shanghai, to the first National People's Congress in 1954; and she was reelected to the second (1958) and third (1964) congresses. She was vice chairman of the Sino-Soviet Friendship Association after 1949, and in 1954 she became chairman of that organization. After 1950 she served as chairman of the China Welfare Institute (the former China Welfare Fund), and after 1951 she was chairman of the Chinese People's National Committee for the Protection of Children. In 1957 she was made honorary chairman of the Women's Federation of China. In 1950, at the second World Peace Congress in Warsaw, she was elected a member of the World Peace Council. In 1951 she was awarded the Stalin Peace Prize.

In her various official capacities, Soong Ch'ing-ling made several trips outside China after 1950. In December 1952 she led the Chinese delegation to the meeting of the World Peace Congress in Vienna, and on her return journey to China, she was received by Stalin in Moscow in January 1953. From December 1955 to February 1956 she headed a Chinese mission to India, Burma, and Pakistan. Later in 1956 she led a Chinese delegation to Indonesia. In February 1964, as a vice chairman of the Central People's Government and accompanied by Chou En-lai as premier, she visited Ceylon.

Soong Ch'ing-ling's position at Peking after 1949 stemmed from her unique personal role as the widow of Sun Yat-sen and from the general Chinese Communist impulse to link the People's Republic of China with the earlier revolutionary movement symbolized by Sun. In important respects, Soong Ch'ing-ling was treated with great deference and respect, though her position was clearly symbolic. She lived in Shanghai, where the house left to her by Sun Yat-sen was thoroughly renovated by the Communist authorities shortly after they gained power in China. Occasionally she broadcast statements and public messages intended for consumption both within China and abroad. She also wrote occasional articles for the English-language magazine *China Reconstructs*, published by the China Welfare Institute. In 1953 a collection of her articles and speeches was published in English under the title *The Struggle for New China*.

The disruption associated with the so-called Cultural Revolution in China affected Soong Ch'ing-ling's life. In September 1966 there were reports that Red Guards accused her of living a luxurious life in contrast to that of common peasants and workers, and ransacked her house in Shanghai. During 1967, however, she made public appearances at Peking, where, in the absence of chief of state Liu Shao-ch'i, she received foreign visitors to China.

Soong Mei-ling   宋 美 齡
West. Mayling Soong

Soong Mei-ling (c. 1897–), wife of Chiang Kai-shek and a leader of Chinese women.

A native of the Wench'ang district of Hainan Island, Kwangtung, Soong Mei-ling was born in Shanghai. She was the fourth of six children and the youngest of the girls in her family. Because her father, Charles Jones Soong (q.v.), was an American-trained Methodist missionary as well as a moderately successful industrialist and merchant, she was brought up in a Christian and highly Americanized environment. She learned English at home and, at the age of five, she enrolled at the McTyeire School, a Methodist missionary school for girls from upper-class Chinese families in Shanghai. She reportedly left school a short time later because she was too young for dormitory life.

In 1908 Soong Mei-ling accompanied her elder sister Soong Ch'ing-ling (q.v.) to the United States. They went to Macon, Georgia, where the eldest sister, Soong Ai-ling, was a junior at Wesleyan College for Women. Because Soong Mei-ling was much too young to attend college, arrangements were made for her registration as a special student. She went with her sisters to Demarest, Georgia, in the summer of 1909 and remained there in the care of a Mrs. Moss, the mother of one of Ai-ling's classmates, to attend eighth grade at the preparatory school of Piedmont College. At the end of the school year, she returned to Macon, where she studied privately under Mrs. Margie Burks, a member of the Wesleyan faculty, for two years.

Soong Mei-ling was admitted to Wesleyan as a regular student in the autumn of 1912. The following year, she transferred to Wellesley College in Massachusetts because both of her sisters had left Georgia and because her brother T. V. Soong (q.v.) had enrolled at Harvard College. Her years in the South left a lasting impression on her speech, coloring her English with a soft Georgia accent. At Wellesley, she majored in English literature, with philosophy as her minor. Among her other courses were French, music, astronomy, history, botany, and Biblical history. In her senior year she was named a Durant Scholar, the highest academic distinction conferred by the college. Throughout this period, she spent her summers attending various summer schools and traveling to other parts of the United States.

By the time of her graduation in 1917, Soong Mei-ling had become thoroughly Americanized. She reportedly said that "the only thing Oriental about me is my face." Nevertheless, she returned to Shanghai, where she learned Chinese again and studied the Chinese classics. As befitted her social position as a Soong, she did church work, engaged in YWCA activities, became a member of a film-censoring committee, and became the first Chinese to be appointed to the child labor commission by the Shanghai Municipal Council.

Both of Soong Mei-ling's sisters had been married in 1914—Ai-ling to H. H. K'ung (q.v.) and Ch'ing-ling to Sun Yat-sen. It was at Sun's home in Canton that Soong Mei-ling met Chiang Kai-shek. He did not seem to be an appropriate suitor, for he was ten years older than she, married, and not a Christian. However, he was persistent. At the end of September 1927, after resigning from his government and military posts, Chiang went to Japan, where Soong Mei-ling's widowed mother was living, in an attempt to win Mei-ling's hand in marriage. He finally overcame the family's objections by promising to study Christianity, and he and Soong Mei-ling were married at Shanghai on 1 December 1927. After taking part in a Christian service in the Soong home at which David Yui (Yü Jih-chang, q.v.) officiated, they were married again in a Chinese ceremony at the Majestic Hotel, with Ts'ai Yuan-p'ei (q.v.) presiding.

After their marriage, Soong Mei-ling accompanied her husband on military campaigns, serving as his secretary and English interpreter. As Chiang became the dominant leader in China, she became a leader of Chinese women. She also held office as a member of the Legislative Yuan in 1930–32. Her influence on her husband was demonstrated by his conversion to Christianity on 23 October 1930. She also helped introduce him to Western culture and ideas. Chiang began to employ such Western advisers as W. H. Donald, an Australian who had been an adviser to Chang Hsueh-liang (q.v.), and such Chinese with Western training as J. L. Huang and K. C. Wu (Wu Kuo-chen, q.v.). In 1934, when Chiang inaugurated the New Life Movement, a program of moral reform based on traditional Chinese virtues, Soong Mei-ling directed its women's department and assumed other important responsibilities. She recruited Western missionaries in rural areas of China to promote the movement. Soong Mei-ling also was concerned with the welfare of military men and their dependants. In 1929 she had founded a school for the orphans of soldiers in the National Revolutionary Army, and she later had helped inaugurate the Officers Moral Endeavor Association to provide recreational activities for servicemen.

Early in 1936 Soong Mei-ling was appointed secretary general of the National Aeronautical Affairs Commission. In this post, she worked to create a modern and effective Chinese air force. During the Sian Incident of December 1936 (*see* Chiang Kai-shek; Chang Hsueh-liang) she acted with courage and determination. She had not accompanied her husband to Sian because of illness. However, when the news of his detention reached her in Shanghai, she immediately went to Nanking, where she used her official position and her influence to help prevent such anxious officials as Ho Ying-ch'in (q.v.) from taking drastic military action. She and H. H. K'ung pointed out that premature military action would endanger Chiang Kai-shek's life and might precipitate a civil war. She then flew to Sian, arriving there on 22 December. Three days later, Chiang Kai-shek was released. In 1937 Soong Mei-ling published a book about this incident, *Sian: A Coup d'Etat.*

The women's advisory council of the New Life Movement was formed under Soong Mei-ling's directorship in 1937. After the Sino-Japanese war began in July, the council trained young women for wartime jobs, established relief programs for refugees and centers for homeless children, and promoted industry by setting up small cooperative factories in rural areas. She also continued to serve as secretary general of the National Aeronautical Affairs Commission until March 1938, when she resigned because of ill health.

Soong Mei-ling also made important contributions to China's war effort through her presentation of her country's cause to Americans. She wrote articles for American magazines and made transoceanic broadcasts to the American people. In 1940 *China in Peace and War* and *This Is Our China* were published in the United States, and in 1941 *China Shall Rise Again* appeared. Soong Mei-ling reached the peak of her prestige in America in 1942–43, when she visited the United States. After arriving in New York on 27 November 1942 and spending two months at the Columbia Presbyterian Medical Center, she accepted an invitation from President and Mrs. Franklin D. Roosevelt to stay at the White House as their guest. On 18 February 1943 she became the first Chinese and the second woman (the other being Queen Wilhelmina of the Netherlands) to address a joint session of the United States Congress. She then traveled throughout the United States, raising funds and making public speeches to large audiences in such cities as New York, Boston, Chicago, Los Angeles, and San Francisco. Newspapers reported her "invasion" of America, saying that she was "taking the country by charm." Her grace and eloquence

helped her to become, as one commentator put it, "the personification of Free China." The effect of her visit was such that every year until 1967 her name appeared on American lists of the ten most admired women in the world. However, some Americans had reservations about her. Mrs. Franklin D. Roosevelt was quoted as saying that Soong Mei-ling "could talk very convincingly about democracy and its aims and ideals, but she hadn't any idea how to live it." After making a three-day trip to Canada in June, where she addressed the Canadian Parliament, Soong Mei-ling returned to China by way of the United States, arriving in Chungking on 4 July.

As cooperation between the United States and China increased during the Second World War, Soong Mei-ling assumed greater political responsibilities, serving as Chiang Kai-shek's interpreter and adviser in his dealings with American officials. She also accompanied him to the Cairo Conference in November 1943. Her actions even won the approval of General Joseph W. Stilwell, a bitter opponent of Chiang Kai-shek. In his diary, *The Stilwell Papers*, published in 1948, General Stilwell described her as "a clever, brainy woman" who had "great influence on Chiang Kai-shek, mostly along the right lines too."

Soong Mei-ling's political influence waned after the Second World War. However, in 1948 Chiang Kai-shek made a final attempt to obtain American aid for fighting the Chinese Communists, and he sent his wife to press the case. She arrived in Washington in November 1948, but, although she was greeted courteously by President Harry S. Truman and other American officials, she could do nothing to alter the American policy of non-involvement in the internal affairs of China. She remained in the United States until January 1950, by which time the National Government had been moved to Taiwan and the Central People's Government had been established at Peking by the victorious Chinese Communists.

In Taiwan, Soong Mei-ling devoted much of her time to directing the Chinese Women's Anti-Aggression League. She made four unofficial visits to the United States (August 1952 to March 1953, April 1954 to October 1954, May 1958 to June 1959, and August 1965 to October 1966) during which she sought medical treatment, visited friends and relatives, and acted as a goodwill ambassador and personal envoy of Chiang Kai-shek.

Honors conferred on Soong Mei-ling over the years included honorary degrees from such American colleges as Wesleyan College for Women and Wellesley College. She was the first and only Chinese woman to receive the highest military and civil decorations awarded by the National Government of China. She served as honorary chairman of such organizations as the American Bureau for Medical Aid to China and as a patron of the International Red Cross Society.

The speeches and writings of Soong Mei-ling were collected and published in Taiwan in 1965 as *Chiang fu-jen yen-lun hui-pien* [collected works of Madame Chiang]. Anecdotal material about her early life and family background is included in Emily Hahn's *The Soong Sisters*, which was published in 1941. Helene Kazangien's *Madame Chiang Kai-shek—Mailing Soong*, the revised edition of which appeared in 1943, is a short but comparatively accurate biography.

Soong, T. V.
Orig. Sung Tzu-wen   宋 子 文

T. V. Soong (4 December 1894–), Harvard-trained financier who was the prime mover in the establishment of a modern financial system in China. He served the National Government in such capacities as minister of finance, vice president and president of the Executive Yuan, governor of the Central Bank of China, and minister of foreign affairs. He also founded and developed such enterprises as the China Development Finance Corporation.

The third child and eldest son of Charles Jones Soong (q.v.), T. V. Soong was born in Shanghai. He received thorough training in both the Chinese classics and modern subjects while a student in the preparatory and college divisions of St. John's University and then went to the United States to enroll at Harvard College. After being graduated from Harvard in 1915 with a B.A. in economics, he went to New York, where he worked at the International Banking Corporation and took courses at Columbia University. He returned to China in 1917 and became secretary of the Han-yeh-p'ing iron and coal complex, which was composed of a steel mill at *Han*yang, iron mines at T*ayeh*, and coal mines at *P'ing*hsiang. Before long, he became active in trade and banking circles in Shanghai.

In October 1923 Sun Yat-sen, who had married T. V. Soong's elder sister Soong Ch'ing-ling (q.v.) in 1914, recruited T. V. Soong to serve as manager of the salt administration in Kwangtung and Kwangi, an important source of revenue for Sun's government. Sun then called on him to investigate the chaotic financial situation in Kwangtung in the hope that he could bring order to it. One result of this investigation was the establishment, in August 1924, of the Central Bank at Canton. Under T. V. Soong's management, the bank made immediate improvements in the financial situation, and in 1926 it undertook the financing of the early stage of the Northern Expedition. In addition to his responsibilities at the bank, Soong served with Chiang Kai-shek, T'an P'ing-shan, Sun Fo, and others on a committee for food control. As a relative of Sun Yat-sen, he was summoned to Peking in late January 1925 to witness Sun's last testament. He attended Sun's funeral in March 1925 before returning to south China.

T. V. Soong was named minister of finance in the newly established National Government at Canton in September 1925, a month after his predecessor, Liao Chung-k'ai (q.v.), had been assassinated. In January 1926, at the Second National Congress of the Kuomintang, he was elected to the Central Executive Committee and was named minister of commerce. Shortly thereafter, he was appointed to the National Government (State) Council. The year 1926 also saw Soong's baptism in international diplomacy: he was sent to Hong Kong to negotiate with British authorities about settlement of the anti-British strike that had paralyzed the colony for several months.

In November 1926, after the Northern Expedition forces had occupied Wuhan, the National Government decided to send a five-man delegation to Wuhan to investigate the possibility of moving the government there. In addition to T. V. Soong, the team included Eugene Ch'en, Hsü Ch'ien, Sun Fo (qq.v.), and Soviet adviser Borodin. Accompanied by Soong Ch'ing-ling, they traveled to Wuhan by way of Nanchang, where they held discussions with Chiang Kai-shek at his military headquarters. After the arrival of the Kuomintang leaders from Canton in December, it was decided at Wuhan to organize a provisional joint session of the Kuomintang Central Executive Committee and the National Government Council to serve as the interim authority pending transfer of the National Government to Wuhan. On 21 February 1927 it was announced that Wuhan would be the seat of the National Government. This decision was confirmed at the third plenum of the second Central Executive Committee of the Kuomintang, held at Hankow from 10 to 17 March. The Wuhan regime, dominated by the left wing of the Kuomintang and strongly influenced by Russian and Chinese Communists, was headed by Wang Ching-wei (q.v.), who returned to China from Europe at the beginning of April. T. V. Soong held many important posts at Wuhan. He was minister of finance, a member of the standing committee of the 28-man Government Council, a member of the 15-man Military Council, and a member of the Kuomintang Political Council.

In April 1927 Chiang Kai-shek and his conservative supporters inaugurated a rival government at Nanking. Just before this development, the Wuhan regime had dispatched T. V. Soong, Eugene Ch'en, and Sun Fo to Shanghai to review the situation and to ask leaders in the Shanghai area to come to Wuhan. Ch'en and Sun turned back mid-way in the journey, but Soong continued on to Shanghai. He tried without success to reconcile the supporters of Wang Ching-wei and the supporters of Chiang Kai-shek. Because he was unable to return to Wuhan—the Nanking regime controlled the Yangtze—he decided to remain in Shanghai.

Chiang Kai-shek retired from office in August 1927 to promote party unity. On 1 December, he married T. V. Soong's sister Soong Mei-ling (q.v.). At the beginning of 1928 he resumed leadership of the National Revolutionary Army, and T. V. Soong was named minister of finance in the National Government at Nanking. His family relationship with T. V. Soong benefitted Chiang in his rise to power, for it was mainly through Soong that the National Government came to have the backing of the powerful bankers and businessmen of Shanghai. Soong also was the key figure in the establishment of a modern financial system.

Soon after T. V. Soong assumed office at Nanking, he revealed that the monthly revenue receipts of the National Government were less than China $3 million, while expenditures exceeded China $11 million. The provinces of Kiangsu and Chekiang, which constituted the richest economic region in China, provided the bulk of the government revenues. Within three months, Soong had increased monthly revenue collections in this region to China $10 million. About this time, the Central Bank of China was established at Shanghai, with Soong as its governor.

In June 1928 at Shanghai T. V. Soong convened a national economic conference, to which he invited China's leading bankers, financiers, and industrialists. A month later, a national finance conference met at Nanking to formulate specific policies on the basis of the general decisions taken at the Shanghai meeting. A program aimed at restoration of China's tariff autonomy also began to take form. On 25 July, Soong and John Van Antwerp MacMurray, the United States minister to China, signed an agreement in principle giving complete national tariff autonomy to China. Similar agreements were signed with other Western nations between November 1928 and May 1930. In February 1930 the National Government officially began to practice tariff autonomy.

Perhaps the most important financial reform instituted by T. V. Soong was the abolition of the likin tax. Although this levy had given rise to many abuses and had long been considered a major instance of bad government, repeated attempts to do away with it had failed. On 31 December 1930 Soong announced its abolition as of 1931, and he enforced that decision. The financial policies of T. V. Soong and the support he won for the National Government played an essential part in the victory of Chiang Kai-shek in a series of civil wars in 1929–30. The importance of Soong's role and the significance of his contributions were reflected in the fact that several attempts were made on his life by rivals. In mid-1931 the Legislative Yuan decided to float a domestic relief bond issue in the amount of China $80 million. When T. V. Soong's strong opposition to this measure was ignored, he resigned in protest.

On 28 May 1931 a group of Kuomintang

dissidents established an opposition national government at Canton as a direct result of the arrest of Hu Han-min (q.v.) by Chiang Kai-shek. Civil war threatened until September 1931, when the contending Kuomintang factions were reunited by a national crisis, the Japanese attack on Mukden. When the National Government was reorganized in December 1931, Sun Fo, the new president of the Executive Yuan, asked T. V. Soong to be minister of finance in his cabinet, but Soong declined. Sun's failure to win the support of Soong and the Shanghai financial community was an important factor in the almost immediate collapse of his cabinet.

Wang Ching-wei (q.v.) succeeded Sun Fo as president of the Executive Yuan on 28 January 1932. That very night, fighting broke out between Japanese troops in the Shanghai area and the Chinese Nineteenth Route Army (for details, see Ts'ai T'ing-k'ai). T. V. Soong played an indirect role in this encounter. As minister of finance, he had built up a well-equipped force of revenue guards for use in intercepting smugglers. This unit later became the New First Army of Burma campaign fame. When hostilities began in Shanghai, the revenue force joined with the Nineteenth Route Army in fighting the Japanese. Ts'ai T'ing-k'ai, the Nineteenth Route Army's commander, later stated that Soong also gave money to the Chinese forces during the crisis.

In February 1932 T. V. Soong was reappointed governor of the Central Bank of China, and in April of that year he became vice president of the Executive Yuan and minister of finance. His active presence in this government was an important factor in the temporary establishment of political equilibrium in Nationalist China and of what became known as the Chiang-Wang coalition, with Chiang Kai-shek in control of the military and Wang Ching-wei at the head of the civil administration of the National Government. In the 1932–33 period T. V. Soong accomplished another major reform in China's fiscal system: the abolition of the tael and the establishment of the silver dollar (yuan) as the standard legal tender of China.

From October 1932 to March 1933, while Wang Ching-wei was in Europe, T. V. Soong served as acting president of the Executive Yuan at Nanking. In April 1933 he went to London to attend the World Economic Conference. After that meeting, he visited Geneva, where he succeeded in stationing a liaison officer for technical aid to China. He then went to the United States, where he secured a cotton and wheat loan of U.S. $50 million on 23 August. Soon afterwards, Soong returned to China.

In October 1933 T. V. Soong resigned from his posts as vice president of the Executive Yuan, minister of finance, and governor of the Central Bank of China. One important reason for his resignation was his disagreement with Chiang Kai-shek over high military expenditures and the issuing of new bonds by the National Government. Soong retained his membership in the standing committee of the National Economic Council, but he devoted most of his time to entrepreneurial endeavors. In June 1934 he founded the China Development Finance Corporation, the stated aim of which was to promote and develop industry and commerce in China by encouraging foreign investment and by developing the domestic money market. Before and during the Sino-Japanese war, the development of rail networks was a prime concern of the corporation, and it negotiated loans on behalf of the National Government with British, French, and other foreign banks for this purpose. None of the railways was completed, however, because of the severe disruptions caused by the Sino-Japanese war. The China Development Finance Corporation also initiated negotiations with American firms in the mid-1930's in the hope of establishing rayon, paper, fertilizer, truck, and rubber factories in China. His resignation from National Government posts notwithstanding, Soong remained close to the centers of power in China. When the Bank of China, the nation's largest and most important private bank, was ordered to reorganize on 1 April 1935 in a move which placed it under the direct control of the National Government, Soong replaced Chang Kia-ngau (Chang Chia-ao, q.v.) as its chairman. He held that post until 1943.

At the time of the Sian Incident of December 1936 (see Chiang Kai-shek; Chang Hsueh-liang), T. V. Soong, as a relative of Chiang and a friend of Chang, played an active role in the negotiations that led to Chiang's release. Afterward, Soong reportedly was greatly angered because assurances of the non-punishment of Chang Hsueh-liang were not honored. Nevertheless, the Sian Incident was the prelude to Soong's re-entry into the political arena. In June 1937 he went to Canton and Wuchow to direct the reorganization of the financial structures of Kwangtung and Kwangsi. He flew to Lushan to report to Chiang Kai-shek just before the Sino-Japanese war broke out in July. Soong moved with the National Government to Chungking, where in March 1938 he became acting chairman of the National Aeronautical Affairs Commission, headed by Chiang Kai-shek. In mid-1940 Soong was appointed Chiang Kai-shek's personal representative in the United States, and in February 1941 he succeeded in negotiating a credit of U.S. $50 million from the United States government against exports of metals. In April 1941 he represented China in negotiations which led to the granting of a second credit of U.S. $50 million.

With the outbreak of the War in the Pacific in early December 1941, China became a wartime ally of the United States and Great Britain. Because of his success as Chiang Kai-shek's representative in Washington, T. V. Soong was made minister of foreign affairs in the National Government. He was still in the United States at the time of his appointment. In January 1942, on behalf of China, he signed the 26-nation agreement at Washington that pledged the Allied powers not to make separate peace treaties with enemy nations. This agreement paved the way for the inclusion of China as one of the so-called Big Four nations, the others being the United States, Great Britain, and the Soviet Union. In February 1942 Soong concluded negotiations for a major credit loan of U.S. $500 million from the United States, and in June of that year he signed the Sino-American Lend-Lease Agreement.

T. V. Soong returned to Chungking in the autumn of 1942 to assume office as minister of foreign affairs (Chiang Kai-shek had been acting as foreign minister pending Soong's return). In January 1943 the United States and Great Britain signed treaties with China in which they relinquished extraterritoriality and other special rights in China. Other Western nations soon followed this precedent. Although executed at a time when much of China was under Japanese control, the new

treaties were widely represented by Chungking as the realization of one of the major aims of the Kuomintang. Soong was particularly gratified that the abolition of the principle of extraterritoriality took place during his tenure of office as minister of foreign affairs. Soong went to Washington again in February 1943 to see President Franklin D. Roosevelt, and in March of that year he met with British Foreign Secretary Anthony Eden while Eden was visiting Washington. After a brief trip to Canada in April, Soong flew to London in July for discussions with the British government on postwar planning. He was received by King George VI on 27 July. In August, he participated in the discussion of the Burma campaigns at the Quebec Conference.

After his return to China in October 1943, T. V. Soong often welcomed and briefed official visitors from the United States. Among these visitors was Vice President Henry A. Wallace, who visited China in June 1944. In September 1944 Major General Patrick J. Hurley and Donald M. Nelson, chairman of the War Production Board, arrived in China on a special mission. Hurley attempted to serve as a mediator in the burgeoning Nationalist-Communist conflict. Soong was among those Nationalist leaders who strongly opposed the concept of coalition government with Communist participation.

In December 1944, when H. H. K'ung left China on a mission to the United States, T. V. Soong became acting president of the Executive Yuan. In March 1945 it was announced that Soong would head the Chinese delegation to the United Nations Conference on International Organization at San Francisco. When that meeting convened on 25 April, he was elected one of its four chairmen. The Chinese delegation at San Francisco was interesting in that one of its members was the Chinese Communist Tung Pi-wu (q.v.), whom T. V. Soong had known at Wuhan in 1927. While in the United States, Soong met with President Harry S. Truman to discuss Far Eastern problems and postwar Sino-American cooperation.

T. V. Soong was appointed president of the Executive Yuan on 31 May 1945. He returned to Chungking on 20 June and assumed office five days later, retaining his post as minister of foreign affairs. His major task at this time was the negotiation of a Sino-Soviet treaty of friendship based on an American commitment to Russian influence in Manchuria during the Yalta Conference. He arrived at Moscow on 30 June, and by 12 July he had met with Stalin several times. At this point, the talks were interrupted and Soong returned to Chungking, where on 20 July he reported to the People's Political Council on the Moscow negotiations. He strenuously objected to concessions to the Soviet Union in Outer Mongolia. On 30 July, he relinquished his foreign ministership to Wang Shih-chieh (q.v.). He returned to Moscow on 5 August, accompanied by Wang. This round of talks led to the signing on 14 August of the Sino-Soviet Treaty of Friendship and Alliance and related agreements which, among other things, established a framework for the independence of Outer Mongolia. Despite strong opposition, the treaty was ratified by the Legislative Yuan.

By this time, the War in the Pacific had ended, with Japan defeated and the military forces of the Soviet Union in control of Manchuria. After General George C. Marshall arrived in China at the end of 1945 to confront the task of mediating between the Nationalists and the Chinese Communists, Soong spent much of his time in consultation with General Marshall and Chiang Kai-shek. But the American mediation effort soon failed—largely because of the bitter mutual suspicion that divided the Kuomintang and the Chinese Communists—and full-scale civil war erupted again in China in the summer of 1946. Meanwhile, the economic situation in Nationalist-controlled areas of China was deteriorating rapidly. T. V. Soong was chairman of the Supreme National Economic Council, and he was forced to introduce emergency measures and restrictions that were unpopular in his attempts to bolster China's sagging economy. His efforts were unsuccessful. Moreover, there was increasing personal criticism of Soong at this time. In March 1947 he resigned as president of the Executive Yuan, though he continued to serve the National Government as a member of the State Council. In September 1947, despite opposition from the Control Yuan, Chiang Kai-shek appointed Soong governor and pacification commissioner of Kwangtung. When Chiang retired from the presidency in January 1949, Soong relinquished his posts at Canton. Soong, whose name was high on the list of so-called war criminals announced by the Chinese Communists, went to the United States and established residence in New York.

T. V. Soong was an unusual figure in Chinese politics during the republican period. His Western ways made him unpopular with many Chinese, and his work was better known and more highly regarded by Westerners than by his compatriots. Because of his Harvard training, fluency in English, and ability to mix socially with prominent Westerners, he was regarded with suspicion by many Kuomintang and National Government officials. At the same time, he was hailed by Western observers as the possessor of the most astute financial mind in China, and he often was praised by Americans for his industry, efficiency, and courage. Soong also was criticized in China because of family relationships. Although he often was on less than cordial terms with Chiang Kai-shek and H. H. K'ung, he nevertheless was invariably associated with them as a target of public censure. The Chinese Communists in particular excoriated Soong as an unprincipled "compradore and bureaucratic capitalist" who utilized official position for personal gain. The extent of Soong's financial interests is unknown, but rumor credited him with a substantial private fortune. In his heyday, he sometimes was referred to as the J. P. Morgan of China. Soong initiated many new enterprises under the aegis of the China Development Finance Corporation and the Bank of China: the China Cotton Corporation, the South China Rice Import Corporation, the Bank of Canton (a private bank with Hong Kong registration), and the Yangtze Electric Company, among others.

In 1927 T. V. Soong married Chang Lo-yi, who was also known as Laura Chang. They had three daughters—Laurette, Mary-Jane, and Katherine—all of whom were raised and educated in the United States. In time, the Soongs also came to have nine grandchildren.

Stone, Mary: *see* SHIH MEI-YÜ.

Su Chao-cheng   蘇　兆　徵

Su Chao-cheng (1885–February 1929), Cantonese seaman who became a labor organizer and a principal figure in the 1922 Canton–Hong Kong strike. He joined the Chinese Communist party in 1925, became chairman of the All-China Federation of Labor in 1926, and served as minister of labor in the Wuhan government in 1927.

Born into a poor peasant family in Hsiangshan (Chungshan), Kwangtung, Su Chao-cheng went to work as a seaman while still in his teens and spent his early life as a working sailor on ocean-going vessels. Like many other Cantonese seamen, Su was attracted to the anti-Manchu movement led by Sun Yat-sen, and he supported the republican revolution of 1911. About 1914–15 Sun sponsored the formation of the Seamen's Friendship Association, headed by Ch'en Ping-shen and Lin Wei-min. Su Chao-cheng served on the association's governing committee.

The notoriously bad working conditions of the Cantonese seamen, little better than that of the poorer coolies, offered splendid opportunities for labor agitation. The sailors had long been exploited by labor contractors, who controlled the market and took a large percentage of the wages as commission. In an effort to improve conditions, Su Chao-cheng and others organized the Chinese Seamen's Union in 1920, with headquarters and registration in the British colony of Hong Kong. In January 1922 the union launched its first strike. The union's chairman, Ch'en Ping-shen, soon resigned, and Su Chao-cheng became acting chairman. Ch'en Chiung-ming (q.v.), then the governor of Kwangtung, reportedly gave financial assistance to the strike committee in an attempt to improve his political position in south China with reference to Sun Yat-sen. The strike, which was settled in March, represented a significant economic and psychological victory for the Cantonese seamen. It demonstrated the strength of organized labor on the China coast, indicated the potency of the strike weapon, and helped prepare the way for political alliance between the Kuomintang and the Chinese Communist party.

At the time of the 1922 strike, Su Chao-cheng had no direct contact with the Chinese Communist party. Indeed, he had tried without success to communicate with the Communists at Canton on behalf of the Chinese Seaman's Union. He apparently encountered the Communist-led international labor movement for the first time in the summer of 1924, when he attended the Pacific transport workers conference held in Hong Kong under Profintern auspices. He joined the Chinese Communist party while at Peking for a labor meeting in the spring of 1925. In two years he rose to become the top Communist labor leader in south China. His prominence was underscored at the second National Labor Congress, held at Canton on 1–6 May 1925, when he was elected to the executive committee of the newly founded All-China Federation of Labor.

Shortly after the Canton congress, the May Thirtieth Incident erupted at Shanghai when police in the International Settlement fired on Chinese. The result was a wave of anti-British agitation, marked in south China by the major strike of 1925–26 in the Canton–Hong Kong area. Su Chao-cheng headed the strike committee, working closely with Teng Chung-hsia (q.v.) and Yang Yin. This strongly organized and vigorously conducted strike seriously affected business and shipping in Hong Kong. As the leader of the strike, Su was elected chairman of the All-China Federation of Labor in May 1926. Because financial support for the strike proved to be a substantial burden for the National Government at Canton to bear, the Kuomintang leaders sought to terminate it. The action ended in the autumn of 1926.

As the National Revolutionary Army moved northward from Canton to central China on the first leg of the Northern Expedition, the principal focus of political activity became Wuhan. When the National Government moved there, Su Chao-cheng was one of two Communists named to ministerial posts, the other being T'an P'ing-shan (q.v.). Su did not assume office as minister of labor until the spring of 1927, when he traveled to Wuhan from Canton with an international delegation which included Jacques Doriot, Earl Browder, and Tom Mann. The group was welcomed on 1 April 1927 by a ceremony at which the young Communist organizer Liu Shao-ch'i (q.v.) spoke. The headquarters of the All-China Federation of Labor was moved to Wuhan at this time. Soon after his arrival at Wuhan, Su attended the Fifth National Congress of the Chinese Communist party, at which he was elected an alternate member of the Political Bureau.

When Kuomintang leaders at Wuhan broke with the Communists in July 1927, Su Chao-cheng was forced to flee to Kiangsi for safety. In August, he took part in the party plenum at which Ch'en Tu-hsiu (q.v.) was removed from office as general secretary and replaced by Ch'ü Ch'iu-pai (q.v.). At that time, Su was elected to full membership in the Political Bureau. Su helped plan the Canton Commune of December 1927 (for details, *see* Chang T'ai-lei), and he was listed as chairman of the Canton soviet government although he was not in Canton during that time.

After presiding over a meeting of the executive committee of the All-China Federation of Labor at Shanghai in February 1928, Su Chao-cheng went to Moscow. He attended the fourth Profintern congress and served on the presidium of its executive committee. At the Sixth National Congress of the Chinese Communist party, held at Moscow in June–July 1928, Su was elected a delegate to the Comintern. In that capacity, he attended the sixth Comintern congress in August 1928 and served on the presidium of its executive committee. He reportedly was the author of a booklet, *An Account of the 1922 Hong Kong Seamen's Strike*, which was published at Moscow during this period.

Persistent hard work and self-neglect over the years finally cost Su Chao-cheng his health. In September 1928 he went to the Ukraine to convalesce after an appendicitis attack. After reporting on the Chinese labor movement to the All-Soviet Federation of Labor, he returned to China by way of Siberia in January 1929. The long journey proved too arduous for him, however, and he died shortly after reaching Shanghai in February 1929. He was survived by his wife, a son, and a daughter.

Su Hsueh-lin   蘇 雪 林
   Orig. Su Mei   蘇 梅
   Pen. Lü Yi   綠 漪

Su Hsueh-lin (1897–), poet, novelist, and short-story writer. She also was noted for her scholarly studies of T'ang poetry and comparative mythology.

Little is known about Su Hsueh-lin's family background or early life except that she was born in Taiping, Anhwei, and that she had three brothers and a sister. She received her early education at home, where she studied the Chinese classics and learned to compose verse in the traditional style. At the age of 15, she enrolled at the Anhwei Provincial First Normal School. After graduation in 1919 and a brief period as a teacher at the Anking Experimental Primary School, she entered the Peking Women's Higher Normal School.

At the Anking Experimental Primary School Su Hsueh-lin had met the writer Lu Yin, (Huang Lu-yin, q.v.), who had quickened Su's interest in writing. The two girls studied together at Peking from mid-1919 to mid-1921. It was the height of the Literary Revolution, and students who had recently returned from study abroad were lionized. Su, desiring to emulate these young intellectuals, applied for and won a scholarship for study and travel in France. So unprecedented for a girl was such a resolve in 1921 that Su did not inform her mother of her plans until the night before her departure.

In the autumn of 1921 Su Hsueh-lin enrolled at the Université d'Outre-Mer de Lyon, where she remained for four years and devoted herself to the study of literature and fine arts. She was successful as a student, but her life in France was marked by a series of crises. First of all, a fellow student proposed marriage to her, but she felt bound to honor the engagement arranged by her parents to a young man she had never met. Next, one of her brothers died. Finally, she became seriously ill. During her illness she was cared for by Roman Catholic nuns and by her friend Pei Lang, a Catholic convert. Pei induced her to study Catholic doctrine. At first Su's interest in Catholicism was almost purely aesthetic. As an artist she admired the Catholic Church's ceremonies and solemn music, but as an intellectual she declined to accept its teachings. In 1924 Su's mother fell ill and was believed to be dying. Su vowed that she would convert to Catholicism if her mother's life were spared. She immediately joined the Catholic Church on hearing of her mother's unexpected recovery. In 1925 Su returned to China and submitted to an arranged marriage.

Having spent four years in France, Su Hsueh-lin was well-qualified to embark on a career of teaching and writing. On her return she went to Soochow, where she taught Chinese at the Laurel Haygood Normal School and the Chen Hua Girls Middle School. She then taught Chinese literature at Shanghai University, Soochow University, and Anhwei University. In 1931 she became professor of Chinese literature at Wuhan University. Except for the war years, which she spent at Loshan, Szechwan, she held the Wuhan post until 1949.

As a teacher of literature Su Hsueh-lin was most interested in poetry. Her first published work of scholarship was *Li Shang-yin lien-ai shih-chi k'ao* [the love life of Li Shang-yin], which appeared in 1927. An epochal work, Su's treatise dispelled much of the obscurity surrounding this T'ang poet's writings. She argued that many of them were love poems addressed to Taoist nuns and other inaccessible women; they thus were couched in heavily allusive language that could be deciphered only through painstaking research into Taoist myth. Su produced a volume of criticism, *T'o-yü ti sheng-huo* [life of a bookworm], in 1929 and two literary studies, *T'ang-shih kai-lun* [introduction to T'ang poetry] and *Liao-Chin-Yüan wen-hsüeh* [literature of Liao, Chin, and Yüan dynasties], in 1934. In 1941, during her wartime exile in Loshan, she published *Nan-Ming chung-lieh chuan* [biographies of Southern Ming loyalists], studies of Ming supporters who had died fighting the invading Manchus in the mid-seventeenth century. A collection of literary studies, the *Ch'ing-niao chi* [bluebird], appeared in 1945. Three years later, she wrote an article in English, "Present-Day Fiction and Drama in China," for a work entitled *1500 Modern Chinese Novels and Plays*. A 40-page history of fiction and drama from the time of the May Fourth Movement to 1948, Su Hsueh-lin's article demonstrated her sound critical sense and her thorough knowledge of modern Chinese literature.

Su Hsueh-lin also achieved recognition as a writer of poetry and fiction. Her earliest published work was a series of poems entitled *Hsiang-ts'un tsa-shih* [home], which appeared in the literary supplement of the *Ch'en-pao* when she was studying in France. On her return to China, Su contributed poems, short stories, and topical articles to *Yü-ssu* [thread of talk] and *Hsin-yüeh yüeh-k'an* [crescent moon monthly]. In 1928 she published *Lü-t'ien* [green skies], a collection of stories about the joys of home and married life. Her most successful work, *Chi-hsin*

[the bitter heart], a fictionalized account of her troubled years as a student in France, appeared in 1928. *T'u-lung chi* [the dragon slayer], a collection of stories, was published in 1941. In 1946 *Chiu-na-lo ti yen-ching* [the eyes of Kunala] was published; it consisted of two plays: the title piece, which was a retelling of the Phaedra myth in an Indian setting; and *Mei-kuei yü ch'un* [roses and spring], an allegory of sacred and profane love. About this time, Su completed her *San-shui chi* [the cicada's shell], in which she retold a number of stories of the old Ming loyalists in the traditional narrative style.

When the Chinese Communists took control of the mainland in 1949, Su Hsueh-lin went to Hong Kong, where she edited tracts for the Catholic Truth Society. In 1950 she went to Paris, where she spent two years studying comparative mythology. She went to Taiwan in July 1952 as professor of Chinese literature at Taiwan Provincial Normal College, later assuming part-time status so as to allow more time for research. In the early 1950's she focussed her attention on the myths of pre-Han China, especially those of the state of Ch'u as reflected in the *Ch'u-tz'u* [elegies of Ch'u]. The *K'un-lun chih mi* [the riddle of K'un-lun] of 1957 advanced the thesis that many of the puzzling myths in the *Ch'u-tz'u*, including mention of the sacred mountain of K'un-lun, can be explained only by reference to myths of the ancient Near East and Europe, a phenomenon which suggests early contact between China and the West. The wars waged by Alexander the Great in the fourth decade of the fourth century B.C. were regarded by Su as being responsible for the migration of peoples eastward and the subsequent enrichment of the culture of the state of Ch'u. In 1957 she published *T'ien-ma chi* [Pegasus], which dealt with Greek mythology. An anthology, *Su Hsueh-lin hsüan-chi*, was published in Taiwan in 1961.

Su Man-shu   蘇 曼 殊
　T. Hsüan-ying   玄 瑛

Su Man-shu (28 September 1884–2 May 1918), poet, translator, journalist, and anti-Manchu revolutionary whose fragments of autobiographical fiction created a legend which captivated a whole generation of Chinese readers.

The son of Su Chieh-sheng, a Cantonese agent of the Wan-lung Tea Company, Su Man-shu was born in Yokohama. His mother was a Japanese called O-sen, and the boy grew up speaking both Chinese and Japanese. In 1894, because of the Sino-Japanese war, Su Chieh-sheng took his son and O-sen to China and settled in Hsiangshan, Kwangtung, where the Su clan had lived for several generations. The sudden appearance in Hsiangshan of a foreign wife and a child of mixed parentage caused consternation, the more so because Su Chieh-sheng's lawful Chinese wife had continued to make her home there during her husband's absence overseas. The next three years were difficult ones for Su Man-shu and his mother, relieved only by the kindness of a serving woman in the Su household who grew attached to the "lady in the old-fashioned dress," as she called Su's mother because of her Japanese attire.

In 1897 Su Man-shu and his mother were sent back to Yokohama, where Su entered the newly established Yokohama Chinese School. He did very badly in classical Chinese, and he suffered from racial snubs administered by members of the school's Chinese staff who objected to teaching Sino-Japanese "half-breeds." In 1899 Su was transferred to the school's English section, where he surprised everyone by making rapid progress. As a result, he was permitted to leave the Yokohama Chinese School in 1900 to enter the high school attached to Waseda University in Tokyo. Little is known about Su's years as a student in Tokyo except that in the autumn of 1902 he joined the Waseda Young Men's Society, a new organized group of revolution-minded young Chinese which supported the radical aims of Sun Yat-sen rather than the reformist policies of K'ang Yu-wei and Liang Ch'i-ch'ao. Su soon rose to prominence in this group because of his knowledge of English and his abilities as a painter in the Chinese style.

Su's activities with the Waseda group resulted in his return to China in 1903. The Shanghai *Su-pao* had been shut down for making anti-Manchu attacks, and a new paper, the *National Daily* (to be of British registry), was contemplated as a successor. Su was appointed a translator on the *National Daily*. He made his way to Shanghai in the autumn of 1903, and he worked for the paper until it was suppressed

late in 1904. During this time, Su collaborated with Ch'en Tu-hsiu (q.v.) on a translation of *Les Misérables* and wrote a number of essays and editorials. Su was sharply critical of the role played by Cantonese in the recent history of China and predicted that if China were ever enslaved the ultimate fault would lie with the Cantonese merchants, whose Chinese qualities had rubbed off by long contact with Westerners and who cared only for profit and nothing for China. Su also wrote approvingly of anarchy and of such proponents of anarchism as Emma Goldman.

By the time the *National Daily* was curtailed, Su had discovered that he liked to write and that he was good at it. He had no difficulty in finding a job with the *China Daily* of Hong Kong. He devoted his entire energies to his new duties to the point of sleeping in the newspaper office, and he soon earned a reputation in Hong Kong that matched the one he had acquired at Shanghai. At the same time, he remained a strong partisan of Sun Yat-sen, and he associated with a number of leading Hong Kong revolutionaries.

Su's success, however, soon bore strange fruit and led to one of the few romantic incidents of his life that can be reasonably verified. Su Chieh-sheng, apparently having been alerted to his son's success, made his way from Hsiangshan to Hong Kong to discuss the important matter of Su's arranged marriage to a girl from his native district. Su learned of his father's plan before he arrived. He consulted his radical cronies about a course of action; to a man they advised him to obey his father and to accept the bride. This solution clearly was not to Su's liking, for he fled the *China Daily* office and refused to meet with Su Chieh-sheng. After several days of moving from place to place, Su disappeared from Hong Kong, leaving his father to return disappointed to Hsiangshan. Su's friends heard nothing from him, and great indeed was their consternation when he returned to Hong Kong several months later displaying the shaved skull and brown robes of a Buddhist monk. By the most reliable accounts, Su had fled Hong Kong for a monastery somewhere in Kwangtung and had taken vows. Monastic discipline apparently had not agreed with him, however, and he had returned to Hong Kong as soon as he could. After a few days in Hong Kong the robe was laid aside except for ceremonial occasions, and Su returned to his old eating and drinking habits. Nevertheless, the question of marriage had been settled once and for all. The only other reminder of Su's monkish interlude was his adoption of the religious name Man Shu, a reference to the chief bodhisattva Manjusri. Su's return to Hong Kong coincided with his father's final illness, and he made a brief trip to Hsiangshan to be with his father and to settle family business after his death.

During 1905 Su seems to have been relatively independent, possibly as the result of a small legacy, and making an adequate living as a journalist while traveling from Shanghai to Nanking to Hangchow. In 1906 he went to Japan to visit his mother, and in 1907 he settled in Tokyo, where he remained for two years, during which time he completed translations of Byron's works which were collected and published in 1908 under the title *Pai-lun shih-hsüan*.

Su's success as a translator made him a sought-after collaborator in revolutionary circles, and he seems to have spent 1909–11 in a series of missions on Sun Yat-sen's behalf in Southeast Asia. In 1909 he accepted a position as teacher of Chinese in the Chinese community at Surabaya, Java, where he resided for two years, with time off for side trips to Singapore and Bangkok. During this period, he helped to foment anti-Manchu feeling among overseas Chinese and to collect funds for the revolutionary cause. He also had an opportunity to witness Western colonialism at first hand, and he acquired a distaste for the Dutch which, along with his impressions of the tropical beauty of Java, was to reappear frequently in his later fiction.

With the establishment of the Chinese republic, Su Man-shu left Southeast Asia for China, where he accepted an editorial post on a Shanghai newspaper. He devoted the following six years, his last, to newspaper work, the writing of poetry and fiction, and the elaboration of the legend of Su Man-shu. This legend, which was to captivate a whole generation of Chinese readers (who believed it true), was set forth in fragments of autobiographical fiction of which the best, according to many critics, was *Tuan-hung ling-yen chi* (*The Lone Swan*), which was published serially in the *Shanghai Pacific Journal* in May–August 1912. In his excellent

biography, *Su Man-shu, a Sino-Japanese Genius*, Henry McAleavy says that the legend represents "a man of the purest Japanese blood, introduced from his childhood into China as a gesture of homage, only to find the confidence abused. Ordained as a monk while still a youth, he is never to know the consolations of family life, but from his solitude he can pass judgement on the society around him, and can see all the more clearly that those who insulted him and his mother are themselves unworthy to bear the name of Chinese. It is he who possesses the true Chinese spirit and who can interpret it to the world, and he is able to do this with all the more authority in that he can bring to the task a wide knowledge of foreign literatures . . . . But when all is said and done, what has Europe, or, for that matter, China herself, to offer that can be compared to the wisdom of India? And to this treasure-house, almost alone of his contemporaries, he has the key." It is in this role of "outsider," able at once to overcome the claims of Western materialism and traditional Chinese values, that Su made his greatest appeal to his readership, providing, vicariously, through his fictional life and adventures, a solution to the commonly felt "crisis of identity." Through the same means, Su himself seems finally to have come to terms with his own mixed heritage and with his inadequacies in leading a normal family life.

A prolific writer and a figure of some romance and mystery, Su lived out his last years elaborating his mystique. His collected letters show, for example, a note to a Señor Lopez in Madrid concerning the publication there in English of Su's translation of *Sakuntalā*, and similar allusions are made to Sanskrit grammars produced early in his youth. No trace of any such works has ever been found. During his last years, Su acquired a gluttonous addiction to sweets, and this may have contributed in 1917 to severe intestinal complaints. When his health failed in early 1918, Chiang Kai-shek gave him a room in his Shanghai house. In April, Su's condition worsened, and he was transferred to a hospital in the French concession, where he died on 2 May 1918. He was interred in a cemetery near the West Lake at Hangchow, in a plot paid for by Wang Ching-wei.

Su's works have been collected and republished at frequent intervals since his death, and

his life and works continue to interest critics.
In 1927 Liu Wu-chi edited *Man-shu i-chu*
[posthumous works of Su Man-shu] and the
year following collaborated with his father, Liu
Ya-tzu (q.v.), on *Su Man-shu nien-p'u chi ch'i-t'a*
[chronological biography of Su Man-shu]. The
latter work is based on a close reading of Su's
writings, and it accepts all aspects of the legend
as true. In 1931 the writer Shih Hsi-sheng
produced four volumes: *Man-shu pi-chi* [Su
Man-shu's notebooks], *Man-shu shih-wen* [prose
and poetry of Su Man-shu], *Man-shu shou-cha*
[holograph letters of Su Man-shu], and *Man-shu
hsiao-shuo* [the fiction of Su Man-shu]. Between
1930 and 1931 there appeared Su's collected
works, which were edited by Liu Ya-tzu and
punctuated by Liu Wu-chi and which bore the
title *Su Man-shu ch'üan-chi*. A second edition
of this five-volume compilation appeared
between 1932 and 1935. A third edition was
published in Hong Kong during the 1940's,
and a fourth in Taiwan in 1961. Selections from
Su's works, under various titles, have been
published even more frequently over the years,
testifying to a continued interest on the part of
the Chinese reading public in this romantic
figure.

Su Yü   粟 裕

Su Yü (c. 1908–), Chinese Communist military
leader who was deputy commander, under
Ch'en Yi, of the New Fourth Army and its
successor, the Third Field Army. After serving
as chief of staff of the People's Liberation Army
in 1954–58, he was made a vice minister of
national defense in 1959.

The Huit'ung district of Hunan was the
birthplace of Su Yü. Although his family
originally came from Fukien, he was generally
regarded in later years as a native of Hunan.
Little is known about his formative years except
that he received his secondary education at one
of the Hunan provincial normal schools.

Su Yü joined the Communist Youth League
in 1926 and became involved in student political
agitation at Ch'angte, Hunan. Having run
afoul of the local authorities for his part in these
activities, he fled to Wuchang, where he joined
the training group associated with the 24th
Division of the National Revolutionary Army.

The divisional commander was Yeh T'ing
(q.v.), and many of the officers had been
trained at the Whampoa Military Academy. In
1927 Su Yü joined the Chinese Communist
party. In June of that year, as Kuomintang-
Communist tensions sharpened, the training
group of the 24th Division was assigned to the
Military Affairs Commission at Nanchang as a
security force. When the Nanchang uprising
(for details, *see* Yeh T'ing) was suppressed after
a few days of fighting in early August, Su Yü,
then a company commander, escaped. He
eventually made his way to the Chingkan
mountains base on the Hunan-Kiangsi border,
where the guerrilla units of Mao Tse-tung and
Chu Teh joined forces in the spring of 1928.

During the early Kiangsi period, Su Yü rose
rapidly in the embryonic Communist military
hierarchy to become a regimental commander.
In 1929, only two years after the Nanchang
incident, he reorganized the Communist forces
in southern Kiangsi into the 64th Division of the
Twenty-second Red Army. After participating
in local operations in central Kiangsi, Su's
division was incorporated into the Fourth Front
Army, headed by Lin Piao (q.v.). When the
Nationalists began their first campaign to wipe
out the Communist base in Kiangsi in early
1931, Su Yü's division was detached from Lin
Piao's command, and he moved eastward to
the Communist base area in northeast Kiangsi
on the Fukien border, where Fang Chih-min
(q.v.) was directing operations as commander
of the Tenth Red Army. In 1934 Su Yü became
chief of staff in Fang's Red Army Anti-Japanese
Vanguard Unit. This force remained in
Kiangsi after the main body of Communist
troops began the Long March in the autumn of
1934. After Fang Chih-min was captured by
the Nationalists and executed in June 1935, Su
Yü succeeded to his command.

With the formation of the Nationalist-
Communist united front in 1937 and the outbreak of the Sino-Japanese war, plans were
made to mobilize guerrilla forces in central
China along the Yangtze to fight the Japanese.
Su Yü's troops thus became an important part
of the New Fourth Army, commanded by Yeh
T'ing. Ch'en Yi (1901–; q.v.) was assigned
to command the 1st column of the New Fourth
Army, with Su Yü as his deputy. From 1939 to
1941 Su served as commander of the 1st
column in Ch'en's south Yangtze command.

The so-called New Fourth Army Incident (for details, *see* Ku Chu-t'ung; Yeh T'ing) of January 1941 resulted in the capture of Yeh T'ing and the death of his deputy, Hsiang Ying (q.v.). Su Yü escaped capture, for he had moved his forces north of the Yangtze before the incident. In the ensuing military reorganization, Ch'en Yi became acting commander of the New Fourth Army, with Su Yü as his deputy and Liu Shao-ch'i as political commissar. For the next three years, this army operated behind Japanese lines, especially in the Shanghai-Nanking-Hangchow area. In 1944 the Chinese Communists established a Kiangsu-Chekiang military district, with Su Yü in command.

After the Japanese surrender in 1945, the Nationalist-Communist struggle for control of the mainland became open and bitter. Su Yü remained in northern Kiangsu, where his army absorbed many of the local Chinese units that had been associated with the Japanese-sponsored regime at Nanking. By this time, Su had acquired a solid reputation as an able and decisive field commander. His performance in campaigns in northern Kiangsu and southern Shantung won him new recognition. These Communist forces were designated the East China People's Liberation Army in 1947 and the Third Field Army in 1948. Ch'en Yi and Su Yü conducted the operations which culminated in the Communist occupation of Shanghai in the spring of 1949. During the civil war period, Su Yü's combat performance was highly regarded by Western military observers in China. He was particularly noted for his ability to make effective use of artillery in conjunction with offensive ground operations.

At the conclusion of the Chinese Communist drive through east China in 1949, the senior military and political officers of the Third Field Army assumed top posts in the regional administrative organizations. Su Yü thus served as deputy to Ch'en Yi at Shanghai and in the east China administrative and military organs during the 1950–52 period. He also became a member of the People's Revolutionary Military Council at Peking. In April 1952 Su was named deputy chief of staff of the People's Liberation Army. He served at Peking under Nieh Jung-chen (q.v.), who was acting chief of staff during the period when Hsü Hsiang-ch'ien (q.v.) was the nominal chief. At the time of the governmental reorganization of 1954, Su was named chief of staff and a member of the National Defense Council. In 1956 he was elevated to full membership in the Central Committee of the Chinese Communist party, having become an alternate member in 1945. During this period, Su also served on a number of military delegations to foreign countries. In February 1958 he served as the ranking military leader accompanying Chou En-lai to North Korea, where arrangements were made for the withdrawal of the Chinese People's Volunteers. In October 1958 Huang K'o-ch'eng (q.v.) replaced Su as chief of staff. Su Yü became vice minister of national defense in 1959.

Sun Ch'uan-fang   孫 傳 芳
T. Hsing-yuan   馨 遠

Sun Ch'uan-fang (1884–13 November 1935), Peiyang warlord who won control of Kiangsu, Chekiang, Kiangsi, Anhwei, and Fukien in the mid-1920's. It was only with the collapse of his power in 1927 that the success of the Northern Expedition became a certainty. Sun was assassinated in 1935.

A native of Linch'eng hsien, Shantung, Sun Ch'uan-fang grew up at a time when the building of a modern army was one of China's major preoccupations. He decided to pursue a military career, and, after receiving a basic military education in China, he went to Japan to enroll at the Shikan Gakkō [military academy]. He was a member of the sixth class, which also included such future leaders as Chao Heng-t'i, Ch'eng Ch'ien, Li Ken-yuan, Li Lieh-chün, T'ang Chi-yao, and Yen Hsi-shan (qq.v.). Although he joined the T'ung-meng-hui during his stay in Japan, he was not an active member. After being graduated in 1909 and receiving a year of field training, Sun returned to China to become the commander of a regiment in the service of the Peiyang militarist Wang Chan-yuan, who controlled Hupeh. Thus Sun became associated with the Chihli clique. He did not distinguish himself during the 1911 revolution or the early days of the republic, and he therefore rose in rank very slowly. In 1917 he became a brigade commander, and in 1921 he was appointed commander of the 18th Division.

His accession to the rank of divisional commander marked a turning point in Sun Ch'uan-fang's career. On 7 August 1921 Wang Chan-yuan relinquished control of Hupeh after being defeated by two army divisions from Hunan. The Peking government appointed Wu P'ei-fu to succeed him as inspector general of Hupeh and Hunan on 9 August. Soon afterwards, Sun Ch'uan-fang was named commander in chief of forces on the upper reaches of the Yangtze, a post created because of an expected attack from Szechwan, where the local military leaders had made an agreement with the Hunan generals for a combined offensive against Wuhan. Wu P'ei-fu and his supporters rapidly suppressed the Hunan-Szechwan coalition.

The first Chihli-Fengtien war broke out in May 1922. The Fengtien forces of Chang Tso-lin (q.v.) were defeated at Ch'anghsintien, near Peking, leaving Wu P'ei-fu dominant in north China. The Chihli clique, formally led by Ts'ao K'un (q.v.), then demanded the resignation of Hsü Shih-ch'ang (q.v.), who held the presidency at Peking. On 15 May, Sun Ch'uan-fang issued a statement advocating the peaceful unification of the northern and southern governments by restoring the constitution of 1912 and the National Assembly of 1913 and by returning Li Yuan-hung (q.v.) to the presidency. When Sun issued a message on 28 May in which he requested the simultaneous resignation of Sun Yat-sen and Hsü Shih-ch'ang, it became clear that Hsü was a principal target of this movement. Hsü resigned on 2 June, and Li assumed office nine days later. Sun Ch'uan-fang's message of 28 May also provided the basis for the demand made by subordinates of Ch'en Chiung-ming (q.v.) at Canton for the resignation of Sun Yat-sen.

In October 1922 Hsü Shu-cheng (q.v.), aided by Hsü Ch'ung-chih (q.v.), established a provisional military government in Fukien. By the time it fell in November, the Peking government had ordered Sun Ch'uan-fang to move his army into Fukien. On 7 March 1923, at the insistance of Ts'ao K'un and of Wu P'ei-fu, the Peking government appointed Sun Ch'uan-fang tuchün of Fukien. After a long campaign, Sun captured Foochow in March 1924. In September of that year, Ts'ao K'un appointed him military rehabilitation commissioner for Chekiang and inspector general of the Chekiang-Fukien area. In these capacities, Sun routed the forces of Lu Yung-hsiang, the Chekiang tuchün. Lu, who had opposed Ts'ao K'un, was forced to flee to Japan on 12 October. When Feng Yü-hsiang (q.v.) staged a coup at Peking in October and ousted Ts'ao K'un, Sun and Kiangsu tuchün Ch'i Hsieh-yuan (q.v.) declared war on Feng. In November, however, Sun sent a message to Peking in which he announced their support of Tuan Ch'i-jui (q.v.), who had become chief executive at Peking. In the meantime, Chang Tso-lin had sent Chang Tsung-ch'ang (q.v.) southward with his Fengtien forces to take control of the Yangtze provinces. The Peking government dismissed Ch'i Hsieh-yuan from his post and appointed Lu Yung-hsiang pacification commissioner of Kiangsu and Anhwei. Chang and Lu entered Nanking with their men on 10 January 1925. Ch'i tried to form an alliance with Sun Ch'uan-fang at this time, but Sun remained neutral and received an appointment as military governor of Chekiang.

The victory of the Fengtien forces led to their control of the rich Shanghai district, but not for long. Sun Ch'uan-fang decided, on the principle that the best defense is a strong offense, to save his Chekiang stronghold from the advancing Fengtien forces by attacking them. In October 1925 he staged a surprise attack on Shanghai, routed the Fengtien forces, and advanced to Hsuchow. Military leaders in Anhwei, Hupeh, and Kiangsi rallied to his support.

Sun Ch'uan-fang now found himself virtually the strongest military leader of the Chihli group, although he still showed deference to Wu P'ei-fu. Accordingly, he appointed himself commander in chief of the allied armies of the five southeastern provinces (Kiangsu, Chekiang, Anhwei, Kiangsi, and Fukien). In December, he returned to Hangchow by way of Nanking and issued a statement declaring that the provinces under his control were not subject to orders from Peking. In the spring of 1926 he attempted to integrate the various Shanghai authorities and jurisdictions into the "Greater Shanghai Municipality." On 5 May 1926 he outlined his plan for the municipality in a speech to the Chinese Chamber of Commerce and appointed V. K. Ting (Ting Wen-chiang, q.v.) executive director of the bureau in charge of planning.

The national scene underwent rapid changes

in 1926. Tuan Ch'i-jui had to step down from his chief executive's post. Chang Tso-lin and Wu P'ei-fu effected a reconciliation to meet the rising threat of the Northern Expedition. Sun Ch'uan-fang declared the neutrality of his five southeastern provinces and put forward his so-called Three-Love Principle—loving the country, loving the people, and loving the enemy. In August, as the Northern Expedition. got underway, Sun took the precaution of sending reinforcements to Kiangsi and re-affirmed his neutrality. At the same time, some of Sun's subordinates were secretly making arrangements to defect to the National Revolu-tionary Army. The Nationalists swept all before them in their advances into Hunan, Kiangsi, and Fukien. By early November, Sun Ch'uan-fang had suffered severe losses in Kiangsi, and both Kiukiang and Nanchang had fallen to the Nationalists. Sun hurried north to Tientsin to confer with Chang Tso-lin.

The meetings at Tientsin led to the election of Chang Tso-lin as commander in chief of the newly created Ankuochün, with Sun Ch'uan-fang, Chang Tsung-ch'ang, and Yen Hsi-shan as deputy commanders. By this time, however, the Nationalists had taken Fukien and many of Sun's generals had defected. By the end of December even Ch'en Yi (q.v.), the governor of Chekiang, had withdrawn his support from Sun. Realizing that Chekiang would soon be lost to him, Sun decided to take his stand against the Nationalists in Kiangsu. In February 1927 Sun and Chang Tsung-ch'ang established a joint headquarters at Nanking and reorganized their armies as the Seven-Province Allied Forces. The Nationalists captured Nanking and Shanghai in March, forcing Sun to retreat to Huaiyin and then to Shantung.

Chang Tso-lin made a last attempt to restruc-ture his military establishment in July 1927. He formed seven group armies, with Sun Ch'uan-fang in command of the First Army Group. In August, Sun recaptured Hsuchow and crossed the Yangtze to take Nanking. In the battle that followed, about 20,000 of Sun's 70,000 men were killed, and about 30,000 were taken prisoner. Faced with the total collapse of his base of power, Sun retired from public life and went to Dairen.

Sun Ch'uan-fang later moved to Tientsin, where he took up Buddhism and became a major supporter of a local Buddhist institution.

He attracted public notice only once in the next few years, and then only because the National Government invited him to the conference at Loyang in 1932 that was held as a result of the Mukden Incident. On 13 November 1935 Sun's peaceful life was shattered. While Sun was attending a service at the Buddhist institute, a girl in her early twenties shot him with a pistol and killed him. She was Shih Chien-chiao, the daughter of Shih Ch'ung-pin, who had served as a brigade commander under Chang Tsung-ch'ang and who had been executed by Sun's supporters in 1925. Public sympathy resulted in a seven-year sentence for Shih Chien-chiao, and she was pardoned in 1936. Among the offspring who survived Sun Ch'uan-fang was Sun Chia-ch'in, who became an artist. He worked as an assistant to Chang Ta-ch'ien (q.v.) and went to live with Chang in Brazil.

Sun Fo　　　　　孫 科
　Alt. Sun K'o
　T.　Che-sheng　　　哲 生

Sun Fo (20 October 1891–), son of Sun Yat-sen. After holding the presidency of the Legislative Yuan from June 1932 to November 1948, he served as president of the Executive Yuan for four months. He then retired from public life and lived abroad in France and the United States before going to Taiwan.

A native of Kwangtung, Sun Fo was born in Hsiangshan hsien, later renamed Chungshan hsien in honor of his illustrious father, Sun Yat-sen. Early in 1896 Sun Fo, then only six sui, and a younger sister born in 1896 left China with their mother to join their father in Hawaii. Sun Fo received his primary and secondary education in Honolulu. He was graduated from a Catholic institution, St. Louis College, in 1910, and in 1908–10 he also worked on a Chinese-language newspaper, the *Liberty News*. In 1911 he went to the United States and enrolled at the University of California. When news of the 1911 revolution and of Sun Yat-sen's return to China reached Sun Fo, he left the United States for China in hopes of joining the repub-lican government. His father had other ideas, however, and he sent Sun Fo back to his studies in America. After being graduated from the

University of California in 1916, Sun Fo went to New York, where he received an M.A. in economics from Columbia University in 1917. Then he hurried back to China to join the military government at Canton.

Sun Fo worked for a time in 1917–18 as a secretary in the offices of the rump parliament at Canton and in the ministry of foreign affairs. When Sun Yat-sen, having lost control of the Canton government to the Kwangsi clique, left Canton for Shanghai in May 1918, Sun Fo remained in Canton. In 1919 he became associate editor of the English-language newspaper *Canton Times*. The following year, however, he moved to Hong Kong.

After Sun Yat-sen was restored to power at Canton through the military efforts of Ch'en Chiung-ming (q.v.), he appointed Ch'en governor of Kwangtung. Ch'en, eager to display himself as an able administrator and as an advocate of local autonomy within the province, entrusted Sun Fo with the task of formulating a set of regulations for a Canton municipal council. When these regulations were promulgated on 15 February 1921, Ch'en appointed Sun Fo mayor of Canton. He held this post from 1921 to 1925, except for a short break in 1922 because of Ch'en Chiung-ming's revolt against Sun Yat-sen. The immediate problems facing the municipal council were the building of roads, the widening of streets, the construction of a sewage system, and the introduction of modern public utilities. The uncertainties of the political situation and the antipathy of property owners to these projects made Sun's task doubly difficult. Despite many obstructions, he prepared the way for the transformation of the old Chinese city of Canton into the greatest modern metropolis in southern China.

In October 1923 Sun Fo was named to the provisional central executive committee of the Kuomintang. It was assigned to draft a constitution, new party regulations, and a manifesto; to oversee the creation of new party branches on the provincial and local levels; and to plan a party congress. At the First National Congress of the Kuomintang, held in January 1924, Sun explicated the proposed constitution and served on the committee which examined reports on the development of Kuomintang activities in various localities.

Sun Yat-sen left Canton for north China in November 1924. When news of his serious illness reached Canton, Sun Fo hurried to his side, arriving in Peking on 2 February 1925. Sun Fo was among those who witnessed the signing of Sun Yat-sen's two wills on 11 March. He returned to Canton after his father's funeral. When the National Government was established at Canton on 1 July, he was elected to the 16-man National Government Council. At the Second National Congress of the Kuomintang in January 1926, he received membership in the Central Executive Committee. At this time, he was regarded by Communists as a rightist. In May, he began his third term as mayor of Canton and became commissioner of reconstruction and acting governor of Kwangtung. He also became a member of the Kuomintang Political Council. Later that year, he was named to head the newly established ministry of communications.

Despite numerous difficulties and setbacks, the National Government in Canton consolidated its position and in July 1926 launched the Northern Expedition, with Chiang Kai-shek as commander in chief of the National Revolutionary Army. After the first stage of the Northern Expedition ended with the capture of Wuhan, the National Government dispatched Hsü Ch'ien, T. V. Soong, Eugene Ch'en (qq.v.), Soviet adviser Borodin, and Sun Fo to Wuhan to investigate the possibility of moving the government there. On 13 December, three days after the group reached Wuhan, it established the provisional joint session of the Central Executive Committee and the National Government Council, which proclaimed itself supreme party and government authority for the time being. Its decision to move the seat of government to Wuhan was opposed strongly by Chiang Kai-shek and his conservative supporters. On 10–16 March 1927 the third plenum of the second Central Executive Committee met at Wuhan and formally established the National Government there. Sun Fo became one of the key figures in the Wuhan regime. He was a member of the five-man Standing Committee of the Government Council, director of the party youth ministry, a member of the Central Executive Committee's Standing Committee, a member of the presidium of the Central Political Council, and a member of the Military Council.

Chiang Kai-shek and his supporters organized a rival government at Nanking in April 1927 and worked to suppress Communists in areas under their control. After Feng Yü-hsiang (q.v.) shifted the balance of power in China by giving his support to Chiang Kai-shek, the Wuhan regime began a purge of Communists in July. This action opened the way for the reunification of the Kuomintang. In the ensuing negotiations, Sun Fo and T'an Yen-k'ai (q.v.) represented the Wuhan faction. Chiang Kai-shek announced his retirement in August, and a unified National Government was established in Nanking on 20 September 1927. Sun Fo served briefly as minister of finance before becoming minister of reconstruction on 3 January 1928. After Chiang Kai-shek resumed power on 9 January, Sun decided to join C. C. Wu (Wu Ch'ao-shu) and Hu Han-min on a trip to India, Egypt, Turkey, and such European countries as France, Germany, Italy, and England. This group left China at the end of January and returned in August.

When the new National Government was established at Nanking in October 1928, Sun Fo became a member of the State Council, minister of railways, and vice president of the Examination Yuan. In 1929 he established the China National Aviation Corporation, China's first civil aviation company. He left Nanking in May 1931 after four senior members of the Central Supervisory Committee of the Kuomintang issued a statement impeaching Chiang Kai-shek for the illegal arrest of Hu Han-min. Sun attended the conference at Canton that led to the formation on 28 May 1931 of an opposition national government at Canton. Among the other participants in the conference were Wang Ching-wei, Eugene Ch'en, T'ang Shao-yi, Ch'en Chi-t'ang, and Li Tsung-jen. Civil war was averted by the Japanese attack on Mukden in September. In the ensuing negotiations, Sun Fo acted as a representative of Canton. Hu Han-min was released; the feuding party factions were reunited; and Chiang Kai-shek temporarily retired from office.

In the December 1931 reorganization of the National Government at Nanking, Sun Fo was made president of the Executive Yuan. Because he and his cabinet failed to win the support of such important men as the Shanghai bankers and T. V. Soong, he resigned on 25 January 1932. In June of that year he was appointed president of the Legislative Yuan, a post he held until

November 1948. It thus was under his direction that the task of drafting modern laws for the republic was carried out. From January 1933 to May 1936 the Legislative Yuan worked on a draft constitution which became known as the 5 May constitution. His high position in the National Government notwithstanding, Sun Fo was among those Kuomintang leaders who opposed Chiang Kai-shek's policies and who advocated immediate and determined resistance to Japanese invasion, the securing of assistance from the Soviet Union, and reconciliation with the Chinese Communists. After the Sian Incident (*see* Chiang Kai-shek; Ch'ang Hsueh-liang) and the formation of a united front against the Japanese, he was chosen to represent China in secret negotiations with Bogomoloff, the Russian ambassador. These talks, which began in March 1937, resulted in the signing of a Sino-Soviet non-aggression pact in August of that year. Sun was sent to Moscow in January 1938 and April 1939 as a special envoy of Chiang Kai-shek. Both times he obtained substantial loans from Stalin, and on the second trip he signed a Sino-Soviet commercial treaty.

In the early years of the Sino-Japanese war, Sun Fo often lectured on the world situation. A collection of his addresses was published in the autumn of 1942 as *Ch'ien-tu*, and an English version was published in the United States in 1944 under the title *China Looks Forward*.

In November 1946, after the war ended and the National Government returned to Nanking from the wartime capital of Chungking, the Kuomintang convened the National Assembly. On 25 December it adopted a constitution, thus ending the Kuomintang's 20-year monopoly on political power in the National Government. The promulgation of this constitution on 1 January 1947 marked the culmination of Sun Fo's career in the Legislative Yuan. Pending the holding of elections, a coalition government was formed in April 1947. Sun Fo was appointed to the newly created post of vice president. He held this office until April 1948, when he was defeated in the race for the vice presidency by Li Tsung-jen. On 17 May, he was elected president of the Legislative Yuan. The Chinese Communists made rapid progress in their campaign for control of the mainland, and in November 1948 Sun Fo was called upon to head the Executive Yuan and form a cabinet. In February 1949, a month after Li Tsung-jen became acting President, Sun Fo moved the Executive Yuan to Canton to express his disapproval of Li's attempts to negotiate with the Chinese Communists. Sun resigned in March, and Ho Ying-ch'in succeeded him.

After 1949, Sun Fo lived for a time in France and then moved to the United States. In October 1964 he went to Taiwan, where he became a senior adviser to the presidential office in December 1965. He received a substantive post as president of the Examination Yuan in May 1966.

Sun Fo was married to Sukying (Kwai Jun-chun). They had two sons and two daughters.

Sun Lan-feng　　　　孫 蘭 峯
T. Wan-chiu　　　　　婉 九

Sun Lan-feng (1896–), north Chinese general who was a long-time subordinate of Fu Tso-yi. In June 1954 he became vice chairman of the Inner Mongolian Autonomous Region People's Government.

Tenghsien, Shantung, was the birthplace of Sun Lan-feng. Little is known about his family background or early career except that he entered military service at the age of 18, that he studied at the Whampoa Military Academy, and that he joined the forces of Fu Tso-yi (q.v.) in the late 1920's or early 1930's. In April 1933, when the Japanese advanced into Jehol and Chahar, Sun led the regiment he then commanded from Kalgan to a point west of Huaijou. He was decorated for his performance in the ensuing battle. In November 1936, by which time he had become a brigade commander, Sun took part in the action, directed by Fu Tso-yi, that resulted in the ouster of the dissident Mongol leader Te Wang (Demchukdonggrub, q.v.) from Pailingmiao. Sun helped occupy Pailingmiao and drive Te Wang's forces into eastern Chahar.

After the Sino-Japanese war began in July 1937, Sun fought the Japanese at Hsinkow, Shansi. His participation in the campaign in southern Suiyuan in the spring of 1938 won him a citation from Chiang Kai-shek. In November 1939 he took part in an attack on the Japanese position at Paotow and received command of a division. He won another

victory in March 1940, at a time when Chinese successes were few and far between. Soon afterwards, he was awarded the Fourth Class Pao Ting decoration. At the time of the Japanese surrender in August 1945, he was designated commander of the vanguard forces charged with the takeover in Suiyuan, Chahar, and Jehol. On 15 August he arrived at Paotow and received the surrender of the Japanese forces in that sector. He reached Tatung with his forces at the end of August, and he flew to Peiping on 8 September. He thus became the first Nationalist to reach the old capital after the Japanese surrender. At the end of September, he was designated to receive the Japanese surrender in Jehol. He flew to Changchun on 12 October to participate in discussions regarding the takeover of Manchuria.

In all of his postwar actions, Sun Lan-feng was associated with Fu Tso-yi, and when Fu negotiated an agreement and surrendered to the Chinese Communists at Peiping in January 1949, Sun followed his commander into Communist service. Sun was a specially invited delegate to the Chinese People's Political Consultative Conference in September 1949, and he became a member of the Suiyuan Military and Administrative Committee. He was elected vice chairman of the Suiyuan People's Government upon its establishment. From March to June 1954 he served on the committee charged with the organization of a government for the projected Inner Mongolian Autonomous Region (IMAR). In June 1954, with the establishment of the IMAR regime, he relinquished his posts to become vice chairman of the IMAR People's Government.

Sun Li-jen　　　　　孫 立 人

Sun Li-jen (1900–), graduate of the Virginia Military Institute who won renown in the Burma campaigns and who rose to become commander in chief of the Chinese Army. He was dismissed from his posts in 1955 on charges of negligence in connection with an alleged plot against the National Government in Taiwan.

Shuch'eng, Anhwei, was the birthplace of Sun Li-jen. After receiving thorough training in both traditional and modern subjects, he enrolled at Tsinghua College. In 1922 he took time out from his studies to serve on the basketball team that represented China in international competition. After being graduated from Tsinghua in 1923, Sun went to the United States, where he studied civil engineering at Purdue University and received a B.S. degree in 1924. He then enrolled at the Virginia Military Institute, from which he was graduated in 1927. After touring England, France, Germany, and Japan to observe military practices, he returned to China and entered the National Revolutionary Army as a corporal.

Sun Li-jen's first military assignment was as commander of a training column at the Central Political Institute. By 1930 he had risen to become a regimental commander with the rank of colonel. In the early 1930's T. V. Soong (q.v.) established under his own command the Salt Gabelle Brigade. Sun was made a regimental commander in this new force. In 1937, while leading his men against the Japanese at Shanghai, he was wounded in 13 places. A student donated blood to save his life, and he was taken to Hong Kong to recuperate.

In 1938 Sun Li-jen was assigned to organize a new unit of Salt Gabelle troops at Changsha. This unit became the New 38th Division in 1942, with Sun as divisional commander. That spring, the division took part in the first Burma campaign, on the Irrawaddy front. The (British) Burma Division had been trapped near Yenangyuang, and Sun was sent to its relief. After initial delays, the Chinese made steady progress toward the beleaguered division, and the Japanese were compelled to shift troops to meet the advancing Chinese. The New 38th Division's attack pushed the Japanese back and enabled the British division to escape. When the Japanese drove combined British and Chinese forces under Lieutenant General Joseph W. Stilwell out of Burma, Sun enhanced his reputation by effecting a skillful evacuation into India. The official U.S. Army history of the China-Burma-India theater, written by Charles F. Romanus and Riley Sunderland, stated that "from the First Burma Campaign the 38th Division and its brilliant commander emerged with their reputations established. To the tactical feat of Yenangyuang, the gallant and capable Sun Li-jen added the unique achievement of bringing his division through

the Chin Hills as an intact fighting unit with discipline and morale unimpaired."

Stilwell's immediate plan was to fight his way back and recover Burma from the Japanese. He soon evolved a plan, approved by both Washington and Chungking, for the training of a basic Chinese force of 30 divisions, the majority of which would be in a Y-force in Yunnan province, with an X-force to be trained at Ramgarh in northeastern India. Stilwell was appointed commander in chief of the Chinese army in India, with Lo Cho-ying as his deputy and Sun Li-jen and Liao Yao-hsiang as Lo's commanders. The training base at Ramgarh was established and the work of creating new Chinese formations began. This task was completed in 1943: the New First Army, composed of the 38th and 30th divisions and commanded by Sun Li-jen, and the New Sixth Army, composed of the 14th, 22nd, and 50th divisions and commanded by Liao Yao-hsiang were ready for action. In December 1943 Chiang Kai-shek gave General Stilwell full authority to use these forces as he saw fit.

After a hesitant beginning on the second Burma campaign, Sun Li-jen experienced his first jungle victory at Taipha Ga at the end of January 1944. With the collaboration of the 3rd Indian Division and Merrill's Marauders, the Chinese forces drove the Japanese 18th Division from the Hukawng and Mogaung valleys in May–June 1944. After hard and tedious campaigning, they finally took the Japanese stronghold of Myitkyina in August, thus ending the first stage of the second Burma campaign. Stilwell termed the action "the first sustained offensive in Chinese history against a first-class enemy."

In the summer of 1944 the (American) Northern Combat Area Command unostentatiously took over from the Sino-American headquarters that had exercised authority over the Chinese troops in Burma. A new offensive, an attack southward from Myitkyina along three routes, was planned for mid-October 1944. With Stilwell's dismissal in October, and the separation of the China theater from the China-Burma-India theater, Lieutenant General Daniel L. Sultan took command of the India-Burma theater. The New First Army of Sun Li-jen achieved its first objective in the three-pronged drive, the occupation of Bhamo, in mid-December. On 6–7 March 1945 the 38th

Division captured Lashio, and on 24 March the 38th and 50th Chinese Divisions met east of Hsipaw. Thus, the whole of the Burma Road from Hsipaw to Kunming came under Chinese control. The mission of the Chinese forces, as defined by Chiang Kai-shek, ended there. The second Burma campaign also served to vindicate Stilwell's belief in the capacities of the Chinese soldier when properly trained, equipped, and led.

Sun Li-jen and his men returned to China in 1945. About this time, General Dwight D. Eisenhower invited Sun to inspect European battlefields. Sun accepted the honor and traveled some 50,000 miles in three weeks. After returning to China, he led his New First Army into Canton and accepted the surrender of the Japanese Twenty-third Army.

When Soviet forces began moving out of Manchuria in March 1946, Sun Li-jen was sent to the Mukden area. The New First Army, now composed of three divisions, moved north from Mukden along the railway and occupied Changtu on 2 April. Ahead lay a roadblock established by the Chinese Communist forces after Soviet troops had moved beyond Ssu-p'ing-kai, an important railway junction that lay halfway between Mukden and Changchun. The Chinese Communists had occupied Ssu-p'ing-kai on 18 March. On 5 April, Sun Li-jen's advance units reached the enemy stronghold, but Sun was obliged to take no action until a Communist threat to the Nationalist rearguard in the Liaosi corridor was eliminated. He finally issued the attack order on 16 April. Strong resistance caused the Nationalists to reinforce the New First Army with the New Fifth and New Sixth armies. Ssu-p'ing-kai finally fell to the Nationalists on 20 May.

In August 1946 Sun Li-jen was appointed deputy pacification commander for the Northeast, with the concurrent assignment, at the head of his New First Army, of Changchun defense commander. At that time, he characterized the Communist People's Liberation Army in Manchuria as "flies attacking a tiger," but his confidence in the Nationalist "tiger" seemed to diminish in the following few months as the Communists chipped away at Nationalist positions. In April 1947 he was replaced as commander of the New First Army by P'an Yü-k'un, a Whampoa graduate, and was made

deputy commander in chief, under Tu Yü-ming (q.v.), of the Northeast Peace Preservation Corps. The New First Army, under new command and renewed Communist attack, abandoned the north bank of the Sungari River. In July, a shakeup of the Nationalist command in Manchuria began. Although Sun Li-jen was the logical replacement for Tu Yü-ming, he was not given that post. Instead, he was removed from field command and was appointed deputy commander in chief of the Chinese Army and commander in chief of army training at Nanking. He held these posts until September 1949, when he became Taiwan defense commander.

In March 1950, after Chiang Kai-shek established the National Government in Taiwan, Sun Li-jen was made commander in chief of the Chinese Army. He was promoted to the rank of full general in May 1951. In Taiwan, however, Sun had to compete for authority and influence with Chiang Kai-shek's son Chiang Ching-kuo (q.v.), whose system of army political commissars was a potential challenge to Sun's authority. That Sun was losing this competition became clear in 1954, when he was removed from his command posts and was appointed personal chief of staff to Chiang Kai-shek. On 20 August 1955 the National Government announced that he had been relieved (on 3 August) of that post as well, having resigned as an "admission of negligence" in connection with an alleged plot by a subordinate, Kuo T'ing-liang. Kuo had been arrested in May, and he was said to have confessed to being a Communist agent. The National Government appointed a nine-man board to investigate, but did not make public the details of the case against Kuo. Available information suggests that the alleged plot consisted in part of a plan for the presentation of a troop petition to Chiang-Kai-shek calling for the abolition of the army political commissar system. Sun Li-jen was not accused of being a Communist agent, but it was assumed that he "may have known what his followers were doing without realizing that the alleged plot was Communist-inspired." He reportedly was placed under house arrest. He later lived in retirement at Taichung. To many Chinese, Sun was known as "the ever victorious general," but in Taiwan, political generals, rather than capable commanders, carried the day.

Sun Lien-chung 孫 連 仲
T. Fang-lu 仿 魯

Sun Lien-chung (1893–), subordinate of Feng Yü-hsiang who entered the service of the National Government in 1930 and became known as an outstanding field commander during the Sino-Japanese war. In July 1945 he became governor of Hopei and commander of the Eleventh War Area, later the Paoting pacification office. In 1948 he served as personal chief of staff to Chiang Kai-shek.

Hsiunghsien, Chihli (Hopei), was the birthplace of Sun Lien-chung. He attended the Paoting Middle School and then, in 1913, joined the regiment commanded by Feng Yü-hsiang (q.v.). He soon rose to become a battalion commander in Feng's 16th Mixed Brigade. After serving with an artillery regiment and receiving advanced military training he rejoined Feng's forces. In the final stage of the Northern Expedition, Feng's armies were reorganized as the Second Army Group. Sun served under Lu Chung-lin (q.v.), the commander in chief of the Northern Route Army of the Second Army Group. This force took the field against the Fengtien troops in northern Honan in April 1928 and played an important role in the final drive northward to Peking. By this time, Sun had risen to the rank of general.

In September 1928 Sun Lien-chung was appointed governor of Tsinghai, and in 1929 he succeeded Liu Yü-fen as governor of Kansu. In the latter post, he was charged with administering the military affairs of Kansu, Tsinghai, and Ninghsia. After participating in the unsuccessful Yen-Feng movement (for details, see Feng Yü-hsiang; Yen Hsi-shan), Sun, like many other officers who had served under Feng Yü-hsiang, entered the service of the National Government. He was given command of the Twenty-sixth Route Army and was appointed Kiangsi director for purging the countryside with responsibility for "bandit-suppression" activities in the rural areas of Kiangsi, Hupeh, Hunan, and Honan. For five years, he was one of the workhorses of the anti-Communist campaigns, and he played a prominent role in the 1934–35 pursuit of the Long March forces. His work in the "bandit-

suppression" campaigns ceased only when the Sian Incident of December 1936 (see Chiang Kai-shek; Chang Hsueh-liang) and the formation of a united front brought these campaigns to an end. Sun's work during this period was recognized by the Kuomintang in 1935 at its Fifth National Congress. Sun was elected to the party's Central Supervisory Committee.

After the Sino-Japanese war began in July 1937, Sun Lien-chung led his Twenty-sixth Route Army to Liuliho, on the southern outskirts of Peiping. His troops gradually were forced into Shansi, which fell to the Japanese in November 1937. Sun then was promoted to commander in chief of the Second Group Army, in which capacity he took part in the battle of Taierhchuang (for details, see Li Tsung-jen) in March-May 1938. For his performance in that critical battle, he was awarded the Blue Sky and White Sun decoration. After withdrawing from east China, he contributed to the defense of Wuhan until October, when he was forced to withdraw northward. In the spring of 1939, he participated in the battle of Tangho, recovering it from the Japanese.

By this time, Sun had established himself as one of the Nationalists' outstanding field commanders. In 1939 he was made deputy commanding officer of the First War Area, and he later held the equivalent post in the Sixth War Area. In July 1945 the National Government appointed him commanding officer of the Eleventh War Area and governor of his native Hopei. At war's end, he was ordered to effect the Nationalist takeover of Hopei, Shantung, and Chahar and to administer matters pertaining to the Japanese surrender. With the aid of American forces in the Chinwangtao, Tientsin, Peiping, and Tsingtao areas, he was able to achieve his objectives with great speed. As the civil war between the Nationalists and the Chinese Communists gained impetus, Chiang Kai-shek began shifting officers and reorganizing civil and military bodies. In March 1947 the Eleventh War Area was reorganized as the Paoting pacification office, with Sun Lien-chung as pacification commissioner and Hopei-Paoan commander. In the autumn of 1947 he participated in the battle of the Peiping-Tientsin-Paoting triangle and won one of the Nationalists' ever-rarer victories. He was appointed commander in chief of defense for the Nanking area in the spring of 1948 and personal chief of staff to Chiang Kai-shek that autumn. When Chiang retired from office in January 1949, Sun also resigned. Sun then went to Taiwan, where he became a member of the strategy advisory commission after the National Government retreated to Taiwan in December 1949.

Sun Pao-ch'i　　　　孫 寶 踦
T. Mu-han　　　　　慕 韓

Sun Pao-ch'i (26 April 1867–3 February 1931), diplomat who represented the Ch'ing government in France and Germany and who served the Peking government as minister of foreign affairs and premier.

The eldest son of Sun Yi-ching, an assistant imperial tutor, Sun Pao-ch'i was born in Hangchow. He received a traditional education in the Chinese classics. Upon completion of his studies, he was awarded the title of second-grade yin sheng. About this time, he married a relative of I-k'uang, who in 1884 became Prince Ch'ing. In 1886 Sun, then 19, was made a junior secretary in the Board of Punishments. He held this post until 1895, when he became expectant tao-t'ai of Chihli (Hopei). In 1898 the Tsungli Yamen, headed by Prince Ch'ing, listed Sun as a candidate for a foreign post, but he did not receive an appointment abroad because of the disruptions caused by the Hundred Days Reform and the Boxer Uprising. After the imperial court fled to Sian, Sun was named telegraph commissioner of the Grand Council. The court returned to Peking in January 1902, and Sun, after a brief period as secretary of legation in Vienna, Berlin, and Paris, received an appointment as minister to France in June 1902.

In 1905 Sun Pao-ch'i demonstrated his sense of honor in a fashion that endeared him to supporters of Sun Yat-sen. At this time, Sun Yat-sen was in Europe to win new members for his Hsing-Chung-hui. Two Chinese students in Paris who had enrolled in the Hsing-Chung-hui became fearful of the possible consequences of their actions—especially because they were studying on government scholarships. To redeem themselves, they went to Sun Yat-sen's lodgings during his absence, took the membership register, and presented it to Sun Pao-ch'i in the hope that he would extricate them from their predicament. Sun Pao-ch'i scolded them for the theft, warned them about the possible consequences of stealing, and ordered them to return the register to Sun Yat-sen.

Sun Pao-ch'i returned to China in the summer of 1906 to become chief secretary of the Grand Council, with responsibility for reorganizing the administrative system. In 1907 he was made minister to Germany. He returned to China in January 1909 after being appointed assistant director of the Tientsin-Pukow railway, and in June of that year he was made governor of Shantung. In 1910, as the clamor for constitutional government increased throughout China, he sent a memorial to the throne urging the prompt establishment of a cabinet system. In November 1911, a month after the Chinese revolution began with the Wuchang revolt, Sun responded to the urgings of his colleagues and of the gentry and merchants of Tsinan by permitting proclamation of the province's independence of Manchu rule. He was acclaimed tutuh [military governor], and he assumed that office on 15 November. In the meantime, however, Yuan Shih-k'ai had won commanding power at Peking. After Yuan demonstrated, by means of the capture of Hanyang from the revolutionaries on 27 November (for details, see Feng Kuo-chang), that he was in control of the situation, Sun Pao-ch'i cancelled Shantung's declaration of independence on 29 November. The imperial authorities magnanimously pardoned him for his temporary dereliction, but accepted his resignation in December.

With the Manchu abdication of February 1912, Sun Pao-ch'i went to Tientsin, where he and Prince Ch'ing went into partnership in a business enterprise. In December 1912 Sun returned to public life as co-director general of the Customs Administration, and in May 1913 he became acting director general. On 11 September, Hsiung Hsi-ling (q v.) appointed him minister of foreign affairs in what became known as the "first caliber" cabinet. Among Sun's first tasks was the negotiation of an agreement with Russia, signed on 5 November, by which Russia recognized China's suzerainty over Outer Mongolia, and China recognized Outer Mongolia's autonomy. Hsiung Hsi-ling resigned in mid-February 1914, and Sun served as acting premier until Hsü Shih-ch'ang (q.v.)

assumed office in May. He continued to serve as minister of foreign affairs until January 1915, when Japan presented the Twenty-One Demands to Yuan Shih-k'ai. Sun resigned, and Lu Cheng-hsiang (q.v.) succeeded him.

Sun Pao-ch'i became director of the bureau of audit in January 1916. From that time on, he was to be concerned chiefly with financial and economic matters rather than with foreign affairs. In April, he became minister of finance in the cabinet of Tuan Ch'i-jui (q.v.), with the concurrent post of director general of the salt gabelle. When the Central Bank of China and the Bank of Communications suspended note exchange operations in June, he resigned his posts. He remained out of office until the summer of 1917, when he was appointed director general of the Customs Administration. He also became director of the audit bureau, and in May 1920 he assumed additional responsibility as director of the economic information bureau. In October 1921 he accepted the chairmanship of the famine prevention commission and the associate directorship of the famine relief bureau, and in January 1922 he was made vice chairman of the Yangtze River commission. He became vice chairman of the commission charged with studying diplomatic questions arising from the Washington Conference and director general of the famine relief bureau in the spring of 1922.

Ts'ao K'un (q.v.) appointed Sun Pao-ch'i premier at Peking in January 1924, but Sun's premiership was compromised from the start because the composition of his cabinet was determined by Wang Lan-t'ing, Ts'ao K'un's chief secretary. Nevertheless, Sun's government achieved the establishment of diplomatic relations with the Soviet Union in May and the successful negotiations of the matter of German debts. Friction between Sun and his minister of finance, Wang K'o-min (q.v.), led to Sun's resignation in July 1924. After Feng Yü-hsiang (q.v.) occupied Peking in October and Tuan Ch'i-jui returned to power as chief executive, Sun became chairman of the foreign affairs committee at Peking. In February 1925, as the Fengtien forces were contending with Sun Ch'uan-fang (q.v.) for mastery of the lower Yangtze region, Sun Pao-ch'i refused the post of director general of the newly created special administrative area of Shanghai. He also refused appointment as ambassador to the Soviet Union. He became instead president of the Han-yeh-p'ing iron and steel complex and of the China Merchants' Steam Navigation Company. In 1926 he was appointed general director of Sino-French University. Sun entered the service of Chang Tso-lin (q.v.) in December 1927 and retired to Dairen when the Northern Expedition reached Peking in 1928.

In 1929 Sun Pao-ch'i, who was suffering from a chronic intestinal disorder, went to Hong Kong for medical treatment. He went to Shanghai in the spring of 1930 and made a trip to his native Hangchow to sweep the graves of his ancestors. After he returned to Shanghai that autumn, his illness became progressively serious. Sun Pao-ch'i died on 3 February 1931. He was survived by six sons and sixteen daughters.

Sun Yat-sen	孫 逸 仙
Orig. Sun Wen	孫 文
T. Ti-hsiang	帝 象
H. Jih-hsin	日 新
I-hsien	逸 仙
Chung-shan	中 山
Alias. Nakayama Shō (Chinese: Chung-shan Ch'iao)	中 山 樵

Sun Yat-sen (12 November 1866–12 March 1925), leader of the republican revolution and of the Kuomintang.

The village of Ts'uiheng (Choyhung) in Hsiangshan hsien, Kwangtung, situated near the coast some 30 miles north of the Portuguese colony of Macao, was the birthplace of Sun Yat-sen. His ancestors had been farmers for generations, and his father, after spending some years in Macao as a tailor, had returned to his native village to resume the family's traditional occupation before Sun was born. At the age of six, Sun Yat-sen began his formal education in the Chinese classics at a village school. In 1879 he was sent to join his elder brother, Sun Mei (1854–1914; T. Te-chang, H. Shou-ping), who had emigrated to Hawaii several years previously and had prospered as a farmer and as a merchant. Sun Yat-sen enrolled at Iolani College, a boys boarding school in Honolulu operated under the auspices of the Church of England. His courses included English, science, and instruction in Christian doctrine. In 1882, after being graduated from Iolani, he returned to Ts'uiheng to live with his family. By that time, his knowledge of the Western world and his Christian training at Iolani had led him to look upon the traditional religious beliefs of the villagers as mere superstitions. Not long after his return, he demonstrated his skepticism by breaking off the finger of an idol in the village temple. This act of youthful bravado aroused the wrath of the local inhabitants and resulted in his expulsion from the village.

Having been banished from the family home, Sun Yat-sen went to Hong Kong in the autumn of 1883. Although detailed information about his life during the next few years is lacking, it appears that he studied for a short time at the Church of England diocesan school and that he entered Queen's College, a school operated by the Hong Kong government, in the spring of 1884. He soon met a young American missionary, Dr. Charles R. Hager, by whom he was baptized a Christian. About the same time as his conversion, he returned home briefly to submit to an arranged marriage to a local girl. In the spring of 1886 he returned to China from a visit to his brother in Hawaii. Having decided to take up medicine as his profession, he went to Canton to become a student at the medical school attached to the Pok Chai Hospital, the oldest Western hospital in China, which then was under the direction of a venerable American medical missionary, Dr. John G. Kerr. Sun left Canton in 1887 and went to Hong Kong to enroll as a student in the college of medicine affiliated with the newly established Alice Memorial Hospital. For the next five years, he studied under the general supervision of Dr. James Cantlie, the dean of the medical school. Upon graduation in June 1892 with a certificate of proficiency in medicine and surgery, Sun moved to Macao, but because he was unlicensed to practice there he was obliged by the Portuguese authorities to leave the colony. In the spring of 1893 he began to practice in Hong Kong.

It was apparently during his years as a medical student in Canton and Hong Kong that Sun Yat-sen began to take a serious interest in China's political affairs and to entertain ideas of overthrowing the ruling Manchu dynasty. According to some sources, his anti-Manchu sentiments had been aroused during his boyhood in Ts'uiheng when villagers had told him tales of the great Taiping Rebellion. Sun himself variously ascribed the origin of his revolutionary tendencies to his early training in Christian principles, to the contrast he observed between the relative efficiency of the British colonial government in Hong Kong and the corrupt and ineffective administration existing in China, and to the failure of the Manchu rulers to defend the frontiers of China from foreign aggression, particularly during the Sino-French hostilities of 1884–85. These early dissatisfactions were reinforced by contact with several young radicals in Canton and Hong Kong. In 1886, while studying medicine in Canton, he became friendly with a fellow student, Cheng Shih-liang (d. 1901; H. Pi-ch'en), who was a member of the Triads (San-ho-hui), one of the largest of the anti-Manchu secret societies in south China. At medical school in Hong Kong, Sun met other students, including Ch'en Shao-pai (q.v.), who shared his anti-Manchu sentiments. After his return from Macao to Hong Kong in 1893, Sun resumed contact with these former schoolmates and with Lu Hao-tung (1868–1895), a boyhood friend from his native village. They held secret meetings and discussed various schemes for China's regeneration, including the possibility of overthrowing the Manchu rulers.

Despite the subversive tenor of these talks, Sun Yat-sen apparently was not yet prepared to commit himself openly to the cause of revolution; he decided instead to work for the reform of existing institutions. In February 1894 he abandoned his languishing medical practice and left for Tientsin to present a letter containing his reform proposals to Li Hung-chang (ECCP, I, 464–71), then governor general of Chihli (Hopei) and one of China's most influential exponents of modernization. The letter, a politically innocuous document, suggested in general terms the ways in which China could be strengthened. It gave special emphasis to the need for adopting Western scientific methods to improve agriculture in China. Li, however, was preoccupied with the hostilities that broke out between Chinese and Japanese forces in Korea that summer and had no time to consider such proposals. A disappointed Sun Yat-sen departed for Hawaii to raise private funds for an agricultural association to carry out the measures he had suggested in his letter. In November 1894, with the help of his brother and others of the overseas Chinese community, he organized the Hsing-Chung-hui [revive China society] in Honolulu. The stated aim of the society was to "revitalize China," and funds for this purpose were raised through the purchase of shares in the society by its members.

During the autumn and winter of 1894, Japanese armies in Korea routed the Chinese forces and advanced rapidly into southern Manchuria, threatening the city of Peking itself. To Sun's friends in China, the prospect of imminent collapse of the imperial forces in north China presented a favorable opportunity for starting a revolt to overthrow the Manchu rulers. In response to an urgent message from China, Sun left Honolulu in January 1895 and, after stopping briefly in Japan, proceeded to Hong Kong. He and his Hong Kong colleagues, Cheng Shih-liang, Ch'en Shao-pai, and Lu Hao-tung, decided to join forces with the Fu-jen Literary Society (Fu-jen wen-she), a secret revolutionary group that had been organized early in 1892 by Yang Ch'ü-yun (1861–1901; T. Chao-ch'un), an employee of a British shipping firm in Hong Kong. The new organization was made the main branch of the Hsing-Chung-hui. Although its ostensible purpose was the establishment of newspapers, schools, and new industries, and the promotion of other measures designed to make China strong and prosperous, the basic aim of the Hsing-Chung-hui was to organize a revolt against the Manchu dynasty and to establish a republican government in China. Its leaders proceeded to work out plans for an attack upon Canton in October. During the spring and summer of 1895, while Yang Ch'ü-yun remained in Hong Kong to raise funds and purchase arms, Sun Yat-sen went to Canton with Cheng Shih-liang and Lu Hao-tung to recruit supporters among former soldiers whose units had been disbanded in accordance with the terms of the Treaty of Shimonoseki, and among members of the secret societies, organizing a Society for the Study of Agriculture (Nung-hsueh-hui) to serve as a cloak for their activities. However, the day before the uprising was scheduled, the plot was discovered by the authorities in Canton, and several of the conspirators, including Lu Hao-tung, were arrested and executed. Sun and a few others escaped to Hong Kong, but, at the behest of the Ch'ing government, the British authorities ordered them to leave the colony. At the end of October 1895 Sun left Hong Kong with a few of his comrades to seek refuge in Japan.

REVOLUTIONARY IN EXILE

The Canton revolt of 1895 marked the beginning of Sun's career as a professional revolutionist. Through his part in this venture he became a political fugitive with a price on his head, and for the next 16 years he was forced to carry on his revolutionary activities outside of China, beyond the reach of the Manchu authorities. On reaching Japan in November, he proceeded to Yokohama, where he set up a branch of the Hsing-Chung-hui under the direction of a local resident and sympathizer, Feng Ching-ju (*see under* Feng Tzu-yu). It was at that time that Sun, seeking to disguise himself as a modernized Japanese, cut off his queue, grew a mustache, and adopted Western-style clothing. He then went to stay with his brother in Hawaii where, in the spring of 1896, he was joined by his family. In Hawaii, Sun began to recruit new members for the Hsing-Chung-hui from among members of secret societies in Hawaii, and he succeeded in establishing connections with the local branch of the Hung-men Society. In June 1896 he went to San Francisco, where he sought to win the support of the Chih-kung-tang and other local Hung-men groups. At that time, however, the Hung-men members in America, despite the anti-dynastic origins of their society, believed that their interests as residents in the United States were best represented by the recognized government of China. Accordingly, they showed little interest in Sun's plans for revolution.

Sun Yat-sen left the United States and went to England to visit his old friend Dr. Cantlie, who had returned from Hong Kong to live in retirement in his homeland. For several months, Sun's movements had been kept under surveillance by agents of the Ch'ing government. As Sun was walking past the Chinese legation on Portland Place on 11 October 1896, he was dragged into the building and was held captive while the Chinese minister and his staff made arrangements to charter a ship to send him back to China for almost certain execution as a rebel. Sun managed to get word to Dr. Cantlie, who prevailed upon the British government to effect his release. The incident was given wide publicity, with the result that almost overnight Sun, up to that time an obscure political fugitive, acquired an international reputation as a notorious revolutionist. Following this adventure, he lived quietly in London for several months. During this time, he was a frequent visitor to the reading room of the British Museum, where he became acquainted with Western socialist literature, including the writings of Karl Marx, as well as the works of the American economist Henry George, whose ideas on taxation and land rents were to exert considerable influence upon the development of his social and economic thought.

In July 1897, after ten months in England, Sun Yat-sen returned by way of Canada to Japan to seek support for the revolutionary cause among the Chinese communities in Yokohama and Tokyo. To conceal his identity from the authorities, he adopted the common Japanese surname of Nakayama. The Chinese pronunciation of this pseudonym, "Chung-shan," was to become the name by which he would be best known to his associates. Although he was able to make but little headway among his conservative countrymen in Japan at that time, he was more successful in enlisting the support of Japanese liberals. Shortly after his arrival in Yokohama, he was approached by Miyazaki Torazō, an adventurer and Sinophile who became one of his most devoted Japanese followers. Through Miyazaki, Sun was introduced to several prominent Japanese liberals, including Miyazaki's patron, Inukai Tsuyoshi (1855–1932), and Okuma Shigenobu (1832–1922). In the interest of Asian unity against the West they were eager to cooperate with Chinese progressives in strengthening China. Inukai was so favorably impressed with Sun that he provided him with living quarters in Tokyo as well as funds to carry on his activities. Another group which received the attention of Japanese liberals was the reform party led by K'ang Yu-wei and his distinguished disciple Liang Ch'i-ch'ao (qq.v.). After the conservative *coup d'état* of September 1898 in China, K'ang, Liang, and other reformers fled to Japan, where they were approached by Sun and his Japanese friends with the proposal that the reformers join with the revolutionary

party in working for the regeneration of China. K'ang, however, was an uncompromising monarchist. He forbade his followers to cooperate with Sun and the Hsing-Chung-hui and in 1899 organized the Pao-huang-hui, a monarchist society that was to become a bitter competitor of the revolutionary party for the support of overseas Chinese in Japan, Southeast Asia, and America.

Meanwhile, Sun Yat-sen, together with Ch'en Shao-pai, Cheng Shih-liang, and other Hsing-Chung-hui members in Japan, had begun to make plans for a new series of uprisings in conjunction with secret societies in central and southern China. During 1899 and 1900 they concentrated on preparations for a revolt at Waichow (Huichow), some 150 miles east of Canton. In Hong Kong, Ch'en Shao-pai established a propaganda newspaper, the *Chung-kuo jih-pao* [China daily], and Cheng Shih-liang enlisted the support of the Triad and other secret societies. Sun arranged with his Japanese collaborators for supplies of arms and ammunition. In October 1900, while Sun was in Taiwan awaiting Japanese military assistance, Cheng Shih-liang led an initially successful revolt in the Waichow area. However, the munitions expected from Japan failed to arrive, and, on receiving word from Sun, Cheng disbanded his forces and fled back to Hong Kong.

After the collapse of the Waichow revolt, Sun Yat-sen returned to Japan and lived quietly in Yokohama for three years. During this period, Tokyo became a center for Chinese political refugees and students seeking a modern education in Japanese colleges and universities. Many of the newcomers were attracted to the cause of constitutional monarchy as presented in the influential publications of Liang Ch'i-ch'ao. However, the successive humiliations suffered by China after the Boxer Uprising caused societies and newspapers organized by Chinese students in Japan to become increasingly radical in their political outlook. In these students Sun saw a new source of support for his revolutionary aims, and while residing in Yokohama he held discussions with a number of young radicals about the desirability of organizing their fellow students into revolutionary groups.

The growing revolutionary sentiment among the Chinese students in Japan led Sun Yat-sen to renew his efforts to extend the membership of the Hsing-Chung-hui in overseas Chinese communities. Early in 1903 he went to Southeast Asia. After establishing a branch of the party in Hanoi, he proceeded to Saigon and to Siam, where he also recruited new members for the revolutionary organization. He returned to Yokohama in July, but set forth again two months later to raise funds and to gain new adherents in America. During his five months in Hawaii and his subsequent travels in the United States (April–December 1904), Sun was vigorously opposed by partisans of K'ang Yu-wei's monarchist party, which had many adherents in overseas Chinese communities. Nevertheless, he succeeded in winning considerable support for the revolutionary cause. In December 1904 he went to England, and during the first six months of 1905 he visited Brussels, Berlin, and Paris, where he set up new branches of his revolutionary organization.

THE FOUNDING OF THE T'UNG-MENG-HUI

In June 1905 Sun left Europe to return to Japan by way of Singapore and Saigon. On arrival in Yokohama in mid-July, he found new political ferment among the Chinese students, whose patriotic feelings had been stirred to a high pitch by the example of Japan's stunning victory over Russia in the war of 1904–5. Also in Japan by that time were such political refugees from China as Huang Hsing and Sung Chiao-jen (qq.v.), the founders of the revolutionary Hua-hsing-hui. Through the introduction of Miyazaki Torazō, Sun made the acquaintance of these and other revolutionary leaders, with whom he discussed plans for the amalgamation of the Hua-hsing-hui, the Hsing-Chung-hui, and the radical student organizations in Japan into a single revolutionary league. A preparatory meeting was held in Tokyo on 30 July, at which the proposed league was named the Chung-kuo T'ung-meng-hui, and some 70 of those attending were enrolled as members. At the first formal meeting, held in Tokyo on 20 August 1905, more than 300 students and young revolutionaries joined the T'ung-meng-hui and, at the suggestion of Huang Hsing, elected Sun Yat-sen as its director.

The new T'ung-meng-hui differed in important respects from Sun's older revolutionary organization, the Hsing-Chung-hui, which had consisted of a number of widely separated and largely autonomous branches with little over-all coordination of purpose or action. In contrast, the T'ung-meng-hui was a more centralized and carefully organized group. Its main headquarters in Tokyo, divided into three separate departments—executive, appraisal, and judicial—was designed to coordinate operations of a network of regional branches in each province of China and in such special areas as Hong Kong and Southeast Asia. In membership as well as in organization, there were significant differences between the two societies. The Hsing-Chung-hui had been composed mainly of members of secret societies in south China and of Chinese merchants and workingmen overseas, while the core of the T'ung-meng-hui consisted of students and young intellectuals from almost every part of China, many of whom, such as Chu Chih-hsin, Hu Han-min, Liao Chung-k'ai, and Wang Ching-wei (qq.v.), were to replace the veterans of the Hsing-Chung-hui as Sun's closest associates. The most notable distinction between the T'ung-meng-hui and the older organization, however, lay in their respective revolutionary programs. The aims of the Hsing-Chung-hui had developed from Sun's early proposals to strengthen China by reform into three revolutionary tenets: expel the Manchus, restore the Chinese, and establish a republican government. By 1905 Sun, whose ideas had been modified by his studies of Henry George and others, had fashioned the san-min chu-i or Three People's Principles—nationalism, democracy, and the people's livelihood. He gave the first indication of the development in his thinking during the spring of 1905 in speeches to Chinese students in Europe. With the formation of the T'ung-meng-hui, a brief outline of Sun's revolutionary program, which was based on the Three People's Principles, was incorporated into the society's constitution. The principles and the program were explained in detail during the next few years in the *Min-pao* [people's journal], which was established in Tokyo in November 1905 as the society's official propaganda organ.

The founding of the T'ung-meng-hui marked the beginning of a period of intensified revolutionary activity by Sun Yat-sen and his colleagues. Almost immediately, they began working to raise funds for the new society and to expand its organization within China and among the overseas Chinese in preparation for new uprisings against the Manchu government. Sun left Japan in October 1905 for Southeast Asia, and during the following year he established branches of the T'ung-meng-hui in Singapore, Kuala Lumpur, Penang, and other places in British Malaya as well as in the Dutch East Indies. After returning to Japan in the autumn of 1906, he gave a rousing address to a rally of several thousand students who had gathered to celebrate the first anniversary of the *Min-pao*. By this time, the increasingly radical tendencies shown by the Chinese students in Japan had become a source of concern to the Japanese authorities, who decided to comply with a demand from the Peking government that Sun Yat-sen be expelled from Japan. His Japanese friends in the government, still wishing to remain on good terms with the revolutionary leader, secretly provided him with funds to continue his activities elsewhere.

Before leaving Japan, Sun Yat-sen conferred with Huang Hsing and other T'ung-meng-hui leaders about future military action against the Manchu regime in China. Although faced with increasing restrictions upon their activities in Japan and Hong Kong, the revolutionaries had learned that the French authorities in Indo-China were sympathetic to their cause and were willing to provide them with a secret base for their activities. Sun and his collaborators decided to set up military headquarters in Indo-China and to concentrate their operations at various points along the southwestern frontier of China. Early in March 1907 Sun left with Hu Han-min, Wang Ching-wei, and others for Hanoi, and with the help of a few French military officers they began to train a small revolutionary force, while at the same time arranging for supplies of arms and ammunition to be sent to them from the T'ung-meng-hui office in Japan. During the spring and summer of 1907 Sun and his staff attempted to take advantage of local unrest in Kwangtung province to foment a number of uprisings. Government troops crushed insurrections near Swatow in May and at Waichow in June. Another unsuccessful uprising broke out in September at Ch'inchow (Yamchow). In December, revolt broke out on the Kwangsi border, and Sun, accompanied by Huang Hsing and Hu Han-min, left Hanoi to join the insurgents, who had captured the frontier

outpost of Chen-nan-kuan. After holding out briefly against imperial forces commanded by Lu Jung-t'ing (q.v.), Sun and his supporters were forced to retire into French territory. In these campaigns the strategy of the revolutionaries was to join forces with the secret societies and bands of local rebels in areas that were accessible from outside China and to infiltrate units of the imperial forces and win over the officers and men to the revolutionary cause. However, the revolutionary forces, consisting at most of a few hundred untrained adventurers and led by amateurs, had little hope of overcoming the well-armed and numerically superior imperial armies. Their strategy was vitiated by their failure to secure the necessary military supplies from Japan and to deliver them to their collaborators within China.

Late in 1907, while Sun was at Chen-nan-kuan, the Ch'ing government had persuaded the French authorities to expel the revolutionary leader from Indo-China; and in March 1908 he departed for Singapore to raise funds for munitions to send to Hu Han-min, whom he left in Hanoi to supervise further military ventures, and Huang Hsing, who returned to China to organize further uprisings. In the spring of 1908, after the failure of uprisings at Ch'inchow and Lienchow in Kwangtung and at Hokow in Yunnan, Hu, Huang, and several hundred of their troops also were deported from Indo-China. Hu and Huang rejoined Sun in Singapore in July 1908. By that time the fortunes of the revolutionary organization had reached a low ebb. Repeated military failure in south China not only had disheartened the revolutionary forces then stranded in Malaya but also had seriously damaged the prestige of the T'ung-meng-hui among the overseas Chinese in Southeast Asia. Thus, when Sun and other T'ung-meng-hui leaders toured Malaya and Siam in 1908 and 1909, they found the Chinese inhabitants reluctant to make further contributions to a seemingly lost cause. Although Sun established a Southeast Asian branch of the party, with Hu Han-min as director, and a Siamese branch, headed by Hsiao Fo-ch'eng (q.v.), his campaign was not a success. Added to these difficulties was the growing discontent with Sun's leadership among some members of the T'ung-meng-hui. Moreover, the Japanese authorities helped stifle the party's activities by banning the *Min-pao* in August 1908.

REVOLUTION

By the late spring of 1909 Sun Yat-sen had become *persona non grata* to the authorities in almost every region of Eastern Asia. Because his movements were restricted, he decided that he could work more effectively for the revolution by going to the West. In May 1909, before leaving for France, he ordered the establishment of a south China bureau of the T'ung-meng-hui at Hong Kong, with Hu Han-min as its director. On his departure, practical responsibility for planning revolutionary activities in China and for building up party support in Southeast Asia passed to Hu Han-min and Huang Hsing.

In Paris, Sun Yat-sen attempted to secure a loan for the T'ung-meng-hui, but without success. After making brief visits to Brussels and London, he left Europe for the United States in October 1909. To refute accusations by Chang Ping-lin (q.v.) and other T'ung-meng-hui dissidents in Japan that he had been misusing the society's funds, he published an itemized accounting of his expenditures in the Chinese-American newspapers. During his five months of travel through the United States and Canada he discovered that the strength of the monarchist party among the overseas Chinese was waning and that they were much more receptive to his arguments for overthrowing the Manchu regime in China than they had been in 1904. Sun raised considerable financial support and established branches of the T'ung-meng-hui in New York, Chicago, and San Francisco. In March 1910 he went to Honolulu, and two months later he returned to Japan to reestablish contact with the T'ung-meng-hui leaders still in Tokyo and to set up a secret organization to coordinate the activities of revolutionary groups throughout China. Although he lived under an assumed name at the Tokyo home of his friend Miyazaki Torazō, his presence in Japan soon came to the attention of the Ch'ing government, which again demanded his expulsion. Thus, after only ten days in Japan, he was asked by the Japanese authorities to leave the country.

Sun sailed for Singapore and then went to Penang. In November, he summoned Huang Hsing, Hu Han-min, and other leaders to a meeting to discuss preparations for another uprising in China. Plans were made for a large-scale revolt in Canton, under the direction of Huang Hsing. Not long after the meeting, however, the British authorities took exception to one of Sun's speeches and ordered him to leave Malaya. Having been excluded from the last remaining refuge in the Far East, Sun embarked upon another tour of North America to raise funds. He left Penang in December and traveled by way of Europe to the United States and Canada, arriving in New York in mid-February of 1911. He was given an enthusiastic reception by the Chinese communities in San Francisco, Vancouver, and Victoria, and within a short time he had raised almost U.S. $80,000 in support of the uprising in Canton. Despite its failure, the Canton revolt, later known as the Huang-hua-kang uprising (for details, *see* Huang Hsing), aroused considerable interest among overseas Chinese. Because of their growing enthusiasm, Sun decided to remain in America to seek funds for further revolutionary attempts in China.

The T'ung-meng-hui and other revolutionary societies in China soon began to concentrate their attention on the Yangtze region, especially the Wuhan cities and Nanking. In July 1911 Chü Cheng, Ch'en Ch'i-mei (qq.v.), Sung Chiao-jen, and others established the central China bureau of the T'ung-meng-hui, with headquarters in the International Settlement at Shanghai. In Hupeh province, allied revolutionary groups infiltrated units of the imperial New Army stationed at the Wuhan cities. Although Sun Yat-sen was not unaware of these developments, he had little direct contact with his colleagues in China. His first knowledge of the Wuchang revolt of 10 October 1911 and the revolution came from reading a newspaper report while traveling on a train from Denver to Kansas City. From subsequent reports in the American press he learned that the revolutionaries in China were planning to establish a republican government with himself as its president. Realizing the importance of the proposed new government's relations with the Western powers, Sun, instead of returning immediately to China, went to Europe and, as the recognized head of the largest revolutionary organization in China, explored questions of diplomatic recognition and foreign loans with European political and economic leaders. He arrived in London at the end of October, where he succeeded in persuading the British government to lift its restrictions on his movements in its territories in the Far East and in obtaining from the Four Power Banking Consortium a verbal promise to suspend further loan installments to the Ch'ing government. He then proceeded to Paris. In an interview with Premier Georges Clemenceau, he broached the matter of French recognition of the republican government in China, but obtained no specific agreement. Sun set sail for China from Marseilles in the latter part of November 1911 in the company of Chang Chi, Li Shih-tseng, Wu Chih-hui (qq.v.), and other revolutionary sympathizers who had joined him in England and France.

By the time Sun Yat-sen arrived in China, Shanghai and Nanking had fallen to the revolutionary armies, and several provinces in succession had declared their independence from the Ch'ing government. In Peking, the Manchu court in desperation had turned the reins of government over to Yuan Shih-k'ai (q.v.); in Nanking, revolutionary delegates from 14 provinces had assembled to discuss the organization of a provisional republican regime; and in Shanghai, truce negotiations had begun, with Wu T'ing-fang (q.v.) representing the revolutionaries and T'ang Shao-yi (q.v.) representing the Peking government. Sun Yat-sen arrived in Shanghai on 25 December 1911 to receive a hero's welcome from a large and enthusiastic crowd of T'ung-meng-hui comrades and other well-wishers. Four days later, the convention of provincial delegates in Nanking elected him president of a provisional republican government, and on 1 January 1912 he proceeded to Nanking, where he assumed office and formally proclaimed the establishment of the Republic of China.

The Republic and the Kuomintang

Sun Yat-sen's inauguration as provisional president of the republican regime in Nanking, after 16 years of exile from China, marked a high point in his revolutionary career. But the political revolution he and his associates had labored to achieve was far from complete. The Manchu emperor still occupied the throne, and the imperial regime in Peking continued to be the government recognized by the foreign powers. Negotiations at Shanghai were deadlocked by the Nanking regime's insistence on the abdication of the Manchus and the establishment of a republic and by the Peking government's objection to Sun Yat-sen as president of a new republic. Furthermore, a stalemate existed between the revolutionary forces and the imperial armies; with foreign loans temporarily suspended, neither side was in a position to finance the military operations necessary to overcome the other. On 22 January 1912 Sun Yat-sen, in an effort to end this impasse, offered to resign his position as provisional president in favor of Yuan Shih-k'ai if the Manchus abdicated and Yuan openly declared his support of the republic. Yuan accepted these conditions, and on 13 February, the day after the announcement of the Manchu abdication, Sun tendered his resignation to the provisional National Assembly (ts'an-i-yuan) which had been established on 28 January 1912 in Nanking. Two days later, on Sun's recommendation, the National Assembly elected Yuan Shih-k'ai as Sun's successor. Yuan was formally inaugurated as provisional president of the republic on 12 March in Peking. In making his decision to relinquish the presidency, Sun was not without misgivings about Yuan's intentions. In an attempt to insure the latter's support of the republic, he had appended certain conditions to his resignation: that Nanking, rather than the old imperial capital, be the new seat of government; and that Yuan agree to be bound by the new provisional constitution then being prepared by the assembly in Nanking. Yuan, however, was reluctant to leave his stronghold in Peking, and by a series of shrewd political maneuvers, he was able to convince Sun and his T'ung-meng-hui associates not only that he should remain in the north but also that the Nanking provisional government itself should move to Peking.

By this time, the T'ung-meng-hui had become an open party, with Sun Yat-sen as its chairman and Huang Hsing as its vice chairman. After his retirement from the presidency, Sun Yat-sen turned his attention from political affairs to the questions raised by the principle of the people's livelihood and began to think about China's economic and social reconstruction. Huang Hsing remained in Nanking when the provisional government moved to Peking, and he held office as resident general at Nanking until 14 June 1912. While its two top leaders were thus engaged, the T'ung-meng-hui began to change. Some of its members in Peking, including Sung Chiao-jen, believed that the revolutionary society, having fulfilled its original aims, should be reorganized to function effectively within the National Assembly so that Yuan Shih-k'ai would be brought under parliamentary control. In the hope of dominating the National Assembly by gaining as many seats as possible in the coming national elections, Sung and his supporters joined with the leaders of four smaller parties—the T'ung-i kung-ho-tang [united republican party], the Kuo-min kung-chin-hui [people's progressive party], the Kung-ho shih-chin-hui [progressive republican party], and the Kuo-min kung-tang [people's public party]—to organize a large federated party called the Kuomintang. Yuan Shih-k'ai, aware of this potential threat to his power, invited Sun Yat-sen and Huang Hsing to Peking for a discussion of national affairs. Sun arrived in Peking on 24 August 1912, and the following day he attended the inaugural meeting of the Kuomintang. He was not overly enthusiastic about the new party because its membership included many ambitious politicians who had little sympathy for the social and economic ideals embodied in his principle of the people's livelihood. Although Sun was elected director of the Kuomintang, he left the management of party affairs to Sung Chiao-jen, for he had comparatively little interest in such political activities.

During Sun Yat-sen's stay in Peking from 24 August to 18 September 1912 he held discussions with Yuan Shih-k'ai about railroad development in China, a subject which had aroused Sun's interest. The cordial reception given him by Yuan dispelled Sun's doubts about the Peiyang leader and led him to endorse Yuan openly as the most suitable person to head the new republic. Yuan listened to Sun's railroad development proposals and, on 9 September, appointed him national director of railroad development. Although some contemporary observers suspected that this appointment was merely a gesture to win Sun's public political support, Sun assumed the duties of his new position with great enthusiasm. At the heart of his scheme for railroad development was a rather grandiose plan for three trunk lines, to be financed by large investments of foreign capital, which would link China to Burma, Tibet, and Sinkiang. In the autumn

of 1912 Sun made an investigative tour of existing rail lines in northern and central China; early in 1913 he went to Japan to investigate its railways and to promote Japanese investment in Chinese railways.

THE SECOND REVOLUTION AND THE CONSTITUTION PROTECTION MOVEMENT

While Sun Yat-sen was touring Japan in the winter of 1912, the struggle for control of the government in Peking led to increasing tension between Yuan Shih-k'ai and the Kuomintang. The national elections of February 1913 resulted in Kuomintang control of the National Assembly, and the party tried to limit Yuan Shih-k'ai's authority by winning control of the cabinet. On 20 March 1913 Sung Chiao-jen was assassinated, apparently by agents of Yuan Shih-k'ai. On hearing of Sung's death, Sun Yat-sen went to Shanghai, where he joined Huang Hsing in demanding a thorough investigation of the case and severe punishment of those reponsible for the assassination. Kuomintang opposition to Yuan was increased by the floating of the "reorganization loan" (for details, *see* Yuan Shih-k'ai) in the spring of 1913. That Yuan intended to suppress the Kuomintang became clear in June, when he dismissed the Kuomintang governors of Kiangsi, Kwangtung, and Anhwei from office and ordered the Peiyang Army to move southward toward the Yangtze. As these forces advanced in a two-pronged drive on Kiukiang and Nanking, Li Lieh-chün (q.v.), the governor of Kiangsi, went to Shanghai to consult with Sun Yat-sen and other Kuomintang leaders. With Sun's approval, he returned to Kiangsi early in July, declared the province independent, and assumed the title of commander in chief of the Kiangsi Anti-Yuan Army [T'ao-Yuan-chün]. Thus began the so-called second revolution. Sun Yat-sen made a public denunciation of Yuan Shih-k'ai, and Yuan responded by dismissing Sun from office as director of railroad development on 23 July. The large and highly trained Peiyang forces soon routed and scattered the Kuomintang troops. Nanking fell to the Peiyang forces of Chang Hsün on 1 September, and orders were issued for the arrest of Sun Yat-sen and other Kuomintang leaders on 15 September. Sun Yat-sen remained in China and worked to organize resistance to Yuan Shih-k'ai until late November, when he decided to seek asylum in Japan. After stopping briefly in Taiwan, he reached Tokyo early in December 1913.

The optimism that had characterized Sun Yat-sen's outlook since the establishment of the republic was replaced by bitterness against Yuan Shih-k'ai and the foreign powers that supported him. Sun determined to overthrow Yuan at any cost, and he decided to reorganize the dispirited and ineffective Kuomintang. On 23 June 1914 the new party, the Chung-hua Ko-ming-tang, was inaugurated in Tokyo. Members were required to take an oath of personal obedience to Sun and to seal this pledge with their right thumbprints. Although such long-time associates of Sun as Chang Chi and Huang Hsing objected to the loyalty oath and refused to join the new party, most of Sun's supporters, including Ch'en Ch'i-mei, Chu Chih-hsin, Liao Chung-k'ai, and Tai Chi-t'ao (q.v.) remained loyal to him. Before long, a new propaganda organ, the *Min-kuo tsa-chih* [republican magazine], had been established and members of the new party had begun working to extend its membership throughout the Chinese communities of Southeast Asia and America. Sun Yat-sen unsuccessfully sought to enlist Japanese support for his anti-Yuan efforts by promising vast concessions in China in the future. He and his associates worked out a revolutionary program (Ko-ming fang-lueh), which provided for the establishment of a revolutionary army and of a military government to rule in China until the revolutionary army had overthrown Yuan's regime. As commander in chief of the new revolutionary army, Sun Yat-sen dispatched Ch'en Ch'i-mei, Chu Chih-hsin and other lieutenants to China to organize armed resistance to Yuan Shih-k'ai.

In December 1915, after Yuan Shih-k'ai had announced his intention to become monarch, Ts'ai O, T'ang Chi-yao (qq.v.), and other military leaders in Yunnan province initiated a revolt against Yuan that soon spread to other provinces in southwest China. Sun Yat-sen's followers in China sought to capitalize on this opposition by staging uprisings in Kwangtung, Anhwei, Kiangsu, and Shantung. In April 1916, when it became apparent that the tide was turning against Yuan, Sun left Japan for Shanghai. The campaigns ended with the death of Yuan Shih-k'ai on 16 June. Sun Yat-sen telegraphed Li Yuan-hung (q.v.),

who assumed the presidency at Peking, and Tuan Ch'i-jui (q.v.), the premier, urging them to restore the provisional constitution of 1912 and the National Assembly that had been dissolved early in 1914. In September 1916 Hu Han-min visited Peking on Sun's behalf and met with Li and Tuan. Sun remained in Shanghai until the summer of 1917, devoting much of his time to setting down his ideas regarding the realization of popular sovereignty in China. Among his writings of this period was a pamphlet arguing against China's entry into the First World War, a question that was a source of bitter contention between Tuan Ch'i-jui, who favored a declaration of war, and the National Assembly. Increasing friction between Tuan and the National Assembly led to the political upheavals of May–July 1917, during which the Parliament was dissolved, Li Yuan-hung was forced to resign in favor of Feng Kuo-chang (q.v.), and control of the Peking government passed into the hands of Tuan Ch'i-jui and his followers.

When Tuan Ch'i-jui decided to convene a new "provisional National Assembly" dominated by his supporters, Sun Yat-sen objected to the dissolution of the old Parliament and to Tuan's seizure of power, saying that both of these actions violated the 1912 constitution. Sun and several members of the old assembly initiated the hu-fa, or constitution protection, movement, their aim being the restoration of the 1912 constitution and the old Parliament. Sun secured the support of the navy, then commanded by Ch'en Pi-kuang (1861–1918; T. Heng-ch'i; H. Yü-t'ang), and assurances of cooperation from the southern military leaders Lu Jung-t'ing and T'ang Chi-yao. In July 1917 Sun left Shanghai with a naval escort and went to Canton, where he and a large number of former members of the Parliament convened a rump parliament and established a military government on 31 August. Although Sun was elected commander in chief (ta-yuan-shuai) of the Canton regime, Lu Jung-t'ing and T'ang Chi-yao, the commanders (yuan-shuai), held the military power. T'ang had little liking for the new regime, and once Lu had gained his own territorial objectives in Hunan in October–November 1917, he, too, began to lose interest in the constitution protection movement.

Because Sun Yat-sen and his adherents were

determined to carry on the struggle against the Peiyang militarists and because they realized that they needed a military power base to do so, they persuaded Chu Ch'ing-lan, the civil governor of Kwangtung, to place 20 battalions of garrison troops under the command of Sun's supporter Ch'en Chiung-ming (q.v.). The Kwangsi militarists made a number of attempts to prevent Ch'en from assuming command, but he finally managed to reorganize them as the Yuan-Min Yueh-chün [Kwangtung army to assist Fukien]. By the spring of 1918 T'ang Chi-yao, Lu Jung-t'ing and other southern military leaders had become dissatisfied with Sun and the military government; with the cooperation of several members of the rump parliament, they effected a reorganization of the government. Sun, instead of being commander in chief, became a member of a seven-man committee of directors general (tsung-ts'ai), which was headed by Ts'en Ch'un-hsuan (q.v.). The other members were T'ang Shao-yi, Wu T'ing-fang, Lin Pao-tse, Lu Jung-t'ing, and T'ang Chi-yao. Sun, having been deprived of his authority, announced his withdrawal from active participation in the Canton regime on 21 May.

After making a brief trip to Japan in an unsuccessful attempt to win Japanese support for the constitution protection movement, Sun Yat-sen established residence in the French concession at Shanghai. During the next two-and-a-half years he wrote some of his most important works, later published as part of the *Chien-kuo fang-lueh* [principles of national reconstruction]. On 1 August 1919 two of his close associates, Chu Chih-hsin and Tai Chi-t'ao, established the *Chien-she tsa-chih* [reconstruction magazine] to expound and discuss party ideology and Sun's proposals for national reconstruction. During this period, Sun also concerned himself with practical party affairs. The Chung-hua ko-ming-tang had failed to capture the popular imagination and thus had exerted little influence upon the political or intellectual life of China. Moreover, many members of the revolutionary organization, especially overseas Chinese, persisted in referring to it as the Kuomintang. To eliminate confusion arising from this problem of nomenclature and to strengthen the structure of the party, on 10 October 1919 Sun announced the reorganization of the party as the Chung-kuo kuo-min-tang.

At Canton, the Kwangsi militarists had been using strong military pressure to increase their control of the military government. Sun had protested their actions by formally resigning from the government in August 1919. The growing dissension within the Canton government between adherents of the Kwangsi militarists and supporters of Sun Yat-sen led to the resignation and departure from Canton of such officials as Wu T'ing-fang, and the situation was complicated further in the spring of 1920 when friction developed between the Kwangsi faction and the Yunnan military clique headed by T'ang Chi-yao. In June 1920 Sun Yat-sen, T'ang Shao-yi, Wu T'ing-fang, and T'ang Chi-yao issued a public telegram declaring all future acts of the Canton military government to be null and void. In August, Ch'en Chiung-ming and his Kwangtung Army left Changchow, Fukien, to return to Kwangtung. After a three-month campaign, the Kwangtung Army, with the help of other pro-Sun units, defeated the Kwangsi militarists and occupied Canton on 26 October 1920. Sun then designated Ch'en governor of Kwangtung. After returning to Canton late in November, Sun reconvened the rump parliament.

THE CANTON GOVERNMENT AND THE REVOLT OF CH'EN CHIUNG-MING

The failure of the constitution protection movement and the disintegration of the military government at Canton had convinced Sun Yat-sen that, rather than persisting in his efforts to wrest control of the Peking government from the Peiyang militarists, he should establish a new national government that would rival, and eventually replace, the northern regime. Kwangtung would be the military base for a campaign to unify the country. Sun believed that once the new government had been recognized by foreign powers as the legitimate government of the Chinese republic, it would receive sufficient loans and revenue from customs receipts to be able to carry out his program of national reconstruction.

In April 1921 the rump parliament at Canton abolished the military government, established a new government (the Chung-hua min-kuo cheng-fu), and elected Sun Yat-sen president extraordinary. On 5 May, when he assumed office, Sun notified foreign powers that the new government, as the only legitimate government of China, would respect all former treaty obligations and would welcome the investment of foreign capital in China; he also announced the intention of the new government to unify all of China under its administration. A few weeks later, he announced plans for a northern expedition against the Kwangsi militarists and ordered Ch'en Chiung-ming's Kwangtung Army to take the field against the forces of Lu Jung-t'ing. The Kwangtung Army pressed steadily into Kwangsi; by the end of September, Lu's armies had been shattered and Kwangsi had been brought under the control of the Canton government. This victory encouraged Sun to make plans for extending the northern expedition into Hunan and Kiangsi. In December, he went to Kweilin, where he established headquarters and assumed personal direction of the campaign. He completed his plans for an invasion of Hunan early in 1922, joining in a military alliance with the Manchurian warlord, Chang Tso-lin (q.v.), and the leader of the Anhwei clique, Tuan Ch'i-jui, against their common enemy, the Chihli clique, headed by Ts'ao K'un and Wu P'ei-fu (qq.v.). At that time the Chihli clique controlled several provinces in north and central China as well as the Peking government.

In the meantime, a rift had occurred between Sun Yat-sen and his top military commander, Ch'en Chiung-ming. After his victorious campaign against the Kwangsi clique in 1920, Ch'en, as governor of Kwangtung and head of the Kwangtung Army, had come to favor consolidating his position within the province under a system, advocated by Chao Heng-t'i (q.v.) and others, of a decentralized federation of provinces, each with an autonomous administration. Accordingly, he had little enthusiasm for Sun Yat-sen's ambitious plans for a northern expedition to unify China under a centralized national government. In particular, he objected to Sun's plans for using Kwangtung as a central military base for this expedition. After the successful Kwangsi campaign of 1921, Ch'en, when informed of Sun's plans to advance into Hunan, opposed this decision. Sun Yat-sen went to Kwangsi and, after an unsuccessful attempt to win Ch'en over to his point of view, reached an agreement whereby he would supervise the Hunan campaign and Ch'en would return to Canton, where he would raise funds for the expedition but otherwise would have a

free hand in Kwangtung. In December 1921, after Ch'en returned to Canton, Sun went to Kweilin and assumed personal direction of the campaign. It soon became apparent, however, that Ch'en was working to obstruct Sun's military plans. When Sun became aware of Ch'en's activities and when his staunch supporter Teng K'eng (q.v.) was assassinated at Canton in March 1922, he withdrew his troops from Hunan for a march on Canton. In April, he relieved Ch'en of his posts as governor and commander in chief of the Kwangtung Army after Ch'en retired from Canton with his personal forces to his stronghold at Waichow.

On 4 May 1922 Sun Yat-sen ordered the resumption of the northern expedition, confident that Ch'en Chiung-ming would trouble him no longer. He moved his troops from the vicinity of Canton to Shaokuan in northern Kwangtung. At this point, Ch'en's troops, led by Yeh Chü (b. 1882; T. Jo-ch'ing), occupied Canton and demanded that Ch'en be restored his posts. Sun hastened to Canton on 1 June to settle the matter personally, but Ch'en's subordinates, with the support of the Chihli clique in north China, on 16 June demanded that Sun resign from the presidency and prepared for an attack on the presidential headquarters in Canton. Sun was warned of their plans in time to escape to a gunboat on the Pearl River, from which he dispatched orders to his forces in Kiangsi to return home and attack Ch'en. They followed his orders, but were repulsed by Ch'en's supporters. After waiting for several weeks aboard the gunboat, where he was attended by a young officer named Chiang Kai-shek, Sun decided that further attempts to dislodge Ch'en would be useless. In mid-August, he went to Shanghai.

After the expulsion from Canton by Ch'en Chiung-ming and the collapse of the northern expedition, Sun Yat-sen was more determined than ever to acquire the power necessary to implement his revolutionary program. Upon arrival in Shanghai on 14 August 1922 he began to work out plans to regain Canton as a military base from which to unify China. He renewed his alliance with Chang Tso-lin and Tuan Ch'i-jui against the Chihli clique and sent emissaries to the remnants of the northern expeditionary forces in Fukien and Kwangsi with instructions to regroup for another campaign against Ch'en Chiung-ming. At the same time, Sun began to prepare for a radical transformation of the Kuomintang. Despite previous reorganizations, the revolutionary party had failed to become an effective political body. Ties with party branches, particularly overseas, had been weak, and some of the older party members, having little understanding of Sun Yat-sen's political and social ideals, often had stood ready to compromise with political groups that opposed Sun's aims. In addition to having defects in organization and discipline, the party lacked effective propaganda techniques. Although it controlled several newspapers and magazines, it had been unable to win firm attention and support from urban groups. Sun hoped to infuse new vigor and revolutionary spirit into the party by attracting new members from among students, merchants, and workers. He considered the support of the students particularly important. Early in September 1922 he called a meeting of the Kuomintang members in Shanghai at which he announced his intention to reorganize the party and named a committee to study the problem. In November, the committee elected Hu Han-min and Wang Ching-wei (q.v.) to draft a declaration on party reform. The process of reorganization was formally set in motion on 1 January 1923 with the announcement of a party manifesto reaffirming Sun's Three People's Principles as the basic aims of the Kuomintang.

During this period, while occupied with problems of reorganization, Sun Yat-sen made what probably was the most crucial decision of his life—to align the Kuomintang with the Soviet Union and the Chinese Communist party. He previously had looked to the Western powers and to Japan for help, but their continued refusals to consider his pleas for assistance had embittered him. After the Russian Revolution, agents of the new Russian government had been sent to China to seek the cooperation of military and political leaders and, later, to supervise the establishment of the Chinese Communist party in July 1921 (*see* Ch'en Tu-hsiu). The following month, Sun Yat-sen had written to G. V. Chicherin, the Russian minister of foreign affairs, to express his interest in Soviet political and military organization. The Comintern representative Maring had visited Sun later that year at his military headquarters in Kweilin to discuss the possibility of Kuomintang-Communist cooperation,

but these discussions, though friendly, were indecisive. When Sun was approached by Russian agents in Shanghai after his flight from Canton in the summer of 1922, however, he firmly agreed to cooperate with the Chinese Communist party to the extent of allowing individual members to join the Kuomintang. He and the Soviet diplomat Adolf Joffe undertook negotiations that resulted in a joint manifesto, signed on 26 January 1923, which, while asserting that the Soviet system was not suitable for China, announced in general terms the willingness of the Soviet Union to cooperate with the Kuomintang in its struggle to unify China. Details of the new alliance, as well as preliminary plans for reorganizing the Kuomintang, were worked out in subsequent discussions, held in Japan, between Joffe and Sun's trusted lieutenant Liao Chung-k'ai.

In deciding to accept the cooperation of the Soviet Union, Sun Yat-sen apparently was influenced less by Communist doctrine, in which he had little interest, than by the need to obtain military assistance in the form of money, arms, and advisers if he were to regain Kwangtung as a revolutionary base for the unification of China. Even before the announcement of the Sun-Joffe manifesto, the East Route Anti-Rebel Army under Hsü Ch'ung-chih (q.v.), together with the Yunnan army of Yang Hsi-min and the Kwangsi army of Liu Chen-huan, had succeeded in driving Ch'en Chiung-ming from Canton. In mid-February 1923 Sun returned to Canton, where he established himself as head of a new military government with the title of ta-yuan-shuai [generalissimo]. To secure his position at Canton, he occupied himself during the spring and summer of 1923 with defensive military operations against the still powerful Ch'en Chiung-ming and against Shen Hung-ying (d. 1935), a former ally who had associated himself with the Chihli clique. The intervention of the Chihli militarists drew bitter condemnation from Sun, who denounced the leader of the clique, Ts'ao K'un, for having bribed his way into the presidency of the Peking government. Sun declared his intention to join with Chang Tso-lin and Tuan Ch'i-jui to overthrow Ts'ao's regime.

REORGANIZATION OF THE KUOMINTANG

With military matters uppermost in his mind, it was not until October 1923 that Sun Yat-sen again directed his full attention to the reorganization of the Kuomintang. In the summer of 1923 he had requested that a Comintern representative be sent to Canton for organizational and advisory purposes. The Soviet adviser Michael Borodin (Grusenberg) arrived at Canton on 6 October and quickly won Sun's confidence. A few weeks later, Sun appointed Borodin special adviser to the Kuomintang, and in the following months Borodin and his staff played a decisive role in guiding the course of Kuomintang political and military reorganization. On Borodin's recommendation, Sun appointed a nine-man provisional central executive committee, which included Lin Sen, Teng Tse-ju, the Communist T'an P'ing-shan (qq.v.), and Liao Chung-k'ai. The purpose of the committee, which was established on 25 October, was to draw up a new set of party regulations, a constitution, and a manifesto; to supervise the organization of new party branches on provincial and local levels; and to prepare for a national party congress to be held early in 1924. The committee completed its tasks in less than three months, and on 20 January 1924 Sun Yat-sen convened the First National Congress of the Kuomintang. During a ten-day session in Canton, the 196 delegates to the congress approved and adopted the new constitution and other reorganization resolutions presented by Sun and the committee.

As constituted by the reorganization of 1924, the new Kuomintang clearly revealed the impress of Soviet policy, particularly in the areas of party organization and revolutionary tactics. The new constitution, drafted for Sun in English by Borodin and then translated into Chinese by Liao Chung-k'ai, transformed the Kuomintang into a tightly disciplined body organized along the lines of the Russian Communist party into a pyramidal structure, with channels of authority descending in successive stages from the highest party organ, the National Congress, down through lesser party organs established at the provincial, county, and local levels. Within the National Congress, which was to meet every two years, power was concentrated in the hands of the Central Executive Committee, elected by the congress and given the authority to act for the congress in the intervals between its sessions. Established by, and under the control of, the Central Executive

Committee were bureaus which directed the various aspects of party activity—organization, propaganda, workers, peasants, youth, women, investigation, and military affairs. Equal in authority to the Central Executive Committee was the Central Supervisory Committee (chung-yang chien-ch'a wei-yuan-hui), elected by the National Congress to inspect and audit the finances of the Central Executive Committee, to review the policies of the party, and to supervise the conduct of all party officials. Only in creating the position of party leader (tsung-li), held for life by Sun Yat-sen, did the new Kuomintang structure differ significantly from its Soviet prototype. Other evidences of Soviet influence were to be found in the restatement of Sun's Three People's Principles in the manifesto of the First National Congress. Without altering the basic tenets of Sun's political philosophy, this new formulation redefined the principle of nationalism as the struggle for liberation from the forces of foreign imperialism and placed new emphasis on the political leadership of a strong, unified party in carrying through the national revolution. Also indicated in the spirit, if not the letter, of the manifesto were those courses of action which the Chinese Communists later referred to as Sun Yat-sen's Three Great Policies (san ta cheng-ts'e): alliance with the Soviet Union, cooperation with the Chinese Communist party, and support of the worker and peasant masses.

In accordance with this new orientation, the First National Congress of the Kuomintang at its final session on 30 January 1924 elected a Central Executive Committee which included three members of the Chinese Communist party; the following day, the Central Executive Committee elected T'an P'ing-shan to head the vitally important party organization bureau and another Chinese Communist, Lin Po-ch'ü (q.v.), to head the peasant bureau. However, Sun and his immediate entourage remained in undisputed control of the party organization even though some Communists held influential positions within the Kuomintang. The strongest challenge to Sun's authority within the party came not from the Communists but from some of his oldest associates. Such conservatives as Chang Chi, Hsieh Ch'ih (q.v.), and Teng Tse-ju, three of the five full members of the Central Supervisory Committee, objected strongly to the decision to admit Communists to the Kuomintang membership. On 16 June 1924 these three men sent a resolution to the Central Executive Committee impeaching the Communists, but it was rejected on 3 July. In an attempt to allay the fears of these conservatives and to halt the growing division of the Kuomintang into right- and left-wing factions, the Central Executive Committee issued a statement on 7 July calling on party members to dispel misunderstandings and reiterating that the Three People's Principles were the sole means to success in the revolution. It was largely to ensure the effectiveness of Kuomintang-Communist cooperation and to keep the right-wing faction in check that Sun Yat-sen decided to increase the centralization of power and his personal authority by establishing, under his personal direction, the 12-man Central Political Council that was to be the ultimate determining authority of basic Kuomintang policies.

MILITARY ESTABLISHMENT

With the reorganization of January 1924 Sun Yat-sen and his advisers laid the foundations of the formidable political-military machine that was to sweep to national power in 1927–28. However, at the time of the reorganization the party's position in Canton was precarious, and Sun, lacking sufficient military power of his own, still was obliged to rely on the uncertain support of the Yunnan and Kwangsi militarists in Kwangtung. Accordingly, one of the first tasks of the reorganized Kuomintang was to recruit and train a military force which would be directly under the authority of the party leadership and which would be dedicated to the party's aim of national revolution. Plans for a party academy had resulted from the 1923 discussions between Liao Chung-k'ai and Adolf Joffe, and the First National Congress of the Kuomintang had approved a proposal to establish the academy at Whampoa, some ten miles downriver from Canton. Early in May 1924, as the first class of cadets was being chosen, Sun designated Chiang Kai-shek the commandant of the Whampoa Military Academy. Because Sun was as concerned with indoctrination in the political principles of national revolution as with military training, he appointed Liao Chung-k'ai party representative to the academy and named Hu Han-min, Wang Ching-wei, Tai Chi-t'ao, and others among his closest followers as political instructors at Whampoa.

As these plans to build up Kuomintang military strength were being put into effect, the very existence of the revolutionary government at Canton was endangered. To the east, Ch'en Chiung-ming remained a constant military threat; in the vicinity of Canton, the leaders of the Kwangsi and Yunnan armies not only ignored the authority of Sun Yat-sen's regime but also expressed increasing suspicion and hostility toward the burgeoning party army being trained at Whampoa; within the city itself, the Kuomintang's position was jeopardized by the Canton Merchants Corps, a powerful militia organization maintained by local Chinese businessmen. Despite these threats, Sun Yat-sen in September 1924 decided to divert the troops then at his disposal to northern Kwangtung in preparation for another northern expedition into Kiangsi and Hunan—a decision prompted in part by Sun's desire to join with Chang Tso-lin, Tuan Ch'i-jui, and other militarists in a renewed attempt to overthrow the hegemony of the Chihli clique of north China. However, after Sun moved to his headquarters at Shao-kuan, his preparations were delayed by an uprising of the Merchants Corps. Acting on orders from Sun, Hu Han-min, then the senior Kuomintang leader in Canton, placed all the forces in the Canton area under the command of Chiang Kai-shek. By mid-October, the Merchants Corps had been crushed and disarmed. However, by the time Sun was ready to launch the northern expedition, the Chihli faction had been defeated by the combined forces of Chang Tso-lin and Feng Yü-hsiang (q.v.), and Ts'ao K'un had been driven from the presidency.

THE FINAL JOURNEY

When Sun Yat-sen received an invitation from Chang Tso-lin and Tuan Ch'i-jui to take part in their deliberations at Peking about national affairs, he perceived in this gesture an opportunity to promote his proposals for a new national convention that would eradicate militarism and imperialism from China and would effect a peaceful unification of the nation. Accordingly, on 13 November 1924, after appointing Hu Han-min acting head of the Canton government, he left for north China in the company of Tai Chi-t'ao, Wang Ching-wei and a number of other followers. Traveling by way of Shanghai and Japan, Sun and his entourage reached Tientsin on 4 December and moved on to Peking at the end of the year. Meanwhile, Tuan Ch'i-jui, as provisional chief executive of the northern government, had already announced his intention of calling an "aftermath conference" in preparation for a national convention. Negotiations between Tuan and Sun, carried on by letter and telegram, soon broke down as Tuan, ignoring Sun's demands that labor, peasant, and merchant groups be represented at the forthcoming convention, moved ahead with his plans to hold the convention against the wishes and without the participation of the Kuomintang.

As he was conducting these fruitless negotiations with Tuan Ch'i-jui, Sun Yat-sen became critically ill. He had been ailing for several months before he had left Canton, and after his arrival in Tientsin his health had deteriorated so rapidly that a special ambulance was required to take him to Peking. On 26 January 1925 he was taken to the hospital of the Peking Union Medical College for exploratory surgery, which revealed inoperable cancer of the liver and other organs. He then was moved to the home of Wellington Koo (Ku Wei-chün, q.v.), where he passed his remaining days attended by close associates and members of his family. On his deathbed he signed both political and personal wills. The document that became known as the "political testament of Sun Yat-sen" was a brief injunction to his followers to carry the national revolution through to completion in accordance with the principles set forth in his major writings; it was drafted in Chinese by Wang Ching-wei. A farewell message to the Soviet Union, drafted by Eugene Ch'en (q.v.), reaffirmed the Kuomintang's policy of cooperation with the Soviet Union in the struggle to liberate China from Western imperialism and expressed "the hope that the day is approaching when the Soviet Union will greet in a free and strong China its friend and ally, and that the two states will proceed hand in hand as allies in the great fight for the emancipation of the oppressed of the whole world." This message later caused controversy within the Kuomintang, some members claiming that the dying Sun Yat-sen had not been able to study its contents adequately. Sun's personal will left his only belongings—his books and a

house in Shanghai—to his second wife. On 12 March, the day after he signed these documents, Sun Yat-sen died at the age of 59. J. Heng Liu (Liu Jui-heng, q.v.) and Paul Stevenson of the Peking Union Medical College undertook to preserve Sun's body for perpetual exhibition. Then, on 19 March, a private Christian funeral service was held in the chapel next to the college's hospital. Tuan Ch'i-jui ordered a state funeral, and after Sun's body had lain in state for several days, it was moved to a temple in the Western Hills.

Sun Yat-sen was survived by his first and second wives, a daughter, and a son, Sun Fo (q.v.). Sun's first marriage, at the age of 18, was to Lu Mu-chen (1867–1952), the daughter of a merchant in his native village. She was the mother of his three children. The elder of their two daughters, Chin-yen, died in 1913; the younger, Chin-yuan (b. 1896), was married in 1921 to Tai En-sai (1892–1955), an American trained diplomat who served as Chinese minister to Brazil. During the greater part of Sun's pre-1911 peregrinations, his first wife, his children, and his mother lived in Hawaii with his elder brother. Later, most of his family moved to Macao. Sun's second marriage, to Soong Ch'ing-ling (q.v.), took place in Tokyo on 25 October 1914. Because he and his first wife had not been divorced and because of the obscure and perhaps irregular nature of the ceremony in Japan, this second union was the subject of controversy and adverse comment, especially among the Christian community in China. Nevertheless, Soong Ch'ing-ling remained Sun's constant companion until the end of his life, and as his widow she came to be esteemed as the living symbol of his doctrines.

THE WRITINGS OF SUN YAT-SEN

Throughout most of his career, Sun Yat-sen was a prophet with little honor in his own country. Although he was highly regarded at the time of the 1911 revolution, public opinion turned against him after the so-called second revolution. In the following years, his preoccupation with military ventures and his involvement in the warlord politics of the period were viewed with little enthusiasm by the war-weary people of China, while his frequent and overblown announcements of new military expeditions won him the derisive epithet "Sun Ta-p'ao" [big gun Sun]. Among his personal following, however, Sun's will was law and his leadership was unquestioned. After his death, the Kuomintang leaders took steps to assure that his memory would be preserved in honor and reverence. At a special meeting of the Central Executive Committee on 16 May 1925, his "political testament" was unanimously adopted as the party's official guide for all future decisions; and at the Second National Congress of the Kuomintang in January 1926 it was decided that, out of respect for the departed chief, no successor should be elected to fill the position of tsung-li. Thus, Sun's posthumous reputation was closely bound to the fortunes of the Kuomintang, and after the establishment under its auspices of the National Government in Nanking, the growing cult of Sun Yat-sen spread from the ranks of the party to the entire country. His bust or portrait began to appear in all public buildings and offices, and his likeness on coins, banknotes, and postage stamps. The name "Chung-shan," by which he had been known to his early followers, became the official designation not only of the hsien in which he had been born but also of innumerable parks, streets, schools, and other institutions throughout China. In 1929 Sun's coffin was transferred from its resting place in the Western Hills to a massive marble mausoleum that had been constructed on Tzu-chin-shan near the tomb of the first emperor of the Ming dynasty. In ultimate tribute to his memory, the National Government decreed on 1 April 1940 that henceforth Sun should be revered by his countrymen as the "father of the republic" (kuo-fu). Sun's long career as a revolutionary leader, the socialistic ideals expressed in his writings, and particularly his policies of alignment with the Soviet Union and the Chinese Communist party, also secured him a place of special honor in the Communist roster of national heroes. After the establishment of the People's Republic of China in 1949, he was accorded by Communist historians the unique appellation of "pioneer of the revolution" (Ko-ming ti hsien-hsing-che), and at many national (as distinguished from Chinese Communist party) functions, his portrait shared the position of public honor beside that of Mao Tse-tung.

Ideologically, the most significant step in the course of Sun Yat-sen's canonization by the Kuomintang was the decision to adopt as the party bible his political testament and his writings mentioned therein: the *Chien-kuo fang-lueh* (*Principles of National Reconstruction*), the *Chien-kuo ta-kang* (*Fundamentals of National Reconstruction*), and the *San-min chu-i* (*Three Principles of the People*). Of these three works, the *San-min chu-i* was unquestionably the most important, both as a source book for Kuomintang propaganda during and after its rise to national power, and as a basic text in school curricula after the establishment of the National Government in Nanking. According to Sun, the formulation of his three principles—nationalism (min-tsu chu-i), democracy (min-ch'üan chu-i), and the people's livelihood (min-sheng chu-i)—was inspired by Abraham Lincoln's famous phrase, "government of the people, by the people, and for the people." They first appeared in writing late in 1905 in Sun's statement introducing the initial issue of the T'ung-meng-hui magazine, the *Min-pao*. However, little more than a vague outline was presented in this statement. Although he frequently referred to these principles in speeches and writings, Sun did little to elaborate upon them until about 1917, when he was living in Shanghai. According to official Kuomintang sources, he took his new writings with him when he moved back to Canton late in 1920 with the intention of completing and publishing them; but following the coup of Ch'en Chiung-ming and Sun's flight from Canton in June 1922 these drafts, left behind in his office, were destroyed by fire. The final version of the *San-min chu-i* consisted of transcriptions of three series of lectures that Sun gave in Canton between January and August 1924. The first six lectures, which concerned the principle of nationalism, were published as a booklet by the Central Executive Committee's bureau of propaganda in Canton in April 1924, with a preface by Sun; the next six, dealing with his principle of democracy, were printed in August; and the final four lectures, expounding the principle of the people's livelihood, appeared in December, one month after Sun had left for Peking. Subsequently, the 16 lectures were published as a single work in innumerable editions.

During the period between their enunciation in 1905 and their final elaboration in 1924, Sun's Three People's Principles underwent several stages of development. In its earliest form, his principle of nationalism was a demand for the overthrow of the alien Manchu dynasty and the restoration of the Chinese as rulers of their own country. After the Manchus had abdicated in 1912, Sun had little to say about nationalism until the time of the 1922–24 Kuomintang reorganization when, as a result of his growing disenchantment with the Western powers and his new orientation toward the Soviet Union, he reinterpreted his first principle in terms of a nationalist revolution against the domination of the imperialists in China, the first step in this revolution being the abolition of the unequal treaties that the foreign powers had imposed upon China.

Sun's principle of democracy also underwent a number of modifications that reflected changes in his political attitudes. As originally outlined in the "manifesto of the military government" of the T'ung-meng-hui in 1905, Sun's concept of democracy closely resembled that of the Western democracies, particularly the United States. However, in traditionally monarchist China, Sun believed, it would be necessary to effect the transition to democratic government in three successive stages: first, a period of military government under the revolutionary party during which the forces of autocracy would be eradicated; second, a period of political tutelage in which the military government would gradually introduce the practice of democratic self-government to each locality in China; and finally, a period of constitutional government, at the beginning of which the military government would relinquish its powers to a national government consisting of a president and a parliament, both elected by the people of the entire country. As Sun became more critical of the West in later years, he revised and expanded his principle of democracy to include a number of concepts which he believed to be improvements upon the Western systems of representative democracy. In the final formulation of his second principle, he argued that the people should possess the rights not only of election but also of recall, initiative, and referendum, and he proposed that governmental functions be divided among five separate and equal bodies, adding to the legislative, executive, and judicial branches of the American system the examination and the control, or censoring, functions that long had existed in Chinese political tradition. Although he stressed the political rights of the people, Sun also placed increased emphasis on the need for concentrating power in the hands of the revolutionary party during the periods of national revolution and political tutelage.

Sun's third principle—the people's livelihood —represented an amalgamation of ideas culled over a period of years from a variety of Western socialist writings. As it first appeared in 1905, it called for the reorganization of China's social and economic system into a socialist state and for the "equalization of land rights," a formula based on Henry George's thesis that private appropriation of increases in land values was the cause of modern social inequities. By 1912 Sun had added the concept of state ownership of railways and major industrial enterprises, an idea which in the next few years was restated in more general terms as the state control of capitalism. Although he claimed that his doctrine of the people's livelihood was both socialism and communism, Sun averred that Marxism, while meriting study as a form of Western socialism, not only was impracticable in China but also was demonstrably erroneous in its theses of surplus value and the class struggle. His own doctrine, Sun maintained, was a special branch of socialism suitable to Chinese conditions—a program by which China, in the course of its modernization, could avoid the social evils and injustices that had attended the industrialization of the capitalist nations of the West.

To the problems of China's modernization, Sun devoted the longest of his writings, the *Chien-kuo fang-lueh*, which was actually a collection of three separate works dealing with various aspects of China's reconstruction. The earliest of these, completed in Shanghai in February 1917, was the *Min-ch'üan ch'u-pu* [first steps in democracy]; it was incorporated into the *Chien-kuo fang-lueh* under the title *She-hui chien-she* [social reconstruction]. Begun shortly after the death of Yuan Shih-k'ai, this work was concerned with the reasons for the past failure of the republic to establish democratic government in China. To Sun, the answer lay in the people's ignorance of the techniques of democratic political organization. The first step toward correcting this shortcoming was to familiarize the people with the practical procedures for organizing and conducting assemblies among themselves; with the experience thus gained, the people would learn how to exercise their political rights in a democratic republic. The next of Sun's three works on reconstruction was a treatise entitled *Sun Wen hsueh-shuo* [the doctrine of Sun Wen], completed at the end of 1918 and later renamed *Hsin-li chien-she* [psychological reconstruction]. An English translation of it appeared in Sun's *Memoirs of a Chinese Revolutionary*. In this work, Sun ascribed the failure of the Chinese people to accept his elaborate revolutionary program to a mental block induced in them by a long-standing belief in the adage "it is easy to know but difficult to do." To counteract this fallacious attitude, which he attributed to the teachings of the Ming dynasty philosopher Wang Yang-ming (1472–1529), Sun sought to prove the validity of his dictum that it is the doing that is easy and the knowing what to do that is difficult. In applying this notion to the problem of China's modernization, Sun stated that once the people were presented with the knowledge of what was to be done, it would be an easy matter for them to carry it out. In the belief that he himself had gained this difficult knowledge, Sun composed his third and longest treatise on China's reconstruction, *Shih-yeh chi-hua* [industrial planning], subsequently renamed *Wu-chih chien-she* [material reconstruction]. Originally drafted in English, this work was translated into Chinese and published serially during 1919 in the Kuomintang magazine *Chien-she tsa-chih*, and in 1920 it was published in English as *The International Development of China*. Sun set forth a series of programs, all conceived on a colossal scale, for the rapid industrialization of China. These included plans for the construction of railroads, roads, canals, modern cities, and port facilities, as well as programs for the development of water-power, steel mills, mines, and agriculture. Adding to the impracticability of these extravagant schemes was Sun's assumption that they would be financed by the investment of astronomical sums by the nations of Europe, which, however, had been exhausted economically by the First World War.

In contrast to this rambling, visionary work was the third of Sun's major writings noted in his political testament, the *Chien-kuo ta-kang*, a short, succinctly worded statement of 25 points outlining his plans for the future government of China. This work, dated 12 April 1924, redefined Sun's concept of the three stages by which the revolutionary party would lead the country from the period of military government through the period of political tutelage to the period of national constitutional government. Although Sun stressed the period of political tutelage, during which the party would instruct the people at the hsien level in the theory and practice of self-government, he also specified that in the final period the people should be governed in accordance with his concept of a five-power constitution, by which the central government would be organized into the five yuan described in his principle of democracy. These political principles later served as the basis for the organization of the National Government in Nanking in 1928.

Sun Yat-sen also was the author of many short writings, for the most part political in nature. These included the *Chung-kuo ts'un-wang wen-t'i* [the question of China's survival], written in 1917 to explain his views concerning China's participation in the First World War, and the *Chung-kuo ko-ming shih* [history of China's revolution], completed in 1923. Also of interest were his very few autobiographical writings. His English-language account of his detention at the Chinese legation in London in 1896, *Kidnapped in London*, was published at Bristol in 1897 and later was translated into Chinese. Another short work, separately published as *Tzu-chuan* [autobiography] but later incorporated in the *Sun Wen hsueh-shuo* as the final chapter, is the most detailed record of his life to be found among all his writings.

Numerous collections of Sun Yat-sen's works have been published. The earliest of these, the four-volume *Chung-shan ch'üan-shu*, published in 1926, included his principal theoretical works and several of his miscellaneous political writings. Much more complete was a five-volume collection edited by Hu Han-min and published in 1930 as the *Tsung-li ch'üan-chi*. In 1960 the *Kuo-fu ch'üan-shu* was published in Taiwan under the general editorship of Chang Ch'i-yün. Both the Hu Han-min and Chang Ch'i-yün editions contain, in addition to Sun's three major works, a large number of his political essays, party manifestoes, lectures, and speeches, as well as hundreds of official telegrams and letters written to his political associates and others prominent in the political affairs of the early republic.

Although Sun Yat-sen in his major writings

touched upon such varied subjects as natural science, psychology, history, and philosophy, his underlying interest was in the general field of political economy—a concern with the administration of the country and the welfare of the people which he shared with a long line of noted Confucian scholars of the past. Sun, however, had but little contact with that Chinese scholarship, and his roots in the intellectual and cultural traditions of his country were shallow. Most of his adult life had been spent either outside or on the periphery of China, and from an early age he had been trained exclusively in Western-operated missionary and medical schools. An eclectic but uncritical thinker, Sun haphazardly borrowed a variety of Western concepts, which he used to elaborate grandiose but unrealistic programs for China's modernization. Lacking intellectual maturity and inner coherence, his writings appear as conglomerations of unrelated facts and absurd inaccuracies, fuzzy reasoning and blatant distortions, interspersed, however, with emotional eloquence, high idealism, and flashes of genuine inspiration. Their positive qualities were sufficient to give Sun's major works, especially his *San-min chu-i*, enormous influence in China. But the sanctification of these writings as the official dogma of the Kuomintang and the nation contributed to an atmosphere of intellectual conformity which had the effect of discouraging truly creative thinking on the part of his followers after his death.

THE CAREER OF SUN YAT-SEN

Well before the end of his life, Sun Yat-sen had established himself as the undisputed leader of the party which, after his death, was to become the dominant political force in China for more than two decades. In attaining this position, Sun showed himself to be a born leader of men. Endowed with great personal magnetism and a gift for profoundly moving oratory, he was able to attract and retain the loyalty of numerous followers and to inspire them with his own unmistakable courage and idealism, his self-assurance and selfless dedication to his cause. Nevertheless, the course of his career as a revolutionary leader was marked by an almost unbroken succession of abortive military ventures, demoralizing defeats, and hasty flights. While these setbacks may well have been due in large part to the magnitude

of the political and military forces against which he pitted himself and his supporters, many of the failures must also be attributed to Sun himself. For all his undeniable qualities of leadership, he had little insight into human character and motivations, and in his dealings with others he was almost incredibly trusting and naive. In planning many of his undertakings he counted heavily and too frequently on vague assurances of support, often with disastrous results. Despite repeated miscalculations of this sort, Sun had the utmost confidence in his own judgment, and in his later years he grew to be convinced of his infallibility, a conviction that made him susceptible to the blandishments of sycophants and impervious to the remonstrances of even his most trusted and intimate associates. Headstrong, impulsive, and impatient for quick, dramatic successes, he plunged into many ventures without really considering the difficulties involved. In consequence, a great deal of effort and money was frittered away in futile, foolhardy escapades. Sun's capricious, unpredictable switches of his party's policies and alliances created bewilderment, confusion, and even resentment among his supporters.

His obvious weaknesses notwithstanding, Sun Yat-sen came to be esteemed by his countrymen as the greatest man of modern China. To understand this evaluation, it is necessary to view Sun's career against the background of his times. In a political atmosphere where lack of principle and scruple, venality and self-seeking, treachery and violence were accepted as matters of course, Sun stood out as a symbol of honesty and sincerity, undaunted idealism, and incorruptible integrity. It was this image of a man who had selflessly devoted his entire life to the cause of China and her people—an image which both time and the efforts of his party had expunged of his personal failings—that captured and held the imagination of his countrymen and that made him in their eyes the preeminent figure of China's long and arduous struggle to become a modern nation.

Sung Che-yuan   宋 哲 元
T. Ming-hsüan   明 軒

Sung Che-yuan (30 October 1885–4 April 1940), subordinate of Feng Yü-hsiang. In 1930 he received command of the Twenty-ninth

Army. As chairman of the Hopei-Chahar Political Council, he was deeply involved before 1937 in Sino-Japanese confrontations in north China.

Loling, Shantung, was the birthplace of Sung Che-yuan. Although he was born into a literary family—since the time of his grandfather, all of his paternal forebears had held sheng-yuan degrees—Sung decided to pursue a military career. He entered the Battalion School of the Left Route Reserve Army, commanded by Lu Chien-chang, the uncle of Feng Yü-hsiang (q.v.). Upon completion of his training, he was given the rank of lieutenant and was assigned to the 2nd Battalion, which was commanded by Feng. When Lu's army was transformed into the Metropolitan Guard Army in 1913, Feng became commander of the 1st Regiment, with Sung as a company commander. In 1914 Sung became a deputy battalion commander in Feng's 16th Mixed Brigade. Sung thus saw service in Honan, Shensi, and Szechwan in 1915–16. After his marriage to Ch'ang Shu-ch'ing in 1916, he was promoted to battalion commander and was assigned the duty of recruitment in Honan. In July 1917, at the time of the restoration attempt by Chang Hsün (q.v.), he spearheaded the attack on Peking that resulted in the defeat of Chang Hsün's troops.

From 1918 to 1921 Sung Che-yuan had the responsibility of guarding Ch'angte, Hupeh. A minor diplomatic incident occurred during this period when Sung's troops wounded three Japanese sailors in a scuffle. Sung's able handling of this incident was praised by Feng Yü-hsiang in *Wo-ti sheng-huo* [my life], published at Shanghai in 1947. In 1921 the 16th Mixed Brigade was reorganized as the 11th Division after its successful campaign against Ch'en Shu-fan in Shensi. Sung became a regiment commander, in which capacity he participated in the first Chihli-Fengtien war of 1922. His performance in the campaign, led by Feng Yü-hsiang himself, against the rebellious military governor of Honan won Sung command of the 25th Mixed Brigade. With the reorganization of Feng's troops as the Kuominchün after the second Chihli-Fengtien war and Feng's coup at Peking on 23 October 1924, Sung received command of the 11th Division. In the autumn of 1925 Sung was removed from field command

and was appointed military governor of Jehol.

In the winter of 1925 war broke out between Feng Yü-hsiang's Kuominchün, now also known as the Northwest Army, and the forces of Chang Tso-lin and Wu P'ei-fu (qq.v.). After Feng's retirement and the evacuation of Peking on 15 April (*see* Lu Chung-lin), Sung Che-yuan went to Kalgan where he joined with Chiang Chih-chiang and Lu Chung-lin in developing a base of operations in the Hopei-Chahar-Suiyuan-Shansi border region. The Northwest Army's stubborn defense of Nankow prevented its dissolution as a fighting force. Although Sung did not participate directly in this action, he played an important part in defending the Nankow region as commander in chief of the northern front and, later, of the western front. After four months of hard fighting, the Northwest Army was forced to retreat to Suiyuan. Sung Che-yuan then became military governor of Suiyuan.

Feng Yü-hsiang rejoined his forces at Wuyuan in September 1926 and announced his support of the Kuomintang. The Northwest Army then became the National Revolutionary Allied Army, and in May 1927 it was redesignated the Second Army Group of the National Revolutionary Army. After Feng decided to support Chiang Kai-shek's regime at Nanking rather than the Left-Kuomintang at Wuhan, Sung Che-yuan received command of the Fourth Area Army in June 1927. That November, he added the governorship of Shensi to his responsibilities. When relations between Feng Yü-hsiang and Chiang Kai-shek became strained early in 1929, Feng went to Shansi and made Sung Che-yuan acting commander in chief of his army at Sian. Sung was among the Kuominchün officers who, on 10 October, addressed a public telegram to Feng Yü-hsiang and Yen Hsi-shan (q.v.) denouncing the policies of the National Government and urging remedial action. The following day, the National Government ordered the arrest of Sung Che-yuan and other Kuominchün officers and announced a punitive expedition. Sung was appointed commander in chief of the Kuominchün, which met the Nationalist forces in mid-October in western Honan. By the end of November, Sung's troops had been driven back into Shensi. He relinquished his post to Lu Chung-lin and took command of the Third Group

Army. In March 1930 Feng Yü-hsiang and Yen Hsi-shan formed the so-called northern coalition against Chiang Kai-shek. The ensuing war lasted from May to September, when Chang Hsueh-liang (q.v.) gave the victory to Chiang. Feng's forces were reorganized as National Government troops. In November 1930 Sung Che-yuan received command of the Twenty-ninth Army.

At the time of the Mukden Incident in September 1931, Sung Che-yuan issued a public telegram proposing war with the Japanese invaders. Although his effort failed to arouse the National Government to resistance, he had occasion to deal with the Japanese threat after he was appointed governor of Chahar in July 1932. On 20 January 1933 the Twenty-ninth Army was ordered to assist in the defense of Jehol, and on 10 February Sung's men established a defensive position at Hsifengkow, one of the important passes. At Hsifengkow and at Lowenyü, the Twenty-ninth Army fought to stem the Japanese advance into Jehol. Although Sung's men were forced to abandon Hsifengkow in April and Kupeikow in May, their resistance ended only with the signing of the Tangku truce on 31 May. By then, Sung had become known as "the hero of Hsifengkow." The Japanese completed their conquest of Jehol and advanced into Chahar, whereupon Feng Yü-hsiang emerged from retirement and established the so-called People's Allied Anti-Japanese Army. He and his men proceeded to clear Chahar of enemy troops at a time when Nanking's chief aim was the avoidance of armed conflict with the Japanese. Sung refused to take sides in the dispute between Feng and the National Government, but worked to resolve it. Feng dissolved his army and retired from the field in August. Sung resumed office as governor of Chahar and held that post until May 1935, when he became Peiping-Tientsin garrison commander. His new appointment coincided with the signing of the Ho-Umezu agreement (see Ho Ying-ch'in). Despite popular opposition to the agreement and to the trend toward autonomy in north China, the National Government abolished the Peiping branch of the Political Council in November. Chief authority in north China was transferred to the newly created Hopei-Chahar Political Affairs Council, with Sung Che-yuan as its chairman. Sung also was appointed governor

of Hopei and Hopei-Chahar pacification commissioner. Chang Tzu-chung, commander of the Twenty-ninth Army's 38th Division, became mayor of Tientsin, and Ch'in Te-ch'un, deputy commander of the Twenty-ninth Army and governor of Chahar, became mayor of Peiping. With the Twenty-ninth Army securely in control of the administrations of Chahar and Hopei, Sung formally assumed his new offices in December 1935.

The Japanese program of this period envisaged the transformation of the provinces of Hopei, Shantung, Shansi, Chahar, and Suiyuan into a Japanese-sponsored autonomous area. The strategy agreed upon by the Twenty-ninth Army and the National Government called for a delaying action which, while giving the Chinese nation additional time to prepare for the impending conflict, would not involve the surrender of additional territory or sovereignty to the Japanese. In this undertaking, Sung worked with Han Fu-chü (q.v.), governor of Shantung. In November 1936 Sung was succeeded as governor of Hopei by his 37th Division commander, Feng Chih-an. During and after the Sian Incident (see Chiang Kai-shek; Chang Hsueh-liang) Japanese pressure on Sung and Han increased. Because Sung would neither yield to the Japanese nor cooperate with the Chinese Communists according to the united front policy adopted by the Chinese Nationalists, he found himself in an untenable position. Accordingly, he left Peiping and went to Loling to sweep the graves of his ancestors.

The Sino-Japanese war began on 7 July 1937 with a clash at Lukouchiao that involved the Twenty-ninth Army's 37th Division. Sung Che-yuan immediately left Loling and went to Tientsin, where be began negotiations with Japanese commanders on 12 July. It soon became evident that the Japanese would resort to military force unless a north China autonomous region were brought into being without reference to Nanking. A strong Japanese column went into action along the Tientsin-Peiping rail line on 25 July, and it occupied Langfeng the following day. Also on 26 July, the Japanese demanded the withdrawal of the 37th Division from the Lukouchiao area by noon of 27 July. Sung Che-yuan rejected the demand. On the night of 28 July, however, he led his men out of Peiping, which fell to the Japanese shortly thereafter. The Japanese then took Tientsin and moved westward and southward. Sung Che-yuan, assuming responsibility for the Japanese successes in north China, submitted his resignation to Nanking on 28 July. The National Government refused his resignation and made him commander of the First Army Group, a conglomerate of the Twenty-ninth Army and other forces. Sung's headquarters at Paoting fell to the Japanese on 24 September, and he was forced to retreat southward once again. Elements of the First Army Group were sent to Linyi and to the Hsuchow front to cover the withdrawal of Chinese forces after the battle of Taierhchuang. The troops remaining under Sung's direct command were concentrated in the Hopei-Shantung-Honan border area around the strategic point of Hsinhsiang. Superior war matériel enabled the Japanese to take Hsinhsiang with relative ease, despite Sung's stubborn resistance. Sung Che-yuan, his once-powerful Twenty-ninth Army scattered and broken, submitted his resignation to Chiang Kai-shek at Chengchow. Chiang accepted it and appointed Sung to the Military Affairs Commission. Sung soon asked for leave from his post on the grounds of illness. In the autumn of 1939 he went to Mienyang, Szechwan, where he had been married many years before. Sung Che-yuan died there on 4 April 1940. The National Government later honored his memory by granting him the rank of full general.

Sung Chia-shu: *see* SOONG, CHARLES JONES.

Sung Chiao-jen		宋 敎 仁
T.	T'un-ch'u	遯 初
H.	Yü-fu	漁 父

Sung Chiao-jen (5 April 1882–22 March 1913), founder of the Kuomintang. He was assassinated by supporters of Yuan Shih-k'ai.

T'aoyuan, Hunan, was the birthplace of Sung Chiao-jen. Little is known about his family background or early education. Sung's father died when the boy was only 12 sui, and thereafter an elder brother supported the family. In the spring of 1899 Sung entered the Chang-chiang shu-yuan. He remained there until the winter of 1902, when he passed the entrance examinations for the Wen-p'u-t'ung chung-hsueh-t'ang, a middle school at Wuchang which had been founded by Chang Chih-tung (ECCP, I, 27–32). Soon afterwards, Russian occupation of large areas in Manchuria aroused strong anti-Russian and anti-Manchu sentiments in Chinese students. Early in 1904 Sung joined the Hua-hsing-hui [society for the revival of China], a revolutionary society organized by Huang Hsing (q.v.) and other Hunanese students who had returned recently from Japan. Sung and some of his schoolmates in Wuchang established the K'o-hsueh pu-hsi so [science study group] in mid-1904 to serve as cover for their recruiting activities on behalf of the Hua-hsing-hui among students and soldiers of the New Army. The young revolutionaries made plans for uprisings at five centers in Hunan during the official celebration of the empress dowager's birthday in November 1904, and Sung Chiao-jen was placed in charge of organizing the uprising at Ch'angte. The discovery by government authorities of this conspiracy early in November forced Sung to flee to Japan.

From mid-December 1904 to June 1905 Sung Chiao-jen studied at the Kobun Institute, which offered short-term courses in law, physics, normal-school training, and political science. He then enrolled at the College of Law and Government. Having become involved in the anti-Manchu revolutionary movement in Japan, he founded the revolutionary magazine *Erh-shih shih-chi chih Chih-na* [twentieth-century China] in June 1905. Sun Yat-sen arrived in Japan in July, and Sung Chiao-jen, Huang Hsing, and other revolutionary leaders met with him to discuss plans for the amalgamation of several anti-Manchu societies into a new revolutionary league, the Chung-kuo T'ung-meng-hui. When the T'ung-meng-hui was inaugurated on 20 August 1905, with Sun Yat-sen as its chairman, Sung Chiao-jen was named to the judicial department. The *Erh-shih shih-chi chih Chih-na* became the organ of the T'ung-meng-hui, but, because an issue of the magazine had been confiscated by the Japanese authorities, its name was changed to *Min-pao* [people's journal].

In February 1906 Sung Chiao-jen enrolled at Waseda University, using the name Sung Lien. By thus concealing his identity he was able to obtain government education stipends through the Chinese legation in Tokyo. He soon became interested in the geography and contemporary history of Korea and Manchuria, and he came to regard the so-called mounted bandits who infested the Korea-Manchuria border areas as potential allies of the revolutionary party. After discussing the matter with Huang Hsing, Sung and a few companions went to Liaotung in an attempt to win the support of the mounted bandits and to gain a territorial foothold for the revolutionaries in Manchuria. However, the vigilance of imperial troops in the area undermined Sung's mission, and he returned to Tokyo.

Another result of Sung's interest in the Korea-Manchuria border region was his indirect involvement in the settling of the so-called Chientao question. Chientao (also known as Kantao or Yenpien), a sizeable area on the Manchurian side of the Tumen River that had been heavily settled by Korean immigrants, had been the subject of several jurisdictional disputes between the Korean government and the Chinese authorities in Manchuria. After the Russo-Japanese war, the Korean government, backed by Japan, reopened the Chientao question and forced the Ch'ing government to negotiate a settlement. Sung Chiao-jen, again using the pseudonym Sung Lien, wrote a pamphlet on the subject, *Chien-tao wen-t'i* [the Chientao question], which was published at Shanghai in August 1908. A copy was sent to Yuan Shih-k'ai (q.v.), then minister of foreign affairs at Peking. According to some sources, the pamphlet proved useful to the Chinese negotiators and Sung was offered a government job. In any event, the matter eventually was settled by the Chientao Agreement of 4 September 1909, which gave the Korean settlers the right to remain in the area, but reaffirmed China's legal jurisdiction over them and the area.

By 1908 the repeated failures of revolutionary attempts in China (*see* Sun Yat-sen; Huang Hsing) had led Chang Chi, Chang Ping-lin (qq.v.), and other T'ung-meng-hui members in Tokyo who were associated with the *Min-pao* to propose the repudiation of Sun as party leader and the election of Huang Hsing as chairman. Sung Chiao-jen supported this proposal, but he and the others were dissuaded from acting on it by Huang Hsing. Sung continued to spend most of his time studying law and government, writing, and translating Japanese works into Chinese. During the

summer of 1910 he met with Chü Cheng (q.v.), T'an Jen-feng (d. 1920; H. Shih-p'ing), and other T'ung-meng-hui leaders in Tokyo to reassess party military strategy, which had been focussed on south and southwest China and which had been markedly unsuccessful. It was decided that the focus of military activity should be shifted to central China and that a central China bureau should be established in Shanghai. T'an Jen-feng was dispatched to the T'ung-meng-hui's south China headquarters in Hong Kong to present these ideas for Huang Hsing's approval, and Huang agreed to support the establishment of a central China bureau if funds could be found for such an undertaking.

At the end of 1910 Sung Chiao-jen left Japan for Shanghai, where, at the invitation of Yü Yu-jen (q.v.) he became chief editor of Yü's newspaper, the *Min-li-pao*. He also made preparations for the establishment of a central China bureau of the T'ung-meng-hui, but his activities were interrupted in April 1911, when he went to Hong Kong in response to a call from Huang Hsing. He helped prepare for the planned assault on Canton and served briefly on Huang's general staff as head of the department dealing with legal matters and the drafting of orders and regulations. After the unsuccessful April revolt in Canton, he returned to Shanghai. On 31 July, he joined with Chü Cheng, Ch'en Ch'i-mei, and others in inaugurating the central China bureau and beginning the task of organizing and coordinating revolutionary uprisings in the Yangtze region, particularly in Wuchang and Hankow.

After the revolt of 10 October 1911 broke out, Sung Chiao-jen accompanied Huang Hsing to Wuchang, then the center of revolutionary activity. Working with Chü Cheng and T'ang Hua-lung (q.v.), the speaker of the Hupeh provincial assembly, he drafted a provisional constitution for Hupeh province and took an active part in planning the convention of provincial delegates called at Wuchang to organize a provisional government. Because Wuchang was still under fire, the convention assembled in the British concession at Hankow on 30 November. By this time, Sung had returned to Shanghai. After the convention moved to Nanking and Sun Yat-sen returned to China, Sung, as a delegate from Hunan, participated in the election of Sun Yat-sen as provisional president on 29 December.

After the provisional government was established in Nanking in January 1912, Sung Chiao-jen was appointed head of the law codification bureau (fa-chih-yuan), which was responsible for the drafting of laws and statutes for the new republic. He believed that the best system for a democratic government in China was a "responsible cabinet" system, under which the cabinet would be answerable to and subject to the approval of the Parliament. The premier, as head of the cabinet, would be the chief executive of the government. The "organic law of the provisional government," formulated in December 1911, had made no provision for a premier or a cabinet and had concentrated power in the hands of the provisional president. When it became apparent that Yuan Shih-k'ai would succeed Sun Yat-sen as provisional president, the presidential system was dropped in favor of a "responsible cabinet" system by the framers of the provisional constitution. It asserted that parliamentary approval was necessary when the provisional president appointed cabinet members and diplomatic envoys, declared war, negotiated peace, or signed treaties. The provisional constitution also provided for the convening of a parliament within ten months of its proclamation.

Before Sun Yat-sen resigned the presidency in favor of Yuan Shih-k'ai, he secured Yuan's assurance that he would abide by the provisional constitution then being drafted in Nanking. On 10 March 1912 Yuan was inaugurated in Peking; the following day, the provisional constitution was proclaimed. Yuan set up a cabinet, in compliance with the constitution, but he insured his control over this body by appointing his old friend T'ang Shao-yi (q.v.) premier and naming trusted subordinates to head the key ministries of war, the navy, and the interior. Sung Chiao-jen and three other T'ung-meng-hui members were named to head less powerful ministries. Although Sung was aware that his position as minister of agriculture and forestry was one of little authority, he was eager to participate in the new government. On 4 April 1912 the provisional Parliament moved to Peking. It soon became apparent, however, that Yuan Shih-k'ai had no intention of sharing power with the premier or the cabinet. His arbitrary appointment of officials brought him into conflict with T'ang Shao-yi, who resigned in the middle of June. Sung Chiao-jen

and the other three T'ung-meng-hui ministers registered their support of T'ang's position by resigning shortly after he left Peking.

Sung Chiao-jen's experience in the short-lived T'ang Shao-yi cabinet strengthened his conviction that a workable cabinet system would have to be imposed on the authoritarian Yuan Shih-k'ai if parliamentary democracy were to succeed in China. To support a cabinet that would be both politically effective and responsible to the Parliament, Sung believed, it would be necessary to create a powerful political party which would win a majority of the seats in the National Assembly in the national elections scheduled for December 1912. Through Sung's efforts and personal influence, the T'ung-meng-hui and four other political groups represented in the provisional Parliament—the T'ung-i kung-ho-tang [united republican party] the Kuo-min kung-chin-hui [people's progressive party], the Kung-ho shih-chin-hui [progressive republican party], and the Kuo-min kung-tang [people's public party]—merged to form the Kuomintang, inaugurated at Peking on 25 August with Sun Yat-sen as its director. When Sun, then more interested in railroad development than in practical politics, left Peking in mid-September he designated Sung to act in his place as general director of the party. As *de facto* leader of the Kuomintang, Sung spent much of the autumn of 1912 in Hupeh, Hunan, Anhwei, and Kiangsu campaigning for the election of party candidates to the new bicameral Parliament and for his own election to the cabinet. The announcement of the election results early in 1913 indicated that the new Parliament surely would be dominated by the Kuomintang, for the new party won 269 of the 596 seats in the National Assembly [chung-i yüan]. The success of the Kuomintang at the polls was also a personal triumph for Sung, and many people expected him to become premier of a new cabinet.

As an ardent admirer of Western parliamentary systems, Sung Chiao-jen had sought to introduce European and American electioneering methods to China during the political campaigns of late 1912 and early 1913. Accordingly, he had made a number of campaign speeches in which he had attacked the Peking government and its policies. Although public criticism of the government and its leaders was an accepted political tactic in the West, it was new to China; and it aroused the bitter animosity of Yuan Shih-k'ai and other powerful conservatives. Moreover, the likelihood that Sung, one of the most forceful proponents of government by party cabinet, would head the new Kuomintang cabinet meant that Yuan Shih-k'ai was faced with the prospect of an intense power struggle. On 20 March 1913, as Sung was boarding a Peking-bound train at the Shanghai railroad station, he was shot twice in the abdomen by an assassin. Two days later, only two weeks before his thirty-first birthday, he died. He was survived by his mother, his wife, a son, and a daughter.

The assassination of Sung Chiao-jen quickly became a *cause célèbre*. Almost immediately after his death, two men were seized by the authorities in Shanghai and charged with the crime. Documents found in their homes implicated Chao Ping-chün, the premier, and Hung Shu-tzu, the secretary of the cabinet, and indicated that Yuan Shih-k'ai had been aware of the plot. Although Yuan was able to avoid direct involvement in the case, the others were less fortunate. One of the assassins died in prison in Shanghai, and the other, after escaping from jail, was murdered by unknown assassins on the Peking-Tientsin train in January 1914. Chao Ping-chün, who had become governor of Chihli (Hopei), died suddenly on 27 February 1914. The last remaining suspect, Hung Shu-tzu, fled to the foreign concession of Tsingtao, where he remained until Yuan Shih-k'ai died in June 1916. He returned to Shanghai under an assumed name in 1917 only to be recognized and apprehended by Sung Chen-lü, the son of Sung Chiao-jen, and Liu Pai, who had been the elder Sung's secretary. Hung was tried in Shanghai, extradited to Peking, and sentenced to death. He was executed on 5 April 1919.

The violent death of Sung Chiao-jen constituted a serious blow to the cause of democratic government in China. The disclosures resulting from the investigation of his assassination brought the conflict of political interest between Yuan Shih-k'ai and the Kuomintang to public attention and helped spark the so-called second revolution of 1913 (*see* Li Lieh-chün). The Kuomintang, deprived of its strongest political leader, split into factions and soon ceased to be an effective political force. Not until its reorganization under Sun Yat-sen a decade later did it regain the strength it enjoyed early in 1913.

Sung Ch'ing-ling: *see* Soong Ch'ing-ling.

Sung Han-chang   宋 漢 章

Sung Han-chang (1872–), banker who devoted almost 50 years of his working life to the Bank of China, many of them as its general manager.

Although his native place was Yuyao, Chekiang, Sung Han-chang was born in Chienning hsien, Fukien, where his father was a merchant. He received his early education at a local private school and then went to Shanghai for study at the Anglo-Chinese Academy. After being graduated in 1889, he obtained a job in the accounts department of the Chinese telegraph service. In 1895 he passed a competitive examination for entrance into the Chinese Maritime Customs Service at Shanghai, and the following year he was transferred to the customs service at Ningpo.

In 1898 Sung Han-chang left the customs service to embark on a banking career. He joined the Commercial Bank of China, which had been established a year earlier at Shanghai under the sponsorship of Sheng Hsuan-huai (q.v.) and which was China's first modern bank. It had two managers, an Englishman who had been a professional banker in his own country and a Chinese who had been important in native banking. British administrative practices were combined with the better features of native banking at this institution, and Sung Han-chang thus gained rich experience during his ten years of service there.

The Hu-pu (Board of Revenue) Bank of the Ch'ing government decided in 1908 to establish a savings department at Peking, and Sung Han-chang was appointed to organize and head it. After the Hu-pu Bank became the Ta Ch'ing Bank, Sung was transferred to Shanghai as branch manager. In 1912, with the establishment of republican government in China, the Shanghai branch of the Ta Ch'ing Bank was reorganized as the Bank of China. The head office of the Ta Ch'ing Bank at Peking later was made the head office of the Bank of China. Sung Han-chang was made assistant manager of the Shanghai branch, and in 1913 he was promoted to be manager, with Chang Kia-ngau (Chang Chia-ao, q.v.) as assistant manager.

Sung Han-chang was mainly responsible for building up the prestige of the Bank of China in Shanghai. Although in later years the Bank of China was to become the virtual leader of Chinese banks, it confronted many difficulties in the early stages of its development. Competition came from foreign banks, native banks, and three modern Chinese banks: the Commercial Bank of China, the Ningpo Commercial Bank, and the National Commercial Bank. Moreover, the Bank of China was a government-operated institution, and the public, because of past experience, had little confidence in it. To overcome these difficulties, Sung Han-chang scrupulously adhered to sound banking practices as followed in Western countries. He rejected, for example, applications for loans, even from government organs, without security. He also resisted the transfer of funds from the Shanghai office of the bank to other areas. Through these and other measures, he gradually won public confidence. This process was accelerated in 1916 when the Bank of China in Shanghai refused to carry out an order from Peking to effect a moratorium on withdrawal against deposits and the cashing of its note issue. At that time, Yuan Shih-k'ai urgently needed funds for his monarchical plans, and he issued the moratorium order to the Bank of China and the Bank of Communications. Chang Kia-ngau strongly advocated the rejection of the order, and Sung Han-chang agreed to the proposal.

At that time, the various branches of the Bank of China handled note issue independently, and the banknotes were identified with the place name of the issuing branch of the bank. This identification system immediately caused a rise of public confidence in the notes issued at Shanghai. In 1922 the branches of the Bank of China in Kiangsu, Chekiang, and Anhwei placed their issues under the control of the Shanghai branch. All their cash reserves against issue were transferred to Shanghai, and the Shanghai notes were circulated throughout these provinces, a clear indication that the Shanghai issue enjoyed greater confidence than the provincial issues. In 1928 the Shanghai branch organized a committee for the inspection of its note issue which included representatives

of the Shanghai Chamber of Commerce, the Shanghai Bankers Association, and the Shanghai Native Bankers Association. By that time the total Shanghai issue was nearly 60 percent of the aggregate national issue of the Bank of China. By 1935, when the currency reform program was introduced and the managed paper currency known as fapi was introduced, the issue of the Bank of China had risen to become about 20 percent of the aggregate issue of all the banks in China.

Sung Han-chang's banking acumen was demonstrated by the policy he used in handling the reserve against note issue. When interest rates rose in the money market, Sung issued the greater part of his reserve in short-term credit loans, against suitable collateral, to the Shanghai banking community. He made use of the bank's reserve of silver dollars to ease prices when dollars were in demand for the purchase of agricultural crops in rural areas after the harvest. From 1915 on, he also made available supplies of the Bank of China's notes to other Chinese banks against security after depositing 40 percent of the value in cash, a system under which the other banks came to share in the benefits from the note issue. That measure greatly promoted the development of the Chinese banking industry and encouraged cooperation among Chinese banks.

The Bank of China was reorganized as a foreign-exchange bank in 1928, and Sung Han-chang was promoted to membership in the standing committee of the board of directors. Soon afterwards, Sung organized the Chinese Insurance Company as a subsidiary of the bank, with a nominal capital of China $5 million. He obtained the services of British insurance experts to organize the new enterprise and to train Chinese personnel. Sung himself soon acquired a solid grasp of the principles and practices of the insurance business. Although the China Insurance Company could not claim to be the largest insurance company in China, it nevertheless enjoyed great prestige.

When the Bank of China was reorganized in 1934–35, with T. V. Soong (q.v.) as its governor, Chang Kia-ngau relinquished his post as general manager to become minister of railways. Sung Han-chang, retaining his seat on the standing committee of the board of directors, again became general manager. He promoted the further development of the bank as a foreign-exchange bank, and he also initiated a savings department. The Bank of China contributed to the economic development of China through extensive help to industrial enterprises manufacturing consumer goods, railways, and cooperative agricultural credit services.

After the Sino-Japanese war began in 1937, the Bank of China moved its head office to Chungking for the duration. Sung Han-chang helped implement the National Government's fiscal policies, established new offices in west China, and operated industrial enterprises. He was named chairman of the board of the Bank of China in 1948, but retired to Hong Kong when the Chinese Communists won control of the mainland in 1949. He went to the United States in 1950, but moved on to Brazil in 1951. There, at the age of 79, he began to build a new life. In 1960, however, he returned to Hong Kong, where he made his home with his youngest son, K. N. Sung, a dental surgeon.

The career of Sung Han-chang was remarkable both for its longevity and for the fact that it was spent entirely in China. He devoted almost 50 years of his working life to the Bank of China and worked assiduously to foster its growth into China's leading banking house. Sung also took part in civic activities: he served on the advisory committee of the Shanghai Municipal Council; helped support the China Foreign Famine Relief Committee of Shanghai, serving as its chairman for more than ten years; and sponsored the Yang-ming Hospital in his native Yuyao, Chekiang.

Sung Hsi-lien   宋 希 濂
T. Yin-kuo   蔭 國

Sung Hsi-lien (b. 1906), Whampoa-trained Nationalist general who commanded the Eleventh Group Army in the early 1940's. After serving as Sinkiang garrison commander in 1946–47, he was transferred to central China. He was captured by the Chinese Communists in 1949.

A native of Hsianghsiang, Hunan, Sung Hsi-lien was born into a family known for its literary men. His father was an official. The young Sung was an able student, and in the early 1920's he was sent to the Chang Chün Middle School, where he was exposed to the doctrines of Sun Yat-sen. With the establishment of the Whampoa Military Academy in 1924, Sung made his way to Canton to become the youngest person in the academy's first class. While at the academy, he participated in both the first and second eastern expeditions, performing with distinction in battle. After graduation, he joined the Northern Expedition as a battalion commander in the 21st Division, which fought in Kiangsi and Chekiang. He was wounded in the battle of Tunglu and was forced out of action by his injuries. After recuperating, he went to Japan for advanced military studies. Although his anti-Japanese activities landed him in jail for a time, in due course he was graduated from the Japanese Infantry School and Staff College.

On returning to China in May 1930, Sung Hsi-lien became a staff officer in the 1st Training Division. He was promoted to battalion commander during the 1930 campaign against the so-called northern coalition of Feng Yü-hsiang and Yen Hsi-shan. After serving briefly as a regimental commander in the 1st Guard Division, he was transferred to the post of commander of the 6th Regiment of the 1st Division. In the winter of 1931 he was promoted to command of the 2nd Brigade of the 1st Division. He continued to serve as a brigade commander when that unit was reorganized as the 87th Division. In January 1932 he participated in the battle against the Japanese at Shanghai. When the fighting ended and the 87th Division returned to its station at Nanking, Sung became its vice commander.

In 1933 Sung Hsi-lien was made commander of the 36th Division, then stationed at Fuchow, Kiangsi. He encountered and defeated Red Army forces at Huwan. Soon afterwards, he was ordered into Fukien to help put down the Fukien revolt of Ch'en Ming-shu and Ts'ai T'ing-k'ai (qq.v.). He then returned to Kiangsi to participate in the campaigns against the Chinese Communists, who soon left Kiangsi to begin the Long March. In the spring of 1935 Sung was transferred to the Shanghai-Nanking sector. At the time of the Sian Incident (*see* Chiang Kai-shek; Chang Hsueh-liang), he and his 36th Division moved northward, prepared for action against the rebellious forces of Chang Hsueh-liang's colleagues Yang Hu-ch'eng and

Yü Hsueh-chung (qq.v.). In February 1937 Sung was appointed Sian defense commander. Soon afterwards, his 36th Division became the first Nationalist unit to enter Sian after the Sian Incident.

When the Sino-Japanese war broke out in July 1937, Sung Hsi-lien was assigned to the Shanghai front. After the Chinese defenses in that area collapsed, ten officers were executed and thirty others were dismissed from their posts for failure to carry out orders. Sung lost command of the 36th Division and was inactive until 1938, when he received command of the Honorable 1st Division. He soon was promoted to command of the Seventy-first Army, in which capacity he fought valiantly against Japanese forces in the Wuhan area. In the winter of 1939 Sung received command of the Thirty-fourth Group Army, becoming, at the age of 33, the youngest group army commander in China. He held this post until November 1941, when he received command of the Eleventh Group Army. In May 1942, when it seemed that the Japanese might occupy western Yunnan, the Eleventh Group Army moved into that area. After initial setbacks resulting in the loss of Lungling and Tengyueh, Sung succeeded in checking the enemy advance at the Nu River.

The Eleventh Group Army's reputation as an able fighting force was diminished somewhat by its performance in the Salween campaign launched in May 1944. The objectives assigned to Sung and his men were the Burma Road and the Japanese positions to the south. In attacking Lungling in June, Sung failed to concentrate his men properly, and they were driven back by a small Japanese force. The setback was compounded by further withdrawals, and the defeat of the Eleventh Group Army by a small Japanese garrison force brought to nothing the attempt by Wei Li-huang (q.v.) to exploit initial gains in the campaign. As a result, Sung Hsi-lien was removed from field command and was made director of a branch of the Central Military Academy. In 1946, however, he was decorated by both the Chinese and American governments. In March of that year, he was transferred to Lanchow to serve as chief of staff to Chang Chih-chung (q.v.). In support of Chang's efforts in Sinkiang province, Sung also became commander in chief of the Sinkiang garrison force in the winter of 1946. He supported the Kirei Kazakh revolt against the Ili regime, and he came to terms with the Kazakh leader Osman (q.v.), who declared his support for the Chinese. The Ili group made an issue of Sung's activities, and Sung was transferred to central China as vice commander in chief for bandit suppression.

The Nationalist position in central and southern China began to crumble as the civil war with the Chinese Communists gained momentum. Early in 1949 Sung Hsi-lien was made chief of the Szechwan-Hunan-Hupeh border region headquarters. Before long, his forces were retreating before the oncoming troops of Liu Po-ch'eng (q.v.). The Communist forces pursued the forces of Sung Hsi-lien and Hu Tsung-nan (q.v.) into the grasslands of the Sikang plateau and overtook them. Sung Hsi-lien was captured. Nothing further is known of him.

Tai Ai-lien 戴愛蓮

Tai Ai-lien (1916–), leading dancer-choreographer who developed traditional dance forms into a truly national art performed by professionals. In 1955 she became principal of the newly established Pei-ching wu-tao hsueh-hsiao [Peking school of dance].

The parents of Tai Ai-lien had migrated from Kwangtung to Trinidad before her birth. As a child, Tai Ai-lien showed great dancing talent, and in 1931 she went to England to study at the Jooss School of Ballet at Dartington Hall in Devon. She also worked under Anton Dolin and Margaret Craske and gained some film and stage experience. In 1940 she left England for China to take up the study of traditional Chinese dances.

Tai Ai-lien made a number of professional appearances in Hong Kong before going on to China proper. The last of these was given at the King's Theater on 22 January 1941. Her program for this benefit performance, "Divertissements," included a new sketch, "East River," which was based on Cantonese folk dancing. From Hong Kong, she went to Kweilin, where she performed twice. She also made appearances at Kweiyang and Chungking. During this period, she began to study local Chinese dance forms, aided by a group of pupil-assistants. Because she had an indifferent command of Chinese, she was forced to conduct her classes in English until she learned sufficient Chinese to communicate easily.

At Chungking, Tai Ai-lien taught at the Kuo-li ko-chü hsueh-hsiao [national academy of opera], the She-hui chiao-yü hsueh-yuan [academy for social education], and Yü-ts'ai hsueh-hsiao [talent-nurturing academy]. The last of these was directed by T'ao Hsing-chih (q.v.). Tai also formed her own troupe, the Chinese Ballet Group, which traveled as widely as wartime conditions permitted to study local dances and adapt them for stage performance at Chungking under the generic title Chung-kuo wu-yang [Chinese dance]. One of Tai Ai-lien's most spectacular successes was her adaptation of certain Uighur dances from Chinese Turkestan. The group also traveled to and brought back dances from such areas as Sinkiang and Tibet. By the end of the War in the Pacific, Tai Ai-lien had gained a national reputation as a dancer-choreographer. In 1946 the name of her troupe was changed to the Dance Group of the Chinese Folk Music and Dance Research Society.

In the summer of 1946 Tai Ai-lien went to the United States with her husband, the painter and cartoonist Yeh Ch'ien-yü (q.v.), whom she had married in Chungking. Yeh had been invited to the United States on a cultural exchange trip sponsored by the United States Department of State. During their year abroad, Tai Ai-lien gave dance recitals in New York. On returning to China in August 1947, she joined some of her former pupils in opening the China School of Dance at Shanghai. In 1949 she moved to north China to pursue her ambition of promoting the study and performance of the dance, an undertaking in which she was given active encouragement by the Chinese Communist authorities.

During 1949 China ushered in the new regime with the yang-ko, a simple rice-planting dance that became the Carmagnole of the Chinese Communist revolution. In every town and city students and children paraded the streets in long and sinuous lines to the insistent beat of the waist drum. For a time, the yang-ko and derivative routines superseded all other forms

of dancing in China. As the initial revolutionary fervor subsided, however, the yang-ko gave way before the first phase of what was to become a notable revival of traditional dancing in China. Tai Ai-lien was a dominant figure in the dance revival. In the summer of 1949 she was a delegate to the initial meeting of the All-China Federation of Literary and Art Circles, the principal organization used to exert Chinese Communist party control in the fields of literature and the fine arts. Thereafter, she held a series of administrative posts in the People's Republic of China, including membership in the National People's congresses.

Early in 1953 Tai Ai-lien, accompanied by two musicians, made an extensive tour to study and record local dance forms throughout China. In 1955 she was appointed principal of the newly established Pei-ching wu-tao hsueh-hsiao [Peking school of dance], the first national academy of its kind in China. Curriculum and training procedures at the school were set up with the help of Russian experts. Selected pupils between the ages of eleven and fourteen were enrolled in a seven-year course in which traditional Chinese choreography was the basic study, although the rudiments of Western ballet dancing also were taught. Much attention was given to the dances of non-Chinese minority groups in the People's Republic of China and to dances of other Asian countries. A strong effort was made to build up a national repertoire drawn from these sources. In 1959 the Pei-ching wu-tao hsueh-hsiao established its own experimental ballet group, and it later sponsored a number of talented troupes. Tai Ai-lien took a leading part in the development of this institution, both as a teacher and as the choreographer of many of the dances performed by the students and the national touring troupes. In the post-1954 period she also served as vice chairman of the board of directors of the China Association for Research in the Art of the Dance.

Tai Ai-lien was a pioneer in her field. Although there had been some experiments in the dance in China before her arrival in 1942, it was only through the thoroughness of her research, her artistic talent, and her choreographic inventiveness that traditional dance forms were developed into a truly national art performed by professionals.

Tai Chi-t'ao   戴 季 陶
  T. Ch'uan-hsien   傳 賢
  H. T'ien-ch'ou   天 仇

Tai Chi-t'ao (6 January 1891–11 February 1949), journalist and personal secretary to Sun Yat-sen who, after Sun's death in 1925, became one of the most authoritative anti-Communist interpreters of the Three People's Principles. He was president of the Examination Yuan from its inception in 1928 until 1948. In his later years he became a devout Buddhist and gradually withdrew from politics.

The forebears of Tai Chi-t'ao migrated late in the eighteenth century from the family home in Wuhsing, Chekiang, to Szechwan, where they operated a business in porcelains in Hanchou (Kwanghan), some 30 miles north of Chengtu. Tai attended a private school in Hanchou, where he received a traditional education in the Chinese classics. After failing the sheng-yuan examinations in 1901, he enrolled at a school in Chengtu for students who intended to study in Japan. His father, a medical practitioner and surgeon, died in 1903 when Tai was only 13. In 1904 Tai obtained a post as the private assistant and interpreter to a Japanese middle-school instructor, and in 1906 he went to study in Japan. The family raised the money for this venture by selling some land. In Tokyo he enrolled in the department of law at Japan University. He made many friends, both Chinese and Japanese, and he soon became active in student groups at the university. In 1908 he founded the Chinese Students Association in Japan and became its president.

After being graduated from Japan University in 1909, Tai Chi-t'ao returned to China, where he served for several months as an instructor in Soochow. Early in 1910 he found employment as editor in chief of a Shanghai newspaper, the *T'ien-to pao*. Writing under the name T'ien-ch'ou, he soon became known as the author of editorials that were bitingly critical of official corruption and mismanagement in the Ch'ing government. Tai also contributed articles to the *Min-hu-pao*, edited by Yü Yu-jen (q.v.). His attacks on local bureaucrats prompted them to secure a warrant for his arrest from the authorities of the International Settlement. He

escaped to Penang, where he joined the T'ung-meng-hui and became the editor of the *Kuang-hua pao*, the local organ of the revolutionary party.

Tai Chi-t'ao returned to Shanghai after the Wuchang revolt of October 1911 to join the revolution. In late December, he met Sun Yat-sen, who had just returned to China, and he accompanied Sun and his party to Nanking for Sun's inauguration as provisional president of the Chinese republic. Tai then returned to Shanghai to attend to the affairs of the *Min-ch'üan pao*, a magazine that he and an associate had established near the end of 1911. After Sun Yat-sen's resignation in favor of Yuan Shih-k'ai, Tai, in contrast to the conciliatory attitude taken by many T'ung-meng-hui leaders, sharply criticized Yuan and his supporters at Peking. In the editorial columns of the *Min-ch'üan pao* he accused Yuan of planning to sabotage the new republic and heaped abuse on T'ung-meng-hui members who, in his view, had compromised with Yuan and had betrayed the ideals of the revolution.

With Sun Yat-sen's appointment as national director of railroad development in September 1912, Tai Chi-t'ao became his personal secretary, a post he was to hold until Sun's death in 1925. After the so-called second revolution of 1913 (for details, *see* Li Lieh-chün), Tai joined the general exodus of republican revolutionaries to Japan. He worked with Sun and such other revolutionary leaders as Ch'en Ch'i-mei, Chu Chih-hsin, Hu Han-min, and Liao Chung-k'ai (qq.v.) in reorganizing the Kuomintang as the Chung-hua ko-ming-tang, inaugurated in June 1914. He then became the editor of the new party's propaganda organ, the *Min-kuo tsa-chih* [republican magazine].

In April 1916, as opposition to Yuan Shih-k'ai increased throughout China, Tai Chi-t'ao returned to Shanghai with Sun Yat-sen. In addition to his secretarial duties, Tai traveled to Peking and to Japan to keep Sun informed of the attitudes of Chinese and Japanese political leaders toward such matters as China's entry into the First World War and the restoration attempt of Chang Hsün (q.v.). In August 1917, following the ouster of Li Yuan-hung (q.v.) from the presidency at Peking by the Peiyang militarists, Sun went to Canton to head an opposition military government as part of the so-called constitution-protection movement. In that new regime Tai became secretary general of Sun's military headquarters, chairman of the law codification committee, and, in April 1918, vice minister of foreign affairs. When Sun withdrew from the Canton government in May 1918, Tai accompanied him back to Shanghai.

For the next two-and-a-half years, while Sun Yat-sen remained in Shanghai formulating his ideas of national reconstruction, Tai devoted much of his time to disseminating these ideas and to popularizing Sun's political and social philosophy. In August 1919 Tai joined with Chu Chih-hsin, Hu Han-min, and Liao Chung-k'ai in establishing the *Chien-kuo tsa-chih* [reconstruction magazine]. He also cooperated with Shao Li-tzu (q.v.) and others in publishing the *Hsing-ch'i p'ing-lun* [weekly review]. Tai's articles for these two magazines reveal his growing interest in Marxism. His introductory exegesis of *Das Kapital* (*Ma-k'o-ssu tzu-pen-lun chieh-shuai*), based on a Japanese translation, appeared serially in the *Chien-kuo tsa-chih* between November 1919 and April 1920; it was one of the earliest Chinese efforts to interpret this work. In "Ts'ung ching-chi shang kuan-ch'a Chung-kuo chih luan-yuan" he attempted to explain Chinese history and contemporary conditions in terms of Marxist economic theory. During this period Tai came to know the group of young Marxist, socialist, and anarchist intellectuals which had formed around Ch'en Tu-hsiu (q.v.). According to Chang Kuo-t'ao (q.v.), one of the earliest Chinese Communists, Tai strongly supported Ch'en's decision to form a Communist nucleus in Shanghai and even attended the organization meeting held in August 1920. However, he refused to join the new organization because of his commitment to Sun Yat-sen, and he soon parted ways with Ch'en and his Communist associates.

While thus engaged in the study and practice of Marxism, Tai also was active as a member of a group of Sun Yat-sen's followers, including Chang Jen-chieh, Ch'en Kuo-fu (qq.v.), and Chiang Kai-shek, which established the Shanghai Stock and Commodity Exchange to raise funds for Sun's revolutionary enterprises in Kwangtung. Their operations were highly successful in 1920–21. In the spring of 1922, however, a business recession wiped out most of their profits.

After his expulsion from Canton by Ch'en Chiung-ming (q.v.), Sun Yat-sen returned to Shanghai in August 1922 to consider plans for the recovery of Canton as a military base from which to unify China. In October, he dispatched Tai Chi-t'ao to Szechwan as his personal emissary to negotiate a peaceful settlement between rival military leaders of that province. On reaching Hankow, however, Tai learned that civil war was already brewing in Szechwan. Overcome, perhaps, by the futility of his mission, he attempted suicide by throwing himself in the river, but he was rescued and brought ashore by river fishermen. Tai reached Chengtu in November and stopped to visit his mother, whom he had not seen for 18 years. His efforts to persuade the local militarists to end the civil war in Szechwan were in vain, and during his eight months in the province the city of Chengtu was attacked four times. It was during this period that Tai took up the study of Buddhism.

By the time Tai Chi-t'ao returned to Shanghai in the autumn of 1923, important decisions had been made about the future of the revolutionary party. Sun Yat-sen, who had succeeded in reestablishing himself at Canton in February 1923, had concluded an alliance with the Soviet Union and had agreed to admit members of the Chinese Communist party to the Kuomintang. An extensive reorganization of the Kuomintang along Leninist lines was under way, and a national party congress was scheduled to convene in Canton early in 1924. Although Tai had previously favored the organization of a Communist party in China, he strongly disapproved of Sun's decision to admit Communists into the Kuomintang and thus was unwilling to attend the congress. However, he eventually was persuaded by Liao Chung-k'ai to go to Canton as one of the three delegates from Chekiang to the First National Congress of the Kuomintang in January 1924. At the congress, he was elected to the party's Central Executive Committee and to the Central Political Council. He also became head of the party's propaganda department, in which capacity he was responsible for the creation of the Central News Agency (Chung-yang t'ung-hsün she). Soon after the congress ended, Tai was appointed chairman of the law codification committee attached to Sun Yat-sen's military headquarters, and in May he was named director of the political department of the Whampoa Military Academy, with Chou En-lai (q.v.) as his deputy. Nevertheless, Tai grew increasingly dissatisfied with his role in the Canton regime. He left Canton for Shanghai early in July. Tai served in the Kuomintang executive headquarters in Shanghai until November, when Sun Yat-sen arrived in Shanghai on his way to Peking. After accompanying Sun to Japan as secretary and interpreter, he returned to Shanghai. However, on learning of Sun's soon-to-be-fatal illness early in 1925, he rejoined the party leader in Peking. Tai was among those who witnessed Sun's political testament on the eve of Sun's death on 12 March 1925.

With the passing of Sun Yat-sen, the cleavage between right- and left-wing elements within the Kuomintang became increasingly pronounced. Although in the past Tai had privately objected to Sun's policy regarding the Communists, he had refrained from publishing his opinions out of deference to Sun's wishes. After Sun's death, however, he had no such inhibitions. He returned to Shanghai in the spring of 1925 and set down his views in two important books. *Sun Wen chu-i chih che-hsueh chi-ch'u* [the philosophical foundations of Sun Yat-senism] was an interpretation of the Three People's Principles in which Tai sought to demonstrate that Sun's thought constituted a moral philosophy that was rooted in the traditional ethical concepts of Confucius and thus was wholly distinct from the alien ideology of Communism. It was in the second work, however, *Kuo-min ko-ming yü Chung-kuo kuo-min-tang* [the national revolution and the China Kuomintang], that Tai made his major attack upon the Communists and their participation in the Kuomintang. He argued that the Three People's Principles formed the sole doctrine of the Kuomintang and that the Kuomintang was the only party working for the national revolution. All those who, like the Communists, were not dedicated to the Kuomintang and its principles should be excluded from membership in the party. He went on to denounce the parasitic policy of the Chinese Communist party, by which Communist members of the Kuomintang used that party's organization to expand the membership and influence of the Chinese Communist party and sought to weaken the Kuomintang by sowing dissension among various groups within the party. Briefly put, Tai called for an end to the policy of Kuomintang-Communist cooperation that had been adopted by Sun Yat-sen during the reorganization of 1923–24.

The publication of these two books in the summer of 1925 elicited a strong reaction from the Communist leaders, who worried about the possible influence of Tai Chi-t'ao's views on non-Communist Kuomintang members. At an enlarged plenum of the Chinese Communist party's Central Committee, held at Peking in October, Tai was singled out for denunciation as the leader of an emerging "new right wing" of the Kuomintang. His theories, later dubbed "Taichitaoism," were deemed the spearhead of a counterrevolutionary movement of the bourgeoisie against the proletariat. Tai had not associated with the Kuomintang old guard before this denunciation, but in November 1925 he accepted an invitation from Lin Sen and Tsou Lu (qq.v.) to attend a plenum of the Kuomintang Central Executive Committee in Peking—a meeting later known as the Western Hills conference. Although he left Peking before the meeting began, Tai permitted the use of his name in the public telegram announcing the conference. In January 1926 the Second National Congress of the Kuomintang was held in Canton. Although disciplinary action was taken by the congress against most of the other participants in the Western Hills conference, Tai Chi-t'ao was reelected to the Central Executive Committee, reportedly with the backing of Chiang Kai-shek. Tai also was warned by the congress to refrain from publishing his views for the next three years.

After the Northern Expedition began in 1926, the National Government at Canton called Tai Chi-t'ao to Kwangtung to serve as the head of National Chung-shan (Sun Yat-sen) University. By the end of 1926 the Kuomintang had split into a left-wing faction at Wuhan and a right-wing faction headed by Chiang Kai-shek. In this period of intra-party dissension Tai found the political atmosphere at Canton far from congenial, and he left his university post in December to join Chiang Kai-shek at Lushan, Kiangsi. Early in 1927, as the Kuomintang's Northern Expedition forces advanced eastward toward Nanking and Shanghai, Chiang Kai-shek and his supporters decided to send a goodwill mission to Japan. Tai was chosen to head the mission because of his knowledge of the country and the language. He left in February and spent more than a month in Japan, where in public lectures and in meetings with Japanese political, military, and industrial leaders he sought to gain Japanese understanding and sympathy for the aims of the Northern Expedition. He returned to Shanghai at the end of March, shortly before the beginning of the so-called party purification movement. Although he did not take an active part in the purge of the Communists from the Kuomintang, his writings of 1925, with their emphasis on party purity and doctrinal orthodoxy, gave the movement ideological justification.

In May 1927 Tai Chi-t'ao went to Nanking, where he joined with Ch'en Kuo-fu, Ting Wei-fen, and Yeh Ch'u-ts'ang (qq.v.) in preparing for the establishment of the Chung-yang tang-wu hsueh-hsiao [central party affairs institute], a civil-service training center for the National Government. In the meantime, Tai had been reappointed president of Sun Yat-sen University, and in July he went to Canton to assume the duties of this post. After the Canton Commune of December 1927 (for details, *see* Chang T'ai-lei), during which the university campus suffered extensive damage, Tai's absences from Canton became frequent, for he found this sort of turbulence difficult to stomach. When at the university, he delivered a series of lectures in which he stressed the need for building a strong and orthodox party ideology based exclusively upon the Three People's Principles and traditional Chinese moral values. The lectures were published early in 1928 as *Ch'ing-nien chih lu* [the road for youth].

Tai Chi-t'ao went to Nanking in February 1928 to attend a plenum of the Kuomintang Central Executive Committee. He was elected to its standing committee and, with Yü Yu-jen and Ting Wei-fen, was chosen to assume responsibility for the affairs of the secretariat of the Central Executive Committee. A few months later, he attended a plenum in Nanking at which he, Hu Han-min, and Wang Ch'ung-hui (q.v.) were appointed to prepare a draft of an organic law incorporating Sun Yat-sen's theories of a five-power system of government. Late in September, Tai was among those who presented the draft to the Central Executive Committee, which adopted it after making some revisions. With the promulgation of the Organic Law in October and the creation of the five-yuan system in the National Government, Tai was designated president of the Examination Yuan, a position he was to hold continuously for the next two decades.

Provision for the establishment of the Examination Yuan was made by Kuomintang leaders in accordance with Sun Yat-sen's concept of a five-power constitution, by which the examination of the qualifications of candidates for government service was to become one of the five independent functions of the National Government (the others being the legislative, executive, judicial, and control functions). Tai and a preparatory bureau spent more than a year in intensive planning to overcome organizational and administrative problems before the Examination Yuan was inaugurated in January 1930. It consisted of two main administrative units, the examination commission (k'ao-hsuan wei-yuan-hui) and the board of personnel (ch'uan-hsü pu). Tai himself was chairman of the commission, which formulated regulations governing the examinations and saw that these regulations were administered properly throughout the country. The functions of the board of personnel were the supervising of registration by successful examination candidates and by men already in the civil service, and the reviewing of the records of officials and of all appointments, promotions, and dismissals.

For all its elaborate organization and large administrative staff, the Examination Yuan was a politically impotent body which was unable to carry out many of its intended duties. During the 20 years that Tai headed the Examination Yuan, the total number of examinations held was relatively small and many of the appointive posts at the higher levels were secured through personal influence or family connections. Moreover, as Tai became increasingly conservative in his outlook, he sought to use the authority of his office to revive both the form and the spirit of the traditional examination system. Like his predecessors in imperial China, he endeavored to tie the aims of education to those of officialdom by emphasizing the candidates' conformity to the ideology of the regime in power. For these and other reasons, many of the more promising graduates of schools and colleges tended to seek careers elsewhere.

In addition to his duties as president of the Examination Yuan, Tai Chi-t'ao took part in various party and government activities. In 1931 he helped prepare for a national convention, held in May, and as a member of the convention's presidium, he chaired the final session. The so-called tutelage constitution of 1 June, adopted during the final session, was said to incorporate many of Tai's views. After the Mukden Incident of September 1931, he served as chairman of a special committee on foreign affairs. In November of that year, he submitted a report recommending that war with Japan be avoided at all cost and that the National Government continue to seek a peaceful settlement by negotiation. Although Tai's recommendations found little favor among the Chinese people, they were approved and adopted as government policy at the Fourth National Congress of the Kuomintang in November. After the Japanese military action at Shanghai early in 1932 and the temporary removal of the National Government to Loyang, Tai was sent on a tour of China's northwestern provinces in the hope that he could propose government measures to encourage the future development of that region. One result of his recommendations was the establishment in 1934 of the Northwest Institute of Agriculture and Forestry in Shensi.

Although Tai Chi-t'ao retained his high rank in the Kuomintang and remained on good terms with Chiang Kai-shek, during the 1930's he receded into the background of Chinese political life. As an "elder statesman" of the Kuomintang, his functions became largely ceremonial in nature. In part, this withdrawal from politics appears to have been Tai's own choice. He had become increasingly preoccupied with the study of Buddhism; and to many in Nanking who knew him well, he seemed more concerned with Buddhist sutras than with party affairs and ideology. His interest in Buddhism and in its origins in India led to efforts to promote Sino-Indian cultural relations. In 1935, with others of similar interests, he organized the Chung-Yin hsueh-hui [Sino-Indian institute] in Nanking. One of its chief purposes was to purchase Chinese Buddhist works and to donate them to centers of Buddhist study in India. Tai's growing preoccupation with the doctrines of China's past was not limited to Buddhism; in the 1930's he promoted the revival of the cultic veneration of Confucius at a number of temples in various parts of China. During this period Tai also became interested in such activities for young people as the Boy Scouts, and he became vice president of the China Boy Scout Association in 1932. He was China's official representative to the 1936 Olympic Games at Berlin, in which capacity he spent four months visiting several European capitals.

After the Sino-Japanese war broke out in 1937, Tai Chi-t'ao moved with the National Government to Szechwan. In 1940 he was sent on a special mission to India soon after the opening of the Burma Road. One of the purposes of his trip was to attempt to ease the tensions that had grown up between Indian nationalists and the British administration in India. He had met Jawaharlal Nehru in Chungking in August 1939, and through Nehru he met Mohandas Gandhi. He also met Rabindrinath Tagore, with whom he had corresponded with reference to the Chung-Yin hsueh-hui and Buddhist studies in India. Tai visited many ancient Buddhist temples and other points of interest in India and Burma before returning to Chungking in December 1940.

During the war years Tai Chi-t'ao's health, which had never been robust, became poor indeed. Because of nervous agitation and insomnia he resorted to sedatives and then to stronger sleeping medicines. After his return from India, his health was impaired further by malaria and dysentery. He had to be carried to and from the plane that took him from Chungking to Nanking in April 1946. Nevertheless, he continued to serve on the Kuomintang's Central Executive Committee and in the National Government until July 1948, at which time he was relieved at his own request of his post as president of the Examination Yuan. At year's end he accompanied the National Government to Canton, where he became increasingly despondent about chaotic conditions in China and the Chinese Communist successes in the north. He took an overdose of sleeping tablets on the night of 11 February 1949 and was found dead the following morning.

Tai Chi-t'ao was a prolific writer, and his shorter articles appeared in the many newspapers and periodicals with which he was associated as a working journalist. A collection of his writings was published in 1921 in Shanghai, together in one volume with a collection of writings by Sung Chiao-jen (q.v.), as the *Sung Yü-fu Tai*

T'ien-ch'ou wen-chi ho-k'an. A four-volume collection of Tai's lectures, speeches, and correspondence, most of which dates from after 1926, was published as the *Tai Chi-t'ao hsien-sheng wen-ts'un* in Taipei in 1959 by the Kuomintang Central Executive Committee. These writings reveal much about his later life as an educator, a government and party official, and a devotee of Buddhism.

Tai Chi-t'ao married Niu Yu-heng in 1911. They had a daughter and a son, Tai An-kuo (1913–). The younger Tai studied mechanical engineering in Germany and during the 1950's served as a director of the Foshing Aviation Company in Taiwan. He then took charge of the West German office of the Central Trust of China, a government trade agency.

Tai Li
T. Yü-nung   戴 笠
                              雨 農

Tai Li (1895–17 March 1946), the chief of Chiang Kai-shek's intelligence services and one of the most powerful and enigmatic men of the republican period.

The eldest of three children, Tai Li was born in Chiangshan, Chekiang. The Tai family was of obscure origin, but in the generation or two preceding Tai Li's birth his forebears had managed to raise themselves from landless peasants to traders. Tai Li's father was a ne'er-do-well and a plague to this family of otherwise industrious entrepreneurs. His mother, on the other hand, was a member of the locally notable Lan family. She took charge of Tai Li's upbringing after his father died in 1900.

Little is known about Tai Li's childhood or youth except that he attended middle school and that he left both school and home in 1909 to join, as a military cadet, a so-called model regiment belonging to the Chekiang Army. From that time until 1926 the record is blank, though in the light of Tai's later activities it is safe to assume that he was not idle and that he probably gained both military and police experience. In 1926 he joined the Kuomintang and became a member of the fourth class at the Whampoa Military Academy. Upon graduation later that year, he joined a cavalry battalion.

During the Northern Expedition, Tai Li discovered his talent for intelligence operations. Although he was not a high-ranking officer, he was sent ahead of the troops to assess public sentiment, to evaluate military and political developments, and to report on the best routes of advance and attack. His success in winning over the powerful gangs and secret societies of Shanghai to Chiang Kai-shek's side helped lay the groundwork for Chiang's entry into Shanghai in April 1927.

For the next several years Tai Li served on Chiang Kai-shek's staff as an intelligence officer. With the deterioration of Sino-Japanese relations which culminated in the Japanese attack on Mukden on 18 September 1931, Tai was appointed head of the second department of the bureau of investigation and statistics of the Military Affairs Commission. This new department was charged with espionage against Japan and counterespionage against Japanese agents in China. Tai conducted these operations with efficiency and vigor, recruiting an expert staff composed largely of Whampoa graduates. Because of the nature of his work, few details about Tai's activities in the 1931-36 period are known. Generally speaking, he carried on clandestine operations against Communists and other domestic foes in addition to his anti-Japanese activities. At the time of the Sian Incident (*see* Chiang Kai-shek; Chang Hsueh-liang), he helped secure the release of Chiang Kai-shek. He later stated that he had gone to Sian in emulation of Chiang Kai-shek himself, for Chiang had gone to the aid of Sun Yat-sen during Ch'en Chiung-ming's revolt at Canton in 1922.

After the Sino-Japanese war began in 1937, Tai Li was sent to Shanghai to organize and direct guerrilla operations against the Japanese. He made use of his connections with the Ch'ing-pang (Green Gang) and with powerful labor groups to organize a guerrilla force known as the Chung-i chiu-kuo chün [loyal and righteous army of national salvation]. When Shanghai fell to the Japanese in November 1937, Tai moved his headquarters to safer territory but retained direction of anti-Japanese operations. He was recalled to Nanking and was appointed deputy director of the Military Affairs Commission's second bureau of investigation and statistics, which had evolved from the second department. In 1938 he became full director, in charge of more than 100,000 agents throughout China. Loyalties were uncertain in the lower Yangtze valley after 1937, and under Tai's command were the men of the second bureau, members of the Shanghai underworld, labor leaders, supporters of the Communist New Fourth Army, and elements of National Government forces commanded by Ku Chu-t'ung (q.v.). The establishment of the puppet Nanking regime in 1939 added another dimension to Tai's complex network of intrigue. Tai Li, a man of unusual aplomb, turned these complications to his own advantage. One notable success was his infiltration of the Nanking administration, particularly of its police and security forces, over which he exerted a measure of control throughout the war. In 1940, in response to problems arising from commodity speculation and smuggling, Tai received additional appointments as director of the chiao-t'ung yün-shu chien-ch'a ch'u [bureau of control for communications], director of the chi-ssu-shu [anti-smuggling bureau], and director of the huo-yün kuan-li ch'u [commodity transport control bureau]. These appointments, together with the directorship of the second bureau, gave Tai virtually complete control of the National Government's intelligence apparatus. With characteristic energy and appetite for action, he did not confine his activities to the direction of the complex services under his command; he also found time to direct important operations and make extensive tours of inspection behind enemy lines.

With the entrance of the United States into the war against Japan at the end of 1941, the China theater assumed new strategic importance for the Allied cause. The United States government recognized the need for joint Sino-American efforts, particularly in the field of intelligence. As a result, in May 1942 Tai Li made several long journeys to enemy-held areas in southeast China in the company of Captain (later Rear Admiral) Milton E. Miles, who had just arrived in Chungking to establish weather stations in China and to secure the cooperation of the Chinese intelligence services for the war effort. Tai's prestige among the Chinese behind Japanese lines and the safety with which the party moved, often virtually under Japanese guns, made a favorable impression on Miles, as did Tai's stamina in sustaining daily marches of up to 30 miles. In October 1942 Captain Miles, in addition to his duties as United States Navy observer at Chungking, was appointed director of the operations of the Office of Strategic Services in China. It was chiefly at his suggestion that ways were explored of assisting Chinese guerrillas and establishing weather stations in parts of China held by the Japanese.

One result of Miles's planning was the Sino-American Cooperative Organization (SACO), which was established under an agreement signed on 15 April 1943 by T. V. Soong (q.v.) for China and Secretary of the Navy Frank Knox for the United States. Tai Li was appointed commander of the new unit, with Miles as his deputy. SACO carried out a variety of important intelligence tasks, including the establishment of weather stations and guerrilla training camps, the observation of weather phenomena, and the planning of guerrilla operations. In return for their aid, the Chinese under Tai Li received radio equipment, arms, and access to general intelligence. SACO ultimately involved some two thousand Americans, of whom none died in combat and only three were captured. Chinese losses numbered over 4,000.

For all of its relatively light casualties, however, SACO had claws. Tai Li's guerrilla forces, with the assistance of American personnel under Miles, destroyed Japanese supplies and ammunition, cut communications lines, and killed substantial numbers of Japanese. Operating behind enemy lines, SACO was the target of great controversy in the bewildering confusion of commands and intelligence services that operated in the China theater during the final years of the Second World War. Perhaps its most important operation was the establishment of some 14 weather stations to assist the United States Pacific Fleet. These stations provided vital information regarding cloud and wind conditions in the far western Pacific and contributed greatly to American naval and air actions aimed at the Japanese home islands.

During the period of SACO's active existence, Tai Li and Miles worked closely together and traveled over much of China to inspect meteorological and guerrilla units. In April 1945 Chiang Kai-shek paid a personal visit to SACO headquarters and publicly commended the Chinese and Americans who had been responsible for the organization's successful record.

By the spring of 1945, it had become apparent that an Allied amphibious invasion of Japan had been scheduled. Tai Li turned his attention to the Japanese-occupied areas of the China coast and along the Yangtze, especially to the metropolitan centers of Shanghai, Nanking, Hankow, and Canton, where enemy troops were concentrated; and he formulated detailed plans for the disruption of attempts he knew would be made to reinforce Japan in the event of an Allied landing. In preparing these plans Tai was aided by the fact that, long before, he had planted or had obtained the support of men in key posts in the Japanese-sponsored government at Nanking.

At war's end, Tai Li assumed the grim duty of running to earth the many puppet officials and other so-called national traitors who had supported the Japanese. In all, his agents were responsible for bringing more than 3,000 such persons to trial. At the Sixth National Congress of the Kuomintang in 1945, Tai was elected to the Central Executive Committee. About this time, Tai turned his attention to the major problem then confronting the National Government: suppression of the Communists. It was probably in connection with this aspect of his work that Tai flew to Tsingtao on 16 March 1946 to confer with the commander of the United States naval forces headquarters there. About noon on 17 March he boarded a Civil Aeronautics Commission plane for the return trip to Shanghai. The plane vanished near Nanking, and its wreckage was found three days later in the mountains near Pangchow. Chiang Kai-shek wept at the news of Tai's death and ordered national mourning. Tai's death caused a great stir, though not all Chinese shared Chiang's grief. Indeed, there were many who refused to believe the news at all, maintaining that it was just another of Tai Li's clever ruses.

Tai Li was married and had two children. His wife, *née* Mao, died in 1939. His son, Tai Tsang-i, was a graduate of Ta-t'ung ta-hsueh (Utopia University) and at the time of Tai's death was principal of the Chien-kuo Middle School in the family's native district of Chiangshan, Chekiang. Tai Li also had a daughter, Tai Shu-chih.

T'ai-hsü　　　　　　　太 虛
Orig.　　Lü P'ei-lin　　呂 沛 林
Religious. Wei-hsin　　唯 心

T'ai-hsü (8 January 1890–17 March 1947), Buddhist monk of the wei-shih [consciousness-only] school who led a movement to reform and modernize his religion. He headed the Wu-ch'ang fo-hsüeh yuan [Wuchang Buddhist institute], edited the *Hai-ch'ao-yin*, and established such organizations as the World Buddhist Association.

Although his native place was in Ch'ungte, Chekiang, T'ai-hsü was born into a poor family in Haining. His father, a bricklayer, died when he was one year old, and his mother remarried when he was five. He spent his childhood in Haining under the care of a maternal grandmother and an uncle. T'ai-hsü received a primary education in the Chinese classics from his uncle, a village school teacher, and he often traveled with his grandmother when she made pilgrimages to Buddhist temples in the area.

At the age of 15, T'ai-hsü was compelled by straitened financial circumstances to go to work as a shop clerk. However, he soon left the job because he wished to become a Buddhist monk. A short time later, he entered the T'ien-t'ung temple near Ningpo, where, from 1906 to 1910, he received basic instruction in Buddhism. He became attracted to the teachings of the T'ien-t'ai and Hua-yen schools, and about 1908 he came to know monks who were sympathetic with reform efforts. At their urging, he began to read works by K'ang Yu-wei, Liang Ch'i-ch'ao, T'an Ssu-t'ung, Chang Ping-lin, Tsou Jung, and Yen Fu, as well as such revolutionary newspapers as the *Min Pao* [people's journal], which then was published secretly in Japan. In 1910 T'ai-hsü went to Nanking, where he studied under Yang Wen-hui (1837–1911; T. Jen-shan), a prominent Buddhist layman who was director of the Buddhist Press. In 1911 he went to Canton, where he was associated with anti-Manchu revolutionaries and developed an interest in anarchism and socialism after reading Chinese translations of works by Tolstoy, Bakunin, Proudhon, and Marx. He participated for a time in a discussion group on socialism and became convinced of the necessity for a social revolution in China.

T'ai-hsü's interest in socialist ideas affected his interpretation of Buddhism and soon led him to formulate plans for a new Buddhist movement in China. He contended that Buddhism and socialism were similar in that both advocated social equality and salvation for all. However, he felt that Buddhism in China had degenerated and had been unable to fulfill its aims because of the relaxation of Buddhist order. Monks had become ignorant, and Buddhist properties were monopolized by a few. Furthermore, the ancient Buddhist doctrines had become outmoded in the new social environment of twentieth-century China. T'ai-hsü believed that the scriptures needed to be redefined with reference to new currents of thought. Buddhism had become an object of popular hostility: temples had been destroyed, and Buddhist properties constantly faced threats of government confiscation. T'ai-hsü therefore aimed at a threefold reform movement: regeneration of the Buddhist clergy, rededication of Buddhist properties, and redefinition of Buddhist doctrines. About 1909 he helped to establish the Association for Monks' Education at Ningpo; in 1910 he founded the Association for the Promotion of Buddhist Education at Canton.

In 1912 T'ai-hsü participated in the formation of the Fo-chiao hsieh-chin hui [Buddhist association]. At the organization's first meeting in Chinkiang, he set forth his principles of religious reform. He believed that Buddhist land holdings were the common property of all followers of the religion and should be dedicated to the promotion of social welfare, particularly education. In a statement that aroused strong controversy, he advocated the adoption in religious communities of the principle that each person should be judged by his abilities and rewarded according to his work. Moreover, he argued for the redefinition of Buddhist doctrine because he believed Buddhism to be a religion for this world. The evolutionary process of religion corresponds with that of political life, and both religion and government should have the same goal: a grand union in which people work according to their abilities and receive according to their needs. In 1913 he wrote: "The evolutionary process of politics is from tribe to monarchy, from monarchy to republic, and from republic to anarchy. The evolutionary process of religion is from pantheism to monotheism, thence to atheism, and finally to no religion. In the ultimate grand union, government becomes anarchy and religion becomes atheism."

T'ai-hsü was so distressed by the unenthusiastic reception of his principles that in 1914 he retired to P'u-t'o Island, where he remained for three years. He secluded himself in the Hsi-ling temple and voraciously read Buddhist literature, Chinese classics, Western logic, philosophy and psychology, and the natural sciences. Among contemporary Chinese writers, he was particularly attracted to Chang Ping-lin and Yen Fu (qq.v.), both of whom were known for their interest in Buddhism. During this period of retreat he also began to study wei-shih, or "consciousness-only," Buddhism, a form of idealism which analyzes the mind into levels of consciousness (*see* Ou-yang Ching-wu). As a result of his years of study and meditation, he decided to "create a new Buddhism based on orthodox doctrines, while at the same time adopting various ancient and modern teachings of both East and West in order to enable it to meet the needs of the time."

The synthetic tendency of T'ai-hsü's thinking became increasingly evident. In order to "combine and transform the various philosophies," he declared, "the world needs the doctrine of idealism." As a follower of the "consciousness-only" school, he believed all sentient things to be the products of consciousness, having no independent existence. In his opinion, this view was confirmed by Einstein's theory of relativity, "that a thing can only be identified by naming its relationship to something else." T'ai-hsü believed that man cannot live alone and that because man shares his lot with society, he must promote public welfare. Civic morality is consonant with the Buddhist view of life that advocates concern for the welfare of others. Like many of his countrymen, T'ai-hsü thought that the First World War testified to the bankruptcy of Western civilization and of Christianity. In order to establish a new moral standard for the world, he said, Buddhists must not use religion as an escape but must enter into the world to practice a new Buddhism which would be humanistic, scientific, demonstrative, and universal.

In 1918 T'ai-hsü made a preaching tour of Taiwan, and he visited Japan before returning to China. His observations during that trip reinforced his conviction that reforms were needed in the Buddhist *sangha*, or order. He called for elimination of commercialism and illiteracy and for higher intellectual and spiritual standards for the clergy. He held that monks should engage in productive labor, religious ceremonies should be simplified, and temples and monasteries should be reserved for meditation and research. A national monastery should be established in China to serve as a model for the new monastic ideals. He also envisaged the building of a national center of Buddhist learning in Nanking and the creation of a network of Buddhist institutes throughout the country, with parishes and chapels for preaching in every city.

Also in 1918 T'ai-hsü, Chang Ping-lin, and Chiang Tso-pin (q.v.) founded the Chüeh-she [enlightenment society], which aimed at propagating the Buddhist faith. It conducted research on Buddhism and on the practice of meditation, and published a quarterly edited by T'ai-hsü, the *Chüeh-she chi-k'an* [enlightenment journal]. T'ai-hsü soon organized a similar group in Hangchow. About 1920 he closed down the Chüeh-she in Shanghai, converted the *Chüeh-she chi-k'an* into the *Hai-ch'ao-yin yüeh-k'an*, and moved to Hangchow to devote himself to editing the *Hai-ch'ao-yin*. It became China's outstanding Buddhist journal and commanded high respect among Chinese scholars of all religions. In 1922 he accepted an invitation to head the newly established Wu-ch'ang fo-hsüeh yuan [Wuchang Buddhist institute], an education center for monks and laymen. The institute, which was famous for its library of over 40,000 books and its lecture program, and the China Institute of Inner Learning, founded by Ou-yang Ching-wu (q.v.), became rival centers of the "consciousness-only" school of Buddhism. During the 1920's T'ai-hsü engaged in polemical debates with Ou-yang Ching-wu, who opposed his synthetic program and advocated strict adherence to traditional Buddhist tenets. In 1922 T'ai-hsü established the Hankow Buddhist Society, which by 1933 claimed a membership of 30,000.

During a symposium on Buddhism held at Lushan, Kiangsi, in 1923, T'ai-hsü announced the establishment of the Shih-chieh fo-chiao lien-ho hui, or World Buddhist Association. In the summer of 1924 a conference of the newly established association called for a meeting of East Asian Buddhists in 1925. In the meantime, T'ai-hsü made plans for establishing a university through which Chinese Mahayana Buddhism might be introduced to the West. He instituted the annual World Conference on Buddhism in Kuling, sent his disciples to study in various Buddhist centers, and invited Buddhist leaders from abroad to lecture at the Wu-ch'ang fo-hsüeh yuan. In the winter of 1925 he led a Chinese delegation of 26 members to the East Asian Buddhist Conference held in Japan, where he delivered a series of lectures on Buddhism. The following year, at the suggestion of Hsiung Hsi-ling (q.v.) and Chang Ping-lin, he founded the Association for Buddhist Education in Asia (later the Association for Buddhist Education in China). He also established the journal *Hsin-teng* [inner light] and, at the invitation of overseas Chinese, gave lectures in Singapore.

Although he was depressed by the recurrent civil wars in China, T'ai-hsü continued his efforts to create a world-wide Buddhist movement. He believed that the West was more dynamic than the East, and he concluded that it would be feasible to influence the East by first influencing the West. Thus, he made a trip to Europe and the United States in 1928–29 to assess the possibilities of introducing Buddhism to the West. He first visited Germany and France with the idea of setting up a world university in Europe for Buddhist studies. This plan failed, but T'ai-hsü did succeed in establishing a branch of the World Buddhist Association in Paris. In England he met Bertrand Russell, with whom he discussed problems of Buddhism; and in the United States, he lectured at Columbia, Yale, and other universities. According to T'ai-hsü, his travels abroad led him to reevaluate Western civilization. He had regarded the West as being superior to the East only in material achievements, but after this trip he decided that this view was an over-simplification.

In 1929 T'ai-hsü founded a new national organization, the Chung-kuo Fo-chiao hui [Chinese Buddhist society], with the aim of enlisting all Chinese temples and monasteries in the cause of reforming the order. He founded the College for Buddhist Teachings at Peiping in 1930, but he soon had to close it because of financial difficulties. In the early 1930's he established the Sino-Tibetan Buddhist Institute at a monastery near Chungking, and in 1935 he founded the College of Pali Tripitaka at Sian. He became head of the Min-nan fo-hsueh yuan [Minnan Buddhist institute] at Amoy in 1937. T'ai-hsü's teaching methods were considered unorthodox, for he encouraged his students to study other subjects besides Buddhism and to attempt to understand the meaning of the Buddhist sutras rather than merely memorize them.

After the outbreak of the Sino-Japanese war, T'ai-hsü moved to Szechwan, where he remained until 1945. His headquarters was at the Sino-Tibetan Buddhist Institute near Chungking. He reestablished the Wu-ch'ang fo-hsüeh yuan and the Chung-kuo fo-chiao hui in Chungking and directed their activities throughout the war years. In 1939 and 1941 he left Szechwan for a short time to lead Chinese Buddhist missions to Southeast Asia, where the group visited Buddhist centers in Burma, Malaya, Ceylon, and India. In addition to lecturing and writing, T'ai-hsü helped organize medical relief work and promoted social welfare projects in Szechwan.

After the Japanese surrender in 1945, T'ai-hsü returned to Nanking and became the chairman of the Buddhist Reform Committee. From 1944 until his death, he also served as an executive director of the Institute of Philosophy of Life, headed by the Roman Catholic bishop Paul Yü Pin (q.v.). In 1947, after a lecture trip to Ningpo, T'ai-hsü retired to Shanghai. He became ill and died on 17 March 1947.

Among T'ai-hsü's important writings are the *Fo-hsüeh kai-lun* [introduction to Buddhology] of 1926, the *Fo-chiao ming-tsung-p'ai yuan-liu* [origins of the most eminent Buddhist sect] of 1930, the *Fo-chiao tui-yü Chung-kuo wen-hua chih ying-hsiang* [influence of Buddhism on Chinese culture] of 1931, the *Che-hsueh* [philosophy] of 1932, and the *Fo-ch'eng-tsung yao-lun* [essential discourse of Buddhist patriarchs] of 1940.

Tan Kah Kee: *see* CH'EN CHIA-KENG.

T'an Chen 覃 振
  Orig. Tao-jang 道 讓
  T. Li-ming 理 鳴

T'an Chen (1885–18 April 1947), founding member of the conservative Western Hills

faction of the Kuomintang. He served the National Government as vice president of the Judicial Yuan (1932–42) and as a member of the Government Council (1943–46).

Born into a farming family in T'aoyuan, Hunan, T'an Chen showed such intellectual promise as a boy that his family decided to excuse him from farm duties so that he could concentrate on his studies. By 1900 he had received a thorough grounding in the Chinese classics. That year, his parents died; Peking was captured during the Boxer Uprising; and T'an met a local secret society leader named Yang. These events combined to transform T'an into a rebel against the prevailing social order in China. In 1902 T'an studied at the local primary school, where he came to know a fellow townsman with revolutionary sympathies, Sung Chiao-jen (q.v.). The following year, he entered the prefectural middle school at Ch'angte. He soon was exposed to anti-Manchu periodicals published by Chinese students in Japan. About this time, the local government established a primary school and a library at the Langchiang Academy. On the opening day, local officials, members of the gentry, and students from various prefectural schools gathered to hear ceremonial oratory. As the last speech ended, T'an emerged from the crowd, jumped onto the platform, and harangued the surprised audience on the need for fundamental changes to save the country, challenging the call for loyalty to the emperor that had been made by a prominent member of the local gentry. The magistrate of Wuling was ready to arrest T'an on the spot, but the prefect of Ch'angte, who was also the superintendent of education, limited T'an's punishment to expulsion from school.

T'an Chen continued to defy the authorities after he left school. He wrote an inflamatory essay entitled *Shih-li chiu-sheng* [how to escape from death] in which he set forth his revolutionary ideas. His friends made copies of the essay and posted them in the busy thoroughfares, thereby attracting large crowds of readers. As T'an's name became widely known, government surveillance of his activities increased. On the advice of friends, he left Hunan and went to Japan, where he enrolled at the Kobun Institute.

In late 1903 or early 1904 Huang Hsing (q.v.)

founded a revolutionary organization in Hunan, the Hua-hsing-hui [society for the revival of China]. When the society made plans with the Ko-lao-hui [society of elders and brothers] to stage an uprising in Hunan during the celebrations of the empress dowager's seventieth birthday in November 1904, Sung Chiao-jen, who was to take charge of the action in Ch'angte, asked for T'an's help. T'an returned to China and helped prepare for the uprising, but premature discovery of the plot forced him to flee Ch'angte. He escaped arrest by hiding in a friendly village. Furthermore, he found time to marry Sung Chih-chao before leaving China again for the safety of Japan. In August 1905 he became a founding member of the T'ung-meng-hui, and he was elected to its legislative council (p'ing-i-pu).

In October 1906 an armed revolutionary force composed of coal miners, secret society members, and disaffected government soldiers invaded P'inghsiang, Liuyang, and Liling in the Hunan–Kiangsi border area. Upon hearing the news, many T'ung-meng-hui members hurried back to China from Japan to participate in the rebellion. T'an returned to Changsha and established contact with revolution-minded students and troops of the New Army. The uprising was suppressed within a month, but T'an managed to escape detection by the authorities. However, he ran afoul of Hunan officialdom again when some educators in Hunan sponsored a public funeral for Ch'en T'ien-hua and Yao Hung-yeh, two Hunanese students who had committed suicide in Japan and Shanghai respectively in protest against the Ch'ing government. Despite official disapproval, the funeral, which T'an helped plan, had a large attendance. The authorities, angered by this show of public defiance, ordered the arrest of the organizers. T'an fled to Japan, where he enrolled at Waseda University.

Huang Hsing sent T'an Chen to Changsha again in 1908. This time, T'an was arrested and sentenced to life imprisonment. He indoctrinated fellow prisoners and, with the help of friends and relatives, kept in touch with other revolutionaries. He later was transferred to a jail in his native T'aoyuan. There he was known to even more people, and, though incarcerated, he virtually ran the local revolutionary group.

At the time of the republican revolution in 1911, T'an Chen was released from jail at the urgent request of Chiao Ta-feng, the newly proclaimed military governor of Hunan. T'an arrived at Changsha to discover that Chiao had been assassinated by supporters of the local gentry in the struggle for control of Hunan. Calling for unity, T'an joined the Hunan–Kwangsi Expeditionary Force that was setting out to help the hard-pressed revolutionary army in Hupeh. When he arrived at Wuchang, he received an appointment from Li Yuan-hung (q.v.) as secretary general in Li's office. It was as Li's personal representative that T'an went to Nanking in December to participate in consultations about establishing a provisional government.

In the spring of 1912, when Yuan Shih-k'ai, who had succeeded Sun Yat-sen as provisional president, presented to the Senate his list of cabinet members, T'an Chen sent a telegram to Yuan in which he strongly criticized his choices. Li Yuan-hung, wishing to avoid offending Yuan, dismissed T'an as his personal representative. T'an then went to Peking to assist Sung Chiao-jen in the creation of the Kuomintang. Early in 1913 T'an was elected to the National Assembly. After Sung Chiao-jen was assassinated by supporters of Yuan Shih-k'ai, T'an mercilessly attacked Yuan's policies in the National Assembly until the Kuomintang was suppressed at Peking and the so-called second revolution (see Li Lieh-chün) against Yuan broke out. When the anti-Yuan movement failed, T'an again sought refuge in Japan.

In July 1914 Sun Yat-sen reorganized the Kuomintang in an attempt to revive the revolutionary spirit of the party. In the meantime, Yuan Shih-k'ai had begun preparing the ground for the realization of his monarchical ambitions. On 23 August 1915 the Ch'ou-an-hui was founded at Peking as a supposedly private society devoted to arousing popular support for Yuan. As a countermeasure, T'an and other Kuomintang leaders in Japan organized public demonstrations against Yuan among the Chinese students. Chiang Shih-li, an agent of Yuan Shih-k'ai, was then in Japan seeking to weaken the influence of the Kuomintang among Chinese students by offering them financial support and political preferment. Because most Chinese students in Japan were living in poverty, Chiang's blandishments succeeded in attracting an increasing number of students and even party members to his side. A young Hunanese, Wu Hsien-mei, presented T'an with a plan to assassinate Chiang which T'an approved. In October, Wu shot Chiang and escaped to Shanghai. T'an was arrested on suspicion of involvement in the crime but was released two weeks later for lack of evidence.

When Yuan Shih-k'ai made public his intention to become monarch, the Yunnan army under the leadership of Ts'ai O (q.v.) marched against Szechwan in revolt. On orders from Sun Yat-sen, T'an Chen left Japan for Shanghai with a group of party members. They plotted with Lung Chang and Chou Chen-lin for the overthrow of T'ang Hsiang-ming, the military governor of Hunan. In February 1916, after several provinces had declared their independence, T'ang asked his brother T'ang Hua-lung (q.v.) to negotiate a settlement with T'an Chen and promised to leave Hunan. T'an refused to enter into an agreement with T'ang Hsiang-ming because of T'ang's past persecution of revolutionaries in Hunan. Nevertheless, T'ang withdrew his support from Yuan publicly on 29 May and left Hunan under pressure on 4 July. Soon afterwards, T'an Yen-k'ai (q.v.) became governor. With a friendly governor in power, the Hunanese members of the Kuomintang returned to their home province in large numbers. T'an then established the Cheng-i-she, with headquarters in Changsha and branches in other cities and towns, to serve as cover for Kuomintang activities. Lung Chang was elected president of the new society, and T'an served as its vice president.

After the July 1917 restoration attempt of Chang Hsün (q.v.) failed, Tuan Ch'i-jui achieved power at Peking and began a campaign to unify China militarily. He dismissed T'an Yen-k'ai from the Hunan governorship and appointed Fu Liang-tso in his place. Fu's appointment was distasteful to many Hunanese. T'an Chen plotted with such Hunanese commanders as Chao Heng-t'i (q.v.) and Lin Hsiu-mei to undermine Fu's position. In the meantime, Sun Yat-sen and others had established an opposition government at Canton. T'an went to Canton to meet with Sun, who appointed him inspector general for Hunan. After returning to Hunan, T'an worked with the Kweichow forces that had come to aid the Hunanese in their campaign against the Peiyang

troops. Fu Liang-tso finally was forced out of Hunan in November 1917.

From 1918 to 1924 T'an Chen devoted himself to the consolidation of a political base for the Kuomintang in south China. At the First National Congress of the Kuomintang in January 1924, he was elected to the Central Executive Committee. That spring, he became a member of the standing committee of the Kuomintang's Hankow executive committee, which had jurisdiction over party affairs in Hunan, Hupeh, Kansu, and Shensi. In consultation with Lin Po-ch'ü, Pao Hui-tseng, and P'eng Su-min, T'an appointed Liu Shao-ch'i (q.v.) preparatory director of the Hunan workers branch and made Hsia Hsi director of the Hunan student branch. Both Liu and Hsia succeeded in greatly increasing Communist influence in Hunan, and T'an soon became suspicious of their intentions and opposed to the policy of Kuomintang cooperation with the Chinese Communists.

T'an Chen went to Peking for Sun Yat-sen's funeral in March 1925. He remained there and organized the T'ung-chih chü-pu, composed of Kuomintang members who had served in the Parliament. In November, he participated in the meeting of anti-Communist members of the Kuomintang known as the Western Hills Conference. The conferees set up a separate Kuomintang central party headquarters in Shanghai. Thereafter, T'an was identified as a member of the Western Hills group.

The Communist issue caused further factionalism in the Kuomintang, and the year 1927 saw the creation of opposing governments at Wuhan and Nanking. By September 1927 the Communists had been purged from the Kuomintang and the stage had been set for the reconciliation of the three major Kuomintang factions. Their representatives met in Shanghai and set conditions for party unity. The Central Special Committee, composed of thirty-two members and nine alternates drawn from all three factions, was established to serve as an interim government at Nanking. T'an became a member of the Central Special Committee and chief of its department of propaganda.

The newly achieved party unity proved extremely fragile. Wang Ching-wei (q.v.), the leader of the Wuhan group, withdrew his support almost as soon as it became known that he would not be able to control the party or the government. In October 1927 T'ang Sheng-chih (q.v.) announced the establishment at Wuhan of a separatist Kuomintang political conference outside the jurisdiction of the Central Special Committee. T'ang's army was routed by Nanking forces in the early part of November. On 22 November, a victory celebration at Nanking turned into a riot, resulting in the death of two students and the wounding of about a dozen other people. For various reasons, the Western Hills members of the Central Special Committee were blamed for this event, and they were dismissed from their posts on 3 December. T'an left Nanking and established residence in Shanghai. In the summer of 1928, the Northern Expedition having ended, he moved with his family to Peiping. In 1930 he participated in the so-called enlarged conference movement (*see* Feng Yü-hsiang; Yen Hsi-shan), and in 1931 he joined the secessionist movement at Canton that began in protest of the arrest of Hu Han-min (q.v.). The Japanese attack on Mukden in September 1931 brought the latter movement to an end; in the face of an outside threat to China, a peace conference was held in Shanghai. As a result of governmental reorganization, T'an was elected vice president of the Legislative Yuan. He resigned this post on 9 May 1932 to become vice president of the Judicial Yuan and chairman of the central civil service disciplinary commission.

In the summer of 1934 T'an toured Europe and North America, spending about six months inspecting the judicial systems of England, France, Germany, Italy, and the United States. Upon his return to China he helped to plan the establishment of the China Law Society, which was inaugurated on 20 September 1935. Following the outbreak of the Sino-Japanese war in 1937, he accompanied the National Government to Chungking. In 1943 he resigned from the Judicial Yuan to become a member of the Government Council. At war's end, T'an, who suffered from chronic asthma, flew to Shanghai for treatment. He died there on 18 April 1947.

T'an Chen-lin   譚震林

T'an Chen-lin (1902–), Chinese Communist political officer who served with the New Fourth Army throughout the Sino-Japanese war.

Thereafter, he held important regional posts in east China. A member of the Secretariat and the Political Bureau of the Chinese Communist party, he helped develop agricultural programs for the People's Republic of China and became director of the party rural work department in October 1962. He also served as vice premier of the State Council and as vice chairman of the State Planning Commission.

Yuhsien, a small town by the Yu River in southeastern Hunan, was the birthplace of T'an Chen-lin. His father was a clerk at a nearby mine. T'an's education was limited to three years' study at an old-style private school. In 1926, at the age of 24, he joined the Chinese Communist party. The following year, he worked with Mao Tse-tung in fomenting what became known as the Autumn Harvest Uprising. When this action failed, he went with Mao and a small number of guerrillas to the Chingkangshan region, where they were joined by Chu Teh (q.v.) in the spring of 1928. The combined fighting forces, designated the Fourth Red Army, remained in the Chingkangshan region until the end of 1928, when they were forced into Kiangsi and Fukien. T'an later became a political commissar in the Twelfth Red Army of Lo Ping-hui.

When the central soviet government was established at Juichin, Kiangsi, T'an Chen-lin, because of his association with Mao Tse-tung, became a member of the central committee. In addition to helping direct military affairs, he aided Li K'o-nung (q.v.) in security matters. When the Long March began in October 1934 T'an and some other trusted activists were left behind with their scattered guerrilla groups to continue spreading Communism in areas held by the National Government. T'an joined Teng Tzu-hui (q.v.) and Chang Ting-ch'eng in organizing a Fukien soviet, with Chang as its chairman and T'an as vice chairman and director of the military department. In 1937 T'an's forces became part of the New Fourth Army of Hsiang Ying and Yeh T'ing (qq.v.). From 1937 to 1941 T'an served as political commissar of its second column. After the so-called New Fourth Army Incident, during which the Nationalists killed Hsiang Ying and captured Yeh T'ing, Ch'en Yi (1901–; q.v.) assumed command of the army's remnant troops. T'an, now working under the assumed name

Lin Chun, was promoted to commander of the 6th Division of the New Fourth Army. In 1944 he also became political commissar of Lo Ping-hui's 2nd Division. T'an soon moved his field of operations to southern Kiangsu, where he served as secretary of the Kiangsu-Anhwei border region committee of the Chinese Communist party and as commander of the south Kiangsu military district. His prominence in the party was confirmed at its Seventh National Congress in April 1945, when he was elected to the Central Committee.

At war's end, T'an Chen-lin moved with elements of the New Fourth Army into Shantung. For the next three years the army, known successively as the East China Field Army (1946–47), the East China People's Liberation Army (1947–48), and the Third Field Army, fought in coastal and central China. T'an served as a political commissar, becoming deputy political commissar of the entire Third Field Army and of the East China Military District in 1948. He held these posts until 1954. In the 1948–49 period he also served as chairman of the Tsinan and Hangchow military control commissions.

After the Central People's Government of the People's Republic of China was established in 1949, T'an Chen-lin became chairman of the Chekiang provincial government, political commissar of the provincial military district, and secretary of the provincial party committee. In 1952 he left Chekiang and moved to become head of the Kiangsu provincial government. That November, he was made vice chairman of the military and administrative committee for east China, serving under Jao Shu-shih (q.v.). He also came to be third secretary in the party's east China regional bureau. After Jao went to Peking at the end of 1952, T'an succeeded him as first secretary of the east China bureau. In 1954 T'an also served as a member of the Standing Committee of the Chinese People's Political Consultative Conference. He was transferred to Peking in March 1956 as deputy secretary general of the Central Committee of the Chinese Communist party, serving under Teng Hsiao-p'ing (q.v.). In September 1956 he was elected to the Secretariat of the Central Committee, and in June 1958 he was elevated to membership in the Political Bureau.

During the 1950's T'an also was in charge of important phases of China's agricultural reform program. From 1950 to 1954 he was chairman of the land reform committee in east China, and in 1952 he became chairman of the ministry of water conservation's committee to harness the Huai River. Shortly after the commune campaign began in 1958, he was identified as a deputy director, under Teng Tzu-hui, of the party's rural work department. He succeeded Teng in October 1962. Beginning in April 1959 T'an served as vice premier of the State Council, to which post he was reappointed in January 1965. In October 1962 he also became vice chairman of the State Planning Commission.

T'an Cheng 譚 政

T'an Cheng (1903–), Chinese Communist political officer who served in the late 1940's as a deputy of Lin Piao in the Northeast and in the Central-South Military Region. In 1956 he became director of the general political department of the People's Liberation Army and a member of the Secretariat of the Chinese Communist party, but he was removed from these offices in 1962.

Little is known about T'an Cheng's early life or family background except that he attended middle school in his native Hunan and then went to Canton to join the National Revolutionary Army, then about to embark on the Northern Expedition. He became a member of the Independent Regiment commanded by Yeh T'ing (q.v.), and he participated in the regiment's march through Hunan in mid-1926 and in the attack on Wuchang that October. Yeh T'ing and his cohorts played a vital role in driving out the forces of Wu P'ei-fu (q.v.) and in establishing Kuomintang control in the Wuhan area. With the establishment of rival regimes at Wuhan and Nanking, the regiment was redesignated the Eleventh Army.

When the Kuomintang and the Chinese Communist party split, the Eleventh Army marched to Nanchang to assist in the Communist coup there on 1 August 1927. With the failure of that takeover, T'an Cheng escaped from Nanchang and joined the straggling guerrilla band led by Mao Tse-tung, which joined forces with Chu Teh (q.v.) at Chingkang-shan on the Hunan–Kiangsi border in

May 1928. During this period, T'an served for a time as Mao Tse-tung's personal secretary. In 1930 T'an was assigned to head the political department of the Twelfth Red Army, in which post he worked to indoctrinate the newly recruited troops which the Yunnanese guerrilla leader Lo Ping-hui had brought over to the Communists the year before. In 1932, after the regrouping of the Chinese Communist forces, he became head of the political department of Chu Teh's First Army Group of the Chinese Workers and Peasants Red Army. He held this post in Kiangsi and during the Long March to Shensi in 1934–35.

At the outbreak of the Sino-Japanese war in 1937, T'an Cheng was appointed deputy director of the general political department of the Eighth Route Army. He served under Jen Pi-shih (q.v.) and played an important role in developing the techniques of political education which made the Chinese Communist military organization an increasingly formidable military-political instrument in northern China during the war years. From 1943 to 1945 T'an also was deputy political commissar and director of the political department of the joint military district which had jurisdiction over the Communist-held areas in the Shansi-Suiyuan and the Shensi–Kansu–Ninghsia border regions. In this post, his immediate superior was Hsiao Ching-kuang, who was in charge of the Communist reserve forces in the Yenan area.

T'an Cheng's performance during the war years resulted in his election in 1945 as an alternate member of the Central Committee of the Chinese Communist party at the party's Seventh National Congress. After the Japanese surrender, T'an was a member of the Communist group assigned to Manchuria, which was recognized by Yenan as a highly strategic area in the approaching power struggle with the Nationalists. During the brief existence of the Executive Headquarters in Peiping, he served as Communist representative on the Northeast truce team, which was responsible for the implementation of the cease-fire agreement of January 1946. With the collapse of the postwar peace negotiations and the onset of general warfare in Manchuria, he became deputy director of the political department of the Chinese Communist forces in the Northeast, under the command of Lin Piao (q.v.).

After the Chinese Communist conquest of Manchuria, T'an Cheng moved southward with Lin Piao's forces (redesignated the Fourth Field Army in 1948) into north China, where he served briefly in the military control structures established by the Communists in Tientsin and Peiping at the beginning of 1949. He accompanied the Fourth Field Army on its drive southward and was one of the principal Communist officials directing the military and civil occupation of Wuhan in the spring of 1949. In the ensuing five years, he played a leading role in the extension of Communist control throughout the area then designated the Central-South Military Region. He held senior political posts in the interwoven military, party, and administrative structures for this region. He was junior to Lin Piao, Lo Jung-huan, and Teng Tzu-hui in the regional party hierarchy, but because Lin and Lo held their positions *in absentia* after 1950, he and Teng were in fact the dominant party leaders residing in Wuhan in the early 1950's.

With the abolition of the regional regimes and the reorganization of the Central People's Government in 1954, T'an Cheng moved to Peking. He attended the National People's Congress in September 1954 as an army representative and became a member of the congress's Standing Committee. Also in 1954 he was appointed a vice minister of national defense, a member of the National Defense Council, and deputy director of the general political department of the People's Liberation Army. He was raised to the rank of full general in the autumn of 1955. At the Eighth National Congress of the Chinese Communist party in September 1956, he reported on political work in the People's Liberation Army and received full membership on the Central Committee and the nine-man Secretariat. In December 1956 he was named to succeed Lo Jung-huan (q.v.) as director of the general political department of the People's Liberation Army. He made his first trip outside China in November 1957, when he was a member of a Chinese Communist military delegation, headed by P'eng Te-huai, which went to Moscow for celebrations marking the fortieth anniversary of the Russian Revolution. In 1962, however, T'an Cheng was removed from the party Secretariat and the directorship of the general political department of the People's Liberation Army. In March 1965 he was removed from office as vice minister of national defense, and he then disappeared from public view.

T'an Hsin-p'ei 譚鑫培

T'an Hsin-p'ei (1847–20 March 1917), leading interpreter of the lao-sheng roles in the Peking drama.

A native of Hupeh, T'an Hsin-p'ei was the only son of T'an Chih-tao (d. 1877), an actor of the lao-tan [elderly woman] roles who went to Peking with his family in the 1850's. T'an Hsin-p'ei received his early training in his father's house in accordance with professional custom. At the age of 11, he was apprenticed to a training troupe, the Chin-k'uei k'o-pan. He studied the male roles, concentrating on the wu-sheng and k'un luan lao-sheng styles. The first of these styles demands a sound knowledge of wu-kung, stage acrobatics, and fighting; and the second requires a command of vigorous expression and gesture as well as singing ability. His early training stood T'an in good stead in later years. When he began to appear in the male roles, his training in wu-kung technique enabled him to combine physical and vocal expression, thereby achieving that complete harmony of stage effect which was of high importance to Chinese playgoers.

After leaving the Chin-k'uei k'o-pan, T'an Hsin-p'ei joined the San-ch'ing-pan, which was headed by the noted actor Ch'eng Ch'ang-keng (d. 1880). Ch'eng was known as "the father of ching-hsi" because his troupe specialized in the new form of entertainment which was the beginning of the style known as Peking drama. T'an Hsin-p'ei quickly attracted the notice of Ch'eng, who came to have a high regard for his new follower. At the beginning of his career, therefore, T'an was closely associated with the master of the newer developments in his craft, and he profited accordingly.

T'an Hsin-p'ei continued to play in the leading Peking theaters until 1879, when he traveled to Shanghai to perform with Sun Ts'ai-chi, a specialist in female roles, at the Ch'üan-kuei Ch'a-yuan theater. The visit was a great success, and T'an's reputation increased proportionately even though he still was acting in wu-sheng roles. He continued to play those roles on his return to Peking until Ch'eng Ch'ang-keng died. Then he succeeded Ch'eng in the lao-sheng roles. In 1884 T'an Hsin-p'ei visited Shanghai again, appearing at the Ta K'uei Kuan theater. Later that year, he appeared at the Hsin Tan Kuei theater. In 1890 he was selected to perform in the theatrical entertainments at the imperial palace, a sure indication of his success as an actor.

Among the plays in which T'an Hsin-p'ei appeared regularly were *K'ung-ch'eng chi* [the strategy of the unguarded city] and *Ssu Lang t'an-mu* [Ssu Lang visits his mother]. He often performed the latter work with Wang Yao-ch'ing (q.v.) in the female role, and their collaboration was a notable one. T'an was also known for his interpretation of the role of Hsieh Jen-kuei in *Fen-ho wan* [at the bend of the river Fen]. The lao-sheng roles in plays of this genre depend heavily on the performer's vocal skill for their success. T'an Hsin-p'ei created an individual vocal style. Chinese critics compared it with the style of two of his distinguished contemporaries, Wang Kuei-fen and Sun Chü-hsien, by saying: "Wang i yün sheng, Sun i ch'i sheng, T'an i ch'ing sheng" [Wang emphasizes the rhyme and Sun stresses the intonation, but T'an emphasizes the tune]. Among those who later followed the T'an-p'ai, or T'an school of dramatic singing, were Ma Lien-liang, T'an Fu-yang, and Yü Shu-yen.

T'an's faultless singing was matched by the hu-ch'in playing of his accompanist, Mei Yü-t'ien, who was an uncle of Mei Lan-fang (q.v.). Although from time to time they fell into disagreement and parted company, they always came together again because each respected the other's abilities. Some very early gramaphone records were made of these two artists performing together in the plays *Mai-ma* [selling the horse] and *Hung Yang Tung* [at the Hung Yang cave]. T'an also experimented with another new medium, motion pictures. In 1908 he was filmed performing in *Ting Chun Shan*.

Although T'an was essentially an actor of metropolitan Peking, he made six visits to Shanghai in the course of his career. In the early years of the twentieth century Shanghai afforded high financial rewards for Peking actors invited to entertain its pleasure-loving merchants. T'an's third visit to Shanghai took place in 1901, when he appeared at the San-ch'ing Ch'a-yuan and at the Ch'üan-kuei

Ch'a-yuan (where he had performed on his first visit). Thereafter, he was in Shanghai in 1910, when he appeared at the Ch'üan-kuei Ch'a-yuan again; in 1912, when he appeared at the Hsin-hsin Wu-t'ai; and in 1915, when he appeared for ten days at a theater managed by his son-in-law. The 1912 visit took place shortly before the Chinese New Year. It was the custom for well-known actors to play a type of role during the last run of the season which was different from their usual parts. T'an was asked to play the comic role of Chu Pa Chieh [piggy], the pig spirit from the famous *Hsi-yu-chi* [monkey] story. In one scene the actor playing this part was supposed to somersault down from the top of a pile of three tables. When T'an came to do this, he feigned consideration of the somersault, shook his head in mock despair, and climbed down exclaiming that he preferred to live. He intended a light-hearted interpretation of what in any case was a piece of seasonal foolery, but the Shanghai audiences, unlike those in Peking, took his joking seriously. There was even some criticism in the press because of his deviation from tradition. Infuriated by this lack of humor, T'an left Shanghai without completing the play's scheduled run. There was a happy reversal of this situation when T'an made his last visit to Shanghai in 1915. On this occasion, he was making a private trip, but he agreed to perform with the local actors for ten days at the behest of his son-in-law. He played to a full house every day, and he had great difficulty in getting through the admiring crowds to his dressing room. The plays in which he appeared during this triumphant visit were the popular *Strategy of the Unguarded City* and *Chu-lien-chai* [the pearl screen fort].

In the spring of 1914 T'an Hsin-p'ei began appearing regularly in evening performances. This innovation became custom after the Ti-i Wu-t'ai theater was opened in 1914. T'an made some of his last Peking appearances with Mei Lan-fang, then a promising young actor. In January and March, they appeared with the Ch'un-ho-she troupe in *Ssu-lang t'an-mu*, *Fen-ho wan*, and *Sang Yuan Chi Tzu*. They also appeared together in a charity show to raise funds for relief work in Fukien. Soon after the charity show, T'an gave a command performance at the home of Li Yuan-hung (q.v.), who then held the presidency at Peking. Although he caught a severe chill there and

became quite ill, he reluctantly appeared at a private party given in March 1917 to honor Lu Jung-t'ing (q.v.). The role he had to play in what proved to be his final appearance was that of the dying general, Yang Yen-chao, in *Hung Yung Tung*. The exertion of acting was more than his weakened constitution could withstand, and he died on 2 March 1917.

T'an Hsin-p'ei had twelve children, eight sons and four daughters, of whom two girls and a boy died in childhood. Five of the remaining seven sons went on the stage. T'an Chia-shan played wu lao-sheng roles. Chia-ch'ing played wu ch'ou [fighting comic] roles before becoming a theater musician; he accompanied his father on several occasions. The third son, Chia-hsiang, played the tan [female] roles, and the fourth, Chia-yung, played the wu lao-sheng parts. The fifth son, Chia-pin, who took the stage name T'an Hsiao-p'ei, played his father's roles. He was the only one of T'an Hsin-p'ei's sons to achieve some reputation as an actor. T'an Hsiao-p'ei's son, who took the stage name T'an Fu-ying, became an extremely popular actor and a fine interpreter of his grandfather's art. T'an Fu-ying remained in China after 1949 and joined the Chinese Communist party in March 1959. The family tradition of playing lao-sheng roles was extended to the fourth generation when T'an Fu-ying's son decided to pursue a stage career.

T'an P'ing-shan   譚 平 山

T'an P'ing-shan (1887–2 April 1956), one of the most influential Communists in the Kuomintang hierarchy during the 1924–26 period of alliance. Upon his expulsion from both parties in 1927, he became a leader of the so-called Third party at Shanghai. He was readmitted to the Kuomintang in 1937, but he later helped organize the dissident San-min-chu-i Comrades Association. After 1949, he held office in the Central People's Government at Peking.

Little is known about T'an P'ing-shan's family background or early life except that his father was a longshoreman and that he was born in Kaoming hsien, Kwangtung. He apparently joined the T'ung-meng-hui soon after its founding, and he took part in the unsuccessful revolt against the Manchu authorities at Chennan-kuan in 1907. Not until the period of the

May Fourth Movement, after he was 30 years old, did he begin to emerge from obscurity. About 1917 he enrolled at Peking University, where he later became an editor of the influential student journal *Hsin-ch'ao* [renaissance]. He and his roommate, Ch'en Kung-po (q.v.), became interested in Marxism and the Russian Revolution, and under the influence of Ch'en Tu-hsiu and Li Ta-chao (qq.v.) they became members of the nascent Chinese Communist organization about 1920.

After graduation in 1920, T'an P'ing-shan and Ch'en Kung-po went to Canton, where they accepted teaching positions (T'an at the Higher Normal College), established a newspaper called the *Ch'ün-pao* [the masses], and organized the Socialist Youth Corps, from which they recruited young intellectuals for membership in a small Communist organization in Canton. In 1921 T'an and Ch'en were associated with Ch'en Tu-hsiu, who had come to Canton at the invitation of Ch'en Chiung-ming (q.v.) to head the Kwangtung provincial education department.

During the first years of Communist activity at Canton, T'an P'ing-shan appears to have been overshadowed by Ch'en Kung-po. Though T'an was secretary of the Kwangtung Communist group, it was Ch'en, the head of its organization department, who represented the Kwangtung group at the First Congress of the Chinese Communist party, held at Shanghai in July 1921. In 1922, with Ch'en Kung-po's withdrawal from the party, T'an emerged as the leader of the party's Kwangtung branch. Although he was obliged to leave the province for a time because of the enmity of Ch'en Chiung-ming, he returned to Canton after Ch'en's defeat early in 1923 by Sun Yat-sen's allies. He then became a member of the propaganda committee at Sun Yat-sen's headquarters. In June 1923 he attended the Third National Congress of the Chinese Communist party as a delegate from Kwangtung.

In January 1924 T'an P'ing-shan was a delegate to the First National Congress of the Kuomintang and was one of three Communists, the others being Li Ta-chao and Yü Shu-te, elected to full membership in the Central Executive Committee. He also was named head of the organization department. In July he was appointed to the 12-man Kuomintang Political Council, organized by Sun Yat-sen to curb the right wing of the Kuomintang, and in October he was named to the Revolutionary Committee to serve as deputy political commissar, under Liao Chung-k'ai (q.v.), of the Kuomintang military units organized to suppress the revolt of the Canton Merchants Corps at Canton. Thus at the height of the period of Kuomintang-Communist collaboration, T'an apparently enjoyed the confidence of the top Kuomintang leadership. As head of the organization department, he did much to further the Chinese Communist plan to infiltrate the Kuomintang hierarchy. He had his protégé Yang P'ao-an appointed secretary of the organization department, and he used his authority to fill many departmental and provincial posts with Communist cadres. By January 1926, when the Second National Congress of the Kuomintang convened at Canton, the Communists had built up a powerful representation within the Kuomintang, led by T'an and Chang Kuo-t'ao (q.v.). At this congress, T'an and six other Communists were elected to the Central Executive Committee. Shortly thereafter, on 22 January, T'an was one of three Communists elected to that committee's Standing Committee. Within a few months, however, his influence waned as the Kuomintang began to split into factions over the question of Communist affiliation. In May 1926 the Central Executive Committee decided that members of the Chinese Communist party should not be allowed to head Kuomintang departments, and T'an was replaced as head of the organization department.

T'an P'ing-shan was among those Chinese Communists who supported the Northern Expedition as a way to promote agrarian revolution in China. In November 1926 he went to Moscow as the Chinese Communist party delegate to the seventh plenum of the Executive Committee of the Comintern. In addressing the committee he declared that Communists should strengthen the Kuomintang's left wing, fight its right wing, and seek to win the support of the faction led by Chiang Kai-shek. When the committee, at the prompting of Stalin and Bukharin, declared its continued support of the Kuomintang as the leader of the Chinese revolution, T'an cautiously pointed to Chiang Kai-shek's anti-Communist coup of 20 March at Canton and to the tactical difficulties inherent in the Kuomintang-Communist collaboration.

Despite his reservations, T'an apparently agreed not to push a policy of agrarian revolution and acceded to the Comintern decision to maintain affiliation with the Kuomintang.

After returning to Canton in February 1927, T'an P'ing-shan found it increasingly difficult to follow the Comintern policy, for friction had increased between Chiang Kai-shek's faction of the Kuomintang and the left wing at Wuhan. With a number of Comintern observers, T'an left Canton for Wuhan, where, at the third plenum of the Kuomintang Central Executive Committee (10–17 March), he was elected to the seven-man presidium of the Political Council and was named minister of agriculture in the new National Government at Wuhan. He also was appointed to the land commission. T'an appears to have followed a cautious policy of conciliating the Kuomintang left wing in agrarian matters. Accordingly, when peasant revolts broke out in Hupeh and Hunan in May, he called for the suppression of peasant "excesses" and on 26 May set out from Wuhan at the head of a committee of five to restrain the peasant forces that had been mobilized by Communist agitators in Hunan for an attack on Changsha. The committee, which included the Russian adviser Borodin, was turned back at the Hunan border by the troops of Ho Chien (q.v.).

T'an's task of reconciling the Comintern line with the policies of the Kuomintang left wing was difficult in the spring of 1927, and by the summer it had become impossible. On 30 June he requested a leave of absence from the Wuhan government on the grounds of ill health. During July and August the Comintern began to call for an increasingly radical policy of agrarian revolt in China and ordered preparations for an armed insurrection of peasants and workers. In response, the Chinese Communist party called a meeting of its leaders late in July, at which T'an was elected to a preparatory committee (including Liu Po-ch'eng, Chou En-lai, Yeh T'ing, and Ho Lung) to plan an uprising at Nanchang. On 1 August, after the fall of Nanchang to the Communist insurgents, T'an became chairman of the short-lived revolutionary committee established there, but with the recapture of Nanchang a few days later by the army of Chang Fa-k'uei (q.v.) T'an was forced to flee with the battered forces of Yeh T'ing and Ho Lung (qq.v.), which retreated southward

through Kiangsi and Fukien to eastern Kwangtung, where they succeeded in seizing Swatow on 24 September. Within a week, however, Yeh and Ho had been defeated by the Nationalists. As the remnants of the Communist forces retired to Haifeng, T'an and other Communist leaders made their way separately to Hong Kong.

In the meantime, T'an P'ing-shan's standing within the Chinese Communist party had been shaken by successive Communist failures. Following the Kuomintang-Communist split, Stalin and the Comintern had shifted onto the Chinese Communists full responsibility for the failure of Comintern policy in Wuhan and had directed the Chinese Communist party to rectify the errors of its leaders. At a secret emergency conference at Kiukiang on 7 August 1927, Ch'en Tu-hsiu was replaced as general secretary of the Chinese Communist party by Ch'ü Ch'iu-pai (q.v.), and T'an P'ing-shan was severely censured. After the unsuccessful uprisings at Nanchang, in Hunan, and in Kwangtung during the summer and autumn of 1927, the Central Committee of the Chinese Communist party met on 9 November to assess these failures. T'an was charged with responsibility for the failure at Nanchang and was expelled from the party for his "Kuomintang Left" illusions.

By that time, however, T'an P'ing-shan had already left the Chinese Communist party. After reaching Hong Kong early in October, he began to form a political group composed mainly of former Communists who, like himself, were dissatisfied with the Comintern's insistence on a policy of armed insurrection and who believed that the goals of Communism could be achieved by less drastic means. The size of T'an's following was increased considerably after the disastrous Canton Commune (see Chang T'ai-lei) of December 1927, when a large number of dissident Communists joined T'an in Hong Kong and went with him to Shanghai in the winter of 1927. At Shanghai, T'an and his followers joined forces with the so-called Third party, a group of former Kuomintang members who opposed the policies of both the Chinese Communist party and the Kuomintang at Nanking and who formed an independent political organization without formally breaking from the Kuomintang.

Assuming leadership of the Third party during the prolonged absence of Teng Yen-ta (q.v.) in Europe, T'an P'ing-shan attempted to reorganize it as a political party. Although T'an reportedly sought a *rapprochement* with the Chinese Communist party, at the party's Sixth National Congress, held in Moscow in 1928, a resolution was adopted which denounced the Third party as a potential "counter-revolutionary tool of the gentry, landlords, and bourgeoisie" that would only "dull the class consciousness of the masses." Moreover, within the Third party itself, T'an's political leanings and his efforts to reorganize the party were criticized by Teng Yen-ta in Europe and by Teng's followers in Shanghai. Late in 1928 T'an reportedly made another unsuccessful attempt to reorganize the Third party into the Chung-kuo she-hui min-chu tang [Chinese social democratic party] with a view to securing recognition of this party by the Comintern. Discouraged by his repeated failures to unite the Third party under his leadership, he returned to Hong Kong.

Little is known about T'an P'ing-shan's activities for several years after 1930. Not until after the outbreak of the Sino-Japanese war in 1937 did he reappear on the national scene. At that time he was readmitted to the Kuomintang, and in 1938 he was invited to serve on the council of advisers of the San Min Chu I Youth Corps at the wartime capital of Chungking. In this capacity he helped organize and direct the activities of the corps while serving in the National Government as a member of the People's Political Council.

During the later years of the war T'an appears to have become restive under the increasing political restrictions imposed by the men who dominated the Kuomintang and the National Government. By 1944 he and Ch'en Ming-shu (q.v.) had become the center of a group of political dissidents in Chungking known as the San-min-chu-i Comrades Forum. In 1945 T'an and Ch'en joined with Liu Ya-tzu, Yang Chieh, and others in forming the San-min-chu-i Comrades Association as a political organization advocating a return to the principles enunciated at the First National Congress of the Kuomintang in 1924. At war's end, T'an left Chungking for Shanghai, where he remained for more than two years. Following the outbreak of full-scale civil war between the Nationalists and the Communists in 1947, T'an's political attitudes moved steadily leftward. In

January 1948 he went to Hong Kong, where he joined other political opponents of the National Government in founding the Kuomintang Revolutionary Committee. He left Hong Kong in August 1948 for Communist-held areas in north China, and in January 1949 at Mukden he announced his support of plans to convene under Communist auspices a conference of all political parties in China. He attended the Chinese People's Political Consultative Conference in September 1949 as a delegate of the San-min-chu-i Comrades Association.

With the formal establishment of the People's Republic of China on 1 October 1949, T'an P'ing-shan was appointed to important posts in the Central People's Government at Peking: he became a member of the Government Council and the Government Administration Council and chairman of the People's Supervisory Committee. He also became an executive board member of the Sino-Soviet Friendship Association. As a delegate from Kwangtung province, he attended the National People's Congress in 1954, and he was appointed to the congress's Standing Committee. In March 1956 he was awarded a vice chairmanship of the Kuomintang Revolutionary Committee. On 2 April 1956 he died at Peking. A public funeral ceremony, attended by several Communist dignitaries, was held in his honor in Peking, at which he was lauded as a "revolutionary patriot." T'an was survived by Sun Sun-ch'uan, whom he had married at Chungking in 1940. Under the name Sun Hsiang-chieh, she had been known as a writer and a professor of Chinese literature at Peking.

T'an Yen-k'ai   譚 延 闓
T. Tsu-an   祖 菴
H. Wu-wei   无 畏

T'an Yen-k'ai (1879–22 September 1930), Hanlin scholar and president of the Hunan provincial assembly who served several times as governor of Hunan in the 1912–20 period. Beginning in 1924 he held high government and Kuomintang posts at Canton, and he directed National Government affairs during the first stage of the Northern Expedition. From October 1928 until his death, he was president of the Executive Yuan at Nanking.

Although his native place was Chaling, Hunan, T'an Yen-k'ai was born at Hangchow. At the time of his birth, his father, T'an Chung-lin (d. 1905; T. Yun-ch'in), was civil governor of Chekiang. The young T'an's mother was a concubine, and he was the third child in the family. A younger brother, T'an Tse-k'ai, in due course would win fame as a calligrapher. T'an Chung-lin later became Liangkwang (Kwangtung and Kwangsi) governor general, and his children received the thorough training in the Chinese classics that was called for by his exalted status and by Confucian tradition. After passing the chü-jen degree examinations in 1902 and the chin-shih examinations in 1904, T'an Yen-k'ai became one of the last Chinese scholars to receive the coveted appointment of compiler in the Hanlin Academy. From 1904 to 1910 he served variously as an educational supervisor, director of the Central Hunan Normal School, and director of the Hunan Ming-te School (see Hu Yuan-t'an). The last of these was a focal point for anti-Manchu agitation.

When the Ch'ing court, moving slowly and painfully in the direction of constitutionalism, inaugurated provincial assemblies in October 1909, T'an Yen-k'ai became president of the Hunan assembly. The following year, he also became a Hunan delegate to the newly inaugurated National Assembly in Peking. When it convened in October, he joined with T'ang Hua-lung (q.v.) and others in petitioning the imperial court to establish promptly a parliament with a responsible cabinet. The imperial decree of November 1910, which shortened the period before the introduction of constitutional monarchy and which provided for the convocation of the new parliament in 1913, left such petitioners as T'an and T'ang dissatisfied. And these two men were among the provincial leaders who established the Hsien-yu-hui [association of friends of the constitution].

The Ch'ing court's railway policies, which included nationalization and using the railways as security for foreign loans, evoked violent opposition from Szechwan and other concerned provinces, including Hunan. T'ung-meng-hui leaders in Japan seized upon the revolutionary opportunity thus offered and sent agents to the central Yangtze provinces to exploit the situation. About this time, T'an returned to Hunan from Peking, apparently to assume additional responsibilities as director of the provincial law codification bureau. He called upon Yü Ch'eng-ko, the provincial governor, who confronted him with a list of suspected revolutionaries. T'an, who had no connection with the T'ung-meng-hui, dismissed charges against those listed, saying they were not worthy of concern. He thus played an unconscious role in easing the way for the republican revolution. The Hunanese revolutionary Chiao Ta-feng by this time had established contact with Chü Cheng (q.v.) in Hupeh; and with the spreading of the railway riots, it had been agreed that Hupeh and Hunan should stage a coordinated uprising. After the Wuchang revolt broke out prematurely and imperial troops were moved from Hunan to the Wuchang area, Chiao and his associate Ch'en Tso-hsin seized Changsha and organized a military government, with Chiao Ta-feng as tutuh [military governor] and Ch'en Tso-hsin as his deputy. In an effort to quell continuing public anxiety and unrest, Chiao appointed T'an Yen-k'ai director of military affairs. A few days later, leaders of the Ch'ün-hsien-tang [constitutional monarchy party] took advantage of the dispatching of revolutionary forces to Wuchang and assassinated both Chiao Ta-feng and Ch'en Tso-hsin. The party leaders then nominated T'an Yen-k'ai as Hunan tutuh, with members of their own party to occupy other important provincial posts. A delegation was sent to T'an's residence to inform him of his election. He refused three times to accept the post (as was the convention), whereupon he was forced into a sedan chair, escorted to his new office, and acclaimed tutuh. It was decided that the deaths of Chiao Ta-feng and Ch'en Tso-hsin should be attributed to "unruly troops." T'an ordered a proper burial for the two revolutionaries and decreed that statues would be erected in their honor.

When Yuan Shih-k'ai succeeded Sun Yat-sen as provisional president of the republican government, he confirmed T'an Yen-k'ai's appointment as Hunan tutuh and gave him the concurrent post of civil governor. At the time of the so-called second revolution (see Li Lieh-chün), however, T'an was among the governors who declared their independence of Yuan Shih-k'ai's rule. After suppressing the movement, Yuan replaced these governors. On 21 October 1913 T'an Yen-k'ai was succeeded by T'ang Hsiang-ming. T'an went to Peking, where he stayed for about three months. In March 1914 he moved his family to Tsingtao; in August, when the Japanese declared war on Germany and attacked Tsingtao, he moved to Shanghai.

Yuan Shih-k'ai died in June 1916, and on 3 August T'an Yen-k'ai was returned to power as Hunan tuchün [military governor] and civil governor. He also received the gratuitous support of a powerful figure in south China, Lu Jung-t'ing (q.v.) of Kwangtung. During a visit to Peking in March 1917 Lu made agreements which established Hunan as a buffer zone by stipulating that it would not be invaded by Liangkwang troops and that it would be governed by a Hunanese. Lu Jung-t'ing was appointed inspector general of Liangkwang before his departure from Peking.

At the time of the so-called constitution protection movement in 1917 and the formation of a military government at Canton (see Sun Yat-sen), Tuan Ch'i-jui (q.v.) replaced T'an Yen-k'ai with one of his Peiyang subordinates, Fu Liang-tso, and sent military units into Hunan as part of his plan to unify China by force. Tuan resigned from office in November under pressure from supporters of Feng Kuo-chang (q.v.), and T'an Yen-k'ai was reappointed governor of Hunan on 7 December. T'an, who had left the province, did not accept the appointment. In the spring of 1918, however, he returned to Hunan by way of Canton at the behest of Sun Yat-sen. By the time T'an arrived in Hunan, however, Tuan Ch'i-jui had been restored to power in Peking as premier; Chang Ching-yao had been appointed military governor of Hunan; and Wu P'ei-fu (q.v.) had occupied Changsha. T'an and a small force were driven into the mountains of southwestern Hunan.

In March 1920 Wu P'ei-fu began to evacuate his troops from Hunan, as did Feng Yü-hsiang (q.v.). T'an Yen-k'ai's force marched at the heel of Wu P'ei-fu's retreating army and took Changsha and Yochow in turn by defeating Chang Ching-yao. T'an became governor again in June, and he spearheaded the federalist (lien-sheng tzu-chih) movement in China by declaring Hunan autonomous on 22 July. Four months later, after a power struggle, he announced the separation of military and civil authority. Chao Heng-t'i (q.v.) succeeded him as commander in chief of the Hunan forces and acting military governor. The provincial assembly elected Lin Chih-yü civil governor. T'an Yen-k'ai left Changsha and went to Shanghai, where he remained until February 1923.

When Sun Yat-sen organized a new military government at Canton in February 1923, T'an Yen-k'ai became minister of the interior. On 7 May, T'an was transferred to the post of minister of reconstruction. He relinquished that post in the summer of 1923 to lead an expedition against Chao Heng-t'i. T'an achieved some success, taking Changsha and other cities, but Wu P'ei-fu came to Chao's aid that autumn and drove T'an's forces back to the Hunan–Kwangtung border. T'an reached the Canton area just in time to help beat back an attack by Ch'en Chiung-ming (q.v.).

With the reorganization of the Kuomintang and the holding of the party's First National Congress in January 1924, T'an Yen-k'ai became a member of the Central Executive Committee and the Central Political Council. In July, he was appointed to the nine-man Military Affairs Commission. He accompanied Sun Yat-sen to Shaokuan in September for Sun's proposed northern expedition, and he was appointed to command the National Construction Army on 6 October. This campaign was abandoned after Feng Yü-hsiang staged his coup at Peking, and Sun Yat-sen accepted an invitation to go to Peking for discussions with Chang Tso-lin (q.v.) and Tuan Ch'i-jui. After Sun's death at Peking in March 1925, T'an joined with Chiang Kai-shek and Hsü Ch'ung-chih (q.v.) in suppressing the threat of open revolt by the Yunnan and Kwangsi mercenary armies of Yang Hsi-min and Liu Chen-huan.

When the Kuomintang-controlled National Government was established at Canton on 1 July 1925, T'an Yen-k'ai became a member of the Government Council and of the council's five-man standing committee, which also included Hsü Ch'ung-chih, Hu Han-min, Liao Chung-k'ai, and Wang Ching-wei. He also became chairman of the Central Political Council and a member of the new Military Council. With the establishment of the National Revolutionary Army in August, his Hunanese forces were reorganized as the Second Army. T'an was reelected to the Central Executive Committee at the Second National Congress of the Kuomintang in January 1926, and he was elected to that body's standing committee. His importance was such that when the Northern Expedition was launched in July 1926, he and Chang Jen-chieh remained in Canton to direct government and party affairs, respectively. After the Kuomintang split into factions, he served the National Government at Wuhan and chaired the controversial third plenary session of the Kuomintang's Central Executive Committee, held at Wuhan in March, which acted to diminish Chiang Kai-shek's authority. After Wang Ching-wei returned to China and took control of the Wuhan regime and Chiang Kai-shek established an opposition government at Nanking, T'an accompanied Wang to Chengchow in June for negotiations with Feng Yü-hsiang, who then held the balance of power in China. The Wuhan negotiators lost to Chiang Kai-shek in the competitive bargaining with Feng, and they then followed Chiang's lead in taking strong action against Communists in areas under their control. In August, Chiang Kai-shek, pressed by the Kwangsi generals and the need for party unity, announced his retirement. T'an Yen-k'ai was a member of the Wuhan group, headed by Wang Ching-wei, that went to Kiukiang on 20 August to meet with Li Tsung-jen (q.v.) and other Nanking leaders to discuss reconciliation. It was agreed that the fourth plenary session of the Kuomintang Central Executive Committee should be held at Nanking and that T'an Yen-k'ai and Sun Fo (q.v.) should go to Nanking before returning to Wuhan. Upon arrival at Nanking, the Wuhan delegates wired Wang Ching-wei recommending the immediate removal of the Central Executive Committee to Nanking. When Wang and other committee members reached Nanking on 5 September, they discovered that T'an and Sun had gone to Shanghai to negotiate with Hsü Ch'ung-chih and other members of the conservative Western Hills faction. T'an and Sun explained upon their return to Nanking that they had undertaken the mission on behalf of Li Tsung-jen and Pai Ch'ung-hsi, and they convinced Wang Ching-wei that he should go to Shanghai for an exchange of views. The delegation that went to Shanghai on 9 September included Li Tsung-jen, Li Lieh-chün (q.v.), Wang Ching-wei, Sun Fo, and T'an Yen-k'ai. At a meeting in Shanghai on 12 September, Sun Fo presented a draft proposal calling for the formation of a committee composed of members of all three Kuomintang factions which would function as an interim government. Although most of the delegates supported this plan, Wang Ching-wei was angered by it, for he believed that his own lieutenants had undermined his hopes for power. He left the conference and Shanghai to return to Kiukiang. On 15 September at Nanking T'an Yen-k'ai chaired the meeting at which the Central Special Committee was established.

Chiang Kai-shek returned to power at Nanking in 1928, and T'an Yen-k'ai became Chairman of the National Government and acting chairman of the Central Political Council. With the victorious end of the Northern Expedition and the establishment of the new National Government at Nanking on 10 October 1928, Chiang Kai-shek assumed the government chairmanship. T'an Yen-k'ai then became the president of the newly created Executive Yuan, a position equivalent to that of premier. At the Third National Congress of the Kuomintang, T'an was reelected to the Central Executive Committee and its standing committee. While attending a military review at Nanking on 21 September 1930 he suffered a stroke, and he died the following day. The National Government proclaimed national mourning for the departed revolutionary veteran. After an elaborate state funeral, as befitted a deceased chief of state, T'an Yen-k'ai was buried at Lingkussu, near the mausoleum of Sun Yat-sen.

T'an Yen-k'ai was survived by two sons and two daughters. Their mother, *née* Fang, had died on 24 June 1918. The elder son, T'an Pei-yu (1900–), known as Beue Tann, became executive director of the International Monetary Fund. A daughter, T'an Hsiang, married Ch'en Ch'eng (q.v.) on 1 January 1932.

T'ang Chi-yao　　　　　　　　唐 繼 堯
T. Hsuan-keng　　　　　　　　萱 賡
H. Tung-ta-lu chu-jen　　　東 大 陸 主 人

T'ang Chi-yao (1881–23 May 1927), military governor of Yunnan who provided military support for the 1915 uprising led by Ts'ai O against Yuan Shih-k'ai. While attempting to extend his power into other provinces after 1916, he nominally supported Sun Yat-sen. After Sun's death in 1925, T'ang made an unsuccessful bid for leadership of the National Government. T'ang continued to rule Yunnan until February 1927, when power in that province passed to Lung Yun.

A native of Huitze hsien, Yunnan, T'ang Chi-yao was born into a scholar-landlord family. He received a good education in the Chinese classics, and in 1904 he obtained a government scholarship for study in Japan. He enrolled at the Shimbu Gakkō [military preparatory academy], where one of his classmates was Li Lieh-chün (q.v.). Like a number of other young Chinese in Japan, both T'ang and Li joined the T'ung-meng-hui soon after its founding. In 1907 they entered the Shikan Gakkō [military academy] as members of its sixth class, which also included Sun Ch'uan-fang and Yen Hsi-shan (qq.v.).

After returning to China, T'ang Chi-yao in 1910 received an appointment as an instructor in the Yunnan provincial military school. He also was given command of a battalion. Li Lieh-chün also came to Yunnan and served in the same school, later becoming principal of a military primary school. In February 1911 Ts'ai O (q.v.) also arrived in Yunnan to assume command of a brigade in the provincial army. At the time of the Wuchang revolt, Li returned to his native Kiangsi, and T'ang joined with Ts'ai O and others to take control of Kunming, where they formed a military government on 31 October with Ts'ai as military governor. T'ang then took command of an expeditionary force and marched northward into Kweichow, where his men suppressed bandits who had exploited the revolution there. As a result, T'ang was elected military governor of Kweichow, and his appointment was confirmed in 1912 by the newly established republican government at Peking.

During the so-called second revolution of 1913 T'ang Chi-yao and Ts'ai O tried to mobilize the forces of Yunnan, Kweichow, Szechwan, and Kwangsi in support of Li Lieh-chün, but their efforts failed. With the collapse of this campaign, T'ang was transferred to the governorship of his native Yunnan. In 1915, as Yuan Shih-kai's monarchical aspirations became increasingly evident, T'ang, acting on instructions from Ts'ai O, expanded his military forces. Toward the end of 1915 such revolutionary leaders as Li Lieh-chün and Hsiung K'o-wu

(q.v.) arrived in Yunnan for discussions of possible actions to be taken against Yuan. Orders were issued to prepare the Yunnanese forces for a revolt, and on 19 December Ts'ai O, who had been working in conjunction with Liang Ch'i-ch'ao (q.v.) on plans for the revolt, arrived in Yunnan. On 23 December, the leaders assembled in Yunnan sent Yuan Shih-k'ai a telegram requesting a clear statement from him in support of the republican system. The following day, an ultimatum was sent to Yuan demanding the execution of 12 men associated with the monarchical campaign and a statement of loyalty to the republic within 24 hours. When Yuan failed to respond, T'ang Chi-yao, Li Lieh-chün, and Ts'ai O issued a joint statement on 25 December declaring the independence of Yunnan and calling on all military and civil authorities in China to join Yunnan in its campaign to save the republic.

The Yunnan forces were reorganized as the National Protection Army, consisting of three armies (commanded by Ts'ai O, Li Lieh-chün, and T'ang Chi-yao), and T'ang Chi-yao was elected military governor of Yunnan. While Ts'ai and Li marched into Szechwan and Kwangsi, respectively, T'ang remained at the Yunnan headquarters. By the end of May, Kwangsi, Kwangtung, Shensi, Hunan, Chekiang, and Fukien had joined the independence movement. Yuan Shih-k'ai announced the abandonment of the monarchy on 22 March 1916, but he retained control as president. In mid-April, T'ang, Li, and Ts'ai demanded that Yuan resign in favor of Li Yuan-hung (q.v.) and that the National Assembly of 1913 be restored. Yuan ignored these demands, and on 8 May, with the aid of Liang Ch'i-ch'ao, the dissident leaders formed a military council at Chaoch'ing (Kaoyao) to act as the government of China until such time as Li Yuan-hung assumed office. T'ang was elected chairman of the council, but because he could not leave Yunnan, Ts'en Ch'un-hsuan (q.v.) acted for him. The death of Yuan Shih-k'ai on 6 June 1916 and the assumption of the presidency by Li Yuan-hung brought the campaign to an end, and the military council was dissolved on 14 July. The new administration immediately confirmed T'ang Chi-yao's appointment as governor of Yunnan.

When the so-called constitution protection movement began in the summer of 1917,

T'ang Chi-yao announced his support of Sun Yat-sen. The rump parliament at Canton established a military government on 31 August, with Sun Yat-sen as commander in chief (ta-yuan-shuai) and with T'ang Chi-yao and Lu Jung-t'ing (q.v.) as commanders (yuan-shuai). T'ang remained in Yunnan, however, and did not assume any official duties. He maintained his nominal association with the southern government after its reorganization in 1918 and refrained from taking sides in the dispute between Sun Yat-sen and the Kwangsi leaders. By this time, it had become evident that T'ang hoped to enlarge his own sphere of influence in southwestern China in accordance with what came to be referred to as Pan-Yunnanism. Neither Peking nor Canton tried to interfere with this plan, for neither government had sufficient strength for such interference. The Szechwanese, however, dashed T'ang's hopes for Pan-Yunnanism by defeating his troops and driving them out of Szechwan. T'ang's sphere of influence never expanded beyond Yunnan, part of Kwangsi, and Kweichow.

In 1920 the old Kwangsi faction was coming to the end of its term of authority at Canton. Before their evacuation of the city in October under pressure of forces supporting Sun Yat-sen, Ts'en Chun-hsuan and Lu Jung-t'ing announced the dissolution of the Canton military government. At this point, T'ang Chi-yao joined with Sun Yat-sen, T'ang Shao-yi, and Wu T'ing-fang in refuting the announcement. With the reestablishment of the government under Sun Yat-sen, T'ang Chi-yao became minister of communications. Although he did not assume the duties of his office, his acceptance of it was implied when, in January 1921, he joined with Sun Yat-sen and other Canton leaders in announcing the willingness of the southern administration to hold peace talks with the northern authorities at Peking.

In February 1921 T'ang Chi-yao suffered the first serious setback of his career when he was ousted from the governorship of Yunnan by his military subordinate Ku Ping-chen. T'ang withdrew with his remnant forces to Liuchow, Kwangsi, where he remained for almost a year before returning to Yunnan and regaining control of the province. After the provincial assembly formally elected him governor, he restructured the Yunnan provincial government in accordance with the federal movement sup-

ported by such leaders as Ch'en Chiung-ming and Chao Heng-t'i (qq.v.). Somewhat contradictorily, in the autumn of 1924 T'ang expressed his allegiance to Sun Yat-sen and assumed the post of commander in chief of the allied forces of Szechwan, Yunnan, and Kweichow, pending joint action with Canton. Because he was chronically short of forces, Sun appointed T'ang deputy generalissimo.

After Sun Yat-sen's death in March 1925, T'ang Chi-yao made a bid for leadership of the Kuomintang government in Canton, but his claim that the deputy generalissimo should succeed the generalissimo was rejected by the Kuomintang authorities. On 20 March, the party's Central Executive Committee issued a statement denouncing T'ang, who responded by appointing Liu Chen-huan to be governor of Kwangsi. The allied army of Liu and T'ang was suppressed by Kuomintang forces, and T'ang made no further attempt to win control of the Canton government until the latter part of 1925, when he supported the unsuccessful attempt of Lu Jung-t'ing to regain control of Kwangsi. In the meantime, he introduced a provincial constitution in Yunnan. Despite such reforms, corruption in the provincial administration, particularly on the part of T'ang's younger brother T'ang Chi-yi, led to a coup in February, when four of T'ang Chi-yao's lieutenants, including Lung Yun (q.v.), presented him with demands for reform of the government. He accepted these demands, and in March the Yunnan government was reorganized with T'ang holding the nominal post of director general. On 23 May 1927, after a short illness, T'ang Chi-yao died, at the comparatively young age of 46.

T'ang En-po　　　　　湯 恩 伯
Orig. K'o-chin　　　　克 勤

T'ang En-po (20 September 1899–29 June 1954), staff officer in the National Revolutionary Army who served during the Sino-Japanese war in such capacities as commander of the Thirty-first Army Group and deputy commander of the First War Area. In 1945 he supervised the Nationalist takeover of Shanghai and the repatriation of Japanese troops and civilians. Four years later, he supervised the Nationalist evacuation of Shanghai. He administered a defeat to the Chinese Communists in the defense of Quemoy in October 1949.

T'angts'unchen, a village formed by the T'ang clan in Wuyihsien, Chekiang, was the birth-place of T'ang En-po. His father, T'ang Te-ts'ai, was an upright and strong-willed peasant. After receiving a primary education at the Wuyi Primary School, T'ang En-po went to Chinhua in 1916 and enrolled at the Seventh Provincial Middle School. He later transferred to a private physical culture school at Hangchow, from which he was graduated in 1920. On his way home in 1920 he learned that the father of a friend was involved in litiga-tion with a notorious local bully, and he stopped to observe the hsien court proceedings. When it appeared that his friend's father was about to be sent to prison, T'ang threw a large rock, which struck the judge. The hsien government issued an order for T'ang's arrest, and he ran away to join the Chekiang Army for Aid to Fukien as a platoon commander.

T'ang's first venture into military life ended disastrously with the rout of the Chekiang forces. Soon afterwards, he encountered a fellow pro-vincial named T'ung, who was looking for a paid companion to study with him in Japan. T'ang accepted the position and accompanied T'ung to Japan in the spring of 1921. Upon arrival in Tokyo, T'ang began to study the Japanese language in hopes of entering the Shikan Gakkō [military academy]. However, he soon learned that a recommendation by a warlord or high official was essential for ad-mission. Because he lacked such a document, he entered the law department of Meiji Univer-sity in March 1922 to study political economy. When T'ung left Japan to return to China, he gave T'ang a gift of money, which T'ang used to open a Chinese restaurant. T'ang's interest was not in law. In May 1924 he abandoned his studies, closed his restaurant, and went to Shanghai.

After spending several months traveling from Shanghai to Hangchow, to Iwu, to Shanghai, and to Japan, T'ang En-po returned to China again in March 1925 and obtained a letter of recommendation to the Shikan Gakkō from Lu Kung-wang, a former military governor of Chekiang. It now remained for T'ang to raise funds for this educational venture. He applied to Ch'en Yi (q.v.), who had been graduated from the Shikan Gakkō in 1907 and

who was serving under Sun Ch'uan-fang (q.v.) as commander of the Chekiang 1st Division. Although Ch'en had never met T'ang, he immediately granted him sufficient funds for enrollment in the eighteenth class at the Shikan Gakkō.

By the time T'ang En-po completed his training and returned to China in the summer of 1927, Ch'en Yi had allied himself with Chiang Kai-shek. Accordingly, T'ang became a staff officer in the National Revolutionary Army. Late in 1928 T'ang received command of the cadet corps of the Central Military Academy's sixth class. He compiled a manual on training infantry companies which was of sufficient merit to bring him to the attention of Chiang Kai-shek. T'ang soon received an appointment as com-mander of the 1st Training Division, in which capacity he participated in the campaign against the so-called northern coalition of Feng Yü-hsiang and Yen Hsi-shan (qq.v.) in 1930. He then became deputy commander of the 4th Division, and in 1931 he received command of the 89th Division. For the next few years he served under Chiang Ting-wen (q.v.), taking part in the action against the Fukien rebels (see Ch'en Ming-shu; Ts'ai T'ing-k'ai) and in the so-called bandit suppression campaigns against the Chinese Communists. After the Communists made the Long March, he was promoted to com-mand of the Thirteenth Army and was trans-ferred to Shensi late in 1935 as director of the north Shensi bandit-suppression and rehabilita-tion office. In November 1936 he aided Fu Tso-yi (q.v.) in the capture of Pailingmiao from Te Wang (Demchukdonggrub, q.v.).

With the outbreak of the Sino-Japanese war in July 1937, T'ang En-po joined with Fu Tso-yi and Liu Ju-ming in the attempt to defend Suiyuan and Chahar. The Japanese, wishing to command the vital northwest China plateau, made a strong drive and overwhelmed that sector with the aid of a combined Manchou-kuo-Mongol force. At the beginning of Sep-tember, T'ang's forces were ordered to proceed to the Hopei-Honan border area for regrouping and expansion into the Twentieth Army Group. T'ang was made commander of the new unit, which was composed of the Thirteenth Army, the Fifty-second Army of Kuan Lin-cheng, and the Eighty-first Army of Wang Chung-lien. Because of Japanese attacks, the organization of the new unit had to be completed at Pohsien in northern Anhwei. The Twentieth Army

Group thus came under the over-all command of Li Tsung-jen (q.v.), who headed the Fifth War Area. In March 1938 T'ang's forces were among those which participated in the famous battle of Taierhchuang. Then, on 24 May, T'ang was appointed commander in chief of the Second Army Group and was charged with directing military operations in the Kweiteh sector of the First War Area, under the direction of Hsueh Yueh (q.v.). The Japanese forces, clearly aiming at the capture of Chengchow, continued their westward advance. Kweiteh fell on 28 May, and Kaifeng was occupied a week later. To check the enemy offensive, the Chinese breached the Yellow River dikes at Huang-tao-k'ou and flooded the area. T'ang then assumed direction of the Chang Tzu-chung Army Group and other units for the defense of the railway lines south of Chengchow The Japanese, however, changed direction and moved up the Yangtze toward Wuhan.

From 1939 to 1942 T'ang En-po served in the Hupeh-Honan region as commander of the Thirty-first Group Army. After the so-called New Fourth Army Incident of January 1941 (*see* Hsiang Ying; Yeh T'ing), he was given the concurrent post of chairman of the committee for the Shantung-Kiangsu-Honan-Anhwei border area, charged with developing Nationalist guerrilla bases in competition with Chinese Communist efforts along the same lines. In 1942 he received the title of commander in chief of that border area. Later that year, he became deputy commander, under Chiang Ting-wen (q.v.), of the First War Area. His forces in Honan were shattered in April 1944, when the Japanese launched the massive operation known as Ichi-go, designed to cut China in two by attacking southward across the Yellow River into Honan. After the Honan debacle, T'ang was ordered to proceed with his remnant forces to Kweichow. In December, he was appointed commander in chief of the Kweichow-Kwangsi-Hunan border area. His old friend Ho Ying-ch'in (q.v.) gave him a new assignment in February 1945 as commander of the Third Front Army, composed of 14 American-equipped divisions. From May to August of that year, he cooperated with the Second Front Army of Chang Fa-k'uei (q.v.) in a drive into Kwangsi. The Chinese recaptured Kweilin on 28 July.

At war's end, T'ang En-po was given the task of disarming the Japanese forces in the Nanking-Shanghai area. When he finished in mid-October, he was made responsible for the repatriation of Japanese troops and civilians through the port of Shanghai. By April 1946 about 80 percent of the more than 850,000 Japanese gathered at Shanghai had been repatriated. Throughout this operation, he attempted to put into practice Chiang Kai-shek's announced policy of "returning good for evil" in dealing with the Japanese. In a farewell address to 20 high-ranking officers of the Japanese Thirteenth Army, he said: "China and Japan occupy the opposite shores of the same sea and mutually support each other. Their peoples are of the same race; the languages are the same. Joined they can both survive; asunder they must both perish. Eight years of bloody warfare have brought grievous wounds to both. Recalling past sufferings we brothers should hold our heads and weep bitterly. Today we cast aside our arms and send you gentlemen home. Some other time we shall welcome your return holding jade and brocades in our arms."

In April 1946 T'ang En-po was appointed commander in chief of the Nanking-Shanghai garrison headquarters and commander of the First Pacification Area, with headquarters at Wusih. In July, as the civil war with the Chinese Communists resumed, he became deputy commander in chief of the Chinese army and garrison commander of the Nanking metropolitan area. He retained these posts until the spring of 1948, when he was made pacification commissioner at Chüchow. When it became apparent that the Communists would emerge victorious from the struggle, Chiang Kai-shek made preparations for retreat to Taiwan, and he appointed T'ang commander in chief of the Nanking-Shanghai-Hangchow area, the emergency exit to Taiwan. After Chiang's retirement from the presidency, T'ang facilitated the removal of funds, troops, and supplies to the island. About this time, his old benefactor Ch'en Yi, now governor of Chekiang, transmitted to T'ang an invitation to surrender to the People's Liberation Army. T'ang reported this offer to Chiang Kai-shek—not to acting President Li Tsung-jen—and arrested Ch'en at Shanghai in February. Ch'en Yi was taken to Taiwan later that year and was executed in June 1950.

With the crossing of the Yangtze by the People's Liberation Army in April and the occupation of Hangchow and Shanghai in May,

T'ang En-po took up a position at Amoy as pacification commissioner. The battle for Amoy began in the last week of September. On 17 October, the day Swatow fell, T'ang withdrew his men from Amoy to the offshore island of Quemoy, where he administered a defeat to the Communist forces on 24 October. T'ang then left Quemoy for Taipei on 29 October. Accompanying him was Japanese Lieutenant General Nemoto, who had assisted him at Amoy and Quemoy. At Taipei, T'ang became a strategy adviser to Chiang Kai-shek, but he held no substantive posts. He went to Japan for treatment of a stomach ailment in January 1953 and returned to Taiwan in July after being entertained royally in Japan by many who remembered his kind treatment of Japanese soldiers and civilians in 1945. In May 1954 he went to Japan again and underwent an operation at the Keio University hospital, but to no avail. T'ang En-po died at Tokyo on 29 June 1954.

| T'ang Erh-ho | 湯 爾 和 |
| T. Liu-sung | 六 松 |

T'ang Erh-ho (1871–8 November 1940), Japanese-trained physician and anti-Manchu revolutionary who founded and served as chancellor of Peking Medical College. In the 1920's he held cabinet posts in the Peking government. He became an official in the Japanese-sponsored government at Peiping in 1937.

Born into a Muslim family in Hangchow, T'ang Erh-ho was the son of Sha Ch'eng-liang. As a youth, he was adopted by a childless maternal uncle, T'ang Hsiao-heng, who seems not to have been a Muslim. The elder T'ang provided him with a belated education. In 1900, at the age of 23 sui, T'ang Erh-ho enrolled at the Yang-cheng School (later the First Chekiang Provincial High School) in Hangchow. The dean of the school, Ch'en Fu-ch'en (1859–1917; T. Chieh-shih), was a prominent scholar and an outstanding teacher who instilled anti-Manchu sentiments in his pupils. Outside of the classroom he introduced interested students to such books as the *Ming-i tai-fang lu*, a trenchant criticism of the Chinese political tradition by Huang Tsung-hsi (ECCP, I, 351–54), and to translations of such Western works as Montes-

quieu's *De l'esprit des lois*, Rousseau's *Contrat social*, and Huxley's *Evolution and Ethics*. T'ang Erh-ho and his good friends Ma Hsü-lun (q.v.) and Tu Shih-chen were so fired by revolutionary enthusiasm that they swore blood-brotherhood and decided to go to Japan for military training. On the eve of their graduation in 1902 the provincial authorities, unaware of their revolutionary bent, awarded them scholarships for study in Japan. Just before graduation, however, Ma and Tu were expelled by the principal for their part in defending several students who had been involved in a verbal fracas with an unpopular teacher. Ch'en Fu-ch'en resigned over the incident. T'ang escaped expulsion only because he happened to be sick in bed.

After graduation, T'ang Erh-ho went to Japan to enroll at the Seika Gakkō, a military preparatory school established by the Japanese to accommodate the many Chinese students who wished to prepare for the entrance examinations of the Shikan Gakkō [military academy]. At this time, the Russians were using the Boxer Uprising as a pretext to invade and occupy Manchuria. In the spring of 1903 the Chinese students in Japan organized the Association for Universal Military Training and sent T'ang Erh-ho and Niu Yung-chien (q.v.) to China as their representatives with the mission of persuading Yuan Shih-k'ai to fight the Russians. Yuan, however, refused to see them.

Having failed in this mission, T'ang Erh-ho went to Shanghai, then a revolutionary center, and joined such anti-Manchu activists as Chang Ping-lin, Wu Chih-hui, and Ts'ai Yuan-p'ei (qq.v.) in the comparative safety of the International Settlement. The Chinese authorities in Shanghai ordered his arrest, but the foreign officials refused to grant permission for his extradition. He soon returned to Japan, where he eschewed military training in favor of medical studies at the Kanezawa Medical School. In 1905 he married a Japanese. Information about the date of his return to China is lacking.

In the summer of 1911 T'ang Erh-ho took a trip to Japan in connection with plans for establishing a medical school in Hangchow. Almost immediately upon his return, he became involved in the events that led to the overthrow of the imperial authorities in Hangchow. At this time, the people of Kiangsu and Chekiang were angry about the imperial government's plans to nationalize the Shanghai-Hangchow-Ningpo railway. The Chekiang section of that railway was under the control of the privately owned Chekiang Provincial Railroad Company. Its general manager was T'ang Shou-ch'ien, a Hanlin scholar who was highly respected by his fellow provincials. His opposition to the nationalization scheme caused his dismissal by the imperial government, which had some control of the company by dint of loans to it. When a stockholders meeting was held to discuss the matter, T'ang Er-ho, Ma Hsü-lun, and Lou Shou-kuang, who had obtained proxy rights from several stockholders, proceeded to dominate the meeting, maneuvering the passage of resolutions opposing the nationalization of the railway and the dismissal of T'ang Shou-ch'ien.

When word of the Wuchang revolt reached Hangchow, T'ang Erh-ho, Ma Hsü-lun, and Lou Shou-kuang suggested to Ch'en Fu-ch'en, then the speaker of the provincial assembly, the organization of militia units in Hangchow. Ch'en endorsed the scheme, as did the local Chamber of Congress. At a meeting of the provincial assembly, T'ang Shou-ch'ien was elected director of the militia, with Ch'en Fu-ch'en as his deputy. The governor of Chekiang, however, refused to grant permission for the arming of the militia, which therefore did not participate in the capture of Hangchow by the republican revolutionaries on 4 November 1911. The next day, T'ang Erh-ho helped negotiate the surrender of the Manchu garrison, and T'ang Shou-ch'ien became the republican governor of Chekiang.

T'ang Erh-ho was one of four Chekiang delegates who went to Wuchang to discuss the formation of a provisional republican government. Because of continuing military action in the area, the first session was held on 30 November 1911 in the British concession at Hankow. Working rapidly, they completed a set of 12 articles governing the organization of the provisional government on 3 December and laid down conditions for peace negotiations with the imperial government on 5 December. Meanwhile, the revolutionary forces from Kiangsu and Chekiang took Nanking on 2 December, which prompted the delegates to make that city the capital of the provisional government. On 29 December, at a meeting in Nanking, 45 delegates from 17 provinces elected Sun Yat-sen president of the provisional government. As the chairman presiding over the election, T'ang Erh-ho was given the honor of presenting to Sun the certificate of office on 1 January 1912.

With the founding of the republic, T'ang Erh-ho withdrew from politics to devote himself to medicine. In 1913 he founded Peking Medical College and became its chancellor. He resigned in 1915 to protest Yuan Shih-k'ai's monarchical ambitions, but he resumed the post after Yuan's death in June 1916. Although he was not active in politics, he maintained close relations with many politicians at Peking. One day in 1916 his old teacher Ch'en Fu-ch'en, then a member of the Parliament, mentioned to T'ang and Ma Hsü-lun that the Chekiang members of the Parliament had sent a telegram to Ts'ai Yuan-p'ei in Europe asking him to become governor of Chekiang. Ts'ai replied that he would like to return to China but not as an official. Ma suggested to T'ang that Ts'ai would be a likely replacement for Hu Jen-yuan, the retiring chancellor of Peking University. T'ang agreed and took up the matter with Fan Yuan-lien (q.v.), the minister of education, who, in turn, secured the approval of Li Yuan-hung (q.v.). Ts'ai accepted the post and returned to China in 1917. He sought T'ang's advice concerning a suitable man to be dean of the college of letters, and T'ang recommended Ch'en Tu-hsiu (q.v.). Thus, T'ang was partly responsible for making Peking University the seedbed of the New Culture movement.

On 5 May 1919 the chancellors of the 13 universities and colleges involved in the May Fourth incident (for details, *see* Lo Chia-lun) met at Peking. They resolved that after they had succeeded in freeing the students imprisoned by the government, they would resign in protest against the arbitrary actions of police and government officials. Telegrams were sent in their names to the educational associations of all provinces, asking their united action in support of the students. Several of the chancellors, including T'ang Erh-ho and Ts'ai Yuan-p'ei, resigned on 9 May, and they did not return to their posts until September.

T'ang Erh-ho became vice minister of education in the Liang Shih-i cabinet on 21 July 1922. When Wang Ch'ung-hui (q.v.) assumed office as officiating premier on 20 September, he appointed T'ang minister of education in what became known as the "cabinet of able men" (hao-jen nei-ko). The cabinet also included V. K. Wellington Koo (Ku Wei-chün), Hsü Ch'ien, and Lo Wen-kan (qq.v.). The wrongful arrest and imprisonment of Lo Wen-kan on 18 November led to the resignation of the entire cabinet on 21 November. T'ang returned to the political scene late in 1926 as minister of the interior in V. K. Wellington Koo's cabinet. In 1927 he was made minister of finance. During this period, Peking was dominated by Chang Tso-lin (q.v.). After the Koo cabinet was dissolved in June 1927, T'ang accepted a post as councillor in the headquarters of the commander in chief of the Northeastern Army, but his precise role in the regional government of Manchuria is not known. His personal interest in that region was clear, however, and he later translated a number of Japanese works about Manchuria. T'ang remained in Manchuria after Chang Tso-lin's death in 1928 and and served under Chang Hsueh-liang (q.v.). He returned to Peiping shortly after the Japanese invaded Manchuria in September 1931. He then was appointed to the Northeast Political Affairs Council.

T'ang remained in Peiping after it fell to the Japanese in July 1937. On Japanese orders a Peking-Tientsin peace preservation committee was established by Chinese collaborators. On 14 December, this body became the so-called provisional government of the Chinese republic. T'ang was chosen to read the declarations of the new government at the inaugural ceremony, an ironic echo of the role he had played on 1 January 1912. In the puppet government T'ang held office as chairman of the legislative commission, a member of the executive commission, minister of education and cultural affairs, chancellor of Peking University, and chairman of the East Asia Cultural Association. When the provisional government was dissolved in March 1940 at the insistence of Wang Ching-wei (q.v.), T'ang became a member of the so-called north China political affairs council and director of its bureau of education. The council, though under the jurisdiction of the puppet regime at Nanking, had considerable autonomy. In June, T'ang also became a member of the standing committee of the commission for the realization of constitutional government. He died at Peiping on 8 November 1940. A biography, *T'ang Erh-ho hsien-sheng*, written by his son Yu-tsung, was published in Peiping.

T'ang Hua-lung   湯化龍

T'ang Hua-lung (27 November 1874–12 September 1918), leader of the movement to establish constitutional monarchy in China. He supported the revolution in 1911. In 1913–14 and 1916–17 he was speaker of the National Assembly. A leader of the Chin-pu-tang [progressive party] and, later, of the research clique, he also held cabinet posts at Peking.

Ch'isui, Hupeh, was the birthplace of T'ang Hua-lung. He came from a family which had lost its wealth during the Taiping Rebellion. His grandfather, T'ang Te-tsao (T. Lan-sheng), was a scholar whose studies finally cost him his eyesight; and his father, T'ang P'ing-hsin (T. I-cheng), was a scholar who had been obliged to go into business to support his family. T'ang Hua-lung received most of his training in the Chinese classics from tutors, and at the age of 19 sui he ranked first in the hsien examinations. Shortly afterwards, his family was brought to financial ruin again by an unjust lawsuit. T'ang helped pay the debt by teaching and by winning prize money in the monthly examinations at the government school.

At the age of 24 sui, T'ang Hua-lung entered the Ching-ku shu-yuan at Huangchou. After passing the examination for the chü-jen degree in 1902, he became an instructor in Chinese language and literature at Shansi University. Upon passing the examinations for the chin-shih degree, he received an appointment as a chu-shih [junior clerk] in the Board of Punishments. Because he believed that national salvation was dependent upon the acquisition of new knowledge which could be used in effecting political reform, he supported his brother T'ang Hsiang-ming in his decision to go to France for naval training and told his youngest brother, T'ang Yu-lung, to enroll at the Hupeh Provincial Industrial School. T'ang Hua-lung himself asked to be sent to Japan for further study and received a Hupeh provincial government scholarship to study law at the Hosei Daigaku. In Japan, he met and became a good friend of Liang Ch'i-ch'ao (q.v.).

About this time, the Ch'ing court, in an attempt to quell popular discontent generated by the Boxer Uprising, was taking its first tentative steps toward constitutional reform. Preparations were made in 1907 for the convening of the Tzu-cheng Yuan [national assembly], an advisory council composed of both appointive and elective members. The administrative structure of the central government was reorganized the following year. Soon after his return from Japan, T'ang Hua-lung was appointed a chu-shih in the newly created ministry of civil affairs. In 1909, the year that provincial assemblies (tzu-i chu) were to be established, Ch'en K'uei-lung, the governor of Hupeh, sent a memorial to the throne requesting T'ang's transfer to Hupeh so that T'ang could take part in the setting up of the provincial assembly. T'ang was elected to the Hupeh provincial assembly in 1909, and he became its speaker in 1910. In the winter of 1909 delegates from 16 provincial assemblies which opposed the Ch'ing court's delaying tactics met in Shanghai and founded the Kuo-hui ch'ing-yuan t'ung-chih hui [association for petitioning the convocation of the national parliament]. A 32-member delegation, which included T'ang Hua-lung, petitioned the court through the Censorate in February and May 1910, but both petitions were rejected. A third petition was presented in October through the newly established Tzu-cheng Yuan, which supported the delegates' objectives. Indeed, many of the petitioners, including T'ang Hua-lung, were members of the Tzu-cheng Yuan.

The Ch'ing court, unable to withstand the rising tide of public opinion, promised in November 1910 to convoke a parliament in 1913. In the intervening years it would complete the reorganization of the administrative system and establish a responsible cabinet. These concessions satisfied some of the petitioners, but T'ang Hua-lung and others remained steadfast in their demand for the immediate convocation of a parliament. The court responded to their renewed demand by sending the recalcitrant delegates home and exiling one of them to Sinkiang. The Tzu-cheng Yuan soon split into factions over this question. Its liberal wing was the Hsien-yu-hui [association of friends of the constitution], which was established on 1 July 1911 as a national organization with branches in ten provinces. T'ang was elected head of its Hupeh branch.

On 11 October 1911, the day after the Wuchang revolt, the republican revolutionaries met with the leaders of the Hupeh provincial assembly and named Li Yuan-hung (q.v.) to head a republican government at Wuchang. T'ang Hua-lung and others persuaded the reluctant Li to accept the appointment. Whatever T'ang's reservations about republicanism may have been, his outward acceptance of the revolution was an important contribution to its immediate success in Hupeh. To bring order out of the general confusion that prevailed in the first days of the revolution, Chü Cheng, Sung Chiao-jen (qq.v.), and T'ang drafted a set of regulations to provide a framework for the military government. After the regulations were promulgated on 16 October, T'ang left Hupeh for Shanghai, where he renewed his acquaintance with advocates of constitutional monarchy. They were joined by Chang Ping-lin (q.v.) in forming the T'ung-i-tang [unification party] in April 1912, thus continuing the rivalry between the republican revolutionaries and the reformers which had begun in the final decade of the Ch'ing dynasty.

After Yuan Shih-k'ai assumed the presidency of the republic and caused the provisional government to be moved to Peking, T'ang Hua-lung was elected vice speaker of the provisional National Assembly on 1 May 1912. By this time, it had become apparent that the T'ung-meng-hui would be the opposition party to the government headed by Yuan Shih-k'ai. Accordingly, Yuan encouraged the formation of a political party capable of challenging the dominance of the T'ung-meng-hui. His wish coincided with the self-interest of the smaller parties, and on 5 May 1912 the T'ung-i-tang combined with four other groups to form the Kung-ho-tang [republican party]. T'ang was named a director of the new party. Although Chang Ping-lin and his followers later withdrew from it and revived the T'ung-i-tang, the Kung-ho-tang was able to claim more than 40 of the assembly's 124 seats.

On 10 August 1912 the provisional National Assembly completed the task of writing the organic and electoral laws for the future parliament. In preparing for the elections, the T'ung-meng-hui combined with other parties to form the Kuomintang. It hoped, among other things, to organize a responsible cabinet system. In October, the Kung-ho-tang was reduced in size by the defection of T'ang Hua-lung and others to the Min-chu-tang [democratic party] organized by Liang Ch'i-ch'ao. The overwhelming victory of the Kuomintang in the parliamentary elections led to the assassination of Sung Chiao-jen on 20 March 1913. When the Parliament convened in April, T'ang Hua-lung was elected speaker of the National Assembly. In May, the Kung-ho-tang, the T'ung-i-tang, and the Min-chu-tang united to form the Chin-pu-tang [progressive party], nominally headed by Li Yuan-hung but directed by Liang Ch'i-ch'ao and T'ang Hua-lung.

The death of Sung Chiao-jen precipitated the outbreak of the so-called second revolution (*see* Li Lieh-chün), which resulted in the enhancement of Yuan Shih-k'ai's political and military power at the expense of the Kuomintang. Yuan pressed his advantage, forcing the suspension of the Parliament by expelling the Kuomintang members. This high-handed treatment of the legislative branch of the government alienated even the Chin-pu-tang, and T'ang publicly denounced Yuan's illegal act. Although T'ang accepted an appointment as minister of education in 1914, he resigned and left Peking for Shanghai when he learned of Yuan's plan to become monarch. T'ang then worked with Liang Ch'i-ch'ao in plotting Yuan's downfall. He also tried to persuade his brother T'ang Hsiang-ming, then governor of Hunan, to desert the would-be monarch. T'ang Hsiang-ming finally declared Hunan independent on 27 May 1916. With the death of Yuan Shih-k'ai on 6 June, T'ang Hua-lung went to Ch'isui for the burial of his mother. She had died on 16 March, but he had not dared to leave Shanghai while Yuan lived.

After Li Yuan-hung assumed the presidency and the Parliament was restored, T'ang Hua-lung resumed his post as speaker of the National Assembly. For a brief time, the Chin-pu-tang split into two factions: the Hsien-fa t'ao-lun-hui [association for the discussion of the constitution], headed by T'ang; and the Hsien-fa yen-chiu-hui [association for constitutional research], headed by Liang Ch'i-ch'ao. On 13 September 1916 the factions reunited to form the Hsien-cheng yen-chiu-hui [association for the study of constitutional government]. Thereafter the T'ang-Liang faction in the Parliament was known as the Yen-chiu hsi, or research

clique. It supported the policies, if not the tactics, of Tuan Ch'i-jui (q.v.), and its members resigned in protest when Li Yuan-hung dismissed Tuan from the premiership on 23 May 1917. During the restoration attempt of Chang Hsün (q.v.), T'ang and Liang joined the successful expedition against Chang that Tuan Ch'i-jui led from Tientsin. They then advised the Feng Kuo-chang–Tuan Ch'i-jui administration to convene a new parliament under new electoral laws. The Kuomintang voiced its opposition to the plan. T'ang was appointed minister of the interior to carry out the scheme, and the Kuomintang responded by launching the so-called constitution protection movement and establishing an opposition government at Canton.

With the downfall of the Tuan Ch'i-jui cabinet and the resignation of T'ang Hua-lung on 30 November 1917, the political influence of the research clique waned. Liang Ch'i-ch'ao withdrew from political activities to devote the remainder of his life to scholarship. T'ang Hua-lung left China on 24 March 1918 for a tour of Japan, the United States, and Canada. On 12 September 1918, after a banquet given by members of the T'ang clan in Victoria, British Columbia, he was assassinated by a Cantonese barber named Wang Ch'ang, who then killed himself. T'ang was survived by a son, P'ei-sung, and a daughter, P'ei-lin.

T'ang Shao-yi 唐 紹 儀
T. Shao-ch'uan 少 川

T'ang Shao-yi (1860–30 September 1938), long-time associate of Yuan Shih-k'ai who became the Chinese republic's first premier in 1912. He broke with Yuan in June 1912 and later allied himself with Sun Yat-sen. After Sun's death, T'ang lent support to various movements within the Kuomintang which opposed the growing authority of Chiang Kai-shek. T'ang was killed by an unknown assassin at Shanghai in 1938.

Hsiangshan (later Chungshan), Kwangtung, was the birthplace of T'ang Shao-yi. Little is known of T'ang's father, but his uncle was the prominent entrepreneur, T'ang T'ing-shu (1832–1892; T. Ching-hsing; West. Tong King Sing), who served as compradore for Jardine Matheson & Co. from 1861 to 1873, and then, under

Li Hung-chang (ECCP, I, 464–71), as director of the China Merchants' Steam Navigation Company from 1873 to 1884, and finally as the principal organizer and director of the K'aip'ing Mining Company from 1877 until his death in 1892. As a boy of ten, T'ang T'ing-shu had entered the Morrison Education Society school in Hong Kong, where he began a life-long friendship with his classmate there, Yung Wing (Jung Hung; ECCP I, 402–5). One result of this friendship was that T'ang Shao-yi was selected as a member of the third contingent of Chinese students to be sent to the United States to receive Western training under the program of the China Educational Mission, headed by Yung Wing. The mission had been proposed by Yung, and had been approved by the imperial court in 1871. Other Chinese students sent under the same program included Chan T'ien-yu, Ts'ai T'ing-kan (qq.v.) and Liang Tun-yen.

Upon arrival in the United States in the autumn of 1874, T'ang's group—which also included M. T. Liang (Liang Ju-hao), who later served as foreign minister, and Chu Pao-k'uei, who became minister of communications—was sent to Hartford, Connecticut, for orientation and preliminary instruction. T'ang later studied at Columbia University and New York University but failed to complete the B.A. degree requirements because he was recalled to China in 1881. The Ch'ing government abolished the China Educational Mission and its program because of reports to the effect that the students were becoming inordinately Americanized and were neglecting their Chinese studies.

Like most of the Chinese students who had studied in the United States, T'ang Shao-yi, after his return to China, was treated with contempt by Ch'ing officials on the grounds that he had lost many essential Chinese characteristics. He was assigned to subordinate clerical work in various offices of the imperial government. Finally, in 1882, he was appointed assistant to the new imperial customs inspector in Korea, P. G. von Möllendorff, in connection with the attempt of Li Hung-chang to buttress China's claim to suzerainty over the so-called Hermit Kingdom. T'ang thus was in Seoul at the time of the disorders there in 1884, and his actions gained him the approbation of Chinese garrison commander Yuan Shih-k'ai. He went with Yuan to Tientsin in April 1885

for consultation with Li Hung-chang, and their discussions with Li and Ito Hirobumi led to the signing of the Tientsin Convention, by which both China and Japan agreed to withdraw their garrisons and military instructors from Korea.

When Yuan Shih-k'ai returned to Seoul in August 1885, T'ang Shao-yi accompanied him as a member of his personal staff. After Yuan assumed the offices of commissioner of commerce and Chinese resident in Korea on 30 October, T'ang served as his deputy, with particular responsibility for handling Chinese political and commercial interests in the port town of Jinsen. In July 1894, as war with Japan over Korea loomed, Yuan Shih-k'ai moved to resign his post. Although his resignation was rejected, he returned to China, saying that he was ill, leaving T'ang Shao-yi to perform his functions at Seoul.

China's ignominious defeat in the Sino-Japanese war marked the beginning of a new phase in the career of T'ang Shao-yi. After serving briefly as Chinese consul general in Korea, he returned to China in 1896 to become secretary to Yuan Shih-k'ai at the headquarters of the Newly Created Army (Hsin-chien lu-chün) in Hsiaochan, Chihli (Hopei). T'ang also became managing director of the northern railways administration. When Yuan was appointed acting governor of Shantung in December 1899, T'ang accompanied him to that province to serve as his chief political officer and head of the provincial trade bureau. They firmly suppressed the Boxer movement in Shantung, and when the crisis ended Yuan recommended T'ang to the throne as "a man of superior talent and perception, well versed in diplomatic affairs." With the death of Li Hung-chang in November 1901 and the appointment of Yuan Shih-k'ai as governor general of Chihli, T'ang was named customs tao-t'ai at Tientsin.

In September 1904, as a result of the crisis precipitated by the Younghusband expedition to Tibet (see Dalai Lama), T'ang Shao-yi was appointed special commissioner for Tibetan affairs and was charged with investigating the situation. On 7 September, however, the British forced the Tibetan Grand Council to sign an agreement that, in effect, established a British protectorate. The Chinese court, which deemed the Lhasa Convention highly unsatisfactory, appointed T'ang minister to the Court of St.

James's and ordered him to Calcutta for negotiations with the British. T'ang and his staff, which included Liang Shih-i (q.v.), arrived in Calcutta in February 1905 with the aim of securing recognition of Chinese suzerainty over Tibet and of the Chinese government as the proper intermediary between Tibet and India. The British proved intransigent, and T'ang returned to China in September 1905. In November, however, he was appointed acting junior vice president of the Board of Foreign Affairs, in which capacity he reopened negotiations on the Tibetan problem with the British minister at Peking, Sir Ernest Satow. On 27 April 1906 the British and the Chinese signed an agreement that acknowledged China's suzerainty over Tibet.

By this time, T'ang Shao-yi had become associate controller general of a new revenue council in the Imperial Maritime Customs, and director general of the Peking–Hankow and Nanking–Shanghai railways. In November 1906 he was appointed senior vice-president of the Board of Communications. He joined with other high officials at Peking to initiate anti-opium legislation which was adopted and proclaimed by the throne on 22 November as the Opium Abolition Regulations. In his communications posts T'ang implemented the throne's policy of primary dependence on loans from abroad for developing a railroad system in China, a policy that drew political criticism. Moreover, his practice of giving preference to foreign-trained Chinese for responsible posts in the Board of Communications caused him to run afoul of its president, Chang Pai-hsi. After T'ang signed a loan agreement with the British in March 1907 for construction of the Canton–Kowloon railway, impeachment proceedings were begun against him. Under heavy political pressure, he resigned all of his posts at Peking in April 1907.

With the reorganization of Manchuria in April 1907 (for details, see Hsü Shih-ch'ang), T'ang Shao-yi became governor of Fengtien. In this post, he again was concerned with railway loans, and he turned to the United States for support against the Japanese and the British. Backed by Yuan Shih-k'ai, then president of the Board of Foreign Affairs at Peking, he negotiated with Willard Straight, the American consul general at Mukden, to secure assistance in the underwriting of currency reform, the establishment of a new bank in Manchuria, and the building of a railroad to compete with the Japanese South Manchurian railway (in defiance of the provision in the Sino-Japanese Protocol of 1905 which prohibited construction of new lines parallel to the Japanese-controlled rail system). T'ang thus became involved in the international railway rivalry that focused on Manchuria. He also was the probable initiator of a policy of colonization of Outer Mongolia by Manchurian peasants in 1908, a policy which soon led to Mongol unrest.

After the accession to the throne of the Hsuan-t'ung emperor, P'u-yi (q.v.), Yuan Shih-k'ai was relieved of his posts and was sent into retirement early in 1909. Yuan's lieutenants also lost power. In 1908 Willard Straight had negotiated preliminary agreements for the establishment of a Manchurian bank and had returned to the United States to work on final arrangements. T'ang Shao-yi had gone to the United States later that year for discussions, but the project had failed because of the political changes in China. T'ang returned to China in mid-1909 only to lose his post as governor of Fengtien because of his association with Yuan Shih-k'ai. He remained in retirement until August 1910, when he was called back to Peking as expectant vice president of the Board of Communications. In October, he became acting president of that board. Because Yuan Shih-k'ai was still in retirement, however, T'ang's position in Peking was not what it had been in previous years, and he resigned early in 1911.

With the outbreak of the republican revolution in October 1911 and the emergence from retirement of Yuan Shih-k'ai, T'ang Shao-yi replaced Sheng Hsuan-huai as president of the Board of Communications. In December, when Yuan Shih-k'ai was appointed premier and was authorized to deal with the republican revolutionaries, he named T'ang head of the imperial delegation charged with negotiating peace. At Shanghai, T'ang Shao-yi and his associates met with a southern delegation headed by Wu T'ing-fang (q.v.). When Sun Yat-sen was inaugurated as provisional president, however, Yuan requested T'ang's resignation from the imperial delegation. The ostensible reason for the request was that T'ang had exceeded his authority in negotiating an agreement regarding the composition of the proposed national assembly, but the actual reason was Yuan's belief that his bargaining position had been compromised by Sun's election to office. T'ang Shao-yi gave up his assignment as requested, but he continued to work on Yuan's behalf.

When Yuan Shih-k'ai assumed office at Peking in March 1912 as provisional president, he appointed T'ang Shao-yi premier. By that time, T'ang apparently had won the confidence of Sun Yat-sen and several other republican leaders. However, Ch'en Chi-mei (q.v.), the military governor of Shanghai and one of the leaders of the 1911 revolution, expressed apprehension about the possibility of T'ang becoming Yuan's tool in the undermining of the republican program. To allay doubts about his devotion to republicanism and his willingness to work with the revolutionaries, T'ang joined the T'ung-meng-hui. Yuan responded to this action by proceeding to undercut Tang's position. Because the government stood in urgent need of funds, T'ang, as responsible head of government under the provisional constitution adapted at Nanking, promptly signed a loan contract with the Banque Sino-Belgique for £1 million. The four-power banking consortium protested the contract as an infringement of its rights. Yuan thereupon asserted that he had known nothing of the matter and left T'ang to put the best face possible on it. Thus began an estrangement between Yuan and T'ang. Then, in June 1912, the Chihli provincial council nominated a Kuomintang official, Wang Chih-hsiang, to command the provincial forces. Both Yuan and the cabinet approved the nomination, but when Wang arrived in north China to assume office and the Chihli forces issued a statement opposing the appointment, Yuan changed his position and sent Wang south to inspect troops. T'ang Shao-yi took this occasion to resign the premiership on 16 June 1912 and leave for Tientsin without bidding Yuan goodbye. Liang Shih-i was sent by Yuan to Tientsin in an effort to change T'ang's mind, but to no avail. T'ang also ignored Yuan's proffer of a sinecure position as "Superior Adviser to the President on State Affairs" and retired to private life in Shanghai, where he became managing director of the Venus Assurance Company.

T'ang Shao-yi continued to oppose Yuan Shih-k'ai's policies, and after Yuan revealed his plan to become monarch, T'ang joined the Kuomintang opposition to Yuan's government. In 1916 T'ang served as special representative in Shanghai of the southern military council based at Chaoch'ing, Kwangtung (for details, see Ts'en Ch'un-hsuan). After Yuan's death in June, Tuan Ch'i-jui (q.v.) named T'ang foreign minister, but strong opposition in north China prevented him from assuming office. T'ang then strengthened his association with Sun Yat-sen and the political forces in south China. Like Sun, T'ang showed some inclination in late 1916 to embrace pan-Asianism as a solution to the problem of Western expansion, suggesting that China should work with Japan and India "for Asian independence against all outside aggression." He also allied himself with Sun in opposing Chinese participation in the First World War and in resisting the idea of changing the provisional constitution of 1912.

In mid-1917 Sun Yat-sen launched the so-called constitution protection movement, and some members of the recently dissolved Parliament at Peking (see Li Yuan-hung) went to Canton for a rump session. A military government was formed at Canton, with Sun at its head. At this point, T'ang Shao-yi and Wu T'ing-fang (q.v.) joined Sun in Canton, where T'ang was named minister of finance and Wu was named minister of foreign affairs. Neither of them formally assumed office, though both remained in Canton to advise Sun. In 1918, when the Kwangsi faction took control of the southern government and Sun departed in disgust for Shanghai, T'ang and Wu remained behind to serve on the seven-man governing board headed by Ts'en Ch'un-hsuan (q.v.). Early in 1919 T'ang left Canton for Shanghai to participate in peace negotiations with northern representatives. After the talks broke down in October 1919, T'ang returned to his native Hsiangshan, where he built an estate called Kung-lo-yuan [garden of common enjoyment] and made plans to live in retirement. He refused an offer from Sun in May 1921 to serve as foreign minister and declined Peking offers of the premiership (August 1922) and the portfolio of foreign minister (November 1924).

When interviewed by a correspondent from the *Chicago Daily News* in 1925, T'ang Shao-yi urged recognition of the "universality of the Chinese soul" and the "domestic heart of China" on the basis of which he believed "the unity of national interests" and the political progress of the country could and should be promoted. In an October 1925 statement expressing his opposition to tariff negotiations in Peking, he advocated general revision of the constitution, local self-government, revival of the civil service as "one of our finest heritages," elimination of "personal" armies, and reduction of foreign influence in China's domestic affairs.

Chiang Kai-shek named T'ang "superior adviser" to the National Government at Nanking early in 1929, but T'ang ignored the appointment. When Chiang's arrest of Hu Han-min (q.v.) in 1931 led to a secessionist movement in south China, T'ang threw in his lot with the Canton coalition led by Wang Ching-wei, Sun Fo, Ch'en Chi-t'ang (qq.v.), and others. Although unity between the Nanking and Canton leaders was restored after the Japanese attack on Mukden in September 1931, T'ang continued to support the semi-independent Southwest Executive Headquarters of the Kuomintang and the Southwest Political Council. During this period, he also served briefly as magistrate of his native hsien, which had been renamed Chungshan in honor of Sun Yat-sen and which had been designated a model hsien under the direct jurisdiction of the National Government. T'ang's magistracy was not a success, however, and he soon relinquished the post.

In 1936 T'ang Shao-yi decided to oppose the increasingly apparent plans of Ch'en Chi-t'ang to stage a revolt against the National Government. Accordingly, he went to Nanking that summer to attend a session of the central committees of the Kuomintang (he had become a member of the Central Supervisory Committee). At the session, he led a group of Cantonese leaders in presenting a resolution calling for the abolition of the Southwest Executive Headquarters and the Southwest Political Council. He also assumed office as a member of the State Council.

After the Sino-Japanese war began, T'ang Shao-yi, burdened by his 77 years, did not follow the National Government to west China but took up residence in the French concession at Shanghai. In 1938 it was rumored that the Japanese had solicited his support. The details of this overture and of T'ang's reaction remain obscure. On 30 September 1938 T'ang was assassinated in his Shanghai home by four axe-wielding men who had gained admission on the pretext of showing him rare pieces of porcelain. Their identities and the motive for the assassination remained mysterious, and the case never was solved. T'ang was survived by his second wife, two concubines, four sons, several daughters, and numerous grandchildren. His son T'ang Liu served for a time as Chinese consul general at Singapore and later became director of the ministry of foreign affairs and consul general at Honolulu. The eldest daughter (d. 1918) had been the wife of V. K. Wellington Koo (Ku Wei-chün, q.v.). T'ang Shao-yi's youngest daughter (by his second wife) married a son of the Singapore multimillionaire K. C. Lee (Li Kuang-ch'ien, q.v.).

T'ang Sheng-chih　　　唐 生 智
T. Meng-hsiao　　　　　孟 瀟

T'ang Sheng-chih (31 October 1890?–), Hunanese militarist whose successes against Wu P'ei-fu were of major importance to the first stage of the Northern Expedition. He dominated Hupeh, Hunan, and southern Honan in 1927, and he was for a time the most powerful man in the National Government at Wuhan. His military career after 1928 was marked by sporadic alliance with and opposition to Chiang Kai-shek. After 1949 he held a variety of posts in the People's Republic of China.

Tungan hsien, Hunan, was the birthplace of T'ang Sheng-chih. His grandfather had been an officer in the Hunan Army, and his father was the director of an industrial bureau. The young T'ang received his early education at home, but with the establishment in 1905 of provincial military primary schools, he enrolled at the Hunan Army Primary School. It may be inferred that he later attended the Wuchang Army Middle School, for in 1912 he enrolled in the infantry course at the Paoting Military Academy, where his schoolmates included Ch'en Ming-shu and Liu Wen-tao (qq.v.). Liu headed a student group which pressed for reform at the academy. T'ang represented the infantry division in this reformist group, and Ch'en represented the artillery division.

Upon graduation from the Paoting Military Academy, T'ang Sheng-chih returned to Hunan to become a probationary platoon commander in the 1st Mixed Brigade. With the death of

Yuan Shih-k'ai in June 1916 and the downfall of the Hunan tutuh [military governor], T'ang Hsiang-ming, Hunan became the scene of a power struggle among such men as T'an Yen-k'ai, Chao Heng-t'i, Ch'eng Ch'ien, Lu Ti-p'ing (qq.v.), and Sung Ho-keng. When T'an Yen-k'ai came to power, T'ang Sheng-chih was appointed a battalion commander serving under Sung Ho-keng. After the Peiyang general Chang Ching-yao became governor of Hunan in 1918, T'ang broke with Sung and joined the forces of Chao Heng-t'i as a regimental commander. Chao emerged as acting governor after the ouster of Chang Ching-yao in 1920. For his part in Chao's rise to power, T'ang was promoted commander of the 2nd Brigade of the 2nd Division. In 1921 he received command of the 4th Division. To instill proper discipline and attitudes in his troops, he sought Buddhist teachers. In 1922 he recruited for this purpose Ku Tzu-t'ung, a native of Yochow who adhered to the mi-tsung [mystic] sect of Buddhism. For the next three decades, Ku exercised considerable influence over T'ang and preached regularly to T'ang's men.

T'ang Sheng-chih figured prominently in the 1923 war between T'an Yen-k'ai and Chao Heng-t'i, remaining loyal to Chao despite offers from T'an. With the aid of forces led by Wu P'ei-fu (q.v.), Chao turned back T'an's troops. By 1926, however, T'ang Sheng-chih had decided to challenge Chao Heng-t'i's rule in Hunan. Having assured himself of National Government support, T'ang began a campaign to maneuver Chao into resigning rather than head a campaign against Wu P'ei-fu. Chao finally resigned on 11 March 1926, appointing T'ang director of the provincial affairs council and acting governor. T'ang assumed office on 25 March. Soon afterwards, Ch'en Ming-shu and Pai Ch'ung-hsi arrived in Changsha to win T'ang's support for the projected Northern Expedition. The combination of this mission and military aid against Wu P'ei-fu bore rich fruit, for on 1 June 1926 T'ang announced his acceptance of the post of commander of the Eighth Army in the National Revolutionary Army.

Supported by forces of the Seventh and Fourth armies, T'ang Sheng-chih launched an offensive against the enemy positions on 5 July 1926. On 9 July, Chiang Kai-shek assumed office as commander in chief of the Northern Expedition and appointed T'ang commander in chief of front-line operations. T'ang thus commanded six Hunan divisions headed by Ho Chien, Li P'in-hsien, Liu Hsing, Chou Lan, Yeh Ch'i, and Hsia Tou-yin; he also had supreme authority over the Fourth Army of Li Chi-shen and the Seventh Army of Li Tsung-jen. His old Paoting classmate Liu Wen-tao was appointed party representative and chief of the political department in the Eighth Army. On 11 July T'ang's forces recovered Changsha, and he formally assumed office there as governor three days later. By the time Chiang Kai-shek arrived in Changsha on 12 August, T'ang had created a strong forward bastion for the Northern Expedition.

In mid-August, T'ang Sheng-chih led a general offensive northward with elements of the Fourth, Seventh, and Eighth armies. His 2nd Division occupied Yochow on 22 August. Wu P'ei-fu, alarmed by the rapid progress of the Northern Expedition armies, arrived at Hankow on 25 August and held a military conference at which it was decided to make a strong stand at Ting-ssu-ch'iao. The battle for that strategic point began on 26 August and ended three days later in a Nationalist victory. By 1 September, divisions of the Fourth Army led by Chang Fa-k'uei (q.v.) and Ch'en Ming-shu had reached the gates of Wuchang. On 6–7 September, T'ang Sheng-chih's forces occupied Hanyang and Hankow. Wuchang finally fell in October, with official credit for its occupation being given to T'ang Sheng-chih, Ch'en K'o-yu (field commander of the Fourth Army), and Teng Yen-ta (q.v.). With the capture of Wuchang and the opening of the Kiangsi front, the Fourth and Seventh armies were moved eastward, leaving T'ang's Eighth Army in effective control of the Hunan–Hupeh area. Chiang Kai-shek accepted his situation and instructed Teng Yen-ta to inaugurate a new Hupeh provincial government in consultation with T'ang. However, Chiang was well aware of the dangers inherent in T'ang's powerful position. In late September, he had reported to T'an Yen-k'ai and Chang Jen-chieh (q.v.) at Canton that "the political situation in Wuhan may not be easy to handle. Unless a few of the government members and Central Executive Committee members come to Wuhan, political power may slip away from the Central authorities . . . . A political council should be formed with Central figures to replace the provincial political council." On 22 October, Chiang suggested that the central Kuomintang headquarters be transferred from Canton to Wuhan.

When the National Government began functioning at Wuhan in January 1927, T'ang Sheng-chih closely associated himself with its leftist political policies. Both Ch'en Ming-shu and Liu Wen-tao were dismissed in March, and T'ang thereafter limited his associations to leftists. After Wang Ching-wei returned from Europe to head the Wuhan regime and Chiang Kai-shek formed an opposition government at Nanking, T'ang became military commander in chief at Wuhan. In late April, even as the break between Wuhan and Nanking was developing, T'ang drove northward into Honan, with the aid of Chang Fa-k'uei's Fourth Army, against strong Fengtien forces. At the beginning of June, T'ang's victorious but battered troops effected a juncture with the Kuominchün of Feng Yü-hsiang (q.v.) in northern Honan. Feng then held the balance of power in China, and the Wuhan leaders ceded Honan to him in hopes of winning his support against Chiang Kai-shek. Feng, however, finally decided to support Chiang. About this time, the Ma Jih Incident (for details, see Ho Chien) caused T'ang Sheng-chih to return to Changsha. His attitude toward Communists began to change when he discovered that his supporters and subordinates in Hunan had become strongly anti-Communist. In mid-July, confronted with strong evidence of Comintern plans to challenge their power, the Kuomintang leaders at Wuhan decided to take action against the Communists. By this time, T'ang's commanders Ho Chien (q.v.) and Li P'in-hsien had moved to Wuhan and had taken action against labor unions in the tri-city area. On 17 July Ho and Li placed Hankow and Hanyang under military rule, suppressing all local Communist organizations. The anti-Communist campaign continued, and by mid-August, Wang Ching-wei and his associates were able to give their full attention to the problem of reconciliation with the Nanking and Shanghai (Western Hills) factions of the Kuomintang. Objections to the composition of the Central Special Committee decided upon to serve as an interim government caused T'ang and Ku Meng-yü (q.v.) to establish the Wuhan branch of the Political Council and to declare the Central Special Committee an illegal body.

The rapid growth of T'ang Sheng-chih's military organization had cost it much of its cohesiveness. Such commanders as Lu Ti-p'ing and Ho Yao-tsu (q.v.) turned against T'ang, and even Ho Chien adopted an equivocal attitude. On 20 October 1927 the Nanking authorities announced plans for an expedition against T'ang and relieved him of all posts; a few days later, the Central Special Committee expelled him from the Kuomintang. In face of the Nanking expedition and the unwillingness of many of his old commanders to support him, T'ang announced his retirement on 11 November and went to Japan. He remained there until the autumn of 1928, when his Buddhist adviser, Ku Tzu-t'ung, interpreted signs as favoring T'ang's return. Soon after his return to China, he effected a coup against Pai Ch'ung-hsi in north China, thereby winning back forces he had commanded before 1927. On 29 March 1929 T'ang's troops were designated the Fifth Route Army for the Suppression of Rebels. On 1 June, he was appointed chief of the military advisory council and director of the organization department of the troop-disbandment conference. In late October, he and his Fifth Route Army took the field against Feng Yü-hsiang in western Honan. T'ang then became acting commander in chief of all National Government forces in Honan. The campaign ended with Feng's withdrawal from Honan in late November. T'ang was awarded for his conduct of the campaign with an appointment to the State Council. On 5 December, however, T'ang announced his intention to oppose Chiang Kai-shek and accepted an appointment from Wang Ching-wei as commander in chief of the Fourth Route of the Party Protection and National Salvation Army. The National Government promptly ordered a punitive expedition against T'ang, causing him to flee to Hong Kong in January 1930.

T'ang Sheng-chih did not return to public life until the spring of 1931, when he joined the secessionist movement at Canton (see Wang Ching-wei; Lin Sen) as a member of its state council. After the Japanese invaded Manchuria in September, T'ang accompanied Wang Ching-wei, Chang Fa-k'uei, and Huang Shao-hung (q.v.) to Shanghai for negotiations with National Government authorities. As part of the arrangements made for reunification, his membership in the Kuomintang was restored on

19 October. In the ensuing reorganization of the party and the National Government he was elected an alternate member of the Kuomintang's Central Executive Committee and was appointed chairman of the military advisory council. In December 1934 he became inspector general of military training; he held that post until the outbreak of the Sino-Japanese war in 1937. In November 1937, on the advice of Ku Tzu-t'ung, he volunteered to lead the defense of Nanking. Upon being appointed Nanking garrison commander, he vowed to achieve victory or die with the city. When Nanking fell on 12 December, however, T'ang moved westward to rejoin the National Government.

Although T'ang was a nominal member of the Military Affairs Commission throughout the war, he played no active role in wartime decision-making. In fact, he left Chungking after a time and returned to his native village in Hunan. In 1948 he was elected to the National Assembly as a delegate from Hunan. T'ang remained in China after the Communist victory in 1949 and held a variety of posts in the People's Republic of China. He served as a member of the National Committee of the Chinese People's Political Consultative Conference, vice chairman of the Hunan provincial government, and a member of the Central-South Military and Administrative Committee. He was a Hunan delegate to the National People's Congress in 1954 and in the ensuing governmental reorganization he was elected to the National Defense Council. In 1956 he became a member of the standing committee of the Kuomintang Revolutionary Committee, and in 1958 he was named to the Standing Committee of the National People's Congress.

T'ang Yung-t'ung   湯 用 彤
T. Hsi-yü   錫 予

T'ang Yung-t'ung (June 1892–May 1964), leading historian of Chinese Buddhism whose major work was the *Han wei liang-chin nan-pei-ch'ao fo-chiao shih* [history of Buddhism during the Han, Wei, Chin, and Northern and Southern dynasties].

Born in Huaiyuan, Kansu, T'ang Yung-t'ung received a sound classical education, including

several years of study with the noted Buddhist scholar Ou-yang Ching-wu (q.v.). He later enrolled at Tsinghua College (later University), from which he was graduated in 1917. From 1918 to 1922 he studied in the United States, returning to China in 1922 to become a professor at Tung-nan University. He taught at Nank'ai University in 1922–23 and at Chungyang University in 1924–30. In 1931 he was honored with an appointment to a professorship of philosophy at Peking University. Despite almost constant political upheaval and the moving of the university to southwest China after the outbreak of the Sino-Japanese war, he succeeded in writing a monumental history of early Chinese Buddhism which was published in 1938. His field of research was one which had received scant attention from earlier Chinese scholars. T'ang remained on the teaching staff of Peking University until 1947, when he went to the University of California at Berkeley to give several specialized courses in the history and doctrines of Chinese Buddhism. He returned to China in 1948 to become dean of the humanities at Peking University, a post he retained after the establishment of the People's Republic of China in 1949. T'ang suffered a stroke in the winter of 1954 which left one side of his body paralyzed. He died at Peking in May 1964.

T'ang Yung-t'ung's first scholarly contribution was an essay, "P'ing chin-jen chih wen-hua yen-chiu" [a critical discussion of research on culture by moderns], which appeared in the *Hsüeh-heng*, one of the early Chinese journals devoted to comparative studies of Western and Chinese culture, in December 1922. He continued to play the role of interpreter of the West to the East by translating Edwin Wallace's *Outlines of the Philosophy of Aristotle*. The result of his labors, "Ya-li-shih-to-te che-hsueh ta-kang," appeared in the *Hsüeh-heng* in 1923. T'ang's next contribution to the *Hsüeh-heng*, "Fo-chiao shang-tso-pu chiu-hsin-lun lüeh-shih" [a summary explication of the nine mental evolvents according to the school of the elders], was the first to reflect his interest in Buddhist studies and comparative methodology. In this article, published in 1924, T'ang analyzed certain doctrines according to one of the early Hinayāna schools and laid a foundation for later comparative studies of Hinayāna and Māhayāna Buddhism.

Turning his attention to historical analysis, T'ang Yung-t'ung wrote a series of notes on the most important work dealing with the period of the introduction and adaptation of Indian or Serendian Buddhism to China—the *Kao-seng chuan* [lives of eminent monks] by the Liang dynasty monk Hui-chiao (479–554). The resulting "Tu-hui-chiao kao-seng chuan cha-chi" appeared in 1931 in the *Shih-hsueh tsa-chih*, a periodical published in Nanking by the Chinese Historical Society. In addition to notes on certain sources used by Hui-chiao, T'ang dealt with specific historical problems posed by some of the biographies: "The Date and Place of Fa-hu's (Dharmaraska's) Death"; "Sanghadeva's *Abhidharma* Studies"; "A Chronology of Kumarajiva"; "Shih Tao-an and Fo-t'u-teng"; "The Year of Tao-an's Escape from the Disturbances"; "A Chronology of Tao-an"; "A Chronology of Shih Hui-yuan"; "Seng-chao's Letter to Liu I-min"; "On Chih T'an-ti"; "On Fo-t'u-teng"; and "The Wei Emperor T'ai-wu's Suppression of Buddhism." Whereas many earlier scholars had simply cited their sources without making any attempt at critical evaluation, T'ang set himself the task of establishing the historical facts (a difficult problem as Buddhists traditionally were ahistorical) and showing how mistakes had arisen in earlier accounts. His insights into the role of doctrinal bias in shaping the traditional accounts pointed the way for later studies of forged texts by other scholars.

Tang's intensive research on the history and doctrines of the formative period of Chinese Buddhism yielded several important articles in the 1930's. "T'ang t'ai-tsung yü fo-chiao" [emperor T'ang T'ai-tsung and Buddhism] appeared in the *Hsüeh-heng* in 1931. Here T'ang studied another important problem in Chinese Buddhist history which had been ignored by almost all traditional Chinese historians, that is, what Westerners would call the church-state problem. The following year saw the publication of "Chu Tao-sheng yü nieh-p'an-hsueh" [Chu Tao-sheng and the studies concerning the Nirvāna-sūtra] in the *Kuo-hsueh chi-k'an*. T'ang brilliantly demonstrated that such fundamental concepts of Ch'an as tun-wu [sudden enlightenment] had been taught at the end of the fourth century A.D., some 175 years earlier than had been supposed by other scholars. Another important contribution was

"Chung-kuo fo-chiao ling-p'ien" [notes on the history of Chinese Buddhism], published in 1937 in the *Yenching Journal of Chinese Studies*. In this article T'ang posed such basic questions as: "How extensive was the reaction among Chinese intellectuals to the introduction of Buddhism from about 100 A.D. on?" "How much of Indian Buddhism was understood by the Chinese, and what modifications were made by them?" "Where does the influence of Buddhism on later generations assert itself?" These questions and Tang's proposed answers, based on painstaking research, provided his readers with a preview of his *magnum opus*, a history of Chinese Buddhism from the Han dynasty to the T'ang.

The *Han wei liang-chin nan-pei-ch'ao fo-chiao shih* [history of Buddhism during the Han, Wei, Chin, and Northern and Southern dynasties] was published at Shanghai in 1938. Almost one-fourth of this 900-page work was devoted to an analysis of the Han dynasty Buddhism. In the first chapter, T'ang sought to separate fact from pious fiction in the various traditional accounts of how and when Buddhism was introduced to China. He then proceeded to a philological analysis of the famous legend that Buddhism was introduced officially under Emperor Ming, concluding that there was indeed a grain of truth in the tradition. This analysis was followed by an investigation of the textual history of the "first sūtra" translated into Chinese, the *Ssu-shih-erh chang ching*. T'ang demonstrated that the so-called Māhāyanistic passages, frequently cited by such scholars as Liang Ch'i-ch'ao (q.v.) to prove the entire work a forgery, were added to the original text by later Buddhists. He concluded that the original form of this "sūtra" was purely Hīnayānistic in inspiration and that in this form it was very old indeed, for it was quoted by an official in a memorial to the throne dated 166 A.D.

Among the other important problems which T'ang discussed in his history were the relationship between Buddhism and Taoism; the sources of Buddho-Taoist metaphysics; the beginnings of various indigenous theories particularly as related to the Prajñā [gnosis] studies of the period of Tao-an (312–385); and the relation of Buddhism to the state in the Northern and Southern dynasties. He also treated such subjects as the revival of gnostic studies, the

San-lun, and the *Ch'eng-shih-lun* under the Southern dynasties and the characteristics of the lü, Ch'an, and Ching-t'u studies pursued during the Northern dynasties.

In many ways, the *Han wei liang-chin nan-pei-ch'ao fo-chiao shih* was a source book for the period it covered. All variant accounts were carefully noted, and controversial statements were documented, usually by title and chapter references to primary sources. The work was not without its limitations: T'ang did not deal with the economic aspects of Buddhism; very little use was made of foreign scholarly works, particularly Indological and Sanskrit studies; and there was no index. Nevertheless, T'ang Yung-t'ung's monumental history was and is essential to anyone studying early Chinese Buddhism, and T'ang's contributions to Chinese Buddhist historical studies easily made him the greatest Chinese scholar of his day in this difficult field.

T'ao Hsi-sheng　　　　陶　希　聖
Orig. Hui-tseng　　　　　彙　曾
Pen. Fang Chün-feng　　方　峻　峯

T'ao Hsi-sheng (30 October 1899–), socio-economic historian and member of the Re-organizationist faction led by Wang Ching-wei. He joined Wang in his efforts to reach a peaceful settlement of the Sino-Japanese war, but he became disillusioned and defected to Hong Kong in 1940 with copies of Wang's secret agreement with the Japanese. He later became a member of Chiang Kai-shek's personal staff and the editor in chief of the *Chung-yang jih-pao* [central daily news].

The T'ao family was of peasant stock, and it was only in the generation of T'ao Hsi-sheng's father that the family began to move toward gentry status. T'ao Hsi-sheng's father, T'ao Chiung-chao, held the sheng-yuan degree, and his mother, *née* Chieh, came from a scholarly family. At the time of T'ao Hsi-sheng's birth in Huangkang hsien, Hupeh, his father was in Peking teaching Chinese to the children of some Bannermen. When the Boxer Uprising began in 1900, T'ao Chiung-chao left Peking and met his family in Sian where he became a proctor at the Hung-tao Academy.

In 1903 T'ao Hsi-sheng moved with his parents to Kaifeng, Honan, and in 1904 he began his formal education under a private tutor. In the next few years the family moved to Hsiayi, Hsinyeh, and Anyang as T'ao Chiung-chao served successively as acting magistrate of these districts. T'ao Hsi-sheng was sent to Wuhan in the summer of 1912 for a year's study at a modern school. He then rejoined his family at Huangp'i, where his father was serving as magistrate. There and later at Huangkang he studied under his father's supervision and developed a deep interest in government, history and law. Early in 1915 he accompanied his father to Peking and became a student at the preparatory school attached to Peking University. After being graduated in 1918, he enrolled in the law department at Peking University. Because he was preoccupied with his studies, the May Fourth Movement had little effect on him. At this time he was particularly interested in Roman law and in Chinese philosophy of the Ming and Ch'ing periods. He also studied Japanese so that he could read works on law in that language.

After being graduated from Peking University in the summer of 1922, T'ao Hsi-sheng joined the faculty of the Anhwei Provincial Law School at Anking. In the winter of 1923 he left Anking for his native district. Through the recommendation of Teng Shao-hsün, he became an editor at the Commercial Press at Shanghai in July 1924, succeeding Chou Keng-sheng as reader of manuscripts on law and political economy. He also continued to do research on social organizations in ancient China. In addition, he found time to contribute articles to the *Hsueh-i tsa-chih* [arts and sciences] and the *Fu-nü tsa-chih* [women's journal].

At the time of the May Thirtieth Incident in 1925, T'ao Hsi-sheng published an article in the *Kung-li pao* in which he demonstrated his knowledge of British law in condemning the militant behavior of the British police in Shanghai. This article led to his appointment as a legal adviser to the Shanghai Students Association. As he became more involved in the movement, his fame grew and he came to know a great many intellectuals. He joined the Hsueh-i she [society of arts and sciences], wrote for the *Ku-chun yueh-k'an* [lone force monthly], and became editor in chief of *Tu-li p'ing-lun* [independent critic]. He also took a teaching post at Shanghai University, then known as a radical institution. About this time, he began reading works on historical materialism. These activities were curtailed in 1926, when he contracted typhoid fever.

In January 1927, possibly at the invitation of Chou Fo-hai (q.v.), T'ao Hsi-sheng went to Wuhan to become an instructor in political science, with the rank of lieutenant colonel, at the Wuhan branch of the Central Military Academy. On orders from Yün Tai-ying (q.v.), he was stationed at Hsienning as director of the department of military justice in the independent division that had been formed to quash the rebellious troops of Hsia Tou-yin. He organized a hsien government and headed its judicial section. Because of Communist dissatisfaction with his work, however, he soon was recalled to Wuhan. He then was appointed secretary of the military academy's political department. After the Communists were purged from the Wuhan regime, he served briefly as secretary of the Kuomintang general political and propaganda departments at Wuhan. As an expeditionary force approached Wuhan in November, he escaped to his native district, from whence he went to Nanchang. After serving for about a month as head of the Kiangsi Party Affairs School, he resigned and left Nanchang for Shanghai.

In February 1928, at the recommendation of Chou Fo-hai, then the director of the political department of the Central Military Academy at Nanking, T'ao Hsi-sheng became senior political instructor and head of the training section of the acdemy's political department. He also became a regular contributor to the *New Life Monthly*, which Chou was editing. In December, T'ao resigned and went to Shanghai, where he joined the Kuomintang kai-tsu t'ung-chih hui [society of comrades for Kuomintang reorganization], founded by Ku Meng-yü (q.v.) and others. This group came to be known as the Reorganizationist faction. In 1930 T'ao published *Chung-kuo feng-chien she-hui shih* [history of Chinese feudal society], *Chung-kuo she-hui chih shih te fen-hsi* [historical analysis of Chinese society], and *Chung-kuo wen-t'i chih hui-ku yü chan-wang* [the China problem: retrospect and prospect]. In these works, which reflected his reading of Marx and Lenin, he argued that feudalism in China had begun as early as 1122 B.C. but had disintegrated gradually during the

early period of the Warring States (403–221 B.C.). Thus, he argued, Chinese society in later years was mercantile capitalist rather than feudal.

T'ao Hsi-sheng's works provoked the publication of *Chung-kuo ku-tai she-hui yen-chiu* [a study of ancient Chinese society] by Kuo Mo-jo (q.v.). Kuo maintained that Chinese feudalism began during the early years of the Warring States and that it reached its full development about 221 B.C. Chinese society, according to Kuo, had never emerged from feudalism. The T'ao-Kuo controversy ignited an animated debate among Chinese intellectuals on the nature of Chinese society.

In 1930 T'ao Hsi-sheng worked briefly as secretary of the general management office at the Commercial Press, which published his *Pien-shih yü yu-hsia* [sophists and knights errant] and *Hsi-Han ching-chi shih* [economic history of the western Han]. He became a professor at Central University in January 1931. That spring, he completed *Chung-kuo she-hui hsien-hsiang shih-lin* [random notes on China's social scene]. He moved to Peking that summer and joined the faculty of Peking University, where he taught Chinese political thought and social history. In 1933 he launched the biweekly magazine *Shih-huo* [economics], which greatly stimulated the study of socio-economic history in China. T'ao also conducted a seminar on the economic history of the T'ang dynasty which resulted in the compilation of an eight-volume work.

With the outbreak of the Sino-Japanese war in July 1937, T'ao Hsi-sheng went to Kuling to attend a meeting of intellectuals who had been called together by Chiang Kai-shek to discuss the national crisis. He then went to Nanking, where he became a member of the National Defense Council, headed by Wang Ching-wei (q.v.). Later that year, he moved the council to Wuhan. When the I-wen yen-chiu hui [literary research society] was organized at Hankow early in 1938, T'ao became its general secretary, serving under Chou Fo-hai. This organization concerned itself with the publication and dissemination of anti-Communist writings. In July, T'ao also became a member of the newly formed People's Political Council, in which capacity he served as an adviser to Wang Ching-wei. He moved with the National Government to Chungking that autumn. By this time, Wang Ching-wei, having become pessimistic about China's ability to sustain a protracted war against Japan, was advocating the conclusion of a peaceful settlement with the Japanese. On 18 December, Wang left Chungking and went to Kunming, where he was joined by T'ao, Chou Fo-hai, and Ch'en Kung-po (q.v.). The group then moved on to Hanoi. Early in 1939 T'ao and Chou went to Hong Kong. They helped conduct a propaganda campaign in support of Wang's peace movement. Wang reached Shanghai on 6 May, and T'ao joined him there in August. On 1 September 1939 Wang convened the so-called sixth national congress of the Kuomintang, at which T'ao was appointed director of the propaganda department of the central party headquarters.

In the next few months, T'ao Hsi-sheng became increasingly disillusioned with the peace movement as he represented Wang in negotiations with the Japanese. He began to make plans to leave Wang. On 30 December 1939 negotiations concerning the Principles for the Readjustment of New Sino-Japanese Relations were completed, and on 4 January 1940 T'ao and Kao Tsung-wu escaped to Hong Kong with copies of the secret agreement. T'ao's family was taken into custody. Tao's wife subsequently was permitted to take her two younger children to Hong Kong after she promised to urge T'ao to return to Shanghai. The three elder children were detained in Shanghai until Tu Yueh-sheng (q.v.) secured their release. In the meantime, publication of the terms of Wang's agreement with the Japanese caused a furor in China.

For the next two years, T'ao Hsi-sheng lived in Hong Kong, where he organized an international news service agency and published the weekly *Kuo-chi t'ung-hsin* [international correspondence]. Toward the end of 1941 T'ao, on the advice of Tu Yueh-sheng, made preparations to leave Hong Kong, then threatened by the Japanese. In February 1942 he arrived in Chungking, where he joined Chiang Kai-shek's staff and took charge of a number of research and writing activities. He also had some responsibility for the content of newspapers, especially the *Chung-yang jih-pao* [central daily news]. In the autumn of 1942 he began collecting materials for Chiang Kai-shek in connection with the writing of *China's Destiny*. This work was published in January 1943. In October of that year, he became editor in chief of the *Chung-yang jih-pao*, a post he continued to hold after the war ended. He was a delegate to the National Assembly in 1946 and deputy director of the central propaganda department in 1946–47. During this period, he also served as Chiang Kai-shek's personal secretary. In 1948, on the eve of the Communist takeover of Peiping, he made arrangements for the evacuation of some prominent professors to Nationalist territory. After Chiang Kai-shek announced his retirement in January 1949, T'ao accompanied him to Fenghua and, eventually, to Taipei.

In Taiwan, T'ao Hsi-sheng continued to edit the *Chung-yang jih-pao*. He became director of the Central Reconstruction Council's planning committee in 1950, a member of the Legislative Yuan in 1951, and a member of the Kuomintang's Central Executive Committee in 1952. In 1955 he retired from the editorship of *Chung-yang jih-pao* to become chairman of its board of directors.

T'ao Hsi-sheng had one daughter, Ch'in-hsün, and six sons: T'ai-lai, Fu-lai, Heng-sheng, Chin-sheng, Fan-sheng, and Lung-sheng.

T'ao Hsing-chih	陶 行 知
Orig. Wen-chün	文 濬
Pen. Ho Jih-p'ing	何 日 平

T'ao Hsing-chih (1891–25 July 1946), educational theorist and reformer who based his ideas on those of John Dewey and Wang Yang-ming. His theories of "life education" were embodied in the mass education and rural education movements of the 1920's and in the work-study and "national crisis education" programs of the 1930's.

Born into a family of small means, T'ao Hsing-chih spent the years from 1896 to 1905 in a traditional Chinese school, where his intelligence and retentive memory made a striking impression. In 1905, possibly because of the abolition of the examination system, he entered a Protestant missionary school. He majored in English and mathematics, completing the four-year course of study in three years. T'ao then entered the Protestant-run Chung-chi Medical School at Hangchow, but because he refused to be baptized and so forfeited a scholarship and because he lost faith in medicine as a career, he soon quit school and went to Soochow. He and a cousin studied together and eked out a meager living by pawning their clothes and other possessions. Finally, in 1911, T'ao entered the literature department of Nanking University.

It was at Nanking that T'ao first became involved with education and politics, the two subjects that were to preoccupy him for the rest of his life. As a student during and after the 1911 revolution, T'ao was an activist, sponsoring a political debating society and organizing a series of patriotic lectures. He also edited the university magazine, the *Chin-ling kuang-hsüeh pao*. Although enrolled in the literature department, T'ao retained his earlier interest in mathematics and developed new ones in the fields of education and philosophy. T'ao and his friends frequently discussed traditional Chinese thought in relation to the modern world. As a result of these explorations, T'ao became absorbed in the philosophy of the unorthodox Neo-Confucian Wang Yang-ming (1472–1529) and especially in Wang's theory of chih-hsing ho-i [the unity of knowledge and action]. He also was struck by Wang's theory of education as set forth in his *Ch'uan-hsi-lu:* "Give children a chance to develop freely. Guide them gently toward desirable ends." This maxim became the basis of T'ao's own theories, and, as an indication of his close identification with Wang, he adopted the courtesy name Chih-hsing [knowledge-action].

In 1914, having again completed a four-year course in three years, T'ao was graduated at the top of his class. With the help of relatives, he set out that summer for advanced study in the United States. Because he then was contemplating a career in municipal government, he enrolled at the University of Illinois as a graduate student in political science. He took a course in educational administration which was taught by a former student of John Dewey, and it was this teacher who gave T'ao his first glimpse of the philosophical and educational system that Dewey was evolving. T'ao was so impressed that he transferred to Teachers College, Columbia University, in 1915, thereby tracing "the Deweyan stream to its source." At Teachers College, where he stayed until the summer of 1917 and where he immersed himself in Deweyan instrumentalism, T'ao decided to devote the rest of his life to education.

In the autumn of 1917 T'ao returned to China, where he began to evolve his own theory of "life education" (sheng-huo chiao-yü), based on the ideas of Dewey and Wang Yang-ming. The next 20 years were to see a working out of these ideas in concrete form, first by gaining a hearing for them and subsequently by embodying them in a series of practical projects which were adapted to meet China's specific needs at various times and which included mass literacy education, rural education, work-study education, education for national crisis, wartime education, nation-wide education, and finally, education for democracy. T'ao received an appointment to the staff of Nanking National Teachers College, but at first he found little audience for his new views. His attempt to reorganize the college on Deweyan principles was voted down; opposition within the education department obliged him to decline its chairmanship; and an eloquent article entitled "The Unity of Teaching and Learning," published early in 1919, received only scant notice. Undiscouraged, T'ao continued to preach the major tenets of Dewey's philosophy, above all the responsibility of the teacher to teach students to learn, to link teaching methods to learning methods, and to continue the pursuit of learning rather than to consider his own knowledge as static or final. The turning point for T'ao came only with the May Fourth Movement. The new tide of thought and action overwhelmed conservative opposition within the college (by then called Southeastern University), and T'ao, at last able to assume the chairmanship of the education department, initiated sweeping reforms.

With his assumption of the chairmanship of the prestigious education department of Southeastern University, T'ao became known as one of the leading interpreters of John Dewey to China. When Dewey toured China in 1919–21 T'ao translated for him during his Nanking lectures, which were sponsored jointly by Southeastern University and Peking University. An outgrowth of this inter-university contact was T'ao's participation from 1919 on in the group associated with the new monthly *Hsin chiao-yü* [new education], whose editor, Chiang Monlin (Chiang Meng-lin, q.v.), also had studied under Dewey at Columbia. T'ao wrote a number of articles on the improvement of Chinese education for the magazine, whose contributors also included Huang Yen-p'ei, Kuo Ping-wen, Lo Chia-lun, Hu Shih, and Ts'ai Yüan-p'ei (qq.v.). In the winter of 1921, this group helped found the Chung-kuo chiao-yü kai-tsao she [Chinese association for the improvement of education], with Ts'ai Yüan-p'ei as chief sponsor. At the association's first meeting in February 1922 at Shanghai, T'ao was chosen executive secretary. At this time, he also became editor of *Hsin chiao-yü*, now the association's official organ.

In the years immediately following Dewey's tour and the founding of the association, T'ao began to promote his first large-scale project, the mass education movement. In June 1923 an association for mass education was formed at Nanking, and within two months the movement had spread to Wuhan and other cities. In August, the mass education association held its organizing convention at Tsinghua University in Peking, and a permanent headquarters was established with the wife of Hsiung Hsi-ling as chairman and James Yen (Yen Yang-ch'u q.v.) as executive secretary. Intensive promotion of the movement began in October, and by June 1924 the campaign had spread into 20 provinces and administrative areas.

T'ao's theories as expressed in his conception of "life education" received characteristic embodiment in the mass education movement. From Wang Yang-ming he had learned that true knowledge must have practical consequences and that knowing and doing are one. From Dewey he had garnered an evolutionary theory of truth, as well as the idea that all forms of human activity are but instruments for problem solving. He also had learned from Dewey that democracy is the primary source of ethical value. With these concepts in mind, T'ao set out to create the vast literate public which alone, he thought, could provide an adequate basis for a democratic China. T'ao's "instrument" was the mass education move-ment—actually a mass literacy project, which was designed to achieve maximum results in the shortest time and thus was centered in the cities. Evening schools were opened, as were "people's reading circles," which consisted simply of any social unit—home, shop, factory, inn, temple—in which the literate could teach the illiterate. In addition, T'ao initiated the "each one teach one" movement, by which each newly literate person undertook to teach at least one illiterate, and he also founded numer-ous centers where itinerant workers, ricksha pullers, and the like could seek instruction.

The mass education movement continued to grow until 1927, and T'ao continued to exhibit that single-minded enthusiasm and energy which Chiang Monlin described as his "mis-sionary spirit." To identify himself with the common people, T'ao wore a plain cotton jacket, a pair of cotton trousers, and a skull-cap. As his colleagues frequently commented, T'ao was one of the "most thoroughly Chinese" of the students who had returned from studying abroad. By March 1927 the mass education movement had proved an unqualified success, but it also had come to be regarded as dangerous by conservative Kuomintang officials and local warlords, especially because T'ao's friends included many leftist writers and intellectuals. Under pressure from these leaders, T'ao took up a new project in March 1927. A month later, the mass education movement went into per-manent decline.

Having seen his efforts stifled in the cities, T'ao now turned to the country and rural education. In March 1927 he and Chao Shu-yü established an experimental teacher-training school at Hsiaochuang, a small village on the outskirts of Nanking. The Hsiaochuang shih-fan hsüeh-hsiao [Hsiaochuang normal school] began operations in the simplest of circumstances with 13 students and tents for shelter. The Hsiaochuang program emphasized teacher training and village renewal. It sought to teach through practice the techniques of running a village school and to immerse the trainees in rural life, transforming their outlook by having them join the peasants in manual labor. The teaching method was entirely learning-by-doing. In addition to serving as a pioneer venture in the training of rural teachers, Hsiaochuang was designed as a prototype of the kind of school that was intended to accom-plish village renewal throughout China. Because T'ao advocated the full gamut of life education and opposed learning exclusively from text books, he opened a new channel in Chinese education. To this end, he formulated such slogans as "life is education," "society is school," "unity of teaching, learning, and doing," and "action is the source of knowledge." By the end of 1927 the school and its principles had achieved popularity and imitation.

Like the mass education movement, the rural education movement continued to flourish until, in 1930, it came under suspicion. In the autumn of 1930 Hsiaochuang was closed by the National Government, and T'ao, who had reason to believe that he was about to be arrested, fled to Japan. About this time, T'ao changed his courtesy name from Chih-hsing [knowledge-action] to Hsing-chih [action-knowledge], possibly signifying that in the future he intended to be less of a cloistered scholar and more of a participant in events. In any case, it was as T'ao Hsing-chih that he subsequently was known.

T'ao returned to China in the spring of 1931. For the next four or five years he engaged in a variety of educational activities. He wrote stories and rhymes for children, compiled a children's science series, and started a children's science correspondence school. He also translated several Western literary works, but the manuscripts perished in the 28 January 1932 bombardment of the Commercial Press by the Japanese. The fire was not a total disaster, however, for it led T'ao to his next major project. Realizing the importance of uniting the Chinese people for their own protection, T'ao organized the Sheng-huo chiao-yü-she [life education association] and started a fortnightly magazine to propagate this idea.

Drawing on his experiences at Hsiaochuang, T'ao developed the concept of the "work-study unit," designed to help the masses support themselves through their own efforts, understand themselves and their lives through study, and protect themselves through their united strength. He established the first work-study unit at Shanghai on 1 October 1932, and within a year the number of students had grown from about 11 to more than 300. Other units soon were formed, and by 1934 the movement had spread to 21 provinces. An important aspect of work-study education was T'ao's initiation of the "little teacher" system, whereby school children became teachers to illiterate adults. As T'ao put it, "The school becomes a power house, and every child a wire reaching out from it to electrify the minds of the people." Accordingly, another association was founded by T'ao, which spread the "little teacher" system extensively among workers and villagers during 1933 and 1934.

By 1935, as the problem of Japan was becoming increasingly acute, T'ao's career began veering more markedly than before toward politics. To meet the national crisis, T'ao advocated what he called "national crisis education," a program of mass mobilization similar to his successful work-study program but geared to produce even quicker results. T'ao also organized an association to propagate the new theory and traveled widely on its behalf.

In the summer of 1936 T'ao was accredited as a delegate to the World New Education Conference in London, at which he reported on aspects of life education and the "little teacher" system. While in Europe, T'ao also functioned as the representative of the year-old National Salvation Association, an organization established to present China's case to the world. A year later, he returned to Europe as a delegate to the World Anti-Aggression Conference in London. On this mission he seems to have traveled with the Communist delegate Wu Yü-chang (q.v.), and together they visited the tomb of Marx.

T'ao was in the United States when he learned that fighting had broken out between China and Japan on 7 July 1937. T'ao rallied overseas Chinese across the United States to the national cause and appealed to the American people to support China in the war of resistance by not supplying Japanese with armaments. He is also said to have enlisted Chinese laundries across the country in the cause of national salvation by having them introduce pro-Chinese propaganda into the pockets of freshly laundered garments. From the United States T'ao went on to visit more than 20 other countries to enlist their support for China, returning home by way of Hong Kong in the autumn of 1938.

Upon his return to China, T'ao threw himself into the war of resistance with all of his customary energy. Having made his way to Kuomintang-controlled territory, he participated in the inauguration of a wartime education association and drafted a program for it. Wartime education was to be based on the principles of life education but adapted to the specific needs of the war, especially the need to preserve and mobilize the masses. At about the same time, T'ao established an emergency headquarters of the life education association at Kweilin and became its interim director general. In 1938 he was appointed to the People's Political Council at Chungking.

T'ao also set about to alleviate the conditions of the thousands of refugee children whom he had encountered on his journey into the interior. In June 1939 he established the Yü-ts'ai hsüeh-hsiao [talent development school] at Peip'ei near Chungking for gifted orphans. The students were divided into eight sections (music, drama, dancing, literature, painting, social science, natural science, and non-specialized) and were submitted to a curriculum which stressed life education. T'ao hoped that the school could become a model for nation-wide education, and, in spite of his other pressing activities and a chronic want of funds, he maintained it.

The school and the People's Political Council were T'ao's major concerns during the war, but with the defeat of Japan his attention focused on the struggle for democracy and the impending civil crisis. He joined the China Democratic League, became a member of its central standing committee, and took charge of two of its publications. For various reasons, the league soon was subjected to harassment, and in January 1946 T'ao was hailed before a court on charges of having incited Yü-ts'ai students to violence. The facts of the case, however, seemed to be that the Yü-ts'ai students, far from provoking violence, had been beaten by Kuomintang agents at a large rally held in Chungking on 10 January 1946 to celebrate the success of the Political Consultative Conference, which had just engineered a shaky truce between the Kuomintang and the Communists. Shortly thereafter, T'ao left Chungking for Shanghai, where he became occupied with the rehabilitation of schools and new educational activities. His most notable project was the She-hui ta-hsüeh [social university] established for and by working-class youths. The students even selected the trustees as well as the president. Life education at this juncture should have a social, and especially a political bias, T'ao thought; and the result, his theory of democratic education, was put into practice at She-hui ta-hsüeh and other schools.

By the middle of 1946 the civil war was again gathering momentum and urban unrest was increasing. In June 1946 T'ao took part in the huge public send-off from Shanghai of a delegation bound for Nanking to petition for peace. A month later, Li Kung-p'u and Wen I-to (q.v.), leaders of the China Democratic League,

were both assassinated. T'ao was much disturbed and stated: "I suggest that if one person is sacrificed for the cause of democracy, ten thousand should be ready to take his place." It was then rumored that T'ao's name now headed the blacklist, and T'ao momentarily expected the "third shot." In an effort to put his affairs in order before the blow fell, T'ao worked day and night despite his tendency to high blood pressure. The strain proved too great, however, and he died at Shanghai of a stroke on 25 July 1946, at the age of 55. Among the many expressions of regret over his passing was one sent from Yenan by Mao Tse-tung and Chu Teh (qq.v.), calling his death a great loss to the people of China. When his body was interred at the top of Mount Lao near Nanking, the old site of Hsiaochuang, no fewer than 53 organizations participated in the official funeral. In 1947 a memorial volume called *T'ao Hsing-chih hsien-sheng chi-nien-chi* was published by a commemoration committee. It contained almost 700 pages of eulogies by more than 100 contributors including John Leighton Stuart, Kuo Mo-jo, Cheng Chen-to, Mao Tun, Ma Yin-ch'u, and Shih Liang.

Coming from a peasant's family and familiar with the hardships of the masses, T'ao maintained an intense interest throughout his life in the lot of the common people of China. He wore their clothes and spoke their language. His vernacular poems, actually folksongs written in the common people's own language, forged a link with the masses. He produced ten volumes of such folksongs, didactic in purpose and dealing with philosophical, political, and educational subjects. Occasions such as birthdays, anniversaries, weddings, and funerals were all grist for his mill. In character T'ao was independent in thought, fearless in speech, and quick in action. He was more dedicated to the masses and the children than to his own family, more concerned about his friends than himself. Outwardly he appeared somewhat cold and quiet, but when he spoke, his thoughts and feelings vied for expression. He lived a very simple life, his only luxuries being peanuts and the theater.

As an author T'ao first won fame as a translator of John Dewey and other Western educators. In 1922 he published *Meng-lu-ti Chung-kuo chiao-yü t'ao-lun* [Paul H. Monroe on Chinese education] and in 1928 *Min-pen chu-i yü chiao-yü*, a Chinese version of Dewey's *Democracy and*

Education. As an original writer, T'ao contributed many articles on education to periodicals. In addition, he wrote a number of books, of which the following are notable: *P'ing-min ch'ien-tzu-k'o* [1000-character basic reader for the masses], of 1924, compiled with the assistance of Chu Ching-nung; *Chung-kuo chiao-yü kai-tsao* [China's education reform], of 1928; *Chih-hsing shu-hsin* [letters of T'ao Chih-hsing], of 1929; *Chiao-yü tso ho-i t'ao-lun* [essays on education in the service of national unity], of 1930; *Lao-shao t'ung ch'ien-tzu-k'o* [1000-character basic reader for young and old], of 1934; *Chung-kuo ta-chung chiao-yü wen-ti* [the question of mass education in China], of 1936; and *Yü-ts'ai hsüeh-hsiao shou-ts'e* [Yü-ts'ai school handbook], of 1944. Works published after his death include: *Hsing-chih shih-ko chi* [poems of T'ao Hsing-chih] and *T'ao Hsing-chih chiao-yü lun-wen hsüan-chi* [selected works of T'ao Hsing-chih on education], both of 1947; *T'ao Hsing-chih hsien-sheng i-chu* [posthumous works of T'ao Hsing-chih], of 1949; *Hsing-chih ko-ch'ü chi* [songs of T'ao Hsing-chih] and *Wei chih-shih chieh-chi* [the class of phoney intellectuals], both of 1950; and *P'u-chi hsien-tai sheng-huo chiao-yü chih lu* [the road to modern life education for all], of 1951. Books about T'ao include Mai Ch'ing's *T'ao Hsing-chih* and Tai Pei-t'ao's *T'ao Hsing-chih-ti sheng-p'ing chi ch'i hsüeh-shuo* [the life and thought of T'ao Hsing-chih], both of 1949; *T'ao Hsing-chih hsien-sheng ssu-chou-nien chi* [a memorial to T'ao Hsing-chih on the fourth anniversary of his death], published by the life education association, and Ho Kung-ch'ao's *Lu Hsün ho T'ao Hsing-chih-ti i-shih* [Lu Hsün and T'ao Hsing-chih], both of 1950; and P'an K'ai-p'ei's *T'ao Hsing-chih chiao-yü ssu-hsiang-ti p'i-p'an* [a critique of T'ao Hsing-chih's theories of education], of 1952.

T'ao was survived by his second wife, Wu Shu-ch'in, four sons, and numerous grandchildren. His first wife, whom he had married in 1914, died in 1936.

Te Wang: *see* DEMCHUKDONGGRUB.

Teng Chung-hsia   鄧 中 夏

Teng Chung-hsia (1897–1933), one of the earliest Communists in China and a leader of the effort to create a unified national labor movement. He is chiefly remembered as the author of the *Chung-kuo chih-kung yün-tung chien-shih* [short history of the Chinese labor movement]. He was executed by the Nationalist authorities.

Born into a prosperous family in Ichang, Hunan, Teng Chung-hsia received a traditional Chinese education. After being graduated from middle school, he went to north China to enroll at Peking University, where he studied Chinese literature. He thus was residing in China's intellectual capital at a time of great ferment. At Peking University he and his contemporary Chang Kuo-t'ao (q.v.) came under the influence of Li Ta-chao (q.v.), who was drawing student interest toward Marxism and toward the possibility of developing a Communist organization in China. The May Fourth Movement of 1919 heightened Teng's interest in these matters, and in 1920 he joined the newly established Ma-k'o-ssu hsüeh-shuo yen-chiu-hui [society for the study of Marxism]. At its meetings, he heard Li Ta-chao and other professors lecture on Marxism. The influence on Teng of these ideas was such that he severed relations with his family so that he would be able to devote himself unreservedly to the cause of revolution.

During the winter of 1920–21 Li Ta-chao organized a group of Peking University students, including Chang Kuo-t'ao and Teng Chung-hsia, and charged them with the mission of introducing Marxist ideas to the railroad workers of north China. Early in 1921 these young intellectuals went to Ch'anghsintien, where they organized a club and a night school for the laborers. They also began publishing a small newspaper, keeping in mind the relatively small vocabularies of most of the workers. Teng also attempted to organize workers in such other industrial and mining centers as Tientsin and T'angshan. In addition to these activities, T'eng found time to participate in the work of the Young China Association (Shao-nien Chung-kuo hsueh-hui), the society established by Li Ta-chao and Tseng Ch'i (q.v.) at Peking in 1918 and dedicated to "rejuvenating China with scientific spirit." At the time the First National Congress of the Chinese Communist party took place in Shanghai in July 1921, he was in Nanking attending the organizational conference of the Young China Association with

Chang Wen-t'ien, Yün Tai-ying (qq.v.), and others.

Chang Kuo-t'ao assumed responsibility for organizing the China Trade Union Secretariat (Chung-kuo lao-tung tsu-ho shu-chi-pu) in the summer of 1921, and Teng Chung-hsia joined him in the effort to create a unified national labor movement. In May 1922 the China Trade Union Secretariat sponsored the meeting at Canton which established the All-China Federation of Labor. Teng was elected to head the new organization's secretariat, which soon was moved to Peking because he also was serving as secretary of the Peking municipal committee of the Chinese Communist party. He led a strike at Ch'anghsintien in August 1922 and another at the mines of the Kailan Mining Administration in October. A general labor union of workers on the Peking–Hankow railroad was organized, and a strike was called in early February 1923 to mark the opening of the union office. Wu P'ei-fu (q.v.), who depended heavily on the rail line for both revenue and troop transport, took action against the strikers. His troops killed some 80 workers and Communist organizers in what became known as the 7 February Incident. Teng was forced to flee the area.

In the late spring of 1923 Teng Chung-hsia went to Shanghai, where he became one of the founders of Shanghai University. Although Yü Yu-jen (q.v.) was its nominal head, it was controlled by such Communist instructors as Teng, Ch'ü Ch'iu-pai (q.v.), and Yün Tai-ying, Teng also became dean of the middle school attached to the university. During this period, he wrote articles on the problems of "the Chinese revolution." In 1924 Teng left Shanghai University to participate directly in the Communist-led labor movement in the city. He was a member of the committee that led the strike of some 40,000 workers in the Japanese-owned textile mills at Shanghai in February 1925, and he was arrested after skirmishes between the striking workers and the concession police. Because he was disguised as a worker, however, his identity was not discovered, and he soon was released.

At the second National Labor Congress, held at Canton in May 1925, Teng Chung-hsia was elected to the executive committee of the All-China Federation of Labor. He was still in Canton when the May Thirtieth Incident occurred in Shanghai. In June, Teng joined with Su Chao-cheng (q.v.) and Yang Yin in leading the Canton–Hong Kong general strike. Teng was the Chinese Communist party's representative on the strike committee. His strategy was to concentrate the propaganda attack on the British and to encourage all non-British vessels to bypass Hong Kong and land their cargoes at Canton. The objective was to isolate the British colony while neutralizing the Chinese business community at Canton. Because no serious economic problems arose at Canton, this major anti-British strike lasted for more than a year. It finally was terminated because the National Government at Canton was anxious to concentrate its resources on preparations for the Northern Expedition.

Teng Chung-hsia probably remained at Canton to direct Communist labor activities in that area when Su Chao-cheng became minister of labor in the National Government at Wuhan. After the Kuomintang-Communist split in 1927, Teng attended the secret emergency conference at Kiukiang on 7 August that was chaired by Ch'ü Ch'iu-pai. Teng had opposed the cautious assessment of Communist activity in the labor field made by Ch'en Tu-hsiu (q.v.) after the 7 February 1923 debacle, and it thus was logical that he should be invited to participate in this meeting, which ended Ch'en's authority as the party's general secretary. Soon after the conference, Teng became secretary of the party's Kiangsu provincial committee. When Chang T'ai-lei (q.v.) was killed in the Canton Commune of December 1927, Teng, because of his previous experience in south China, was transferred to Canton as secretary of the party's Kwangtung provincial committee. He was arrested and imprisoned, but he was released after three months because the authorities failed to discover his identity. He then went to Hong Kong, where he worked with Yün Tai-ying in editing *Hung-ch'i-pao* [red flag].

In 1928 a number of Communist leaders from south China, including Su Chao-cheng, Teng Chung-hsia, and Teng Fa (q.v.), went to the Soviet Union. When the Sixth National Congress of the Chinese Communist party was held at Moscow that summer, Teng Chung-hsia was elected a delegate to the Sixth Congress of the Comintern and a delegate of the All-China Federation of Labor to the Fifth Congress of the Profintern. He was elected to the Profintern's executive committee.

Teng Chung-hsia returned to China in the summer of 1930 to become party representative in the western Hunan–Hupeh soviet area and political commissar of the Second Red Army, commanded by Ho Lung (q.v.). In 1932 he went to Shanghai to work in the Chinese Communist party underground, serving as director of the party's "mutual aid head-quarters," to assist party cadres in distress. While helping to organize anti-Japanese activities in Shanghai, Teng was arrested by the French concession police on 15 May 1933. He was extradited to Nanking, where he was executed by National Government authorities. He was survived by his wife and by at least one child.

A number of Teng Chung-hsia's polemical articles were published in *Chung-kuo ch'ing-nien* [China youth], edited by Yün Tai-ying, in the early 1920's. As early as 1923 he openly criticized Ch'en Tu-hsiu, then the dominant figure in the Chinese Communist party. Teng's *Chung-kuo chih-kung yün-tung chien-shih* [short history of the Chinese labor movement], written when he was in Moscow and published there in 1930, came to be regarded by the Chinese Communists as a classic work.

Teng Fa   鄧發

Teng Fa (1906–8 April 1946), Chinese Communist political worker and labor organizer. He was senior Communist official in Sinkiang in 1937–38 and head of the central party school in 1939–42. He also served at Yenan as chief of the workers' committee.

Yünfou, the native place of Teng Fa in Kwangtung, is just west of Canton in an area where seafaring vessels long have plied the lower reaches of the Pearl River. Teng, who was born into an obscure peasant family and who received no formal education, went to work on British ships owned and operated by Butterfield and Swire Company. By 1922 he had become a Western-style cook on river steamers operating between Canton and Hong Kong.

The Cantonese seamen's strike directed by Su Chao-cheng (q.v.) in 1922 made a strong impression on Teng Fa, who joined the Chinese Seamen's Union and became known to its leaders. When the major anti-British strike of 1925–26 in the Canton–Hong Kong area began, he was placed in charge of propaganda work for the strike committee headed by Su Chao-cheng. His performance won him entrance into the Whampoa Military Academy, where many volunteers from the ranks of the striking workers were rallying to the cause of nationalism and anti-imperialist revolution in south China. In the winter of 1925 Teng joined the Chinese Communist party.

When the Northern Expedition began in July 1926, Teng Fa remained in south China, where he was assigned to youth work and later, toward the end of 1927, to organizing laborers in the vegetable oil industry in Kwangtung. He participated in the Canton Commune of December 1927 (*see* Chang T'ai-lei), but received no special notice. After its suppression, he continued to work as a Communist labor organizer. He held various party posts in the Canton–Hong Kong area and gradually established himself as a reliable party worker. His name began to appear in *Hung-ch'i* [red flag], the organ of the party's Central Committee. The party rewarded him for his services in south China during this period of anti-Communist suppression by sending him to study in the Soviet Union in 1929. At Moscow, Teng had the opportunity to study Russian and to become familiar with the basic doctrines of Marxism-Leninism.

Teng Fa returned to China in the summer of 1930. At the enlarged third plenum of the sixth Central Committee of the Chinese Communist party in August-September 1930 at Lushan, Kiangsi, he was elected to the Central Committee. That autumn, he became secretary of the party's Fukien–Kwangtung–Kwangsi committee and chairman of its military subcommittee. From 1931 to 1934 he worked in the Communist-held areas of Kiangsi. When the central soviet government was established at Juichin in November 1931, he was elected to its executive council. About that time, he became chief of the Chinese Communist party's political security bureau, a position he retained throughout the Long March period in 1934–35.

After making the Long March, Teng Fa served as a political worker and organizer in northwest China. He was at Sian for a time before the Sian Incident of December 1936 (see Chang Hsueh-liang; Chiang Kai-shek). In 1937 after the outbreak of the Sino-Japanese war in July and the signature of the Sino-Soviet non-aggression pact in August, arrangements were made with Sheng Shih-ts'ai (q.v.) of Sinkiang to send a group of Chinese Communist cadres to that province. The Communist top command at Yenan assigned Teng Fa to duty in Sinkiang, with concurrent responsibilities as the Urumchi representative of the Eighth Route Army and of the party Central Committee. Teng served as the senior Chinese Communist official in Sinkiang until 1939, when he was replaced by Ch'en T'an-ch'iu (q.v.).

Teng returned to Yenan to become head of the central party school and chief of the party's workers committee. He thus was responsible for the publication of the *Chung-kuo kung-jen* [Chinese worker]. After leaving his school post about 1943, he worked to organize handicraft and industrial workers in the Communist-controlled areas in north China. In the spring of 1945 he headed the preparatory committee of the Communist-led Industrial Workers Association. Teng won membership in the party's Political Bureau during the war years, but for reasons that are not clear, he failed to be reelected to the Central Committee at the party's Seventh National Congress at Yenan in 1945.

In August 1945 Teng Fa went to Chungking as representative of labor unions in Communist areas to the China Association of Labor, headed by Chu Hsueh-fan (q.v.). Shortly thereafter, he and Chu went to Paris to attend the September–October organization meetings of the World Federation of Trade Unions (WFTU), at which they were elected to the new body's executive committee. After touring Western Europe, Teng returned to Chungking in January 1946 by way of Southeast Asia. On 8 April, he left Chungking on a plane bound for Yenan. The plane, apparently off course, crashed in northwestern Shansi, killing Teng Fa and such other prominent Communists as Ch'in Pang-hsien, Wang Jo-fei, and Yeh T'ing (qq.v.).

Teng Hsi-hou　　　　　鄧 錫 候
　T. Chin-k'ang　　　　晉 康

Teng Hsi-hou (1889–30 March 1964), Szechwanese militarist who in 1936 became the first

independent commander in that province to hand over his defense area to the National Government authorities. During the Sino-Japanese war he commanded the Fourth and the Twenty-second Group armies. He governed Szechwan in 1946–47. In 1949 he declared allegiance to the Chinese Communists.

Jungshan hsien, Szechwan, was the birthplace of Teng Hsi-hou. He received his education at the Szechwan Army Primary School, the Nanking Army Middle School, and the Paoting Military Academy. Upon graduation from Paoting in 1912, he returned to Szechwan to become a training officer under Liu Tsun-hou. He rose steadily in the Szechwan forces, becoming a regimental commander. In 1916 he participated in the campaign against Yuan Shih-k'ai which resulted in the declaration of Szechwan's independence. When Liu Tsun-hou became military governor of Szechwan in 1917, he elevated Teng to the rank of brigadier general and appointed him commissioner for purging the countryside. After Hsiung K'o-wu (q.v.) ousted Liu Tsun-hou and assumed office as military governor, Teng served with the forces of Liu Ch'eng-hsun. In 1920 he received command of the 6th Division, with the concurrent post of Shunking-Suiting garrison commander.

About 1921 Teng Hsi-hou took command of the 3rd Division. The following year, he joined with such leaders as Liu Ch'eng-hsun, Tan Mou-hsin, Lai Hsin-hui, T'ien Sung-yao, and Liu Pin in driving Yang Sen and Liu Hsiang (qq.v.) out of Szechwan. In February 1923, however, Teng came into conflict with Liu Ch'eng-hsun and aided the return of Liu Hsiang and Yang Sen to Szechwan. Ts'ao K'un (q.v.) appointed Teng civil governor of Szechwan in May 1924. He took part in an attempt to unseat Yang Sen as military rehabilitation comissioner in March 1925, but formed an alliance with Yuan Tsu-ming in February 1926 to support Yang's return to power. In May of that year Wu P'ei-fu (q.v.) appointed Yang Sen civil governor of Szechwan, with Teng as military governor and Yuan Tsu-ming as Szechwan–Kweichow defense commissioner.

At the end of 1926 Teng Hsi-hou, like Yang Sen, decided to declare allegiance to the Nationalists, and in 1927 they sided with Chiang Kai-shek against the Nationalist regime at Wuhan. After serving as commander of the

Twenty-eighth Army of the National Revolutionary Army, in late 1927 Teng became a member of the Military Affairs Commission at Nanking and commander in chief of the Seventh Route Army.

On 31 October 1928 the new National Government at Nanking appointed Teng Hsi-hou commissioner of civil affairs in the reorganized Szechwan provincial government headed by Liu Wen-hui (q.v.). He also became deputy chairman, under Liu Hsiang, of the Szechwan–Sikang military reorganization commission. He assumed these posts in the spring of 1929. In the autumn of 1932 he joined with Liu Hsiang and Yang Sen in a campaign to unseat Liu Wen-hui. By October 1933 Liu Wen-hui had been driven into Sikang. Liu Hsiang assumed office as governor of Szechwan in 1934. In 1935, when the Communist Long March forces threatened the stability of Szechwan, Liu Hsiang assumed the concurrent post of peace preservation commissioner, and Teng received command of the Forty-fifth Army and took the field as commander of the First Route of the Szechwan Bandit-Suppression Army. The following year, Teng became the first semi-independent Szechwanese militarist to hand over his defense area to the National Government authorities, thus aiding the National Government's effort to strengthen its influence in Szechwan. For this action, he received the rank of full general and the Cloud and Banner decoration. He also received command of the Sixth Route Army.

Soon after the Sino-Japanese war began in July 1937, Teng Hsi-hou's army was redesignated the Fourth Group Army and was sent to the Shansi front. It later was transferred to the Hsuchow-Haichow front, where it performed brilliantly in the battle at Tenghsien in March 1938. That month, Teng was appointed commander of the Twenty-second Group Army and pacification commissioner for Szechwan and Sikang. He held those posts for the rest of the war. In 1946 he was named acting governor of Szechwan, and he was confirmed as governor in May 1947. He assumed the office on 2 June, but was removed from it in April 1948 on charges of misappropriating funds. At that time he was appointed pacification commissioner for the Szechwan-Shensi-Kansu area.

As the Nationalists were preparing to abandon Szechwan, their last stronghold on the Chinese mainland, to the Chinese Communists in December 1949, Teng Hsi-hou and Liu Wen-hui declared allegiance to the Communists. Teng subsequently became a member of the Southwest Military and Administrative Committee. He later held such posts in the People's Republic of China as vice chairman of the Szechwan provincial government, central committee member of the Kuomintang Revolutionary Committee, delegate to the National People's Congress, and member of the National Defense Council. He died at Chengtu on 30 March 1964, at the age of 75.

Teng Hsiao-p'ing 鄧小平

Teng Hsiao-p'ing (c.1902–), Chinese Communist political officer who rose to become the chief executive officer of the Chinese Communist party, a vice premier in the Central People's Government, and a vice chairman of the National Defense Council. In 1966 he became one of the prime targets of Red Guard criticism in the so-called Cultural Revolution.

Little is known about Teng Hsiao-p'ing's family background or early years except that his native place was Chiating (Loshan), Szechwan. He probably attended one of the new middle schools established at Chiating after the abolition of the imperial examination system in 1905. Although the 1911 revolution had little if any impact on Teng's political consciousness, the May Fourth Movement of 1919 evidently did, for he joined the work-study movement (for details, *see* Li Shih-tseng). After attending classes at a special preparatory school in Chengtu, he went to Shanghai and thence to Europe early in 1920. There is no record of Teng's having attended classes at any school or university in France; nor is it clear what type of work he did there. Throughout the five years he spent in Europe he remained an obscure figure in the Chinese student politics of the day. From 1920 to 1925 he apparently was in Paris, where he learned French and joined the French branch of the Chinese Communist party. His only known political activity in Paris was producing the mimeographed Chinese Communist party weekly *Ch'ih-kuang* [red light], a task which earned him the title "doctor of mimeograph-ing."

After leaving France in 1925, Teng Hsiao-p'ing went to the Soviet Union, where he re-portedly spent several months attending classes at Sun Yat-sen University in Moscow. He may have returned to China in August 1926 in the company of Feng Yü-hsiang (q.v.). In any event, by late 1926 Teng had become a political instructor at the military school that Feng had established at Sanyuan, Shensi. Beginning in 1927 Teng was associated with the Li Li-san (q.v.) group in the Chinese Com-munist party at Shanghai. In July 1929, how-ever, he was assigned to work in Kwangsi province, an inhospitable area because of its backwardness and because of the anti-Com-munist activities of Pai Ch'ung-hsi (q.v.). By year's end, Teng and other Communist organiz-ers had organized the Seventh Army of the Chinese Workers and Peasants Red Army, with headquarters at Paise (Poseh). During 1930 that unit, commanded by Chang Yün-yi with Teng Hsiao-p'ing as party representative, expanded its control in the mountainous districts of western Kwangsi. Working with Chuang tribal leaders in the infertile area along the Indo-China border southwest of Nanning, the Communists also succeeded in establishing a smaller soviet area on the right bank of the Yü River which provided the territorial base for the Eighth Red Army. Teng then returned to Shanghai to report on his progress. In the summer of 1930 he was ordered to return to Kwangsi to direct the transfer of the Communist forces there to Kiangsi, apparently in prepara-tion for a push on the Wuhan cities. By the time he arrived there in September, however, the Eighth Red Army had been destroyed by the Kwangsi authorities. Leaving a Chuang guer-rilla force behind, Teng and Chang Yün-yi made their way to the central soviet base area in Kiangsi. Beginning in 1932 Teng served as an official in the propaganda section of the general political department of the Communist military headquarters, editor of the army newspaper *Hung-hsing* [red star], and instructor at the Red Army Academy. He also held office as party secretary of Juichin hsien and, later, of Kiangsi. During the Kiangsi period he became associated with the Mao Tse-tung faction within the Chinese Communist party.

He remained with Mao throughout the Long March of 1934–35.

Upon arrival at Shensi in the autumn of 1935, Teng was made political commissar with the First Front Army troops of P'eng Te-huai. With the outbreak of the Sino-Japanese war and the reorganization of the Chinese Commu-nist forces in north China as the Eighth Route Army, Teng became political commissar in the 129th Division of Liu Po-ch'eng (q.v.). The 129th Division moved into Shansi in September 1937 and established a base in the T'aihang mountains north of Ch'angchih. This base, which provided the springboard for expansion southward into Honan and eastward into Shantung, gradually developed into what be-came known to the Communists as the Shansi-Hopei-Shantung-Honan Border Liberated Area. The major Communist achievement of the 1938–45 period was the phenomenally rapid expansion of a competing administrative system behind the Japanese lines which showed itself to be more effective, more responsive to popular opinion, and more concerned with basic reforms than was the National Government, then isolated in west China.

The role of Teng Hsiao-p'ing in this process of wartime expansion is unclear. All that is certain is that he was appointed to the Chinese Communist party's north China bureau in 1938, that he was made political commissar of the T'aihang military region in 1940, and that he was assigned to Yenan in 1943 to direct the general political department of the People's Revolutionary Military Council, then the top planning group in the Chinese Communist military establishment. At the Seventh National Congress of the Chinese Communist party in 1945, Teng was elected to the party's Central Committee for the first time. He spent the 1946–49 civil war period as political commissar to Liu Po-ch'eng. Beginning in November 1948 he also served as secretary of the new general front command established by the Communists in the Hwai-Hai area. The Hwai-Hai engage-ment, which began on 7 November, ended in overwhelming victory for the Communists and cleared the way for their advance on Nanking and Shanghai.

Teng Hsiao-p'ing served at Chungking from 1950 to 1952 as vice chairman (under Liu Po-ch'eng) of the Southwest Military and

Administrative Committee and secretary of the party's southwest bureau. In addition to his regional posts, he held membership in the Central People's Government Council and the People's Revolutionary Military Council. Teng was transferred to Peking in 1952 as a vice premier in the Central People's Government. In this post, he increasingly appeared as substitute spokesman for Chou En-lai when Chou was out of the country. From November 1952 to October 1954 Teng was a member of the State Planning Committee, and from September 1953 to June 1954 he also held office as minister of finance. He played an important role in the preparations for the 1954 reorganization of the central government, acting as secretary general of the Central Election Committee and serving on the committee charged with drafting the constitution and the national election law. At the time of the reorganization he was made a vice premier of the State Council and a vice chairman of the National Defense Council.

The most significant aspect of Teng Hsiao-p'ing's career in the middle and late 1950's was his emergence at the top level of command in the Chinese Communist party. In May 1954 he was identified for the first time as secretary general (mi-shu-chang) of the Central Committee of the Chinese Communist party. When a national conference of the party was convened in March 1955 to deal with problems of leadership, political discipline, and economic planning, Teng gained national notice by delivering a major speech on the "anti-party faction" of Kao Kang and Jao Shu-shih (qq.v.). The following month, Teng and Lin Pao were elected to the party's Political Bureau. At the party's Eighth National Congress, held in September 1956, Teng presented a report on the new party constitution and emerged fourth (after Mao Tse-tung, Liu Shao-ch'i, and Lin Po-ch'ü) in the Central Committee rankings. On 28 September 1956 Teng was chosen general secretary (tsung shu-chi) of the party's Central Committee. He also was reelected to the Political Bureau, ranking sixth—after Mao, Liu, Chou En-lai, Chu Teh and Ch'en Yun.

In addition to his responsibilities as the chief executive officer of the Chinese Communist party, Teng Hsiao-p'ing became increasingly prominent in the handling of Peking's day-to-day

relations with the international Communist movement. He met with virtually every major Communist leader who visited the People's Republic of China in the late 1950's and early 1960's, and he frequently journeyed to Moscow. In February 1956 he served as Chu Teh's deputy at the momentous Twentieth Congress of the Communist Party of the Soviet Union, and in November 1957 he accompanied Mao Tse-tung to Moscow for the fortieth anniversary celebrations of the Bolshevik Revolution. Three years later, he served as deputy leader of the Chinese delegation, headed by Liu Shao-ch'i, to the forty-third anniversary celebrations. On 14 November 1960, at a gathering in Moscow for leaders from 81 Communist parties, Teng called Nikita Khrushchev a liar and proclaimed that the Chinese Communist party was duty-bound to break ranks and develop a new line on international policy if the "present Soviet leadership" continued to stray from the high road of orthodox virtue. Sino-Soviet party relations continued to deteriorate in the early 1960's, and in July 1963 Teng flew to Moscow for talks with Mikhail A. Suslov. Although the meetings were fruitless, Teng was welcomed at the airport on his return to China by virtually all Peking's major leaders.

As the so-called Cultural Revolution began to take form early in 1966, Teng Hsiao-p'ing was singled out as a prime target of Red Guard criticism. In 1968 the *Jen-min jih-pao* [people's daily] officially termed him "the other biggest head taking the capitalist road." Like Liu Shao-ch'i, designated as the "biggest head" of Chinese revisionism, Teng was downgraded in the party hierarchy, not officially removed from his government and party posts.

Little is known about Teng Hsiao-p'ing's private life except that his wife's maiden name was Cho Lin.

Teng K'eng 鄧鏗
T. Chung-yuan 仲元

Teng K'eng (1885–23 March 1922), revolutionary leader in Kwangtung who later played a key role in the organizing and training of the Kwangtung Army. His assassination in 1922 marked the beginning of an open contest between Sun Yat-sen and Ch'en Chiung-ming for control of Kwangtung.

The second of six brothers in a merchant family, Teng K'eng was born in Meihsien, Kwangtung. His father, Teng Li-chuan, had inherited the family business at Tanshui, and it was there that Teng spent his childhood and received his early education. Through the influence of teachers and friends, he became an enthusiastic supporter of the anti-Manchu revolutionary movement. In 1905, at the age of 21 sui, he was admitted to the Chiang-pin hsueh-t'ang, a military officers training school at Canton. After graduation in 1906, he remained at the school as an assistant instructor. He held that post until 1908, when he was appointed dean of the Whampoa Military Primary School, newly established as part of the Ch'ing government's program of military reorganization. He made use of his new position to instill revolutionary ideas in the cadets, several of whom, such as Chang Fa-k'uei, Hsueh Yueh, Teng Yen-ta, and Yeh T'ing (qq.v.), later became prominent military leaders.

By 1910 Teng K'eng had become directly involved in the underground activities of the revolutionary T'ung-meng-hui in Kwangtung. Early that year he went secretly to Hong Kong to help in planning the unsuccessful New Army uprising in Canton led by Chao Sheng. He also took part in the famous Huang-hua-kang revolt of 27 April 1911, following which he fled with several of his comrades to Hong Kong. After the Wuchang revolt of 10 October 1911, Hu Han-min (q.v.) and other revolutionary leaders in Hong Kong planned an attack on Canton from four different routes. In accordance with this plan, Teng K'eng and Ch'en Chiung-ming (q.v.) were assigned to raise an army in the East River region of Kwangtung. Teng left for his family home at Tanshui, while Ch'en departed for his native Haifeng. Combining their forces to capture Waichow, they formed a single army, with Ch'en as its commander and Teng as chief of staff. At the same time, Teng reorganized four battalions of the imperial garrison which surrendered at Waichow to form a regiment under his personal command. With these forces, Ch'en and Teng marched to Canton, where the revolutionaries had already declared Kwangtung independent of the Manchu regime and had elected Hu Han-min provincial governor.

Ch'en Chiung-ming became acting governor of Kwangtung in December 1911, and Teng K'eng, as director of military affairs in the Kwangtung provincial government, reorganized and expanded the revolutionary military forces into two divisions. For a brief period in 1913 Teng also served as garrison commander and rehabilitation commissioner of Hainan Island. With the outbreak of the so-called second revolution (see Li Lieh-chün) against Yuan Shih-k'ai in the summer of 1913, the revolutionary forces in Kwangtung were routed by Yuan's supporter, Lung Chi-kuang (q.v.), and Teng fled to Hong Kong with other adherents of the defeated Kuomintang. Soon afterwards he went to Japan. During the next two years Teng was active in support of Sun Yat-sen's efforts to overthrow Yuan Shih-k'ai. In 1914 he returned secretly to Kwangtung, where, working with Chu Chih-hsin (q.v.) and other lieutenants of Sun, he sought to organize armed resistance to Lung Chi-kuang, but without success. He also traveled to Malaya with Chu Chih-hsin, Hsü Ch'ung-chih (q.v.), and others to seek support among the overseas Chinese for the Kuomintang and the anti-Yuan movement.

In 1916 Teng K'eng was again in Kwangtung where, from a base at Sheklung, he led several military forays against Lung Chi-kuang. After being defeated and forced again to find refuge in Hong Kong, he went to Japan and for a brief period took up the study of military and political science. In 1917 his father's death brought him back to Kwangtung where Sun Yat-sen, with the help of Lu Jung-t'ing (q.v.) and other Kwangsi military leaders, had established himself as head of a military government and had launched the so-called constitution protection movement against the Peiyang militarists and their allies in south China. However, since Kwangtung and the Canton military government were under the domination of the Kwangsi clique, Sun Yat-sen desired to organize an independent military force under his own control. In the winter of 1917 the civil governor, Chu Ch'ing-lan, placed some 20 battalions of his garrison troops at Sun's disposal. These were hastily organized under the command of Ch'en Chiung-ming to form the Yuan-Min Yuehchün [Kwangtung army to assist Fukien], in which Teng K'eng became Ch'en's chief of staff. In the spring of 1918 this force moved into eastern Kwangtung in preparation for an advance into the neighboring province of Fukien. By August, it had established its headquarters at Changchow (Lung-ch'i), west of the coastal port of Amoy.

During the next two years, while encamped at Changchow, Teng K'eng concentrated upon building up the Kwangtung Army into a seasoned fighting force. Selecting the most energetic and dedicated revolutionary youth from among these troops, he set up a model independent squad. After rigorous training under Teng's personal supervision, this squad was expanded into an independent company and then into an independent battalion. During this period, Teng made frequent trips to Shanghai to report to, and receive instructions from, Sun Yat-sen. In the summer of 1920 Sun decided that the time was opportune for the Kwangtung army to wrest control of Kwangtung from the Kwangsi militarists. Although Ch'en Chiung-ming was reluctant to leave Changchow, Teng K'eng and Hsü Ch'ung-chih persuaded him to comply with Sun's wishes. In August, the Kwangtung Army advanced into Kwangtung in three columns, with Ch'en commanding the center, Hsü the right flank, and Teng the left flank. The ill-disciplined and demoralized Kwangsi troops were soon defeated, and in October Teng's crack independent battalion spearheaded the Kwangtung Army's successful assault upon Canton.

In November 1920, with the return of Sun Yat-sen to Canton and the reestablishment of the military government, Ch'en Chiung-ming became governor of Kwangtung province, retaining his position as commander in chief of the Kwangtung Army. Teng K'eng, as Ch'en's chief of staff, reorganized several units of the Kwangtung Army into its 1st Division, of which he became commander. Its officers included Li Chi-shen, Ch'en Chi-t'ang, Ch'en Ming-shu, and Ts'ai T'ing-k'ai (qq.v.), as well as his former students Chang Fa-k'uei, Hsueh Yueh, and Teng Yen-ta. In the summer and autumn of 1921, units of the 1st Division played an important part in the Kwangtung Army's northern expedition against Lu Jung-t'ing's forces in western Kwangtung and Kwangsi. Teng himself, who remained behind in Canton to protect the army's rear, was successful in beating back an attack from northern Kwangtung by Shen Hung-ying, an ally of Lu Jung-t'ing.

With the occupation of the entire province of Kwangsi by the victorious forces of the Canton government, a disagreement arose between Ch'en Chiung-ming and Sun Yat-sen over the latter's decision to continue the northern expedition into Hunan and Kiangsi. As a result, a compromise was reached by which Sun took over personal command of the forces in Kwangsi, while Ch'en returned to Canton with the understanding that he would raise funds and secure supplies for the expeditionary forces in the north. However, once he reached Canton, Ch'en became increasingly uncooperative and began to work secretly to impede the progress of Sun's northern campaign.

Teng K'eng, because of his long association with Ch'en Chiung-ming and his strong personal loyalty to Sun, was appointed by Sun to serve as the chief liaison officer between the northern front and the rear in Canton, with the added responsibility of ensuring that military supplies from Canton reached the expeditionary forces. Caught in the middle of a widening rift between Sun and Ch'en, Teng endeavored to provide supplies for Sun's forces and at the same time to dissuade Ch'en from obstructing the northern campaign. However, Teng's efforts in support of Sun's military expedition irritated Ch'en and his followers, and during the winter of 1921–22 relations between the two men grew increasingly strained.

In March 1922 Teng K'eng went to Hong Kong with C. C. Wu (Wu Ch'ao-shu, q.v.), the vice minister of foreign affairs for the Canton government, to purchase arms for the northern expeditionary forces. He returned to Canton with Wu on 21 March. On arrival at the railway station in Canton, Teng was shot three times. In the ensuing confusion the assassin escaped. Teng died of his wounds on 23 March 1922, at the age of 38 sui. During his last moments, Teng was said to have described to Hu Han-min a heated quarrel he had recently had with Ch'en Chiung-ming over support for Sun Yat-sen and to have further stated that the assassin's face was familiar to him. On the basis of these statements, reports began to circulate that Ch'en was the man behind Teng's assassination. However, these reports were never proven, and Ch'en himself later denied with vehemence any connection with the death of his subordinate.

Teng K'eng was buried in the northern suburbs of Canton, not far from the grave of

Chu Chih-hsin, who before his death in 1920 had been one of Teng's closest and most respected associates. Following the defeat of Ch'en Chiung-ming in 1922, the Canton government erected a library on Kuanyin Hill dedicated to the memory of Teng K'eng.

Teng Tse-ju   鄧 澤 如

Teng Tse-ju (19 March 1869–14 December 1934), tin miner and supporter of Sun Yat-sen who was best known for his fund-raising activities in Southeast Asia on behalf of the Kuomintang.

A native of Hsinhui hsien, Kwangtung, Teng Tse-ju was born into a peasant family. Because he went to work at an early age to help support the family, he received very little schooling. As a young man in his early twenties, he migrated to Singapore, where he worked as a shop assistant. A few years later, he left the island colony for mainland Malaya to join the "tin rush." He became a fairly successful tin miner in the Kinta valley in the state of Perak.

It is not known precisely when Teng Tse-ju first became interested in anti-Manchu revolutionary activity. In December 1907 he became chief of the Malayan branch of the T'ung-meng-hui, and thereafter he quickly emerged as a strong leader and fund-raiser. To counter the effect of military failures in south China, Sun Yat-sen, Hu Han-min, and Wang Ching-wei (qq.v.) visited Singapore and Malaya in 1908. By this time, Teng Tse-ju had moved his home and business to Seremban in the state of Negri Sembilan. The T'ung-meng-hui leaders visited him there before going on to such cities as Kuala Lumpur, Ipoh, and Penang to raise funds and to boost morale through public lectures given by Hu and Wang.

In addition to his fund-raising activities, Teng Tse-ju now took up the task of providing shelter for revolutionaries who were forced to flee China because of their activities. Moreover, in 1909 the general branch of the T'ung-meng-hui for the British and Dutch colonies in Southeast Asia was moved from Singapore to Penang, and Sun Yat-sen entrusted Teng with the task of supervising its activities. At the time of the Wuchang revolt of October 1911 Teng launched a new fund-raising campaign. Sun Yat-sen passed through Penang and Singapore on his way back to China from Europe, and he met with Teng on board ship at Singapore on 16 December. After Sun became provisional president of the new republic, he sent a message to Teng asking for funds to be considered a subscription to state bonds for the republic. For once, Teng's task was easy—a Chinese millionaire in Kuala Lumpur pledged the entire amount. In February 1912, at Sun's request, Teng traveled to China with members of Sun's family who had been living in Penang. After visiting Nanking, Shanghai, and Hangchow, he spent several months in Kwangtung, where he investigated mining possibilities. On 24 July he returned to Malaya to resume his own mining operations.

Early in 1913 Hu Han-min, then the military governor of Kwangtung, summoned Teng Tse-ju to China. When Teng arrived at Canton, Hu tried to persuade him to develop tin mining in the province and to serve as general manager of the provincial bank. Teng expressed interest in the mining part of the proposition and proceeded to tour areas alleged to have mineral deposits. In June, he agreed to head a mining enterprise which would be financed by the Kwangtung branch of the Kuomintang. Before arrangements could be made to establish this enterprise, however, Yuan Shih-k'ai appointed Ch'en Chiung-ming (q.v.) to succeed Hu Han-min as military governor of Kwangtung. Before relinquishing his post, Hu created an office to liquidate the Kuomintang's financial obligations to overseas Chinese and placed Teng in charge of it. Because the funds for this office and its activities came from the provincial treasury, a number of Kwangtung leaders objected to it. Ch'en Chiung-ming finally yielded to them, and the office was closed. When Ch'en was forced out of Kwangtung by Lung Chi-kuang (q.v.) during the so-called second revolution, Teng Tse-ju returned to Malaya. From September 1914 to November 1916 he served as chief of the finance department in the reorganized Kuomintang. He raised funds for the anti-Yuan movement in 1914–15 and for the so-called constitution protection movement in 1917.

When Teng reached the age of 50 sui in 1918, his Kuomintang colleagues honored him. Hu Han-min composed a congratulatory message; Liao Ch'ung-k'ai wrote it; and such leaders as Wang Ching-wei, Ch'en Chiung-ming, Chü

Cheng, Lin Sen, Hsü Ch'ien, Hsü Ch'ung-chih, Teng K'eng, Tai Chi-t'ao, and Chu Chih-hsin signed it. Sun Yat-sen sent him a tablet on which he had inscribed the characters meaning "long life for the benevolent."

In 1921 Teng Tse-ju went to Kwangtung, where he served for a time as provincial salt commissioner. He also helped develop tin mines in Kwangsi. At the time of Ch'en Chiung-ming's revolt against Sun Yat-sen in June 1922, Teng escaped to Hong Kong. He immediately set to work raising funds to meet this emergency. Sun, then in Shanghai, appointed Teng head of the Kwangtung branch headquarters of the Kuomintang. A special office was established at Hong Kong to plan action against Ch'en Chiung-ming. Hu Han-min was the nominal head of this office, which was composed of a liaison section headed by Ku Ying-fen (q.v.), a military affairs section headed by Lin Chih-mien, and a finance section headed by Teng Tse-ju. In October, Sun appointed Teng his special finance commissioner at Hong Kong. With Sun's return to power in February 1923, Teng became minister of reconstruction in the Canton government.

In the autumn of 1923 Sun Yat-sen began to implement plans to reorganize the Kuomintang along Leninist lines. On 25 October, he appointed a nine-man provisional central executive committee, which included Teng Tse-ju, Lin Sen, Liao Chung-k'ai, and the Communist T'an P'ing-shan (q.v.). Its task was to carry out the party reorganization. To the surprise of everyone, Teng, who hitherto had never expressed any political opinion other than complete support of Sun Yat-sen, began to speak out against cooperation with the Communists. Nevertheless, the reorganization of the Kuomintang proceeded according to plan. At the First National Congress of the Kuomintang in January 1924, Teng was elected a full member of the Central Supervisory Committee along with Chang Chi, Hsieh Ch'ih, Li Shih-tseng, and Wu Chih-hui (qq.v.). On 16 June, Teng, Chang, and Hsieh sent a resolution to the Central Executive Committee impeaching the Chinese Communists, but it was rejected on 3 July. Four days later, the Central Executive Committee issued a directive calling on party members to dispel misunderstandings and reiterating the Kuomintang's requirement that all who joined it must submit themselves to party discipline. After Sun Yat-sen's death in March 1925, the Kuomintang decided to reorganize the Canton government. Teng Tse-ju took exception to the proceedings leading to that decision, and on 30 June he submitted, in the name of the Central Supervisory Committee, an impeachment of the Central Political Council and requested postponement of the reorganization. Despite his objections, the National Government was inaugurated at Canton on 1 July 1925. Although Teng did not participate in the activities of the so-called Western Hills faction of the Kuomintang, he reportedly gave financial support to this conservative group.

Teng Tse-ju was reelected to the Central Supervisory Committee at the Second National Congress of the Kuomintang in January 1926. After the Northern Expedition began and the Kuomintang split into factions, Teng gave his support to Chiang Kai-shek. On 9 April 1927 he joined with several other members of the Central Supervisory Committee in denouncing the left-Kuomintang government at Wuhan. This statement paved the way for the purge of radicals carried out by the Kuomintang at Shanghai on 12 April. Teng then joined the opposition government formed by Chiang Kai-shek at Nanking. When the Kuomintang at Nanking organized a party purge committee on 5 May, he became one of its seven members. At the time of Chiang Kai-shek's temporary retirement in August in the interests of party unity, Teng resigned his posts and took a trip to Japan with Ku Ying-fen. Soon after their return to China, the Canton Commune (*see* Chang T'ai-lei) took place. On 16 December the National Government asked Teng and Ku to investigate Wang Ching-wei's role in this incident. The report they submitted on 31 December 1927 was highly critical of Wang. Teng then returned to Canton, where he lived in virtual retirement even though he retained membership in the Central Supervisory Committee of the Kuomintang and the National Government Council. He appeared on the political scene again, however, in April 1931 when he joined Hsiao Fo-ch'eng, Ku Ying-fen, and Lin Sen in issuing a statement which called for the impeachment of Chiang Kai-shek for Chiang's action in placing Hu Han-min under house arrest. In May, a secessionist government was established at Canton by such political leaders as Sun Fo, Wang Ching-wei, and Eugene Ch'en. It lasted until September 1931, when the national emergency created by the Japanese attack on Mukden led to a settlement with Nanking. At this time, Teng Tse-ju received appointments as a standing committee member of the Southwest Executive Headquarters of the Kuomintang and the Southwest Political Council. He died at Canton on 19 December 1934.

Teng Tzu-hui　　　　鄧 子 恢

Teng Tzu-hui (c.1893–), early leader of the Communist movement in Fukien. He served as a political and liaison officer during the Sino-Japanese war and the war with the Nationalists. In 1949–52 he dominated the party's Central-South bureau. He then became director of the Central Committee's rural work department, and he held such posts at Peking as deputy director of the State Council.

Little is known about Teng Tzu-hui's family background or early years. Available sources state that he was born into a merchant family in Lungyen, Fukien; that he studied for a year in Japan after graduation from an army middle school about 1916; and that in 1925 he joined the Kuomintang and entered the Whampoa Military Academy. Teng's political career began when he joined the Chinese Communist party about 1926. He was assigned to work in his native province. By about 1928 he and such other Communists as Chang Ting-ch'eng had established a base in western Fukien with headquarters at Lungyen. He continued to work in this area for three more years, establishing a soviet government which encompassed eight hsien, with himself as its chairman. During this period, he and his associates established contact with Mao Tse-tung and Chu Teh (qq.v.), whose guerrilla forces were carving out a territorial base in southeastern Kiangsi. When the central soviet government was established at Juichin in November 1931, Teng became a member of its executive council and director of its finance department.

Teng Tzu-hui did not take part in the Long March of 1934–35. He remained behind in Kiangsi to continue guerrilla activities. By early 1935 Nationalist military pressure had

forced the Communist guerrillas to retreat from Kiangsi into Fukien. In February 1935 Teng's group was intercepted by Nationalist forces near Ch'angting. Ch'ü Ch'iu-pai (q.v.) and several others were captured, but Teng managed to escape. He later joined forces with Chang Ting-ch'eng, and they established a new Communist base in Fukien. Chang served as chairman of the Fukien soviet government, with Teng as vice chairman and director of the finance department and with T'an Chen-lin (q.v.) as vice chairman and director of the military department. In October 1936 the Communist guerrilla troops in Fukien were divided into two columns, with Teng Tzu-hui directing the 1st column.

When the Sino-Japanese war began in July 1937, the Communists in southwest Fukien renamed their forces the Anti-Japanese People's Volunteers and made informal arrangements with the Nationalist authorities in the province to suspend domestic hostilities. When the New Fourth Army was established in January 1938 to organize the scattered guerrilla troops in central and east China for anti-Japanese operations, Yeh T'ing (q.v.) designated Teng Tzu-hui's forces the 2nd column of the New Fourth Army. Some of these troops were moved to southern Anhwei and southern Kiangsu. After the so-called New Fourth Army Incident of January 1941 (see Yeh T'ing; Hsiang Ying), the remnants of the army were reorganized. Ch'en Yi became acting commander, with Liu Shao-ch'i (q.v.) as political commissar and Teng Tzu-hui as deputy director of the political department. The New Fourth Army was expanded gradually to include seven regular divisions, and Teng continued to serve as a senior political officer of these forces during the remaining years of the Sino-Japanese War. His achievements during this period were recognized at the Seventh National Congress of the Chinese Communist party in 1945, when he was elected to the Central Committee.

At war's end, Teng Tzu-hui played an important liaison role among the Communist military commanders who were responsible for the extension of Communist control after the Japanese surrender. In the autumn of 1946 he was appointed political commissar of the Communist forces in the Shansi-Hopei-Shantung-Honan Border Liberated Area, then commanded by Liu Po-ch'eng (q.v.). Teng also assumed responsibility for liaison between Ch'en Yi and Liu Po-ch'eng, in which capacity he helped coordinate Communist military movements in the rural areas north of the Yangtze in 1947–48. Late in 1948 the principal Communist forces on the mainland were redesignated: the units under P'eng Te-huai (q.v.) became the First Field Army; those under Liu Po-ch'eng, the Second Field Army; those under Ch'en Yi, the Third Field Army; and those under Lin Piao (q.v.), the Fourth Field Army. Lin Piao's troops moved from Manchuria into north China proper, occupied Tientsin and Peiping, and continued southward. At this point, Teng Tzu-hui was assigned to liaison duties between Liu Po-ch'eng and Lin Piao to ensure that the Second Field Army would provide maximum support to the Fourth Field Army in the drive along the Peiping-Hankow railway line to Wuhan. Teng Tzu-hui thus became a deputy political commissar in the Fourth Field Army.

When the Fourth Field Army continued its drive southward after occupying Hankow in mid-1949, Teng Tzu-hui remained behind to help guide the consolidation of Communist control in central China. For about three years (1949–52), he dominated the Chinese Communist party's Central-South bureau. Lin Piao and Lo Jung-huan (q.v.), though senior to Teng in the regional hierarchy, were absent from Wuhan for most of this period. Teng also served as a vice chairman of the Central-South Military and Administrative Committee, in which capacity he produced long and authoritative policy statements on economic and political affairs. At the national level, he was a member of the Central People's Government Council and the People's Revolutionary Military Council.

Teng Tzu-hui moved to Peking late in 1952 to become a vice chairman of the financial-economic committee of the Government Administration Council and a vice chairman of the State Planning Commission. In 1952 he was made director of the rural work department of the party Central Committee. With the reorganization of the Central People's Government in 1954, he became a vice premier of the State Council and director of that body's staff office in charge of agriculture and water conservation. In the spring of 1955 he made his first trip outside China as head of the Chinese delegation to the tenth anniversary celebrations of Hungary's Communist regime. He was appointed director

of the central famine relief committee in July 1957, and he became director of the State Council's office of agriculture and forestry in September 1959. Three years later, he was removed from the latter office to become deputy director of the State Council. In December 1964 Teng was elected to membership in the Standing Committee of the Chinese People's Political Consultative Conference. Throughout this period, he retained his position as head of the rural work department.

Teng Yen-ta   鄧 演 達
T. Tse-sheng   擇 生

Teng Yen-ta (1895–29 November 1931), director of the general political department of the National Revolutionary Army during the Northern Expedition. Beginning in 1927 he opposed Chiang Kai-shek's leadership, and in 1930 he organized the Provisional Action Committee of the Kuomintang, known as the Third Party. He was executed by the Nationalists as a traitor in 1931.

Huichou (Waichow), Kwangtung, was the birthplace of Teng Yen-ta. At the age of 12 sui he enrolled at the Whampoa Military Primary School in Canton, where such other future leaders as Hsueh Yueh and Yeh T'ing (qq.v.) also received their first military training. Teng was the youngest cadet in his class, but his prowess as a student soon brought him to the attention of the school's dean, Teng K'eng (q.v.).

In 1911, with the outbreak of the republican revolution, Teng Yen-ta interrupted his military studies to join the revolutionary forces of Yao Yü-p'ing. After the establishment of the republic in 1912, he returned to Canton to continue his military education. He entered the Kwangtung Short-Term Military School, from which he was graduated in 1914. After studying at the Second Military Preparatory School in Wuchang from 1914 to 1916, he spent the years from 1916 to 1919 at the Paoting Military Academy. In 1919 he was assigned to field duty as a junior officer in the Northwest Frontier Defense Army of Hsü Shu-cheng (q.v.).

By this time, Teng K'eng had risen to the position of chief of staff, under Ch'en Chiung-ming (q.v.), of the Kwangtung Army, which in 1918 had established its headquarters at

Changchow in southern Fukien. In 1920 Teng K'eng summoned his former pupil to Changchow and placed him in command of a unit there. Following the reoccupation of Canton by the Kwangtung Army in October 1920, Teng K'eng was made commander of the 1st Division of the reorganized Kwangtung Army, with Teng Yen-ta as a staff officer and commander of an infantry battalion.

Teng Yen-ta and his battalion were assigned in late 1921 to serve as a garrison unit guarding Sun Yat-sen's field headquarters at Kweilin. After the assassination of Teng K'eng at Canton in March 1922, the subsequent attempt of Ch'en Chiung-ming to gain sole control of the province, and the flight of Sun Yat-sen to Shanghai, Teng Yen-ta and such other officers as Chang Fa-k'uei and Ch'en Chi-t'ang (qq.v.) worked to preserve the integrity of the 1st Division as an effective military force in support of Sun Yat-sen against Ch'en Chiung-ming. In the winter of 1922, the 1st Division joined with armies from Yunnan and Kwangsi in driving Ch'en Chiung-ming out of Canton. During this period, Li Chi-shen (q.v.) became the commander of the 1st Division, and Teng Yen-ta was named commander of its 3rd Regiment.

Early in 1923 Sun Yat-sen returned to Canton, determined to reorganize the Kuomintang. Teng Yen-ta strongly supported the policies of collaboration with the Communists and establishment of a Kuomintang military training school. In January 1924 he was appointed by Sun to a seven-man preparatory committee for the projected military academy at Whampoa, and with the inauguration of the Whampoa Military Academy in May, he was named assistant director, under Li Chi-shen, of its training department. Teng thus played an important part in the academy's initial training programs, designed to imbue the cadets with patriotism and political discipline. Although his energy and enthusiasm for the revolutionary cause made him a popular figure among the Whampoa cadets, he incurred the enmity of such leaders as Wang Po-ling, head of the academy's department of instruction. In late 1924 or early 1925 Teng suddenly resigned his posts and went to Germany.

In Berlin, Teng Yen-ta became acquainted with Chu Teh (q.v.) and with Kao Yü-han and other Chinese Communists there who held regular meetings to study and discuss the doc-trines of Marxism. He returned to China, by way of the Soviet Union, in time to attend the Second National Congress of the Kuomintang in January 1926, at which he was elected to alternate membership in the Central Executive Committee. At Chiang Kai-shek's request, he returned to Whampoa to serve as dean of the academy. During Chiang's 20 March coup at Canton, however, he was arrested along with a number of Chinese Communist representatives. He was released soon afterwards and was transferred to Ch'aochou in Kwangtung, where he was placed in charge of the local branch of the party military school.

Within a few months, however, Teng was recalled to Canton to assume the most important position of his career: director of the general political department of the National Revolutionary Army. When the Northern Expedition was launched in the summer of 1926, Teng dispatched teams of propagandists in advance of the armies to mobilize the support of the peasants and to investigate peasant conditions as a preliminary step toward agrarian reforms in accordance with Sun Yat-sen's economic doctrine of equalization of land holdings. Teng demonstrated great skill in mass agitation and political organization, and he played a prominent part in the political warfare that contributed to the rapid succession of military victories won by the Northern Expedition in Hunan and Hupeh. With the assistance of Teruni, a Russian adviser attached to the general political department, Teng also acted as chief liaison officer between Chiang Kai-shek and his field commanders, especially T'ang Sheng-chih (q.v.), the commander of the Eighth Army. As the National Revolutionary Army advanced steadily against the opposing forces of Wu P'ei-fu (q.v.) in Hunan and Hupeh, Teng was virtually the deputy of Chiang Kai-shek in directing military operations, and during the siege of Wuchang, he personally supervised the assault upon the walls of the city. While the offensive against Wuchang was still under way, Chiang appointed Teng chairman of the Hupeh political affairs committee, sharing authority in that province with Ch'en Kung-po (q.v.). After the capture of Wuchang on 10 October, Chiang sent Teng a telegram urging the speedy establishment of the political administration of Hupeh province in consultation with T'ang Sheng-chih.

Up to the conclusion of the military campaigns in Hupeh late in 1926, it appears that close, even cordial, relations were maintained between Chiang Kai-shek and Teng Yen-ta. Teng was able to keep Chiang informed of the activities of T'ang Sheng-chih, who had become the most powerful Nationalist commander on the central front and whom Chiang suspected of independent political ambitions. Toward the end of 1926, however, relations between Chiang and Teng became more strained as growing tension arose between the Kuomintang leaders at Nanchang, headed by Chiang Kai-shek, and those members of the Kuomintang, including Teng Yen-ta, who had set up their headquarters at Wuhan.

Three initial points of disagreement between these two factions were collaboration with Communists, the location of the new capital, and the future military strategy of the Northern Expedition. Following the capture of Wuchang, Teng Yen-ta had flown to Canton to press for the immediate transfer of the Kuomintang Central Executive Committee to Wuhan. Teng was a member of the joint session, chaired by Hsü Ch'ien (q.v.), of the Central Executive Committee and the National Government Council, established on 13 December 1926 to function as a temporary government until the National Government and Kuomintang organs were transferred from Canton to Wuhan. However, after the party and government staff arrived at Nanchang on 31 December, Chiang Kai-shek decided that the temporary capital should be located at Nanchang. This political disagreement was heightened by conflict over the military strategy proposed by the party leaders at Nanchang. At a conference of military commanders held at Nanchang on 1 January 1927 Teng Yen-ta, speaking for the Wuhan leaders, vigorously opposed Chiang's plan to move the Nationalist forces against Nanking and Shanghai instead of pushing directly north toward Peking.

As the Nanchang-Wuhan controversy deepened during the early months of 1927, Teng Yen-ta emerged as one of the most influential leaders of the Kuomintang-Communist coalition at Wuhan. After the third plenary session of the Kuomintang's Central Executive Committee, held in Hankow on 10–17 March 1927, the left wing gained ascendancy over Chiang Kai-shek's faction. Teng, retaining his post as head of the general political department, was elected to full membership on the Central Executive Committee and was appointed head of the peasant department of the Kuomintang and a member of the presidium of the reconstituted Military Council. At the end of March, he also was named head of the new Wuhan branch of the Central Political-Military Academy.

As the split between Chiang Kai-shek and the Wuhan regime developed into an open test of strength, Chiang summoned an emergency meeting of the Kuomintang Central Supervisory Committee in Shanghai on 2 April, which decided to launch a "party purification movement" against the Communist and other left-wing leaders of the Kuomintang. Teng Yen-ta was singled out for criticism by Chiang, who, in a "proclamation closing the general political department," accused Teng of packing the department with men who wished to destroy the national revolution. In the following months, documents issued by the government established by Chiang at Nanking in April charged Teng with subverting the Wuhan regime under the Russian adviser Borodin's direction and referred to Teng as the leading exponent of Lenin's policy of armed insurrection by the workers and peasants.

Early in July 1927 the *Chung-yang jih-pao* [central daily news] at Wuhan carried an article by Teng Yen-ta in which he branded Chiang Kai-shek and Tai Chi-t'ao (q.v.) as traitors to Sun Yat-sen's Three People's Principles and called for a punitive expedition against Chiang and "all reactionary elements." By this time, however, many members of the Kuomintang left wing in Wuhan, then headed by Wang Ching-wei (q.v.), had begun to seek a *rapprochement* with the Nanking regime. One reason for this action was that Feng Yü-hsiang (q.v.), who held the balance of power in China, had decided to support Chiang. At an informal meeting of the presidium of the Military Council in Wuhan, it was decided to expel the Communists from the Kuomintang. Vigorously protesting this decision, Teng Yen-ta resigned immediately from his posts as head of the general political department and the peasant department. He publicly denounced the Wuhan leaders for compromising with Chiang Kai-shek and for distorting the Three People's Principles.

Throughout this period, Teng Yen-ta had supported Sun Yat-sen's policies of cooperation with the Soviet Union and the Chinese Communists. He had worked closely with his Russian adviser, Teruni, and many of his colleagues and protégés had been Communists. He appears to have adopted Communist techniques and policies of indoctrination and mass organization of peasants. Moreover, his political pronouncements of mid-1927—calling for social revolution against "exploiters and the ruling class" and urging the founding of a socialist state—revealed the influence on him of Marxism-Leninism. Despite his close connections with Communist personnel and doctrine, however, Teng Yen-ta's principal allegiance was to Sun Yat-sen's ideal of national revolution and the Three People's Principles. He regarded Chiang Kai-shek's policies as a betrayal of what he believed to be Sun's political and social ideals, but he also came to view with disfavor certain activities of the Communists at Wuhan. He came to suspect that the Communist policies of political agitation, which threatened to disrupt the vital economic life of the Wuhan cities, were determined less by the national interests of China than by the interests of the Comintern and the Soviet Union. Confronted with the open break between the Kuomintang and the Chinese Communist party, and the impending collapse of an independent left wing of the Kuomintang, Teng began to consider a new possibility: the creation of a third party which would integrate the economic and social ideals of the two existing major parties within the context of Sun Yat-sen's theories.

Teng Yen-ta left Wuhan in the early summer of 1927. Disguised as a laborer, he proceeded on foot along the Peking-Hankow rail line to Chengchow and then moved westward into Shensi. After reaching T'ungkuan, he joined the automobile caravan which was taking Borodin and other Soviet advisers back to Moscow. Teng arrived at Moscow on 15 August 1927. He was welcomed by delegates of the Third International, and on 17 August he was invited to lecture on the "Origins of the Recent Grave Situation in the Chinese Revolution." Teng stated that although the Chinese people welcomed the friendly assistance of the Third International, the Chinese revolution was an entirely Chinese affair and should not be shaped to serve the purposes of the Comintern. The Communist revolution, he argued, applied only to the capitalist nations of Western Europe. In China, a feudal, semi-colonial country, the revolution would be prolonged indefinitely unless the problems of agrarian reform were solved. These views found little favor with Stalin, and Teng secretly left the Soviet Union for Berlin after making a brief visit to the Caucasus.

Despite his disagreements with Nanking, Teng Yen-ta regarded himself as an orthodox member of the Kuomintang. On 1 November 1927 he issued a formal manifesto urging his colleagues in China to organize a provisional action committee of the Kuomintang to function as the legitimate heir to Sun Yat-sen's revolutionary mission and to expose the political heresies of the "spurious" Kuomintang organization at Nanking. In the summer of 1928 he made a trip to Spitsbergen and there turned to a more prosaic itinerary, embarking on a tour to study social and economic conditions in a variety of countries. Between 1928 and 1930 he visited Scandinavia, England, France, Austria, and Italy, as well as Poland, Lithuania and Hungary. In February 1930 he visited Bulgaria, and he later reported that the period he spent there was the happiest of his European sojourn. He considered Bulgaria a worthy model for the future development of China and urged Chinese students to spend time there. After visiting Turkey, Iraq, and India, he arrived at Shanghai in May 1930.

Teng Yen-ta immediately began to work with the so-called Kuomintang provisional central action committee, which had been established at Shanghai in 1928 by a small group of Teng's former associates at Shanghai. Although the affairs of this group had been managed by Chi Fang and others at Shanghai, Teng Yen-ta had been considered its leader since its inception. After T'an P'ing-shan (q.v.) and other former Communists had attempted to reorganize the group into a new party, some of Teng's followers had sent telegrams to Germany urging him to return to China and assume personal direction of the movement. Upon his return to China in 1930, Teng reorganized his forces and drafted a new political program. An organizational conference on 1 September adopted the program, elected a 25-member central executive committee, and issued a manifesto announcing the formation of a new party called the Provisional Action Committee of the Kuomintang. Two weeks later, Teng issued a public statement accusing the Kuomintang at Nanking of betraying the people of China and of becoming the tool of the militarists, bureaucrats, landlords, and financiers. In the same document he criticized the Chinese Communist party for subservience to the Comintern, citing the Canton Commune of December 1927 and the attack on Changsha of July 1930 as instances in which the Chinese Communists had sacrificed the success of the Chinese revolution to the interests of the Soviet Union. He reiterated these charges in an introduction to the new party organ, *Ko-ming hsing-tung* [revolutionary action].

As the leader of the Third party, as the Provisional Action Committee generally was called, Teng Yen-ta devoted much of his time to writing political essays. The purpose of the Third party, according to Teng, was to carry forward the revolution begun by Sun Yat-sen so that it would become a truly national revolution. It should be a thoroughgoing social upheaval supported by all the "common citizens" [p'ing-min] of China, including the oppressed and exploited elements of the lower middle class. The goal of the revolution was the creation of a socialist state which, through a planned national economy and a policy of land nationalization, would strive to solve the agrarian problem. Although Teng shared some of these aims with the Chinese Communist party, he strongly opposed the concepts of class struggle and the dictatorship of the proletariat.

Because of his outspoken criticism of Chiang Kai-shek and his political activities, Teng Yen-ta incurred the bitter animosity of the Nationalist authorities in Nanking. In 1931 he further angered them by supporting the secessionist movement at Canton. On 17 August 1931 Teng was arrested in the International Settlement at Shanghai and was extradited to Nanking. After some months of imprisonment, he was tried by a military tribunal on charges of treason. On 29 November 1931 he was executed near Nanking.

Teng Yen-ta left a political legacy of essays and pronouncements which were collected by his followers and published in a memorial volume entitled *Teng Tse-sheng hsien-sheng chi-nien chi*. Chang Po-chün (q.v.) succeeded him as head

of the Third party, which in 1947 became the China Peasants and Workers Democratic party. It was one of the minor parties which participated in the establishment of the Central People's Government at Peking in the autumn of 1949. A special meeting to commemorate the "thirtieth anniversary of the murder" of Teng Yen-ta was held at Peking on the evening of 28 November 1961, with such notables as Chou En-lai and Soong Ch'ing-ling in attendence. Peking's official appraisal of Teng Yen-ta said: "A supporter of Dr. Sun Yat-sen's program of the bourgeois democratic revolution, Teng Yen-ta made certain contributions to the cause of the Chinese People's Revolution."

Teng Ying-ch'ao   鄧 頴 超

Teng Ying-ch'ao (1903–), wife of Chou En-lai (q.v.) and one of the few women to survive the Long March. She held important posts in the All-China Federation of Democratic Women and other Communist women's organizations. In 1956 she was elected to the Central Committee of the Chinese Communist party.

Hsinyang, Honan, was the birthplace of Teng Ying-ch'ao. Her father, an imperial army officer who had become magistrate of Hsingyang, died when she was very young. After his death, her mother was forced to find work as a teacher in order to support herself and her daughter. Teng received her education in Peking and Tientsin. In 1919, while a student at the First Girls Normal School of Tientsin, she became involved in the student political activities that characterized the May Fourth period. In September of that year, students from her school and from Nankai University established the Chueh-wu she [awakening society], which embraced humanitarianism, socialism, and anarchism and which dedicated itself to the belief that social progress should be based upon the self-awakening of the individual. One of the organizers of this society was Chou En-lai (q.v.), then a student at Nankai University. He and Teng worked together and spent some time in jail together in the winter of 1919.

After being graduated in 1920, Teng Ying-ch'ao taught school in Peking and Tientsin. She joined the Communist Youth League in

1924, and the following year she became a member of both the Chinese Communist party and the Kuomintang. By this time, Chou En-lai, who had gone to France on the work-study program (*see* Li Shih-tseng) in 1920, had returned to China to serve at Canton as a secretary of the Kwangtung provincial committee of the Chinese Communist party and deputy director of the political department of the Whampoa Military Academy. He and Teng were married in 1925. Teng held office in 1926 as secretary of the women's activities committee of the Chinese Communist party's Kwangtung-Kwangsi district committee. At the Second National Congress of the Kuomintang, held in 1926, she was elected to alternate membership in the Central Executive Committee.

Teng Ying-ch'ao spent 1927 in Wuhan, where she served under Ho Hsiang-ning (q.v.) as vice chairman of the Kuomintang women's department. In July, when Kuomintang leftists at Wuhan began to purge Communists in the areas under their control, Teng and other Communist leaders were forced into hiding. Nothing further is known of her activities until 1928, when she and Chou En-lai went to Moscow as delegates to the Sixth Congress of the Comintern. They also attended the Sixth National Congress of the Chinese Communist party, at which Teng was elected head of the party's women's activities department. After their return to China in 1929, Teng worked in Shanghai. She was elected to alternate membership in the Central Committee in January 1931. Because of increased police vigilance, it became almost impossible for the Chinese Communist central apparatus to operate in Shanghai. Accordingly, Teng and Chou left Shanghai in the spring of 1931 for the central soviet area in Kiangsi. Teng thus became one of the few women to make the Long March to Shensi in 1934–35. After doing some party work among women in northern Shensi, in 1937 she was forced to spend some time in a Peiping sanatorium because she had contracted tuberculosis. She was still in Peiping when the Sino-Japanese war broke out, but managed to get back to Shensi with the help of Edgar Snow, then a foreign correspondent in Peiping.

During the Sino-Japanese war Teng Ying-ch'ao spent most of her time in areas controlled by the Nationalists. In 1938 she became one of seven Communist representatives to the People's Political Council. She and Chou, who had become deputy director of the political department of the Military Affairs Commission, lived for a time at Hankow, the temporary seat of the National Government. When Hankow fell to the Japanese, they returned to Shensi. In September 1939 they went to Moscow, ostensibly because Chou required medical treatment, and remained there until March 1940. Soon after their return to China, they went to Chungking, the wartime capital of the National Government. While Chou served as Chinese Communist liaison officer and a member of the Supreme National Defense Council, Teng represented the Communist Eighth Route Army in Chungking. At war's end, they moved with the National Government to Nanking, where they remained until November 1946. Then, because Nationalist-Communist negotiations had broken down, they returned to Yenan.

Teng Ying-ch'ao served as vice chairman of the preparatory committee of the Liberated Areas Women's Federation until April 1949, when the Chinese Communists began to activate a powerful mass organization, the All-China Federation of Democratic Women. Teng became its first vice president. In December 1948 she gained new recognition in the field of Communist-sponsored women's activities by being elected to the board of directors of the International Federation of Democratic Women.

When the Central People's Government of the People's Republic of China was established in October 1949, Teng Ying-ch'ao was named to the political and legal affairs committee of the Government Administration Council and to the Standing Committee of the Chinese People's Political Consultative Conference. In 1950 she went to Warsaw as a delegate to the World Peace Congress. Beginning in 1951 she was vice chairman of the Chinese People's Committee for the Protection of Children. In 1953 she attended the Asian Peace Conference held at Peking in October. At the time of the governmental reorganization of 1954, she served on the committees charged with implementing the new marriage laws and with supervising the elections. In addition, she served as a delegate from Honan and a Standing Committee member of the National People's congresses. Teng was elected to full membership in the Central Committee at the Eighth National

Congress of the Chinese Communist party in September 1956.

T'ien Han
T.   Shou-ch'ang

田 漢
壽 昌

T'ien Han (13 March 1898–), playwright and pioneer of the modern theater movement in China and a founder of the Nan-kuo she (South China Society) and the League of Left-Wing Dramatists. He was also known for his film scenarios and song lyrics. During the Sino-Japanese war he revised and adapted the traditional Peking drama for modern production. In 1966 T'ien Han became a major target of criticism in the so-called Cultural Revolution.

Born into a peasant family in T'ien village, Changsha hsien, Hunan, T'ien Han received his early education at local schools. At the Changsha Normal School, which he entered in 1914, he performed in school productions and wrote plays, two of which were published in the literary magazine. After being graduated, he went to Japan to study at the Tokyo Higher Normal School where he remained until 1921; in this time his training as a teacher became less important to him than literature, the theater, and films—he saw all the foreign films that came to Tokyo while he was there. His stay in Japan coincided with the most active period of the Modern Dramatic Society of Kamiyama Sojin and Matsui Sumaku and with the rise of the art forum movement of Shimamura Hogetsu.

Among the Chinese students then in Japan were Kuo Mo-jo and Chang Tzu-p'ing (qq.v.), who decided in 1918 to join with Yü Ta-fu (q.v.) and Ch'eng Fang-wu in starting a new literary magazine. T'ien Han decided to join this group after talking with Kuo Mo-jo, who had been introduced to him by Tsung Pai-hua, the editor of the *Shih-shih hsin-pao* (*China Times*). In 1921 the members of this group went to Shanghai, where they founded the Creation Society (Ch'uang-tsao she). The first issue of the society's *Ch'uang-tsao chi-k'an* (Creation Quarterly) appeared in May 1922 and contained two plays by T'ien Han: *Chia-fei tien chih yeh* [a night at a tea house] and *Wu-fan chih ch'ien* [before lunch]. The publication of these plays

won him widespread recognition as a talented playwright.

In 1925 T'ien Han quarreled with Ch'eng Fang-wu, left the Creation Society, and became a professor at the Shanghai i-shu ta-hsueh (Shanghai College of Fine Arts), which he made his base for plays and the film projects that he began in 1926. The Hsin shao-nien ying-p'ien kung-ssu (New Youth Motion Picture Company) was the first organization to invite him to participate in its endeavors. In the latter part of 1926 T'ien Han organized the South China Film Drama Society, wrote its charter, and wrote and directed *To the People!*, the society's first film. In 1928, having resigned from the Shanghai College of Fine Arts because of a dispute with the principal, he founded the Nan-kuo i-shu hsueh-yuan (South China Academy of Fine Arts). The academy was forced to close six months later because it lacked funds. Nevertheless, it was important as the progenitor of the Nan-kuo she (South China Society), a dramatic club under T'ien Han's direction which became the center of a new theater movement. The South China Society enabled students to make some kind of living as actors while studying new dramatic methods. Performances were staged regularly in Shanghai, Nanking, and Canton. At first, the company's repertoire consisted of romantic French pieces and T'ien Han's new plays. Such works as *Su-chou yeh-hua* [night talk in Soochow] and *Nan-kuei* [return to the south] achieved great popularity. T'ien Han also served as editor of the society's publications. The bi-weekly *Nan-kuo pan-yueh-k'an* ceased publication after four issues; it was succeeded by a monthly magazine, *Le Midi yueh-k'an*. The South China Society was closed down in 1930 by the central party headquarters of the Kuomintang, which also banned *Le Midi yueh-k'an*.

During this period, T'ien Han wrote *Three Modern Women* and *Survival of the Nation* for the Lien-hua ying-p'ien kung-ssu (Lotus Motion Picture Company). In addition, he lectured on dramatic art at Chinan, Ta-hsia, and Futan universities, and he served as an editor at the Chung Hua Publishing Company, which issued the *Shao-nien Chung-kuo yueh-k'an* [young China monthly]. In 1930 he presided at a conference attended by members of the South China Society, the Creative Dramatic Society, and the Shanghai Art Drama Association which led to the formation of the League of Left-Wing Dramatists in 1931, the year in which T'ien Han joined the Chinese Communist party. Two plays staged by T'ien to emphasize contemporary social and political problems were *Hung-shui* [flood] and *Huo-chih t'iao-wu* [a dance of fire]. When war broke out in Shanghai in February 1932, the League of Left-Wing Dramatists conducted a propaganda campaign against the Japanese. It soon became too vocal for the National Government, which arrested a number of the league's leading members, including T'ien Han. Information about the date of T'ien's release is lacking, but it is known that by June 1932 he was free and writing for a new and influential literary monthly, the *Wen-hsueh yueh-pao*.

While working for the Lotus Motion Picture Company, T'ien Han collaborated on a number of film songs with the composer Nieh Erh (q.v.). Their first effort was "The Miners Song" for the film *Glorious Motherhood*. In 1934 they wrote and produced an opera, *Storm on the Yangtze*. The best-known product of this creative association was the song "March of the Volunteers," written for the film *Children of the Storm*. This song later became the national anthem of the People's Republic of China.

After the Sino-Japanese war began in July 1937, T'ien Han went to Kweilin, where he established a theatrical training school for children. In 1938 he joined the political training board of the Military Affairs Commission at Chungking. He held office as director of the cultural work committee of the third department until 1945, and he also served as head of the propaganda section of the Military Affairs Commission's general affairs department. During the war, he devoted much attention to revising and adapting the traditional Peking drama for modern production. He experimented with several plays, working to modernize stage techniques and make archaic dialogue intelligible to modern audiences without destroying the old forms or altering their basic style. He was strongly criticized by traditionalists, but he received the sympathetic cooperation of such actors as Mei Lan-feng (q.v.) and Chou Hsin-fang. His version of the *Pai-she chuan* [white snake legend] achieved great popularity, and he organized theatrical troupes which

presented this and other plays in the northwestern provinces. Of his several wartime film scenarios the most important was for *Victory March*, an episodic film about the war effort in northern Hunan.

At war's end T'ien Han returned to Shanghai, where he taught at the Municipal Experimental Drama School. He then moved to Hong Kong and remained there until December 1948, when he went to Manchuria to join the Chinese Communists. After the Central People's Government was established, he became a member of the national committee of the All-China Federation of Literary and Arts Circles and the Union of Chinese Writers, chairman of the Union of Chinese Dramatists, director of the drama improvement bureau of the ministry of culture, and a member of the culture education committee of the Government Administration Council. From 1951 to early 1958 he headed the art affairs bureau in the ministry of culture. He was a delegate from Szechwan to the First and Second National People's congresses, and at various times he served on the executive board of the Sino-Soviet Friendship Association, the China Peace Committee, and the Chinese People's Association for Cultural Relations with Foreign Countries.

A prolific playwright, T'ien Han began his literary career as a proponent of romanticism and moved through reformist realism to advocacy of class struggle. Throughout his career, however, he remained first and foremost a practical man of the theater. Among his greatest contributions to the modern Chinese theater were his encouragement of new teaching and training methods and his insistence on improving the technical aspects of Chinese stage production. His own plays reflect his careful attention to construction and detail. In the 1950's and early 1960's he continued to experiment with traditional Peking drama and Western stage techniques, and he wrote several costume plays based on historical figures. In 1966, however, he became a major target of criticism in the so-called Cultural Revolution.

T'ien Han married three times. His first wife, I Shu-yü (d.1923), was a dramatist. After a brief union with a Miss Lin, about whom nothing further is known, he married a Cantonese actress named Ah O in 1925. T'ien Han had one son, Hai-nan.

T'ien Keng-hsin   田 耕 莘

Religious. Thomas

T'ien Keng-hsin (24 October 1890–24 July 1967), the first Chinese to become a cardinal of the Roman Catholic Church.

The second son in a family of five children, T'ien Keng-hsin was born in Changch'iuchen, in the Yangku district of Shantung. His native place was a prosperous commercial center which was known for its uncommonly large variety of temples and shrines. Little is known about T'ien's mother except that her maiden name was Yang and that she came from Kochiachuang. His father, T'ien K'o-liang, the son of a prosperous merchant, was a sheng-yuan, a teaching scholar, and a poet. He supervised T'ien Keng-hsin's early training in the Chinese classics.

In 1896 T'ien K'o-liang began teaching Chinese at the Po-li-chuang Minor Seminary, a training center supported by Changch'iuchen's small Roman Catholic community. He was baptized in 1898, a year before his death. In 1901, at the age of 11, T'ien Keng-hsin was baptized, at which time he took the name of Thomas. The rest of the family converted to Roman Catholicism in later years. Beginning in 1904 T'ien studied in local Catholic seminaries for 12 years. He later characterized this educational experience as labored and considerably hampered by inept teaching and inadequate textbooks. Moreover, at its conclusion his ordination into the priesthood almost was sacrificed to the vagaries of illness and inner doubt. When tuberculosis caused him to be absent during the last critical months of his training, an unsympathetic bishop—possibly interpreting these lapses as signs of indecision as much as illness—threatened to deny him ordination. However, he finally entered the priesthood in June 1918.

From 1919 to 1929 Father T'ien served in seven different districts of the Shantung diocese. Local problems were compounded by dilemmas arising as a result of the First World War. At one point, all German priests were threatened with expulsion from Shantung and were assembled at a transfer center for evacuation, only to be returned to their posts at the urging of Chinese priests and parishioners. Foreign national interests were reflected in conflicts between French and German orders. Moreover, some foreign priests in Shantung tended to be contemptuous of Chinese priests. In two districts Father T'ien founded and administered schools. By appealing to Catholics in Shanghai, Hong Kong, and Southeast Asia, he raised about China $10,000, which enabled him to establish many training classes, to provide needy students with room and board, and to organize a variety of religious programs and organizations.

In March 1929 Father T'ien joined the Society of the Divine Word. After two years of special study and training, he took the final vows on 7 February 1931. Upon his return to pastoral work in August 1932, he was assigned to a missio dependens comprised of Yangku, Shou-chang, Ch'aoch'eng, Kuanhsien, and Fanhsien. It was designated an apostolic prefecture on 14 December 1932, and Father T'ien was appointed the apostolic prefect on 24 February 1933.

Father T'ien made his first journey outside China in February 1937, when he participated in the International Eucharistic Congress in Manila. The occasion for his second trip, in 1939, was a summons to be blessed personally by Pope Pius XII on the occasion of Father T'ien's appointment by the Curia Romana as apostolic vicar of Yangku. The Sino-Japanese war did not deter Father T'ien. He made his way through the Japanese lines to Shanghai and boarded a German liner bound for Europe, only to be turned back in mid-journey when war came to Europe. By changing ships, however, he finally reached Italy and the Vatican. He was consecrated a bishop by Pope Pius XII on 29 October 1939. After his return to China and three years of effective evangelism in Yangku, Bishop T'ien was appointed apostolic vicar of Tsingtao. On 24 December 1945 Pope Pius XII announced the appointment of Bishop T'ien to the college of cardinals, and on 18 February 1946 he became the first East Asian to be enthroned as a cardinal. China was designated a hierarchy of 20 sees on 11 April 1945, and Thomas Cardinal T'ien was named archbishop of Peiping.

Upon assuming his new duties on 29 June 1946, Cardinal T'ien promptly turned his attention to education. He urged young priests to undertake a period of university study and transformed a department at Fu-jen (Catholic) University in Peiping into St. Thomas College of Philosophy. He arranged for the schooling of young Catholic refugees, who swarmed into Peiping as the Communists advanced in north China. In the autumn of 1947 he founded the Keng-hsin Middle School, which was in fact a minor seminary. To improve the production and dissemination of Catholic literature, he established the Institutum St. Thomas as a publishing center and founded the Catholic Broadcasting Association. When an eye ailment forced him to seek medical treatment in Shanghai, Cardinal T'ien took what proved to be final leave of Peiping in June 1948. He went to the United States in the spring of 1949 and underwent medical treatment in Chicago. Before leaving China he was instrumental in sending ten young priests and more than twenty seminarians abroad to continue their studies.

Throughout the 1950's Cardinal T'ien lived in Chicago. In 1950 he made a trip to Rome for the issuing of the papal bull *Munificentissemus Deus*, which defined the dogma of the Assumption of the Virgin Mary. At the urging of the National Government in Taiwan, he paid a visit to Taiwan in September–November 1957. The following year, he took part in the papal elections. In December 1959 Pope John XXIII appointed him apostolic administrator of the Archdiocese of Taipei. Cardinal T'ien arrived in Taiwan in March 1960 to assume his new duties.

Cardinal T'ien made his last trip to Rome in 1962, when he participated in the Second Vatican Council and in the election of Pope Paul VI. On 24 July 1967 he died at St. Martin de Porres Hospital in Chiayi, Taiwan, at the age of 76.

Ting Fu-pao   丁 福 保
T. Chung-yu   仲 祐

Ting Fu-pao (4 August 1874–1952), prominent Shanghai physician who also made important scholarly contributions in the fields of Buddhism, traditional Chinese literature, and philology.

Wusih, Kiangsu, was the birthplace of Ting Fu-pao. His grandfather, Ting Wen-ping, a minor official at Haiyen, Chekiang, had been killed during the Taiping Rebellion. His eldest son, Ting Chieh-an, was Ting Fu-pao's father. Although the family owned more than 100 mou of land, Ting Chieh-an had to teach school to supplement the family income, for the district had not yet recovered from the ravages of the Taipings. Ting Fu-pao began school at the age of seven and received additional instruction from his elder brother, Ting Pao-shu, who also taught Wu Chih-hui (q.v.). At first Ting Fu-pao progressed slowly in his studies, for he found kite-flying in winter and fishing in summer more congenial than the Chinese classics. In 1889 he entered the local academy at Wusih, and in 1895 he transferred to the Nanching Academy in nearby Chiangyin, then headed by the celebrated scholar Wang Hsien-ch'ien (q.v.). Wang advised Ting to work intensively on the *Erh-ya*, *Shuo-wen chieh-tzu*, *Wen-hsüan*, and *Shui-ching-chu* and to collate all the annotations to each text. Ting compiled with his teacher's instructions, concentrating on the *Shuo-wen chieh-tzu* and thus laying the foundations for his later achievements as a compiler and editor.

Ting Fu-pao passed the sheng-yuan examinations in 1896, but failed the chü-jen examination the following year. His father died of consumption in September, and Ting decided to fulfill his filial obligation by making no further attempts at competitive examinations. In 1898 he returned to the Nanching Academy, specializing in mathematics under the authoritive guidance of Hua Heng-fang and Hua's younger brother Hua Shih-fang. He also taught at another school to supplement the family income. In 1899 Ting's sister died, also of consumption, and Ting found himself without funds. It was at this point, he asserted later, that he set about studying the chapter on wealthy merchants in the *Shih-chi* of Ssu-ma Ch'ien. In 1900 he produced his first work of scholarship, *Suan-hsueh shu-mu t'i-yao* [an annotated bibliography of mathematical books]. From 1900 to 1902 he studied medicine and chemistry in Soochow. He then entered the Tung-wen hsueh-she, which had been established by Sheng Hsuan-huai (q.v.). He became fluent in Japanese and in 1902 published the *Tung-wen-tien ta-wen* [questions and answers on Japanese], which proved so popular that an edition of 5,000 copies soon was exhausted. Later that year, he joined with Li Yuan-i and Hua Wen-ch'i in founding the Wen-ming Book

Company. Over the years this company published no fewer than 83 medical treatises translated and edited by Ting under the series title *I-hsueh ts'ung-shu* [the medical library].

In 1903 Ting Fu-pao went to Peking to teach mathematics and physiology at both Ching-shih ta-hsueh-t'ang [imperial university] and the I-hsueh-kuan [bureau of translation]. He returned to Wusih in 1906 and established the I-shu kung-hui [book translation company], which, however, failed within a year. Also in 1906 Ting published the first of a series of compilations, the *Han Wei Liu-ch'ao ming-chia chi* [collected writings of illustrious writers of the Han, Wei and Six Dynasties]. He went to Shanghai in 1908 to practice medicine, and in 1909 he passed a medical qualifying examination in Nanking. Later in 1909 he was sent to Japan by Tuan-fang (ECCP, II, 780–82), who wanted him to study Japanese medical schools and hospitals, and by Sheng Hsuan-huai, who sought information about the organization of orphanages. After a month's stay in Japan, Ting returned to Shanghai and established the Chung-hsi i-hsueh yen-chiu hui [Sino-Western medical research society]. The organization enjoyed the official sanction of the local government and maintained a membership of several hundred medical men. About this time, Ting also began to publish a medical journal, the *Chung-hsi i-hsueh pao* [Sino-Western medical bulletin].

From his medical practice, publishing ventures, and writings, Ting Fu-pao soon accumulated the wealth he had desired as a young man. In 1916, after recovering from a serious illness, he began to turn his attention to Buddhist studies. That year saw the publication of his continuation of the standard *Li-tai shih-hua* [discussions of poetry through the ages] under the title *Li-tai shih-hua hsü-pien,* and of the *Ch'üan Han San-kuo Chin Nan-pei-ch'ao shih* [collected poetry of the Han, Three Kingdoms, Chin, and Northern and Southern Dynasties periods]. He adopted a vegetarian diet in 1918 and assumed the status of a chü-shih, or lay monk. In 1921 he published the *Fo-hsueh ta-tz'u-tien* [dictionary of Buddhism], based on the *Bukkyō daijiten* of Mochizuki Shinkō. His preoccupation with Buddhism persisted until 1924, when his interest in compiling and editing revived.

In 1925 Ting completed and published his philological study of the *Wen-hsüan,* entitled *Wen-hsüan lei-ku* [philological notes on the *Wen-hsüan* categorically arranged], a rearrangement by stroke-order of the commentaries of Li Shan (658–718) and others. Two years later he produced his *Ch'ing shih-hua* [Ch'ing dynasty discussions of poetry]. These two works were dwarfed, however, by Ting's monumental *Shuo-wen chieh-tzu ku-lin* [collected glosses on the *Shuo-wen chieh-tzu*], published in 1932. Basically a compilation of photolithographed clippings from 182 separate works of commentary on the first great Chinese dictionary of Hsü Shen (c.100), the *Shuo-wen chieh-tzu ku-lin* was over three decades in the compilation. In the field of numismatics, which began to absorb his interest in the early 1930's, Ting produced the *Ku-ch'ien ta-tz'u-tien* [dictionary of ancient coinage] in 1938, with a supplement in 1939.

Ting Fu-pao died in 1952 at Shanghai. Four of his works, edited by his disciple Chou Yün-ch'ing, appeared after his death. These were the *Ssu-pu tsung-lu i-yao pien* [medicine and remedies in the classics] of 1955, *Ssu-pu tsung-lu t'ien-wen pien* [astronomy in the classics] of 1956, *Ssu-pu tsung-lu man-fa pien* [mathematics in the classics] of 1957, and *Ssu-pu tsung-lu i-shu pien* [the arts in the classics] of 1957.

Ting was also noted in his later years as a philanthropist. He made many donations of cash and books to public and private schools and libraries, particularly those in Wusih and Shanghai. Little is known about his personal life except that he married in 1897 and that his wife bore him seven children, five sons and two daughters. Ting's wife died in 1920.

Ting Hsi-lin   丁　西　林
T.   Sun-fu   巽　甫
H.   Hsieh-lin   燮　林
Pen. Hsi Lin   西　林

Ting Hsi-lin (1893–), director of the Academia Sinica's institute of physics. He was best known as a writer of theatrical comedies. After 1949 he held a number of important cultural posts in the People's Republic of China.

A native of T'aihsing, Kiangsu, Ting Hsi-lin traveled abroad as a young man and earned a

M.Sc. degree from the University of Birmingham in England. He then returned to China and embarked on an academic career, receiving appointments in 1928 as professor of physics at Peking University and as the director of the Academia Sinica's instutute of physics. He held these posts until 1945. Although he was a teacher-administrator rather than a scientist of outstanding achievement, he did achieve a certain professional recognition for his article, "A Proposed Method of Absolute Determination of 'g' by a New Pendulum," which appeared in 1930 in the first issue of the *Bulletin of the Research Institute of Physics, Academia Sinica*. In 1945, in company with Kuo Mo-jo (q.v.), he went briefly to Moscow for the anniversary celebrations of the Russian Academy of Sciences.

It was as a playwright and not as a scientist, however, that Ting Hsi-lin made a national reputation. In 1923 he completed his first work, *I-chih ma-feng* [a hornet]. Although not his best play, *I-chih ma-feng* is fairly typical of Ting Hsi-lin's style. It is a one-act comedy about the problems besetting an engaged couple. The action is swift, with many surprises and revelations; and the dialogue, the outstanding feature of all of Ting Hsi-lin's plays, is bright, pointed and witty. Ting Hsi-lin's output over the years was steady but small. In 1947 he published a collection of seven one-act plays entitled *Hsi-lin tu-mu chü-chi*. In addition to *I-chih ma-feng*, this collection contains *Ch'in-ai-ti chang-fu* [dear husband], a farce in which an ideal young bride turns out to be a man; *Chiu-hou* [after the wine], an adaptation of a story by Ling Shu-hua; *Pei-ching-ti k'ung-ch'i* [the air of Peking], which details the adventures of some small boys in Peking; *Hsia-le i-chih yen-ching* [blind in one eye], a conjugal comedy; *Ya-p'o* [oppression], another comedy of betrothal and perhaps Ting Hsi-lin's best-known play in the West; and *San-k'uai-ch'ien kuo-pi* [three dollars, please], a humorous account of a quarrel over nothing. Ting Hsi-lin had a true feeling for comedy and satire, but his plays were unpretentious and made a direct appeal to his audiences. His simplicity of style and lightness of touch made his plays particularly popular among school and college dramatic societies, and such pieces as *I-chih ma-feng*, *Ch'in-ai-ti chang-fu*, and *Pei-ching-ti k'ung-ch'i* were at one time staged in schools all over China.

Ting Hsi-lin occasionally attempted longer pieces, of which the best known is his four-act comedy *Miao-feng-shan*, of 1945. In this play, a university professor turned bandit, Wang Lao-hu (Tiger Wang), first is arrested, and then is released through the aid of a young girl, Miss Hua. Wang conducts her, his former captors, and his friends to remote Miao-feng-shan, in which district his gang operates. Under Miss Hua's influence, Tiger Wang softens, and the play ends with his marriage to Miss Hua and with the determination of Miss Hua and the others to remain at Miao-feng-shan and help Wang's band in the resistance to Japan. The play was clearly a "patriotic" work as called for by the prevailing literary doctrines of the time, but Ting Hsi-lin's dialogue and sure sense of comedy kept it from becoming a mere propaganda exercise.

After the Central People's Government was established in Peking in 1949, Ting Hsi-lin functioned in a number of high cultural posts. He served as vice minister of culture from 1949 to 1958. In 1954 he was appointed vice chairman of the Chinese People's Association for Cultural Relations with Foreign Countries, and in 1955 he became director of the Peking National Library. Ting Hsi-lin also led or participated in several cultural delegations to foreign countries. In 1951 he headed a cultural group on a tour of India and Burma; from December 1953 to February 1954 he served as head of a delegation to the India-China Friendship Conference. He was also the leader of cultural delegations sent to North Viet Nam in 1954 and to Cambodia in 1957. In 1955 he participated in the Asian Countries Conference at New Delhi, in 1958 in the Korean-Chinese Friendship Month festivities in North Korea, and in 1960 in the international commemoration of the fiftieth anniversary of Working Women's Day.

After 1949 Ting Hsi-lin seems not to have been productive either as a scientist or as a playwright, and most of his posts carried more prestige than power. As vice minister of culture he participated in the writing of *Han-tzu-ti cheng-li ho chien-hua* [the orderly arrangement and simplification of Chinese characters] in 1954. A collection of his plays, *Ting Hsi-lin chü-tso hsüan* appeared in 1955, and a smaller selection, entitled *Ya-p'o*, was published in 1963.

Ting Ling　　　　　　　　丁　玲
Orig. Chiang Wei-wen　　蔣　禕　文
Pen. Ting Ping-tzu　　　丁　冰　姿

Ting Ling (c.1902–), novelist and short story writer who gained fame during the 1920's. She was known for her vivid descriptions of rebellious youth. Her later career centered on the Chinese Communist party, which she joined in 1933. She was an early critic of Mao Tse-tung's decrees on art, but received a Stalin prize for literature in 1951. In 1957 she was expelled from the Chinese Communist party as a rightist.

The Chiang family into which Ting Ling was born was in many ways typical of the declining gentry of the late Ch'ing period. Ting Ling's father was a sheng-yuan degree holder who had studied political economy in Japan. He was a liberal and generous man, traits which Ting Ling inherited, but impractical in managing his affairs. As a result, when he died about 1911, Ting Ling, her younger brother, and her mother were left in somewhat straitened circumstances. Fortunately for the family, Ting Ling's mother, an intelligent and strong-willed women with a healthy physique and a cool disregard for the conventional reticences of widowhood, was able to cope with the immediate crisis by depositing Ting Ling and her younger brother with her family at Changteh. She then took a step which in its day was remarkable for both a widow and a woman of the "advanced" age of 30—she left for Changsha and the Provincial First Girls' Normal School to prepare herself for the teaching profession. Ting Ling's long and moving story, "Mu-ch'in" [mother], completed in 1933, retells the story of her mother's extraordinary courage and resourcefulness.

While her mother was at Changsha, Ting Ling was growing up at Changteh in the house of her cousins, the Yü's. When her mother returned several years later, she established two elementary schools in Changteh, one for boys and one for girls, and it was at the latter that Ting Ling started her formal education. It was also during this period that her younger brother died, a great blow to both her and her mother.

In 1917 Ting Ling was sent to the Provincial Second Girls' Normal School at Taoyuan, where she stayed for two years. Taoyuan was an important city, and "new ideas" such as the independence of women and the equality of the sexes, which were virtually unheard of in Changteh, were openly studied and debated. Ting Ling took to these liberating ideas passionately, and when, in 1919, the May Fourth Movement gave them coherent expression and a measure of public approval, she ran away from Taoyuan to a coeducational school at Changsha. Ting Ling's rebellion shocked even her liberal-minded mother and let to a rupture between them that lasted several years. At Changsha, Ting Ling was involved for two years with the work-study program. By 1921, however, even the provincial capital seemed stale; and so, with a close friend, Wang Chien-hung, Ting Ling at last made her way to China's greatest metropolis, Shanghai.

At this stage Ting Ling was still a student, and she probably still contemplated a career similar to her mother's. Accordingly, upon arrival at Shanghai she enrolled in the P'ing-min nü-hsiao [people's school for girls], which had been founded by Ch'en Tu-hsiu (q.v.). Ting Ling now led a wholly "emancipated" existence and seems to have spent little time on her school work. She studied her schoolfellows closely, however, as her subsequent writings demonstrate, and for a time became deeply absorbed with anarchism, which was then much in vogue among young intellectuals. For all these varied activities and interests, Ting Ling's first sojourn in Shanghai did not last long. After a few months she and her friend Wang Chien-hung left for Nanking, where the two led a carefree but impecunious existence. Ting Ling's wanderings finally terminated when she and her friend became reconciled with their families, and thereafter Ting Ling's mother provided her with a small allowance.

The summer of 1923 found Ting Ling and Wang Chien-hung once again in Shanghai and enrolled at Shanghai University, which had been recently founded by Yü Yu-jen (q.v.) and others. Ting Ling enrolled in the department of literature, but, as usual, spent most of her time in extracurricular affairs. She retained an interest in anarchism, but seems not to have been politically minded. She was described by a contemporary as a "romantic liberal" who valued freedom and individuality above all else and who showed a distaste for

Communist propaganda and agitation despite her friendship with some Communist party members. Shanghai University at this time was noted both for its left-wing faculty, which included Ch'ü Ch'iu-pai, Yün Tai-ying, Li Ta, and Teng Chung-hsia (qq.v.), and for the freedom with which faculty and students fraternized. Wang Chien-hung became the fiancée of Ch'ü Ch'iu-pai, and Ting Ling spent much time with Ch'ü's younger brother. However, in early 1924, when Wang and Ch'ü were married, Ting Ling left Shanghai for Peking.

In Peking Ting Ling determined to continue her education and enrolled in a school which prepared students for university entrance examinations. She also took private lessons in painting. It was as a student that Ting Ling in the spring of 1925 met Hu Yeh-p'in (q.v.), a young poet who had just been relieved as editor of *Min-chung wen-i* [popular literature], a not too thriving literary supplement. Ting Ling, according to her later reminiscences, was impressed immediately by Hu's courage, obstinacy, and optimism, all qualities which she regarded as essential in a man. Before long, the two set up a small household in the Western Hills outside Peking.

The couple was poor, but they had abundant leisure in which to read, write, and admire the beauty of nature. It was during this period that Ting Ling began her active literary career. Except for daily chores, she spent most of her time reading in their small library, which consisted of some volumes of Chinese poetry, a few translations of Western novels, and several works in English. The two books which she read and reread were Flaubert's *Madame Bovary* and Dumas' *La Dame aux camélias*. She also began to read Hu Yeh-p'in's manuscripts and to offer advice. According to Shen Ts'ung-wen (q.v.), even before Ting Ling herself was a published writer she exhibited keen perception in matters of literary criticism. In the meantime, however, Hu remained without prospects, and without some cash the Western Hills idyll could not continue indefinitely. Accordingly, Ting Ling attempted to find a job, first as a secretary, next as a primary school teacher, and finally as an actress in the Shanghai cinema, but none of these ventures proved successful. As a last resort, Ting Ling decided to try her hand at writing. By now she had read enough modern Chinese

literature and had met enough "new" writers to have a certain confidence in her own efforts.

The result was her first short story, "Meng-k'o," which utilized her own experiences in trying out in the movie business in Shanghai and which was published in the December 1927 issue of *Hsiao-shuo yüeh-pao* [short story magazine]. Encouraged by the editor of the magazine, Yeh Sheng-t'ao (q.v.), she wrote a second story, "Sha-fei nü-shih te jih-chi" [the diary of Miss Sophie] in which she depicted a willful and sensual girl dying of tuberculosis and explored with unexampled honesty the quickening of her physical appetites. *Tsai hei-an-chung* [in the darkness], Ting Ling's first collection of stories, was warmly greeted in 1928 by readers and critics alike. In addition to "Meng-k'o" and "Sha-fei nü-shih te jih-chi," the volume contained "Shu-chia-chung" [summer recess], a series of incidents in the lives of several young teachers who are obliged to choose between their careers and their destinies as women, and "A-mao ku-niang," the gloomy account of a young bride's dreams of luxury, disappointment, progressive apathy, and suicide. When first published, "Meng-k'o" and "Sha-fei nü-shih te jih-chi" earned Ting Ling 140 yüan. These stories, written in a fresh and spontaneous style, presented a new type of Chinese heroine—daring, passionate, and independent, gentle and essentially feminine, but bewildered and emotionally unsatisfied. Readers familiar with Ting Ling as a person could not fail to detect autobiographical elements in the fictitious characters of her highly successful early writing.

The time was propitious for Ting Ling's success. Hsieh Wan-ying (q.v.), recuperating from an illness, was lethargic. Yüan-chün had turned her interest to the study of traditional Chinese lyrics. And although Su Hsüeh-lin (q.v.) and Ch'en Hsüeh-chao still attracted a large number of female readers, their work was not to be compared with Ting Ling's, which had a more general appeal. There was no necessity to pioneer, since a ready market existed for works by women. But while Ting Ling became successful with her stories, Hu Yeh-p'in remained a frustrated poet. Disturbed by this situation, they moved to Shanghai in the spring of 1928, planning to start a magazine of their own in which Hu's work could be published. Together with Shen Ts'ung-wen, they started several unsuccessful ventures (for details, *see*

Hu Yeh-p'in). During this period Ting Ling compiled a second collection of stories, *I-ko jen te tan-sheng* [birth of an individual], published in 1929, and wrote a long story, "Wei-hu," published in September 1930. "Wei-hu" concerns a Bolshevik revolutionary who loves a non-Communist girl but eventually has to leave her because of the conflict between love and revolution. The hero, Wei-hu, apparently is a portrayal of Ch'ü Ch'iu-pai in 1923, and many characteristics of the heroine, Li-chia, are reminiscent of the girlish Ting Ling during the days spent in Nanking and Shanghai. It is uncertain, however, to what extent the fictional story is identifiable with life. In 1930 Ting Ling also published *I-ko nü-jen* [a woman], a collection of six stories on the theme of feminine fascination and coldness.

Because he needed money, Hu Yeh-p'in left for Tsinan in the spring of 1930 to take a teaching position, and Ting Ling joined him there a month later. In May, the two had to flee to Shanghai under threat of arrest, for Hu's teachings on proletarian literature had created a stir among his students. Hu soon joined the League of Left-wing Writers (*see* Chou Shu-jen), but Ting Ling did not take an immediate interest in the league's activities. She believed that a literary career demanded as much devotion as a revolutionary one. She was still trying to remain primarily a writer, although her sympathies were with the revolutionary efforts, as indicated in *I-chiu san-ling-nien ch'un Shang-hai* [Shanghai, spring 1930], a novelette in two parts written to illustrate how intellectuals discover the meaning of their lives in a mass movement.

In November 1930 Ting Ling gave birth to a boy, Hsiao-p'ing, also called Wei-hu after her short story of that name. About this time, Hu Yeh-p'in became a member of the Chinese Communist party and substituted underground party activities for his unsuccessful writing career. Ting Ling became active in the League of Left-wing Writers and served as secretary of the group, but she still entertained anarchist rather than Marxist sentiments. In the course of their dangerous work they seem to have relied too much on the semblance of security offered by the foreign concessions in Shanghai, and Hu especially had many narrow escapes. Finally, on 17 January 1931, Hu was arrested by the Nationalist authorities. Despite all the efforts of Ting Ling and Shen Ts'ung-wen, who

even went to seek the help of Shao Li-tzu and Ch'en Li-fu (qq.v.), Hu was executed on 7 February 1931. The desolate Ting Ling took her infant son to Hunan, left him in her mother's care, and returned to Shanghai. The bitterness resulting from Hu Yeh-p'in's death seemed to have led her to cross the borderline between literature and revolution, and a sense of revenge propelled her to serve the cause for which he had given his life. Now Ting Ling became active in the League of Left-wing Writers. Together with Hu Feng (q.v.), she edited the league-controlled magazines *Pei-tou* [the big dipper], *Wen-i hsin-wen* [literary news], and *Shih-tzu chieh-t'ou* [crossroads]. She became a member of the Chinese Communist party, probably in early 1933, reportedly through the introduction of Feng Hsüeh-feng, and she also wrote for party journals.

Ting Ling's conversion to Marxism was reflected in her writings. *Shui* [flood] may be taken as representative of her work during this period. Written in 1931, it was acclaimed by the Communists as a milestone in the development of Chinese proletarian literature. Both in intent and in technique, it may be regarded as a forerunner of socialist-realist fiction in China. Inspired by the flood situation in China in 1931, Ting Ling attempted in this story to show the impact of a flood on the political consciousness of a group of peasants, who, according to the author's contention, embodied the Marxian theme of group heroism.

In May 1933 Ting Ling's Communist activities led to her abduction by Kuomintang underground agents in Shanghai. Her abduction evoked protests from writers and intellectuals outside of China, thus becoming an international incident. Though her life was spared, she was imprisoned for a time, and she then lived on parole in Nanking for about three years. Meanwhile her whereabouts were a mystery and she was thought to be dead, a circumstance which resulted in the publication of collections of her works. Disguised as a Manchurian soldier, Ting Ling managed to escape to Peking and then to Sian, where she stayed for a short time before joining the Communists at Yenan at the end of 1936. She became friendly with Mao Tse-tung, who composed two poems in her honor, and became romantically involved with P'eng Te-huai (q.v.), to whom she reportedly was engaged just before the Sian Incident of

December 1936. She was appointed deputy director of the Red Army garrison and was given responsibility for political training. She also lectured on Chinese literature at the Red Army Academy, headed by Lin Piao (q.v.). In 1936 Ting Ling published *I-wai chi* [the unexpected], a collection of eight stories.

After the outbreak of the Sino-Japanese war, Ting Ling went to the front, first as a secretary attached to the Eighth Route Army, and later as a leader of the Northwestern Front Service Corps. Probably because of her political work, Ting Ling wrote little between 1937 and 1940. Stories written during this period, which include "I-k'o wei-ch'u-t'ang te ch'iang-tan" [an unfired bullet] of 1937 and "Hsin te shin-nien" [new confidence] of 1939, are pedantic and didactic, while a volume of plays on which she collaborated, *Hsi-pei chan-ti fu-wu-t'uan hsi-chü-chi* [northwestern front service corps plays] of 1938, is readable only as crude propaganda. And yet Ting Ling was not so dogmatic as to idealize the Communist fighters completely. In "Chi-ts'un chih yeh" [a night at Chi village], written shortly after Ting Ling reached the front in 1937, a guerrilla band is described emerging as a group of fallible men bound together by patriotic feeling and a sense of solidarity. Exhausted by her journeys and tours, Ting Ling returned to a village near Yenan in March 1941. However, on being informed that she was needed to edit the literary supplement of the forthcoming *Chieh-fang jih-pao* [liberation daily], she returned to Yenan where she worked closely with Po Ku (Ch'in Pang-hsien, q.v.), then editor in chief, and Ai Ssu-ch'i (q.v.). Ting was much taken with the personality of Po Ku, and she soon found herself reading his collection of translations of Russian literature and learning to appreciate Tolstoy and Andriev, the influence of whose novels was discernible in her later writings.

Despite her efforts to conform with Communist doctrine, Ting Ling was unable to restrain herself from expressing dissatisfaction with certain aspects of revolutionary life. In 1941, in a story called "Tsai i-yüan-chung" [in a hospital], she sadly described the bleak poverty of Yenan life, and on 9 March 1942, on the occasion of international woman's day, she lamented the fate of women under the Communist government in an editorial in the literary supplement of the *Chieh-fang jih-pao*. Following

her editorial there appeared in the same paper a series of critical articles by Ai Ch'ing, Hsiao Chün, Wang Shih-wei, and others. Mao Tse-tung immediately called a literary conference, at which he delivered the famous "Talks at the Yenan Forum on Art and Literature." Ting Ling was censured and secretly punished for her criticisms. As the war drew to a close in 1945 she was sent to Kalgan and then to Harbin in connection with propaganda and education activities, and in 1946 she published *Ying-hsiung-chuan* [stories of heroes].

Like most Chinese Communist novelists, Ting Ling turned her attention after the war to the peasants' struggle against the richer farmers. *T'ai-yang chao-tsai Sang-kan-ho-shang* [the sun shines over the Sangkan river], published in 1948, is a novel concerned with this subject. In preparing this work Ting Ling joined the land-reform corps in Chahar for the summer of 1946 and observed the land reform in Hopei for four months in 1947. This novel, which won a Stalin Prize in 1951, tells the story of peasants' struggles against the richer farmers in a village along the Sangkan River.

After the establishment of the People's Republic of China, Ting Ling held a number of official posts. She was a member of the committee on culture and education, director of the Central Research Institute of Literature, and member of the committee for world peace. In 1953 she was a member of the presidium of the Second All-China Congress of Democratic Women, an executive member of the All-China Federation of Democratic Women, and vice chairman of the All-China Association of Literary Workers. She was vice chairman of the executive committee of the Association of Chinese Writers and a delegate from Shantung province to the National People's Congress. In 1951 she was a delegate to the congress of the World Federation of Democratic Women in Budapest. In 1952 she went to Russia to receive the 1951 Stalin Prize for Literature. She was in Moscow again in 1954 to attend the second All-Russia Writers' Congress.

Although Ting Ling wrote little fiction after her successful novel of 1948, she continued to produce a number of books in her capacity as a leading writer and party member. These include *Fang-Su yin-hsiang* [impressions of a visit to the Soviet Union] and *Tsai ch'ien-chin-te tao-lu-shang* [on the progressive road], both of 1950;

Ou-hsing san-chi [miscellaneous notes on a trip to Europe], of 1952; *K'ua-tao hsin-te shih-tai lai* [onward to the new age], of 1953; *Tao ch'ün-chung ch'ü lo-hu* [abide with the masses], and *Yen-an-chi* [Yenan anthology], both of 1954; *Tso-chia t'an ch'uang-tso* [writers on writing], of 1955, in collaboration with Lao She (Shu Ch'ing-ch'un, q.v.) and Chou Li-po; and *Wu-nien chi-hua sung*, [songs of praise for the five-year plan], of 1956, in collaboration with many others. Her contribution to the latter work deserves special attention, because it contains one chance sentence which sheds much light on Ting Ling: "The five-year plan is too rich for my blood." Ting Ling even in 1956 was experiencing some difficulty in adjusting to the new society.

As early as 1955 Ting Ling was in political trouble once again. When she had been in Moscow at the end of 1954, the case against Hu Feng was already brewing. After Hu Feng's imprisonment, the so-called Ting Ling-Ch'en Ch'i-hsia clique became the target of a purge directed by Chou Yang (q.v.). In August and September 1955 Ting Ling was censured by the party nucleus of the Writers' Association for the alleged crimes of rejecting party guidance, fostering factionalism, and promoting capitalist-individualist thought. The case was not publicized, probably because of her prominence. However, after a long silence during which her "collaborators" freely confessed their "crimes" and Mao Tun publicly attacked her as retaining the ideology of "Miss Sophie," she was reported to have confessed her "errors."

Ting Ling was too outspoken a woman to remain quiet for long, and the slogans of the Hundred Flowers campaign were enticing to a discontented writer. During the campaign Ting Ling joined the chorus of dissidence in voicing the demand for freedom of literature from state control. When the Central People's Government reversed its policy in June 1957, Ting Ling became a prime target of party criticism. From June to September the party nucleus of the Writers' Association held 27 meetings to combat the so-called Ting-Ch'en clique, which also included Ch'en Ming, Ting Ling's husband since about 1942, and Feng Hsüeh-feng. As a result, Ting Ling was expelled from the party on January 1958 and was deprived of her rights as an author and a citizen on charges of conspiracy against the party during the Hundred Flowers campaign. She and her "clique" were accused of trying to exonerate themselves from the censure of 1955; of collaborating with Lo Lung-chi, Chang Po-chün (qq.v.), and other "rightists" of the Shanghai *Wen-hui-pao;* and of attempting to cause dissension by launching a magazine to rival the *Wen-i pao.* Ting Ling was also accused of fostering a petit-bourgeois mentality through her writing, and of posing as "a poor tenant-peasant in the literary field" (being oppressed), and in so doing, "setting fire" (inciting dissatisfaction) wherever she went.

In 1958 Ting Ling was reported to have been working as a charwoman in the Peking headquarters of the Writers' Association. According to an American journalist, she was in Manchuria in 1959 serving a two-year term of reform through labor. On 10 August 1960, a *Jen-min jih-pao* dispatch stated that she had written a letter to the Chinese Writers' Association promising to reform and to engage in self-criticism.

Ting Ling was a popular writer for a period of about 30 years. During this time a number of anthologies of her works appeared. These include *Ting Ling hsüan-chi* [selections from Ting Ling], edited by Yao P'eng-tzu in 1934; a second collection bearing the same title, edited by Hsü Ch'en-ssu and Yeh Wang-yu in 1935; *Ting Ling wen-chi* [Ting Ling's prose], edited in 1936 by Shao-hou (pseud.); a collection bearing the same title, published over 1948–49; another *Ting Ling hsüan-chi*, of 1951; and *Ting Ling tuan-p'ien hsiao-shuo chi* [Ting Ling's short stories], of 1954.

Ting, V. K. : *see* TING WEN-CHIANG.

Ting Wei-fen 丁 惟 汾
　　T. Ting-ch'eng 鼎 丞

Ting Wei-fen (6 November 1874–12 May 1954), founding member of the T'ung-meng-hui who directed revolutionary activities in Shantung. He later served as director of the Kuomintang's Peking office, director of the Kuomintang youth department, dean of the Central Political Institute, secretary general of the Central Executive Committee, and vice president of the Control Yuan. After 1937 he devoted his attention to the study of phonetics with reference to the Chinese classics.

The ancestors of Ting Wei-fen had been scholars and officials in Jihchao, Shantung, since the early Ming dynasty. His father, Ting I-tz'u, was a profound classical scholar and the author of the *Mao-shih cheng-yün* [classification of rhymes in Mao's edition of the *Book of Odes*]. The young Ting Wei-fen, however, proved to be more interested in contemporary political affairs than in the Chinese classics. After graduation from the Paoting Normal School, he went to Japan, where he enrolled at Meiji University. In Tokyo, he joined the T'ung-meng-hui and joined with other party members from Shantung in publishing the *Ch'en-chung chou-k'an* [morning bell weekly]. After returning to Shantung in 1908, he established a provincial T'ung-meng-hui headquarters and founded schools—the Shantung Academy in Tsinan, the Tung-mou Academy in Chefoo, and the Chen-tan Academy in Tsingtao—for the purpose of propagating revolutionary ideas.

At the time of the Wuchang revolt in October 1911, Ting Wei-fen went to Shanghai for consultations with Huang Hsing (q.v.). He later accompanied Hu Ying to Chefoo. They drove out the Manchu officials and installed Hu as tutuh [military governor] of Shantung. With the establishment of the Chinese republic in 1912, Ting became director of party organization in Shantung, a member of the provincial assembly, and the chancellor of the Shantung Provincial Law School. Late in 1912 he was elected to the National Assembly. At Peking he joined with such other Kuomintang members as Sung Chiao-jen (q.v.) in attempting to strengthen the democratic system.

At the time of the so-called second revolution (*see* Li Lieh-chün) in 1913, Ting Wei-fen returned to his native district. In 1915, when Yuan Shih-k'ai's plot to create a monarchy became apparent, Ting went to Shanghai and joined with other former members of the Parliament in condemning Yuan's actions and intentions. After the conference, he returned to Shantung, where he and Chü Cheng (q.v.) began preparations for a revolt against Yuan Shih-k'ai. Their forces captured Weihsien in May 1916 and moved on to other points along the Kiaochow-Tsinan railway. The hostilities ended with the death of Yuan Shih-k'ai in June 1916 and the restoration of Parliament under Li Yuan-hung (q.v.). Ting went to Peking to take his seat in the reconvened National Assembly. In 1917, however, the National Assembly's refusal to yield to Tuan Ch'i-jui (q.v.) on the question of China's entry into the First World War led to its dissolution and the seizure of power at Peking by Tuan and his adherents. Ting and other members of the Parliament then gathered at Canton for a so-called extraordinary congress called by Sun Yat-sen. This congress established a military government at Canton, with Sun as its commander in chief.

In the 1917–26 period Ting was active at various times in party and parliamentary affairs at both Canton and Peking. One of his major responsibilities was the propagation of Kuomintang principles in north China. Late in 1923, on orders from Sun Yat-sen, Ting established at Peking a north China executive office of the Kuomintang. At the First National Congress of the reorganized Kuomintang in January 1924, he was elected to the Central Executive Committee and was confirmed as director of the party's Peking office. He returned to Peking and remained there until the Northern Expedition was launched in mid-1926. At that time, he went to Canton to serve the Kuomintang as director of the youth department, member of the Central Executive Committee's standing committee, and member of the Central Political Council. He soon returned to Peking, however, because he believed that the very existence of the Kuomintang in north China was being threatened by its Communist membership. Li Ta-chao (q.v.) and his colleagues had a strong hold on the Kuomintang at Peking. To counterbalance the effects of Communist propaganda, he established an association, the Chung-shan-chu-i t'ung-meng-hui, which later became known as the Ta-t'ung-meng.

Ting Wei-fen supported Chiang Kai-shek in the 1927 split of the Kuomintang into factions at Wuhan and Nanking. Because he believed that to combat Communist influence it was necessary to have capable cadres with orthodox political understanding, in mid-1927 he proposed to the Central Executive Committee of the Kuomintang the establishment in Nanking of the Central Party Affairs School. It was inaugurated on 8 August 1927, with Chiang Kai-shek as president, Ch'en Kuo-fu (q.v.) as director of general affairs, and Ting as director of training. Because Ting then was devoting most of his time to the work of the Central Executive Committee, most of his school duties fell to Ku Cheng-kang, the deputy director of training. With the reorganization of the Central Political Institute in the summer of 1929, Ting was named its dean. He held the title until 1941, but the work of the deanship during that period fell to Lo Chia-lun, Ch'en Li-fu, and Ch'en Kuo-fu. From 1931 to 1934 he served as secretary general of the Kuomintang's Central Executive Committee, and from 1932 to 1937 he was vice president of the Control Yuan. It gradually became evident after 1928, however, that he was withdrawing from active participation in politics.

With Ting's withdrawal from public life came a wholehearted devotion to the study of phonetics with reference to the Chinese classics and their meanings. He completed six books in this field: *Mao-shih shih-yun* [the narrative on the rhymes in Mao's edition of the *Book of Odes*], *Mao-shih chieh-ku* [the interpretation of ancient words in Mao's edition of the *Book of Odes*], *Erh-ya ku-yin-piao* [the charts of ancient phonetics in *Erh-ya*], *Fang-yen-yeh* [the interpretation of Yang Hsiung's *Fang-yen*], and *Li-yü-cheng-ku* [rustic expressions as evidenced in ancient classics].

When the Chinese Communists won control of the mainland in 1949, Ting Wei-fen moved to Taiwan, where he was a member of the Control Yuan and of the Kuomintang's Central Appraisal Committee. He died at Taipei on 12 May 1954. Ting was survived by his wife (who died on 17 December 1959, at the age of 85 sui), and by three daughters and a son.

Ting Wen-chiang   丁 文 江
   T.   Tsai-chün   在 君
   Pen. Tsung-yen   **宗 淹**
   West. V. K. Ting

Ting Wen-chiang (13 April 1887–5 January 1936), known as V. K. Ting, professor of geology at Peking University (1931–34) and secretary general of the Academia Sinica (1934–36) who was best known for his achievements as founder and first director (1916–21) of the China Geological Survey.

Born into a gentry family in T'aihsing, Kiangsu, V. K. Ting received a traditional education in the Chinese classics. He came to the attention of the hsien magistrate, Lung Chang, who persuaded Ting's parents to allow their 15-year-old son to go to Japan in the company of the Hunanese scholar Hu Yuan-t'an (q.v.). In Tokyo, Ting met many other Chinese students who were interested in politics, and in the 18 months he spent in Japan he devoted his time to political pursuits and did not enroll at any school. One of Ting's student friends was in correspondence with Wu Chih-hui (q.v.), who was then in Edinburgh, Scotland. After Wu wrote that opportunities for education in Great Britain were superior to those in Japan, Ting persuaded his parents to allow him to go to Great Britain. He sailed for Europe in the spring of 1904.

After spending some time at Edinburgh studying English, V. K. Ting left Scotland for a preparatory school in England. In 1906 he attended classes at Cambridge University briefly, but found it too expensive. He then went to Glasgow, where he prepared to take the entrance examinations for the medical school of the University of London. After failing the examinations, he enrolled in 1908 at the University of Glasgow, where he majored in zoology and geology. He was graduated in 1911, by which time he had become a Social Darwinist and a scientific positivist.

During his seven years in Great Britain, Ting became an enthusiastic traveler and made several tours of Western Europe. Having decided that on his return to China he would travel through the interior provinces, he left England in the spring of 1911 and arrived in Indo-China early in May. Traveling on the newly completed Haiphong-Kunming railway, he entered China by way of Yunnan province and, proceeding through Kweichow and Hunan to Hankow, reached Shanghai and his native district late in July, less than three months before the outbreak of the revolution that ended Manchu rule in China.

After the establishment of the republic early in 1912, V. K. Ting spent a year in Shanghai teaching at the Nanyang Middle School. In February 1913 he went to Peking to serve as head of the geology section in the department of mining administration of the ministry of industry and commerce. In that capacity he took part in the first intensive geological investigation of southwest China, departing early in 1914 for Yunnan province by way of Hong Kong and Annam. In his extensive geological surveys in Yunnan, Kweichow, and parts of Szechwan, Ting paid close attention not only to the coal, tin, and copper resources but also to fossil remains and to the tribal customs of the non-Chinese peoples of the region.

Upon his return to Peking early in 1915, Ting wrote up his findings, including a study of the Chinsha (Kinsha) River, which flowed from the Tibetan plateau through Yunnan province to the Yangtze. In the final years of the Ming dynasty, this river had been described by the famous geographer and explorer Hsü Hung-tsu (ECCP, I, 314–16), in a diary entitled *Hsü Hsia-k'o yu-chi*. Ting had become deeply interested in Hsü's diary and had taken a copy of it with him to Yunnan in 1914. In the course of his geological investigations, Ting had passed by many of the sites noted by Hsü in his diary and had confirmed Hsü's claim that the Chinsha River was the true source of the Yangtze. Some years later, as a result of his continuing interest in Hsü Hung-tsu, Ting published a revised edition of the *Hsü Hsia-k'o yu-chi* in three volumes (1928), which included his chronological biography of Hsü and an atlas indicating the routes taken by Hsü in his explorations of the region.

In 1916, largely through the efforts of V. K. Ting and his associates, the China Geological Survey (Chung-kuo ti-chih tiao-ch'a-so) was set up by the ministry of agriculture and commerce. Ting became its first director and held that post until 1921, when he was succeeded by the Belgian-trained geologist Wong Wen-hao (q.v.). The Geological Survey soon achieved an international reputation. Not only did it succeed in its dual purpose of training competent personnel and conducting geological and mineralogical surveys throughout China, but it also began in 1919 to publish valuable scientific reports on its findings in a bulletin (*Ti-chih hui-pao*) and in two series of its memoirs (*Ti-chih chuan-pao*].

In the winter of 1918–19, V. K. Ting joined a group which accompanied Liang Ch'i-ch'ao (q.v.) on his trip to Europe as an unofficial delegate to the Paris Peace Conference. The party also included Carsun Chang (Chang Chia-sen), Chiang Fang-chen, and Hsü Hsin-liu

(qq.v.). This trip marked the beginning of a close friendship between Ting and Liang Ch'i-ch'ao, and the broadening of Ting's interests to include government and philosophy may well have stemmed from it.

Among the geological investigations conducted by V. K. Ting as head of the Geological Survey was a mining survey in southeastern Jehol province, near the site of the abandoned Pei-p'iao coal mine. The survey indicated that the mine would be operated profitably, and in 1921 a group organized the Pei-p'iao Coal Mining Company as a private enterprise. Ting resigned from office to become general manager of the new company, which soon grew into a flourishing industry with an annual output of 144,758 tons. He soon was drawn into closer contact with political and military affairs. The colliery was located within the sphere of influence of the Fengtien military clique, headed by Chang Tso-lin (q.v.), and Ting had to learn to be alert to the frictions between rival warlords and political factions. He traveled regularly among Pei-p'iao, Mukden, Peking, and Tientsin, and he recorded his observations in a number of articles, signed with the pen name Tsung-yen, which appeared first in the *Nu-li chou-pao* [endeavor] and later as a book entitled *Min-kuo chün-shih chin-chi* (1928).

Ting's association with the *Nu-li chou-pao* marked his entrance into the field of political journalism. Because they were deeply disturbed by the tendency toward political chaos in China, Ting, Hu Shih (q.v.), and others began publishing this weekly magazine, which was devoted to the discussion of political questions and reforms in the government. In the second issue (14 May 1922) there appeared a statement entitled "Wo-men ti cheng-chih chu-chang" [our political proposals], written by Hu Shih and signed by 16 intellectuals with such divergent opinions as Ts'ai Yuan-p'ei, Wang Ch'ung-hui, Liang Shu-ming, Li Ta-chao (qq.v.), and Ting. Stressing the need for "good government" in which "good men" should take an active part, the statement proposed a peace conference between the various factions in north and south China, the reconvening of the 1917 National Assembly, and the drafting of a new constitution. In a later issue of the magazine (No. 67), Ting elaborated on this theme. Influenced to some extent by the Confucian political ideal of the nineteenth-century scholar-statesman Tseng Kuo-fan (ECCP, II, 751–56), Ting argued that good government depended upon the vigorous leadership of a few men of the utmost integrity and ability. He attributed the then current political evils in China to the fact that truly talented and virtuous men were neither willing nor able to assume an active role in the government.

Political and military affairs were not the only topics which claimed V. K. Ting's attention. In February 1923 his friend Carsun Chang published in the *Tsinghua Weekly* a lecture entitled "Jen-sheng kuan" [philosophy of life], in which he stated that the development of science in the West had resulted in a materialistic and morally degenerate civilization. Declaring that science, with its orientation to the external world of matter, was powerless to solve the basic spiritual problems of human life, Chang asserted that a philosophy of life must rely not on the determination of scientific laws but on man's intuition, his free will, and the cultivation of his inner mind. V. K. Ting, angered by this attack on scientific method, published in the *Nu-li chou-pao* (15 and 22 April 1923) a refutation of Chang's arguments entitled "Hsuan-hsueh yü k'o-hsueh" [metaphysics and science]. Citing the Austrian physicist Ernest Mach and the English mathematical statistician Karl Pearson, Ting sought to defend the role of scientific method in intellectual life and to deny that it was a cause of moral decay in the West. He argued that a scientific outlook was essential rather than detrimental to a philosophy of life. The controversy between Chang and Ting came to involve many of the leading minds of the day. By the end of 1923 a two-volume collection of articles written by Ting, Chang, and the later participants in this debate had been published as *K'o-hsueh yü jen-sheng-kuan* [science and the philosophy of life].

As his reputation as an astute observer of conditions in north China grew, V. K. Ting began to consult with prominent military and political leaders. In July 1925, through the introduction of Lo Wen-kan, he had an interview with Wu P'ei-fu (q.v.) at Yochow, and in August of that year he spent a week at Hangchow in consultation with Sun Ch'uan-fang (q.v.). Ting resigned as general manager of the Pei-p'iao Coal Mining Company in the winter of 1925 and then served briefly as one of the three Chinese members of the advisory committee of

the Anglo-Chinese Boxer Indemnity Commission headed by Lord Willingdon. In May 1926 he was invited to Shanghai for further consultation with Sun Ch'uan-fang, who prevailed upon Ting to assist him in a project to develop a "Greater Shanghai." With the official title of director of the port of Woosung and Shanghai, Ting proceeded with plans to organize the hitherto separately administered districts in the Chinese part of the city as a single entity under a single municipal government, which would be in a better position to develop new port facilities and to negotiate for the abolition of foreign concessions in the city. Within the next eight months (May-December 1926) Ting also introduced modern sanitation systems and secured an agreement with the foreign consular corps in the International Settlement by which control of the Shanghai Mixed Court was restored to China. The "Provisional Agreement for the Rendition of the Shanghai Mixed Court" (31 August 1926), negotiated on the Chinese side by Ting and Hsü Yuan, the Kiangsu provincial commissioner of foreign affairs, extended Chinese jurisdiction into the International Settlement and thereby constituted a step toward the eventual abolition of extraterritoriality in China.

On 31 December 1926, as the Northern Expedition forces marched toward Shanghai, V. K. Ting resigned from office and went to Dairen, where he worked on his edition of Hsü Hungtsu's travel diary. He returned to his geological pursuits in 1928, when he went to Kwangsi to make a survey of the tin and coal resources in the northern and central parts of the province and to make a detailed study of the limestone formations at Map'ing. In November 1928 the China Geological Survey commissioned him to make the most comprehensive survey of his career, a geological investigation of southwest China. Early in 1929, after organizing a team of investigators, Ting proceeded southward from Chungking through Kweichow province to the Kwangsi border, and thence back to Chungking. In addition to supervising extensive surveys of the mineral resources and compiling detailed geological maps of the region, he found time to study the non-Chinese tribes of the region, particularly the Lolo of Kweichow. From the materials he began to gather while on this expedition, he later compiled a book of Lolo texts with Chinese translations. A part of this work was published posthumously in 1936 as the *Ts'uan-wen ts'ung-k'o*, the first volume in a monograph series of the Academia Sinica's institute of history and philology.

In 1931 V. K. Ting was appointed professor of geology at Peking University by the new chancellor, Chiang Monlin (Chiang Meng-lin, q.v.). Although his three years (1931–34) there were among the happiest of his life, Ting, like many of his colleagues, became increasingly apprehensive about the course of events after the Japanese occupation of Manchuria. In the spring of 1932 he joined with Fu Ssu-nien, T. F. Tsiang (Chiang T'ing-fu, qq.v.), Hu Shih, and other professors in organizing the society that began, on 22 May, to publish the *Tu-li p'ing-lun* [independent critic]. Ting contributed sixty-four articles to the *Tu-li p'ing-lun* during its three years of publication. The majority of these articles described his travels, but some were devoted to discussions of Japan and of plans to resist a Japanese invasion.

During the summer vacation of 1933 V. K. Ting attended the sixteenth congress of the International Geological Society in Washington, D.C. On the way back to China he spent some six weeks in the Soviet Union. While traveling through the United States at the onset of the New Deal and in the Soviet Union near the end of the first Five Year Plan, he noted with interest the large-scale experimentation in government economic planning in these countries. These observations wrought a change in his thinking which began to be reflected in his writings in 1934. He sought to adapt his earlier concept of an able and virtuous ruling minority to his new political ideal of a "modern dictatorship," pressing for a rapid and systematic modernization of the country under vigorous, centralized leadership. He argued that such modernization could only be achieved by a unified government headed by a decisive leader and administered by efficient technocrats. Under the supervision of an enlightened and public-spirited dictatorship, teams of scientifically trained experts selected on the basis of their specialized abilities would be able to study, coordinate, and execute plans for the scientific reconstruction of China.

It was, perhaps, with such ideas in mind that Ting gave up teaching at Peking University and in June 1934 accepted Ts'ai Yuan-p'ei's invitation to succeed Yang Ch'uan (q.v.) as secretary general of the Academia Sinica in Nanking.

According to Hu Shih, Ting saw in the Academia Sinica an organ which could assist China's national development by stimulating and coordinating scientific research throughout the country. The Council of the Academia Sinica was established to coordinate the research activities of the academy's various institutes with those of other academic institutions and government agencies. On 27 May 1935 the National Government promulgated the constitution of this council; on 20 June some 30 members representing China's leading scholarly bodies were elected to the council; and on 7 September V. K. Ting was elected honorary secretary.

In addition to his administrative duties at the Academia Sinica, Ting was called upon to assist the National Government in plans to develop China's resources and to strengthen its defenses. As one of the planners of the Canton-Hankow railway, then in the late stages of construction, Ting concerned himself with the development of coal resources near the railway in Hunan. After arriving in Changsha from Nanking on 2 December 1935, he went to the T'an-chia-shan colliery in Hsiangt'an hsien to inspect the mines. He spent the night of 8–9 December at an inn in Hanyang in an unventilated room which was heated by a charcoal stove. On the morning of 9 December he was found unconscious from coal-gas fumes and was taken to a local hospital. A week later he was moved to Hsiang-ya Hospital in Changsha, where he died on 5 January 1936. He was survived by his wife, *née* Shih Chiu-yuan, and by six brothers, the most prominent of whom was Ting Wen-yuan (d. 1957; T. Yueh-po), president of T'ung-chi University in Shanghai from 1947 to 1950.

V. K. Ting was active in a variety of fields, but was best known as one of China's leading geologists. As founder of the China Geological Survey, he helped to bring into being China's first institute of modern scientific research; and as its first director he not only promoted the professional study of geology but also stimulated the development of the allied fields of paleontology and archaeology. Working with such colleagues as Wong Wen-hao and Li Ssu-kuang and with such Western advisers as the Swedish geologist J. G. Andersson and the French scientist-priest Teilhard de Chardin, Ting helped to create the conditions that made China a center for research on the neolithic period and led to the discovery of Sinanthropus Pekinensis (*see* P'ei Wen-chung) in 1927. Even after his resignation from the Geological Survey in 1921, he continued to take an interest in its development. In 1929, with financial assistance from the Rockefeller Foundation, he helped to found the Geological Survey's Cenozoic Research Laboratory, of which he became honorary director; and he later was instrumental in setting up the Soil Laboratory, Fuel Laboratory, and Hsi-shan Seismological Station.

Apart from his activities in the Geological Survey, the Academia Sinica, and other official institutions, Ting played a leading role in organizing a number of learned societies and publications in China. He was one of the founders of the Geological Society of China (Chung-kuo ti-chih hsueh-hui) in January 1922, and he took part in editing and publishing its bulletin (*Chung-kuo ti-chih hsueh-hui chih*). Also in 1922 he arranged for funds to publish a bulletin of paleontology (*Chung-kuo ku-sheng-wu chih*), which he edited, and in 1929, he helped found the China Paleontological Society (Chung-kuo ku-sheng-wu hsueh-hui).

A practicing scientist with broad experience in his field, V. K. Ting was the author of numerous articles on the subject of geology, of both general and technical nature, which appeared in a variety of scholarly journals both in China and abroad. As a geologist, however, Ting's best known work was an atlas of China, the *Chung-hua min-kuo hsin ti-t'u*, which he compiled in collaboration with Wong Wen-hao and Tseng Shih-ying. Among the best modern atlases ever printed in China, it contained both physical and political maps based on thousands of Chinese and foreign maps of China and supplemented by the findings of the Geological Survey. Published at Shanghai in 1934 by the *Shun Pao* in commemoration of the newspaper's sixtieth anniversary, this work was commonly known as the "Shun Pao Atlas."

Among Ting's non-technical writings was a draft chronology of Liang Ch'i-ch'ao, which Ting began to compile after Liang's death in 1929. In was published in 1958 in Taiwan under the title *Liang Jen-kung hsien-sheng nien-p'u ch'ang-pien ch'u-kao* (3 volumes). Ting was also the author of two works relating to his travels abroad and in China: the *Man-yu san-chi*, miscellaneous field notes on his travels through interior China; and the *Su-o lü-hsing chi*, a collection of essays describing his journey through Russia in 1933. Both of these works were later (1956) reprinted in Taiwan as part of the third volume of the *Chung-yang yen-chiu-yuan yuan-k'an* [annals of the Academia Sinica], a volume published in commemoration of the twentieth anniversary of Ting's death.

Tong, Hollington: *see* TUNG HSIEN-KUANG.

Ts'ai Ch'ang 蔡暢

Ts'ai Ch'ang (c.1900–), ranking woman member of the Chinese Communist party and sister of Ts'ai Ho-sen (q.v.).

Born in Hsianghsiang hsien, Hunan, Ts'ai Ch'ang was the younger sister of Ts'ai Ho-sen (for information about the family, *see* Ts'ai Ho-sen). Her mother sent her to live with relatives in Changsha about 1912 to avoid an arranged marriage between Ts'ai Ch'ang and a local landlord's son. Ts'ai enrolled at the Chou-nan Girls School, where the principal was Hsü T'e-li (q.v.) and where her schoolmates included Hsiang Ching-yü (q.v.). When her brother and Mao Tse-tung organized the Hsin-min hsueh-hui [new people's study society] in 1918, she became a member. The following year, she and Hsiang Ching-yü organized a group of young women to participate in the work-study program in France (*see* Li Shih-tseng). They sailed to Europe late in 1919 along with a group from Hunan which also included Ts'ai Ho-sen. In France, Ts'ai Ch'ang studied political science, worked in a factory, and joined the French branch of the Chinese Communist party. She married Li Fu-ch'un (q.v.) in 1923. They returned to China in late 1924 after spending some time in Moscow studying at the Communist University for Toilers of the East.

In 1924–26 Ts'ai Ch'ang worked to organize women workers in Shanghai and then in the Canton–Hong Kong area. This was the period of Kuomintang-Communist collaboration, and Ts'ai held such posts at Canton as executive secretary of the Kuomintang women's department and secretary of the propaganda section of the National Revolutionary Army's general political department. She also served as head of the women's department of the Chinese Communist party's Kwangtung provincial committee. After the Northern Expedition was launched in 1926, she headed a women's propaganda team which entered Wuhan with the military forces. She remained in Wuhan until the Kuomintang-Communist split of 1927, when she went to Shanghai and disappeared from public view. In 1928 she served as a delegate to a Comintern conference in Moscow. She rejoined her husband in Shanghai after making a brief tour of Eastern Europe. They moved to the central soviet area in Kiangsi in mid-1931. Ts'ai then became head of the women's department and a member of the Kiangsi provincial committee of the Chinese Communist party. Early in 1934 she was elected to alternate membership in the party's Central Committee. She was one of the few women who survived the rigors of the Long March in 1934–35, but the hardships she experienced undermined her health. After working briefly in the Shensi-Kansu area, she went to Moscow for rest and medical treatment.

Ts'ai Ch'ang returned to China in 1937. During the Sino-Japanese war she emerged as the senior woman Communist at Yenan and the leader of Chinese Communist efforts to mobilize women in the Shensi-Kansu-Ninghsia Border Region. At the Seventh National Congress of the Chinese Communist party, held at Yenan in 1945, she was the only woman elected to regular membership on the Central Committee. At that time, she also became secretary of the women's work committee, with responsibility for political and propaganda programs for women. Her work to organize all women in China under firm Communist control culminated in 1949 with the establishment of the All-China Federation of Democratic Women with Ts'ai as chairman.

With the establishment of the People's Republic of China in 1949, Ts'ai Ch'ang became a member of the Central People's Government Council. Beginning in 1954 she was a member of the Standing Committee of the National People's Congress. A member of the executive committee of the All-China Federation of Trade Unions since 1948, she was elected to the presidium of that organization in 1957. Ts'ai was one of the leading Chinese participants in the Communist-dominated International Federation of Democratic Women, serving as its

vice chairman after 1948. She attended meetings of the federation in such foreign capitals as Prague, Budapest, Rome, and Copenhagen. Throughout the 1950's and early 1960's Ts'ai Ch'ang continued to play an important part in the formulation and direction of all programs affecting women in the People's Republic of China.

Ts'ai Ho-sen   蔡和森
T. Lin-pin   林彬

Ts'ai Ho-sen (c.1890–1931), close friend and political associate of Mao Tse-tung. He helped organize the French branch of the Chinese Communist party, after which he returned to China to become a prominent party propagandist and the first editor of the *Hsiang-tao chou-pao* [guide weekly]. He was executed by the Nationalists in 1931.

Hsianghsiang hsien, Hunan, was the birthplace of Ts'ai Ho-sen. His mother, *née* Ko Chien-hao, was distantly related to the illustrious scholar-statesman Tseng Kuo-fan (ECCP, II, 751–56), and his father was a scholar and small landlord who by the end of the Ch'ing period had been reduced to working in the Kiangnan Arsenal in Shanghai. Ts'ai's parents were not happy together, and his father left home when Ts'ai was still a child. Thus, the burden of raising six children fell on Ts'ai's mother, a strong-willed woman who learned to read with her children and went on to become a teacher. Because of the family's financial situation, Ts'ai Ho-sen went to work at an early age, toiling at various times as a cowherd, a shop apprentice, and a farm hand. Little is known about his early education, but his later writings indicate that he received good training in the Chinese classics.

In 1913 Ts'ai Ho-sen passed the entrance examinations for the Hunan First Normal School at Changsha. That autumn the school absorbed the Hunan Fourth Normal School; Ts'ai thus became a schoolmate and a close friend of Mao Tse-tung. The First Normal School was the largest school in Changsha, with an enrollment of about 1,200. Competition for entrance was keen, for the school offered free tuition, board, lodging, books, and even clothing. One of the school's new faculty members in 1913 was Yang

Ch'ang-chi (q.v.), who taught logic, ethics, and education. Ts'ai, who became one of Yang's favorite students, was strongly influenced by his teachings. Ts'ai soon began to advocate the reform of Chinese society through the introduction of certain Western principles and institutions. He also became concerned with the reform of the Chinese language, an interest apparently stimulated by articles carried in the *Hsin ch'ing-nien* [new youth] of Ch'en Tu-hsiu (q.v.). Yang strongly supported the *Hsin ch'ing-nien* and regularly distributed copies of it to Ts'ai and other students. Ts'ai also emulated his teacher in matters of self-discipline: he practiced meditation, slept on a wooden door board, and became a physical culturist.

After spending two years at the Hunan First Normal School, Ts'ai Ho-sen transferred to the Yueh-lu-shan Higher Normal School. Upon graduation in 1917 he was unable to find a teaching job. He spent the summer with his mother and his sister Ts'ai Ch'ang (q.v.), who had rented a house at the foot of the Yueh-lu mountain. He maintained his friendships with his former schoolmates from the First Normal School, some of whom were now teaching at the Ch'u-i School. They corresponded with one another, and they occasionally met at Ts'ai's house or the Ch'u-i School. According to Mao Tse-tung, in the summer of 1917 he and his friends decided to form a student organization dedicated to "strengthening China through strengthening Chinese youth." The resulting Hsin-min hsüeh-hui [new people's study society] was inaugurated at Ts'ai's house on 18 April 1918, with a membership of 13, including Mao Tse-tung, Ts'ai Ho-sen, and Ho Shu-heng (q.v.). Its rather vague constitution stipulated that members should practice "personality building and scholarly research" to prepare themselves for the work of saving their country. They should refrain from gambling, visiting brothels, and loafing. New members would be recruited on the basis of their moral and intellectual qualities, which would be assessed by the organization's deliberation committee (p'ing-i hui). Ts'ai Ho-sen was elected one of the five secretaries of the committee, and Mao Tse-tung became its deputy secretary general.

In June 1918 the Hsin-min hsüeh-hui sent Ts'ai Ho-sen to Peking to investigate the work-study program. Through the introduction of Yang Ch'ang-chi, now a professor at Peking University, he met with Li Shih-tseng and Ts'ai Yuan-p'ei (qq.v.), who were in charge of the work-study program in France. Ts'ai Ho-sen soon wrote Mao Tse-tung and other friends in Hunan, urging them to come to Peking and to bring with them other students who wanted to go to France. He hoped that the presence of a large Hunanese group in Peking would lead the authorities to provide support for them, and he believed that "only when a large group engages in fishing will there be enough fish to eat." He also wrote his sister Ts'ai Ch'ang urging that she organize women for the work-study program. In sum, he saw the work-study program as a way of preparing members of the Hsin-min hsüeh-hui for the task of reforming Chinese society. In September 1918 Ts'ai was joined in Peking by Mao Tse-tung, Siao Yü, Lo Hsueh-tan, Hsiung Kuang-ch'u, Chang K'un-ti, and other young Hunanese. They crowded themselves into a two-room apartment on Three Eyes Well Street near Peking University. By then about 50 Hunanese students had arrived in Peking, the largest group to join the work-study program. On the advice of Li Shih-tseng, Ts'ai Ho-sen and others began to organize classes for these students to study French and to learn a trade. Under the auspices of the Franco-Chinese Association, three such classes were set up—in Peking, Paoting, and Lihsien. Ts'ai Ho-sen, Mao Tse-tung, and Siao Yü were among those who attended the training class at Peking and who helped other Hunanese students to find scholarship money and to make arrangements for their passports.

About this time, the study of Marxian socialism and anarchism became the fashion at Peking University. Such publications as the *Hsin ch'ing-nien* began to speak for "the Russian type of social revolution." According to Lo Hsueh-tan, with whom Ts'ai Ho-sen and Mao Tse-tung shared lodgings, Mao and Ts'ai spent a great deal of time reading magazines and newspapers and discussing "the latest theories." Mao left Peking in the spring of 1919, but Ts'ai was there for the May Fourth Movement, which undoubtedly enhanced his enthusiasm for Marxism and intellectual revolution.

In October 1919 Ts'ai Ho-sen led a group of Hunanese students to Shanghai on the first leg of their journey to France. At Shanghai, the group was joined by Ts'ai's mother and by a group of young Hunanese women which had been organized by Ts'ai Ch'ang and Hsiang Ching-yü (q.v.). In the course of the voyage to France Ts'ai Ho-sen and Hsiang Ching-yü fell in love. They began to exchange love poems; these later were collected and published as *Hsiang-shan t'ung-meng* [toward a brighter day]. Because both of them were determined to devote themselves to patriotic work, they resisted the idea of marriage until 1921.

The Hunanese group arrived in Paris on 2 February 1920 and immediately proceeded to Montargis, where they would study French. Because living and school expenses were provided by the Societé Franco-Chinois d'Education in the form of a loan, there was no immediate necessity for the students to begin work in a factory. Ts'ai Ho-sen planned to stay in France for five years, alloting the first two to language study. In accordance with this plan, he began to read newspapers and magazines in French with a dictionary. Before long, he was translating articles on Communism and trade-unionism to send to Mao Tse-tung. In his letters to Mao he described in some detail the theoretical foundations of Marxism and the structure of the Soviet Communist party. The theme of these letters was that the social doctrine and party organization of the Soviet Union were the only suitable models for China to adopt in achieving national reconstruction. To achieve revolution, he urged the employment of four tools: a party, trade unions, cooperatives, and soviets. He explicitly suggested to Mao that a Chinese Communist party be organized and that it be a tightly knit organization with a carefully selected membership and a precisely formulated platform. When established (hopefully within two years), the party would become the nerve center of a Chinese revolution. Ts'ai also recommended alliance with the Soviet Union and participation in the Comintern. His suggestions won the hearty approval of Mao Tse-tung, who was influenced during this period by Ts'ai as well as by Li Ta-chao (q.v.) and Ch'en Tu-hsiu.

While trying to convince his friends at home by letters, Ts'ai also worked to convert Chinese students in France to Communism. As might be expected, Hsiang Ching-yü and Ts'ai Ch'ang were among his first converts. He talked about his convictions to his friends at Montargis and won over Li Fu-ch'un, Li Wei-han (qq.v.),

and others. In mid-1920 he and his old friend Chang K'un-ti organized the Kung-hsueh shih-chieh she [work-study cosmopolitan club], ostensibly to promote the work-study program but actually to disseminate Communist propaganda. Such activities soon brought him into conflict with Siao Yü, and their differences of opinion came into the open at a meeting of the Hsin-min hsüeh-hui held at Montargis in July 1920. Siao opposed the concepts of class struggle and revolution and spoke for the socialization of China through education, trade-unionism, and other peaceful means. This dispute split the membership of the Hsin-min hsüeh-hui, and it was a major cause of that organization's dissolution in early 1921.

Ts'ai Ho-sen's efforts were aided by the economic crisis among Chinese students in France in 1921. At the beginning of the year, the Societé Franco-Chinois d'Education announced that because its funds had been exhausted it no longer could provide Chinese students with loans. About the same time, the French economy sagged, and the Chinese students found themselves unable to work. On 8 February, a crowd of Chinese students demonstrated in front of the Chinese legation in Paris, demanding the right "to study, to get jobs and bread." Ts'ai and his wife were among the organizers of this demonstration. Later that year, they helped establish the Chung-kuo ch'ing-nien kung-ch'an-t'uan [young Chinese Communist corps] and a branch of the Socialist Youth Corps, both of which were predecessors of the French branch of the Chinese Communist party established at Paris in 1922. In September 1921 a group of about 100 work-study students— including Chou En-lai, Ch'en Yi (1901–), Li Li-san (qq.v.), and Ts'ai Ho-sen—forced their way into the Institut Franco-Chinois at Lyon (for details, *see* Li Shih-tseng) to protest their exclusion from its first class. They were arrested and expelled from France as a result of this action.

Upon arrival at Shanghai, in either late 1921 or early 1922, Ts'ai Ho-sen immediately made contact with the Central Committee of the Chinese Communist party and gave his support to Ch'en Tu-hsiu. A militant Marxist-Leninist, he opposed the so-called democratic minority within the party, led by Ch'en Kung-po (q.v.) and Li Han-chün, which maintained that the party should pursue only legitimate activities, that is, research and propaganda. Chinese Communist historians later credited Ts'ai with "expelling the Li Han-chün faction from the party." At a Central Committee meeting on 18 June 1922 Ts'ai supported Ch'en Tu-hsiu's policies of concentration on mass education work until the time came for the proletariat to seize power and of pursuit of a united front in the revolutionary movement. The Central Committee decided to regard the Kuomintang as an ally but did not specify the nature of the alliance. Ts'ai was elected to the Central Committee at the Second National Congress of the Chinese Communist party, held at Shanghai in July 1922. He reportedly proposed that the party follow Comintern directives, expand the revolutionary movement, and carry out the strategy of a united front. These proposals were passed unanimously. In August, Comintern representative Maring called a special plenum of the Central Committee at Hangchow and proposed that Chinese Communist party members join the Kuomintang, a proposal the Central Committee finally accepted with great reluctance. Ts'ai, Ch'en Tu-hsiu, and others feared that the alliance would cost the Chinese Communist party its identity as the party of the proletariat. It is ironic that Ts'ai, one of the earliest advocates of Comintern membership for the Chinese Communist party, should be faced so soon with a situation in which the Comintern line conflicted with his principles.

In keeping with the new Comintern policy, Ch'en Tu-hsiu founded the *Hsiang-tao chou-pao* [guide weekly] in September 1922 to replace the *Kung-ch'an-tang yueh-k'an* [Communist party monthly]. Ts'ai Ho-sen became the editor of the new journal, which promoted the Kuomintang-Communist alliance as a means of effecting a national anti-imperialist revolution in China. Under Ts'ai's guidance, the journal's circulation soared. He also headed the propaganda department of the Central Committee of the Chinese Communist party, while his wife headed the women's department. They worked to organize students and factory workers in Shanghai, and their house was a favorite meeting place of Chinese Communists. At the time of the May Thirtieth Incident of 1925, they played important roles in the attempt to direct political unrest into channels useful to the Chinese Communist party. It was Ts'ai who suggested the demonstration that resulted in

the injury or death of a number of Chinese who were fired on by police in the International Settlement. And it was Ts'ai who suggested the ensuing strike movement (*see* Li Li-san). Ts'ai's activities throughout the 1922–25 period were almost exclusively Communist; he remained aloof from the Kuomintang and critical of its leaders.

Ts'ai Ho-sen and Hsiang Ching-yü left China for the Soviet Union toward the end of 1925 so that Ts'ai could attend the sixth plenum of the Executive Committee of the Comintern (17 February–15 March 1926). Ts'ai spent the next year in Moscow as a Chinese Communist delegate to the Comintern, returning to China with his wife in April 1927 to attend the Fifth National Congress of the Chinese Communist party. In August, after Ch'ü Ch'iu-pai (q.v.) replaced Ch'en Tu-hsiu as general secretary of the party, Ts'ai became secretary of the north China bureau. Hsiang Ching-yü was assigned to work underground in Hankow, where she was arrested and executed in the spring of 1928.

Although Ts'ai Ho-sen was reelected to the Central Committee and the Political Bureau (positions he had lost when Ch'ü Ch'iu-pai came to power) at the Sixth National Congress of the Chinese Communist party, held in Moscow in 1928, he did not return to a position of influence within the party. He was sent to Moscow again in 1929 because of disagreements with Li Li-san, then the *de facto* head of the party, returning to China in the summer of 1930 (after testifying against Li to the Comintern) to take part in the Central Committee meeting at which Li's policies were reconsidered and rejected. In the summer of 1931 Ts'ai was sent to Hong Kong as secretary of the party's Kwangtung and Kwangsi provincial committee. Within two months, he had been arrested by the Hong Kong police and extradited to Canton. It is known that he was executed, but the precise circumstances of his death are unclear.

Ts'ai O   蔡　鍔
   Orig. Ken-yen   根　寅
   T.   Sung-p'o   松　坡

Ts'ai O (18 December 1882–8 November 1916), able and scholarly Hunanese military commander who served as military governor of

Yunnan after the revolution. In 1913–15 he held posts at Peking while laying plans for a revolt against Yuan Shih-k'ai, who hoped to become monarch. The anti-Yuan campaign began at Yunnan in December 1915 and ended with Yuan's death in June 1916.

Paoch'ing (later Shaoyang), Hunan, was the birthplace of Ts'ai O. He was the eldest son in a prosperous peasant family. Until he was 15, he received a classical education under the guidance of private tutors in preparation for the civil service examinations. In 1895 he passed the examinations for the sheng-yuan degree. He sat for the chü-jen examination two years later, but failed them.

Ts'ai was introduced to reformist thought by his tutor Fan Chui, with whom he studied from 1894 to 1897. Fan was a close associate of T'ang Ts'ai-ch'ang (1867–1900), who taught at the newly established Shih-wu hsueh-t'ang (Academy of Current Affairs) at Changsha, and of T'an Ssu-t'ung (ECCP, II, 702–5). In 1897 Ts'ai O entered the academy, where he was strongly influenced by the new chief lecturer, Liang Ch'i-ch'ao (q.v.). When the academy was closed in September 1898 following the failure of the Hundred Days Reform, Ts'ai applied for admission to the Liang-hu shu-yüan but was denied entrance because of his association with the defeated reformers.

In 1899 Ts'ai and several of his former classmates traveled to Japan at the invitation of Liang Ch'i-ch'ao. In Tokyo he studied for a time with Liang and T'ang Ts'ai-ch'ang before entering the Great Harmony Secondary School, established by Liang and others in Tokyo for students whose schools in China had been closed. In 1900 Ts'ai and other students returned to China to assist in the preparations being made by T'ang Ts'ai-ch'ang for an uprising at Hankow. Ts'ai was sent to persuade officers in Hunan's New Army to cooperate in their revolutionary plans. He thus escaped the fate of 18 of his fellow conspirators, who were executed at Hankow when their plot was discovered by the imperial authorities. Ts'ai returned to Japan and enrolled at the Seijo Military Preparatory School, an action which reflected his preoccupation with the question of national power.

Two complementary ideas had come to dominate the thinking of Ts'ai O: an urgent sense of China's backwardness and weakness in a starkly competitive world, and an awareness of the imperative need for the development of China's national power. Japan was Ts'ai's model for the transformation of China into a strong military power. In an article entitled "A Militant Citizenry," published in the *Hsin-min ts'ung-pao* [renovation of the people] in 1902, Ts'ai centered his attention on the need to develop a martial spirit in China. He traced the absence of a martial spirit to several sources: an educational system in which the energies and talents of young Chinese were exhausted and dissipated in learning "useless formalities and ornamental phrases"; a perversion of Confucianism by such scholars as Liu Hsiang (77–6 B.C.) and Chu Hsi (1130–1200), who, Ts'ai asserted, were really Taoists; the low social status accorded the military in China; and the failure of Chinese literature and music to glorify martial qualities. Ts'ai noted with admiration that the Japanese system of education developed the qualities of the soldier almost unconsciously in students—art classes, for example, were devoted to the drawing of warships and artillery pieces. He also noted the high social status of the military in Japan and the contributions of Japanese literature, philosophy, and music to the development of a martial spirit, stating that China would have to emulate Japan in order to survive. Ts'ai's concern with national power also extended to political institutions, where it served as his rationale for supporting republicanism. He argued that in a republic all the people bear limitless duties and obligations and that all human resources can be mobilized in the struggle for national survival, whereas in a monarchy only the monarch has rights and only he has a sense of responsibility to the country.

After being graduated from the Seijo Military Preparatory School in 1902 and from the Shikan Gakkō [military academy] in 1904, Ts'ai O returned to China, where he held a series of military posts in Kiangsi, Hunan, Kwangsi, and Yunnan. He spent most of the 1904–10 period in Kwangsi, where his posts included superintendent of the Kwangsi Middle Military School, supervisor of the Academy of Military Instruction, and assistant director of the provincial military bureau. During the five years he served in Kwangsi, he faced many obstacles in his efforts to retrain and modernize the provincial forces. His letters of the period convey the impression that he conceived of himself as waging a personal struggle of great importance to his country against nearly overwhelming odds. His efforts to restore order to a critically deteriorating provincial army won him a reputation as a stern disciplinarian, and his practice of appointing Hunanese rather than natives of Kwangsi to positions of importance in the Kwangsi military training programs aroused the hostility of Kwangsi military men. In 1910 a protest movement calling for the removal of Ts'ai from office was begun by military school students. It culminated in the impeachment of Ts'ai by the Kwangsi provincial assembly. He later was exonerated, but by that time he had accepted an appointment from Li Ching-hsi, the governor general of Yunnan, as commander of the 37th Brigade and instructor at the Yunnan Military Academy.

When Ts'ai arrived in Yunnan in the spring of 1911, he was ordered to make a compilation of inspiring and instructive maxims relating to the command of military forces. The result was the *Tseng Hu chih-ping yü-lu*, a collection of writings by Tseng Kuo-fan and Hu Lin-i. In his accompanying commentary to these writings, Ts'ai cited five qualities which he considered the essentials of military leadership: knowledge, sincerity, humaneness, discipline, and courage. He attributed the military successes of Tseng and Hu, "two scholars with no practical experience in military affairs," wholly to the absolute sincerity with which they undertook their task. Ts'ai used the term humaneness to refer to the Confucian concept of the relationship that should exist between father and son, applying the concept to superiors and subordinates in a military organization. Ts'ai's commentary was his most traditional piece of writing—his emphases and modes of expression were Confucian in tone, and his comments on sincerity and humaneness were Confucian in substance.

In the 1904–10 period Ts'ai O was not a professional revolutionary, nor was he involved in any of the uprisings associated with the T'ung-meng-hui. However, he was associated on several occasions with preparations made by fellow Hunanese for revolutionary uprisings, and while serving as a training officer in various provinces he did not hesitate to appoint known T'ung-meng-hui activists to important posts.

A striking feature of his activities both during this period and later was his ability to cooperate, within limits, with sharply disparate groups. His dual loyalty to a revolutionist, Huang Hsing (q.v.), and to a constitutional reformer, Liang Ch'i-ch'ao, grew out of the strongly personal character of his loyalties and his concept of himself as a leader who should draw factions together. Although his personal qualities of caution and reserve drew him to the reformers, his beliefs about national power made him sympathetic to the aims of the republican revolutionaries.

On 30 October 1911 Ts'ai O led his 37th Brigade in a successful revolt against Manchu authority in Yunnan, thus joining the revolution of 1911. The foundations of the revolt in Yunnan had been laid several years earlier. In 1908–10 more than 20 Yunnanese graduates of the Shikan Gakkō, all of whom were T'ung-meng-hui activists, had returned to Yunnan to receive important military posts. Some of them had become instructors at the Yunnan Military Academy in Kunming, and others had been given field commands. At the time of the revolution, therefore, Ts'ai O's 37th Brigade, the largest military unit in the Kunming area, had one regimental commander and six battalion commanders who were graduates of the Shikan Gakkō and members of the Tung-meng-hui. On hearing of the Wuchang revolt of 10 October 1911, Ts'ai called a meeting of his regimental and battalion commanders to determine the course of action they would take. The composition of this group made revolution in Yunnan inevitable. On 31 October an independent military government was established at Kunming, and Ts'ai O was elected military governor.

In his new position Ts'ai O soon demonstrated considerable skill in maintaining order among competing military factions. His success was the result of his administrative abilities, his carefully cultivated reputation for impartiality, and his well-developed flair for the dramatic. He served as military governor of Yunnan until the summer of 1913, when he resigned on the understanding that he would be appointed to a similar position in his native Hunan. Yuan Shih-k'ai, however, decided to deprive the popular and ambitious Ts'ai of his military power and did not make the promised Hunan appointment. Instead, he appointed Ts'ai to a series of prestigious but politically innocuous posts at Peking. In 1913 Ts'ai became assistant director of the translation bureau of the ministry of war and a member of the political conference established by Yuan Shih-k'ai to determine the duties to be assumed by those members of the Parliament who remained at Peking after Yuan's cancellation of the Kuomintang's parliamentary membership on 4 November. The following year he served as a member of the political council, a sort of legislative yuan, and as director of the land measurement bureau.

As soon as Ts'ai O learned of Yuan Shih-k'ai's plans to become monarch, he began working to overthrow Yuan's regime. To allay Yuan's suspicions, he affected a life of debauchery, living, drinking, and feasting with the sing-song girl Hsiao Feng-hsien. He also quarreled publicly with his wife, Liu Hsieh-chen, and divorced her so that he could send her back to Hunan in safety. Yuan, who had kept Ts'ai under surveillance since Ts'ai's arrival in Peking, was taken in by these deceptions. The surveillance was relaxed, leaving Ts'ai relatively free to plot and to plan his escape from Peking. During this period, Ts'ai also cultivated the acquaintance of such loyal Yuan adherents as Yang Tu, whom he frequently entertained at the home of Hsiao Feng-hsien. On 16 August 1915 he was sent by Yang to Tientsin to persuade his former teacher Liang Ch'i-ch'ao to support Yuan. Unknown to Yang, Ts'ai and Liang had been in communication for some time and had been making plans for a revolt against the monarchists. They were supported in this effort by Ts'ai's friend T'ang Chi-yao (q.v.), the governor of Yunnan, and they agreed that Yunnan should be the base of military operations against Yuan. It also was agreed at Tientsin that Ts'ai would try to remain in Yuan's confidence for several months so that preparations could be made for the Yunnan uprising. Ts'ai then returned to Peking, his feigned debauchery, his revolutionary plans. Kuomintang leaders began to arrive in Yunnan to support the movement, and important preparations for war had been made by the time Ts'ai finally escaped from Peking in December.

Ts'ai O arrived in Yunnan on 19 December 1915. Four days later, a telegram was sent to Yuan requesting a clear statement from him in support of the republican system. On 24 December, an ultimatum was telegraphed to Yuan, giving him 24 hours to make a statement of loyalty to the republic and to execute 12 men who were closely associated with the monarchical movement. Yuan failed to reply, and on 25 December T'ang Chi-yao, Ts'ai O, and Li Lieh-chün (q.v.) issued a statement declaring Yunnan's independence and announcing that military action would be taken against Yuan. At a military conference, the armed forces in the area were organized as the National Protection Army (Hu-kuo chün). Ts'ai O became commander in chief of its First Army, with Lo P'ei-chin as chief of staff and with Liu Yun-feng, Chao Yu-hsin, and Ku Pin-chen as divisional commanders. The Second Army was led by Li Lieh-chün, and the Third Army was commanded by T'ang Chi-yao, who also served as military governor of the independent province.

At the beginning of 1916 Ts'ai O led his First Army into southern Szechwan; Li Lieh-chün moved into Kwangsi; and part of the Third Army under Tai K'an marched into Kweichow. Their progress was such that on 22 March, Yuan Shih-k'ai announced the abandonment of the monarchy, though he retained control as president. By this time, Kweichow and Kwangsi had joined the ranks of independent provinces. On 31 March a ceasefire agreement was signed by the commanders on the Szechwan-Kweichow front. The National Protection Army wished to regroup its forces, and Yuan's commanders, disheartened by his announcement, were not eager to continue fighting. In general, however, compromise was not reached, for the leaders of the independent provinces insisted that Yuan resign in favor of Li Yuan-hung (q.v.) and that the National Assembly of 1913 be restored. In April and May 1916 Kwangtung, Szechwan, Chekiang, Shensi, Hunan, Fukien, and even Heilungkiang declared independence.

When Yuan Shih-k'ai persisted in his refusal to step down, a military council was established at Chaoch'ing (Kaoyao) on 8 May 1916 for the stated purpose of serving as the legitimate government of China until Li Yuan-hung succeeded Yuan. The council's members were: T'ang Chi-yao (chairman), Ts'en Ch'un-hsuan (acting chairman), Ts'ai O, Liu Hsieh-shih, Lu Jung-t'ing, Ch'en Ping-kun, Lu Kung-wang, Lung Chi-kuang, T'ang Hsiang-ming, Li Lieh-chün, T'ai Kan, Lo P'ei-chin, Li Ting-hsien, and Liu Chuan-hou. Liang Ch'i-ch'ao was chief of the political committee; Chang Shih-chao was secretary general; and Li Ken-yuan was staff officer to the allied northern expeditionary forces and liaison officer in Shanghai. The foreign relations representatives were T'ang Shao-yi, Wang Ch'ung-hui, and Wen Chung-yao; and the representatives in Shanghai were Fan Yuan-lien, Ku Chung-hsiu, and Niu Yung-chien. After Yuan Shih-k'ai died on 6 June and Li Yuan-hung succeeded him, the council dissolved itself on 14 July. Thus ended the anti-Yuan movement which Ts'ai O fostered.

On 6 July 1916 Li Yuan-hung appointed Ts'ai O governor of Szechwan. Ts'ai assumed office at Chengtu in late July, but resigned two weeks later when it was discovered that he had an advanced case of throat cancer. He went to Japan for treatment and died in Tokyo on 8 November 1916.

Ts'ai T'ing-k'ai　　蔡 廷 鍇

Ts'ai T'ing-k'ai (15 April 1892–25 April 1968), field commander of the Nineteenth Route Army who won international fame as a result of that force's brave stand against the Japanese at Shanghai in 1932. In late 1933 he participated in the so-called Fukien revolt against Nanking. After 1949 he held a variety of posts in the Central People's Government of the People's Republic of China.

Loting hsien, Kwangtung, was the birth-place of Ts'ai T'ing-k'ai. He was the second of four children born to Ts'ai Tien-ming, a peasant farmer who also was a tailor, a herbalist, and a geomancy expert. Because his father was somewhat enlightened, Ts'ai T'ing-k'ai was allowed to attend school in 1901–3. His formal education came to an end, however, when his mother died and his father remarried in 1904. The young Ts'ai helped his father work the land and took over the tailoring business so that his father could devote more time to his practice as a herbalist. In 1908, at the age of 16, Ts'ai married P'eng Hui-feng (d.1937). In time, they had two sons, Shao-chang and Shao-hui, and two daughters, Shao-lu and Shao-min.

For several years Ts'ai had considered an army career, and in 1910 he enlisted. He stayed in the army for but a few months, however,

and did not join the other recruits at the training base. His father died in 1911, and Ts'ai then joined a small local force which supported the republican revolution. He remained with this unit until 1915, when he enlisted in a force near the river port of Sanlo. His association with this force ended when he participated in an abortive attempt to turn it against Yuan Shih-k'ai in support of the Kuomintang revolutionaries. Ts'ai then returned to his native village. In 1919 the people of Lochiang market organized a volunteer corps for protection against bandits and appointed Ts'ai its deputy commander. When the volunteers were incorporated into a regular army unit in the area, he became a platoon leader. In 1920 he was sent to the military academy in Canton for formal training. Upon graduation, he was assigned to the 4th Regiment, commanded by Ch'en Ming-shu (q.v.), in the 1st Division of the Kwangtung Army. He remained with this division until 1923, when he left after being passed over for promotion. He then joined the 1st Battalion, commanded by Teng Shih-tseng, of the special regiment attached to Sun Yat-sen's head-quarters. When Teng was promoted to regimental commander, Ts'ai succeeded him.

When the National Revolutionary Army was established in 1925, the Kwangtung Army became the Fourth Army, with Li Chi-shen (q.v.) as its commander. Ts'ai's regiment was renamed the 28th Regiment and was placed under the 10th Division, commanded by Ch'en Ming-shu. When the Northern Expedition began in 1926, the 10th Division formed part of the vanguard force in the drive on Wuhan. The capture of the Wuhan cities brought the first stage of the Northern Expedition to an end. In the ensuing reorganization of the National Revolutionary Army, Ch'en Ming-shu became commander of the Eleventh Army, composed of the 10th Division and a new 24th Division. Chiang Kuang-nai (q.v.) commanded the 10th Division, and Tai Chi commanded the 24th, with Ts'ai T'ing-k'ai as deputy commander. At the time of the Wuhan-Nanking split in 1927, Ch'en, Chiang, and Tai all left their posts. Chang Fa-k'uei (q.v.) then assumed command of the Eleventh Army, with Ts'ai T'ing-k'ai heading the 10th Division.

By the summer of 1927, relations between Wuhan and Nanking had deteriorated to such an extent that armed conflict seemed inevitable.

T'ang Sheng-chih (q.v.), having assumed the position of commander in chief in the Wuhan government, appointed Chang Fa-k'uei commander of the Second Front Army, which included the Fourth Army, the Eleventh Army, and the Twentieth Army. The Second Front Army moved eastward to the Nanchang area. On 1 August, the Communist commanders in the Wuhan forces—Yeh T'ing (q.v.), who commanded the 24th Division, and Ho Lung, who commanded the Twentieth Army—joined with Chu Teh (q.v.) in staging the insurrection at Nanchang that later was celebrated as marking the birth of the Chinese Communist army. When Chang Fa-k'uei forced them to evacuate the city a few days later, they took Ts'ai T'ing-k'ai along with them. Ts'ai managed to escape, and he led units of the Eleventh Army into Fukien. At his urgent request, Ch'en Ming-shu resumed command of the Eleventh Army.

Ts'ai T'ing-k'ai spent much of 1928 suppressing local banditry on Hainan Island. With the reorganization of Kwangtung military units in 1929, he became commander of the 60th Division and Chiang Kuang-nai became commander of the 61st Division. After helping to repel the forces of Chang Fa-k'uei and Li Tsung-jen (q.v.) in 1930, these divisions were transferred to north China to take part in the campaign against the so-called northern coalition of Feng Yü-hsiang and Yen Hsi-shan (qq.v.). The Nineteenth Route Army was created at this time, with Chiang Kuang-nai as commander in chief and Ts'ai T'ing-k'ai as field commander. In 1931 the Nineteenth Route Army took part in the National Government's first encirclement campaign against the Chinese Communists in Kiangsi. In the meantime, Chiang Kai-shek had placed Hu Han-min (q.v.) under house arrest at Nanking. In response, a secessionist government was established at Canton by such dissident leaders as Eugene Ch'en, Sun Fo, T'ang Shao-yi, and Wang Ching-wei (qq.v.), with the military support of Ch'en Chi-t'ang (q.v.) and Li Tsung-jen. Although the southern regime bid for the support of the Nineteenth Route Army, it remained loyal to Nanking despite the possibility that its men would be called upon to fight their former comrades of the old Fourth Army. The Japanese invasion of Manchuria in September 1931 averted the threat of civil war and led to the

dissolution of the Canton government. The Nineteenth Route Army then was transferred to the Shanghai area for garrison duty.

The early months of 1932 saw Ts'ai T'ing-k'ai's phenomenal rise to international fame. On the night of 28 January, the Japanese marines attacked Shanghai. The Nineteenth Route Army stubbornly held its ground against tremendous odds for more than three months. During this period, world attention focused on the Nineteenth Route Army and its leaders, and contributions of supplies and money poured in from many countries. Later in 1932, the Nineteenth Route Army was transferred to Fukien, where Ts'ai became its commander in chief and Chiang Kuang-nai became pacification commissioner at Foochow. At year's end, Ts'ai again succeeded Chiang when the latter became governor of Fukien.

On 20 November 1933 the so-called Fukien revolt began with the establishment of an opposition government at Foochow. The principal instigator of this movement was Ch'en Ming-shu, and the leaders of the Nineteenth Route Army remained loyal to their old associate. Although Ts'ai T'ing-k'ai showed some reluctance about supporting the movement, he served on the 11-man government council at Foochow and as commander in chief of the First Direction Army (a slightly enlarged Nineteenth Route Army). The Fukien rebels called for democratic government in China and strong resistance to Japanese aggression. The National Government suppressed the revolt quickly and easily, for the governors of provinces and even the Chinese Communists refused to support the rebels. The Foochow regime collapsed in January 1934, and the remnants of the Nineteenth Route Army fled into Kwangtung to be absorbed by Ch'en Chi-t'ang. By February, almost all the leaders of the Foochow debacle had taken refuge in Hong Kong.

The misadventure in Fukien hardly impaired the personal popularity of Ts'ai T'ing-k'ai, especially among overseas Chinese. In April 1934 Ts'ai left Hong Kong on a world tour. Traveling on an Italian vessel, he stopped at Singapore, Penang, Colombo, Bombay, Suez, Cairo, and Venice, and everywhere he was warmly received by Chinese residents. In Rome, he was received by Mussolini and invited to visit military establishments. He then went on to Geneva, Vienna, Budapest, Prague, Berlin,

Copenhagen, Stockholm, Amsterdam, Brussels, Paris, and London. In August, he went to the United States, where he stayed for 160 days and visited 63 cities. When his ship arrived in New York on 28 August, he received a hero's welcome from a crowd of more than 3,000. A grand banquet in his honor was held at the Hotel New Yorker on 30 August. Among the major cities Ts'ai visited in the United States were Boston, Chicago, Philadelphia, Washington, Detroit, Los Angeles, and San Francisco. He reached San Francisco on 4 November 1934 and remained there until 5 February 1935. He then went to Australia by way of Honolulu, the Fiji Islands, and New Zealand. He reached Melbourne on 9 March and remained in Australia for a month. He made the final leg of the journey back to Hong Kong by way of the Philippines, where he stayed for 12 days. He reached Hong Kong on 19 April 1935, exactly one year and one week after his departure.

In the course of his tour, Ts'ai was called upon to make many public addresses. He displayed considerable skill in handling his audiences. In the United States for instance, where most of his Chinese hosts were Cantonese, he dealt generally with the patriotism and generosity of overseas Chinese and emphasized that most of the men of the Nineteenth Route Army had been Cantonese. In the Philippines, where most of the Chinese residents had come from Fukien, Ts'ai apologized for not having done much for the welfare of the Fukienese. He took pains to explain that the Foochow secessionist movement had been forced on the Nineteenth Route Army and that the army immediately had withdrawn under military pressure from Nanking. Had it not done so, he explained, the people of Fukien would have suffered the extreme ravages of war.

On his return to Hong Kong, Ts'ai joined with Li Chi-shen, Ch'en Ming-shu, and Chiang Kuang-nai in forming a new political party, the Chinese People's Revolutionary League. Li Chi-shen was its chairman, and the ranking members included Feng Yü-hsiang, Hsü Ch'ien (q.v.) and Eugene Ch'en. Its newspaper, the *Ta-chung Pao*, set forth its platform of resistance to the Japanese and "overthrow of the traitor government and establishment of the people's state power." During the 1935–36 period, Ts'ai spent his time promoting the party and studying.

In 1937 Ts'ai T'ing-k'ai made a trip to the Philippines. When he learned that the Sino-Japanese war had broken out, he returned to Hong Kong, arriving there on 22 July. He soon received a summons from Chiang Kai-shek and went to Nanking, where he was appointed a councillor in Chiang's headquarters. At this time, Ts'ai, Li Chi-shen, Ch'en Ming-shu, and Chiang Kuang-nai decided to dissolve the Chinese People's Revolutionary League on the grounds that it had accomplished the task of mobilizing the Chinese people to fight Japan.

Ts'ai's wife died in Hong Kong in September 1937. Before that year was out, Ts'ai himself met with a serious automobile accident. He was taken to Hong Kong for medical attention. He remained inactive until mid-1938 when he directed operations in southwestern Kwangtung as a member of the Kwangtung Self-Defense Forces Command. In January 1939 Chiang Kai-shek called him to Chungking and appointed him deputy commander of the Sixteenth Army Group in Kwangsi. That July, Ts'ai married Lo Hsi-ou, and in September, he was made commander in chief of the Sixteenth Army Group. In April 1940 he was appointed commander in chief of the Kwangtung and Kwangsi border areas. However, he soon discovered that his army had been moved away for reasons unknown to him. He thus became a soldierless commander, and he responded to this situation by resigning in September. Toward the end of 1940, he was named to the Military Council at Chungking. He visited Hong Kong in 1941, where he met with Eugene Ch'en and Madame Sun Yat-sen (Soong Ch'ing-ling, q.v.). He then retired to Kweilin, where, with the exception of occasional trips to Yunnan and Kweichow, he spent the next three years. At the end of 1944 he moved to his native village of Loting, and at war's end in 1945 he moved to Canton.

In 1946 Ts'ai helped organize the Kuomintang Democracy Promotion Association, a group composed mainly of former Kuomintang military officers who had become severely critical of the National Government. This group later was incorporated into the Kuomintang Revolutionary Committee, of which Li Chi-shen was chairman. Ts'ai then became a vice chairman of that committee. Ts'ai left Hong Kong for the Northeast in September 1948, and he arrived in Peiping in February 1949. He was a delegate to the Chinese People's Political Consultative Conference in September 1949.

With the establishment of the Central People's Government of the People's Republic of China in October 1949, Ts'ai T'ing-k'ai became a member of the People's Revolutionary Military Council and the Overseas Chinese Affairs Commission. In 1954 he was appointed to the National Defense Council. He was on successive National Committees of the Chinese People's Political Consultative Conference and served as a delegate to the 1954 and 1958 National People's congresses. In 1958 he was promoted to deputy chairman of the National Defense Council. He died at Peking on 25 April 1968.

Ts'ai T'ing-kan 蔡 廷 幹
T. Yao-t'ang 耀 堂

Ts'ai T'ing-kan (1861–29 September 1935), naval officer and long-time associate of Yuan Shih-k'ai. He held protocol, customs, and other foreign-affairs posts at Peking until 1927.

Although Ts'ai T'ing-kan considered himself a native of Tahsing, Chihli (Hopei), he was born at Hsiangshan (later Chungshan), Kwangtung. He received his early education in the Chinese classics at local village schools and then, in 1870–71, studied at the Chinese Educational Mission School established by Yung Wing (Jung Hung, ECCP, I, 402–5) at Shanghai. In 1873, after completing the school's course of study, he went to the United States as a member of the second group of 30 young Chinese sent abroad on the China Educational Mission program (for further information, see Chan T'ien-yu).

In the United States, Ts'ai enrolled at the Hartford Grammar School in Connecticut. He later studied at the New Britain High School and lived at the home of a Mrs. MacLean in Springfield, Massachusetts. He soon gained a reputation for mischief-making, and his school companions dubbed him the "Fighting Chinee." At the request of Mrs. MacLean, he was transferred before graduation to study practical mechanics in the machine shops at Lowell. At that time, for purely utilitarian reasons, he cut off his queue. He returned to China in 1881 when the Ch'ing government abolished the China Educational Mission on the grounds that the students were becoming excessively Americanized and were neglecting their Chinese studies. Upon his return, he enrolled at a torpedo school established by Li Hung-chang (ECCP, I, 464–71) at Taku. In addition to torpedo theory and practice, from 1882 onward he also studied electrical engineering, mining, and surveying under American and French instructors. After completing the basic course at Taku in 1884, he studied navigation under British officers while serving a period of apprenticeship with Li Hung-chang's fledgling Peiyang fleet.

In 1888, at the age of 27, Ts'ai was commissioned a junior lieutenant in the Chinese navy. The following year, he received the rank of acting senior lieutenant. In 1891 he was given command of a torpedo boat and was assigned to patrol duties. The next year, he was given the substantive rank of commander, awarded the Peacock Feather decoration, and put in charge of a newly acquired squadron of torpedo boats, stationed at Port Arthur. He and his squadron played an active role in the September 1894 engagement known as the Battle of the Yellow Sea. Although the Chinese fleet of Admiral Ting Ju-ch'ang was heavier than the Japanese fleet of Admiral Ito Yuko, it was handicapped by inferior command capacities and by the disabilities imposed upon it by the empress dowager's diversion of naval funds to other purposes. Accordingly, the Japanese won a decisive victory. The Chinese lost five ships, and several others were damaged. When the wounded fleet retired to Port Arthur for repairs, Ts'ai's squadron accompanied it.

After making temporary repairs, the Chinese fleet sailed for the Weihaiwei base and took up a defensive position there. It was a strong position, with the anchorage shielded by two fortified islands. In late January 1895, however, the Japanese army of General Oyama captured the forts on the mainland opposite Ting Ju-ch'ang's refuge. Ting's officers refused to attempt a breakout, and, when he finally decided to surrender, they refused to destroy their ships. With the fleet in general mutiny, ten torpedo boats led by Wang Teng-yun sped out of the western harbor entrance on 7 February in a break for safety. These boats, which included Ts'ai T'ing-kan's own craft, were fired upon by Chinese ships, by the forts on the mainland, and by pursuing Japanese vessels.

Although Wang Teng-yun managed to reach Chefoo, Ts'ai's boat was sunk under him. Ts'ai was fished from the sea by the Japanese and held as a prisoner of war. On 13 February, Ting Ju-ch'ang surrendered the remainder of the fleet at Weihaiwei to Admiral Ito. Ting then took poison.

With the signing of the Treaty of Shimonoseki in the aftermath of that inglorious affair and of China's defeat in the Sino-Japanese war, Li Hung-chang was in disgrace. The officers of Li's Peiyang fleet, including Ts'ai T'ing-kan, were degraded in rank. In 1901, when Li died and Yuan Shih-k'ai succeeded to his posts, the degraded naval officers began to be employed in connection with Yuan's plans for the military rehabilitation of north China. Through the introduction of T'ang Shao-yi (q.v.), Ts'ai T'ing-kan entered Yuan's service and gradually became a favorite of Yuan. In 1908 Yuan successfully petitioned the throne to restore the naval officers' ranks.

When Yuan Shih-k'ai was forced into retirement in 1909, Ts'ai T'ing-kan also withdrew from public life. Yuan returned to power at the time of the revolution in 1911, and Ts'ai promptly was appointed chief of the department of naval administration in the Navy Board, with the rank of rear admiral. After Yuan arrived in Peking, Ts'ai was made expectant metropolitan officer of the third rank in December. In January 1912 he was transferred to Yuan's staff as naval aide de camp. In that post, he helped Yuan to achieve the abdication of the Manchu authorities and Yuan's accession to power at Peking as provisional president of the new republic. Ts'ai's efforts won him promotion to vice admiral on 20 November 1912.

Early in 1913 Ts'ai was awarded the Fourth Order of Merit and was appointed chief inspector of the salt gabelle. On 1 October, he became associate director general of the customs revenue council. He continued to perform various functions in the presidential office, especially with regard to the reception of foreign visitors, and in May 1914 his informal position in that office was dignified with the title of assistant master of ceremonies.

Ts'ai suffered a temporary political setback, because of his close association with Yuan Shih-k'ai, when Yuan died in June 1916. However, in October 1917 Tuan Ch'i-jui (q.v.) awarded Ts'ai the Paokuang Chiaho decoration,

second class, and in 1918 Tuan appointed him chairman of the tariff revision commission. Later in 1918 Ts'ai was reappointed to his old position in the presidential office at Peking, with the title of assistant grand master of ceremonies. He became associate director of the enemy subjects repatriation bureau in January 1919, and the work involved in this post caused him to relinquish his protocol duties the following month.

In 1921 Ts'ai attended the Washington Conference as an adviser to the Chinese delegation. In accordance with agreements reached at that conference, a tariff revision conference was convened in Shanghai at the end of March, with Ts'ai as its chairman. Agreement finally was reached in September for the establishment of a revised tariff schedule which would go into effect the following January. At the end of 1922 Ts'ai officiated as master of ceremonies at the wedding of P'u-yi (q.v.), the last Manchu emperor. His chief responsibility on that occasion was the introduction of foreign guests to the imperial couple. Throughout this period, Ts'ai had maintained close ties with the foreign community at Peking, and his official functions continued to have something to do with foreign affairs.

Ts'ai T'ing-kan also was known for his participation in civic affairs. In April 1919 he became vice president of the Chinese Red Cross Society. The following year he assumed the duties of chief of the transportation section of the China International Famine Relief Commission. He became the treasurer of that organization in January 1923. Ts'ai was president of the Peking Rotary Club in 1924–25, and for years he served as president of the American-Returned Students Club.

In 1923, with the initial work of tariff revision done, Ts'ai became a member of the commission for the reorganization of China's domestic and foreign debts. On 30 June he was appointed chairman of the commission charged with preparing for a special customs tariff conference, and in the autumn of 1924 he became director general of the customs revenue council. He held that office for more than two years despite changes of administration at Peking (see Feng Yü-hsiang). In 1925 he was one of three high commissioners appointed to investigate the May Thirtieth Incident at Shanghai. And when the Special Customs Tariff Conference finally convened at Peking on 26 October 1925, he served as one of the delegates. Because of the war between Feng Yü-hsiang (q.v.), on one side, and Chang Tso-lin and Wu P'ei-fu (qq.v.), on the other, the conference found it impossible to proceed with the work at hand. By the spring of 1926 only two of the five chief Chinese delegates, Ts'ai and W. W. Yen (Yen Hui-ch'ing, q.v.), were still in Peking. On 3 July, the frustrated foreign delegations issued a statement expressing their desire to proceed with consideration of the problems before the conference whenever the Chinese delegates were in a position to do so.

Tu Hsi-kuei had succeeded W. W. Yen as premier at Peking in June 1926. At the first meeting of his cabinet on 6 July, he appointed Ts'ai T'ing-kan foreign minister. A mandate issued on 14 July appointed a new delegation to the tariff conference, with Ts'ai at its head. Ts'ai soon encountered new difficulties, for the Peking government's authority to represent China at the conference was challenged by Feng Yü-hsiang and by the National Government at Canton, which had just launched its Northern Expedition. The conference adjourned "for the summer" in the absence of a responsible Chinese government, and it did not resume that fall. As foreign minister, Ts'ai continued to pursue the general matter of treaty revision, but the weakened condition of the Peking government made negotiation impossible.

With Wu P'ei-fu heavily engaged on the southern front, Chang Tso-lin's forces and influence became dominant at Peking. At the beginning of October 1926, Tu Hsi-kuei abandoned the premiership and Ts'ai T'ing-kan resigned as foreign minister. V. K. Wellington Koo (Ku Wei-chün, q.v.), who then became acting premier and foreign minister, assumed the duties of chairman of the Chinese delegation to the dormant tariff conference. Ts'ai thus was left only with the position of director general of the customs revenue council. In May 1927, as the Peking regime's financial situation became critical, Ts'ai resigned from his last official post and retired to Dairen and private life. He remained there until the time of the Japanese attack on Mukden in September 1931. He then moved back to Peiping, where he devoted his attention to the Chinese classics, poetry, and calligraphy. He translated the *Tao-te-ching* and ancient Chinese poems into English, and in 1932 a collection of his translations of T'ang poems

was published by the University of Chicago Press as *Chinese Poems in English Rhyme*. Ts'ai T'ing-kan died at Peiping on 29 September 1935.

Ts'ai Yuan-p'ei   蔡 元 培
  T. Ho-ch'ing   鶴 卿
  H. Chieh-min   孑 民

Ts'ai Yuan-p'ei (January 1868–5 March 1940), the last of the Hanlin scholars to have major influence in twentieth-century China, was the leading liberal educator of early republican China and an important synthesizer of Chinese and Western intellectual patterns. After the overthrow of the Ch'ing dynasty, he served as minister of education (1912–13), chancellor of Peking University (1916–26), and founder and president of the Academia Sinica.

Shanyin, then the chief hsien of Shaohsing prefecture in Chekiang province, was the birthplace of Ts'ai Yuan-p'ei. Both his grandfather and his father were merchants. His father, Ts'ai Kuang-p'u, was a successful manager of a native bank. Generous by nature, Ts'ai Kuang-p'u invariably came to the aid of needy relatives and friends. As a result, when he died in 1877, his widow and three sons (of whom Ts'ai Yuan-p'ei, then eleven sui, was the second), found themselves in straitened circumstances. Some of Ts'ai Kuang-p'u's former beneficiaries suggested raising a fund to help to educate the Ts'ai children, but his widow, *née* Chou, declined the offer. She brought up the children by dint of diligence and frugality. Ts'ai Yuan-p'ei inherited both the instinctive generosity of his father and the independence of his mother, qualities which did much to shape his personal development in later years.

Ts'ai began his education in the Chinese classics at the age of 6 sui. Among his tutors was an uncle, Ts'ai Ming-en, a chü-jen who had an excellent private library which he let his nephew use. Ts'ai Yuan-p'ei took the sheng-yuan degree in 1883, at the age of 17 sui. In 1889 he gained the chü-jen degree, and in 1890 he passed the metropolitan examinations for the chin-shih degree, thus becoming one of the youngest candidates to gain the top degree in the imperial examination system. Ts'ai was selected in 1892 as a scholar of the Hanlin

Academy, and in 1894 he was promoted to the rank of compiler. During this period, he became friendly with a fellow Chekiang provincial, Chang Yuan-chi (q.v.).

Ts'ai Yuan-p'ei's success in the metropolitan examination and at the Hanlin Academy was in a sense a surprise. After he had gained the sheng-yuan degree in 1883, Ts'ai had lost interest in the stereotyped form of Chinese literary composition characterized as the eight-legged essay and had devoted his full attention to study of Chinese language and history, which did not contribute directly to success in the examination system of the time. He continued to study these subjects even after his admission to the Hanlin Academy and became one of the most erudite classical scholars of his day.

China's ignominious defeat at the hands of Japan in the war of 1894–95 and the failure of the reform effort of 1898 had significant effects on Ts'ai's career. Because he believed that the backwardness of Chinese education was the principal cause of China's patent weakness, he resigned his positions and left Peking to return to Chekiang and devote himself to education. For a long time, he served at Shaohsing as principal of the Chung-hsi hsueh-t'ang [Sino-Western school], which boasted a modern curriculum. A student in the school at that time was Chiang Monlin (Chiang Meng-lin, q.v.), who was later to become an associate of Ts'ai at Peking University. In 1901 Ts'ai left his native district for Shanghai, where he taught at the Nan-yang kung-hsueh [Nanyang public school], a government-supported academy. Chang Yuan-chi was its principal. Among Ts'ai's students there were Huang Yen-p'ei and Shao Li-tzu (qq.v.), and a fellow teacher was Wu Chih-hui (q.v.). In 1902 Wu Chih-hui, who had gone to Japan with young Chinese government scholars from Kwangtung, came into conflict with the Chinese minister in Tokyo, who refused to recommend some of Wu's charges for admission to Japanese military schools. In the ensuing fracas, Wu was taken into custody by the Japanese authorities, who planned to deport him. Wu attempted suicide but was rescued by the Japanese police. Ts'ai Yuan-p'ei, then on a holiday trip to Japan, cut short his visit and volunteered to accompany Wu back to Shanghai to ensure that he would not make another suicide attempt.

On his return to Shanghai in August 1902,

Ts'ai Yuan-p'ei participated in the organization of the Chung-kuo chiao-yü hui (China Education Society) and became its first president. The association was an anti-Manchu revolutionary organization, and its leaders included Chang Ping-lin (q.v.), Huang Yen-p'ei, and Wu Chih-hui. It soon organized its own school at Shanghai, the Ai-kuo hsueh-she [patriotic study society], established chiefly for students who had been expelled from the Nan-yang kung-hsueh. Another institution established about that time was the Ai-kuo nü-hsueh [patriotic girls school], financed by Mrs. Silas Hardoon; the girls school also was related to the China Education Society in that Ts'ai Yuan-p'ei and his colleagues taught there and Ts'ai served as its principal for a time. Because the girls' school was not directly involved in revolutionary activities, however, it was not curbed by the authorities. Eventually it developed into one of the leading girls' schools of Shanghai.

In 1903, when a dispute arose between the China Education Society and the Ai-kuo hsueh-she, Ts'ai, disgusted with the petty strife, left for a visit to Tsingtao. When the case of the *Su-pao*, a revolutionary newspaper (*see* Chang Ping-lin), broke in Shanghai, Ts'ai was among those whose name was included in the first list of men wanted by the authorities. The juxta-position of circumstances led to rumors that Ts'ai had gone to Tsingtao to escape trouble. Actually, he returned to Shanghai almost immediately and took part in the founding of the *Ching-chung jih-pao*, a new journal that was regarded as a continuation of the efforts made by such papers as the *Su-pao* and the *Kuo-min jih-pao* to publish and disseminate anti-Manchu propaganda.

In the autumn of 1904, a new revolutionary organization, the Kuang-fu-hui [restoration society] was organized by young patriots from Kiangsu and Chekiang, particularly the latter province. Ts'ai Yuan-p'ei helped in the founding of the new group and was elected its first president. Other leaders included Chang Ping-lin, T'ao Ch'eng-chang, Ch'iu Chin, and Hsü Hsi-lin. The Kuang-fu-hui was the third-largest organized revolutionary group at that time, coming after the Hsing-Chung-hui of Sun Yat-sen and the Hua-hsing-hui of Huang Hsing (q.v.). Most of the members of these three groups became adherents of the T'ung-meng-hui when it was formed in Tokyo in August 1905.

Ts'ai Yuan-p'ei was appointed head of the Shanghai branch of the society and was charged with recruiting new members in that area.

Ts'ai's role as practicing revolutionary was abandoned during the final years of the Ch'ing dynasty. In 1906 he returned to Peking with the hope of gaining a government scholarship for study abroad. When he discovered that scholars then were being sent to Japan, while he himself wanted to go to Europe, he accepted a post as teacher in the I-hsueh kuan [translation institute]. In 1907 Sun Pao-ch'i (q.v.) was appointed minister to Germany. Sun agreed to guarantee Ts'ai a monthly subsidy of 30 taels of silver; the Commercial Press in Shanghai, where Chang Yuan-chi directed the office of compilation and translation, also promised him a modest salary for translation work. Ts'ai thus went to Berlin, where he studied German for a year. From 1908 to 1911 he attended the University of Leipzig, where he attended lectures on philosophy, literature, ethnology, European history, experimental psychology, and aesthetics.

Ts'ai Yuan-p'ei returned to China in November 1911, shortly after the Wuchang revolt. When Sun Yat-sen assumed the provisional presidency of the republic in January 1912, he appointed Ts'ai minister of education. After Sun resigned in favor of Yuan Shih-k'ai, Ts'ai and Wang Ching-wei (q.v.) led a delegation to north China to discuss arrangements for Yuan's inauguration at Nanking. Yuan insisted, however, that the government be moved to Peking. In the first cabinet under Yuan headed by T'ang Shao-yi (q.v.) as premier, Ts'ai retained the post of minister of education. Growing friction between T'ang and Yuan Shih-k'ai led to the resignation of that cabinet in June 1912. Ts'ai then left for Germany and studied for a year at Leipzig. He returned to China in 1913, but he soon became disheartened over the failure of the so-called second revolution against Yuan Shih-k'ai and went to Europe again.

After a period in Germany, Ts'ai moved to France, where he associated himself with Li Shih-tseng (q.v.), Wang Ching-wei, Wu Chih-hui, and others in developing plans to enable young Chinese to study in France. In 1915, this group organized the Societé Franco-Chinois d'Education at Paris, with Ts'ai as its Chinese president, and they also sponsored a work-study program in which some 2,000 Chinese students participated. In the course of this French interlude during the First World War, Ts'ai, removed from the turmoil of Chinese politics, matured intellectually, and he found time to write a general outline of the principles of philosophy and a study on Kantian aesthetics. He also had sufficient leisure to renew friendships with Chang Jen-chieh (q.v.), Li Shih-tseng, and Wu Chih-hui. In later years the four men were widely known as the "four elder statesmen of the Kuomintang."

Late in 1916, after the death of Yuan Shih-k'ai and the accession of Li Yuan-hung (q.v.) to the presidency, Ts'ai Yuan-p'ei was appointed chancellor of Peking University. The appointment aroused controversy within the Kuomintang, as many of its leaders felt that acceptance of the post by Ts'ai would be tantamount to defection from the revolutionary ranks. Sun Yat-sen, however, favored the appointment on the ground that a scholar like Ts'ai who combined practical experience with intellectual excellence would in fact be an ideal man to disseminate the spirit of the republican revolution in north China.

The incumbency of Ts'ai Yuan-p'ei as chancellor of Peking University (or Peita as it was conventionally shortened in Chinese) from 1916 to 1926 coincided with a critical period in recent Chinese history which was marked both by intellectual ferment and by the emergence in China of a new spirit of modern nationalism and social reform. Peking University played a major role in this process of experimentation and change. The leadership of Ts'ai Yuan-p'ei, and his devotion to independent thinking, innovative experimentation, and encouragement of young talent, helped to develop Peking University into China's premier institution of higher education. Ts'ai nurtured by both advocacy and example an atmosphere at Peking University which encouraged first-class scholarship and permitted espousal of heterodox opinions in the faculty and political activism on the part of the students. The university served as a center of the May Fourth Movement, and it was also the institution where Li Ta-chao (q.v.), the young Mao Tse-tung, and others became interested in the tenets of Marxism-Leninism. While personally moderate in temperament, Ts'ai was implacable when moral or ethical principles were involved in an issue. When student leaders were arrested in Peking after the May Fourth Movement in 1919, for example, he left Peking for Hangchow as a gesture of protest against official persecution. Public opinion forced the Peking authorities to release the students, and Ts'ai returned to his post in September.

During his tenure as head of China's ranking university, Ts'ai Yuan-p'ei made several trips abroad. In November 1920, commissioned by the Chinese ministry of education to survey educational conditions in Europe and the United States, Ts'ai traveled with Lo Wen-kan (q.v.), who was on a special mission to investigate judicial systems. In France Ts'ai received an honorary doctorate from the University of Paris; and he and Lo Wen-kan then visited several other Western European countries. In July 1921 they visited the United States, where Ts'ai received an honorary degree from New York University and raised funds for the construction of Peking University library. On the way back to China, he attended the Pacific Educational Conference in Honolulu.

In November 1922, when internecine political struggles at Peking led to the arrest of Lo Wen-kan, who was then minister of finance, on charges of corruption, Ts'ai again left his post in protest. After an interlude of retirement at Soochow in 1923, he went to Europe, where he lived for a time in Brussels. In 1924 he spent time in Belgium and France, where he assisted Li Shih-tseng and Wu Chih-hui with Sino-French cultural and educational exchange problems, and in 1925 he went to Germany, where he studied ethnology at the University of Hamburg. Because of this absence in Europe, he did not participate in the reorganization of the Kuomintang at its First National Congress, held at Canton in January 1924. He was, however, elected to alternate membership in the Central Supervisory Committee.

In February 1926 Ts'ai received a cable from the ministry of education urging him to return to Peking University, where Chiang Monlin (Chiang Meng-lin, q.v.) had served as acting chancellor of the institution during his absence. Ts'ai returned to China only to discover that the Northern Expedition had been launched from Canton. He then joined the Kiangsu-Chekiang-Anhwei Joint Association, an organization designed to mobilize support for the National Revolutionary Army. That winter, when he went to Ningpo to attend a meeting of the association, he found the situation in Chekiang to be dangerous. Accordingly, he fled to Foochow, where he remained for several months. During the period of conflict between the Nationalist governments at Nanking and Wuhan in 1927, Ts'ai Yuan-p'ei sided with his fellow-provincial Chiang Kai-shek. He attended meetings of the Central Political Council and became a member of the Central Supervisory Committee of the Kuomintang. At the same time he was appointed acting minister of justice at Nanking, and he later became a member of the State Council. In the autumn of 1928, when the National Government at Nanking inaugurated a five-yuan system of government in accordance with the formula stipulated by Sun Yat-sen, Ts'ai was appointed president of the Control Yuan, but he soon resigned.

Although he did not return to Peking University after 1926, Ts'ai Yuan-p'ei's basic role in national affairs continued to be directly related to higher education. In 1927 he was named president of the Ta-hsueh-yuan [board of universities], which replaced the former ministry of education. The new system, patterned after the French model, had been recommended by Chang Jen-chieh, Li Shih-tseng, and Wu Chih-hui, who had been influenced by their residence in France. The system called for creation of so-called university districts in various parts of China, and as a start three such districts were inaugurated in Peking and in Kiangsu and Chekiang provinces. After an initial year of experimentation, the system was found to be unsuitable for China; it was abolished in 1929, and the ministry of education was restored.

Early in 1928 Ts'ai helped to found the Chung-yang yen-chiu-yuan, or Academia Sinica, designed to be the highest institution of advanced study and research in China. The Academia Sinica, with Ts'ai as its first president, did much to raise the level of research in China, and certain of its institutes gained international recognition. Serving under Ts'ai as secretary general of the Academia Sinica was Yang Ch'uan (q.v.), an able academic administrator trained in the United States. Yang was politically active in China, and in late 1932 he was a prominent figure in the organization of the China League for Civil Rights, which was supported by Sun Yat-sen's widow, Soong Ch'ing-ling (q.v.), and other public figures.

Ts'ai Yuan-p'ei was active in efforts to safeguard civil rights in China, and in 1932 he participated in an unsuccessful appeal to gain the release of Ch'en Tu-hsiu (q.v.), who had served under him at Peking University as dean of the college of letters. In June 1933, Yang Ch'uan was assassinated at Shanghai. The impact of that event on Ts'ai Yuan-p'ei was such that after extended consideration he resigned all official posts in 1935 and issued a public statement expressing disgust with the restrictive political and intellectual controls exercised by the Nanking authorities.

After retirement from public life, Ts'ai fell ill in 1936 at Shanghai. When the Sino-Japanese war erupted in mid-1937, he did not accompany the National Government on its westward exodus, a decision caused partly by poor health, partly by dissatisfaction with Nanking politics. Instead he went to Hong Kong in late 1937 and was joined there by his family in February 1938. Ts'ai lived the final months of his life in virtual anonymity. He made only one public appearance—to attend an exhibition of Chinese art sponsored by the vice chancellor of the University of Hong Kong, when he was persuaded to make a speech. His health continued to decline, and his physical condition was aggravated by an accident at home on 3 March 1940. He was rushed to the hospital, but he died two days later.

Ts'ai Yuan-p'ei married three times. His first wife, née Wang, died in 1898. In 1901 he married Huang Chung-yu, a highly educated young woman from a scholarly family in Kiangsu. She died in Peking in 1921 while Ts'ai was on a mission to Europe. On 1 July 1923 while in retirement in Chekiang, he married Chou Chun, who survived him. She had been a student of Ts'ai at the Ai-kuo nü-hsueh in Shanghai and had become a prominent educator. Ts'ai had four sons. The eldest, Ts'ai Wu-chi, studied agriculture and veterinary medicine and at one time headed the bureau of commodity inspection and testing in Shanghai. The other three sons were Pai-ling, Huai-hsin, and Ying-to. Ts'ai had two daughters, Wei-lien (d. 1939), who studied art in France, and Tsu-ang.

Ts'ai Yuan-p'ei's reputation rests on his performance and integrity as the leading liberal educator of pre-1928 China. Although a product of the classical system and an eminent scholar of traditional Chinese culture, he was also imbued with the spirit of independent inquiry characteristic of modern Western scholarship. He was especially interested in problems of philosophy, was an enthusiastic exponent of aestheticism, and produced a succinct but comprehensive history of Chinese ethics, *Chung-kuo lun-li-hsueh shih*, in 1931. That year he contributed a chapter on painting and calligraphy to the *Symposium on Chinese Culture* edited by Sophia H. Chen Zen (Ch'en Heng-che, q.v.). Ts'ai was a product of the Confucian system, but he was critical of the formality of Confucianism and encouraged critical study of its basic texts at Peking University. As chancellor of Peking University and founder of the Academia Sinica, Ts'ai Yuan-p'ei had a deep influence on higher education in republican China.

Ts'ao Ju-lin　　　　曹　汝　霖
　T. Jun-t'ien　　　　潤　田

Ts'ao Ju-lin (1876–4 August 1966), pro-Japanese official at Peking who was one of the principal targets of the May Fourth Incident of 1919.

Born at Shanghai, Ts'ao Ju-lin was the son of Ts'ao Yü-ts'ai, a scholar who held the sheng-yuan degree. The young Ts'ao was given a thorough grounding in the Chinese classics. At the age of 13, he also began to study French. He abandoned classical studies in 1895, after China's defeat in the Sino-Japanese war, because he believed that the old system of education had failed to prepare China for the new problems it faced. He then enrolled at the Hupeh Railway School in Wuhan. In 1897 he married Wang Mei-lin. Two years later, he went to Japan, where he studied law at Waseda University and then at Chuo University in Tokyo.

Upon his return to China in 1904, Ts'ao passed the special examinations for students returning from abroad and received the degree of chin-shih in law from the Ch'ing government. In 1905 he became an apprentice secretary in the Board of Agriculture and Commerce and a lecturer in law at Imperial University (later Peking University). He also helped organize the bureau of constitutional research and compilation and the bureau of law codification.

When Komura Jutaro, the Japanese foreign minister, came to Peking in November 1905 for negotiations regarding Manchuria, Ts'ao because of his Japanese educational training was transferred to the Board of Foreign Affairs as an apprentice secretary. He served as an attaché to the Chinese delegation in the negotiations that resulted in China's acceptance of the territorial disposition made in the Treaty of Portsmouth, which had ended the Russo-Japanese war. The agreement signed between China and Japan on 22 December also granted Japan the right to hold concessions in Mukden and other Manchurian cities. Ts'ao thus was introduced to international diplomacy. He then became a junior secretary in the Board of Foreign Affairs.

It was natural, given Ts'ao's legal training, that he should be involved in the establishment of provincial assemblies in 1909 and in the inauguration of a national assembly in 1910. Also during this period, he was sent to Manchuria to conduct investigations which apparently had something to do with the "rehabilitation" of the region as set forth in the Sino-Japanese agreement of 1905. He submitted detailed recommendations regarding Manchurian administration, and his proposals were well received by the Ch'ing court. About 1910 he was appointed junior vice president of the Board of Foreign Affairs.

After the revolution of 1911 and the establishment of republican government in China, Ts'ao Ju-lin became a personal adviser to Yuan Shih-k'ai. When the new Parliament convened at Peking in 1913, Ts'ao was present as a senator representing Mongolia. He was a member of the Chin-pu-tang [progressive party], which supported Yuan in his struggle with the Kuomintang. In July, he was named to the 60-man committee which was responsible for drafting a permanent constitution. The following month, he was appointed vice minister of foreign affairs. After Japan declared war on Germany in August 1914, attacked at Tsingtao, and advanced to take over Germany's privileged position in Shantung, Ts'ao acted as chief aide to Sun Pao-ch'i (q.v.) in negotiations with Japan. The Japanese presented their Twenty-One Demands to Yuan Shih-k'ai's government in January 1915, whereupon Sun Pao-ch'i resigned and Lu Cheng-hsiang (q.v.) was reappointed minister of foreign affairs. Although

Lu signed the agreement with the Japanese on 25 May, Yuan Shih-k'ai and Ts'ao Ju-lin were responsible for the Chinese side of the negotiations leading to that agreement. Lu and Ts'ao both came under popular attack for their roles in this matter, but Yuan refused to accept their proffered resignations.

When Yuan Shih-k'ai launched his campaign to become monarch in the summer of 1915, Ts'ao Ju-lin supported him. That October, Yuan bestowed a title upon Ts'ao which in effect gave him a rank equal to that of the foreign minister. And in December, Ts'ao became a member of the enthronement preparations office. Yuan's monarchical plan failed, and in March 1916 he turned to Tuan Ch'i-jui (q.v.) for help. Tuan became premier in April and organized a cabinet in which Ts'ao was minister of communications. When Lu Cheng-hsiang resigned in May, Ts'ao also became acting foreign minister. However, with the death of Yuan Shih-k'ai in June and the accession of Li Yuan-hung (q.v.) to the presidency, Ts'ao lost his cabinet posts and temporarily retired to private life.

In the autumn of 1916 Ts'ao Ju-lin gained the interest and confidence of Tuan Ch'i-jui by presenting him with a master plan for the military unification of China. According to this plan, the Japanese would provide funds for the strengthening of Tuan's military establishment, and Ts'ao would handle the negotiations with the Japanese through his friend and schoolmate Chang Tsung-hsiang (q.v.), then the Chinese minister to Japan. Tuan appointed Ts'ao managing director of the government-operated Bank of Communications. Lu Tsung-yü, who was a friend of Ts'ao and who had preceded Chang Tsung-hsiang as minister to Japan, also became associated with the bank. Thus the stage was set for the implementation of Ts'ao's plan to obtain Japanese aid.

In January 1917 Ts'ao negotiated a loan of ¥5,000,000 from a consortium of three Japanese banks and agreed that the Bank of Communications would engage Japanese advisers. But this loan was of minor importance. For the full implementation of Tuan's scheme, China would have to declare war on Germany so that Peking could turn to Tokyo for "war loans" for the building up of the Peiyang armies. These armies then could be used to effect the unification of China. Li Yuan-hung, however, opposed the idea of participation in the First World War. In February, Ts'ao was made a member of the "International Affairs Study Association," organized by Tuan for the nominal purpose of deliberating upon China's policy with reference to the war. While applying pressure on the Parliament through this and other groups, Tuan continued, through Ts'ao, to negotiate secretly with Japan.

Japanese leaders perceived that the situation developing in Peking might prove advantageous to them, and in early March a delegation headed by Nishihara Kamezo as personal representative of Premier Terauchi arrived in Peking for negotiations on the matter of financial aid. Ts'ao's proposals in the secret discussions that followed, according to revelations made by Eugene Ch'en (q.v.) in his *Peking Gazette*, aimed at securing a loan of as much as ¥100,000,000, munitions, training officers, and arsenal technicians.

The struggle between Tuan Ch'i-jui and Li Yuan-hung reached a new stage with the dismissal of Tuan from the premiership in late May 1917. However, the situation was reversed with Li's abandonment of the presidency and Tuan's return to power in July after the restoration attempt of Chang Hsün (q.v.). On 17 July, Ts'ao Ju-lin became minister of communications in Tuan's reorganized cabinet. Tuan promptly declared war on Germany, and in September the first of the so-called Nishihara loans was negotiated. Although Tuan was forced once more, in November, to relinquish the premiership, he retained much of his power, and Ts'ao was able to keep control of the ministry of communications. When Tuan returned to the premiership in March 1918, he gave Ts'ao the additional post of acting minister of finance. By this time, Ts'ao had established himself firmly as the leader of the so-called new communications clique—as distinguished from the old communications clique of Liang Shih-i (q.v.)—and he became a prominent member of the Anfu Club, organized in March by Hsü Shu-cheng (q.v.). That September, four more Japanese loans were negotiated, bringing the total of the Nishihara loans (according to a Japanese source) to some ¥177,000,000. Given the circumstances under which they were negotiated and the fact that the National Government of 1928 claimed to have come into possession of no records of the transactions, the exact total may

never be known. In any event, the loans were never paid.

In return for these loans, the Peking government made valuable concessions to Japanese interests in connection with mining, banking, the construction of railroads and telecommunications systems, the supply of military equipment, and "rehabilitation projects." Moreover, on 24 September 1918 in an exchange of notes with the Japanese foreign minister, Chang Tsung-hsiang made an unfortunate lapse in stating that "the Chinese government gladly agrees" to Japan's proposal regarding her position in Shantung.

In October 1918 Ts'ao Ju-lin became commissioner of a new currency bureau, with Lu Tsung-yü as his director general. He then resigned as acting minister of finance but continued to serve as minister of communications. In January 1919 he also gave up the currency bureau post. That month, the Paris Peace Conference convened. How this conference dealt with the Shantung question was of major importance to China. As the conference progressed and the extent of Chinese concessions to Japan became known, however, it became apparent that China would be unable to dislodge Japan from its position as the inheritor of Germany's privileged position in Shantung. Chinese public fury mounted as a result of these revelations, and Ts'ao Ju-lin was, of course, a target of this wrath. The arrival of Chang Tsung-hsiang in Peking on 30 April and the fact that he chose to stay at Ts'ao's home rather than his own gave rise to rumors and to the organization of Peking students for protest action (for details, *see* Lo Chia-lun). The demonstrations on 4 May began peacefully enough, but after the student march was halted at the entrance to the Legation Quarter, some of the demonstrators marched to Ts'ao Ju-lin's house, where they believed that Ts'ao, Chang, and Lu Tsung-yü were holding a secret conference. They shouted such slogans as "death punishment for the traitors, Ts'ao, Lu, and Chang." The students stormed the house. Lu was not in the house; Chang was beaten into insensibility; and Ts'ao escaped through a window and took refuge in the Legation Quarter. His house was burned, and a number of students were arrested. The indignation which resulted from the arrests transformed the incident into the beginning of the May Fourth Movement.

Because of continued agitation against the "three traitors," Ts'ao, Chang, and Lu were dismissed from their posts on 10 May.

Ts'ao Ju-lin retired from public life to become manager of the Exchange Bank of China and a director of the Industrial Bank of China. In January 1922 he was made special commissioner for the promotion of industries, but he was removed from office that June when Li Yuan-hung returned to the presidency. Thereafter, Ts'ao confined himself to his business interests. He remained in Peiping throughout the Sino-Japanese war and the Nationalist-Communist civil war until 1949, when he moved to Taiwan. After living with a daughter in Taipei for a year, he moved to Japan and lived in Tokyo for seven years. In October 1957 he went to the United States to live with his youngest daughter. Ts'ao Ju-lin died in Detroit, Michigan, on 4 August 1966.

Ts'ao K'un 曹　錕
T. Chung-shan 仲　珊

Ts'ao K'un (12 December 1862–17 May 1938), Peiyang general who served as governor of Chihli (Hopei) in 1916 and inspecting commissioner of Chihli, Shantung, and Honan in 1920. With Wu P'ei-fu's support, he headed the Chihli clique in 1920–23. Ts'ao held the presidency at Peking from October 1923 to November 1924.

The third son born into an impoverished family in Tientsin, Ts'ao K'un in his youth made a living as a cloth-goods peddler. According to one source, it was during this period that he became a friend and drinking companion of the high-spirited young Yuan Shih-k'ai (q.v.), while plying his trade in Yuan's native town of Hsiang-ch'eng, Honan. When he was about 20 years old, Ts'ao enlisted in the Huai-chün [Anhwei army] as a private. He later enrolled at the Tientsin Military Academy (Wu-pei hsueh-t'ang), becoming an instructor there upon graduation in 1890. During the Sino-Japanese war of 1894–95 he served in Korea and Manchuria under Sung Ch'ing (ECCP, II, 686–88). At war's end, Ts'ao was assigned to Hsiaochan, headquarters of the Newly Created Army (Hsin-chien lu-chün) that had recently been placed under the command of Yuan Shih-k'ai.

Ts'ao helped direct the army's field training programs at Hsiaochan and, after the Boxer Uprising, at Yuan's new military quarters at Paoting. He rose rapidly in rank, becoming a regimental commander in 1901, a brigade commander in 1902, and commander of the 3rd Division of the Peiyang Army at Ch'angch'un in 1906.

After the republican revolution began in October 1911, Yuan Shih-k'ai transferred Ts'ao K'un and his 3rd Division to Peking to preserve order in the metropolitan area and to bolster his own position in the struggle for power with both the Manchus and the revolutionaries. Late in February 1912, when the revolutionary party's delegates were about to escort the reluctant Yuan to Nanking for his inauguration as provisional president, Ts'ao, presumably at Yuan's bidding, engineered a "mutiny" among his well-disciplined troops. The disturbance helped convince the delegates that Yuan's presence was required in north China to maintain order and that he should be allowed to assume the presidency at Peking.

In September 1913, after the collapse of the so-called second revolution (see Li Lieh-chün), Ts'ao K'un was named commander in chief of the Ch'ang-chiang shang-yu tsung-ssu-ling [upper Yangtze region] and was transferred with the 3rd Division to Yochow, Hunan. At the height of the monarchist movement in 1915, he was created an "earl" in Yuan Shih-k'ai's new monarchical hierarchy. With the outbreak of the anti-monarchist revolt led by Ts'ai O (q.v.), Ts'ao was ordered on 5 January 1916 to proceed upriver to Szechwan and then to advance southward on Ts'ai O's forces, which were moving northward from Yunnan. Units of Ts'ao's 3rd Division engaged Ts'ai O's army at points along the Szechwan-Yunnan border, but they were fought to a standstill. This stalemate ended only with the death of Yuan Shih-k'ai in June 1916. At that time, Ts'ao moved the 3rd Division back to its permanent headquarters at Paoting.

Soon after his return to Paoting, Ts'ao K'un became tuchün [military governor] of Chihli (Hopei) on 16 September 1916. As governor of this metropolitan province and commander of one of the most highly trained divisions of the Peiyang Army, he was a powerful leader in north China. With the passing of Yuan Shih-k'ai, the Peiyang military machine gradually split into competing cliques as rival generals began to jockey with one another for military and political advantage. During the early stages of the struggle between the developing Anhwei and Chihli cliques, Ts'ao K'un was identified with the Chihli group. For the most part, however, his actions appear to have been determined by political expediency, and more often than not he supported the policies of Tuan Ch'i-jui (q.v.), the leader of the Anhwei faction and then the dominant figure at Peking. In July 1917 Ts'ao joined Tuan and other Peiyang leaders in opposing the attempt of Chang Hsün (q.v.) to restore the Manchu monarchy. Ts'ao's troops constituted a large part of the force that defeated Chang, and Tuan rewarded him with the civil governorship of Chihli. Later, during the period of political rivalry between Tuan and the acting president at Peking, Feng Kuo-chang (q.v.), who was head of the Chihli clique, Ts'ao sought to remain on good terms with both factions. In December 1917, at a conference held in Tientsin, Ts'ao and other military governors decided to launch a campaign against the Hu-fa-chün [constitution protection army], which had been dispatched by the military government at Canton and which had overrun most of Hunan. Ts'ao K'un became commander in chief of a military force that was to descend upon Hunan from Hupeh while a second force, commanded by Chang Huai-chih, attacked Hunan from the east. In February 1918, after ordering the 3rd Division and other units to move southward, Ts'ao transferred his military headquarters to Hankow. Within two months his troops had captured Changsha and had advanced as far as Hengchow in southern Hunan.

It was at this time that a notable change took place in relations between Ts'ao K'un and the Anhwei clique under Tuan Ch'i-jui. Ts'ao, who had been one of the strongest advocates of Tuan's policy of military unification, suddenly lost his enthusiasm for the war and grew cool to Tuan's regime at Peking. Ts'ao's change of attitude was due in part to his suspicion that Tuan's deputy, Hsü Shu-cheng (q.v.), was secretly planning to remove him from his post as military governor of Chihli. Another reason was the stand taken by Ts'ao's subordinate Wu P'ei-fu (q.v.), who had distinguished himself as field commander of the 3rd Division during the fighting in Hunan. Because Wu believed

that his victories had not received the recognition they merited from Tuan's government, he ordered his troops to cease fighting. Fearing the collapse of their policy of military unification, Hsü Shu-cheng, and subsequently Tuan himself, hastened to Hankow in an effort to placate the two commanders. To regain Ts'ao's support, Tuan offered him the resounding title of ching-lueh-shih [high commissioner] of Szechwan, Kwangtung, Hunan, and Kiangsi, and further promised him, in secret, the vice presidency at Peking. These gestures failed to satisfy Ts'ao, and at the end of May he transferred his headquarters back to Chihli, thereby dashing Tuan's hopes of subduing the southern military leaders.

The tension between Ts'ao K'un and Tuan Ch'i-jui was heightened by the increasingly independent line taken by Wu P'ei-fu. In the summer of 1918 Wu, still in acting command of Ts'ao's 3rd Division, made verbal attacks on the Peking government which aroused the ire of Tuan Ch'i-jui. Tuan put increasing pressure on Ts'ao K'un to keep his unruly subordinate in line. Ts'ao found himself in an awkward situation, for the 3rd Division, the core of his military strength, was stationed in Hunan under a subordinate whose actions had become increasingly difficult for Ts'ao to control. During the next two years, as Tuan Ch'i-jui and his subordinates continued to build up the military strength of the Anhwei clique, Ts'ao K'un's position in Chihli became insecure. To counter Tuan's military might, Ts'ao effected an agreement between the Fengtien faction of Chang Tso-lin (q.v.) and the Chihli clique, which then included the Yangtze military governors Li Ch'un (Kiangsu), Wang Chan-yuan (Hupeh), and Ch'en Kuang-yuan (Kiangsi). About this time, Wu P'ei-fu withdrew his troops from Hunan and moved them northward to support Ts'ao K'un in Chihli. On 13 July 1920 Ts'ao joined Chang Tso-lin in announcing plans to oust Tuan and his government from Peking, and the Chihli-Anhwei war began two days later. By 18 July Tuan Ch'i-jui's forces had been defeated and the power of the Anhwei clique had been shattered.

With the victory of the Chihli faction, Ts'ao K'un became its undisputed leader. On 2 September 1920 he was appointed inspector general (hsün-yueh-shih) of Chihli, Shantung, and Honan in recognition of his authority in north China. Soon, however, personal antagonism between Wu P'ei-fu and Chang Tso-lin set the stage for a power struggle between the Chihli and Fengtien military cliques. In this developing contest, it was Wu, rather than Ts'ao, who took the initiative within the Chihli group. Ts'ao was reluctant to challenge the growing influence of Chang Tso-lin in north China, but because he was almost entirely dependent on Wu P'ei-fu for military backing, he did not challenge Wu. However, Ts'ao's conciliatory attitude gradually hardened as a result of Chang Tso-lin's steady encroachment upon his territory in Chihli. In April 1922 Ts'ao joined Wu and other leaders of the Chihli clique in opposing the advance of Chang's troops into north China. Early in May, in the first Chihli-Fengtien war, troops under the command of Wu P'ei-fu routed Chang's forces and forced them back to Chang's stronghold in Manchuria.

The defeat of Chang Tso-lin left the Chihli clique in control of the government at Peking and of most of north China. To achieve peaceful unification of China, their announced goal, they found it expedient to agree to the reconvening of the old National Assembly of 1917 and the restoration of the 1912 constitution. They also favored a proposal whereby Hsü Shih-ch'ang (q.v.) and Sun Yat-sen, presidents of the rival regimes at Peking and Canton, would resign simultaneously so that a new president of a unified national government could be selected. After the resignation of Hsü Shih-ch'ang on 2 June 1922 (Sun was driven from Kwangtung by supporters of Ch'en Chiung-ming later that month), Ts'ao K'un and the other Chihli leaders induced Li Yuan-hung (q.v.) to take office again as president on 11 June. In September, the "able men" cabinet of Wang Ch'ung-hui (q.v.) was installed in Peking to implement a policy of peaceful unification.

In the autumn of 1922, however, differences of opinion began to arise within the Chihli clique. Ts'ao K'un had long coveted the presidency at Peking, and he now believed that he was in a position to realize that ambition. Wu P'ei-fu, on the other hand, preferred to maintain the then current administration in office until peaceful unification had been achieved. Other factors also served to strain relations between Ts'ao K'un and Wu P'ei-fu. Even before the Chihli-Fengtien war, the two

men had become the foci of rival factions within the Chihli clique, one centered at Wu's camp at Loyang and the other at Ts'ao's headquarters at Paoting and Tientsin. As Wu's power and prestige began to overshadow those of his nominal superior, members of the Ts'ao faction grew resentful of Wu's predominance within the Chihli clique. They became openly impatient with Wu's policies, and they lost no opportunity to embarrass Li Yuan-hung and the "cabinet of able men." Ts'ao K'un and his partisans succeeded in having Wang's minister of finance, Lo Wen-kan (q.v.), arrested on false charges of bribery. Wu, fearing open dissension within the Chihli clique, reluctantly bowed to Ts'ao's wishes and withheld his support from the administration he formerly had endorsed, thereby causing the collapse of the "cabinet of able men" in November 1922.

During the spring and summer of 1923 Ts'ao K'un's political supporters intensified their drive to gain control of the government at Peking. In June, they succeeded in bringing about the fall of the Chang Shao-tseng cabinet and in forcing Li Yuan-hung to leave Peking and to resign. Turning next to the National Assembly, they sought to persuade its members to remain in Peking and to elect Ts'ao K'un to the presidency. The cooperation of some members was secured by assurances that they would be allowed to complete their work on the draft of a permanent constitution. Nearly 500 members of the National Assembly voted for Ts'ao K'un, and on 10 October 1923 he was inaugurated. The newly drafted constitution that was promulgated soon afterwards became known as the "Ts'ao K'un constitution."

In assuming the presidency, Ts'ao K'un seemingly attained the pinnacle of his career, but his power rested entirely on the military strength of Wu P'ei-fu. It was not at Peking but at Wu's Loyang headquarters that most of the important governmental decisions were made. Outside of Peking, Ts'ao's authority received token recognition in the areas controlled by militarists of the Chihli clique, but it was challenged or ignored in the provinces of south and west China, in Chekiang, and in Manchuria. Moreover, the unabashed bribery and coercion employed by Ts'ao's partisans to secure control of the government at Peking lost Ts'ao whatever public respect and support he had formerly enjoyed. The greed of these

National Assembly members who sold him their votes earned them the appellation of "piglings" (chu-tzu).

During the period of about a year that Ts'ao K'un held the presidency, Wu P'ei-fu's newly adopted policy of armed unification of China led to hostilities which culminated in the second Chihli-Fengtien war of September-October 1924. In mid-September, Chang Tso-lin, after denouncing Wu P'ei-fu and accusing Ts'ao K'un of being Wu's puppet, began moving his troops southward from Manchuria to challenge the power of the Chihli clique. In response, Ts'ao hurriedly summoned Wu to Peking to assume command of the Chihli armies. However, after Wu had advanced almost to Shanhaikuan and had engaged the Fengtien forces in heavy fighting, Feng Yü-hsiang (q.v.) and other subordinates of Wu revolted against him. In accordance with a prearranged scheme, Feng went to Peking with his troops on 23 October and issued a telegram calling for an end to the war. The surprised Ts'ao K'un was left defenseless at Peking. Surrounded by Feng's troops at the presidential mansion, he was forced to proclaim a cease-fire and to issue orders on 24 October relieving Wu P'ei-fu of his military command. Ts'ao was compelled by Feng to announce his resignation from the presidency on 2 November 1924.

The overthrow of Wu P'ei-fu in October 1924 brought Ts'ao K'un's public career to an end. After his enforced resignation, he was held under house arrest at Peking until 9 April 1926, by which time Feng Yü-hsiang had been driven from the capital. Ts'ao then moved to Wu P'ei-fu's headquarters at Chengchow, but in the spring of 1927, when Wu retreated westward, he went to Tientsin, where he lived in complete retirement for the remainder of his life. In 1937 he was reported to have rejected Japanese overtures to secure his participation in a Japanese-sponsored regime in north China, and after his death on 17 May 1938 the National Government at Chungking, in recognition of his refusal to cooperate with the enemy, issued a special mandate of commendation on 18 June 1938 and designated him a full general of the first class.

Two younger brothers of Ts'ao K'un had minor public careers, principally as his protégés. Ts'ao Jui (c.1866–1924; T. Chien-t'ing) began his career as a legal officer in the imperial army and then as judicial commissioner of Chihli province. In 1912 he served briefly as financial commissioner of Chihli, and sometime after 1917 he became civil governor of that province, a post he held until June 1922. Ts'ao Ying (b. 1873; T. Tzu-chen) was attached to the staff of Hsü Shih-ch'ang in 1907 and in 1910 was transferred to the Military Survey School, of which he became director in 1912. He became chief military adviser to Ts'ao K'un at Paoting in 1916, commander of the 4th Mixed Brigade in 1917, garrison commander of the Chihli troops at Shanhaikuan in 1918, and commander of the newly organized 26th Division in 1920. After Ts'ao K'un's election to the presidency, he became a full general (November 1923) and director general of forestry affairs in Jehol (January 1924). He retired after his brother's downfall in November 1924.

Ts'ao Yü: *see* WAN CHIA-PAO.

Tsen, Philip Lindel: *see* CHENG HO-FU.

Ts'en Ch'un-hsuan	岑 春 煊
Orig. Ch'un-tse	春 澤
T. Yün-chieh	雲 階
H. Chiung-t'ang lao-jen	炯 堂 老 人

Ts'en Ch'un-hsuan (1861—March 1933), prominent Ch'ing official and rival of Yuan Shih-k'ai. He played a leading role in the anti-Yuan campaigns of 1915–16. He later joined the southern military government at Canton, serving as its head in 1918–19.

A native of the Hsilin district of Kwangsi, Ts'en Ch'un-hsuan was the third of seven children in his family. His father was the illustrious official Ts'en Yü-ying (ECCP, II, 742–46), best known for his work in suppressing the Muslim uprisings in Yunnan and for participation in the Sino-French war of 1884–85. As a boy Ts'en Ch'un-hsuan accompanied his father on the elder Ts'en's tours of duty in Fukien and Kweichow as governor and in Yunnan as governor general. In 1879, at the age of 20 sui, Ts'en Ch'un-hsuan was sent to Peking to study at the imperial academy for two years. He returned to Kwangsi in 1881 to continue his studies, and he obtained the chü-jen degree in 1885. Soon afterward, he went to Peking again, where he served in the Board of Works. Not unwilling to join in the corrupt practices of the period, he gained promotion to the rank of senior secretary in return for "contributions" to the Chinese navy, which were, in fact, donations to the empress dowager to help finance the construction of her sumptuous new summer palace. The Kuang-hsü emperor was married that year, and Ts'en was appointed an assistant in the office in charge of preparations for the wedding. In return for his efforts, he was exempted from the normal term of service for a senior secretary and was allowed to proceed to the next higher rank as soon as a post was available. His success in ingratiating himself with the imperial family at this time was to be of no small importance in his later career.

When Ts'en Yü-ying died in June 1889, Ts'en Ch'un-hsuan joined his brothers in hastening to Kunming for the funeral. They took their father's remains home to Hsilin for burial, and Ts'en Ch'un-hsuan remained there for three years in mourning. In April 1892 he returned to Peking, where he became a sub-director of the Kuang-lu ssu. After holding junior posts in the imperial bureaucracy for two years, he volunteered for military service in 1894 following the outbreak of the Sino-Japanese war. He was ordered to Shantung to take part in the defense of Chefoo. With the conclusion of a peace treaty between China and Japan, he returned to his native Kwangsi.

In 1898 Ts'en took his youngest brother, Ts'en Ch'un-yin, to Peking to sit for the imperial examinations. In accordance with established practice, Ts'en Ch'un-hsuan paid a courtesy call at the palace. He was summoned for an imperial audience, and he took advantage of the occasion to express his views on the defeat China had just suffered at the hands of the Germans, who had occupied Kiaochow in Shantung. The emperor was impressed with Ts'en, who thereupon submitted a written memorial setting forth his views on the crisis in detail. A few days later, he was rewarded with an appointment as provincial treasurer of Kwangtung. He took office at Canton in June 1898, but he soon came into conflict with the governor general of Kwangtung-Kwangsi, T'an Chung-lin, by accusing T'an of sheltering a

corrupt tao-t'ai. The quarrel resulted in Ts'en's transfer to Kansu as provincial treasurer.

Ts'en had been in Kansu for only a few months when the Boxer Uprising broke out. On learning that an Allied expeditionary force was moving toward Peking, he mustered a small force, despite objections from the governor general of Shensi-Kansu, and hastened to the capital. Shortly after their arrival, Ts'en and his men were ordered to help the forces under Tung Fu-hsiang dig trenches in the suburban areas around Peking. As the Allied military force neared Peking, Ts'en escorted the emperor and the empress dowager on their flight to Taiyuan and thence to Sian in Shensi. By these gestures of loyalty to the court, Ts'en earned the gratitude of the empress dowager, which manifested itself in his appointment as governor of Shensi. He assumed office in March 1901 and held that post for a year.

When the imperial court returned to Peking in 1902, Ts'en escorted it from Shansi to the capital. In July of that year, he was appointed governor of Kwangtung. Just at that time, Szechwan reported uprisings of Boxers and local bandits, and the Ch'ing court rescinded Ts'en's Kwangtung appointment and sent him to Szechwan as acting governor. He succeeded in restoring order to that troubled province within a few months. In April 1903 he was appointed governor general of Kwangtung-Kwangsi and military superintendent of Kwangsi, which then was being preyed upon by bandits. This appointment was particularly significant because only one other Kwangsi man in the entire Ch'ing period, Ch'en Hung-mou (ECCP, I, 86–87), had been named governor general of a region that included his own native province. In bringing the Kwangsi situation under control, he raised Lung Chi-kuang and Lu Jung-t'ing (qq.v.) to high military posts. Both men later became important leaders in south China. Ts'en Ch'un-hsuan's tenure as governor general of Kwangtung-Kwangsi marked the zenith of his official career in the late Ch'ing period, when he was one of the men most trusted by the empress dowager.

In 1906 Ts'en received orders to leave Canton and to take up the post of governor general of Yunnan-Kweichow, an office which his father had held with distinction. During his tenure of office at Canton, Ts'en had dealt drastically with several cases of corruption in the maritime customs administration. Because the chief culprit was a protégé of Prince Ch'ing (I-k'uang, ECCP, II, 964–65), it is hardly surprising that Ts'en was removed from his post at Canton. Rather than going to Kunming, Ts'en requested leave and went to Shanghai. In March 1907 he was ordered to Szechwan as governor general, an appointment which he viewed as another attempt to remove him from the political mainstream. He sent a petition to Peking requesting an audience with the emperor and left for the capital without waiting for a reply. Upon arrival at Peking, he was received in audience. He took the opportunity to report to the empress dowager details he had learned from Sheng Hsuan-huai (q.v.) of the widespread corruption associated with Prince Ch'ing. Under the protection of the empress dowager, Ts'en was appointed president of the newly created Board of Communications at Peking.

Another opportunity to remove Ts'en Ch'un-hsuan from Peking came soon, however, with reports of disturbances in Kwangtung. Yuan Shih-k'ai, a rival of Ts'en and a strong supporter of Prince Ch'ing, reportedly exaggerated these reports of unrest. For his part, Prince Ch'ing informed the empress dowager that the situation in south China was so threatening that only an official of Ts'en Ch'un-hsuan's caliber could deal with it effectively. Accordingly, Ts'en was appointed governor general of Kwangtung-Kwangsi once again and was ordered to Canton immediately. Apparently resigned to his fate, Ts'en traveled southward. When he arrived at Shanghai, he learned of the dismissal of privy councillor Ch'ü Hung-chi (1850–1918), who had been regarded as the one man in high office at Peking who had dared to oppose Prince Ch'ing and Yuan Shih-k'ai. Ts'en then recognized that his own position was hopeless, and he remained in Shanghai, requesting sick leave. Yuan Shih-k'ai, however, was intent upon humbling his antagonist further. He resorted to the ingenious ruse of having a composite photograph made which showed Ts'en Ch'un-hsuan with the reformers K'ang Yu-wei and Liang Ch'i-ch'ao (qq.v.) in front of a newspaper office in Shanghai. When this photograph was shown to the empress dowager, she became very angry. Nevertheless, she recalled Ts'en's loyalty at the time of the Boxer Uprising and limited herself to relieving

him of his substantive appointment at Canton. Ts'en then established residence at Shanghai. Soon afterward, Yuan Shih-k'ai himself was dismissed from office following the deaths of the empress dowager and the Kuang-hsü emperor.

After the Wuchang revolt of October 1911, the Ch'ing government found itself in desperate straits and without competent officials in high office at Peking. It turned to Yuan Shih-k'ai and Ts'en Ch'un-hsuan in its extremity. Yuan was appointed governor general of Hupeh-Hunan, and Ts'en was made governor general of Szechwan. However, the spread of the revolution prevented Ts'en from assuming office. He advised the Manchu rulers to abdicate, an idea that was opposed by the intransigent loyalists at Peking. When Yuan Shih-k'ai achieved a new position of authority at Peking as provisional president of the republican government, he adopted a conciliatory attitude toward Ts'en and offered him new positions. In the autumn of 1912 Ts'en assumed office as pacification commissioner of Fukien, where he succeeded in removing from office a venal official who had exploited the situation there during the republican revolution. His actions, which earned him the gratitude of the Fukienese, soon made Yuan Shih-k'ai suspicious of his intentions.

Ts'en soon became active in the so-called second revolution of 1913 and in subsequent movements directed against Yuan's power. He hoped to mobilize support in south China, but he found that his former subordinate and protégé Lung Chi-kuang of Kwangtung had become a firm supporter of Yuan. Ts'en and Li Ken-yuan (q.v.), who had gone to Canton to win Lung to their cause, were forced to flee to Macao and Hong Kong. Ts'en then went to Penang, where he remained for three years as the guest of Hu Tzu-ch'un, a local millionaire.

In 1915, when Yuan Shih-k'ai's monarchical aspirations became apparent, the republican revolutionaries began to rally their forces against him. In December of that year, Ts'ai O, T'ang Chi-yao, and Li Lieh-chün (qq.v.) led an anti-Yuan uprising in Yunnan. Lu Jung-t'ing, the military governor of Kwangsi and an erstwhile associate of Yuan, prepared to join the Yunnan revolutionaries; and Ts'en was invited to return to Kwangsi to take charge. In

January 1916 Ts'en arrived in Shanghai where he met with Li Ken-yuan, Liang Ch'i-ch'ao, and others to discuss plans and requirements. Accompanied by Chang Shih-chao (q.v.), Ts'en went to Japan, where he negotiated a loan and obtained sufficient weapons to outfit two divisions. Ts'en then went to Chaoch'ing, Kwangtung, where on 1 May 1916 he became the nominal commander of the anti-Yuan National Protection Army of Kwangtung and Kwangsi.

One week later, the leaders of the anti-Yuan movement organized a military council at Chaoch'ing which claimed to be the legitimate government of China until such time as Yuan Shih-k'ai was removed from the presidency. T'ang Chi-yao was elected chairman of the council, with Ts'en as vice chairman; but because T'ang remained in Yunnan, Ts'en assumed the duties of acting chairman. Yuan Shih-k'ai died the following month, and Ts'en derived great satisfaction from this final resolution of his long feud with Yuan. In July 1916, following the accession to the presidency of Li Yuan-hung (q.v.), the southern military council was dissolved, and Ts'en retired to live in Shanghai.

In 1917, after the seizure of power at Peking by Tuan Ch'i-jui (q.v.), an opposition movement called the "constitution protection" campaign was organized by Sun Yat-sen. With the co-operation of T'ang Chi-yao and Lu Jung-t'ing, Sun became head of a new military government at Canton. In 1918 this military regime was reorganized, largely through the influence of Lu Jung-t'ing and the powerful Kwangsi military faction in Kwangtung, and Sun was forced to share leadership with six other directors, including T'ang Chi-yao, Lu Jung-t'ing, and Ts'en Ch'un-hsuan. After Sun's resignation as head of the regime in May 1918, Ts'en was elected chairman of the board of directors; and with the backing of the Kwangsi faction he again became head of a military regime in south China.

During the next two years, increasing friction in the Canton military government arose among the Kwangsi military clique (then predominant in Kwangtung), the Kuomintang followers of Sun Yat-sen, and local commercial interests. In August 1919 Sun, in protest against the Kwangsi faction, announced his complete withdrawal from the regime, and in June 1920 he and several other Kuomintang leaders joined T'ang Chi-yao in declaring all actions of the Kwangsi-dominated Canton regime to be illegitimate. Despite this growing opposition, Ts'en, with the support of the Kwangsi generals, continued to head the Canton government until 1920, when the Kwangsi forces were routed and driven from Canton by the Kwangtung Army under Ch'en Chiung-ming (q.v.). Deserted by his former military backers, Ts'en on 24 October 1920 announced the dissolution of the Canton military government and fled the city. Two days later, Ch'en Chiung-ming and his troops entered Canton.

This time Ts'en Ch'un-hsuan completely retired from public life and took up residence in Shanghai. He remained in close contact with Chang Shih-chao, Li Ken-yuan, and Yang Yung-t'ai (q.v.), but these contacts were purely personal and had no political implications. In 1922, accompanied by the Shanghai speculator Silas A. Hardoon and Hardoon's wife, Lo Chia-ling, Ts'en visited Soochow, where he bought a house. In 1930, on his seventieth birthday, he prepared an account of his life entitled *Lo-chai man-pi* in which he took pains to describe how the Ts'en family had for generations been favored by the Ch'ing court and how he had devoted himself to loyal service to the Manchus.

Ts'en Ch'un-hsuan died at Shanghai in March 1933. His wife, *née* Liu, had died many years before in 1902. Their eldest son, Ts'en Te-ku, obtained the chü-jen degree in Hupeh. A younger son, Ts'en Te-kuang, served as special foreign affairs commissioner in Kwangsi and as superintendent of the Wuchow customs. He later headed the famine relief commission in the Japanese-sponsored government at Nanking headed by Wang Ching-wei after 1940.

The place of Ts'en Ch'un-hsuan in modern China's history is difficult to assess. His official career between 1902 and 1911 was marked by determined efforts to expose corruption, actual or alleged, and he was generally regarded more with fear than with affection by the people of the areas he administered. Although he prided himself on his close personal and family ties with the ruling Manchu house, he was perhaps the highest-ranking official in China to recommend abdication in 1911. His role in the internecine rivalries of the early republican period in China is equally paradoxical, though it clearly resulted more from Ts'en's personal feud with Yuan Shih-k'ai than from genuine conversion to republican principles.

Tseng Ch'i
T. Mu-han

曾 琦
慕 韓

Tseng Ch'i (5 August 1892–7 May 1951), leader of the Young China party.

Although Tseng Ch'i was born in Lungch'ang, Szechwan, he spent his childhood in Kwangsi, where his father, Tseng Yu-san, served as a minor government official. He was orphaned while still a boy, whereupon he and his elder brother, Tseng Chao-yü, returned to Szechwan to live with a maternal uncle, Sung P'ing-chou. After completing his basic education in the Chinese classics, Tseng Ch'i enrolled at the Chengtu Higher Middle School, where he was known for his excellence in Chinese composition and for his inferiority in other subjects. He became particularly interested in works by such seventeenth-century scholars as Wang Fu-chih, Ku Yen-wu, and Huang Tsung-hsi (ECCP, I, 351–54), who expressed anti-Manchu attitudes. He also dabbled in journalism, contributing articles to the *Ch'eng-tu shang-pao* [commercial gazette of Chengtu] and the *Szuch'uan kung-pao* [gazette of Szechwan] and editing the *Min-kuo hsin-pao* [a new gazette of the republic] and the *Ch'un pao* [newspaper for the people].

In 1912 Tseng Ch'i enrolled at the Szechwan Law School in Chengtu. With the firm establishment of the Chinese republic, he reportedly was elected to the National Assembly. In 1913 he participated in the so-called second revolution against Yuan Shih-k'ai. The failure of this movement caused Tseng to flee Szechwan in the late summer of 1913, leaving behind his cousin and bride of three months, Sung Ching-yi. He made his way to Shanghai with the intention of going to France to study. By the time he reached the port city, however, the First World War had broken out. Because he could not go to France, he enrolled at Aurora University, a French Jesuit institution in Shanghai. There he met Li Huang (q.v.) and Tso Shun-sheng, with whom he would collaborate in later years.

Tseng Ch'i went to Japan in 1916 to become a student of government and law at Chuo (Central) University. He devoted much of his time to Chinese student politics. In 1917 he helped found the Overseas Chinese News Service (Hua-yin t'ung-hsin she) at Tokyo to report on the secret negotiations between the Tuan Ch'i-jui (q.v.) government at Peking and the Japanese. The following year he was a founder of the Liu-Jih hsueh-sheng chiu-kuo t'uan [corps of Chinese students in Japan for national salvation] and a leader of the Chinese students in Japan who decided to return home to protest the so-called Nishihara loans and the Sino-Japanese Military Mutual Assistance Conventions. Upon arrival in Shanghai, Tseng and others established the *Chiu-kuo jih-pao* [save-the-nation daily], in which Tseng published a series of articles urging Chinese students to join the salvation movement.

In late June 1918 Tseng Ch'i was in Peking. On 30 June, he helped organize the Shao-nien Chung-kuo hsueh-hui [young China association] to organize opposition to Tuan Ch'i-jui's pro-Japanese regime. Tseng was in Shanghai at the time of the May Fourth Incident (*see* Lo Chia-lun). Late in May he went to Peking, as a representative of the Liu-Jih hsueh-sheng chiu-kuo t'uan, to support the student movement at Peking. He played a significant role in the attempt to organize a boycott of Japanese goods.

Sometime in the latter part of 1919, Tseng Ch'i went to Paris. He and Li Huang founded the Paris News Service as a branch office of the Shanghai *Hsin-wen-pao*. Under the pen name Yü Kieng, he wrote regularly for the *Hsin-wen-pao* to support himself. As a student and journalist in France, Tseng Ch'i was politically active. Because of arguments with the Chinese Communists, on 2 December 1923 Tseng and Li Huang, having returned to Paris from a tour of Germany, became the principal founders of the Young China party, and Tseng was elected secretary general of the organization. However, not until September 1929 was the formation of this party announced publicly. Until then, its members referred to it as the Chinese Youth Corps of Nationalism (Chung-kuo kuo-chia chu-i ch'ing-nien tuan). It advocated nationalism and democracy, with emphasis on "expelling internal traitors and resisting external powers." The "internal traitors," in Tseng's view, were the Chinese Communists.

In August 1924 Tseng Ch'i returned to Shanghai, where he taught at Ta Hsia University, Shanghai Law College, and T'ung-chi University. He was a founder of the Hsueh-i ta-hsueh [art and sciences college], where Kuo

Mo-jo (q.v.) also taught. The years from 1924 to 1927 were also years of strenuous political activity for Tseng. In October 1924 he and his group founded in Shanghai the *Hsing-shih chou-k'an* [awakened lion weekly], which became a forum for advocates of nationalism. More than 30 societies to promote nationalism were founded in China's major cities, with total membership reportedly reaching about 50,000. These organizations published such magazines as *Independent Youth, Self-Strengthening* (*Tzu-ch'en*), the *New Nation* (*Hsin kuo-chia*), *Patriotic Youth* (*Ai-kuo ch'ing-nien*), and *Light of the Nation* (*Kuo-kuang*). The over-all aim of these magazines was to promote nationalism in opposition to Communism. They argued that all classes of Chinese society should join together instead of struggling against one another. Because Tseng and his colleagues believed that there was no such thing as an international proletariat, they opposed Sun Yat-sen's policies of collaboration with the Chinese Communist party and alliance with the Soviet Union. Tseng attempted to win over Sun Yat-sen to the views of the Young China party in the winter of 1924, but he failed. After Sun's death Tseng gave his full support to the conservative Western Hills group (*see* Lin Sen) in the Kuomintang. In the summer of 1927 he was arrested and imprisoned in Shanghai by the Kuomintang authorities. Upon his release later in 1927, he went to Japan, where he lived for several years.

It is uncertain when Tseng Ch'i returned to China. He probably was in Hunan in 1933 helping the Kuomintang in propagandizing against the Chinese Communists. In 1934 he went to Szechwan, where he supported Chiang Kai-shek's encirclement campaigns. In 1937 he visited Chiang Kai-shek at Fenghua and participated in the Lushan Conference. Tseng was appointed to the National Defense Council, and in 1938 he became a member, representing the China Youth party, of the People's Political Council. He accompanied the National Government to Chungking in 1938 and remained there until late 1941, when illness forced him to return to Shanghai. He lived in the French concession at Shanghai until the winter of 1944, when he went to Peiping on the first leg of the journey back to Chungking. He arrived in Chungking in 1945 just in time for the celebrations of the victory over Japan. That winter, he took part in the Political Consultative Con-

ference at Chungking, and later in 1946 he returned with the National Government to Nanking. When a coalition government of the Kuomintang, the Social Democratic party, and the Young China party was established in the spring of 1947, Tseng was appointed an adviser to Chiang Kai-shek. In 1948 he participated in the National Assembly as a delegate from the Lungch'ang district.

In the autumn of 1948, when it seemed certain that the Chinese Communists would win control of the mainland, Tseng Ch'i left China for the United States, where he underwent medical treatment. He made speeches to overseas Chinese communities in the United States, calling for the organization of a "Chinese League of Democracy and Freedom." In 1950 he toured Europe, where he advocated the organization of an "Anti-Communist League of All Religions." That trip lasted only two months, for Tseng's health had begun to fail as a result of anemia. He returned to the United States. In May 1951 his condition was complicated by appendicitis which turned into peritonitis. On 7 May 1951 he died at George Washington Hospital in Washington, D.C., having been converted to Roman Catholicism in his last hours. He was survived by his second wife, Chou Jo-nan, and by a son, Tseng Hsien-pin.

Tseng Chung-ming   曾 仲 鳴

Tseng Chung-ming (1 March 1896–22 March 1939), scholar and official who was a long-time associate of Wang Ching-wei (q.v.). He was killed at Hanoi in 1939 by assassins whose intended victim may well have been Wang.

Born into a scholarly but impoverished family at Foochow, Tseng Chung-ming was brought up by his widowed mother and by his elder sister Tseng Hsing, who also was a widow. About 1900 Tseng Hsing accompanied her deceased husband's two younger brothers, Fang Sheng-t'ao and Fang Sheng-tung, and a younger sister, Fang Chün-ying, to Japan. They all later became members of the T'ung-meng-hui, and it was through their activities that the young Tseng Chung-ming became involved with the republican revolution and with some of its most prominent leaders.

After the republic was established in 1912,

Tseng Hsing and Fang Chün-ying, who had received government money to study in France, set out for Europe with Fang Chün-pi (a younger sister of Fang Chün-ying), Tseng Chung-ming, Wang Ching-wei (q.v.), and Ch'en Pi-chün (q.v.), Wang's new wife. The group settled at Paris and made ends meet by pooling the scholarship funds. Tseng Chung-ming enrolled at a secondary school, from which he went on to the University of Bordeaux and a B. Sc. degree. He then exchanged science for literature, and in 1921 he was awarded the degree of Docteur ès Lettres by the University of Lyon. Throughout this period, he kept up his Chinese studies, working under Wang Ching-wei's direction whenever Wang was in France. And at some point, Tseng married Fang Chün-pi, who pursued a career as a painter while Tseng continued his studies. In 1921–24 Tseng served as chief secretary of the Sino-French University at Lyon, which had been organized as part of the work-study movement (see Li Shih-tseng). Early in 1925 he and his wife returned to China, where Tseng found work teaching French at Chung-shan (Sun Yat-sen) University at Canton. When the National Government was established at Canton in July 1925, Tseng was appointed a secretary in one of the new ministries. He evidently owed this appointment to Wang Ching-wei, and from this time on he followed Wang through all of his political and personal vicissitudes.

In 1927 Tseng Chung-ming served as senior secretary in the Wuhan regime under Wang Ching-wei and as chief secretary of its central political council. In 1930 he again served under Wang, this time as secretary general of the so-called enlarged conference of the Kuomintang at Peiping (see Feng Yü-hsiang; Yen Hsi-shan). The next year, 1931, also saw anti-Chiang Kai-shek intrigues instigated by Wang, who joined T'ang Shao-yi, Sun Fo (qq.v.) and various members of the Kwangtung and Kwangsi military cliques in organizing a secessionist movement at Canton. The Japanese attack on Mukden in September 1931 served to unite the party, however, and Tseng followed Wang back into the fold. At the Fourth National Congress of the Kuomintang, Tseng was elected to alternate membership in the Central Executive Committee. Soon afterwards, he also became deputy secretary general of the Central Political Council.

Tseng Chung-ming assumed the post of administrative vice minister of railways, serving under Ku Meng-yü (q.v.), in 1932. He proved an able administrator, and it was under his direction that the Pukow ferry service was inaugurated at Nanking to provide a much-needed connection between the Tientsin-Pukow and Nanking-Shanghai railways. In addition, the ministry extended the Lunghai line and completed the Canton-Hankow railway. In 1935 Tseng also served as vice minister of communications.

In March 1936 Tseng Chung-ming resigned his posts to accompany Wang Ching-wei to France for treatment of wounds which Wang had incurred when an attempt had been made on his life in 1935. When news of the Sian Incident of December 1936 (see Chiang Kai-shek; Chang Hsueh-liang) reached France, they hurriedly returned to China, where Wang resumed office as chairman of the Central Political Council, with Tseng as the council's deputy secretary general. With the outbreak of the Sino-Japanese war in July 1937, the National Government organized the Supreme National Defense Council. Tseng served on this body as senior secretary under Wang, its deputy chairman. When the National Government moved to Chungking in 1938, Tseng and Wang accompanied it. On 18 December 1938, however, Wang, Tseng, and Fang Chün-pi left Chungking for Hanoi, traveling by way of Kunming. On 28 December Wang issued his famous peace message, and he continued his efforts to secure peace with Japan. Possibly as a result of Wang's actions, in the early hours of the morning of 21 March 1939 assassins entered Wang's residence at Hanoi and shot and fatally wounded Tseng Chung-ming, as well as injuring Fang Chün-pi and three others. Tseng died the next day, 22 March 1939.

The assassination caused a sensation and much speculation in China, but the murderers were never apprehended. The most commonly held theory was that Wang was the target of the assassins and that Tseng was killed by mistake. A second explanation held that Tseng was killed as a warning to Wang to abandon his peace moves. Wang wrote a moving eulogy for his fallen colleague which appeared as the first article in *Tseng Chung-ming hsien-sheng hsing-chuang* [an account of the late Mr. Tseng Chung-ming], published in 1939.

Throughout his political career, Tseng Chung-ming was active as a writer and translator. His works in Chinese included a history of Chinese poetry and a volume entitled *I-shu yü k'o-hsüeh* [art and science], which was published in 1930. His French translations of Chinese works ranged from a rendering of the *T'ang-shih san-pai-shou* [300 poems of the T'ang] to Kuomintang political tracts.

After Tseng Chung-ming's death, Fang Chün-pi and their children went to live in Nanking, where Fang continued to paint in the kuo-hua, or traditional, style. Typical of her production is *Ch'iu-t'ing ch'en-k'o t'u* [morning lesson in an autumnal courtyard], published in collotype facsimile in 1934, which depicts Wang Ching-wei and his mother as they might have appeared when Wang was nine sui and accustomed to receiving instruction from his mother early in the day. After the War in the Pacific ended, Fang Chün-pi took up residence in the United States. A collection of reproductions of her paintings, *Fang Chün-pi kuo-hua chi*, has been published.

Tsiang, T. F.: *see* CHIANG T'ING-FU.

Tsien, H. S.   錢 學 森
Orig. Ch'ien Hsueh-sen

H. S. Tsien (2 September 1909–), American-educated scientist and professor at the California Institute of Technology who was known for his important work in the fields of jet propulsion, rocketry, and space physics. He was permitted to leave the United States in 1955 after five years of confinement to Los Angeles county for security reasons. He then went to the People's Republic of China, where he played a leading role in Peking's ballistic missile development program.

The native place of H. S. Tsien's family was the Hangchow district of Chekiang. He spent his boyhood in Shanghai, where his intellectual potential soon was recognized. He thus received his secondary education in Peking at the practice school attached to the National Normal University, a school then generally regarded as one of the best middle schools in China. He then matriculated at Chiaotung University in Shanghai, where he received an undergraduate degree in mechanical engineering in 1934. Tsien was awarded a Tsinghua fellowship for study abroad, and he went to the United States in 1935. He first studied at the Massachusetts Institute of Technology, where he received an M.S. in aeronautical engineering in 1936. Tsien then transferred to the California Institute of Technology to study under the Hungarian-born engineering scientist Theodore von Karman. His fields of concentration were aerodynamics and applied mechanics, and he conducted his early scientific experiments in the aeronautical laboratories at Pasadena. Von Karman, impressed with the brilliance of the young Chinese graduate student, noted that Tsien possessed unusual strength in mathematics and theoretical physics, combined with great ability to visualize accurately the physical characteristics of natural phenomena. Von Karman later (1967) wrote that Tsien, while a graduate student, had "helped me to clear up some of my own ideas on several difficult topics."

As a graduate student, Tsien also began to publish professional papers, notably in the *Journal of the Aeronautical Sciences*, dealing with such specialized topics as supersonic flow over an inclined body of revolution, flight analysis of a sounding rocket with special reference to propulsion by successive impulses (the "Karman-Tsien method"), and two-dimensional subsonic flow of compressible fluids. After receiving the Sc.D. at the California Institute of Technology in 1939, Tsien remained at Pasadena as a research fellow in aeronautics. With von Karman and L. G. Dunn, he wrote "The Influence of Curvature on the Buckling Characteristics of Structure," which was published in the *Journal of the Aeronautical Sciences* in 1940.

During the period of early experimentation with guided missiles, Tsien recognized their potential importance and suggested informally that the United States create a new service which would concentrate on jet weapons. He pointed out that the skills required for developing and operating remote-controlled missiles were different from those needed for other types of weaponry and that their operation required new modes of organization and planning in the military services.

During the Second World War, H. S. Tsien remained at the California Institute of Technology, where he contributed substantially to the JATO (jet-assisted takeoff) program and other research conducted under United States government sponsorship. In 1943 he was promoted from research fellow to assistant professor in aeronautics and chief research analyst at the Jet Propulsion Laboratory headed by von Karman. He contributed to several basic memoranda prepared by the laboratory during the later wartime period, notably "The Possibilities of Long-range Rocket Projectiles" (November 1943) and "Comparative Study of Jet Propulsion Systems as applied to Missiles and Transonic Aircraft" (March 1944).

In 1944 von Karman, under United States Army Air Force sponsorship, organized a special Scientific Advisory Group. Tsien was invited to serve as a consultant to that group, and he participated in an important meeting held under Air Force auspices at Woods Hole, Massachusetts, in 1945 to assess long-range problems and prospects of space flight technology. A major report stemming from the work of the Scientific Advisory Group, entitled *Toward New Horizons*, dealt with a broad spectrum of problems, including flight in the atmosphere, guided missiles, and orbital flight. It became a basic document in United States long-range aeronautical programming. Near the end of the Second World War, Tsien accompanied von Karman to Europe to inspect rocket installations in Germany, including the Kochel and Otztal wind tunnels, which later served as models for similar equipment in the United States. Tsien was with von Karman when he interrogated his former professor, Ludwig Prandtl, the prominent aerodynamicist of the Göttingen institute who had remained in Germany under the Nazi regime.

During his first decade in the United States, Tsien thus had unique opportunities for personal contact not only with von Karman but also with the talented group of pioneers in rocket research and development then largely centered at Pasadena, a group which included L. G. Dunn, Clark Millikan, William H. Pickering, William Duncan Rannie, Homer Joe Stewart, and others. He gained unusual insight into the problems involved in design and development of missiles and space vehicles. In 1945 Tsien was promoted to the rank of associate professor in aeronautics at the California Institute of Technology. He was regarded as von Karman's most talented student and he reciprocated, in the traditional Chinese manner, by addressing his professor as "revered teacher."

In addition to rockets and jet propulsion problems, Tsien's interests embraced rarefied gases, the dynamics of compressible fluids, and the theory of elastic thin shells. His scientific papers gained international recognition from colleagues in aerodynamics and related fields. In 1946 he published what was regarded as the first analysis made in the United States of the theoretical potential of nuclear fission and fusion for interplanetary and interstellar flight. In the same year, his article on "Superaerodynamics, Mechanics of Rarefied Gases," published in the *Journal of the Aeronautical Sciences*, was another innovating inquiry which defined and systematically explored problems occurring in very high altitude and orbital flight and in atmospheric entry. (Then a new branch of aerodynamics, this research area quickly expanded at an exponential rate. By the 1960's there were several thousand scientists working in the field, with an International Symposium on Rarefied Gas Mechanics meeting biennially.) Tsien's "Similarity Laws of Hypersonic Flows," published in the *Journal of Mathematics and Physics* in 1946, was also a pioneering paper. Other research papers of the early postwar period dealt with a variety of specialized topics: lifting-line theory for a wing in non-uniform flow, the Glauert-Prandtl approximation for subsonic flows of a compressible fluid, two-dimensional irrotational mixed subsonic and supersonic flow of compressible fluids and the upper critical Mach number, and a generalization of the Alfrey theorem for viscoelastic media. Tsien also continued to serve as a member of the Scientific Advisory Board of the United States Air Force.

In 1946 Tsien returned to Cambridge to join the faculty of aeronautical engineering at the Massachusetts Institute of Technology. After a year there as associate professor of aerodynamics, he was promoted in 1947 to the rank of professor, one of the youngest scientists ever to gain that rank at the institution. In the summer of 1947 he returned to China for family reasons. He was offered the post of president of Chiaotung University, his alma mater in Shanghai, but he declined it and returned to the Massachusetts Institute of Technology.

Tsien's internationally recognized distinction was confirmed in 1949 when he was named Robert H. Goddard Professor of Jet Propulsion and director of the Daniel and Florence

Guggenheim Jet Propulsion Center of the California Institute of Technology. In June 1950 his important survey article on programs of instruction and research at the Jet Propulsion Center, published in the *Journal of the American Rocket Society*, dealt with the entire range of problems involved in development of missiles and spaceships: finance, research, development, experimentation, and engineering.

In August 1950, after the outbreak of the Korean War but before the intervention of Chinese Communist military forces, H. S. Tsien decided to return to his native land. He purchased airplane tickets and delivered luggage, books, and research materials to a forwarding agent for shipment to the Far East. Two days before he was scheduled to depart from Los Angeles, Tsien received notification from United States immigration authorities that, because of the outbreak of the Korean conflict, he would have to remain in the United States for an indefinite period. Although the notice was a routine announcement sent to Chinese students and others in the United States who planned to return to the mainland of China, the scientific distinction of H. S. Tsien quickly made his case a *cause célèbre*. Agents of the Federal Bureau of Investigation searched his luggage, and his books and research notes were impounded by the United States customs. In September 1950 the immigration authorities notified Tsien that he had violated United States laws.

Tsien then was arrested on charges that he was or had been a member of the Communist party and that he was attempting to leave the United States for the People's Republic of China with allegedly secret scientific documents dealing with rocketry and space physics. These allegations were based on unidentified reports that Tsien, while a graduate student in Pasadena, had been acquainted with American students who had been members of or associated with the Communist party and that he therefore had supported the overthrow of the government of the United States by violent means. After two weeks of confinement, Tsien was released on $15,000 bail, which was provided by the California Institute of Technology. The case quickly attracted widespread attention. Faculty colleagues and other scientists attested to Tsien's personal integrity and professional reputation. Although a United States federal court later upheld the deportation order for

Tsien, the security authorities of the United States government took the position that Tsien possessed so much information on classified research programs directly related to American national security interests that it would be inadvisable to permit him to leave the country.

From late 1950 until 1955 H. S. Tsien was forbidden to travel outside the boundaries of Los Angeles county and was required to report monthly to the United States immigration authorities. The Federal Bureau of Investigation kept him under constant surveillance during the entire period. In his autobiographical volume *The Wind and Beyond* (1967), Tsien's mentor von Karman wrote: "I was convinced, as were virtually all of my associates . . ., that Tsien was not a member of the Communist party or had had anything more than social association with some individuals who were later identified as Communists or Communist sympathizers. A number of us felt, however, that while such 'evidence' against Tsien as was available could not be acceptable in a court of law, the Immigration Service tended to act on hearsay, and on relatively flimsy evidence."

Despite, or perhaps because of, personal tensions created by the unusual security precautions, Tsien buried himself in work and produced a fantastic flow of scientific papers, many of which were published in the *Journal of the American Rocket Society*. These papers dealt with a wide variety of topics: transfer functions of rocket nozzles, linear systems with time lag, automatic guidance of long-range rocket vehicles, properties of pure liquids, take-off from satellite orbit, a similarity law for stressing rapidly heated thin-walled cylinders. He also wrote on problems of education in the engineering sciences and sought to promote a new interdisciplinary science which he labeled "physical mechanics."

Like many other first-class scientists, H. S. Tsien wrote many papers but few books. While in Cambridge in the late 1940's, he had been impressed with the work of Norbert Wiener at the Massachusetts Institute of Technology. Wiener then was completing the manuscript for his book *Cybernetics*, published in 1948, which formulated the new science of the organization of mechanical and electrical components for stability and purposeful actions. Tsien was struck by the fact that a distinguishing feature of Wiener's system was total absence of considerations of energy: the primary concern of cybernetics was the qualitative aspects of interrelations among various components of a system and the synthetic behavior of the total mechanism. Tsien was so impressed with the potential significance of this line of conceptualization that he wrote a book entitled *Engineering Cybernetics*, which was published in 1954. His major objective was to study those aspects of the new science of cybernetics which had direct application to the control and guidance of mechanical and electrical systems that were of vital importance to modern weaponry systems and warfare. Writing in 1954, Tsien suggested that at the then current level of development in the field there were significant advantages in formulating engineering cybernetics as a new interdisciplinary approach designed to embrace the entire field of control and guidance engineering in a systematic way, to suggest new vistas, and to probe new approaches to new problems. Because he had little personal interest in (or patience with) routine engineering problems. Tsien's concern was primarily conceptual. He stressed the fact that while servo-mechanics was an engineering practice, engineering cybernetics was an engineering *science*, dominated by theoretical analysis and utilizing the tools of advanced mathematics. In discussing control of error, for example, he recognized that the subject was in a primitive stage of development and noted that theory was then based almost entirely on a series of lectures, "Probabilistic Logics and the Synthesis of Reliable Organisms from Unreliable Components," given by John von Neumann at the California Institute of Technology in 1952.

During his period of confinement, Tsien continued to hold the Goddard chair at the California Institute of Technology. On 4 August 1955, more than two years after the ceasefire arrangements that terminated the Korean conflict (superficially, the obstacle to his planned departure in 1950), Tsien was notified by the United States government authorities concerned that he would be permitted to leave the country. He then terminated his affairs at Pasadena and sailed from San Francisco on 17 September aboard the President Cleveland. His disenchantment at that point with aspects of government security operations in the United States, where he had spent two decades, was scarcely

concealed. After disembarking at Hong Kong, where the British authorities took special precautions, he proceeded by rail to Canton on 8 October 1955. There he was greeted not only by representatives of the Chinese Academy of Sciences but also by his 74-year-old father, who celebrated the return of his distinguished son by presenting him a set of copies of major Chinese paintings. Tsien then proceeded to Shanghai, where he was welcomed by prominent Chinese scientists. He reached Peking on 28 October 1955. Two days later he held a press conference at which he openly condemned the United States government for his extended detention, expressed sympathy for Chinese students still in the United States, and stated his determination to serve the Chinese people. On 3 November, it was announced that Tsien had accepted the invitation of the Academy of Sciences to direct its program of research in applied mechanics. Tsien himself stated that he hoped to place his scientific knowledge and research experience at the service of China and to help train younger scientists in the People's Republic of China.

As director of the institute of mechanics of the Academy of Sciences, Tsien occupied a key position in Peking's advanced research apparatus. In January 1957 the academy announced that Tsien had been given a first-class award for the outstanding work on fundamental problems of automatic control and guidance embodied in his 1954 volume on engineering cybernetics. In 1958 he was permitted to join the Chinese Communist party at the same time that Ch'ien San-ch'iang (q.v.) and several other prominent Western-educated scientists gained membership. Tsien also served as chairman of the China Dynamics Society and of the China Automation Society; and he was chairman of the department of modern mechanics at the University of Sciences and Technology in Peking. He represented Kwangtung province as a deputy to the National People's Congress.

Little was known of the work of H. S. Tsien at Peking during the 1960's. He did write a technical paper, "On the Basic Equations of Soil Dynamics," which appeared in the English edition of a volume entitled *Problems of Continuum Mechanics* (1961), issued in honor of the seventieth birthday of N. I. Muskhelishvili of the Soviet Academy of Sciences. During the mid-1960's Tsien was called upon to support the then current Peking position that it was necessary for Chinese intellectuals to demonstrate both political reliability and professional competence, or, in the phrase used by the Communists, to be "both red and expert." In a leading article in June 1965 in *Chung-kuo ch'ing-nien-pao* [China youth newspaper], Tsien stressed that political considerations were dominant in all societies, whether socialist or bourgeois, and stated that scientists in the United States, even those who professed to do pure research, were involved in politics and shaped by the constraints of the capitalist system. Although his nominal responsibilities in China were limited to problems of applied mechanics in the Academy of Sciences, Tsien's larger contributions to Peking's ballistic missile development program were suggested by the announcement in October 1966 that China had successfully landed a missile bearing a nuclear warhead on target at a distance of 400 miles.

On his return to China from the United States in the summer of 1947, H. S. Tsien married Chiang Ying (Tsiang Yin), the third daughter of a prominent intellectual and specialist on military strategy, Chiang Fang-chen (q.v.). Tsien dedicated *Engineering Cybernetics* to her.

Tsien San-tsiang: *see* CH'IEN SAN-CH'IANG.

Tso Ch'üan　　　　左 權
T. Tzu-lin　　　　　　字 林

Tso Ch'üan (1906–3 June 1942), Chinese Communist who was deputy chief of staff of the Eighth Route Army from 1937 until his death in 1942.

A native of Liling, Hunan, Tso Ch'üan was born into a family of landowners. While a middle-school student in his native province, he was influenced by the nationalistic ideas engendered by the May Fourth Movement of 1919. In 1923, at the age of 17, he went to Kwangtung, where he enrolled at the Hunan Cadets School and became a member of the Kuomintang. He there entered the Whampoa Military Academy as a member of its first class and came to know such Communist officials at the academy as Chou En-lai and Nieh Jung-chen

(qq.v.). After graduation, Tso became a battalion commander in the Kuomintang forces under Chiang Kai-shek.

By mid-1926 Tso Ch'üan had joined the Chinese Communist party. After qualifying in examinations at Canton, he went to Moscow to attend the Communist University for Toilers of the East. He remained in the Soviet Union for about four years, transferring to the Frunze Military Academy in 1928. One of his fellow students at the academy was Liu Po-ch'eng (q.v.).

Upon returning to China in 1930, Tso Ch'üan went to the central soviet area in Kiangsi. He served as an instructor at the Red Army Academy and later as deputy to Liu Po-ch'eng, who then was chief of staff of the Communist general military headquarters at Juichin. After Lin Piao (q.v.) became commander of the First Army Group of the Chinese Workers and Peasants Red Army, Tso became his chief of staff. Tso held that position throughout the Long March of 1934–35. After the arrival of the Communist forces in Shensi, Tso became acting commander of the First Army Group when Lin was named head of Anti-Japanese Military and Political University.

When the Chinese Communist military units were reorganized after the outbreak of the Sino-Japanese war in 1937, Tso Ch'üan became deputy chief of staff of the Eighth Route Army. Because Yeh Chien-ying (q.v.), the chief of staff, was frequently absent from north China, Tso often worked as senior staff officer under Chu Teh and P'eng Te-huai (qq.v.). From the time the Eighth Route Army began its push against the Japanese in Shansi in 1937 until his death five years later, Tso Ch'üan was in the field with the Chinese Communist forces. For a time in 1938, when Chu Teh and P'eng Te-huai were at Yenan for meetings of the Central Committee of the Chinese Communist party, he assumed complete responsibility for Eighth Route Army operations in north China. Tso Ch'üan was killed in action on 3 June 1942 in a battle with Japanese units along the Ch'ingchang River.

Tso Ch'üan wrote several articles on military subjects and translated *Combat Rules and Regulations of the Soviet Red Army*. A precise and conscientious professional soldier, he did not participate in the formulation of major political policies in the Chinese Communist party.

Tsou Lu　　　　　　　　鄒　魯
T. Hai-pin　　　　　　　海　濱

Tsou Lu (2 February 1884–13 February 1954), conservative Kuomintang leader who became chancellor of National Chung-shan University (1932–39) and leading authority on the 1911 revolution and the early history of the Kuomintang.

A native of Tap'u, Kwangtung, Tsou Lu was born into a poor Hakka family. His father reportedly was a tailor and a peddler. As the only child in the family, Tsou received his early education at private schools. In 1903, at the age of 19, he enrolled at the Han-shan shu-yuan, a semi-modern school at Ch'aochou. After a few years of both studying and teaching, he went to Canton in 1907 to enroll at the Kwangtung Fa-cheng hsueh-t'ang [college of law and government]. The nature of Tsou's early connection with the revolutionary movement is not entirely clear. In any event, he is said to have participated in the Huang-hua-kang uprising of 27 April 1911 (see Huang Hsing) and to have served on the staff of the *K'o-pao*, a revolutionary newspaper at Canton of which Ch'en Chiung-ming (q.v.) was a leading sponsor. After the revolution began in October 1911, he took part in the capture of Anhwei and advance to Nanking. He then supervised the campaign which resulted in the withdrawal of Chang Hsün (q.v.) from the Kiangsu area.

In 1913 Tsou Lu was elected to the Parliament at Peking, but he soon abandoned his seat in protest against Yuan Shih-k'ai's policies and returned to Canton. With the failure of the so-called second revolution (see Li Lieh-chün), he fled to Japan, where he enrolled at Waseda University. He also played an active role in reorganizing the Kuomintang as the Chung-hua ko-ming-tang and helped edit the *Min-kuo tsa-chih* [republican magazine]. In 1915 he traveled to Southeast Asia to raise funds for Sun's cause. Late that year he returned to China, where he helped Chu Chih-hsin and Teng K'eng (qq.v.) organize local forces in Kwangtung. These forces joined Li Lieh-chün's units in the thrust against Lung Chi-kuang (q.v.) in 1916. In 1917 Sun Yat-sen, then at Canton, appointed Tsou military commander for the Ch'ao-mei (Chaochow-Mei-hsien) district in eastern Kwangtung and ordered him to bring the rebellious troops of Mo Ching-yu under control.

Military and administrative duties absorbed Tsou Lu's energies during the next few years as Sun Yat-sen attempted to consolidate a territorial base in south China. In 1920–21, as salt commissioner in Kwangtung-Kwangsi, Tsou was in charge of an important element in the public finance structure of those two key provinces. In 1921 his familiarity with local military leaders in Kwangsi helped him to win the allegiance of Liu Chen-huan, who had been a division commander under Lu Jung-t'ing (q.v.). During 1922 Tsou traveled to Peking and Shanghai on Kuomintang business. The following year, he became commissioner of finance of Kwangtung. At this point, Tsou began to return to his earlier interest in the educational field. He was assigned to amalgamate the Kwangtung Higher Normal School with two other institutions to form Kwangtung University (later National Chung-shan University). It was at this university that Sun Yat-sen in January–August 1924 delivered three series of lectures on the *San-min chu-i* [three principles of the people]. The transcript of these lectures— the final draft of Sun's great work — was edited and proofread by Tsou Lu before publication.

At the First National Congress of the Kuomintang in 1924, Tsou Lu was elected director of the party's youth department and a member of the Central Executive Committee's standing committee. Because he was strongly opposed to radicalism and to the Kuomintang-Communist coalition, he made determined efforts to check Communist political infiltration of schools in the Canton area.

Tsou Lu went to Peking in 1925 to attend Sun Yat-sen in his final illness and to witness his will. After Sun's death, Tsou returned to Canton in May with other Kuomintang leaders. In September, the National Government at Canton ordered Tsou and Lin Sen (q.v.) to direct party activities in north China and to lead a "diplomatic delegation" to Peking for negotiations with the Peking government. Tsou and Lin soon decided to launch an anti-Communist campaign within the Kuomintang. In November they and eight other anti-Communist members of the Central Executive Committee held a meeting in the Western Hills near

Peking. At this Western Hills conference, as it became known, they passed resolutions calling for the ouster of all Communists from the Kuomintang and the impeachment of Wang Ching-wei. In answer, the Second National Congress of the Kuomintang, meeting in January 1926, passed a resolution calling for disciplinary action against the Western Hills leaders and threatening their dismissal from the party if they did not desist. Far from being deterred by this resolution, the Western Hills leaders convened an opposition second congress at Shanghai and elected their own central executive committee in April. Tsou Lu remained in Shanghai throughout 1926, working on behalf of the Western Hills faction and compiling a history of the Kuomintang. In the early months of 1927 the Communist question further divided the Kuomintang, with opposition governments being established at Wuhan and Nanking. By September, the Communists had been expelled from the Kuomintang and plans had been made for the restoration of party unity through the formation of the Central Special Committee.

In January 1928 Tsou Lu embarked on a world tour which lasted for a year. He recorded his impressions in a volume entitled *Erh-shih-chiu kuo yu-chi* [travels in 29 countries]. After his return to China, he spent a year in Shanghai doing further research on Kuomintang history. In 1929 he visited Japan. He resumed political activities in 1930, when he returned to China to join the so-called enlarged conference movement (*see* Feng Yü-hsiang; Yen Hsi-shan; Wang Ching-wei). He prepared the draft constitution for the opposition government which was to be established at Peiping. This document was known as the Taiyuan constitution because it was completed at Yen Hsi-shan's headquarters in Taiyuan, Shansi.

With the failure of the enlarged conference movement, Tsou Lu returned to south China. He soon joined another opposition government, this time at Canton. It took form as a result of Chiang Kai-shek's arrest of Hu Han-min (q.v.) in February 1931. Hsiao Fo-ch'eng, Ku Ying-fen, Teng Tse-ju (qq.v.), and Lin Sen issued a statement proposing the impeachment of Chiang Kai-shek on 30 April, and they joined with such other dissident leaders as Sun Fo, Eugene Ch'en, T'ang Shao-yi, Ch'en Chi-t'ang (qq.v.),

and Wang Ching-wei in establishing a government at the end of May. Tsou Lu served on the standing committee of the Southwest Political Council. Civil war threatened until mid-September, when the Japanese attacked Mukden. The ensuing national crisis led the Nanking and Canton leaders to hold peace talks at Shanghai. Tsou participated in these negotiations, which led to the release of Hu Han-min.

Tsou Lu became chancellor of National Chung-shan University in 1932, and he held this post at Canton until 1940. Although he was named to the State Council in 1935, he increasingly turned away from politics to devote his attention to academic administration. In 1936, in recognition of his contributions to modern higher education in China, he was invited to Germany to attend the World University Education Conference and the five-hundred-fiftieth anniversary celebrations of the University of Heidelberg. He received an honorary LL.D. degree from Heidelberg.

During the Sino-Japanese war, Tsou Lu was relegated to the position of an elder statesman in the Kuomintang. At Chungking, he served on the Supreme National Defense Council; and at Nanking after the war, he was elected a commissioner of the Control Yuan. He left Canton for Taiwan shortly before the Chinese Communists entered Canton in October 1949. On 13 February 1954 he died in Taiwan, at the age of 70.

Tsou Lu's most lasting contributions probably were made in the areas of education and political history. In the 1930's he did much to develop National Chung-shan University into south China's most influential academic institution. His first-hand knowledge and diligent research combined to make him a leading authority on the 1911 revolution and the early history of the Kuomintang. His important works included *Kuang-chou san-yueh erh-shih-chiu ko-ming shih* [history of the 29 March revolt in Canton], the *Chung-kuo kuo-min-tang shih-kao* [draft history of the Kuomintang], and the *Chung-kuo kuo-min-tang shih-lüeh* [brief history of the Kuomintang].

Tsou Lu was survived by two wives, six sons, and three daughters. One of his sons, Tsou Tang, became a professor of political science at the University of Chicago.

Tsou T'ao-fen   鄒 韜 奮
Orig. En-jun   恩 潤

Tsou T'ao-fen (5 November 1895–24 July 1944),
journalist known for his editorship (1926–33) of
the *Sheng-huo chou-k'an* [life weekly] and for his
leadership in the national salvation movement.
After working at Chungking in support of the
Chinese war effort, he went to Hong Kong in
1941 because of difficulties with Kuomintang
press censorship. He spent some time in the
Communist-held areas of Kiangsu, but went
to Shanghai in March 1943 because of illness.

Although his native place was Yüchiang,
Kiangsi, Tsou T'ao-fen was born in Foochow,
Fukien. He was the eldest of six children born
to Tsou Kuei-chen, a scholar-official who worked
in various salt bureaus in Fukien and, after
1915, in the ministry of finance in Peking. At
the age of five, Tsou T'ao-fen began to study
the Chinese classics with a private tutor, and in
1910 he entered the Foochow Engineerng
School. In 1912 his father, who wanted him to
pursue an engineering career, sent him to the
elementary school attached to Nanyang College
in Shanghai. Within a year he had been promoted to its middle school, where he spent four
years. In 1919, having had a one-year course
in electrical engineering at Nanyang College,
he decided to transfer to St. John's University
as an English major.

After being graduated from St. John's in
1921, Tsou T'ao-fen worked as an English
secretary in the Hou-sheng Textile Factory and
the Shanghai Cotton Stock Exchange. He also
taught English at a middle school sponsored by
the YMCA. It was his ambition to become a
journalist, and in 1922 he was appointed director
of the editorial board of the China Vocational
Education Society, headed by Huang Yen-p'ei.
He also taught English at the China Vocational
Institute and participated in other vocational
guidance activities.

In October 1926 Tsou T'ao-fen became the
editor of the *Sheng-huo chou-k'an* [life weekly]
which the China Vocational Education Society
had founded a year earlier. He transformed the
magazine, which had dealt primarily with
vocational guidance, into a forum on social and
political issues. He even created a column
called "Hsin-hsiang" [mail box] to answer
readers' questions. The effect of these changes
was testified to by its rapid increase in circulation from 2,800 in 1925 to 80,000 in 1930. This
expansion compelled Tsou to relinquish his
posts as general manager and an editor of the
Shih-shih hsin-pao. In October 1930 the *Sheng-
huo chou-k'an* set up a department to supply
books and periodicals to its readers. In July
1932 this department was reorganized as the
Sheng-huo shu-tien [life publications com-
pany], and by the late 1930's it had 55 branches
in major cities of China. Tsou ran both the
magazine and the publications company on a
cooperative basis, giving additional benefits and
incentive to his staff.

At the time of the Japanese attack on Mukden
in September 1931, Tsou T'ao-fen strongly
criticized the conciliatory policy of the Kuomintang and urged strong resistance to the
Japanese. His readers enthusiastically responded, and circulation jumped to 120,000.
Under Tsou's direction, the magazine launched
a fund-raising campaign in November, to which
its readers contributed some China $129,000.
The money was sent to Ma Chan-shan (q.v.),
who was fighting the Japanese in Manchuria.
In 1932 Tsou undertook another fund-raising
campaign, this time in support of the Nineteenth
Route Army (*see* Chiang Kuang-nai, Ts'ai
T'ing-k'ai). He also ordered his staff to organize a hospital for Chinese soldiers wounded at
Shanghai. That year, the popularity of the
Sheng-huo chou-k'an reached its pinnacle, with a
circulation of 155,000. The Kuomintang began
to impose censorship on the magazine. In
January 1933 Tsou joined the China League for
the Protection of Civil Rights (Chung-kuo
min-ch'üan pao-chang t'ung-meng), which denounced the methods of the Kuomintang. He
soon became a member of its executive committee. His activities soon placed him in a
position where he stood in danger of reprisal.
At the urging of friends, he left China. The
Sheng-huo chou-k'an was closed by the Kuomintang on 16 December.

After leaving Shanghai, Tsou T'ao-fen went
to Italy, Switzerland, and France. In September 1933 he arrived in London. He remained
there until February 1934, when he went to
Belgium, Holland, and Germany. In July,

he went to the Soviet Union, where he attended the summer session at Moscow University and toured southern Russia and the Crimea. He then returned to London before going on to the United States, which he toured in May–July 1935. In August, he returned to Shanghai. During his travels, Tsou paid close attention to the social and political conditions of the countries which he visited, and he recorded his impressions in a series of articles which he sent back to China. These articles later were collected and published: *P'ing-tsung chi-yü* [words from the wandering duckweed], a three-volume work on his travels in Europe and Russia; and *P'ing-tsung i-yü* [reminiscences of the wandering duckweed], on his experiences in the United States. He was more favorably impressed by the Soviet Union than by Western Europe and the United States. The changes that had taken place in his thinking during his trip soon were reflected by the new weekly which he started in November 1935, the *Ta-chung sheng-huo* [life of the masses]. Its aims were "achievement of national liberation, eradication of feudal remnants, and suppression of individualism." He continued to call for a united front against the Japanese.

In December 1935 Tsou T'ao-fen was elected to the executive committee of the Shanghai National Salvation Association, and in January 1936 he joined a group of more than 200 writers, newspapermen, and lawyers in forming the Cultural Workers' National Salvation Association. On 31 May 1936 he was elected to the executive committee of the All-China Federation of National Salvation Associations. The greater part of his work on behalf of the movement was carried on through the *Ta-chung sheng-huo*, which, however, was banned by the Kuomintang on 29 February 1936, after having reached a circulation of 120,000. In March, he established another weekly called *Yung-sheng* [eternal life], which was forced to suspend publication in June. He then went to Hong Kong, where, on 7 June 1936, he founded the *Sheng-huo jih-pao* [life daily]. Because of technical and financial difficulties, he was forced to discontinue publication after only 55 days. He returned to Shanghai and started publishing the *Sheng-huo hsing-ch'i-k'an* [Sunday life], but it was banned by the Kuomintang in December.

Tsou T'ao-fen joined with Chang Nai-ch'i, Shen Chün-ju and T'ao Hsing-chih (qq.v.), who also were leaders of the national salvation movement, in publishing a petition in July 1936 entitled "A Number of Essential Conditions and Minimum Demands for a United Resistance to Invasion." It was addressed to all Chinese political parties, but in particular to the Kuomintang and Chiang Kai-shek. It called for the cessation of Kuomintang-Communist civil war and a united front against Japan. This document and Tsou's other pronouncements led to his arrest in Shanghai on 23 November 1936. Apprehended at the same time were Li Kung-p'u, Wang Tsao-shih, Sha Ch'ien-li, Shen Chün-ju, Chang Nai-ch'i, and Shih Liang, all of whom were members of the executive committee of the All-China Federation of National Salvation Associations. The charges were "Communist behavior" and "suspicion of having instigated a strike in the Japanese-owned cotton mills." Because of insufficient evidence, they were released on bail, but within 24 hours they were rearrested on charges of having committed "acts with intent to injure the Chinese republic." They were handed over to the bureau of public safety of the Chinese municipal government in Shanghai. On 4 December, they were escorted to Soochow for trial before the Kiangsu provincial high court. In spite of efforts to keep the arrests and trial proceedings secret, the news spread quickly and aroused widespread shock and indignation. The group became known as the ch'i chün-tzu [seven gentlemen]. The trial began in April 1937, but it was suspended and the seven were released on bail after the Sino-Japanese war began that July.

During the months of imprisonment that followed his arrest, Tsou T'ao-fen made use of the enforced leisure to set down his memoirs in a volume entitled *Ching-li* [experiences]. It was also at this time that he wrote the last few chapters of *P'ing-tsung i-yü* and completed the *Tu-shu ou-i* [miscellaneous translations]. All of these were published by the Sheng-huo shu-tien between April and July 1937. On being released, Tsou and his associates went to see Chiang Kai-shek to pledge their support to the war effort. When the Japanese occupied Shanghai, Tsou left with Ho Hsiang-ning, Kuo Mo-jo (qq.v.), and others and joined the National Government in Wuhan, later following it to Chungking. Tsou became a member of the People's Political Council, but did not accept a position in the government. In the council, he presented a number of motions requesting freedom of the press and abolition of censorship. He centered his efforts on "whipping up popular enthusiasm for the war" through his new magazines: *K'ang-chan* [war of resistance], also known for a time as *Ti-k'ang* [resistance], which had been published in Shanghai and which then moved its headquarters to Hankow; and its successor, *Ch'üan-min k'ang-chan* [total war of resistance], published in Hankow and later in Chungking. Tsou also made a number of trips to the front to bolster the morale of the troops.

As the Kuomintang reinstituted a policy of censorship, Tsou T'ao-fen, with his repeated demands for political democracy and freedom of the press, became one of the first targets of repression. By June 1940 all but six branches of the Sheng-huo shu-tien had been closed and about fifty of its employees had been put in prison. When the remaining branches of the company were banned in February 1941, Tsou went to Hong Kong, where he wrote for a newspaper and revived the *Ta-chung sheng-huo*. That May, he joined with eight other leaders of the National Salvation Association in publishing a petition entitled "Our Stand and Opinion on National Affairs." In October, he urged the formation of a "League of Chinese Democratic Political Groups" (Chung-kuo min-chu cheng-t'uan t'ung-meng). The articles he wrote during this period, which were severely critical of the Kuomintang policies and practices in Chungking, later were collected and published as *K'ang-chan i-lai* [since the war of resistance].

Following the Japanese occupation of Hong Kong, Tsou T'ao-fen fled to Kwangtung in January 1942. He planned to proceed directly to Chungking, but wartime conditions forced him to remain for three months in Kwangtung with Communist guerrillas. He then learned that he was *persona non grata* at Chungking. Accordingly, he remained in a village on the Kwangtung-Kwangsi border during the summer of 1942, and in September he set out for northern Kiangsu, to the regions behind Japanese lines held by Chinese Communists. He reached Shanghai in October, by which time he had developed a serious ear infection. He went on to northern Kiangsu in November, where he was welcomed by the New Fourth Army and the local people. In spite of increasing illness, he went about delivering speeches and writing articles. He seems to have been impressed by

what he saw in the Communist-held regions. But when his health continued to deteriorate and he was found to have cancer of the ear, he was taken back to Shanghai in March 1943.

Though confined to a sick-bed, Tsou continued to be deeply concerned with the affairs of the nation. In September 1943 he published an "Appeal on National Affairs," advocating continuation of the united front until the achievement of victory over Japan, the immediate establishment of democratic government, and the promotion of popular education in an atmosphere of freedom. In January 1944 he began work on his last book, *Huan-nan yü-sheng chi* [records of a troubled life]. On 2 June, in the presence of some friends and relatives, he set forth his political testament, in which he emphasized the same points as in the "Appeal on National Affairs." He also expressed three personal wishes: that his body be given to a hospital for dissection; that his body then be cremated and the ashes sent to Yenan; and that he be made a member of the Chinese Communist party. Tsou T'ao-fen died on 24 July 1944. The Central Committee of the Chinese Communist party granted his dying wish for membership on 28 September.

As a journalist for almost two decades, Tsou T'ao-fen wrote copiously. In 1949 a collection of his articles written between 1925 and 1937 was edited by his friend Hu Yü-chih and published in Shanghai as *T'ao-fen wu-lu* [T'ao-fen's essays]. In 1959 his collected works were published in three volumes as the *T'ao-fen wen-chi* by the San-lien Publishers in Hong Kong.

Tsou T'ao-fen married twice. His first wife, *née* Yeh, died less than two years after their marriage. He married his second wife, Shen Ts'ui-chen, in 1926. They had two boys and one girl.

Tsu, Y. Y.
Orig. Chu Yu-yü   朱 友 漁
West. Andrew Y. Y. Tsu

Y. Y. Tsu (18 December 1885–), Chinese Episcopal bishop known for his work during the Sino-Japanese war as executive representative of the House of Bishops of the Chinese Episcopal Church. He later directed the Church's central office in China and served as executive secretary of its Home Mission Board. Upon his retirement in 1950, he went to live in the United States.

The son of Yu-tang Tsu (d. 1903), a Chinese Episcopal minister, Y. Y. Tsu was born near Shanghai. He had two elder sisters, a younger brother, and three younger sisters. When he was baptized, his parents christened him Yu-yue [friend of fishermen], and he later adopted the Western name Andrew. When Y. Y. Tsu was a year old, his family moved to Shanghai, where his father served as assistant chaplain at St. John's College (later St. John's University) and later as vicar of the Church of Our Savior. The young Tsu was graduated from St. John's College in 1904. His class, which consisted of four young men, was the first at that institution to be awarded B.A. degrees.

In 1904–7 Y. Y. Tsu received theological training at St. John's College, after which he was appointed to serve under the Reverend Gouverneur F. Mosher as a deacon at St. Andrew's Mission in Wusih, Kiangsu. After two years at Wusih, Tsu received a scholarship to the General Theological Seminary in New York. In addition to his studies at the seminary, he did graduate work in the social sciences at Columbia University. In June 1911 he was ordained an Episcopal priest in a ceremony at the Cathedral of St. John the Divine, and in June 1912 he received a B.D. from the General Theological Seminary and a Ph.D. from Columbia University. He then returned to China, where he joined the faculty at St. John's University.

In the years following his return to China, Tsu became interested in the pai-hua movement of Hu Shih (q.v.) and others and in the efforts of such prominent Chinese as T'ai-hsü (q.v.) to reform Buddism. In 1918 he was among those who advised Sun Yat-sen in the writing of his book *International Development of China*. The group, which also included David Yui (Yü Jih-chang, q.v.) and Chiang Monlin (Chiang Meng-lin, q.v.), met weekly at Sun's house in Shanghai.

In 1920 Y. Y. Tsu received a fellowship for a year's graduate study at Union Theological Seminary in New York. In 1921–24 he served in the United States as executive secretary of the Chinese Students Christian Association. Before returning to China, he married Caroline Huie. She was the daughter of the Reverend

Huie Kin, founder and pastor of the First Chinese Presbyterian Church in New York. In the summer of 1924 the couple left the United States and went to Peking, where Tsu accepted an invitation from Roger S. Greene, executive secretary of the China Medical Board, to become chaplain at the newly established Peking Union Medical College. In 1925 Y. Y. Tsu officiated with Timothy Lew (Liu T'ing-fang, q.v.) at the Christian memorial service held for Sun Yat-sen in the college's auditorium. In the summer of 1928, when Suiyuan province in Inner Mongolia was suffering from a long drought, he became a member of the China International Famine Relief Commission and volunteered to spend his summer vacation doing famine relief work. He was assigned to quarters in the Hai Lung Huang Miao, or the Temple of the Sea Dragon King, and his work involved the registration for corn rations of Chinese and Mongols in the region.

Tsu went to the United States for the academic year of 1931–32 as a visiting lecturer on oriental religions and cultures; he spent the fall term at the Pacific School of Religion in Berkeley and the spring term at the General Theological Seminary. In addition to his teaching duties, he engaged in a number of debates with prominent Japanese in America on the question of Japanese aggression in Manchuria. Although he was asked to become rector of St. Clement's Episcopal Church in Berkeley, he refused the offer and instead accepted a position with the National Christian Council and returned to China. His work with the council required him to attend many conferences. He traveled to south China for a meeting on cooperation among churches, and to the Philippines for the biennial meeting of the Federation of Churches. He also attended a meeting of the Federation of Christian Missions in Karuizawa, Japan, where he also addressed, along with Japanese Ambassador to the United States Sato and General Araki, the Oriental Culture Summer Institute on the question of Manchuria.

Although Y. Y. Tsu was offered the post of general secretary of the National Christian Council, he declined the invitation and rejoined the faculty of St. John's University in the spring of 1935. When St. John's admitted its first girl students, Tsu's wife was named dean of women. After the Sino-Japanese war broke out in the summer of 1937 and the Japanese bombed and captured Shanghai, the Tsu family was forced to abandon their house and move to the International Settlement. The state of affairs at St. John's University was precarious because the campus was situated on the border of the International Settlement; thus, for a time during the war the campus had to be relocated inside the settlement. In order to deal with the thousands of refugees who were entering the International Settlement, an International Red Cross Society was established, with Tsu as Chinese executive secretary.

In the summer of 1938 Colonel J. L. Huang sent a message to Tsu, asking him to travel to Hankow to discuss war work with Chiang Kai-shek and asking the university for his services. Tsu went by way of Hong Kong to Hankow, where Chiang requested that he and W. Y. Ch'en become his advisers for six months to help establish a youth training corps to prepare young men for military service during the war and for reconstruction work afterwards. However, Tsu was to serve much longer as an adviser to the project, for Chiang Kai-shek renewed the half-year period of service many times. As a result of his numerous trips to the warfront, Tsu became concerned about the lack of adequate medical facilities, and he began to devote most of his time to rectifying that situation. He served as a liaison official between the recently formed Shanghai Medical Relief Committee and parts of China not under Japanese occupation. In late October 1938 he was forced to evacuate Hankow with the National Government and move to Changsha and then to Chungking. He continued his wartime activities, which included personally meeting every medical unit that the Shanghai Medical Relief Committee sent. In 1939, in order to meet a unit sponsored by St. John's University, he traveled to Haiphong; the group then made the rigorous trip to Kweilin. Tsu was joined in Changsha by his wife, who was president of the Young Women's Christian Association Board. Another one of Tsu's many jobs was to inspect and make suggestions to the supervisors of the Burma Road, then being constructed by the National Government.

In 1940 the Chung Hua Sheng Kung Hui, or Chinese Episcopal Church, decided to create a new missionary diocese that would include the provinces of Yunnan and Kweichow, and Tsu was named bishop of the new diocese. He flew to Kunming to discuss the duties of the post and then traveled to Shanghai, where, on 1 May 1940, he was consecrated as Assistant Bishop of Hong Kong, serving as Bishop of Kunming, in charge of the new Yunnan-Kweichow Missionary District. He left immediately for Kunming, where he set up headquarters in St. John's Church. Because of wartime conditions, the House of Bishops was unable to provide him with either funds or staff, and these problems were complicated by the fact that the Episcopal Church had made few converts among the people of Yunnan. However, he was able to find funds to keep St. John's Church operating, and many other missionaries soon came to the city. By the end of 1940 the new district had seven ordained Chinese priests and several Western missionaries. During this period, Tsu also took on the duties of pastor at St. John's Church. In February 1941 he interrupted his work to attend a meeting of the House of Bishops, at which he was named special delegate of the House of Bishops for the Dioceses of Free China (later changed to executive representative of the House of Bishops). He returned to Kunming by way of Hong Kong, where he attended a meeting of the standing committee of the Dioceses of South China and Hong Kong, and by way of Rangoon, from which he traveled on the Burma Road.

In his capacity as special delegate of the House of Bishops, Bishop Tsu undertook a journey to Shanghai in October 1942 for the purpose of communicating with occupied dioceses throughout China. To escape possible detention by the Japanese, he disguised himself as a farmer. Upon his arrival in Shanghai, he contacted Bishop E. S. Yui and the Shanghai Medical Relief Committee and then paid a visit to his mother. Immediately after he completed the long and dangerous trip back to Kunming, which was further lengthened by a month spent in a hospital in Changsha, Tsu traveled at the behest of T. V. Soong (q.v.) to Chungking, where he learned that Chiang Kai-shek had included him in a group of scholars and educators who were to go to the United States for the purpose of creating goodwill between the peoples of the two nations. He left China in June 1943 for the United States, and he spent over a year making speeches on behalf of Nationalist China to various organizations.

Before Bishop Tsu left China, the bishops of the Episcopal Church in Nationalist-controlled territory met and decided, among other things, to recommend to Church authorities in the United States, Great Britain, and Canada that the Chung Hua Sheng Kung Hui be free to elect bishops regardless of nationality. As executive representative of the House of Bishops, Tsu was delegated to present a memorandum to the meeting of the Archbishops of the Anglican Church in Canada at Toronto in September 1943. He also presented the memorandum at the Triennial General Convention of the American Episcopal Church, at which recognition was given to the authority of the Chung Hua Sheng Kung Hui to elect its own bishops; in September, he flew to England, where he met with the Archbishop of Canterbury, received support from British missionaries for his memorandum, and preached in Westminster Abbey. He then returned to the United States, and he was joined there by his family.

In January 1945 Bishop Tsu accepted an invitation from the United States Army Headquarters in China to become a civilian chaplain for army personnel in the Burma Road area. He was the only Chinese chaplain in the United States Army in China, and, at the end of the War in the Pacific, he was awarded a Citation for Meritorious Civilian Service by the Chaplain-General. In March 1945 Tsu had been asked by bishops in Nationalist areas of China to set up a provisional central office in Chungking for the Chung Hua Sheng Kung Hui; his first job as director of the new office was to secure the return of church property which had been seized by the Japanese and then taken over by Nationalists. He discussed the problem with Chiang Monlin, then secretary general of the Executive Yuan, and Chiang issued an order charging all authorities to return church property. At the meeting of the House of Bishops in March 1946, it was decided that the central office would be moved to Nanking and that Bishop Tsu would be made its general secretary. Tsu thus found it necessary to give up his post as Bishop of Yunnan and Kweichow. He traveled by jeep to Nanking in May 1946. As general secretary, Tsu was in charge of the August 1947 General Synod meeting of the Chung Hua Sheng Kung Hui, at which he was named chairman of a special committee to draft a clergy pension plan.

Bishop Tsu was also appointed executive secretary of the Home Mission Board, and in that capacity he traveled to Sian, Shensi, to install the new bishop of the province. In the summer of 1948 he attended the Lambeth Conference of the Bishops of the Anglican Communion in England and the Amsterdam Assembly of the World Council of Churches in the Netherlands. He addressed the Lambeth Conference on "The Significance of the Younger Churches in the Life of the Church Universal," and he spoke at the Amsterdam Assembly on "The Chinese Church in Action." The Amsterdam Assembly voted to create a World Council of Churches, and Tsu was named to the central and executive committees of the new organization. He then spent two months in the United States, doing missionary deputation work for the National Council of the American Episcopal Church. He returned to Nanking in late November, only to find the city in a chaotic state as a result of the Kuomintang-Communist civil war. It was necessary to relocate the national office of the Chung Hua Sheng Kung Hui in Shanghai, but the move was not effected until April 1949, when Tsu traveled by jeep to Shanghai. However, Shanghai was taken by Communist forces in May. At first, some Episcopal leaders in China were favorably inclined toward the Communists and the People's Republic of China. However, when the "Christian Manifesto" was issued (see Wu Yao-tsung), dissatisfaction began to grow. In this delicate situation, the bishops of the Chung Hua Sheng Kung Hui sent members of their church a letter which affirmed the Christian faith, but which also stressed duty to one's nation.

In July 1950 Bishop Tsu left China to attend the semi-annual session of the central committee of the World Council of Churches in Toronto and to visit his family in the United States. In August he traveled to Hong Kong, from whence he went to Shanghai. Because he would be 65 in December, he announced his retirement. He left Shanghai on 7 December for the United States to rejoin his family. He and his wife later settled in Pennsylvania. In April 1951, as part of the Three-Self Movement (see Wu Yao-tsung), Tsu and 13 other Chinese church leaders were denounced by a group of Christian and Communist leaders as "imperialist agents under the cloak of religion." Tsu himself was branded as "a heartless renegade of our people, a wholehearted follower of

American imperialism," and he was denounced by Bishop Robin Ch'en, chairman of the House of Bishops.

Y. Y. Tsu and his wife had four children: David, who attended Yale University; Robert, who became an Episcopal clergyman; Carol, who married Dr. Monto Ho, professor of microbiology at the University of Pittsburgh; and Kin, who attended Princeton University. Tsu's autobiography, *Friend of Fishermen*, was published in the United States after his retirement.

Tsur, Y. T.: *see* CHOU I-CH'UN.

Tu Chung-yuan   杜 重 遠

Tu Chung-yuan (1895–1943), liberal journalist associated in Shanghai with Tsou T'ao-fen (q.v.) in dissemination of anti-Japanese materials before 1937, for which action he was arrested by the National Government. He later went to Sinkiang, where he served under his fellow-Manchurian Sheng Shih-ts'ai (q.v.), who in 1943 had him executed as a "leftist."

The Kaiyuan district of Liaoning in southern Manchuria was the native place of Tu Chung-yuan. After receiving his early education at local schools in Manchuria, he went to Japan where he came to know Sheng Shih-ts'ai, also a native of Kaiyuan. Little is known about Tu's career during the 1920's except that he established himself in business at Mukden, where he operated a plant that manufactured chinaware.

The Japanese invasion of Manchuria in 1931 brought an abrupt change in Tu Chung-yuan's life. Rather than remaining in Mukden under Japanese rule, he abandoned his business and moved to Shanghai. He soon established contact with Tsou T'ao-fen (q.v.), editor of a popular liberal Chinese journal called *Sheng-huo chou-k'an* [life weekly]. In October 1933, while Tsou was abroad, the magazine was suppressed by the Nationalist authorities. Shortly thereafter, Tu Chung-yuan resumed publication under a slightly different name, *Hsin-sheng chou-k'an* [new life weekly]. With Tu as editor and publisher, the new journal gave emphatic expression to anti-Japanese views. In the inaugural issue of February 1934, Tu remarked

that the fervent anti-Japanese sentiment of 1931–32 had subsided; and he said that his periodical would articulate a new call to arms. The Chinese phrase used, na-han [call to arms], evoked memories of the famous collection of short stories under that title written by Lu Hsün (Chou Shu-jen, q.v.) a decade earlier.

On 2 July 1935 Tu Chung-yuan was arrested and called before the high court of Kiangsu province. On 8 July, after having been denied the right of appeal, he was sentenced to 14 months in prison on charges that the *Hsin-sheng chou-k'an*, in its issue of 4 May 1935, had published an article derogatory to the Japanese emperor. The article under attack had stated, with reference to emperors in general, that the institution had become meaningless, and it had concluded that the most pitiable of emperors was P'u-yi (q.v.), the putative emperor of Manchoukuo. The Japanese authorities, then pressing hard to extend control over the five provinces of north China, inflated the charge into an international issue, made official representations at Nanking, and moved the flagship of their eleventh destroyer flotilla from Hankow to Nanking. In fact, the article that aroused Japanese attention was probably another one entirely: an editorial by Tu Chung-yuan that appeared in the 22 June 1934 issue of the journal. In that editorial Tu had spoken out strongly against growing Japanese imperialism in China since 1931 and had sternly criticized the official "forbearance" policy of the Chinese government. The Chinese, Tu stated, "have nothing to lose but the chains of imperialism." Nanking, again bowing to Japanese pressure, had responded by suspending the *Hsin-sheng chou-k'an*, jailing Tu Chung-yuan in a manner that violated normal legal procedures, dismissing seven members of the Kuomintang censorship committee at Shanghai, and issuing new warnings to the Chinese press to adhere to earlier regulations that prohibited acts "obstructing friendly relations" between China and foreign powers. In November 1935 Tsou T'ao-fen, after his return to China, launched another new journal, the *Ta-chung sheng-huo* [life of the masses] to replace the *Hsin-sheng chou-k'an*. Tu remained in prison at least until September 1936; and Tsou T'ao-fen and other members of the National Salvation Association were arrested in November of that year.

In September 1937, after the Sino-Japanese war began, he journeyed overland to Sinkiang province, where Sheng Shih-ts'ai had gained power. Tu spent several months in Sinkiang gathering materials on political and economic developments. After Tu returned to Hankow, Tsou T'ao-fen urged him to publish his findings. The result was a volume, *Sheng Shih-ts'ai yü hsin Hsin-chiang* [Sheng Shih-ts'ai and the new Sinkiang], with a preface written by Tsou T'ao-fen which lauded Tu as "a most loyal comrade" in the national salvation movement. Tu's book, originally published in 1938, went through several editions and provided useful information on developments in Sinkiang, where Sheng Shih-ts'ai, with Soviet assistance, was then introducing significant changes in the economic and social life of the province.

Two of Sheng Shih-ts'ai's major political precepts at that time were anti-imperialism and friendship with the Soviet Union. As a frustrated patriot disillusioned with the National Government, Tu Chung-yuan believed that he could better serve China in Sinkiang than in China proper. Accordingly, late in 1938 he returned to Sinkiang, where Sheng Shih-ts'ai had appointed a number of Chinese Communists from Yenan as officials and advisers (*see* Ch'en T'an-ch'iu, Mao Tse-min) in the provincial government. At Urumchi he was named chancellor of Sinkiang Academy, where the prominent novelist Mao Tun (Shen Yen-ping, q.v.) was serving as dean of studies. Tu attempted to develop an institution that would reflect the complex racial and linguistic composition of the population of Sinkiang and offer new facilities for non-Chinese previously denied equal educational opportunities.

Sheng Shih-ts'ai later moved away from his pro-Soviet orientation and began to apply stringent political controls throughout Sinkiang. Two of Tu Chung-yuan's colleagues at the Sinkiang Academy, Liu Kuei-pin and Hsing Kuo-wen, were arrested; and Mao Tun left in the spring of 1940 for Yenan. Tu and some other associates also requested permission to leave, but Sheng Shih-ts'ai denied the request. During 1940, according to Sheng Shih-ts'ai's account, his security police unearthed an extensive conspiracy in which Tu Chung-yuan, as well as Soviet advisers and technicians, were implicated. Despite this development, Tu Chung-yuan continued for a time to hold his post at Urumchi as chancellor of the Sinkiang Academy. Late in 1941, however, Tu and others were arrested on charges of plotting Sheng Shih-ts'ai's downfall. This action was taken partly in response to the changed international situation after the German invasion of the Soviet Union in June 1941, an attack which led Sheng to reconsider the logic of maintaining a pro-Russian orientation. He soon began to arrest Communists and fellow-travelers within his domain to justify a shift of allegiance to the Chinese National Government. Many of the human pawns held in Sheng's Sinkiang prisons later died. Among them was Tu Chung-yuan, who apparently perished in 1943. Sheng Shih-ts'ai's version of the case was that Tu had poisoned himself in fear of Chinese Communist reprisals. Another estimate is that Tu was poisoned by Sheng's military medical service.

Paradoxically, Tu Chung-yuan had some posthumous influence outside China. *Sheng Shih-ts'ai yü hsin Hsin-chiang* was one of the Chinese sources used by Martin R. Norins in his book *Gateway to Asia: Sinkiang, Frontier of the Chinese Far West*, published in New York in 1944. The Norins book provides a useful selection of English paraphrases translated from Tu Chung-yuan's earlier volume on Sheng Shih-ts'ai's Sinkiang of the 1937 period.

Tu Yü-ming   杜聿明
　T. Kuang-t'ing   光亭

Tu Yü-ming (1903–), Whampoa graduate who was one of Chiang Kai-shek's favorite commanders. In 1945 he helped strengthen Nationalist control of Yunnan by ousting Lung Yun (q.v.). In the civil war with the Chinese Communists he served in Manchuria and at Hsuchow in the decisive Hwai-Hai battle. He was captured by the Chinese Communists in January 1949.

The son of Tu Tou-yuan, a teaching scholar who held the chü-jen degree, Tu Yü-ming was born in Michih, Shensi. After the republic was established in 1912, Tu Tou-yuan taught at the Yülin Middle School, and the young Tu studied there. In 1924, having completed his course of study at Yülin, Tu Yü-ming went to Canton and enrolled in the first class at the

Whampoa Military Academy. He served in one of the training regiments and participated in the second so-called eastern expedition (*see* Chiang Kai-shek). After graduation, he participated in the Northern Expedition, gradually working his way up from company commander to vice commander of a division.

Little is known about Tu Yü-ming's activities in the early 1930's. In May 1937 Tu was charged with the creation of an armored corps. It is doubtful that he was able to complete this task, for the Sino-Japanese war broke out two months later and a Chinese biographer has stated that Tu participated in the battles of Woosung-Shanghai, Hsinkow, and Nanking. Because his name does not appear on the official order of battle as a unit commander in any one of those engagements, it may be assumed that he served as a staff officer or (in the lower Yangtze sector) as commander of the embryo armored force. In any event, in January 1938 he became the commander of the 200th Division, in which capacity he participated in the 1938 battles of Taierchuang, Lanfeng, Hsinyang, and Sanhaikow. With the loss of the Wuhan area and the removal of the National Government to Chungking, the 200th Division was expanded into the Fifth and New Eleventh armies. Tu was appointed commander of the Fifth Army.

After the War in the Pacific began in December 1941, the United States and Great Britain, hard pressed by the Japanese in the new war theater, called upon China to send troops into Burma to relieve pressure on the British forces by the advancing Japanese. The National Government in March 1942 designated the Fifth, Sixth, and Sixty-sixth armies for use in that expedition. The over-all Chinese commander was Lo Cho-ying, but the Fifth and Sixth armies in particular were to be subject to the direct orders of Lieutenant General Joseph W. Stilwell as commander of U.S. forces in the China-Burma-India theater and Chiang Kai-shek's chief of staff.

The expedition had a good beginning. Tu Yü-ming's Fifth Army at this time was composed of the 22nd, the 96th, and the 200th divisions. Stilwell judged him to be "O.K. Solid on tactics. Ready to fight." The Japanese took Rangoon on 8 March and moved north. The 200th Division under Tai An-lan had taken up a position at Toungoo the day before, and it stubbornly resisted the Japanese 55th Division

for 12 days. The 22nd Division had moved into position to attack the Japanese in a pincers movement. Stilwell, seeing the opportunity for an important victory, ordered a concerted attack. He soon realized that he was not in field command after all: the official American history of the war records that "Tu was prolific with excuses as to why an attack was impossible"; and it soon became evident that Chiang Kai-shek in distant Chungking was retaining direct control over the troops he had nominally placed under Stilwell. His orders to both Lo Cho-ying and Tu Yü-ming bypassed Stilwell. Tu did not move the 22nd Division, and the 200th Division was forced to retire on 29 March.

Plans for further operations envisaged a trap to be laid by coordinating the Fifth Army's three divisions in a series of moves. The first part of the plan was smoothly and successfully accomplished, and in April 1942 the trap was ready to be sprung. At that juncture, however, British withdrawals and defeats evidently gave rise to second thoughts at Chungking. Chiang Kai-shek issued a series of conflicting orders which hopelessly snarled the command situation. Stilwell's orders to Tu Yü-ming went unobeyed, heavy losses were suffered by some of the Chinese units, and the Irrawaddy front was lost. At the end of April, the Japanese took Lashio, cutting off the Burma Road. The perilous retreat of British and Chinese units from Burma into India and China then began. The 200th Division retreated from Taunggyi in the direction of the China border, but the rest of the Fifth Army moved toward India. The 22nd and 96th divisions were within a few days' march of the Indian border and safety when Tu Yü-ming received orders from Chungking to withdraw to China. The two divisions changed direction, received new conflicting orders, parted company, and attempted to make their separate ways back to China. The 22nd Division arrived in China in fairly good shape, but the 96th Division fared less well.

In January 1943 Tu Yü-ming was made commander in chief of the Y-Force reserve (the Fifth Group Army) at Kunming, Yunnan. He commanded this American-equipped unit for the rest of the war. At the time of the Japanese surrender in 1945, the Yunnanese forces of Lung Yun (q.v.) were sent to Indo-China to take over from the Japanese in that area. The Nationalist authorities took advantage of this opportunity to strengthen their control of Yunnan. Tu staged a coup at Kunming late in 1945, and Lung Yun was replaced as military governor by Lu Han (q.v.).

On 15 October 1945 Tu Yü-ming was appointed peace preservation officer for the Northeast. At this time the National Government was trying to reestablish its authority in Manchuria. On 29 October, Tu flew to Changchun to join his superior officer, Hsiung Shih-hui (q.v.), the director of the Northeast headquarters of the Military Affairs Commission. The Manchurian operation was not a success, and by early November the Nationalists at Changchun had been confined to their headquarters by the Chinese Communists. The Nationalist officials withdrew by air to Peiping on 17 November. Manchuria continued to be a major theater of Nationalist-Communist conflict in 1946–47. By the summer of 1947, following an offensive led by Lin Piao (q.v.), the Chinese Communists had seized the initiative. Chiang Kai-shek declared the Communists to be in a state of rebellion and ordered national mobilization. At the end of August, he replaced Hsiung Shih-hui with Ch'en Ch'eng (q.v.). Tu Yü-ming was removed from field command in Manchuria at the same time. He was reappointed to this post in October 1948, but the Nationalists were forced to abandon their Manchurian effort in November of that year.

In November 1948 Tu Yü-ming was appointed deputy field commander, under Liu Chih (q.v.), at Hsuchow. The decisive Hwai-Hai battle began in that sector on 6 November 1948 with a half-million troops committed on each side. This massive battle was a disaster for the Nationalists almost from the beginning. On 28 November, Liu Chih, Chiang Wei-kuo (q.v.), and Li Mi of the Thirteenth Army Group flew out of Hsuchow to Pengpu. Tu Yü-ming remained behind. On 1 December, he led the Nationalist rearguard forces out of Hsuchow in an effort to break through Communist lines and join forces with the Twelfth Army Group, which had been trapped nearby. However, Tu's 130,000-man force was similarly trapped by the Communists about 20 miles west of Hsuchow. It managed to hold out for a time, despite strong Communist attack, but it finally was forced to surrender on 10 January 1949. Tu Yü-ming was captured while trying to escape from the battleground in the guise of a common soldier.

Tu Yü-ming was among the 33 former Nationalist leaders who, having been held as "war criminals," were pardoned by the Central People's Government at Peking in December 1959. They were said to have "repented, acknowledged their crimes, and shown that they were turning over a new leaf."

Tu Yueh-sheng   杜 月 笙
Orig. Yung   杜 庸

Tu Yueh-sheng (22 August 1888–16 August 1951), Shanghai secret society leader, banker, industrialist, philanthropist, and social celebrity who also was known for his personal contributions to the Nationalist war effort during the Sino-Japanese war.

The village of Kaochiao on the southern bank of the Whangpoo across from Shanghai was the birthplace of Tu Yueh-sheng. He was orphaned at an early age and was brought up by relatives who were poor peasants. As a youth of about 20, Tu, like many of his fellow villagers, crossed the river to seek his fortune in the great metropolis of Shanghai. He apprenticed himself to a fruiterer whose business was located near the waterfront of the French concession, a waterfront dominated by the Ch'ing-pang (Green Gang). He began to associate with members of this secret society, and his resourcefulness, dexterity, and capacity for making friends soon came to the attention of its leaders. He soon became a protégé of Huang Chin-jung, who then operated most of the smuggling syndicates. At this time (about 1912), opium smuggling was the most lucrative business in which the Chinese underworld engaged, and Huang was, therefore, a man of tremendous importance. He placed Tu in charge of one of the syndicates, and Tu made the most of this opportunity, becoming a powerful leader in the Green Gang.

In 1924 a civil war developed between Ch'i Hsieh-yuan, the military governor of Kiangsu, and Lu Yung-hsiang, the military governor of Chekiang and a personal friend of Tu Yueh-sheng. Lu controlled Shanghai even though it was part of Kiangsu. In September 1924, at his request, Tu raised a force of nearly 2,000 men to maintain order in Shanghai. Tu's abilities and influence thus came to the attention of political and military leaders in other parts of China. In 1925, after Lu finally lost the war, Tu organized a society for the relief of refugees.

The National Revolutionary Army reached Shanghai on the Northern Expedition in March 1927. At this time, Tu Yueh-sheng came to the support of the conservative faction of the Kuomintang, led by Chiang Kai-shek. With the temporary rank of major general, Tu organized his secret society followers in opposition to the Communist-dominated labor movement at Shanghai. On 12 April, Tu and other supporters of Chiang, including the Twenty-sixth Army, undertook a bloody anti-Communist purge in which more than 100 were killed and several hundred were arrested and executed later. The incident made Tu a hero in some quarters and a villain in others.

By this time, Tu had proved himself to be a successful enterpreneur in legitimate business activities. He controlled the Chung Wai Bank, the Tung Wai Bank, and the Pootung Savings Bank; and he became a director of the Chinese Stock Exchange and the Chinese Cotton Goods Exchange in Shanghai. In 1928 he won the gratitude of a large part of the Shanghai population for his successful mediation in a dispute between the workers and the management of the electric and water utility in the French concession. Perhaps because of this episode, he was listed in the *China Year Book* as "the most influential resident in the French Concession, Shanghai."

In January 1932 the Japanese attacked Shanghai. The stubborn resistance of the Nineteenth Route Army (*see* Chiang Kuang-nai; Ts'ai T'ing-k'ai) to this attack brought world-wide renown to that Chinese force. Tu Yueh-sheng was a sponsor of the campaign to provide the Nineteenth Route Army with supplies and equipment, and he personally donated the money for two tanks. When the hostilities ended, the leaders of this campaign organized the Shanghai Civic Federation, with Shih Liang-ts'ai (q.v.) as its chairman and Tu as a vice chairman. When Shih was assassinated, Tu succeeded him as chairman.

Tu Yueh-sheng's fame and influence reached their peak in the years immediately preceding the Sino-Japanese war. In 1936 he built an ancestral temple in his native village of Kaochiao. The inauguration ceremonies recalled scenes of the days of imperial pageantry, so great was the splendor. Guests and senders of gifts included National Government leaders, provincial governors, businessmen, industrialists, and bankers.

When the Sino-Japanese war, which began in July 1937, spread to Shanghai that August, Tu used the Shanghai Civic Federation to spearhead a resistance movement. He also offered the entire fleet of the Ta-ta Steamship Company, of which he was the chairman, to the National Government for blockading the lower reaches of the Yangtze. Toward the latter part of 1938 Tu was forced to leave Shanghai. He then went to Hong Kong, where he resided until the end of 1941 and continued to contribute to the Chinese war effort. As vice president of the Chinese Red Cross, he attended to the care of refugees from the Japanese-occupied areas. He also gave assistance to Chinese secret agents in occupied areas and helped coordinate their activities. In 1940, after T'ao Hsi-sheng (q.v.) and Kao Tsung-wu escaped to Hong Kong with a copy of Wang Ching-wei's secret agreement with the Japanese, Tu secured the release of three of T'ao's children, who were being held hostage in Shanghai. Fortunately for Tu, when the War in the Pacific began in December 1941 he was on one of his occasional trips to Chungking. He remained there for the rest of the war. Because he had established a textile mill and a flour mill in Chungking and a paper mill in Kunming in 1939, he was able to devote some of his attention to business. He held a few nominal posts in the National Government, but his chief interests were these mills and the development of the China Bank of Commerce. He also continued his work with the Chinese underground, and his activities in this area brought him into close association with Tai Li (q.v.).

At war's end, Tu Yueh-sheng returned to Shanghai on 3 September 1945. Because of his wartime efforts, he received a hero's welcome. He resumed his banking and industrial activities and became chairman of the board of directors of the *Shun Pao*. Early in 1949, on the eve of the Chinese Communist occupation of Shanghai, he moved to Hong Kong. He died there on 16 August 1951, at the age of 64 sui. His dying wish, that he be buried in Taiwan, was honored on 28 June 1953, when his remains were taken to Taiwan and buried in a village near Taipei.

Tu Yueh-sheng was survived by his second wife, three secondary wives, eight sons, and three daughters.

In his lifetime, Tu Yueh-sheng became an almost legendary figure. He has been described as a gangster, a knight errant, a protector of the weak, a patron of the talented, and a patriot. He was, perhaps, a little of each.

Tuan Ch'i-jui 段 祺 瑞
   T. Chih-ch'üan 芝 泉
   H. Cheng-tao lao-jen 正 道 老 人

Tuan Ch'i-jui (6 March 1865–2 November 1936), Peiyang military leader and head of the Anhwei clique. He served at Peking as minister of war (1912–14), premier (April–June 1916; June 1916–May 1917; July-November 1917; March–October 1918), and as provisional chief executive at Peking from November 1924 to April 1926.

The eldest of three brothers, Tuan Ch'i-jui came from a family with a long tradition of military service. His grandfather, Tuan P'ei (d. 1879; T. Yuan-shan), had joined Liu Ming-ch'uan (ECCP, I, 526–28) and other natives of Hofei, Anhwei, in organizing militia bands under the over-all command of Li Hung-chang (ECCP, I, 464–71) to fight the Taipings. Tuan P'ei subsequently rose to the rank of brigade commander in the army of Liu Ming-ch'uan, and beginning in 1872 he was stationed at Such'ien, Kiangsu. That year, Tuan Ch'i-jui, then a boy of seven, went to Such'ien, where he studied under his grandfather's supervision until the latter's death in 1879.

In 1881, at the age of 16, Tuan joined one of his father's cousins at the army camp at Weihaiwei, Shantung. He held a minor military post there until 1884 when he passed the entrance examination for the newly established Peiyang Military Academy (Pei-yang wu-pei hsueh-t'ang), becoming a member of its first class. After three years of training in modern military methods under foreign instructors, he was graduated at the top of his class in 1887 and was assigned to supervise repairs in the gun batteries at Port Arthur. Late in 1888 Tuan was one of the five graduates of the Peiyang Military Academy selected by Li Hung-chang for military study abroad. Tuan arrived in Germany in the spring of 1889, studied military science in Berlin, and later received practical training in artillery engineering at the Krupp armament works. Upon his return to China in the autumn of 1890, he was placed in charge of the Peiyang Arsenal (Pei-yang chün-hsieh-chü). In 1891–94 he served as an instructor at the military school attached to the army base at Weihaiwei.

Late in 1895 Tuan Ch'i-jui was transferred to the army camp at Hsiaochan, near Tientsin, where Yuan Shih-k'ai had just begun to organize the Newly Created Army. As commander of the army's artillery battalion and director of the artillery training school attached to the base, Tuan made important contributions to the building up of the military machine that became known as the Peiyang Army. When Yuan Shih-k'ai was transferred to Shantung late in 1899 as acting governor, Tuan and the army (which had become the Right Division of the Guards Army) went with him to garrison the provincial capital of Tsinan. Two years later, when Yuan was moved to Chihli (Hopei) as governor general, he took Tuan with him and had him promoted to the civil rank of expectant prefect. In July 1902, again on Yuan's recommendation, Tuan was promoted to expectant tao-t'ai in recognition of his part in restoring calm to southern Chihli, which had been plagued by bands of outlaws.

As one of Yuan Shih-k'ai's chief military aides, Tuan Ch'i-jui played an important role in the Ch'ing government's program to expand and modernize China's military establishment. Yuan carried out an administrative reorganization of the military forces under his command in the summer of 1902 and set up a provincial department of military administration (chün-cheng-ssu), placing Tuan at the head of its staff section in charge of military planning. In December 1903 the Ch'ing government followed Yuan's lead and established a commission for army reorganization, with Yuan as associate director and Tuan as head of the military command department (chün-ling-ssu) in charge of military planning, cartography, and military stores. Yuan was ordered to increase the number of Peiyang Army divisions, and Tuan became commander of a number of these new units as they were formed. Tuan took command of the 3rd Division when it was activated in June 1904; he was transferred to the 4th

Division in February 1905; and he received command of the 6th Division in September 1905.

Early in 1906, while briefly serving again as commander of the 3rd Division, Tuan was appointed supervisor of the Peiyang Military Academy, and for the next three years he devoted himself to military education. Although he was appointed brigade general at Ting-chouchen, Fukien, in March 1906, he remained in Chihli and became director of the staff officers college (chün-kuan hsueh-t'ang) attached to Yuan Shih-k'ai's camp at Paoting. Late in 1909 Tuan resumed command of the 6th Division, and at the end of December 1910 he became acting commander in chief of the Chiangpei region in Kiangsu. After the republican revolution began with the Wuchang revolt of 1911, he was transferred to Peking. On 27 October, Yuan Shih-k'ai replaced the Manchu Yin-ch'ang as high commissioner of the imperial forces in Hupeh, and Tuan became commander of the Second Army. After Yuan had established control over the government at Peking, he appointed Tuan acting governor general of Hupeh and Hunan on 17 November, with full military authority in the Wuhan area. Tuan also replaced Feng Kuo-chang (q.v.) as commander of the First Army.

During the final years of the Ch'ing empire Tuan Ch'i-jui, like most senior Peiyang military officers, appears to have been loyal primarily to Yuan Shih-k'ai rather than to the Ch'ing dynasty. He thus was prepared to give his full support to Yuan as the provisional president of the republican government. On 20 March 1912 Tuan became minister of war at Peking, a post he held, with only brief interruptions, through a succession of cabinets in the next three years. From May to July 1913 he also served as acting premier. He went to Hankow in December 1913 to demand that the reluctant Li Yuan-hung (q.v.) go to Peking and assume office as vice president. After Li complied, Tuan remained in Hupeh for a time as military governor and brought the province under the complete domination of Peiyang troops. In February–March 1914 Tuan served as military governor of Honan so that he could assume direction of military operations against the bands of outlaws led by Pai-lang [white wolf] which were causing widespread unrest in central China.

By 1914 Tuan Ch'i-jui had become the most powerful of Yuan Shih-k'ai's lieutenants. Because he had assumed such functions as the training and transfer of troops and the selection and promotion of officers, many of the younger officers in the Peiyang Army regarded him, rather than Yuan, as their principal patron. In the spring of 1914 Yuan took steps to regain many of the powers which, because of the pressure of government affairs, he had delegated to Tuan. Early in May, Yuan reorganized the top military command, transferring a number of powers and responsibilities from the ministry of war to a new generalissimo's office under his personal control. Tuan, chagrined by this curtailment of his authority, began to absent himself from the war ministry, leaving much of his work to his vice minister, Hsü Shu-cheng (q.v.). He later decided to oppose Yuan's plan to become monarch and resigned from office on 31 May 1915.

Yuan Shih-k'ai's monarchical campaign went badly, and in March 1916 he was obliged to turn to Tuan Ch'i-jui for help in salvaging his regime. Tuan agreed to serve as chief of general staff on the understanding that Yuan would restore the republican form of government. On 22 April, after Yuan had indicated that he would relinquish his powers, Tuan also consented to act as premier. The next day, Tuan announced his new cabinet, in which he held the key post of minister of war. However, as Yuan continued to circumvent Tuan's demands that full military authority be restored to the ministry of war, it became apparent to Tuan that Yuan had no intention of yielding any real authority to him. There followed a silent struggle for power between the two men that ended only with Yuan's death in June 1916.

Although Li Yuan-hung succeeded Yuan Shih-k'ai as president at Peking, much of the power held by Yuan passed into the hands of Tuan Ch'i-jui, who acted quickly to change the governmental system so that the cabinet, with himself as premier, would be the center of executive authority. On 10 June 1916, he dissolved the generalissimo's office and transferred its powers to the ministry of war, and by the end of the month he had ordered the repeal of many laws made during Yuan's presidency. Although he had little understanding of parliamentary government, he reluctantly yielded to southern political and military leaders and agreed to abolish Yuan's constitutional compact of 1914, to order the restoration of the provisional constitution of 1912, and to call for a meeting of the old National Assembly that had been dissolved by Yuan Shih-k'ai in January 1914.

Tuan Ch'i-jui was confirmed as premier by the president and the reconvened National Assembly on 1 August 1916. Before long, his open impatience with the legal restraints on his power aroused opposition from Li Yuan-hung, who had never been on good terms with him, and from factions within the National Assembly. To control this opposition, Tuan relied on the Peiyang military clique. At conferences of provincial representatives called by Chang Hsün (q.v.) at Hsuchow in 1916 and 1917, the leading Peiyang military governors, headed by Ni Ssu-ch'ung, affirmed their support of Tuan's regime. In the spring of 1917 the Peking government's attention focused on the question of China's relations with Germany. In February 1917 the United States began to press the Peking government to enter the First World War on the side of the Allies; and Japan, which previously had opposed China's participation in the war, changed its position and urged Peking to declare war on Germany. Tuan moved quickly to sever diplomatic ties with Germany, a measure which was approved by the National Assembly on 14 March 1917. Tuan then worked to achieve a formal declaration of war, but on this question opinion within the National Assembly and even within the Peiyang clique was divided. On 25 April, Tuan summoned the military governors to Peking for a conference and succeeded in obtaining their unanimous agreement to a declaration of war. Having secured this backing, Tuan exerted heavy pressure on the National Assembly to pass the war participation bill. The assembly members, incensed by their harassment by "citizens groups" organized by Tuan's supporters and further angered by the recently disclosed loan agreements that Tuan was negotiating with the Japanese, demanded Tuan's resignation as their price for passing the bill. Because Tuan apparently was no longer in control of the political situation at Peking, Li Yuan-hung took advantage of the situation to dismiss Tuan from the premiership on 23 May.

After denouncing Li Yuan-hung's action as illegal, Tuan Ch'i-jui withdrew to Tientsin, where he and his followers began to organize military support for a plan to drive Li Yuan-hung from office and to take control of the Peking government. At Tuan's suggestion, Ni Ssu-ch'ung and several other northern governors declared their provinces independent and prepared their troops for an assault on the capital. Although Tuan remained silent on the question, his followers, to gain the military backing of the monarchist Chang Hsün, feigned agreement with Chang's demands that the Manchu emperor be restored to the throne. But after Chang Hsün arrived in Peking and announced the restoration of the emperor on 14 June, Tuan publicly denounced this move. He then declared himself commander in chief of an army which included the troops of Ts'ao K'un (q.v.), the 16th Mixed Brigade of Feng Yü-hsiang (q.v.), and the 8th Division of Li Ch'ang-t'ai. This army quickly routed Chang Hsün's forces, and on 14 July Tuan entered Peking in triumph. He promptly announced the end of the restoration and ordered the arrest of its leaders. He also assumed office once again as premier and minister of war. On 17 July he announced the composition of his new cabinet, which, in addition to his supporters, included such representatives of the so-called research clique as Liang Ch'i-ch'ao and T'ang Hua-lung (qq.v.). By this time, Li Yuan-hung had resigned under strong pressure from Tuan's followers, turning the presidency over to Feng Kuo-chang.

Because he no longer was hampered by the opposition of Li Yuan-hung and the National Assembly, Tuan Ch'i-jui had little difficulty in pushing through a declaration of war on Germany, which was announced on 14 August 1917. Regarding domestic matters, however, his regime faced complex problems. When a new National Assembly, dominated by his supporters, was convened at Peking, dissident leaders in south China undertook the so-called constitution protection movement in opposition to Tuan's government and organized a military government at Canton headed by Sun Yat-sen, Lu Jung-t'ing, and T'ang Chi-yao. Tuan and several other Peiyang leaders favored the use of military force to eliminate this opposition and to unify China. In the summer of 1917 he had replaced T'an Yen-k'ai (q.v.) as military governor of Hunan with one of his own trusted subordinates, Fu Liang-tso, and had transferred additional Peiyang military units to Hunan in preparation for an invasion of Kwangsi and Kwangtung.

Opposition to Tuan's policy of military unification came from members of the Peiyang clique as well as from the southern leaders. Feng Kuo-chang and his supporters in the Yangtze provinces favored peaceful unification. Feng's opposition was caused, in part, by his rivalry with Tuan for leadership of the Peiyang military faction. This power struggle led to the formation within the Peiyang faction of rival groups which became known as the Chihli clique (led by Feng Kuo-chang) and the Anhwei clique (led by Tuan Ch'i-jui). In the autumn of 1917 Tuan's efforts to subjugate Hunan and Szechwan met with failure, and Feng Kuo-chang's supporters circulated telegrams calling for a peaceful settlement of the civil strife in south China. Tuan responded by resigning from office and retiring to his stronghold in Tientsin.

While Feng Kuo-chang and Tuan's successor as premier, Wang Shih-chen (q.v.), sought to implement a policy of peaceful negotiation with the southern leaders, Tuan's supporters gathered about him to plan his return to power. Under the direction of Hsü Shu-cheng, a conference of military leaders was called at Tientsin on 3 December 1917. Three days later, Ni Ssu-ch'ung, Chang Tso-lin (q.v.), and other military chiefs presented Feng Kuo-chang with a joint demand that he declare a punitive war on the southwestern provinces. This display of Tuan's strength forced Feng to yield ground. On 18 December, he appointed Tuan commander of China's forces participating in the European war. Tuan used this position to exert increasing pressure on Feng to reverse his policy of conciliation, forcing him to resume the war with the south and to send reinforcements under Ts'ao K'un and Chang Huai-chih into Hupeh and Hunan. Toward the end of February 1918, Tuan's influence was augmented when Chang Tso-lin agreed to loan Hsü Shu-cheng some Fengtien forces. On 19 March a telegram signed by a majority of the Peiyang generals, including some 18 military governors, demanded that Feng Kuo-chang reappoint Tuan premier. Feng had no alternative to compliance, and Tuan assumed office on 23 March.

Throughout his fourth and final term as premier (March–October 1918) Tuan dominated the government at Peking through two powerful new organs. The first of these was the war participation bureau (tu-pan ts'an-chan shih-wu ch'u). Its purpose was the organization and training of a new military force, ostensibly to serve in Europe but actually to carry out the military unification of China under Tuan's direction. The second organization, the Anfu Club, was mainly political in character. It came into being on 7 March 1918 through the efforts of Hsü Shu-cheng and Wang I-t'ang (q.v.), and its aims were to influence the election of the new National Assembly in June and thereafter to manipulate the new body in favor of Tuan's policies.

The operations of the war participation bureau and the Anfu Club reflected the close ties between Tuan's regime and Japanese interests. In 1917–18 Tuan's government concluded a number of agreements, known as the Nishihara loans (see Ts'ao Ju-lin), by which Japan obtained vast railroad, mining, and other concessions in China. Although most of the loan funds were earmarked for economic development, much money was spent to pay for Tuan's military campaigns against the southern provinces and to finance the political machinations of the Anfu Club. Tuan also used a share of the Japanese loan money to build up a new army. Under the direction of the war participation bureau, the Chinese government signed secret mutual military assistance agreements with Japan (25 March and 16 May) by which the Japanese agreed to finance, train, and equip a new Chinese military force, the War Participation Army (Ts'an-chan-chün), in return for such concessions as the right to station Japanese troops in Manchuria and Mongolia. Through these and other agreements, Japan's influence in China reached a new peak.

On 10 October 1918 Tuan Ch'i-jui's foremost rival, Feng Kuo-chang, turned over the presidency to Hsü Shih-ch'ang (q.v.) and retired from public life. That same day, as a concession to popular sentiment, Tuan also resigned. His resignation, however, in no way diminished his personal power; and through his control of the war participation bureau and the Anfu Club he was able to dominate the Peking government for almost two years. On 28 September, he had secured an additional loan from Japan to finance China's participation in the First World War, and he continued to enlarge the War

Participation Army after the war ended. During the peace conference of northern and southern delegates at Shanghai early in 1919, the southern delegates demanded the disbandment of the War Participation Army and the dissolution of the military agreements with Japan. To avoid criticism on these points, the Peking government on 24 June reorganized the war participation bureau as the frontier defense bureau (tu-pan pien-fang shih-wu ch'u), with Tuan Ch'i-jui as director and redesignated the War Participation Army as the Northwest Frontier Defense Army (Hsi-pei pien-fang chün), with Hsü Shu-cheng as commander in chief. With continued Japanese assistance, the Northwest Frontier Defense Army became a formidable military machine which aroused the apprehension of some Peiyang generals as well as the military leaders in the southwestern provinces of China.

The Peking regime soon became the object of growing public disfavor. The high-handed conduct of the Anfu Club earned it and the National Assembly it controlled an unsavory reputation. The prominent role of Japanese officers in the training of the Chinese army caused student agitation, as did the vast concessions granted Japan in return for the Nishihara loans. Reports from the Paris Peace Conference to the effect that Tuan's government had secretly agreed to transfer German rights in Shantung to Japan touched off a burst of indignation which resulted in the student demonstrations of May 1919. More significant for Tuan's power position, however, were signs of disaffection among the northern militarists, in particular, Ts'ao K'un and his redoubtable subordinate Wu P'ei-fu (q.v.). Wu, who nursed a grievance against Tuan, became increasingly critical of Tuan's regime, denouncing its policy of military unification and finding fault with such activities as the secret loan agreements with Japan. At the same time, the rapid expansion of Hsü Shu-cheng's power in Outer Mongolia challenged the interests of Hsü's former ally Chang Tso-lin, thus creating further antagonism to Tuan's regime.

By July 1920 Tuan Ch'i-jui's enemies were ready to move against him. The Chihli clique, led by Ts'ao K'un, had made an agreement with the Fengtien faction of Chang Tso-lin, and Wu P'ei-fu had begun moving northward toward Peking. To counter the impending attack, Tuan Ch'i-jui on 6 July announced the formation of the National Pacification Army (Ting-kuo-chün), composed of three divisions of the Northwest Frontier Defense Army, one of Hsü Shu-cheng's brigades, and the 15th Peiyang Division. On 14 July, these troops clashed with Chihli forces, thus beginning the Chihli-Anhwei war. With the aid of units dispatched by Chang Tso-lin from Fengtien province, the Chihli forces defeated Tuan's army in a number of clashes south of Peking. On 19 July, Hsü Shih-ch'ang announced the end of the five-day conflict, and on 28 July he accepted Tuan's resignation from the frontier defense bureau, which then was abolished. The following month brought the dissolution of the Northwest Frontier Defense Army and the Anfu Club.

The Chihli-Anhwei war marked the end of Tuan Ch'i-jui's hegemony in north China. As effective control of the Peking government passed to his adversaries, Tuan withdrew to Tientsin, where he bided his time in retirement for the next four years. It was not until the autumn of 1924 that he reentered political life. After the defeat of Wu P'ei-fu and the removal of Ts'ao K'un from the presidency, the victorious Feng Yü-hsiang and Chang Tso-lin looked about for another man to head the Peking government. Tuan, as senior member of the Peiyang militarists, still commanded considerable prestige but had little military strength of his own. Thus he was acceptable to Feng, Chang, and the powerful military chiefs in the Yangtze provinces. On 24 November he became provisional chief executive (lin-shih tsung chih-cheng) of the Peking government.

The military leaders in Peking gave careful consideration to the type of government which would replace the discredited administration of Ts'ao K'un. As a gesture of conciliation to the Kuomintang, Tuan Ch'i-jui joined Feng Yü-hsiang and Chang Tso-lin in inviting Sun Yat-sen to Peking for discussion about governmental organization. Sun called for a national convention to determine the future government of China; and, in apparent agreement with Sun's ideas, Tuan announced that within a month he intended to convene a preliminary "aftermath conference" (shan-hou hui-i), to be followed two months later by a national congress of people's representatives. However, by the time Sun Yat-sen reached Tientsin early in December, Tuan had promulgated the articles of his provisional government. It soon became clear that Tuan had no intention of allowing Sun or the Kuomintang to interfere in the organization or workings of the new regime. Negotiations between Tuan and Sun about the composition of the aftermath conference quickly broke down. Despite strong protests from Sun and his colleagues, Tuan proceeded to hold the conference, beginning on 1 February 1925, without the formal participation of the Kuomintang. In subsequent meetings the conference adopted regulations providing for the organization of a national assembly of people's representatives. During the spring and summer of 1925 Tuan's regime went through the motions of preparing for a new National Assembly, providing for a committee to draft a new constitution, and fixing the dates for the election of representatives to the assembly. However, these provisions apparently were no more than token gestures to appease public opinion.

Beginning in the autumn of 1925, the struggle for power between Feng Yü-hsiang and Chang Tso-lin made Tuan's position insecure. Because he found it impossible to placate both of them at the same time, Tuan Ch'i-jui sought to maintain his position by siding with whoever happened to have the upper hand at a given moment. But by April 1926, Tuan had lost the support of the victorious Chang Tso-lin, and after resigning his position on 20 April, he hastily left the capital for the safety of the Japanese concession in Tientsin. Thereafter, he devoted himself to the study of Buddhism and to giving financial encouragement to poor but promising students. After the Japanese seizure of Manchuria in 1931, many once-prominent Chinese were urged to participate in a Japanese-sponsored puppet government in north China. Although he had followed a pro-Japanese policy as premier, Tuan now resisted all Japanese attempts to win his support. He left Tientsin in January 1933 and moved to Shanghai, where, on 2 November 1936, he died of gastric ulcers.

Tuan Ch'i-jui had two younger brothers, Tuan Ch'i-fu (1873–1921), and Tuan Ch'i-hsün (1874–1927). The latter was a graduate of the Shikan Gakkō in Japan who served as director of military training under Hsü Shih-ch'ang when Hsü was governor general in Manchuria under the Ch'ing dynasty. Tuan Ch'i-jui married his first wife, *née* Wu, in 1886;

a year after her death in 1900 he married a member of the Chang family. Two sons lived to maturity, Tuan Hung-yeh (b. 1887) and Tuan Hung-fan (b. 1918).

Tuan Hsi-p'eng 段 錫 朋
   T. Shu-i 書 詒

Tuan Hsi-p'eng (1896–26 December 1948), a leader of the May Fourth demonstrations of 1919 and the first chairman of the Student Union of China. He taught history at Wuchang University in 1925 and at Kwangtung University in 1926. In 1932–37 he was vice minister of education, and in 1938 he became chairman of the education committee of the Kuomintang Central Training Corps.

Born into a scholarly family in Yunghsin, Kiangsi, Tuan Hsi-p'eng received his early education in the Chinese classics at home. He then enrolled at a normal school near Yunghsin, where he learned English. After graduation in 1916, he received a scholarship which enabled him to go to Peking and enroll at the law school of Peking University. Thus, he was a student at Peking University during its golden era under the chancellorship of Ts'ai Yuan-p'ei (q.v.)

Secret negotiations between the government of Tuan Ch'i-jui (q.v.) at Peking and the Japanese gave rise to student unrest in 1917–18. The floating of the so-called Nishihara loans (*see* Ts'ao Ju-lin) and the signing in May 1918 of the Sino-Japanese Military Mutual Assistance Conventions led to massive student demonstrations at Peking on 21 May 1918. Tuan Hsi-p'eng was among the 13 student representatives who met with Feng Kuo-chang (q.v.) that day in an attempt to learn the contents of the Sino-Japanese agreements and to press for the annulment of these and other agreements. Although the students failed to achieve their aims, the 1918 demonstrations were not insignificant. They served to unite the students and prepare the way for such significant joint actions as the May Fourth Incident of 1919 (for details, *see* Lo Chia-lun).

Tuan Hsi-p'eng helped organize the demonstrations of 4 May 1919, as a result of which 32 students were arrested. On 5 May, he presided at a meeting of some 3,000 students. The students called for the release of the 32 who had been arrested and resolved that they would boycott all classes until this demand was met. They also passed resolutions asking for the punishment of pro-Japanese officials and the restoration to China of Tsingtao. To promote the patriotic May Fourth Movement, they established the Student Union of Peking, with Tuan as one of its chief representatives. Because their demands were refused by the government, Tuan and his colleagues went to Shanghai to organize a nation-wide student union. The Chung-hua-min-kuo hsüeh-sheng lien-ho-hui (Student Union of the Republic of China) was established on 16 June at a meeting, held in the Ta Tung Hotel in Shanghai, which was attended by more than 30 student representatives and some 200 guests. Two days later, Tuan Hsi-p'eng was elected to a one-year term as chairman of this organization. As one of the best organized bodies of its day, the Student Union of China was a highly effective pressure group. It helped secure the release of the arrested students and the dismissal of several pro-Japanese officials.

After graduation from Peking University, Tuan Hsi-p'eng went abroad. In 1920–24 he studied successively at Columbia University, the University of London, Berlin University, and the University of Paris. Upon his return to China in the autumn of 1925, he joined the faculty of Wuchang University as a professor of history. The following year, he went to Canton, where he was appointed chairman of the history department at Kwangtung University.

In 1926 Ch'en Kuo-fu (q.v.) brought Tuan Hsi-p'eng into the organization department of the Kuomintang as part of his attempt to limit Communist influence in that body. Ch'en sent Tuan to Kiangsi in November to oversee party activities in that province. Tuan soon discovered that the provincial Kuomintang organization was dominated by such Communists as Fang Chih-min (q.v.). To counter Communist influence, Tuan organized the A. B. (anti-Bolshevik) Corps. His efforts were hindered by the establishment of the left-wing Kuomintang regime at Wuhan, for it supported the policy of collaboration with the Communists. On 1 April 1927 the Kiangsi provincial government and party organs were ordered reorganized, and anti-Communist officials were dismissed. A number of these anti-Communists were arrested the following day. On 4 April, Tuan fled Kiangsi in disguise. He went to Shanghai. Subsequently, he played an important role in the purge of the Communists from the Kuomintang.

Tuan became chief of the office of party guidance at Chiang Kai-shek's field headquarters at Nanchang in 1930 and a member of the Huai River Conservation Commission. In June 1932, having become vice minister of education, he was appointed acting president of National Central University in Nanking. Because of student opposition, the university had lacked a president for some time. When Tuan tried to assume office, the students assaulted him. The Executive Yuan then ordered the temporary dissolution of the University. Tuan continued to serve as vice minister of education until the end of 1937.

In February 1938 Tuan Hsi-p'eng became a member of the Central Executive Committee of the Kuomintang and chairman of the education committee of the Central Training Corps, the leading training center for Kuomintang cadres. Throughout the Sino-Japanese war, he devoted his attention to the activities of the Central Training Corps. He died of lung cancer on 26 December 1948 at Shanghai. Newspapers in Shanghai and Hong Kong eulogized Tuan as a righteous statesman who never lost his revolutionary spirit.

Tung Ch'i-wu   董其武

Tung Ch'i-wu (c.1899–), Shansi general and long-time subordinate of Fu Tso-yi (q.v.). Tung became governor of Suiyuan in 1947 and, because of Fu's surrender arrangements with the Chinese Communists, retained that post until July 1952.

Hochin hsien, Shansi, was the birthplace of Tung Ch'i-wu. In his boyhood he studied with a maternal uncle, Fan Pi-ying, who instilled in him ideas of political change. Tung attended a nearby middle school and then entered the Pin-yeh School at Taiyuan, a military school. Upon graduation in 1924, he left Shansi and went to Canton. The following year, he joined the newly established National Revolutionary Army. In the course of the Northern Expedition, he rose in rank from platoon commander to regimental commander.

In the summer of 1928 Tung Ch'i-wu became a staff officer at the Tientsin garrison, commanded by Fu Tso-yi (q.v.). Thus began an association which was to last for many years. Tung served under Fu as a commander in the Tenth Army, and, in 1931, as commander of the 36th Regiment in the Thirty-fifth Army. After Fu became governor of Suiyuan later in 1931, Tung and Sun Lan-feng (q.v.) undertook the task of ridding eastern Suiyuan of bandits. Tung and Sun also took part in the 1933 campaign against the Japanese advances in Inner Mongolia and the fighting at the Great Wall. In 1934 Tung received advanced instruction in the Lushan Training Corps and then became a brigade commander. He and Sun Lan-feng, under Fu Tso-yi's direction, took part in the November 1936 action that resulted in the ouster of Te Wang (Demchukdonggrub, q.v.) from Pailingimiao.

After the Sino-Japanese war began in July 1937, Tung fought under Fu Tso-yi's command in Suiyuan and Shansi. Tung was wounded in the battle of Ni Ho, but he did not retire from the field. He participated in the effort to defend Taiyuan, but the Japanese captured it in November. Tung's performances in battle won him command of the 101st Division. Fu Tso-yi became deputy commander of the Eighth War Area in 1939, and that winter he deployed his forces against the Japanese at Paotow, Suiyuan. When the Japanese launched a major counterattack in the spring of 1940 Fu's forces won an important victory at Wuyuan — with Tung Ch'i-wu's 101st Division making a major contribution to that victory by engaging Japanese reinforcements in a flank attack. Tung then became commander of the Fourth Cavalry Army, and in 1944 he received command of the Thirty-fifth Army.

Suiyuan and Ninghsia became the Twelfth War Area in July 1945, with Fu Tso-yi as commander and Tung Ch'i-wu as director of political affairs. At war's end Tung was ordered to Paotow to receive the Japanese surrender and to hold it against Communist attack. He was decorated for his performance in repulsing the forces of Ho Lung and Hsiao K'o (qq.v.). The disarming of Japanese units in Suiyuan was completed in September 1945. In April 1946 Tung also became commander of the Temporary Third Army. In September, he led the Twelfth War Area forces in a cam-

paign which achieved the recovery of Tsining, the lifting of the Communist siege of Tat'ung, and the occupation of Kalgan. The National Government then appointed him garrison commander at Kalgan. In November, Fu Tso-yi was made governor of Chahar, and Tung Ch'i-wu was made governor of Suiyuan.

When Fu Tso-yi surrendered Peiping to the Chinese Communists in January 1949, he made provisions for the preservation of his troops in Suiyuan and for the protection of Tung Ch'i-wu and Sun Lan-feng. Tung was made a delegate to the Chinese People's Political Consultative Conference in September, and in December he was confirmed as governor of Suiyuan and made a vice chairman of the Suiyuan military and administrative committee. In January 1952 he received the rank of commander of a corps in the People's Liberation Army. At that time, he also became a member of the north China administrative committee. With the removal of the Inner Mongolian Autonomous Region People's Government to Kweisui in July 1952, he was replaced as governor of Suiyuan by Ulanfu (q.v.), but he continued to serve on the provincial administrative committee until June 1954. He then served as a delegate to the National People's Congress. In the ensuing governmental reorganization, he gave up his position on the north China administrative committee and became a member of the People's Revolutionary Military Council. He was a delegate to the 1959 National People's Congress and a member of its National Committee. Also in 1959, he was appointed to the National Defense Council. By this time it had become apparent that his posts in the People's Republic of China were more honorary than substantive.

Tung Hsien-kuang   董 顯 光
West. Hollington K. Tong

Tung Hsien-kuang (9 November 1887–), known as Hollington Tong, American-trained journalist and biographer of Chiang Kai-shek who served during the Sino-Japanese war as vice minister of information at Chungking and a principal source of news for Western correspondents stationed there. Tong served as Chinese Nationalist ambassador in Japan from

1952 to 1956 and in the United States from 1956 to 1958.

Born into a family of some means in Yinhsien, Chekiang, Hollington Tong received his early education at a missionary school in Soochow. He remained a devout Presbyterian throughout his life. Tong later attended the Lowrie High School, the Shanghai High School, and Anglo-Chinese College, all of which were in Shanghai. In 1905 he taught at the Chien-chiu School in Ningpo, where one of his students was "a grave-minded, ambitious, unforgettable youth from near-by Chikow, named Chiang Kai-shek." The two young men, who had been born less than a month apart, became friends. In 1906 Tong left Ningpo for Shanghai and a job at the Commercial Press.

Having decided to further his education abroad, Hollington Tong went to the United States in 1907, where he enrolled at Park College in Missouri. The following year, he transferred to the newly founded School of Journalism at the University of Missouri, from which he was graduated in 1912. He then became a member of the first class at the School of Journalism at Columbia University. Among Tong's 12 classmates was Carl W. Ackerman, who later became the school's dean. In New York, Tong also worked as a reporter on *The New York Times* and the *World* and as an assistant editor on the *Independent*.

Upon his return to China in 1913, Hollington Tong became the Peking correspondent for several Shanghai newspapers and, for a brief period, the English secretary of the Senate. After the so-called second revolution (*see* Li Lieh-chün), he was assistant editor of an English-language daily at Shanghai, the *China Republican*, which was owned by the Kuomintang. In 1914–16 he was again in Peking as editor of the English-language *Peking Daily News*. During this period, he also served as English secretary for the National Petroleum Administration and made a brief trip to the United States. In 1917 he became the Peking correspondent for the well-known Shanghai English-language weekly, *Millard's Review* (later the *China Weekly Review*). A year later, he was promoted to assistant editor, though he continued to work in the Peking-Tientsin area. He also found time to serve as secretary to the Chihli river commission in 1918 and as adviser to Yang Yi-te (the Chihli police commissioner)

and Chu Hsing-yuan (the Tientsin foreign affairs commissioner) in 1920.

In August 1920 Hollington Tong joined the ministry of communications in the Peking government as a junior adviser. Later that year, he was made executive secretary of the ministry's railway finance commission, and in May 1922 he was promoted to acting councillor of the ministry. He became secretary to Admiral Y. L. Woo, then minister of communications, in 1923. For his services to the ministry, he was awarded three decorations by the Peking government in 1923: the third class Chia-ho, the second class Chia-ho, and the second class Tashou Paokuang. After leaving government service, he was editor of the Tientsin *Yung-pao* from 1925 to 1931. In 1926 he served briefly as foreign affairs adviser to Wu P'ei-fu (q.v.), and in 1929–30 he accompanied Admiral Tu Hsi-kuei on a world inspection tour as his English secretary.

By this time, the Kuomintang had succeeded in unifying most of China through the Northern Expedition, and the center of political activity had shifted from Peiping in the north to the Nanking-Shanghai area in the lower Yangtze valley. Accordingly, in 1931 Hollington Tong accepted an offer to become managing editor of a Shanghai English-language daily, the *China Press*. Though founded by Wu T'ing-fang (q.v.) and controlled by Chinese interests, the paper had an American registration. Tong secured the services of such active and promising young American reporters as Tillman Durdin and Harold Isaacs. In mid-1931 he was made managing director of the paper. He held that post until 1935, when he became managing director of a group which had acquired a controlling interest in four journalistic enterprises in Shanghai: the *China Press*, the *Shih-shih hsin-pao* [China times], the *Ta-wan pao*, and the Shun Shih News Agency.

In 1935 W. H. Donald, an Australian correspondent who had been an adviser to Chang Hsueh-liang (q.v.) and who then was an adviser to Chiang Kai-shek, informed Tong of Chiang's wish that Tong become chief censor of all outgoing foreign press messages. Donald appealed to Tong's patriotism, pointing out that "inefficient press censorship was responsible for an increasingly bad press abroad." Accordingly, Tong agreed to undertake this function, assuming the title of secretary of the Military Affairs Commission's Shanghai office. When the

Sino-Japanese war began in July 1937, it soon became clear that in addition to the fighting on the battlefronts, a war of international publicity had to be fought. Thus, when the Military Affairs Commission was reorganized to cope with wartime needs, Tong was appointed vice minister of its fifth board, which was responsible for national and international publicity. While hostilities still were going on in the Shanghai area, Tong took the initiative to form an anti-Japanese committee in the International Settlement to publicize the Chinese cause. It was composed of C. L. Hsia (principal of Anglo-Chinese Medhurst College), Wen Yuan-ning (later Chinese ambassador to Greece), Herman Liu (Liu Chan-en, q.v.), and H. J. Timperley (correspondent of the *Manchester Guardian*). After Shanghai fell to the Japanese late in 1937, Hsia went to the United States, Wen went to Hong Kong, and Timperley went to Great Britain to take charge of overseas information operations under Tong's direction. Liu remained in Shanghai, where he was assassinated, probably by Japanese agents, on 7 April 1938.

Toward the end of 1937, Tong's department was transferred to the ministry of information. Tong then became vice minister of information, a post he held for the rest of the war. He set up a modest office at Hankow with a staff of 20–30 people and appointed the veteran newspaperman Tseng Hsü-pai as his deputy. The few foreign correspondents who had followed the National Government to Hankow included Freda Utley, Agnes Smedley, Lily Abegg, John Gunther, and Tillman Durdin. Tong remained in Hankow for ten months. In addition to censorship and publicity functions, he was often called upon to handle tasks connected with other aspects of foreign relations. He was among the last of the National Government personnel to leave Hankow, which he did on the evening of 25 October 1938, as the Japanese troops were entering the city. He then made a ten-day hike to Changsha, where he operated a temporary office until headquarters could be established for him at the wartime capital of Chungking.

As the war developed, more foreign correspondents were drawn to Chungking. Early in 1939 Hollington Tong conceived the idea of building a press hostel to accommodate foreign correspondents. He obtained a small grant from H. H. K'ung (q.v.) and built a simple dormitory consisting of 13 rooms. The popularity of "Holly's Hotel" increased as Japanese bombings reduced accommodations elsewhere. Among those who spent time at this hostel were Brooks Atkinson, Theodore H. White, Spencer Moosa, and Tillman Durdin. In speaking of this period, Durdin said that Tong was "without official stuffiness or arrogance. He was always approachable. In Chungking, correspondents could get him out of bed at 4 in the morning to argue a point of censorship or check up on a news story, and he would show no impatience. He lived with his wife in a little plaster-walled cabin in the same compound as the correspondents' hostel.... He was indefatigable in getting facilities and interviews for correspondents." In addition to working with the Kuomintang Central News Agency (*see* Hsiao T'ung-tzu) to furnish the foreign correspondents with news dispatches, Tong's department published a general magazine entitled *China at War* and maintained the radio station XGOY, which was operated by Mike Peng (P'eng Lo-shan). Tong's efforts helped draw to Chungking such important American visitors as the publishers Roy Howard and Henry R. Luce.

In the course of the war years, Tong took three trips abroad. In February 1942 he accompanied Chiang Kai-shek on a two-week trip to India for discussions with Gandhi and Nehru. He accompanied Madame Chiang Kai-shek (Soong Mei-ling, q.v.) on her November 1942–June 1943 visit to the United States. And in November 1943 he was included in Chiang Kai-shek's entourage at the Cairo Conference.

While in the United States, Tong held discussions with his old Columbia classmate, Carl W. Ackerman, who had become dean of the Graduate School of Journalism, about establishing a training school for journalists at Chungking. With the assistance of Columbia University, a two-part program was established in 1943. Four journalists were employed by the United States Department of State and sent to Chungking to serve as guest experts in information agencies; one of the four was Floyd Taylor, who later became head of the American Press Institute. The second part of the program was the establishment of a Chinese-administered school of journalism at Chungking with an American staff. Harold Livingston Cross, then professor of newspaper law at the School of Journalism, went on leave to serve in 1943–44 as the Chungking school's dean. His teaching staff of four (later increased to seven) included Richard T. Baker, who in 1968 became acting dean of the School of Journalism. The Chungking school, which was affiliated with the Central Political Institute, trained more than 60 young journalists before it suspended operations in the summer of 1945. Dean Ackerman's 1945 report on the Chungking school spoke of its achievements "in helping the State Department's cultural cooperation program in China, in breaking down the hesitancy of Chinese officialdom to give out information and news, in spreading the gospel of freedom of the press, in teaching the responsibilities of men and women engaged in journalistic enterprises, and in training young Chinese to follow American methods in collecting and disseminating news through newspapers and by radio." Thus, the Chungking journalism school helped realize Hollington Tong's ambitions for Chinese journalism.

In recognition of his wartime achievements, Tong was elected to the Central Executive Committee of the Kuomintang in 1945. After a short respite from official life, he assumed office as director of the Executive Yuan's government information office in 1947. The following year, he became minister without portfolio in the Executive Yuan. When the Chinese Communists won control of the mainland, he moved to Taiwan. From 1950 to 1952 he was managing director of the Broadcasting Corporation of China and a member of the Kuomintang Central Advisory Committee. He then spent four years as ambassador to Japan. From April 1956 until September 1958 he was ambassador to the United States, where he was much in demand as a public speaker. On his retirement from public activity in 1958, Chiang Kai-shek appointed him a senior adviser to the presidential office in Taiwan. Tong remained in Taiwan until 1961, when he came to the United States for a Moral Rearmament conference. He suffered a stroke and, after partial recuperation, went to live with a daughter in California.

Hollington Tong was married to Sally Chao (Chao Hsiang-ying), and they had three sons and three daughters. The youngest son died in an airplane crash in 1960.

The best known of Hollington Tong's published works in English are the authorized biography *Chiang Kai-shek, Soldier and Statesman* (1937) and *Dateline: China* (1950), an account of Tong's experience during the war years.

Tung K'ang   董 康
  T. Shou-ching   綏 經
  H. Sung-fen chu-jen   誦 芬 主 人

Tung K'ang (16 April 1867–1947), leading authority on Chinese law and jurisprudence who served as a cabinet minister and as chief justice of the Supreme Court at Peking during the Peiyang period. He also was known as a scholar of early Chinese drama who contributed a number of special collections of rare works to the available literature on the subject.

A native of Wuchin, Kiangsu, Tung K'ang studied as a youth at the Nan-ching Academy in Chiangyin where he took particular interest in traditional Chinese literature. In 1889 he became a chü-jen and in the next year a chin-shih, which led to his immediate appointment as a junior official in the Board of Punishments. During the Boxer Uprising, he was an assistant secretary in the same board, taking charge of judicial affairs for Shensi province. After the entry of the Allied forces into Peking and at the request of civic leaders in the southern quarter of the capital, he helped establish the Hsieh-hsün kung-so [patrol authority], which did much to maintain order. In recognition of the patrol's accomplishments, the occupation forces soon returned its full administrative authority to Chinese officials of the Board of Punishments. Tung K'ang was subsequently promoted to be chief warden of the prison of the Board of Punishments and a judge of the Supreme Court, and he was one of the officials who supervised the executions of Ch'i-hsiu (ECCP, I, 407) and Hsü Ch'eng-yü (ECCP, I, 408) on 26 February 1901.

After the death of his mother in 1902, Tung K'ang remained at home beyond the required mourning period. However, upon his subsequent return to Peking, he became the editor in chief of the law codification bureau. In close cooperation with another Nan-ching graduate, Wang Jung-pao, he completed a new code which was promulgated by the Ch'ing government after being approved by the National Assembly.

Tung K'ang served briefly as minister of finance in 1912 but was obliged to resign his post and leave for a tour of Europe, the United States, and Japan when he incurred the displeasure of Tuan Ch'i-jui (q.v.) and his followers for looking too closely into the foreign loans which had been floated by Tuan. After returning to China, Tung K'ang served as chief justice of the Supreme Court from 1914 to 1918, president of the law codification bureau in 1918, and minister of justice in 1920.

Near the end of 1926 the feud between Tung K'ang and Tuan Ch'i-jui again came into the open. Tuan induced Sun Ch'uan-fang and Chang Tsung-ch'ang (qq.v.), military governors of Kiangsu and Shantung respectively, to order Tung's arrest. Tung fled to Japan, where he stayed until April 1927. Prior to this episode, as a distinguished authority on Chinese law, Tung K'ang had received in 1925 an honorary degree of LL.D. from Soochow University Law School in Shanghai and had served as a professor there in 1926. After his return from Japan to Shanghai in 1927, he practiced law and headed a technical school for training judicial officers which was known as the Shanghai fa-hsüeh-yüan. Tung visited Japan during 1934 and 1935 to lecture on the history of law. After the Sino-Japanese war began in 1937, he took an active part in the Japanese-sponsored government at Peiping as chairman of the judicial court, chairman of the judicial committee, and chief justice of the supreme court. Tung's postwar career is obscure, but it is likely that he was taken into custody because of his collaboration. He died in 1947.

In addition to being a lawyer and an official, Tung K'ang was a scholar of early Chinese drama who contributed a number of special collections of rare works to the available literature on the subject. These include both photolithographical reproductions of the collections *Tsa-chü shih-tuan-chin*, by Chu Yu-tan (d. 1439); *Su-men hsiao*, by Fu Ch'ing-mei; and *Mao Hsi-ho lun-ting hsi-hsiang-chi*, a critical study of the *Hsi-hsiang-chi* [romance of the western chamber], by Mao Ch'i-ling (ECCP, I, 563–65); as well as editions of old plays prepared by Tung himself: *Shih-ch'ao ch'uan-ch'i ssu-chung*, containing the texts of the four extant plays of Juan Ta-ch'eng (ECCP, I, 398–99), and *Sheng-ming tsa-chü*, a collection of dramas written by the leading playwrights of the Ming and early

Ch'ing periods. Tung also edited the *Ch'ü-hai tsung-mu t'i-yao*, a descriptive catalogue of 684 titles of dramas written during the Yüan, Ming, and early Ch'ing periods, originally compiled by Huang Wen-yang (fl. 1780), and the *Sung-fen-t'ang ts'ung-k'an*, a collectanea of the most important texts and critical works relating to traditional drama.

T'ang was an aesthete and a perfectionist, noted for his collections of stone monuments, rubbings, and ancient coins. He was a congenial man, and, despite his wartime associations with the Japanese, retained the nickname of Tung Sheng-jen or "Tung the Sage" to the end of his life.

Tung Pi-wu   董 必 武

Tung Pi-wu (1886–), Chinese Communist liaison officer with the Kuomintang (1936–45) and the only Communist member of the Chinese delegation to the United Nations Conference on International Organization in 1945. After 1949 he held such high posts at Peking as vice premier, president of the Supreme People's Court, vice chairman of the People's Republic of China, and head of the party's Central Control Commission.

Huangan hsien, Hupeh, was the birthplace of Tung Pi-wu. His father and an uncle were scholars and teachers, and the Tung family has been described as "landless gentry." Tung Pi-wu received his early education in the Chinese classics at home and passed the sheng-yuan examinations in 1901. He then went to Wuchang to attend a junior middle school which had a modern curriculum. It was during his years in Wuchang that he first was exposed to reformist and revolutionary political views. In 1911, after attending senior middle school for a few months, he accepted a position as a schoolmaster in Huangchou.

When the Wuchang revolt began in October 1911, Tung immediately left his teaching post and hastened to join the republican forces. He arrived in Wuchang on 13 October, and, according to his own account as told to Nym Wales, "from that day on" was "constantly engaged in revolution as a profession." Then 25, Tung went to work in the financial department of the republican regime established at Wuhan.

Near the end of 1911 he joined the T'ung-meng-hui, becoming a member of its Hupeh branch council in 1912. Tung later served as head of the salt tax bureau at Ich'ang. At the time of the so-called second revolution in 1913 (*see* Li Lieh-chün), he was among those Kuomintang leaders who were forced to flee to Japan. He studied jurisprudence at Tokyo Law College and reportedly supported the 1914 reorganization of the Kuomintang (for details, *see* Sun Yat-sen). On orders from Sun Yat-sen, he returned to Hupeh in 1915 to organize resistance to Yuan Shih-k'ai's rule. Tung's activities were discovered, and he was arrested and imprisoned late in 1915. He was released soon after Yuan Shih-k'ai's death in June 1916, whereupon he went back to Tokyo to complete his law studies.

Upon graduation from Tokyo Law College in 1917, Tung returned to China to take part in the so-called constitution protection movement, attempting to influence troops on the Hupeh-Szechwan border to support Sun Yat-sen and his associates at Canton. Sun Yat-sen withdrew from the Kwangsi-dominated Canton regime the following year and went to Shanghai. Tung arrived at Shanghai in the spring of 1919 to report to Sun and found the intellectuals there already affected by the "new culture" spirit emanating from Peking. The heady intellectual atmosphere of the May Fourth period and personal association with the intellectual Communist Li Han-chün caused Tung to decide that Sun Yat-sen's attempts to influence military leaders were essentially impractical and that political action, to be effective in a technologically primitive and largely illiterate country like China, required popular support. Thus, in 1920, with seven other teachers and little money, Tung returned to the Wuhan area to open a middle school for the teaching of pai-hua [the vernacular]. In the winter of 1920–21, he with Ch'en T'an-ch'iu (q.v.) and the secretary of Comintern representative Gregory Voitinsky formed a Communist group at Wuhan. The various local groups, including that of Mao Tse-tung at Changsha and that of Li Ta-chao at Peking, were brought together at the First National Congress of the Communist Party of China, held at Shanghai in July 1921. Shanghai was, of course, the home of the first Communist nucleus organized by Ch'en Tu-hsiu (q.v.). Tung Pi-wu and Ch'en T'an-ch'iu represented Wuhan at the congress. Of those

present at that historic meeting, only Mao Tse-tung and Tung Pi-wu survived to hold high office at Peking after 1949.

Tung Pi-wu and Ch'en T'an-ch'iu returned to Hupeh after the party congress and began the work of creating an organizational framework for the Hupeh branch of the Chinese Communist party (for details, *see* Ch'en T'an-ch'iu). Following a short trip to Szechwan, a venture described as an attempt to "revive some of my old tactics of winning over the military forces to revolution," Tung returned to Wuchang to raise money for the Wuhan Middle School, still an important center of Communist influence. In 1922 he accompanied his ailing father from Wuchang to the family home in Huangan, where the old man soon died. Tung returned to Wuchang before the outbreak of the workers' strike on the Peking-Hankow line in February 1923, organized by Chang Kuo-t'ao (q.v.) and suppressed by Wu P'ei-fu (q.v.).

During the early 1920's Tung Pi-wu, relying on his T'ung-meng-hui background, was known publicly as a member of the Kuomintang, which, like the Chinese Communist party, was still a clandestine organization in the Wuhan area. After the formation of the Kuomintang-Communist alliance, he worked in the Hupeh provincial headquarters of the Kuomintang, and he attended the Second National Congress of the Kuomintang, held in Canton in January 1926. Early in 1926, when final plans were being made for the Northern Expedition, the Kuomintang sent Pai Ch'ung-hsi, Ch'en Ming-shu (qq.v.), and Tung Pi-wu to Changsha to win the support of T'ang Sheng-chih (q.v.). Their success enabled the Northern Expedition forces to launch a much stronger campaign than would have been possible without T'ang's support. After the occupation of the Wuhan cities in September–October 1926, Tung continued to be important in the Hupeh provincial headquarters of the Kuomintang. During the period when the National Government was at Wuhan, he also served as director of the Hupeh provincial department of agriculture and industry.

When the left wing of the Kuomintang at Wuhan (*see* Wang Ching-wei) began purging Communists in areas under its control in mid-1927, Tung Pi-wu escaped to the Japanese concession at Hankow. In December, he disguised himself as a sailor, made his way down-river to Shanghai, and sailed to Japan, where he went into hiding in Kyoto. Several months later, repressive measures by the Japanese security police forced him to flee again, this time to the Soviet Union. Traveling by way of Siberia, he reached Moscow in September 1928. He returned to China in 1932, after four years of study at Lenin University, and went to the central Soviet area in Kiangsi, where he became the first director of the Communist party school. In January 1934 he was elected an alternate member of the party Central Committee. With the reorganization of the Juichin government that month, he became a member of its central executive committee and head of the provisional supreme court. During the Long March to Shensi he served as principal health officer. Upon arrival at Wa-yao-pao in northern Shensi late in 1935, he again became head of the Communist party school. He continued to hold that post in 1936–37 as the Communists moved their base to Paoan and finally to Yenan. In December 1936 he was a member of the Communist delegation, headed by Chou En-lai (q.v.), which went to Sian for the negotiations with Chang Hsueh-liang (q.v.) that led to the release of Chiang Kai-shek.

After the Sino-Japanese war began in July 1937, Tung Pi-wu accompanied Chou En-lai to the final negotiations which led to the formation of the united front with the Nationalists, announced that September. In 1938 Tung was appointed to the People's Political Council, the consultative body established to mobilize popular support for the war effort. With the National Government's withdrawal to Chungking in October 1938, Tung went to the wartime capital to serve with Chou En-lai and Lin Po-ch'ü (q.v.) in a small Communist liaison mission. In the aftermath of the New Fourth Army Incident of January 1941 (see Yeh T'ing; Ku Chu-t'ung), the Chinese Communists withdrew all their members from the People's Political Council except Tung Pi-wu, who continued to make token appearances.

On 26 March 1945 the National Government announced that T. V. Soong (q.v.) would head the Chinese delegation to the United Nations Conference on International Organization in San Francisco, California. Tung Pi-wu, who had known T. V. Soong at Hankow in 1927, was the only Communist named to the ten-man delegation. At San Francisco, however, he took no active part in the conference discussions and made little impression on the gathering.

His public and press relations were handled by his two English-speaking Chinese secretaries, Chang Han-fu and Ch'en Chia-k'ang. With their assistance, Tung produced a *Memorandum on China's Liberated Areas*, published in San Francisco on 18 May, which described government, economics, education, the army, and the workers' movement in the Communist-controlled areas of China. After the conference closed, Tung and his aides toured the United States. In press interviews, Tung called on the United States to help avert civil war in China by calling for a unified, democratic government in China, by investigating Chiang Kai-shek's "misuse of lend-lease supplies against the Chinese Communists," and by planning effective measures to halt civil war if it should break out. In November, he also called for the withdrawal of American troops from China, asserting that they were helping to train and equip Nationalist units to fight the Communists.

Tung returned to Yenan in December 1945 having become the only Chinese Communist of rank to have traveled extensively in the United States after the Second World War. His senior position in the Chinese Communist party had been confirmed in his absence at the Seventh National Congress of the Chinese Communist party with his election as the seventh-ranking member of the Central Committee and as a member of the Political Bureau. On his return, he immediately became involved in the American mediation effort, the major external force then affecting Chinese politics, and with the preparations for the Political Consultative Conference in Chungking. Late in December, he and Yeh Chien-ying (q.v.) accompanied Chou En-lai when Chou first called upon General George C. Marshall, special representative of the President of the United States. In January 1946 Tung was a member of the Chinese Communist delegation to the Political Consultative Conference (for details, see Chou En-lai). During 1946 and early 1947 Tung continued to act as Chou En-lai's deputy in the stormy Kuomintang-Communist negotiations. Despite the American mediation effort, the bitter mutual suspicions which divided the two parties led inexorably to civil war rather than civil compromise. The negotiations moved to Nanking in 1946 after the National Government returned there, and they remained in Nationalist territory even after civil war broke out that summer. Chou En-lai left Nanking for Yenan on 19 November, stating that the early resumption of negotiations seemed an impossibility. To preserve a channel of communications, however, a small Communist mission headed by Tung Pi-wu remained in the Nanking area.

With Chou En-lai gone and military campaigns developing in north China, Tung Pi-wu initiated no new political approaches. As chairman of the China Liberated Areas Relief Association, he was the ranking Communist spokesman in efforts to channel United Nations Relief and Rehabilitation Administration (UNRRA) supplies into Communist areas, which desperately needed medical facilities, supplies, and services. However, difficulties created by both the Nationalists and the Communists frustrated UNRRA efforts to a very great extent. Finally, as military factors came to outweigh relief and rehabilitation considerations, Tung Pi-wu's protests about interference with supply deliveries became increasingly pointless. Early in 1947 he and the other Communists at Nanking withdrew from the Nationalist capital and went to Yenan.

On 18 August 1948 Tung Pi-wu became chairman of the North China People's Government, established at Shih-chia-chuang in southern Hopei and designed to unify all areas in north China then under Communist control. The veteran Shansi Communist Po I-po (q.v.) was the first vice chairman of this regime. Following the Communist capture of Tientsin and Peiping at the beginning of 1949, the North China People's Government moved to Peiping on 20 February. Tung continued to serve as its chairman until its dissolution at the end of October. He also played an active role in the preparatory meetings for the establishment of a new national government. In September, he was named to the Chinese Communist party delegation to the Chinese People's Political Consultative Conference. On 22 September, he reported on the drafting of the Organic Law of the Central People's Government, which in effect provided the legal basis of national government in China until 1954. With the establishment of the Central People's Government, Tung became a member of the Government Council, one of four vice premiers—the others being Ch'en Yun, Kuo Mo-jo, and Huang Yen-p'ei (qq.v.)—and chairman of the Government Administration Council's committee on political and legal affairs. He also continued to hold prominent welfare posts, becoming director of the central flood control headquarters and vice chairman, under Madame Sun Yat-sen (Soong Ch'ing-ling, q.v.), of the People's Relief Administration. In 1953 he was elected chairman of the China Society of Political Science and Law.

As senior vice premier at Peking, Tung often presented official reports when Chou En-lai, the premier and foreign minister, was absent from Peking. He also wrote significant theoretical statements on the evolving structure and operation of government in the People's Republic of China. At the time of the governmental reorganization in 1954, he was elected president of the Supreme People's Court. He continued to hold this senior judicial post until the spring of 1959. In 1956 he presented a major report on the Chinese Communist legal system. As an elder statesman of the Chinese Communist party, he also continued to hold important party posts. In addition to his continuing membership in the Central Committee and the Political Bureau, he served as head of the Central Control Commission, which was established as a result of the breach represented by the case of Kao Kang and Jao Shu-shih (qq.v.). It was the top organ in a nationwide hierarchy of control commissions which were established in 1955 to replace the discipline inspection committees and which were designed to identify, investigate, and punish infractions of political standards.

Despite his advanced years, Tung did not avoid travel on public business. In 1954 he headed the Chinese delegation to the tenth anniversary celebrations in Sofia of the People's Republic of Bulgaria. He visited Urumchi in September 1955 as Peking's representative at the establishment of the Sinkiang-Uighur Autonomous Region. And in 1958 he headed the Chinese Communist delegation which attended party conferences in Bulgaria, Czechoslovakia, and East Germany.

In April 1959 Tung Pi-wu and Soong Ch'ingling were elected to the newly created vice chairmanships of the People's Republic of China. In this capacity, Tung greeted visiting government delegations, received the credentials of foreign diplomats, and performed other ceremonial duties. In the early and middle 1960's he also continued to head the party Central Control Commission.

Tung Tso-pin   董 作 賓
  Orig. Tso-jen   作 仁
  T.   Yen-t'ang   彥 堂
  H.   P'ing-lu   平 廬

Tung Tso-pin (20 March 1895–23 November 1963), leading authority on chia-ku-wen, the study of oracle bone and turtle shell inscriptions of the Shang-Yin period. He first suggested the systematic excavation of the Anyang site. He served as director of the Academia Sinica's institute of history and philology in 1950–54, during which time he also was a professor at Taiwan University. Tung's reconstruction of the Yin chronology was a major research achievement.

About the time that Tung Tso-pin was born into a storekeeper's family in the Nanyang district of southern Honan, the villagers of Hsiaot'un in the northern Honan district of Anyang found in their fields fragments of shoulder blades of oxen and turtle shells, some of which were inscribed with curious forms of writing. The peasants scraped off the inscriptions and sold these fragments to apothecaries as the medicinal dragon bones of the traditional Chinese pharmacopoeia. In 1899 a number of these bones and shells came to the attention of scholars, who realized that the inscriptions were in an early form of Chinese writing current during the Yin (Shang) dynasty and who began to collect them. The significance of this discovery was known to very few people, least of all to the small storekeepers of such a conservative town as Nanyang.

When Tung Tso-pin was six sui, his father sent him to a traditional private school, where he learned to read and write. As he grew older, he was taught the Chinese classics. Because the family was poor, he had to help his father in the shop after school. His talent as a calligrapher must have been recognized during his childhood, for during the New Year holiday he sold paper scrolls calligraphed by himself to the townspeople, who pasted them over their doorways. When Tung was about 11 or 12, his interest in Chinese writing manifested itself in another direction. A seal engraver who lived across the street from the Tung family agreed to teach the boy his craft. Tung learned to engrave the seal characters on tiles, and by the time he was 14, he was engraving stone seals for customers at four copper coins per character. During this period, he developed what was to be an abiding interest in ancient Chinese writing.

In 1910 Tung entered the Yuan-chung Higher Primary School, which boasted a modern curriculum. Unfortunately for him, his brother died the following year, and his father, needing help in the shop, took Tung Tso-pin out of school. The boy tutored children in his spare time to earn extra money, and in 1913 he began selling books in the family shop, an arrangement which enabled him to read new books without spending money. To improve his writing ability, he joined with some friends in organizing a literary society. They set up a monthly schedule of independent study and, with the help of older scholars, worked to improve their literary styles.

In the spring of 1915 Tung Tso-pin decided to resume his formal education. He passed the entrance examination for the teacher training school established by the county government. Before leaving for the county seat he cut off his queue. He was graduated the following year with highest honors and was asked to stay on as a teacher. Because his father had died in late 1915, Tung had to find someone to manage the family business before he could pursue his own career. In the spring of 1917, having been unable to find a manager, he sold the shop and went to Kaifeng, the provincial capital, to study at the Yü-ts'ai kuan, an institute for the training of government personnel. It was there that he learned of the existence of inscribed oracle bones and turtle shells. After graduation in 1919 Tung and some classmates founded a newspaper, the *Hsin-yü jih-pao*, and he served as its editor for two years.

Tung's thirst for knowledge led him in 1922 to Peking, where he spent a year auditing the classes of such philologists as Ch'ien Hsuan-t'ung (q.v.) at Peking University. He devoted some of his spare time to tracing on thin paper the ink rubbings in the *Yin-ch'ü shu-ch'i ch'ien-pien* [Anyang inscriptions], a work by Lo Chen-yü (q.v.) which had appeared in 1911. When Peking University established a research institute in 1923, Tung enrolled as a student in its sinology department. He studied philology, archaeology, ethnology, and history. To defray his living expenses, he served as editor of the

Folksong Weekly. In the winter of 1924 he joined his teachers and fellow students in participating in the classification and cataloguing of the treasures of the imperial palaces in Peking.

In the spring of 1925 Tung accepted an invitation to teach Chinese at Fukien Christian University. That winter, he returned to Honan to become a lecturer at Chung-chou University in Kaifeng. He went to Peking in the summer of 1927 to accept an appointment as an executive secretary in the department of sinology at the research institute of Peking University. He remained there until August, when he and many other Peking University teachers and students left the old capital for Canton to protest the Peking government's attempt to amalgamate nine universities in Peking. At Canton, he joined the faculty of National Chungshan University and became a close friend of Fu Ssu-nien (q.v.), then acting dean of the college of arts and chairman of the departments of Chinese and history. Tung became a member of the institute of history and philology which Fu founded. In August 1928 Fu became director of the institute of history of the Academia Sinica. By this time, Tung had returned to Honan because his mother was ill and had taken a job at the Nanyang Middle School. During his summer vacation he visited Anyang and discovered that the villagers still were digging up oracle bones and shells from the Yin site and selling them. He suggested to Fu that the Academia Sinica sponsor a systematic excavation of the Anyang site. Fu agreed and appointed Tung editor of the institute of history and philology. Tung began field work on 13 October and continued digging until 30 October. This first systematic excavation of the Yin site yielded 784 pieces of oracle bones and shells. From then until the outbreak of the Sino-Japanese war, Tung participated in most of the 15 Anyang excavations, under the direction of Li Chi (q.v.). In November 1930 he took part in the Ch'eng-tzu-yai excavation in Shantung (for details, *see* Li Chi) which led to the discovery of the Lungshan culture. Tung became a full member of the research staff of the institute of history and philology in 1932.

Tung Tso-pin's epochal *Chia-ku-wen tuan-tai yen-chiu li* was published in March 1932. In this work, he set forth ten criteria for dating a given piece of inscription within the Yin dynasty: genealogy of the Yin kings; terms of address used by the divining king to his ancestor; name of the diviner; position of the pit in which the artifact was discovered; the name of any foreign country mentioned in the inscription; persons mentioned in the text; events related in the text; grammatical construction; ideographical construction; and calligraphical style. By creating this classification system, Tung paved the way for scholars who wished to collate authentic biographical and historical information on the Yin rulers; to examine the institutional, calendrical, and geographical data of the Yin dynasty in chronological order; to date the other cultural relics that were discovered with the oracle bones; and to establish the authenticity of information on Yin culture in ancient and more modern books.

In addition to his field work in connection with the Anyang excavations, Tung directed the T'eng-hsien excavation in Shantung in the autumn of 1933, planned the repair project for the Chou-kung ts'e-liang t'ai, and investigated the foundation of the old Soochow wall in 1936. In the spring of 1935 he began the arduous task of preparing the Anyang oracle bone inscriptions for publication. By the spring of 1937 the manuscript had been sent to the Commercial Press in Shanghai. Publication was suspended, however, when the Japanese invaded Shanghai in August. In 1940 Tung sent another copy of his manuscript to the Hong Kong printing plant of the Commerical Press. The printing and binding of this long-awaited book, the *Yin-ch'ü wen-tzu, chia p'ien* [texts from Anyang, first collection], were completed in the autumn of 1941. By then, the Japanese had occupied almost the entire coast of China, and the books could not be shipped to the interior. When Hong Kong was occupied later in the war, the books were either lost or destroyed. Not until 1947 was the book finally published for general circulation.

During the war years, Tung moved with the institute of history and philology from Nanking to Changsha to Kweilin to Kunming to Nanhsi. Because Fu Ssu-nien was occupied with other tasks, Tung administered the affairs of the institute. He also continued to do research on the Yin calendar. He had begun this work about 1931, the year he had written "Pu-tz'u-chung so-chien-chih Yin-li" [the calendar of Yin as glimpsed in oracle bone texts]. In 1943 he completed the *Yin-li-p'u* [the calendar of Yin]. When this product of over a decade's labor appeared in 1945, it was hailed as a monumental achievement.

In 1946 Tung returned with the institute of history and philology to Nanking. He then accepted an invitation to lecture on chia-ku-wen and chin-wen [bronze inscriptions], and in January 1947 he embarked from Shanghai on his first trip abroad. He served as a visiting professor at the University of Chicago and gave lectures at Yale University. He was elected *in absentia* to the Academia Sinica in March 1948. Late that year he returned to China by way of Hawaii and Japan. Almost immediately he set to work on the evacuation to Taiwan of the institute of history and philology. He moved to Taipei as the Communists came to power on the mainland, and he became professor of ancient Chinese writing and history at Taiwan University. In the summer of 1950 he and several of his friends founded the academic journal *Ta-lu tsa-chih*. After Fu Ssu-nien's death in December 1950, Tung succeeded him as director of the institute of history and philology. That winter, Tung published "Wu-wang fa Chou nien yueh jih k'ao" [the day, month, and year of Chou Wu-wang's attack on the last king of Shang], which placed the date of this invasion, a subject of controversy for more than 2,000 years, at 1111 B.C. His *Hsi-Chou nien-li p'u* [the calendar of Western Chou] appeared in 1951. In 1953 the *Yin-ch'ü wen-tzu, yueh p'ien* [texts from Anyang, second collection], was published. Tung was honored for these and other scholarly achievements in 1954, when the ministry of education awarded him a prize and a medal.

Tung resigned from the institute of history and philology in August 1955 and took a leave of absence from Taiwan University so that he could accept an invitation to do research at the institute of oriental culture at Hong Kong University. In 1956 he became honorary professor of history at Hong Kong University and professor of history at the Ts'ung-chi Academy. The following year, he also taught at New Asia College. While in Hong Kong, he completed his *Chung-kuo nien-li tsung-p'u*, a much-needed reference work in Chinese and English on the chronology of Chinese history. In the winter of 1957 he delivered a paper entitled *Chung-kuo shang-ku-shih nien-tai* [the most ancient period

of China's history] at the Ninth Pacific Science Congress in Bangkok. He returned to his post at Taiwan University in the autumn of 1958. The following spring, the institute of history and philology celebrated his sixty-fifth sui by issuing a *festschrift*. In August 1960 he was appointed research professor of chia-ku-wen at Taiwan University, a post he held until his death on 23 November 1963. Tung was survived by the child of his first marriage, Yu-ching (1932–); by his second wife, *née* Hsiung Hai-p'ing, whom he had married in 1935; and by the five children of his second marriage: Hsiao-min (1936–), Hsiao-hsing (1937–), Hsiao-p'ing (1939–), Hsiao-i (1944–), and Hsiao-wu (1946–).

Scholars agree that Tung Tso-pin's most important contributions to historical knowledge were his studies of oracle bone inscriptions. He discovered five stages in the evolution of the chia-ku-wen and two schools of calendrical construction during the Yin dynasty, thus facilitating the dating of individual inscriptions. He increased modern knowledge of ancient Chinese writing by identifying and interpreting individual characters in the chia-ku-wen. He compiled the ritual calendars of many Yin kings, reconstructed the astronomical calendar of the Yin dynasty, and correlated the Yin calendar with the record of lunar eclipses. Furthermore, he worked out a complete system of ancient Chinese chronology which must be taken into account in any study of the Yin and Chou civilizations.

Tung Yuan-feng   董 遠 峯
  T. T'ien-chi   天 驥

Tung Yuan-feng (1883–4 November 1941) was one of the first serious philatelists of twentieth-century China. He made technical studies of the Nanking and Foochow neutrality issues of 1912 and of the stamp series depicting Kuomintang martyrs first issued by the National Government in 1932.

The Kan-ch'üan district of Kiangsu was the birthplace of Tung Yuan-feng. Born into a family of respectable lineage and comfortable means, he was a nephew of the Ch'ing scholar and official Tung Hsün (ECCP, II, 789–91). His father was interested in local history and was an active proponent of the views of the Ming loyalist Wang Fu-chih (ECCP, II, 817–19), whose patriotic outlook found favor with the anti-Ch'ing movement at the turn of this century.

Tung Yuan-feng received a traditional education in the Chinese classics from tutors. His father died early, and the young Tung took charge of the family's property interests. He also devoted himself to revising his uncle's *Kan-t'ung hsiao-chih* (1855), a topographical work on the clan's native town in Kiangsu; to preparing an annotated catalogue of the family library; and to collecting samples of the calligraphy of prominent Kiangsu natives.

On a visit to Shanghai in 1908 Tung met Ch'en Chin-t'ao (q.v.), who had been sent abroad by the imperial government to investigate methods for improving the manufacture of Chinese postage stamps. Ch'en had concluded that the techniques used in the United States were least subject to counterfeiting, a highly developed art in China; and he had invited two American experts, William A. Grant and Lorenzo J. Hatch, to China to advise the bureau of printing and engraving at Peking. After meeting in Shanghai with Grant, who had been in charge of the engraving room of the American Bank Note Company, Tung developed an interest in the technical problems involved in the production of bank notes and postage stamps with inscriptions in Chinese characters.

During the next decade Tung developed into a serious philatelist and became one of the first Chinese to study Chinese philatelic history, which dates back to 1878. In September 1918 he published notes gleaned from his research on stamp issues of the Chinese treaty ports, notably those of Amoy, Chefoo, Hankow, Ningpo, Swatow, and Weihaiwei. Written in elegant classical Chinese and supplemented with hand-drawn reproductions of stamp designs in complete detail, the work was privately printed for circulation among members of the Nan-she, or Southern Society (*see* Liu Ya-tzu). The small community of Chinese stamp collectors, then clustered in the Shanghai area, recognized it as a work of the first caliber. Tung was one of the first Chinese philatelists to appreciate the significance of watermarks, perforation scales, and varieties of paper and ink in stamp classification.

In the 1920's and 1930's, Tung Yuan-feng spent most of his time in Shanghai, then the principal stamp market in China. His precise knowledge of early Chinese issues made him an invaluable consultant, though his personal interests remained more in research than in stamp merchandising. Building on experience gained in his early work on treaty port issues, Tung became a leading authority on the rare provisional neutrality overprint issues of 1912, and his study of the many forgeries of these rare stamps was published in several installments in 1924–25 in the *Philatelic Bulletin*, issued by the Chinese Philatelic Society of Shanghai.

Tung's stamp interests were comprehensive, but he was most interested in aspects of Chinese history and culture that were visually or otherwise documented through postage stamps and postal covers. Utilizing Chinese stamps and stamps used by foreign post offices in China, he sought to record and verify historical events through philatelic evidence, especially by studying dates and places of cancellation. A major interest of Tung's was philatelic portraits, an interest which caused him in 1935 to go to great lengths to obtain a Communist stamp issued several months earlier in the remote Szechwan-Shensi border area (*see* Chang Kuo-t'ao, Hsü Hsiang-ch'ien) which boasted a picture of Karl Marx. Because possession or circulation of Communist materials was suspect in Nationalist-controlled areas of China, Tung was arrested, and the offending stamp was confiscated by the authorities at Nanking. Released after two weeks because of his impeccable record and lack of genuine evidence of Communist sympathies, Tung Yuan-feng emerged furious at the loss of the stamp which, according to acquaintances in the Shanghai stamp trade, had found its way into the possession of a senior Nationalist official without philatelic sophistication. Tung immediately appealed to a family friend, Chang Jen-chieh (q.v.); and Chang, though politically inactive at the time, intervened with Chiang Kai-shek and arranged the return of the offending stamp. Nevertheless, this incident may have played a part in Tung's disillusion with the post-1928 Kuomintang and his decision to remain in Shanghai after the outbreak of war with Japan in 1937.

Tung's continued residence in Shanghai after 1937 was also motivated by a sense of patriotism and by a desire to prevent Japanese philatelists from acquiring some of China's "national treasures" during a period when many Chinese stamp dealers were forced by financial pressures to sell their collections. During the 1937–41 period, Tung did much preclusive buying in the Shanghai area and acquired many rare or unique items. One of his long-range research interests was the so-called martyrs' issue, which depicted Chinese patriots who had given their lives in the republican revolutionary movement associated with Sun Yat-sen. This group included such figures as Ch'en Ch'i-mei, Chu Chih-hsin, Huang Hsing, Liao Chung-k'ai, Sung Chiao-jen, Teng K'eng (qq.v.), and others. Tung compiled a list of 109 differences in design and printing details between the basic Peking printing (1932) of these stamps and the later (1939–41) Hong Kong printing. He was engaged in expanding this list when he succumbed to pneumonia in Shanghai in late 1941. Just before his death Tung also was engaged in research on overprinted surcharges of the martyrs' issue that appeared in Japanese-controlled areas of China beginning in 1941. Conservative in instinct, Tung generally eschewed political polemics. One of his last articles, however, boldly suggested that certain contemporary Japanese postage stamps were aesthetically superior to Chinese stamps. Published posthumously in a Chinese weekly in Shanghai early in 1942, the article was later appropriated and reprinted by the Japanese-sponsored government headed by Wang Ching-wei at Nanking in its cultural offensive against the National Government of Chiang Kai-shek at Chungking.

In interests and style, Tung Yuan-feng was a man who preserved the Chinese tradition of eccentricity in connoisseurship. Always an enthusiastic amateur, he nevertheless made distinctive contributions to the development of professional standards in twentieth-century Chinese philately. Tung was uninterested in the accoutrements of Western civilization with the exception of the postage stamp, and that only in its Chinese incarnation. At the same time, his detachment from prevailing radical nationalist tendencies in republican Chinese philately led him to study treaty port issues, often denounced by both Nationalist and Communist as bogus relics of Western imperialism in China. After the Second World War, some items in Tung Yuan-feng's philatelic trove were sold privately, with the approval of members of the Tung family, to the prominent

British collector Sir Percival David. Chung Hsiao-lu (H. L. Chung), who was the editor of the *Chin-tai yu-k'an (Modern Philatelic Monthly)* at Shanghai and who was regarded by Western collectors as the dean of Chinese philatelists, reportedly facilitated that transaction. Certain of these items were sold at auction in London in 1964.

Tung Yuan-feng's detailed knowledge of the varieties of Chinese postage stamps of the late imperial and early republican periods assisted the preliminary cataloguing efforts of two fellow philatelists in Shanghai; Ma Zung-sung (Ma Jun-sheng) and his son Ma Ren-chuen (Ma Jen-ch'uan). Ma Zung-sung died at Chungking in October 1945, but his materials were supplemented and prepared for publication by his son. The resulting bilingual catalogue, published at Shanghai in July 1947, is entitled *Ma's Illustrated Catalogue of the Stamps of China (Ma-shih kuo-yu t'u-chien)*. It is generally regarded as the most authoritative pre-Communist catalogue of Chinese postage stamps.

Ulanfu   鳥 蘭 夫
Alt. Yün-tse   雲 澤

Ulanfu (1903–), Tumet Mongol who joined the Chinese Communist party in 1927 and rose to become its principal representative in Inner Mongolia. In the 1950's and early 1960's he dominated party, government, and military structures in that region. Ulanfu became a target of criticism during the so-called Cultural Revolution and was removed from his posts in 1967.

Little is known about Ulanfu's family background or childhood except that he was born in the village of Taputs'un in Inner Mongolia and was raised among the Tumet Mongols. The Tumet Banner, a numerically small and culturally sinicized group of Mongols, occupied the area west of Kweisui near the great bend of the Yellow River in what later became Suiyuan province. In contrast to other Mongol groups of Inner Mongolia, which retained nomadism and remained relatively free of Chinese infiltration, the Tumet Mongols at the turn of the century were largely sedentary, agricultural, and Chinese-speaking. Both cultural and linguistic factors made them closely related to Chinese influences.

Like many other young Mongols who became active in Inner Mongolian political affairs during the republican period, Ulanfu went to Peking to attend the Mongolian-Tibetan Academy. There, about 1923, he gained initial exposure to radical ideas. This exposure came through contact with Li Ta-chao, Teng Chung-hsia (qq.v.), and other members of the north China bureau of the infant Chinese Communist party who were attempting to stimulate interest in Marxism among student groups in the Peking area. In 1924, while a student at the Mongolian-Tibetan Academy, Ulanfu joined the Communist Youth League. The following spring he participated in anti-imperialist demonstrations organized by Peking students after the May Thirtieth Incident, when British police in the International Concession at Shanghai fired on Chinese.

The year 1925 also marked Ulanfu's entry into political activity in Inner Mongolia. In October he participated in a Communist-planned gathering of Mongolian nationalists held at Kalgan which brought into being the Inner Mongolian People's Revolutionary party. This group diverged from the moderate political line adopted by the Young Mongols, of which Te Wang (Demchukdonggrub, q.v.) was an active leader. The Young Mongols aimed at establishment of an autonomous Inner Mongolian government within the framework of the Chinese nation. The Revolutionary party, as a united front organ of the Chinese Communist party, espoused a program which called for abolition of feudalism in Mongolian society, active resistance to Chinese rule over Mongolian territory, independence for Inner Mongolia, and close relations with the Mongolian People's Republic, which had been established in 1924 in Outer Mongolia under Soviet influence.

The position of Ulanfu and the Inner Mongolian People's Revolutionary party in 1925 reflected the political alliance between the Chinese Communists and the Kuomintang and the common antagonism which both felt toward the Peking government which then ruled Inner Mongolia. Earlier that year a new party called the Inner Mongolian Kuomintang (*see* Buyantai) had also been formed, and it was that party which recruited many young Mongols for study at Ulan Bator (Urga) and Moscow. In the winter of 1925 Ulanfu was sent to the Soviet Union to study at Sun Yat-sen University, opened that year for training revolutionary cadres from China. While a student in Moscow, Ulanfu became a Communist in 1927. It is also possible that it was during this period in Russia that he dropped his original name, Yün-tse, and adopted that of Ulanfu, which, it has been suggested, may have been derived from that of Ulyanov, the family surname of Lenin. After graduation, Ulanfu worked for a period as a translator in the Soviet Union.

After four years in the Soviet Union, Ulanfu left Moscow in 1929 and went to the Mongolian People's Republic. He was briefly involved in an abortive movement, based at Choibalsan, aimed at achieving independence for the Hulunbuir Mongol area in eastern Mongolia (western Manchuria). In 1930 he returned to China, where a northern coalition of Kuomintang leaders (*see* Feng Yü-hsiang; Yen Hsi-shan) had been formed in opposition to Chiang Kai-shek's growing power at Nanking. Ulanfu became attached to the staff of one of Yen Hsi-shan's commanders, Fu Tso-yi (q.v.), and served as political officer in a cavalry regiment under Fu. With the defeat of the northern coalition, Fu Tso-yi became associated with Chang Hsueh-liang, who had become the dominant figure in north China. After Fu Tso-yi became governor in Suiyuan in 1931, Ulanfu remained for a time in Fu's entourage and thus returned to his native province.

During the next few years, Ulanfu pursued a dual career as pro-Communist and anti-Japanese propagandist. The Japanese military occupation of Manchuria in 1931, followed by penetration of Jehol and Chahar in 1932–33, evoked a complex series of challenges and responses throughout Inner Mongolia. Because the National Government at Nanking made no serious effort to resist Japanese aggression, some Mongol leaders began to search independently for measures to ensure maximum protection of their interests. One group, led by Te Wang and the Young Mongols, attempted to organize an Inner Mongolian autonomous government under the general supervision of Nanking but outside the jurisdiction of the provincial governments of Chahar and Suiyuan. In April 1934 the Mongolian Local Autonomous Political Council, designed to provide partial recognition of these Mongol aspirations, was established at Pailingmiao. Within a few months, Te Wang, for a variety of reasons, had developed closer relations with the Japanese. During these years

Ulanfu had been working in Inner Mongolia to organize resistance against Japan. As provincial governor of Suiyuan, Fu Tso-yi was strongly opposed both to Japanese aggression and to Inner Mongolian autonomy. Fu thus encouraged Ulanfu, a Tumet Mongol, to mobilize Mongols of the Ikechao League in an attempt to counter the activities of Te Wang and his supporters, many of whom were of the Silingol and other Mongol leagues.

Chinese Communist policy during this period aimed at formation of a united front composed of all anti-Japanese forces in the country. Neither the Communists nor the Kuomintang could condone the growth of a variety of Inner Mongolian autonomy which might further weaken China and which would strengthen the position of Japan on the mainland. As a result of the agitation directed by Ulanfu and other political heirs of the People's Revolutionary party, the Chinese Communists were able to gain footholds in Inner Mongolia after 1935. In February 1936 Ulanfu was involved in an uprising at Shiramuren near Pailingmiao which was designed to split the Mongol membership of the Political Council there. When Te Wang and his associates, with Japanese support, launched an attack on Suiyuan in November 1936, Ulanfu reportedly was with the forces of Fu Tso-yi, which participated in the resistance and in the capture of Pailingmiao. Early in 1937, after the Sian Incident (*see* Chiang Kai-shek; Chang Hsueh-liang) temporarily eased relations between the Nationalists and Communists, Ulanfu emerged as political commissar of a Mongolian peace preservation corps in Suiyuan commanded by Pai Hai-feng, a Mongol long associated with the Kuomintang. After the outbreak of full-scale war between China and Japan in July 1937, Ulanfu was assigned to lead an independent brigade formed of Mongols of the Ikechao League.

After the Japanese military drive into Suiyuan, Ulanfu escaped to Yenan, the wartime capital of the Chinese Communists in northern Shensi, where for the first time he established relations with the central party apparatus. During the war years he headed the so-called Mongolian Cultural Association at Yenan and was active in the Nationalities Institute, the organ primarily responsible for political training of Mongol and other non-Chinese cadres. He served concurrently as director of the nationalities affairs commission of the Shensi-Kansu-Ninghsia Border Region Government and thus was involved with Communist plans and policies in this realm. When the Seventh National Congress of the Chinese Communist party met at Yenan (April-June 1945), Ulanfu was elected to alternate membership on the Central Committee.

From 1944 to 1946, just before and after the close of the Second World War, Inner Mongolia was the scene of growing political competition. The Kuomintang, the Chinese Communists, the Mongols of Inner Mongolia, and the Mongols of Outer Mongolia all vied for influence and power within a new and sharply altered framework of Sino-Soviet-Mongolian relations. Various Mongol autonomy movements, some old, some new, appeared both in eastern Mongolia (western Manchuria) and in Inner Mongolia proper. In the early autumn of 1945 Soviet military forces moved southward to occupy Manchuria and parts of Inner Mongolia for a period. But the decisive new element in the situation was the fact that the Chinese Communists, partly through the ineptness of the Kuomintang and partly through the efforts of Ulanfu, now possessed a framework for political and military action aimed at winning control of all of Inner Mongolia.

Ulanfu himself occupied a key position, not in the Inner Mongolian nationalist movement, but in the major radical force in Chinese national political life. In 1944, before the Japanese defeat, he organized a so-called democratic anti-Japanese government in the Ikechao League which served to harass Japanese-held territories. In this effort and in later operations, Mongolian cadres trained by Ulanfu at Yenan played a key role in helping him to consolidate his new position in Inner Mongolia. In November 1945, as the military contest between the Nationalists and Communists brewed, this Yenan group took the lead in organizing the Inner Mongolian Autonomy Association, a group based at Kalgan and headed by Ulanfu, which was designed to provide firm Chinese Communist direction of indigenous desire for self-determination in western Inner Mongolia. In March 1946 another conference, with Ulanfu again in a dominant position, met at Chengteh in Jehol. This meeting brought together representatives from both western and eastern Inner Mongolia, and Ulanfu succeeded in effecting a merger of the two groups in a new joint committee under Chinese Communist direction. The Chengteh meeting reflected this direction by denouncing the Chinese Nationalists and by announcing support for creation of a new "democratic" autonomous government in Inner Mongolia. These pronouncements were premature, however, for during the latter part of 1946 the Nationalists made significant military advances in Suiyuan and Jehol as well as in north China and Manchuria.

Ulanfu and his supporters then moved to eastern Mongolia. There, on 1 May 1947, the "People's Government of the Inner Mongolian Autonomous Region" was established at Wang-yeh-miao (renamed Ulanhot, or Red City, in Mongolian). This regime, controlled by Mongols who were strong supporters of the Chinese Communists, was headed by Ulanfu, who was also identified as secretary of the Inner Mongolia sub-bureau of the Chinese Communist party and as commander and political commissar of a new Inner Mongolian People's Self-Defense Army. The significance of this new regime was not immediately apparent even though cavalry units associated with the Ulanhot regime fought with regular Chinese Communist armies in the Manchurian campaigns of 1947–48. These units later were incorporated into the People's Liberation Army. Representatives from the Communist-controlled Inner Mongolian regime also attended the meeting at Mukden in August 1949 at which a new regional Northeast People's Government (see Kao Kang) was established.

In September 1949, when the People's Political Consultative Conference met at Peiping, it became evident that the Inner Mongolian Autonomous Region would be an integral political unit in the new People's Republic of China. With the establishment of the Central People's Government in October 1949, it was confirmed that Ulanfu would continue to lead the effort to extend Chinese Communist authority throughout Inner Mongolia. In addition to regional responsibilities, Ulanfu now held senior posts at the national government level: member of the Central People's Government Council, president of the Central Institute of Nationalities, deputy director of the Nationalities Affairs Commission, and others.

For several years after its formation at Ulanhot in the spring of 1947, the development of the Inner Mongolian Autonomous Region was marked by two trends: steady growth in the geographical area embraced by the region and increasing consolidation of effective Chinese Communist authority. Reflection of these processes was seen in early 1950 in the movement of its capital from Ulanhot to Kalgan in Chahar province. The most important Mongolian areas not included in the Inner Mongolian Autonomous Region in 1949–50 lay in Suiyuan, which then had been governed for some two decades by Fu Tso-yi. Although Fu had surrendered Peiping to the Communists without a fight at the beginning of 1949, two of his subordinate generals, Tung Ch'i-wu and Sun Lan-feng (qq.v.), had retained control of substantial elements of Fu's troops in Suiyuan itself. Because of this situation, the Communists permitted Tung Ch'i-wu to remain as governor for some time after the formal surrender of the province.

In mid-1952, in a series of new moves designed to consolidate direct control over Suiyuan, Peking announced major changes. On 1 July 1952 the principal organs of the government of the Inner Mongolian Autonomous Region, together with the Inner Mongolia regional apparatus of the Chinese Communist party, moved from Kalgan to Kweisui (Huhehot) in Suiyuan. (The Communists officially changed the name of Kweisui to Huhehot, or Blue City in Mongolian, in the spring of 1954). Peking then announced that Ulanfu, head of the Autonomous Region government, had been named concurrently governor of Suiyuan, replacing Tung Ch'i-wu. On 1 August, the Suiyuan and Inner Mongolia military districts were merged into a unified (Sui-Meng) military district. The full merger of Suiyuan into the Inner Mongolian Autonomous Region was approved by the Peking authorities in January 1954, and the two areas were amalgamated in March. Two years later, in the spring of 1956, the territories inhabited by the Alashan and Edsingol Mongols in Ninghsia were similarly incorporated into the Inner Mongolian Autonomous Region.

Throughout these administrative changes during the decade after 1947, Ulanfu remained the most active Chinese-oriented Mongol Communist in Inner Mongolia, and he dominated party, government, and military structures in that region. As first secretary of the Inner Mongolian Communist party committee, head of the government, and commander of the Inner Mongolian military district, Ulanfu held an apparently undisputed position. When an Inner Mongolia University was established in 1957, he became first president of that institution. And in May 1962 he presided over the celebrations at Huhehot which marked the fifteenth anniversary of the Inner Mongolian Autonomous Region.

At the same time, Ulanfu held senior positions at Peking. In 1953 he was a member of the commission charged with drafting a new constitution for the People's Republic of China. After the reorganization of the Central People's Government in 1954, he served as a member of the State Council and as member of the National Defense Council with the rank of general in the People's Liberation Army. He was concurrently chairman of the Nationalities Affairs Commission, in which capacity he announced official policies toward non-Chinese minority groups. He represented Inner Mongolia as a deputy to the first, second, and third sessions of the National People's Congress. In 1956, at the Eighth National Congress of the Chinese Communist party, Ulanfu was elected to membership on the party Central Committee and to alternate membership on its Political Bureau.

As senior-ranking non-Chinese member of the Chinese Communist hierarchy, Ulanfu also occupied a prominent position in Peking's international political programs. Because of the importance of relations between China and Outer Mongolia, he headed Peking's delegations to Ulan Bator to observe successive congresses of the Mongolian People's Revolutionary party: the twelfth (1954), the thirteenth (1958), and the fourteenth (1961). In 1955 he headed China's delegation to Czechoslovakia to attend celebrations marking the tenth anniversary of the ending of the German occupation; in 1961 he went to France to observe the sixteenth Congress of the French Communist party. In 1956 he headed the Chinese delegation to attend the coronation ceremonies of King Mahendra of Nepal. And late in 1957 he was a member of the major delegation that accompanied Mao Tse-tung to Moscow for the observance of the fortieth anniversary of the Bolshevik revolution.

For 20 years after his participation in the establishment of the Inner Mongolian People's Revolutionary party in 1925, Ulanfu served as principal Chinese Communist activist in that region. For another 20 years after 1945 he was the leading individual involved in implementing Chinese Communist policies in Inner Mongolia. These assignments were made difficult because of long-standing political and economic tensions between the pastoral Mongol nomads and the agricultural Chinese and because of dilemmas in balancing national requirements as set by Peking against local attitudes and aspirations. Mongol-Chinese antagonisms with respect to collectivization and other programs of socio-economic reorganization were complicated after 1955 by significant Chinese migration into the region (where Mongols comprised only about one-sixth of the total population in 1954). Despite these obstacles, Ulanfu and his Chinese Communist associates were successful in their efforts to bring a measure of stability to that strategically important borderland region.

For a period, Ulanfu's ability to curb anti-Chinese local nationalism in the Inner Mongolian Autonomous Region was related to Peking's willingness to tolerate gradualism in implementation of radical reforms in non-Chinese minority areas. Yet the very measure of stability attained in Inner Mongolia made Ulanfu a target of bitter attacks during the Cultural Revolution after 1966. The turmoil associated with the Cultural Revolution in Inner Mongolia led to heavy pressure upon entrenched bureaucracy and upon individuals alleged to have followed policies castigated *ex post facto* as creations of Liu Shao-ch'i (q.v.). An obvious scapegoat because of his virtual monopoly of senior bureaucratic positions in Inner Mongolia, Ulanfu was publicly condemned by revolutionary activists in August 1967. Near the end of that year, he was denounced for "towering crimes" against the people of Inner Mongolia and was removed from official positions.

Unenbayin
Chinese. Wu Ho-ling

Unenbayin (8 February 1896–), also known as Wu Ho-ling, leading intellectual in the Inner Mongolian autonomy movement. After serving as head of the Mongolian section of the Mongolian-Tibetan Affairs Commission from 1930 to 1936, he returned to his native region. In 1942–45 he headed the political affairs department of the Mongolian Federated Autonomous Government.

A Mongol of the Right Kharchin Banner of the Josuto League, Unenbayin was the son of Lamajab (Wu Feng-sheng), a commoner who was commander of the banner's forces. Unenbayin received his early education at home under the tutelage of Chang Kung-chien, a Shantung Chinese who held the chü-jen degree. He then attended the Normal School at Chengteh, Jehol, after which he entered the Cheng-fa ta-hsueh [university of politics and law], from which he was graduated in 1917. In 1926 he became the first Mongol to be graduated from Peking University, where he majored in Chinese literature.

While studying at Peking, Unenbayin taught, beginning in 1918, at the Mongolian-Tibetan Academy. This school for young Mongols had been founded in 1912 by Gungsang Norbu, the prince of the Right Kharchin Banner, and its graduates included Buyantai (q.v.), Merse, and Fumingtai. Unenbayin also assisted Gungsang Norbu at the bureau of Mongolian-Tibetan affairs and held a position in the ministry of the interior at Peking. In addition, after 1924 he taught at the Chu-shih Middle School, worked at the Ching-kuan kao-teng hsueh-hsiao, and served as vice president of the Peking YMCA.

Unenbayin was a conscientious student, and his thinking was influenced by new trends in China. Still, he remained aloof from the radical and revolutionary currents of the day. While such young Mongols as Merse, Buyantai, Fumingtai, and Ulanfu (q.v.) pressed for social revolution in Mongolia, Unenbayin advocated the unification and strengthening of Mongolia through gradual reforms. He favored the attainment of Mongolian autonomy purely through political means, and, although pan-Mongolism appealed to him emotionally, he believed that Inner Mongolia had lost its opportunity for independence from China and unification with Outer Mongolia at the time of the 1911 revolution. Because of this belief, he consistently worked for political self-determination and cultural preservation of the Mongols through

the complex and tedious process of strengthening the legal position of Mongolian autonomy within the administrative structure of the Chinese republic. At the same time, he urged reforms in the quasi-feudalistic administration of the Mongol banners.

After the successful completion of the Northern Expedition in June 1928, Buyantai was given responsibility for the reorganization of the Mongolian-Tibetan affairs office at Peking. Unenbayin and other Mongols at Peking were distressed by this decision, and their unease increased when the Kuomintang Central Political Council on 29 August 1928 passed a proposal to convert the Mongolian special districts of Jehol, Chahar, and Suiyuan into provinces. Accordingly, Unenbayin and other Mongolian banner representatives at Peking formed a delegation which went to Nanking in November to press for the autonomy that Sun Yat-sen had promised China's minority peoples in *Principles of National Reconstruction*. The delegation did not achieve its aims, and all of its members except Unenbayin left Nanking. Because he believed that he could accomplish more for the Mongols by staying at the capital, he established residence at Nanking and set up the Capital Office of Allied Mongolian League and Banner Affairs. Through this office, he was able to assist Mongol students and to exert pressure on the National Government in the cause of Mongolian autonomy.

The National Government established the Mongolian-Tibetan Affairs Commission at the end of 1928, and Yen Hsi-shan (q.v.) assumed office as its chairman on 1 January 1929. Buyantai became a member of the commission, and Unenbayin joined the staff of its Mongolian affairs section, becoming section head in 1930. He soon proposed the convening of a Mongolian conference to consider outstanding problems. Over 40 representatives met at Nanking in May 1930, and among the results of the conference was a concession from the National Government for 15 Mongolian representatives to be taken into the new National Assembly when it met the following year. Agreement also was reached on a proposal for a "Basic Law for the Organization of Mongolian Leagues and Banners." When the National Assembly met in 1931, the 15 Mongol representatives went to great lengths to gain ratification of their proposals. Led by Unenbayin, they congregated and threatened mass suicide if their demands were ignored. The Law for the Organization of Mongol Leagues and Banners was passed by the National Assembly on 12 October 1931 and subsequently was approved by the Central Executive Committee of the Kuomintang. The passage of this law was one of Unenbayin's most cherished accomplishments. It provided a legal basis for preserving the integrity of Mongol banners and leagues, for their relationship to the Chinese provinces in Inner Mongolia and to the National Government, and for the reform of banner administration through the abolition of hereditary rule and succession. The law fell short of Unenbayin's hopes, however, because it made no provision for uniting the separate and isolated Mongol banners.

In August 1933 a new crisis arose when the ruling princes of western Inner Mongolia sent a telegram to Nanking which announced their intention of establishing an autonomous Mongolian government. The National Government sent a delegation to Pailingmiao, which included Huang Shao-hung (q.v.) and Unenbayin, for talks with Te Wang (Demchukdonggrub, q.v.) Yun Wang (Prince Yun), and other Mongol leaders. With Unenbayin and the Panchen Lama (q.v.) working essentially as mediators, agreement finally was reached. However, the dispute began again when the terms of the agreement were modified at Nanking and the Kuomintang Central Political Council passed an act on 17 January 1934 which omitted much of the substance of the Pailingmiao agreement. Because of Unenbayin's objections and the threat of an Inner Mongolia-Manchoukuo alliance, this act was repealed almost immediately. On 28 February, the Central Political Council passed the Eight Principles of Mongolian Autonomy (Mengku tzu-chih yuan-tzu pa-hsiang), drafted by Unenbayin, which provided for the establishment of the Mongolian Local Autonomous Political Council and for an end to Chinese migration into Mongolian lands.

In the mid-1930's Unenbayin was forced to make a crucial personal decision with reference to Inner Mongolia and its relationships with China and Japan. By early 1936 it had become obvious that a Japanese takeover of Inner Mongolia was inevitable, for the Chinese authorities at Nanking would do nothing to counter increasing Japanese influence in that area. Because Unenbayin believed that he could accomplish nothing if separated from other Mongols by a Japanese occupation, he decided to return to Inner Mongolia. In a private meeting with Chiang Kai-shek, he persuaded Chiang to let him go without suspicion of treachery. According to their agreement, in the event of Unenbayin's death a public announcement would be made to scotch any accusation of treason. Unenbayin's decision was a difficult one. For the next decade he would be regarded by some Japanese as a Chinese agent, by some young Mongols as a compromising conservative, and by some Chinese as a war criminal.

When Te Wang inaugurated the so-called Inner Mongolian Government at Tehua (Coptchil) on 28 June 1936, Unenbayin became its chief counselor. Later, after a sort of exile in Japan (1939–41), Unenbayin became head of the political affairs department of that regime's successor, the Mongolian Federated Autonomous Government. At Kalgan, the government headquarters, Unenbayin was responsible for day-to-day administration in guiding the government under Japanese occupation. With the full support of Te Wang, he also served as a buffer between idealistic Mongol nationalists and harsh Japanese military authorities. Although he did not stir young men to ambition for Mongolian independence, he did much to encourage young Mongols to prepare themselves for service to their people. He was the leading planner and patron of a special school in Kalgan which prepared hundreds of Mongol youths for advanced study in Japan.

One of Unenbayin's proudest achievements during this period was the development of the horisha, an adaptation of the cooperative. This economic institution had several purposes: liberating Mongols from traditional financial bondage to Chinese merchants, establishing standard selling prices for goods, increasing Mongol economic power during the Japanese occupation, and producing increased revenue for national development and the strengthening of Mongol autonomy. In addition to cooperative marketing, Unenbayin and other Mongol leaders promoted the use of modern techniques in gathering and processing milk products and animals in nomadic areas.

Unenbayin held office at Kalgan until the

Second World War ended and the Chinese Communists began to take control in that area. Rejecting the Communist alternative, he moved south and evacuated his family to Taiwan. Then, at the behest of Te Wang, he flew to Ninghsia to assist in another attempt to organize Mongolian resistance. The attempt failed, partly because the Communist advance, led by P'eng Te-huai (q.v.), was unexpectedly rapid. Unenbayin and a number of other Mongol leaders then escaped to Taiwan. There, despite heart attacks and other severe illnesses, he continued to urge the National Government to follow progressive policies which would win Mongol support.

Wan Chia-pao　　　　萬 家 寶
Pen. Ts'ao Yü　　　　　曹 禺

Wan Chia-pao (1910–), known as Ts'ao Yü, playwright whose best-known work was *Lei-yü* [thunderstorm]. After 1949 he devoted himself to cultural activities in the People's Republic of China. Wan joined the Chinese Communist party in 1957.

Born in Ch'ienchiang, Hupeh, Ts'ao Yü came from a well-to-do family. He attended the Nankai Middle School in Tientsin, where he became an enthusiastic member of a dramatic club directed by Chang P'eng-ch'un, the younger brother of Chang Po-ling (q.v.). Ts'ao Yü appeared in several stage productions during his school days and collaborated with Chang P'eng-ch'un in translating John Galsworthy's play *Strife*. In 1930 Ts'ao Yü entered Tsinghua University, where he studied Western literature. He was graduated in 1933 but stayed on at the university for another year. His first play, *Lei-yü* [thunderstorm], was staged in 1935 by the Futan University Dramatic Club under the direction of Ou-yang Yü-ch'ien and Hung Shen (qq.v.) in Shanghai. When taken on tour by the Chung-kuo lü-hsing chü-t'uan [China traveling dramatic troupe], *Lei-yü* was an outstanding success in every city visited. Ts'ao Yü wrote five more successful plays within the next six years. These were *Jih-ch'u* [sunrise], of 1935, awarded the *Ta Kung Pao* drama prize in 1936; *Yuan-yeh* [wilderness], of 1936; *Shui-pien* [metamorphosis], of 1940; *Pei-ching jen* [Peking man], of 1940; and *Chia* [family], of

1941, adapted from the novel of the same title by Pa Chin (Li Fei-kan, q.v.).

In 1934 Ts'ao Yü was a professor of English at Tientsin Normal College for Women, and in 1935–40 he served as professor and dean of the National Academy of Dramatic Art at Nanking and, after the Sino-Japanese war began, at Chiangan. He also lectured in the English department of Futan University, which moved to Peip'ei near Chungking. At war's end, Ts'ao Yü returned to Shanghai. In March 1946 he and Lao She (Shu Ch'ing-ch'un, q.v.) went to the United States on a cultural cooperation grant from the Department of State. Ts'ao Yü attended a writers conference at the University of Denver, visited Canada at the invitation of its government, and collaborated with Reginald Lawrence on an adaptation of *Pei-ching jen*. He remained in the United States until December 1946, when he returned to Shanghai because his mother was ill. Upon his return he went to work as a script writer for the Wen-hua film studio. In addition to his film work, he lectured at the Municipal Experimental Drama School and wrote a play entitled *Ch'iao* [the bridge], which was published in the *Wen-i fu-hsing* [literary renaissance].

A supporter of the Chinese Communist effort to win control of mainland China, Ts'ao Yü attended the conference of Chinese writers and artists which was held at Peiping in July 1949 and served on its presidium. He also served on the Chinese delegation to the World Peace Conference at Prague. Upon his return to China, he was elected to the standing committee of the All-China Federation of Literary and Art Circles, the national committee of the Chinese Association of Literary Workers, and the standing committee of the China Association of Dramatic Workers. In 1950 he became vice president of the Academy of Dramatic Arts and director of the Peking People's Art Theater. He was a delegate from his native district in Hupeh to the National People's Congress in 1954. In 1956 he attended the Congress of Asian Writers at New Delhi and the World Congress for Banning Atomic and Hydrogen Bombs at Nagasaki. He joined the Chinese Communist party in 1957, when membership was being expanded to include older intellectuals. In the mid-1950's Ts'ao Yü also participated in a number of campaigns against "rightists" and "anti-party" writers, including

Hu Feng and Ting Ling (qq.v.) in 1955 and Wu Tsu-kuang and Hsiao Ch'ien in 1957. He served as vice president of the Sino-Mongolian Friendship Association in 1958. That October, he was appointed to the board of editors of *Shou-huo* [harvest]. In August 1960 he became vice chairman of the China Dramatists Association.

Apart from abortive attempts to rewrite his early plays according to Marxist tenets, Ts'ao Yü remained creatively inactive until 1956, when his first new play in ten years, *Ming-lang-ti t'ien* [a brighter day], was staged in Peking. The plot concerns a bacteriologist on the staff of the former Peking Union Medical College, now transformed on Communist lines, who volunteers for the Korean front when germ warfare shatters his belief in the dedication of the scientist. This play was awarded a prize by the Central People's Government, although by contemporary Western standards both the dialogue and stage production were undistinguished and were marked by obsessive anti-American propaganda. In 1958 he published *Ying-ch'un chi* [welcome, spring], miscellaneous essays of his collected from newspapers and periodicals. In 1962, in collaboration with other writers, he published the five-act historical drama *Tan-chien p'ien* [Kou-chien's revenge] based on the legend of the struggle between King Fu-ch'a of Wu and King Kou-chien of Yüeh in pre-Ch'in times and the eventual conquest of Wu by Yüeh after many defeats and humiliations. Selections of Ts'ao Yü's plays, published under the title *Ts'ao Yü chü-pen hsüan*, were published in Peking and elsewhere in 1952, 1954, and 1961.

Ts'ao Yü's reputation as a dramatist rests on his early plays, which were probably the most significant contribution of any single writer to the modern or Western-style Chinese drama (hua-chü). Although his early promise was not fulfilled in later years, his youthful achievements have become theater history. *Lei-yü*, his masterpiece, is a long four-act drama with prologue and epilogue. It depicts the disintegration of a wealthy middle-class family through the adultery of various members, whose spiritual destruction is dramatically accented by setting the action of the play against the physical menace of a gathering storm. The characterization is clever, the dialogue is convincing, and the plot is well constructed. These three elements were the dominating factors in all of Ts'ao Yü's plays, which also owed a great deal of their stage success to their author's skill in adapting modern Western stage methods to Chinese themes. Henrik Ibsen and John Galsworthy inspired his realism as did the Greek dramatists' somber sense of fatalism, which runs through all of Ts'ao Yü's work. By his emphasis on human tragedy and degradation, Ts'ao Yü exposed the corruption of society, but he also held out the promise of redemption. In *Jih-ch'u*, for example, he tells the story of a girl whose life is spent among the evils and temptations of the city and who is about to attempt suicide when her faithful lover arrives from the country to encourage her to face a new future. Family revenge and murder color the theme of *Yüan-yeh*, in which the dramatist symbolizes human struggle against fate through tortuous family complications arising from the arranged marriage system. *Pei-ching jen* is a satire on the decadence of traditional family life and the ineffectiveness of the student who has returned from study abroad. Beneath the Chinese theme is a suggested condemnation of the whole civilization. *Shui-pien* concerns a woman doctor who reforms a corrupt wartime hospital, where her son, a resistance hero, undergoes a serious operation. In this conflict of public duty and personal emotion, Ts'ao Yü symbolizes the regeneration of China. *Chia* is a stage tragedy of unfulfilled love and a condemnation of traditional Chinese ethics.

Ts'ao Yü had a perceptive grasp of Chinese psychology, and his characters sprang to life for his audiences. When he wrote his first play, the modern Chinese theater movement was in a period of active expansion, its days of pioneering experiments having ended. Receptive middle-class intellectual audiences had grown enormously in the major cities. With this potential support, Ts'ao Yü, with his talent for uncompromising realism dramatically stated and backed up by a sound practical knowledge of stage requirements, was assured of immediate success. Besides his main works, Ts'ao Yü wrote several one-act plays and made some translations, of which the most important was Shakespeare's *Romeo and Juliet*, produced during the Sino-Japanese war.

Ts'ao Yü married Cheng Hsiu, a fellow student at Tsinghua and the daughter of a jurist.

Wan Fu-lin   萬 福 麟
T. Shou-shan   壽 山

Wan Fu-lin (1880–July 1951), Manchurian military commander who served as military governor of Heilungkiang in 1929–31. He commanded the Fifty-third Army from 1932 to 1938, when he was charged with dereliction of duty. In 1941 he became a member of the Military Affairs Commission.

The Nungan district of Kirin province was the native place of Wan Fu-lin. Little is known of his family background or early years except that he began his career as a soldier in Manchuria. By 1906 he had risen from the ranks to become a patrol officer in a unit of the Fengtien cavalry forces. He later rose through the battalion and regimental commander grades and received command of the 57th Brigade of the 29th Division. In 1921 Wu Chün-sheng, commander of the 29th Division in Manchuria, was named by Chang Tso-lin (q.v.) to be military governor of Heilungkiang province. Wan Fu-lin, still heading the 57th Brigade, was assigned to command the Harbin-Manchouli sector of the Chinese Eastern Railway guard forces and the garrison in the Manchouli-Hailar area.

During the early 1920's Wan commanded the 17th Division and headed peace preservation forces in Heilungkiang. In 1926 he was given command of the Eighth Army, with concurrent authority over the 17th Division. The following year, when the combined forces of Chang Tso-lin and Wu P'ei-fu (q.v.) took action against the Kuominchün of Feng Yü-hsiang (q.v.), Wan campaigned against Fu Tso-yi (q.v.) in north China. Wu Chün-sheng, Wan Fu-lin's senior officer in the Manchurian military forces, was among the Northeastern officials who accompanied Chang Tso-lin on his retreat from north China in June 1928. Wu died in the bomb explosion that killed Chang Tso-lin and others when their train was blown up near Mukden on the return journey. Chang Tso-lin's eldest son, Chang Hsueh-liang (q.v.), succeeded to his position, and Wan Fu-lin then was named acting military affairs commissioner of Heilungkiang, succeeding Wu Chün-sheng. In December 1928 Chang Hsueh-liang pledged the allegiance of Manchuria to the new National Government at Nanking. The situation in the Northeast remained unstable, however, for Chang Hsueh-liang's rise to power brought him into direct conflict with his father's former chief of staff, Yang Yü-t'ing (q.v.). Chang resolved the issue by ordering Yang's execution in January 1929. The ensuing consolidation of the Manchurian power structure left Chang Hsueh-liang's authority resting on three main supports: Wan Fu-lin in Heilungkiang, Chang Tso-hsiang in Kirin, and T'ang Yü-lin in Jehol. Chang Hsueh-liang himself controlled Liaoning province in southern Manchuria. Chang (chairman), Wan, T'ang, and Chang Tso-hsiang constituted the new Northeast Political Council. Wan Fu-lin also was named deputy commander, under Chang Hsueh-liang, of the Northeast Border Defense Army and was confirmed as military head of Heilungkiang. He was usually at loggerheads with Chang Yin-huai, the civil governor of Heilungkiang.

In 1930, at the time of the so-called northern coalition against Chiang Kai-shek (see Feng Yü-hsiang; Yen Hsi-shan), Wan Fu-lin followed Chang Hsueh-liang in refusing to participate in that coalition. In a joint telegram to Chiang Kai-shek, Wan and Chang Tso-hsiang declared their allegiance to and support of the National Government at Nanking. Despite verbal protestations of loyalty to Nanking, Chang Hsueh-liang in September 1930 attempted to capitalize on the situation by moving Northeastern troops south of the Great Wall and into Hopei province. Some of Wan Fu-lin's troops were moved into north China in this operation, and a measure of political agreement, based on military realities, was reached between Chang Hsueh-liang and Chiang Kai-shek.

Worsening Sino-Japanese relations in Manchuria reached a critical stage in the following year. In September 1931, only a year after Chang Hsueh-liang's intervention in north China, the Japanese Kwantung Army began the occupation of Manchuria with the so-called Mukden Incident. At the time of the Japanese attack, Chang Hsueh-liang, many of his senior officers, and some 100,000 Northeastern troops were in north China. Wan Fu-lin was in Peiping with Chang Hsueh-liang, having left affairs in Heilungkiang in the hands of his feckless son, Wan Hai-p'eng. Instead of returning to his post, Wan Fu-lin designated Ma Chan-shan (q.v.), garrison commander at Taheiho on the Amur River, to take military action on his behalf. The Japanese occupation quickly progressed from Liaoning to Kirin province, and the invading forces soon began to exert heavy pressure on Heilungkiang. Chinese strategic policy in this crisis, determined by Nanking, was one of non-resistance to the Japanese aggression. Wan Fu-lin did not return to Manchuria to take action against the Japanese, and in due course the authorities at Nanking named Ma Chan-shan to succeed him as acting governor of Heilungkiang.

Tacit acceptance by Nanking and the Northeastern leaders of the probable durability of Japanese occupation of Manchuria then led to certain organizational changes in north China. Chang Hsueh-liang emerged from the debacle with his reputation badly damaged. In August 1932 the Kuomintang authorities accepted Chang's resignation as pacification commander at Peiping. Chang was assigned to new positions at Peiping, though these did nothing to compensate for the loss of his homeland. Wan Fu-lin was named to membership on the new Peiping branch of the Military Affairs Commission, serving under Chang Hsueh-liang. Also in 1932, in connection with the reorganization of Manchurian forces in north China, Wan's troops were reorganized as the Fifty-third army, composed of three infantry divisions, one cavalry division, and an artillery brigade.

The reorganized military establishment was soon put to the test when Japanese military planning turned to Jehol province. There the main responsibility rested with the governor of Jehol, T'ang Yü-lin, but Wan Fu-lin's Fifty-third Army also was assigned to participate in the defense. Late in February 1933 the Japanese issued an ultimatum to Chang Hsueh-liang and the National Government at Nanking demanding the withdrawal of all Chinese troops from Jehol. This action was followed by a rapid advance of Manchoukuo-Japanese forces. The Northeastern defense collapsed almost at once, and Japanese occupation of Jehol province was completed in about a week. Chang Hai-p'eng, formerly a close associate of Wan Fu-lin, became the new governor of Jehol under Manchoukuo-Japanese administration. Under

heavy political pressure, Chang Hsueh-liang met with Chiang Kai-shek at Paoting in March 1933, submitted his resignation, and transferred control of his remaining troops to Chiang.

With the loss of Manchuria and Jehol to the Japanese and the departure of Chang Hsueh-liang from the political scene, Wan Fu-lin associated himself with the new Chinese structure of power in north China, where the situation deteriorated under steady Japanese pressure. For a time he served under Ho Ying-ch'in (q.v.), who took over the Peiping branch of the Military Affairs Commission; and in 1935 he became a member of the Hopei-Chahar Political Affairs Commission under Sung Che-yuan (q.v.). When Chang Hsueh-liang returned to China and was assigned to handle anti-Communist operations in the northwest, a portion of Wan Fu-lin's Fifty-third Army was transferred to the Shensi-Kansu area. In December 1936, at the time of Chang Hsueh-liang's arrest of Chiang Kai-shek at Sian, Wan's position became equivocal. Wan then sent a telegram to Nanking to voice loyalty to the Kuomintang (he had become a member of the Central Executive Committee) and to assert his willingness to urge his former chief to release Chiang.

When the Sino-Japanese war broke out in July 1937, Japanese forces quickly drove southward along the Peiping-Hankow rail line. Wan Fu-lin's Fifty-third Army, based at Paoting, performed no better than it had in Jehol and soon suffered heavy losses and defeat. In January 1938 Wan was among a number of Nationalist commanders charged with dereliction of duty (*see* Han Fu-chü), but he escaped serious punishment. The remnants of his military command were virtually wiped out in the fighting in the Wuhan sector in 1938, and Wan retired to Chungking with neither troops nor honor.

Perhaps because of personal connections with Ho Ying-ch'in, minister of war in the National Government, and other senior Nationalist military officers, Wan Fu-lin regained a measure of authority during the wartime period. In 1941 he was made a member of the Military Affairs Commission at Chungking. After the Japanese surrender in 1945, Chiang Kai-shek's initial effort was to establish firm National Government control of postwar affairs in Manchuria and to eradicate the authority of indigenous Northeastern leaders. When the conflict with the Communists for control of that critical region ran into difficulties, however, Chiang belatedly attempted to enlist a number of Northeastern leaders to buttress his cause. In 1948 Wan Fu-lin was thus named chairman of the political affairs commission of the Generalissimo's Northeastern headquarters. But the Nationalist effort was already nearing its end; and all Manchuria had been lost to the Communists by the late months of that year.

After the collapse of Nationalist authority on the mainland in 1949, Wan Fu-lin retreated to Taiwan, where he was appointed to membership on the National Policy Advisory Committee. He died in July 1951 at Taichung, Taiwan, at the age of 71.

Wang, C. C.: *see* WANG CHING-CH'UN.

Wang Chao-ming: *see* WANG CHING-WEI.

Wang Chen					王震

Wang Chen (1909–), Chinese Communist guerrilla leader and political commissar who was one of the leading figures in the political-military administration of the Sinkiang region in 1949–53. In 1954 he became a member of the National Defense Council at Peking, and in 1956 he was appointed minister of state farms and land reclamation. Beginning in 1966, he was a target of Red Guard criticism.

The eldest of ten children, Wang Chen was born in Liuyang, Hunan, where his father was a tenant farmer. Wang received about three years of primary education before leaving home at the age of 12. He worked in 1921 as an orderly in the army garrison at Changsha and then became a servant in the local station master's office on the Canton-Hankow railroad. This was his introduction to the life of a railroad laborer, and he worked successively as switchman, oiler, repairman, and locomotive fireman on the Canton-Hankow line.

In 1924 Wang Chen joined the railroad workers union led by the Communist Kuo Liang. In June 1925 Wang participated in a strike led by the union in protest against the May Thirtieth Incident, when British police

in the International Settlement at Shanghai fired on Chinese. After the strike ended, he joined the Kuomintang, which then was preparing for the Northern Expedition. He became increasingly active in union affairs, and, at the age of 16, he was elected to the executive committee of the Changsha branch of the Hunan General Labor Union, a branch which claimed to represent some 3,000 workers. When the National Revolutionary Army occupied Changsha in 1926, railroad workers under the leadership of the executive committee took charge of operating trains in support of the Nationalist forces.

Wang Chen joined the Chinese Communist party in 1927. He enrolled in a training class for labor leaders at Changsha which, though sponsored by the Kuomintang, was conducted by men who were Communist party members or sympathizers. In this class Wang evidently received some military training, which, though rudimentary, provided a basis for his subsequent shift from labor organizing to soldiering. In May 1927 he was wounded in the anti-Communist coup at Changsha led by Hsü K'o-hsiang, a regimental commander in the army of T'ang Sheng-chih (q.v.). The termination of the Kuomintang-Communist alliance forced the Communist-led labor movement underground. After working in Hunan for a time, Wang served in the army of Li Tsung-jen in 1928–29.

In the autumn of 1929 Wang Chen returned to his native Liuyang and participated in Communist efforts to mobilize the peasants of the area. He established a party branch at Liuyang and built up a small guerrilla force. When the central apparatus of the Chinese Communist party at Shanghai, then directed by Li Li-san (q.v.), ordered military operations against cities in the summer of 1930, Wang led his partisan band in an unsuccessful attack on Liuyang. He then joined forces with P'eng Te-huai (q.v.) in a briefly successful attack on Changsha. By this time, Wang's father had joined the Communist guerrilla forces; he fought in the skirmishes around the Changsha area until his death in 1932.

After P'eng Te-huai's retreat from Changsha, Wang Chen was ordered to eastern Hunan. Upon arrival, his force was amalgamated with other units to form the Independent 1st Division, commanded by Liu Po-ch'eng (q.v.).

Wang became a political commissar at the regimental level in the Hunan-Kiangsi border area. In November 1931 he was a delegate representing Hunan to the All-China Congress of Soviets at Juichin, Kiangsi. In 1932 he was made political commissar of the Independent 1st Division, which subsequently became the Eighth Army of P'eng Te-huai's Third Army Group. While recovering from a battle wound in the winter of 1932–33, Wang served in the Hunan-Hupeh border area as political commissar of the 22nd Division in the Sixth Red Army of Hsiao K'o (q.v.). In January 1934 Wang was a delegate to the second All-China Congress of Soviets.

Accompanied by Jen Pi-shih (q.v.), who then was serving as political commissar of the Sixth Red Army, Hsiao K'o and Wang Chen started on the Long March in July 1934, three months before the main body of Communist forces left the central soviet base in Kiangsi. In October, the Sixth Red Army joined forces in Kweichow with the Second Red Army of Ho Lung (q.v.) to form the Second Front Army, with Ho Lung as commander and Jen Pi-shih as political commissar. The Second Front Army established a base in the Hunan-Hupeh-Szechwan-Kweichow border district before moving on. Wang Chen reportedly was responsible for the successful negotiations with Miao groups in Kweichow that eased the way for the march through that province. The Second Front Army joined the Fourth Front Army of Chang Kuo-t'ao and Hsü Hsiang-ch'ien (qq.v.) at Kantzu, Sikang, in June 1936, and the two forces marched on to Shensi, arriving at the Communist base in northern Shensi in October.

After the outbreak of the Sino-Japanese war in 1937, the Communist forces in the northwest were reorganized as the Eighth Route Army, composed of three divisions, Wang Chen, then only about 27, became commander of the 359th Brigade in Ho Lung's 120th Division. Wang's troops, spreading out in Shansi and Hopei, became nuclei around which local guerrilla units were formed to harass the Japanese and to extend Communist influence. In the winter of 1939 Ho Lung assigned Wang Chen and his troops to the Shensi-Kansu-Ninghsia region to defend the central Communist base. Wang apparently remained near Yenan for four years, with his troops stationed

along the line from Yülin through Michih to Suite in northeast Shensi. In 1944 he was sent to the Hupeh-Honan area, where he served as a political commissar under Li Hsien-nien (q.v.) and helped develop the soviet area in the Hupeh-Honan-Anhwei-Hunan-Kiangsi border region. Shortly before the war ended, Wang led a southward march into Kwangtung. When the Japanese surrendered, he withdrew to Hupeh again.

During the postwar negotiations between the Nationalists and the Chinese Communists, Wang Chen was a member of the Hankow field team of the Peiping Executive Headquarters. When negotiations failed and civil war broke out, he assumed responsibility for the defense of the Yenan area. In 1946–47 he was chief of staff of the Shensi-Kansu-Ninghsia and Shansi-Suiyuan military districts and commander of the central Shensi garrison headquarters. In 1948–49 he was commander of the 2nd Column of the Northwest People's Liberation Army (later the First Field Army).

After Communist troops moved into Sinkiang in 1949, Wang Chen became one of the leading figures in the political-military administration of that complex area. Between 1949 and 1952 he was secretary of the Sinkiang sub-bureau of the party's Central Committee. He also was deputy commander (1949–50) and then acting commander (1951–52) of the Sinkiang Military District, a member of the Sinkiang provincial government council, and a member of the Northwest Military and Administrative Committee. When the Central People's Government was reorganized in 1954, Wang was transferred to Peking. He represented the People's Liberation Army at the National People's Congress and became a member of the National Defense Council. From May 1954 to August 1957 he also was commander and political commissar of the Railway Corps of the People's Liberation Army. He was raised from alternate to full membership in the Central Committee of the Chinese Communist party in 1956. That May, he became minister of state farms and land reclamation. From October to December 1957 he led an agricultural-technical delegation to Japan. He was appointed a member of the Sungari River Planning Commission in January 1958 and vice chairman of the Committee for Receiving and Resettling Returned Overseas Chinese in February 1960. In 1958 and

1960 he represented Heilungkiang at the second and third National People's congresses. Beginning in 1966, Wang was a target of Red Guard criticism in the so-called Cultural Revolution.

Wang Chen married four times. He reportedly had three sons by his fourth wife.

Wang Cheng-t'ing　　王 正 廷
T. Ju-t'ang　　　　儒 堂
West. C. T. Wang

Wang Cheng-t'ing (25 July 1882–21 May 1961), known as C. T. Wang, minister of foreign affairs and one-time acting premier of the Peking government in the early 1920's. He served as minister of foreign affairs in the National Government in 1928–31. In 1937–38 he was ambassador to the United States.

Fenghua, Chekiang, was the birthplace of C. T. Wang. His father had become a Methodist minister in suburban Shanghai shortly before his birth. The young Wang received his early education at local Fenghua schools and then at missionary schools in Shanghai. In 1895, at the age of 13, he entered Anglo-Chinese College at Tientsin, and the following year he matriculated at the preparatory school of Peiyang University. At the time of the Boxer Uprising in 1900 he left his studies to teach at Anglo-Chinese College and then went to Hunan, where he taught in the Provincial High School at Changsha until 1905. He then went to Japan to study, and while in Tokyo he served as secretary of the Chinese YMCA.

In July 1907 C. T. Wang went to the United States, where he enrolled at the University of Michigan. The following year, he transferred to Yale University. He served as president of the Chinese Students' Alliance and as traveling secretary in charge of religious work among Chinese students in the United States. At the time of his graduation from Yale in 1910, he was elected to Phi Beta Kappa. After a year of graduate study, he returned to China in June 1911.

Upon arrival at Shanghai, Wang accepted a position as secretary of the local YMCA. One of his chief functions was to help students returning from abroad to find employment. Soon, however, his life was changed by the revolution of 1911. After the Wuchang revolt of 10 October, a republican regime was established at Wuchang with Li Yuan-hung (q.v.) at its head. The revolutionary Hu Ying was appointed chief of the regime's department of diplomatic affairs. Because Hu lacked knowledge in this field and spoke no foreign language, he sent an agent to Shanghai to obtain the services of an interpreter-assistant. Li Teng-hui (T. H. Lee), a Yale alumnus who was serving as principal of Futan College in Shanghai, recommended C. T. Wang, who accepted the appointment. Wang arrived at Wuhan in late November, when the imperial forces recaptured Hanyang and threatened Wuchang. Because of the fluctuating political situation, Wang's appointment was changed, and he became a representative of Hupeh to the conference held at Hankow to organize a provisional national government. On 2 December, he was elected to a committee charged with drafting an organizational outline for the government. He was one of the signers of the resulting Organizational Law when it was adopted on 3 December. Soon afterwards, he and Hu Ying were designated representatives of the Wuchang regime to accompany T'ang Shao-yi (q.v.), then serving as head of an imperial delegation, to Shanghai for negotiations with Wu T'ing-fang (q.v.), representing the southern revolutionaries.

After Yuan Shih-k'ai succeeded Sun Yat-sen as provisional president of the republican government, C. T. Wang served at Peking as vice chairman of the Senate, under Lin Sen (q.v.). On 29 March 1912 Wang was appointed vice minister of industry and commerce by T'ang Shao-yi, the premier. Because Ch'en Ch'i-mei (q.v.) remained in Shanghai and did not assume the ministership, Wang was appointed acting minister of industry and commerce in May. He outlined his policies on 13 May to the cabinet, but before he could put any programs into effect, T'ang Shao-yi resigned the premiership in June. In mid-July Wang also resigned and went to Shanghai. He returned to Peking in April 1913 to serve as vice speaker of the Senate, under Chang Chi (q.v.), and as chairman of the committee for review of the constitutional convention. He also became the Kuomintang's representative at Peking and director of the Peking headquarters of the national railway development administration, then headed by Sun Yat-sen. Wang remained in Peking until the Kuomintang was outlawed after the so-called second revolution of 1913 (*see* Li Lieh-chün). He then went to Shanghai, where he became general secretary of the national committee of the YMCA and governor of the Eighty-first District (China and Hong Kong) of the Rotary International.

With the death of Yuan Shih-k'ai in June 1916 and the accession of Li Yuan-hung (q.v.) to the presidency, the Parliament was reconvened at Peking. Wang again served as vice speaker of the Senate, holding that post until June 1917, when the Parliament was dissolved. He then went to Canton, where he served as vice speaker of the rump parliament which established a military government at Canton, with Sun Yat-sen at its head. After that government's reorganization in April 1918 and Sun Yat-sen's withdrawal to Shanghai, Wang and two other representatives of the Canton regime were sent to the United States to seek diplomatic recognition and financial aid. While in the United States, Wang was designated to represent the Canton government on China's delegation, headed by Lu Cheng-hsiang (q.v.), to the Paris Peace Conference. C. T. Wang and V. K. Wellington Koo (Ku Wei-chün, q.v.) played prominent roles in the presentation of the case for the return of Shantung to China and in the decision not to sign the Treaty of Versailles because it provided for the transfer to Japan of Germany's treaty rights in Shantung.

Upon his return to China in February 1920, C. T. Wang established residence in Shanghai. In 1920–21 he established a brokerage house, an import-export company, and the Hua Feng Cotton Mill at Woosung. He was appointed president of China College at Peking in 1921, and he retained that chiefly honorary post until the 1940's. About this time, he became an ardent advocate of the sinification of the various Christian clerical hierarchies in China. In 1921 he reentered political life as a member of the Chinese delegation to the Washington Conference. The Nine-Power treaty of February 1922 and the settlement of the Shantung issue were measures of the success of the Chinese delegation, which was headed by Sao-ke Alfred Sze (Shih Chao-chi, q.v.) and which also included Wellington Koo. Wang returned to China in March 1922 to become head of the Shantung Rehabilitation Commission. In June,

he was made China's chief representative on a Sino-Japanese commission charged with handling problems in connection with the transfer of political authority in Shantung. He also served as commissioner for takeover of the Kiaochow-Tsinan railway and as commissioner of the Tsingtao commercial port.

At the end of November 1922 C. T. Wang succeeded Wellington Koo as minister of foreign affairs at Peking. Early in December, he went briefly to Tsingtao to complete arrangements for the creation of a Chinese administration there. From mid-December 1922 to mid-January 1923 Wang served as acting premier at Peking. He relinquished that post to Chang Shao-tseng and refused Chang's offer of the justice portfolio in the new cabinet. In March 1923 the Peking government gave him responsibility for handling Sino-Soviet relations. After extensive negotiations with Soviet envoy Leo M. Karakhan beginning in September 1923, two agreements were signed in March 1924. Among the provisions were the immediate establishment of Sino-Soviet diplomatic relations and the setting up of a provisional administration for the Chinese Eastern Railway. Because the agreements contained no provisions for the cancellation of Soviet-Mongol treaties or the withdrawal of Red Army forces from Outer Mongolia, the Chinese cabinet refused to ratify the agreements. Wellington Koo, then foreign minister, repudiated Wang's signature and dismissed him. Ironically enough, Koo signed an agreement with similar provisions on 31 May.

Wang left Peking in March 1924 to become managing director of the Liuhokou Mining Company in Honan. He was recalled to Peking by Feng Yü-hsiang (q.v.) at the time of Feng's October 1924 coup. Wang served in the interim cabinet of Huang Fu (q.v.) as minister of foreign affairs and minister of finance, resigning on 24 November after Tuan Ch'i-jui (q.v.) assumed office as provisional chief executive. Wang was politically inactive until the spring of 1925, when he again was given responsibility for Sino-Soviet diplomatic relations. He also was appointed a delegate to the special tariff conference which ended in March 1926 with a preliminary agreement guaranteeing China tariff autonomy by 1 January 1929. In the Peking cabinet reorganization of 31 December 1925 Wang again became minister of foreign affairs, and he held that post until 4 March 1926. That September, having also shed his Sino-Soviet responsibilities, he returned to private life in Shanghai.

In Shanghai, Wang became chairman of the board of directors of the Liuhokou Mining Company, chairman of the Chinese Ratepayers Association of Shanghai, president of the National Highways Association, and chairman of the Far Eastern Olympics. In August 1927, on Feng Yü-hsiang's recommendation, he was made managing director of the Lunghai railway administration. It was also through Feng that Wang established ties with Chiang Kai-shek and the National Government at Nanking. In 1928 Wang became a member and then chairman of the Central Political Council's foreign affairs committee. He succeeded Huang Fu as minister of foreign affairs in June. By March 1929 he had reached a settlement of the May Third Incident at Tsinan (*see* Ho Yao-tsu) in 1928; and in June 1929 Japan formally recognized the National Government at Nanking. Also in June 1929 a crisis arose as a result of Nationalist moves against Soviet interests in Manchuria. A Chinese search of Soviet consular premises at Harbin and arrests of consular personnel at the end of May were followed by Soviet diplomatic protests. On 11 June, Wang offered to have an investigation made. On 10 July, however, the Nationalists seized the Chinese Eastern Railway and Soviet shipping interests on the Sungari River. Wang issued a statement asserting that the National Government did not intend to solve the problem of the Chinese Eastern Railway by force, that it had assumed temporary administrative control of the railway because the Soviet administrators had abandoned their duties, and that it hoped to maintain friendly relations with the Soviet Union. Soviet military pressure eventually forced the National Government to sign the Khabarovsk Protocol of 22 December 1929, restoring the *status quo ante* with regard to Soviet rights and interests in the Chinese Eastern Railway and in navigation of the Sungari River.

C. T. Wang was foreign minister from June 1928 until September 1931, during which time he effected more than 40 important treaties and agreements. By mid-1930 he had negotiated the restitution of Weihaiwei by Great Britain, an agreement with France regarding Tonkin, tariff agreements with Japan and 12 other countries, and commercial treaties with Greece, Poland, and Czechoslovakia. His aims were tariff autonomy and the elimination of other inequities in China's position with reference to other nations. Despite these achievements, popular opinion turned against him after the Japanese invasion of Mukden in September 1931. Student opinion in particular blamed him for the National Government's policy of non-resistance and for its failure to persuade the League of Nations to take forceful action. On 28 September, a large group of students invaded Wang's office, demanded an immediate declaration of war against Japan, assaulted Wang, and wrecked the premises. Foreign office personnel intervened, removed Wang to a gunboat, and took him to Shanghai for hospitalization. On 30 September, the National Government announced his resignation.

After his recovery, C. T. Wang did not take an active part in politics for a time, although he retained his membership in the State Council, the Central Political Council, and the Central Committee of the Kuomintang. In August 1936 he was appointed ambassador to the United States. He did not reach Washington until May 1937, by which time the outbreak of the Sino-Japanese war had put a new complexion on his mission. He retained that post until September 1938, when he was succeeded by Hu Shih. Wang then went to Hong Kong, where he helped the Bank of Communications shift some of its capital and property to Manila. About six months later, he moved to Chungking, where he spent the rest of the war in virtual retirement. In late 1944 he was appointed chairman of the Executive Yuan's war crimes investigation commission, and after the Japanese surrendered he served at Shanghai in that capacity. He also became a member of the Shanghai Municipal Council and the Legislative Yuan.

C. T. Wang's wife died in 1944, and in 1946 he married a daughter of Sir Shouson Chow (Chou Ch'ang-ling, q.v.). When the Chinese Communists won control of the mainland in 1949, Wang did not follow the National Government to Taiwan. In 1952 he established residence in Hong Kong, where he served as chairman of the board of directors of the Pacific Insurance Company. He died at Hong Kong on 21 May 1961.

Wang Chia-hsiang   王 家 祥

Wang Chia-hsiang (1907–), Russian-trained Communist leader who directed the general political department of the Chinese Workers and Peasants Red Army in Kiangsi and headed the Academy for Military and Political Cadres in Yenan. In 1949–50 he was ambassador to the Soviet Union, and in 1956 he was elected to the Secretariat of the Chinese Communist party.

Born into a relatively well-to-do farming family in Chinghsien, Anhwei, Wang Chia-hsiang received his early education at missionary schools. In 1924, while an upperclassman at St. Jacob's Senior High School in Wuhu, Anhwei, he led a student protest against compulsory Bible reading and prayer. This activity was part of an anti-Christian movement in China in the 1920's which, spurred on by the May Thirtieth Incident in Shanghai in 1925, culminated in the formation of the Anti-Christian Federation of China and the closing of many missionary schools, including St. Jacob's.

Wang Chia-hsiang subsequently went to Shanghai and enrolled at Shanghai University, where he came under the influence of such Communist instructors as Ch'ü Ch'iu-pai and Yün Tai-ying (qq.v.). He soon joined the Chinese Communist party, which selected him to go to the Soviet Union to study at the Communist University for Toilers of the East and the Red Institute for Teachers. Wang spent three years at Moscow, where he came to know Ch'en Shao-yü and Ch'in Pang-hsien (qq.v.). Thus, although he never studied formally with Pavel Mif at Sun Yat-sen University, he was regarded as part of the group known as the 28 Bolsheviks.

After attending the Sixth National Congress of the Chinese Communist party at Moscow in 1928, Wang Chia-hsiang returned to China by way of Europe. He then worked in Shanghai as an underground agent of the Chinese Communist party. According to a Japanese source, he did liaison work for the All-China Federation of Labor and propaganda activity among the Shanghai textile workers. By 1930 he had become a member of the Kiangsu provincial committee of the Chinese Communist party.

About this time, he founded the *Workers' Bulletin*.

In the summer of 1930 Pavel Mif was made Comintern delegate to China. He arrived in Shanghai accompanied by Ch'en Shao-yü and several of his other Chinese protégés. In the ensuing intra-party struggle, Wang Chia-hsiang supported this group's bid for power and opposed the leadership of Li Li-san (q.v.). The 28 Bolsheviks won control of the central party organs in January 1931, at which time Wang was elected to the Central Committee. Later that year, he also received membership in the Political Bureau. In November 1931 he participated in the All-China Congress of Soviets. He was elected to the central executive council of the central soviet government at Juichin, and he later became that government's commissioner of foreign affairs. Because the regime had virtually no foreign dealings, he occupied himself with problems of ideological training and control of the Chinese Workers and Peasants Red Army. As vice chairman of the military council and director of the army's general political department, he set up a system of political work in the army. His achievement was such that one Communist source praised him as "the soul of the Workers and Peasants Red Army."

In 1934 Wang Chia-hsiang was wounded in a Nationalist air raid. He participated in the Long March despite considerable physical pain and difficulty. After arriving in northern Shensi in October 1935, he went to the Soviet Union for medical treatment. Wang returned to China in 1937 when the Sino-Japanese war began. He founded Anti-Japanese Military and Political University and later headed the Academy for Military and Political Cadres and the staff of the Eighth Route Army's magazine. He was responsible for the training of hundreds of cadres who were sent to various parts of China and for the syllabi used in teaching them. In 1941 he published a pamphlet entitled *The Chinese Communist Party and the Revolutionary War*, which was circulated widely. He contracted tuberculosis about 1941 and had to resign his posts. By 1945 he was well enough to serve as secretary of the party Secretariat. At the Seventh National Congress of the Chinese Communist party, held at Yenan in 1945, he became an alternate member of the Central Committee. He was promoted to full membership in 1946.

At war's end, Wang was one of the first high-level Communist officials to reach Manchuria, where he headed the propaganda bureau of the party's Northeast bureau. There he met and married Chu Hsi, a medical doctor who in 1948 was superintendent of the Harbin Municipal Hospital. Wang remained in Manchuria until September 1949, when he went to Peiping as a Chinese Communist party delegate to the Chinese People's Political Consultative Conference. He was elected to the conference's National Committee.

With the establishment of the Central People's Government in October 1949, Wang Chia-hsiang was appointed ambassador to the Soviet Union and deputy foreign minister. In Moscow, he participated in the negotiations, along with Mao Tse-tung and Chou En-lai (qq.v.), which led to the signing, on 14 February 1950, of the 30-year Sino-Soviet Treaty of Friendship, Alliance, and Mutual Assistance. He was recalled to Peking for reasons of health in the spring of 1951 and was replaced by Chang Wen-t'ien (q.v.). He accompanied Liu Shao-ch'i (q.v.) to the Nineteenth Congress of the Communist Party of the Soviet Union in October 1952, Chou En-lai to the Geneva Conference in April-June 1954, and Chu Teh (q.v.) to the Twentieth Congress of the Communist Party of the Soviet Union in February 1956. In 1957 he went with Chou En-lai to Moscow, Warsaw, and Budapest on a mission to seek the reestablishment of Communist bloc solidarity. That November, he accompanied Mao Tse-tung to Moscow for the fortieth anniversary celebrations of the Russian Revolution. When Nikita Khrushchev visited Peking in July-August 1958, Wang took part in the official talks with the Soviet premier. The four other Chinese participants in these discussions were Mao Tse-tung, Chou En-lai, P'eng Te-huai, and Ch'en Yi (1901–; q.v.). In March 1959 Wang was a member of the Chinese delegation to the Third Congress of the Polish Communist party in Warsaw. After this congress, he and Wu Hsiu-ch'üan went to England for the Twenty-sixth National Congress of the British Communist party.

In addition to his many trips abroad, Wang Chia-hsiang often received foreign Communist leaders at Peking. Although he lost his foreign ministry post when the State Council was reorganized in September 1959, he continued to make official appearances in connection with the visits of foreign dignitaries. In 1956 he was elected to the Secretariat of the Chinese Communist party, and he represented the party at the Chinese People's Political Consultative Conferences in 1959 and 1964. His participation in government and party affairs was gradually curtailed in the 1950's and early 1960's by failing health.

Wang Ching-ch'un   王 景 春
T.   Chao-hsi   兆 熙
West. C. C. Wang

Wang Ching-ch'un (30 June 1882–16 June 1956), known as C. C. Wang, had a long and distinguished career in railroad administration in China during the period before 1928. From 1931 until 1949 he served abroad as director of the Chinese Government Purchasing Commission in England.

Born into a Christian family in Luanhsien, Chihli (Hopei), Wang Ching-ch'un received his early education at a school operated by the local Methodist mission, where his father, Wang Zy-yan, served as a pastor. When the Boxer Uprising engulfed the Luanhsien district in 1900, Wang took refuge in Peking. Because he was proficient in English, he found employment there as an interpreter at the American legation. In 1904 he made his first trip to the United States, serving as a representative of north China merchants at the International Exposition held at St. Louis. K. P. Ch'en (Ch'en Kuang-fu, q.v.), was also in St. Louis at that time attached to the Hupeh provincial delegation to the exposition. After Wang completed his mission, he remained in the United States, with financial aid from the Chinese government, for further education.

After studying science at Ohio Wesleyan University in 1905–6, Wang went on to Yale. He was graduated with honors in civil engineering in 1908. Wang then moved to the University of Illinois, where he gained an M.A. in 1909 and a Ph.D. in economics and railway administration in 1911. His thesis, which dealt with "Legislative Regulation of Railway Finance in England," was later published in the series entitled Illinois Studies in the Social Sciences. While a graduate student at the

University of Illinois, Wang won recognition from the prominent Chinese diplomat Wu T'ing-fang (q.v.), who awarded him a special scholarship. Wang was also active in Chinese student affairs in the United States, serving as president of the Chinese Students Alliance in 1907–8 and as editor of the *Chinese Students' Monthly* in 1908–9. During his last two years at Illinois, he was a fellow in railway administration and lecturer on commerce and Oriental history.

Wang Ching-ch'un's sojourn in the United States from 1904 to 1911 coincided with the formative years of the republican revolutionary movement led by Sun Yat-sen. After returning to China by way of Europe, Wang was appointed by Sun Yat-sen to work as a foreign affairs secretary in the newly inaugurated provisional republican government at Nanking. When Sun Yat-sen relinquished the provisional presidency, Wang resigned. In 1912 he began his career as a professional railway administrator when he was named vice director of the Peking-Mukden railroad. In 1913 he was transferred to the post of vice director of the Peking-Hankow line. It was mainly through Wang's recommendation that the ministry of railways at Peking in 1912 created a special commission, with Wang as acting chairman, to work on the problem of unification of accounts and statistics for China's rail system. The commission invited H. C. Adams, professor of economics at the University of Michigan, to come to China as its principal Western adviser. The group's investigations quickly confirmed the existence of serious administrative and fiscal confusion, due principally to the fact that, prior to the First World War, China's railroads had been built with foreign loans that represented diverse national interests, operating procedures, and languages. After more than seventy meetings, the commission formulated nine sets of accounting and statistical regulations to govern capital investment, operating receipts and expenditures, annual budgets, statistics on rolling stock, and other basic matters. The commission also prescribed standard procedure and format for annual reports on railway operations; these came into effect in 1915. With these new regulations, it became possible for the ministry of communications at Peking to exercise effective administrative control over China's rail system and to simplify and streamline operations.

As a result of his service as acting chairman of the special unification commission, Wang was assigned in 1914 to direct the department of railway finance and accounts of the ministry of communications. Two years later he became controller general of the ministry. From 1917 to 1919 he served as managing director of the Peking-Mukden and Peking-Hankow railroad lines. His professional competence and personal integrity soon won him the confidence of Chinese colleagues and subordinates and also the respect of foreign staff and associates. Despite political and military strife in China, China's national railway service began to attain a measure of professionalism and administrative integrity; and Wang's public spirit did much to raise morale in that service.

Wang Ching-ch'un was assigned as technical expert attached to the Chinese delegation to the 1919 Paris Peace Conference when it was envisaged that railroad questions in Shantung province would be on the agenda. Also in 1919, because of the chaotic situation that prevailed in Siberia after the Bolshevik revolution, an Inter-Allied Technical Board was established to manage the Chinese Eastern Railway in Manchuria. Wang was named to represent China on that board. In November 1920, after the return of the Chinese Eastern Railway to China under a special agreement, the Chinese government at Peking named Wang deputy director general of that line. After a year (1921) as chief of the railway department of the ministry of communcations, he was promoted in 1922 to director general and chairman of the board of the Chinese Eastern Railway. He held that important post until 1924, when he became special adviser to the ministry of communications. In 1927 Wang held his final governmental position in China; chief of the postal department and director general of postal services. During the 1920's Wang also represented the Chinese government at several conferences, notably the International Telegraph Conference (Paris, 1925) and the International Radio Conference (Washington, 1927). He also was active in educational and social work; he served as chairman of the board of directors of the Peking YMCA and chairman of the board of the Huiwen School in his native Luanhsien district of Hopei.

After leaving the field of railway administration, Wang went to the United States in 1928 and spent three years there as director of the Chinese Educational Mission, supervising Chinese students studying abroad. Previously, he had been associated with the work of a special committee created in 1926 to advise the Sino-British Boxer Indemnity Commission headed by Lord Willingdon. Other Chinese members of the advisory committee were V. K. Ting (Ting Wen-chiang) and Hu Shih (qq.v.). After studying the problem of British Boxer indemnity funds returned to China, the commission recommended that the bulk of these funds should be used to develop and rehabilitate China's railroads and to develop other productive enterprises, while the interest should be spent on educational and cultural undertakings. After extended deliberations, a board of trustees of the Sino-British Boxer Indemnity Fund was created in 1931.

Under the board's auspices, the Chinese Government Purchasing Commission was established in England, with Wang Ching-ch'un as managing director. Wang's principal mission after 1931 was the procurement of essential railway and other materials on behalf of the ministry of communications and the National Resources Commission. Wang and his tiny staff in London handled the purchase of materials (paid for by the British share of the Boxer indemnity) for construction of the Canton-Hankow and Nanking-Kiangsi rail lines; overhaul of the Tientsin-Pukow, Kiaochow-Tsinan, and Shanghai-Hangchow-Ningpo lines; and materials for the river ferry across the Yangtze at Nanking. These transactions involved the outlay of an estimated £7 million. In addition, his office handled transactions totaling over £5 million for the National Resources Commission, including steamships and telecommunications equipment for the ministry of communications. Wang's tasks were greatly complicated by the outbreak of full-scale war between China and Japan in 1937 and of general war in Europe beginning in 1939.

After 18 years as head of the Chinese Government Purchasing Commission in London, Wang closed his office in 1949 when the Chinese Communists established the People's Republic of China. He then moved to the United States, where he settled in Claremont, California. During retirement, Wang was given a sinecure position by the Chinese National Government as special adviser on railways attached to the Chinese Embassy at Washington. In California, he was active in Methodist activities, and he became an honorary consultant on Asian studies to the Claremont Graduate School.

Wang's primary activity during his later years, however, was the preparation of a new Chinese dictionary with romanized transcriptions of Chinese ideographs suitable for use in telegraphic communication. Because Chinese is not an alphabetical language, the so-called telegraph code system normally used in China for wireless communications identified individual Chinese ideographs by numerical compounds which were then transmitted in Morse, with coding and decoding required at each end of the process. International conventions, however, prevented acceptance of messages written in numerals for cable transmission as open messages. Wang had been concerned with this problem for many years, and as early as 1928 he had supervised preparation of a phonetic Chinese telegraphic dictionary. While in England during the Second World War, he had continued to work on an improved method for indexing Chinese ideographs. In 1940–41 he had published articles on that topic in the *Chinese Social and Political Science Review* and the *Tung-fang tsa-chih* [eastern miscellany]. In 1944 he had published in Chinese a detailed description of his so-called Sinhanzyx method of indexing characters and romanization. The system Wang developed in the United States to facilitate telegraphic transmission of Chinese messages in plain-language communications was called the Gueeyin system. Wang described it in a preliminary publication, "The Gueeyin System of Indexing," issued by the College Press of Claremont, California, in 1955. The system of indexing represented, in its author's view, an improved version of the radical system. Instead of grouping Chinese ideographs under 214 basic elements known as radicals, Wang's system presented a new method of indexing based on amalgamation of radicals, cross-entry of characters, location of characters through two radicals, and other special techniques.

Long afflicted with chronic asthma, Wang Ching-ch'un died at the Pomona Valley Community Hospital in California on 16 June 1956, only two weeks short of his seventy-fourth birthday. The local Claremont *Courier*, in its obituary notice, paid tribute to Wang as a representative of the best type of government official of pre-Communist China. "He combined the cultural background of old China with technological training in the Western world." Perhaps more notable to Chinese residents of the United States was the modest size of Wang's estate, which was taken as conclusive evidence of personal integrity.

Wang was survived by his wife, Meng Wen-jung, whom he had married in September 1903, and by two sons, Howard Wang of Toronto and David Wang of Pasadena, and two daughters, Mrs. Frances Chin of Berea, Kentucky, and Mrs. Lois Guo of Philadelphia.

Wang Ching-wei   注 精 衞
Orig. Wang Chao-ming   注 兆 銘

Wang Ching-wei (4 May 1883–10 November 1944), Kuomintang leader and intimate political associate of Sun Yat-sen. At the time of the Sino-Japanese war, after more than a decade of feuding with Chiang Kai-shek for top authority in the Kuomintang, Wang became head of a Japanese-sponsored regime established at Nanking in 1940.

Although born at Canton and generally regarded as a Cantonese, Wang Ching-wei had his ancestral home at Shaohsing, Chekiang, the native province of Chiang Kai-shek. For financial reasons his father, Wang Shu, moved south to Kwangtung in the late Ch'ing period to take a position as legal secretary, personally employed by an official of the imperial civil service. The youngest of ten children, Wang Ching-wei received his childhood education in the Chinese classics at home under his father's tutelage. The boy's ethical and aesthetic standards during his formative years were conventionally Chinese, his later reminiscences referring particularly to the philosophy of Wang Yang-ming (1472–1529) and to the poetry of T'ao Ch'ien (365–427) and Lu Yu (1125–1210). Like other sensitive young Chinese growing up in the 1890's, Wang Ching-wei, in the course of reading Chinese history, became impatient of China's weakness and resentful of the alien Manchu dynasty then ruling at Peking.

Penury was a constant dimension to life in the Wang family, for Wang Ching-wei's father was in straitened circumstances and thus was forced to continue working until he was over 70. A rapid series of deaths left the family financial situation precarious about this time. Wang's mother died when the boy was about 13; his father died a year later; and two of his three elder brothers died soon thereafter. Wang was admitted to an academy at Canton in 1898; he also worked as a tutor to help support his brothers and sisters. He continued to study independently with the help of an uncle's well-stocked library and in 1903 passed the Kwangtung provincial examination. He won a government scholarship for study in Japan the following year. Meiji Japan opened new vistas for Wang Ching-wei. In Tokyo he found a congenial group of fellow-Cantonese students, including Hu Han-min (q.v.) and others. He learned Japanese rapidly, supplemented his government stipend by doing translations, and studied constitutional law and political theory at Tokyo Law College, where he obtained a degree in 1906.

Before graduation, Wang joined the new Chinese patriotic society, the T'ung-meng-hui, formed in Japan in 1905 by Sun Yat-sen, Huang Hsing (q.v.), and other anti-Manchu activists. Elected chairman of one of the three key councils of the T'ung-meng-hui, Wang, then only 22, began a close personal association with Sun Yat-sen. In the Chinese student communities of Tokyo and Yokohama, Wang soon established a reputation as a brilliant polemicist. In November 1905 the pro-republican group in Japan established the *Min Pao* to disseminate Sun Yat-sen's precepts and to promote anti-Manchu sentiment. The T'ung-meng-hui's principal political competitor in Japan was another refugee group, led by K'ang Yu-wei and Liang Ch'i-ch'ao (qq.v.), which advocated constitutional monarchy for China. Wang Ching-wei wrote the leading article in the first issue of the *Min Pao* (10 November 1905) and soon proved himself an eloquent controversialist in a literary duel with Liang Ch'i-ch'ao. Drawing upon theories absorbed at Tokyo Law College, Wang grew in stature as an interpreter of "nationalism," later canonized as the first of Sun Yat-sen's Three People's Principles.

Sun Yat-sen was forced to leave Japan in 1907. Accompanied by Hu Han-min and Wang Ching-wei, he moved to Southeast Asia to expand the T'ung-meng-hui organization and to enlist financial support in the overseas Chinese communities. There Wang continued to demonstrate his talents not only as forceful journalist but also as persuasive public speaker on behalf of a political movement which had as yet won scant success in the effort to rid China of Manchu rule. Wang's oratorical brilliance played an important role in attracting new overseas Chinese support to the T'ung-meng-hui and in establishing new branches, the most important of which were at Singapore and Penang.

When Sun Yat-sen left Singapore for Europe in 1909, Wang returned to Japan, where he edited a short-lived clandestine edition of the revived *Min Pao*, ostensibly published in Paris by young Chinese anarchists sympathetic to Sun but actually printed in Tokyo. The Chinese revolutionaries in Japan then were greatly influenced by the ideas of Russian anarchists, many of whom had fled to Japan after the failure of the Russian revolution in 1905. Wang Ching-wei's editorial tone in this period was distinctly militant. In the 1 February 1910 issue of *Min Pao*, he wrote a fiery discourse, "On the Revolutionary Current," advocating assassination to spark the overthrow of the dynasty.

During the 1907–10 period, the T'ung-meng-hui suffered a series of setbacks. Six revolutionary attempts were suppressed by the Ch'ing government and resulted only in the arrest and execution of the leaders. In addition to these failures, the T'ung-meng-hui was faced with an internal crisis: two prominent members, Chang Ping-lin (q.v.) and T'ao Ch'eng-chang, challenged the authority of Sun Yat-sen's leadership. The prospects of the republican revolutionary cause were hardly bright. It was at this juncture that Wang Ching-wei decided to stimulate the movement by drastic measures. He decided to sacrifice himself for the good of both party and nation. Thus he journeyed incognito to Peking early in 1910 and led an attempt to assassinate the prince regent, Ts'ai-feng, by placing a bomb under a bridge over which the prince was scheduled to pass. An error on the part of the conspirators upset the plot and aroused the police, who combed the city and apprehended Wang in April 1910. When interrogated, Wang freely admitted his identity and voiced his hope that this sensational act, if consummated in the imperial capital, would rouse the Chinese people to revolution. The Manchu authorities were struck by Wang's forthright stand and courageous bearing. Moreover, the weak position of the dynasty during its final days led Ts'ai-feng to attempt to placate the revolutionaries by dealing gently with political criminals. Thus Wang was only imprisoned, though he himself had been prepared for execution and a martyr's death. When released in the wake of the Wuchang revolt in October 1911, Wang, then 28, found himself a national hero in China.

Despite his position as the golden boy of Chinese nationalism, Wang Ching-wei remained aloof from Chinese politics after the establishment of the republic. He was influenced by anarchist ideas then current in emancipated intellectual circles in China. In 1912 he helped establish the Society for the Promotion of Virtue, dedicated to the propositions that basic social reforms had to accompany political change and that China, if she were truly to create a new society, first had to build a new morality. That same year he was one of the organizers of the movement to encourage and assist Chinese students to go to France for a combined work-study program (*see* Li Shih-tseng).

Also in 1912, Wang Ching-wei married Ch'en Pi-chün (q.v.), daughter of a prosperous overseas Chinese family from Penang and ardent admirer of the dashing young revolutionary in his T'ung-meng-hui days. After their marriage in Shanghai, the couple left China on a wedding trip to the Straits Settlements and Europe. Wang spent the years of the First World War in France, intermittently involved with the training of Chinese students there but relatively uninvolved with political maneuverings at home. His relation to China during this interlude of comparative leisure and detachment was, rather, at the literary level. Wang was a member of the Nan-she, or Southern Society (*see* Liu Ya-tzu), which included many former T'ung-meng-hui members. It was the major society advocating and using traditional Chinese literary forms during the early republican period. Although a radical nationalist intellectually, Wang's connection with the Southern Society exposed a romantic stratum in his personality. His poetry, collected as the *Shuang-chao-lou shih tz'u-k'ao*, reveals an aspect of the man which is sensitive, contemplative, oriented to nature in the classical Chinese manner. Its style and serenity stand in marked contrast to the political tumult which dominated his later career.

Wang returned to China late in 1917 and joined Sun Yat-sen, who was then at Canton leading an opposition regime and attempting to rally military support. During the next seven years Wang was a member of the personal entourage which served Sun as he sought new theoretical and organizational formulae to guide the nationalist cause. The patriotic outburst stemming from the May Fourth Movement of 1919, combined with Sun Yat-sen's contacts with Soviet representatives in China after the Russian Revolution, led in 1922–23 to Sun's decision to collaborate with the infant, Comintern-dominated Communist Party of China. Although he played no direct role in the negotiations leading to the alliance between the Chinese nationalist movement and Soviet communism, Wang Ching-wei occupied a prominent political position at Canton. At the First National Congress of the Kuomintang in January 1924, he was elected second-ranking member of the Central Executive Committee, following Hu Han-min in the number of votes received.

National unification remained Sun Yat-sen's primary objective, and late in 1924 he made a final journey northward to confer with the men holding power at Peking: Chang Tso-lin, Feng Yü-hsiang, and Tuan Ch'i-jui (qq.v.). Sun and his entourage left Canton in November, with Wang Ching-wei serving as confidential Chinese secretary to the Kuomintang leader. From Shanghai, Sun proceeded to the north by way of Japan, while Wang went direct by rail to Tientsin to work out arrangements for the talks. Sun Yat-sen arrived in north China at the end of 1924, only to discover that Tuan Ch'i-jui, then chief executive at Peking, had no intention of permitting the Kuomintang to interfere in the operation of the new regime there. Sun's health was rapidly deteriorating, and in January 1925 he was admitted to the hospital of the Peking Union Medical College with cancer. After two decades of association with Sun Yat-sen, Wang Ching-wei was the most senior and trusted Kuomintang leader then in Peking. Except for Sun's young second wife, Soong Ch'ing-ling (q.v.), and his

son, Sun Fo (q.v.), probably no person was closer to the dying man than Wang. On 24 February, Wang drafted Sun's final political testament, a brief injunction to Sun's followers to carry the national revolution through to completion in accordance with the principles set forth in his major writings. Sun signed this document on 11 March 1925, the day before his death.

After Sun Yat-sen's death, it appeared that Wang Ching-wei might succeed to Sun's position as leader of the Kuomintang, though Hu Han-min and Liao Chung-k'ai (q.v.) were also contenders for the honor. Wang appeared to consolidate his supremacy when he was elected Chairman of the National Government formed at Canton in July 1925. The assassination of Liao Chung-k'ai in August placed him in an even more advantageous position, for Hu Han-min was involved vicariously in that incident and had to resign his post in the party. Thus two of Wang's political rivals were removed from competition. Chiang Kai-shek, another rival of Wang, was relatively junior in experience in the Kuomintang, though he held key positions at Canton as head of the newly founded Whampoa Military Academy and commander of the First Front Army. With this control of military power, Chiang was in an increasingly strong position to challenge Wang Ching-wei.

During his period of authority in 1925–26, Wang Ching-wei was regarded as a leader of the left wing of the Kuomintang, which advocated collaboration with the Communists, while Chiang Kai-shek was identified with more conservative interests. On 20 March 1926, in the so-called Chungshan Incident, Chiang ordered the arrest of Communists under his command. Various interpretations have been placed on that incident, but one element was Chiang's desire to erode the position of Wang Ching-wei and his supporters. A resolution of the meeting of the Kuomintang Central Executive Committee after the incident held that "in view of the present situation, the comrades of the left should temporarily retreat." Wang Ching-wei was forced to resign, and he left for France in May 1926.

Personal strife inside the Kuomintang evolved within the larger context of the alliance between that party and the Chinese Communists, one of the more ambiguous sections of Sun

Yat-sen's political legacy. The Nationalist-Communist entente lasting from 1923 to 1927 marked a complex period, of interest both because of the mutual antipathy of the partners and because of the effect which that alliance had on the political rise of the Nationalists. After the Northern Expedition reached the Yangtze valley in central China, the Kuomintang was sufficiently split on the issue of continued collaboration with the Communists that two separate regimes emerged at the beginning of 1927: a right-wing group centered about Chiang Kai-shek at Nanking, and a left-wing group at Wuhan. As the breach between the two factions widened, the government at Wuhan, anxious to offset the growing military authority of Chiang Kai-shek, who had grown in power and prestige during the military push northward, called for the return of Wang Ching-wei from Europe. Wang, distrustful of Chiang Kai-shek, returned at once. Upon arrival at Shanghai, he conferred with Ch'en Tu-hsiu (q.v.), general secretary of the Chinese Communist party, about Kuomintang-Communist relations. On 5 April 1927 they issued a joint statement in which they reiterated their intention to maintain collaboration between the two parties. Wang then proceeded to Wuhan to become the dominant figure in the coalition regime there which embraced both Communists and the left wing of the Kuomintang.

In April 1927 Chiang Kai-shek broke the alliance with the Communists by undertaking a bloody coup at Shanghai. At Wuhan, Wang Ching-wei's cooperation with the Russian advisers and the Chinese Communists also proved to be short-lived. In late May 1927 it became clear to Wang that the Communists intended to follow a radical land policy and to maintain autonomous political positions, both of which policies he regarded as contradictory to Sun Yat-sen's principles. Moreover, on 1 July, M. N. Roy, the Comintern representative at Wuhan, indiscreetly informed Wang of Moscow's aggressive plans for China and the Chinese revolution. Wang then severed relations with the Russian advisers and ordered the expulsion of Communists from both the government and the Kuomintang. From that point onward in his political career, Wang Ching-wei firmly opposed the Communists, for he regarded them as a major obstacle to national unification and economic reconstruction in China. All

factions of the Kuomintang now agreed on an anti-Communist line, but personality clashes continued. Wang Ching-wei believed that he should hold undisputed leadership but found himself increasingly harassed by criticism from antagonists on the party's right wing. Such criticism was especially heavy at the time of the Communist-led Canton Commune in December 1927 (see Chang T'ai-lei); and Wang, disturbed by the turn of events, abruptly left Shanghai to return to France.

From 1928 to 1931, whether abroad or in China, Wang Ching-wei headed the so-called Association for Reorganization of the Kuomintang, shortened in Chinese to Kai-tsu-p'ai. This was a group within the Kuomintang which opposed the growing power of Chiang Kai-shek over both the National Government and the Kuomintang. This control was demonstrated at the Third National Congress of the Kuomintang, which met at Nanking in March 1929. Dominated by Chiang Kai-shek supporters, that congress leveled charges of political deviationism at Wang Ching-wei and expelled several of Wang's associates from the party. Wang's opposition to Nanking's authority evoked response from several military leaders who were dissatisfied with Chiang Kai-shek's policies, suspicious of his intentions, and jealous of his rising star. Among Chiang's leading rivals were Feng Yü-hsiang and Yen Hsi-shan (q.v.), who controlled substantial forces in north China and who had begun a brief but destructive war with Nanking. In 1930 Wang Ching-wei joined these men in attempting to establish a rival national government at Peiping, a move which failed because of Nanking's success in gaining the support of the Young Marshal, Chang Hsueh-liang (q.v.), who controlled Manchuria. Following the collapse of the anti-Chiang coalition at Peiping, Wang again found himself a political refugee, a dissident with a cause but little support. He moved south, where, during the early months of 1931, he became the senior Kuomintang leader active in a new opposition movement at Canton, sparked by Chiang Kai-shek's house arrest of Hu Han-min at Nanking and sustained by the political ambitions of Kwangtung and Kwangsi military leaders. This Canton movement, though not successful in dislodging Chiang Kai-shek, restored Wang's position and paved the way for his *rapprochement* with Nanking.

These domestic dissensions sapped the energies of the National Government and frustrated its efforts to achieve nation-wide unification. The grave challenge posed by Japanese military aggression in Manchuria beginning in September 1931 forced many of the feuding factions in the Kuomintang to set aside their differences in the interests of the nation. Temporary political compromises on the part of all Kuomintang leaders followed, though personal frictions continued into the war years. Wang Ching-wei made his peace with the Nanking authorities, and with the reorganization of the National Government in the winter of 1931 he was named president of the Executive Yuan. He assumed office on 28 January 1932. That very night, the Japanese garrison at Shanghai launched an undeclared attack against Chinese troops in the area. Wang Ching-wei was not to see peace again in his lifetime.

From February 1932 until November 1935, Wang sustained an uneasy collaboration with Chiang Kai-shek, heading the government at Nanking while Chiang supervised military operations aimed at extirpating the Communist bases in Kiangsi and elsewhere. During the early 1930's, it appeared to some independent observers that a new nation was emerging in the lower Yangtze valley and attracting the loyalty of many patriotic Chinese. The dimensions of reconstruction and expansion were varied: fiscal and financial reform; development of communications, including civil aviation; rural rehabilitation; modernization of university education; revitalization of public morals and morale. From 1932 to 1935, when Wang Ching-wei headed the Executive Yuan at Nanking, his political authority and personal incorruptibility did much to make that period the most progressive in the history of the National Government. However, his position at Nanking was not without personal frustrations. Although Wang was prime minister, Chiang Kai-shek placed his own relatives by marriage, H. H. K'ung and T. V. Soong (qq.v.), in key posts at Nanking to guarantee appropriate checks on Wang. Irritated by suspicion and surveillance, Wang went on leave in October 1932. He visited Europe for six months, allegedly for medical reasons, while T. V. Soong acted in his place at Nanking.

In March 1933, when Wang passed through Hong Kong on his return to China, he called on Hu Han-min and attempted to persuade Hu of the validity of his views on the national political situation. The meeting of the two former friends, which proved to be their last encounter, was not a success. Wang returned to Nanking to resume the presidency of the Executive Yuan and to serve concurrently as acting foreign minister. Wang soon became involved in negotiations with Japanese diplomatic and military authorities regarding the establishment of railway and mail communications between China proper and Manchoukuo, and the legal arrangements defining the Japanese position on the mainland of China. While attempting to defend China's territorial and administrative integrity, Wang nevertheless found himself in an increasingly vulnerable political position as the man most closely associated in the public mind with the policy of yielding to Japan, the individual censured by all patriotic groups in China which advocated positive resistance. The climax came on 1 November 1935, when, at a meeting of the Central Executive Committee of the Kuomintang at Nanking, he was wounded by an assailant who disguised himself as a photographer, with a revolver concealed in his camera. Surgery in Shanghai failed to remove all the bullets, and Wang was forced to resign all official posts in December to seek medical care abroad.

When Wang left for Europe in February 1936 after four years as administrative head of the National Government, medical exigencies appeared paramount. Beneath the surface, however, lay a deeper malaise. Wang was being ruined politically by the long, agonizing process of appeasement, for which Chiang Kai-shek was ultimately responsible, during the uneasy years between the Mukden Incident of 1931 and the Lukouchiao attack in 1937. Throughout this period, forces of reform, patriotism, liberal opinion, Communist pressure, student sentiment, and national self-respect fed the opposition to Nanking's cautious line. Wang Ching-wei found himself the civilian leader of a government pursuing an intensely unpopular policy, losing popularity while he shielded Chiang Kai-shek from anti-appeasement criticism. Following the Sian Incident of December 1936 (*see* Chang Hsueh-liang), a move designed to force Chiang to take a firm stand against Japan, Wang Ching-wei hastened back to China from Europe. But Chiang Kai-shek continued to hold the high cards; and when the Sino-Japanese war began in mid-1937, he gained full power as top commander of the Nationalist war effort. When the Kuomintang held a special wartime congress at Hankow in March 1938, Chiang's position as party dictator was confirmed when he was elected tsung-ts'ai [leader], with Wang Ching-wei as his deputy. Wang's personal power was now more nominal than real, and his political associates were excluded from key offices in favor of Chiang Kai-shek's intimates.

During the first year of the war, Wang Ching-wei became discouraged about the eventual outcome and proposed that the National Government negotiate a peaceful settlement with Japan. When the National Government was forced to evacuate, first to Wuhan and then to Chungking after the fall of Wuhan in October 1938, Wang became increasingly dubious about China's ability to sustain a protracted war against the Japanese. He was further disillusioned by the Chinese scorched-earth policy after the tragic burning of Changsha in November (see Chang Chih-chung).

On 16 December 1938 Wang met with Chiang Kai-shek. During this interview he made no mention of his private pessimism regarding the military situation. Two days later, he flew to Chengtu for a ceremonial occasion. He then flew to Kunming, and on 21 December he arrived at Hanoi in French Indo-China. On 22 December, Prince Konoye, the Japanese premier, issued a statement announcing that Japan would collaborate with a new Chinese regime in order to readjust Sino-Japanese relations on the basis of a "new order in East Asia." Chungking immediately refused the Konoye offer. On 29 December 1938 Wang issued a public declaration of his advocacy of peace in a telegram to the National Government at Chungking requesting Chiang Kai-shek to halt armed resistance and to work out a peaceful settlement with Japan.

In the early morning hours of 21 March 1939, Nationalist secret agents entered his residence in Hanoi and fired dozens of shots. Wang himself was uninjured, but his long-time personal protégé and confidant, Tseng Chung-ming (q.v.), was fatally wounded. The mystery of the shooting was never solved, but the most prevalent theory was that the gunmen were aiming for Wang Ching-wei but shot Tseng by mistake. Whatever the facts, Wang regarded the murder of his friend as a personal outrage. Infuriated to the point of no return, he spent the last years of his life working actively with his country's major foreign enemy. After proceeding from Hanoi to Shanghai in the spring of 1939, he conferred with Chinese who were active in the north China puppet regime and in the so-called reform government at Nanking to arrange a merger of the various Chinese administrations in Japanese-occupied China. He visited Tokyo twice, in May and again in October of 1939, and worked out a joint statement with the Japanese authorities covering the "new relations between China and Japan." It was signed secretly at the end of 1939.

Wang's movement suffered a setback in January 1940 when his associates Kao Tsung-wu and T'ao Hsi-sheng (q.v.) defected to Hong Kong with copies of Wang's secret agreement with Japan. The leak failed to deter Wang's preparations, although publication of the terms of the secret agreement created a furor in China. On 30 March 1940 a new "national government," patterned on the five-yuan structure of the legitimate central government, was formally established at Nanking with Wang Ching-wei as its ranking official. He immediately issued a general invitation to all civil servants and Kuomintang party officials in Chungking to participate. In April, discussions were initiated for a treaty to govern relations between Nanking and Japan. Because Japan's original intention in supporting Wang had been to force Chungking to enter peace negotiations, the Japanese government delayed granting formal recognition to the Nanking regime until it became apparent that the National Government would not negotiate. Tokyo did not sign a basic treaty with Nanking and accord formal diplomatic recognition to that government until 30 November 1940, almost two years after Wang had first left Chungking, and eight months after his regime had been established. The November 1940 agreement, contrary to what Wang and his followers had hoped, maintained strong Japanese military and economic domination over the occupied areas while granting the Chinese authorities at Nanking only token responsibility for internal administration.

Wang's pessimism regarding China's prospects

for effective resistance against the Axis powers was intensified during 1940 by military developments in Europe, particularly the fall of France and the desperate position of England in the face of the German air assault. Within the context of Chinese politics, Wang Ching-wei took the position that his government was the legitimate national government of China, his party was the Kuomintang, his flag was the Kuomintang flag, and the principles of his government were the Three People's Principles of Sun Yat-sen. Wang believed himself to be Sun's rightful heir. Prior to the outbreak of war with the United States, the ideology underlying the Nanking government—a pan-Asian, anti-Western mystique—was not unattractive to many Chinese. In Tokyo's eyes, the Nanking government and the doctrine of Asian solidarity which lay behind it offered the greatest potential for securing a settlement of the "China Incident" on terms favorable to Japan.

China during the early 1940's was divided into three major political parts. One section was Nationalist China, the areas in the west extending from Kansu through Yunnan which were controlled by or nominally loyal to the legitimate National Government located at Chungking. Another was Communist China, a series of expanding enclaves behind and between the ports and railway lines of north, east, and central China which were controlled by or loyal to the Communist insurgent government at Yenan in Shensi province. The third division was Japanese-occupied China, a series of semi-autonomous regimes stretching from northern Manchuria to the Gulf of Tonkin in the south. This third division was itself subdivided into Manchoukuo, the Manchurian regime which had been established in 1932; a north China puppet regime at Peiping; Mengchiang, the Japanese-controlled government in Inner Mongolia; and Wang Ching-wei's regime at Nanking.

The outbreak of the War in the Pacific in December 1941 brought little immediate change in the political geography of China. The expansion of conflict did, however, enhance the role of the Nanking regime in Tokyo's China policy as that policy developed during the war between Japan and the Allied powers. Militarily, the Japanese settled into a holding operation on the mainland of China, with main efforts and power committed farther south. Yet,

despite the prizes gained in Southeast Asia during 1942, China remained of vital economic importance to Japan as a source of coal, iron ore, and other essential raw materials. In late 1942 and early 1943 Japan made moves designed to ease the more glaring inequalities in the original position of the Nanking government. Wang Ching-wei again went to Tokyo, where he had conversations with Tojo and other members of the Japanese government, as well as an audience with the emperor. As a result of these negotiations, Japan relinquished her concessions in China and the right of extra-territoriality, while the Nanking government on 9 January 1943 formally declared war on the United States and Great Britain.

During the summer of 1943, following a visit by Tojo himself to China and Japanese pressure upon the representative of the Vichy French regime in Nanking, agreements were signed under which Nanking assumed administrative control over the International Settlement and the French concession at Shanghai. On 1 August 1943 the Nanking authorities took formal possession of these areas, long the heart of Western control in China's major trading and financial metropolis. Following the return to Tokyo of Shigemitsu Mamoru, who had been Japanese ambassador at Nanking, to become foreign minister in 1943, Japan's "New China Policy" took more definite shape. Aimed at achieving a settlement with Chiang Kai-shek, this policy embodied the concept that Japan would modify her earlier ambitions for dominant control of East Asia while at the same time blocking the return of the Western powers to their former position of influence.

Japan's gambit had the corollary effect of conceding to Wang Ching-wei's government at least the nominal status of an ally and an equal. When a new treaty of alliance between Nanking and Tokyo was concluded on 30 October 1943, voiding the treaty of November 1940, its preamble expressed the resolve of the two governments to cooperate as equal and independent neighbors in the establishment of Greater East Asia. But the key aspect of Tokyo's China policy was not so much its psychological effect on the prestige of Wang Ching-wei's government as its potential political effect upon individuals and groups in Chiang Kai-shek's government at Chungking. Through the October 1943 treaty with Wang Ching-wei and through covert overtures to Chungking channeled through Tai Li (q.v.), Japan pressed the line that Chiang's true interests lay in severing relations with the United States and Britain and in collaborating with Nanking to liquidate the Chinese Communist movement, then steadily growing in strength in the countryside. During 1944, even as Japan encountered mounting disaster in the Pacific campaigns and Germany was retreating on the western front, growing political frustration at Chungking found outlet in renewed alarm over the threat of Mao Tse-tung. And the idea of joint Chungking-Nanking operations against the Chinese Communists reportedly gained some support from conservatives in the Kuomintang who viewed the Communists as a greater long-term threat than the Japanese.

Still in ailing health from the bullet wounds received several years earlier, Wang Ching-wei was again forced to go to Japan for medical treatment in 1944. He died at Nagoya on 10 November 1944. Ch'en Kung-po (q.v.), who had been close to Wang since 1927, succeeded him as head of the Nanking government, but Ch'en lacked the prestige that Wang had enjoyed in Nationalist circles. Another individual prominent as political strategist at Nanking was Chou Fo-hai (q.v.), who had been the most widely read Kuomintang theorist in China before 1937. Despite the efforts of these men, it soon became obvious that the Nanking government had been held together by Wang Ching-wei's seniority and reputation for probity. By the end of 1944, when Wang died, Japan's hopes of bringing Chinese resistance to an end had dimmed, and the outcome of the Second World War was no longer seriously in doubt.

For millions of Chinese who had no practical alternative to life under Nanking's administrative control, Wang Ching-wei's regime did provide a measure of Chinese protection against the Japanese from 1940 to 1945. In dealing with the Japanese, Wang attempted to maintain integrity, to protect Chinese rights, and to assure that there would be no more incidents like the rape of Nanking in December 1937. There was notably little public remonstrance or violence directed against the puppet authorities when Japan surrendered in August 1945.

Together with his other principal associates, Wang Ching-wei's widow, Ch'en Pi-chün, was tried for treason following the Japanese defeat.

In testimony given at her trial, she stressed Wang's sincerity and patriotism in believing that a peaceful accommodation with Japan was the only realistic method of preserving Chinese national interests.

Wang Ch'ung-hui   王 寵 惠
T. Liang-ch'ou   亮 疇

Wang Ch'ung-hui (1881–15 March 1958), foreign minister in the provisional republican government in 1912. He subsequently held various ministerial posts and served briefly as acting premier at Peking in 1922. He later was president of the Judicial Yuan (1928–30; 1948–57), foreign minister (1937–40), and secretary general of the Supreme National Defense Council (1942–46). Wang also served as deputy judge (1923–24) and as judge (1931–36) on the Permanent Court of International Justice at The Hague.

Although his native place was Tungkuan, Kwangtung, Wang Ch'ung-hui was born in Hong Kong, where his father was a Protestant minister. When Wang was a boy, Sun Yat-sen and Ch'en Shao-pai (qq.v.) often came to the Wang home to discuss Christian theology and anti-Manchu revolutionary ideas. Wang received a bilingual education at Hong Kong, where he attended St. Paul's College and Queens College and studied classical Chinese with a tutor. In 1895 he went to Tientsin and enrolled at Peiyang University, newly founded by Sheng Hsuan-huai (q.v.). He was graduated *cum laude* from its law school in 1900.

Because of the Boxer Uprising in north China, Wang Ch'ung-hui went to Shanghai in 1900 to teach at Nanyang College. The following year, he went to Japan to become an editor of the anti-Manchu *Kuo-min-pao*. He remained in Tokyo until late 1902, when he went to the United States for advanced education in law. He enrolled at the University of California but soon transferred to Yale University, where he received an LL.M. degree in 1903 and a D.C.L. degree in 1905. It was while Wang was at Yale that Sun Yat-sen went to the United States, and the two men met in New York to discuss politics. Wang drafted Sun's first public statement on the aims of the Chinese revolution, "The True Solution of the Chinese Question."

During this period, Wang also served as an editor of the *Journal of the American Bar Association*.

In 1905 Wang went to Europe for advanced study in jurisprudence and international law in England and Germany. He translated the German Civil Code of 1900 into English, and his translation, published in 1907, became the standard English version. In 1907 he was called to the bar at the Middle Temple, London. Soon afterwards, he was appointed an aide to Lu Cheng-hsiang (q.v.) at the Second Hague Conference. When the conference ended, he returned to London. In 1908 he wrote Sun Yat-sen in Singapore to ask for financial aid, and Sun sent him money, to the dismay of his T'ung-meng-hui colleagues, who were strapped for funds and who did not understand why any available money should not be used for specifically revolutionary purposes. Sun justified his action by saying that Wang was an eminent scholar whose services might later be important to the revolutionary cause.

Wang Ch'ung-hui returned to China in the autumn of 1911. When the revolution began, he became an adviser to Ch'en Ch'i-mei (q.v.), the revolutionary military governor of Shanghai. As a delegate from Kwangtung, Wang participated in the convention at Nanking which elected Sun Yat-sen provisional president of the Chinese republic. He and T'ang Erh-ho (q.v.) then were dispatched to Shanghai to inform Sun officially of his election. Wang was designated minister of foreign affairs in the provisional government. After Yuan Shih-k'ai succeeded Sun as president, Wang became minister of justice in the cabinet of T'ang Shao-yi (q.v.) at Peking. T'ang resigned in June 1912 and Wang followed suit in July. He then went to Shanghai and became chief editor of the Chunghua Book Company and vice chancellor of Futan University.

Although Wang did not take part in Kuomintang activities during the so-called second revolution of 1913, he later joined the anti-Yuan Shih-k'ai movement, becoming deputy commissioner of foreign affairs in the military council established at Chaoch'ing, Kwangtung, on 8 May 1916 (for details, *see* Liang Ch'i-ch'ao; Ts'ai O). With Yuan's death and the dissolution of the council, Wang went to Peking to be chairman of the Law Codification Commission, with Lo Wen-kan (q.v.) as vice chairman.

In 1920 he was appointed chief justice of the Supreme Court. As China's leading jurist, he was one of ten men designated in 1921 to participate in the work of revising the League of Nations Covenant. On his way to that meeting, he made a public statement at Vancouver, British Columbia, in April 1921 to the effect that China had three important enemies: Article 21 of the League Covenant, the Anglo-Japanese alliance, and the Lansing-Ishii agreement of 1917. Wang was one of China's delegates to the Washington Conference convened that autumn, in the course of which the Anglo-Japanese alliance was dissolved and the Lansing-Ishii agreement was rescinded.

In the meantime, in December 1921, Wang Ch'ung-hui had been appointed minister of justice in the cabinet headed by Liang Shih-i (q.v.). In January 1922, because of opposition from Wu P'ei-fu (q.v.), Liang was forced to resign in favor of W. W. Yen (Yen Hui-ch'ing, q.v.), who became acting premier. A struggle began between Wu P'ei-fu and Chang Tso-lin (q.v.) for control of the premiership, with Wu backing W. W. Yen and Chang supporting Liang Shih-i. In February, as the struggle continued, Wang Ch'ung-hui was named deputy judge on the Permanent Court of International Justice at The Hague. The struggle between the two warlords resulted in the first Chihli-Fengtien war in April, the defeat of Chang Tso-lin in May, and the return of Li Yuan-hung to the presidency at Peking. On 11 June Li designated W. W. Yen premier. Wang Ch'ung-hui became minister of justice in Yen's cabinet, and he became acting premier when Yen requested a leave of absence at the end of July. On 20 September, Wang was named officiating premier. He formed a cabinet, known as the "cabinet of able men" (hao-jen nei-ko), in which Lo Wen-kan was minister of finance, V. K. Wellington Koo (Ku Wei-chün, q.v.) was minister of foreign affairs, and Hsü Ch'ien (q.v.) was minister of justice. Before long, however, Wang's cabinet was caught in another power struggle. This time the chief antagonists were Wu P'ei-fu and Ts'ao K'un (q.v.). In November, the speaker of the National Assembly, Wu Ching-lien, and the deputy speaker, Chang Po-lieh, charged that Lo Wen-kan had accepted a bribe in connection with the adjustment of an Austrian loan contract. After Lo was arrested on these trumped-up charges, Wang Ch'ung-hui and his entire cabinet resigned on 21 November. It was with some relief that Wang left China in 1923 to assume his post on the World Court. On the recommendation of Lu Cheng-hsiang, he also represented China at the League General Assembly meeting in September 1923. Wang served on the World Court until 1925 and then became a member of the League Committee for the Progressive Codification of International Law.

Upon his return to Peking in 1925, Wang Ch'ung-hui became a delegate to the Special Customs Conference, chairman of the commission for investigation of extraterritoriality, and director general of the Law Revision Office. In January 1926 he was elected to the Central Supervisory Committee of the Kuomintang at that party's Second National Congress. In May, he was named minister of education in W. W. Yen's cabinet, but the cabinet was dissolved at its first meeting in June. Because of his continued association with the Peking government, Wang was removed from the Kuomintang Central Supervisory Committee in March 1927. Two months later, he left Peking and joined Chiang Kai-shek's regime at Nanking as minister of justice. He retained that post until mid-1928. When the Judicial Yuan was established on 16 November 1928, Wang became its president. He was reelected to the Kuomintang Central Supervisory Committee in 1929, and he was appointed chairman of the commission for rehabilitation of domestic and foreign loans in November of that year.

Wang Ch'ung-hui served as president of the Judicial Yuan and as a member of the State Council from 1928 to 1931. He worked to rid China of extraterritoriality and to inaugurate a system of political tutelage which, according to Kuomintang doctrine, would lead to constitutionalism in China. Wang played an important part in formulating the principles underlying both the civil and the criminal codes. He had participated in the drafting of the provisional constitution of 1912; he had helped Sun Yat-sen evolve the concept of a five-yuan government; and he now guided the drawing up of the provisional constitution of 1931.

In 1930 Wang had been elected judge of the Permanent Court of International Justice. His domestic commitments had caused him to defer acceptance of the post, but he went to The Hague in April 1931 after an opposition movement had begun in protest against Chiang Kai-shek's arrest of Hu Han-min (q.v.). He completed his term on the World Court in 1936 and then returned to China, where he reportedly served as a moderating influence at Nanking during the Sian Incident of December 1936 (*see* Chiang Kai-shek; Chang Hsueh-liang). In March 1937 he became minister of foreign affairs. On 21 August 1937 he and the Soviet ambassador, Bogomoloff, signed a Sino-Soviet non-aggression pact which granted aid to China from the Soviet Union at a time when such support from other countries was difficult to obtain. He held the foreign ministership until April 1941, when he was succeeded by Quo Tai-chi (Kuo T'ai-ch'i, q.v.). In 1942 he became secretary general of the Supreme National Defense Council, in which capacity he accompanied Chiang Kai-shek to India in 1942 and to the Cairo Conference in 1943. Beginning in 1943 he also served on the People's Political Council.

Wang Ch'ung-hui was a member of the Chinese delegation to the United Nations Conference on International Organization at San Francisco in 1945. Upon his return to China, he served as director of the Far Eastern Branch Committee of the Commission for the Investigation of Pacific War Crimes. He also supervised the preparation of an authorized English translation of Chiang Kai-shek's *Chung-kuo chih ming-yün*. The translation was published in the United States in 1947 as *China's Destiny*. During this period, Wang also helped to frame the constitution that was promulgated on 1 January 1947. He then served on the State Council, and in June 1948 he again became president of the Judicial Yuan. Also in 1948 he received membership in the Academia Sinica. When the Chinese Communists won control of the mainland in 1949, he moved with the National Government to Taiwan.

At Taipei, Wang Ch'ung-hui was a member of the Kuomintang Central Reform Committee and of its successor, the Central Advisory Committee. Despite chronic illness, he also continued to serve as president of the Judicial Yuan until his death on 15 March 1958. Wang was survived by his wife, *née* Chu, and by a son, Ta-hung.

Wang Hsien-ch'ien   王 先 謙
T. I-wu   益 吾

Wang Hsien-ch'ien (6 August 1842–8 January 1918), scholar, educator, and government official. He was best known for his monumental compilations, including the *Han-shu pu-chu* [supplementary notes to the *Han-shu*] and the *Hou-Han-shu pu-chu*.

The third son in an impoverished gentry family, Wang Hsien-ch'ien was born in Changsha, Hunan. He became a sheng-yüan in 1857 and passed the chü-jen examination in 1864, having in the meantime served as secretary to a commander of river flotillas at Wuchang and at Anking, Anhwei. In 1866 he became a chin-shih and thus began a career of service to the Ch'ing court which extended to 1888. In 1881 he received the signal honor of appointment as president of the Kuo-tzu-chien or Imperial Academy.

In 1885 Wang went to Chiangyin, Kiangsu, to serve as provincial director of education. There he also headed the Nanching Academy, which he put on a sound financial basis by acquiring more than 50,000 mou of reclaimed swamp land. The revenues from this land kept the school going until the Second World War. At the Nanching Academy, Wang was associated with a number of illustrious scholars, including Miao Ch'üan-sun (q.v.).

As an official, Wang was noted for both his probity and his scholarship, and during his last decade of public service he acquired a reputation as a fearless remonstrant of imperial abuse. In 1881 he memorialized the court in criticism of Hsü Chih-ming's handling of the belligerent Muslims of Yunnan. In 1885 he boldly submitted a memorial urging the discontinuance of construction work on the pleasure lakes in the Forbidden City, a cherished project of the Empress Dowager Tz'u-hsi (ECCP, I, 295–300), who was diverting a large proportion of the naval appropriation to this end. In 1888 he again memorialized the throne, asking that the powerful eunuch Li Lien-ying (ECCP, I, 298) be placed under strict surveillance. This last remonstrance, an audacious affront to the Empress Dowager Tz'u-hsi, caused fear for his safety among Wang's friends but won him

fame and sympathy throughout China. It also hastened his retirement. He left government service the same year to devote himself to scholarship and teaching in his native province.

As a retired official, Wang first taught at the Ssu-hsien School, an institution founded by Kuo Sung-t'ao (ECCP, I, 438–39) in honor of Wang Fu-chih (ECCP, II, 817–19). There he established a printing concern, financed from surpluses in the local salt sales. In 1889 Wang left the school for the Ch'eng-nan Academy, where he remained until 1894. He spent the next decade at the Yüeh-lu Academy, leaving when it was converted into a modernized normal school. Thereafter Wang confined his activities to private scholarship, although in 1907 he did receive the purely honorary title of president of the bureau of educational affairs in Hunan.

Wang held no political post of substance after 1888 but remained politically active as a widely respected "elder statesman" of pronouncedly conservative views. In 1897, at the height of the reform movement in Hunan sponsored by Ch'en Pao-chen (ECCP, II, 703), Wang publicly demanded suspension of the *Hsiang-hsüeh-pao*, the organ of the Hunan reformers. During that period he also had his disciple, Su Yü (d. 1914), compile the *I-chiao ts'ung-pien*, [collected works to defend China's civilization], a repository of polemical materials useful for the discomfiture of the reformers. In 1904–5 Wang was a leader in the successful movement to nullify a contract signed by the Hunan provincial government with an American company to build a railway linking Hankow and Canton through Hunan.

In 1910 Wang played his last scene on the political stage, again in opposition to the Hunan provincial government. For a number of years Hunan had suffered crop failures, in the course of which Wang had repeatedly suggested to the provincial authorities that supplies of grain should be kept at hand in granaries for use during emergencies. His advice, however, was not heeded, and no action was taken. In April 1910 a hungry and disorderly mob rioted at Changsha and burned the governor's palace. Alarmed civic leaders jointly petitioned the governor general in Wuchang, charging that the Hunan governor was directly responsible for the disturbance and demanding his immediate dismissal. Wang's name somehow found its way to the top of the list of signers.

As a result and upon the recommendation of the governor general, Jui-chang (ECCP, I, 128), Wang was deprived of his residual honors and ordered cashiered from the civil service. Subsequent attempts by Wang to establish his innocence and restore his titles failed, and he died a private citizen eight years later, on 8 January 1918, at Changsha.

The abiding import of Wang's life is to be found, however, not so much in his political activity as in his works of scholarship. In breadth of learning and in organizational capacity he may be compared with the greatest Chinese scholars of the eighteenth century, the heyday of Han-hsüeh, or textual research. His work divides itself conveniently into four categories: historical, classical, and literary scholarship, and polemical and other writings including his own literary efforts. His *Tung-hua-lu*, and the companion compilation, *Tung-hua-hsü-lu*, based on the *shih-lu*, or "veritable records," stored in the Bureau of National History, remain among the most important primary sources for the study of Ch'ing history from its inception to the middle of the nineteenth century. His most monumental contribution to historical scholarship and what is generally considered his greatest work is the *Han-shu pu-chu* [supplementary notes to the *Han-shu*], in 100 chüan, published in 1900. The book synthesizes the findings of 47 earlier works in defining each phrase or term in the *Han-shu*, normally concluding with Wang's own comments. A similar work for the *Hou-Han-shu*, entitled *Hou-Han-shu pu-chu*, appeared in 1915, but is generally less valued than the earlier work. In both enterprises Wang was assisted by Su Yü.

Wang was also active in bringing together important collections of traditional literature. In 1882 in continuation of the *Ku-wen-tz'u lei-tsuan* [classified compilation of ancient literature] by the eighteenth-century scholar Yao Nai (ECCP, II, 900–1), Wang compiled the *Hsü ku-wen-tz'u lei-tsuan*, which included samples of the work of 38 scholars of the post-Ch'ien-lung (1736–1795) period. Although the work was intended to glorify the achievements of the conservative T'ung-ch'eng school, of which Yao Nai was a leading figure, Wang's anthology included several essays by writers of the rival and less rigidly orthodox Yang-hu school, a circumstance which aroused much unfavorable

criticism of Wang at the time of publication. In 1889 he produced the *Shih-chia ssu-liu wen-ch'ao* [selected rhyme-prose of the "Ten Geniuses"], a collection of rhyme-prose by master writers mostly of the nineteenth century with a preface by Wang in the same style. In 1900, in collaboration with Su Yü, he completed his *Lü-fu lei-tsuan* [anthology of metrical fu] and followed this a year later with another anthology of rhyme-prose, *P'ien-wen lei-tsuan*.

As a classicist and editor, Wang also made important contributions to Chinese scholarship. One of the best editions of classical texts extant had Wang as its editor in chief. The works he edited include the *Shih-shuo hsin-yü* and the *Yen-t'ieh-lun*, both published in 1891, the *Hsün-tzu chi-chih* of 1901, and the *Chuang-tzu chi-chih* of 1909. In 1907 he published a collection of his correspondence on questions of the day under the title *Hsü-shou-t'ang shu-cha*. His literary works were collected under the title *Hsü-shou-t'ang wen-chi*, and his poetry as *Hsü-shou-t'ang shih-ts'un*.

Wang I-t'ang　　王 揖 堂
Alt. I-t'ang　　　　一 堂

Wang I-t'ang (6 October 1878–September 1946), political associate of Yuan Shih-k'ai and Tuan Ch'i-jui who later served on the Hopei-Chahar political council. Wang was among the first of the Peiyang politicians to cooperate with the Japanese in 1937. He served as minister of relief and later as chairman of the Japanese-sponsored government in north China. In 1946 Wang was tried and executed for treason.

Hofei, Anhwei, was the birthplace of Wang I-t'ang. He was the second son of Wang Hsi-yuan (d. 1907; T. Tse-chai) and the younger brother of Wang Chih-yü. After receiving a traditional education in the Chinese classics, Wang I-t'ang passed the examinations for the chü-jen degree in 1903 and achieved the chin-shih degree in 1904. He then went to Japan, where he received military and legal training. Upon his return to China in 1907, he came to the attention of Hsü Shih-ch'ang (q.v.), the governor general of the Three Eastern Provinces, who appointed him to the military staff in Fengtien. Wang rose to the rank of brigade commander and served for a time in the Kirin military training headquarters.

In 1909 Wang I-t'ang was selected to accompany Tai Hung-tz'u, an imperial commissioner, on a courtesy mission to Russia. With the completion of that mission, Wang went to Germany for additional military training. He toured Europe and the United States before returning to China late in 1910. In March 1911 he became military councillor at the Kirin military training headquarters, with the rank of expectant tao-t'ai. At the time of the 1911 revolution Wang, on the recommendation of Hsü Shih-ch'ang, joined Yuan Shih-k'ai's secretariat. And when Yuan succeeded Sun Yat-sen in 1912 as provisional president of the Chinese republic, Wang became his political adviser and a lieutenant general in the army. At Peking, Wang founded a college of law, the Fa-cheng ta-hsueh, which later became the Chung-hua ta-hsueh.

Wang I-t'ang soon became an active organizer and official of the Kung-ho-tang [republican party]. In the parliamentary elections held early in 1913 he became a senator representing Tibet. Because the Kung-ho-tang emerged a poor second to the Kuomintang in these elections, it merged with the Min-chu-tang [democratic party] and the T'ung-i-tang [united party] to form the Chin-pu-tang [progressive party]. This party, which sided with Yuan Shih-k'ai in his struggle with the Kuomintang and supported his plans for the Reorganization Loan from an international banking consortium, was led by such men as Liang Ch'i-ch'ao, Chang Chien, Wu T'ing-fang, T'ang Hua-lung (qq.v.), and Wang I-t'ang. The Chin-pu-tang, however, was still a minority party. The Kuomintang dominated the constitution drafting committee, whose work was of greatest concern to Yuan Shih-k'ai. Wang I-t'ang and the other Chin-pu-tang representatives on the committee could not control its deliberations. The failure of the so-called second revolution (see Li Lieh-chün) provided Yuan with a pretext for ordering the dissolution of the Kuomintang and the expulsion of its members from the Parliament. The speakers of both chambers on 13 November 1913 announced the suspension of the Parliament for want of a quorum. On 10 January 1914 Yuan formally proclaimed its dissolution.

Yuan Shih-k'ai then organized the Political Conference (Cheng-chih hui-i), which, in turn, convened a conference on the provisional constitution. It was composed of 60 members representing Peking, various provinces, and the National Federation of Chambers of Commerce. Wang I-t'ang was elected to the conference as a representative of Anhwei province. It convened on 18 February 1914 and completed its work on 29 April. The resulting Hsin yueh-fa [new provisional constitution] incorporated all of Yuan's recommendations and gave the president virtually dictatorial powers. The Hsin yueh-fa, in effect from 1 May 1914 to 12 December 1915, provided for a unicameral legislature called the Li-fa yuan. Prior to its establishment, the Ts'an-cheng yuan [council of state], an advisory body created by Yuan, would replace the Political Conference. The appointment of Wang I-t'ang to the Ts'an-cheng yuan was announced on 26 May 1914.

In August 1915 Wang I-t'ang resigned his Peking post to become governor of Kirin. By this time, Yuan Shih-k'ai's plans to become monarch were well advanced. In December, Wang became a baron in the new order. Soon afterwards, however, Yuan was forced to abandon his plans. On 22 April 1916 Tuan Ch'i-jui (q.v.) was appointed premier at Peking in an attempt to salvage Yuan's regime. Wang I-t'ang was recalled to Peking as minister of the interior. At Peking, he also founded Kuo-min and Chung-hua universities. Wang resigned from office after Yuan Shih-k'ai's death in June, and in the autumn he went to Europe. He returned to China in April 1917. When a new provisional National Assembly was convened at Peking in November, Wang was elected its speaker.

On 7 March 1918 Wang I-t'ang and Hsü Shu-cheng (q.v.) established the Anfu Club to influence the election of the new Parliament in June. Elections were held in only 14 provinces —the others did not participate either because of opposition to Tuan Ch'i-jui or because of civil war conditions. The Anfu Club won an overwhelming victory, and when the new Parliament convened on 12 August, Wang I-t'ang was elected speaker of the National Assembly. Thereafter, Wang worked to manipulate the National Assembly in favor of Tuan's policies, and he represented Peking for a time in the unsuccessful peace negotiations with representatives of Sun Yat-sen at Shanghai.

The struggle for power between the Chihli

clique of Ts'ao K'un and Wu P'ei-fu (qq.v.) and the Anhwei clique of Tuan Ch'i-jui finally led to open warfare in July 1920. The Chihli clique joined forces with Chang Tso-lin (q.v.) to administer a decisive defeat to Tuan, who resigned the premiership. Wang I-t'ang was removed from his posts, and orders were issued for his arrest on 29 July. The Anfu Club was dissolved on 4 August. Wang fled to Japan, where he remained until November 1924, when Tuan Ch'i-jui became provisional chief executive at Peking. Upon his return to China, Wang was appointed governor of Anhwei and director for the readjustment of military affairs. In 1925, however, he was compelled to give up the governorship by Chang Tso-lin. Wang retired to Tientsin, where he devoted his time to the study of Buddhism. When the Northern Expedition reached Peking in 1928, his arrest was ordered. He then moved to the Japanese concession in Tientsin.

In 1931 Wang I-t'ang was plucked from obscurity to become a member of the Peiping political affairs council. In 1935 he and other former Peiyang politicians received membership in the Hopei-Chahar political council, which functioned as a buffer between the National Government at Nanking and the Japanese militarists in north China. After the Sino-Japanese war began, the Japanese sponsored the establishment of a puppet government at Peiping on 14 December 1937. Wang and many of his council colleagues moved smoothly into the new regime.

Wang I-t'ang belonged to the small group of men who controlled the Japanese-sponsored government at Peiping through interlocking membership in all its important organs. He was a member of the executive and legislative councils and minister of relief. In 1938 he participated in the conference in Dairen at which representatives of the Peiping and Nanking puppet governments came to an agreement on the means of cooperation between the two regimes. When the Nanking government headed by Wang Ching-wei (q.v.) was established in 1940, an attempt was made to give an appearance of unity by appointing Wang I-t'ang to the presidency of the examination yuan at Nanking, but he never assumed that office. In March 1940 he became chairman of the Peiping regime (then known as the north China political council), and director of its

bureau of the interior. He held the chairmanship until February 1943, when he resigned in favor of Chu Shen. After the Japanese surrender in 1945, Wang I-t'ang was arrested. He was imprisoned in Peiping and was tried and executed for treason in September 1946.

Wang I-t'ang's writings include a book on poetry, *Chin-ch'uan-shih-lou shih hua*, of 1933; a monograph on the Shanghai concessions, *Shanghai tsu-chieh wen-t'i*, of 1924; and a travel book on Japan, *Tung-yu chih-lueh*, of 1934.

Wang Jo-fei   王 若 飛
Alt. Huang Ching-ling   黃 敬 齡

Wang Jo-fei (1896–8 April 1946), founding member of the European branch of the Chinese Communist party. In the 1920's he organized workers in Shanghai. In 1931 he went to Inner Mongolia, where he was arrested by Nationalist agents. After his release in 1937, he held important staff positions' at Yenan. From 1944 until his death in 1946 he served in the Communist liaison mission at Chungking.

Anshun hsien, Kweichow, was the birthplace of Wang Jo-fei. When Wang was only seven, he, a younger sister, and their mother went to live with his mother's brother, Huang Ch'i-sheng, a well-known educator. Wang began his formal education in the institution his uncle headed, the Ta-te Academy in Kweiyang. The school administration was progressive and was sympathetic to the revolution of 1911. After being graduated from the academy in 1912, Wang worked for two years in a Kweiyang bookstore owned by Ts'ai Heng-wu, a former teacher for whom he had great respect.

In the meantime, Huang Ch'i-sheng had entered politics as commissioner for external affairs for Kweichow province, and Huang's younger brother had become commissioner of industry. In 1914 Wang Jo-fei worked for a time in a mining company which was under his younger uncle's jurisdiction. In 1915, when Yuan Shih-k'ai's monarchical ambitions became apparent, Huang Ch'i-sheng and Wang Jo-fei went to Shanghai to participate in the anti-Yuan movement. Wang returned to Kweichow in 1917 and became a teacher at the Ta-te Academy. Toward the end of that year, he won a government scholarship for study in

Japan. In the spring of 1918, accompanied by Huang Ch'i-sheng, he went to Japan and enrolled at Meiji University. Because of the Russian Revolution, interest in socialism was intense, and Wang soon became so absorbed in the study of socialist literature that he completely neglected his courses. He returned to China in 1919, at the time of the May Fourth Movement.

Wang Jo-fei soon became interested in the work-study movement in France (*see* Li Shih-tseng). Accompanied by Huang Ch'i-sheng, he left Shanghai for France in October 1919 in a group which also included Ts'ai Ho-sen (q.v.). On arrival in France, the group proceeded to Montargis to study French. Three months later, Wang began working in factories to support himself. Work was not easy to find, and Chinese officials in Paris could do nothing to alleviate the students' hardships. Early in 1920 Ts'ai Ho-sen and Wang Jo-fei decided to organize a mutual aid society. At its inaugural meeting, Wang made a speech in which he called on his fellow students to "take to the road of the working class of the Soviet Union."

As his devotion to Marxism increased, Wang Jo-fei began to travel throughout France in an attempt to turn the hitherto anarchistic tendencies among Chinese students into socialist channels. In the winter of 1921 he helped organize the China Socialist Youth Corps in France. Its members included Chou En-lai, Chao Shih-yen, Ch'en Yen-nien, Hsiang Ching-yü, Li Fu-ch'un, and Nieh Jung-chen (qq.v.). Wang Jo-fei also joined the French Communist party in 1922. That summer, the Socialist Youth Corps was reorganized as the European branch of the Chinese Communist party. Wang and a group which included Chao Shih-yen and Ch'en Yen-nien then went to the Soviet Union to study at the Communist University for Toilers of the East. During his two years in Moscow, Wang served as head of the Chinese Communist party branch at the university.

Upon his return to China in 1925, Wang Jo-fei was appointed secretary of the Chinese Communist party's Honan-Shensi committee. That May, he attended the All-China Labor Congress at Canton, after which he concentrated on organizing the workers on the Peking-Hankow and Lunghai rail lines. About this time, he met and married Li P'ei-chih. Toward the end of 1925, he was called to Shanghai to become the first chief executive officer (mi-

shu-chang) of the Chinese Communist party's Central Committee. When the Central Committee was moved to Wuhan early in 1927, Wang was transferred to the Kiangsu provincial committee of the party with the special assignment of directing the organization of workers in the Chinese city of Shanghai. Wang joined with Chou En-lai and Chao Shih-yen in directing the general strike that aided the Nationalist occupation of Shanghai. At the Fifth National Congress of the Chinese Communist party, held at Wuhan in May 1927, Wang was elected to the Central Committee. Because of the Kuomintang purge of Communists in the Shanghai area, for a brief period he was the only active Communist leader there. That autumn, after leading an unsuccessful peasant uprising at Wusih, he fled to the Soviet Union.

In the summer of 1928 Wang Jo-fei attended the Sixth National Congress of the Chinese Communist party, held at Moscow. He was elected a delegate of the Chinese Communist party to the Comintern, and in that capacity he lived in Moscow for the next three years. Upon his return to China in the summer of 1931, he was assigned to work with Ulanfu (q.v.) in Inner Mongolia, the immediate task being the organization of Mongols in Shensi, Kansu, Ninghsia, and Suiyuan. At the beginning of November, Wang was arrested at Paotow by Nationalist agents and sent to a prison in Kweisui, Suiyuan. He was not tried until 1934, when the Suiyuan Higher Court sentenced him to a prison term of 15 years. In June 1936, because of the Communist threat to Suiyuan, he was moved to Taiyuan. When a new period of Kuomintang-Communist cooperation began with the Sian Incident of December 1936 (*see* Chiang Kai-shek; Chang Hsueh-liang) and the outbreak of the Sino-Japanese war in July 1937, Wang was released. He had spent five years and seven months in prison.

Wang Jo-fei immediately went to Yenan, where he was appointed director of the propaganda department of the Shensi-Kansu-Ninghsia Border Region committee of the Chinese Communist party. In 1939 he became deputy chief of staff of the Eighth Route Army (Eighteenth Army Group). His next assignment was as secretary general of the Central Committee's north China–central China work committee. When this committee's work was done, he became the Central Committee's chief executive officer and director of its party affairs research bureau. In 1944 he was sent to Chungking to serve in the Communist liaison mission there with Chou En-lai and Lin Po-ch'ü (q.v.). He returned to Yenan in August 1945 to accompany Chou and Mao Tse-tung to Chungking for discussions as part of the American effort to mediate the Kuomintang-Communist conflict. In January 1946 he participated in the Political Consultative Conference, at which a Kuomintang-Communist truce agreement was signed. On his way back to Yenan on 8 April 1946, the plane in which he was traveling crashed, and he was killed. Other victims of this tragedy included Ch'in Pang-hsien, Teng Fa, Yeh T'ing (qq.v.), and Wang's uncle Huang Ch'i-sheng. Wang was survived by his mother, his wife, and a son born in 1939.

Wang K'ai-yün 王闓運
T. Jen-ch'iu 壬秋
H. Hsiang-i hsien-sheng 湘綺先生

Wang K'ai-yün (19 January 1833–October 1916), distinguished Hunanese classical scholar who was also known for his nonconformism. His best known work was the controversial *Hsiang-chün-chih* [history of the Hunan Army].

Born in Hsiangt'an, Hunan, Wang K'ai-yün was orphaned at an early age and was brought up by relatives. He studied at the Ch'eng-nan Academy and passed the examinations for the chü-jen degree in 1857. Two years later, he went to Peking and sat for the chin-shih examinations, but he failed them. On the recommendation of friends from the Ch'eng-nan Academy, he was granted an interview with Su-shun (ECCP, II, 666–68), then president of the Board of Revenue. Wang served Su-shun as a secretary-adviser for several months.

On his way back to Hunan in 1860, Wang K'ai-yün visited Su-shun's protégé Tseng Kuo-fan (ECCP, II, 751–55) at the headquarters of the Hunan Army (Hsiang-chün) in Ch'imen, Anhwei. The cordial relationship which developed between the two men in due course determined Wang's career and the subject of one of his major works of scholarship. In 1861 Su-shun was executed for his part in the co-regency attendant upon the accession of the

T'ung-chih emperor. Wang later raised money for Su-shun's impoverished heirs by editing Su-shun's writings and publishing them in 1871.

In 1878, on the recommendation of Ting Pao-chen (ECCP, II, 723-25), then governor general of Szechwan and formerly a general in the Hunan Army, Wang was appointed director of the Tsun-ching Academy in Chengtu. He held this post until Ting's death in 1886. Wang then returned to Hunan, where he taught successively at the Chao-ching Academy and the Ch'uan-shan Academy. In 1903 Hsia Shih, the governor of Kiangsi, appointed Wang a lecturer at the Yü-chang Academy in Nanchang. Three years later, the Ch'ing court awarded Wang an honorary chin-shih degree and a brevet appointment as reader of the Hanlin Academy.

Unlike many degree holders of the Ch'ing dynasty, Wang K'ai-yün accepted political appointments from the republican government established at Peking in 1912. He participated in meetings of prominent officials and scholars called in 1912 and 1914 by Yuan Shih-k'ai, and after the second meeting he accepted appointments as director of the bureau of national history and political consultant to the government. Later in 1914 he took part in a lavish gathering, sponsored by Yuan, for holders of Hanlin appointments. Wang soon wearied of life at Peking, however, and he returned to Hsiangt'an at the end of 1914. He died there in October 1916.

Wang K'ai-yün's lasting fame derives not from his political career but from his distinguished literary scholarship and from his dogmatic and frequently bizarre nonconformism. Few among his acquaintances escaped his pointed criticisms in matters of morals or manners, but he rarely applied these critical standards in judging his own behavior. Nevertheless, he managed to retain his position in society, partly because of Chinese admiration for the nonconformist style and spirit known as feng-lin, and partly because of his relationships with men of power. For all his eccentricity, Wang was a recognized authority on the Chinese classics and a competent historian. He wrote extensively on the *Shu-ching* [book of documents] and the *Li-chi* [book of rites], and he was a leading scholar of the chin-wen [new text] school. His work on the *Kung-yang* and *Ku-liang* commentaries to the *Ch'un-ch'iu* [spring and autumn annals] broke new ground. This work later was carried on by his disciple Liao P'ing (q.v.). Wang also wrote commentaries on other classic philosophical writings.

Wang K'ai-yün's best known work was the controversial *Hsiang-chün-chih* [history of the Hunan Army], published in 1881. Originally proposed by Wu Min-shu and supported by Kuo Sung-t'ao (ECCP, I, 438–39), the compilation of a work devoted to a full account of the achievements of the Hunan Army had been under consideration even as the Taipings surrendered. Tseng Kuo-fan favored the proposal and suggested that Wang K'ai-yün compile the work. Accordingly, in 1874 Tseng's eldest son, Tseng Chi-tse, commissioned Wang to take charge of the compilation. Wang seems to have given this assignment his personal attention. He completed a first draft in 1879 and the final version in 1881. When it appeared in 1881, the *Hsiang-chün-chih* was denounced vehemently by some Hunanese leaders. They were outraged by its failure, in their estimation, to give full credit to the military achievements of Tseng Kuo-fan and Tso Tsung-t'ang (ECCP, II, 762–67) and by its lack of objectivity. A strong critic of the work was Tseng Kuo-fan's younger brother, Tseng Kuo-ch'üan (ECCP, II, 749–51). With only 30,000 soldiers at his command, he had withstood the attack at Nanking by 300,000 soldiers directed by the renowned Taiping general Li Hsiu-ch'eng (ECCP, I, 459–63). His successful, 46-day defense had marked a turning point in the campaign against the Taipings. The cursory treatment given this campaign in Wang's book so enraged Tseng Kuo-ch'üan that he personally scolded Wang and called the book slanderous. Wang then sent the printing blocks of the *Hsiang-chün-chih* to Kuo Sung-t'ao, who destroyed them. However, some of Wang's students produced another edition in Chengtu, which was published in 1886. Meanwhile, Tseng Kuo-ch'üan commissioned Wang Ting-an to write the *Hsiang-chün-chi* [record of the Hunan Army], which was published in 1889 with a preface by Tseng. Kuo Sung-t'ao, his son Kuo Cho-ying, and his brother Kuo K'un-t'ao each wrote essays attacking Wang's book. These were collected and published by Kuo Chen-yung, a son of Kuo Cho-ying, in 1921 as *Hsiang-chün-chih p'ing-i.*

From a purely literary viewpoint, however, Wang K'ai-yün's *Hsiang-chün-chih* was a classic of its kind. It was, perhaps, for this reason that Li Shu-ch'ang, a follower and chronicler of Tseng Kuo-fan, included five of Wang's sixteen chapters in his *Hsü ku-wen tz'u-lei-tsuan* of 1889. Li compared Wang's impartiality to that of ancient China's first great historian, Ssu-ma Ch'ien.

Collections of Wang K'ai-yün's works include the *Hsiang-i-lou ch'üan-shu* and the *Hsiang-i-lou wen-chi.* His diary for the period from 1869 to 1916 was published in 1927 as *Hsiang-i-lou jih-chi.* Wang's son Tai-kung wrote a chronological biography of his father entitled *Hsiang-i-fu-chun nien-p'u.*

Wang Kan-ch'ang　　　王淦昌

Wang Kan-ch'ang (1907–), outstanding nuclear physicist and a discoverer of the anti sigma minus hyperon, played a leading role in the development of the People's Republic of China's nuclear capabilities. His field of specialization was high energy physics, the study of mesons, hyperons, cosmic rays, and heavy unstable particles.

The son of a prosperous and renowned physician, Wang Kan-ch'ang was born in Ch'angshou, Kiangsu. Little is known of his life before 1929, when he was graduated from Tsinghua University in Peiping at the top of his class. He then went to Germany, where he studied nuclear physics under the noted scientist Dr. Lise Meitner at the University of Berlin and did research on beta rays. After receiving a Ph.D. degree from Berlin in 1934, he returned to China to teach physics at Shantung University in Tsingtao. In 1936 he joined the faculty of Chekiang University in Hangchow. With the advent of the Sino-Japanese war in 1937, he moved with the university to Kiangsi, Kwangsi, and Kweichow. Throughout the war period, he carried on teaching and research work with limited equipment and under difficult circumstances. At war's end, Chekiang University sent Wang abroad for further study. He was a research associate in physics at the University of California at Berkeley in 1947–48. He then returned to China.

After the People's Republic of China was established in 1949, Wang Kan-ch'ang rose to become one of the country's outstanding research scientists. He served under Ch'ien San-ch'iang (q.v.) as deputy director of the institute of modern physics of the Chinese Academy of Sciences from November 1953 to July 1958. In February 1955 he was elected to the organization committee for popular lectures on atomic energy, and in June of that year he received membership on the committee of the department of mathematics, physics, and chemistry of the Chinese Academy of Sciences. That summer he attended the International Conferences on the Peaceful Uses of Atomic Energy, held at Geneva and Moscow.

In March 1956 Wang Kan-ch'ang led a group of 21 Chinese nuclear physicists to the Soviet Union to participate in advanced research at the newly established Joint Nuclear Research Institute (JNRI) at Dubna, near Moscow. Wang was made deputy director of the JNRI and a member of its scientific council. As a delegate to the Conference on High Energy Particles at Moscow in May 1956, he presented a paper on atomic research in China. That September, he signed the JNRI constitution on behalf of China at the JNRI Conference in Moscow. In November 1957 Wang served as an organization committee member and a delegate to the International Conference on Certain Physical Phenomena, also held in Moscow.

At the JNRI in Dubna, Wang Kan-ch'ang worked with Dr. Bruno Pontecorvo, who had defected from the West in 1950. In May 1958 *The New York Times* reported that "with the Chinese physicist Wang Kan-ch'ang, Dr. Pontecorvo was said to have headed a team that increased several times the intensity of the beam of accelerated protons produced by the synchroton and found new particles caused by their collision with nuclear targets." A Peking press release of March 1960 described Wang as one of the discoverers of the anti sigma minus hyperon and quoted his statement that this was the first discovery of a charged anti-hyperon and an advance in knowledge of the basic particles of the micro world. Referring to his four years of research at the JNRI, Wang praised the Russian director of the institute, D. I. Blokhintsev, and the Russian director of the laboratory of high energy particles, V. I. Veksler—as well as the cooperating Soviet, Chinese, Vietnamese, Rumanian, Polish, Czech,

and Korean scientists—for their contributions to this discovery, "which testified once more to the superiority of the socialist system." Wang also declared that the excellent equipment at Dubna was a factor of importance in this discovery and that the discovery could not have been made without the gigantic ten bev synchro-phasotron.

Wang returned to Peking in February 1960 to assume office as a deputy director of the institute of atomic energy of the Chinese Academy of Sciences. This institute had replaced the institute of modern physics in May 1957, and Wang had been named to a deputy directorship in July 1958. At the time of his return to China in 1960, it was rumored that he also would be in charge of a project to install equipment for the manufacture of atomic bombs in Sinkiang province.

Despite the demands placed upon him by his scientific research and administrative responsibilities at the institute of atomic energy—which had control over all aspects of nuclear physics, radiological chemistry, radiobiology, isotope apparatus, cosmic ray experiments, reactors, and accelerators in China—Wang appears to have been relatively active in political affairs. In the 1950's he had been a delegate and a National Committee member of the Chinese People's Political Consultative Conference. At the third meeting of this body, he served as a delegate of the Scientific-Technical Association and won reelection to the National Committee. In September 1964 Wang was elected a delegate from Kiangsu to the National People's Congress. He became a member of the presidium of the National People's Congress in December 1964 and a member of the congress's Standing Committee in January 1965. Wang was present on the rostrum for the National Day celebrations of 1967.

Little is known about Wang Kan-ch'ang's personal life except that he was married and the father of five children.

Wang K'o-min 王 克 敏

Wang K'o-min (1873–26 December 1945), sometime minister of finance at Peking and governor of the Bank of China who later became a member of the Hopei-Chahar political council. From December 1937 to March 1940 he headed the Japanese-sponsored government in north China.

Little is known about Wang K'o-min's family background or early life except that he was a native of Hangchow. After passing the examination for the chü-jen degree, in 1900 he received an appointment as a supervisor of the Chinese students sent by the Chekiang provincial government to study in Japan. His performance in that position earned him an appointment as councillor to the Chinese legation in Tokyo in 1902.

Upon his return to China in 1907, Wang K'o-min worked for a time in the ministry of finance and the ministry of foreign affairs at Peking. Late that year, he joined the staff of Chao Erh-sun (q.v.), then governor general of Szechwan. He left Chao's service in 1908 to take a foreign-relations post in the secretariat of Yang Shih-hsiang, the governor general of Chihli (Hopei). In 1910 he became acting commissioner of foreign affairs in the Chihli government, and his appointment was confirmed in 1911. After the revolution, he was commended for his role in maintaining order and in protecting the safety of foreign nationals in Tientsin.

In the spring of 1913 Wang K'o-min resigned from office and went to Europe. He returned to China that October to become the Chinese managing director of the Banque Industrielle de Chine, a joint Sino-French undertaking which gave assistance to the Peking government. The bank's main office was located in Paris, but it possessed the right of note issue in China. Its capitalization was two-thirds French and one-third Chinese. Wang K'o-min's success in the managing directorship was such that in July 1917 he was appointed governor of the Bank of China. That December, he became minister of finance and director general of the salt administration in the cabinet of Wang Shih-chen (q.v.) at Peking. He resigned with the rest of the cabinet on 29 March 1918. Wang's next official assignment was as a Peking government representative to the unsuccessful peace negotiations with representatives of Sun Yat-sen at Shanghai early in 1919.

Wang K'o-min was reappointed governor of the Bank of China in 1922. Soon afterwards, he became involved in the so-called Gold Franc dispute. The French government de-

manded Boxer Indemnity payments in gold instead of the much-depreciated paper franc and persuaded the governments of Italy, Spain, and Belgium to make similar demands. Because of the heavy financial losses such an arrangement would entail, the Peking government was reluctant to yield to the demand. As an inducement to compliance, the French government promised to reopen the Banque Industrielle de Chine, which had been ordered closed in 1921 by its main office in Paris. The Chinese financiers who had deposited funds in the Banque Industrielle de Chine put pressure on the Peking government to accept the French demand. At this point, in December 1922, the Peking government referred the case to Wang K'o-min. He recommended acquiescence to the French demand, and his suggestion was approved by the cabinet on 9 February 1923. The decision caused a public furor, and the Parliament passed a resolution condemning the decision. Negotiations concerning payment were suspended until 1925, when the dispute was resolved in favor of payment in gold. The Banque Industrielle de Chine then was reorganized as the Banque Française-Chinoise pour le Commerce et l'Industrie.

In October 1923 Wang K'o-min resigned from the Bank of China. He then became acting minister of finance at Peking. When Sun Pao-ch'i (q.v.) assumed the premiership in January 1924, Wang was appointed minister of finance and director general of the salt administration. That October, when Feng Yü-hsiang (q.v.) staged a coup at Peking, he ordered Wang's arrest for his role in the Gold Franc case. Wang then fled to Manchuria, where he came under the protection of Chang Tso-lin (q.v.). He later became a financial adviser to Chang's son Chang Hsueh-liang (q.v.).

In May 1933 Wang K'o-min was appointed to the Peiping political affairs council, under the chairmanship of Huang Fu (q.v.). The council, with jurisdiction over the five northern provinces of China, had the delicate task of preserving the authority of the National Government in that area while dealing with Japanese demands and moves for greater control in north China. At the end of May, Ho Ying-ch'in (q.v.) and Huang Fu signed the Tangku Truce, which, by creating a demilitarized zone in east Hopei in exchange for Japan's withdrawal of its troops beyond the Great Wall, weakened China's ability to defend the vital Peiping-Tientsin area and created an opportunity for the Japanese to sponsor a puppet government in the demilitarized zone. Huang Fu left Peiping in the spring of 1935, and Wang K'o-min succeeded him as chairman of the council. Chinese sovereignty in north China was further undermined that summer with the conclusion of the so-called Ho-Umezu agreement (see Ho Ying-ch'in). The Peiping political affairs council was abolished in September 1935. Its functions were taken over in December by the Hopei-Chahar political council, chaired by Sung Che-yuan (q.v.). Wang I-t'ang, Ch'i Hsieh-yuan (qq.v.), Wang K'o-min and other former Peiyang officials who were known for their pro-Japanese sentiments were members of the council.

After the Sino-Japanese war began in July 1937, Wang K'o-min went to Hong Kong. In December, he returned to north China to head the so-called provisional government of the republic of China, which was established at Peiping under Japanese sponsorship on 14 December. It was composed of an executive committee, a legislative committee, and a judical committee. The executive committee, chaired by Wang, dominated the government, and its members held all the important posts in every department of administration. The legislative committee was composed of Wang K'o-min; T'ang Erh-ho (q.v.), who was minister of education; Chu Shen, who was minister of justice; Tung K'ang (q.v.), who was chairman of the judical committee; and Wang I-t'ang, who was minister of relief.

On 20 January 1938 the hitherto autonomous east Hopei provincial government was incorporated into the provisional government of Peiping. On 10 March, the Peiping regime issued its own currency through the newly organized China United Reserve Bank. The new currency was expected to finance the government's operations, to undermine the value of the National Government's currency, and to secure raw materials for the Japanese at no greater cost than that of printing notes. The Peiping regime appointed a representative to Tokyo in March. Similar agents were appointed to Kobe in June, to Yokohama in July, and to Nagasaki in October. In the meantime, on 28 March 1938, the Wei-hsin, or reformed, government of China was established under Japanese auspices

at Nanking. It was headed by Liang Hung-chih (q.v.). That autumn, representatives of the two puppet governments met in Dairen and established a joint committee of the governments of China, headed by Wang K'o-min. It was to meet alternately at Peiping and Nanking and to coordinate and control communications, postal service, education, foreign affairs, customs, and transportation.

The Japanese soon came to realize that Wang K'o-min and Liang Hung-chih lacked the personal prestige to compete successfully with Chiang Kai-shek for the loyalty of the Chinese people. After negotiations with Wang Ching-wei (q.v.) in May 1939, the Japanese decided that Wang would head a central government of occupied China at Nanking but that the provisional government at Peiping would retain its autonomy. Wang K'o-min and Liang Hung-chih met with Wang Ching-wei on 18–20 September, and the joint committee announced its unanimous support of Wang Ching-wei on 21 September. In January 1940 a conference was held at Tsingtao to draft the organic laws for the new government at Nanking, which was established on 30 March 1940. The provisional government at Peiping became the north China political council, with Wang I-t'ang as its chairman. He was succeeded by Chu Shen on 8 February 1943. When Chu died on 2 July 1943, Wang K'o-min became the council's chairman. He held that post until the regime fell in August 1945.

At war's end, Wang K'o-min was arrested. He died in a Peiping prison on 26 December 1945.

Wang Kuo-wei　　　　　王　國　維
　T. Ching-an　　　　　　靜　安
　　Po-yü　　　　　　　　伯　隅
　H. Kuan-t'ang　　　　　觀　堂
　　Yung-kuan　　　　　　永　觀

Wang Kuo-wei (23 December 1877–2 June 1927), eminent classical scholar and ultra-royalist. Although he made contributions to several branches of humanistic studies, Wang was essentially a student of ancient Chinese history, a field in which he combined the highest traditions of Ch'ing scholarship with an awareness of the relevance of new data and modern techniques.

The Haining district of Chekiang province was the native place of Wang Kuo-wei. His father was Wang Nai-yü (d. July 1906), an amateur painter who gave up classical studies to become a merchant during the Taiping Rebellion. The elder Wang, author of the *Yu-yueh-lu* and the *Yü-lu shih-chi*, tutored Wang Kuo-wei in the Chinese classics. In 1892 Wang Kuo-wei entered a local academy in Chekiang and passed the sheng-yuan examinations. Two years later and again in 1897, he attempted but failed the examination for the chü-jen degree. He then returned to his native place to become a private tutor.

In 1898 Wang went to work in Shanghai as clerk and proofreader for the *Shih-wu-pao*, founded two years earlier by Wang K'ang-nien (ECCP, II, 822). To make maximum use of his free time, Wang Kuo-wei studied Japanese and some European languages under Fujita Toyohachi and Taoka Reiun at the Tung-wen hsueh-she [eastern culture society], which had been founded by Lo Chen-yü (q.v.) to train translators for his Nung-hsueh-she [agronomy society], which, in turn, was designed to introduce non-Chinese literature on agriculture into China. Impressed by the young Wang Kuo-wei's abilities, Lo Chen-yü appointed him general manager of the Nung-hsueh-she. This accidental association of Wang with Lo Chen-yü proved to be long-lived and was very influential on Wang's career, political thinking, and scholarly work.

At the suggestion of Lo Chen-yü, Wang Kuo-wei went to Japan in 1901, where he studied physics in Tokyo. The following year he returned to Shanghai, where he assisted Lo in editing the *Nung-hsueh-pao* [agronomy bulletin] and the *Chiao-yü shih-chieh tsa-chih* [education magazine]. In 1903 Wang became a teacher of ethics and psychology at the Nant'ung Normal School, where he attempted to introduce Western concepts both through his lectures and through translations of philosophical works by Kant and Schopenhauer.

In 1906 Wang received appointment as a junior officer in the general affairs section of the Board of Education and moved to Peking, where he developed an interest in literature. He became absorbed in the study of Chinese poetry, notably the tz'u form, and the drama of the Sung and Yüan periods. Some of his writings of this period were collected by Shen Tsung-ch'i

as *Ch'en-feng-ko ts'ung-shu* [collectanea from the tower of dawn breezes], published in 1909. It was also during these years in Peking that Wang became acquainted with many prominent scholars, including K'o Shao-min, Miao Ch'üan-sun, Tung K'ang (qq.v.), Liu Shih-heng (ECCP, I, 523), Wu Ch'ang-shou (ECCP, I, 434), and the French sinologist Paul Pelliot.

Shortly after the revolution of 1911, Wang Kuo-wei and Lo Chen-yü moved to Japan, where Wang lived mostly at Kyoto until 1916 investigating oracle bones, bronze inscriptions, bamboo strips discovered in Kansu, and other historical data. After returning to China, he edited a catalogue of the collection of tortoise-shell inscriptions belonging to Silas A. Hardoon; and in 1918 he became professor at a private university in Shanghai founded by Mrs. Hardoon (*née* Lo Chia-ling). During this period he became a devoted student of Shen Tseng-chih (1850–1922; T. Tzu-p'ei), from whom he learned much about phonology and the geography of Mongolia. He was also associated with Chang Erh-t'ien (q.v.) and with the Confucianist Sun Te-ch'ien (1869–1935; T. I-an); and both Wang and Chang Erh-t'ien worked under Shen Tseng-chih on compilation of a revised edition of the *Che-chiang t'ung-chih* [gazetteer of Chekiang].

As early as 1919, Wang Kuo-wei was approached by Peking University about a possible appointment as professor of Chinese. He repeatedly declined the offer, but in 1921 he agreed to become an adviser for its newly established graduate school of Chinese studies. In 1923, through his relations with Shen Tseng-chih and K'o Shao-min and on the recommendation of Sheng-yün (1858–1931), Wang was appointed a tutor on the staff of the deposed Manchu monarch P'u-yi (q.v.). Only a year later, however, P'u-yi was expelled from the imperial palace in Peking and forced to seek temporary refuge in the Japanese embassy compound in the Legation Quarter of Peking. As a Ch'ing loyalist, Wang Kuo-wei frequently went there to pay homage to the man whom he regarded as emperor of China.

About this time, Tsinghua College was considering the establishment of a research institute of sinological studies in Peking, and Wang Kuo-wei was invited to be its first dean. Wang declined at first, but he agreed in 1925 to join the Tsinghua graduate faculty as a professor after he had received authorization from P'u-yi. While at Tsinghua, Wang worked particularly on the history and geography of Mongolia, and he produced a substantial body of work between 1925 and 1927 in which he used documentation from non-Chinese sources to verify Chinese historical writings. His scholarly career seemed to be at a new peak. In late May 1927, however, word reached Peking that the advance of the National Revolutionary Army into Honan had placed Chiang Kai-shek's forces in a position to threaten Shantung and north China. On 2 June 1927 Wang quietly left the Tsinghua campus and went to the nearby Summer Palace, where he drowned himself in Kunming Lake. He left only a brief testament addressed to his third son, Wang Chen-ming, which read in full: "Now at the age of 50, all I owe to myself is death. Having passed through so many political upheavals, as a matter of principle I see no reason why I should be humiliated once again. After my death and subsequent simple funeral rites, I wish to be buried in the graveyard of Tsinghua. If you can not return to the south, you may as well live temporarily in Peking. Your elder brother need not come north for my funeral, partly because of the disruption of communication systems and partly because he has had no traveling experience. As for my books, they should be entrusted to Wu Mi and Ch'en Yin-k'o (qq.v.). There must be someone to look after the other members of our family who would in any case not find it impossible to go back to the south. In spite of the fact that I leave no inheritance of money or property to you, you will not starve to death, providing that you are careful, industrious, and thrifty."

The news of Wang Kuo-wei's suicide caught the scholarly world, both in China and abroad, completely by surprise. Many theories were later adduced in an effort to analyze the causes of his tragic death; and the autobiography of P'u-yi published many years later suggested that the reasons were financial pressures and friction with Lo Chen-yü. On balance, however, the contemporary observations of the prominent sinologist Ch'en Yin-k'o seem most plausible: "A man who has absorbed the best elements of a given cultural pattern finds it most difficult to adjust himself to a new and changing pattern, particularly if the latter is totally different from the former. The more elements of an older pattern that a man has absorbed, and the more he has identified with that pattern, the more he feels pain when that pattern draws to a drastic end. Eventually it reaches a point of no return, whereupon suicide is the only way out."

Wang Kuo-wei was generally regarded in China as a many-sided genius who provided fresh insights into a variety of specialized fields. Before 1911, he was a pioneer in critical studies of Sung poetry and Yuan drama, the latter a topic held in low esteem by most traditional Chinese scholars. His *Jen-chien tz'u-hua* [commentaries on the various schools of tz'u], published in 1910, remained an authoritative work; and his influential *Sung Yuan hsi-ch'ü shih* [history of Sung and Yuan drama], originally published in the same year, has never been wholly superseded. Wang himself wrote two collections of tz'u, later published together under the title *T'iao-hua tz'u*. He was not modest about his personal poetical accomplishments and once reportedly observed that only one or two poets since the Southern Sung (1127–1280) period had excelled him.

After 1912 Wang Kuo-wei relinquished earlier interests in literature and philosophy, including Western ideas, and devoted himself completely to serious study of ancient Chinese history. In this demanding field, Wang came to be regarded as perhaps the most brilliant Chinese scholar of the twentieth century. He and Lo Chen-yü were among the first Chinese to work on decipherment and analysis of inscribed fragments of bone and tortoise shell discovered in 1899 at Anyang in Honan. These proved to be records of divination from the Shang period (c.1500–1100 B.C.) and established the historical existence of that dynasty. Wang Kuo-wei demonstrated that information deduced from these inscriptions confirmed many statements in ancient Chinese texts which had become suspect as forged or otherwise untrustworthy sources. In *Studies in Early Chinese Culture* (1937), H. G. Creel described this labor of textual and historical criticism as one of the major achievements of twentieth-century world scholarship. Wang Kuo-wei also paid close attention to bronze inscriptions of the Shang period; and he and Lo Chen-yü worked jointly on Han dynasty records on bamboo strips, discovered at Tunhuang in Kansu, which proved to be of great importance in reconstruction of certain aspects of Chinese history and literature.

In connection with his scholarly work, Wang Kuo-wei went to great pains to study phonology, etymology, and the evolution of the Chinese written script. Unlike Chang Ping-lin (q.v.), Wang believed in the relevance of newly discovered sources such as the oracle-bone inscriptions for study of ancient history. He never reached conclusions without critical examination of all available evidence. He combined the highly sophisticated k'ao-cheng methodology developed by major Ch'ing scholars such as Ku Yen-wu (ECCP, I, 421–26), Tai Chen (ECCP, II, 695–700), and others with the use of fresh archaeological and other evidence: a combination that offered far broader scope for historical hypothecation than had been characteristic of traditional Chinese textual criticism.

Partly because of early training received from his Japanese mentor, Fujita Toyohachi, Wang was indirectly influenced by German historiographical methods, which emphasized the importance of primary source materials. It was through Wang's urging that Lo Chen-yü rescued a huge archival depository of late Ming and early Ch'ing cabinet records discovered at Peking in the course of repairs in one of the buildings of the imperial palace. This unique collection was preserved to form an important element in the documentary collection of the institute of history and philology of the Academia Sinica.

Wang Kuo-wei's collected scholarly writings were published twice. In 1940 his younger brother, Wang Kuo-hua (1887–), supervised preparation of the *Hai-ning Wang Ching-an hsien-sheng i-shu* [collected works of the late Wang Kuo-wei of Haining], which was edited with far greater precision than an earlier edition under the same title that had been hastily compiled in 1927 immediately after Wang's death.

Wang Kuo-wei married twice. His first wife, whom he married in 1897, bore him three sons, the youngest being Wang Chen-ming. About 1909 Wang Kuo-wei married again, and seven children were born of that union.

Wang Ming: *see* CH'EN SHAO-YÜ.

Wang P'eng-sheng   王芃生
Orig. Ta-chen   大楨
H.   Yueh-sou   曰叟

Wang P'eng-sheng (5 March 1893–17 May 1946), leading Kuomintang expert on Japanese affairs. During the war years in Chungking, he headed the Military Affairs Commission's institute of international relations, an intelligence-gathering body. He was closely associated with Tai Li (q.v.).

A native of Liling hsien, Hunan, Wang P'eng-sheng was the son of a scholar, Wang Chang-chih. After learning to read and write at home, in 1906 Wang P'eng-sheng enrolled at the Liling Higher Primary School, a modern institution staffed by teachers who had studied in Japan. About this time, the Hsing-min Book Company was established in Liling by a T'ung-meng-hui member, Ning Tiao-yuan. It published revolutionary literature, some of which Wang read. Because of family financial difficulties, Wang transferred to the tuition-free Liling Porcelain Industry School, where he studied porcelain painting and porcelain chemistry. Some of his teachers were Japanese, and he soon became interested in Japanese studies. After graduation, he worked for the porcelain company for 18 months. In the spring of 1909 he enrolled at the Army Primary School at Changsha, and that autumn he joined the T'ung-meng-hui.

When the republican revolution began with the Wuchang revolt of October 1911, Wang P'eng-sheng fought at Hanyang on behalf of the revolutionaries. He was forced to withdraw from active duty when he received a telegram informing him of his mother's critical illness. He returned to Liling, arriving there eight days after her death. Because one of her last wishes had been that he wed before her shrine, he married a local girl, *née* Chang. He remained at home in mourning until February 1912, when he went to Nanking to rejoin the students of the Changsha Army Primary School. By order of Huang Hsing (q.v.), these students had gone to

Nanking to be organized into a cadet corps. Because of his nearsightedness, Wang was assigned to the Military Supplies School. He and the school were moved to Peking in May. During his two years at the Military Supplies School, he came under the influence of Liu Yen, who taught international law. At the same time, he joined the Kuomintang and became a strong admirer of Sung Chiao-jen (q.v.). Wang soon began to devote every available moment to the study of international affairs and Japanese. He translated a number of Japanese legal documents into Chinese for the Anhwei Law Society. After graduation in 1914, he became an assistant instructor at the school.

In the winter of 1916 Wang P'eng-sheng went to Japan on a government scholarship to study at the Japanese Army Commissariat School. Because that school did not have separate classes for Chinese students, Wang was able to read certain war histories and reports which usually were not made available to Chinese. Upon graduation in 1918, he was assigned to field duty for three months. He then managed to have himself attached to the Japanese expeditionary force being sent to Siberia. He met several Japanese commanders and collected extensive information about Japanese units in the Ussuri River region. When he reached Manchouli, Wang discovered that the Japanese had placed him under surveillance. He immediately gave the documents he had collected to a Chinese YMCA official who was going to Mukden. Wang later went to Peking by way of Mukden and wrote a report for the Peking government. Upon receipt of the report, the Peking government sent him to Outer Mongolia as a member of an investigating mission. He returned to Peking two months later and wrote *Things Seen and Heard in Outer Mongolia*.

The Military Supplies School sent Wang P'eng-sheng to Japan again in the spring of 1920. He became a special student in the economics department of Imperial University in Tokyo. He spent much of his time studying the Japanese political system and collecting information about Japanese ambitions with reference to China. He soon became acquainted with another Chinese student, Kung Te-po, who shared his belief that the Peking government's intelligence efforts in Japan were dangerously weak. Wang and Kung began working together, and Wang soon completed the manuscripts for such works as the *Scientific Study of the History of Sino-Japanese Relations: Secret Record of the Truth About Negotiations over Taiwan*. When the Washington Conference was announced, Wang and Kung decided to use their knowledge to help the Peking government work out sound diplomatic policies. Accordingly, Wang wrote an essay entitled "Conjectures on the Washington Conference and What Items China Should Prepare to Take Up." Kung took the essay to Peking, where he gave it to his former teacher Hu Yuan-t'an (q.v.) for transmission to the Peking government. When the essay came to the attention of W. W. Yen (Yen Hui-ch'ing, q.v.), the head of the Chinese delegation to the Washington Conference, he appointed Wang and Kung advisers to the delegation.

While Wang P'eng-sheng was in the United States for the Washington Conference, his talents and thorough knowledge of Japanese affairs won him the admiration of Wang Ch'ung-hui (q.v.), who recommended him to C. T. Wang (Wang Cheng-t'ing, q.v.). Upon his return to China, Wang P'eng-sheng was made deputy chief of the investigation department of the Shantung Rehabilitation Commission, headed by C. T. Wang. He held this and other posts at Peking until February 1924, when he went to Shanghai and took a teaching job at the Shanghai Statistical Institute. In the summer of 1925 he took part in a plot to overthrow the military governor of Shantung, Chang Tsung-ch'ang (q.v.). The plot was exposed, however, and Wang fled to Japan. He studied ancient Japanese texts and wrote such articles as the "Discourse on Japanese History" and "The Forgery of Japan's Ancient History." By this time, he had become known as China's foremost "Japanologist."

Wang P'eng-sheng returned to China in the summer of 1926 to become chief of staff, with the rank of colonel, in the 2nd Division of the Eighth Army of the National Revolutionary Army. The division was commanded by Ho Chien (q.v.). With the completion of the first stage of the Northern Expedition and the split of the Kuomintang into factions based at Wuhan and Nanking, Ho Chien was made commander of the Thirty-fifth Army of the Fourth Front Army, with Wang as his chief of staff. When Ho became acting governor of Anhwei in September, Wang was appointed acting commissioner of civil affairs for that province. Later that year, Ho sent Wang to Shanghai to call on Chiang Kai-shek, then in temporary retirement, and express Ho's loyalty to Chiang. At Chiang's invitation, Wang remained in Shanghai as a member of Chiang's staff.

In June 1928 C. T. Wang, then minister of foreign affairs at Nanking, sent Wang P'eng-sheng to Japan on a secret mission to convince Japanese officials not to obstruct negotiations on the revision of Chinese treaties with foreign powers. Wang's success in this mission and in preparing the way for Japanese recognition of the National Government (achieved in June 1929) was such that C. T. Wang later sent him a letter in which he said: "Had it not been for your struggles in Japan for half a year, at least the negotiations over tariff autonomy would have been sabotaged by Japan. It was largely due to your efforts that we here in Nanking have been able to make some smooth progress." After returning to China, Wang P'eng-sheng served for three years as an adviser to the Hunan provincial government. By mid-April 1931 his continued observation of Japanese politics had convinced him that Japan was about to invade Manchuria. He went to Peiping in an attempt to persuade Chang Hsueh-liang (q.v.) to make preparations for the defense of Manchuria, but he failed to convince Chang of the immediate peril. The Japanese occupation of Manchuria began with the Mukden Incident of 18 September 1931. In the aftermath of this incident, V. K. Wellington Koo (Ku Wei-chün, q.v.) was attached to the Lytton Commission, which was sent to Manchuria by the League of Nations to investigate the Sino-Japanese dispute. At Koo's request, Wang supplied the commission with a large amount of information and documentary evidence in support of China's case.

Also in 1932, Wang P'eng-sheng divorced his wife and married Charlotte D. Tsung, a Wellesley graduate. In September, they were appointed to the Chinese delegation to the General Assembly of the League of Nations. After the meetings ended, they toured Europe and then spent six months in London, where Wang spent most of his time studying Japanese materials at the British Museum. They left London in February 1935 for Ankara, Turkey, where Wang served for a year as counselor of the Chinese legation under Ho Yao-tsu (q.v.). From February to November 1936 Wang served in Tokyo as adviser to Hsü Shih-ying (q.v.), then the Chinese ambassador to Japan. Wang returned to China in November 1936 convinced that war was imminent.

After the Sino-Jaanese war began in July 1937, Wang P'eng-sheng was appointed vice minister of communications in the National Government. He soon went to Kunming to discuss the construction of the Burma Road with Lung Yun (q.v.), the governor of Yunnan. After these discussions, he went on a good-will mission to Burma, Thailand, Viet Nam, and Singapore. Before the war had begun, Wang had proposed the establishment of an international problems research institute to strengthen China's intelligence efforts. Late in 1937 he was summoned to Hankow by Chiang Kai-shek and was appointed director of the Military Affairs Commission's institute of international affairs. By 24 November 1941, the information collected by the institute (then at Chungking) from sources throughout the world had convinced Wang that the Japanese were about to launch a major attack in the Pacific. The War in the Pacific began with the bombing of Pearl Harbor on 7 December 1941. The efficiency of Wang's intelligence-gathering operation brought him to the attention of Allied intelligence services, and he became closely associated with them. In China, he was identified with Tai Li (q.v.) and his intelligence operations.

At war's end, Wang P'eng-sheng went to Peiping and Tientsin to deal with problems concerning Japanese prisoners of war and civil residents. By this time, his health had deteriorated because of wartime strains. He rejoined the National Government at Nanking on 16 May 1946. The following day, he suffered a heart attack and died. He was survived by his second wife and by their sons, Hsiao-peng and Yu-peng.

Wang Shih-chen　　　　王 士 珍
　T. P'in-ch'ing　　　　聘 卿
　H. Kuan-ju　　　　　冠 儒

Wang Shih-chen (1861–1 July 1930), one of Yuan Shih-k'ai's three chief assistants (with

Tuan Ch'i-jui and Feng Kuo-chang) in organizing and training the Peiyang Army. In 1917 he served as premier and minister of war at Peking, and in 1922 he became president of the college of marshals.

Chengting, Chihli (Hopei), was the birthplace of Wang Shih-chen. The Wang family had been well-to-do and had produced officials and military officers. However, Wang's father and uncle both died when he was a young child, and the family finances quickly diminished. Because he was a sickly child, Wang was late in starting to school. After a few years of traditional education, about 1876 he began to train himself in archery and horseback riding to develop the proficiency required by the military examinations. In 1877 he enlisted in the Chengting garrison force. It later was transferred to Shanhaikuan, the strategic pass between China proper and Manchuria.

In 1885, when Li Hung-chang (ECCP, I, 464–71) established a military academy in Tientsin, Wang Shih-chen became a member of its first class. After three years of modern military training, he was graduated in 1888 and was sent back to Shanhaikuan to take charge of artillery instruction. He and his students went to Korea in 1894 to take part in the Sino-Japanese war. Because of the humiliating defeat sustained in that war, China embarked on a program of military reorganization. In 1896 Wang Shih-chen became chief assistant to Yuan Shih-k'ai in the Newly Created Army and commander of the engineering corps. He also participated in various teaching and course development programs at the Tientsin Military Academy. In 1900, when Yuan Shih-k'ai was appointed governor of Shantung, Wang was entrusted with the arrangements for the transfer of his troops from Tientsin to Shantung. When Yuan became governor general of Chihli in 1902, he instituted a new army program in which Wang played an important role. After the establishment of a provincial training center at Paoting, Wang was made commander of the 1st Infantry Brigade and was given general responsibility for training.

A commission for army reorganization was established at Peking in 1903, and Wang Shih-chen became chief of its department of military training. He later was appointed chief of the department of military administration and

commander of the 6th Division of the New Army. When the commission for army reorganization was brought under the Board of the Army, Wang was made acting vice president of that board. He was confirmed in that office in mid-1907, at which time he also became provincial commander in chief of the garrison force in northern Kiangsu. After he had made several requests for relief because of ill health, Wang was allowed to resign from these offices in 1910. When the revolution began in 1911, he was recalled to serve as governor general of Hupeh and Hunan and, later, as minister of war. When the republic was established, he retired to his native Chengting.

In the summer of 1914 Yuan Shih-k'ai, who then held the presidency at Peking, persuaded Wang Shih-chen to come out of retirement and to hold office in the Peking government. Wang was made resident director of the office of the supreme commander of military forces and head of the model corps at Peking, Yuan's personal elite force. In 1915 Wang became acting minister of war, and in 1916 he was appointed chief of general staff. He evidently remained aloof from Yuan Shih-k'ai's monarchical movement.

The death of Yuan Shih-k'ai in June 1916 did not damage Wang Shih-chen's career. In June 1917 he was appointed minister of war. During the restoration attempt of Chang Hsün (q.v.), he was appointed grand councillor. When the forces of Tuan Ch'i-jui (q.v.) moved against Chang Hsün at Peking, Wang led the cadets of the model corps in support of Tuan's troops. Later in 1917, after Feng Kuo-chang (q.v.) became acting president, Wang served as premier and minister of war. He resigned in 1918. In 1922 he was made a marshal and was appointed president of the college of marshals.

Early in 1925 Tuan Ch'i-jui, then provisional chief executive at Peking, convened the so-called rehabilitation conference. Wang Shih-chen served as a delegate to this conference and as chairman of the military reorganization committee. Later, when Chang Tso-lin and his Fengtien forces entered Peking in 1926 and when the Northern Expedition forces won control of Peking in 1928, Wang attempted to preserve peace and order in the city. Thereafter, until his death on 1 July 1930, he led a quiet life in the old capital.

During a militarist-dominated period in

north China, Wang Shih-chen showed little interest in the struggle for personal position, territorial control, or private fortune. It is said that he always refrained from talking about his own achievements. When asked, he would say: "These are all 'mirrored flowers' and 'reflections of the moon in water' which are highly illusory. What good does it do to reminisce?" On his deathbed he said that the death of a man is like the fading of smoke, and his last wish was that his funeral would be a simple one.

Wang Shih-chieh　　　王 世 杰
T. Hsüeh-t'ing　　　　雪 艇

Wang Shih-chieh (10 March 1891–), chancellor of Wuhan University (1929–32) and minister of education (1933–36) who served during the Sino-Japanese war as secretary general of the People's Political Council and minister of information. In 1945–48 he was minister of foreign affairs. He served as secretary general of the presidential office in Taiwan in the early 1950's. In 1962 he became president of the Academia Sinica.

Little is known about Wang Shih-chieh's family background or early life except that he was born in Ch'ungyang, Hupeh, and that he received his primary and secondary education in his native province. In 1911, the year of the republican revolution, he entered Peiyang University in Tientsin. Upon graduation, he went to England and enrolled at the University of London. After receiving a B.S. in economics and political science in 1917, he enrolled at the University of Paris, from which he received the degree of Docteur en Droit in 1920.

Wang Shih-chieh returned to China in 1921 to become professor of comparative constitutional law at Peking University. About 1923 he was made dean of the law school. He wrote scholarly articles for the *Pei-cheng ta-hsueh she-hui k'o-hsueh chi-k'an* [journal of social sciences of Peking University] and produced a two-volume work, *Pi-chiao hsien-fa* [comparative constitutional law], which later was adopted as a standard textbook in many colleges in China. During this period, he gradually became interested in contemporary politics, and in 1924 he and several friends founded the *Hsien-tai p'ing-lun* [modern critic]. He contributed several

articles to the magazine criticizing the ineptitude and corruption then prevailing in the capital. The Peking government responded by banning the magazine in 1926. Wang and some of his collaborators, presumably fearful of arrest and imprisonment, fled Peking. By February 1927, Wang had returned to his native Hupeh.

Early in 1927 the National Government at Wuhan appointed Wang Shih-chieh to its foreign treaty commission. With the reunification of the Kuomintang and the establishment at Nanking of a new National Government in September 1927, he moved to Nanking and became director of the legislative bureau. In the governmental reorganization of 1928, he was appointed to the newly established Legislative Yuan. Also in 1928 Wang was elected to the Permanent Court of Arbitration at The Hague, a post he retained until 1938 even though he spent little time at The Hague. About 1929 he was made director of the legislative section of the National Central Institute of Social Sciences at Nanking.

Beginning in Feburary 1929 Wang Shih-chieh devoted much of his time to a new office, that of chancellor of Wuhan University. In 1930 he founded the *Wuhan ta-hsueh she-hui k'o-hsueh chi-k'an* [Wuhan University social science quarterly]. He lost his membership in the Legislative Yuan in 1931 but took on new responsibilities as Hupeh provincial commissioner of education in April 1932. He left Wuhan in 1933 to become minister of education in the National Government. In this capacity, he initiated a series of important reforms to strengthen the school system and to spur the nation's intellectual growth. He worked to increase the number of science courses offered at all levels and to expand the hitherto underdeveloped normal and vocational schools. In 1934–35 regulations governing postgraduate research and the granting of degrees were promulgated, and the National Government began to give financial assistance to private universities. Wang vigorously promoted closer cooperation between the Academia Sinica and various institutions of higher education. At the same time, he launched a nation-wide compulsory education program. In 1935–36, in the interest of efficiency, he restructured the entire ministry of education. After the outbreak of the Sino-Japanese war and the removal of the National

Government to Wuhan, Wang was replaced by Ch'en Li-fu (q.v.), an expert in doctrinal training, as minister of education.

In April 1938 Wang Shih-chieh became secretary general of the People's Political Council. After the National Government moved to Chungking at the end of 1938, he received such additional posts as those of counsel to the Military Affairs Commission, minister of information, secretary general of the standing committee of the San Min Chu I Youth Corps, president of the Central Cultural Association, and head of the Anglo-Chinese Cultural Association. In 1941 he received the additional office of secretary general of the Supreme National Defense Council's central planning board. In 1942, however, he was relieved of one of his many posts—that of minister of information. He was elevated to the presidium of the People's Political Council in May 1943. That November, he headed a good-will mission which visited England on the invitation of the British government. After being received by King George VI, Wang presented a personal letter from Chiang Kai-shek to Prime Minister Winston Churchill, a message from the People's Political Council to the British Parliament, and greetings from the Chinese National Press Association to the British press. After spending forty-four days in England, the mission split into two groups. Wang led one group back to China by way of the United States in February 1944. After his return, he was reappointed minister of information. On 30 July 1945 he succeeded T. V. Soong (q.v.) as minister of foreign affairs, and on 14 August of that year he signed the Sino-Soviet Treaty of Friendship and Alliance. According to this treaty, which was based on the Yalta pact, China yielded various rights in Manchuria and in the Chinese cities of Dairen and Port Arthur, and the autonomy of Outer Mongolia was recognized. When the terms of the treaty became known in China in 1946, a public outcry ensued. In September 1945 Wang attended the Big Five Foreign Ministers Conference in London, where he argued that China should have a preferred position with respect to Japanese reparations because of the length of time China had been engaged in the war and the losses it had sustained.

Between his trips to Moscow and London, Wang Shih-chieh participated in negotiations with the Chinese Communists. At the end of August 1945 Mao Tse-tung went to Chungking for negotiations with Chiang Kai-shek. Chang Ch'ün, Shao Li-tzu (qq.v.) and Wang Shih-chieh held working-level conferences with Chou En-lai, Wang Jo-fei (q.v.), and other Communist representatives. After he returned from London, Wang Shih-chieh participated in the Political Consultative Conference held at Chungking in January 1946 as part of the American effort to mediate the Kuomintang-Communist conflict.

After the failure of the American mediation effort in China and the resumption of the civil war between the Kuomintang and the Chinese Communists, Wang Shih-chieh pursued a strongly America-oriented foreign policy. In January 1948, when the United States government was addressing itself to the problem of how to buttress the deteriorating Nationalist position in China, he sent a mission to Washington to press for financial aid. With the passage of the China Aid Act of 1948, he became a member of the Council for United States Aid to China, which was set up under the Executive Yuan to control the utilization of American economic aid. The military situation in China, however, was not waiting on American aid; the Nationalist troops suffered repeated defeats. The efforts of Chang Ch'ün, Madame Chiang Kai-shek (Soong Mei-ling), Chiang T'ing-fu (qq.v.), and Wang Shih-chieh in the area of foreign policy could not offset the military defeats and the galloping inflation plaguing the Nationalists. Wang was replaced as foreign minister by Wu T'ieh-ch'eng (q.v.) at the end of 1948, but he continued to be closely associated with Chiang Kai-shek's plans and projects. Before retiring from the presidency early in 1949 in favor of Li Tsung-jen (q.v.), Chiang had begun to create a new political organization on Taiwan, and Wang became chief of the central planning committee of the Kuomintang party leader's office there. He accompanied Chiang to the important meeting with Li Tsung-jen at Hangchow in April 1949 and on trips to the Philippines and South Korea that summer.

When Chiang Kai-shek resumed the presidency of the National Government in Taiwan in March 1950, Wang Shih-chieh became secretary general of the presidential office and a member of the Kuomintang Central Advisory

Committee. He held these posts until 1954, when he retired to private life. He emerged from retirement in July 1958 to become minister without portfolio in the cabinet of Ch'en Ch'eng (q.v.). In April 1962 he succeeded Hu Shih (q.v.) as president of the Academia Sinica.

Little is known about Wang Shih-chieh's personal life except that he was married to Hsiao Te-hua.

Wang Tsao-shih   王 造 時

Wang Tsao-shih (1903–), a leader of the National Salvation Association who gained national prominence as one of the Ch'i-chün-tzu [seven gentlemen] arrested by the National Government in November 1936 for advocating formation of a united front with the Chinese Communists against the Japanese.

Little is known about Wang Tsao-shih's family background or early years except that he was born in Anfu hsien, Kiangsi. He was a student at Tsinghua College at the time of the May Fourth Movement of 1919, and he became a student leader. After the May Thirtieth Incident at Shanghai in 1925, when British police fired on Chinese, he was sent by Peking students to Shanghai to support the ensuing strikes and demonstrations. During his student days at Tsinghua he was known for his oratory, and at one time he reportedly served as chairman of the student government. Upon graduation, he went to the United States and enrolled at the University of Wisconsin. He obtained a Ph.D. in political science, did some work at the University of Chicago, and became a research fellow at the University of London.

Wang Tsao-shih returned to China about 1930 and began teaching at Kuang-hua University, later becoming dean of its school of arts. He became an advocate of constitutional government for China about the time that the Japanese attacked Mukden in September 1931, and he began publishing articles on government and politics in Shanghai newspapers. As Japanese encroachment on Chinese territory continued, he became increasingly outspoken, expressing his criticisms of the National Government's policy of non-resistance in such publications as the *Tung-fang tsa-chih* and the *Hsin*

Chung-hua tsa-chih. As a result of these articles, he no longer was able to supplement his income by lecturing at institutions which were supported by the National Government. Accordingly, he opened a law practice in Shanghai. He retained his position at Kuang-hua University without difficulty, for it was a private institution.

In 1935 Wang Tsao-shih helped organize the Shanghai Writers' Association and became a member of its standing committee. In January 1936 he helped Shen Chün-ju and Tsou T'ao-fen (qq.v.) establish the Cultural Workers' National Salvation Association. That May, the All-China Federation of National Salvation Associations (usually referred to as the National Salvation Association) was formed, and Wang became a member of its standing committee. The new organization issued a statement entitled "The First Political Principles in Resisting Japan and Saving the Nation." Two months later, Chang Nai-ch'i, T'ao Hsing-chih (qq.v.), Shen Chün-ju, and Tsou T'ao-fen published "A Number of Essential Conditions and Minimum Demands for a United Resistance to Invasion." These National Salvation Association leaders called for an end to civil strife with the Chinese Communists, the release of political prisoners, and the establishment of a united front against the Japanese. Because the Chinese Communists responded favorably to this proposal, some National Government officials came to believe that the National Salvation Association was working with the Chinese Communists.

Toward the end of 1936, strikes broke out in Japanese-owned factories in Shanghai. Although the leaders of the National Salvation Association did not instigate these strikes, they supported them by creating a relief committee to provide financial aid to the strikers. As a result, the National Government took action against the National Salvation Association. On 22 November 1936 Wang Tsao-shih was arrested at his home in Shanghai on charges of endangering the nation by weakening the people's confidence in the National Government and propagating ideas that were detrimental to the *San-min chu-i*. Also arrested were Shen Chün-ju, Tsou T'ao-fen, Chang Nai-ch'i, Li Kung-p'u, Sha Ch'ien-li, and Shih Liang. They became known collectively as the Ch'i-chün-tzu [seven gentlemen]. Not long after their arrest, the

Sian Incident occurred. Among the demands put forth by Chang Hsueh-liang (q.v.) was the release of political prisoners, specifically the Ch'i-chün-tzu. Because of this demand, Wang and his fellow prisoners were suspected of having been associated with Chang in planning the Sian Incident.

The Ch'i-chün-tzu were held under surveillance at the Shanghai municipal police station and, after 4 December 1936, in the detention house of the higher court at Soochow. They did not come up for trial until April 1937. Wang passed the time by revising the manuscript of his book *An Analysis of the China Problem*, which had been scheduled to appear in 1935 but which had encountered censorship problems. He also worked on the manuscript of *Huang-miao chi*. Wang fully exhibited his knowledge and oratorical skill during the trial in April 1937. He accused the National Government spokesman of being ignorant of the principles of political power and modern government. The government, he argued, should be differentiated from the nation. Moreover, the government derived its power to rule from the people. In so arguing, Wang challenged the official indictment, which presupposed that to criticize the National Government was to endanger the Chinese nation. The Ch'i-chün-tzu were released on bail without sentence on 31 July, after the Sino-Japanese war had begun. They immediately announced that "one is not wrong for wanting to save the country" and plunged vigorously into anti-Japanese activities. Wang Tsao-shih became a member of the People's Political Council at Wuhan in July 1938, and from 1938 to 1942 he was chief editor of the *Ch'ien-hsien jih-pao* in Kiangsi.

Information is lacking about Wang Tsao-shih's activities from 1942 to 1949. He was identified in 1949 as the publisher of the Freedom Press. After the People's Republic of China was established in 1949 he served on the cultural and education committee of the East China Military and Administrative Committee. During the 1957 anti-rightist campaign, Wang was accused of collaborating with Lo Lung-chi and Chang Po-chün (qq.v). It was reported that he had attacked the Central People's Government's judicial work, had attempted to control the *Hsin-wen jih-pao*, had "peddled democracy of the American brand,"

and had tried to revive the National Salvation Association in order to influence and control students and overseas Chinese. Wang then disappeared from public view.

Wang Tsao-shih was married to Chu T'ou-fang. They were known to have four children.

Wang Yao-ch'ing   王 瑤 卿
T. Chih-t'ing   稺 庭

Wang Yao-ch'ing (1882–1954), actor noted for his portrayal of the ch'ing-i-tan roles in Peking drama and for his stage partnership with T'an Hsin-p'ei (q.v.). Wang was a teacher of Mei Lan-fang (q.v.).

The eldest son of Wang Ts'ai-lin, a noted actor of the sheng [male] roles in Peking drama, Wang Yao-ch'ing received the traditional training required for actors. In 1904 he was registered in the imperial household bureau of theatrical entertainment (Sheng-p'ing-shu). Wang played the ch'ing-i-tan [female] roles, and during his years of stage partnership with T'an Hsin-p'ei (q.v.) he often was seen in such plays as *Wu Chia P'o, Nan T'ien Men, Fen-ho wan*, and *Ssu-lang t'an-mu*. In the last-named play, he wore a stylish Manchu lady's costume with such flair that he established a precedent for future interpreters of the role. Singing is very important in the ch'ing-i roles, and actors usually had paid little attention to expression and movement. Wang Yao-ch'ing was the first Chinese actor to break with this tradition and to introduce greater fluidity into the old ch'ing-i forms. During his heyday on the Peking stage, Wang developed his own singing style by drawing upon older methods and techniques and combining them in new ways to produce the effects he desired.

Unfortunately for Wang, his voice deteriorated before he reached the peak of his career. He retired from the stage in 1911 to become a teacher and adviser. Although his was a power behind the scenes after 1911, he nevertheless made a significant contribution to traditional Chinese dramatic art. The famous stage musician Mei Yü-t'ien arranged for his nephew Mei Lan-fang (q.v.) to have private lessons with Wang. It was largely due to Wang's experiments and teaching that Mei Lan-fang was able to perfect his new approach to older acting forms. Wang's attention to facial expression and stylized body movements, for example, prepared the way for Mei's later mingling of the wu-tan, hua-tan, and ch'ing-i acting methods, which previously had been rigorously separated. Mei Lan-fang never failed to acknowledge his debt to Wang Yao-ch'ing. Wang was also one of the first Chinese acting teachers who was willing to instruct girls. A number of the promising young actresses who came to the fore in the 1930's were students of Wang. During the last years of his life, Wang was associated with the Hsi-chü hsueh-hsiao, a training school at Peiping for actors of the traditional drama. He died in 1954.

When he lost his singing voice, Wang had won recognition for his innovative interpretations of the roles that were his specialty. Had he not suffered that professional tragedy, he might have gone on to become one of the great actors of the period. However, his distinctive talents were perpetuated in the achievements of his pupils.

Wang Yao-ch'ing's younger brother Wang Feng-ch'ing was an actor of the sheng roles who often appeared with Mei Lan-fang after 1912.

Wang Yin-t'ai　　　　王 蔭 泰
T. Meng-ch'ün　　　　孟 羣

Wang Yin-t'ai (14 July 1888–15 December 1961), German-trained lawyer who was counselor of the law drafting bureau at Peking in 1914–19. He later held a variety of positions at Peking, becoming minister of foreign affairs in 1927. During the Sino-Japanese war, he held office in the Japanese-sponsored government in north China.

Born in Shaohsing, Chekiang, Wang Yin-t'ai received his early education in the Chinese classics at local schools. In 1902 he went to Japan and entered the First Higher School. Upon graduation in 1906, he went to Germany, where he enrolled in the law department of Berlin University. In 1909 Tuan-fang (ECCP, II, 780–82) commissioned him to make a study of the German constitutional system and local government, thus providing Wang with an opportunity to pursue practical research beyond that usually done by an undergraduate. Wang received his LL.B. degree from Berlin University in 1912, the year that the Chinese republic was established. Upon his return to China early in 1913 he was engaged as an editor-translator in the law drafting bureau of the Peking government. He soon was promoted to the post of editor-compiler of the law compilation commission and then was made counselor of the law drafting bureau. For a time, he also was professor of law at Peking University.

Wang served as counselor of the law drafting bureau for seven years, from 1914 to 1920. The degree of his participation in the bureau's work varied, for he also served at various times on government commissions concerned with the civil service and the diplomatic and consular service. In 1917, when the question of China's participation in the First World War became a political issue at Peking (for details, *see* Tuan Ch'i-jui), Wang's own role in the government took on a partisan character. After war was declared by China in August, Wang became a legal adviser to the office of the custodian of enemy property. He thus was closely associated with the powerful pro-Japanese elements in Tuan Ch'i-jui's coterie, particularly Ts'ao Ju-lin and Hsü Shu-cheng (qq.v.). Later that year, he was attached to the mission in Japan that was negotiating matters pertaining to the so-called Nishihara loans. He remained in Japan until mid-1919.

Upon his return to China in 1919, Wang Yin-t'ai was appointed legal counselor to the office of the high commissioner for northwestern frontier development, serving under Hsü Shu-cheng. In October, he accompanied Hsü to Urga (Ulan Bator), where Hsü forced the Mongol leaders to "petition" Peking to accept the renunciation of Mongolian autonomy and to organize a new government at Urga. Hsü was made rehabilitation commissioner for Outer Mongolia, and in 1920 Wang became the director of the general affairs office of the commander in chief of the Northwest Frontier Defense Army, the commander in chief being Hsü. Wang appears to have remained in Urga after Hsü's downfall in 1920, and he presumably retreated to Siberia at the time of the White Russian occupation of Urga, led by Baron von Ungern-Sternberg, in February 1921. He then went to Manchuria and entered the service of

Chang Tso-lin (q.v.). After assisting Yang Yü-t'ing (q.v.) in the organization of the Mukden arsenal, Wang became an adviser to Chang Tso-lin in the headquarters of the Fengtien Army.

In January 1922 Wang Yin-t'ai returned to Peking to become counselor to the civil service bureau in the cabinet headed by W. W. Yen (Yen Hui-ch'ing, q.v.). Power struggles and changes of administration notwithstanding, he remained in Peking. In November 1922 he resumed his old post of counselor of the law drafting bureau. He served as a member of the Chinese delegation to the Customs Tariff Revision Conference at Peking in late 1925 and early 1926. He also held office as vice minister of foreign affairs in the short-lived regency cabinet of Tu Hsi-kuei. In June 1927 Chang Tso-lin, who then held power at Peking, proclaimed himself Ta-yuan-shuai, or general-issimo of China. On 20 June, Wang became minister of foreign affairs in the new cabinet organized by P'an Fu. He assumed the post of minister of justice in June 1928, just a few days before the Northern Expedition reached Peking. At the time of the Nationalist victory, Wang accepted a post as managing director of the Exchange Bank of China. In 1930 he went to Shanghai and established a private law practice.

Wang Yin-t'ai returned to public life in 1938 as minister of industries in the Japanese-sponsored provisional government at Peiping. He also served on that regime's economic consultative commission. With the establishment of the Japanese-sponsored government at Nanking headed by Wang Ching-wei (q.v.) in 1940, the Peiping regime was reorganized as the north China political council. Wang served as director general of the board of industries and as a member of the council's standing committee. He held those posts until the Japanese surrender in 1945.

In October 1945 Wang Yin-t'ai was arrested at Peiping on charges of collaboration. He later was sentenced to death, but the sentence was reduced to life imprisonment by Chiang Kai-shek. As a political prisoner, he was left in jail at the time of the Nationalist downfall, and he remained there under the Communists for more than a decade until his death on 15 December 1961. During his lengthy confine-

ment, Wang became an assiduous student of Buddhism. He also worked on a German-Chinese dictionary.

Wang Yin-t'ai was married to Ruth Kettner, the daughter of a German Lutheran minister. They had six daughters: Suzanne, Ruth, Linda, Didi, Billa, and Liana. All of the children went to live in the West.

Wang Yün-wu   王 雲 五
Orig. Chih-jui   志 瑞

Wang Yün-wu (9 July 1888–), editor in chief (1921–29) and general manager (1930–45) of the Commercial Press, republican China's largest publishing house. From May 1946 to April 1947 he was minister of economic affairs, and in 1948 he served as minister of finance during the ill-fated gold yuan currency conversion. In Taiwan, he was vice president of the Examination Yuan in 1954–56 and vice president of the Executive Yuan in 1960–63.

Although his native place was Hsiangshan (Chungshan), Kwangtung, Wang Yün-wu was born in Shanghai. He was the fourth of five children born to the merchant Wang Li-tang. His eldest brother, ten years his senior, passed the examinations for the sheng-yuan degree in 1896, at the comparatively early age of 19 sui. It was this brother who taught Wang Yün-wu to read. The premature death of this brother in 1898 and Wang Yün-wu's own delicate state of health as a child caused his father to delay sending him to school. It was not until 1899, when he was 11 sui, that Wang Yün-wu was admitted to a Shanghai private school. His education was interrupted a year later, when his father sent the family to the ancestral home at Hsiangshan because of the Boxer Uprising. Wang returned to Shanghai and to school in 1901, but in 1902 his father apprenticed him to a merchant. Thereafter, Wang had to content himself with studies at a night school, where he learned English. Because of his phenomenal progress in English, in 1905 he was allowed to go to a private school, the Tung-wen-kuan, operated by the English missionary Charles Budd. Wang soon became a teaching assistant to Budd, who gave the young man free access to his fine collection of books.

In 1907 Wang Yün-wu became a teacher of English at the New China Academy and he retained this post after the academy was reunited with its parent institution, the Chungkuo kung-hsueh. Among his pupils were Hu Shih, Chu Ching-nung (qq.v.), and Yang Hsing-fo. At the end of 1911, Wang was appointed by the Cantonese community in Shanghai to deliver the address of welcome at a reception for Sun Yat-sen. Sun responded by appointing Wang a secretary in the provisional government established at Nanking in 1912. Wang soon submitted a memorandum on education to Ts'ai Yuan-p'ei (q.v.), who appointed Wang to the ministry of education. After the provisional government moved to Peking, Wang became a section chief and then a division director. He left the ministry of education in May 1913 to become a working journalist and a teacher at Kuo-min and Peking universities. In 1914 he accepted a part-time post as head of the compilation and translation division in the national petroleum bureau, headed by Hsiung Hsi-ling (q.v.). Throughout the 1912–15 period, Wang also pursued his own studies. He enrolled in the International Correspondence School, taking courses in civil engineering and applied chemistry. At the same time, he completed the law course offered by the La Salle Correspondence School.

Wang Yün-wu returned to Shanghai in 1916. After serving for a time as special commissioner of Kiangsu, Anhwei, and Kiangsi for prohibiting opium, he turned once more to compilation and translation. In 1921 he joined the Commercial Press, China's leading publishing firm, as editor in chief and head of the compilation and translation department. Among the projects he undertook was the *Chiao-yü ta-tzu-tien* [educational dictionary], the first specialized dictionary of professional quality to be published in China. In 1924 he developed the "four corner numeral system" for the identification and classification of Chinese characters. This system came to be used by a number of lexicographers in China. During this period, Wang also became the librarian of the Tung-fang t'u-shu-kuan, or Oriental Library. It was an expansion of the Han-fen-lou collection, which had been built up for the Commercial Press by Chang Yuan-chi (q.v.). After Wang was elected chairman of the Shanghai Library Association, he opened the Oriental Library to the public, with the approval of the Commercial Press, and recatalogued the collection according to the Dewey Decimal system. To encourage the establishment of new libraries throughout China, he undertook the production of such series as the Pai-k'o-hsiao-ts'ung-shu [miniature encyclopedia] and the Wan-yu-wen-k'u [universal library]. The latter series, which included both Chinese classics and translations of foreign works, was composed of 1,010 titles bound in 2,000 volumes.

In the summer of 1929 Wang Yün-wu resigned from the Commercial Press and accepted an appointment from the Academia Sinica as a researcher. Six months later, upon the death in November 1929 of Pao Hsien-ch'ang, the general manager of the publishing house, Wang was asked to succeed Pao. He accepted the offer on the condition that he first go abroad to study scientific management. In March 1930 he left China on a tour of Japan, the United States, England, France, Germany, Belgium, the Netherlands, and Italy. He visited factories, called on experts, and studied every book he could find on scientific management. On his return to China in early September 1930, Wang Yün-wu assumed the general managership of the Commercial Press and began to use the techniques of scientific management. His innovations attracted the attention of businessmen throughout Shanghai. Before he could justify his efforts, however, the offices of the Commercial Press, the Oriental Library, and the dormitories for workers were destroyed in the Sino-Japanese hostilities of January 1932.

The period immediately following this disaster was necessarily a trying one for Wang Yün-wu. The Commercial Press had established printing plants in Hong Kong and Peiping, and the fullest use possible was made of these facilities in order to produce the large quantities of textbooks needed in schools that autumn. The restoration of production in Shanghai was, of course, gradual, and it was attended by serious labor disputes. Despite these difficulties and the death of his father in April 1932, Wang persisted in his efforts. By autumn, Commercial Press operations in Shanghai were at 30 percent of capacity. Wang thoroughly reorganized the Shanghai plant, achieving greater labor efficiency and lower production costs. Late in 1932 he embarked on the compilation of the Ta-hsueh ts'ung-shu [university library], a series intended for China's institutions of higher learning, which hitherto had relied mainly on foreign textbooks. By July 1937 more than 260 titles in this series had been published. During this period, Wang also continued to produce facsimile editions of rare classical works (*see* Chang Yuan-chi). Another important project was the Ts'ung-shu-chi-ch'eng series, a collection of over 3,000 volumes of writings selected for reduplication from rare *ts'ung-shu* [collectanea].

When the Sino-Japanese war began in July 1937, Wang Yün-wu moved some of the Commercial Press equipment from Shanghai to the Hong Kong plant. In 1938 he entered political life as a member of the People's Political Council. Wang moved to Chungking in February 1942, soon after the War in the Pacific broke out, and established a Commercial Press office in the wartime capital. He became increasingly interested in economics, and in October 1942 he was appointed chief of the Yunnan-Kweichow regional office of the economic mobilization promotion committee. After spending a month at Kunming, he returned to Chungking in February 1943 and wrote an article on price control. That November he was appointed to the People's Political Council's good-will mission to England. In London, Wang made public speeches, visited bookstores and met with leading British intellectuals. On his way back to China in January 1944, he visited Portugal, Egypt, Iran, Iraq, and Turkey. After reporting to the resident committee of the People's Political Council, he published his *Diary of the Chinese Mission in Great Britain* and *Impressions of Wartime Britain*.

In January 1946 Wang Yün-wu was one of the nine unaffiliated delegates to the Political Consultative Conference held at Chungking as part of the American effort to prevent civil war by mediating between the Nationalists and the Chinese Communists. Wang left Chungking in April 1946 to reestablish the Commercial Press at Shanghai. A month later, Chiang Kai-shek appointed Wang minister of economic affairs in the National Government. Wang accepted the appointment and in October he turned over the general managership of the Commercial Press to Chu Ching-nung (q.v.).

As minister of economic affairs, Wang often found himself at loggerheads with T. V. Soong (q.v.), and he tendered his resignation three times in 1946. He finally relinquished that post in April 1947, when he became a member of the State Council. In May 1948, when Wong Wen-hao (q.v.) became the first president of the Executive Yuan to be chosen under the new 1947 constitution, Wang was appointed minister of finance in Wong's cabinet. That July, Wang undertook a currency reform with the introduction of the chin yuan chuan [gold dollar note], fixed at the value of US $0.25. This reform, which was expected to curb the ever-increasing inflation that was plaguing China, proved disastrous. The gold yuan fell within three months, taking with it the savings of the many thrifty Chinese who had been required to convert all holdings in gold, silver, and foreign currency into the new currency. Wang Yün-wu resigned from office as a result of this fiasco.

Wang went to Hong Kong at the end of 1948 and founded the Hua-kuo Publishing House, which later was moved to Taiwan. After the Chinese Communists won control of the mainland in 1949 and the National Government moved to Taiwan, he went to Taipei to serve as an adviser in the presidential office. In 1954 he was appointed vice president of the Examination Yuan, serving under Mo Te-hui (q.v.). In 1957 he was a member of the Chinese delegation to the United Nations General Assembly. At the bequest of Chiang Kai-shek he undertook a study of the Hoover Commission recommendations on the organization of the executive branch of the United States Government. He returned to Taiwan and reported on his findings on 10 February 1958. That day, he was assigned to organize a committee for administrative reform. The committee submitted its recommendations to the National Government in September. In May 1960 Wang became vice president of the Executive Yuan, serving under Ch'en Ch'eng (q.v.). Both men resigned on 15 December 1963 because of the increasing power of Chiang Ching-kuo (q.v.). Wang, who had been teaching part time in the graduate school of Chengchih University since 1955, then became a full-time professor at that university.

Little is known about Wang Yün-wu's personal life except that he was married and that he had seven sons and daughters.

Wei Cho-min   革卓民
West. Francis C. M. Wei

Wei Cho-min (1888–), leading Chinese Christian scholar and educator who for many years was president of Huachung University.

Born into a prosperous Cantonese clan of bankers and merchants, Wei Cho-min received his early education in the Chinese classics. In addition, he studied English with private tutors in 1902–3. His father, then a tea merchant at Hankow, in 1903 sent his son to the Boone School, an Episcopalian mission institution in Wuchang. The young Wei was admonished by his father to pay attention to his studies but to ignore the religious ideas of the Westerners.

In 1907 Wei Cho-min completed his secondary education and enrolled at Boone University. He was graduated with honors in 1911, at which time he was baptized a Christian. Because of his superior academic record, he was invited to remain at Boone University as an instructor in mathematics and Chinese. He accepted the position and also enrolled as a graduate student at Boone. In 1915 he received his M.A. degree after completing a thesis on the political principles of Mencius. During the years of the First World War, he worked in close association with the Reverend Alfred A. Gilman, the president of Boone University and later Wei's predecessor as president of Huachung University, and with the Reverend Arthur M. Sherman, then dean of St. Paul's Divinity School in Boone University.

After seven years of teaching at Wuchang, Wei Cho-min went to the United States for graduate study. He enrolled at Harvard University in 1918, received his M.A. in philosophy in 1919, and completed all requirements for the Ph.D. except the thesis in 1920. At the same time, he took courses at the Episcopal Theological School in Cambridge. Its dean characterized Wei as the ablest student then enrolled. William E. Hocking, professor of philosophy at Harvard, later said of his former student that "Dr. Wei is not a person whom one is likely to forget, having once known him. As a graduate student at Harvard, he impressed us by his power and seriousness of purpose.... He is impressive in his personality, grave in speech, quiet, deeply conscious of the difficulties of the time both in China and elsewhere. In person, he is slender and graceful and gives the impression of bring tall .... His personal appearance is attractive and the charm of his character speaks through his face and manner."

Wei Cho-min returned to China in 1920 without completing his doctorate. He explained this action by saying that he did not wish to spend a year doing possibly inconsequential research in the United States when China had a pressing need for men of his training. Upon his return to Wuchang, he became professor of philosophy at Boone University. He also lectured on Christian evidence at the divinity school.

The Burton Educational Commission, as a result of an extensive survey of education in China in 1921–22, recommended the merging of several small mission institutions in central China to increase their efficiency and educational influence. Stimulated by that recommendation and by the need for consolidation in face of increasingly hostile anti-Christian feeling, Boone University, Wesley College, and the London Missionary Society joined together to form Huachung University at Wuchang in 1924. Wei Cho-min was named dean of the faculty of arts and sciences, vice president in charge of administration, professor of philosophy, and temporary chairman of the department of Chinese. After the university's acting president, Bishop Alfred Gilman, left China in October 1926 for a short stay in the United States, Wei also assumed the duties of the presidency.

After the fall of Wuhan to the Northern Expedition forces and the establishment of the National Government at Wuhan under the control of the Kuomintang left wing and the Chinese Communists, student unrest increasingly disrupted the operations of Huachung and other universities in the area. Western faculty members at Huachung were forced out, and the Chinese staff came under attack by students who wanted to take over the university. In May 1927, because of great personal danger, Wei Cho-min went to Hankow and boarded a British steamer bound for Shanghai. Wei's enemies sent word to the Shanghai police that he was a Communist, and he was arrested upon arrival at Shanghai. Fortunately for Wei, his old colleague Dr. Arthur M. Sherman, then of the American Episcopal Mission, was traveling on the same steamer and was a witness to the arrest. He protested Wei's arrest to the police and eventually secured his release.

Wei Cho-min then went to England, where he studied with L. T. Hobhouse at the University of London and with the Reverend B. H. Streeter at Oxford. He received a D. Phil. degree from London in 1929. During the 1927–28 period, he also studied briefly at the University of Berlin and at the Sorbonne in Paris. He returned to China in 1929 to become president of the newly reopened Huachung University, now composed of Boone University, Griffith John Institute, Huping College, Wesley College, and Yale-in-China. Wei was to devote most of his remaining career to developing Huachung into one of the leading centers of Christian higher education in republican China.

For the next two decades, Wei Cho-min continued to make occasional visits to the West for academic and ecclesiastical purposes. In August 1934 he participated in a seminar on education and culture contacts held at Yale University. Before leaving the United States for the return trip to China, he delivered the Woodward lectures at Yale, the Schermerhorn lectures at Columbia, and the Haskell lectures at the graduate school of theology at Oberlin. In 1937 he attended the Conference on Life and Work at Oxford in July and the Conference on Faith and Order at Edinburgh in August. He then proceeded to the United States to serve as visiting professor of ethics at the Yale Divinity School. He returned to China in the summer of 1938, crossing the Pacific by air and preaching on successive Sundays in Honolulu and Manila.

After a short stay in Hong Kong, Wei Cho-min went to Kweilin to rejoin his university, which had been forced to move there in July 1938 because of Japanese advances. Huachung University soon was forced to move again, first to Kunming and then to the small town of Hsichou, near Tali. From March 1939 until the end of the Second World War the university campus consisted of three temple buildings and some temporary structures in the temple courtyards which were used as laboratories and classrooms. The faculty and students lived in rented family temples and courtyards in Hsichou. Wei Cho-min declined all government appointments during the war years, but from 1938 to 1942 he did serve on the People's Political Council. He also made periodic trips to Chungking to consult with government officials and to bring the wartime plight of private universities to their attention.

Wei Cho-min suffered a severe illness in the winter of 1944, but at war's end he went abroad as the first holder of the Henry W. Luce visiting professorship of world Christianity at Union Theological Seminary in New York. He also held an appointment under the Hewett Foundation to lecture at the Andover-Newton and Episcopal Theological seminaries in the Boston area. His Hewett lectures were published in the United States in 1947 as *The Spirit of Chinese Culture*. In July 1946, on his way back to China, Wei preached before a congregation of 3,000 in York, England, at the opening of the Archbishop's Fund for China. That August, the tenth synod of the Sheng-kung-hui, or Chinese Episcopal Church, elected Wei chairman of its house of delegates.

With the Communist military victory in the civil war with the Nationalists, the position of all Christian institutions of higher learning became directly involved with the demands of political revolution. Despite increasing interference from the new authorities and other difficulties following the Communist takeover of the Wuhan cities in 1949, Huachung University managed to survive for a period under Wei Cho-min's leadership. By January 1951 Western teachers had stopped meeting their classes and were leaving China; some students had been recruited for service in Korea; and remittances to Huachung from abroad had been forbidden. In the summer of 1951 it was announced that Huachung University and the Government Teachers College would be combined to become the normal school in the Wuhan area for the training of middle-school teachers. Wei Cho-min reportedly became a faculty member at the new institution. He was publicly denounced in 1957 during the anti-rightist drive, but no punishment was reported. In 1962 he was identified as a member of the board of directors of the United Theological Seminary at Nanking.

As one of the leading Chinese educators of the republican period who was also an outspoken Christian and an active churchman, Wei Cho-min consistently stressed his belief that the distinctive feature of Christian, in contrast to state or secular, education was its deliberate emphasis upon the building of character as the primary objective of the process of education.

In inviting Western missionaries as educational colleagues, he specified that they possess those active and contagious qualities of personal character which he believed could best assist them in achieving their end. At the same time, Wei insisted that the professional competence of Western faculty members at Huachung University should be such as to qualify them for appointment to academic faculties in the United States. He laid great stress upon high academic standards in order to establish and maintain proper prestige for Christian education in China. Moreover, he worked continually at the task of raising the level of academic requirements and performance in theological education and contributed as much as any other educator in China to the quality of Chinese clerical training.

Wei Cho-min attempted to interpret Christianity in Chinese terms, for he believed that "if Christianity is to take root in China, it must assume a Chinese form, congenial to the Chinese cultural heritage." On the basis of that conviction he insisted that Chinese Christian leaders receive their basic education in their homeland in order to appreciate Chinese culture as well as Christian values. Wei's major contribution was the establishment and direction of Huachung University as an institution designed to educate Christian leaders in China.

Wei Li-huang   衞 立 煌

Wei Li-huang (1897–17 January 1960), Nationalist military commander who rose to become commander in chief of the First War Area in 1938 and of the Chinese Expeditionary Force in 1942. In 1948 he was acting director of the Nationalist operations in the Northeast, and his career was ruined by the loss of that strategic area. Wei later held sinecure posts in the People's Republic of China.

Born in Hofei hsien, Anhwei, Wei Li-huang began his military career as a volunteer in the forces of Wu Chung-hsin (q.v.). He soon became Wu's bodyguard, and in this capacity he accompanied Wu to Canton about 1920. At Canton, Wei joined the Second Army of Hsü Ch'ung-chih (q.v.) as a squad leader. Wei rose steadily in rank, and in 1926 he received command of the 3rd Division in the First Army of the National Revolutionary Army. In 1927, after participating in the first stage of the Northern Expedition, he was appointed commander of the 3rd column of the northern Anhwei garrison forces. With the full-scale resumption of the Northern Expedition in 1928, Wei became deputy commander of the Ninth Army of the First Group Army. In the military reorganization that followed the successful completion of the Northern Expedition, he was made commander of the 45th Division (later the 10th Division) and commander in chief for "bandit suppression" in northern Anhwei. In 1930 he was designated garrison commander for northern Anhwei.

In connection with the 1931 campaign against the Communists in central China, Wei Li-huang took command of the Fourteenth Army and participated in the operations in central Kiangsi. In 1932, by a surprise stroke, he succeeded in capturing the Chinese Communist base at the market town of Chinchiachai in the Tapieh mountains in southwestern Anhwei. Chiang Kai-shek was so pleased by this victory that he renamed the town Lihuang and named the area around it Lihuang hsien. By reason of his victories over the Chinese Communists, Wei Li-huang won the nickname "ch'ang-sheng chiang-chün" [ever-victorious general]. At this juncture, he was given some formal military education, as befitted one of his accomplishments and promise. In 1933–34 he took a short course at the Central Military Academy.

In 1934 the National Government launched its fifth campaign against the Chinese Communists, the campaign which forced them out of their Kiangsi stronghold and on the Long March to Shensi. Wei Li-huang served as commander in chief of the eastern route of the Kiangsi-Kwangtung-Fukien-Hunan-Hupeh Bandit-Suppression Army. In 1935 he was elected to the Central Executive Committee of the Kuomintang. At year's end, he was appointed commander in chief of the Nationalist forces on the Hunan-Hupeh-Anhwei-Kiangsi border.

After the Sino-Japanese war began in July 1937, Wei Li-huang became deputy commander of the Second War Area in Shansi. In October, he deployed the troops of Liu Mao-en, Li Mo-an, and Wang Ching-kuo against the advancing Japanese north of Taiyuan. In the ensuing battle of Hsinkow, they inflicted heavy losses on the Japanese. Taiyuan finally was captured by another Japanese force, which moved on it from the east in November. Late in 1938 Wei became commander in chief of the First War Area (Honan and southern Shensi), with concurrent command of the Third Group Army. In the spring of 1939 he also became governor of Honan. That May, he was promoted to full general. He received the concurrent posts of commanding officer of the Hopei-Chahar War Area and chief of the Hopei-Chahar party-government field committee in 1940. At that time, Hopei and Chahar were under Japanese occupation. At the end of 1941, Wei was relieved of his posts, reportedly because of his reluctance to take action against Chinese Communist forces after the New Fourth Army Incident (*see* Hsiang Ying; Yeh T'ing). In 1942, however, he was made a member of the Military Affairs Commission and was appointed commander in chief of the Chinese Expeditionary Force, with headquarters at Kunming, which was charged with participation in the joint Anglo-American-Chinese campaign for the recovery of Burma.

Wei Li-huang was in command of five Chinese armies which crossed the Nu River in May 1944 and attacked in the direction of Tengchung and Lungling, in coordination with forces which had been trained and stationed in India. This, the Second Burma Campaign, planned by Lieutenant General Joseph W. Stilwell, achieved its objective in January 1945 after hard fighting. With the capture of Wanting and the recovery of control of the entire Burma Road, the work of the Chinese Expeditionary Force came to an end. Wei Li-huang, who had been appointed deputy commander in chief of the Chinese ground forces in 1944, experienced a period of military inactivity after this campaign. In 1946 he was sent to Europe and the United States on an inspection tour. He did not return to China until the end of 1947, by which time the Nationalists had suffered serious defeats at the hands of the Chinese Communists in Manchuria.

In January 1948 Wei Li-huang succeeded Ch'en Ch'eng (q.v.) as acting director of the Northeastern headquarters and commander in chief for bandit-suppression in the Northeast. He assumed office on 18 January, by which time the Communists had long since taken the initiative in that area. Nevertheless, when the Nationalists were forced to abandon their

Manchurian effort in October, Wei received much of the blame for the loss of the Northeast. He was stripped of all titles and posts and was imprisoned at Nanking to await trial on charges of corruption. After Li Tsung-jen (q.v.) became acting President in 1949, Wei was released in April. He then went to Hong Kong, where he lived in virtual retirement.

On 15 March 1955 Wei Li-huang went to Peking, the capital of the People's Republic of China. He was a delegate to the Chinese People's Political Consultative Conference in January 1956, and he was elected to the conference's National Committee. After the conference, he entered the Socialist Academy at Peking. He soon became a member of the standing committee of the Kuomintang Revolutionary Committee, a post he retained until 1959. In November 1958 he represented Anhwei at the National People's Congress. He was appointed a vice chairman of the National Defense Council in April 1959. Soon afterwards, he was elected to the Standing Committee of the Chinese People's Political Consultative Conference. By this time, arteriosclerosis and heart disease had undermined Wei's health. He died at Peking on 17 January 1960.

Wei Li-huang married four times. The first of these unions was an arranged marriage. When he was a regimental commander at Kweilin, he took a new wife, *née* Sung. In 1936 he married a nurse at the Chinkiang Children's Hospital, Chu Lu-ssu. Finally, in the postwar period, he married Han Ch'uan-hua, a graduate of Tsinghua University who had studied in the United States. After 1955, she taught at the Peking Normal College for Girls. Wei had six children by his first three wives: three sons—Tao-chieh, Tao-shu and Tao-jan—and three daughters—Tao-ch'ung, Tao-ching, and Tao-yun.

Wei Tao-ming 魏 道 明
  T. Po-ts'ung 伯 聰

Wei Tao-ming (c.1899–), government official who served as minister of justice (November 1928–April 1930), mayor of Nanking (1930–31), secretary general of the Executive Yuan (1938–41), ambassador to the United States (1942–46), and governor of Taiwan (1947–48). After living in the United States in the 1950's, he returned to Taiwan, where he became minister of foreign affairs in the National Government in 1966.

The son of Wei Tiao-yuan, an affluent educator who took part in the republican revolution of 1911 and later became a member of the Parliament at Peking, Wei Tao-ming was born in Kiukiang, Kiangsi. He received his early education in a missionary school and then matriculated at the Kiangsi First Middle School, from which he was graduated about 1918. After studying French for a year at Peking, he went to France in 1919 to study law at the University of Paris. He received the degree of Docteur en Droit in 1926, and his dissertation, *Le cheque en Chine*, was published in Paris that year. Wei then returned to China, where he established a law practice in the French concession of Shanghai with Cheng Yü-hsiu (q.v.), also a law graduate of the University of Paris.

In May 1927 Wei Tao-ming was appointed secretary general of the ministry of justice at Nanking. That August, having dissolved their law partnership, he married Cheng Yü-hsiu. Both of them were regarded as protégés of Wang Ch'ung-hui (q.v.). In December, Wei was promoted to the post of vice minister of justice. Early in 1928 he received a concurrent appointment as a member of the National Reconstruction Commission, in which capacity he went to Europe and the United States on an investigating mission. At the same time, Cheng Yü-hsiu was given responsibility for working out a preliminary understanding with the French government with respect to the rapidly changing situation in China. Their first son, Tchow-mei, was born in Paris in May. They returned to China by way of the United States in August.

Wei Tao-ming was appointed minister of justice in the National Government in November 1928. At this time, he also received membership in the Central Political Council, the Boxer indemnity committee, and the national education fund committee. Wei soon established courts of appeal in such distant provinces as Sinkiang, Suiyuan, and Chahar so that each of China's provinces would have its own higher court. He also established 21 new district courts and initiated special training

courses for lawyers who wished to be judges. Although prison reform was one of Wei's concerns, his plans for the construction of new prisons were not realized because of inadequate funds. Changes in the system of extraterritoriality occurred during Wei's term of office, and he thus became responsible for the replacement of foreign judicial administrations in Shanghai with the new Kiangsu Court of Appeals and the District Court of the Shanghai Special Area. The smoothness and effectiveness of this transfer of authority won Wei the appreciation of Chinese and foreigners alike.

In April 1930 Wei Tao-ming left the ministry of justice to become mayor of Nanking, which had the status of a special municipality because it was the nation's capital. He held that important post until the end of 1931, when he was succeeded by Ma Ch'ao-chün (q.v.). In April 1932, a month after the creation of Manchoukuo (*see* P'u-yi), Wei was sent to Europe to win foreign support for China with reference to the Sino-Japanese situation. Upon his return to China in 1935, he became general manager of the *Shih-shih hsin-pao*, the *Ta-lu pao*, and the *Ta-wan pao*, three influential Shanghai newspapers. He also was made a trustee of the *China Press*. He held those posts until the Sino-Japanese war broke out in 1937. Then, in November 1937, he returned to the service of the National Government as secretary general of the Executive Yuan. He retained that post after H. H. K'ung (q.v.) assumed the presidency of the Executive Yuan in 1938.

Wei Tao-ming was appointed ambassador to France in April 1941. He and his wife left China in July and traveled to the United States on the President Madison. Upon arrival at San Francisco, they learned that Japanese forces had occupied parts of French Indo-China, and they decided to wait in the United States until the situation became clear. Wei took the opportunity to visit several Latin American countries to promote support of the Chinese cause. He then went to Washington to serve in the Chinese embassy under Hu Shih (q.v.), the Chinese ambassador to the United States. He was named to succeed Hu in September 1942, and he presented his credentials to President Franklin D. Roosevelt on 6 October of that year. Among his achievements as ambassador was the signing, on 11 January 1943, of the Sino-American treaty by virtue of which the

United States renounced extraterritorial privileges in China. Early in 1944 Wei returned to Chungking for consultation. He returned to Washington in April. That autumn he was a member of the Chinese delegation to the Dumbarton Oaks Conversations, and the following year he was a member of the Chinese delegation to the United Nations Conference on International Organization at San Francisco.

In September 1945, because of reports that V. K. Wellington Koo (Ku Wei-chün, q.v.) was to replace him, Wei Tao-ming submitted his resignation as ambassador to the United States. The National Government refused his resignation, and he soon received an additional appointment as Chinese representative on the Allied Far Eastern Advisory Commission, established at war's end to formulate joint policies with respect to Japan. Early in January 1946 Wei returned to Chungking once again for consultation. Upon arrival back at Washington in mid-March, he was named vice chairman of the Far Eastern Commission. In July 1946 he returned to China after being succeeded as ambassador to the United States. Wei then became vice president of the Legislative Yuan, serving under Sun Fo (q.v.).

Late in February 1947 riots broke out in Taiwan as a result of the oppressive rule of Ch'en Yi (q.v.). In suppressing them, Ch'en massacred several thousand Taiwanese. The Executive Yuan responded to this crisis by recalling Ch'en, establishing a Taiwan provincial government, and appointing Wei Tao-ming governor in April. When he assumed office as the first civilian governor of Taiwan in mid-May, Wei ended martial law, abolished censorship of the mails, and affirmed the principle of freedom of the press. He then worked to strengthen the island's economy by curbing inflation, procuring more goods and supplies from the mainland, increasing rice and sugar production, and improving the efficiency of electric power plants. Civilian administration of Taiwan lasted until the end of 1948, when Ch'en Ch'eng (q.v.) was named to replace Wei Tao-ming as governor. Ch'en, a military man, assumed office on 5 January 1949 and undertook the task of preparing for the Nationalist evacuation from the mainland. Because a Chinese Communist victory in the contest for the mainland seemed inevitable, Wei Tao-ming and his wife went to the United States, where they lived first in New York and later in southern California.

After his wife's death in December 1959, Wei Tao-ming made a brief visit to Taiwan. He emerged from retirement in the early 1960's to become Chinese Nationalist ambassador to Japan. On 7 June 1966 he assumed office at Taipei as minister of foreign affairs in the National Government.

Wen I-to	聞 一 多
T. Yu-san	友 三
H. Yu-shan	友 山

Wen I-to (24 November 1899–15 July 1946), leading Chinese poet of the 1920's . In the 1930's he devoted himself to classical studies and to teaching at Tsinghua University. The outbreak of the Sino-Japanese war galvanized him into political activity, and he became a leader of the China Democratic League. Wen was assassinated in 1946.

Born into a large family of some affluence in Hsishui, Hupeh, Wen I-to received a closely supervised traditional education under the guidance of his father, who held the sheng-yuan degree. English was added to the classical curriculum when Wen was 10. Under the influence of the ideas behind revolution of 1911 and the writings of Liang Ch'i-ch'ao (q.v.), the boy, to his father's displeasure, developed an aversion to classical ethics and a fondness for history, poetry, and art.

In 1913, when he was 13, Wen I-to entered Tsinghua Academy (later a college) at Peking. Although he chose Western literature as his major field, it was his excellent classical Chinese training that first made him known among his teachers and fellow students. In 1915–16 he was an editor of the student magazine *Ch'ing-hua chou-k'an* [Tsinghua weekly], for which he also wrote literary essays and poems in the traditional style, and in 1919 he served as a student editor of the *Ch'ing-hua hsueh-pao* [Tsinghua journal].

In the period preceding the May Fourth Movement of 1919, Wen I-to opposed the use of pai-hua [the vernacular] in writing. His ideas began to change, however, at the time of the May Fourth Incident (*see* Lo Chia-lun). On the morning of 5 May 1919 the students at

Tsinghua discovered that a copy of the well-known patriotic poem "Man-chiang-hung," by the gallant Sung general Yueh Fei (1103–41), had been posted on the wall of a dining hall in a gesture by Wen I-to of support for the students' cause. Two days later, when the Tsinghua students organized themselves to support the movement, Wen was given responsibility for preparing materials to incite the students to action. He soon began to write in pai-hua, and his first poem in this style, "Hsi-an" [the western bank], appeared in the *Ch'ing-hua chou-k'an* in July 1920. Wen was graduated from Tsinghua in June 1921. In protest against the school administration's imposition of an extra examination on graduating students who normally would have been sent abroad automatically to study, Wen postponed his projected trip to the United States and remained at Tsinghua for an additional year.

Wen I-to left China for the United States in July 1922, arriving in Chicago early in August. He enrolled at the Art Institute of Chicago, specializing in Western painting. Although he was deeply impressed by the institute's art collection and by the American aesthetic sensibilities which underlay it, he found urban life in Chicago extremely distasteful. He quickly encountered racial discrimination and later wrote a poem, "The Laundryman's Song," to express his indigation about the inferior social and economic status of Chinese in the United States. Wen soon began to sacrifice his class work at the Art Institute to his growing interest in poetry. He became very enthusiastic not only about such great Chinese poets as Tu Fu and Lu Yu but also about the English Romantics. He met such American luminaries as Harriet Monroe and Amy Lowell and read the works of such American poets as John G. Fletcher and Carl Sandburg. In 1922 he corresponded frequently with Liang Shih-ch'iu (q.v.) and other friends in China, telling them of his new ambitions for a literary career. He wrote that for him, literature was "a faith, a vision, and an ideal, not merely a medium for the expression of emotion."

His new dedication to literature did not keep Wen I-to from being lonely and homesick in Chicago. In the autumn of 1923, therefore, he joined Liang Shih-ch'iu at Colorado College in Colorado Springs. Although he continued to major in fine arts and painting, his time was spent on literature. He took courses in Victorian and modern poetry. In September, his first volume of poems, *Hung-chu* [red candles], was published at Shanghai. Liang Shih-ch'iu and Kuo Mo-jo (q.v.) were instrumental in securing publication of this collection of lyrics. Wen's poems were acclaimed in China for their technical excellence and for the richness of their imagery. When Liang Shih-ch'iu went to Cambridge, Massachusetts, in the summer of 1924, Wen moved to New York, where he joined the Art Students League and became a dedicated theater-goer. He also joined the Ta-chiang-she [great river society], a political group organized by Chinese students in the United States to support the development of a strong Chinese state. Wen became a fervent cultural nationalist, particularly intent upon the rejuvenation of Chinese painting, poetry, and drama. At this time he was an admirer of Sun Yat-sen, but he did not join the Kuomintang.

After nearly three years in the United States, Wen I-to returned to China in May 1925 with the dramatist Yü Shang-yuan. Upon his return, Wen became dean of the National Academy of Fine Arts in Peking. He was greatly distressed by the political and social situation he found in China and expressed his despair in poems. He joined a group of anti-Communist intellectuals devoted to building a strong Chinese nation, but he soon dropped out, deciding that the political situation was hopeless.

In the spring of 1926 Wen I-to and such other young poets at Peking as Hsü Chih-mo, Chu Hsiang (qq.v.), and Liu Meng-wei began to meet regularly at Wen's house for discussions about the new poetry. On 1 April 1926 they launched the *Shih-chien* [poetry weekly]. Although the magazine ceased publication in June, it had a strong influence on the technical development of the new forms of Chinese poetry which the group advocated. Wen I-to's poems of this period were collected and published in January 1928 as *Ssu-shui* [dead water]. The title poem, which may be interpreted as a symbolic description of China in the late 1920's, depicts a "ditch of dead and hopeless water" on which "no breeze can raise a ripple" and where "beauty can never stay." The poet then states: "Better abandon it to evil—/then, perhaps, some beauty will come out of it."

Wen I-to resigned from the Peking Academy of Fine Arts and went to his home in Hupeh in the summer of 1926. That autumn, he went to Shanghai to become dean of students at National Political University (*see* Chang Chia-sen). In 1927, after the National Government had moved to Wuhan, a friend secured a position for him as chief of the art section in the general political department under Teng Yen-ta (q.v.). After a month in that post, Wen resigned and returned to Shanghai. The Kuomintang at Shanghai closed National Political University, and Wen then went to Nanking, where he accepted a minor post in the Chiang Kai-shek regime. In the autumn of 1927 he was appointed chairman of the department of foreign languages and literatures at National Fourth Chungshan (Sun Yat-sen) University at Nanking, the predecessor of National Central University.

In March 1928 Wen I-to joined such longtime friends as P'an Kuang-tan, Lo Lung-chi, Hu Shih (qq.v.), Hsü Chih-mo, and Liang Shih-ch'iu in founding the literary monthly *Hsin-yueh* [crescent moon] at Shanghai. This journal sought to introduce Western literature to Chinese readers and to promote an appreciation of pure aesthetics. Wen I-to, Hsü Chih-mo, and Jao Meng-k'an edited the journal and contributed translations to it. By mid-1928, however, Wen I-to had give up the writing of poetry and other creative endeavors. That autumn, he left Nanking for Wuchang to become dean of the school of arts at Wuhan University and chairman of the department of Chinese language and literature. He resigned from the *Hsin-yueh* in April 1929, and thereafter his relationship with the Crescent Moon group gradually came to an end. He began to devote his attention to classical Chinese literature. In 1930 he moved to Tsingtao University, and in 1932 he became professor of Chinese literature at Tsinghua University. He remained on the Tsinghua faculty until his death.

After 1928 Wen became increasingly depressed about political and social conditions in China and increasingly introverted because of his depression. He neglected most of his friends and immersed himself in classical studies and in teaching. His intensive research in the history of Chinese classical literature and in T'ang and ancient poetry led him to the study of philology, ancient arts, and mythology. His major works in these fields include *Shao-ling hsien-sheng nien-p'u hui-chien* [a chronological biography of Tu Fu], of 1930–31; *Ts'en Chia-chou hsi-nien k'ao-chang* [a chronological biography of Ts'en Ts'an], of 1933; *Shih-ching hsin-i* [new interpretation of the *Book of Odes*], of 1934–37; *Ch'ü-tz'u chiao-pu* [a textual study of Ch'ü Yuan's poetry], of 1934–42; *Chou-i i-ching lei-tsuan* [interpretation and authentication of the *Book of Changes*], of 1941; and an article, "Fu-hsi k'ao" [a study of the legend of Fu Hsi], of 1942.

The outbreak of the Sino-Japanese war in 1937 interrupted Wen's quiet academic life. He moved with Tsinghua University to Changsha and then, in February–April 1938, he traveled with a group of more than 200 students through the mountainous areas between Changsha and Kunming. The trip revived his interest in art, and he made over 100 landscape drawings. At Kunming, Wen resumed his regular teaching and research work. Like all other professors at this time, he was caught in the accelerating wartime inflation. To support his family he had to augment his income by carving seals and by teaching in a middle school.

In the autumn of 1943 a nephew who just had left a student volunteer army group visited Wen, told him of the miserable life led by common soldiers in the Nationalist forces, and painted a dark picture of the military and political situation confronting China. Wen I-to was so shocked by this account that he retired into seclusion for a week to consider the right course for his own future career. He resolved to give up his isolated life and turn his attention to political and social problems facing China. He began to discuss contemporary affairs with his students and to read leftist literature. He reversed his previously unfavorable attitude toward the works of such radical writers as Lu Hsün (Chou Shu-jen, q.v.). In 1944, as the Japanese pressed forward into Kwangsi and Kweichow, Wen made speeches and published articles demanding that the National Government adopt "democratic measures" and mobilize "the masses of the people" to strengthen resistance to the Japanese. In December of that year, he was made an executive member of the China Democratic League's Yunnan provincial committee and an editor of the *Min-chu chou-k'an* [democratic weekly]. He became a member of the league's central committee, its Yunnan propaganda director, and president of the *Min-chu chou-k'an* in September 1945. During this period his office usually was crowded with liberal and leftist students and professors.

After the Second World War ended, Wen I-to opposed the resumption of civil conflict between the Chinese Communists and the Nationalists. He denied baseless rumors that he had joined the Chinese Communist party. On 9 July 1946 Li Kung-p'u, one of his colleagues in the Democratic League, was assassinated in Kunming. An anti-Communist group alleged that Li had been killed by the Communists and warned that Wen would be the next victim. On the morning of 15 July 1946 Wen, disregarding these warnings, attended Li Kung-p'u's funeral and made a speech accusing National Government agents of committing the murder. On his way home late that afternoon, Wen I-to was shot and killed by assassins. He was survived by his wife, three sons, and two daughters.

As a poet, Wen I-to contributed to the development of a new poetic form in China by fusing Western techniques, Chinese and Western images, and classical Chinese poetic diction in a new vernacular style. As a scholar, he combined orthodox Chinese and Western methodology. His complete works were collected and edited by Chu Tzu-ch'ing (q.v.) and others and were published in four volumes in 1948 as *Wen I-to ch'üan-chi.*

Wong Wen-hao　　　　翁 文 灝
　T.　Yung-ni　　　　詠 霓
　Alt. Weng Wen-hao

Wong Wen-hao (1889–), pioneer in the development of geological research in China as director of the China Geological Survey and head of the geological research institute at Peiping. In 1938–45 he served the National Government as minister of economic affairs. He was the first president of the Executive Yuan to be elected under the 1947 constitution, but he resigned after the disastrous failure of the 1948 currency reform. In the 1950's he undertook prospecting expeditions for the People's Republic of China.

Ningpo, Chekiang, was the birthplace of Wong Wen-hao. Little is known about his early life except that he studied for his doctorate in physics and geology at Louvain University in Belgium and received his degree in 1912. Upon his return to China in 1912, he became chief of the mining section of the ministry of agriculture and commerce. Knowledge of China's natural resources was far from adequate at the beginning of the republican period, and Wong soon made major contributions to the development of geological research in China.

In 1921 Wong Wen-hao succeeded V. K. Ting (Ting Wen-chiang, q.v.) as director of the China Geological Survey (Chung-kuo ti-chih tiao-ch'a-so), which conducted mineralogical surveys throughout China and which became known throughout the world. In 1922 and 1929 he attended the Pacific Science Conference. During this period, he also taught at Tsinghua University, becoming chairman of its geology department in the late 1920's For a brief period in 1931 he served as acting president of Tsinghua. With the establishment of the Academy of Sciences at Peiping, the China Geological Survey joined with the academy in 1929 to establish a geological research institute. Wong headed the institute for many years. Despite all of these responsibilities, Wong found time to write many articles and two books, *Mineral Resources of China* and *Earthquake Sequences in China.*

In October 1932 Wong Wen-hao made a brief foray into politics as minister of education in the National Government He soon resigned and returned to geology. In collaboration with V. K. Ting and Tseng Shih-ying, he compiled an atlas of China, the *Chung-hua min-kuo hsin ti-t'u,* which was published in 1934 in commemoration of the sixtieth anniversary of the Shanghai *Shun Pao.* This work, which drew on the findings of the Geological Survey and on thousands of Chinese and foreign maps of China, contained both physical and political maps.

Chiang Kai-shek appointed Wong Wen-hao secretary general of the Executive Yuan in 1935. That year, Wang also became chairman of the National Resources Commission, which controlled such key mineral resources as tin, tungsten, and antimony, and secretary general of the national defense planning commission, established to cope with the probable result of deteriorating Sino-Japanese relations. In 1938, after the Sino-Japanese war began, the National Government organized the ministry of economic affairs to unify control of industrial, mining, commercial, and agricultural activities. Wong headed this important ministry throughout the war years. In 1943, with the aid of various scholars, he drafted an outline of postwar industrial policy, urging the development of state capital, the regulation of private capital, and the promotion of foreign investment in China. The Kuomintang Central Executive Committee approved his proposals in August 1943.

After the war ended, Wong Wen-hao served in 1946 as vice president of the Executive Yuan. He continued to head the National Resources Commission after it came under the authority of the Executive Yuan. Wong sent the economist Chang Hsin-fu to Manchuria for a survey of Japanese industrial and commercial properties there. Chang, however, was killed by Soviet forces near Fushun. Wong went to Manchuria to investigate the case. He was discouraged by the complicated international situation affecting that strategic area, and he was shocked by the corruption prevailing among Nationalist officials assigned to take over Japanese property. Upon his return to Chungking, he resigned from all of his posts.

In 1948 Wong Wen-hao returned to political life as the first president of the Executive Yuan to be elected under the new 1947 constitution. However, his tenure of office was a short and unhappy one, in large part because of the disastrous failure of the currency reform introduced by his minster of finance, Wang Yün-wu (q.v.). Wong resigned in the autumn of 1948. A few months later, he went to Hong Kong with his father and his wife, leaving his three sons on the mainland. After the Chinese Communist occupation of Shanghai, Ch'en Yi 1901– ; q.v.) sent Wong's eldest son, Wong Hsin-yuan, to Hong Kong with an invitation to return and serve the People's Republic of China. Wong sent his father and his wife back to Shanghai, but he did not accept the invitation at that time.

Wong remained in Hong Kong until mid-1950, when he went to Paris. Early in 1951 he returned to Hong Kong and then crossed the border into the People's Republic of China. He arrived in Peking on 6 April 1951. On arrival he was met at the railroad station by Kuo Mo-jo, Chang Chih-chung, Yeh Kung-cho (qq.v.), and others. Soon afterwards, Chou En-lai (q.v.) gave a dinner in Wong's honor. Two weeks later, Wong reportedly left Peking for Sinkiang in connection with a project for

the prospecting of uranium deposits. In 1952–54 he made three trips to Tibet to look for uranium and other mineral deposits. On each of these trips he headed a team of several hundred geologists and workers.

Information is lacking about Wong Wen-hao's precise status in the People's Republic of China. He received membership in the standing committee of the Kuomintang Revolutionary Committee in 1958, and in the National Committee of the Chinese People's Political Consultative Conference in 1959. However, he seems to have held no other posts. Even more puzzling to Western observers was his omission from such scientific organizations as the Academy of Sciences and the Chinese Geological Society.

Wu, Butterfly: *see* HU TIEH.

Wu Ch'ao-shu　　　　　伍 朝 樞
T. T'i-yün　　　　　　　梯 雲
West. C. C. Wu

Wu Ch'ao-shu (23 May 1887–2 January 1934), known as C. C. Wu, Western-educated official at Peking who went to Canton in 1917 with his father, Wu T'ing-fang, to join the Canton regime of Sun Yat-sen. He later served as minister of foreign affairs at Canton and Nanking. In 1928–30 he was minister to the United States, and in 1929–30 he also represented China at the League of Nations.

The only son of Wu T'ing-fang (q.v.), C. C. Wu was born in Tientsin, where his father was serving as director of the China Railway Company. He received his early education in the Chinese classics at Tientsin. In 1897 he went to the United States with his father, who had been appointed Chinese minister to the United States, Spain, and Peru. The young Wu studied at the Force School, the Western High School, and the Atlantic City High School. Upon graduation from the last-named institution in 1904, he returned to China and became a secretary in the Kwangtung provincial board of works at Canton. In 1907 he served as a minor official in the Kwangtung board of agriculture, industry, and commerce. He continued to study throughout this period, and in 1908 he went to England, where he entered the law department of the University of London. He held Inns of Court Students and University scholarships, and he was graduated at the head of his class in 1911.

C. C. Wu returned to China in May 1911. At the time of the republican revolution, he became commissioner for foreign affairs in the Hupeh provincial government. He held that post until September 1912, when he went to Peking as chairman of the foreign ministry's treaty commission. In 1913 he was elected to the National Assembly. After Yuan Shih-k'ai dissolved the Parliament in January 1914, Wu became a member of the Constitutional Conference and of its constitution drafting committee. In May, he was named to the newly created council of state [cheng-shih t'ang], headed by Hsü Shih-ch'ang (q.v.). He also served as chairman of the treaty revision committee. When Wu became aware of Yuan Shih-k'ai's plans to became monarch, he resigned from his posts. Yuan granted Wu three months' leave but insisted that he remain in Peking. Wu thus lived in seclusion in Peking until Yuan's death in June 1916. After Tuan Ch'i-jui (q.v.) became premier at Peking, Wu served as a councillor in the cabinet and as counselor to the ministry of foreign affairs, serving under his father. In the wake of the disagreement between Tuan and Li Yuan-hung (q.v.) and the restoration attempt of Chang Hsün (q.v.), Wu and his father left Peking for Canton and the so-called constitution protection movement of Sun Yat-sen.

When Wu T'ing-fang became a director and foreign minister of the reorganized government at Canton in 1918, C. C. Wu was appointed vice minister of foreign affairs and chief of the general affairs department of the administrative council. Late in 1918 C. C. Wu was made head of the southern section of China's delegation to the Paris Peace Conference. Upon his return to China in mid-1919 he resumed office at Canton even though the government then was in the hands of the Kwangsi militarists. He retained the vice ministership of foreign affairs after Sun Yat-sen regained power at Canton. In 1922 Sun sent him to Mukden for negotiations with Chang Tso-lin (q.v.). At the time of the June 1922 coup at Canton by supporters of Ch'en Chiung-ming, Wu's father died. Wu accompanied Sun Yat-sen to Shanghai and returned with him to Canton after Ch'en was

ousted in 1923. He became minster of foreign affairs in Sun's government that March.

At the First National Congress of the Kuomintang, held at Canton in January 1924, C. C. Wu was elected to the Central Political Council. Soon afterwards, he became secretary general of the council and head of the merchants department in the Kuomintang central headquarters. He succeeded Sun Fo (q.v.) as mayor of Canton later that year. In October 1924 there occurred at Canton a clash with the Canton Merchants Corps. Conservative British interests in Shameen and Hong Kong were involved in the affair, and although it was brought to a successful conclusion by the Canton government's use of force, it was damaging to the position of C. C. Wu. Sun Yat-sen thought that Wu had played too feeble a role as foreign minister and mayor, and Wu's influence began to be eclipsed by that of the more radical Eugene Ch'en (q.v.), Sun's foreign affairs adviser.

In the general strike and anti-British boycott that hit Hong Kong and Canton after the May Thirtieth Incident of 1925, C. C. Wu again showed himself to be a moderate in his dealings with British and French officials. When the National Government was established at Canton in July 1925, Hu Han-min (q.v.), not Wu, received the post of foreign minister. Wu, however, became a member of the Military Council and chairman of the judicial committee. He also retained office as mayor of Canton. When Hu Han-min resigned from office after the assassination of Liao Chung-k'ai (q.v.), Wu succeeded him as foreign minister in September. In January 1926 Wu was elected to the Central Executive Committee. That spring, he reportedly became involved in activities directed against the leftist-oriented Canton regime, and he was relieved of his government posts in May.

After the first stage of the Northern Expedition and the transfer of the National Government to Wuhan, Chiang Kai-shek established an opposition government at Nanking in April 1927. The following month, Wu became foreign minister in Chiang's government. With the end of the Kuomintang-Communist alliance and the retirement of Chiang Kai-shek in August, Wu became one of the intermediaries in the effort to reunite the Wuhan, Nanking, and Shanghai factions of the Kuomintang. He retained the foreign ministership when a reorganized National Government was established at Nanking in September. He resigned at the end of December, saying that he did so because he was unable to accomplish anything in a government which could not "compel enforcement of orders within and without."

In January 1928 C. C. Wu accompanied Hu Han-min and Sun Fo to Europe for the purpose of making political and economic studies. The party stopped at Singapore for receptions given by the local Chinese community. On his way to a reception on 8 February, Wu was the object of an assassination attempt, but he escaped death. It later became evident that the would-be assassins had mistaken Wu for Hu Han-min, who had not gone to that reception. By the time of the Tsinan incident in May 1928 (*see* Ho Yao-tsu), Wu had reached Paris. Huang Fu (q.v.), then minister of foreign affairs, asked that he go immediately to the United States to seek American mediation if need be and perhaps also to take up the matter of treaty revision.

C. C. Wu reached Washington in late May 1928. Upon arrival, he stated that "the only way to bring the belligerent factions in China together would be for the whole country to accept the Nationalist principles." However, Wu occupied an anomalous position in undertaking his new mission: Peking's incumbent, Sao-ke Alfred Sze (Shih Chao-chi, q.v.) still held the post of Chinese minister to the United States. Wu opened a separate office and established contact with the Department of State, but he was received only in Sze's company. After the Peking government was overthrown in June, Sze continued to serve as minister, and Wu's representations regarding treaty revision continued to be ineffectual. It was Sze who negotiated the new Sino-American treaty of July 1928.

In November 1928 C. C. Wu finally succeeded Sao-ke Alfred Sze as Chinese minister to the United States. He retained that post until 1931 and performed a number of other duties during that period. In February 1929 he acted as Chinese plenipotentiary in negotiations for a new Sino-Turkish treaty of friendship. That September, he represented China at the League of Nations Assembly in Geneva, where he was elected a vice president. With reference to China's plea for the abolition of unequal treaties, he strongly argued the case for applic-

ability of the doctrine of *rebus sic stantibus*. In March 1930, he attended the Hague Conference for Codification of International Law as China's representative. He argued that China would not be held accountable for damages within its territory to the property or persons of foreigners beyond equality of treatment with Chinese citizens. In June 1930 he negotiated a treaty of arbitration with the United States. That September, he again represented China in the League Assembly.

The illegal arrest of Hu Han-min (q.v.) in March 1931 led to the formation of an opposition government at Canton in May. When the National Government instructed C. C. Wu to request arms from the United States for use against the dissidents, he resigned, saying that "I am a Cantonese." He returned to China and joined the Canton government as head of its judicial department and chief justice of its supreme court. After the Japanese attack at Mukden in September and the subsequent release of Hu Han-min at Nanking had paved the way for a reconciliation between the two Kuomintang factions, Wu went to Shanghai as one of the Canton regime's delegates to the peace talks. Agreement was reached on the basis of Chiang Kai-shek's temporary retirement from office and a redistribution of power at Nanking. Wu was appointed president of the Judicial Yuan and a member of the State Council, but he resigned in May 1932 without having assumed the duties of these offices. He then became governor of Kwangtung and Hainan reclamation commissioner. He soon resigned from these posts because of a clash between Ch'en Chi-t'ang (q.v.) and Admiral Chan Chak (Ch'en Tse).

C. C. Wu embarked on a tour of China in mid-1932. In the autumn of 1933 Sun Fo, then president of the Legislative Yuan, invited Wu to serve as an adviser to the constitutional drafting committee. Although Wu refused the post, he took the opportunity to stress again that it was important for China to incorporate the principle of *habeas corpus* into its judicial system. On 2 January 1934 C. C. Wu died suddenly at his Hong Kong residence of a cerebral hemorrhage, at the age of 46. He was survived by his wife, three sons, and five daughters. He was eulogized by a former associate as "a scholar, a writer of English prose, a first-class diplomat who understood revolutionary diplomacy but was prevented by political turmoil from fulfilling his mission to the Chinese people "

Wu Chien-hsiung   吳 健 雄
Alt. Wu Chien-shiung
West. C. S. Wu

Wu Chien-hsiung (31 May 1912–), known as C. S. Wu, outstanding physicist and professor at Columbia University who was best known for her experimental investigations of nuclear beta decay.

A native of Liuho, Kiangsu, C. S. Wu was brought up in a scholarly atmosphere. Her father, Wu Zong Yee, was the principal of a school in Liuho. He instilled in his children a love of reading and a deep respect for Chinese tradition, along with an awareness of the Western values and ideas which then were reaching China.

After receiving her early education at a local elementary school, C. S. Wu entered the Kiangsu Second Girls School in Soochow (later the Soochow Girls Normal School), which was famous for its emphasis on discipline and for its experiments with modern subjects and teaching techniques. It was while attending this school that C. S. Wu became strongly interested in mathematics and the sciences, especially physics. She also began to study English and German. In 1930, having completed her secondary education, she enrolled at National Central University in Nanking. She took all the available mathematics and physics courses and utilized her knowledge of German and English to keep up with the research in physics then being done in Europe and the United States. After being graduated in 1936, she worked for a short time as an assistant in the university's physics department.

Because C. S. Wu wished to pursue the study of physics and because opportunities for graduate work in that field were lacking in China, she went to the United States in the autumn of 1936 to enroll in the University of California at Berkeley. Her choice of Berkeley attests to her awareness of developments in physics at the time and of the institutions which were in the vanguard of research. Under the leadership of E. O. Lawrence, the winner of the 1939 Nobel Prize in physics for his development of the

cyclotron, the Radiation Laboratory at Berkeley was one of the foremost centers of experimental nuclear physics research in the world. Beginning with the second semester, C. S. Wu held a teaching assistantship until she completed the Ph.D. degree in 1940. She then was given a position as research assistant to Dr. Lawrence.

When the War in the Pacific began, pure research was pushed aside at Berkeley, and defense research became the order of the day. In 1942 C. S. Wu left Berkeley to become an assistant professor at Smith College. She spent the following year at Princeton University as an instructor. In March 1944 she joined the scientific staff of the Division of War Research (Manhattan Project) at Columbia University. After the war, she stayed on at Columbia as a research associate, becoming an associate professor in 1952 and a full professor in 1958.

C. S. Wu was best known for the accurate and extensive experimental investigations of nuclear beta decay which she carried out. Nuclear beta decay is the transformation of the nucleus of an atom of some particular element to that of another element by the spontaneous emission of positive or negative particles known as beta particles. A positive beta particle is called a positron; a negative beta particle, an electron. This transformation of a nucleus into another nucleus is characterized by the probability that it will occur in a certain interval of time and by the energy spectrum of the emitted beta particles. A successful theory of nuclear beta decay must predict these two characteristics correctly in any particular case. C. S. Wu's investigations in this field began with a study of the X rays which are excited by beta particles. This study, as well as a study of the decay schemes of some radioactive noble gases from uranium fission, was performed at Berkeley as her doctoral thesis. She later demonstrated the existence of a dependence of the beta spectrum upon the thickness of the source, a problem which before identification had caused some misinterpretation of the theory of beta decay. She also made a systematic study of various types of nuclei for which the beta spectra are quite different, providing the necessary evidence of the correctness of the theory of beta decay.

In 1956 two theoretical physicists, T. D. Lee of Columbia and C. N. Yang of the Institute for Advanced Study at Princeton, carried out a thorough survey of the existing experimental evidence concerning the conservation of parity in processes involving the weak interaction. This survey was prompted by the existence of a peculiar phenomenon: the existence in nature of two sub-nuclear particles which were identical in all respects except in the way they decayed. The assumption that these were but one particle with two different modes of decay required, however, that parity not be conserved. Parity conservation in a physical process is equivalent to saying that a distinction between left and right is not possible in such a process. For example, when a charged particle is accelerated, it emits electromagnetic radiation. If it emits more radiation on the left side of its path than on the right side, one would say that parity is not conserved. The survey of Li and Yang showed that evidence for parity conservation existed for all processes except those involving the weak interaction. They therefore postulated that in such processes parity is not conserved, and suggested some experiments which could be attempted in order to test their hypothesis.

One of the processes which involves the weak interaction is the beta decay of atomic nuclei. Lee and Yang, aware of C. S. Wu's experimental work in this field, asked her to carry out an experiment which would test their theory. The experiment, which C. S. Wu carried out in collaboration with scientists of the National Bureau of Standards, was essentially the following: The nuclei of radioactive cobalt-60 were aligned in the direction of a magnetic field while at a temperature close to 273°C below zero. The reason for using such a low temperature was to reduce the amount of thermal agitation which at higher temperatures causes a group of nuclei to be aligned randomly. The electrons from the decay of cobalt-60 which came out forward and backward along the direction of alignment then were counted. The results, announced early in 1957, showed that the electrons were emitted preferentially in one direction, differentiating right from left, and, hence, proving that parity was not conserved in nuclear beta decay. Within a few weeks, other results, obtained at Columbia and the University of Chicago, showed that parity was not conserved in other physical processes involving the weak interaction.

In 1963, in collaboration with Columbia research physicists Y. K. Lee and L. W. Mo,

C. S. Wu reported the experimental confirmation of a new fundamental theory of beta decay. This theory, proposed in 1958 by Richard Feynman and Murray Gell-Man of the California Institute of Technology, is known as the theory of conservation of vector current.

For her part in the overthrow of the principle of parity conservation, as well as for her work in nuclear beta decay and other fields, C. S. Wu was awarded many honors. Among these were the 1958 Research Corporation Award, the 1962 John Price Wetherill Medal of the Franklin Institute, the 1964 Cyrus B. Comstock Award of the National Academy of Sciences, and the 1965 Award for Achievement in Science from the Chi-Tsin Cultural Foundation in Taiwan. In 1958 she received the first honorary doctorate in science given to a woman by Princeton University. She also received honorary Sc.D. degrees from Smith College (1959), Rutgers University (1963), and Yale University (1967). She was the author of many research papers and co-author with S. A. Mozkowski of *Beta Decay*, published in 1966.

C. S. Wu married the physicist Luke Chia-liu Yuan, a grandson of Yuan Shih-k'ai, in 1942. They had one son, Vincent.

Wu Chih-hui　　　　　吳 稚 輝
　Orig. Ching-heng　　　敬 恒

Wu Chih-hui (25 March 1864–30 October 1953), scholar and educator, social reformer and revolutionary, anti-Communist and long-time associate of Ts'ai Yuan-p'ei, Chang Jen-chieh, and Li Shih-tseng. They came to be identified as the "four elder statesmen" of the Kuomintang. Wu was also known for his efforts to standardize the Chinese spoken language.

Yanghu hsien (Wuchin), then the seat of Changchow prefecture in Kiangsu province, was the birthplace of Wu Chih-hui. Yanghu had a great literary tradition in the Ch'ing dynasty which almost rivalled that of T'ung-cheng, Anhwei. Wu came from a scholarly family, and his mother was a member of the Tsou clan of Wusih. She died in 1870, leaving her bedridden husband, Wu Chih-hui, and a daughter. Two other children had died in infancy. Because Wu Chih-hui's father, who died in 1900, was unable to care for Wu and his sister, they went to live with their maternal grandmother in Wusih. The young Wu received a traditional education in the Chinese classics. In 1887, at the age of 23 sui, he passed the examination for the sheng-yuan degree. Two years later, he was admitted to the Nan-ch'ing Academy at Chiangyin. The director of the academy was the well-known scholar Huang I-chou, whose motto, "stick to the truth, and never be a compromiser," so impressed Wu that he adhered to it throughout his life.

In 1891 Wu Chih-hui achieved the chü-jen degree. He sat for the chin-shih examinations the following year, but failed them. Two more attempts, in 1894 and 1895, also brought no success. After the third failure, Wu went to Shanghai and became a tutor in the household of the noted scholar Lien Ch'üan. In 1897 Wu went to Tientsin to teach Chinese at Peiyang University, where he made the acquaintance of K'ang Yu-wei and Liang Ch'i-ch'ao (qq.v.), leaders of the constitutional reform movement. Although Wu agreed with many of the precepts of the constitutional reform movement, he still clung to the traditional concept of unswerving loyalty to the reigning sovereign. In any event, he resigned from the university just before the Hundred Days Reform began in 1898. He returned to Shanghai and joined the staff of the Nan-yang kung-hsueh, the predecessor of Chiao-t'ung University.

The Boxer Uprising and its aftermath brought Wu Chih-hui to a more radical way of thinking. He formulated three slogans in 1901: in any dispute between the emperor and the subjects, help the subjects; in any dispute between teachers and students, help the students; and in any dispute between fathers and sons, help the sons. In line with these slogans, he proposed to Chang Yuan-chi (q.v.), the new principal, that the school be administered jointly by the faculty and the students. When Chang refused the suggestion, Wu resigned. Chang then awarded him a fellowship for study in Japan. Wu went to Tokyo in May 1901, where he shared living quarters with Niu Yung-chien (q.v.), whom he had known at the Nan-ch'ing Academy. When Niu went to call on Sun Yat-sen, Wu refused an invitation to go along, for he was still far from being a revolutionary.

Late in 1901 Wu and Niu were recommended by Liu Erh-k'uei (later the editor of the *Tsu-yuan*) to go to Canton to help T'ao Mo, the governor general of Kwangtung and Kwangsi, establish a college and a military school. After completing this task, Wu and Niu were assigned by T'ao in April 1902 to escort a group of 26 students from Canton to Japan. One of the members of this group was Hu Han-min (q.v.). In July, Wu came into conflict with Ts'ai Chün, the Chinese minister to Japan, who refused to recommend some students for admission to Japanese military schools. As a result of this quarrel, the Japanese authorities decided to deport Wu. On his way to Kobe, under police escort, Wu attempted suicide by jumping into a canal, but the police rescued him. At this time, Ts'ai Yuan-p'ei (q.v.), a former colleague of Wu at the Nan yang kung-hsueh, was vacationing in Japan. Fearing that Wu might attempt suicide again. Ts'ai cut short his holiday to accompany Wu back to Shanghai.

Soon after his arrival in Shanghai, Wu Chih-hui joined with Ts'ai Yuan-p'ei, Chang Ping-lin (q.v.), and others in forming the Chung-kuo chiao-yü hui [China education society] to promote modern education in China. The society soon became a center for clandestine revolutionary activity. In November, it established a school, the Ai-kuo hsueh-she [patriotic society], with Ts'ai Yuan-p'ei as its principal and Wu as a member of its teaching staff. One of the students at the school was Chang Shih-chao (q.v.), who became editor in chief of the *Su-pao* in May 1903. The staff of the Ai-kuo hsueh-she contributed articles to the *Su-pao* which reflected strong anti-Manchu sentiment. As a result, the Ch'ing government ordered the suppression of the newspaper and the arrest of Chang Ping-lin, Tsou Jung (1885–1905; ECCP, II, 769), and others associated with it. Wu Chih-hui managed to escape from Shanghai, but Chang and Tsou were arrested.

Wu Chih-hui made his way to Edinburgh, Scotland, where he spent about six months. Early in 1904 he moved to London. The following year, he met Sun Yat-sen and Chang Jen-chieh (q.v.) in London and became a member of the T'ung-meng-hui. He moved to Paris in 1906 and joined Chang Jen-chieh and Li Shih-tseng (q.v.), whom he had met in Shanghai in 1902, in founding the Shih-chieh-she [world society], a revolutionary publishing house with an affiliated printing establishment. In June 1907 they began publishing the *Hsin shih-chi* [new century]. It was edited by Wu, and it reflected the flirtation he and Li were having with anarchism. The magazine issued 121 numbers before suspending publication on 21 May 1910. By the time it ceased publication, Wu had returned to London. With financial aid from Chang Jen-chieh, he had brought his family out of China in May 1909. His wife and their son and daughter—Wu Shu-wei (1896–) and Wu Meng-fu (1899–)—lived in London for the next 17 years.

After the republican revolution began in October 1911, Wu Chih-hui helped Sun Yat-sen draft various documents during Sun's short stay in London on his way back to China. Wu went back to China in January 1912, after Sun was installed as provisional president of the republican government. He stayed at Sun's headquarters for a time. In June, he went to Peking at the invitation of Ts'ai Yuan-p'ei, then minister of education, to promote the adoption of phonetic symbols for Chinese characters. Wu later was appointed director of the conference on the unification of pronunciation which convened at Peking on 15 February 1913. Also in 1912, Wu helped launch the thrift-study program in France (for details, *see* Li Shih-tseng). With the collapse of the so-called second revolution in September 1913, Wu Chih-hui and other Kuomintang leaders were forced to flee China. Wu rejoined his family in London. In 1915 he went to France to help Li Shih-tseng launch the work-study movement. Wu returned to China after Yuan Shih-k'ai's death in June 1916 to become editor of the *Chung-hua jih-pao* at Shanghai. The following summer, Fan Yuan-lien (q.v.), then minister of education, gave Wu a grant for the compilation of a dictionary with phonetic aids. Wu completed the project in the summer of 1918. The publication of the dictionary in September 1919 spurred new interest in the phoneticization of the Chinese language.

From 1918 to 1920 Wu Chih-hui taught Chinese at the T'ang-shan School of Railways and Mining. In 1920 he helped Li Shih-tseng and Ts'ai Yuan-p'ei found Sino-French University near Peking and the Institut Franco-Chinois de Lyon in France. Wu obtained financial aid from the Canton government of Ch'en Chiung-ming (q.v.), and he accompanied a group of about 100 students from Kwangtung and Kwangsi to Lyon, where he assumed the presidency of the Institut Franco-Chinois. He remained at Lyon until 1923, when he returned to China to find intellectuals engaged in the spirited science-philosophy debates (for details, *see* Chang Chia-sen; Ting Wen-chiang). Wu joined the fray on the side of the supporters of science with a long article entitled "A New Cosomology and Philosophy of Life Based Upon a New Belief."

At the First National Congress of the Kuomintang in 1924, Wu Chih-hui was elected to the party's Central Supervisory Committee. That spring, he made an unsuccessful attempt to reconcile the continuing differences between Sun Yat-sen and Ch'en Chiung-ming. He then went to Peking as a member of the commission, headed by Li Shih-tseng, taking inventory of the palace treasures. Wu thus was in Peking at the time of Sun Yat-sen's final illness and death in 1925, and he was one of the witnesses to the signing of Sun's political testament. Wu remained at Peking after Sun's death and operated a small private school at Nanhsiao-chieh for the children of Kuomintang leaders. Among his students was Chiang Ching-kuo (q.v.), the elder son of Chiang Kai-shek. During this period, Wu became increasingly opposed to Communist participation in the Kuomintang. He participated in the so-called Western Hills conference in November 1925. In 1926 he moved to Shanghai after a brief sojourn in Canton to take part in the launching of the Northern Expedition. He reopened his school at Shanghai and worked with Niu Yung-chien as a special Kuomintang agent. While helping prepare for the Nationalist takeover of Kiangsu, he became even more opposed to the Chinese Communists than he had been previously. Wu, Ts'ai Yuan-p'ei, Chang Jen-chieh, and Li Shih-tseng (who became known collectively as the "four elder statesmen" of the Kuomintang) were among the members of the Central Supervisory Committee who met in Shanghai in April 1927 and demanded the expulsion of all Communists from the Kuomintang. Wu and his associates strongly supported Chiang Kai-shek's government at Nanking, established in opposition to the Wuhan regime of Wang Ching-wei (q.v.).

After the reunification of the Kuomintang and the expulsion of Communists from that party, a new National Government was established at Nanking. Although Wu Chih-hui was offered high posts in the government, he declined them all, for he believed that he could work more effectively for Chiang Kai-shek as an adviser. After 1927 he devoted much of his time to the standardization of spoken Chinese as chairman of the preparatory commission for the unification of the national language. In 1930 he supported Chiang Kai-shek's plan to hold a national convention to adopt a provisional constitution, a plan strongly opposed by Hu Han-min. When Hu refused to accept Wu's arguments in favor of the constitution, he was placed illegally under house arrest on 28 February 1931. Wu presided over the constitutional convention in May 1931. About that time, he also became a member of the Central Political Council. At the end of May, supporters of Hu Han-min formed an opposition government at Canton, and civil war threatened until the Nanking and Canton leaders held peace talks after the Japanese attacked Mukden in September.

During the Sino-Japanese war, Wu Chih-hui lived in semi-retirement at Chungking. After his residence was destroyed by Japanese bombs in June 1940, he shared a house with his old friend Niu Yung-chien. He devoted much of his time to calligraphy and supported himself by selling examples of his calligraphic art. At war's end, he returned to Shanghai. In November 1946 he was elected to the presidium of the National Assembly, which drew up a constitution for the Chinese republic. On 20 May 1948, representing the National Assembly, he administered the presidential oath to Chiang Kai-shek. He left the mainland for Taiwan in April 1949 after destroying the papers, political documents, and other material he had collected assiduously for 60 years so that this valuable collection would not fall into the hands of the victorious Chinese Communists. He died in Taiwan on 30 October 1953, at the age of 89 sui. In accordance with his will, a box containing his cremated remains was lowered into the sea at Quemoy. In March 1964 a bronze statue of Wu was unveiled at Taipei on the occasion of the centenary of his birth.

Wu Ching-hsiung 吳経熊
West. John C. H. Wu

Wu Ching-hsiung (28 March 1899–), known as John C. H. Wu, lawyer, juristic philosopher, educator, and prominent Catholic layman. He was president of the Special High Court at Shanghai, vice chairman of the Legislative Yuan's constitution drafting committee, founder of the *T'ien Hsia Monthly*, translator of the Psalms and the New Testament, and Chinese minister to the Holy See (1947–48).

Ningpo, Chekiang, was the birthplace of John C. H. Wu. His father, Wu Chia-ch'ang (1847–1909), born into a modest family and with little formal education, had become a prominent banker and philanthropist in Ningpo. He also served as the first chairman of the Ningpo Chamber of Commerce. The youngest of three children, John C. H. Wu began his Chinese education at the age of six. After studying under a tutor at home for two years, he entered a Western-style school in Ningpo. In April 1916, while attending a Western-style secondary school, he submitted to an arranged marriage. Both he and his bride, Li Yu-t'i, were 17 years old. Also in 1916 Wu went to Shanghai to enter the Shanghai Baptist College for scientific studies. A schoolmate, Hsü Chih-mo (q.v.), urged Wu to join him at the Peiyang University Law School in Tientsin. Wu agreed and studied at Peiyang during the spring term of 1917. That autumn he returned to Shanghai and registered at Soochow University's Comparative Law School of China, then headed by Dean Charles W. Rankin. Wu thus came into contact with Western missionaries and, under the influence of Dean Rankin, became a Methodist. He was graduated at the top of his class in 1920.

In the autumn of 1920 Wu sailed for the United States to enroll as a candidate for the LL.M. degree at the University of Michigan Law School. Because of his exceptional academic record of 10 straight A's in Ann Arbor, he was awarded an advanced J.D. degree in June 1921. During that year he also published his first professional article in English, "Readings from Ancient Chinese Codes and Other Sources of Chinese Law and Legal Ideas," in the *Michigan*

Law Review. The article discussed universal legal ideas in the context of comparative law, stated that the Chinese legal mind was well prepared to accept contemporary Western sociological jurisprudence, and argued that foreign powers should be prepared to give up extraterritorial rights in China. He sent a copy of the article with a note requesting critical comment to Oliver Wendell Holmes, an act that initiated an extended correspondence and warm friendship. Holmes was then already 80; Wu, barely 22. The two men met only briefly and at long intervals, but with each exchange of letters their mutual affection deepened. The letters Holmes sent to Wu over a period of 11 years were among the best letters written by Holmes. Throughout his later legal career in China, Wu was strongly influenced by Holmes's legal philosophy.

Wu was recommended by his professors at Michigan to Judge James Brown Scott of the Carnegie Endowment for International Peace, which awarded him a traveling fellowship to visit Europe for advanced work. At Paris in 1921 he composed a treatise entitled "Les transformations des conceptions fondamentales du droit des gens," an effort to provide international law with a broader juridical basis through philosophical, rather than merely factual, analysis. In Berlin he attended lectures by the prominent neo-Kantian philosopher of law Rudolf Stammler, whom he came to know and admire. As in his relations with Holmes, the young Wu retained notable independence of mind. He sought to strike a middle course between the perceptual, intuitive approach to law of Holmes and the logical, conceptual approach of Stammler.

In March 1923 Wu's study of "The Juristic Philosophy of Justice Holmes" appeared in the *Michigan Law Review*. That article discussed juristic philosophy, which Wu defined as "man thinking about generalities in connection with law," in relation to problems of epistemology and ethics. It then examined the manner in which Holmes had contributed to resolution of these problems. Judge Benjamin Cardozo, in 1923 lectures at the Yale Law School, took note of Wu's article and indicated that his own thinking was similar; the Cardozo lectures were published in 1924 as *The Growth of the Law*. In 1923–24 Wu returned to the United States to accept a research scholarship in jurisprudence at the Harvard Law School, then under the direction of Dean Roscoe Pound. An article by Wu on "The Juristic Philosophy of Roscoe Pound" appeared in January 1924 in the *Illinois Law Review*. In December 1923 Wu visisted Washington, where he met Justice Holmes for the first time.

John C. H. Wu returned to China in the spring of 1924. That autumn he joined the faculty of his alma mater in Shanghai, the Comparative Law School of China, as professor of law. Three years later, on the resignation of Dean W. W. Blume, Wu was one of the most popular candidates for the deanship. For practical reasons, Wu, who was deemed by some people connected with Soochow University to be a brilliant but somewhat unpredictable person, instead was promoted to a new position, that of principal, while Robert W. H. Sheng became the new dean. Later in 1927, when the new National Government regained jurisdiction over Chinese nationals in the International Settlement of Shanghai and established its own courts there, Wu was named judge of the civil division of the Shanghai Provisional Court. In writing to Holmes of the appointment, Wu declared that he would do his best to "Holmesianize the law of China." As the first Chinese to dispense justice in an area still under foreign administration, Wu laid down the principle that "the law of nations is a part of the common law of China." In the spring of 1928 he was appointed to membership on the codification commission attached to the ministry of justice at Nanking. That summer he became presiding judge of the criminal division of the Court of Appeals. *Judicial Essays and Studies*, a collection of his papers on aspects of legal and judicial philosophy, was published by the Commercial Press in Shanghai in 1928.

The year 1929 brought Wu's promotion to the presidency of the Special High Court at Shanghai. Late in the year, however, he resigned his judgeship to accept offers from institutions in the United States. In January 1930 he delivered the Julius Rosenwald Foundation lectures at the Northwestern University Law School in Chicago, where he discussed China's traditional and modern legal systems. He then took up a research fellowship at the Harvard Law School during the spring term. During his stay in Cambridge in 1930, he went to call on Justice Holmes at Beverly, Massachusetts. This proved to be their final meeting. Wu returned to China that summer to collect Chinese materials for a new course on commercial law which he was to offer at Harvard; but the illness of his wife forced him to cancel the course and remain in Shanghai.

In the autumn of 1930 John C. H. Wu began the practice of law in Shanghai. He was immediately, almost notoriously, successful, receiving more in fees during his first month of practice than he had earned in all his previous years as professor and judge. His academic qualifications and professional prominence combined to make him one of the most sought-after Chinese lawyers of the day. Despite his success, Wu found only minimal intellectual challenge in broken contracts, torts, and disputes over legacies and became increasingly frustrated and depressed by his situation. Thus, when Sun Fo (q.v.) invited him to join the Legislative Yuan in 1933, Wu quickly accepted. Sun Fo, who had been named president of the Legislative Yuan in 1932, held that post until 1948. During most of this period Wu served successively as vice chairman of the constitution drafting committee, chairman of the general committee, and chairman of the foreign relations committee of the Legislative Yuan. As vice chairman of the constitution drafting committee, he was entrusted with responsibility for the first draft of a new national constitution scheduled for 1936. He singlehandedly prepared the draft in four weeks, and he then was authorized to publish it under his own name for public comment. The original draft went through manifold revisions before it was adopted by the National Government in 1946, but the section of the document in which Wu had most interest, the chapter on basic rights and duties of the citizen, was preserved almost intact when the constitution finally was promulgated.

While serving in the Legislative Yuan, Wu also took an active part in the affairs of the Sun Yat-sen Institute for the Advancement of Culture and Learning. In May 1935, under the institute's auspices, he founded the *T'ien Hsia Monthly*, an English-language magazine devoted to increasing East-West cultural communication. Wu invited Wen Yuan-ning, a British-trained scholar of English literature (later Chinese ambassador to Greece), to become chief editor and asked Lin Yü-t'ang (q.v.) and T. K. Ch'uan (Ch'uan Tseng-ku) to be co-editors. This journal published many contributions of lasting significance by both Chinese and Western writers before it suspended publication in 1941. Wu devoted much of his energies to literary and editorial matters and delved deeply into both Chinese and Western literature.

Shortly after the Sino-Japanese war began in 1937, John C. H. Wu became a Roman Catholic. His conversion was sparked by a chance reading of the autobiography of St. Theresa of Lisieux, translated into Chinese by Ma Liang (q.v.). The Theresian message of God's love, together with unbounded faith in God's mercy, struck him with the force of a revelation. Wu had found the Methodist brand of Protestantism emotionally cold and had investigated Confucianism, Buddhism, and Taoism. The problem of sin deeply disturbed him, for, like Boswell in London, Wu in Shanghai had oscillated between bouts of dissipation and pangs of conscience. The door opened by the life of St. Theresa led to a passage of many turnings—mysticism and dogma, philosophy and asceticism—and Wu found himself intrigued by each new discovery. It was not the intellectualism of Catholicism that attracted Wu; rather it was the simplicity of the Catholic message, its admission of the inscrutable mystery of God's love, and its demand for child-like faith. Wu's submission to the Catholic Church was as dramatic as it was genuine. He was baptized in December 1937 and was confirmed two years later. Within a few months, his wife (baptized Mary Teresa) and their children had followed Wu into the Catholic Church.

In 1938 Wu moved to Hong Kong, where the *T'ien Hsia Monthly* was edited until its demise three years later. When Japanese troops invaded Hong Kong in December 1941, Wu was interned for several weeks but later released through the intercession of Sir Robert Kotewall. He escaped from Hong Kong in May 1942 and sailed up the East River to Kweilin. After several weeks of rest, he went to Chungking, where he was a guest of Fu Ping-ch'ang, then vice minister of foreign affairs. He was commissioned by Chiang Kai-shek to translate the Psalms into Chinese. Wu returned to Kweilin in late 1942 and spent two secluded but happy years preparing a metrical rendering of the Psalms which would have the flavor of classical

Chinese poetry. In the autumn of 1944 a new Japanese offensive forced him to move to Kweiyang and then to Chungking. Wu's translation, in which Chiang Kai-shek and his wife, Soong Mei-ling (q.v.), took direct personal interest, was later published by the Commercial Press in 1946. The work was widely acclaimed for its elegance, and Wu himself rated it his happiest literary production in Chinese.

In the spring of 1945 John C. H. Wu served as adviser to the Chinese delegation to the United Nations Conference on International Organization at San Francisco. He returned to Chungking to attend meetings of the Political Consultative Conference in early 1946. Later that year Chiang Kai-shek named Wu Chinese minister to the Holy See, and Wu presented his credentials to Pope Pius XII in February 1947. During his mission to the Vatican, Wu completed a Chinese translation of the New Testament, also rendered in the classical Chinese style (published in Hong Kong in 1949). But he found the rigors of diplomatic life in Rome hardly more congenial than law practice in Shanghai. After returning to China briefly in early 1949, he returned to Rome. Soon afterward, he resigned his diplomatic post.

In 1949 Wu moved to Honolulu to become visiting professor of Chinese philosophy at the University of Hawaii, where he remained for two years. There he wrote the autobiographical volume *Beyond East and West*, published in 1951. Despite its undisguisedly ambitious title, the book drew wide attention for its summation of Wu's 30-year spiritual odyssey, his search for an immutable scale of values suitable for all men. A second book, *The Interior Carmel*, also written in English, was a study of the Christian path of perfection.

In 1951 Wu was invited to join the law faculty of Seton Hall University in South Orange, New Jersey. Legal philosophy had been an early intellectual love, and he returned to the subject as though discharging a debt of honor. As a youth he had been a tentative champion of the natural law; in maturity, he viewed it as the basis of all law. The author of natural law was God, who either promulgated it through an agent (*e.g.* Moses) or imprinted it in men's hearts. This concept is indeed orthodox Catholic teaching, of which Aquinas was the ablest expositor; but Wu articulated it with the authority of an academically trained

jurist. *Fountain of Justice* (1955) and *Cases and Materials on Jurisprudence* (1958) presented Wu's mature thinking. In 1957 he received the honor of appointment as a member of the Permanent Court of Arbitration at The Hague.

As a Catholic writer who lived his later years in the United States, Wu became better known in the English-speaking world than in China. His classical Chinese renderings of the Psalms and the New Testament could not achieve the general utility or popularity of versions written in modern vernacular Chinese. His poetical English verson of the *Tao Te Ching* of Lao-tzu, published in 1961, was praised as a graceful translation prepared by a man for whom the famous Taoist text "represents a living tradition, not a philological exercise." A collection of his essays, *Chinese Humanism and Christian Spirituality*, edited by Paul K. T. Sih, appeared in 1965. Wu was a panel member at the East-West Philosophers' conferences held in Hawaii in 1959 and 1964, and two of his papers prepared for those meetings, "Chinese Legal and Political Philosophy" and "The Status of the Individual in the Political and Legal Traditions of Old and New China," appeared in *The Chinese Mind: Essentials of Chinese Philosophy and Culture*, edited by Charles A. Moore and published in 1967. Wu held honorary degrees from a number of institutions, including Portland University (Oregon), Boston College, and St. John's University (New York); and he was an honorary member of the American Academy of Arts and Sciences and the Academy of Living Catholic Authors.

After 1937 John C. H. Wu was generally regarded as one of China's chief lay exponents of Catholic ideas. Some observed that, as in the case of Hsü Kuang-ch'i (baptized Paul Hsü; 1562–1633; ECCP, I, 316–19), the Catholic Church had found a true intellectual convert in China. Others responded that Wu was the greater gain to the Church since he was far better equipped than the Ming dynasty scholar and official to appreciate and interpret the Catholic faith.

Wu's first wife died in the winter of 1959. During their more than 40 years of marriage, 13 children had been born to them. One son, Peter (b. 1934) became a priest of the Maryknoll Society. In June 1967 Wu visited Taiwan, where he married Chu Wen-ying (baptized Maria Agnes) from Hong Kong.

Wu Chung-hsin   吳 忠 信
T. Li-ch'ing   禮 卿

Wu Chung-hsin (15 March 1884–16 December 1959), military and political associate of Sun Yat-sen and Chiang Kai-shek who served as governor of Anhwei (1932) and Kweichow (1935), chairman of the Mongolian and Tibetan Affairs Commission (1936–44), and governor of Sinkiang (1944–45).

Ancestors of Wu Chung-hsin had moved from Kiangsi to Lochiakang in the northern part of Hofei, Anhwei, in the early years of the Ch'ing dynasty. They had taken up farming as a livelihood. At the time of the Taiping Rebellion, his paternal grandfather, Wu Yung-pi, had established a hsien defense militia, thus enabling the inhabitants to enjoy a measure of peace. Because Lochiakang was far from any market town, Wu Yung-pi established a small store. Lochiakang soon became known locally as Wuchiatien. Wu Yung-pi's son, Wu Chi-lung, had five sons, of whom Wu Chung-hsin was the youngest. When Wu Chung-hsin was barely two, his father died; his mother died five years later. Thus, the young Wu was reared and educated by his four elder brothers.

Wu Chung-hsin decided to pursue a military career, and in 1901 he enrolled at the Kiangnan Military Academy. Upon graduation in 1905, he was sent to Chinkiang to handle troop conscription there. His performance was such that he soon received command of a battalion in the Kiangnan Army. In 1906 Yang Cho-lin, a member of the T'ung-meng-hui, returned to China from Japan to promote the revolutionary cause in the Kiangnan Army. Wu soon joined the T'ung-meng-hui. After Yang was executed in 1907 Wu, then at Nanking, began disseminating revolutionary ideas in the army to avenge his friend's death. As a result, Wu was transferred to Chinkiang, where he served as judge advocate in the headquarters of the 15th Regiment. At the time of the republican revolution in 1911, he served as chief executive legal officer and inspector general of military depots in the Kiangsu-Chekiang-Shanghai revolutionary forces.

With the establishment of the Chinese republic in 1912, Wu Chung-hsin was appointed super-intendent of the Nanking police force. He held that post until June, when he received command of forces in the Nanking-Chinkiang-Kiangyin-Woosung sector. Soon afterwards, he resigned and went to Shanghai to serve under Yü Yu-jen (q.v.) as general manager of the *Min-li pao*. At the time of the so-called second revolution (*see* Li Lieh-chün) in 1913, Wu resumed office as Nanking police superintendent at the request of Huang Hsing (q.v.). When the anti-Yuan Shih-k'ai campaign failed, he fled to Japan, where he studied political economy. He supported the reorganization of the Kuomintang as the Chung-hua ko-ming-tang, with headquarters in Japan.

In October 1915 Ch'en Ch'i-mei (q.v.) returned to China accompanied by Chiang Kai-shek, Ch'en Kuo-fu, Ch'en Li-fu (qq.v.), and Wu Chung-hsin to plan moves against Yuan Shih-k'ai. This group staged the spectacular but unsuccessful Chao-ho gunboat affair on 5 December in an attempt to recapture Shanghai. Ch'en Ch'i-mei and his supporters were forced to flee from their headquarters in the French concession at Shanghai to escape arrest. At the time of Ch'en Ch'i-mei's assassination on 18 May 1916, Wu narrowly escaped death. He was just entering the room when the shots were fired. Wu lost a tooth in the subsequent confusion but otherwise was unharmed.

In 1917, when Sen Yat-sen established a military government at Canton, Wu Chung-hsin joined the Kwangtung forces. By the end of 1921 he had risen to become garrison commander of Kweilin and had become acquainted with such young Kwangsi leaders as Li Tsung-jen and Pai Ch'ung-hsi (qq.v.). Throughout this period, however, Wu was plagued by dysentery and other intestinal troubles. In April 1922 he resigned from his military post and went to Shanghai for medical treatment. He then went to Soochow to recuperate, remaining there until the Northern Expedition began in mid-1926.

Chiang Kai-shek invited Wu Chung-hsin to Nanchang in the autumn of 1926 and appointed him an adviser in his headquarters there. The National Revolutionary Army captured Shanghai in March 1927, and Wu was made a member of the Kiangsu provincial council. He then became chief of the Woosung-Shanghai police department. Because Shanghai had no municipal administration, the police department also had to perform the functions of a municipal government. Both before and after the anti-Communist purge in April, Wu was confronted with many problems. He handled them pragmatically with the help of Tu Yueh-sheng (q.v.). In August, when Chiang Kai-shek temporarily retired in the interests of party unity, Wu resigned and returned home. He returned to public life in February 1928, when he became a member of the newly established National Reconstruction Commission (*see* Chang Jen-chieh). In October of that year, Chiang Kai-shek sent him to north China to reorganize the Hopei armies. After completing that task, Wu left China with K. P. Ch'en (Chen Kuang-fu, q.v.) in February 1929 for a tour of Southeast Asia, Europe, the Unites States, and Japan. Wu and Ch'en returned to China in October.

After serving as a member of the Control Yuan in 1931, Wu Chung-hsin became governor of Anhwei in the spring of 1932. Because of the great difficulties he encountered in attempting to govern his native province, he tendered his resignation in December 1932, but it was not accepted until May 1933. He then became chief adviser to Chiang Kai-shek's Nanchang headquarters and participated in planning the campaigns that forced the Chinese Communists out of Kiangsi on the Long March. In 1935 he was appointed governor of Kweichow, and he was made a member of the Central Executive Committee of the Kuomintang.

In August 1936 Wu Chung-hsin succeeded Huang Mu-sung (q.v.) as chairman of the Mongolian and Tibetan Affairs Commission. At that time, the Panchen Lama (q.v.) was attempting to return to Tibet. Because of British and Tibetan protests and the political complexities caused by the outbreak of the Sino-Japanese war in July 1937, Wu urged the temporary postponement of the Panchen's return to Tibet. The matter came to an end with the Panchen's death that December. In 1938 Wu recognized a new opportunity for the adjustment of Sino-Tibetan relations in the forthcoming confirmation of the fourteenth incarnation of the Dalai Lama. That December, the National Government designated Wu Chung-hsin and Radreng Rimpoche, the Tibetan regent, to be in charge of the confirmation ceremony. After some difficulty, Lhasa finally decided to accept Wu's mission when assurances

were given about its political scope. The confirmation ceremony was held on 22 February 1940. At that time, the staff of the Chinese liaison office at Lhasa consisted of one radio operator. After extended negotiations with the Lhasa authorities, on 1 April Wu established a Tibetan branch of the Mongolian and Tibetan Affairs Commission. On 14 April, he left Lhasa. On his way back to Chungking, he stopped in India, where he visited Rabindranath Tagore and Jawaharlal Nehru. Wu reached Chungking in July 1940 and made his report. Many years later, in 1959, his report was published in Taipei as *Hsi-tsang chi-yao* [record of important facts about Tibet]. Chinese influence in Tibet diminished again in 1941, when the pro-Chinese Radreng Rimpoche was replaced as regent by the pro-British Jung-tseng. Chinese plans for a supply route through Tibet then had to be abandoned.

Wu Chung-hsin succeeded Sheng Shih-ts'ai (q.v.) as governor of Sinkiang in October 1944. After his arrival at Urumchi, he released a large number of political prisoners, including Burhan (q.v.) and several National Government officials. Sheng Shih-ts'ai's oppression of Sinkiang's non-Chinese inhabitants and the overzealous efforts of Kuomintang workers to sinicize the province after their arrival at the beginning of 1943 had given rise to intense anti-Chinese feeling in Sinkiang. Kazakh and Turki peoples, with some Soviet support, staged a revolt in November 1944; won control of the Ili, Chuguchak, and Altai districts; and established the so-called East Turkestan Republic. The rebellion continued, and in the late summer of 1945 Chang Chih-chung (q.v.) was sent to Urumchi to aid Wu. Arrangements were made for Soviet mediation, and a preliminary agreement with the Ili rebels was signed in January 1946. Chang Chih-chung then succeeded Wu as governor of Sinkiang in March.

When the National Government was reorganized in April 1947, Wu Chung-hsin was elected to the State Council. In December 1948 he was appointed secretary general in the presidential office, charged with handling the delicate matter of the transfer of presidential authority from Chiang Kai-shek to Li Tsung-jen. He resigned on 21 January 1949, when Chiang Kai-shek announced his retirement from office and Li Tsung-jen became acting President. Thereafter, he served as a liaison officer between Chiang and Li. In May, as the war for control of the mainland was coming to an end, Wu went to Taiwan, where he helped prepare that island as a base for retreat. After Chiang Kai-shek resumed the presidency of the National Government in Taiwan on 1 March 1950, Wu became a member of the board of directors of the Central Bank and a member of the Kuomintang Central Advisory Committee. In July 1952 he was appointed chairman of the Kuomintang Central Disciplinary Committee. He held these posts until his death on 16 December 1959. Wu was survived by three sons and a daughter. His eldest son, Shen-shu, studied art in France. His younger sons, Yung-shu and Kuang-shu, and his daughter, Hsun-shu, all studied in the United States.

Wu Han　　　　　　　　吳　唅

Wu Han (1909–), historian and university professor, was known before 1949 primarily as a leading authority on the Ming dynasty. He served after 1952 as a deputy mayor of Peking and as vice chairman of the China Democratic League until his political disgrace in 1966.

The Iwu district of Chekiang was the native place of Wu Han. He was the eldest of four children in the family of a local school teacher and small landowner who had obtained the sheng-yuan degree. Wu stated that his grandfather had been a tenant farmer, but this contention was challenged in a Communist investigation of his background made in 1966. Utilizing the Wu family genealogy and making inquiries among local poor peasants in Chekiang, the investigators charged that Wu's grandfather had been a usurer and suppressor of the Taiping rebels and that his father had been a well-to-do landowner and local police official characterized by the Communists as reactionary.

Wu Han's early interest in history was stimulated by the only set of books his family possessed, the *Yü-p'i t'ung-chien*, by which is probably meant the *Yü-p'i t'ung-chien chi-lan* (1767), an edition of Ssu-ma Kuang's *Tzu-chih t'ung-chien* [comprehensive mirror for the aid of government] with moral criticisms of historical characters supplied by the Ch'ien-lung emperor himself. After graduation from a local middle

school, Wu taught for a year as a primary school teacher. With clan aid and money from the sale of his mother's jewelry, he was then able to continue his studies in a college preparatory school at Hangchow and at the university section of the Chung-kuo kung-hsueh [China institute] in Shanghai. Toward the end of his two-year stay there, Wu attended a course of lectures given by Hu Shih (q.v.), then president of the institute, on Chinese civilization and wrote for him a paper entitled *Hsi Han-ti ching-chi chuang-k'uang* [the economic situation of the western Han]. Hu Shih liked the paper, but he could do nothing about it, for he then was forced to resign his post. Wu was able to sell the treatise to a local publisher and to travel to Peking on the proceeds. On the recommendation of Ku Chieh-kang (q.v.), Wu was given a job as a research cataloguer in the Yenching University library.

In 1931, after passing the entrance examinations, Wu Han entered Tsinghua University as a second-year student in the history department. On the recommendation of Hu Shih, he was given a work scholarship by the departmental chairman, T. F. Tsiang (Chiang T'ing-fu, q.v.). At the same time, Wu began writing articles on historical subjects for money; and from 1933 on he was able to get his articles accepted by such prestigious scholarly journals as the *Ch'ing-hua hsueh-pao* and the *Yen-ching hsueh-pao*. It was at this time that Wu's father died, leaving heavy debts. Because Wu was responsible for the upkeep of a brother and sister who were also studying in Peking, he was unable to enter graduate school. Accordingly, he stayed at Tsinghua as a teaching assistant. Tsinghua was known in these years as a jumping-off place for people seeking advanced study in the United States, but because Wu's specialty was Chinese history, he had no reasonable excuse for going there. Consequently, as he later asserted, he felt downgraded and out of touch with the intellectual mainstream in China.

During his early years at Tsinghua (1931–37), Wu Han made important contributions to knowledge of the Ming period. Utilizing techniques and critical tenets absorbed from his mentor Hu Shih, he demonstrated an acute faculty for detecting tendentious or falsified documentation. Wu's first important article on Ming history, a study of the Hu Wei-yung affair, appeared in the *Yenching hsueh-pao* in

June 1934; it argued that virtually all of the "crimes" charged to Hu Wei-yung were in fact fabrications. Wu concluded that the real aims of the early Ming purges, of which the Hu Wei-yung case was the greatest, extending over 14 years and claiming some 40,000 lives, were to eliminate any possibility of an anti-dynastic coup on the part of the founder's old followers after the former's death; to create an entirely docile official and intellectual class; and to fill the state treasury through confiscations of the victims' properties. It was perhaps ironic that the author himself became involved in a political purge some 30 years after the writing of this article. Subsequent contributions published in 1935 were an essay on the disputed issue of the identity of the Yung-lo emperor's mother, and a competent discussion of the Yung-lo usurpation. Wu's treatment of Ming maritime relations before the sixteenth century, published in 1936, became a standard reference, as did his 1937 article on the Ming military system.

After the Sino-Japanese war began in July 1937, Wu accompanied the migration of the universities from Peking to southwest China. From 1937 to 1946 he was a professor in the department of history of Southwest Associated University at Kunming. During the summer and autumn of 1943 he wrote a full-length biography of Chu Yuan-chang, the founder of the Ming dynasty, which was published in 1944 under two different titles: separately as *Yu seng-po tao huang-ch'üan* [from begging bowl to imperial power], and under the name of *Ming t'ai-tsu* [the first emperor of the Ming] as one of a series of biographies of the great heroes of China's past edited by P'an Kung-chan (q.v.), who had been vice director of the Kuomintang central propaganda department. Revised and expanded as *Chu Yuan-chang chuan* [biography of Chu Yuan-chang] and published at Shanghai in 1947, this work is considered by many writers to be the best biography written by a modern Chinese.

During the war years, Wu developed an active interest in current affairs. Because the Kuomintang suppressed open discussion of contemporary problems and forbade criticism of government officials, it was necessary to approach these topics through indirect means. Thus some of Wu's scholarly articles were rather timely in their choice of topic: papers published in 1939, 1943, and 1944, for example, focused attention on the growing inflation in wartime China (a forbidden topic) through discussion of paper currency problems in the Yuan, Ming, and Ch'ing dynasties. Wu also began contributing to Yunnan newspapers short satirical articles using historical allegory to refer to current issues. Most of these essays were collected and republished in Peiping in 1946 as *Li-shih-ti ching-tzu* [the mirror of history]. In politics, Wu became a supporter of the generally liberal coalition group known as the China Democratic League, which aimed at steering a middle course through the Communist–Kuomintang struggle and reconciling conflicting interests through a Western-style rule of law. It was in this connection that in January 1946 he joined the anthropologist Fei Hsiao-t'ung (q.v.) and others in addressing a letter to General George C. Marshall, supporting Marshall's efforts at mediating the civil conflict in China. Wu also was closely associated with Wen I-to (q.v.), who was assassinated at Kunming in July 1946.

By the autumn of 1946, Wu Han had returned to Peiping and had accepted a position as professor of history at Tsinghua University. He led a group of junior professors in an unsuccessful attempt to place one of their number on the university senate, which was dominated by older faculty under the president of Tsinghua, Y. C. Mei (Mei Yi-ch'i, q.v.). Simultaneously, Wu and his colleagues from Tsinghua and the other universities in Peking—many of them members of the Democratic League and the Democratic Youth League or underground members of the Chinese Communist party—held frequent meetings on their own, during which they discussed the current situation in China, drafted proclamations, and distributed news bulletins which they secretly picked up on radio from the Communist-held areas. After the Kuomintang outlawed the Democratic League in October 1947, Wu Han and his friends cooperated with the Communists, mainly by clandestinely funneling young intellectuals, badly needed by the Communists at that time, from Peiping to the so-called liberated areas. Wu's scholarly output as this time included an excellent article published in 1948 on the horrors of the early Ming schools, a subject admittedly prompted by what the author saw of the oppressed and undernourished students of Peiping. Another article published in the same year on the scholar Ch'ien Ch'ien-i (ECCP, I, 148–50) was intended as an attack on Wang Yün-wu (q.v.), the head of the Commercial Press.

When the Kuomintang began in August 1948 to arrest individuals regarded as subversives, Wu Han fled Peiping with a group of students and professors from Tsinghua and by an indirect route reached Communist-controlled territory. The group sent a letter to Y. C. Mei, promising to return in the spring of 1949 and requesting him to remain in charge at Tsinghua to prevent the dispersal or destruction of its holdings and personnel. Mei received the letter, but he elected to depart for Taiwan.

After arrival in Communist territory, Wu Han at first professed a distaste for the cult of Mao Tse-tung. After some ideological remolding, he began to see things in a different light. The magazine *Chung-kuo ch'ing-nien* [China youth] during 1949 carried Wu's interim report on his progress in the study of Marxist thought; in February 1950 the same magazine published his triumphant "Wo k'o-fu-le 'ch'ao chieh-chi' kuan-tien" [I overcame the "supra-class" viewpoint]. In this latter piece—later included in the pamphlet *Tsen-yang kai-tsao* [how to reform] together with similar statements by Fei Hsiao-t'ung, the philosopher Feng Yu-lan (q.v.), and others—Wu reviewed his family and personal background and classed himself as a petty bourgeois intellectual with selfish, individualistic, and escapist tendencies. The pernicious influence of Hu Shih, he said, had prevented him from using Marxism–Leninism in his historical writings. An evening's interview with Mao Tse-tung, who had read his *Chu Yuan-chang chuan* and who discussed it with him, made him realize the relevance of Communism to contemporary conditions, the importance of Mao's guidance of the party, and the significance of the techniques of criticism and self-criticism.

Wu Han held a variety of posts in the People's Republic of China. His first appointment, as one of the directors of the Democratic League, came in May 1949. In September 1949 he was made a delegate to the Chinese People's Consultative Conference, which established the new regime, and in August 1952 he was selected for the post of deputy mayor of Peking. Numerous other temporary and subsidiary appointments followed in later years. In 1953 he was vice director of an official delegation to

North Korea; in 1956 he visited India as the leader of a delegation from the Sino-Indian Friendship Association. Wu's official duties were not so burdensome as to put an end to his writing. Prior to the Hundred Flowers campaign of 1957, he confined himself to scholarly pursuits. In 1955 he published papers on the development of the early Ming economy and on the question of the beginnings of capitalism during the Ming period; in 1957 some of his old articles were gathered and published as *Tu-shih cha-chi* [notes on reading history]. His politically punctilious behavior during the Hundred Flowers period and his contribution to an attack on Lo Lung-chi (q.v.) during the subsequent anti-rightist campaign apparently convinced him of his own ideological orthodoxy and personal immunity, for from 1959 onward his writing became voluminous and directed toward the general public. In 1959, Wu collected his pre-1949 topical essays, many of which had been meant as veiled attacks on contemporaries and some of which had appeared in *Li-shih-ti ching-tzu*. He revised and reprinted them as *T'ou-ch'iang chi* [javelin throwing]. He followed this with *Teng-hsia chi* [under lamplight] in 1960, which reprinted a large number of essays in popular style on historical subjects. In 1951 there appeared *Ch'un-t'ien chi* [spring], a large miscellany, and the historical play, *Hai Jui pa kuan* [the dismissal of Hai Jui], which was published in *Peking Literature and Art* in January.

After 1959 Wu Han's main intellectual concern centered about the general problem of the significance of China's past for its present. After giving due attention to the past statements of Mao Tse-tung on the subject, Wu opted for the formula "emphasize the present at the expense of the past; use the past for the sake of the present." By the phrase "present" in the first part of the formula, Wu meant Chinese history since the Opium War of 1840, but with emphasis on the history of the Chinese Communist party and especially China after 1949. The first half of the formula constituted an attack on antiquarians and historians of traditional China for whom the year 1840 stood as a *terminus post quem*, while the other half attacked the modernists for whom traditional history had no meaning. The past, said Wu, must be studied and explained scientifically from the standpoint of Marxism–Leninism.

That part of the past which is worthy of study is the history of the masses, the history of revolutionary struggle (*i.e.*, popular uprisings), and the history of production relationships. Yet, objective historical study must also consider the dark, unprogressive side of the picture—the history of the ruling classes; and any study of the struggle of the masses must include also a consideration of these heroic personages who were able to advance the cause of progress for the ages in which they lived. Wu proposed eight tentative principles for describing and judging the great men of the past. First, to be judged great, a man's action had to be of benefit to the majority of the common people or had to serve to raise the general level of culture. Second, the historical sources used in such judgments had to reflect the majority opinion of the common people and not that of the landlord bureaucrats. Third, not only a man's class origins but also his individual development had to be taken into account, for it is always possible for good men to have bad (i.e. landlord-feudal) backgrounds. Fourth, a man's public achievements are of overriding importance; his private life does not matter. Fifth, epithets such as "democratic," applicable to the heroes who help build socialism, cannot properly be ascribed to heroes living in slave-owning or feudal societies. Sixth, judgments and descriptions have to conform to objective reality; exaggerations or fabrications must be avoided. Seventh, the useful experiences of previous generations of Chinese in the class struggle have to be given significance for the present, so that by studying these experiences the past can be made to serve current revolutionary struggle. Finally, any judgment of the goodness or badness of any hero has not only to take into consideration the man's own time but also all of subsequent history; thus the builder of the Grand Canal increased the people's burdens in building it, but this factor is outweighed by the benefits of the canal to later generations.

On the basis of these principles, Wu selected four representative heroes of the past for analysis in a talk which he gave at Nankai University in October 1959. The first, Ts'ao Ts'ao (155–220), had been the subject of recent controversy; the second and third, the T'ang Empress Wu (d. 705) and Hai Jui (d. 1587), were ripe subjects for discussion; and the fourth, the late Ming historian T'an Ch'ien (d. 1657),

was practically unknown. Ts'ao Ts'ao was praiseworthy in having sought to unify the empire. Although he failed in his effort, he did bring peace to north China, and under his rule production developed, population rose, culture flourished, and barbarian attacks were thwarted. He struck at a number of large landlord-officials and their families and replaced them with intellectuals of obscure background. His bad side, however, is shown in his cruel methods of commanding troops and in his defeat of the Yellow Turban rebels. Whether the good outweighs the bad in Ts'ao Ts'ao must await a total reexamination of medieval Chinese history. The Empress Wu likewise acted against the interests of the feudal ruling circles by opening government office to obscure men of talent through the examination system, and thus set the stage for the heyday of the T'ang empire during the first half of the eighth century. The resulting cultural splendor is not to be dismissed; the feudalistic age was not an unrelieved period of darkness. The irregularities of the private life of the empress have no historical significance, and she should not be judged on this basis. Hai Jui represents the upright, model bureaucrat with distinguished accomplishments to his credit. He led the minority left wing within the feudal ruling class and gained the support of young intellectuals, peasants, and townspeople. While upholding the feudal order, he actively sympathized with middle and poor peasants in their struggle with the large landowners and the feudal reactionaries. In southeast China (responsible for a third of the Ming dynasty's quota of taxes), Hai Jui acted against the large landholders by carrying out a survey of their holdings, making them return all illegally occupied land to the rightful owners, and forcing everyone to bear his fair share of the tax burden. These measures, plus Hai Jui's implementation of the "single-whip" tax reform (which generally simplified tax-collecting procedures by making all dues payable as a lump sum in silver), lightened the peasants' burdens and reduced their exploitation by the landlords. Hai Jui's tenacity of purpose is shown in one of his legal cases. In proceedings brought against a retired official who when prime minister had done a personal favor for Hai Jui (Hai Jui was in prison for criticizing the emperor, and the prime minister helped get him out), Hai Jui decided for the plaintiff even though he knew it would lead to his own dismissal from office. As for T'an Ch'ien, he is an exemplar for the historian of the present day. A poor and lowly secretary to an official during the last years of the Ming period, he expressed dissatisfaction with the few histories he had chanced to see and devoted the rest of his life to the patriotic task of writing a voluminous annalistic account of the Ming, enduring all kinds of hardship in his quest for accurate source materials.

A concern for Chinese history and its heroes made Wu Han an ardent promotor of mass popularization. In his introduction to *Teng-hsia chi* he urged all ideological workers to publish simplified expositions of their particular specialties for the enlightenment of children, cadres, workers, and peasants. For popularizing his own specialty, Wu hit upon the medium of the stage. He attempted to create what he regarded as a new genre—the historical play, which aims to portray as accurately as possible real events and real characters drawn from history. Wu explained his purposes and answered his critics in a series of articles on the historical play. *Hai Jui pa kuan*, rewritten some half-dozen times before it was staged in 1961, was his first attempt to compose one.

Hai Jui was becoming a controversial figure even before the appearance of Wu's play about him. Although he had flourished in the mid-sixteenth century, Hai Jui was a figure well known and highly regarded by the common people in twentieth-century China; there were even popular stories about his courage in criticizing imperial authority. Did the fact that he had actually been a feudal bureaucrat mean that he must be condemned by people living in an age of socialist construction? Wu Han thought not. In September 1959 he averred that Hai Jui's qualities of consistency and persistence were models for emulation during socialist construction, though he went on to argue that these qualities could only achieve genuine fulfillment under the changed conditions of China since 1949. Those (like Hai Jui) who adopted the standpoint of the working class were needed at present in China to combat bureaucratism and to lead the masses in the struggle for socialism. At this time and again a month later, however, Wu warned against people who were adopting the pose of Hai Jui for improper purposes. Some insincere imita-

tors of Hai Jui were constituting themselves an "opposition," criticizing certain shortcomings of the government at Peking and dampening the ardor of the masses for building socialism. "Right opportunist" elements were even appropriating Hai Jui's reputation for candid speaking to denounce the backyard steel production and the people's communes instituted during the Great Leap Forward of 1958. Such denunciation was wrong because it substituted a "good" (socialist) target for a "bad" (feudal) one and in effect favored the large landowning class against which the real Hai Jui had struggled all his life.

During 1962 and 1963 Wu Han was involved in a heated logomachy which resulted from his publication of two articles on traditional morality in *Ch'ien-hsien*, the party theoretical journal edited at Peking by Teng T'o. In these articles Wu had called for a selective revival of the feudal virtues of loyalty, filial piety, honesty, perseverance, and courage. He argued that these virtues had a place even in a period of socialist construction. Attacks and replies were featured primarily in the *Kuang-ming jih-pao*.

In 1963 and 1964 Wu edited a series of pamphlets under the general title *Chung-kuo li-shih ch'ang-shih* [Chinese history for everyman]. In his preface (which appeared in each pamphlet), Wu noted that in spite of a great interest in Chinese history among urban and rural youth, People's Liberation Army troops, and organizational cadres, most young people were unable to handle the old dynastic histories or even more recent general histories of China. This new cooperative effort to produce simplified history was intended to inculcate both patriotism and a basic grasp of historical materialism.

By taking definite stands on several subjects of contemporary controversy, Wu Han had made himself conspicuous and vulnerable to attack. The attack began on 10 November 1965 in the Shanghai *Wen-hui-pao* (reprinted 30 November in *Jen-min jih-pao*) with a critique of *Hai Jui pa kuan* by one Yao Wen-yüan. Yao's charges were serious: Wu had made an ideological error by portraying the struggle within the feudal ruling class and neglecting the masses and their struggle with the ruling classes as a whole; worse, Hai Jui's redressing of the people's grievances reflected Wu Han's own support of those who were calling for a return to individual farming during the economic crisis

China was undergoing in 1961, the year the play was staged. Wu Han wrote a lengthy answer, which appeared in the *Pei-ching jih-pao* of 27 December 1965, in which he admitted that he had forgotten the class struggle and thanked Yao for exposing his serious relapse into bourgeois-feudal ways of thought. He denied, however, that his motive for writing the play was counterrevolutionary; rather, he said, it was "indistinct and foggy."

Hai Jui pa kuan was debated in the Chinese press through February 1966. Wu's motives were defended by certain academicians and by friends on the Peking municipal party committee—chiefly Teng T'o, who on 13 December called an informal meeting of some 20 university students for a discussion of Hai Jui. After a month's silence, the attack on Wu Han resumed with exposés in *Jen-min jih-pao* and *Hung-ch'i* during the first week in April and continued through early May. First, *Hai Jui pa kuan* was alleged to have been written in support of certain "dismissed" right-opportunist opponents of the Great Leap Forward, particularly P'eng Te-huai (q.v.). It was no mere historical drama, but "a vicious blast against Party and Socialism" with implied criticism of Mao Tse-tung. The exposés went further. A careful analysis of *T'ou-ch'iang chi* showed that Wu had made extensive revisions of the original articles, deleting direct anti-Communist statements in order to hide his former open support for Chiang Kai-shek. The actual target of the "javelins" was the Chinese Communist party itself. A complete investigation of Wu's background, especially his activities during the 1940's, followed. This investigation reportedly brought to light the facts that Wu had desired all along to become Chiang Kai-shek's "upright official," and that all his writings during those years were meant to help Chiang "rectify his rule." After the Communist victory, Wu wanted to "right wrongs" for his own landlord class, and in order to disguise his aims, he had falsified the true facts of his own landlord class origins in his writings. Under the pretext of "popularizing historical knowledge," he praised the emperors and great ministers of the past in order to turn the people away from Mao Tse-tung. Finally, from 1961 to 1964 he had joined with two of the top aides of Peking mayor P'eng Chen (q.v.)—Teng T'o and Liao Mo-sha—in writing a column which was featured in Teng's Peking party theoretical journal, *Ch'ien-hsien*. This column, it was charged, attacked the party through the use of fables and historical allusions. The movement that developed into the Cultural Revolution then dropped the attack on Wu Han to move on to Teng T'o and to bigger game, including some of the most senior figures of the Chinese Communist party.

Wu Ho-ling: *see* UNENBAYIN.

Wu Hsien   吳 憲
　T. T'ao-min   陶 民

Wu Hsien (24 November 1893–8 August 1959), internationally known biochemist who between 1917 and 1920, with Otto Folin of Harvard University, developed the Folin-Wu method of blood analysis. Wu's research interests were primarily in protein chemistry and nutrition. He was also known for his contribution to modern medical education in China as head of the department of biochemistry at Peking Union Medical College (1924–41).

A native of Foochow, Fukien, Wu Hsien was born into a scholarly family. He received his early education in the conventional Chinese curriculum. In 1906 he entered the Fukien Provincial High School, where he completed the course of study in four years. He competed successfully in government examinations for study abroad in 1910 and went to the United States. In September 1911 he enrolled at the Massachusetts Institute of Technology in naval architecture, an appropriate field for a son of Fukien province, which had a strong naval tradition. However, while spending the following summer on a farm in New Hampshire, he read Thomas Huxley's essay on "The Physical Basis of Life" and decided to change his major to chemistry. Wu obtained a B.S. degree from M.I.T. in 1916.

After spending another year at M.I.T. as a graduate student and assistant in organic chemistry, Wu entered the graduate school of Harvard University in September 1917 and gained his Ph.D. in biochemistry two years later. While at Harvard he did research under the direction of Dr. Otto Folin of the Harvard Medical School. Wu's thesis, "A System of

Blood Analysis," presented a new method for preparing a protein-free blood filtrate suitable for quantitative determination of all important constituents of blood within a single sample of 10 c.c. The method was more convenient and accurate than earlier techniques and permitted analysis from a single drop of blood. During 1919–20, as a research fellow, Wu continued work with Folin on research which came to be designated the Folin-Wu system of blood analysis. Among other contributions, this system permitted determination of blood sugar, a procedure of value to investigators of insulin, the new hormone of the 1920's.

In the summer of 1920 Wu Hsien returned to China to join the staff of the newly organized Peking Union Medical College (PUMC) as an associate professor. In 1924 he was appointed organizer and first head of its department of biochemistry, a post which, with advancement to the rank of professor in 1928, he held until the seizure of the institution by the Japanese in early January 1942.

During these years Wu Hsien participated in a wide variety of professional and public activities. In the summer of 1925 he went to Europe to visit laboratories and to consult with biochemists. In addition to teaching and administrative responsibilities, Wu established and headed a nutrition research laboratory at the PUMC. From 1921 to 1927 he was connected with the chemistry division of the national committee on standardization of scientific terminology, one of the major early tasks in the serious introduction of Western science into China. In 1926 he worked with his colleague Robert K. S. Lim (Lin K'o-sheng, q.v.), professor of physiology at the PUMC, to found the Chinese Physiological Society. Wu served as a member of the editorial board of its journal, the *Chinese Journal of Physiology*, from 1927 to 1941, when it was forced to cease publication. In 1930 he served as adviser to the Academia Sinica, China's highest organization for advanced research, in establishing its institute of physiology, and Wu himself was elected to membership in the Academia Sinica. From 1935 to 1937 Wu Hsien served as a member of a three-man committee in charge of the administration of the PUMC. Results of his research were published in numerous scientific papers as well as two books: *A Treatise on Nutrition* (in Chinese, Shanghai, 1929) and

Principles of Physical Biochemistry (in English, Peking, 1934). After the Japanese invasion of Manchuria in September 1931, Wu Hsien joined with a prominent group of political independents in founding a journal of opinion, the *Tu-li p'ing-lun* [independent critic], which began publication in May 1932 and gained widespread recognition and influence.

Japanese seizure in early 1942 of Western-controlled organizations in north China, including the Peking Union Medical College, temporarily ended Wu Hsien's active career, and for two years he lived in retirement. In March 1944 he left north China and made the hazardous trek through Japanese lines to Szechwan. After arrival at Chungking in April, he was assigned to establish and direct a new nutrition institute to meet wartime exigencies. After completing plans for the new organization, Wu Hsien left China for the United States in July 1944 to serve as nutrition expert attached to a commission sponsored by the United Nations Relief and Rehabilitation Administration (UNRRA) to study China's postwar problems. In that capacity, Wu traveled widely in the United States to visit nutrition and public health institutes, medical schools and hospitals, research laboratories-pharmaceutical houses, and food processing plants. In consultations with American nutritionists, who proposed using soybean preparations instead of dried milk in China, Wu insisted that Chinese children needed cow's milk and won his point—food shipments later sent to China under UNRRA auspices included milk powder. After his return to Chungking at war's end in 1945, Wu reported to National Government agencies on nutrition advances in the United States and expanded plans for the new Nutrition Institute. Late in the year, he returned to Peiping.

In the summer of 1946 the National Government at Nanking, again the capital of China, summoned Wu to make plans for organizing a branch of the National Institute of Health at Peiping. Wu was appointed branch director while holding the concurrent post of director of the Nutrition Institute at Nanking. In July 1947 Wu left for England as one of China's six delegates to the International Physiological Congress at Oxford. After the congress, Wu planned to return to China through the United States. In New York he talked with an old friend, T. P. Hou (Hou Te-pang, q.v.), formerly a contemporary of Wu Hsien at the Massachusetts Institute of Technology who had become China's foremost chemical engineer and general manager of the Yungli Chemical Industries Company. Wu proposed the establishment in China of a new institute of human biology under Yungli auspices. This new interest dictated resignation at the end of 1947 from his post with the National Institute of Health at Peiping. In January 1948 he accepted an invitation to become visiting scholar in the department of biochemistry at the College of Physicians and Surgeons of Columbia University in New York. With the requirements of the proposed new institute of human biology in mind, Wu began to acquire new techniques involved in isotope research. During the 18 months (1948–49) which Wu spent at Columbia, he presented a paper on "Nutritional Deficiences in China and Southeast Asia" at the Fourth International Congress of Tropical Medicine and Malaria; participated in meetings of the advisory committee on nutrition of the Food and Agriculture Organization (FAO) of the United Nations; and maintained contact with the American Bureau for Medical Aid to China (ABMAC) regarding China's most urgent requirements.

Meanwhile, the balance in the Chinese civil war had swung in favor of the Communists. In January 1949, on the eve of the entry of Communist troops into Peiping, Wu Hsien's family, still in north China, fled to Shanghai and thence to Hong Kong and San Francisco. Wu accepted an appointment in the autumn of 1949 as visiting professor of biochemistry at the medical college of the University of Alabama in Birmingham. During 1949–50 he also participated in meetings of the committee on calorie requirements of the United Nations. In October 1952 Wu Hsien suffered a coronary thrombosis which led to his resignation from the University of Alabama faculty as of August 1953. He then moved with his family to the Boston area.

At his residence in Brookline, Wu Hsien continued to work on problems connected with publication of the results of research carried out at Alabama. He also completed the first draft of a manuscript entitled "A Guide to Scientific Living" (published by the Academia Sinica in Taiwan in 1953) and began others dealing with

Chinese calligraphy, Chinese phonetics, and world peace. The study of mathematics and Spanish occupied leisure moments.

In the summer of 1959 he enjoyed a happy reunion with the surgeon and public health expert J. Heng Liu (Liu Jui-heng, q.v.), who was in Cambridge to participate in the fiftieth reunion of his Harvard class. The two men, along with Robert K. S. Lim, had been the first three Chinese to attain professorial rank at the Peking Union Medical College. On 8 August 1959, after suffering a new series of heart attacks, Wu Hsien died in the Massachusetts General Hospital at Boston.

Among other organizations, Wu was a member of the American Society of Biological Chemists, the Society for Experimental Biology and Medicine, and Sigma Xi. He was an honorary fellow of the Deutsche Akademie für Naturforschung (Halle) and an advisory board member of *Biochimica et Biophysica Acta*. His career is recorded in *American Men of Science* (9th edition) and the *International Who's Who in World Medicine*.

Shortly after Wu Hsien's death, his widow prepared and published privately (Boston, 1959) a memorial volume containing tributes to Wu by a large number of friends and professional colleagues throughout the world. The bibliography of Wu's publications between 1919 and 1959 contains 159 items. His chief fields of research were clinical chemistry, nutrition, immunochemistry, the metabolism of amino-acids, and gas and electrolytic equilibria. Political events and governmental demands increasingly kept Wu Hsien from the laboratory during his later years, as is indicated by the fact that only 20 scientific research papers were published after 1942. However, his reputation as a sound and original biochemist was secure before the dislocations of international and civil war, and he is remembered as one of the pioneering Chinese scientists of his generation.

Wu Hsien's first marriage, arranged by his paternal grandmother, took place before he went to the United States in 1911. After his return to China in 1920, attempts to find common ground with that wife failed, and the marriage was terminated. There were no children. In December 1924 at Shanghai Wu Hsien married Daisy Yen, who then held an assistantship in biochemistry at the Peking Union Medical College. The daughter of a prosperous silver merchant of Shanghai, she had been ranking student in the class of 1921 at Ginling College at Nanking, had received an M.A. from Columbia University, and had become a nutritionist interested in food chemistry. Husband and wife collaborated in research and publication on protein chemistry during the early years of their marriage in China and later worked together on amino-acids at the University of Alabama.

Five children were born to Wu Hsien and his wife. The eldest son, Ray Jui Wu, with Ph.D. in biochemistry from the University of Pennsylvania, engaged in cancer research in New York; the younger son, Ying Victor Wu, Ph.D. from M.I.T., became a physical chemist at Cornell University. The three daughters were: Evelyn Wan-hsien Wu, dietician and science teacher with M.S. from the University of Alabama; Dorothea Wan-lien Wu, music librarian with M.S. from Simmons College; and Christine Wan-ming Wu, M.D., radiologist at the Yale Medical School.

Wu Hsien-tzu   伍 憲 子
  Orig. Chuang   莊

Wu Hsien-tzu (1881–7 October 1959), Confucian scholar who studied under K'ang Yu-wei and Chien Ch'ao-liang. He was long associated with Li Ta-ming in publishing the *Chinese World* in San Francisco, and he became head of the Constitutionalist party and chief bearer of the political heritage of K'ang Yu-wei.

A native of Shun-te (Shuntak), the richest and perhaps the most culturally developed district in Kwangtung province, Wu Hsien-tzu was born into a merchant family. His grandfather had been a successful trader in the northern parts of the province near the Hunan border. His father was less active, though he had business enterprises in Canton. Although his father died in 1886, when the boy was only six sui, the family remained in comfortable circumstances. Wu Hsien-tzu began his traditional education at the village school in 1887. In 1892 his mother arranged for him to be admitted into the family school of the Mak (Mai) family in the neighboring village, where facilities for more advanced study were available. Two youths of the Mak family were pupils of

K'ang Yu-wei (q.v.), and it was through them that Wu first came into contact with the ideas of the prominent reformer.

Wu Hsien-tzu spent four years studying the Chinese classics in the Mak family school. His mother, a free-thinking woman for that period, did not cherish the idea of her son seeking an official career through the imperial examinations. She believed it more practical, and also more profitable, for the boy to follow in the footsteps of his forebears and to pursue a business career. Accordingly, in 1896 she sent him to Canton to work in a cotton firm which his father had founded and in which the family retained a financial interest. Because he had been trained to observe the Confucian virtue of filial piety, the boy did not question his mother's decision.

Wu was, however, temperamentally unable to abandon his books, and he spent his leisure time reading. Noting this, a friend of the family convinced his mother that it would be unfortunate for the lad to interrupt his studies when he could afford to continue them. She was quick to respond to this plea. In 1897 Wu was accepted as a pupil by Chien Ch'ao-liang (1851–1933; T. Chi-chi; H. Chu-chü). Both Chien Ch'ao-liang and K'ang Yu-wei had been students of Chu Tz'u-ch'i (1807–1882; ECCP, I, 91), one of the leading Cantonese scholars of the nineteenth century. Though the two were close personal friends, they held opposing political views. Wu Hsien-tzu already had been converted to the reformist ideas of K'ang Yu-wei, and, during his first year as a student under Chien, he took two months off during the summer to attend lectures given by K'ang at his famous school, the Wan-mu ts'ao-t'ang [cottage of ten thousand trees], near Canton. K'ang left for Peking in the autumn of 1897; and in 1898 he made an abortive attempt to oust the empress dowager. After the failure of the attempt, he was forced to flee from China, and Wu Hsien-tzu had no opportunity for direct contact with him for several years. Wu did, however, continue to enjoy the benefit of personal instruction from Chien Ch'ao-liang, under whom he studied for about six years, from 1897 to 1903.

During his student days at Canton, Wu began writing newspaper articles. In 1900, at the age of 20 sui, he married Huang Shu-fen. In 1902 he went to Kaifeng, Honan, to take the special imperial examination for the chü-jen degree. On his return to Kwangtung from the north, Wu was invited in 1903 to teach in the Yu family school. He moved with the school to Hong Kong the following year.

With that move, Wu Hsien-tzu became involved in journalism. K'ang Yu-wei requested that Wu assist Hsü Ch'in, another disciple of his, in running the *Shang Pao*, a Hong Kong newspaper which advocated constitutional monarchy for China. Wu Hsien-tzu soon was appointed editor of the *Shang Pao*, a post he held from 1905 through 1911. During these years, the paper conducted a continuing editorial battle with the *Chung-kuo jih-pao*, the Hong Kong organ of the T'ung-meng-hui. Although K'ang Yu-wei's monarchist organization was initially the stronger, it steadily lost ground in the competition for overseas Chinese allegiance during the final years of the Ch'ing dynasty. During that period, Wu Hsien-tzu played one spectacular role which even his political foes applauded. In 1908 the Chinese authorities got into difficulties with the Japanese over the handling of a Japanese vessel which had been caught smuggling arms. The Japanese government presented harsh demands for settlement of the case. The Chinese in Hong Kong began a boycott of Japanese goods, and Wu Hsien-tzu, through his writings, kept the movement going. The Japanese first attempted, unsuccessfully, to buy him off. They then applied pressure on the Hong Kong government, which ordered Wu's deportation. Wu, however, fought his case in the courts, and he won.

In 1909 Wu visited Southeast Asia, where he served for a brief period with the reformist newspaper in Singapore. There he had to battle formidable editorial opposition from Hu Han-min and Wang Ching-wei (qq.v.), both of whom were then in Singapore writing for the revolutionary *Chung-hsing jih-pao*. After returning to China in 1910, Wu visited Shanghai and Peking, taking an active part in the organization of the federation of provincial advisory councils that was agitating for the early promulgation of the constitution promised by the Ch'ing government.

After the republican revolution began in October 1911, Wu Hsien-tzu went to Japan to join K'ang Yu-wei, who was launching a new campaign against republicanism. Because K'ang

was ill late in 1911, he dictated to Wu his *Kung-ho cheng-t'i lun* [on the republican system of government], which argued that China could only avoid prolonged and disastrous chaos by establishing a constitutional monarchy. In 1912, the year the Chinese republic was founded, Wu Hsien-tzu left Japan and visited Canada, where he spent a month at Vancouver, British Columbia. His original plan to tour other parts of Canada and the United States was interrupted by a message of recall from Liang Ch'i-ch'ao (q.v.), who had decided to accept Yuan Shih-k'ai's invitation to return to Peking. In 1913, when a cabinet was formed by Hsiung Hsi-ling (q.v.), Liang was named minister of justice. Wu Hsien-tzu was appointed director of the civil affairs division of the provincial government in his native Kwangtung. He served there for only a short time, however, and had no time to institute administrative reforms before he was transferred to a similar post in Hupeh province early in 1914. Wu did not take up the Hupeh appointment, however, and he later declined an appointment to be superintendent of the Chinese Maritime Customs at Lungchow.

In 1914 Wu established residence at Peking. Although he was made an adviser in the finance ministry and also a counselor in the presidential headquarters, he took no active part in politics. As Yuan Shih-k'ai's monarchical aspirations became increasingly clear in 1915, Liang Ch'i-ch'ao and Ts'ai O (q.v.) decided to take action against Yuan. Ts'ai proceeded to Yunnan where, with the aid of T'ang Chi-yao, the famous Yunnan revolt of December 1915 was staged. Early in 1916 Liang Ch'i-ch'ao went to Kwangsi to secure the collaboration of Lu Jung-t'ing (q.v.). Hsü Ch'in, who was later to head the Constitutionalist party, was assigned to Kwangtung to mobilize opposition against Lung Chi-kuang. Wu Hsien-tzu was assigned to work with Hsü, but because he was detained in north China, he did not leave for the south until later.

After the death of Yuan Shih-k'ai in 1916, Li Yuan-hung (q.v.) succeeded to the presidency at Peking. Wu Hsien-tzu then served as a counselor in the headquarters of the vice president, Feng Kuo-chang (q.v.). The abortive attempt of Chang Hsün (q.v.) in July 1917 to restore the Manchus to the throne led to a total political split between K'ang Yu-wei and Liang

Ch'i-ch'ao, with K'ang supporting the restoration attempt and Liang playing a major role in its suppression. Wu Hsien-tzu later claimed that he made a fruitless attempt at that time to dissuade K'ang Yu-wei from supporting Chang Hsün.

After remaining in Peking for about three years, Wu Hsien-tzu went down to Hong Kong again in the autumn of 1919 and took over the operation of the newspaper *Kung-ho jih-pao* [republican daily]. When it suspended publication in 1922, he returned to Peking, where he was given a sinecure position with the state council. He paid two visits to Loyang in an unsuccessful attempt to dissuade Wu P'ei-fu (q.v.) from precipitating a civil war with the Fengtien clique led by Chang Tso-lin (q.v.). He also visited Canton, Amoy, and Hainan Island during 1923 and 1924. Early in 1925, on instructions from K'ang Yu-wei, he journeyed to Yunnan, where he saw T'ang Chi-yao (q.v.) and tried to urge him to take a stand against the Canton government. Exploiting the death of Sun Yat-sen, T'ang had assumed the post of acting generalissimo in the hope of rallying support from the southern provinces. But the National Government which was formed at Canton in that year quickly denounced him.

When K'ang Yu-wei died at Tsingtao in March 1927, Liang Ch'i-ch'ao, Wu Hsien-tzu, and Hsü Ch'in met in Tientsin, where Liang then was living, to discuss the continuation of K'ang's work. It was decided that Liang Ch'i-ch'ao should remain in China to supervise the affairs of the Constitutionalist party, that Wu Hsien-tzu should assume charge of the party's organizations abroad, and that Hsü should go to Mexico to reorganize the bank that the party owned there. The plans were more impressive than their implementation: Hsü was unable to go to Mexico, and Liang Ch'i-ch'ao died at Peking early in 1929. Wu Hsien-tzu, however, did go to San Francisco in the summer of 1928. There he took charge of the newspaper *Chinese World*, the organ of the Constitutionalist party, which was committed to preserving the political legacy of K'ang Yu-wei. Wu remained in the United States for eight years carrying on a solo crusade, with the aid of his newspaper, against the policies of the Kuomintang, which was rapidly consolidating power in China. In the spring of 1935 he was hospitalized for three months as the result of an automobile accident in San Francisco. After his recovery, he made an extensive tour of the Chinese communities in the United States.

Wu Hsien-tzu returned to China in the summer of 1936. At the invitation of Sung Che-yuan (q.v.), he visited Peiping. There he met Carsun Chang (Chang Chia-sen, q.v.), with whom he discussed the possibility of merging Chang's National Socialist party and the Constitutionalist party. A tentative agreement was reached. The leaders of the two groups taking part in the discussions and signing the draft agreement included Chang Tung-sun, Hsü Ch'in, and Lo Lung-chi. Wu was in Peiping in July 1937 when the Sino-Japanese war began. As hostilities spread in north China, Wu moved to the British concession in Tientsin to await developments. He remained in Tientsin until 1940, when he decided to move to Hong Kong.

On his journey south, Wu stopped at Nanking, where Wang Ching-wei had established a Japanese-sponsored regime in March 1940. Wu Hsien-tzu had already refused Wang's invitation to join the regime, but he did call on Wang three times to attempt to convince him of the futility of his so-called peace movement. Wu compared Wang Ching-wei's advocacy of Sino-Japanese cooperation with K'ang Yu-wei's advocacy of the preservation of the monarchy and the theory that both Han Chinese and Manchus were "one family" in the twilight years of the Ch'ing dynasty. Although Wu Hsien-tzu had been an adherent of K'ang Yu-wei, he emphasized that the constitutional monarchists had failed in 1911, while the revolutionaries had succeeded. Similarly, he told Wang Ching-wei, the concept of Sino-Japanese cooperation could not stand up against the more popular principle of Chinese resistance sparked by the Japanese military invasion.

After his arrival in Hong Kong, Wu Hsien-tzu established contact with the leaders of the various minor parties then active in that British colony, particularly Liang Shu-ming (q.v.), who then was editing the *Kuang-ming pao* [light]. Wu joined the opposition elements which in 1941 formed the League of Chinese Democratic Political Groups (*see* Chang Lan). He placed little credence in the persisting rumors that the Japanese would attack Hong Kong. Events soon proved him wrong, however, but he nevertheless remained in Hong Kong throughout the years of Japanese occupation.

When Hsü Ch'in, head of the Constitutionalist party, died at Tientsin after a long illness early in 1945, Wu Hsien-tzu became the chief bearer of the political heritage of K'ang Yu-wei. That position was confirmed in the immediate post-war period when, at a meeting held at Montreal, Canada, in November 1945, the Constitutionalists reorganized their party as the Chinese Democratic Constitutional party. The use of the word "democratic" was intended to stress that the party, though committed to the fight for sound constitutional government in China, no longer had royalist tendencies. Wu Hsien-tzu was elected chairman of the reorganized party, with Li Ta-ming (q.v.) as his deputy and head of the American overseas headquarters. Despite the general jubilation in China following the end of the war with Japan, Wu Hsien-tzu took a dim view of the domestic political situation. Writing in the magazine *Tsai-sheng* [renaissance] in Hong Kong, he warned the Chinese people against the reemergence of civil conflict between the Kuomintang and the Chinese Communists. During the summer of 1946, as United States mediation efforts in China disintegrated, Wu participated in an attempt to create a stronger alternative to both the Kuomintang and the Chinese Communist party. In August of that year, at a meeting in Shanghai, his Democratic Constitutional party and the National Socialist party of Carsun Chang combined to form the new Democratic Socialist party. Carsun Chang was chosen to be chairman of the new organization, with Wu Hsien-tzu as vice chairman, At that time, the National Government at Nanking was attempting to broaden its base of power and to undercut Communist influence by offering posts to members of minor political parties. Wu thus was named to the State Council at Nanking, but he did not assume office.

Early in 1947, internal dissension wracked the newly formed Democratic Socialist party. After Wu Hsien-tzu had made an unsuccessful attempt to mediate in the dispute, the Democratic Constitutionalist party decided to withdraw from the coalition and to resume its independent status. Meanwhile, a dissident group within the Democratic Socialist party formed a so-called reform committee and elected Wu Hsien-tzu its chairman. Wu, however, was not responsible for the formation of that group and never became actively associated with the move.

In 1949, when Wu Hsien-tzu was 69 sui, his mother died at the advanced age of 86 sui. In keeping with Confucian tradition, he remained inactive during the conventional period of mourning. At the end of 1951, he paid a brief visit to Taiwan at the invitation of the National Government, but soon returned to Hong Kong. Wu then retired from political life, though he occasionally wrote newspaper articles and delivered lectures in the Chinese colleges of the colony. He died of a heart ailment in Hong Kong on 7 October 1959.

Wu Hsiu-ch'üan   伍修權

Wu Hsiu-ch'üan (4 March 1908–), Russian-trained Chinese Communist who held important staff positions in Kiangsi in the 1930's and in the Northeast in the 1940's. In 1949–51 he served as director of Soviet and Eastern European affairs in the ministry of foreign affairs at Peking. He then became deputy foreign minister. In 1955–58 he was ambassador from the People's Republic of China to Yugoslavia.

Little is known about Wu Hsiu-ch'üan's family background or early life except that he was born in Wuchang, Hupeh. He attended middle school in the Wuhan area, where he became active in the student radical movement. From 1927 to 1930 he studied in France and the Soviet Union, where he attended Sun Yat-sen University and an artillery school. He joined the Chinese Communist party in 1927 and came to know many of its members who took refuge in Moscow during the years following the Kuomintang-Communist split in China.

On his return to China, Wu taught briefly at Futan University in Shanghai. He then went to the central soviet base area in Kiangsi, where he served as a staff officer in the headquarters of the Red Army and instructor in the Red Army Academy at Juichin. He rose to become a regimental commander and deputy chief of staff of the Third Army Group, led by P'eng Te-huai (q.v.), in the First Front Army. Wu left Kiangsi on the Long March in October 1934 with the main forces of Mao Tse-tung,

Chu Teh, and P'eng Te-huai. After arrival in Shensi, he headed a reception center at Yenan run by the Chinese Communist party's united front department. In 1938 he became secretary general of the Shensi-Kansu-Ninghsia Border Region government, headed by Lin Po-ch'ü (q.v.). From 1938 to 1940 he directed the office of the Eighth Route Army at Lanchow, Kansu.

At war's end, Wu Hsiu-ch'üan went to Manchuria, where he became deputy chief of staff of the Northeast Democratic Alliance Army, headed by Lin Piao (q.v.). He soon became chief of staff of the Chinese Communist Northeast military district and held that post until 1949. In 1946 Wu was connected with the tripartite Executive Headquarters, established at Peiping as part of the United States mediation effort in China, to monitor and enforce Nationalist-Communist ceasefire arrangements worked out in January of that year. Yeh Chien-ying (q.v.) was assigned as chief Chinese Communist delegate to the Executive Headquarters, and in late 1946 Wu served as the Communist representative at its Changchun office. The Executive Headquarters effort proved fruitless, however, and military operations resumed in Manchuria. When Lin Piao's forces occupied Mukden in November 1948, Wu became vice chairman of the Mukden military control commission and commander of garrison forces there. In August 1949 he became a member of the Northeast People's Government Council, the first regional authority established by the Chinese Communists in that area.

With the establishment of the Central People's Government at Peking in October 1949, Wu Hsiu-ch'üan became director of the division of Soviet and East European affairs in the ministry of foreign affairs headed by Chou En-lai. He held this post until 1952 and made good use of his knowledge of Russian. During this period Wu also carried out important assignments abroad. In January 1950 he accompanied Chou En-lai to Moscow for the later stages of the negotiations that led to the signing in February of the Sino-Soviet Treaty of Friendship, Alliance, and Mutual Assistance and related agreements. He remained in Moscow with a Chinese Communist trade mission until April. The outbreak of the Korean war in June 1950 was followed in late

October by the intervention of Chinese Communist troops and by an invitation to Peking from the United Nations Security Council to participate in discussions of the Far Eastern situation. Wu Hsiu-ch'üan was selected to head Peking's delegation, the first to appear at the United Nations from the People's Republic of China. On 28 November 1950, he delivered a blistering 20,000-word speech to the United Nations Security Council in New York in which he stated that that body should penalize the United States for its "armed aggression" against China, Taiwan, and Korea. He added that the People's Republic of China intended to "liberate" Taiwan and to aid the Communist movements in Vietnam, the Philippines, and Japan. "The Chinese people," Wu concluded, "have arisen."

From January 1951 until March 1955, Wu Hsiu-ch'üan served as a vice minister of foreign affairs at Peking. He visited the Mongolian People's Republic in February 1952 and was a member of the Chinese delegation headed by Chou En-lai that flew to Moscow in March 1953 to attend Stalin's funeral. He also served as a director of the Chinese People's Institute of Foreign Affairs, and he represented Szechwan at the National People's Congress in 1954.

In 1955 Wu Hsiu-ch'üan was named the first ambassador from the People's Republic of China to Yugoslavia. He remained at Belgrade until mid-1958, when Peking launched a new attack on Tito's revisionism and recalled Wu. In 1956 Wu had been elected for the first time to the Central Committee of the Chinese Communist party at its Eighth National Congress. After his return from Yugoslavia, he became extremely active in the international liaison work of the Central Committee of the Chinese Communist party, and during the next few years he greeted and conferred with almost all senior Communist party leaders from abroad who visited Peking. He also traveled frequently to represent the Chinese party at Communist party congresses abroad: in Poland and Great Britain in 1959, and in Rumania in June 1960. In August 1960 he flew to Cuba to observe the ninth congress of the Cuban People's Socialist party, a trip that paved the way for the establishment of diplomatic relations between Peking and Havana. In the spring of 1961 he participated in discussion at Peking with Souvanna Phouma, premier of Laos.

With the deterioration of relations between the Communist parties of China and the Soviet Union after 1960, Wu Hsiu-ch'üan traveled widely throughout the Communist bloc to press Peking's case against the Russian party leadership. He visited North Korea in September 1961 and Eastern Europe (Bulgaria, Hungary, and Czechoslovakia) in November–December 1962. Chinese and Soviet differences were plainly apparent in January 1963 at the sixth congress of the East German Communist party in East Berlin. That congress was attended by 70 delegations from national Communist parties, most of whom sided with Nikita Khrushchev. On 18 January 1963 Wu delivered a vigorous rebuttal to Khrushchev while other delegates shouted and attempted to disrupt his presentation.

In March–April 1963 Wu accompanied Chou En-lai and Teng Hsiao-p'ing (q.v.) in talks with the Soviet ambassador to China regarding arrangements for negotiations between their two Communist parties. In July he served as a member of the Chinese delegation headed by Teng Hsiao-p'ing which flew to Moscow for abortive talks with the Soviet leaders. In September 1963 he accompanied Liu Shao-ch'i to North Korea. In November 1964 he was a member of the delegation led by Chou En-lai to Moscow for observance of the forty-seventh anniversary of the Russian Revolution; he also visited Tirana with Li Hsien-nien (q.v.) to attend the celebrations marking the twentieth anniversary of Communist rule in Albania. During 1964–65 Wu continued to be an active figure at Peking in discussions with Communist leaders from abroad who visited China. He was also a member of the standing committee of the National Committee of the Chinese People's Political Consultative Conference.

Wu, John C. H.: *see* Wu CHING-HSIUNG.

Wu Kuo-chen   吳 國 楨
    West. K. C. Wu

Wu Kuo-chen (21 October 1903–), known as K. C. Wu, government official who served as mayor of Hankow (1932–38), mayor of Chungking (1939–41), political vice minister of foreign affairs (1943–45), mayor of Shanghai (1946–48), and governor of Taiwan (1950–52). He resigned in 1953 and went to the United States, charging that Taiwan was becoming a police state.

Chienshin, Hupeh, was the birthplace of K. C. Wu. His father, Wu Ching-ming, was director of military training in the ministry of war at Peking, and the young Wu grew up in the capital. From 1913 to 1917 he studied at the Nankai Middle School in Tientsin, where he was a classmate of Chou En-lai (q.v.). In 1917 he enrolled at Tsinghua University, from which he was graduated in 1921. Wu then went to the United States for graduate work. In 1923 he received an M.A. from Grinnell College in Iowa, after having been elected to Phi Beta Kappa. Wu left Grinnell for Princeton, where in due course he was elected Nova Caesaria scholar, fellow in politics, and Elizabeth Proctor fellow. He received his Ph.D. in 1926, and his dissertation, *Ancient Chinese Political Theories*, later was published by the Commercial Press at Shanghai.

K. C. Wu returned to China in 1926 to teach at the National Political Science Institute in Peking. In 1927 he joined the National Government at Nanking as a secretary in the ministry of foreign affairs. He was sent to Shanghai as a secretary and chief of protocol in the office of the commissioner of foreign affairs for Kiangsu province. In 1928 he was made a deputy section chief and a member of the treaty revision commission in the foreign ministry at Nanking. Later that year, as a result of proposals he had made for reforms in the Hupeh tax structure, he became director of the Hupeh wine and tobacco tax bureau. In 1929 he was appointed counselor, director of the land administration bureau, and director of finance in the Hankow special municipal government. He held those posts until 1931, when he served for ten months as Hupeh commissioner of finance and then became secretary to Chiang Kai-shek at Nanking.

In 1932 K. C. Wu returned to Hupeh as mayor of Hankow. Depressed economic conditions in Hupeh, Communist activities, and the problems presented by foreign political and commercial interests made the Hankow mayor's task an unusually complicated and difficult one. Wu succeeded in gradually reducing opium traffic, and he played a major role in saving Hankow when it was threatened by floods in 1936. After the Sino-Japanese war began, Wu remained at Hankow until the Wuhan cities fell to the Japanese in October 1938. He then proceeded to Chungking, the wartime capital of the National Government.

After serving briefly as chief of the second section of the Supreme National Defense Council, K. C. Wu was made mayor of Chungking in 1939. Wartime Chungking, its population swollen by hundreds of thousands of refugees from other parts of China, presented even greater administrative problems than Wu had encountered at Hankow. His efforts with respect to civil defense were largely responsible for Chungking's survival under sustained Japanese bombing raids. However, when nearly 1,000 people died in an air raid shelter panic in June 1941, Wu was removed from office.

In 1943 K. C. Wu was appointed political vice minister of foreign affairs, serving under T. V. Soong (q.v.). At the Cairo Conference in 1943, Wu acted as official interpreter for Chiang Kai-shek. Because T. V. Soong spent much of his time in Washington, Wu was acting foreign minister for much of the remaining war period. At war's end, in August 1945, he was appointed Kuomintang minister of propaganda.

The Nationalist return to areas which had been under Japanese occupation presented many difficulties. In May 1946 K. C. Wu was appointed mayor of China's largest and most turbulent city, Shanghai. Politicians and businessmen thronged back into the city from west China, UNRRA and military supplies poured into the port, and masses of hungry refugees converged on the city. Shanghai was beset by carpet-bagging, graft, sky-rocketing inflation, blackmarketing in rice and other foodstuffs, and the anger of restless workers and students. His fight to maintain order in the face of these chaotic conditions won Wu recognition as "the La Guardia of China."

In the spring of 1949, as the Chinese Communist forces approached Shanghai, K. C. Wu withdrew to Taiwan. That December, he was made governor of Taiwan, minister without portfolio in the Executive Yuan, and a standing committee member of the Kuomintang Central Executive Committee. As governor of Taiwan, Wu faced such problems as Taiwanese resentment caused by the earlier administration of Ch'en Yi (q.v.), the many difficulties caused by

the influx of some two million Nationalist refugees, and the saddling of the island's population with the support of the National Government. He helped stabilize the island's financial position by selling 20,000 Japanese houses at 70 percent of their assessed value and by sacking surplus officials; he strove to lessen antipathy to the Nationalists by securing passage of a law guaranteeing free elections for municipal and district officials; and he continued the implementation of the land reform program initiated in August 1949 by his predecessor, Ch'en Ch'eng (q.v.). Elections held in the eastern coastal region of Taiwan in May 1950 gave the native Taiwanese a large measure of representation.

K. C. Wu was allowed to proceed with his liberalizing programs while the Nationalists were *in extremis* and without foreign military aid. The situation changed, however, after the Korean conflict began in 1950. The increased importance of Taiwan in American military planning in the Far East, the moving of the United States 7th Fleet into the Taiwan Strait, and the new American program of large-scale military and economic assistance to the Nationalists markedly improved the National Government's hopes and prospects. Despite Wu's efforts, the freedom of elections in Taiwan diminished. Wu was given new titles—commander of the Taiwan peace preservation headquarters, director of the anti-Communist protection and mobilization committee, chairman of the Taiwan production board—but his authority dwindled. In particular, there was increasing interference by the Nationalist secret police, controlled by Chiang Ching-kuo (q.v.), in the maintenance of public order and the processes of justice and education.

In the early spring of 1953 Wu submitted his resignation. Chiang Kai-shek refused to accept it, granting Wu a month's "sick leave." Wu and his wife were refused passports even though he had received several invitations to speak in the United States. After much difficulty, Wu was permitted to resign in April. Passports were issued to himself and his wife, but his son Hsiu-huang was not allowed to leave Taiwan. Wu and his wife arrived in the United States in May 1953 for the nominal purpose of obtaining treatment for his asthma. On 14 March 1954 he held a press conference in Evanston, Illinois, at which he announced that he had broken with the National Government. He charged that the National Government was endangering support from foreign countries for the effort to recover the mainland because of the undemocratic practices of its personalized one-party rule, because of damage to troop morale by the political department of the ministry of national defense and because of the activities of the secret police. The National Government responded by stripping Wu of his posts and party membership and by demanding that he return to Taiwan to face charges. Wu announced that he would return if a United States court, after consideration of the evidence, were to agree to extradition. The National Government chose not to accept the challenge. Wu then charged that his son was being detained in Taiwan, reiterating his request for a passport. The National Government acceded to his request in principle but stipulated that Wu would have to submit evidence that he would be employed and able to support his son in the United States for the next two years. Wu satisfied this requirement with a three-year contract of employment as Far Eastern consultant to the *Chicago Tribune.* And on 24 June 1954 his article "Your Money Has Built a Police State in Formosa" appeared in *Look.* In mid-July, his son left Taipei by plane for the United States.

K. C. Wu and his wife, the former Edith Cho-ch'ün Huang, lived in Evanston until 1967. They then moved to Savannah, Georgia, where Wu joined the faculty of Armstrong College. The Wu's, who married in 1930, had two sons, Hsiu-kuang and Hsiu-huang, and two daughters, Hsiu-jung and Hsin-hui.

In addition to his doctoral dissertation, Wu wrote a political novel, *The Lane of Eternal Stability,* which was published in the United States in 1962.

Wu Lien-teh   伍 連 德
    Alt. Ng Leen-tuck
          Gnoh Lean-tuck
    West. G. L. Tuck

Wu Lien-teh (10 March 1879–21 January 1960), pioneer in modern medical research and administration in China. He gained international recognition for his measures to end the disastrous plague in Manchuria in 1910–11, and

he directed the Manchurian Plague Prevention Service from 1912 to 1930. In 1930–37 he headed the National Quarantine Service at Shanghai.

The son of a Cantonese goldsmith and his Malaya-born Hakka wife, Wu Lien-teh was born and raised at Penang amid contrasting Malayan, Chinese, and European influences. His education, however, was wholly British. After being graduated from the Penang Free School in 1896, he received a Queen's Scholarship for study at Emmanuel College, Cambridge. He decided to study medicine, and his progress in England was rapid and distinguished.

In 1897 Wu Lien-teh took his first professional M.B. examination, and two years later he received a B.A. degree and became a Foundation Fellow of Emmanuel College. In the autumn of 1899 he won a scholarship to St. Mary's Hospital, London, where he was the first Chinese student to be enrolled. His name appeared on the records at St. Mary's, as at Cambridge, as G. L. Tuck. At St. Mary's, Wu was awarded the Kerslake Scholarship in pathology in 1901 and the Cheadle gold medal for clinical medicine in 1902. Also in 1902 he assumed a housemanship at Brompton Hospital for Consumption and Diseases of the Chest, and he received a research scholarship from Emmanuel College. After receiving the degree of MB. Bch. in 1903, he traveled and studied briefly with Ronald Ross at the Tropical Diseases Institute at Liverpool, Karl Fraenkel at Halle-an-der-Salle, and Elie Metchinikoff at the Institut Pasteur. In September 1903 he returned to Malaya.

Wu worked for a year at the newly established Institute for Medical Research at Kuala Lumpur. Because the prospects for a Chinese in colonial government service were poor, he entered private practice in 1904. St. Mary's Hospital, London, awarded him the M.D. degree in 1905. That year, he married Ruth Huang (Huang Shu-chiung) whose sister was the wife of the first Malayan Chinese to have qualified in Western medicine, Lim Boon Keng (Lin Wen-ch'ing, q.v.). Wu's major outside interest at this time was the anti-opium movement. In 1906 he organized the first Anti-Opium Conference for the Straits Settlements and Federated Malay States, held at Ipoh. It was with the keenest bitterness, therefore, that he found himself charged with possessing in his surgery a quantity of tincture of opium later that year. He was convicted and fined, although he maintained that the charges were false and that the British authorities were singling him out to teach him a lesson. The incident did nothing to alter Wu's advocacy of anti-opium legislation, but it led him to reconsider his career in Penang. In 1907 he went to London to address an anti-opium rally and to reconsider his future. After returning to Penang, he went to China in 1908 and, at the behest of Yuan Shih-k'ai, became vice director of the Army Medical College at Tientsin.

The climactic opportunity of Wu's life then presented itself. In November 1910 plague had reached epidemic proportions in Harbin, decimating the population and threatening to spread throughout the whole of Manchuria and north China. Abruptly, in late December, Wu was summoned from Tientsin by Sao-ke Alfred Sze (Shih Chao-chi, q.v.) then serving in the ministry of foreign affairs, and was asked to proceed to Harbin to take charge of plague control measures. Wu left Peking on 24 December 1910, accompanied by a single assistant, Lin Chia-swee, a senior student from the Army Medical College.

On arrival at Harbin, Wu quickly saw that the plague was spreading for two reasons: tradition-bound local officials declined to take elementary hygienic precautions, such as the destruction of diseased corpses by cremation; the vectors of the infection had been misidentified by the Western-trained doctors on the scene. Wu immediately memorialized the throne for permission to destroy disease-ridden corpses, and obtained it. At the same time, he studied the plague and discovered that it was not spread by rats. Rather, it originated in the infected lungs of the tabagan, a species of marmot valued for its pelt, which in turn passed the deadly virus on to hunters and trappers and thence to the population at large. Appalled by the absence of any properly organized preventive service and the inadequacy of local sanitary arrangements, Wu set to work to get the plague under control with his own methods. He encountered initial opposition, but his ideas soon prevailed as the death rate started to decline. Helped by a considerable body of medical personnel, he enforced drastic disciplinary measures in the plague area and

ordered the wholesale cremation of corpses. The last case of plague was registered on 1 March 1911, after an epidemic of five months and 60,000 deaths. In April Wu was ordered to make his report to the emperor and was made a major in the imperial army.

His success in Harbin brought Wu Lien-teh recognition as the leading Chinese authority on plague. In the same month in which he received his army commission, he was sent to Mukden, where he organized an international conference on plague control. He was appointed medical adviser to the ministry of foreign affairs, but almost immediately he was granted leave to form a special anti-plague service in Manchuria. Wu established his headquarters at Harbin and ordered construction of a modern hospital and laboratories. Wu's new organization soon grew into the Manchurian Plague Prevention Service, of which he served as director from 1912 to 1930. During the years of its existence the service was credited with the suppression or control of a number of diseases and the significant lowering of the death rate throughout its jurisdiction.

Immediately after completing the organization of the service, Wu made the first of a long series of trips abroad to attend the International Opium Conference held at The Hague. There, in 1912, he was one of the chief signatories to the First Convention for Control and Suppression of Narcotics. In August–September 1913 Wu attended the International Congress of Medicine in London and from there went on to Buffalo, New York, where he spoke at the International Conference on School Hygiene. Upon his return to China at the end of the year, he submitted a long memorandum on medical education to the republican government at Peking. As a result, a presidential mandate was issued legalizing dissection of corpses for teaching purposes.

In 1915 Wu was elected honorary secretary of the newly formed National Medical Association. He edited its journal from 1915 to 1921 and served as its president from 1916 to 1920. In 1924 he was awarded a Rockefeller Foundation Fellowship in Public Health, and he spent a year of research at The Johns Hopkins University. He represented China at the Far Eastern Association of Tropical Medicine conference held at Tokyo in October 1925, and in 1927 he studied health organizations in Europe as the recipient of a League of Nations traveling fellowship.

On 1 November 1928 the National Government inaugurated a new ministry of health at Nanking. A year later, plans for a National Quarantine Service were announced. Wu was selected to head the new service, and he assumed office on 1 July 1930, with headquarters on the Bund at Shanghai. The new organization steadily increased its scope and responsibilities, and for the first time a systematic rat-flea service was established in all of the principal Chinese ports. The Manchurian Plague Prevention Service, on the other hand, did not long survive Wu's departure. It ceased operations after the Japanese advanced into Manchuria in 1931.

Wu served as director of the National Quarantine Service until the invasion of China by Japan in 1937 caused the cessation of health services in Shanghai. Unwilling to remain in Japanese-occupied Shanghai but equally unwilling to make the long trek to Chungking, Wu returned to Malaya, where he set up practice at Penang and later in Ipoh.

After the war, Wu played no significant role in the Malayan independence movement, although at one time he was identified with the "Queen's Chinese" as being opposed to the federation. Wu was not a political man, and he seems to have taken no part on either side in the Chinese civil war. Shortly after the Communist capture of Peiping, he presented his house there to the Chinese Medical Association for use as its headquarters. Wu Lien-teh died quietly at Penang on 21 January 1960.

Wu was richly honored during his lifetime, receiving honorary degrees from Cambridge, Johns Hopkins, Peking, St. Johns (Shanghai), Hong Kong, and Tokyo. He was also a member of the Academia Sinica, a foreign member of the Society of Microbiology (U.S.S.R.), and physician extraordinary to successive presidents of the Chinese Republic. Wu wrote many monographs and several books, of which the last was his autobiography, *Plague Fighter*, published in 1959. Wu married twice. His first wife, Huang Shu-chiung, died in 1937. His second wife was Li Shu-chen, who survived him. Wu had three sons by his first marriage and two sons and three daughters by his second.

Wu Mi　　　　　　吳 宓
T. Yü-seng　　　　雨 僧

Wu Mi (August 1894–), founder and editor of the *Hsüeh-heng* [critical review], an important literary journal which opposed the literary revolution in China in the 1920's. A disciple of Irving Babbitt, he taught Western literature at Tsinghua University in 1924–44.

The Chingyang district of Shensi was the birthplace of Wu Mi. His father, Wu Chungch'i, a landholder who was known as a scholar of traditional Chinese literature and as a skilled swordsman, served as deputy military governor of Chahar province during the late Ch'ing period. After receiving a conventional Chinese education as a boy, Wu Mi studied at Tsinghua College in Peking. Upon graduation in 1916, he went to the United States to continue his studies, first at the University of Virginia and then at Harvard University.

Wu received a B.A. *cum laude* from Harvard in 1920 and an M.A. in 1921. During that period in Cambridge, he came under the influence of Irving Babbitt, the stimulating professor of comparative literature and leader of the New Humanism movement, which was dedicated to upholding the values that Babbitt and his associates believed to be the abiding elements in literature in the face of unbridled experimentalism and romantic subjectivism. After a brief sojourn at Oxford, Wu Mi returned to China, where he attempted to apply Babbitt's theories regarding the importance of discipline and tradition to the chaotic literary scene during the period following the May Fourth Movement.

While serving as professor of English at Southeastern University (after 1927, Central University) at Nanking in 1922, Wu Mi became one of the founders and chief editor of *Hsüeh-heng* [critical review], one of the most important periodicals opposed to the literary revolution. Mei Kuang-ti (q.v.), who also had studied with Irving Babbitt at Harvard, was a close associate of Wu in this endeavor. Although they received the ill-deserved epithet of "fake antiques," the *Hsüeh-heng* writers were not fighting literary reform in a spirit of blind reaction; many among them were perhaps better informed about Western literature than the zealous Chinese advocates of "total Westernization." The aims of the *Hsüeh-heng* were stated in English in every issue: "(1) to study, elucidate, and systematize the Chinese learning with critical method and scholarly equipment; (2) to introduce and to assimilate what is best and most important in the literature, philosophy, art, etc., of the West, presenting Western Civilization in its entirety and most salutary aspects; (3) to be a literary magazine of high standard . . . by employing a pure, elegant and pleasing style, . . . by publishing in each issue a strictly selected number of essays, poems, and stories . . . to create a model style of Chinese prose . . . ."

To illustrate its principles, the *Hsüeh-heng* prefaced its first issue with portraits of Confucius and Socrates, neither of whom were heroes to the Chinese intellectuals of the 1920's. In this and subsequent issues, there appeared essays criticizing the new literary movement for its shallowness, its opportunism, its ignorance of the Chinese past, and its lack of understanding of the West which it was attempting to imitate. As a corrective, Liu I-cheng (q.v.) contributed a comprehensive history of Chinese culture; and other Chinese writers translated selections from Plato, Aristotle, and Voltaire. An ambitious plan to translate all the works of Irving Babbitt, referred to by Wu Mi as the most significant writer of modern times, was carried out in part. Wu Mi himself wrote the initial chapters of a projected history of Western literature, beginning with Homer. He compiled lists of reference books for Chinese students of English literature. In addition, he translated English poems into classical Chinese verse, adding detailed notes on their historical background, literary allusions, and prosodic features.

Although the *Hsüeh-heng* made an important contribution to the stream of translations of and introductions to Western literature, it did not noticeably affect the particular course that Chinese creative writing was already beginning to take in its attempts to imitate the West. The *Hsüeh-heng*, in fact, deplored the then current emphasis on "social realism" and the admiration for such writers as Tolstoy, Balzac, Zola, and Ibsen. Wu Mi and his group failed to take sufficient account of the fact that the modern Chinese literary revolution was motivated largely by a desire for social and political reform. The demand of the times was not so much for the development of a new literature in itself as it was for the recruitment of literature into the service of social action. Zola therefore, was more "useful," more relevant, and more popular than Vergil. For similar reasons, fiction and drama, the two forms most adaptable to the detailed documentation of social conditions, attained the status of serious literature for the first time in Chinese history. However, examples of these genres were conspicuously absent from the pages of the *Hsüeh-heng*, in part because they were not highly regarded by the American-educated New Humanists. Poetry written in the classical language and based on classical conventions was a central concern of *Hsüeh-heng* contributors. Their belief, expounded earlier by the poet and reformer Huang Tsunhsien (ECCP, I, 350–51), was that modern poetry should use traditional language and forms while attempting to embody contemporary ideas. In 1935 Wu Mi published a volume of poems written in accordance with this principle.

The journal *Hsüeh-heng* is remembered and vilified by its critics chiefly for its opposition to the use of colloquial language in prose as well as in poetry. Any views on literature, no matter how liberal or judicious, would have been unlikely to gain a sympathetic hearing among the new intellectuals and writers of twentieth-century China if couched in a language already widely labeled as "dead" or "reactionary." The classical style employed by *Hsüeh-heng* writers had been stripped of archaisms and empty rhetoric, but in their hands it did not become a vigorous instrument of debate and did not lend itself to the formulation of appealing slogans or rousing battle cries. During a period of tumultuous change, the voice of moderation, if not conservatism, is likely to go unheeded; and the *Hsüeh-heng* failed to provide a rallying point for effective opposition to the new literature. It nevertheless was able, under the indefatigable editorship of Wu Mi and in a period marked by the proliferation of short-lived literary magazines, to appear monthly for five years and intermittently thereafter for another twenty or so issues.

Wu Mi continued to edit the *Hsüeh-heng* after he left Nanking in 1924 to begin two decades of teaching Western literature at Tsinghua University in Peking. In 1929 he also assumed the editorship of the literary supplement of the influential daily *Ta Kung Pao* at Tientsin. At various times he also held teaching or administrative positions at Northeastern University, Peking University, Peking Normal University, and Yenching University. During the Sino-Japanese war he migrated with Tsinghua to Changsha, and then to Kunming, where the university became part of the Southwest Associated University. He remained at Kunming until 1945, with the exception of a year as visiting lecturer at Wuhan University, then at Chungking.

Chinese acquainted with Wu Mi observed that he was a classicist in intellectual conviction but a romantic in temperament and sensibility. He was known for his lectures on the *Hung-lou-meng* (*Dream of the Red Chamber*), on which he published several studies; his gallant attention to female students; and his ill-concealed amorous involvements. Perhaps frustrated by the apparent contradiction between intellectual ideals and personal hedonism, Wu Mi became increasingly attracted to the study of metaphysics. At war's end he returned to north China, but in 1948 he moved from Peiping to Szechwan. There he studied Buddhism at Chengtu and later became chairman of the department of Western languages at Southwest Normal College.

These manifestations of romantic temperament and metaphysical yearnings in his later years reveal how far Wu Mi had moved from the New Humanist position of his youth. In one sense, however, he was continuing the search for unity and harmony between East and West, between old and new. In 1947 he published a *Table of the One and the Many*, written in English and then translated into Chinese, which summarized the conclusions of this search. Borrowing, as he explained, the terms "One" and "Many" from Greek philosophy and the Buddhist scriptures, he used them to classify all truth, knowledge, and experience into two opposite categories. His examples ranged from Plato to the Sung Neo-Confucians and the *Hung-lou-meng*.

To what personal synthesis of ultimate truths these investigations would have led Wu Mi will perhaps never be known, for in 1952 he became engulfed in the Communist program of "thought reform" of the intellectuals. He published a confession article in Chungking in which he renounced his previous intellectual positions and announced that he would dedicate himself to the study of Marxism-Leninism. The account he gave of his intellectual development followed the pattern of self-criticism and repentance prevalent in hundreds of similar confessions. His chief ideological fault, he wrote, had been his "feudal" respect for native Chinese culture. He had venerated China's cultural past while ignoring its ruthless and ugly aspects; he had loved ancient art objects without considering that they actually represented the fruits of the blood and toil of the oppressed masses. He acknowledged further as proof of his "criminal deeds" and "vicious influence" that few if any of his large number of students later became Communists or sacrificed their lives to the cause of revolutionary Communism in China. Wu Mi confessed also to erroneous romantic ideas about relations between the sexes. He had separated from his wife in 1929 and had engaged in various meaningless amorous activities. Fatigue and disillusionment then had led him to embrace Buddhism in an effort to "drug himself" and to alleviate his personal suffering through the "narcotic effects" of religion. When the Communists came, he had first attempted to fuse his old views with the new philosophy of dialectical materialism, but he now promised to reform his ideology more thoroughly in order to become a true teacher of the people. He would, he concluded, continue to study dialectical materialism and historical materialism, to accept Marxism-Leninism and Mao Tse-tung's theory of the Chinese revolution, to uproot idealism, and to discard all reactionary ideas.

Wu P'ei-fu   吳 佩 孚
T. Tzu-yü   子 玉

Wu P'ei-fu (22 April 1874–4 December 1939), warlord and leader of the Chihli military faction who became the dominant military leader in north China in 1922. Although his control of the Peking government was broken by Feng Yü-hsiang in 1924, he continued to dominate the Honan-Hupeh-Hunan area until 1926, when he was defeated by the Northern Expedition forces.

The son of a tradesman, Wu P'ei-fu was born in Tengchow on the northern coast of Shantung province. At the age of five, he began his early education in the Chinese classics at a local school. Because his father's death in 1887 left the family in straitened circumstances, the young Wu enrolled as a cadet attached to the naval station at Tengchow. He continued his studies in his spare time, and in 1896 he became a sheng-yuan. Because of a misdemeanor, he was deprived of this degree in the following year and was forced to flee to Peking, where he supported himself for a time by telling fortunes. He went to Tientsin in 1898 and obtained a position as clerk in the partially modernized army of Nieh Shih-ch'eng through the influence of a relative. Subsequently, he was admitted to a military preparatory school at K'aip'ing, where he remained for five months until the school was closed during the Boxer Uprising of 1900.

In 1902 Wu P'ei-fu was admitted to Paoting Military Academy, then recently established by Yuan Shih-k'ai (q.v.); and in this manner he began his long association with the Peiyang military clique. After specializing for a year in cartography and surveying, Wu was graduated in 1903 as a lieutenant and was assigned to a Japanese Army intelligence group based at Chefoo. During the Russo-Japanese war of 1904–5 he made several reconnaissance missions in Korea and Manchuria for the Japanese army, and at war's end he was decorated for his services by the Japanese government. One of the Japanese officers with whom Wu collaborated at that time, Okano Masujiro, later became one of Wu's military advisers, as well as one of his principal biographers.

At the conclusion of the Russo-Japanese war Wu P'ei-fu, by then a captain, was assigned to the Peiyang Army's crack 3rd Division. Late in 1906 Ts'ao K'un (q.v.) succeeded Tuan Ch'i-jui (q.v.) as division commander, and the 3rd Division was transferred to Changchun. After the republican revolution in 1911, the 3rd Division was recalled and was stationed in the Nanyuan quarter of Peking to support Yuan Shih-k'ai in his political maneuvering against the Nanking provisional government. To convince the delegates of Nanking that Yuan's presence was necessary in Peking to maintain order, the 3rd Division dutifully staged a "mutiny." For his part in the affair, Wu received command of the 3rd Division's 3rd Artillery Brigade, with the rank of colonel.

For the next eight years, Wu P'ei-fu's career was closely linked with the 3rd Division and its commander, Ts'ao K'un. In March 1912 the division was sent by Yuan Shih-k'ai to Hunan to restrain the activities of the revolutionaries in central China. During the so-called second revolution of 1913 (*see* Li Lieh-chün), Wu's brigade was assigned to protect communications along the southern section of the Peking-Hankow railway. In 1915, when Ts'ai O (q.v.) led a revolt against Yuan Shih-k'ai in southwest China, Yuan ordered the 3rd Division to Szechwan to crush it. After the failure of Yuan's monarchical movement and Yuan's death in June 1916, Wu returned with Ts'ao K'un and the 3rd Division to Paoting. With Ts'ao's appointment as military governor to Chihli (Hopei) province, Wu was left in temporary command of the division. In 1917 the 3rd Division was transferred back to Hunan, where the Peiyang forces were faring badly against the "constitution protection" forces of the southwestern military leaders. During the spring of 1918 Wu P'ei-fu, in acting command of the Peiyang forces, advanced as far as Hengchow in southern Hunan and recovered most of the province for the Peking regime.

Wu aspired to the military governorship of Hunan, but his hopes were dashed by Tuan Ch'i-jui, then the premier at Peking, who awarded the post to one of his own followers. This rebuff to his ambitions probably was one of the factors which turned Wu P'ei-fu against Tuan Ch'i-jui. Already Wu's loyalty to Tuan's leadership of the Peiyang military establishment had been undermined by the split of the Peiyang group into the rival Anhwei and Chihli factions: Wu and his immediate superior, Ts'ao K'un, were identified with the Chihli faction, while Tuan was the leader of the then dominant Anhwei faction. Also, while his forces were bogged down near the Hunan-Kwangsi border, Wu was approached by emissaries of the opposing Hunanese leaders, who urged him to consider the advantages to China of bringing the war in Hunan to a peaceful conclusion. Impressed by their arguments, resentful of Tuan, and in personal command of a powerful army well beyond the reach of Tuan's authority, Wu P'ei-fu decided to embark upon a course of action which would bring increasing independence from the military leadership of Tuan in Peking.

The change in Wu's attitude became apparent in August 1918. At that time he circulated the first of many open telegrams proposing an end to the civil war and the unification of north and south China by peaceful means. In this and later telegrams, though not attacking Tuan Ch'i-jui by name, Wu voiced his disapproval of Tuan's policy of uniting China by military force. He also denounced the Nishihara loans and other secret agreements which Tuan's government was negotiating with Japan, in particular the agreements concerning Japanese concessions in Wu's native province of Shantung. After the student demonstrations of the May Fourth Incident of 1919 in Peking, Wu sent an open telegram to Hsü Shih-ch'ang (q.v.), the president, expressing his sympathy for the students' opposition to the government's dealings with Japan.

Tuan Ch'i-jui responded to Wu's criticism by warning him about the consequences of disobeying orders from the Peking government. On the advice of Ts'ao K'un, Wu restrained his verbal attacks for a brief period. By mid-January 1920, however, he was ready to chart a more aggressive course. He telegraphed Peking for permission to return north from Hunan with the troops of the 3rd Division. After several such requests had been refused, Wu publicly announced his intention to withdraw his troops from Hunan. At the time, he was reported to have made a secret agreement with the Canton military government to turn over the areas he vacated in Hunan to the southern allies of Sun Yat-sen in return for large quantities of military supplies. On 25 May 1920, in defiance of the Peking government, Wu began to transfer his forces to Hankow and thence northward up the Peking-Hankow railway to Paoting. Aroused by this open challenge of his authority, Tuan Ch'i-jui dismissed Wu and Ts'ao K'un from office. On 14 July, Tuan's National Pacification Army (Ting-kuo chün) took to the field against the 3rd Division. Assisted by a large detachment sent from Manchuria by Chang Tso-lin (q.v.), the Wu-Ts'ao forces bested the National Pacification Army in a series of engagements along the Peking-Hankow railway. Tuan hastily resigned from office and took refuge in the Japanese concession in Tientsin.

As a result of this conflict, known as the Chihli-Anhwei war, Wu P'ei-fu became the dominant figure in the Chihli military clique, overshadowing his nominal chief, Ts'ao K'un. However, Ts'ao's ally Chang Tso-lin, regarded Wu's growing power as a challenge to his own ambitions in north China and sought to curb Wu's influence. Thus, at a conference of warlords held in Tientsin in April 1921—attended by Chang Tso-lin; Ts'ao K'un; Chin Yün-p'eng (q.v.), the premier; and Wang Chan-yuan (1861–1934), the military governor of Hupeh—Chang insisted that Wang Chan-yuan, rather than Wu P'ei-fu, receive the coveted post of inspector general (Hsün-yueh-shih) of Hupeh and Hunan.

When Wang Chan-yuan returned to Wuchang as inspector general, he immediately was confronted with threats of mutiny among his troops and by an invasion of Hunan by independent Hunanese militarists. Wang sent urgent pleas to Wu P'ei-fu for military assistance, but Wu kept his troops standing by at Loyang and waited for his rival to be overthrown by the Hunanese armies. Two days after Wang was driven from his post on 7 August 1921, the Peking government appointed Wu to succeed him as inspector general of Hupeh and Hunan. At the same time, Wu's subordinate Hsiao Yao-nan (1875–1926; T. Heng-sheng) was made military governor of Hupeh, and Sun Ch'uan-fang (q.v.) became commander in chief of the upper Yangtze region. With the ouster of Wang Chan-yuan, Wu P'ei-fu and his colleagues moved quickly against the Hunanese. Wu advanced from Loyang to Hankow and dispatched a fleet of warships upriver against Yochow, in northern Hunan. Yochow fell on 27 August and the Hunanese armies, confronted on two sides by Wu's troops, soon were defeated. Despite this success, Wu was reluctant to extend himself southward into Hunan, for he was suspicious of Chang Tso-lin's intentions in north China. On 1 September 1921 Wu concluded a truce with the Hunanese leaders, leaving them in control of much of their native province. The following month, he succeeded in driving back an attack by Szechwanese troops in western Hupeh. Having thus secured his flanks to the south and west, Wu was ready to turn his attention to north China and his chief antagonist, Chang Tso-lin.

While Wu had been strengthening his

position in central China, Chang Tso-lin had been working to extend his influence over the government in Peking. In December 1921, with the backing of the communications clique and the Anhwei faction, he succeeded in installing his candidate, Liang Shih-i (q.v.), as premier. To counter Chang's influence, Wu P'ei-fu resorted to tactics similar to those he had used against Tuan Ch'i-jui. He issued a series of public telegrams attacking the Liang Shih-i government for its financial dealings with Japan. In particular, he denounced Liang for having undermined the position of the Chinese delegation to the Washington Conference by negotiating separately with the Japanese government regarding the question of former German concessions in Shantung. Wu's campaign against the Liang government gained the support of several military and civil governors and also a large segment of public opinion, and after only a month in office, Liang Shih-i was obliged to resign under fire. Thwarted by Wu's tactics in the political sphere, Chang Tso-lin began to move troops from Manchuria into Hopei province and announced his intention of unifying China by force of arms.

The ensuing struggle between Wu P'ei-fu and Chang Tso-lin, known as the first Chihli-Fengtien war, broke out in January 1922, but for some months the fighting was carried on in desultory fashion. Playing for time in order to concentrate his scattered forces, Wu at first confined hostilities on his part to a "war of telegrams," criticizing Chang's policy of unifying China by military force and urging Chang to withdraw his troops north of the Great Wall. Wu secretly ordered his subordinate Feng Yü-hsiang (q.v.), then military governor of Shensi, to rush his troops eastward to Honan; and to offset an alliance between Chang Tso-lin and Sun Yat-sen, Wu reportedly made secret arrangements with Sun's lieutenant Ch'en Ch'iung-ming (q.v.) to obstruct Sun's plans for a northern expedition from Kwangtung into Hunan and Kiangsi. By the end of April, both Wu and Chang were prepared for an open test of strength. Although inferior in numbers and equipment to Chang's Japanese-trained forces, Wu's troops gained the upper hand in a number of engagements near Peking and forced the Fengtien army to retreat northward to its base in Manchuria.

As a result of his victory over Chang Tso-lin, Wu P'ei-fu became the dominant military figure in north China. His past pronouncements against Japanese interference in China and in favor of peaceful unification of the country, as well as his support of the "able men" cabinet of Wang Ch'ung-hui (q.v.), earned for him a reputation as a public-spirited leader of patriotic and liberal leanings. During the latter part of 1922, however, Wu's plans for peaceful unification under the "able men" cabinet were frustrated by the designs of his old chief, Ts'ao K'un. Wu's failure to back the Wang Ch'ung-hui cabinet against the scurrilous and unscrupulous attacks of Ts'ao's partisans, and his unwillingness to dissociate himself openly from Ts'ao's schemes to make himself president, soon disenchanted many of his admirers in liberal circles.

Early in 1923 Wu P'ei-fu suddenly reversed his former stand in favor of peaceful unification and began preparations to unite China by military force. The chief obstacle to his plans was Chang Tso-lin, who, since his defeat at Wu's hands the year before, had been building up his military forces in Manchuria for another move into north China. While Wu was engaged in assembling troops and equipment for another encounter with his adversary to the north, he also tried to extend his influence into the provinces of south China. In the spring of 1923 he forced the Peking government to appoint Sun Ch'uan-fang military governor of Fukien and Shen Hung-ying, an allied Kiangsi militarist, military governor of Kwangtung. At the same time, he encouraged a young subordinate, Yang Sen (q.v.), to invade Szechwan. Although Sun Ch'uan-fang eventually succeeded in taking over Fukien, Yang Sen was only partially successful in establishing himself in Szechwan, and Shen Hung-ying was badly defeated by Sun Yat-sen's forces in Kwangtung.

During 1923–24 Wu P'ei-fu was visited regularly at his military headquarters in Loyang by Chinese and foreign dignitaries who recognized that he, rather than Ts'ao K'un's shadow government in Peking, was the actual center of power in north China. As inspector general of Chihli-Shantung-Honan (a post held by Ts'ao K'un until he became president in October 1923), Wu controlled a large territorial base extending from Peking to the Yangtze province of Hupeh (under his subordinate Hsiao

Yao-nan). It was from this large domain rather than from the Peking government that Wu derived the revenues needed to maintain his large armies and to finance his plans for military unification of China. Apart from the land tax, the salt gabelle, and periodic "squeeze" extracted from wealthy merchants of Hupeh, Wu's greatest source of income was the Peking-Hankow railway. Beyond its economic significance, the railroad constituted Wu's major line of communication and transport by which he could rapidly move men and supplies between north and central China. It was, therefore, vital to Wu's military plans that the line be kept in operation. It undoubtedly was this consideration that prompted Wu, who formerly had shown a paternalistic benevolence toward labor organizations, to suppress the Peking-Hankow railway workers' strike of February 1923. This incident, in which some 80 workers were killed by Wu's troops, together with his undisguised espousal of a policy of military unification and his toleration of Ts'ao K'un's unsavory regime in Peking, contributed to a rapid decline in Wu's popularity after 1922. For quite different reasons, Wu had also become unpopular with his military associates. A stern disciplinarian, he stood aloof from his officers and frequently treated even senior subordinates with a brusqueness bordering on contempt. As a result, he alienated many of the officers under his command, the most important being Feng Yü-hsiang, upon whose support Wu had relied heavily in his victory over Chang Tso-lin in 1922.

In September 1924 Chang Tso-lin began to move his troops southward from Manchuria. In response to an urgent plea from Ts'ao K'un, Wu hurried from Loyang to Peking, where he announced that he would field an army of 200,000 men. It was at that point that Wu committed the gravest error of his career. Although he realized that Feng Yü-hsiang was not entirely trustworthy, he nevertheless placed him in command of the 3rd Division and assigned him to the Jehol front. Wu reasoned that he could ensure Feng's reliability by ordering two of his other subordinates, Hu Ching-i (d. 1925; T. Li-seng) and Wang Ch'eng-pin (b. 1873; T. Hsiao-po), to keep watch on Feng's movements. Wu was unaware that Hu, Wang, and Peking garrison commander Sun Yueh (1878–1928; T. Yü-hsing)

had joined Feng in a conspiracy against him. On 23 October 1924, while Wu was personally commanding his forces near Shanhaikuan, Feng Yü-hsiang suddenly returned with his army to Peking, imprisoned Ts'ao K'un, and circulated a telegram calling for an immediate end to the war. The following day, Ts'ao K'un was forced to order a truce and to dismiss Wu P'ei-fu from the post of inspector general of Chihli-Shantung-Honan.

When Wu P'ei-fu learned of Feng's betrayal, he hastened south to Tientsin to engage Feng in battle. His troops were hopelessly outnumbered, however, for they had been cut off from reinforcements in central China and badly defeated by Chang Tso-lin's forces at Shanhaikuan. As Feng's army advanced toward Tientsin, Wu boarded a navy transport at Tangku and on 7 November 1924 sailed south to Woosung and thence upriver to Hankow. There he sought to enlist the aid of Hsiao Yao-nan, Sun Ch'uan-fang, and other Chihli generals. These erstwhile subordinates, seeing that Wu's power had been broken, refused to join him and recognized instead the new "executive government" of Tuan Ch'i-jui in Peking. Wu then proceeded to his former headquarters at Loyang, but the occupation of Honan by Feng's newly organized Kuominchün and the growing coolness of Hsiao Yao-nan in Hupeh forced Wu to retire with only a small bodyguard to one of his gunboats in the Yangtze. Early in March 1925, at the invitation of Chao Heng-t'i (q.v.), then governor of Hunan, he sailed upriver to Yochow, where he announced his retirement from military life.

In the summer and autumn of 1925 Chang Tso-lin succeeded in extending his power southward from Peking to the Yangtze, thereby precipitating the so-called Fengtien-Chekiang war with Sun Ch'uan-fang and his allies. During this conflict, Hsiao Yao-nan and other Chihli militarists invited Wu P'ei-fu to take part in the war on the side of Sun Ch'uan-fang. Presented with this opportunity to recoup his losses, Wu hurried from Yochow to join Hsiao in Hankow. Assuming the title of commander in chief of the allied "anti-bandit" forces, he hastily assembled an army to act in conjunction with Sun Ch'uan-fang. Sun, however, had no desire to serve again under Wu's authority and, politely declining Wu's overtures, succeeded in defeating the Fengtien armies in Kiangsu and Shantung with his own forces.

Thereafter, Wu P'ei-fu and Sun Ch'uan-fang pursued their ambitions independently. In November 1925, with the outbreak of hostilities between Chang Tso-lin and Feng Yü-hsiang in the north, Sun Ch'uan-fang favored an alliance with Feng to check the power of Chang Tso-lin. Wu, on the other hand, was intent upon avenging the treachery of his former subordinate. Irked by Sun's refusal to support him in an attack on Feng, Wu joined forces with his old antagonist Chang Tso-lin against their common enemy. With the defeat of Feng Yü-hsiang early in January 1926 and his retirement to the Soviet Union, Wu P'ei-fu regained some of his prestige among the militarists of the Chihli clique, who urged him to lead them in a renewed attack upon Chang Tso-lin. Wu, reluctant to turn against his new ally and determined to continue his vendetta against Feng, attacked Feng's generals in Honan and Hopei. After several months of fighting, Wu's forces regained most of Honan province. By June, Wu again controlled the entire length of the Peking-Hankow railway.

As Wu P'ei-fu was engaging the remnants of Feng Yü-hsiang's armies in the north, events were taking place in Hunan that would endanger his entire southern flank. In March 1926 Wu's ally, Chao Heng-t'i, was forced to resign as governor of Hunan in favor of T'ang Sheng-chih (q.v.). T'ang's subsequent efforts to establish his control over all of Hunan were opposed by Wu P'ei-fu, who sent a strong force southward from Hupeh under the command of Yeh K'ai-hsin, one of T'ang's Hunanese rivals. After being pushed back into southern Hunan by Wu's forces, T'ang joined the National Revolutionary Army at Canton as commander of its Eighth Army. With the help of the Fourth and Seventh Armies of the National Revolutionary Army, T'ang was able to advance into central and northern Hunan. By 21 August, he had taken Yochow.

When Wu P'ei-fu learned of the reverses in Hunan, he left the Peking area to assume personal command of his battered forces in the south. Because he could not stem the advance of the Northern Expedition in southern Hupeh, he fell back to defend the Wuhan cities. On 6 September 1926 he abandoned Hankow to the victorious Nationalist forces and withdrew up the Peking-Hankow railway to Chengchow in northern Honan, where he remained with the remnants of his forces until the spring of 1927. By May of that year, however, Wu's position had become untenable. Pressed on the north and east by the armies of Chang Tso-lin, threatened from the west by Feng Yü-hsiang's advancing forces, and confronted to the south by T'ang Sheng-chih's Eighth Army, he fled southwestward through Honan with the remainder of his troops. Wu evaded the forces of Feng Yü-hsiang in western Hupeh, reached the Szechwan border in July with about 100 followers, and took refuge with his former subordinate Yang Sen. For all practical purposes, his career as a military leader had come to an end.

For the next four years, Wu P'ei-fu remained in Szechwan under the protection of Yang Sen. Although Yang had joined the National Revolutionary Army in 1926 as commander of its Twentieth Army, he had retained a large degree of independence from the National Government in Nanking. He thus was able to ignore repeated orders from Nanking to arrest his former chief. Wu, for his part, announced his retirement from public affairs and took up the study of the Buddhist canon and the Confucian classics. In the autumn of 1931, he moved with his family and a few retainers from Chengtu to Peiping, arriving there in January 1932.

In Peiping, Wu's life of retirement soon was disturbed as a result of Japanese aggression in north China. After the Japanese occupation of Manchuria, General Doihara Kenji and the Kwantung Army became increasingly interested in establishing a Japanese-controlled "autonomous" government in north China, and in 1935 Doihara made the first of many unsuccessful attempts to persuade Wu P'ei-fu to head such a regime. Wu also refused counter-offers from the National Government late in 1936, but he assured Nanking that he would never serve the interests of another nation.

After the Sian Incident of December 1936 (see Chiang Kai-shek, Chang Hsueh-liang), Wu's attitude underwent a noticeable change. Expressing alarm over the spread of the "red evil" and "foreign influences" at work in Nanking, he indicated interest in cooperating with the Japanese against what he believed to be the growing power of Communism in China.

After the outbreak of the Sino-Japanese war and the establishment of the Japanese-sponsored regimes under Wang K'o-min (q.v.) in Peking and Liang Hung-chih (q.v.) in Nanking, it soon became apparent to the Japanese that they needed a leader of greater prestige than either Wang or Liang to induce the Chinese populace to collaborate with the Japanese authorities. In 1938 Doihara's agents again approached Wu P'ei-fu. Although Wu appeared willing to consider their proposals, his price for co-operation was impossibly high. He demanded not only a free hand in mobilizing a Chinese anti-Communist army of 500,000 men, supplied and equipped by Japan, but also the gradual withdrawal of all Japanese troops from Chinese soil. When the Japanese proved unwilling to grant his demands, Wu resisted all further efforts to enlist his participation. By November 1938 the Japanese had decided to look else-where. Late in 1939, while under considerable pressure to collaborate with the new Japanese candidate, Wang Ching-wei (q.v.), Wu P'ei-fu developed blood-poisoning from an infected tooth. He died in Peiping on 4 December 1939, at the age of 67. With the permission of the Japanese occupation authorities, Wu's friends and former adherents gave him an elaborate funeral in Peking, while the National Government in Chungking honored him for his refusal to serve the Japanese. At war's end, Wu's remains were disinterred and reburied in a state ceremony. Although his overbearing manner and fierce temper had antagonized many of his military colleagues and subordinates, his personal honesty and his indifference to wealth and high political office had won the admiration of many contemporaries, both Chinese and foreign.

Wu P'ei-fu married twice. He was survived by his second wife, *née* Chang. Because he had no son of his own, he adopted as his heir Wu Tao-shih, the son of his deceased younger brother, Wu Wen-fu.

Wu P'ei-fu was something of a writer and a patron of the traditional culture. Following his flight to Szechwan in 1927 he had ample leisure to reflect upon his past experiences as well as the chaotic state of his country. As one who respected the military traditions of loyalty exemplified in such martial heroes of the past as Kuan Yü and Yueh Fei, Wu concluded that both his own and his country's misfortunes were due to the breakdown of the traditional moral order. It was in this vein that he composed a brief treatise entitled *Hsun-fen hsin-shu* (1930) in which he extolled such traditional virtues as filial obedience, loyalty, sincerity, and propriety and their importance in maintaining social order and discipline. In a manner reflecting, perhaps, his military background, Wu admonished his readers to be content with their appointed station and to fulfill but not exceed the duties of their position. After his departure from Szechwan for Peking in 1931, Wu gave a number of speeches and lectures on various aspects of traditional moral philosophy. These were collected and printed in such works as the *P'eng-lai Wu-kung chiang-hua lu* (1932) and the *Cheng-i tao-ch'üan* (1936). A commemorative collection of his writings, together with his biography and nien-p'u, was published by his old friends and associates in Taiwan as the *Wu P'ei-fu hsien chi* (1960).

Wu T'ieh-ch'eng   吳 鐵 城

Wu T'ieh-ch'eng (9 March 1888–19 November 1953), aide to Sun Yat-sen who later served as mayor of Shanghai (1932–36) and secretary general of the central headquarters of the Kuomintang (1941–48).

Although his family's native place was Hsiangshan (later Chungshan), Kwangtung, Wu T'ieh-ch'eng was born at Kiukiang, Kiangsi. After receiving his early education in the Chinese classics from private tutors, he began to study English at the age of about 14 sui, and he was graduated from the Methodist T'ung-wen School at Kiukiang in 1906. Plans were then made for him to go to Japan for further study, but his father insisted that Wu should be married before leaving China. Because of the death of the Kuang-hsü emperor in 1908, Wu's marriage to Ma Fang-chi had to be postponed until 1909. In the same year Wu came to know Lin Sen (q.v.) and participated in clandestine anti-Manchu activities. He joined the T'ung-meng-hui in 1910.

In 1911 Wu T'ieh-ch'eng again made plans to go to Japan. A Chinese merchant guild delegation was then to visit Tokyo at the invitation of the Japanese government, and Wu, whose father was deputy chairman of the

Kiukiang merchants guild, was chosen to represent Kiukiang. News of the Wuchang revolt in October reached Wu in Shanghai as he was about to embark. He then abandoned his plans and returned to Kiukiang to aid Lin Sen in the revolutionary effort. After a republican government had been established in Kiangsi, he and Lin Sen went to Nanking as members of the Kiangsi delegation to the assembly that elected Sun Yat-sen provisional president of the Chinese Republic.

With the failure of the so-called second revolution in 1913 (*see* Li Lieh-chün), Wu T'ieh-ch'eng was forced to seek refuge in Japan, where he studied briefly at Meiji University. In 1914 Sun Yat-sen sent him to Honolulu to take charge of Kuomintang affairs and to run a newspaper there. Upon his return to China in 1916 Wu became an aide to Sun Yat-sen. He later became Sun's chief aide. In 1922 Wu was elected magistrate of Hsiangshan hsien, his and Sun's native place, in the first popular elections held there. The following year, he was appointed to the committee charged with carrying out the reorganization of the Kuomintang. He also became municipal director of public security for Canton, commissioner of public security for Kwangtung, and gendarmerie commander for Kwangtung. After the Kuomintang reorganization in 1924 he also served as an executive member of the Kuomintang headquarters at Canton.

During the turbulent period that followed Sun Yat-sen's death in March 1925, Wu T'ieh-ch'eng occupied a sensitive position in Canton as public security director and commander of the 1st Independent Division (later the 17th Division) of the National Revolutionary Army. For reasons that are unclear, he was imprisoned in May 1926, allegedly for negligence of duty, but he was released in October. Little is known about his activities during 1927. He returned to Canton in 1928 as commissioner of reconstruction. In the spring of 1929 he was elected to the Kuomintang Central Executive Committee and to the newly established Legislative Yuan. During this period, he also began to demonstrate his abilities as a negotiator. During the 1929 Sino-Soviet dispute over the Chinese Eastern Railway and other matters, Wu went to Mukden as Chiang Kai-shek's personal emissary to Chang Hsueh-liang (q.v.). In 1930, when the National Government was

being threatened by the northern coalition of Feng Yü-hsiang and Yen Hsi-shan (qq.v), Wu went to Mukden once again for discussions with Chang Hsueh-liang. Although Chang did not openly support the National Government, his refusal to intervene on behalf of Feng and Yen doomed the northern coalition. In 1931 Wu was among the Nanking representatives to the successful peace talks with such leaders of the Canton secessionist government as Wang Ching-wei, Eugene Ch'en, and Tsou Lu (qq.v.).

In 1932 Wu T'ieh-ch'eng was named mayor of Shanghai. The difficult task of administering that great metropolis required both political sagacity and diplomatic tact. Wu handled both the domestic and the international aspect of the position with deftness and cordiality. His term of office (1932–36) was a period of steady accomplishment in municipal construction despite Japanese military pressure. In March 1937 Huang Mu-sung (q.v.) died suddenly, and Wu was appointed to succeed him as governor of Kwangtung.

After the Sino-Japanese war began, Wu T'ieh-ch'eng was transferred to Hong Kong in 1938 as director of Kuomintang affairs in Hong Kong and Macao. He also was appointed minister of overseas affairs in the central party headquarters. In this capacity, he went on a special mission to Southeast Asia in 1940 to mobilize support for the Chinese war effort. Upon his return from that mission in the spring of 1941, he went to Chungking to assume office as secretary general of the central party headquarters. He held that high administrative post until 1949. He also served as a member of the Kuomintang Central Executive Committee's standing committee. In 1946 he was a Kuomintang delegate to the Political Consultative Conference, and in 1946–48 he was vice president of the Legislative Yuan. In December 1948 his old friend Sun Fo (q.v.) prevailed upon Wu to serve as vice president of the Executive Yuan and minister of foreign affairs in Sun's short-lived emergency cabinet. With the Chinese Communist victory in the contest for control of the mainland, Wu went to Taiwan, where he served as a presidential adviser and as an appraisal member of the Kuomintang Central Executive Committee. In Taipei, he devoted himself to working for the People's Foreign Relations Association and to writing a volume of memoirs, *Ssu-shih-nien-lai chih*

Chung-kuo yü wo [40 years of China and I]. On 19 November 1953, at the age of 66 sui, he died at his residence in Taipei. He was survived by two sons, Yu-ling and Yu-liang, and by three daughters, Mei-yün, Lo-yün, and Ai-po.

Wu Ting-ch'ang 吳 鼎 昌
T. Ta-ch'uan 達 詮

Wu Ting-ch'ang (1884–August 1950), banker, newspaper publisher, and government official. After holding banking and financial posts at Peking in 1912–19, he headed the Yien-yieh Bank and the Joint Treasury of north China's four leading banks. In 1926–34 he also was chairman of the board and director of the *Ta Kung Pao* and the Kuo-wen enterprises. Wu then served as minister of industries (1935–37), governor of Kweichow (1938–44), and chief secretary of the National Government (1945–47).

Although his native place was Wuhsing, Chekiang, Wu Ting-ch'ang was born in Suiting, Szechwan, where his father was serving as an officer. After receiving his early education in the Chinese classics under private tutors, he entered the Tsun-ching shu-yuan in Chengtu in 1896. Soon afterward, he passed the examinations for the sheng-yuan degree. In 1901 he went to Japan and enrolled at Tokyo Higher Commercial College, from which he was graduated in 1909. When the T'ung-meng-hui was established in 1905, Wu was one of its founding members. He returned to China in 1911 to become general manager of the Penhsi Coal Company in Manchuria. He later served as branch manager of the Ta Ch'ing Bank in Kiangsi.

In 1912, soon after the establishment of the Chinese republic, the Ta Ch'ing Bank was reorganized as the Bank of China in accordance with suggestions made by Wu Ting-ch'ang. The new scheme envisaged the continued recognition of private stocks subscribed by investors, the expansion of private capital through new subscriptions, and the cancellation of the bank's government shares, which were used to compensate for losses sustained during the revolution. Sun Yat-sen appointed Wu director of the new bank in February 1912. Unfortunately for Wu, Yuan Shih-k'ai succeeded Sun as provisional president soon

afterwards, and Yuan's minister of finance, Chou Hsueh-hsi (q.v.), refused to adopt many of Wu's suggestions. In December 1912 Wu resigned from the directorship of the Bank of China.

For the next seven years, Wu Ting-ch'ang served the Peking government as director of the Central Mint (1913–14), vice minister of agriculture and commerce (1914–15), and vice minister of finance (1917–19). He was removed from office in 1920 when the government of Tuan Ch'i-jui (q.v.) fell. Wu then became chairman of the board and general manager of the Yien-yieh Bank. His interest in the American banking system led him to advocate the cooperation of private banks to centralize reserves and thereby bolster public confidence in note issuance. In January 1923 the Yien-yieh Bank, the Kincheng Banking Corporation, the Continental Bank, and the China and South Seas Bank pooled their resources to establish the Joint Treasury and the Joint Savings Society. The four banks, which came to be known as the pei ssu-hang [four northern banks], helped circulate the banknotes which they alone, under the new arrangement, had the power to issue. Wu served as general manager of the Joint Treasury until 1935.

In 1926 Wu Ting-ch'ang entered the field of journalism. He formed a holding company, the Hai-chi Company, which purchased and reorganized the *Ta Kung Pao* in Tientsin and the Kuo-wen enterprises. Wu served as chairman of the board and director of the *Ta Kung Pao*, with Hu Lin (q.v.) as general manager and Chang Chi-luan (q.v.) as chief editor. The new enterprise was a financial as well as a journalistic success, and a Shanghai edition of the *Ta Kung Pao* was established in April 1936.

Wu Ting-ch'ang joined the National Government in 1935 as minister of industries and director of the National Economic Reconstruction Movement Association. In keeping with his personal credo, he severed all of his connections with banks, newspapers, and other private enterprises. Wu made a number of significant contributions to the economic reconstruction of China. He helped establish an agricultural credit administration to promote rural marketing cooperatives and to supply farm credit loans, and he expanded the activities of the national bureau of agricultural research (*see* Shen Tsung-han). To promote foreign trade, he established the China Vegetable Oils Corporation and the China National Tea Corporation, and he streamlined the operations of the bureau of commodity inspection in order to standardize exports. He also founded the national bureau of industrial research and promoted the establishment of new industries. In his economic policy, Wu was guided by the principles of equalization of wealth and localization of enterprises in order to curb state capitalism, state monopolies, and the overconcentration of capital. To achieve these goals, he arranged for the sinking fund of the agricultural credit administration to be supplied by various banks. Similarly, banks and private industry supplied the capital for a joint company for marketing manufactured goods, and the capital of the vegetable oils and tea companies was subscribed by the ministry of industries, provincial governments, and private merchants.

At the end of 1937 Wu Ting-ch'ang was appointed governor of Kweichow. In addition to being land locked and poor in natural resources, Kweichow was plagued by illiteracy, opium cultivation, and malnutrition. Wu instituted a crash program to replace the production of opium poppies with wheat and tobacco, to establish public health services in every hsien, and to set up some 5,000 public schools. With funds from the National Government, the Kweichow provincial government, banks, and private investors, he established the Kweichow Enterprise Company. It managed utilities, mines, manufacturing of consumer goods, agricultural processing industries, transportation, insurance, and construction industries, but it did not interfere with the operations of private enterprises in the province. Agricultural cooperatives were established at the hsien level. Wu made great strides in Kweichow, but at considerable cost to his health. His ailments finally forced him to resign in the winter of 1944.

In 1945–47 Wu Ting-ch'ang served as chief secretary of the National Government and the Central Planning Board. He became chief secretary of the presidential office after the elections of 1948. Ill health forced him to resign at the end of 1948, and he went to Hong Kong at the beginning of 1949. Wu died of cancer at Hong Kong in August 1950.

Wu Ting-ch'ang's writings included *Chung-kuo hsin ching-chi cheng-ts'e* [China's new economic policy], published as a pamphlet in 1926; "Chung-kuo hsin chin-jung chih-tu" [China's new fiscal system], which appeared in the *Kuo-wen chou-pao* in 1926; and *Hua-ch'i hsien-pi*, a volume of reminiscences about his life as an administrator which was written and published while he was governor of Kweichow.

Wu T'ing-fang   伍 廷 芳
T. Chih-yung   秩 庸
H. Wen-chüeh   文 爵

Wu T'ing-fang (9 July 1842–23 June 1922), English-educated lawyer who gained international prominence as the Ch'ing government's diplomatic representative in the United States in 1897–1901 and in 1907–9. He also served as co-chairman of the fa-lü pien-tsuan-kuan [bureau for the compilation of the law]. Wu was chief delegate for the revolutionaries in the peace negotiations that led to Manchu abdication and the establishment of the republic in 1912. He later served as foreign minister at Canton.

Although Wu T'ing-fang was born at Singapore, his native place was Hsinhui (Sunwui), Kwangtung, where his father, Wu Jung-chang, had been a merchant for many years. When Wu T'ing-fang was only three, his family returned to China and established residence at Fangts'un, an islet in the Pearl River near Canton.

After receiving his early education in the conventional Chinese curriculum, Wu was sent to Hong Kong to enroll at the British Central School (later Queen's College), a secondary school operated by the Hong Kong government. He was graduated in 1860. For the next decade he held various positions in the colony, including the post of interpreter in the Hong Kong courts. He was also associated with the *Chung-ngoi san-po (Chung-wai hsin-pao)*, the first modern daily newspaper to be published in Chinese. Although it is unclear whether he was a founder of this paper, which appeared in 1858, Wu played a leading role as an editor of the *Chung-ngoi san-po* during its early years. In 1873 he joined Wang T'ao and Huang Sheng in founding another early Hong Kong newspaper, the *Tsun-wan yat-po (Hsün-wan jih-pao)*, which became the most successful Chinese-owned paper of that period.

In 1874 Wu T'ing-fang went to London to read law. He was called to the English bar in 1876, becoming the first Chinese barrister. Soon afterward, his father died, and Wu returned to Canton in 1877 to observe the prescribed period of mourning. He then became the first Chinese to practice law in Hong Kong, where he was known by his Cantonese name, Ng Choy, and became active and influential in civic affairs. Sir John Pope Hennessy, the governor of Hong Kong, was making efforts to broaden representation in the colony's administrative apparatus through appointment of some non-European members. Wu T'ing-fang was thus appointed an acting magistrate, the first Chinese to hold this post. In 1880 the governor, despite opposition from some other officials of the Hong Kong government, appointed Wu to membership in the Legislative Council. The first Chinese in the colony's history to be elevated to this post, Wu owed his appointment partly to the fact that he was a British subject through his birth in Singapore and partly to favorable support from the "wealthy and better Chinese" in the colony. With his brother-in-law Ho Kai, he was also active in the establishment in Hong Kong of a college of medicine attached to the Alice Memorial Hospital; it was there that Sun Yat-sen studied medicine a few years later.

In 1882 Wu T'ing-fang left Hong Kong to join the secretariat of Li Hung-chang (ECCP, I, 464–71) at Tientsin. Wu soon took part in the negotiating and signing of a Sino-French treaty in April–June 1885. He also gained experience in a number of other fields of activity, including the establishment of such schools as Peiyang University, the Peiyang Military Academy, and the Tientsin School of Telegraphy. In 1887 Wu was made director of the China Railway Company, charged with the construction of a rail line between Tientsin and the nearby port of Tangku. When the line was completed the following year, he became its managing director. In 1889 Wu's mother died, and he returned to his home in Canton to observe the three-year mourning period, returning to Tientsin in 1891. He was active in diplomacy during the Sino-Japanese war. In 1895 he aided Li Hung-chang in the treaty negotiations at Shimonoseki, and later that year he officiated at the exchange of treaty ratifications.

Wu T'ing-fang was appointed minister to the United States, Spain, and Peru in 1897. He established legation headquarters in Washington and worked to spread correct knowledge of China, then something of a mystery to the Western world. It was through his personal assistance that the Library of Congress began to give serious attention to the systematic collecting and cataloguing of Chinese materials. On 14 April 1898 he and Senator Calvin Brice, head of the American China Development Company, signed a loan agreement for the financing of the Canton-Hankow railway. In 1899 he negotiated a Sino-Mexican treaty, securing most-favored-nation status for China for the first time. During the Boxer Uprising, he took a moderate stance and worked to get the United States to take the initiative in bringing the hostilities to an end.

In 1902 Wu T'ing-fang was recalled to China and was appointed a co-commissioner for the revision of treaties. He established residence at Shanghai and concluded new commercial treaties with Great Britain, the United States, and Japan. Before long, Wu was transferred to Peking as vice president of the Board of Commerce, in which capacity he assumed jurisdiction over the newly opened treaty ports and formulated the Company Law to bring order to commercial enterprises in these areas. Also during this period, Wu served as vice president of the Board of Foreign Affairs and as co-chairman of the fa-lü pien-tsuan-kuan [bureau for the compilation of the law]. The other co-chairman was Shen Chia-pen (q.v.). Wu and Shen proceeded slowly, hiring Chinese and Japanese scholars and establishing a law school (for details, see Shen Chia-pen). In April 1905 Shen and Wu proposed a series of changes in the Ch'ing legal code. Most of these changes concerned the abolition of corporal punishment, and they were accepted. Early in 1906 Wu was appointed vice president of the Board of Punishments. When the Ch'ing court refused to consider sweeping reforms in criminal procedures, Wu resigned his government posts on the grounds of illness. He returned to government service in 1907 as Chinese minister to the United States. Although his faith in the Ch'ing court had been shaken by its refusal to move quickly toward constitutionalism and a modern legal structure, he continued to send memorials to the throne proposing such reforms as the removal of the queue. He was recalled in 1909. Upon his return to China by way of Europe in early 1910, he settled in Shanghai and turned his attention to community affairs.

After the Wuchang revolt of October 1911, Wu T'ing-fang gave active support to the republican revolutionaries. On 3 November 1911 he convened the emergency meeting of public-spirited residents and officials that established the Shanghai revolutionary government, with Ch'en Ch'i-mei (q.v.) as military governor. Wu and Wen Tsung-yao served as secretaries for foreign affairs. Wu also became foreign minister and diplomatic representative in Shanghai of the central republican government at Wuhan. He repeatedly communicated with the diplomatic and foreign press corps in Shanghai, calling for Manchu abdication and describing the Chinese revolution as the "least sanguinary in the history of the world." Wu also was designated chief delegate to negotiate a settlement with the Peking authorities. His first meeting with T'ang Shao-yi (q.v.) was held at Shanghai in December 1911.

With the establishment of the Chinese republic in January 1912, Wu T'ing-fang became minister of justice. He remained in Shanghai, however, to participate in the negotiations which led to the abdication of the Manchu emperor (see P'u-yi) and to Sun Yat-sen's resignation in favor of Yuan Shih-k'ai. After Yuan assumed the presidency, Wu retired to his home in Shanghai. He established a group, the T'ien-jen ming-tao hui, to study and discuss Confucianism, Buddhism, Christianity, and other religions. Although Wu was a political moderate, he received membership in a wide variety of political parties by virtue of his status as an elder statesman. At the time of the so-called second revolution against Yuan Shih-k'ai in 1913, Wu considered Yuan's policy "dangerous," but he blamed both sides for refusing to compromise. He opposed Yuan's plan to become monarch and declined to serve as a mediator after Yuan renounced his monarchical ambitions. After Yuan's death, Wu, then in his seventies, accepted the foreign ministership in the cabinet of Tuan Ch'i-jui (q.v.) in November 1916.

Early in 1917 Tuan Ch'i-jui encountered parliamentary opposition to his proposal that China enter the First World War on the side of the Allies. When Tuan threatened to dissolve the Parliament, his cabinet resigned. Li Yuan-hung (q.v.), the president, issued an order (countersigned by Wu T'ing-fang) on 23 May dismissing Tuan and naming Wu acting premier. Five days later, Li Ching-hsi became premier. These actions resulted in the so-called revolt of the tüchuns (see Tuan Ch'i-jui), and on 13 June Li was forced to dissolve the Parliament by Chang Hsün (q.v.), who hoped to restore the Hsuan-t'ung emperor to the throne. On 9 July, Feng Kuo-chang (q.v.), who had become acting president, dismissed Wu T'ing-fang from the foreign ministership. Wu then went to Canton to join the so-called constitution protection movement of Sun Yat-sen. Sun appointed Wu minister of foreign affairs in the new military government at Canton, but Wu did not assume office formally.

With the reorganization of the Canton government early in 1918, Wu T'ing-fang became a member of its seven-man directorate. The other members were Lu Jung-t'ing, Ts'en· Ch'un-hsuan, T'ang Chi-yao (qq.v.), Sun Yat-sen, T'ang Shao-yi, and Lin Pao-tse. Sun withdrew from the government in May (though he did not resign until August) and went to Shanghai. Wu, who also was serving as foreign minister, eventually found cooperation with the Kwangsi warlords impossible, and he left Canton with Lin Sen (q.v.) in March 1919 for Shanghai. In October 1920 Ch'en Chiung-ming (q.v.) drove the Kwangsi clique from Canton and prepared the way for Sun's return to power. Sun returned to Canton in November, accompanied by Wu T'ing-fang and T'ang Shao-yi. Wu resumed office as foreign minister, and in May 1921 he also became minister of finance when Sun Yat-sen took office as president extraordinary.

Ch'en Chiung-ming, who initially had opposed the plan to reorganize the Canton government, also opposed Sun Yat-sen's plans for a northern expedition. As a result of their continuing differences of opinion, Sun removed Ch'en from office as governor of Kwangtung in April 1922 and appointed Wu T'ing-fang to succeed him. On 16 June, Ch'en's supporters staged a coup at Canton. Sun escaped to a gunboat in the Pearl River. On 17 June Wu went to see Sun. Exhausted and frustrated in his long struggle for Chinese unity, Wu T'ing-fang died a week later, on 23 June. He was survived by his wife and by his son, C. C. Wu (Wu Ch'ao-shu, q.v.).

Wu T'ing-fang's writings included *Rustic Opinions on Planning Government for the Republic*, in which he set forth his general philosophy of cultural conservatism and political liberalism. He was a firm believer in physical fitness and wrote a book on physical culture called *New Methods for Extending Life*. Descriptions of his character and examples of his wit were collected and published in 1924 as *Anecdotes about Wu T'ing-fang*.

Wu T'ing-hsieh   吳 廷 燮
  T. Hsiang-chih   向 之
  H. Tz'u-k'uei   次 夔

Wu T'ing-hsieh (3 January 1866–14 December 1947), government official at Peking who was best known as a scholar and historian. His systematic arrangement of widely scattered data into chronologically ordered compilations greatly facilitated the research of later scholars.

Although the ancestral home of the Wu family was in Chiangning (Nanking), Wu T'ing-hsieh was born in Shansi province where his father, Wu Shih-ch'i (d. 1884), a chü-jen of 1844, was serving as a magistrate. Under his father's guidance he received a traditional education in preparation for the civil service examinations. He was also given training in the elements of bibliography and historical research, and he acquired some knowledge of world history and geography. After 1882, he participated in the provincial examinations six times before he succeeded in becoming a chü-jen in 1894. After serving as a copyist in the office of military archives at Peking, he was appointed an assistant sub-prefect in Shansi province in 1895. He remained in Shansi for almost a decade, rising in the Shansi provincial administration to the position of acting prefect of Taiyuan prefecture.

In 1904 Wu was summoned to Peking to become assistant chief in the Bureau of Government Affairs (cheng-wu ch'u), and he continued to hold posts in various departments of the central government until the abdication of the Manchu emperor in February 1912. After Yuan Shih-k'ai (q.v.) had been installed as president of the new republic, Wu T'ing-hsieh

became a secretary in the presidential office. From 1914 until the fall of the Peking regime in 1928 he headed the central bureau of statistics. During these years he occasionally held concurrent posts, such as those of compiler in the bureau of compilation of Ch'ing history and secretary to the provisional chief executive, Tuan Ch'i-jui (q.v.), whose government lasted from November 1924 to April 1926.

Wu T'ing-hsieh remained in Peking until 1928, when the occupation of the northern capital by the National Revolutionary Army brought the Peking regime to an end. Wu then retired from government service and went to Manchuria, where he was professor of history at the Ts'ui-sheng Academy in Mukden from 1928 to 1931. After the Mukden Incident of September 1931 and the Japanese occupation of Manchuria, Wu returned to Peiping. He lived quietly in retirement at his residence at Peiping and in Nanking until the end of the Second World War. After the return of the National Government to Nanking, he was invited to become a compiler in the national history compilation bureau in 1947. He died in December 1947, at the age of 81.

Wu was described as short and stout. Even in the summer he was in the habit of wearing long gowns with wide sleeves, a mode of dress which, among the people of Shansi, earned him the nickname of "Big-sleeves Wu."

As scholar and historian, Wu T'ing-hsieh followed Ch'ing traditions of scholarship in both methodology and presentation. His principal scholarly contribution was the systematic arrangement of widely scattered data into chronologically ordered compilations which greatly facilitated the research of later scholars. Most of Wu's work was in the field of history, ranging from supplements to the dynastic histories to a study of the Sino-Russian boundary and a chronology of important events in his native Kiangsu province. He prepared a list of his writings and compilations which, though not complete, included 51 titles; some 20 of these works dealt with the Ch'ing period. Not all of these titles were published, and many of his early publications were issued in limited editions or in mimeographed form.

Among Wu's better known works were his chronological tables (nien-piao) of military governors under the Chin, Eastern Chin, Northern Wei, T'ang, Sung, Southern Sung,

Liao, Chin, Yüan, and Ming dynasties. Originally published as the *Li-tai fang-chen nien-piao*, these ten works were included in the *Erh-shih-wu-shih pu-pien* (1936–37), a collection of materials supplementing the 25 dynastic histories which was published by the K'ai-ming Bookstore at Shanghai. One of these tables, the *Chin fang-chen nien-piao*, also appeared in the collectanea *Liao-hai ts'ung shu* (1935), published at Dairen. While serving in the bureau of compilation of Ch'ing history, Wu was chief editor of the piao [tables] section of the *Ch'ing-shih kao*. He compiled useful charts of high officials in the metropolitan and provincial administrations.

At the invitation of Hsü Shih-ch'ang (q.v.), Wu assisted also in the compilation of a local history of Manchuria. A segment of this projected work was his *Tung-san-sheng yen-ko piao*, which was privately printed by Hsü Shih-ch'ang at Tientsin in 1922. Another of Wu's works, a chronology of Tuan Ch'i-jui (q.v.) entitled *Ho-fei chih-cheng nien-p'u ch'u-kao* (1937), was received with unfavorable criticism. Wu seems to have been aware of its shortcomings, both in quality and comprehensiveness, for he included in the title the words "ch'u-kao" [preliminary draft].

After Wu's death, the national history compilation bureau at Nanking printed two of his works in its official publication, the *Kuo-shih-kuan kuan-k'an*. These were an autobiographical chronology, the *Ching-mu tzu-ting nien-p'u* (November 1948), which ended with the year 1937; and a chronology of railroad development in China from 1864 to 1932, entitled *T'ieh-lu ta-shih chi* (January 1949).

Wu Yao-tsung   吳 耀 宗
West. Y. T. Wu

Wu Yao-tsung (c. 1893–), known as Y. T. Wu, head of the publication department of the YMCA in China in the 1930's and 1940's. Beginning in 1950 he led the so-called Three-Self Reform Movement of Protestantism in the People's Republic of China.

Little is known about Y. T. Wu's family background or early life except that he was born in Canton. From 1908 to 1913 he received his secondary education at the Customs College in Peking. He then was employed for seven years in the Chinese Customs Service at Canton, Newchwang (Yingkow), and Peking.

A major turn in Y. T. Wu's career was made with his conversion to Christianity in 1920. He was baptized by an American missionary, Rowland Cross, at Peking. Wu then began his long career with the Young Men's Christian Association as one of its secretaries assigned to work among students in Peking. At this time, he was also an active member of the Mi-shih Chinese Christian Church, which had been developed by Ch'eng Ching-yi (q.v.) into a strongly independent congregation. The church attracted a large number of Chinese Protestant laymen who preferred association with it rather than with one of the many mission-related churches in Peking. In 1921 Wu was also appointed executive secretary of the Christian Student Work Union.

Y. T. Wu traveled to the United States for study at Union Theological Seminary at New York in the autumn of 1924. In February 1925 he also enrolled as a graduate student in philosophy at Columbia University. He was strongly influenced by the social gospel movement. After the completion of his thesis, which was entitled "William James's Doctrine of Religious Belief," he received the M.A. degree for his combined studies at the two institutions in October 1927. Wu was not ordained a minister, however, and he worked entirely as a layman in later years.

Upon his return to China in 1927, Wu became a secretary of the student division of the YMCA's National Committee, and from 1930 to 1932 he was the student division's executive secretary. In 1932 he was appointed editor in chief of the Association Press, the publication department of the National Committee of the YMCA in Shanghai. The press had been developed by H. L. Zia (Hsieh Hung-lai, q.v.) into one of the most effective publishing houses of the International YMCA, and in China it was the foremost publisher of liberal Protestant Christian literature during a period of steadily increasing demand for translations of Western works as well as for original texts by Chinese leaders.

Y. T. Wu was known for his zealous concern for translation of works in English on Christian thought, ethics, social problems, and institutional development. Eugene E. Barnett, for many years the associate general secretary of the YMCA in China, spoke highly of his careful planning in the publication field. By 1940 the Association Press had completed a three-year plan of translation and production and had launched a five-year program for supplying books and pamphlets in translation and for the promotion of books on Christianity.

During this period, Wu was also the author or co-author of many articles in Chinese Christian periodicals. He edited a short volume, *The Jesus I Know*, with contributions by himself and several other Chinese Christians; the Association Press published the Chinese version in 1932, and an English edition was published privately by the Christian leader T. Z. Koo. Wu's volume *She-hui fu-yin* [the social gospel], published in 1935, reflected his sustained concern with the application of Christianity to rectification of economic and social injustice and his long-range commitment to social progress. During the 1930's Wu was also active as translator of the *Autobiography* of Gandhi (*Kan-ti tzu-chuan*, 1933), of *Pacifism and Social Reconstruction* (*Wei-ai chu-i yü she-hui kai-tsao*, 1934), and of John Dewey's *A Common Faith* (*K'o-hsueh ti tsung-chiao-kuang*, 1936).

In the early period of his career with the YMCA, Y. T. Wu was strongly pacifist in outlook. He was an early member of the Fellowship of Reconciliation in China and was for some time chairman of that group and editor of its magazine. But the Japanese invasion of Manchuria beginning in 1931 and continued Japanese aggression in China in later years changed his outlook. In 1937 Wu traveled to England, where he spoke as a representative from China at meetings of three Christian organizations: the World Committee of the YMCA, the executive committee of the World Student Christian Federation, and the Oxford Conference of the World Council of Churches on the Life and Work of the Church. He then went to New York, where he again studied for a period in late 1937 under a mission fellowship at Union Theological Seminary. There Wu was exposed to the political and social activism enunciated by Reinhold Niebuhr, professor of applied Christianity. After his return to China, Wu was a delegate in 1938 to the Madras (India) Conference of the International Missionary Council.

During the Sino-Japanese war, Y. T. Wu continued to direct the publication department

of the YMCA, which had been moved to Chengtu in Szechwan. Despite wartime stringencies, he succeeded in publishing a large number of books, magazines, and articles, many of them focused on the acute international and social problems of the time. His personal attitude, reflecting deep concern with the inequities which he saw in wartime China, was marked by increased disenchantment with Chiang Kai-shek and the Kuomintang and by growing support of the political and social policies of the Chinese Communist party. Serious interest in Marxism-Leninism led him to attempt to formulate a Christian response to the radical challenges raised by socialist theory. In 1940 he edited *Chi-tu-chiao yü hsin Chung-kuo* [Christianity and the new China], a symposium in which his own contribution was important. A major statement of Wu's views came with publication of *Mei-yu jen k'an-chien-kuo shang-ti* [no man hath seen God] in 1943, a significant effort to square Christian precepts and devotion with Marxist understanding of human society and its requirements. Because of his critical and outspoken views, he was placed under surveillance by the National Government security police. After the Japanese surrender and his return to Shanghai, he was a member of a group of delegates from the Shanghai Federation of People's Organizations which was assaulted by a mob in June 1946 as it was traveling to Nanking to protest continuation of the civil war between the Nationalist and Communist forces.

Y. T. Wu was a member of the Chinese delegation to the World Conference of Christian Youth held at Oslo, Norway, in July 1947, and in August of that year he attended the YMCA's World Alliance meeting at Edinburgh, Scotland. Upon his return to China, Wu wrote an article in which he charged that a world-wide revolution was developing in religion as well as in economics. This article, "The Present-Day Tragedy of Christianity," appeared in the 10 April 1948 issue of the well-known Chinese Christian periodical *T'ien-feng*, of which Wu was editor. In it he equated the downfall of capitalism with that of Protestantism. "Historically speaking," he wrote, "the religious and the industrial revolutions are just two expressions of the same society. The religious revolution created Protestantism, and the industrial revolution created capitalism . . . ." Because the two institutions are so intimately related, Wu argued, contemporary Protestantism is in effect a crusade to uphold capitalism, and the United States, as the foremost capitalist nation, is the leading force behind Protestantism. Wu's article aroused such widespread indignation, particularly from the Christian Literature Society, which was one of the sponsoring institutions of *T'ien-feng*, that Wu was forced to resign his position.

When the People's Republic of China was established in October 1949, Y. T. Wu, as one of China's foremost activist Christians, enthusiastically welcomed the new regime. He participated in the establishment of the Central People's Government and held a number of posts in the new political structure: member of the National Committee of the Chinese People's Political Consultative Conference, the political and legal affairs committee of the Government Administration Council, the East China Military and Administrative Committee, and the executive committee of the Sino-Soviet Friendship Association. During the 1950's he frequently traveled to Europe and other parts of Asia for meetings of the World Peace Council. At various times he was also an official of the Chinese People's Relief Administration and the Chinese People's Association for Cultural Relations with Foreign Countries. He was a delegate to the National People's Congress after 1954.

By far the most important role of Y. T. Wu in the People's Republic of China, however, was as a dominant figure in the institutional realignment of the Protestant Church. In a sense, his 1948 article on "The Present-Day Tragedy of Christianity" foreshadowed the pattern of change after the consolidation of Communist authority in China. In July 1949, at the request of the editors of the *Ta Kung Pao*, he produced a three-part article, "The Reformation of Christianity: On the Awakening of Christians," designed to give more definite form to criticism of Christianity and Christian missions which that newspaper had received in letters from readers. In this article, Wu alleged a close connection between missionary work and imperialism in China and charged that American and British imperialism had utilized the Chinese Christian Church to further their political purposes. As society progressed from feudalism to capitalism to socialism, Wu argued, so must the Christian Church pass through the stages of Roman Catholicism and Protestantism to become a reformed socialist body. To achieve this third stage, the church must disassociate itself from the capitalist and imperialist order. "Protestantism today," Wu wrote, "is still living on capitalism, and separation from it will spell the death of Protestantism economically and materially. But this death is precisely its rebirth."

Beginning in 1950 Y. T. Wu became the leading Chinese Christian in the major development affecting Protestantism in China under Communism, the so-called Three-Self Reform Movement. That movement officially began in July 1950 with the proclamation of a "Christian Manifesto," a document prepared largely by Wu and signed by 40 prominent Chinese Christian leaders. The manifesto, entitled "Direction of Endeavor for Chinese Christians in the Construction of the New China," had as its principal objective the cooperative participation of Christian organizations in the Chinese Communist program for national development. Chinese Christian churches were to develop three definite characteristics: self-propagation, self-government, and self-support. These objectives had long been promoted by many Westerners in the missionary enterprise, but they now were enforced in nationalist and Communist definitions. Christian leaders were thus to help the Communist party liquidate the missionary enterprise in China, cut off the dependence of Chinese churches upon foreign funds and foreign personnel, and set up a new central organization designed to link support of the new regime with patriotism. It was later reported that the 1950 manifesto had gained more than 400,000 Protestant Christian signatures in China as a result of a mass campaign for public endorsement.

A second important event in the evolution of the Three-Self Movement was the April 1951 meeting in Peking of Chinese Christian leaders with Chou En-lai (q.v.), premier of the Central People's Government and high-ranking official of the Chinese Communist party. Y. T. Wu became head of a 25-member preparatory council which was to direct the work of the movement until a national conference of Christians could organize a new governing body. This national conference, with Wu as chairman, met in Peking in July 1954. At that time Wu made a report emphasizing that though so-called imperialist influences still remained in Chinese Protestantism, the churches were demonstrating a new spirit of "Love-country Love-church." The national Three-Self Reform Committee, headed by Wu, was established. This committee, which ostensibly received authority through a mandate from the Chinese churches, became the organization, responsible to the government authorities at Peking, for policy formulation and executive control of Protestant churches in the People's Republic of China. In March 1956 an enlarged meeting of the Three-Self Committee was held at Peking. Two years later worship in all Protestant denominations was unified. In 1961 Wu again presided over the National Conference of Christian Churches in China.

In addition to responsibilities as chairman of the Three-Self Committee, Wu also held other posts in the religious field: president of the board of directors of the Nanking Theological Seminary, and moderator of the Church of Christ in China, the largest of the Protestant groups. His sustained effort to relate Christian doctrine with Marxist presuppositions was reflected in his *Chi-tu-chiao chiang-hua* [talks on the Christian faith], a volume including 11 earlier articles from *T'ien-feng*, published in 1950, and in other works dealing with dialectical materialism and with the Christian reform movement.

The publication department of the YMCA, in which Wu continued to serve as chief editor of the Association Press, took part in the Three-Self Movement by issuing a series of publications entitled "Books for the New Age." After 1950 Wu continued to produce many articles dealing with both religious and political topics. Three of these, linked by the theme of "freedom through truth," appeared in *T'ien-feng* in 1954 and dealt with faith and works, the death of Jesus, and God as the source of all good. In a later article, "My Recognition of the Communist Party," which appeared in *T'ien-feng* on 30 June 1958, Wu emphasized that the Chinese Communist party "does not believe in religion, but it protects religion and respects religious faith." In later articles, some appearing in the official *Jen-min jih-pao* [people's daily] in the early 1960's, he continued his vigorous attacks on the alleged imperialist aspects of the American Protestant missionary movement in China.

Because of Y. T. Wu's sustained effort to relate Christianity to practical social problems and to Marxism, he was a controversial figure in the eyes of Westerners in the YMCA and the Protestant mission effort in China. Most, however, respected his Christian faith and personal sincerity. Frank W. Price, a veteran American missionary, commented in his book *China: Twilight or Dawn?* of 1948, that "Y. T. Wu is like an Old Testament prophet; his soul is seared by the social sins and injustices that he sees around him, and his words, though quietly spoken and written, lash and cut. He has made a thorough study of socialist and communist theories and seeks a truly Christian answer to their challenge; some, therefore, think of him as a radical. But he is also mystical and a man of prayer."

Y. T. Wu and his wife, Yang Su-lan, a physician, were known to have two children, a son and a daughter.

Wu Yi-fang　　　　　　吳 貽 芳

Wu Yi-fang (26 January 1893–), distinguished Christian educator who was the first woman college president in China. She headed Ginling College from 1928 to 1952.

Although her family's native place was Hangchow, Chekiang, Wu Yi-fang was born in Wuchang, Hupeh, where her father, Wu Shou-hsün (T. Hsiao-ying), was stationed as a Ch'ing government official. She was the third of four children, and she received her early education at home with her elder brother. In 1904, at the age of 11 sui, she accompanied her elder sister to Hangchow, where they enrolled at a newly established girls school. Two years later, they went to Shanghai and enrolled at the Morning Star School, a Catholic institution for non-Christian pupils, but they returned home after only one term to study English and mathematics with a private tutor. In the spring of 1908 they entered the Laura Haygood Girls School, a Methodist institution at Soochow, but they returned home in 1910 when their father died. The family then moved to Hangchow. At the time of the revolution in 1911 they joined some relatives in Shanghai. Wu Yi-fang's elder brother died suddenly, and her mother and elder sister died about a month later. Wu Yi-fang and her ten-year-old sister went to Hangchow to live with the family of her maternal aunt. In 1913 she attended the Hangchow Union Girls School as a special student. The following year, her aunt and uncle moved to Peking, and Wu taught at the Girls Normal School. In 1915 they went to Shanghai, and in February 1916 Wu enrolled at Ginling College, at Nanking, thus becoming a member of the first class at the first college for women in China.

At Ginling, Wu Yi-fang became a convert to Christianity and joined the Methodist Church in 1918. She was graduated in 1919 and was offered an assistantship at Ginling, but she declined the offer to become head of the English department at the Peking Higher Normal School for Girls. She remained there until 1922, when she was awarded a Barbour scholarship for study at the University of Michigan. She received an M.S. in biology in 1924 and a Ph.D. in 1928; her dissertation was entitled "A Contribution to the Biology of Simulium." During this period she also served as chairman of the Chinese Student Christian Association in the United States (1924–25) and as vice chairman of the Chinese Student Alliance in North America (1925–26).

Wu Yi-fang returned to China in 1928 to become president of Ginling College. She was the first Chinese woman to hold a college presidency. In the next nine years the campus and the curriculum were enlarged, and the enrollment was doubled. Wu proved herself a capable administrator and a determined and resourceful educator. She also became increasingly involved in international good-will and national Christian work. She served as chairman of the National Christian Council in China in 1935 and in 1938–48, and she was a Chinese delegate to the Institute of Pacific Relations conferences in the United States in 1929, 1931, and 1933. Also in 1933 she was a delegate to the International Congress of Women and the United Foreign Missions Conference in the United States and to the meeting of the International Missionary Council in England. In 1936 she represented Ginling at the Harvard tercentenary celebrations.

After the Sino-Japanese war began in July 1937, Ginling College was forced to close. Temporary arrangements were made for students to study in other Chinese cities. In 1938 Wu Yi-fang collaborated wih Madame Chiang Kai-shek (Soong Mei-ling, q.v.) in founding the women's advisory committee of the New Life Movement, which coordinated women's activities and assisted war orphans. When the National Government moved to Chungking, Wu reopened Ginling on the West China Union University campus in Chengtu, which Ginling shared with three other refugee colleges throughout the war. Despite difficult wartime conditions, the student body grew to 300. The students put their studies to practical use by setting up nutrition, sanitation, and child care projects in Szechwan. A record of the war years in west China, China Rediscovers Her West, was published in 1940. Wu edited this symposium with the American Presbyterian missionary Frank W. Price and wrote one of its chapters, "Women in the War."

In 1938 Wu Yi-fang was appointed to the People's Political Council at Chungking, and in 1941, when Chou En-lai (q.v.) withdrew, she was elected to its five-member presidium. In December 1938 she led China's delegation to the International Missionary Council Assembly at Madras, India, and she was elected vice chairman of the International Missionary Council. She visited the United States late in 1942 as the only woman member of an educational mission studying international relations and postwar reconstruction. Before her return to China in 1943, she was awarded an honorary LL.D. degree by Smith College, which for many years had helped support Ginling College. Throughout the war years, she sat on advisory boards, conferred with Szechwan government officials, and received a steady procession of government officials and war committee workers who sought her advice and support for their projects.

Wu Yi-fang was the only woman member of the Chinese delegation to the United Nations Conference on International Organization at San Francisco in 1945. While in California, she received honorary degrees from Mills College and the University of Southern California. Upon her return to China, she undertook the onerous task of moving Ginling College back to its Nanking campus. In 1946 she was a member of the National Assembly, which met to draw up a constitution. As the Nationalist-Communist civil war increased in intensity, student unrest in Nanking mounted. Wu urged her students to attend to their studies and did all that she could to keep Ginling running smoothly. When the Chinese Communist forces occupied Nanking in April 1949, Wu formed a Nanking citizens' protection committee to maintain order during the transfer of power. Although many Chinese and Western friends urged her to leave the mainland, she refused to abandon Ginling and chose to remain in Nanking.

In September 1949 Wu Yi-fang attended the Chinese People's Political Consultative Conference at Peiping. After the Central People's Government was established, she was named to the editorial board of the English-language periodical *China Reconstructs*. Upon her return to Nanking she began working to change the curriculum and the administrative organization of Ginling so that the new regime would accept the college. Ginling operated much as it always had until 1952, when the Peking authorities decided to combine it with the University of Nanking to form National Ginling University. Wu was appointed vice president of the new institution. In 1956 she became vice chairman of the National Christian Council, vice president of Nanking Normal College, and commissioner of education for Kiangsu province. The following February, she was appointed vice chairman of the Kiangsu provincial government. In September 1957 she received an additional appointment as an executive committee member of the Women's Federation of the People's Republic of China. She also served as a delegate to the first and second National People's congresses and as a delegate to conferences abroad, including the World Peace Conference in Finland in 1955 and the Fourth Congress of the International Federation of Democratic Women in Vienna in 1958.

Throughout her career Wu Yi-fang played a leading role in improving the lot of Chinese women. She consistently upheld the rights of her sex, saying that "if a Chinese woman is well trained and qualified, she may compete equally with men for any position from the highest government office down. Only as women become educated can we expect them to step into their places as leaders." Wu's work as an outstanding educator, stateswoman, and Christian leader provided many new opportunities for Chinese women.

Wu Yü   吳虞

Wu Yü (1872–1949), scholar and poet whose intensely anti-Confucian writings contributed to the revolution in Chinese thought at the time of the May Fourth Movement. He taught at Peking and Szechwan universities.

Little is known about Wu Yü's family background or early life. In his youth he apparently received a traditional education in the Chinese classics. After the death of his mother, Wu married in 1893 and took up residence apart from his father. Part of the time he lived in his own establishment in Chengtu, which he named Ai-chih lu; at other times he resided on part of the family estate situated in a secluded area some 15 miles north of the city. In the years that followed, he devoted himself to supervising the farm tenants and to pursuit of literary and historical studies, becoming particularly interested in poetry and in the philosophy of Lao-tzu and Chuang-tzu. Wu came to know the scholar Liao P'ing (q.v.) and became familiar with the teachings of the celebrated Hunanese scholar Wang K'ai-yün (q.v.), one-time head of the Tsun-ching Academy in Chengtu.

Stimulated by the new ideas that spread throughout China during the Hundred Days Reform of 1898, Wu Yü's attention turned to the world outside of China. Late in 1905 he left Chengtu to study law and political science in Japan. By this time he had grown impatient with certain aspects of Chinese social life, particularly the family system, which were still governed by Confucian ethical sanctions. In 1906, while in Japan, he composed a series of verses entitled *Chung-yeh pu-mei o-ch'eng* in which he expressed criticism of the traditional Confucian political and social order in China.

After he returned to China, Wu Yü continued his studies privately in his native province. Under the influence of such Western authors as Montesquieu, Herbert Spencer, John Stuart Mill, and Edward Jenks, and of the Japanese scholars Endo Ryūkichi and Kubo Tenzui, Wu devoted himself to a comparative study of the legal institutions of China and the West. He examined the classical Chinese texts of the books of rites and the law codes of the T'ang and

Ch'ing dynasties, as well as the literature available in Chinese dealing with Western constitutions and penal codes. As a result of these comparative studies, he concluded that, in contrast to the liberty and freedom existing in the West, inequality and rule by force had been the principles governing the state and society of China for 2,000 years. In Wu's opinion, the responsibility for the unfortunate conditions in twentieth-century China rested entirely upon Confucius and the Confucians.

Although Western concepts were important in the shaping of Wu Yü's attitudes, those concepts served more to confirm than to inspire his deep opposition to Confucianism. Essentially his thinking remained rooted in Chinese philosophical traditions. To support his anti-Confucian convictions, he relied largely upon the traditional Chinese opponents of the Confucians—Mo Ti, the Legalists Shang Yang and Han Fei-tzu, and particularly the Taoists Lao-tzu and Chuang-tzu. Wu also sought confirmation for his views in the arguments of later critics of Confucianism, such as the later Han sceptic Wang Ch'ung and the T'ang dynasty critic of historiography Liu Chih-chi. Most important for Wu was the heterodox late Ming scholar Li Chih. During his lifetime, Li Chih had enjoyed fame and popular favor, but toward the end of his life his writings had been banned as "heretical" by the state-supported Confucian orthodoxy. Few of his works survived the literary inquisitions of the eighteenth century. In Li Chih, Wu Yü found a kindred spirit whose arguments could be used to buttress his own anti-Confucian position. Not long before the 1911 revolution, a newspaper in Chengtu published some of Wu's writings in which there appeared quotations from Li Chih. The Ch'ing government ordered Wu's writings banned and ordered his arrest. He escaped arrest by leaving Chengtu and hiding in a nearby rural area.

Late in November 1911, when the government officials in Chengtu threw their support to the republican revolution, Wu Yü returned to the city and again published some of his writings. In his poetry as in his prose, he continued to express anti-Confucian sentiments. In 1911, for example, he published a collection of 96 poems, *Hsin-hai tsa-shih*, which clearly revealed his antipathy toward orthodox Confucianism. The forces of tradition remained powerful in the remote and relatively isolated province of Szechwan, and the anti-Confucian tone of Wu's writings aroused the antagonism of conservative and influential scholars of the region. In 1913 a periodical which had published some of Wu's works was banned, and for several years thereafter no local newspapers or magazines in Chengtu ventured to print articles disparaging the Confucian doctrines.

Although denied publication, Wu persevered privately in elaborating his arguments against the traditions of Confucianism. During the early years of the republic he composed a number of essays attacking Confucianism as the perpetrator of the evils of autocratic government and a fixed class sysem. Among his works of this period was a biography of Li Chih, *Li Cho-wu pieh-chuan*, which Wu was eventually able to publish in 1916 in the *Chin-pu tsa-chih* at Shanghai. By drawing public attention to the life of Li Chih, Wu was in part responsible for a revival of interest in this long-forgotten figure. Li Chih's tomb outside the north gate of T'ung-chou, east of Peking, was refurbished; some of his works later were reissued; and he became the subject of a series of scholarly studies in China, Japan, and the West.

In 1916 Wu came upon a series of anti-Confucian articles published by Ch'en Tu-hsiu (q.v.) in the *Hsin ch'ing-nien* [new youth]. These articles had been written in response to the proposals of the Confucian scholar K'ang Yu-wei (q.v.) that the republican government adopt Confucianism as the state religion of China. Wu Yü wrote to Ch'en about the writings that he had been unable to publish in Chengtu. In this way Wu became a contributor to the *Hsin ch'ing-nien*, and his articles appeared in five successive issues of this magazine in March–July 1917. The climax of Wu's attack on Confucianism was reached in November 1919, at the height of the May Fourth Movement, when his essay "Ch'ih-jen yü li-chiao" [cannibalism and the doctrine of ritual propriety] appeared in the *Hsin ch'ing-nien*.

In 1917, at the invitation of Ts'ai Yuan-p'ei (q.v.), Ch'en Tu-hsiu had become dean of the College of Letters of Peking University. In 1919 Wu Yü also accepted a call to join the university's faculty of literature. He remained there until 1925, when he returned to Chengtu. About 1926, he became a member of the faculty of Chengtu University, one of the three institutions which merged to form National Szechwan University in 1931.

After his return to Chengtu, Wu maintained his uncompromising attitude toward Confucianism. In 1928, in an essay entitled "My Opinions on the Question of Confucian Worship," he accused such intellectuals as Chang Ping-lin and Liang Ch'i-ch'ao (qq.v.) of softening their former anti-Confucian views. In 1932 he urged the graduates of National Szechwan University to disregard the Confucian humbug of "virtue" and "righteousness" and to undertake such useful pursuits as enriching the nation, strengthening the country's military power, and protecting the common people. Wu was often a thorn in the flesh of the ultra-conservative Confucian scholars who, because of their connections with local military leaders, were able to exert considerable influence upon the educational policies of the universities in Szechwan. In the face of such opposition, Wu retired to a private residence, which he named the I-yin-t'ang, situated in the former Manchu quarter of Chengtu. There, until Wu's death in 1949, a visitor would find the rooms of his small establishment crowded with books arranged in meticulous order; and would see Wu Yü himself, a gaunt figure with white hair and a thin white beard, leaning on a tall bamboo staff, his outward appearance calling to mind the Taoist hermits of old. Inwardly, too, Wu's thinking had been molded by the Taoist philosophy, but his pugnacious opposition to Confucianism indicated that he did not interpret Taoism as a purely passive philosophy.

Wu Yü wrote his many essays attacking Confucianism and the traditional moral values in a simple but eloquent style. He held that Confucius and Confucianism should be judged pragmatically by the political and social consequences of the Confucian doctrine, not theoretically by the ethical principles articulated in the *Analects*. The essence of the Confucian doctrine, according to Wu, lay not in the *Analects* but in the code of ritual propriety (li), which separated members of society and of the family into two classes; those who ruled and those who obeyed. Confucianism was based upon a system of inequality and lack of freedom, whereby the head of the state and the head of the family possessed absolute authority over those under them. In his essay entitled "Shuo hsiao" Wu was particularly severe in his condemnation of the Confucian virtue of obedience towards the elders: "[The Confucians] teach obedience toward the elders and hence they teach loyalty, too. This means that they instruct people to be humble and meek; to let themselves be led about by the nose by their superiors and to be loath to rebel against those above them. They have converted China into a 'huge factory to manufacture docile people.' This has been the function of the word, obedience toward the elders." Wu Yü inveighed against the past 2,000 years of China's history as an age which, under the influence of Confucius, had been characterized by barbarous cruelty and rule by force. In one passage he compared Confucius with the robber Chih, a famous figure of the *Chuang-tzu*: "The robber Chih was a menace to only one period; the robber Confucius has been a source of suffering for ten thousand generations." Wu sought to show that the lofty ethical precepts of the Confucian teaching often served merely as a cloak to hide unbridled selfishness: the august majesty of the emperor and the awesome authority invested in his officials afforded excellent opportunities for self-aggrandizement in wealth and power; the reverence for elders, esteemed as the foundation of the traditional family system, allowed the family patriarch to oppress and exploit the younger members of his family; and the general assumption that women were inferiors of men, illustrated in the institution of concubinage, opened the door to concupiscence on the part of the male.

Wu Yü's attack upon what he regarded as the falseness of the traditional social system and its moral values reached its peak intensity in his 1919 essay "Ch'ih-jen yü li-chiao." Drawing inspiration from "A Madman's Diary," a famous short story by Lu Hsün (Chou Shu-jen, q.v.), Wu argued that beneath the cloak of Confucian decorum, the upper classes of China had been living off the flesh of the common people. Citing several historical sources, Wu sought to reveal how Confucius's teachings of ritual propriety had led to actual instances of cannibalism among his followers.

Through his writings published in the *Hsin ch'ing-nien*, Wu Yü helped turn the minds of Chinese students and younger intellectuals against the Confucian traditions, then still held in high esteem by many of China's government leaders and military rulers. Hu Shih (q.v.)

compared Wu to the Peking street-cleaners who wet down the dusty streets with water ladled from water-carts, only to have the dust stirred up again when the water dried. To Hu Shih, Wu was the "street-cleaner of the Chinese world of thought," who tried to lay the dust of Confucian refuse with water of enlightenment; for this unrewarding task he was berated by the people of the old school because he failed to appreciate the delectable fragrance of Confucian refuse. Tired and discouraged, Wu Yü wanted to give up his work as hopeless, when suddenly at the other end of the street he saw another group of street-cleaners (Ch'en Tu-hsiu and his followers) performing the same task, and from this he gained fresh courage to continue his work.

A collection of Wu Yü's essays was published in 1921 in Shanghai as the *Wu Yü wen-lu;* in 1936 this collection was republished in Chengtu by Wu himself in a traditional woodblock edition. Also in 1936 he printed a woodblock edition of a small collection of writings, *Wu Yü wen pieh-lu.* In 1937 a collection of his essays and other writings was published as *Wu Yü wen hsü-lu.* Although a great many of his essays were written in pai-hua [the vernacular], Wu's poems were all in the classical style. A collection of his verse, *Ch'iu-shui chi,* appeared in 1913.

In 1893 Wu Yü married Tseng Lan (1876–1917; T. Chung-shu; H. Hsiang-tsu), a daughter of a chü-jen in Chengtu. She shared her husband's interest in literature and Taoist philosophy, as well as his anti-Confucian leanings. She wrote many essays, one of which, "Nü-ch'üan p'ing-i," on the subject of equal rights for women, appeared in the *Hsin ch'ing-nien* in June 1917; other essays were published in the *Fu-nü tsa-chih* and the *Hsiao-shuo yüeh-pao.* Her collected writings were published as the *Ting-sheng-hui-shih i-kao.* The marriage resulted in one son, who died as a child, and four daughters. Wu Yung-ch'üan, the younger brother of Wu Yü, studied law in Japan and was a professor and dean of the faculty of law at National Szechwan University during the 1930's and 1940's.

Wu Yü-chang   吳 玉 章
Alt. Yung-shan   永 珊

Wu Yü-chang (1878–14 December 1966), republican revolutionary and educator who later became a Chinese Communist official. He was known for his leadership of the movement to romanize the Chinese written language.

Born in Yunghsien, Szechwan, Wu Yü-chang was the second of three sons born into a well-to-do gentry family. After receiving his early education in the Chinese classics, in 1903 he went to Japan to enroll at the Shimbu Gakkō [military preparatory academy]. He joined the T'ung-meng-hui when it was established in 1905, and two years later he began publishing a journal, *Szechwan.* The Japanese authorities banned the journal in 1908 and sentenced Wu to six months in jail. He avoided imprisonment because of his student status. In 1910 Wu was associated with the attempt made by Wang Ching-wei (q.v.) to assassinate the Manchu prince regent. After the plot went awry and Wang was arrested, Wu went to Peking in an unsuccessful attempt to rescue Wang. Early in 1911 Wu was in Canton working with Huang Hsing (q.v.) on plans for the 27 April revolt which became known as the "Three Twenty-nine Revolution" or the Huang-hua-kang uprising. When it failed, Wu escaped to Japan, where he tried to secure arms for revolutionaries. He returned to his native Szechwan in May to head a group of young revolutionaries which proclaimed its independence of Manchu rule in September. When the revolution began in October, he joined the forces of Hsiung K'o-wu (q.v.).

With the establishment of the republic, Wu Yü-chang became a secretary in the presidential office of Sun Yat-sen and a Szechwan delegate to Sun's headquarters. He later returned to Szechwan to assist in the reorganization of the provincial government. After the so-called second revolution of 1913 (*see* Li Lieh-chün), he fled to France. In 1915 he helped establish the Societé Franco-Chinois d'Education and the Societé Rationelle des Etudiants-Travailleurs Chinois en France, or Ch'in-kung chien-hsueh hui (for details, *see* Li Shih-tseng). In 1916 he returned to China with another leader of the work-study movement, Ts'ai Yuan-p'ei (q.v.). From 1917 to 1922 Wu worked in the military government at Canton as a representative of Szechwan. He then became principal of a higher normal school in Chengtu, the predecessor of Szechwan University. By this time, his political sympathies must have moved far to the left, for in 1923 he helped organize the Chung-kuo ch'ing-nien kung-ch'an-tang, an independent Communist youth group in Szechwan.

At the First National Congress of the Kuomintang, held at Canton in January 1924, Wu Yü-chang served as secretary to Sun Yat-sen. In 1925, at the behest of the Szechwanese Communist Chao Shih-yen (q.v.), Wu and his independent Communist group formally joined the Chinese Communist party. For the next two years, Wu was active in Szechwan as head of the province's branch of the Kuomintang and as the founder of a Sino-French school for revolutionary workers who wanted to study in France. In 1926 he served as secretary general of the Second National Congress of the Kuomintang, at which he was elected to the Central Executive Committee. He also taught at the Peasant Movement Training Institute, of which Mao Tse-tung was principal. In July, when the Northern Expedition began, he went to Canton, and late in 1926 he accompanied the leftist leaders of the National Government to Wuhan. After participating in the short-lived Communist takeover of Nanchang (*see* Ho Lung; Yeh T'ing) in August 1927, he fled to the Soviet Union.

From 1928 to 1930 Wu Yü-chang studied in Moscow at the Communist University for Toilers of the East. He soon became interested in the work being done on the romanization of the Chinese language by Ch'ü Ch'iu-pai (q.v.) and the Russian Sinologist Kolokolov, a teacher at the university (for details, *see* Ch'ü Ch'iu-pai). In 1930 Wu went to Vladivostok to teach at the Far Eastern Workers School of Leninism. He wrote an essay on "The Principles and Regulations of the Chinese Latinized New Written Language" which was used as the opening declaration at the First Conference on the Romanization of Chinese, held at Vladivostok in September 1931. By the time the conference opened, Wu was in Moscow launching the *Chiu-kuo shih-pao* [national salvation times], a Chinese Communist newspaper which was published in Moscow from 1931 to 1935 and in Paris from 1935 to 1937. In the 1931–35 period Wu seems to have divided his time between Paris and Moscow. He is known to have attended the 1935 Comintern congress in Moscow, and in 1936 he taught at Far Eastern University in the Russian capital.

After the Sino-Japanese war began in July 1937, Wu Yü-chang was sent to Paris to do propaganda work on behalf of the Kuomintang-Communist united front against Japan. After attending the Anti-Aggression Conference at London in February 1938, he made his way back to China, where he became a member of the People's Political Council. Soon after the council's first meeting, he went to Yenan to recuperate from an illness. From 1941 to 1945 he served at Yenan as president of the Lu Hsün Academy of Arts, the School for the New Written Language, and Northwest Associated University. He also chaired the Yenan branch of the Sino-Soviet Cultural Association and the cultural association of the Shensi-Kansu-Ninghsia Border Region. In addition, he helped found the Sin Wenz Society in 1940 to promote the new alphabetized Chinese system of writing, and he published an edition of the Chinese Communist party's official organ, the *Chieh-fang jih-pao* [liberation daily]. In 1945 he was elected to the Central Committee of the Chinese Communist party.

In September 1949 Wu Yü-chang was a delegate to the Chinese People's Political Consultative Conference, which prepared the way for the formal establishment of the People's Republic of China. When the Central People's Government was inaugurated in October, he received membership in the Government Council, the political and legal affairs committee of the Government Administration Council, and the Sino-Soviet Friendship Association. With the governmental reorganization in 1954, he became a member of the administrative committee of the Central School of Administrative and Legal Cadres and a Standing Committee member of the National People's Congress. Throughout this period, Wu's greatest usefulness to the Chinese Communist party was in the areas of education and culture. He was president of North China University in 1948-49 and president of the Chinese People's University from 1950 until his death. In addition, he was honorary president of the All-China Federation of Scientific Societies and the Chinese Association for the Advancement of Science and Technology. In 1954 he became a member of the philosophy and social sciences department of the Chinese Academy of Sciences. He chaired the All-China Educational Workers Trade Union and served on the executive committee of the All-China Federation of Trade Unions. Wu maintained his interest in the romanization of the Chinese language, serving as vice chairman of the Government Administration Council's committee for the reform of the Chinese written language in 1951–54. Wu participated in the 1961 celebrations in Peking that marked the fiftieth anniversary of the Wuchang revolt of October 1911. An English-language version of his short book, *The Revolution of 1911: A Great Democratic Revolution of China*, was published by the Foreign Languages Press at Peking in 1962. Wu died in Peking on 14 December 1966, at the age of 88 sui.

Little is known about Wu Yü-chang's private life except that he married in 1896 and had two children.

GENERAL BIOGRAPHICAL
REFERENCE WORKS

Biographies of Prominent Chinese, ed. by A. R. Burt, J. B. Powell, and Carl Crow. Shanghai, no date.

Chang Yüeh-jui. *Chin-jen chuan-chi wen-hsüan*. Changsha, 1938.

張越瑞。近人傳記文選。

Chao Chia-chin and Chang Sheng-chih. *Ming-jen chuan-chi*. Hong Kong, 1947.

趙家縉。張聲智。名人傳記。

Chin-shih jen-wu chih, ed. by Chin Liang. Taipei, 1955.

近世人物志。金梁。

Chin-tai Chung-kuo ming-jen ku-shih, ed. by Yü Ling. Shanghai, 1949.

近代中國名人故事。俞凌。

Chin-tai ming-jen chuan-chi hsüan, ed. by Chu Te-chün. Shanghai, 1948.

近代名人傳記選。朱德君。

Chin-tai ming-jen hsiao-chuan, ed. by Wo-ch'iu chung-tzu (pseud.). 3 vols. No place, 1926.

近代名人小傳。沃丘仲子。

China Handbook, 1937–1945, with 1946 Supplement, ed. by the Chinese Ministry of Information. New York, 1947.

China Handbook, ed. by the China Handbook Editorial Board. Taipei, 1951–.

The China Year Book, ed. by N. G. W. Woodhead. Tientsin, 1921–39.

The Chinese Year Book, ed. by the Council on International Affairs, Ministry of Foreign Affairs. Shanghai, 1935–41.

Ch'ing-tai ch'i-pai ming-jen chuan, ed. by Ts'ai Kuan-lo. Kowloon, 1963.

清代七百名人傳。蔡冠洛。

Chuan-chi wen-hsüeh. Taipei, 1962–.

傳記文學。

Chūgoku bunkakai jimbutsu sōkan, ed. by Hashikawa Tokio. Peking, 1940.

中國文化界人物總鑑。橋川時雄。

Ch'un-ch'iu. Hong Kong, 1957–.

春秋。

Chung-hua min-kuo jen-shih lu. Taipei, 1953.

中華民國人事錄。

Chung-hua min-kuo ming-jen chuan, ed. by Chia I-chün. 2 vols. Peiping, 1932–33.

中華民國名人傳。賈逸君。

Chung-kung jen-ming tien, ed. by Chang Ta-chün. Kowloon, 1956.

中共人名典。張大軍。

Chung-kung jen-wu chih, ed. by *Jen-min nien-chien*. Hong Kong, 1951.

中共人物誌。人民年鑑。

Chung-kuo jen-wu hsin-chuan, ed. by Hsü Liang-chih. Hong Kong, 1954.

中國人物新傳。徐亮之。

Chung-kuo kung-ch'an-tang lieh-shih chuan, ed. by Hua Ying-shen. Hong Kong, 1949.

中國共產黨烈士傳。華應申。

Chung-kuo li-tai ming-jen nien-p'u mu-lu, ed. by Li Shih-t'ao. Shanghai, 1941.

中國歷代名人年譜目錄。李士濤。

Chung-kuo ming-jen chuan, ed. by T'ang Lu-feng. Shanghai, 1932.

中國名人傳。唐盧鋒。

Chung-kuo ming-jen tien, ed. by Li Hsi-keng and Fang Cheng-hsiang. Peking, 1949.

中國名人典。李希更。方正祥。

Chung-kuo pai-ming-jen chuan, ed. by Ch'en I-lin. Shanghai, 1937.

中國百名人傳。陳翊林。

Chung-kuo tang-tai ming-jen chuan, ed. by Fu Jun-hua. Shanghai, 1948.

中國當代名人傳。傅潤華。

Chung-kuo tang-tai ming-jen i-shih, ed. by Chang Hsing-fan. Shanghai, 1947.

中國當代名人逸事。張行帆。

Directory of Party and Government Officials of Communist China, ed. by the Bureau of Intelligence and Research, U.S. Department of State. 2 vols. Washington, 1960.

Eminent Chinese of the Ch'ing Period (1644–1912), ed. by Arthur W. Hummel. 2 vols. Washington, 1943–44.

Erh-shih chin-jen chih, ed. by *Jen-chien-shih* she. Shanghai, 1935.

二十今人志。人間世社。

Feng Tzu-yu. *Ko-ming i-shih*. Changsha, 1939.

馮自由。革命逸史。

Gendai Chūgoku Chōsen jimmei kan, ed. by Gaimushō Ajia-kyoku. Tokyo, 1953.

現代中國朝鮮人名鑑。アジア局。

Gendai Chūgoku jimmei jiten, ed. by Kasumigaseki-kai. Tokyo, 1962.

現代中國人名辭典。霞關會。

Gendai Chūgoku jiten, ed. by Chūgoku kenkyū-jo. Tokyo, 1950.

現代中國辭典。中國研究所。

Gendai Chūka minkoku Manshu teikoku jimmei kan, ed. by Gaimushō jōhōbu.

現代中華民國滿洲帝國人名鑑。外務省情報部。

Gendai Shina jimmei jiten, ed. by Tairiku bunka kenkyū-jo. Tokyo, 1939.

現代支那人名辭典。大陸文化研究所。

Gendai Shina jimmei kan. Tokyo, 1928.

現代支那人名鑑。

Hatano Kenichi. *Gendai Shina no seiji to jimbutsu.* Tokyo, 1937.

波多野乾一。現代支那の政治と人物。

Hemmi Juro. *Chūkaminkoku kakumei nijishunen kinen shi.* Keijo, 1931.

逸見十郎。中華民國革命二十週年紀念史。

Hsien-tai shih-liao, ed. by Hai-t'ien ch'u-pan-she. 4 vols. Shanghai, 1935.

現代史料。海天出版社。

Hsin Chung-kuo fen-sheng jen-wu chih, ed. by Sonoda Ikki; tr. by Huang Hui-ch'uan and Tiao Ying-hua. Shanghai, 1930.

新中國分省人物誌。園田一龜。黃惠泉。刁英華。

Hsin Chung-kuo jen-wu chih, ed. by Chou-mo pao. Hong Kong, 1950.

新中國人物誌。週末報。

Hsüeh Chün-tu. *The Chinese Communist Movement, 1921–1937.* Stanford, 1960.

———. *The Chinese Communist Movement, 1937–1949.* Stanford, 1962.

Hua-ch'iao hsing-shih hsien-hsien lieh-chuan, ed. by Hai-wai wen-k'u. Taipei. 1956.

華僑姓氏先賢列傳。海外文庫。

Huang Fen-sheng. *Pien-chiang jen-wu chih.* Chungking, 1945.

黃奮生。邊疆人物誌。

Huang Kung-wei. *Chung-kuo chin-tai jen-wu i-hua·* Taipei, 1949.

黃公偉。中國近代人物逸話。

Hu-nan ko-ming lieh-shih chuan, ed. by Chung-kung Hu-nan sheng-wei hsüan-ch'uan-pu. Changsha, 1952.

湖南革命烈士傳。中共湖南省委宣傳部。

I-chiang-shan hsün-chih chiang-shih chung-lieh lu, ed. by Tsung-ssu-ling-pu shih-cheng-ch'u. Taipei, 1959.

一江山殉職將士忠烈錄。總司令部史政處。

I-ching. Shanghai, 1936–37.

逸經。

Jen-chien-shih. Shanghai, 1934–35.

人間世。

Klein, Donald W. *Who's Who in Modern China.* New York, 1959.

Ko-ming hsien-lieh chuan-chi, ed. by Wang Shao-tzu. Shanghai, no date.

革命先烈傳記。王紹子。

Kuo-shih-kuan kuan-k'an. Nanking, 1947–49.

國史館館刊。

Liu Ts'un-jen. *Jen-wu t'an.* Hong Kong, 1952.

柳存仁。人物譚。

Lu Man-yen. *Shih-hsien pieh-chi.* Chungking, 1943.

陸曼炎。時賢別記。

Lu Tan-lin. *Tang-tai jen-wu chih.* Shanghai, 1947.

陸丹林。當代人物志。

Min-kuo ming-jen t'u-chien, ed. by Yang Chia-lo. 2 vols. Nanking, 1937.

民國名人圖鑑。楊家駱。

Ming-jen chuan, ed. by Hai-wai wen-k'u. Taipei, 1954.

名人傳。海外文庫。

Pei-chuan chi-pu, comp. by Min Erh-ch'ang. Peiping, 1932.

碑傳記補。閔爾昌。

Saishin Shina kanshin roku, ed. by Shina kenkyū-kai. Tokyo, 1919.

最新支那官紳錄。支那研究會。

Saishin Shina yōjin den, ed. by Tōa mondai chōsa-kai. Osaka, 1941.

最新支那要人傳。東亞問題調查會。

Sekai jimmei jiten: Tōyō-hen, ed. by Ōrui Noburu. Tokyo, 1952.

世界人名辭典：東洋篇。大類伸。

Shin Chūgoku jiten, ed. by Chūgoku kenkyū-jo. Tokyo, 1954.

新中國事典。中國研究所。

Shina jinshiroku, ed. by Sawamura Yukio and Ueda Toshio. Osaka, 1929.

支那人士錄。澤村幸夫。植田捷雄。

Shina mondai jiten, ed. by Fujita Chikamasa. Tokyo, 1942.

支那問題辭典。藤田親昌。

T'an-tang-tang-chai chu (pseud.). *Hsien-tai Chung-kuo ming-jen wai-shih.* Peiping, 1935.

坦蕩蕩齋主。現代中國名人外史。

Tang-tai Chung-kuo jen-wu chih, ed. by Chung-liu shu-chü. Shanghai, 1938.

當代中國人物誌。中流書局。

Tang-tai Chung-kuo ming-jen chih, ed. by Hsiao Hsiao. Shanghai, 1940.

當代中國名人誌。蕭瀟。

Tang-tai Chung-kuo ming-jen lu, ed. by Fan Yin-nan. Shanghai, 1931.

當代中國名人錄。樊蔭南。

Tang-tai Chung-kuo ming-jen tz'u-tien, ed. by Jen Chia-yao. Shanghai, 1947.

當代中國名人辭典。任嘉堯。

Tang-tai jen-wu, ed. by Su Chi-ch'ang. Chungking, 1947.

當代人物。蘇季常。

T'ang Tsu-p'ei. *Min-kuo ming-jen hsiao-chuan*. Hong Kong, 1953.

唐租培。民國名人小傳。

T'ao Chü-yin. *Chin-tai i-wen*. Shanghai, 1945.

陶菊隱。近代軼聞。

T'o Huang. *Chin-jih ti chiang-ling*. Shanghai, 1939.

拓荒。今日的將領。

Tso Shun-sheng. *Chung-kuo hsien-tai ming-jen i-shih*. Kowloon, 1951.

左舜生。中國現代名人軼事。

Tsui-chin kuan-shen lü-li hui-lü. Peking, 1920.

最近官紳履歷彙錄。

Tsurumi Yūsuke. *Danjō shijō gaijō no hito*. Tokyo, 1928.

鶴見祐輔。壇上紙上街上の人。

Tzu-yu Chung-kuo ming-jen chuan, ed. by Ting Ti-sheng. Taipei, 1952.

自由中國名人傳。丁滌生。

Wang Sen-jan. *Chin-tai erh-shih-chia p'ing-chuan*. Peiping, 1934.

王森然。近代二十家評傳。

Who's Who in China, ed. by the China Weekly Review. Shanghai, 1926-50.

Who's Who in Communist China, ed. by the Union Research Institute. Hong Kong, 1966.

Who's Who in Modern China, ed. by Max Perleberg. Hong Kong, 1954.

Who's Who of American Returned Students, ed. by Tsing Hua College. Peking, 1917.

Wu, Eugene. *Leaders of Twentieth-Century China*. Stanford, 1956.

Yü Hsüeh-lun. *Ch'i-ch'ing-lou tsa-chi*. 2 vols. Taipei, 1953, 1955.

喻血輪。綺情樓雜記。